Richard A. Wheeler.

HISTORY

OF THE

TOWN OF STONINGTON,

COUNTY OF NEW LONDON, CONNECTICUT,

FROM ITS

FIRST SETTLEMENT IN 1649 TO 1900,

WITH A

GENEALOGICAL REGISTER

OF STONINGTON FAMILIES.

BY RICHARD ANSON WHEELER,

Member of the New England Historic Genealogical Society; Life Member and one of the
Vice Presidents of the Connecticut Historical Society, and Life Member
of the New London County Historical Society.

"*I have remembered the days of old and the years that are passed.*"

NEW LONDON, CONN.
PRESS OF THE DAY PUBLISHING COMPANY.
1900.

Notice

In many older books, foxing (or discoloration) occurs and, in some instances, print lightens with wear and age. Reprinted books, such as this, often duplicate these flaws, notwithstanding efforts to reduce or eliminate them. The pages of this reprint have been digitally enhanced and, where possible, the flaws eliminated in order to provide clarity of content and a pleasant reading experience.

Copyright © 1900, by Richard Anson Wheeler

Originally published
New London, Connecticut:
1900

Reprinted by:

Janaway Publishing, Inc.
732 Kelsey Ct.
Santa Maria, California 93454
(805) 925-1038
www.janawaygenealogy.com

2001, 2007, 2011

ISBN: 978-1-59641-065-7

Made in the United States of America

DEDICATION.

To my daughters,
Miss Emily Avery Wheeler
and
Miss Grace Denison Wheeler,
who have greatly assisted me
in its compilation,
I affectionately dedicate this Book.

Richard A. Wheeler.

CORRECTIONS AND ADDITIONS.

Page 58. Seventh line from the top, insert Wheeler after Paul.

Page 58. Seventh and fifth line from the bottom, read said, in place of d meeting.

Page 59. Fifteenth line from the top, read said inhabitant, instead of d inhabitant.

Page 61. Fifth line from the top, read brave, instead of grave.

Page 223. Ninth line from top, read Jane Willis, instead of Wissis.

Page 229. Second line from top, read d. Oct. 22, 1691, instead of married.

Page 303. For Eunice (No. 291), read Junice.

Page 319. Eleventh line from top, read she was living in 1770, instead of she died childless in 1755.

Page 407. Eighth line from top, read Almy, not Amy.

Page 439. Seventh line from top, read Kemp, not Kempt.

Page 446. Read Rev. William Hyde (No. 37), and omit Rev. from Charles Hyde (No. 36).

Page 490. In the Note about Col. Joseph Noyes, read several months, instead of years.

Page 497. Read Jennie, not Jessie, Page.

Page 541. No. 2, Dea. Medad, not Medid.

Page 612. Mary Swan (No. 57) m. Thomas Wheeler (No. 74), not 54.

Page 668. Read Abel H., instead of Abel N. Simmons.

Page 250. Hannah Brewster, b. ———, m. 1st, John Thompson; 2nd, Samuel Starr, Dec. 15, 1664. She is the dau. of Jonathan Brewster (No. 2), that family, and is omitted in his family.

ABBREVIATIONS.

b.   means born.
bapt.   "   baptized.
m.   "   married.
d.   "   died.
dau.   "   daughter.

PREFACE.

Having been frequently requested by my friends to write and publish a History of Stonington, from its first settlement in 1649 to the present time, has induced me to undertake the task of its compilation and in so doing have spared no labor of research into all of the available sources of historical information, including the Connecticut Charters and records of the Town and Churches here and regret that from their imperfect records, I have not been able to produce a more perfect book.

There are but few of our early planters here whose lineal descendants can be accurately traced by our local records to the present time. For reasons not now generally understood the graves of many of our early settlers have no headstones to mark their last earthly resting places, and in many instances their names do not appear on our town or church records, which has greatly embarrassed me in my work and with all its imperfection, with grateful acknowledgements to all persons who have assisted me in its compilation, this book is now submitted to the public, with the hope that they will kindly excuse all errors that may appear therein.

HISTORY OF STONINGTON.

The territory embraced in the boundaries of the original Town of Stonington was included in the first patent of Connecticut, granted by Robert, Earl of Warwick, in 1631 to William, Viscount Say and Seal, the right honorable Robert, Lord Brook and others, acting therein by authority vested in him by Lord Charles, King of England, Scotland, France and Ireland. The colony of Massachusetts having furnished men and munitions of war for the conquest of the Pequot Indians in 1637,[1] claimed an interest by right of conquest in all the lands held by the Pequots before their overthrow, and determined to occupy it in advance of any settlement on the part of the Connecticut authorities, though they had asserted jurisdiction as early as

---

[1] "At a General Corte, at Boston, the 6th, 3rd mo, 1646, Whereas John Winthrope, Junior, & othrs have by alowance of this Corte, begun a plantation in ye Pequod country, wch appertaines to this jurisdiction, as pt of or pportion of ye conquered country, & whereas this Corte is informed yt some Indians, who are now planted upon ye place where this said plantation is begun, are willing to remove from their planting ground for ye more quiet & convenient settleing of ye English there, so that they may have anothr convenient place appointed—It is therefore ordred, yt ye said Mr. Winthrop may appoint unto such Indians as are willing to remove to othr lands or ye othr side, yt is, or ye east side of ye great ryver of the Pequod country, or some othr place for their convenient planting & subsistence, wch may be to ye good likeing and due sitisfaction of ye said Indians, & likewise to such of ye Pequod Indians as shall desire to live there, submitting themselves to ye English governt, (reserving to ye commissionrs of ye United Colonies what pply belongs to their disposing concrning ye said Pequods), & also to set out ye place for ye said plantation, & to set out lots for such of ye English as are there already planted, or shall come to them, and to governe ye people according to lawe, as occasion shall require, untill this Corte shall take further ordr therein; & whereas Mr. Thom: Peter is intended to inhabite in ye said plantation, this Corte doth think fit to joyne him to assist ye said Mr Winthrope, for ye better cariing on ye worke of ye said plantation according to this ordr."
—Records of the Governor and Company of the Massachusetts Bay, vol. i, 160, 161."

1640-41-42 by granting lands thereof to Capt. John Mason and others. But notwithstanding all this, Mr. John Winthrop, Jr., located himself at Pequot as early as 1645. The next year the Massachusetts General Court gave Mr. Winthrop a commission to begin a plantation there in behalf of that colony. Connecticut resisted the claims of Massachusetts, and in order to reach a peaceable settlement of all questions in dispute relative to jurisdiction, both colonies united in referring the whole matter to the Commissioners of the United Colonies, who, after an exhaustive hearing in the premises decided in favor of Connecticut.[2]

---

[2] "At a meeting of the Commissioners for the United Colonies of New England at New Haven, September 9, 1646.

"An English plantation being lately begun by Mr. John Winthrop junior at Pequat, a question grew to which Colony the jurisdiction should belong. The Commissioners for the Massachusetts propounded an interest by conquest, the Commissioners for Connecticut by patent, purchase and conquest. It was remembered that in a treaty betwixt them at Cambridge 1638, not perfected, a proposition was made that Pequat River in reference to the conquest should be the bounds between them, but Mr. Fenwick was not then there to plead the patent, nor had Connecticut then any title to those lands by purchase or deed of gift from Uncas. But the plantation is on the west side of Pequat, and so within the bounds at first propounded for Connecticut. The Commissioners jointly agreed that an English plantation there being well ordered may in sundry respects be of good use to all the Colonies, and thought fit it should have all due encouragements, only they conceived unless hereafter the Massachustts shew better title the jurisdiction should belong to Connecticut."— C. J. Hoadley.

[3] "At a Meeting of the Commissioners for the United Colonies of New England, held at Boston the 26th of July, 1647.

"The question concerning the jurisdiction of the English plantation lately settled on the east side of Pequat River was again taken into consideration by the Commissioners.

"Mr. John Winthrop now present exprest himself as more indifferent but affirmed that some of the planters sat down there in reference to the government and in expectation of large privileges from the Mattachusetts, and should be much disappointed if that plantation fall and be settled under any other jurisdiction.

"The Commissioners considering what passed at New Haven last year, and that in all the Colonies though the title to land may be several ways acquired, yet jurisdiction goeth constantly with the patent, they told Mr. John Winhrop that they doubted not but Connecticut would tenderly consider and afford such privileges as may suit a plantation so remote, but concluded that the jurisdiction of that plantation doth and ought to belong to Connecticut."— C. J. Hoadley.

Mr. Winthrop's planting at Pequot, or Nameaug, now New London, was the first settlement in Eastern Connecticut, and after the last decision of the Commissioners he recognized the jurisdiction of this colony, who in 1649 established the boundaries of his new township at four miles wide on the east side of the river Thames, and six miles from the sea northwardly. During that time Mr. Winthrop was engaged in the settlement of New London he became acquainted with William Chesebrough, then a resident of Rehoboth, in the Plymouth Colony, and invited him to join in the settlement of his new plantation.

Mr. Chesebrough visited the place during the year 1645, but finding it unsuitable to his expectations, did not conclude to settle there. On his way home he examined our town and selected a place for his future residence, and on which he erected a dwelling-house, and removed his family there during the year 1649, supposing that his new home was within the jurisdiction of Massachusetts.

Connecticut having assumed jurisdiction and asserted authority over all the territory embraced within her chartered limits, summoned Mr. Chesebrough to appear before Capt. Mason at Saybrook, or some other magistrate upon Connecticut River, to give an account to him or them of what he was doing alone in the wilderness outside the limits of any recognized township. Mr. Chesebrough at first disregarded this order, claiming that his new home was within the jurisdiction of Massachusetts, but, subsequently, acting under the advice and assurance of Mr. Winthrop and other friends at Pequot, he so far yielded to the authority of the colony of Connecticut as to appear at the General Court at Hartford in March, 1651, and in answer to their summons said that he was not engaged in any unlawful trade with the Indians, and also assured them that his religious sentiments were in accordance with those of the General Court; that it was not his intention to remain alone and lead a solitary life in the wilderness, but that he should endeavor to induce a suitable number of his friends to join him and establish a new township.

On hearing his statement, the court so far changed its determination as to permit him to remain, on condition that he would give bonds not to engage in any unlawful trade with the Indians, and furnish to the court before the next winter the names of such persons as he might induce to settle with and around him at Wequetequock, as hereinafter more particularly described.

The planters at New London were friendly with Mr. Chesebrough, and did not want him to remove unless he went there to live, nor did they like the idea of a new township in this region. After repeated conferences with him, they engaged that if he would put himself on the footing of an inhabitant of that town, they would confirm to him the title to his lands at Wequetequock.

To this proposition he acceded, but the townsmen of New London soon discovered that they were making pledges that they had not the power to fulfill for the eastern boundary of their then township, did not extend but four miles east of the river Thames.

However, on request, the General Court extended the eastern boundary of New London to Pawcatuck River, and then New London gave to Mr. Chesebrough a home-lot over there, which he never occupied.

In January, 1652, the town of New London redeemed its promise to him, and gave a grant of confirmation to Mr. Chesebrough and his sons of all the land they claimed in Stonington. Previous to the agreement of the General Court with Mr. Chesebrough, and the confirmation of his land to him and his sons by the town, Thomas Stanton, in 1650, procured of the General Court a license to erect a trading-house at Pawcatuck, with the exclusive right of trade in that region for three years. He immediately built and occupied the trading-house, but did not bring his family to Stonington until 1658. Thomas Miner, a former resident of Charlestown, Mass., and then of Hingham, came to New London in 1645, received a home-lot there, and built a house on it the same year. He continued to reside there until 1652, when he came to this place, and took up a tract of land east of and adjoining Wequetequock Cove, and during that year and in the next erected a house thereon, which is more at large hereinafter described.

On the 30th day of June, 1652, the town of New London granted a tract of three hundred acres of land to Governor Haynes for a farm lying together on the east side of Wequetequock Cove.

When Walter Palmer (yielding to the request of his old friend Chesebrough to join him, in settling the new township) came here and purchased this tract of land of Governor Haynes, but, before he took his deed he found it covered and embraced the house and lands of Thomas Miner. So he and the governor entered into a written agreement that Palmer should give a hundred pounds for the place and such cattle as Mr. Haynes should select out of Palmer's stock. If any disagreement should arise, as to the price of the stock, it should be decided by indifferent persons. This contract recognized the title to the house and lands occupied by Mr. Miner and was dated July 15th, 1653. Mr. Miner was selected to put Mr. Palmer in possession of the land purchased of Governor Haynes and did so by a written instrument, embodying therein a conveyance of his own land and dwelling-house (included in the boundaries of the Haynes land) to Mr. Palmer, reserving the right, however, to occupy his said house until he could build another at Mistuxet, now Quiambaug. The western boundary of Governor Haynes' land sold to Walter Palmer, including the house and lot of Thomas Miner, rested on Wequetequock Cove and the rivulet that enters the cove. The other grants and purchases of land to and by Walter Palmer lay south of this purchase and on the eastern slope of Taugwonk or Togwonk, crossing Anguilla Brook, embracing the large farms of the late Col. William and Dudley Randall, in all, some twelve hundred acres. Mr. Thomas Miner built his new house at Mistuxet in 1652-3. Capt. George Denison and family joined the new settlement in 1654, erecting his house near Pequotsepos Brook. Capt. John Gallup and Robert Park, with their families, came the same year, and settled near Mystic River. The new settlement being composed of men of note, progressed as rapidly as could be expected under the circumstances. Mr. Chesebrough was now surrounded by a sufficient number of inhabitants to claim corporate powers from the General Court. The first local name that the settlement received was Mystic and Pawcatuck; Mystic embracing the territory between Mystic River on the west and Stony Brook on the east; Pawcatuck embracing the territory between Pawcatuck River on the east and Stony Brook on the west. It being understood by the planters here, as a condition precedent to the new settlement that as soon as a suitable number had joined them, they should be incorporated as a new town. So in 1654 they applied to the General Court for corporate powers. But no sooner made than it was opposed by New London, embracing Groton, and defeated. The planters did not rest satisfied with their defeat, and resolved to agitate the matter until they succeeded sooner or later. They were of the independent Puritan stamp, and ready to make any sacrifice in defense of the right to worship God according to the dictates of their own conscience. But to to be taxed for a minister at New London, some twelve miles away, with two rivers to cross to get there, and no ferry-boats, was a little too much for their Puritanism, so they were determined to have a town and a church of their own, and continued to ask for them of the General Court, but were denied as often as they applied. In the early part of 1657, the Rev. William Thompson came here to reside, and preached to the planters a part of the time, and the rest of the time to the Pequot Indians. He was employed by the Commissioners of the United Colonies, who were acting as the agents of the London Missionary Society. The first religious services were held at the dwelling-house of Walter Palmer, March 22, 1657. Services were subsequently held at the dwelling-houses of the planters, whose efforts were continued with unremitting determination to break loose from New London and organize for themselves a new town and church. They remembered that Massachusetts had previously claimed a part or all of the Pequot territory, embracing Groton, Stonington, and Westerly, so they sought the friendship of Massachusetts in their contests, and in October the planters, joined by the Rev. Mr. Thompson, prepared a memorial to the Massachusetts General Court,[4] complain-

---

4 "To the Honoured Governour, Deputy Governour & Magistrates, together with the Deputies now assembled in the General Court a petition of the Inhabitants of Mistick & Pawquatuck, humbly sheweth that whereas we have taken several grants of lands that we are now possessed of, from the Goverment of Coneticot, lying upon the east side of the Pequid River, being conquered land from the Pequids; & since understanding, that the Jurisdiction their of, belongs not unto them but is claimed by your selves & and as we conceive, justly, as appears by the acts of the Commissioners in forty six, & forty seaven, we therefore humbly request the confirmation of those grants from this Honoured Court unto the present inhabitants: & that you would please to accept us under your Goverment & grant unto us the Liberties &

ing of the course pursued against them by the General Court of Connecticut.[5] Massachusetts notified Connecticut, who appointed a committee to confer with the planters here and bring the contest to an issue if possible.

---

priveledges of a Townshipp, their being allready settled in this place about twenty families: and this conquered land being accepted of & owned by you, we hope may not be unprofitable to this common-wealth, it being sufficient to afford accommodations for another towne-shipp, which may (if it should seeme good to your Honoured Courte so to dispose of it), be sufficient to gratify such persons as have beene deserving in the conquest of that land; besides the commodity of one of the most conveinent harbours in the land. And will we hope be a means conducing much to our settlement & comfort, which we humbly expecting, under your Government, whereof we have had former experience shall heartily pray: etc.

"October: 15th (57)
"GEORGE DENISON,
"WM. THOMPSON,
"WALTER PALMER,
"JOHN GALLUP,
"THOMAS STANTON.

"In the name of the rest of the Inhabitants & with their consent."

"The deputties desire our honoured magistrates would be pleased to give answer to this petition in the first place.
"WILLIAM TORREY, Cleric."

"20 8mo. 57, In answer to this petition ye magistrates Judge meet yt ye letter here to Anext should be sent from ye Court to ye Genll. Court of Connecticut if theire brethren the depts. Consent thereto.
"EDWARD RAWSON, Secrety."
"Consented to by the deputies.
"WILLIAM TORREY, Cleric."

[5]"Answer to Capt. Denison's Petition.
"Court Records, vol., page 266.

"In answer to the peticon of George Denison, William Thompson, Walter Palmer, Tho Stanton and Jno Gallup, the Court judgeth it mete to order, that the letter here under writt be sent to the Generall Court of Conecticott by ye secretary.

"Gentn—Wee cannot but take notice of your claime unto and disposing of the lands in the Pequot country wherein wee have alwaies challenged an interest, and yet see not reeson to laydowne the same wee have perused the judgment of the Comissrs. in 46 and 47 that the Jurisdiction on the west side of the Pequot river ought to belong to Conetticut till the Massatusets shew reasons to the contrary, against wch we shal not at prest object conceiving there by our title to the lands on the east side the river to be (at least tacitely) yielded to us, notwithstanding wch you have proceeded to dispose of these lands to diverse persons and to exercise Jurisdiction over them,

What was done in the premises cannot now be ascertained, for no records of their proceedings have been preserved.

In May, 1658, William Chesebrough, Thomas Stanton, and Walter Palmer, in behalf of the planters, petitioned the Massachusetts General Court again, stating that some of them were settled here by Governor Winthrop in 1649, by virtue of a commission from the court, notwithstanding which they had been called to account for their doings under their authority, and asking for relief from such interferences from the Connecticut authorities, and also for confirmation of their lands.[6]

---

wch desire and expect you doe friendly yield up these aforesd lands on the east side of the Pequot river unto us, and that you doe not further procede to exercise authority over the Inhabitants there, or to be grievous to them, without their owne consent till the matter be determined according to the articles of confederation if (at least) your owne justice shall not prevaile with you to yield it to us wthout that trouble wee are moued at present to make knowne our claime to you by a petition presented to us from the Inhabitants thereof, supposing it will not be unacceptable to you that this business be issued peaceably & friendly, accordinge to the relation wherein wee mutually stand engaged, we shall not ad further at present, but Comitt you to God & rest.

"October 21st. 1657."

—Massachusetts Archives, vol. xxx, pages 66 and 67, by William B. Trask.

6 "To the Honorable Generall Court Assembled at Boston, the Humble petition of the Inhabitants of Mistic and Pawcatuck: May it pleas you,—Whereas your pore Petioners by the provydec of God are settled in theas pts of the Pequit Country Soomn of Vs being settled hear in the yeare 1649 by the Honnered John Winthrop Esquire now Governor of the Collony at Connectycoat by Vertu of a Coition from your honerable Court but in short tyme we weare Caled to the Court at Conctcoat to give acount by what athoryty we heare settled we ansered as aforesaid but the Court answered that theas parts did belong to them by Patent & Purchase & the agrement of the Comiconers & did require our subjection but now all of vs vnderstanding that it doth of right belong to this Jurisdiction & that you have beene pleased gratiously to accept a petition from vs alredy we are bould still to petition that you will please to Confarme our lands and Possestions & to grant vs the liberty of a Township & the privyledges thearof & likewise Charrytably to Consider our remoatnes as also being surrounded with many indyans & many malignant percons often passing this way as quakers and others that you will be pleased thearfore to establish soomm such athoryty among vs that we may be preserved in righteousnes & peac we have with this our peticon sent our Honnered Friend Capt. George dennysoun home, we Judge Faithfull, he knos well in what stait we are to hose Care and Faithful-

But this was denied them, accompanied, however, by a suggestion that the whole matter in dispute be referred to the Commissioners of the United Colonies, and meantime to order their affairs by common agreement until provision be made in their behalf. In answer to the suggestion of the Massachusetts General Court they organized the following association for their own protection:

"The Asotiation of Poquatuck peple, June 30th 1658: Whereas thear is a difference betwene the 2 Collonyes of the Matachusetts and Conecticoate about the government of this plac, whearby we are deprived of Expectation of protection from either, but in way of Curtecy, & wheareas we had a command from the generall Court of the Matachusetts to order our own busines in peac with common consent till further provition be made for us, in obedyience to which commuand we have addressed our selvs thearunto, but connot atain it in regard of soomm distractions among ourselves, and thear hath bene injurious insolencys done unto soom persons,—the cattell of others threatened

---

nes we Comit the transaction of all our matters with the Honnorable Court thus Craueing Pardon For the rudenes of our lynes with desire you may Find more vertu in our actions we rest & wait your Charatable answer. Your peretitioners.

         "WILLM CHESEBROUGH
         "WALTER PALMER
         "THO. STANTON
         "in the prsance of the Rest.
"May 10th 1659."

"In Answer to ye Petition of the Inhabitants of Misticke, The Court Considering there hath bene no Answer Retourned from the Generall Court of Conecticott to our letter directed to them which Giues vs Cawse to Imagine they are not Resolved to give vp theire Claime to those lands so that the matter in likely to Come to be Judged by the Commissionrs, The Court thinks meete to forbeare further Acting therein till the meeting of the Commissionrs and doe expect & Require the Inhabitants to Carry themselves & order theire Commissioners and doe expect & Require the Inhabitants to carry themselves & order theire affaires peacably & by Comon Agreement in the meane while and till other provision be made in thir behalfe: And further doe desire our Commissioners to be mindfull of this busines & endeavor Issue thereof at the next meeting. The magists have past this wth Reference to ye Consent of theire brethren the deputys thereto.

         "EDWARD RAWSON, Secrety
"Consented to by the deputies
         WILLIAM TORREY, Cleric
"25th 3d 1659"
—Mass. Archives, vol. 112. pp. 105, 106, by William B. Trask.

to be taken away,—and the chattell of soom others already taiken away by violence.

"We haveing taken into consideration that in tymes so full of danger as theas are, unyon of our harts and percons is most conducing to the publick good & safety of the place,—thearfore in pursuance of the same, the better to confirm a mutual confydence in one another & that we may be perserved in righteousness and peac with such as do commenc with us, & that misdemeanors may be corrected and incorrygable persons punished:—We hose names are hereunto subscribed do hearby promis, testify & declare to maintain and deffend with our persons and estait the peac of the plac and to aid and assist one another acoarding to law & rules of righteousness acoarding to the true intent & meaning of our asociation till such other provition be maide ffor us as may atain our end above written, whereunto we willingly give our assent, & nether ffor ffear hoape or other respects shall ever relinquish this promis till other provition be maide ffor us. And we do not this out of anny disrespec unto either of the afoarsaid governments which we are bound ever to honnor, but in the vacancy of any other aforesaid.

       "GEORGE DENISON,   "MOSES PALMER,
       "THOMAS SHAW,   "WALTER PALMER,
       "NATHANIEL CHESEBROUGH,   "THO. STANTON,
       "ELIHU PALMER,   "WILLM CHESEBROUGH,
       "THOMAS STANTON,   "SAMUEL CHESEBROUGH,
       "ELISHA CHESEBROUGH,

"Upon the request of severall among us to enter into this association with us they are admitted and have accordingly subscribed thear names.
"June 30, 1658.

"By virtue of this association, that justice may not be obstructed &c, the peac preserved,—we maid choise of Captain Gorg Dennyson and Willm. Chesebrough to be comytioners to issue out warrants & to cause to be brought before them anny suspitious percons, or ffor any misdemeanor, & to hear & to determine the casses, and to pronounce sentence upon them & to see the judgment executed, provided it extended not to the los of life or limb or banishment or stigmatizing; in such casses as thear power will not reach due punishment ffor the crime, then to taik order that their percons may be secured, and sent whear Justice may procede against them.

"And ffurthur, they are to issue all other differences, whether of debts or cases, and to kepe a register of thear actions providid allwaies the action excede not fforty pound.

"This choise is the act of the whole body of the Asociates.
                                          "WALTER PALMER
                                          "THOMAS STANTON."
—Stonington Records.

Following out these suggestions, George Denison and his associate planters assembled on the 30th day of June, 1658, and formed a compact called by them "The Association of Pawcatuck People," which was organized for municipal purposes only, and not in defiance of the laws of either colony, but was established by them with a firm purpose to maintain it until some provision adequate to their wants should be made for them. The question in dispute between the Massachusetts and Connecticut colonies as to jurisdiction was referred to the Commissioners of the United Colonies, who in 1658 rendered a decision[8] that all the Pequot territory west of Mystic River belonged to Connecticut, and all the territory east of it, including Stonington, North Stonington and part of the town of Westerly, belonged to Massachusetts. In order to bring the Pequot territory

---

[8] "September 1658.—The Issue of the difference betwixt the two Colonies of the Massachusetts and Conecticott about the Pequot Country being jointly referred to the Commissioners of the other colonies.

"Whereas there is a controversy again revived betwixt the two colonies of Massachusetts and Connecticut concerning their interest in the Pequott country, and many pleas have been made on both sides for their greater interest; we having seriously weighed what hath been by each of them alledged, conceive the determination doth arise only from their several rights by conquest, the which for ought we can understand is not greatly different yet being tender of any inconveniency or disturbance that may accrue to thos that are already possessed either by commission from the Massachusetts or Connecticut in any part thereof (should they now be put off their improvements) and also upon inquiry finding that the Pequot country which extendeth from Nianticke to a place called Wecopaug about ten miles eastward from Mistick river may conveniently accommodate two plantations or townships we therefrom (respecting things as they do now stand) do conclude that Mistick River be the bounds between them as to proprietie and to jurisdiction so far as conquest may give title thereunto; always provided that such as are already accommodated by commission from either of the governments, or grants of any tracts of land on any side of the said Mistick river be not molested in their possessions or rights by any after grants, and that all due care be had that Christian society and ordinances may be provided for and upholden according to God, in each plantation.

"THOMAS PRENCE,
"JOSIAS WINSLOW,
"FRANCIS NEWMAN,
"WILLIAM LEETE.

"Boston 16th of Septem. 1658.

"By bounding it by Misticke River we intend that river shall be the bounds so far as the pond by Lanthorn Hill, and thence from the middle of the said pond to run away upon a north line."—Records of the United Colonies. Plymouth Colony Records. vol x, p. 209.

HISTORY OF STONINGTON.

east of Mystic River under the jurisdiction of Massachusetts, the General Court adopted the following resolution:

"At the second session of the General Court held at Boston the 19th of October, 1658. In answer to the petition of the inhabitants of Mystic and Pawcatuck the Court judgeth it meet to grant that the English plantation between Mystic and Pawcatuck be named Southertown and to belong to the County of Suffolk and order that all the prudential affairs thereof be managed by Capt. George Denison, Robert Park, William Chesebrough, Thomas Stanton, Walter Palmer and John Meinot sen., til the court take further order and that Capt. George Denison, William Chesebrough and John Minot (Thomas Miner meant) be commissioners to end small causes there and to deal in criminal matters as one magistrate may do, and that Walter Palmer be constable, Capt. Denison Clerk of the writs, and he also is hereby empowered and authorized to solemnize marriages between such as are published according to law; that the said Capt. Denison taking his oath be empowered to give the oath to the other two, provided always the bounds of the town is not hereby determined (at the same court.)

"In answer to petition of Inhabitants of Southertown, humbly desiring for several reasons that the bounds of their plantation may extend into the country northward between Weacapauge and Mystic river eight miles from the mouth of Mystic River.

"The Court judgeth it meet to grant request."—Mass. Archives. Wm. B. Trask.

At the next session of the Massachusetts General Court, after this decision was rendered, they passed an act that the English plantation between Mystic and Pawcatuck Rivers should be named Southerton, and belong to the county of Suffolk, Mass., and appointed Capt. George Denison and others to manage the prudential affairs thereof until the court take further orders.

Walter Palmer was appointed constable, and the bounds of the plantation were extended into the country northward eight miles from the mouth of Mystic River.[10]

---

10 "We whose names are vender written being chosen by the Towne of Southertown to lay out the bounds according to the Courts grant, the which we did as followeth, ffirst we began at Misticke Rivers mouth, and ffrom thence we run six miles to the north, northeast to the pond lying by Lanthorne Hill, where we marked a chestnut tree with six noches right against the middle of the pond, which pond we found to be seuen chains and one pole wide, and ffrom thence we run two miles due north to an ash tree which we marked ffouer ways and set eight noches ffor the eight miles lying by a little still brooke, and we run from thence due east tenn miles and one quarter and twelve chains to white oake tree marked with X and SV. and ffrom

Thus, after a severe and protracted struggle, they succeeded in obtaining a local government. It should be borne in mind that the Massachusetts General Court did not create or even organize a new township, but simply declared that the English plantation between Mystic and Pawcatuck Rivers should be called Southertown. They recognized in part the local association of the people, and extended and confirmed their bounds.

During the years 1659, 1660 and 1661 several town-meetings were held for the purpose of building and locating a meeting-house, which was raised May 13, 1661, and was so far completed as to be ready for use in September of that year, when the Commissioners of the United Colonies being in town attended worship there, and were addressed by that stern old warrior statesman, Capt. John Mason. This, the first meeting-house of Stonington, stood a short distance southwest of the residence of Mr. Henry M. Palmer.

It is not known how large it was or what its shape or style, but from some facts that may be gleaned from the old town records, it is probable that it was a small building and but partially finished, for as early as 1667, six years after it was raised, a vote was passed in town meeting to repair it and make it more comfortable; and even after it was repaired the people did not use it in cold weather, but held their meetings at the house of Amos Richardson, which was situated a little way east of the meeting-house.

Rev. Mr. Thompson remained here until 1659 when he removed to New London, September 30th of that year. The Rev. Zachariah Brigden of Boston, Mass., preached here by invitation of the town, which subsequently held a meeting for the purpose

---

thence we run due south six miles and three quarters, there we crossed Poquatuck River and ffrom thence vpon the same line to a place called Quanaquatag which line poynted vpon Block Island which Quanaquatag lies east of Weeckapoug two miles and quarter, which two miles a quarter we took possession ffor the countrie to dispose of either for us or as the countrie shall cause.

"GEORGE DENISON, THOMAS MINER,
"THOMAS PARKE, THOMAS STANTON,
 SAMUEL CHESEBROUGH.

"Dated the 2nd. of March 1659."
—Stonington Town Records."

of securing his services. Mr. Brigden labored here until his death, which took place April 24, 1662. After his death Mr. Chauncey and Fletcher preached for the town until the spring of 1664, when the town appointed a committee to go to the Bay (Massachusetts) and procure a minister for the town, who invited Mr. James Noyes of Newbury, to become their gospel-preaching minister. He accepted the invitation, and came here in the latter part of June, 1664, and continued his labors preaching as a licentiate until 1674, when he was ordained. In 1660-61 an old Pequot captain, known as Soche, laid claim to that part of Southertown called Misquamicut, and lying east of Pawcatuck River, and sold it to a number of planters from Newport, Middletown and Portsmouth, R. I., who took possession and held it as part of Rhode Island Colony. The planters here were greatly vexed by the conflict of jurisdiction, and serious trouble grew out of it. In some instances the same territory was granted by each of the then colonies to different persons, and long years of litigation was the result.

Sorely pressed by these difficulties, and annoyed by the apprehension that the Connecticut Colony meditated their subjection, the selectmen, or townsmen, as they were then called, in behalf of the town, under January 19, 1662, again petitioned the Massachusetts General Court for redress of grievances,[1] to

---

[1] "To the Honored Governor deputye Governor and magistrates together with the Counsell of Generall Court of the mattachusetes the petition of the inhabitants of southertowne humbly sheweth that whereas by the Good providence of God we have bin orderly put vnder your Goverment by the cometioners of the vnighted Collonies, acording vnto articles of confederation: by which means through your Faviour we have ffor this several years enjoyed our peace, with many other liberties and privilidges both sivell and spirituall, which we could not formerly injoy, or bee made pertakers of, notwithstanding all our indevers and adresses made vnto those, who claimed a proprietye in thes parts, the which peace of ours, together with your authoritye amongst vs hath bin much interrupted, and your authoritye together with all our priviledges much impugned by the authoritye of Coneticots sending downe amongst vs these warrants, and prohibiting vs the exersice of any authoritye amongst vs but such as shall be deriued from them; indevering to make a faction, or to incorage the same amongst vs, that so thay might attaine there owne eandes, which how reguler it is we leaue vnto your visdoms to judge,—these things haue ocationed vs to make seuerall adreses vnto your honored selues and we have had your faiourable acseptance therein, as manifestly apears by

which no response seems to be made. On the 22d of April, 1662, Governor Winthrop succeeded in obtaining a new charter of Connecticut from King Charles II. The eastern boundary of the colony was therein fixed at Pawcatuck River, thus placing a large part of the town of Southertown under the jurisdiction of Connecticut, leaving that part east of Pawcatuck River under the control of Rhode Island.

Massachusetts gracefully yielded obedience to the new charter.

At the October session of the General Court for that year the charter was publicly read to the assembled freemen of Connecticut, and from that time forward became the recognized law of the land.

At the same session it was ordered that "ye inhabitants of Mystic, and Pawcatuck, not Southertown, shall from henceforth forbear to exercise authority by virtue of Commissioners from any other Colonies, and in case any differences that may arise, they repair to our Dept. Governor for help, and they choose a constable for the year ensuing, and ye said constable to repair to the Dept. Governor for his oath. And they are required to pay unto Mr. James Noyes, Lt. Samuel Smith, and Ensign Avery, for in behalf of the Charter, the sum of twenty pounds as their towns proportion, two-thirds in wheat at four

---

your letters vnto Coneticot, and orders vnto your selues, for the preservation of our peace and the retaining vs vnder your Goverment (which faviour we cannot but thankfully take notis of, and doth Firther oblidg vs vnto your service and our owne fidellitye and dutye): yet not withstanding all your indevers and letters vnto Coneticut, for the preservation of our peace, etc. it doth two manifestly apear that thay doe slight boh your letters, and power, for thay still continue to trouble vs with there warrants, requireing our obedienc, and seeke to tirrifye vs with there threats if we shall not attend there orders, which may apear in part vnto your selues, by sum letters or orders which of leate came vnto sum of our facktions persons, the which we thought meete to sease, and send downe with these, for your better information; what their intentions are we know not, for it is giuen out and we have cause to feare, that they will not at least willingly be tryed by the cometioners, but that they will force vs by power, it haueing bin Giuen out that they will have Capt. denison alive or dead, and that there will bee many widowes and fatherless Children amongst vs are long, together with there Countinancing and complyanc with those vnreasonable men of road iland now at Paquatuck one of these cheefe saying openly that thay had rather the road Ilands should haue that land than the bay, with many high and slighting

shillings, and one-third in peas at three shillings eight pence, by the last of November next." It does not appear that the town of Southertown was represented in the General Court of Massachusetts while it was under the jurisdiction of that colony; nor were the planters represented in the General Assembly of

---

wordes respecting the bay and the interest, thretening the nullifying of what ever the bay hath done hear, respecting privilidges or proprietyes; things being thus, or thus apearing vnto vs, we being weeke and vnexperienced in the manageing of cases of this natures, causeth vs with all humilitye to sped these things before your worships and this Honerable assembly, humbly begging your firther faviour and countenanc in thes respects, for our incoragement in the manifestation of our fidellitye, vnto which we haue ioyntly bound our selves: wherefore we doe earnistly intreat that since we haue bin and are orderly vnder your care and Government, that you would be pleased to doe your vtmost for vs to contenew us. So, and that we may not bee left vnto the mercyes of those of coneticote, whose wordes and actions speaks (unto vs) nothing but our ruin, who haue aproued our selues faithfull, yee and the ouerturning of the authoritye of the bay to there vtmost power: and becaus we doe not know how soone they may macke sum further attemtes against vs, we doe earnistly craue sum further orders and instructions may be sent unto vs, by this messenger if posably, that so we may not be in the darke what to do, if such attemts should be made against vs, which the lord in mercy prevent, by your wisdome, and if that purpose you would send any letters unto coneticot our mesenger can speedily convey them vnto there deputys Governor, which posably may abate there furye, and may be a means to prevent our further truble and of the continuance of our peace, together with your authoritye and interest: pardon we beseech you our bouldness, and let our presing nesesitye, together with our earnest desire after peace, and order, and the attending your orders and instrucktions to that end speake for vs: and if the lord shall macke your worships instrumentall for the preservation of our peace and comfort, by the improuement and vpholding your authoritye amongst vs, we and ours shall haue caus as to owne his Goodnes so to acknowledg youre favioure, and shall continue to pray.

"Yours in all Loyallty, though vnworthy to be owned,

      "GEORGE DENISON
      "WILLIAM CHESEBROUGH
      "THO. STANTON
      "SAMUEL CHESEBROUGH
      "ELIHU PALMER
           "Townsmen

"From Southertown: this: 19 of January 1662.
"In the name and with the consent of the towne."
—Mass. Archives, vol. ii, page 34 by William B. Trask.

Connecticut until the October session for 1664, when William Chesebrough was elected, and at the commencement of the session presented a petition[1] in behalf of the planters, asking their pardon for past offenses, and their favor for the future, which was granted to all except Capt. Denison.[2]

In 1665 the name of Southertown was by the General Court changed to that of Mystic, in memory of that victory God was pleased to give this people of Connecticut over the Pequot Indians. In May, 1666, an act was passed as follows: "The town of Mystic is by this Court named Stonington, the Court doth grant to the plantation to extend the bounds thereof ten miles from the sea up into the country northward, and eastward

---

[1] "To the Honorable Genrall Court now asembled at Hartford in the Collony of Connectycoat, Hounorable may it pleas you—We your poore petitioners being summoned by the Hounored Counsel of this jurisdiction to yield our obedience & subjection to this jurisdiction acording to his majestyes letters patent gratiously granted to this Collonie & to make choise of a percon to be a Comishonor & to atend the servis of this present Court in obedience to this summons we have yielded our selves & sent vp one to be a Comishonor to atend the servis of the Court. We humbly besech you thearfore that you will pardon all such mistaiks or miscariges wch through humain frailty hath bene offencive or grievous vnto you & receaue vs with a loving aspect & renue your former favor vnto vs that we may be remembered with equall priviledges of other Townes acording to our Capacite that we maie be preserved in truth & peace & that scandals may be removeed for the forme we may not be so bould as to prescrib knowing the wisdom & prudenc of the Hounered Court hose wisdom & favor we do commit ourselues vnto.

"We humbly do be besech allso that the bounds of our plantation may be confirmed wch was granted vnto vs by the Bay, thus being loath to trespas vpon your patenc we humbly taik our leave & rest your pore petichoners.

WILLM CHESEBROUGH in the name of the rest

"October 14: 64"
—Conn. Archives.

[2] "Mystic & Pawcatuck haveing by Mr. Chesebrough petitioned this Court for their fauoure to pass by their offences the Court haueing considered the same doe hereby declare that what irregularties or abusiue practices haue proceeded from them, whereby they haue seemed to offer contempt to the authority here established it shall be forgiuen and buryed in perpetuall oblivion and forgetfullness, and this to extend it selfe to all ye members of the afoarsayd plantation, Captayn Denison onely excepted whoe hath neglected or refused to submit himselfe peaceably to the order of the Councill of this Colony."—Trumbull's Colonial Records, vol. i., p. 499.

to the river called Pawcatuck. This Court doth pass an act of indemnity to Capt. George Denison upon the same grounds as was formerly granted to other inhabitants of Stonington."

Mr. Noyes did not at first make arrangements to remain for any given length of time, but subsequently, in 1668, the town passed a vote that they would freely contribute, or give towards his building a dwelling-house among them in order to his settling in the town, and carrying on the work of the ministry among them. They also voted to give him a salary of fifty pounds currency annually for seven years, and in 1671 the town added the use of the ministry land to Mr. Noyes' salary, and subsequently raised it to one hundred pounds, with several grants of land and other donations. About this time a movement was set on foot to build a new and better meeting-house, to lay out public lands for the support of the gospel ministry, and to form a church in accordance with the established religion of the colony. In 1667 the planters convened in town-meeting and decided to set apart and lay out five hundred acres of land, to be styled the ministry land, the avails of which were to be applied to the support of the gospel ministry. In July of the same year the town established what they called a town plot, and appointed a committee to lay out as many lots as there were inhabitants then living in the town. Their home-lots contained twelve acres each, and were so arranged that each lot had a street front. Two hundred acres of this ministry-land was laid out around the place where the Road meeting-house now stands, the eastern line of which extended along a few feet east of said meeting-house, running nearly north and south. The western boundary was Mistuxet Brook. The northern and southern lines cannot now be traced, but the form of the plot can nearly be seen when we look at the distance between the east and west lines and the number of acres that were laid out. The home-lots were laid out around and upon each side of the ministry land. They extended as far east as Stony Brook, and south as far as Smith's Mill; one tier was located north, and the remainder west and south of said land. In 1668, a census of the inhabitants of the town was ordered to be taken, embracing those only who were inhabitants or heads of families. February 2d there were found to be forty-three inhabitants, viz., Thomas Stanton, George Denison, Thomas Miner, John Gallup,

Amos Richardson, Samuel Cheesebrough, James Noyes, Elisha Cheesebrough, Thomas Stanton, Jr., Ephraim Miner, Moses Palmer, James York, John Stanton, Thomas Wheeler, Samuel Mason, Joseph Miner, John Bennett, Isaac Wheeler, John Denison, Josiah Witter, Benjamin Palmer, Gershom Palmer, Thomas Bell, Joseph Stanton, John Fish, Thomas Shaw, John Gallup, Jr., John Frink, Edmund Fanning, James York, Jr., Nathaniel Beebe, John Reynolds, Robert Sterry, John Shaw, John Searls, Robert Fleming, Robert Holmes, Nathaniel Chesebrough, for Mrs. Anna Chesebrough, his mother, Gershom Palmer for Mrs. Rebecca Palmer, his mother, Henry Stevens, and Ezekiel Main. A home-lot was laid out for each inhabitant, and the title was obtained by lottery on the following conditions, namely: If built upon within six months and inhabited, the title would be complete, except that each proprietor must reside on his lot two years before he could sell it, and then he must first offer it to the town and be refused, before he could sell the same to any person and give good title. How many of these home-lots were built upon by the then inhabitants cannot now be ascertained.

Up to this time all religious services had been provided for and conducted by the authorities of the town. Ministers were employed by the selectmen, and paid from the town treasury. The town also appointed committees to examine candidates for the ministry, to see if they were sound in the fundamentals. "They did not by their acts recognize Councils, Assemblies, or ecclesiastical machinery in any way until 1669, when they preferred a petition to the General Court of the colony asking liberty to settle themselves in church order, which was granted at once;" but the church was not formed until 1674. During the time that these preliminary steps were moving for church organization, the inhabitants were worshipping at Pequot, in their dwelling-houses and the old meeting-house. They had repaired it several times in pursuance of town votes. It was also occupied by the town for holding town meetings.

At a meeting held therein in June, 1670, it was voted, with a joint consent, "That a bigger and better meeting-house should be built." Nothing appears to have been done about building a new house, for the reason that they could not agree upon a location. In April, 1671, another meeting was held, which voted, "That the meeting-house agreed upon shall stand upon the most convenient place of the ministry land," and the selectmen were directed "to view said land and approve the place where they find it most convenient, according to the order of the town, to set the meeting-house."

The selectmen could not agree upon a location, and called another town meeting, which was held Thursday, December 14, 1671. At this meeting, after spending most of the day in fruitless motions and discussions, it was voted, "That the meeting should continue until Friday night, and that all the inhabitants meet Friday morning by nine of the clock at the meeting-house, and to go from thence to view a place to set the new meeting-house on."

They met the next day, and looked over the ministry land, and unanimously agreed upon a location for their new house, and then went back to the old meeting-house and passed the following votes, viz.: "That the New Meeting-House shall for time to come be set up and stand without removing upon the hill called Agreement Hill, so named by the town at the same place." The dimensions of this house were agreed upon at this meeting, and were as follows: "Forty feet long, twenty-two feet wide, and fourteen feet posts from joint to joint." It was also voted at this meeting, "That the present minister, Mr. James Noyes, for the time that he continues to be the minister of this place, shall have the use of all the ministry land to himself, besides his fifty pounds currency per annum, and at his death or departure to leave it wholly to the town." A committee of five were appointed to superintend the erection of the new meting-house. It was built by subscriptions of timber, planking, shingles, ceiling, nails and labor of men and teams, etc. At the time the meeting-house was located upon Agreement Hill by the town, the hill was covered with heavy timber, which was removed by the inhabitants by voluntary labor, who then laid the foundations for the new house, and raised it Jan. 15, 1673. This house stood a few rods west of the present meeting-house at the road. It was not finished for several years. At first there were no slips or pews, except for the deacons, magistrates, and minister's family; benches were used by all people, and a committee was appointed to seat them according to their notions of propriety. This state of things did not last long, for the town voted the next year to have the floor of the house and of the gallery assigned to the inhabitants for pews. A committee was appointed to make the assignment, who encountered much opposition, but finally agreed upon a plan which was submitted to the town and accepted. Those who were dissatisfied with the section assigned them did not make their pews, and occupied the old benches. Some of them after a while reconsidered their determination and built them. The inside of the house was never lathed and plastered. After the pews were built the space between them and the gallery was ceiled, and this was done by sections, which had been assumed by some of the wealthier inhabitants. When this house was dedicated is not known. Religious meetings were held there in the summer of 1673, and ever after that until it was taken down to make way for a larger one, which was erected in 1729. Soon after this town was incorporated by the General Court of Massachusetts, the planters became apprehensive of trouble with the Narragansett and Wampannoag Indians, whose western limits bordered along on the eastern boundary of Southertown. The danger of the planters here had been increased by a union with the Massachusetts Colony, for the reasons that it was with that and the Plymouth Colony that the trouble originated that finally culminated in King Philip's war. Becoming a part of the Massachusetts Colony, they were regarded by the Indians as their enemies. Their isolated condition and the neutral position of Rhode Island marked them as an easy prey for savage vengeance. Nor did the new charter in 1662 and their annexation to the colony of Connecticut better their condition, for as the difficulties with the Indians increased the whole of New England became involved in the conflict.

King Philip's emissaries visited the remnant of the Pequot Indians, and besought them to join in the grand plan of exterminating the English.

They were partially successful at first in their endeavors, but the influence of Chesebrough, Stanton, Denison, Gallup and others prevailed with the Pequots and they remained friendly with the English and rendered them most important services when the war actually commenced. They participated in the great swamp-fight in Kingston, R. I., which took place Dec. 19, 1675. Capt. James Avery, of New London, commanded the Pequots and Mohegans, who, urged on by Oneko, fought with unyielding determination. Capt. John Gallup was among the slain, but how many of lesser grade, and of the rank and file of our town, were killed and wounded cannot now be ascertained. Almost all of the able-bodied men of Stonington were engaged in the Indian wars of their time. Capt. George Denison raised and mustered into service from the colony a large force of English and Indians. He was provost-marshal for New London County and Rhode Island. He had a stockade fort just west of his dwelling-house in Stonington, where his soldiers encamped previous to their forays into the Indian territory. During the year 1676, Capt. Denison organized three expeditions, which pursued with unrelenting vengeance the shattered remnants of King Philip's forces. It was during the third of these expeditions, which began March 28, 1676, and ended April 10, 1676, that the brave Narragansett chieftain, Canonchet, was taken prisoner. He was brought to Stonington, where a council of war was held at Anguilla, near the present residence of Gideon P. Chesebrough. He refused to negotiate for peace, or for the cessation of hostilities on any terms, so the council decided that he must die, and when told of his fate, replied "That he liked it well, and should die before his heart had grown soft, or he had said anything unworthy of himself." He was executed after the Indian mode, being shot by Oneko and two Pequot sachems, the nearest to his own rank among his conquerors. This was done by his captors without consulting, or advice from any one superior to them in authority. No list or roll of the Stonington men who participated in the early Indian wars has been preserved. The nearest approach to which may be found in "list of the English volunteers in the late Narragansett war," as prepared by a committee for that purpose in order to secure a grant of land for their services, as follows: Capt. George Denison, Sergt. John Frink, Capt. John Stanton, Capt. Samuel Mason, Rev. James Noyes, Lieut. Thomas Miner, Samuel Youmans, John Fish, George Denison, Jr., William Denison, Nathaniel Beebe, Henry Stevens, Edmund Fanning, Thomas Fanning, John Bennett, William Bennett, Ezekiel Main, William Wheeler, Gershom Palmer, Samuel Stanton, Daniel Stanton, Manasseth Miner, Joseph Stanton, James York, Henry Bennett, Capt. James Pendleton, Robert Holmes, Thomas Bell, Henry Elliott, Isaac Wheeler, John Gallup, Nathaniel Chesebrough,

Ephraim Miner, Joseph Miner, Samuel Miner, John Ashcroft, Edmund Fanning, Jr., John Denison, William Billings and Samuel Fish.

After the close of King Philip's war nothing occurred to interrupt the progress of the settlement. Some matters, however, connected with the contests between the colonies of Connecticut and Rhode Island, relative to the boundary line between them, lingered, to make trouble for the adjoining towns of Stonington and Westerly. The boundaries between Connecticut and Rhode Island as fixed by the new charter were not satisfactory to the Connecticut people, nor entirely so to the Rhode Island people, but after years of contention and litigation measures in the interest of peace prevailed, and the present boundary line was established. The attempted overthrow of the charter of the colony by Sir Edmund Andros, acting in pursuance of the policy of King James II., did not particularly affect the interest of the planters here, though they were bitterly opposed to the measures adopted by the king for the purpose of consolidating all of the New England colonies into one, shorn of the liberties granted them by the charter of 1662. The sudden collapse of King James, his abdication of the government of England in 1688, the arrest of Andros in Massachusetts, and his forced return to England gave great satisfaction to the inhabitants of this town, as well as to all of New England; and when William and Mary ascended the throne in 1689 they were hailed with universal respect and esteem. Their beneficent policy was felt on this side of the Atlantic, and with the restoration of the charter and the assurance of the protection of the mother-country, the planters here went on from year to year electing their town and colonial officers, levying and collecting taxes for church, town and state and furnishing without dissent their quota of men to resist the invasion of the French and Indians from the north. During the latter part of the Rev. Mr. James Noyes' pastorate his health began to fail him, and the people of his charge were anxious to afford him all the assistance in their power. By this time the northern part of Stonington, now North Stonington, had become settled, and the old place of worship at Agreement Hill was felt to be too remote for them to attend. So they began to take measures to divide the town into two societies for religious purposes, pending which the town held a meeting in 1715, and voted and agreed to call the Rev. Joseph Noyes[1] to assist his father in the work of the ministry, one of whom was to preach to the people remote from the old meeting-house. Mr. Joseph Noyes did not accept of this call, anticipating one from New Haven, which he subsequently received and accepted. Another town meeting was held in 1717 and adopted measures for the division of the town, which was consummated by the General Assembly in 1720.[2] The legal effect of these proceedings thus far was to divide the town into societies and leave them without authority to assemble and elect their officers, there being no general statutes at the time providing for calling the first society meeting for that purpose. Whereupon a petition was preferred to the Governor and Council in December, 1720, asking that a time might be

---

[1] "At an adjourned Town Meeting held April the 14th, 1715, It was voted and agreed to call Mr. Joseph Noyes to be helpfull to the Rev. Mr. James Noyes in carrying on ye work of ye Ministry amongst us in thiss town, and that one of ye two Ministers shall preach to the People living remoat from the Meeting House at sum convenient Place where they, ye people agrived shall unanimously agree upon, and that after the death, removal or inability of either of the two ministers, to carry on the work of ye ministry, or so soon after as the uper people shall so cause the Town to be divided into two Societies for carrying on ye work of ye ministry; And ye Town to be divided so as may be consistant with ye rule of justice and righteousness and the Northern Society when set out as above shall have an equal part of the ministry land, in this town and for incuragement of ye uper society, the lower society shall when divided as aforesaid, pay unto them the sum of one hundred pounds towards ye settleing of a minister amongst them. It was voted that if Mr. Joseph Noyes shall accept of a call of this town to be minister with his father the Rev. Mr. James Noyes, that then ye town will give him, ye sd Mr. Joseph Noyes for his incuragement ye sum of one hundred pounds towards settling him amongst us and to pay him annually ye sum of seventy pounds as money so long as they ye sd Mr. James and Mr. Joseph Noyes shall carry on ye work of ye ministry amongst us in this town, and if it pleased God that Mr. Joseph Noyes shall succeed ye Rev. Mr. James Noyes and doe continue to carry on ye work of ye ministry amongst us that then, he shall have his salloroy raised to make it a comfortable and credeble maintanance from this Town."—Stonington Town Records."

[2] "Generall Assembly May Session A. D., 1620. Holden at Hartford.—Upon consideration of the petition of the inhabitants dwelling in the northward part of Stonington, praying that a Committee may be appointed to settle and establish a line that shall divide Stonington into two societies. Ordered, by this Assembly, that Mr. John Plumb of New London Conn., John Sprague of Lebanon, Conn., Joseph Bacchus of Norwich, and Lt. Timothy Pierce

fixed for a meeting of the inhabitants of said parish qualified to vote in the affairs therein. The petition was granted and the 28th day of December, 1721, at the old meeting-house, at twelve o'clock noon, was designated as the time and place for said meeting and three men were selected to warn it by giving five days' notice thereof, and when assembled either of said persons was to preside and lead the parishioners to a choice of society officers.[3]

of Plainfield, or any three of them be a committee to settle the line desired and make return of their doings therein to the Assembly in October next and that the Towne of Stonington be at the charge of it.—Hoadley's Colonial Records, vol. v, page 180.

"Whereas the Generall Assembly held in May 12th. 1720. Did appoint us ye subscribers to fix and settle a line in Stonington to divide it into two societies, and we having heard ye Parties, what they had to offer in ye premises and viewed ye list of estates as also taken a view of severall Quarters in ye sd. town and seriously considered ye same, do fix and settle ye aforesaid line which divides ye sd. Town into two societies as follows. Beginning at ye house and farme of Mr. William Wheeler, from thence west north-west line to Mystick River brook about one mile and from ye sd. house of William Wheeler a line easterly to ye house and farm of Mr. Josiah Grant, and from thence a line eastwardly to ye house and farm of Mr. John Brown, and thence a line easterly to ye house and farm of Mr. Thomas Brown, and from thence a line easterly to ye house and farm of Mr. John Randall, and from ye sd Mr Randall's house, an east line to Shoonuck River and so by Shoonuck River to Pawcatuck River, the aforesaid line taking in ye sd Mr William Wheeler, Mr Josiah Grant, Mr John Brown, Mr. Thomas Brown, and Mr John Randall with their present improvements into ye North Society and to be a part of it as witness our hands.

          "JOHN SPRAGUE,
          JOHN PLUMB,
          JOSEPH BACHUS,
          TIMOTHY PEIRCE,
             Committee.

"Stonington, June 25, 1720."—Society Records.

[3] "At a meeting of the Governor and Council in New London, December 20, 1720. Present, The Honorable Gurdon Saltonstall Esq. Governor Richard Christophers Esq., Assistant: Jonathan Prents Esq., John Picket, Christopher Christophers, Jonathan Star. Upon application made by several inhabitants of the societies or parishes in Stoningtown, lately established by the General Court, desiring that a time may be appointed for the meeting of the inhabitants of said parish, qualified to vote in the affairs thereof, and an order given for notifying them of the time for their convening for that end.

"Ordered that Wednesday the 28th of this instant December at 12 of

The meeting assembled in response to the notice and elected Samuel Stanton, Jr., clerk; Samuel Stanton, Sr., Daniel Palmer, James Miner, Joseph Denison and Samuel Chesebrough, Sr., committee, and Nehemiah Williams, collector. These proceedings completed the organization of the First Ecclesiastical Congregational Society of Stonington. Ministers' rates were no longer laid and collected by the town, that duty devolved upon the society; also the settling of ministers in connection with the church, building of meeting-houses, and all the temporal matters of the church. Pending the proceedings that were instituted in England for the subversion of the charter of 1662 and the overthrow of the colonial government established by virtue thereof, the General Court in May, 1685, enacted that "This Court, for the prevent of future trouble, and that every township's grants of land, as it hath been obtained by gift, purchase, or otherways of the natives and grants of this court, may be settled upon them, their heirs, successors, and assigns forever, according to our charter granted by his late majesty of happy memory, this court doth order that every township in this colony shall take out patents, for their said grants of the Governor and company, which this court doth hereby order shall be granted unto them, for holding of such tracts of land, as have been formerly or shall be hereafter granted to them by this court, and to their heirs and successors and assigns firm and

---

the clock at noon, and at the old meeting house in said parish, be the place and time for the meeting of the said inhabitants.

"Ordered, That Capt. Manassah Miner, Mr Adam Gallup, and Mr Sylvester Baldwin, all of the said parish, or either of them, do give at least five days notice to the inhabitants within the precinct of said parish, who are qualified voters in the said society, that on the said Wednesday the 28th instant at twelve o'clock at noon, at the old meeting-house in said parish, a meeting of the said society is appointed and ordered by this board for choosing a clerk and committee, and for managing other affairs of the said society or parish. And the said Capt. Miner, Mr. Gallup, and Mr. Baldwin, or either of them, are appointed to lead the said parishioners at the said meeting to the said choice.

"Ordered, That the clerk of the council inclose in a letter to the said Messrs. Miner, Gallup and Baldwin or either of them, a copie of this order, attested by him, which shall be a sufficient warrent for their attending to the service which they are herein directed to."—Hoadley's Colonial Records, vol. v., pages 228, 229.

sure, according to the tenure of our charter in free and common vocage, and not in capite nor by knight service, which patent shall be sealed with the seal of the colony, and signed by the Governor, and by the secretary in the name of this court and entered upon record, which patent or record of the court shall be sufficient evidence for all and every township that hath the same to all intents and purposes, for the holding of the said lands firm to them, their heirs, successors, and assigns forever."

The town of Stonington, for reasons not now understood, did not take out a patent under the act aforesaid until 1716, which is as follows, viz.:

"To all persons to whom these presents shall come. The Governor and company of his majesties colony of Connecticut, in General Court assembled, send Greeting. Whereas, we ye said Governor and company, by virtue of Letters Patents to us, granted by his Royal Majesties Charles ye Second of England &c King, bearing date ye (23d) twenty third day of April in ye fourteenth year of his Reign, Annoque Domini 1663, Have firmly by certain acts and grants passed in General Assembly, given and granted to Thomas Stanton Esq., Ephraim Miner Esq., Nehemiah Palmer Esq., Nathaniel Chesebrough Esq., the Revend. Mr James Noyes, Mr Daniel Mason, Mr John Gallup, Mr Daniel Denison, Mr Isaac Wheeler, Mr. Stephen Richardson, Mr John Frink, Mr William Bennet, Mr Robert Stanton, Mr Samuel Stanton, Mr Joseph Stanton, Mr Gershom Palmer, Mr Moses Palmer, Daniel Palmer Esq., Lieut. Ichabod Palmer, Joseph Palmer, William Palmer, George Palmer, Walter Palmer, Samuel Stanton Secundus, Samuel Stanton Jr., Daniel Stanton, Capt. Mannassah Miner, Capt. Ephraim Miner, Mr Joseph Miner, Ensign Elnathan Miner, Ensign Samuel Miner, James Miner, John Miner, Thomas Miner, Mr Samuel Chesebrough, Mr William Chesebrough, Mr Elihu Chesebrough, Elisha Chesebrough, Samuel Chesebrough Secundus, Ebenzer Searle, Thomas Noyes, John Noyes, Mr Benadam Gallup, Lieut. William Gallup, William Denison, William Denison Secundus, William Wheeler, Capt. John Mason, Samuel Mason, Mr Benjamin Hewitt, Mr Henry Stephens, John Frink Jun., Mr Ebenezer Billings, Jeremiah Main, Daniel Shaw, Thomas York, Mr George Denison, and to their heirs and assigns or such as shall legally succeed or represent them or either of them a just and legal propriety in a certain tract of land, now commonly called and known by the name of Stonington, lying and within ye Colony aforesaid (to us by ye said letters Patents granted to be disposed of,) and bounded as hereinafter followeth. And ye said Thomas Stanton, Ephraim Miner, Nehemiah Palmer, Nathaniel Chesebrough, Mr James Noyes, and ye rest of ye above named persons, with such other persons, as are at this present time by virtue of ye aforesaid grants and acts, proprietors of the said tract of land, having made application to us for a more ample confirmation of their propriety in ye sd. tract of land (which they are now in possession of) by a good and sufficient instrument, signed and sealed with ye seal of this corporation. Therefore, know ye that we, ye sd. Governor and company in General Court assembled by virtue of ye aforesaid letters Patents and for divers good causes and considerations pursuant to ye end of said letters Patent, us hereunto moving, have Given, Granted, Rattified and confirmed and by these presents do further, fully, clearly and amply, Give, Grant, Rattifie and Confirm unto ye aforesaid Thomas Stanton, Ephraim Miner, Nehemiah Palmer, Nathaniel Chesebrough, Mr James Noyes, with ye rest of ye above named persons aforesd. and to all other persons at this present time proprietors with them of this said tract of land, now being in their full and peaceable possession and seisen and to their heirs and assigns, or such as shall legally succeed or represent them or either of them, forever ye aforesaid tract of land commonly known by ye name of Stonington, lying in ye colony aforesaid and boundeth as followeth. Beginning at ye mouth of Mystic River, and northerly up said river and brook, falling in ye sd. river to ye pond by Lanthorn Hill to ye north end ye pond, where ye pond in seven chains and one pole wide, thence north to an ash tree formerly marked with eight notches, standing by a still brook, thence north to a white oak tree, formerly marked with ten notches known by ye name of Stonington north-west corner tree, from thence extended a little due east by heaps of stones, marked trees and monuments in ye line, nine miles to a rock about four feet high, of ye form of an ovell, marked with a letter S on ye south side and a white oak standing by it, marked with with ye letter R which rock is about one hundred rods to ye southeast of a cedar swamp and from said rock south somewhat westerly to ye south of Ashoway River, where said river falls into Pawcatuck River, and by ye middle of the stream of said Pawcatuck River unto the sea, taking in ye small adjacent islands to ye mouth of Mistick River aforesaid, together with all and singular ye messuages, tennements, meadows, pastures, commons, woods, underwood, fishing, small islands, islets and herridittaments whatsoever being, belonging or anywise appurtaining to ye said tract of land aforesaid, and do hereby grant and confirm to ye said proprietors, their heirs and assigns, or such as shall legally succeed them or represent them, his or their several, particularly respective proprietors in ye premises, according to such alotments or divisions as ye ancestors of ye said present proprietors or said proprietors themselves, have already made by virtue of any gifts or grants of said town or townsmen of Pequot, now called New London, or shall hereafter make of ye same. To have and to hold the said tract of land, with ye premises aforesaid to them ye said Thomas Stanton, Ephraim Miner, Nehemiah Palmer, Nathaniel Chesebrough, James Noyes, and all others, ye present proprietors of ye said tract and premises, their heirs and assigns or such as shall legally represent them forever, as a good, sure, rightful, perfect, absolute and lawful estate in fee simple according to the aforesaid letters Patent, after ye most free tenure of His Majesties manner of East Greenwich, in ye County of Kent. To ye sole, only, proper use and behoof of them, ye said Thomas Stanton, Ephraim Miner, Nehemiah Palmer, Nathaniel Chesebrough, James Noyes, with all other ye present proprietors of ye said tract and premises, their heirs and assigns or such as shall legally succeed or represent them forever, as a good, sure, rightful estate in manner as aforesaid, reserving only to his Majestie, Our Sovereign, Lord George of England, King, and his successors forever, one fifth part of all gold or silver mines or ore that have been or shall be found within ye premises so granted and confirmed and further we, ye said Governor and Company, the aforesaid tract of land and premises and every part and parcell thereof hereby granted and confirmed to ye said Thomas Stanton, Ephraim Miner, Nehemiah Palmer, Nathaniel Chesebrough, James Noyes, Daniel Mason, John Gallup, Daniel Denison, Isaac Wheeler, Stephen Richardson, John Frink, William Bennet, Robert Stanton, Samuel Stanton, Joseph Stanton, Gershom Palmer, Moses Palmer, Daniel Palmer, Ichabod Palmer, Joseph Palmer, William Palmer, Samuel Stanton Secundus, Samuel Stanton Jun, Daniel Stanton, Manassah Miner, Ephraim Miner, Joseph Miner, Elnathan Miner, Samuel Miner, James Miner, John Miner, Thomas Miner, Samuel Chesebrough, William Chesebrough, Elihu Chesebrough, Elisha Chesebrough, Samuel Chesebrough Secundus, Ebenezer Searle, Thomas Noyes, John Noyes, Benadam Gallup, William Gallup, William Denison, William Denison Secundus, William Wheeler, John Mason, Samuel Mason, Benjamin Hewitt, Henry Stephens, John Frink Jr, Ebenezer Billings, Jeremiah Main, Daniel Shaw, Thomas York, George Denison, and to ye rest of ye present proprietors thereof, their heirs and assigns, or such as shall legally succeed or represent them to their own proper use in ye manner and under ye limitations above expressed against us and all and every other person or persons lawfully claiming by, from or under us, Shall and Will Warrant and forever Defend by these Presents. In witness whereof we have agreed and concluded that this present instrument be signed in our name by ye Governor and Secretary of this corporation as also that our common seal be affixed hereunto.

"Dated in New Haven ye 24th day of October Anno. Domini 1716. Annoque, Regne Regis, George Magnes Britanies, Tertia.

"By order of ye Governor,

"G. SALTONSTALL, Gov."

In 1726 the first and south society in Stonington decided to build a new meeting-house and to locate it at the Centre, at a place now known as Putnam's Corners, about half mile east of the old meeting-house. The action of this meeting gave dissatisfaction to a large number of the members of the society, who preferred the old site at Agreement Hill. Other town-meetings followed relative to the location of the proposed new house, the result of which was that no definite action was reached for several years. Petition after petition was addressed to the General Assembly until 1731 when an agreement was reached to divide the society north and south. Previous to this, two new meeting-houses had been raised, one on Agreement Hill and the other at Putnam Corners, neither of which were completed for a number of years. After this the east and west societies acted wholly independent of each other. The meeting-house at the Putnam Corners was the largest, with two tiers of galleries, one above the other, with an immense sounding board. After the division of the old society, Mr. Rossiter, who was the second settled pastor here, continued his labors until his death, which took place in 1762. Previous to his death and during his pastorate, the town sold the old ministry land and divided the avails of the sale equally among the then three societies of the town. After the death of Mr. Rossiter some of the more prominent men in the two south societies favored a reunion, which was approved of by the pastors of the neighboring churches and was subsequently adopted.[1]

---

1 "Terms of the Union.—1st. That the two meeting-houses now standing in said society shall be common property and joint interest of ye two parishes to be united. When they are united and as ye peues in each meeting-house are a personal property, we ye sd. committee agree to give up our right and title to sd. peues that they may become a common stock with said houses and also to recommend it to ye other proprietors of ye peues to do the same that they may become ye legal property of all in common and improved as such with the said two meeting-houses.

"2nd. We agree that after ye sd. society's are united as aforesaid and by their legal vote think it convenient and best to build another meeting-house for public worship in ye room and stead of the sd. two meeting-houses now standing in said societyes for ye better accommodation of sd. society that ye said meeting-house shall be built on that acre of land that Nathan Chesebrough, Esq, has generously given to erect a meeting-house on, near ye dwelling house of Mr Nathaniel Hewitt's, sd. Nathan Chesebrough Esq. having first given a deed of sd. land for ye purpose aforesaid.

"3rd. It is also agreed that the ministry and school money of both ministry land money in each society be made equal by each Society if either be wanting, and that ye school money, in ye sd. east society be improved in ye sd. east society on the east side of Stoney Brook, and that ye school money in ye sd. west society be improved in said society on ye west side of Stoney Brook, and this be a standing rule for said societies when made one, but to be so understood as not to hinder any that desire to take benefit of ye whole.

"4th. That ye Rev. Nathl. Eells shall have ye pastoral charge and care of said societies when united and ye Church of Christ therein, with ye same jurisdiction and authority over ye whole as he is now vested with over ye sd. east society and that his annual salary shall be raised and paid him at ye joint charge of ye sd. united Society.

"5th. It is agreed ye two societies shall assemble at ye east meeting-house to worship six months each year and ye west meeting-house the other six months and when a meeting-house is erected on ye place agreed on, then said societies so united as aforesaid shall meet and worship in said house as aforesaid.

"6th. It is also agreed in order to confirm each and every article of ye

In 1763 the matter was brought before both societies, and finally a plan of union was prepared and agreed upon and subsequently adopted by both parishes, and accepted by the churches. The Assembly established the same[2] with such provisions as

foregoing articles of ye foregoing terms of agreement, offered to ye consideration of sd. societies that they may be certain and unchangeable, that ye sd. societies by their agents address ye Honorable and General Assembly in May next by a proper memorial to ratify and confirm their aforesaid proposals and agreement, that we may by their authority established our own acts herein be again one united ecclesiastical society, which is ye sincear and harty wishes and desire of all.

"Dated Stonington Jan. ye 17th A. D. 1765 all ye aboue and fourgoing articals was agreed on and voted by ye afoursd. Comtee. in ye affermative.

"JOHN HALLAM "SIMON RHODES,
"ELIHU CHESEBROUGH "PHINEAS STANTON,
"NEHEMIAH WILLIAMS "JOHN DENISON YE 3RD.
"AMOS CHESEBROUGH "JOSEPH PAGE
"NATHAN PALMER, "JOSEPH MINER
"JOSEPH DENISON "DANIEL DENISON
"JOHN WILLIAMS "NATHLL. GALLUP

"Voted, That said report with ye additions to & alterations of ye 3rd Paragraph in said Report following, be inserted in said report, viz., That all ye school moneys belonging to sd. east society at this time, shall when sd. societyes are united and became one intire ecclesiastical society, be improued within ye limmits theirof or ye east side of Stoney brook, and that ye school moneys now belonging to said west society be improved within ye limmits thereof on ye west side of Stoney brook, and that be a sure and unalterable rule.

"Dated March 25th. 1725."—Society Records.

2 "At a General assembly of the Governor and company of the Colony of Connecticut holden at Hartford May Second Thursday, A. D. 1765, Upon the memorial of the East and West Society's in Stonington, shewing to this Assembly that on the Death of the Revd Mr Ebenezer Rosseter, Pastor of the Church in said West Society being advised by the Revd. Benjamin Lord, Asher Rosster, and Jonathan Barker Associations Committee again to unite into one Ecclesiastical Society, and the said East and West Society's having accordingly agreed thereupon, and made application to this Assembly for that purpose as pr. Memorial on file, &c.

"Resolved by this assembly that the said East and West Society's in said Stonington, be again united and become one entire Ecclesiastical Society, to be for the future called and known by the name of the first Society, in said Stonington, and they are hereby united, created, and made one entire Ecclesiastical Society with all the Priviledges and Immunities by Law allowed to other Ecclesiastical Society's in this Colony, vested with and enjoyed the same Priviledges and Advantages which the said East and West Society's

were necessary to enable the old societies to merge and hold their property, and then directed the mode of organizing the new society. After the reunion they called the Rev. Nathaniel Eells the pastor of the east society to become the pastor of the reunited societies, which he accepted, and for several years preached alternately for six months in the east house, and for six months in the west house. A majority were looking forward to the erection of a new meeting-house at the place designated by the terms of the union. But they were doomed to disappointment. Long Point, now Stonington Borough, was not settled until 1752, but the settlement increased so rapidly that they demanded and secured the afternoon service of Mr. Eells; this produced great dissatisfaction in the east and northern part of the society, and various society meetings were held, and petitions to the General Assembly were preferred without satisfactory results. Finally eighty-three of the inhabitants of the village[1] in 1774

have heretofore severally had and enjoyed,— and that they the said East and West Society's be and they are hereby enabled and empowered as separate and distinct Society's to act and transact any society or Parish affairs to compleat the settlements referred to in said memorial until the first day of December next, and Joseph Denison Esqr. of said Stonington shall be, and he is hereby fully empowered, authorized by himself or other Person by him for that purpose appointed and directed after said first day of December next, and during said month of December to give legal warning to all the inhabitants of said first Society that are qualified by Law to vote in Society affairs to meet at such time and place as he the said Joseph shall for that purpose in said first society, appoint, and being so met, that he preside as Moderator of such meeting, in the forming of said Society, and choice of all officers, and other Prudentials of sd. society as Occasion may require."

"A true copy of Record, examined by George Wyllys, Secretary, Conn. Colonial Records.

[1] "To the Honorable General Assembly of the Colony of Connecticut to be held at Hartford on the second Thursday of May instant. The memorial of William Morgan, Benjamin Park, John Denison 4th, Joseph Denison 2d, Oliver Hillard, Edward Hancox, Oliver Smith, and the rest of the subscribers hereto in behalf of themselves and the professors of the established Religion of the Colony, living at a place called Long Point in Stonington in the County of New London, humbly sheweth, that they are scituate near four miles from any meeting-house and that the inhabitants living at sd. Long Point are generally poor, they living principally by the whale and cod-fishery, there carried on, to the public advantage, by which means within a few years said place has increas'd to upwards of eighty families among which are twenty widows, seventeen of which have children as families there that the whole number of

addressed the Assembly for liberty to build a meeting-house by lottery, which was granted at the October session of 1774, limiting the amount to be raised thereby to four hundred pounds.[2]

inhabitants are nigh to five hundred, that there is not among them more than one horse to ten families so that but very few are able to attend meeting at the meeting-house except those that are robust hardy and used to travel on foot, which are very few, the greater number of said inhabitants consisting of women and children, that thereupon the society have for several years consented to have one sermon preached at sd. point every sabbath by their Rev. Pastor which he has performed and is still willing to continue, but their number has so increased that it is very inconvenient for those that do attend public worship (as they have no where to convene but in a small school house or private houses) and many more than at present do attend, would there were room to accommodate them, that for the want of a proper place to meet in for celebrating divine service, many who means the sabbaths are misspent and may be more and more misspent and prophaned, that those who would be glad to build a house and maintain preaching and good order among them, have been and continue unable of themselves to bear the expense by which the cause of religion much suffers there, and the good people among them greatly fear the increase of vice and irreligion. That the town of which ye memorialists are a part, have lately paid and are liable to pay upwards of one thousand pounds for the deficiency of several collectors, that have lately failed that your memorialists from great necessity, by their being very remote from any constant grist mill, have lately contributed £70 as an incouragement to an undertaker to build a wind mill at sd. Point, which, with about the same sum lately subscribed by sd. inhabitants for a school house, with the great labour and expense they have been at to make roads and Causeways to said point, all of which with the poor success that attended the last year's fishery and the lowness of markets and the various and different sentiments in the religious denomination of Christians among them, viz: First day Baptists, Seven day Baptists, and the Quakers or those called Friends, are such real grief and great discouragement to your memorialists who are of the established Religion of this Colony that they can no longer think of obtaining a meeting-house by subscription or any other ways among themselves.

"Wherefore they humbly pray that liberty may be granted to build a meeting-house for public worship at said Long Point, and that your Honours would in your great goodness grant them a Lottery for raising a sum sufficient for the purpose aforesaid, or so much as your Honours shall think proper under such restrictions and regulations as your Honours shall think fit and your memorialist as in duty bound shall ever pray.

"Dated at Stonington May 10th 1774.

[2] "At a General Assembly of the Governor and Company of Connecticut in New England in America holden at New Haven in said Colony on the second Thursday of October being the 18th. day of said month and continued by several adjournments to the fourth day of November next following, Anno Domini, 1774. Upon the memorial of Nathaniel Miner Esq., William Morgan

The managers of the lottery did not at once inaugurate their scheme, nor did they accomplish it until 1777, which was successfully drawn and the necessary funds secured. But the Revolutionary war so absorbed the means of the people that a large part of this sum was used for the defense of the place, and balance invested in Continental bills, which after the close of the war became worthless. Whereupon in 1785,[3] another petition was preferred to the Assembly, for liberty and authority to raise by lottery money enough to make up the four hundred pounds,

and others, inhabitants of the first society in Stonington, shewing that they lived at Long Point in said society and are far remote from the place of public worship there, that said place has greatly increased in numbers within a few years past, that the inhabitants of said point and thereabouts are generally poor and unable to build a house to meet for public worship, that if they had a house to meet in for that purpose they apprehend the growth of irreligion and impiety would be prevented &c, praying for a lottery to build a meeting-house, on which a committee have been appointed who have reported in favour of said memorials and affixed a place for building, which report is accepted and thereupon Resolved by this assembly that the memorialists have liberty and they are hereby authorized to raise by way of lottery the sum of £400..0..0 lawfull money to be applied for the purpose mentioned in said memorial and also the further sum of £30..0..0 lawfull money, to defray the expense of such lottery, and Nathaniel Miner Esq., Joseph Denison 2nd, John Denison 4th, Peleg Chesebrough, and John Brown Jun, all of said Stonington, or any three of them accepting said trust, are hereby appointed managers and directors of said lotteries who should be jointly holden to make good all benefit tickets drawn in such lotteries and shall be sworn to a faithful discharge of their said trust and the adventurers in said lotteries, shall have their remedy against said managers for the benefit tickets by them drawn in manner aforsaid and the monies so raised by said lotteries shall be laid out and applied to the purposes aforesaid and account thereof be rendered to the General Assembly when demanded."—Conn. Archives, by C. J. Hoadley.

3 "At a General Assembly of the State of Connecticut, holden at Hartford in said State on the second Thursday of May, being the 12th. day of said month, and continued by adjournments until the ninth day of June next following Anno. Dom. 1785. Upon the memorial of Nathaniel Miner, John Denison 3rd. & Joseph Denison 2nd. all of Long Point in Stonington, setting forth that they with others of the first Society in said Stonington were on the second Thursday of October, 1774, appointed Managers of a Lottery granted by the Honorable General Assembly to your Memorialists William Morgan and others of the established Religion of the then Colony of Connecticut for the purpose of raising the sum of £400, to build a Meeting-house at said Point. That said Managers proceeded by way of Lottery to raise said sum in Continental Bills towards the close of the Summer of 1777, when your Memorialists for whom the Grant was made, not being apprehensive of the depre-

which was granted, and the money raised. Instead of building a new house at the Point they took down the old meeting-house at the Putnam Corners and took it down there and with their lottery fund, old meeting-house and subscription erected a meeting-house at Stonington Point in 1785-6, which work was done under the superintendency of Col. Joseph Smith.

ciation that would attend said Bills and considering the great scarcity and dearness of materials for building said House and the danger they were then exposed to from the enemy who were then at New York, Newport and Long Island, thought best for the Grantees not then to proceed in building said House, since which the Bills in the Hands of your Memorialists have depreciated to almost nothing except a part which has been turned into Public Securities, Praying that a Judicious Committee may be appointed to examine into the matters of said Memorial and the true State and Circumstances of the money which they held in trust, put a just value thereon, and that said committee be, enabled to direct said managers, to raise on said Grant such Sums with what they already have as to make up the £400 granted by your Honors as per memorial, &c.

"Resolved, by this Assembly that said Nathaniel Miner, John Denison 3rd, Joseph Denison 2nd, be continued as managers of said Lottery with the addition of James Rhodes and Elijah Palmer of said Stonington, and that the Honorable William Hillhouse and Benjamin Huntington Esqrs, Elisha Lathrop Esq, be and they are hereby appointed a committee to inquire into the state and circumstances of said Lottery and liquidate and settle the accounts thereof, and ascertain the value of the avails thereof in the Hands of said Managers, and in case said Committee shall judge it to be reasonable, they may and they are hereby Authorized and impowered to direct that said Managers proceed to Issue and draw such further numbers of tickets in said Lottery as to raise such sum of money for the purpose of building a meeting-house at said Point as shall be thought by said committee to be proper, not exceeding £400, including what is already on hand as aforesaid and exclusive of the cost of said Lottery, said managers to be accountable to the General Assembly when requested for their Doings in the premises."—Conn. Archives by D. W. Edgcomb.

REVOLUTIONARY WAR.

Pending the agitation that preceded the Revolutionary war in all of the colonies, that subsequently united in the Declaration of Independence the town of Stonington was not indifferent to the momentous struggle and in order to give force and effect to their political sentiments assembled in town-meeting, and passed patriotic resolutions.[1] Whereupon the meeting elected a Committee of Correspondence who addressed Major General

---

[1] At a legal town-meeting held in Stonington the 11th day of July 1774, the following resolution was passed:

"Deeply impressed with the alarming and critical situation of our Publick affairs, by the many repeated attacks upon the liberties of the English American Colonies, by sundry acts of parliament, both for the purpose of raising a revenue in America, as well as the late most extraordinary act for blocking up the port of Boston. Think it our indispensable duty to manifest our sentiments upon the important occasion and are most clearly of the opinion that they are repugnant to the spirit, freedom and fundamentals of the British Constitution, and in direct violation of Magna Charter. Their surprising exertion of power which so remarkably distinguished the inauspicious times and necessarily alienate the affections of the Americans from their Mother Country, and the British Merchants and manufacturers will of course be extreme in losing the most beneficial commerce that they derive from any part of the Globe, We recommend as our best advice to the publick, that a General convention of delegates from all the colonies be convened with all possible dispatch and what they in their wisdom, upon the most mature deliberation shall agree upon as most expedient for the interest of this growing fertile and extensive continent; shall be adopted by us, and that in the interim, as a necessary step to open the eyes of the present administration, and to obtain that justice that is due to the worthy descendants of Great Britain, which has of late through an extreme misguided policy been denied, we Wherefore recommend a suspension of all commerce with Great Britain, to immediately take place.

"We are bound in justice to ourselves to declare, that we have ever manifested (and are still ready on all occasions) the most affectionate loyalty to the illustrious house of Hanover; which we are truly sensible consists in nothing more evidently than in a well regulated zeal for liberty and the Constitution.

"A sense of real honor grounded upon principals of religion, and experience,

Warren of Boston, who replied in a letter glowing with the loftiest sentiments of patriotism.[2]

The people of Stonington not only sympathized with the inhabitants of Boston in their resistance to British aggression, but furnished men and means to enable them to maintain their liberties. They were represented at the battle of Bunker Hill by true and determined men as they were afterwards, in almost every battle field, of the Revolution. After the battle of Bunker Hill, the American army pressed close around Boston and cut off the supplies of the British army to such an extent that they com-

---

will warrant us to affirm that their endowments of loyalty public spirit of honor, and religion are no where found in higher perfection than in the British Colonies. Notwithstanding what is past, we are still desirous to remain upon our former good understanding, with the mother country, and continue to them their gainfull commerce, provided a repeal of those grievous acts take place.

"We heartily sympathize with our distressed brethren, the Bostonians, who we view as victims sacrificed to the shrine of arbitrary power, and more immediately suffering in the general cause. We rejoice to see so many of the neighboring colonies and even towns vieing with each other in their liberal benefactions to the distressed and injured town of Boston. Wherefore we have opened a subscription for the relief of the inhabitants of the town of Boston, which the Committee of Correspondence, viz. Charles Phelps Esq., Dr. Dudley Woodbridge, Col. Henry Babcock, Joseph Denison Esq., Mr. John Dean, Paul Wheeler Esq., Nathaniel Miner Esq., Capt. Daniel Fish, Joseph Palmer Esq., Mr. Benjamin Clark, and Mr. Samuel Prentice are appointed to receive and forward to the selectmen of the town of Boston, and said committee are instructed to correspond with the committees of the different colonies and transmit a copy of this vote to the corresponding committee of Boston, whose well timed zeal, vigilance, and watchful fidelity in the great and most interesting cause of liberty, we cannot sufficiently thank."

Passed in a very full town-meeting without a single dissenting voice.

[2] Boston, August 24th, 1774.

"Gentlemen,—Your elegant and benevolent favor of the first instant yielded us that support and consolation amid our distresses which the generous sympathy of assured friends can never fail to inspire. 'Tis the part of this people to frown on danger, face to face, to stand the focus of rage and malevolence of the inexorable enemies of American freedom.

"Permit us to glory in the dangerous distinction and be assured that, while actuated by the spirit and confident of the aid of such noble auxiliaries we are compelled to support the conflict.

"When liberty is the prize, who would shun the warfare? Who would stoop to waste a coward thought on life? We esteem no sacrifice too great, no

pelled them to forage for supplies all along the coast of New England, and farther west and south.

Some of the Tories of this region round about had notified Com. James Wallace of the English navy, who had been appointed and commissioned by Admiral Graves of Boston, and given command of three small frigates, "that Stonington was rich in the requisite food for an army and navy, and was also in receipt of a large number of neat stock from Block Island, which had been brought here in a vessel and landed at Long Point, and driven back into the country."

Upon the receipt of this information Com. Wallace came to Long Point, in Stonington, in the frigate "Rose," Aug. 30, 1775, and sent a boat ashore with a peremptory demand for a delivery of said cattle to him, threatening terrible vengeance in case of non-compliance. Refusal having been returned as peremptory as the demand, Com. Wallace sent his tender sloop up the harbor to seize and bring off the cattle and whatever else they could find. Before they could accomplish their object news of their approach spread through the town which aroused the people, and a large number of men from the country had arrived at the Point, and co-operated with the inhabitants of the village, in its defense. A company of men at the time rendezvoused at or near the Road Meeting House, under the command of Capt. William Stanton, marched directly to the Point and joined the men there under the command of Capt. Oliver Smith. Sergt. Amos Gallup, William and George Denison and others to the number of twenty

---

conflict too severe to redeem our inestimable rights and priviledges. 'Tis for you, brethren, for ourselves, for our united posterity, we hazard all; and permit us humbly to hope, that such a measure of vigilance, fortitude, and perseverance will still be afforded us, that by patiently suffering and noble daring, we may evenually secure that more precious than Hesperian fruit, the golden apples of freedom.

"We eye the hand of Heaven in the rapid and wonderful union of the colonies; and that generous and universal emulation to prevent the sufferings of the people of this place, give a prelibation of the cup of deliverance. May unerring wisdom dictate the measures to be recommended by the Congress. May a smiling God conduct this people through the thorny paths of difficulty and finally gladden our hearts with success.

"We are, gentlemen,
"Your friends in the cause of Liberty.
"JOSEPH WARREN, Chairman.

men composed the company of Capt. Stanton. They were armed with Queen Ann muskets which were very effective at long range. Our troops were at first stationed in the Robinson pasture, a tract of land just north of the old Wadawanuck Hotel, and from there marched down to Brown's wharf, where they opened a very effective fire upon the enemy, which compelled them to leave the harbor as fast as they could with a severe loss, when they reported their ill success to their commander. Com. Wallace had for his pilot, a tory, Stephen Peckham, by name, and he succeeded in mooring the frigate "Rose" in a favorable position, with springs on her cables, from which a severe cannonade was opened upon the village, and kept up for several hours. Some of the inhabitants for protection went down into the cellars of their dwelling houses and others sought safety by placing themselves behind large rocks and others fled into the country. The greater part of the houses were more or less injured by the cannonade, but no lives were lost, and only one man was wounded. Com. Wallace did not venture to land and burn the village as he designed, being deterred by the formidable appearance of matters on shore as well as by the drubbing his tender had received. He hovered on our coast for about a week and then disappeared. Long Point was the only place that resisted successfully this prince of marauders, whose operations partook of the nature of both land and sea piracy. During the bombardment Mr. James Tripp, a friend Quaker, then a resident of the village, though a man of peace, felt his patriotism stir within him as he witnessed the injury to the houses by the shot of the enemy, seizing a musket, he said to those near him, "Can you all bear this, I cannot." He than ran down to the shore and discharged his gun at the frigate "Rose" in token of defiance and resistance to the attack of the enemy. During the Revolutionary war there was a large sycamore (buttonwood) tree standing a little southwest of the store now owned by Mr. James H. Brown, then owned and occupied by the Hon. Nathaniel Miner, who was one of the leading patriots of Stonington, at the time. That tree was called Liberty Tree, because the association of young men, styled "Sons of Liberty" and other patriots were accustomed to meet under it and discuss war measures and pass resolutions relative thereto. Evidence of the attack of Com. Wallace upon the village of Stonington Point remained for a long time; traces of cannon shot through some of the houses were plainly visible when the village of Stonington Borough was attacked by Capt. Hardy in 1814. A fort or water battery was erected during the Revolutionary war in the southern part of the village not far from where the lower school house used to stand, with an armament of several long six and nine pounders and one twelve pound carronade. A barrack was also erected for the accommodation of soldiers, which stood between the present edifice of the Baptist church and the residence of the late Mrs. Fanny Kean. No other attack was made on the village during the Revolutionary war. After its close, the battery was allowed to remain without any care and soon run down and went to ruin, and the cannon became dismounted and sunk into the ground. Before the State authorities caused them to be removed, the barrack was altered into a dwelling house, which was afterward burned down. So passed away the forts and barracks of the Revolutionary war in the Borough. During the early days of the Revolution the Stonington Point fort was garrisoned by a strong force and supplied by cannon and munitions of war, for the attack on Long Point had aroused the people of Connecticut to a sense of their danger, especially those residing near the seacoast, which resulted in a special session of the General Assembly, which was convened and held at New Haven in April, 1775, the first act of which was "The appointment of a council of safety," consisting of the Hon. Matthew Griswold, Hon. Eliphalet Dyer, J. Huntington, William Williams, N. Wallace Jr., J. Elderkin, Joshua West, and Benjamin Huntington Esq., to assist the Governor when the Assembly was not in session, with power and authority to direct the marshals and stations of the troops, to be raised for the defence of the colony, as they should judge best, and to see that they were furnished in every respect and for every purpose. At a session of the Governor and Council at Lebanon, Mr. Huntington reported "That he had found one small vessel that could be purchased for two hundred pounds of Edward Hancox of Stonington." After due consideration thereof by the Council he was directed to purchase Mr. Hancox's vessel, which was a schooner called the "Britannia," and in connection with Capt. Deshon and Capt. Niles were authorized to have her speedily rigged and fitted with guns and munitions of war, which was done, and Robert Niles of Norwich was appointed the commander. In session

Sept. 4, 1775, Col. Saltonstall and Capt. Deshon were present as a committee from New London and Major Oliver Smith and Capt. Palmer of Stonington. Capt. Palmer stated that Stonington had been lately attacked and bombarded by Com. Wallace and asked the Governor and Council for some military company to be stationed there, and both committees prayed for aid to erect works for defence. Again in session, "Sept. 14th, 1775, it was ordered to enlist 50 men under Maj. Oliver Smith for the defence of Stonington, and for carrying on the works begun there until the 29th of Oct. 1775."

The widow Smith of New London stated that the prisoners who had lately been driven to New London by stress of weather in a vessel piratically taken from Stonington by Com. Wallace of the "Rose," man-of-war, were confined at Windham, and prayed that said prisoners might be exchanged for her son, Amos Smith, B. Green and N. Comstock, who had been taken by said Wallace in New London, which was agreed to and so ordered and done. The General Assembly in session at New Haven Oct. 2, 1775, granted a bounty or pension as follows: Jonathan Weaver Jr., of Stonington, who was a musician in the company of Capt. Oliver Smith was dangerously wounded at Long Point, was allowed £12 4s. and 4d. The Assembly also promoted Capt. Oliver Smith to the office of major.

At a session of the General Assembly at New Haven Dec. 14, 1775, it was ordered that the battery at Stonington should be supplied with six cannon, two 18 and four 12-pounders. At a session of the Governor and Council Feb. 2, 1776, they having been authorized by the Assembly to supply the batteries at Groton, Stonington and New Haven with cannon and munitions of war, which would be very difficult to do unless they should be cast in the furnace of Mr. Smith of Salisbury, Conn. Thereupon Col. Elderkin was appointed to go immediately to Salisbury and give the proper orders and directions.

In session Feb. 23, 1776, Maj. Smith of Stonington urged an addition be made to his men in Stonington for the defense of the town and harbor. The Governor and Council ordered said company of forty men to be augmented to ninety men by voluntary enlistment and to be continued in service until the first day of December (next) unless sooner discharged and to be stationed at or near the fortification in Stonington. Nathan Palmer, Jr., was appointed first lieutenant, John Belcher second lieutenant and Clement Miner, ensign of the company above mentioned under Maj. Oliver Smith, who was authorized to enlist said men with all speed. Nathaniel Miner, Esq., was appointed commissary to provide supplies for the company at said fort.

In session March 23rd, 1776, Capt. Theophilus Stanton of Stonington was appointed captain of the row galley (then building at Norwich, Conn.)

In session April 10th, 1776, an order was given Nathaniel Miner, Esq., for one hundred and fifty pounds as commissary to the troops at the fort, at Long Point, in Stonington. The order was delivered to Nathaniel Gallup.

In session April 29th, 1776, Mr. Miner, the commissary for the company at Stonington, asked for a further sum of money, and the sum of two hundred and fifty pounds was allowed him to provide for said company.

Zadoch Brewster was appointed lieutenant of the row galley under the command of Capt. Theophilus Stanton, of Stonington.

At a session of the General Assembly held in May, 1776, Rev. Nathaniel Eells of Stonington was appointed chaplain of the regiment to be stationed at or near New London.

At a session of the Governor and Council held July 2, 1776, Oliver Smith of Stonington was appointed lieutenant colonel of the regiment at New London in place of Col. Mott, promoted. Nathan Palmer was appointed captain of the company stationed at Stonington in the place of Col. Oliver Smith, promoted. John Belcher, first lieutenant, Clement Miner, second lieutenant, Moses Palmer, second ensign of said company. N. Shaw was ordered to deliver to the commanding officer at New London, or to Col. Oliver Smith, for the use of the fort at Stonington five hundred pounds of cannon powder. The delay in procuring the necessary means of defence and the detention of some of the heavier guns designed for the place caused great dissatisfaction among the people of Stonington, who memorialized the General Assembly as follows, viz.:

"To the Hon, the General Assembly, now setting at New Haven.

"The memorial of the committee of correspondence and inspection of the town of Stonington and sundry of the inhabitants of said town most humbly sheweth That whereas your Honors thought fit in your last Session in May, to grant for the defence and protection of this place, a Capt. and 90 men, since which one half have been ordered to New London. Your Honors may remember that this Town, is the only one in this State, that has received any damage from those sons of tyranny and despotism sent by that more than savage tyrant George, the Third, to deprive us of those unalienable rights that the Supreme Gov. of Heaven and Earth has invested us with.

"Your memorialists therefore pray that the number of men ordered and destined as above may still be continued and that the two 18 pounders and four 12 pounders and shot etc. that were ordered in your former session for this place, may be delivered as soon as possible as the harbor is perhaps more used by coasters and vessels bound to sea, than any harbor in this State, and is a place of great consequence, not only to this, but other States. We therefore beg leave to inform your Honors, that several vessels have lately been chased into our Harbor by the King's ships and have here been protected. Your memorialists further pray, that the three large cannon (now at New London) belonging to this town, be likewise ordered to this place and the two field pieces that were lent by this town to the town of New London, be ordered back to the town of Stonington. We therefore flatter ourselves that this our most reasonable request will be granted.

"And your memorialists as in duty bound will ever pray."

Signed by   NATHANIEL MINER,   PAUL WHEELER,
                     JOHN BROWN JR,   JOHN DENISON,
                     HENRY BABCOCK,   SIMON RHODES.
                                                       Comm. of Safety.

and the same was indorsed by 92 men of the inhabitants of Stonington who appended their names thereto.

At a session of the Governor and Council of Connecticut February 15, 1777, Capt. William Ledyard of Groton and Capt. Nathan Palmer of Stonington were sent for to consult about raising artillery companies. General Parsons was desired to draw on Cols. Huntington's and Durkee's regiments at the posts and forts at New London, Groton, and Stonington for defense at those places. Capt. Nathan Palmer, at Stonington, was directed to dismiss his company as soon as General Parsons should send to that place a sufficiency of Continental troops for the defense of that post. The Governor and Council also voted to raise a company of artillery to be stationed at Groton and Stonington until Feb. 1, 1778. Capt. William Ledyard was appointed captain of said company.

In session March 20, 1777, an order was given to Nathaniel Miner to purchase or seize ten thousand pounds of cheese in Stonington for the State. Capt. Nathan Palmer, of Stonington, was directed to purchase twenty thousand weight of cheese to supply the State troops at the price fixed by law; provided, he should be unable to purchase the same, and found in the hands of any person more than was sufficient for their family use, he was authorized to seize and take the same for the purpose aforesaid, and pay them the price fixed by law, and make report of his doings.

In session March 26, 1777, Capt. Nathan Palmer seized eleven thousand six hundred and eighteen pounds of cheese per order of the Governor and Council, the property of Church & Hakes, at six-pence per pound, with one and a half per cent. for commissions, being £299 16s. 6d; cheese sent to Norwich; also, for services about the fort at Stonington, £15 7s. 6d.

In session May 12, 1777, Capt. Palmer was directed to remove the public stores at Stonington back into the country to a place of safety. Orders were also given to the commanding officers of the forts of New London and Groton to order the troops, drafted from northern companies in Stonington, to march directly to the forts at Stonington, to man that place for defense, and those drafted from northern companies in Connecticut, to return home and hold themselves in readiness to move on the shortest notice for the defense of those posts.

In session May 31, 1777, it was ordered that one half of the militia at the forts of New London and Groton were ordered to be drawn off by lot and dismissed, and all the militia companies at Stonington dismissed, and the officers at those posts were directed to execute the same. Their orders were not executed fully, and before the troops were dismissed at Stonington they were ordered to remain by Governor Trumbull.

In session Sept. 26, 1777, it was ordered that a lieutenant and thirty men were to continue at Stonington. Sept. 26, 1777, a ship of two hundred tons, prize to Capt. Conklin, of the privateer "Revenge," arrived at Stonington, laden with seventy-five thousand feet of mahogany and thirty tons of logwood. About an hour after his prize came to anchor, Capt. Conklin was chased by a man-of-war and schooner of twelve guns belonging to the English fleet, and the English vessels, in attempting to head Capt. Conklin and cut him off from land, ran on Watch Hill reef, about one mile from Capt. Conklin, who came to anchor within Watch Point, now known as Sandy Point. A brisk fire was kept up between them for several hours, and the man-of-war came to anchor just without the schooner, to protect her against Capt. Conklin. The schooner remained on the reef until the next morning, when the British set her on fire in the hold, and then went on board the man-of-war's boat and left her, and she was blown up by her magazine. The guns, some small-arms and anchors were saved, and a man found dead by the side of her. Capt. Conklin escaped unhurt.

At a session of the Governor and Council, Nov. 18, 1777, orders were sent to Gen. Tyler to send from his brigade (by draft) twenty men, to be stationed at Stonington, to serve for two months from the time of their arrival there.

In session Feb. 6, 1778, Capt. William Ledyard, in pursuance of an act of the General Assembly, on the second Thursday of January, A. D. 1778, was appointed captain of a company of fifty men, including one captain, one lieutenant, one second lieutenant, fireworkers, two sergeants, and two corporals, to be stationed at Stonington and Groton and to be continued in service until Jan. 1st, 1779, unless sooner discharged.

In session March 25, 1778, William Ledyard Esq., was appointed to command the forts at New London, Groton and Stonington, with the rank and pay of major. Achors Sheffield was appointed first lieutenant of the company of twenty men at Stonington.

In session April 21, 1778, Henry Denison of Stonington was appointed second lieutenant of the artillery company under Col. Latham at Groton, and commissioned. It was resolved that four men should be allowed in addition to the number of artillery men under Lieut. Achors Sheffield at Stonington and said Sheffield was ordered to enlist them. Twelve hundred pounds of cannon powder for William Ledyard, to be used at Groton, New London and Stonington. Capt. Nathan Palmer was directed to deliver to Lieut. Sheffield as many guns, over and above the eight guns he had, to arm his whole party of twenty-four men. Owing to the scarcity of the munitions of war, it was with the greatest difficulty that the troops could be properly armed and equipped. The fort or battery at Stonington never received the cannon designed for it; they were used at New London and Groton. Some of the British ships lay off in sight of the town during the greater part of the war, but made no further attempt to take or destroy the place. Towards its close the danger of invasion was not considered so imminent and the detail of the men at the fort was discontinued. There is no perfect roll or list of the men of Stonington who served in the army of the Revolution, but from the most reliable information now in existence I have compiled the following list:

Rev. Nathaniel Eells, chaplain, Col. Giles Russell, Col. Oliver Smith, Col. Samuel Prentice, Sergeant Christopher A. Babcock, Capt. Elnathan Rossiter, Capt. James Eldredge, Capt. Richard Hewitt, Capt. Lemuel Lamb, Capt. Thomas Holmes, Capt. Thomas Wheeler, Capt. Joseph Gallup, Capt. William Stanton, Capt. John Williams, Capt. Ebenezer Prentice, Capt. Ichabod Palmer, Capt. Jonathan Palmer, Capt. Elijah Palmer, Capt. Amos Hallam, Capt. John Breed, Capt. Peleg Noyes, Capt. John Maine, Capt. Christopher Brown, Capt. Sanford Billings, Capt. Oliver Grant.

Subordinate Officers, Musicians and Privates.—Nathan Avery, Nathaniel Fellows, John Wheeler, Peleg Denison, Nathan Denison, Thomas Leeds, William Roe Miner, David Wheeler, Oliver Babcock, Jesse Prentice, Clement Miner, Jonathan Palmer, John Palmer, Samuel Prentice, Jr., Joseph Hewitt, Ebenezer Billings, Samuel Graves, Joseph Hancox, Allen York, Paul Bromley, Thomas Brown, Nathaniel Williams, Nathaniel Maine, Jabez Dewey, Silas Hewitt, James Starkweather, Zebulon Stanton, Eliphalet Hobart, David Niles, Amos Chesebrough, Simon Babcock, Joshua Miner, David Hilliard, Sands Niles, William Fellows, Abel Palmer, Joshua Weaver, David Babcock, William Stewart, Sterry Hewitt, Nathaniel Baldwin, Timothy Coates, John Hilliard 2nd, Charles Brown, Randall Billings, Thomas Coates, James Billings, Elisha Stewart, Christopher Billings, Edward Coates, Samuel Darrow, Gershom Breed, Melvin Parks, John Allyn, Abraham Lewis, Caleb Hakes, James Stevens, Joseph Babcock, John Palmer, Rufus Brown, Thomas Palmer, Nathaniel Chesebrough, Elisha Billings, Zebulon Chesebrough, Peter Chesebrough, James Chesebrough, John Davids, John West, Jonathan Palmer, Daniel Brown, Elias Carpenter, Henry Worden, James Alexander, Amos Latham, John Monroe, Samuel Rogers, Thomas Tripp, William Collins, Daniel Fellows, George McKenzie, Nathaniel Plumb, James Satterlee, William Brumley, Abel Brown, Samuel Billings, Benajah Billings, George Buttolph, Oliver Brown, Samuel Brown, Elisha Boardman, Chanler Barnaby, Azariah Babcock, Daniel Butler, Jacob

REVOLUTIONARY WAR. 47

Button, Simeon Cardwell, Charles Clark, Joshua Chappell, Nathan Cottrell, David Crouch, Henry Thomas, Joseph Hewitt, John Hudson, Ebenezer Hill, Hezekiah Ingraham, Valentine Lewis, James Phillips, William Peck, Joseph Peck, Timothy Pierce, William Paul, Roswell Parish, Samuel Shelly, Simon Rouse, Daniel Smith, James Somers, John Satterlee, Reuben Wells, Walter Worden, Jesse Worden, Wait Worden, John White, Prince Williams, Joseph Westland, Jabez Breed, Nathaniel Hewitt, Robert Hewitt, Charles Miner, Elisha Wilcox, Stephen Wilcox, John West, Edward S. Coleman, Andrew Gay, Jeffry Hazzard, Jonathan Peters, Simon Carew, Ebenezer Stanton, Sirus Fish, Reuben Brown, David Willard, Joseph Freeman, Lewis Hart, Elisha Hancock, Elias S. Palmer, Joseph Smith, Eliakim Fitch, Jonathan Dunning, Joshua Brown, Daniel Brown, Jesse York, Stephens Hall, Shepard Wheeler, Jesse Palmer, Samuel Peabody, Collins Wilcox, James York, Zebulon Brown, Jephtha Brown, Stephen Main, Nathaniel Main, Jedediah Brown, John Utley, Thomas Swan, Stephen Hull, Jr., Nathaniel Babcock, Daniel Denison, Edward Swan, Daniel Prentice, Benajah Billings, Michael Palmer, Samuel Brown, Jonas Prentice, Cornelias Walch, Amos Morgan, John Ayer, Jr., Jonathan Morgan, George Swan, Thomas Smith, Jeremiah Wheeler, John Wheeler Gear, John Hallam, Jr., Wareham Williams, Simeon Whipple, Abel Bailey, Timothy Filley, Levi Gallup, Beebe Denison, Nathan Hancox, Oliver H. Dennis, Eleazer Williams, Samuel Stanton, Ebenezer Williams, Charles Williams, Gilbert Williams, Amos Williams, Andrew Denison, Perez Miner, Jabez Dean, Gilbert Denison, John Price, Valentine Lewis 2nd, Frederick Denison, Ezra Gallup, David Bailey, Jr., Joshua Wheeler, Daniel Stanton 2nd, Thomas Williams, Edward Stanton, Jedediah Chesebrough, Sanford Palmer, Elisha Williams, Henry Chesebrough, Isaac Frink, Roswell Holmes, Reuben Hewitt, George Gallup, Benoni Brown, Billings Burch, Ezekiel Bentley, Asa Baldwin, Perez Chesebrough, Simeon Miner, Joseph Noyes, Jonathan Wheeler, Caleb Cuff, Ichabod Dickinson, William Robinson, Jedediah Austin, Nathan Belcher, Elisha Prentice, Gideon Ray, Enoch Baker, Elisha Palmer, Amos Wheeler, Jedediah Randall, Joseph Wheeler, Joshua Grant, William Halsey, Nathan Stanton, Jabez Holmes, Daniel Hill, Manassah Miner, Joshua Wilcox, Isaac Williams, Amos Miner, David Miner,

Nathaniel Williams, Isaac Williams 2nd, Thomas Gardiner, Benedict Arms, Amos Solomon, Isaac Geer, Elijah Boardman, Jeremiah Holmes, Joseph Witter, Randall Billings, Elnathan Miner, Robert Hewitt 2nd, Thomas Miner, Enoch Stanton, Daniel Stanton, William Noyes, Charles Hewitt, Benjamin Park, Nathaniel Palmer, Eleazer Prentice, Amos Denison, Robert Hempstead, Amos Gallup, Manassah Miner 2nd, Lester Wheeler, Park Williams, Daniel Denison 2nd, Joshua Williams, Azariah Stanton, Joseph Whipple, John Dean, Jr., Israel Denison, Ebenezer Wilcox, John Murphy, George Denison 3rd, Daniel Stanton 3rd, Christopher Dewey, James Thompson, Philemon Baldwin, Jeremiah York, Gershom Ecclestone, Daniel Miner, Oliver Avery, Nathaniel Palmer, Nathaniel Miner, Elihu Hancock, Fortune Black.

The following are true copies of the records of Stonington showing the deep interest manifested by the inhabitants thereof for her patriotic soldiers in the armies of the Revolutionary war:

Att a Town Meeting Legally warned and held in Stonington, this 28th day of March, 1777.

The same Day Charles Phelps Esqr., was chosen Moderator of said meeting. The Same Day, Voted that a Committee be Appointed to Provide Necessaries for the Families of those Persons who shall voluntarily enlist into the Service of the United States, at the Prices Affixed by law, According to the Advice of the Governor and Council of Safety.

The same Day, Capt. Phin Stanton, Charles Phelps Esqr., Mr. Sands Niles, Mr. Jonathan Palmer, Mr. Henry Minor, Capt. Daniel Fish, Mr. Joseph Smith, of the Colony, were chosen Committee Men for the above Purpose. The Same Day, Voted that the Laws Regulating Prices shall be strictly adhered to, & Prosecuted against the Egressor. The same Day, Voted that the Captains of Every Company in the town be called together as Soon as may be at some Convenient place agreed on in Order that the Recruiting Officers may fill up their

Quota Of men for said town, & said meeting was Accordingly Adjourned to the 7th Day of April next at two of the Clock afternoon.

Att a Town meeting Legally held by adjournment this 7th Day of April, 1777.

The same Day, Voted that the clerks of Each Respective Company in the Town Procure a List of all the Persons in their Companies as well as the Alarm List as Militia Roll and Deliver the Same to the Select Men & Authority on Thursday, the 10th day of April, Instant, and said Meeting was accordingly Adjourned to sd. 10th day of April at two of the Clock in the Afternoon.

Att a Town Meeting held by Adjournment this 10th Day of April, 1777, Resolved by this Meeting that a Committee be Chosen to Ascertain the Number of Men within the Limits of Each Company, and Proportion to Each Company the Number of Men to be Raisd in Each Company, & that Each Company Shall Raise their Quota.

Capt. Peleg Noyes,
Capt. John Swan,
Capt. John Breed Junr,
Capt. Thomas Wheeler,
Capt. Willm Stanton,
Lieu Elias S. Palmer,
Capt. Amos Main,

Were Chosen a Committee & in Case of Failure next in Command.

The same Day, Resolved that all Men Living within the Limits of Each Company Subjected to pay a Tax, Shall not be Exempted from being Proportioned as Well as Militia, and said meeting was Adjourned to the 21st Day of April, Instant, at 2 O'Clock Afternoon.

Att a Town Meeting Legally Warned and Held in the North Society, in said Stonington, this 9th Day of September, 1777.

The same day Capt. John Randall was chosen Agent for the town to Buy and Procure Provisions for the families of the enlisted Soldiers that are in the Continental Service Belonging to this Town, the town Supplying him with money for that Purpose, and he Refused Serving, and the Same Day Joshua Randall was Chosen Agent for the Above Purpose and Accepted.

Att a Town meeting Legally Warned and Held in Stonington this 13th Day of Oct. 1777, the Same Day Joseph Denison Esqr, was Chosen Moderator of said meeting. The Same Day, Voted that the Several Commanding Officers of the Several alarm Companies & Militia Companies in this Town be appointed a Committee Forthwith to Purchase or procure at least 1 Pair of Good Shoes, 1 pair of Good Yarn Stockins, 1 Good Flannel or linnen Shirt, 1 Good hunting Shirt or Frock, and 1 pair Good Overhalls for Each of the Soldiers now in the Continental Service from this Town and that said Committee on the 21st day of Octr. instant, Deliver all said Goods to Messrs. John Breed Junr., Joshua Prentice, George Denison, Junr., and Coll. Oliver Smith, who are Appointed a Committee to Receive said Goods and Apprize them at the Present true Value thereof in money, take an Exact amount thereof and Deliver the Same with said Goods to the Select-men, who are Appointed to Forward them to Elijah Hubbard at Middletown or Royale Flint at Peekskill, and take his or their Rect. for the Same—also Voted that in Case the Committee appointed to Purchase and Procure apparel for the Soldiers in the Continental army, in Case they Cannot otherwise procure the same that each of said Commanding Officers Class the men in his Particular Company in such case as Will Furnish 1 pr Shoes, 1 pair Woolen Stockins, 1 Pair Woolen Overhalls & 1 Good hunting Shirt or Frock for Each Class, and Deliver Agreeably to the Vote aforesaid. Also Voted that the Soldiers' Wives and others in this town Expecting any Benefit of Being Supplyed with necessaries at the Stated Price Forthwith send in the number of their Respective familys and what Each Expected Provided for them for the year ensuing to the Selectmen, or Committee for Supplying said Wifes and Familys that the same May be laid Before the town. Also Voted that the Committee Chosen in march or April last to Procure Necessarys for the Soldiers' Wives and Familys be Impowered to hire One Hundred and Fifty Pounds for that Purpose and said meeting was dissolved.

Att a Legal Town Meeting of the Inhabitants of the town of Stonington Oct. ye 20th, 1777, Voted to Grant and it is hereby Granted a Rate or tax to Be Levyed on the Poles and Ratable Estate of the inhabitants of this town the sum of Seven Pence on the Pound on the list of said town for the year 1776. Forthwith to Be Collected by the Collector or Collectors of town Rates heretofore Chosen for the Year 1777, for the Purpose of Raising money to Purchase Clothing &c. for Soldiers Belonging to this town now in the Continental Service. Also, Voted that the Commanding Officers of the Several Alarm and Militia Companies in this town Be a Committee forthwith to Procure and Purchase Clothing &c for the Soldiers Belonging to this town now in the Continental Service Agreeably to the Resolve of the Governor and Council and Deliver the Same to the Selectmen of this town: and the said Committee are Impowered to Receive money of Capt. Simon Rhodes, the town Committee, to Purchase the same and in Case any Persons shall see Cause to let said Committee have any of the said Articles towards their part of the town Rate last Granted, the said Committee are Impowered to Agree With them therefor and Give them an Order on the treasurer of said Town for the Same, which shall Answer so much of their Rate. Also Voted that Capt. Simon Rhodes be appointed a Committee to hire on interest for and Behalf of the town the sum of One thousand Pounds Lawfull money for the Purpose of Purchasing Clothing for the Soldiers in the Continental Service and that he Deliver out the Same to the Committee appointed to Purchase said Clothing, taking their Rect. for the Same. Said meeting was accordingly dissolved.

Att a Legal Town Meeting held in Stonington Decem. 2, 1777, it was Voted that the School Committees in the Several Districts be appointed a Committee to Provide necessaries for the Soldiers' Wives & families Living Within their Districts.

Att a Town meeting Legally Warned and held in Stonington this 1st day of January. 1778. The Same day Maj. Charles Phelps was Chosen moderator of said meeting, the same Day the Articles of Confederation and Perpetual Union was Read & said meeting was Adjourned to the 5th Day of January.

Att a Legally Warned Town meeting held by adjournment January 5th, 1778. The same Day the Confederation & Perpetual union was Universally Consented to by the town & said meeting was Accordingly Dissolved. The same Day Voted that Capt. Simon Rhodes be appointed a Committee man to Procure Clothing &c. for the Soldiers in the army; also Voted that Capt. Simon Rhodes be impowered to Borrow the money for the purpose above mentioned upon interest till the Debt Can be Discharged.

Att a Town meeting Legally Warned and held in Stonington this 23d Day of march, 1778. The same Day Voted that Capt. Simon Rhodes be appointed a Committeeman to Procure Clothing &c. for the Soldiers Belonging to this town in the Continental army.

Att a Town Meeting Legally Warned and held in Stonington this 8th day of September A. D. 1778. Voted that the Representatives Chosen to attend the General Assembly in Octr. next are Directed by the Town to have the Law altered in Regard of Taxation in Case it Can be altered for the Better, and said meeting was Dissolved.

Att a Town Meeting legally warned and held in Stonington this 15th day of December Anno Domini 1778. The same Day Voted that Capt. James Eldridge be a Committee to Procure a sufficient Quantity of the Necessaries of life for the Use of the familys of the Officers & Soldiers of the Continental army that this town are Directed by law to Provide for, and that Capt. Elisha Denison hire Such Sums of money and Deliver to sd Eldridge as he Shall need for that Purpose and that said Eldridge Deliver said necessaries out to the School Committee in the Several Societys or their orders and that they be an Issuing Committee to Deliver the same out to the familys of said Officers & Soldiers according to law and keep proper account of what they shall so Deliver out and to whom & Render an account thereof to the Selectmen who is to transmit the same to the Committee of paytable of this State & draw the money therefor & Appropriate the same for paying money so Borrowed & the Necessary Expense &c. & that the money Borrowed & Expenses arising more than may be drawn from the Treasurer of this State (if any) be paid out of the Treasurer of this town.

Att a Town Meeting Legally Warned and Holden in Stonington this 18th day of February Dominus 1779. The Same Day Voted that Mr. Joshua Prentice and Mr. William Woodbridge Be a Committee to Purchase this Town's Quota of Blankets, Woolen over hawles and Stockins Agreeably to a Resolve of Assembly at their Sessions in January last and Deliver them to the County Commissary and take his Receipt therefor and present their Accounts of Expense and Trouble to the Committee of paytable and if their should be any Defalcation of what the Paytable shall allow them for their Cost and Trouble the same shall be made up by this town together with their Interest till paid—the same day John Denison 3rd & John Haley was Chosen a Committee to se that the Soldiers Familys are Supplyed with Provisions & said Meeting was Dissolved.

Att a Legal Town meeting of the Inhabitants of Stonington at West meeting House in the South Society in said Town August 24th, 1779, Capt. Wm. Williams was Chosen moderator of sd meeting. The Distressing Situation of Publick Affairs occasioned by the Rapid Depreciation of the Currency has Ingaged the Attention & Exercised the Speculations of many Protectors of our Liberties, the Continental Congress have manifested those feeling Sensations, which the Importance of such an Affair naturally Inspires, indeed every Generous Bosom in which the Pulse of Liberty yet Beats must be most Sensibly Affected with those Dismal Consequences (which to human Apprehension) must necessarily attend. (Voted) that in Obedience to the Call of the Guardian of our Country to the example of numerous towns in this & other United States & Especially to the many most important Demands of Virtue & our Country's Sacred Cause, we Will according to our Ability Readily Co-operate with our Brothren of the other Towns in this Country, State or States, in any Salutary measures for Preventing any Further Depreciation of the Currency & Supporting its Credit by Regularly Reducing & Determining the Prices of necessaries & Conveniences of life—Encouraging loans & thereby Prevent the necessity of Further Emissions and the Following Persons (Viz): Docr. Dudley Woodbridge, Paul Wheeler Esqr., Capt. Elnathan Rossiter, & Capt. James Eldridge are appointed a Committee to Correspond with whom it may Concern on the Premises & said meeting was Dissolved.

Att a Town Meeting Legally warned and held in Stonington this 16th day of Decemr. 1779. The same Day Wareham Williams was Chosen in the Room of Paul Wheeler Esqr., a Committee man to Supply the Soldiers Familys.

Att a Town Meeting Legally warned and held in Stonington June 26th, 1780. Also Voted that the Soldiers that shall Inlist into the Continental Army for three Years or During the war shall be paid as a Bounty of 60 Dollars in Silver or Gold Exclusive of the Bounty Given by this State or Congress Including the Light horse to be paid out of the Treasury of this Town.

Also Voted the 40s. per month given by this State to the Soldiers that shall enlist into Service shall be made Equal to 40s. in Silver or Gold; also Voted that the Soldiers that shall enlist into the Continental army for Six months shall have a Bounty of £6 Exclusive of State or Congress Bounty. Also Voted that the Soldiers that shall inlist into the service for three months shall have a Bounty of £4.10—45s. to be paid upon the enlistment & the other 45s. at the end of Sd Term in Case they serve the time out; also Voted that Coll. O. Smith, Capt. John Randall & Paul Wheeler Esqr., be a Committee to Reserve the money Lent to the Town for the purpose of Inlistment to Give their Receipt to the Lenders of sd money & Devote the same to the purpose above mentioned.

Att a Town meeting Legally Warned and held in Stonington July 8th, 1780; the same day Charles Phelps was Chosen Moderator of said Meeting. The same day Voted that the Present men Called for the Continental service be allowed 18 pounds for an Incouragement for three years service or During the War. Also Voted that Six Pounds Lawfull money be allowed to those that shall inlist into the Continental Service for Six months or the last of Decemr next. Also Voted that Capt. Christopher Brown be Joyned to the other Committee to Borrow on the Credit of the Town the hard money for the above Purpose.

Att a Town meeting Legally Warned and held in Stonington Nov. 10th, 1780. The same Day Majr. Phelps was Chosen moderator. The same Day Granted a Rate of Six pence on the Pound upon the Polls & Ratable Estate of the Inhabitants of Stonington upon the List of 1779 to be paid in Provisions at the Prices set in the Resolves of the General Assembly of Oct. 1780. Also Voted that Paul Wheeler Esqr., Capt. Elisha Denison, Capt. Amos Palmer, Lieut. Daniel Collins, Capt. Amos Main and Mr. Joshua Prentice be a Committee to Reserve the Provisions & Salt them up &c. Also Granted a further Tax of 3 pence the Pound upon the Polls & Ratable Estate of the inhabitants of Stonington upon the List of 1779 to be paid in Silver by those persons that neglect paying the Provision Tax & sd meeting was Adjourned to the first monday of December next.

Att a Town Meeting Legally Warned and held in Stonington

this 21st day of Novemr, 1780. The same Day Charles Phelps Esqr., was Chosen Moderator of sd meeting. The same day the Question was put whether the town would accept of the Resolve of Assembly Requesting Clothing for the Army, Past in the affirmative. The Same day the Question was put Whether they would Choose a Committee to Class the Inhabitants of said town & Proportion their Lists, that Each Class should Procure their men to fill up the Continental Army, Past in the Affirmative. The same day Charles Phelps Esqr., Paul Wheeler Esqr., Henry Minor, Nathl Gallup, Peleg Chesebrough, Joshua Babcock, Capt. Jno. Randall Joshua Prentice & Jno. Davis was Chosen a Committee to Class the Inhabitants of said town & Proportion their Lists. Also Granted a Silver Tax of one penny on the pound upon the Polls & Ratable Estate of the Inhabitants of said town upon the List of 1779 to be paid in male Clothing for the Army & the prices of the Clothing Stated in the following manner Viz: Flannen Shirt of 3½ Yd Shirting Width a 3 Dollars in Silver, Linnen Shirts 3½ Yds Shirting Width a 2 Dollars, Shoes a 10s, Woollen Stockins a 6s, Mittens 2s. Also voted that the Persons that Neglect paying their Rates in above mentioned Clothing by the First monday in Decemr next shall be Subjected to pay it in money. Also Voted that Capt. Amos Main, Capt. Wm. Stanton & Mr. Joshua Prentice be a Committe to Receive the Clothing & forward the Same to the Army. Also Voted that in Case the inhabitants of said town neglect paing in the Clothing by the 1st monday of December next that the above Committee borrow the Money upon the Credit of the town and immediately Purchase the Clothing & forward the same to the Army.

Att a Town Meeting Legally warned and held in Stonington this 12th day of February, 1781. Also Voted that Col. Oliver Smith, Capt. James Eldridge & Paul Wheeler Esq., to fill up the Recruits in the several Neglecting Classes. Also Voted that the head of each neglecting Class has Liberty from this time till the 19th of this instant to Procure their Recruit to fill up the Continental Army & not give to Exceed 120 Silver Dollars & the states Bounty & the Neglecting Individuals in each Class shall be assessed double the sum that it shall Cost to that part of the Class that advances sd money to hire said Recruit, which sum assessed shall be for the Benefit of that part of the Class that advances the money & that the head of Each Class make Return of their doings to the adjourned town meeting. Also Voted that Gilbert Fanning be a Committee in addition to the Committee heretofore Chosen to take Care of the Soldiers families.

Att a Town Meeting Legally held in Stonington on the 19th day of February, 1781, by adjournment. The same Day that the Several Classes that have Procured a Recruit for their Class & no Collector appointed for them in any of the above Votes that the head of such Classes be the Collector to Collect of Neglecting Individuals in such Class their Proportion of Monies due. The Same Day Col. Oliver Smith, Capt. James Eldridge & Paul Wheeler, Esqr., was Chosen a Committee to asses the Neglecting Classes or Neglecting individuals in said Classes Agreeable to an Act of the Assembly holden at Hartford on the second Thursday of October, 1780, for filling up the Continental Army & Also to make Return of such Recruits to his Excellency the Governor as shall be Raised by said town & also the Number & Names of the Soldiers now in the army Belonging to said town. The same Day Paul Wheeler Esq., & Capt. Oliver Grant were Chosen a Committee to make Out the Rate Bills for the Provision Rate & also for the Clothing Rate. The Same Day Lieut. Joseph Smith was Chosen Collector to Collect of such neglecting Classes as have not Procured their Recruits. The same Day Mr. John York was chosen Committeeman to Supply Soldiers familys. Paul Wheeler moderator of meeting.

Certified Pr Joshua Prentice, Clark Pro Tempore.

Att a Town Meeting Legally Warned and held in Stonington this 12th day of March, 1781. The Same Day Voted that they would Raise Ten Men for the State Service by Classing the inhabitants agreeable to an Act of Assembly. Also Voted that this Committee be impowered to put the Act of Assembly into Execution according to Law Respecting the Raising the State Soldiers & to asses the neglecting Classes, or the Nelecting individuals in Each Class. Also Voted that the Surplussage Money Raised from Each Neglecting Class shall be put into the town treasury & be for the Benefit of the Town, & that the Surplussage money Raised from Each Neglecting individuals in Each Class shall be for the Benefit of the Class to which he Belongs.

Att a town meeting Legally Warned and held in Stonington April 9th, 1781. The Same Day Paul Wheeler Esq. was Chosen Agent by said Town to meet a Committee Appointed by the General Assembly of the State of Connecticut (in order) to Lay in our Several inter Claims, with the Different towns, Respecting our Soldiers in the Continental Army the Same Day Capt. Amos Main, Joshua Prentice & Wm. Stanton was appointed a Committee to Receive the Clothing Requested by the Assembly for the Continental Soldiers & forward the Same to the Army & affix the Price & Notify the Collector what Proportion Each person shall pay upon the last tax granted for on the pound. Also Voted that Col. Oliver Smith be appointed a Committee to go to Hartford to get the State's Bounty due to the Several Classes.

Att a Town Meeting Legally Warned and held at the North meeting House in Stonington on Thursday, the 26th of June, 1781. The same Day Voted a tax of 4 pence on the Pound in Gold, Silver or Beef Cattle be paid by the inhabitants of said Stonington Monthly Agreable to Act of Assembly passed May last Requiring a Silver Tax on Beef. Voted that Joshua Brown be a Collector for the above Tax. Also Voted that Capt. Amos Main be a Committee to Receive the town clothing.

Att a Town Meeting Holden by Adjournment this 25th day of September, 1781. The same day Elisha Denison was appointed Receiver of Clothing, in addition to Capt. Amos Main. Also Voted that Messrs. Paul Wheeler Esqr. and Mr. Henry Minor is appointed to Procure Orders from the Men that went out of this town in the Six months Continental Service in the year 1780 and Prepare their Returns and for them Receive their Wages and pay the same to the men Respectively at the charge of this town that the town may as Soon as may be able to pay out what they have to make up to Each Soldier according to the Vote of this town made this 26th day of June, 1780. Also Voted that Selectmen Liquidate and adjust the amounts of the Committee Chosen by this town at their meeting in November last to Receive and Put up Provisions for the army for their trouble & Expense in Receiving and Securing the Same and Draw Orders on the Treasurer for what shall be found Equitably due to them Over and above what the pay Table Committee hath or may allow to them for said Service.

Att a Town meeting Legally Warned and held in Stonington this 2nd day of December, 1781. The Same day Peleg Chesebrough was Chosen T. Clerk & Sworn. The Same Day Voted that the Receivers of Provisions, Clothing, &c. be impowered to Receive untill the 1st day of January next.

Att a Town meeting Legally warned and held in Stonington the 4th day of march A. D. 1782. The same Day Paul Esqr. was Chosen Agent to meet a Committee at New London Appointed by ye General Assembly. Also Voted that the town will Raize & inlist a Guard for the Defense of long Point to Consist of Twelve Privates, Two Corporals & a Commander, such Persons as the Selectmen shall think proper to appoint to Commence from ye first of april next ensuing & to Continue till ye 1st of December next unless soner Dischargd. Also Voted that the Commander of the Guard shall have three Pounds Pr month, the Corporals 45s Pr month & the Privates 40s Pr month to be paid when Discharged.

Att a Town meeting Legally Warned and held in Stonington April 8th, 1782. Also Voted that the Soldiers Ordered to be Raized by the Assembly to fill up the Continental army shall have a Bounty of £10.00 Lawful money, Three pounds of sd Bounty to be paid down upon their enlistment or Detachment and the Remaining Seven Pounds ye Selectmen is Ordered to give their Security to the Soldiers inlisted or Detached to be paid when their time Expires & said Rate was Granted & ordered to be Collected immediately for that purpose. Also Voted that Mr. Henry Minor & Mr. Jno. Denison at point be a Committee to hire the money that ye town has promis to pay down & the town is to pay them for their service and the money Borrowed or hird when Soldiers service Shall Expire which will be ye last of December next & sd meeting was Dissolved.

Att a town meeting Legally Warned and held in Stonington June 10th, 1782. The Same Day Col. James Rhodes was Chosen moderator of d meeting. The Same Day Mr. Gilbert Fanning was Chosen Agent to Defend in the Case against Jonathan Palmer Junr in a Suit against d township in the County Court. The same Day Mr. Henry Minor was chosen a Committee to inspect into the Classes that were Deficient in Raising their men for the Defense of their Guards at Horse neck & made His Report to the Selectmen to the ajournd town meet-

REVOLUTIONARY WAR.   59

ing which will be this day fortnight & said meeting was Adjourned to Mr. Fishes meeting house to the 24th of this instant June, 2 O'clock Afternoon.

At an adjourned Town Meeting Legally held this 24th June, 1782. The same Day Granted a Tax of one penny half penny Lawfull money upon the pound upon the Polls & Ratable Estate of the inhabitants of said town upon the List of 1781. The said Paul Wheeler Esqr. & Mr. Henry Minor was appointed a Committee to make a Settlement with the 9 month & 3 month Soldiers in Regard to making good their wages as heretofore promised by a former Vote of said Town & sd Committee to make Report of what they find due and the Selectmen are Directed to draw Orders upon the Town treasurer for the Balance due. Also Voted that Mr. Gallup may fill up his guard at long point out of d inhabitants on d Point. Also Voted that Mr. Gallup may draw Powder & Ball out of the town treasury; first take Esqr. Wheeler's directions in the matter.

Att a Town meeting legally Warned & held in Stonington Septemr 10th, 1782. The Same Day The Question was put whether the Town would or not Continue the Guards Stationed at Long point at the Expense of said town after said 10th of September. Passed in the Negative.

Att a Town meeting Legally warned & held in Stonington Decemr 9th, 1782, Capt. Akors Sheffield is appointed to take Care of the Guns, Stores, &c. at long Point. Paul Wheeler Esqr. & Mr. Henry Minor is Appointed a Committee to Settle With the three months men Respecting their wages.

I have no reliable information, showing how many of the patriot soldiers of Stonington, who entered their country's service, lost their lives on the battle fields of the American Revolution, or died from wounds or sickness while in their country's service. The companies and regiments to which they were assigned participated in nearly all of the great battles of the war, and some of them must have fallen, but no record shows that any of them deserted or turned traitor to freedom's cause.

Lieut. Enoch Stanton and his brother, Daniel Stanton, and Thomas Williams of this town, fell in the battle and massacre of Fort Griswold, Sept. 6th, 1781, and their cousins, Edward and Daniel Stanton of Stonington, were dangerously wounded in that inhuman massacre. They both rallied and recovered after long continued suffering.

WAR OF 1812.

Nothing of especial interest occurred in this town after the close of the Revolutionary war and the ratification and adoption of the Constitution of the United States, by a convention assembled at Hartford, Conn., by authority of the General Assembly of the State Jan. 9th, 1788, wherein this town was ably represented in the affirmative by its representatives, Nathaniel Miner Esq. and Dr. Charles Phelps, beyond the annual election of town officers and representatives to the General Assembly and laying of taxes to defray the cost of the Revolution, until the war clouds again appeared between the United States and Great Britain. The embargo acts of Congress, which were so severely denounced and resisted in the Courts of New England found active and influential defenders. In order to give force and expression to their views on that subject a town meeting was called and held in Stonington March 27th, 1809, which adopted a preamble and resolutions, denouncing all opposition to the embargo acts of Congress and all who did not approve of them, closing with an order to send a copy of their proceedings to the then President of the United States. The determination of the British government to impress American seamen into their service, and other belligerent acts on her part, led to several armed collisions and finally culminated in a declaration of war by the United States government against Great Britain, June 18, 1812. Very little had ever been done by the general government for the defense of our seacoast. Long Point since the close of the Revolution had materially increased in population and wealth. The General Assembly had incorporated the place into a Borough in 1801. Mystic was but a small village at the time, composed largely of enterprising, seafaring men. Before the embargo, the foreign trade of the town of Stonington was almost entirely with the West Indies, and generally productive of large gains. During the war, and especially after the spring of 1813, our seacoast was blockaded by a British squadron, which at first well nigh annihilated all our commerce, but a few grave, resolute, enterprising men ran the blockade and carried on business with New York. Privateers were fitted out and were successful in most cases in capturing English vessels. We lost the sloop "Fox" in 1813, which was taken by the privateer "Hero," fitted out at Mystic and manned by Stonington and Groton men. Other feats of heroism and successful daring, by Groton and Stonington men combined, took place on the ocean before the close of the war. During its first year England had her hands full with European conflicts, but in the spring of 1813 she managed to send a formidable fleet to our shores and blockaded Long Island Sound. Stonington Borough had received two eighteen pounders from the General government for the defense of the place. A battery had been erected there during the Revolution which had almost disappeared. But the inhabitants, with the guards stationed there, drafted from the militia of the State, had erected another battery, the north end of which terminated at the northeast corner of the Messrs. Atwood's silk manufacturing establishment. So apprehensive were the people of Stonington Borough that their village would be attacked and burned by the British fleet that they sought the aid of the State, and the Governor of Connecticut ordered detachments from the militia to be drafted and stationed there. There were six of these detachments of militia who served at Stonington Borough, four of which were commanded by Lieut. Horatio G. Lewis, one by Lieut. Samuel Hough, and one by Sergt. Peleg Hancox. On the 19th day of June, 1813, a portion of the British fleet, under the command of Commodore T. M. Hardy, approached New London, creating fearful apprehension on the part of the people of that place and Groton Bank. Memories of the battle and massacre at Fort Griswold, Sept. 6th, 1781, intensified the excitement and alarm. Brig. Gen. Jirah Isham, then in command, immediately summoned his brigade by orders borne by postriders, directed to the lieutenant colonels commanding the regiments of his brigade. The following is a copy of the order directed to Lieut. Col. Randall, then in command of the Thirtieth regiment, composed of eight companies of infantry, four from Stonington and four from North Stonington:

"To Lieut. Col. William Randall, commanding the 30th Regiment, 3rd Brigade, Conn. Militia:

"Sir—You will immediately on the receipt of this, order the regiment under your command to march to the defence of New London, Groton and vicinity, giving them notice to be armed and equipped according to law. Lose no time as those places are in such imminent danger of invasion as will admit of no delay.

"Headquarters at New London, June 19th, 1813.
"JIRAH ISHAM,
Brig. Gen. 3rd Brigade Commanding.
"By order of Geo. A. Perkins, Maj. 3rd Brigade."

Immediately on receipt of this order, Col. Randall, though living in the country and widely separated from his staff and from most of the officers of his regiment, acted with such energy and dispatch that his whole regiment paraded on Groton Bank the next morning, after marching nearly all night in a raging tempest to assemble and reach the place some fifteen miles away. The roll-call showed the presence of Lieut. Col. William Randall, First Maj. Nathan Wheeler, Second Maj. Nathan Pendleton, Adjutant Cyrus Williams, Paymaster Samuel Chapman, Quartermaster Latham Hull, Surgeon's Mate John Billings, Sergt. Maj. Nathan Smith, Quartermaster's Sergt. John P. Williams, Drum Maj. Augustus A. Williams, Fife Maj. Christopher Dewey, six captains (one absent, and one vacancy), seven lieutenants, eight ensigns, twenty-six sergeants, twenty-one corporals, two hundred and nine privates; total, three hundred and eighty-eight men. This muster of a regiment that made up a roll at its review, and dress parade in October following of only two hundred and forty-two men shows something of the spirit of our citizens and soldiers in the face of the threatened invasion, and of the confidence reposed in their commander. Col. Randall was a brave, efficient and energetic officer, and during the whole war commanded the Thirtieth regiment, who were proud of him and most cheerfully obeyed his orders under all circumstances.

The British fleet, after making a showy demonstration at the mouth of the Thames, went back to their anchorage ground in Gardner's Bay, relieving the inhabitants of Groton Bank and New London of their impending danger. Gen. Isham's brigade remained in camp at New London and Groton Bank for several days awaiting another demonstration from Commodore Hardy, who wisely kept his fleet at their old anchorage. On the morning of June 25th, Gen. Isham ordered the lieutenant colonels commanding each regiment of his brigade to detach about one half of the officers and men of their respective regiments to remain in service, the remainder thereof to be discharged and to return to their homes. In pursuance thereof, Col. Randall issued the following order:

"Regimental Orders, 30th Regiment, 3rd Brigade Conn. Millitia.

"I am directed by Brig. Gen. Jirah Isham to detach from the regiment under my command now in service at Groton Bank (omitting in said detachment the eighth company, who were from Stonington Borough, and were then needed for defense of that place), thus, 1 major, 1 adjutant, 1 quartermaster, 1 chaplain, 1 surgeon's mate, 2 captains, 2 lieutenants, 2 ensigns, 8 sergeants, 8 corporals, 120 privates, who are to remain in service until further orders.

Gen. Isham, after ordering Col. Randall to detach his officers and men as aforesaid, tendered to him, his subordinate officers and soldiers his warmest thanks for their "alacrity and unusual promptitude, manifested by them while disregarding the tempestuous state of the weather, they appeared in defence of the rights and sovereignty of their country, when threatened with immediate danger.

"Dated at headquarters, June 25th, 1813.

"WILLIAM RANDALL, Lieut.-Col. Commanding.

"By order Cyrus Williams, Adjutant."

Towards the end of June, 1813, Gen. Burbeck arrived in New London and assumed the military command of the district, which had been assumed by the general government. The troops then on duty probably did not exceed eight hundred men, and belonged to the militia of the State, and were under no orders but those of the Governor. The refusal of Connecticut to place her militia under the orders of the United States to be marched away from her protection to Canada and elsewhere had greatly vexed the general government, who had determined on a change. So Gen. Burbeck on the 12th day of July, 1813, in pursuance of an order from the Secretary of War, dismissed the whole force, and our Stonington men then on duty at New London returned to their homes, but General Burbeck did not dismiss the guard at Stonington then under the command of Lieut. Horatio G. Lewis. But the evacuation of Forts Griswold and Trumbull, without a man on duty to protect the property there, and at a time, too, when the British fleet in the Sound was largely augmented, created a panic, not only among the inhabitants over there but at Stonington, who felt the protection of a large force at New London and Groton Bank. By some underground communication the officers of the British squadron had learned of the discharge of our military force, and the next day the "Ramillies" and her consorts came up to the mouth of the harbor and saluted the panic stricken inhabitants with a tremendous cannonade. General Burbeck realizing the danger of the situation, on his own responsibility applied to the Governor for a temporary force, who authorized Maj. Gen. William Williams to call out as large a body of militia as emergencies should demand. But no additional requisition was made on Col. Randall for any more troops from Stonington. During the latter part of July, August and September, the British squadron were so much engaged in blockading the river Thames and the eastern approach of Long Island Sound through the Race, and in pursuing the Yankee privateers that vexed their commerce, that they did not molest the village of Stonington; but during October their threatening attitude alarmed the inhabitants, who petitioned the Governor under the approval of Brig. Gen. Burbeck, commanding the United States troops at New London, who in reply issued the following order:

"New Haven, 29 October, 1813.
"Col. William Randall, 30th Regiment of Militia:
"Sir—Pursuant to a request of certain inhabitants of the Town of Stonington, and of Brigadier Gen. Burbeck, commanding the United States troops at New London, I do hereby, in conformity to advice of the Council, direct you to detach from your Regiment one subaltern, two sergeants, two corporals, and twenty-six privates, for a guard at Stonington Point, to serve from the first day of November next to the 30th of the same month, inclusive, unless sooner discharged. Application must be immediately made to Brigadier-General Burbeck, at New London, for provisions, to whom also the subaltern commanding the detachment will apply for orders, and to whom he must make a report from time to time as he shall be directed.
"I am, Sir, your Obt. servant,
"JOHN COTTON SMITH, Capt. General."

Pursuant to the order of Governor Smith, Col. Randall detached the requisite number of men from his regiment, which he put under the command of Lieut. Horatio G. Lewis, and they served at Stonington Borough during the time ordered by the Governor, receiving their army rations from Gen. Burbeck of New London. During the winter months of 1813 and 1814 no alarming demonstrations were made by the enemy, but as soon as the spring opened of 1814, unusual activity was observed on their part, which became so formidable that another draft upon the militia was made for a detachment of forty-one men to be stationed at Stonington, under the command of Lieut. Horatio G. Lewis. This detachment served from May 31st to June 30th, 1814, when they were dismissed, and another detachment of forty-one men were drafted from the militia in the northern part of the State, took their places and served from June 29th to August 29th, 1814, when they were dismissed. This detachment was under the command of Lieut. Samuel Hough.

The war thus far had progressed with varying success. The navy of the United States had immortalized itself upon the ocean, while on the land our armies, though small in numbers, had performed prodigies of valor. The early part of this year was marked by some of the most momentous events of the world's history. Napoleon was overthrown after a fearful struggle and the treaty of peace at Fontainebleau, which was concluded April 4, 1814, between France and the allied powers of Europe, released the larger part of the British army from active service there; and as soon as the exigencies of the case would admit were transported to this country and employed against the United States. So all-pervading was the apprehension of an attack from the enemy on our seacoast that the captain-general of our State, in the early spring of 1814, issued orders to the militia, through their superior officers, as follows, viz.:

BRIGADE ORDERS.
"3d Brigade, Conn. Militia.

"Pursuant to orders and instructions from his Excellency the Commander in chief. The Brigadier General directs that an inspection be made without delay of the troops under your command, and you will see that they are in every respect prepared, as the law directs, for immediate service. If orders cannot be furnished to the respective Captains in season to have the inspection made on the first Monday in May next, it is the pleasure of the Captain General that the inspection may be performed by the commissioned officers at the dwellings of the men to prevent burdensome meetings of the militia. The Captain General relies with confidence on the zeal and fidelity of the several officers in the performance of the duty so essential at the present juncture. From the recent movements of the Hostile Squadron in our waters, there is reason to apprehend that further attempts will be made to invade the territory of the State, as well as to destroy the vessels in our harbor. For these reasons the Brigadier General is directed by his Excellency the Commander in Chief, to call upon all officers and soldiers, of the 3rd Brigade to hold themselves, in readiness to march at a moment's warning, completely equipped and furnished for immediate and actual service. The respective Lieut. Cols. Commandant of Regiments will immediately on the receipt of this, establish some suitable place, on the most elevated ground and as near the center of their Regiment, as possible, which they will provide at the expense of the state (for a signal to give notice to their men, in case of an alarm), several Tar Barrels to be raised one at a time on the end of a pole to be erected for that purpose, and burnt in succession as circumstances will require, the Barrels to be furnished with such a quality of tar and other articles as to burn the longest time practicable, and emit the largest quantity of fire and smoke, particularly the latter, if fired in the day time, and have them so arranged that fire may be put to them in a moment, and some proper officer must be entrusted with this duty residing near the spot. Let this be done without delay in each Regiment, and notice given as soon as possible to the brigadier of the place where these signals are erected, and also the names of the officers who are appointed to take charge of them. Should an alarm first come to the knowledge of the Brigadier, he will send expresses to the officer who has charge of the signal in these regiments whose services may be required, and the Commandant will do the like, in their respective regiments should the alarm first reach them, and should the signals be made at any time of day or night, the troops in the Regiment will forthwith and without further order, assemble at some alarm post (as near the southern limits of their Regiments as can be with convenience), to be previously designated by the respective commandants and notified in their orders, from which alarm posts (to be also communicated to the Brigadiers) the men will march as soon as a company or part of a company has assembled, to such point as the Commandant of Regiments shall direct, if they first notify the alarm, or as shall be directed by the brigadier, in case he gives notice, and in that case he will by express, at the same time he notifies the officer in charge of the signals, also gives notice to the colonel where to march his men. In addition to these signals a Capt. commanding artillery companies will, when the signals are made, immediately fire three alarm guns in quick succession.

"Given under my hand at New London this 28th day of April one thousand eight hundred and fourteen. "JIRAH ISHAM, Brigadier General.

"By order: George L. Perkins, Brig. Maj.

"To William Randall, Esq., Lieut. Col. Command 30 Regt. Militia, Stonington.

"General Jirah Isham:

"Sir—Your order of the 28th of April, 1814, came to hand the 9th of May, and I have given the necessary orders as therein directed. I have established the place for the signals near the dwelling-house of Maj. Nathan Wheeler, on what is called Grant's Hill, and have directed him to erect a pole and procure tar barrels to burn in case of alarm; who will also take charge of the signals and give notice to the Brigadier should an alarm take place in this Regiment and the quartermaster and quartermaster sergeant of the regiment will also attend to their orders and assist in giving the signals, and such other duties as circumstances may require. "WILLIAM RANDALL,

"Lieut. Col. Commanding 30th Reg. Conn. Militia.

"Dated at Stonington, May 15th, 1814.

By the 1st of July, 1814, the British squadron in Long Island Sound was largely augmented, and so imposing was their armament and so imminent was the danger of invasion, and so divided were the American people relative to the origin and mode of prosecuting the war, that President Madison, on the 8th of August, 1814, issued a proclamation calling an extra session of Congress.

The language of the proclamation indicates the danger apprehended by the President, for he said: "Whereas great and weighty matters claiming the consideration of the Congress of the United States form an extraordinary occasion for convening them," etc. The blockade of the harbors on the Connecticut coast was so close and effectual that it was almost impossible for an American vessel to leave or enter our ports, but now and then a privateer would slip by, or through the British fleet.

On the 30th of July, 1814, a privateer disguised as a merchant vessel, with a crew of fifty men, made her appearance in Long Island Sound, running in for the north shore. She was discovered, and a British barge, under the command of Midshipman Thomas Barret Powers, was dispatched in pursuit. Not knowing her true character, and seeing but a few men on deck, not more than were necessary for the navigation of the vessel, Powers pressed on for a prize. The wind being light he soon overhauled her, and when within short musket-range the men rushed upon deck, and Powers immediately took off his hat in token of surrender. A Dutchman among the crew without orders leveled his musket and shot Powers through the head, killing him instantly. The barge surrendered and was brought into Stonington Borough. The remains of the young midshipman were buried with military honors in the burial place now embraced in the Stonington cemetery. The Rev. Ira Hart, then chaplain of the Thirtieth regiment, delivered an appropriate address on the occasion, which was listened to with deep feeling, drawing tears from many an eye unused to weep.

This unfortunate young officer was but eighteen years of age, and great sympathy was manifested for his untimely end.

After peace took place with England, late in the summer of 1815, a grave and elderly gentleman came to Stonington and quietly took lodgings at the hotel kept by Capt. Thomas Swan. Soon after he arrived he inquired for the clergyman of the place, who was sent for and introduced. He then revealed to him his name and his mission, telling him that he had come all the way from England to visit the grave of his only son, and to thank him and other kind friends for the Christian burial extended to his dear boy. Mr. Hart, who was a man of strong sympathies, was deeply moved for his stranger friend, and procuring a carriage took him to the burial place of his son.

Before the British fleet left our waters, the Hon. Capt. Piget and his brother officers of the ship "Superb" erected a monument to the memory of the fallen midshipman. When the monument that marked the last resting place of his son came in view, he requested Mr. Hart to remain, as he wished to be alone by the grave. Slowly and with reverent steps he approached it, when, overpowered with the agony of his own sorrows, he fell upon the grave and wept with unrestrained emotion until the fountains of nature were exhausted. Composing himself at length, he rejoined Mr. Hart, who had witnessed his grief, when together they returned to the hotel. Before leaving Mr. Powers expressed himself in grateful terms for the kindness and consideration to his feelings which Mr. Hart had manifested, and warmly shook his hand at parting.

When the British fleet was seen in motion, sailing easterly, August 9th, 1814, the people of Stonington Borough did not believe that ships of such size would dare to venture in Fisher's Island Sound, on account of its water depth and reefs; but when those ships were seen coming in between Fisher's Island and the mainland their object became apparent, which was soon disclosed by a flag in charge of an officer from the ship "Pactolus," who approached the place in a boat, which was met by a boat from the shore which received this note from the officer in command of the fleet:

"His Majesty's Ship "Pactolus,"
9th of August, 1814, half-past 5 o'clock p. m.

"Not wishing to destroy the unoffending inhabitants residing in the town of Stonington, one hour is given them from the receipt of this to move out of town.

"T. M. HARDY, Captain H. B. M. Ship 'Ramillies.

"To the inhabitants of the Town of Stonington."

From the date of this communication it will appear that Commander Hardy was himself on board the "Pactolus" to direct the attack, the "Ramillies" then lying at anchor at the west of

Fisher's Island. The people assembled in great numbers to hear what was the word from the enemy, when the above was read aloud. The enemy in the barge lay upon their oars a few moments, probably to see the crowd and if some consternation might not prevail.

Whatever effect was produced, this we know, that Sir Thomas's unoffending inhabitants did not agree to give up the ship, though threatened by a force competent, in a human view, to destroy them, when compared with the present means of defense in their power. It was exclaimed from old and young, "We will defend." The male citizens, though duly appreciating the humanity of Sir Thomas in not wishing to destroy them, thought proper to defend their wives and their children, and, in many instances, all their property, and we feel a pleasure in saying that a united spirit of defence prevailed, and during the short hour granted us, expresses were sent to Gen. Cushing at New London and to Col. Randall, whose regiment resided nearest to the scene of danger. The detachment stationed here under Lieut. Hough was embodied; Capt. Potter residing within the Borough gave orders to assemble all the officers and men under his command that could be immediately collected. They cheerfully and quickly assembled, animated with the true spirit of patriotism. The ammunition of our two 18-pounders and 4-pounder was collected at the little breastwork erected by ourselves. The citizens of the Borough assisted by two strangers from Massachusetts manned the 18-pounders at the breastwork, and also the 4-pounder. One cause of discouragement only seemed to prevail, which was the deficiency of ammunition.

Whatever opinion the majority of the people of Connecticut might have expressed as to the propriety of declaring war with England in 1812, without adequate preparation for the same, when the war was declared, were united in defending their State from invasion of the enemy. But as soon as the British fleet were seen approaching Stonington harbor, Aug. 9th, 1814, then the tar barrel signals of danger were soon ablaze. Col. Randall ever on the alert, though living about five miles away, reached the Borough before dark and issued the following orders, which did not reach but a small number of his regiment, some of whom lived fifteen miles away from the Borough. It was the blazing tar barrels, so erected as to be seen all over the area of his regiment, that set the patriotism of his soldiers on fire, who rushed by every possible means of conveyance and on foot to the scene of conflict, eager to meet the enemy who they expected would land and before daylight of the 10th of August, the whole regiment, officers and soldiers, had reached the Borough.

The following is a copy of Col. Randall's order issued as aforesaid:

"To the 30th Regiment Connecticut Militia:

"In consequence of an attack on Stonington Borough, and in pursuance of orders received from the Brigadier, this Regiment is called into active service, and will assemble at the Public House of Oliver York forthwith, and officers and soldiers will attend to this order and warn others and assemble accordingly.

"Given under my hand at Stonington Borough this 9th day of August, 1814.

"WILLIAM RANDALL, Lieut. Col. Com."

The public house of Oliver York was situated on the southeast corner of the Wadawanuck Hotel grounds. Col. Randall's regiment had been mainly summoned by the tar barrel signals, and without stopping to form as companies went immediately to Stonington Borough, were organized out of reach of the enemy's guns and held in readiness to repel any landing that they might attempt.

The militia of the State of Connecticut at the time of the last war with England were organized with conformity to a law of Congress enacted in 1792, consisting of divisions, brigades, regiments, battalions, and companies. The eastern division of the State militia was at that time commanded by Maj. Gen. Williams, assisted by staff officers Maj. Francis Richards, Maj. Thomas Shaw Perkins, aides-de-camp; Lieut. Col. Coddington Billings, inspector; Robert Coit, quartermaster. The Third Brigade of said division was commanded by Brig. Gen. Jirah Isham, assisted by staff-officers Martin Lee, aide-de-camp; George L. Perkins, brigade major; Henry Wheat, quartermaster.

The Thirtieth regiment of said brigade was commanded by Lieut. Col. William Randall, and the following is a correct roll of the field and staff officers of said regiment and their attendants at the battle of Stonington, Aug. 10, 1814:

William Randall, lieutenant colonel; Nathan Wheeler, first major; Nathan Pendleton, second major; Henry Chesebro, adjutant; Samuel Chapman, quartermaster; Giles R. Hallam, paymaster; Ira Hart, chaplain; William

Lord, surgeon; John Billings, surgeon's mate; Nathan Smith, sergeant-major; John P. Williams, second sergeant-major; Augustus L. Babcock, drum-major; Christopher Dewey, fife-major; John Champlain, Henry Newgear, Giles Wheeler, Ira R. Wheeler, Nathan S. Pendleton, John Frink, Charles T. Hart, Thomas Brooks, waiters.

The following roll-copies of the eight companies of said regiment show the names of the men who responded to their country's call and marched to Stonington Borough to defend the place when attacked by the British fleet, Aug. 9th and 10th, 1814:

THIRTIETH REGIMENT.

First Company—Denison Noyes, captain; Reuben Palmer, Jr., lieutenant; Ephraim Williams, ensign; William S. Bradford, sergeant; George Sheffield, second sergeant; Joseph Noyes, 3rd sergeant; Isaac Wheeler, third, fourth sergeant; John Yeomans, Eleazer Wheeler, Jr., Perry Barber, Jr., corporals; Privates, John Davis, Charles Palmer, John Noyes, Samuel Holmes, Benjamin F. Stanton, Nathaniel M. Noyes, Peleg West, Constant Taylor, Samuel Chesebrough, 2nd, Thomas B. Stanton, Elihu Robinson, Charles P. Noyes, Elias Stanton, Stephen E. Stanton, Ezra Witter, John Dodge, Nathaniel Robinson, Paul Bradford, William Chesebrough, Ross Austin, Stiles Stanton, Jabez Swan.

Second Company.—Asa A. Swan, captain; Samuel Prentice, lieutenant; George W. Baldwin, ensign; Ephraim Meech, John Prentice, sergeants; John S. Hewitt, drummer; Elias Wheeler, fifer; Privates, Andrew Baldwin, Edward Coats, Jr., James Wheeler, Stephen P. Stewart, Avery Prentice, Coddington Swan, Samuel W. Prentice, Stephen Main, William Jackson, Christopher Avery 3rd, Joseph Ayer, Jr., Gurdon Chapman, Charles Church, Denison Swan, Sanford Brown, Eldridge Whipple, John Wilkinson, Levi Meech, Gardner Morey, John Stewart, Thomas Davidson.

Third Company.—Jesse Breed, captain; William Frink, lieutenant; Dudley Brown, ensign; Daniel Bentley, Perez Wheeler, Roswell R. Avery, Ralph R. Miner, sergeants; Elias Miner, Isaac Burdick, corporals; Privates, Asa Baldwin, Jr., Prentice Cook, Jonas Breed, Roswell Breed, Samuel Frink, Stephen Babcock, Roswell Breed, Thomas Hinckley, Jr., Simeon Baldwin, Roswell Brown, Oliver Miner, William Crandall, John Davis, Oliver Denison, Peleg L. Barber, James Bliven, John Breed, Oliver Wheeler, William S. Frink, Benjamin F. Frink, Christopher Bill, Shepherd Brown, Thomas B. Miner, David Bromley, Peleg Wheeler, Cyrus W. Brown, Samuel Clark (drummer), Charles P. Randall, Jesse Breed, Jr., Pitts D. Frink.

Fourth Company.—John W. Hull, captain; Silas Chesebrough, ensign; Henry Grant, Russell Wheeler, Elias Hewitt, Jr., sergeants; David Coats, Gilbert Miner, John D. Gallup, corporals; Joshua Clark, fifer; Stephen Wilcox, drummer; Privates, John Breed, Ezra Stanton, Denison Miner, William Coggswell, Elijah Kenyon, James Holmes, Jr., Dudley Denison, Gilbert Brown, Luther Miner, Ansel Coates, Moses Palmer, Coddington Brown, John L. Berry, Obadiah Mathewson, William Alexander, Robert Miner, Caleb Green,

Nathan Stanton, Sanford Brown, Elias Irish, Joseph Tift, Benjamin F. Breed, William Chesebrough.

Fifth Company.—John Hyde, lieutenant; Noyes Palmer, ensign; Joseph D. Mason, Daniel Hobart, William Bailey, sergeants; William Wheeler, Jonathan Wheeler, corporals; Edwin Lewis, drummer; Privates, Amos Miner, Amos Gallup, Jr., Andrew Chesebrough, Amos Chesebrough, Andrew Denison, Cyrus Peckham, Daniel Wheeler, Daniel Mason, Elisha Frink, Elisha Brown, Elam Denison, Edward C. Williams, Frederick Denison, Frederick Denison 2nd, Gilbert Williams, Hazard Holmes, Henry Denison, Henry Lewis, Isaac Morgan, Jeremy Crandall, Jabez Gallup, John Leroy, John Miner, Justin Denison, John Bennet, Jesse Wheeler, Nathaniel Lewis, Noyes Lewis, Paul Miner, Robert Fellows, Samuel Stanton, Jr., Samuel Wheeler, Thomas Leeds, Theophilus Rogers, Gilbert Wheeler, Franklin Chesebrough, Franklin Palmer.

Sixth Company.—Daniel Carr, Gideon Chapman, Nathan Chapman, Henry Babcock, Moses Thompson, Jr., Simeon Pendleton, sergeants; Reuben York, Cyrus Palmer, corporals; Privates, Horace Grant, Henly Grant, Julius Palmer, James York, Jr., Andrew Breed, Charles Chapman, Elias Chapman, Sanford Chapman, Palmer Chapman, Freeman Pierce, Lewis Chapman, Amos Chapman, Robert Thompson, Jesse Chapman, Reuben Chapman, John Grey, Jr., Luke C. Reynolds, Gershom Breed, Robert Palmer, Jeffrey Chapman, Zebulon York, Amos Thompson, George L. Chapman, Thomas Geer, Ezra Geer, George Geer, Jr., Lyman Wilcox, Noah Wilcox, Elisha Coon, John W. Ecclestone, Rowland Ecclestone, Amos Maine, 2nd, Elijah Perry, Simeon P. Kenyon, Joshua H. Thompson, Israel Palmer, Jr., Joseph Burton, Daniel Palmer, Richard Slocum.

Seventh Company.—Daniel Miner, 2nd, captain; Amos Holmes, lieutenant; Phineas Wheeler, ensign; Thomas Partelo, Chandler Maine, Jesse Maine, sergeants; Joshua Brown, Avery Brown, Prentice Holmes, Benadam Palmer, corporals; Arnold Crumb, drummer; Privates, James Brown, Latham Brown, Sanford Brown, Joshua Brown 3rd, Matthew Brown, Peter Eldredge, Jonathan Allen, Jr., Isaac Partlo, Jonas Partlo, Samuel Maryott, Amos Brown, Cyrus L. Park, Gurdon Ingraham, J. Ross Burdick, Isaac R. Taylor, John Allen, Allen Wheeler, Nathan York, John Main, Daniel Dewey, John Brown, Beriah Lewis, Royal Main, Joseph Kennedy, Nathan Kenyon, James Crandall, Joseph Holmes, Shepard Wheeler, Rufus Wheeler.

Eighth Company.—William Potter, captain; Horatio G. Lewis, lieutenant; Daniel Frink, ensign; Francis Amy, Charles H. Smith, Peleg Hancox, sergeants; Gurdon Trumbull, Azariah Stanton, Jr., Junius Chesebrough, Joshua Swan, Jr., corporals; Privates, Phineas Wilcox, Hamilton White, Henry Wilcox, Nathan Wilcox, Samuel Burtch, Jonathan Palmer, Andrew P. Stanton, James Stanton, Thomas Breed, Amos Loper, Samuel Bottum, Jr., Benjamin Merritt, Elihu Chesebrough, Jr., Christopher Wheeler, Amos Hancox, Zebediah Palmer, Nathaniel Waldron, Thomas Spencer, Nathaniel M. Pendleton, Simon Carew, Elisha Faxon, Jr., Ebenezer Halpin, Asa Wilcox, Jr., Warren Palmer, Joseph Bailey, Jr., Nathaniel Lewis.

The day after the battle the following orders were issued by the commanding officer:

"Headquarters, Aug. 11, 1814.

"Sir—By order of the Gen. commanding you will detach one company of (about 30 men) from the regiment under your command to stand guard at or near the bridge during the night, from which a patrolling party will be kept out, and be relieved from time to time. The party will be extended about one mile from the west end of the bridge to give information of the movements of the enemy, and communicate the same to headquarters.

"By order GEORGE L. PERKINS, Brig. Maj.

"To Col. William Randall, 30th Regt."

"Headquarters, Stonington, Aug. 12th, 1814.

"Sir—By order of the Gen. commanding, you will please detach Maj. Wheeler, of the 30th Regt., to take command of the guards to be stationed conformable to the enclosed order, which you will please hand to him, at the same time direct that he repair to this place at an early period for the above purpose.

"Major Wheeler will not neglect to station the said detachment before sun-setting, and report from time to time during the night, as is required by the enclosed order directed to Lieut.-Col. Tracy, of the 20th Regiment.

"GEO. L. PERKINS, Maj. Brig.

"Lieut.-Col. Wm. Randall, 30th Regt."

"Sir—The General commanding has directed Col. William Belcher to furnish forty men to be put under your command for the purpose of extinguishing fires. You can call on him for the whole or any part of that number of men at any time when they are required.

By order: MARTIN LEE, Aide-de-Camp.

"Capt. William Potter.

"August 12, 1814."

There have been several accounts of the battle of Stonington written and published, none of which gave as an accurate description thereof as the letter addressed by the Hon. Amos Palmer of Stonington to the Secretary of War at Washington, D. C., which was as follows:

"Stonington Borough, Aug. 21, 1815.

"To the Hon. William H. Crawford, Secretary of War:

"Sir—The former Secretary of War put into my hands as chairman of the committee of defence, the two eighteen-pounders and all the munitions of war that were here belonging to the general government, to be used for the general defence of the town, and I give my receipt for the same. As there is no military officer here, it becomes my duty to inform you of the use we have made of it. That on the 9th of Aug. last (year) the "Ramillies," seventy-four, the "Pactolus" forty-four, the "Terror" bomb-ship, and the "Despatch," gun-brig anchored off the harbor. Com. Hardy sent a boat with a flag, we met him with another from the shore, when the officer of the flag handed me a note from Com. Hardy informing us that one hour was given to the unoffending inhabitants before the town would be destroyed.

"We returned to the shore, where all the male inhabitants were collected. When I read the note aloud, they all exclaimed they would defend the place to the last extremity, and if it was destroyed they would be buried in the ruins.

"We repaired to the small battery that we had hove up; nailed our colors to the flag-staff. Others lined the shore with their muskets. About seven in the evening they put off five barges and a large launch, carrying from thirty-two to nine-pound carronades in their bows, and opened fire from their shipping with bombs, carcasses, rockets, round grape and canister shot, and sent their boats to land under cover of their fire. We let them come within small grape distance, when we opened our fire upon them from our two eighteen-pounders with round and grape shot. They soon retreated out of grape distance and attempted a landing on the east side of the village. We dragged a six-pounder that we had mounted over and met them with grape, and all our muskets opened fire on them. So they were willing to retreat the second time. They continued their fire till eleven at night. The next morning at seven o'clock, the brig "Despatch" anchored within pistol shot of our battery and they sent five barges and two large launches to land under cover of their whole fire (being joined by the "Nimrod," twenty-gun brig). When the boats approached within grape distance we opened our fire on them with round and grape shot. They retreated and came round the east side of the town. We checked them with our six-pounder and muskets till we dragged over one of our eighteen-pounders. We put in it a round shot and about forty or fifty pounds of grape, and placed it in the center of their boats as they were rowing up in a line and firing on us. We tore one of their boats all in pieces, so that two, one on each side, had to lash her up to keep her from sinking. They retreated out of grape distance, and we turned our fire upon the brig and expended all our cartridges but five, which we reserved for the boats if they made another attempt to land. We then lay four hours, being unable to annoy the enemy in the least, except from muskets on the brig, while the fire from the whole fleet was directed against our buildings. After the third express from New London, some fixed ammunition arrived. We then turned our cannon on the brig, and she soon cut her cable and drifted out. The whole fleet then weighed and anchored nearly out of reach of shot, and continued this and the next day to bombard the town. They set the buildings on fire in more than twenty places, and we as often put them out. In the three days' bombardment they sent on shore sixty tons of metal and strange to say, wounded only one man. We have picked up fifteen tons, including some that was taken up out of the water and the two anchors that we got. We took up and buried four poor fellows that were hove overboard out of the sinking barge.

"Since peace, the officers of the "Dispatch" brig have been on shore here. They acknowledged they had twenty-one killed and fifty wounded, and further say, had we continued our fire any longer, they would have surrendered for they were in a sinking condition, for the wind then blew from the southwest directly into the harbor. Before the ammunition arrived it shifted around to the north, and blew out of the harbor. All of the shot suitable for the cannon we have reserved. We have now more eighteen-pound shot than was sent us by the government. We have put the two cannon in the arsenal and housed all the munitions of war.

"AMOS PALMER."

Major Gen. Williams of Stonington, living in New London at the time, isssued an order to Brig. Gen. Jirah Isham to call out his brigade for the defense of Stonington, which was immediately done.

The following is a copy of the order issued by him to Col. Randall, of the Thirtieth regiment, which did not reach him until long after he had issued his orders and nearly all of his regiment had reached the scene of trouble:

"New London, Aug. 9th, 1814, half past eight P. M.
"Lieut. Col. Wm. Randall, Com. of the 30th Regt. 3rd Brigade Conn. Militia:

"Sir,—Pursuant to orders from the Major General of the 3rd Division, you will immediately call your Regt. into service in addition to the signals to be given at your signal pole (if not already done), you will use every exertion to get all your Regt. out as soon as possible and march them immediately to Stonington Point, that place being in imminent danger of invasion. Lose no time.

"Yours Respectfully,
"JIRAH ISHAM, Brig. Gen. 3rd Brigade."

The battle of Stonington was not a victory for the British fleet. They doubtless intended to burn the place, in fact they declared that, having ample means in their possession, they would destroy it and that they did not, was owing to the bravery of its defenders. From some unaccountable neglect on the part of the authorities of the State or Nation there were not a dozen rounds of ammunition for our cannon on hand at the time of the attack. It seems almost incredible that a place as much exposed as the Borough, with a succession of military detachments detailed for its protection, with three cannon and a battery erected for defense, should all have been provided without ammunition for an hour's fight. But so it was and but for the powder obtained from New London during the bombardment, and some gathered from Capt. George Fellows and others, our battery with its guns would have been well-nigh useless. Sergt. Maj. Nathan Smith, then residing in the Borough, communicated to Col. Randall the approach of the hostile fleet, who gave the alarm through his signals on Grant's Hill, and hastened to the Borough with all the men he could rally on his way, some five miles.

Capt. William Potter, then in command of the Eighth company of the Thirtieth regiment, immediately assembled all of his command in reach, consisting of twenty-one men, including officers, out of a roll of thirty-four men. He joined Lieut. Hough with his detachment, numbering forty-two men, which added to the militia under the command of Col. Randall, assisted by a number of volunteers, defended the place as best they could during the evening of August 9th until nearly midnight, when the enemy ceased firing; and but for the spirited resistance that the barges and launches received from the militia and volunteers under the command of Col. Randall, the enemy would have landed and burned the place. During the remainder of the night a large part of Col. Randall's regiment, observing the signals, hastened to the place, and before the break of day two hundred and twenty-seven men, including officers, had reached headquarters, and were assigned to their respective companies, which, added to Capt. Potter's and Lieut. Hough's men, aggregated a force of two hundred and ninety men, not including Col. Randall's staff. Thus marshalled they awaited the coming day, and at the early dawn of Aug. 10th another attempt was made by the enemy to land from their barges and launches, coming around on the east side of the Borough, firing shot and shell into the place. As soon as the approach of the enemy was discovered some of the volunteers drew the four-pounder across the Point to prevent the enemy from landing. Col. Randall, observing the movement of the enemy, ordered his whole force down to the lower end of the Point to meet them, and when he reached the battery he ordered a detachment of his men and the volunteers who were acting under military orders to draw one of the eighteen-pounders across the town, so as to repel the apprehended landing. The gun was manned and directed by **Ensign Daniel Frink**, of Capt. Potter's company, and so well was it handled that the enemy was compelled to recede and seek safety in flight. The prompt assembling of Col. Randall's regiment and their presence at this moment prevented the enemy from attempting another landing during the bombardment of the place.

This attempt of the enemy to attack the village on the east side thereof was designed to effect a landing there and burn the place, the result of which was so well described by Mr. Amos Palmer in his letter to the then Secretary of War, that I will not attempt to repeat it. The battery was manned by volunteers, some of which belonged to the militia, some were sea-faring men and others residents of the town.

It is difficult to say at this distance of time from the battle, how many men actually entered the battery and handled the guns on the 9th and 10th of August, 1814, or how many and who assisted in bringing ammunition to them in the battery, or making cartridges for their use. From the best attainable information on hand the Stonington Borough men were: Capt. George Fellows, Capt. William Potter, Lieut. Horatio G. Lewis, Ensign Daniel Frink, Alexander G. Smith, Amos Denison, Jr., Elihu Chesebrough, Jr., Rev. Jabez S. Swan, Luke Palmer, George Palmer, Thomas Wilcox and Asa Lee.

The Mystic men were Silas E. Burrows, Capt. Jeremiah Holmes, Capt. Jeremiah Haley, Frederick Denison, Capt. Nathaniel Clift, Capt. Simeon Haley, Isaac Denison, Ebenezer Denison, and Frederick Haley. From the rural districts of Stonington were John Miner, Jesse Dean, John Dean Gallup, Charles T. Stanton, Charles P. Wheeler, and Jonathan Denison, who refused to enter the battery, but fought the enemy from the shore with his musket at long range.

The Groton men were Ebenezer Morgan, Stanton Gallup, Alfred White, Frank Daniels, Giles Moran; the New London men were Maj. Simeon Smith, Capt. Noah Lester, Maj. N. Frink and Lambert Williams; the Massachusetts men were Capt. Leonard, Wm. G. Bush, and Mr. Dunham, and no doubt others. The fire from the battery on the 9th was under the command of Capt. George Fellows, and under the command of Capt. Jeremiah Holmes on the 10th of August. Both were brave men and true. Capt. Holmes' three years' service on board of a British man-of-war, the greater part of which he served as captain of a gun, enabled him to direct the guns in the battery with great precision. He double-shotted the eighteen-pounders, and sent the shot plunging through the brig below her water lines. There were other volunteers who rendered important services in extingishing fires, and in other ways, which the government has recognized, and granted to the participants land warrants under a law of Congress enacted in 1856, viz.: Henry Smith, Benjamin T. Ash, Pitts D. Frink, William C. Moss, Charles R. Randall, and Jesse Breed, and perhaps others.

Edward Stanton, a Revolutionary hero, who was fearfully and dangerously wounded at Fort Griswold, Sept. 6, 1781, living some five miles away from the scene of action, immediately on hearing the first gun, took his trusty musket and marched for the Borough, saying, with emphasis, that he had shed a part of his blood for his country in the Revolution, and if necessary was fully prepared to shed the last drop of it in defense of his country.

It was plainly evident that the enemy were determined to burn the village of Stonington, not only from the declared purpose of Capt. Hardy, but from the use of rockets and carcasses in the bombardment. In order to prevent the consummation of this purpose, Col. Randall, on the evening of the 9th, detached Charles H. Smith, then the second sergeant of Capt. Potter's company (and afterwards its captain), and twenty men of the regiment to follow up and extinguish all the fires that might be kindled by the missiles of the enemy. This service was bravely and efficiently done, and a large number of fires extinguished. This duty was as perilous as a place in the battery. It is to be regretted that a list of these brave men has not been preserved. They were daily relieved by detachments taking their places. Gen. Isham and staff arrived from New London about noon, August 10th, and took command, fixing his headquarters at the dwelling house of Capt. Nathaniel Palmer. Col. Randall's headquarters were at the hotel of Oliver York, that stood on the southeast corner of the Wadawanuck Hotel grounds. The glory of the battle of Stonington cannot all be showered upon the men who worked the guns in the battery, though they immortalized themselves by their heroic conduct and Spartan bravery. Col. Randall, his staff, and the officers and men of his regiment for their prompt and energetic behavior in meeting and repelling the enemy's boats in their efforts to land and burn the place on the evening of the 9th and the morning of the 10th of August, entitles them to the highest honors. Especially should that brave band of soldiers who watched the carcasses and rockets in their fiery circles, and extinguished them before they could kindle a flame be remembered with everlasting gratitude. To every one who participated in the defense of Stonington in August, 1814, Stonington cheerfully awards a full measure of praise, and will cherish their memory and gratefully appreciate their heroic services.

A HEROINE.—An elderly lady, by the name of Huldah Hall, lived at Stonington Borough during the last war with England. She was in feeble and rapidly declining health, when Capt. Hardy, on the 9th of August, 1814, gave one hour's notice for the unoffending inhabitants of the place to be removed. She was attended by an only daughter bearing her name, who had been her sole companion during her weary declining years. During the excitement and alarm caused by Capt. Hardy's order, and the hasty departure of the unoffending, there were no efforts made for the removal of Mrs. Hall. Nor is it certain that she was able to be removed at the time, if an effort for that purpose had been made. The house occupied by Mrs. Hall stood close in the rear of the battle, and was dangerously exposed to the shot and shell of the enemy. During the evening of the 9th of August it became apparent that Mrs. Hall was rapidly sinking, doubtless hastened by the bombardment of the place, and on the 10th of August, amid the thunders of the bombardment and the deafening roar of the guns in the battery, she breathed her last. Beside her bed during all of the excitement and dangers of battle stood the brave-hearted daughter, tenderly watching with loving ministrations her dying mother, though shot and shell crushed through the house, and through the room where they were. No sooner was life extinct than the daughter, throwing a light shawl over her head, went down to the battery amid the flying shot and shell to get assistance to remove and bury her mother. When seen approaching by the men in the battery they were awe-struck, trembling for her safety, though reckless of their own. When informed of her errand, four men were detached and went with her to the house, carefully and tenderly inclosed her remains in the bed and bed-clothes where she lay and bore her to the old Robinson burial place, in the Borough, attended by the daughter. In a deep cut made by the explosion of a bomb-shell, without any form or ceremony, except the thunders of the bombardment, they buried her remains. While cheerfully awarding the highest honors to the men who so bravely defended Stonington, let us drop a tear to the memory of this heroic child, believing that the viewless artists of the skies have woven for her garlands of immortal glory.

In pursuance of the order of Maj. Gen. William Williams issued August 9, 1814, addressed to, and directing Brig. Gen.

Jirah Isham to call out his brigade, which consisted of four regiments, comprising all of the infantry militia of New London County, to march to Stonington Borough forthwith, for its defense, which order was immediately complied with by Gen. Isham, and all four regiments assembled at Stonington Borough as soon as possible. Col. Randall's Thirtieth regiment assembled before the break of day Aug. 10th. The Eighth regiment, commanded by Lieut. Col. William Belcher, was the next on the ground. The Thirty-third regiment, commanded by Lieut. Col. Asa Comstock, and the Twentieth regiment, commanded by Lieut. Col. Charles Thomas, living remote from the Borough, was notified by post riders, and came as soon as possible. No railroads or telegraphs were then in existence and much more time was then required to assemble two regiments at Stonington Borough from the northern and western towns of our County than now, but they came as soon as notified, by teams and on foot, ready and eager to meet and repulse the enemy. These four regiments remained on duty at the Borough until they were dismissed by order of Gen. Isham (except a few drafted men) as follows: The Twentieth regiment was dismissed on Tuesday, the 27th of August, 1814; the Eighth regiment was dismissed on Wednesday, the 24th inst.; the Thirty-third regiment was dismissed on Thursday, the 26th inst.; the Thirtieth regiment was dismissed Friday, the 26th inst.; the brigade and regimental staff was dismissed on Saturday the 27th inst.

The British fleet did not again attempt to destroy the village of Stonington Borough during the war, but an apprehension on the part of the people of the place that they might again do so, caused them to apply to Col. Randall for another detachment of militia to act as guard, and he complied with their request and detached Sergt. Peleg Hancox with fourteen men from Capt. Potter's company, who served from Sept. 27th to Nov. 15th, 1814. Peace with Great Britain came in February, 1815, and with it unusual prosperity. In celebrating the event, a young man by the name of Thomas Stanton, of Pawcatuck, was instantly killed at Stonington Borough by the premature discharge of a cannon, which was being fired in honor of peace.

WAR OF 1861-5.

Stonington was largely interested in commerce before the war of 1812, which revived after its close. Manufacturing was introduced and successfully pursued on a large scale in the State of Connecticut, this town having a full share. Nothing of importance beyond the yearly routine of town and State elections, with a Presidential election every four years, happened in our midst to attract particular attention, until the Mexican war. But that did not materially affect our interests, it only served to stimulate the politics of the day. Later on the acquisition of territory, resulting from the war, brought to the surface again the irrepressible conflict between slavery and freedom. The conflict of opinions between the North and South began to assume a more violent form and finally culminated in open rebellion by the slave-holding states. After the election of Abraham Lincoln, as President of the United States in 1860, the slave-holding states began to secede. This town favored the restoration of the Union by coercive measures and sent to our armies many of our best and bravest sons. The following list shows the Stonington Roll of Honor:

INFANTRY.

First Regiment.

Company G.—James B. Anderson.

Second Regiment.

Rifle Company B.—Peter McEwen.
Rifle Company C.—James H. Latham, William W. Latham, Herbert E. Maxson, Theodore C. Smith, Robert P. Wilbur.

Third Regiment.

Rifle Company D.—Charles J. Edwards.

Fifth Regiment.

Company G.—Albert L. Gavitt (sergeant), George W. Wilcox, Albert C. Burdick, Albert C. Andrews, John C. Briggs, Charles C. Brightman, George Bedford, William H. Noyes (pro. to 1st lieut.), Isaac E. Norman, Frank Vanauken, Francis Alrey.

Company K.—Joseph N. Banks, Edward L. Cordner, John H. Nye, Erastus O. Smith, Nathaniel P. Wolfe.

Eighth Regiment.

Company D.—Horace Burton.

Company E.—Thomas D. Sheffield (pro. to lieut. col.), Lafayette Starr.

Company G.—1st. Lieut. Thomas D. Sheffield (pro. to captain), Henry E. Morgan, 2nd lieut. (pro. 1st lieut.); Sergeants Andrew M. Morgan (pro. capt.); Joseph C. Langworthy; Corporals Leonidas A. Barter, William H. Lamphere, Francis V. D. Sloan, Thos. C. Curtis, John H. Smith, Oscar W. Hewitt, John B. Averill, Franklin H. Crumb, James A. Peabody, Isaac Allen, George H. Barney, Charles Baird, Thomas Bedford, Henry Brannan, Thomas Brannan, Sanford P. Burdick, Horace Burton, David S. Bryant, Thomas Casey, Charles W. Clark, William P. Clark, Patrick Conlon, Ethan A. Collins, James P. Conlon, Charles H. Culver, Benjamin Crossley, Alpheus G. Davis, Alfred Dixon, Oliver A. Eccleston, Albert S. Edwards, Charles J. Edwards, John L. Edwards, George W. Foster, Marius E. French, Edward Gavin, Denis Geary, Wm. Geary, Charles W. Hall, Henry Hallam, Hazzard Holland, James E. Holdredge, Francis Jager, Henry G. Knowles, Charles D. Lamphear, Clark F. Lamphear, Wm. Lamphear, Michael Lombard, Thomas H. Lord, John McCarthy, Franklin Mason, John M. Maynard, Erastus D. Miner, Joseph D. Nye, Stephen F. Nye, Jerome A. Palmer, Wm. R. Palmer, Wm. H. Potter, David W. Price, Jr., Wm. Reed, Ebenezer Rose, Patrick Shay, Horace Slocum, Henry Staplin, George H. Shepard, Charles Stebbins, Wm. Terwilliger, Nehemiah D. Tinker, George Usher, Charles B. Wilcox, John Walker, Wm. D. Wilcox, Edward Willis, John F. Cory, Courtland H. Durfee, Michael Farley, John C. Knowles, Benjamin A. Kempton, Ebenezer Rose, Ebenezer Rose, Jr., George Randall, Jr., Barney Sisson, Henry E. Wells, John Miner, Joseph Milners, Wm. C. Macomber.

Ninth Regiment.

Company G.—Oswald Reed, Thomas McGregor.
Company H.—Corporal Dudley Lewis.

Tenth Regiment.

Company F.—Samuel Bentley.
Company H.—William Pond.

Twelfth Regiment.

Company K.—1st Lieut. James D. Roach (pro. capt.); Sergeants William B. Lucas, George W. Stedman (pro. 1st lieut.); Stanton Allyn, Gurdon Green, Patrick Barnes, Charles W. Bicknell, Cornelius Burgoyne, William Butterworth, Ori E. Chapman, Levi A. Clarke, Charles H. Comstock, Edmund Congdon, James Crowley, Nathan Davis, George Fitzgerald, Richard Lever, John Lucy, Felix McArdle, Hugh McColligan, John Murphy, Henry B. Pinney, Michael Ryan, William H. Reynolds, William Scott.

Thirteenth Regiment.

Company K.—Clarence D. Payne, John E. Wheelock.

WAR OF 1861-5.   83

Fourteenth Regiment.

Company A.—William Brown, Charles F. Chester, George H. Snyder.
Company B.—Thomas Holt, George Harris.
Company D.—Andrew Lovejoy, James Needham.
Company E.—Samuel Steele.
Company F.—Michael Henderson.
Company G.—Thomas Kain, George W. Starr.
Company H.—Charles Duncan, Charles E. Jones, John McDonald.
Company I.—1st Lieut. William Thompson.
Company K.—Corporal Paul P. Noyes, Frank Coleman.

Eighteenth Regiment.

Company K.—John Loonnun, George Williams.

Twentieth Regiment.

Company A—Joseph Lombra.
Company G.—Maurice L. Nunan.

Twenty-first Regiment.

Company E.—Capt. Charles T. Stanton, Jr. (pro. maj.); 1st Lieut. Henry R. Jennings; 2nd Lieut. Franklin H. Davis; Sergeants James B. Vanderwater, James H. Carter, Howard E. Miner, John F. Trumbull (pro. 1st lieut.), Walter P. Long (pro. capt.); Corporals Seth Slack, John L. Hill, William R. Targee, Jr., Charles H. Crumb, Nelson Wilcox, John J. McMillen, Joseph H. Newberry, Erastus Holmes, Charles G. Avery, Jesse Bennett, William C. Burdick, Oliver A. Brown, Alfred L. Burdick, Joseph L. Burdick, Denison Brightman, Joseph W. Carpenter, William W. Crandall, William Conway, Charles L. Cordner, William Dunham, John C. Douglas, Samuel Denison, Elias N. Davis, George W. Eldridge, George Ecclestone, George W. Frazier, Jr., William H. Frazier, Arvin A. Frazier, Lewis H. Gerry, Lyman Green, William Gardner, John Hevy, Amos F. Heath, William F. Hancox, Amos S. Hancox, Albert F. Harris, Joseph E. Harrington, Palmer Hulet, Ranson Jackson (pro. 1st lieut.), Robert Kulbert, Leonard O. Lamphere, Richard Lever, Patrick H. Mulligan, Benedict W. Morgan, Charles L. Miner, Francis J. Musgrave, George R. Newberry, Nathan Noyes, Wait W. Ridabock, George Root, William H. Robinson, Henry D. Smith, Gardner B. Smith, Charles Smith, Daniel D. Tift, John L. Tift, Frederick O. Tucker, Charles H. Taylor, Abram Vanauken, Leonard Wilcox, Harlan H. Wilcox, Rufus C. White, Charles H. Williams.
Company F.—Stafford Holland.
Company G.—Robert Sutcliff.
Company H.—Charles F. Brown.
Company K.—Alexander Buchanan.

Twenty-sixth Regiment.

Company H.—Capt. David Champlin; 1st Lieut. John F. Jencks; 2nd Lieut. Samuel K. Tillinghast (pro. 1st lieut.); Sergeants Henry H. Packard, John H. Morgan, Thomas W. Grace, William M. Sherman, Thomas W. Gardiner; Corporals George E. Brayton, Frank W. Gard, Jacob R. Lockwood, Charles H. Burdick, George D. Edwards, Charles Bennett (2), George H. Burgess, Andrew

H. Brown, Elias L. Maynard, Pardon L. Babcock, John R. Prentice, Erastus D. Appleman, Elias Babcock, Jr., Richard A. Brown, Horace F. Burdick, Amos D. Barnes, Thomas H. Brown, Orville M. Briggs, Henry L. Babcock, Amos A. Crandall, Joseph W. Coleman, Thomas Crowley, William F. Eccleston, Samuel R. Eccleston, Alexander B. Frazier, Charles H. Gladding, John E. Holberton, Shubael Holmes, Philip A. Irons, George A. Latham, Christopher A. Lyman, James A. Lord, David S. Merritt, John C. Moore, Stephen D. Merritt, Jr., Charles A. Miller, John M. Mosher, Samuel M. Macomber, John Nye, Avery E. Parks, Chauncey D. Rice, Elisha K. Rathbun, Edwin N. Shirley, Nathan S. Sheffield, James W. Targee, Warren P. Thompson, James O. Thompson, Charles W. Taylor, Thaddeus M. Weems.

Twenty-ninth Regiment.

Company D.—Isaac J. Hill.
Company H.—Isaac H. Antone.

Thirtieth Regiment.

Company A.—Corp. Courtland Thomas, Henry Demarist, James W. Darrell, George Fisher.
Company B.—Henry Hall.
Company C.—Augustus Jackson.

ARTILLERY..
First Regiment.

Company C.—Ichabod B. Slates, Chas. E. Staplis.
Company D.—Courtland F. Hall, Joseph H. Pendleton, John P. Trant.
Company F.—John Merklee.
Company G.—Elias Babcock, Jr., Dennis S. Gillmore, James McCaffery, Hiram P. Shaw.
Company H.—George Walker.
Company I.—2nd Lieut. William C. Faxon (pro. capt.).

Second Regiment.

David Bradford.

CAVALRY.
First Regiment.

Company C.—Capt. William S. Fish (pro. col.); 1st Lieut. Charles P. Williams, Jr., died; Q. M. Sergt. William T. Cork (pro. 1st lieut.); Sergt. Edwin W. French (pro. capt.); Corporals George H. Lord, John G. Williams, William C. Harris (pro. Q. M.); John Bentley, George Braman, John H. Bliven, Isaac T. Bliven, Henry D. Bennett, Alfred V. Barnum (pro. 1st lieut.), James L. Eggleston, Charles W. Sheffield, James A. Edwards, John O'Rourke, Joshua Perkins, Thomas I. Price, Christian Pflaum, Zachariah Patterson.
Company D.—John McGovethy, Peter Maines.
Company I.—Peter Wright, Reuben G. Weeks.
Company K.—Lyman Doolittle, John N. Mitchell.
Company L.—Myron H. Crandall.
Company M.—John Smith, Michael Begg, John Burgan.

Since the close of the Rebellion, our town has suffered its full measure from the inflation and contractions of the currency. Since specie payment has been restored, business has revived and confidence in business circles has been established. Thus the town of Stonington, where William Chesebrough first built his forest home in 1649, has grown to be a community of 7,353 inhabitants with a grand list of $5,390,130. The people for intelligence and enterprise are the equal of any township in this State. The soil is strong, rugged and hard to cultivate, but when properly cared for yields remunerative crops.

SPANISH-AMERICAN WAR.

April 21st, 1898, war was declared by the Congress of the United States against Spain, which continued until August 11th, 1898, when Spain accepted terms of peace, proposed by the American government. April 23rd, 1898, the President called for 125,000 volunteers, which was increased to 200,000 May 25th, 1898, and was nobly responded to by the patriotic young men of the United States. Two full companies of volunteers were recruited in Stonington, Conn., one by Captain Hadlai A. Hull, who was promoted to Major, Sept. 23rd, 1898, and after peace was concluded. resigned October 17th, 1898. The other was recruited at Pawcatuck, Conn., by Cornelius Bransfield, who retired after the close of the war. The heroism displayed by the American volunteers brought the war to a close in a very short time.

ECCLESIASTICAL HISTORY.

The first church organized in the town of Stonington was formed June 3, 1674. The preliminary steps taken for the organization of the church originated in the following vote, passed at a town meeting held at Stonington, on the 6th day of April, 1669: "It was voted that those of the inhabitants whose hearts God shall move that way, may have liberty to address themselves to the General Court for liberty to erect and gather a church among us."

It was legally passed by vote, "That there should be another town meeting on Thursday, next come a seven night, being the 15th day of April next ensuing the date thereof, for any who have a desire to propound themselves as to be beginners of the Church, may give in their names to Mr. Noyes at that meeting at the Meeting house, about nine of the clock in the forenoon."

Whether this adjourned meeting assembled or not does not appear from the record, but a petition to the General Court was preferred, asking liberty to associate in church order, which after due consideration was passed upon as follows, viz.: Several inhabitants of Stonington petitioning this Court for their approbation that they might settle themselves in church order, this Court grants them their petition. But before they organized themselves into church order they (the town) set out five hundred acres of land for the support of the ministry, met and agreed to build a new meeting-house and fixed the site, and laid out home lots of twelve acres each for every inhabitant around it. Built the meeting house in 1672-3, dedicated it and on the 3rd day of June, 1674, organized the church with nine members, viz.: Mr. James Noyes, Mr. Thomas Stanton, Mr. Nathaniel Chesebrough, Mr. Thomas Miner, Mr. Nehemiah Palmer, Mr. Ephraim Miner, Mr. Thomas Stanton, Jr., Mr. Moses Palmer, Mr. Thomas Wheeler. They established a covenant when they formed the church, in harmony with the Savoy confession.

Previous to the organization of the church, all of the religious services here were held and conducted by ministers, called by a vote of the town and paid for from its treasury. Such services were at first held at the dwelling-houses of the planters. In 1661 the town erected a meeting-house which stood a short distance west of Mistuxet avenue, southwest of the residence of Mr. Henry M. Palmer. This house was used for religious and town meetings until 1672-4 when the town voted to build, and did build a large edifice for religious and town service and located it on Agreement Hill, so named by the town as a compromise settlement between the (then) inhabitants of the town. This meeting-house stood until 1729, when it was taken down and another house was built on its enlarged site. These two meeting-houses stood a few rods west of the present church edifice at the road on the original Agreement Hill. Rev. James Noyes was called by the town to preach here as a licentiate in 1664, and so continued until Sept. 10th, 1674, when he was ordained, and labored successfully with the church as its pastor until his death, which took place Dec. 30, 1719. Before the close of Mr. Noyes' pastorate the people who had settled in the north part of the town became anxious to have religious services held in their vicinity. As early as 1722 the town was divided into two religious societies for the public worship of God. Subsequent proceedings show that a controversy arose about the location of the dividing line, which was referred to the General Assembly in 1720, who appointed a committee to arrange it, but their report was set aside by the Assembly on a remonstrance of certain persons, and another committee was appointed in 1721, who came to Stonington and established the dividing line, which is substantially the dividing line between the towns of Stonington and North Stonington. The Rev. Ebenzer Rossiter of Guilford, Conn., by ordination, succeeded Mr. Noyes as the pastor of the church Dec. 19, 1722. During his pastorate the Second Congregational Church of Stonington, now the North Stonington Congregational Church, was formed. Owing principally to the location of the site of a new meeting-house which the church and society had in contemplation, a serious controversy arose, which resulted in a division of both and the erection of a meeting-house at the center farm or Putnam Corners, and the call and settlement of the Rev. Nathaniel Eells of Scituate, Mass., who was ordained June 14th, 1733. Mr. Rossiter and Mr. Eells preached in their respective parishes in Stonington until the death of Mr. Rossiter. The church and society became reconciled and were again united under the pastorate of Mr. Eells, who preached for six months alternately to each church for a while, when yielding to the wishes of his parishioners, who resided at Stonington Point he commenced preaching at the Road meeting-house Sunday mornings and at the Academy at the Point in the afternoon, and so continued while he lived, and just before his death the meeting-house at the Putnam Corners was taken down and rebuilt at Stonington Point.

Mr. Eells was succeeded in the pastorate of the First Church by the Rev. Hezekiah N. Woodruff, of Farmington, Conn., who was ordained July 2nd, 1789, and continued pastor of the church until June, 1803, when he was dismissed by a mutual council. After him, came the Rev. Ira Hart, of Bristol, Conn., who was installed Dec. 6th, 1809, and labored with them successfully as their pastor until his death, which took place Oct. 29th, 1829.

Next came Mr. Joseph Whittlesey, of Washington, Conn., who was ordained May 27th, 1830, and continued their pastor until Dec. 14, 1832, when he was dismissed at his own request by mutual council. He was succeeded by the Rev. N. B. Cook, of Long Island, followed by the Rev. Pliny F. Warner, Rev. Paul Couch, Rev. John C. Wilson, and the Rev. John O. Barrows, the present pastor by installation.

The Second Congregational Church of Stonington, now North Stonington, was organized in 1727. The controversy over the boundary line, dividing the town of Stonington into two religious societies, and the location of their first meeting-house, served to divide the people as to the choice of a pastor for the church. After calling Mr. William Worthington, Mr. Thomas Craghead and Mr. Jabez Wight, they finally agreed upon Mr. Ebenezer Russell as and for their gospel preaching minister, who was ordained Feb. 22, 1727, at which time the church was organized. Rev. Mr. Russell continued pastor of the church until his death, which took place May 22, 1731.

The church and society then invited Mr. Joseph Fish, who was ordained Dec. 27th, 1732, and for a few years Mr. Fish's pastorate was eminently successful. "The new light" awakening, as it was generally called by the people, served to divide the church, which resulted in the organization of a strict Congregational or Separatist Church, Sept. 11, 1746. These two Congregational churches maintained separate religious worship until March 16th, 1827, when they were reunited under the ministrations of the Rev. Joseph Ayer.

The next church in the town of Stonington was the Baptist Church, organized at Pung-hung-we-nuck Hill in 1743, and was the outcome of the great awakening (so called) which commenced under the preaching of Drs. Edwards and Whitfield. Mr. Wait Palmer, one of the awakened converts, became their first pastor, but for something not now fully known he was excluded from the church after nearly twenty years' service. He has been succeeded by pastors worthy of their calling.

The next church organized in Stonington was formed in 1765, and its meeting-house was erected on Shunuck Hill. Simeon Brown was ordained their first pastor in March, 1763. He was a native of Stonington, and a man of sterling worth, but not a pulpit orator. Other ministers, natives of Stonington, succeeded him in the pastorate of this church.

The next church of Stonington was the Baptist Church, organized in 1775 at Long Point (now Stonington Borough), where most of its members resided. During the years of its organization Sir James Wallace bombarded the place, which with the events and scenes of the Revolutionary war, doubtless, delayed the progress of the church. This church was gathered under the pastorate of the Rev. John Rathbone. Its first meeting-house was not built until the close of the Revolutionary war and was a substantial building, some forty feet square. This church has had twelve pastorates and a membership at one time of three hundred and fifty. The present house of worship was erected during the pastorate of the Rev. Albert G. Palmer, and is a magnificent building of modern architecture, and most admirably arranged. Owing to the want of a proper title to the site of its former meeting-house, and the questionable authority of using its funds in the purchase of the site of its present church, and in order to vest the property entirely in the church, independent of trustees or societies, the members of the church were in 1889 constituted and created by the Legislature of Connecticut a body politic and corporate by the name of the First Baptist Church of Stonington Borough, with full power to receive, hold and mortgage any and all, both real and personal, that may be given or descend to said church. The present pastor of the church is the Rev. Henry Clark, who was called to the pastorate in 1891.

No more churches were organized in Stonington before the division of the town in 1807. Pending the agitation and controversial feeling between the inhabitants of the northern and southern sections of the town of Stonington, relative to the old mail stage route, and the layout of the new highway from Stonington Borough to Old Mystic, and the construction of the bridge over Lambert's Cove, Pine Tree Point to Quana duct, in order to give the electors of the town an opportunity to decide the matter in question, a town meeting was legally warned and held at the old meeting-house at the Road, April 5th, 1807, for the express purpose of dividing the town of Stonington so as to relieve the taxpayers of the northern section of the town from the cost of the new highway and bridge. The meeting was largely attended, and after an animated and heated discussion of the matter in question, it was voted, by a small majority thereof, to divide said town into separate townships by the old society line, and that the north part shall be called Jefferson. When the General Assembly met the May following, the division of the town was duly considered and adopted and divided on the line suggested, but the name of Jefferson for the new town was not adopted for the reason that the society of North Stonington had been so named by the General Assembly, and had had charge of the schools therein for a great many years, and the name had become identified with its vital interests, so it was considered not best to change it, and the new town was called North Stonington.

The first church organized in Stonington after the division of the town was the Methodist Episcopal Church at Old Mystic.

As early as 1816 several Methodist clergymen visited Old Mystic, and preached occasionally; but no efforts were made to organize a class, preparatory to the promotion of a church until 1824, when a class was organized consisting of seven persons. No minister was stationed at Old Mystic until 1826, when the Rev. Newell S. Spauding was assigned to that place. The first Quarterly Conference was held Aug. 13 and 14, 1828. The first house of worship erected by the Methodist Society was dedicated January, 1849. Prior to this time they had worshipped in the

Union meeting-house, now used as a livery stable. The first house of worship (Methodist Episcopal) was forty-two by thirty-three feet, costing about eighteen hundred dollars. Unfortunately it was destroyed by fire Feb. 17th, 1851. The loss was very severe, but undismayed the church and society resolved to build another and a better church, which was completed before the close of the year, and the people were again worshipping God under their own vine and fig tree. In 1882 it was renovated and re-dedicated, and again in 1894. This church has been under the pastoral care of eminent ministers, and is now enjoying the pastorate of the Rev. A. E. Legg.

The Second or Third Congregational Church and Society of Stonington was organized as follows: The First Congregational Society of Stonington, after several unsuccessful attempts to divide itself into two societies by metes and bounds, called a meeting to assemble on the 28th day of September, 1833, and after mature deliberation took a new departure and adopted a plan for organizing a new church and society in Stonington, viz.: "That whenever forty members of the First Society should withdraw and organize a new Congregational Society at the Borough and elect society officers, and shall give notice to the old society of their doings within thirty days from the day of the meeting, the new society shall then be regarded as organized and receive $1,825 of the old society's fund." The conditions were immediately complied with at the meeting. Forty-five members of the society withdrew, formed a new society, and took their money and invested it in a new meeting-house. As soon as the new society was formed, ninety-three members of the First Church seceded and organized the Second Church in connection with said society Nov. 11th, 1833. Their first settled pastor was the Rev. John C. Nichols, who was called and installed May 17th, 1834. After laboring with that people for about five years, he was dismissed by a mutual council. Since then that church has had a succession of pastors, whose labors have been blessed to them as follows: Rev. Jonathan Erskine Edwards was ordained and installed April 7th, 1840, and was dismissed by a mutual council, April 13th, 1843. He was followed by Rev. William Clift, who was ordained and installed Dec. 17th, 1844; dismissed by a mutual council April 21st, 1864. He was succeeded by Rev. Edward Whiting Gilman, who was installed Sept. 14th, 1864, dismissed by a mutual council April 25th, 1871. After him came the Rev. Henry Wheaton Wales, who was installed Oct. 18th, 1871, and dismissed by a mutual council Aug. 2nd, 1874. Following him was the Rev. Henry Barnes Elliott, who labored with the church as acting pastor thereof until April 1st, 1880, when the Rev. Henry B. Mead was called to the pastorate of the church, and was continued as such until the Rev. Charles J. Hill was called to the church to become the pastor, which he accepted, and was installed May 19th, 1888, and labored with that church until his dismissal by a mutual council. The present clergyman officiating as the pastor of the church is the Rev. William C. Stiles, who was installed by a mutual council in 1898.

The Methodist Episcopal Church at Mystic, Conn., was organized in 1835, under the labors of a circuit preacher, the Rev. Hermon Perry. The first house of worship was built, and the Rev. Wm. S. Simmons was the first pastor. In 1867 this present church edifice was built. They sold the first church building to the Roman Catholics. The Rev. Wm. S. Simmons has been succeeded by eminent clergymen, whose labors have been most acceptable to the people of their charge. The present pastor is the Rev. John McVey.

Pawcatuck Congregational Church.—During the year 1843 six members of the First, with sixteen members of the Second Congregational Church of Stonington residing in the vicinity of Pawcatuck Bridge united, with the advice and consent of a council of neighboring churches with them assembled, and formed a new church there, Feb. 14th, 1843, under the name and title of the Pawcatuck Congregational Church. Their first public religious services were held at the old Union meeting-house and in the hall of the Academy until 1849, when they erected their new meeting-house which, to accommodate their increasing congregation has since been twice enlarged.

The first settled minister was the Rev. S. B. Goodenow, who was called and settled April 1st, 1843. He remained but one year. The next pastor was the Rev. Joshua Brown, settled May 1st, 1844, and after two months' labor terminated his connection with the church. Rev. James D. Moore commenced his labors with the church July 21st, 1844, and remained until 1846, when Mr. Whitmore came and remained for one year. Rev. A. L.

Whitman was settled in 1847, and continued to labor with the church until 1866, when he resigned, and was dismissed by a mutual council that year. Mr. Whitman was followed by the Rev. E. W. Root, who came in 1867, and remained until 1870. Then came the Rev. A. H. Wilcox, who was settled in 1872, but whose failing health compelled him to resign. He was succeeded by the Rev. D. N. Beach, who in turn was followed by the Rev. John P. Hawley, who resigned Sept. 30th, 1883, and was dismissed by a mutual council soon after. March 18th, 1884, a call was extended to Rev. George L. Clark, which he accepted by letter April 9th, 1884, and was installed by mutual council May 29th, 1884, and continued his labors with the church successfully until he resigned his pastorate August 15th, 1888, which was accepted by the church August 27th, 1888, after which he was dismissed by a mutual council.

April 15th, 1889, the church voted to extend a call to Rev. Hiram L. Kelsey, of Boston, Mass., which was accepted by him, April 23rd, 1889, when he came to Westerly and commenced his labors with the church and so continued until April 6th, 1890, when he tendered his resignation, which the church declined to accept. On May 7th, 1891, Mr. Kelsey again resigned, to go into effect July 1st, 1891, which resignation was accepted by the church May 29th, 1891, after which he was dismissed by mutual council.

During the fall of the year of 1891, Mr. D. L. Moody recommended a young man, Mr. Samuel M. Cathcart, to supply the church for a while, and the church formally requested him to come and remain with them one month, which was acceeded to by him, and on the 26th day of October, 1891, the church voted to invite Mr. S. M. Cathcart to remain with them for an indefinite period. After the expiration of the month, Mr. Cathcart consented to remain as supply for an indefinite period, but upon further reflection and consideration with the church, decided to give his preparatory studies his entire attention, so the church on Dec. 14th, 1891, gave a call to Rev. Samuel H. Woodrow, of Yale Divinity School of New Haven, Conn., which was accepted by him Dec. 30th, 1891, and he was ordained and installed by a mutual council, and remained with the church as their pastor, preaching with great acceptance until Oct. 15th, 1895, when he resigned his pastorate and was dismissed by a mutual council.

On Feb. 29th, 1896, a call was extended to Rev. Edgar L. Warren, of North Attleboro, Mass., and by him accepted March 11th, 1896, after which he was installed pastor of the church, and continued as such until his dismission by a mutual council. He has been succeeded by Rev. Frank H. Decker, who was installed by a mutual council in 1898 as pastor of the church.

The Third Baptist Church of Stonington.—This church was gathered and organized Oct. 14th, 1846. Their pastors have been Rev. Flint, Rev. Joseph Lewis, Rev. William Spellman, of New York, William Smith of Groton Bank, Conn., Rev. Erastus Denison of Mystic, Conn., D. B. Bailey of Mystic, Rev. G. N. Hamblin of Providence, Rev. Solomon Gale of Mystic preached nearly 12 years; Rev. William L. Francis of Brooklyn, N. Y.; Rev. William J. Nayter of Florida was with the church for a time; just now the church has no settled pastor.

Greenmanville Seventh-Day Baptist Church.—This church was organized in 1850, consisting of about forty members. Their meeting-house was erected in 1851. The Rev. Sherman S. Griswold was the first regular pastor, and held the position for about fifteen years. During his pastorate he became interested in our common schools, and held the position of school visitor for several years, laboring very successfully for the promotion of public education. He was succeeded by Rev. L. E. Livermore, whose pastorate commenced in 1866. He was succeeded by Rev. Charles A. Burdick, whose pastorate commenced in 1869. He was followed by Rev. S. L. Gardiner, whose pastorate commenced in 1875. He was followed by Rev. O. D. Sherman in 1880.

Calvary Episcopal Church.—The Calvary parish, under the Protestant Episcopal Church of the United States, diocese of Connecticut, was formed May 31st, 1847. The corner-stone of this beautiful little stone church (built from plans by Upjohn, the celebrated architect) was laid Sept. 3, 1847. This church went forward to completion, and was consecrated May 31, 1849. The Rev. Junius Marshall Willey was the first rector, being called to the rectorship March 23rd, 1847. He remained till 1854, when Rev. W. W. Bronson entered upon his rectorship, and remained till 1856. The third rector was the Rev. Daniel C. Weston, D. D., who continued till the spring of 1863. Upon his resignation, the Rev. J. C. Middleton became its rector and continued till 1871. He was followed by the Rev. Rufus Emery until 1873, when the Rev. W. C. Hyde became the rector and remained till 1874. He was succeeded by the Rev. Thomas Mallaby, who remained five years. In 1880 the Rev. Alfred Goldsborough took charge and remained till 1884. After him came the Rev. Stevens Parker, D. D., until 1888, when the Rev. S. H. Gallaudet came, who remained only a few months, and he was succeeded by the Rev. Charles Westerman. After his resignation in 1890, the parish was in charge of the Rev. Joseph Hooper, rector of St. Mary's Church at Mystic, until 1892, when the Rev. Edward W. Babcock became rector, resigning Feb. 1st, 1896, upon the same Sunday the Rev. Erit B. Schmitt, the present rector, assumed charge.

Pawcatuck Catholic Church, St. Michael's.—About fifty years ago, Father Felton, of Boston, came to Pawcatuck to celebrate mass, and preach for the benefit of the Catholics then residing at Pawcatuck and Westerly. There being no church edifice of that order then at Pawcatuck, he held and conducted his services in the open air. The trustees of the Union meeting-house tendered him the use of that building for religious services as he might have occasion to use it. He continued his ministrations for about five years, and was succeeded by Father Daley for one year, who was followed by Father Duffy, under whose regime the Roman Catholic Church at Stonington Borough was erected and dedicated by Bishop O'Reilly in the year 1851, who afterwards perished at sea in the ill-fated "Pacific." Father Duffy remained pastor for two years, and was succeeded by Father Thomas Dray, who remained for six years, who in turn has been succeeded by several priests, whose ministrations have been acceptable to the people of their charge. During these years, the present church building, parsonage and convent school have been erected on Berry Hill at Pawcatuck.

Mystic Congregational Church.—This church was organized by thirty-seven seceding members from the First Congregational Church of Stonington, with five persons from other churches, on the 30th day of January, 1852, under the approval of a committee of the Consociation of Congregational Ministers and Churches of New London County, consisting of Rev. Messrs. A. McEwen, D. D., moderator, Timothy Tuttle, Jared R. Avery, William Clift, and Myron N. Morris, clerk. For the first year the pulpit was supplied by several ministers of the gospel. A call to settle was first extended to the Rev. D. R. Austin, which was declined. An invitation was then extended to the Rev. Walter R. Long to become the pastor of the church, which he accepted, and was duly installed Sept. 15th, 1853. He continued with the church for about ten years, preaching very acceptably to the people of his charge. He was dismissed by a ministerial council March 29th, 1863. He was succeeded by the Rev. Charles H. Boyd, who was settled as the second pastor of the church in May, 1859, and continued to labor with the church and people until May 6th, 1865, when, on account of failing health he was obliged to resign. He was formally dismissed by mutual council in January, 1866, and died soon after. Mr. Boyd was succeeded by Rev. Algernon Goodnough, who was settled pastor of the church, and was installed June 3rd, 1866, and dismissed by mutual council Feb. 26th, 1867. Rev. William Clift succeeded Mr. Goodnough. He was installed March 9th, 1869, and after laboring with the people of his charge until Nov. 13th, 1879, he was dismissed by a mutual council. Rev. Charles H. Oliphant commenced his labors with this church as its acting pastor June 1st, 1879, and continued as such until Aug. 31st, 1884, when he closed his labors with them. Rev. Herbert S. Brown succeeded Mr. Oliphant. He was installed June 23rd, 1886, and labored with the people of his charge until Aug. 11th, 1890, when he was dismissed by a mutual council. Rev. Austin H. Burr began his labors with the church Oct. 1st, 1890, as their acting pastor, and continued with them until failing health compelled him to resign his charge, dying Dec. 5th, 1891. J. Romayn Danforth succeeded Mr. Burr, and was ordained and installed Oct. 25th, 1892, by a mutual council. Mr. Danforth's labors with the church have been productive of the best results, with flattering prospects of increasing usefulness in the future. The cornerstone of their present church edifice was laid with appropriate ceremonies Nov. 24th, 1859, and went on to completion and dedication. It was enlarged in 1869 by the addition of fourteen feet to its length. The present officiating clergyman with the church is the Rev. Claire F. Luther.

The Advent Christian Association was organized in Stonington Borough September 1st, 1874, by Capt. George S. Brewster, William H. Smith, William F. Tanner, and Benjamin C. Brown, who commenced religious services at the dwelling-houses of the associated brethren, until they secured the rooms of the Young Men's Christian Association, where they now worship. The organization of this association was brought about by a few conscientious, devoted men, whose efforts have been blessed until their members have increased beyond their expectations. Like all of the primitive churches of New England, they started with a fixed purpose, disregarding all opposing forces, and with unshaken faith trusted in Him who doeth all things well. They have no settled pastor, but enjoy a stated supply from neighboring churches. The church is greatly indebted to Capt. George S. Brewster for his unselfish devotion to its interests.

St. Patrick's Roman Catholic Church at Mystic.—The church edifice was purchased from the Methodist Episcopal Society, and dedicated in 1870. Rev. P. P. Lawlor, first pastor, was succeeded by Rev. Wm. Hart, Nov. 18, 1872, who remained until April 9th, 1873. He was followed then by Father John Flemming, who remained until Sept. 11th, 1881. He was succeeded by Rev. J. F. Dougherty, who remained until Sept. 19th, 1895, when Rev. J. F. Murphy took charge, and is now the present pastor.

Quiambaug Chapel.—Formerly religious meetings and Sunday schools were held in Quiambaug school-house in Stonington, composed of all religious denominations in that region roundabout. Some of the people in that vicinity had repeatedly expressed an opinion that a school-house was not a proper place for such meetings, especially during school terms, so an effort was made and generally concurred in to raise by subscription money sufficient to build a chapel of adequate dimensions to accommodate the people of that vicinity. The money was raised, a site was procured and the corner-stone of the chapel was laid December 27th, 1889, and the building was erected and dedicated in April, 1890. Sunday school sessions and other religious services have been held in the chapel to the present time, productive of great and lasting good.

Wequetequock chapel.—Sunday School sessions were formerly held at the Wequetequock school-house, later on at the chapel there, erected by the Calvary Episcopal Church of Stonington for mission services; but for reasons not generally well understood the Sunday school services were transferred to, and held in the parlors of the Second Congregational Society's dwelling-house at Wequetequock, where they were held until the Episcopal chapel was purchased Nov. 9th, 1893, by the Wequetequock Chapel Association, a corporation organized and existing on the basis of a union non-sectarian, joint stock association, since which time the Sunday School sessions have been in the chapel, where other religious services have been held by clergymen and other prominent men of the surrounding parishes.

The Sunday School sessions have been held under the superintendence of Dea. Joshua Haley of the Second Congregational Church of Stonington for eighteen years and have been productive of great and lasting good to all attending and participating. A union association of ladies has been formed, whose influence has enlarged the patronage of the association. Since its purchase the chapel has been repaired and beautified, and with gifts from those interested now presents an attractive appearance with ample sheds, all showing the progress of the association.

St. Mary's Roman Catholic Church at Stonington Borough.— This church was formed in 1851, and the edifice was erected the same year by subscriptions from the Catholics of Stonington, Westerly and the Mystics, under the supervision of Rev. P. Duffy, who was the first pastor. At present it is joined to Mystic as an out-mission and attended by the priests at Mystic, the Rev. Father Murphy being its present pastor.

COMMON SCHOOLS.

The men who settled Connecticut left their homes in England and emigrated to this country not to acquire wealth or worldly honor, so much as to enjoy civil and religious liberty and freedom; so as soon as the population was sufficient, teachers were employed to instruct the youth of the colony.

This was done in advance of any colonial legislative enactments on the subject of common schools, and in fact when laws were passed in relation to them they did little more than to make obligatory the practices which had grown up and been established by the founders of the several towns which composed the original colonies of Hartford and New Haven.

The founders of this State were educated men, and seeking for the best opportunities of educating their children the common school system was introduced in Connecticut. The first law upon the subject was enacted by the town of New Haven March 25, 1641, which provided for a free school under the care and management of the minister and magistrates. The next law was enacted by the town of Hartford, seven years after, appropriating thirty pounds for its schools. In 1646 Roger Ludlow, Esq., compiled a body of laws for the colony of Connecticut, which provided that every township of fifty families shall maintain a school for the education of all their children, and as soon as such township shall contain one hundred families, they are to maintain a grammar school. Various public acts were passed relative to common schools up to 1700, when the Connecticut code was revised and embraced the following, that "Every town having seventy householders shall be constantly provided with a sufficient schoolmaster to teach children and youth to read and write, and every town having a less number shall provide a teacher for one-half of the year, also that there shall be a Grammar school set up in every shire-town of the several counties."

In 1766 a law was passed authorizing each town and society to divide themselves into necessary districts for keeping their schools, which district shall draw their proportion of all public moneys belonging to each town according to the lists of each district therein.

In 1786 Connecticut surrendered to the general government for the benefit of the people, all its claim to a vast territory west of Pennsylvania and New York, from the sale of which we derived our present school fund. For ten years it was controlled by a board of managers, but in 1810 Hon. James Hillhouse was appointed sole commissioner of the school fund, and by his management its value was greatly increased.

In 1836, the town deposits fund came into existence from the general government, by a distribution of surplus revenues between all the States, this State receiving $764,670.60, which was divided amongst the several towns according to the population, and one-half of the income by a law of our State was annually appropriated for the benefit of common schools education. And in 1845 another law was passed, devoting all of this income to common schools. The amount received by this town was $8,734.91.

Notwithstanding the repeated acts of Legislature, relative to common schools, they were so much neglected in this town that the friends of education induced the selectmen to call a town meeting Oct. 31, 1853, and after a long discussion the town voted to levy a tax of one cent on a dollar of the grand list for the benefit of common schools in the town, and the money should be expended under the direction of B. F. Langworthy, Charles H. Mallory and Richard A. Wheeler, for the benefit of schools; first, in paying lectures for them, second to bring up the funds of the small districts to seventy-five dollars; third, to divide the rest among the children of all the districts equally. So after various provisions, revisions and enactments of laws, the Legislature dissolved the school societies and placed the schools under the care of the town, thus returning to the first system of common schools established in Connecticut. At the present time there are forty teachers employed in the fifteen districts in this town, in fourteen of which are schools well taught and regularly attended. One district has not the requisite number of scholars within its limits to sustain a school, but the town pays for transporting the few children to the next nearest school.

The amount of money expended for the forty teachers is

$15,269.85, and the total expenditure by town and district for educational purposes is $20,505.78, for the 1,754 scholars instructed.

The Liberty Street school, called No. 16, has within its limits a parochial school, which takes the larger number of pupils in that district.

The new schoolhouse at Pawcatuck, called the West Broad Street school, is reputed to be the finest school building in the State, costing about $40,000.

HIGHWAYS.

Highways in Connecticut were established and laid out by an act of its General Court in the year 1638, which was amended in 1640, and in 1643 surveyors thereof were authorized to be appointed by the several towns, who were empowered to call out certain persons to repair the same. These laws were enlarged and perfected by the code of laws of Connecticut, enacted by the General Court in the year 1650 as follows:

"Whereas the maintaining of highways in a fit condition for passage according to the several occasions that occur is not only necessary for the comfort and safety of man and beast, but tends to the profit and advantage of any people, in the issue. It is therefor thought fit and ordered, that each town within this jurisdiction shall every year choose one or two of their inhabitants as Surveyors, to take care of, and oversee the mending and repairing of the Highways within their several Towns respectively, who have hereby power allowed them to call out the several cartes or persons fit for labor in each town, two days at least in each year, and so many more as in his or their judgments shall be found necessary for the maintaining of the afore mentioned end, to be directed in their works by the said surveyor or surveyors, and it is left to his or their liberties to require the labor of the severall persons in any family, or of a team and one person, where such are, as he finds most advantageous to the public occasions, he or they giving at least three days' notice or warning beforehand of such employment; and if any refuse or neglect to attend the service in any manner aforesaid, he shall forfeit for every day's neglect of a man's work two shillings sixpence, and of a team six shillings; which said fines shall be imployed by the Surveyors to hire others to work at the said wages: and the Surveyors shall within four days after the several days appointed for worke deliver in to some Magistrate a true presentment of all such as have beene defective, with their several neglects, who are immediately to grant a distress to the Marshall or Constable, for the levying of the incurred forfeiture by them to be delivered to the Surveyor for the use aforesaid, and if the Surveyor neglect to perform the service hereby committed to him, either in not calling out all the inhabitants in their several proportions as before or shall not return the names of those that are deficient, he shall incur the same penalties as those whom he so passes by are liable to, by virtue of this order, which shall be imployed to the use aforesaid, and to be levied also by distress upon information and proof before any one Magistrate."

In 1674 the General Court passed an act fixing the liability of persons to repair the highways, between sixteen and sixty years of age. In 1679 an act was passed by the General Court, ordering all the towns of the colony to clear their roads of brush at least one rod wide. In 1698 the General Court of Connecticut passed an act by which the General Court (which up to that time had acted as one body) should for the future consist of two houses, the first shall consist of the Governor, or in his absence of the Deputy Governor and assistants, which shall be known by the name of the upper house, and the other shall consist of such deputies as shall be returned by the several towns within this colony to serve as members of this General Assembly which shall be known as the lower house.

In 1699 the General Court passed an act, giving authority to the county courts to lay out and establish and repair highways, with power to assess damages therefor. But it was not until 1795, that a general law of Connecticut was enacted authorizing towns to build and repair highways by a tax on their polls and ratable estate. The privilege to do so was previously conferred upon several towns when thereto by them specially requested.

The office of selectmen of Connecticut was created by its General Court in the year 1639, with authority to lay out and repair highways, but no reference of their proceedings in laying out highways was required to be passed upon by the towns after the layout thereof.

The town of Stonington acting under and by virtue of the laws of the Connecticut Colony proceeded by its selectmen to lay out and establish certain highways as follows:

"At a town meeting legally warned and held on the second day of March, 1669, it was voted that the Selectmen with Capt. George Denison, Thomas Park, senior, and John Bennet, are chosen to seek out the country highway and other highways that are needful for the Towns use and to lay them out or the major part of these chosen are to lay out the country highways, by the first of May next; provided that the Selectmen give notice that all may know the time and place where to meet."

"At a town meeting held March 25th, 1669, it was voted that the country highway shall be laid out by the men chosen for that purpose from the head of Mystic (now Old Mystic), to Kitchamaug, so near as may be according to the old footpath lies, provided it meet with London highway at Mystic River, having respect to the public good and the convenience of the particular proprietors through whose lands this country highway shall run, and this highway to be allowed four-pole (rod) wide."

HIGHWAYS.

The committee authorized to lay out said country highway as aforesaid made the following report:

"The country highway beginning at Mystic River on the west, four rod wide; lying between a white oak and a little beech tree marked on three sides, and so running through the Indian field at Quaquataug to Mistuxet Brook in or near to the old footpath and from thence running on the north side of John Reynolds, his house as the trees are marked to the Stoney Brook near to the old path; the path lying on the south a little distance, and from the Stoney Brook to Goodman York, his house in the old footpath, and from Goodman York, his house four pole wide through the said York's land; next unto Mr. James Noyes his land to the old footpath, and if the little swamp proves not passable, that is in the said York's land then the said York is to repair it, or else to suffer it to lie on the old footpath, because it is said he has sixteen pole allowed him the whole length of his land for that purpose and end; and from that leaving the old footpath a little to the south by reason of a foul swamp till we come to the top of the hill called Petequack and from thence to the wading place at Pawcatuck river known as Kitchamaug, above the Indian wares in the common traveled highway.

"And this was laid out by us, whose names are under written, on the first day of April, 1669, and the way is to be four pole wide from Mystic to Pawcatuck, according to the town order, the 25th of March, 1669.

"As witness our hands this fifth day of April, 1669.
THOMAS STANTON
GEORGE DENISON,
THOMAS WHEELER,
SAMUEL CHESEBROUGH,
NEHEMIAH PALMER,
THOMAS PARK,
JOHN BENNET."

"At a town meeting legally warned and held April 6th, 1669, it was passed by vote that Captain George Denison should be employed to make a directory, and set it upon a tree or post at this the wading place at Pawcatuck river, Kitchamaug, where the country highway is laid out, that strangers and travellers may know how to find the country highway through the town to London highway at Mystic River and another at Mystic (now Old Mystic). The same day it was voted that there shall be a country highway laid out, the present month at the furtherest and that the Selectmen should appoint the time and day and the persons to accompany the Selectmen in the work, to lay out the said country highway from where they left off at Kitchamaug to the east end of the town at Wecapaug and on the fifteenth day of March, 1670, the said country highway was laid out from the wading place at Kitchamaug on the Pawcatuck river, where we ended the country way from Mystic to Pawcatuck and from Pawcatuck river to Wecapaug through the town four pole wide through a field where John Reynolds dwells, and so through the part of the field where the Tinker did dwell and so throughout."

This was done by the selectmen and constables to the number of fourteen men. A few of the early grants of land here were given by the town, subject to necessary highways for the improvement thereof, but a majority of the land grants contained no such condition. Prior to 1699, there were no legal provisions in the statute laws of Connecticut, by which towns were liable for damages accruing by the layout of a highway by the selectmen thereof, the natural consequence of which was that the landholders, over which highways were laid by the selectmen, fenced in, plowed and planted the roads at pleasure, which so obstructed the travel thereon that the town took further action in the premises as follows, viz.:

"At a Town Meeting March ye 9th, 1686, the following highways, considered of ye sundry inhabitants appointed by order of the town, were legally voted, viz.: That the country highway lie from Mystic river head, between Major Winthrop and Deacon Park, their land to ye end of said York's his land, and then as ye way now runs to ye meeting-house, and so as we now go to ye brook Anguilla by Mr. Noyes his house, where it goes into ye former country way to the wading place at Pawcatuck river."

This proceeding of the town did not improve the condition of the highways nor satisfy the landholders whose interests were disregarded by the town, nor did they remove their fences across this old post road and throw it open to travel except in the winter season.

Traveling in those days was on horseback and by ox-teams, the highways were not graded, nor were the rivers and brooks bridged. The town of Stonington was not alone in poor roads, bridgeless brooks and rivers. The whole colony was suffering from the same cause and so much so that the General Assembly took the matter in hand as follows, viz.:

"Complaint being made that Post and other travellers meet with great difficulty in journeying as they pass through this Colony, especially in the town of Stonington, difficulty doth arise either for want of stated highways or for want of clearing and repairing highways when stated and erecting and maintaining sufficient bridges when needing repairs: For remedy whereof the Selectmen in each town in this Colony situate in the accustomed roads are hereby required upon sight or publication hereof forthwith to take effectual care that convenient highways as may be for the advantage of Posts and others travelling in their journeying as aforesaid be laid out through their townships."

A committee was also appointed by the General Assembly to see that the foregoing order was duly complied with and carried into effect by the selectmen of the several towns. The town of Stonington had passed several votes relative to the survey and repair of its highways, but for some reason not now understood they were not carried into effect, and the roads were well nigh impassable. When the said order of the General Assembly was received, the selectmen proceeded to re-examine the old post road, which was the only established highway of the town at the time; the other roads were private ways or bridle paths, so called, and by their own act relaid it and caused the same to be recorded as follows, viz.:

" In attendance of an act of the General Assembly bearing date May 12th & 25th, 1698, the Selectmen of Stonington have for settlement of the country Road made search in our town records and have viewed and considered the road as far as we can find it hath been laid out and recorded. And we find that Stephen Richardson hath fenced the way on this side of Pawcatuck River at two places by his house and corn field; Now we order the said Stephen to repair and clear the way at those places, till his corn is off the land, and the way turned again where it was laid out. We find that Mr. Noyes hath turned the way at the west end of his land at the bridge; we order the said Mr. Noyes forthwith to repair the bridge and keep it in repair till his crop bee off and the way returned where it was laid out; That James Babcock hath turned the road where his fields are; We order the said Babcock to maintain sufficient way there, till his present crop be off, and then to pull down his fences and let the road be open according to law and town order, where it was laid out. We find that Elihu Chesebrough hath stopped the way by two gates and we do order the said Elihu to repair and mend the said gate till his present grass is off the land and then to take away his gates and let the way be open where the town has laid it out; and we find the rest of the way, as convenient as we know it how it was laid out, from Elihu Chesebrough's land to the meeting house at the road, and from the said Meeting-House to Reynolds his path on the east side of Quaquataug hill and then finding the way hath not been fully settled, we have laid out the way from the foot of the hill where the road crosseth Reynolds his path straight as the ground will allow it to go, going on the west of the ground, where it is most free from rocks then it is to pass through the upper end of said Park's his land as the trees were marked till it came into the lane and it is to go in the lane to the brow of the upper part of the hill, near the gate and pass thence down the hill where the road way is now trod and taking the best advantage for the ground because the hill is steep; We do order that from the brow of the hill near the gate down to the little pasture the way is to be left eight pole wide because the ground is wet and springy land, and then it is to pass through the pasture and through the southward part of the uppermost little cornfield by Mystic River side and then it is to go along, by the River as it is now travelled, to the place where it passes through Mystic River. And this way for a country road is to be four rods wide; and where there are any lanes for this way to pass through they are to be left four pole wide; and we do order the surveyors for the highways forthwith to call the town to repair the road according to law.

"By the Selectmen, date August 12th, 1698.

NEHEMIAH PALMER,
JOSEPH MINER,
JOSEPH SAXTON,
ADAM GALLUP,
Selectmen.

This road remained unfenced, except as against improved lands for a good many years, and was the principal thoroughfare between New London and Newport for more than one hundred years, and until it was superceded by turnpikes and railways. It has never been materially changed in its course since 1698. It has been reduced to its present grade by continued repairs little by little, and the bridges over Anguilla, Stoney and Mistuxet Brooks were made by special vote of the town.

The want of a law in our colony to enable the selectmen to lay out highways and cause damages to be assessed therefor to the proprietors of land taken for the same, which must be paid by a tax on the polls and ratable estate of the towns, finally resulting in petitions to the courts of the county, which had ample authority for laying out and establishing highways, so in 1752 a petition was presented to the County Court for a highway from Long Point to the town of Preston, which was granted, and the highway was laid out and established. The next year a highway was so laid out, on petition by authority of said court, from Pawcatuck Bridge to Voluntown. Later on highways were so laid out from Pistol Point to the old Road meeting-house. Also a highway was so laid out from Long Point to Wequetequock, and on northerly to the old post road at Anguilla, thence easterly by and with said post road a short distance, from thence northerly and northeasterly to the said Voluntown highway. Also another highway was so laid out from the town landing at Old Mystic northerly and northeasterly to the said Preston highway, near the residence of the late Deacon Charles Wheeler.

After the enactment of the law of 1795, giving the selectmen of the several towns of our State authority to lay out highways, the entire expense of which was to be paid by a tax on the polls and ratable estate of the towns, the larger number of our highways has been laid out by the selectmen subject to ratification or rejection by action of said town, in lawful meeting assembled.

After the close of the Revolutionary war the mails between New York and Boston via New London and Newport were to be carried by mail stages and passed over this old post road until Long Point, now Stonington Borough, claimed and obtained a diversion in their favor, previous to which their mail matter had been mostly carried by coasting vessels. When the mail stages passed through Long Point, their route lay from the head of Mystic to the farm residence of the late Thomas W. Palmer, thence down to Long Point and over the highway to Pawcatuck Bridge. In 1784 Dr. Charles Phelps and William Williams, Esq., representatives of Stonington for that year, were instructed as agents of the town to prefer a memorial to the General Assembly at New Haven, praying for a lottery scheme, to be granted said town, to raise three hundred pounds lawful money, to enable them to build a bridge across the cove, called Lambert's Cove, from Pine Point to Quanaduct; also voted at said meeting to instruct Messrs. Paul Wheeler, Phineas Stanton and Edward Hancox, to measure the highway from Long Point to New London, by the contemplated road, via said bridge, so as to enable Messrs. Phelps and Williams to show the Assembly the saving by the bridge route.

In 1785 the General Assembly of Connecticut passed the following preamble and act as follows, viz.:

"Whereas the congress of the United States have directed that the public mails in future shall be carried by stages and it is necessary that the public roads be repaired immediately on the routes used by the stages; Therefore,

"Be it enacted by the Governor, Council and Representatives in general Assembly convened, and by authority of the same that the Selectmen of the several towns through which the stages charged with the mails pass; do immediately mend and repair the bridges and roads used by the stages and keep the same in good repair; and when complaint is made to the County Court of any neglect in either County such county shall order necessary repairs and grant a warrant against the Selectmen of the town where such neglect is found, to collect the sum to be expended in repairs from the selectmen of the town or towns so neglecting their duty."

The town of Stonington did not readily comply with the requirements of this law, nor did the towns generally throughout the State; the principal reason that induced this town to disregard its provisions were, that the stage route through this town was so circuitous that it was deemed advisable by some to lay and build a more direct road, for the stages from the head of Mystic to Long Point; the necessity for such a highway had been previously considered by the town. The year before a committee was appointed to apply to the General Assembly for a lottery scheme to raise money to build a bridge over Lambert's Cove from Pine Point to Quanaduct, which did not succeed. The inhabitants living in the southern part of the town favored the new road, those residing in the northern part were opposed to it. Both sections agreed in one thing, and that was that the stages being the property of companies, they did not think it right to tax the people to build and repair roads for their benefit.

Aside from such considerations, the people at Long Point and Mystic felt the necessity of the proposed highway for common convenience and the general good. The difference of opinion relative to the repairs on the old post mail stage road, and the building of a new highway from Mystic to Stonington, resulted in a serious controversy between the inhabitants residing in the upper and lower sections of the town. Similar controversies arose from the same cause in other towns in the colony, and the result in general was that the stage routes were not much improved. The expense of building a bridge over Lambert's Cove was the tug of war in this town, that prevented anything of consequence being done toward repairing the old stage route; other objections were but secondary considerations.

In 1794 another effort was made to procure a lottery scheme for building said bridge, which resulted in failure. The pressure was so great upon the General Assembly of that year and the next, in favor of improving the stage routes, that a committee of three, consisting of Samuel Mott, Joshua Huntington and Simeon Baldwin, Esq., were appointed in 1795, to straighten by a new lay the great post road from New Haven by Dragon's Bridge eastward to New London Ferry, and so on to Pawcatuck Bridge. This committee proceeded to discharge the duties of their appointment, and so far as their survey went, straightening said road, it may be called a success, but nothing was ever done in this town or in pursuance of their survey or the act of the Assembly to straighten or repair the old post road or any other road, nor can their survey be found in our town records or files, or in our State archives.

The town in 1796 remonstrated in the most solemn manner against said lay, appointing a committee of their ablest men to oppose and defeat the same if possible. Uniting with other towns similarly situated, they defeated it and succeeded in creating so strong a current of feeling against the mail stage companies that no further direct action was taken by the Assembly to compel the towns to build and repair highways for their special benefit. Some of the mail stage companies had by this time petitioned the Assembly for liberty and authority to lay out and construct highways of their own, with the right to place turnpike or toll gates thereon. During the latter part of the year 1796, Elijah Palmer and others of this town made application to the County Court, for a new road from Long Point to Mystic, now Old Mystic, which did not succeed. Stonington as a whole did not favor said road, for the town at a legally warned meeting thereof, appointed a committee to oppose said application, and also directed the selectmen to view the road from Mystic River to Pawcatuck Bridge, for the purpose of straightening and repairing the same, and report their doings to the next town meeting. To what town meeting they reported is not known, but in the year 1800 the town voted in legal meeting assembled, to expend the sum of four hundred dollars on the road used by the mail-stages from Old Mystic to Pawcatuck Bridge via Stonington Point, and directed the selectmen to straighten the same, which they did and reported their doings to the town, without stating how much of the appropriation they had used in straightening and repairing said mail stage route, through this town.

The mail stage companies or the town were not satisfied with the proceedings of the selectmen. The stage companies gave up their efforts to compel the town to keep up their route here and turned their attention to the construction of a turnpike road for the use of their mail stages. But the controversy over the Mystic Road and Pine Point Bridge over Lambert's Cove was continued with unabated energy. In 1801 a petition was preferred to the Court of Common Pleas, signed by Noyes Palmer and others, for a highway from the Baptist meeting-house in Stonington Borough to the old post road, at the town landing at Old Mystic. The court ordered an investigation of the matter in question, and appointed Benjamin Coit, John G. Hillhouse and Ezra Bishop, Esq., to hear and report upon the feasibility of the proposed road. The protracted sickness and death of Mr. Bishop delayed the proceedings of the committee until the next year, when the court appointed Mr. Joshua Huntington in the place and stead of Mr. Bishop, who upon a thorough examination of the proposed route for said highway, and evidences pro and con relative to the same, proceeded to lay out a road from the Borough of Stonington to Mystic, substantially as the road is now travelled, except near the head of Mystic, where a subsequent change, placed it where it now is. The remonstrances of Mr. Joshua Brown, and a plea for a jury to re-assess damages to him occasioned by the lay of said road over his premises, delayed the proceedings in court until 1803, when the layout thereof was accepted and declared by the court. The opposition to this road by the inhabitants of the north part of the town increased to such an extent that an effort was made to divide the town, which did not prevail at the time. The opponents of the road were in the majority, and pending the proceedings connected with the layout of the same, the town remonstrated again and again in the most solemn manner and petitioned the General Assembly to interpose in its favor, but all to no purpose. The town repeatedly asked the Assembly for a lottery scheme to defray the expense of building the bridge over Lambert's Cove and finally obtained one which from bad management resulted in a failure and was finally sold for a mere trifle. Some of the inhabitants headed by Mr. Amos Wheeler associated themselves together and petitioned the General Assembly for a Ferry charter over Lambert's Cove from Pine Point to Quanaduct. After a full hearing thereon the petitioners were given liberty to withdraw. But their defeat before the Assembly did not abate the opposition to the building of the highway and bridge, but rather increased it, and to such an extent that it resulted in the division of the town in 1807.

The town of Stonington did not give up the idea of defeating this new road, after their northern neighbors had left them alone to fight it. They continued to oppose it by remonstrance, and by every conceivable obstruction that they could invent they delayed its opening until 1815, when it was in part built and opened by the sheriff of the county. So from 1784 to 1815, this town was more or less engaged in a bitter contest about this road and bridge. It was traversed by the hated mail stages as soon as opened and gave them a more direct and level route from Mystic to Westerly.

The bridge first built over Lambert's Cove was barely wide enough for a single team to pass, with a long wooden span, in the middle; subsequently it was widened and a middle pier constructed, leaving two spans. Those interested in the mail stage companies, in 1816 petitioned the General Assembly for a turnpike charter from Groton Ferry to Westerly, designing to pass over the new road.

The town did not oppose the grant of the charter, it only asked that the committee appointed to lay out the turnpike road should not be confined to any particular route through this town. Owing to a variety of causes, the charter for the said turnpike company was not granted until 1818, when the request of the town was complied with, giving the committee appointed to lay out the road, liberty to select any route they might prefer. The committee, after examining the proposed route defined in the petition, and other routes, concluded to follow the direction of the old post road, in the town of Groton, changing it for the better in several places. But when they reached the head of Mystic, now Old Mystic, instead of following the new mail stage route through Stonington to Westerly as prayed for, they turned to the left, following in part the country road from the town landing at Mystic to North Stonington, until they reached Wolfneck, thence turned easterly through Stonington and North Stonington to Hopkinton city, connecting with a turnpike from thence to Providence, R. I. When the turnpike road was completed, it became the through mail stage route from New London to Providence and Boston, carrying also passengers to the full extent of their ability.

The construction of the new road from the head of Mystic to Stonington Borough, and the turnpike road from Mystic to North Stonington and Hopkinton city, deprived the old post road of its importance as a postal route, though post riders carried newspapers and private mail matter over its long beaten tracks for a good many years, and until the railroads and steamboats diverted the transmission of such matter to other routes. The old post road was first laid along the track of the Indian path, between Narragansett and Pequot (now New London).

It was followed by Capt. John Mason and his famous seventy-seven men in 1637, until they reached Taugwank Hill, where they held their council of war, the afternoon before the battle. After leaving Taugwank they deployed to the north somewhat to avoid Quaquataug Hill, for fear of exposing themselves to the keen eye of the Pequots on Mystic Hill and fort in Groton. It was on the north side of this road at Anguilla that Canonchet, after refusing to treat with the English for peace, was executed by the friendly Indians acting under the orders of the English officers. The layout of the town lots on both sides of this road on Agreement Hill in Stonington, and the erection of the meeting-house there in 1673-74 made it the business center of the town, and in consequence thereof it received the name of the Road, which is still applied to the region around the town hall and the present meeting-house there. It was at the Road in the first meeting-house there, that the King's commissioners met repeatedly to hear and determine the matter of jurisdiction between Rhode Island, Connecticut and Massachusetts. The commissioners to hear and report to the king the evidence in the celebrated case between the colony of Connecticut and the Mohegan Indians as supported by the Mason family, relative to various land titles, met and held their sessions for several days in this meeting-house in 1704. Such Commissioners' Courts were called the King's Courts and were regarded with great respect and consideration and the occasion of their sitting drew together almost the entire population of the town at the time to witness their proceedings.

The General Court of Connecticut in recognition of the gallant services of Major John Mason in the Pequot war of 1637, granted him in September, 1651, an island in Mystic Bay, then called Chipachaug (now known as Mason's Island), with one hundred acres of upland and ten acres of meadow, near Mystic River, where he should make choice.

November 15, 1651, the town of New London gave him a grant of one hundred acres of land to adjoin his colonial land. Major Mason located both of those one hundred-acre grants of land on the main land east and northeast of his island. The layout thereof by the town surveyor was very liberal and embraced more land than is now contained in the large farms of Mr. Nathan S. Noyes and of the heirs at law of Mrs. Mary Fish, deceased. Subsequently the town of New London gave him a right of way to the then contemplated meeting-house in Stonington, which was afterwards erected on the west slope of Palmer's Hill. This right of way was laid out to Major Mason sixteen rods wide, beginning at Pequotsepos Brook, a little way below the old county road, east of the village of Mystic, thence easterly along the south side of Capt. George Denison's second grant of land in Stonington, now known as the south boundary line of the farm that belonged to the late Mr. Oliver Denison, deceased; through the field next north of Mr. Jefferson Wilcox's dwelling-house, following the south line of said Denison land to Mistuxet Brook above where it falls into Quiambaug Cove, thence still further east over Palmer's Hill, leaving south of it one hundred and two acres of the late Deacon Noyes Palmer and other lands, passing just south of the Palmer burial place, and on east to Blackmore's Head (a rock so called), a short distance southerly of the junction of the Flanders with the old Stonington and Mystic road.

This sixteen-pole rightofway was bequeathed by Major Mason to his sons, Hon. Samuel Mason and Lieut. Daniel Mason. That part of it between Pequotsepos Brook and the land of the emigrant, Thomas Miner, was held by Mr. Samuel Mason, his heirs and assigns. That part of said way, from the west side of the said Thomas Miner land to Blackmore's Head, was held by Lieut. Daniel Mason, his heirs and assigns.

It has hitherto been claimed that this sixteen-pole highway, with slight variations, furnished a tract for the highway now leading from the village of Mystic to the Road meeting-house, but such a claim is a wild guess, for the only place where said highways ran along together was a short distance between the Pequotsepos Brook and a point a few rods east of the old school-house site. Nor did the sixteen-pole highway extend west of this brook into the village of Mystic. The present highway from Mystic to the old meeting-house at the Road, with slight variations made therein by the town of Stonington, is a county highway, laid from Pistol Point to the old Road meeting-house, which stood at the time a few feet west of the present church edifice there.

BRIDGES AND FERRIES.

Stonington being situated between Pawcatuck River on the east and Mystic River on the west, required bridges to enable people to travel east and west therefrom. The first bridge was built over Pawcatuck River as early as 1712, the funds to pay the cost thereof was raised by Capt. Joseph Saxton of Stonington and Capt. John Babcock of Westerly. The Governor and Council of Connecticut, sitting officially at New London April 8th, 1712, gave their consent for the erecting of the bridge as per the subscription briefs of Capts. Saxton and Babcock, which provided for its completion in eighteen months. In 1720 this bridge began to need repairing and the Connecticut Assembly sitting at New Haven, in October of that year passed an order:

"That there be paid out of the Public treasury the sum of ten pounds towards the good repairing of the west half of said bridge between the towns of Stonington and Westerly, in such manner in specie as the rates of this Colony for defraying the public charge shall hereafter be paid in, and the remainder of the charge of the repairing of the said one half shall be paid by the town of Stonington; and that the selectmen of said town shall take effectual care that the said half part of said bridge be well repaired forthwith.

"And whereas the town of Stonington are at no great charge about the bridges in the county and within their own town, in comparison of what many other town are, 'tis therefor ordered by this court, that after the said half part of the bridge is well repaired, it shall always be maintained, and kept in good repair by the said town, untill the Court shall order otherwise."

The town of Stonington not relishing the idea of being compelled to keep the bridge in repair, and believing it to be the duty of the colony and not the town, neglected to repair it, nor did the colonial authorities move in the matter at all until the October session of the General Assembly of 1721, when they passed this act:

"Whereas this Assembly has been certified that the bridge between Stonington and Westerly is so far gone out of repair, that the limbs and arms of travellers are endangered thereby, notwithstanding the provision made formerly by this Assembly for repairing it in conjunction with the Government of Rhode Island, upon which nothing has yet been done, and whereas the Governor upon Correspondence with the Government of Rhode Island, for that end has received a letter from Isaac Thompson, Esq., of Westerly, a justice of the peace, signifying that the Assembly of Rhode Island has offered fifteen pounds to be drawn out of the Treasury of that colony for repairing half the said bridge, and that he has the order of that government to cause the said money to be applied to that service, if this government shall agree to repair the other half of the same. It is therefore ordered that fifteen pounds in the whole shall in like manner be drawn out of the Treasury of this Colony for the said end, and that it shall be put into the hands of Mr. John Noyes and Mr. Stephen Richardson of Stonington, who are hereby empowered to apply the said money to the said end, in conjunction with the said Thompson, or any other person who shall be empowered, to apply the like sum to the repair of the said bridge on the behalf of the Government of Rhode Island.

"And the said Mr. Noyes and Mr. Richardson are hereby ordered to use their best endeavors to cause the said repairs to be made as soon as may be, and in the meantime to endeavor that the said bridge may be so constructed at each end as to prevent the hurt which travellers are in danger of."

Though the government of Rhode Island had assumed the liability of repairing one-half of said bridge, yet the colony of Connecticut did not intend by the act of their Assembly to expend more than ten pounds in repairing the bridge, so they supplemented their act of 1721 by the following proviso:

"And whereas it was ordered by this Assembly in October last, that the town of Stonington should be at all the charge for repairing one half of the said bridge above the sum of ten pounds, which was then ordered to be drawn out of the public treasury for that end.

"It is now ordered that instead thereof the townsmen or selectmen of said Stonington do raise, in the usual manner upon the inhabitants of said town the sum of five pounds in money, and cause the same to be paid into the treasury of this colony at or before the first of May next."

In obedience to the order of 1721, the selectmen of Stonington, acting in conjunction with the Rhode Island authorities, repaired the bridge so as to make it passable. It was a slim concern, barely wide enough for a single ox-team to pass, but as all the travel of those days was on horseback (except by ox-team), it answered very well the purpose for which it was designed. The bridge then repaired lasted for about ten years. The town of Stonington still adhering to their belief that a bridge uniting two colonies should be erected and kept in repair by the colonies, and not by the town, that simply furnished the ground for the abutments thereof to rest upon, so they refused to repair the west end of the bridge, until it became unsafe and almost impassable, when, in 1731, the General Assembly of the colony of Rhode Island passed an act relative to said bridge as follows: "Upon the petition of Capt. Oliver Babcock and Capt. William Clark, setting forth to the Assembly the necessity of rebuilding Pawcatuck bridge, which is now quite gone to decay, and rendered impassable either for man or horse; and praying that a sufficiency of money may be drawn out of the general treasury for rebuilding this government's part thereof. It is voted and enacted that there be allowed and drawn out of the general treasury a sufficiency of money for building the one half of said bridge, in case the colony of Connecticut will build the other half, and that the colony of Connecticut be acquainted therewith." This act of the Assembly of Rhode Island was transmitted to Connecticut, and at the May session of its General Assembly the following act was passed: "Upon consideration had on the act of the General Assembly of the colony of Rhode Island, respecting the building of a bridge over Pawcatuck River, ordered by this Assembly, that the secretary of this colony send a copy of that act of this Assembly to the secretary of the colony of Rhode Island, made at this session in October, 1720, wherein the town of Stonington is ordered for the future to keep in repair one half of the bridge over Pawcatuck River at their own charge; and that the town of Stonington take notice thereof and conform themselves accordingly." The town of Stonington did not readily yield to the act of the Assembly, nor did they repair the bridge as ordered for several years. They were strengthened in their position by the act of the General Assembly of Rhode Island in assuming the entire expense of one half of the bridge on the part of that colony. They reasoned that if the colony of Rhode Island should build or repair the east end of the bridge, then the colony of Connecticut should build and repair the west end of the bridge; but the colony of Connecticut thought otherwise; they said that because the town of Stonington was subject to less expense than most other towns in the colony on account of bridges that they should build and maintain one-half of the bridge over Pawcatuck River, no matter what the colony of Rhode Island should do in the premises. The town of Stonington still refused to repair said bridge, but the colony of Connecticut was equally determined that they should repair it at their own expense. This state of things continued until 1734, when at the October session of the General Assembly, and after a protracted discussion of the subject-matter, the following preamble and act was passed:

"Whereas this Assembly did at their session at New Haven, in October, 1720, order the sum of ten pounds to be paid out of the public treasury of this Colony toward repairing the half of the bridge between the towns of Stonington and Westerly, and the remainder of the charge thereof to be paid by the town of Stonington, and that the Selectmen of said town should take effectual care that said half part of said bridge should be always maintained and kept in good repair by said town of Stonington until this Assembly should order otherwise. And whereas the said selectmen of Stonington have been very negligent in said affair, for want of some suitable provision in said act to enforce it, notwithstanding the little charge they are at to maintain any other bridges on the country roads. Be it therefore enacted by the Governor, Council, and Representatives, in General Court assembled, and by the authority of the same. That in case the said town of Stonington shall not meet and complete the one half of said bridge within nine months next after, any one of their selectmen being duly certified of the readiness of the Government of Rhode Island, or town of Westerly, to join with them in said affair, then the treasurer of this Colony upon due certification thereof shall immediately send forth his warrant directed to the Constable of said Stonington, requiring him to levy and collect of the inhabitants of said Stonington the sum of three hundred pounds, which sum so collected shall be paid to said treasurer by said Constable of Stonington within three months after his receiving said warrant, in order to be improved to the use aforesaid, and in case the said town of Stonington shall not maintain and keep in due repair according to the aforesaid act, the one half of said bridge, after it is thus erected, they shall forfeit the sum of fifty shillings per week, to be collected in manner aforesaid, and it is further enacted that a copy of this act be forthwitth transmittted to the Governor of Rhode Island."

This act of the General Assembly of Connecticut settled the matter.

MYSTIC BRIDGE.—During the early settlement of the towns of Stonington and Groton, Mystic River was crossed by ferry-boats from Elm Grove Cemetery, in Stonington, to the Burrows' Half-way House, in Groton. Later, and down to the present century, the crossing was by ferry-boats from Packer's village, in Groton, over the river to Pistol Point, in Stonington. At the General Assembly of 1819 the Mystic Bridge Company was chartered as follows:

"Resolved by this Assembly, That George Haley, Nathaniel Clift, Jeremiah Haley, Ebenezer Denison, Manasseh Miner, William Stanton, Ambrose D. Grant, Jeremiah Holmes, and such others as may be associated with them, be and they are hereby incorporated and made a body politic, by the name of 'Mystic Bridge Company,' and by that name may sue and be sued; that said company shall have a clerk, who shall record all votes and by-laws of said company, and be sworn to a faithful discharge of his duty, and who shall be appointed by the president and directors of said company; that the said company shall choose a president and two directors, who, or a major part of them, shall manage all the concerns of said company. The stockholders of said company shall hold their first meeting on the second Monday of July next, at the dwelling-house of Ebenezer Denison, in said Stonington; and said meeting shall be warned by the petitioners before named, by publishing notice thereof in the Connecticut Gazette, printed in New London, two weeks successively before said second Monday of July; and when met, the said company shall choose the aforesaid officers, who shall continue in office until others are chosen in their place and accept their appointment, and said company, when so as aforesaid formed, shall immediately raise sufficient money to erect a bridge across said river at the place already designated by the committee who have reported thereon; and when the commissioners on said bridge shall have accepted the same, they shall give the company a certificate of the same, adjust the accounts and all the expenses incurred relative to said bridge, and give them a certificate of the amount due said company; and said company shall continue to keep up and maintain said bridge in good repair; and to reimburse them their expenses, with ten per cent. interest on the sums extended in erecting said bridge, shall have right and they are hereby authorized and empowered to erect a gate on or near said bridge, at which gate said company shall have right to collect for crossing said bridge the following toll, viz.:

	cts.	m.
"For each coach or hack, or other four-wheeled carriage, drawn by two horses abreast	25	0
Each additional draft horse	3	0
Each chaise, sulkey or other wheeled carriage drawn by one horse	12	5
Additional draft horse	3	0
Each wagon drawn by two horses, loaded	12	5
" " " " " empty	6	2
Each light wagon drawn by one horse, with two persons or less	8	0
Additional horse	3	0
Each loaded cart or wagon drawn by four beasts	12	5
" empty " " " " " "	6	2
Additional draft beast, each	2	0
Man or horse	5	0
Foot person	2	0
Draft horse	3	0
Neat Cattle	2	0
Mules	2	0
Sheep or swine, each	1	0

"Resolved, however, and it is hereby resolved, that the aforesaid rates of toll shall not be collected from persons traveling to attend public worship, funerals, or town, society or freemen's meeting, and returning therefrom;

BRIDGES AND FERRIES.   121

officers and soldiers going to or returning from military duty; persons going to or returning from mill for the use of their families; all of which persons shall be exempted from paying toll, as aforesaid.

"Bonds shall be given to the Treasurer of this State to his acceptance on or before the last day of August next, in the penal sum of five thousand dollars, conditioned that said bridge shall be built by said company to the acceptance of said commissioners by the first Monday of September next, and in default of such bond this grant shall be void.

"The stock of said company shall consist of fifty shares, which shall be transferable on the books of said company, and each member of said company, present at any legal meeting thereof, shall have power to give one vote for each share standing in the name of such member, and the said stockholders, at any legal meeting, shall have power to direct, by major vote, the amount to be paid from time to time on the shares of said capital stock; provided, that this act may be altered, revoked, or amended at any time hereafter at the pleasure of the General Assembly.

"The road on the west side of Mystic River, leading from the Mystic bridge to the old road, as laid and reported by the committee to this Assembly at the last session, remain as laid by said committee till it comes six rods on the land of Ambrose H. Grant, and be thence discontinued; that the former committee, viz.: Moses Warren, William Randall, and John O. Miner, be reappointed to lay a road from the place last mentioned, where said road is discontinued, to the village at Parker's Ferry, four rods wide, and assess the damages to the owners of the land over which the road may pass, and report to this or some future Assembly."

The bridge was erected under the charter, and maintained by the company as a toll-bridge down to 1854 when the towns of Stonington and Groton, at town meetings legally warned and held for that purpose, voted to buy the bridge and franchises of the company for eight thousand dollars, two thousand dollars in addition having been subscribed by the citizens of the villages of Mystic Bridge and Mystic River. Deacon B. F. Langworthy and Capt. John Holdridge, the representatives of the town of Stonington for that year, were charged with the management of the matter before the Legislature in connection with the representatives of the town of Groton. During the session of the General Assembly for 1854 the following enabling act was passed, "authorizing the Mystic Bridge Company to sell their bridge:"

"Resolved, That the towns of Stonington and Groton be, and they hereby are authorized to purchase of the Mystic Bridge Company their bridge and drawbridge over the Mystic River, between said towns, at the price of eight thousand dollars; and in case said bridge shall be so purchased, the president of said company shall lodge a certificate to that effect in the office of the Secretary of State. And from and after the time said purchase shall be made, said bridge shall be and remain a public bridge, free for public travel, and shall be forever supported, and maintained by said towns of Stonington and Groton together, with the draw therein, at their joint expense; and said draw shall always be maintained at not less than its present width, and the same facilities shall be afforded for the navigation of said river through said draw at the like joint expense of said towns as are now furnished by said bridge company.

"And after said purchase shall be perfected, and said certificate lodged on file as aforesaid, the said bridge company shall be discharged from all liability for or on account of said bridge, and deprived of all right to collect toll for the passage of the same."

At a town-meeting legally warned and held in Stonington on the 7th day of August, 1854, it was voted that Asa Fish and Richard A. Wheeler be a committee to join with the selectmen or committee of the town of Groton, appointed for the purpose of receiving the transfer of the Mystic Bridge and all of its appurtenances from the Mystic Bridge Company to the towns of Groton and Stonington, in pursuance of a special act of the Legislature for that purpose, and in accordance with the vote of this town, passed May 12, 1854; also that they pay to the said company the sum of four thousand dollars, with interest from the 1st day of April, 1854, deducting the net tolls for the same time, and that the selectmen are to draw their orders on the town treasurer for the necessary amount to liquidate and pay the liability of the town of Stonington for the purchase of said bridge, and to employ a suitable person in connection with the town of Groton to tend the draw in said bridge and care generally for the same.

During the years 1734 and 1735 the said Pawcatuck bridge was widened and substantially rebuilt by the colony of Rhode Island and the town of Stonington, which stood for a good many years. About ninety-five years ago the Stonington approach was raised and one of the sluices removed, shortening the wood-work some twenty-five feet. With repairs of timber and plank, the bridge so remained until 1873, when it was widened and sidewalks appended and in that condition remained until 1886, when the old wooden bridge was removed, and an iron bridge substituted in its place with protected sidewalks on each side thereof.

SHIP BUILDING.

The first ship-builders in this region were Thomas Wells and George Denison, Jr. They resided in what is now Westerly, though at the time claimed as a part of the present town of Stonington. Joseph, the son of Thomas Wells, was also a shipbuilder. On the 3d day of January, 1680, Joseph Wells signed a contract to finish up a vessel then on the stocks at Pawcatuck. On the 20th of May, 1680, he signed another contract for the building of a vessel, wherein he describes himself as of Mystic, Conn. He married Hannah Reynolds, of Stonington (Mystic), Dec. 28, 1681, and settled in Groton, where he died Oct. 26, 1711. Joseph Wells, soon after his location at Mystic, built a ship for Amos Richardson, of Stonington, which ended in litigation. To what extent ship-building was carried on in Stonington from the days of Joseph Wells down to the Revolution it is now impossible to tell, for no known record thereof exists.

Several small craft were built at Stonington, Long Point, and on the Mystic River before and during the war of the Revolution, but their owners and tonnage is not certainly known. Before the Revolution the accumulated wealth of the inhabitants was largely invested in commerce, building most of their vessels. Long before the Revolution, Col. Joseph Pendleton, of Westerly, built a brig on the west bank of the river below Pawcatuck bridge, which was launched and floated down the river with much difficulty. She was sent to New York under command of his son, Capt. Joseph Pendleton, and was loaded with a cargo for the West Indies, which was carried in safety. After discharging and reloading with molasses, etc., she started on the home voyage, after which nothing was heard of the vessel or crew. The General Assembly of Rhode Island, in consideration of his heavy loss and other misfortunes equally as great, gave him a lottery grant of a tract of land, on part of which is now located

Avondale village. This land waslaid out in one hundred and twenty-six house-lots, and put up in a lottery, each successful ticket-holder drawing a house-lot. The grant was dated Feb. 27, 1750, and was executed by Isaac Sheffield and Elias Thompson, aided by W. Babcock as surveyor. Near the old Tristam Dickens house, on the west bank of Pawcatuck River, opposite said village, there was built in 1823 the schooner Julia Ann, 60 tons, Capt. Nathan Barber.

The following vessels were built by Mr. George Sheffield, of Pawcatuck:

1818, sloop Connecticut, 50 tons; Capt. Stephens.
1823, brig Rimack, 175 tons; Capt. Basset.
1824, brig Pomona, 225 tons; Capt. Newton.
1825, schooner Phoenix, 150 tons; Capt. Spicer.
1826, schooner William, 175 tons; Capt. Peleg Wilbur.
1829, brig Christopher Burdick, 165 tons; Capt. Burdick.

He built two vessels at Stonington Borough.

1821, ship Stonington, 250 tons; Capt. Hull.
1822, brig Pomona, 175 tons; Capt. Barnes.

George Sheffield & Sons built the following vessels:

1830, sloop Caspian, 50 tons; Capt. William C. Pendleton.
1832, sloop New York, 60 tons; Capt. Wilcox.
1833, sloop Pioneer, 75 tons; Capt. Wilbur.
1838, sloop George Eldredge, 75 tons; Capt. Eldredge.
1839, brig George Moon, 250 tons; Capt. Moon.
1840, brig Edward, 275 tons; Capt. Magna.
1842, sloop Pawcatuck, 30 tons; Capt. Ethan Pendleton.
1843, ship Ann Welsh, 450 tons; Capt. Dunham.
1844, sloop China, 40 tons; Capt. Ethan Pendleton.
1845, three-masted schooner Arispa, 100 tons; Capt. Gates.

H. & F. Sheffield built the following vessels:

1847, schooner Phoenix, 80 tons; Capt. James R. Dickens.
1849, schooner Frances, 130 tons; Capt. Hawley.
1850, Water Lily, 75 tons; Capt. J. A. Robinson.
1851, schooner Nebraska, 200 tons; Capt. Blake.
1852, brig Escambra, 250 tons; Capt. Magna.
1852, steamer Tiger Lily, 100 tons; Capt. J. A. Robinson.
1853, schooner Hannah Martin, 230 tons; Capt. Morgan.
1854, schooner Sarah Starr, 250 tons; Capt. Bunnell.
1856, sloop Tristam Dickens, 70 tons; Capt. J. R. Dickens.

1856, schooner George Sheffield, 260 tons; Capt. Stiles.

The following vessels were built by Mr. John Brown.

1821, sloop Flying Fish, 30 tons; Capt. Brown.

1822, sloop Franklin, 30 tons; Capt. E. Brown.

1825, sloop Fame, 46 tons; Capt. E. Brown.

All three built where C. Maxon & Co.'s carpenter-shop is now located.

1830, schooner Fox, 60 tons; Capt. Elias Brown; built where C. Maxon & Co.'s barn is now located.

1832, sloop John Brown, 50 tons; built for a Mr. John Brown, of Fall River, Mass., on the lot formerly occupied by Hall & Dickinson as a lumber-yard.

1832, schoooner Flash, 75 tons; Capt. Elias Brown, built at the same place as the above.

There was framed in the yard in the rear of the late Jesse Breed, West Broad street, a small sloop named Willie Sheffield, between 20 and 30 tons, which was conveyed to the river and launched in April, 1867, commanded by Capt. N. M. Card.

In 1867, June 12th, there was launched near the residence of Timothy Gavitt the sloop Glide, 24 tons; Capt. Gavitt.

There were built west of C. Maxon & Co.'s barn, West street, and launched sideways, the following:

1855, schooner Niantic, 80 tons; Capt. George P. Barber.

1865, schooner Josephine, 50 tons; Capt. Charles A. Maxon.

There were built on the lot formerly occupied by Hall & Dickinson as a lumber-yard, Mechanic street, by Stephen L. Dickerson, for Oliver D. Wells, the following vessels:

1842, schooner Urbana, 137 tons; Capt. Small.

1843, schooner Tallahassee, 120 tons; Capt. Oliver Gavitt.

1842, ship Wabash, 500 tons; Capt. Charles T. Stanton. This vessel was built near "Cuff's house," below Pawcatuck Rock.

Christopher Leeds built several small vessels at Old Mystic after the close of the last war with England, viz.: Brig Hersilia, schooner ———, and others. He built two small steamboats for Silas E. Burrows, viz.: Cadet and New London.

Messrs. Greenmans commenced ship-building at the head of Mystic in 1827, where they built a number of small vessels, mostly smacks and sloops. When they moved down to their present location, in 1838, then called Adam Point, they commenced building fishing vessels, schooners, and brigs for Southern coasting trade. As business increased, the demand came for larger vessels, and they built a number of ships for European trade, and finally, when the California trade opened, they built several large ships for that and other trades, building for one house in New York fifteen large ships, averaging about 1,500 tons each. They have also built quite a number of screw-steamers and side-wheel steamboats, three-masted schooners, yachts, pilot-boats, and in fact, all kinds and descriptions of vessels, both sail and steam, as many as one hundred and twenty-five in all.

The following is an incomplete list:

Ship Silas Greenman, for Everett & Brown.
Ship William Rathbone, for Everett & Brown.
Ship John Baseon.
Ship E. C. Scranton, for Everett & Brown.
Ship Caroline Tucker, 1853.
David Crocket, 1853.
Ship Belle Wood, 1854.
Ship Leah, 1856.
Ship Atmosphere, 1858.
Ship Prima Donna, 1858.
Bark Texana, built in 1859.
Screw-steamer New London, built in 1859.
Bark Lucy E. Ashby, built in 1859.
Bark Heiress, built in 1860.
Brig Belle of the Bay, built in 1860.
Bark Diadem, built in 1861.
Screw-steamer Blackstone, built in 1861.
Screw-steamer Thames, built in 1861.
Screw-steamer Oriole, built in 1861-62.
Side-wheel steamer San Juan, built in 1862.
Screw-steamer Delaware, built in 1862.
Side-wheel steamer Escort, built in 1862.
Ship Favorite, built in 1862.

Screw-steamer Constitution, built in 1862-63.
Screw-steamer Weybossett, built in 1863.
Side-wheel steamer Rafael, built in 1863.
Screw-steamer Montauk, 1863.
Side-wheel steamer Ann Maria, built in 1863-64.
Screw-steamer Idaho, built 1864.
Side-wheel steamer W. W. Coit, built in 1864.
Side-wheel steamer Fountain, built in 1864.
Side-wheel steamer City Point, built in 1864.
Steam-tug George, built 1864.
Brig William Edwards, built in 1865.
Brig Amanda Guion, built in 1865.
Ship Cold Stream, built in 1866.
Bark Cremona, built 1867.
Ship Frolic, built 1868-69.
Schooner G. P. Pomeroy, three-masted, built in 1872.
Three-masted schooner Nellie Lamper, built in 1873.
Two steam-lighters, built 1874.
Schooner William H. Hopkins, three-masted, built in 1876.
Side-wheel steamer G. R. Kelsey, and others.

SHIP BUILDING. 127

Vessels built by Charles Mallory, Esq., at Mystic:

STEAMERS.

	Launched.	Ton.		Launched.	Ton.
Penguin	1859	400	Ella, side-wheel	1864	246
Varuna	1860		Ariadne	1864	792
Owasco, U. S. gov't	1861	575	Euterpe	1864	824
Falcon	1861	875	Loyalist	1864	335
Eagle	1861	198	Twilight	1865	644
Haze	1861	210	A. J. Ingersoll	1865	803
Thorne	1861	210	Varuna	1869	670
Stars and Stripes	1861	410	8 Spanish gunboats	1869	173
Union	1862	1100	Bolivia	1869	509
Oreole	1862	1056	City of Galveston	1870	1110
August Dinsmore	1862	727	City of Austin	1871	1492
Mary Sanford	1862	721	Carondelet	1873	1461
Governor Buckingham	1863	912	Aurora	1874	869
Yazoo	1863	1285	Sisson	1875	94
Varuna	1863	1007	Aeronaut	1875	94
Victor	1863	1340	Gerett Polhimus	1875	78
General Sedgwick	1864	817	Telegram	1876	45
Atlanta	1864	1054			

CLIPPER-SHIPS.

	Launched.	Ton.		Launched.	Ton.
Eliza Mallory	1851	647	Constitution	1857	500
Alboni	1852	916	Twilight (1)	1857	1482
Pampero	1853	1376	Haze	1859	800
Hound	1853	714	Twilight (2)	1866	1303
Samuel Willets	1854	1300	Annie M. Small	1869	1054
Elizabeth F. Willets	1854	825	Part of his whaling fleet.		
Mary L. Sutton	1855	1448			

BARKS.

	Launched.	Ton.		Launched.	Ton.
Ann	1854	700	Tycoon	1860	735
Frances	1855	600	Galveston	1866	622
Lapwing	1859	590			

SCHOONERS.

Eliza A. Potter..1857 247

Vessels built by Irons & Grinnell, Mystic Bridge, in and after 1840:

	Tonnage.		Tonnage.
Brig Almeda	250	Andrew Jackson, clipper-ship	1500
Ship Harriet Hoxie	700	Racer, ship	800
Ship Charles Mallory	800	4 brigs, East, West, North and South	400
Ship Asa Fish	400		
Cavalo, bark	300	6 schooners, names and tonnage not preserved.	
Electric, clipper-ship	1200		
Harvey Burtch, ship	1500	Ship Montauk	400

Mr. Dexter Irons died in 1858, and a firm of Hill & Grinnell was established, who carried on the business.

Vessels built by Hill & Grinnell at Mystic:

	Built.	Tonnage.
Steamer Linda	1864	450
" Relief	1865	300
Bark Mary E. Packer	1866	800
" Aquidnic	1865	350
" Moro Castle	1868	450
Five Spanish gunboats	1868	200 (each.)
Schooner Nellie M. Rogers	1870	50
" Raven's Wing	1870	230
Pilot-boat Eclipse, schooner	1870	70
Ferry-boat Union	1872	125
Sloop-smack Florida	1873	60
Bark George Moon	1874	1000

Vessels by Mason C. Hill:

	Built.	Tonnage.
Steamer Gipsey	1876	70 (about.)
" Annie L. Wilcox	1877	130
" G. S. Allen	1877	130
" Manhanset	1879	128

VESSELS BUILT AT STONINGTON BOROUGH—Peleg Brown and Elisha Denison were in their day engaged in ship-building and in the West India trade, but the names and tonnage of the vessels built and employed by them has not been preserved. Mr. Brown, in his will, dated in 1796, provides for finishing a vessel on the stocks in which he was interested. In 1811, Capt. Nehemiah Palmer and Mr. Morrill built the ship "Volunteer," which was sold in New York. The ship "Cotton Planter" was built by Mr. Giles R. Hallam, which was also sold in New York. Ship "Hydaspy" was built in 1822 by Capt. Edmund Fanning. He also built the ship "Almyra," which was sold in New York. The schooner "George" was built by William Miller. Gen.

William Williams built ships "General Williams," "Robert Brown," and "Pomona." Brig "Seraph," "Othello," and "Bogatar" were built by Captain Edmund Fanning. The brigs "Bunker Hill" and "Dandy" were built by Mr. William A. Fanning. The following vessels were built by various parties, viz.: Ships "Charles Phelps" and "Glen," brigs "James," "Lawrence," and "Tampico," schooners "Joseph Warren," "J. C. Waldron," "Breakwater," "Pacific," "Defence," "Hancox," "James I. Day," and "Williams." Sloops "Hero," "James Monroe," "Paulino," and "Deacon Fellows." The ship "Betsey Williams" was built by Charles P. Williams in 1846. Schooners "Juliet" (yacht), by N. B. Palmer; "White Wing" (yacht), by C. P. Williams; "Josephine," "America," 60 tons, "Madgie," 112 tons, "Palmer," 194 tons, "Madgie," 164 tons (yachts), by R. F. Loper; "Nora" (yacht), by N. B. Palmer; and "Juliet" (yacht), by N. B. Palmer (2). There were built at Quiambaug, by Jesse Wilcox, sloops "Hattie," "Inthia," and several others.

Before the Revolution, and when the West India trade was so profitable, vessels of all sorts and descriptions were pressed into the business. Vessels from fifteen tons and upwards were used, and some of them were framed and set up in the woods where the timber grew, and then taken down, carried to some suitable place on the shore, completed, and launched. Four such vessels were framed in the woods of Deacon Joseph Denison, and two in the woods of Mr. Jonathan Wheeler, besides others in different parts of the town. The "Royal Limb," a famous canoe, was made from the limb of a tree so large that a barrel of molasses could be easily rolled on the inside from one end to the other. The butt of the tree from which the limb was taken was forty-eight feet in circumference. The heart rotted out in its old age, leaving an aperture in the south side, and before it fell a score of sheep could easily find shelter from the weather in the cavity of the tree.

COMMERCE.

The license granted by the General Court of Connecticut in 1650 to Thomas Stanton for the exclusive trade of Pawcatuck River for three years laid the foundation of the commercial relations of this town with the West Indies. Parties in New London became interested with Thomas Stanton & Sons, and carried on a successful trade with the Indians and the West Indies, principally with Barbadoes. Trade was carried on with Boston and the Plymouth Colony to a considerable extent. Thomas Hewitt, of Hingham, came into Mystic River with his vessel in 1656 and bought up the surplus produce of the planters in that region. He subsequently married Hannah, daughter of Walter Palmer, in 1659, bought and built him a house on the grounds of the Elm Grove Cemetery and continued his coasting trade, and left for the West Indies in 1661 and was never again heard of, vessel or crew. The Messrs. Stanton continued and increased their fur trade, and in order to reap all of its advantages Daniel Stanton, one of the firm, went and resided at Barbadoes, where he remained until his death. Edward Denison, son of the ship builder, George Denison of Westerly, removed to Stonington and built the house lately occupied by the town clerk's office at the Road, in 1714, where he remained until 1752, when he built the first house in Stonington Borough, and that year built the first wharf of the place, and he and his son, John Denison, continued their West India trade, in which they had previously been engaged at Pawtucket. Samuel Stanton soon sold out his real estate at Pawcatuck, and with his son Nathan came over to the borough and built the Polly Breed house, and engaged in the West India trade, which was followed by Capt. Ebenezer Stanton, son of Nathan Stanton.

William Williams, living near Mystic, became largely interested in commerce. His son William commanded one of his vessels, and died at sea in 1770. His wife died at home a few days after, leaving two children, William, the late Maj. Gen.

William Williams, and Eunice, first the wife of Rufus Wheeler, and after his death the wife of the Hon. Coddington Billings, and mother of his sons, Noyes and William, and daughter, Mrs. Eunice Farnsworth, of Norwich, Connecticut. Deacon Joseph Denison was also interested in commerce, and later the Haley family participated. The Revolutionary war almost annihilated commerce. After its close it slowly recovered, but before it had assumed its former proportions the embargo acts of Congress and the complications with European powers prostrated it again.

Then came the last war with England, with a close blockade of our harbor, crippling our commerce. After the close of the war commerce again revived, and has been prosecuted with great success in almost every department of trade. Fishing and the whaling business very early attracted the attention of our people. In 1647 the General Court enacted this: "If Mr. Whiting, with any others, shall make trial and prosecute a design for the taking of whale within these liberties, and if upon trial within the term of two years they shall like to go on, no others shall be suffered to interrupt them for the term of seven years." Whether Mr. Whiting engaged in the business or not does not appear. As early as 1701, and for several years thereafter, whales were taken and brought on shore at Wadawanuck, the oil tried out and sold in Boston and the West Indies. After the close of the Revolution a law was passed exempting all vessel property engaged in the fish and whaling business from taxation. Also the polls of the men employed four months on board a fishing or whaling vessel was exempted from taxation.

After 1790 the exemption of the vessel property was repealed, but the exempting of poll-tax was continued. Under the patronage of the State, whaling was carried on principally at and from New London, but nothing of the kind was done here until some time after the close of the last war with England. On and after 1830 several prominent business men in Stonington gave their attention to the whaling business, viz., Capt. Charles P. Williams, Charles Mallory, John F. Trumbull, Francis Pendleton, Joseph E. Smith and Moses Pendleton, aided by a most intelligent and able set of captains and subordinates, successfully prosecuted the business, and for several years it was the most lucrative business of the town. The following is a list of the vessels employed in whaling:

132   HISTORY OF STONINGTON.

Vessels.	Tonnage.	Owners and Agents.
America	464	Charles P. Williams
Bolton, bark	220	" "
Charles Phelps	362	" "
Caledonia	446	" "
Corvo	349	" "
Calumet	300	" "
Eugene	297	" "
Fellowes	268	" "
George	251	" "
Herald	241	" "
Thomas Williams	340	" "
United States	244	" "
Mary and Susan	392	" "
Autumn	220	" "
Betsey Williams	400	" "
Cavalier	295	" "
Rebecca Groves, brig	128	" "
Beaver	427	" "
Prudent	398	" "
S. H. Waterman, bark	480	" "
Uxor, brig	100	" "
Francis, brig		" "
Acasto	330	" "
Henrietta, schooner	139	" "
Colossus, schooner	85	" "
Pacific, schooner	96	" "
Penguin	82	" "
Sovereign	95	" "
Byron, bark	178	John F. Trumbull.
Cabinet	305	" "
Cynosure	230	" "
Tiger	311	" "
Pheletus, bark	278	" "
Richard Henry, bark	137	" "
Tybee	299	" "
Sophia and Eliza	206	" "
Sarah E. Spear, bark	150	" "
Flying Cloud, schooner	100	" "
Toka	145	" "
Aeronaut, ship	265	Charles Mallory.
Bingham, ship	375	" "
Blackstone, ship	280	" "
Leander, ship	213	" "
Romulus, ship	365	" "
Vermont, ship	292	" "
Coriolanus, ship	268	" "

Vessels.	Tonnage.	Owners and Agents.
Eleanor, ship	301	Charles Mallory.
Leander, ship	213	" "
Robinhood, ship	395	" "
Prescott, ship	341	" "
Vermont, ship	292	" "
Bolina	200	" "
Tampeco, brig	225	" "
Uxor, brig	180	" "
Wilmington, schooner	100	" "
Lyon, schooner	150	" "
Cornelia, schooner	150	" "
Frank, schooner	200	" "
Mercury, schooner	305	Pendleton & Trumbull, and Jos. E. Smith & Co.
Newburyport, schooner	341	Pendleton & Trumbull.
Autumn, schooner	181	Elisha Faxon, Jr.
Boston, schooner	200	" "
Cincinnati, schooner	457	F. Pendleton & Co., and Stanton & Pendleton.
Warsaw, schooner	332	Pendleton & Stanton.

In July, 1819, the brig "Hersilia" sailed from Stonington on an exploring and sealing voyage under command of Capt. James P. Sheffield, William A. Fanning supercargo, and Nathaniel B. Palmer mate, for Cape Horn and the South Shetlands and the Antarctic Circle, made a splendid voyage and returned safely to Stonington. The next season a fleet of vessels consisting of the brig "Frederick," Capt. Benjamin Pendleton, the senior commander; the brig "Hersilia," Capt. James P. Sheffield; schooners "Express," Capt. E. Williams; "Free Gift," Capt. F. Dunbar; and sloop "Hero," Capt. N. B. Palmer, was fitted out at Stonington, Conn., on a voyage to the South Shetlands. They reached a place known as Yankee Harbor, Deception Island, during the season of 1820 and '21, where, from the lookout of an elevated station on a very clear day, the discovery of a volcano in operation was made.

To examine the newly discovered land Capt. N. B. Palmer was dispatched in his sloop "Hero" for that purpose. He found it to be an extensive mountainous country, sterile and dismal, loaded with snow and ice, though it was in the midsummer of that hemisphere, and a landing was difficult. On his way back he got becalmed in a fog between the South Shetlands and the newly discovered continent, but nearest the former; when the fog began to clear away, Capt. Palmer was surprised to find his little bark between a frigate and a sloop-of-war, and instantly ran up the United States flag.

The frigate and sloop-of-war then set the Russian colors, and sent a boat to the "Hero," and when alongside the lieutenant presented an invitation from his commander for Capt. Palmer to go on board, which he accepted, and found that their ship was on a voyage of discovery around the world, sent out by the Emperor Alexander of Russia After an interesting interview, followed by an invitation from Capt. Palmer to the Russian admiral to visit Yankee Harbor, where the American fleet lay, where he might procure water and refreshments, which he declined, complimenting Capt. Palmer on the fine appearance of his vessel, adding that he thought he had discovered some new land, but now here we are in the presence of an American vessel. But his astonishment was yet more increased when Capt. Palmer informed him that away in the dim distance might be seen an immense extent of land. Capt. Palmer, while on board the frigate, was treated in the most friendly manner, and the commodore was so forcibly struck with the circumstances of the case that he named the coast far away to the south Palmer's land, and by this name it was recorded on the Russian and English charts and maps. The Stonington fleet returned richly laden in fur, and went back again the next season to the same latitude. Capt. Palmer, in the sloop "James Monroe," a vessel of eighty tons or more, traced his new-discovered land, finding the shore barred by fast ice firmly attached to the shore; after coasting eastward he returned to the fleet, and with them to Stonington, richly laden with furs. Soon after Capt. Palmer was joined by his younger brother, Alexander S. Palmer, who accompanied him on several voyages, and both became distinguished navigators. Capt. Nathaniel Palmer rose to a high position among the importers of New York, and gained their confidence to an unlimited extent, superintending the construction of their ships for the European and China trade, notably the "Great Republic." He was known and respected not only in this country but in Europe.

The sealing business, so successfully begun by Capt. Fanning, Capt. Palmer, Charles T. Stanton, and others, did not prove to be

COMMERCE.

as profitable as the whaling business. The following is an incomplete list of the vessels employed by Stonington and Mystic men in the sealing business:

Brig Frederick	Capt. Benjamin Pendleton.	
" Hersilia	" P. Sheffield.	
" Bogartar	" E. Fanning.	
" Sarah	" "	
Schooner Free Gift	Charles P. Williams.	
" Express	" "	
Brig Enterprise	Stiles Stanton and Joseph E. Smith.	
Schooner Eveline	Joshua Pendleton.	
" Courier	Edward Phelps.	
" Carolina	Edward Phelps.	
" Summerset, elph. oil	Pendleton & Faxon.	
" Thomas Hunt	Joseph N. Hancox.	
" Express	" "	
Charles Shearer		
Brig Henry Trowbridge		
Schooner Montgomery	Joseph Cottrell, Agent.	
" Plutarch	" " "	

J. C. Smith and Stanton Sheffield owned and successfully operated a marine railway at Stonington Borough for several years, and finally sold it to the railroad company for terminal facilities.

MILLS AND MANUFACTURING.

The first mill for any purpose erected in the town of Stonington was built in 1662, under the following stipulations, viz.:

"Articles of Agreement between us whose names are here underwritten as followeth this 10th day of December, 1661. We, Thomas Stanton senior, Samuel Chesebrough, Nathaniel Chesebrough, Elihu Palmer, Nehemiah Palmer, Elisha Chesebrough, Thomas Miner, Sen., & Clement Miner, do bind ourselves each to the other in a bond of twenty pounds to build a grist mill at We-que-te-quock upon the river that runs by Goodman Chesebrough's between this and Michaelmas next, each man to be at equal charges, either in good pay or work, & each man to have equal shares in the Mill & benefits thereof, when it is built, and no man to sell his share to any other person, if any of those will give as much for it as another will; & hereto we set our hands interchangeably this 10th of December, 1661.

"THOMAS STANTON, NEH. PALMER,
"SAMUEL CHESEBROUGH, ELISHA CHESEBROUGH,
"NATH'L CHESEBROUGH, CLEMENT MINER,
"ELIHU PALMER, THOMAS MINER."

This agreement was followed by another between the proprietors of the land to be used in building and was as follows:

"We, William Chesebrough & Elihu Palmer, do hereby engage for ourselves & our relations, that whatever land is taken up for the Dam of the Mill before mentioned, or for any trench work, or that the water in draining overflows or for the setting of the Mill & Mill house shall go free without cost or pay to the undertakers of ye work as witness our hands this 10th day of Dec. 1661 & this land is to remain to the mill & undertakers as long as the mill continues in use; if it be defective and not sold, to return to the above mentioned William Chesebrough & Elihu Palmer, as witness our hands.

"WILLIAM CHESEBROUGH,
"ELIHU PALMER.

"Witness: THOMAS MINER."

This mill has been kept up and in operation ever since, and is now the property of Mr. John F. Chesebrough. Farther up stream Mr. Chauncey Johnson, a few years ago, built another grist-mill, on lands purchased of Capt. Charles P. Williams. The second grist-mill was on the Pawcatuck River, and was built before 1666.

MILLS AND MANUFACTURING.

During the early settlement of the town the wives and daughters of the planters spun and wove all of their linen and woolen cloth, and at first and along dressed the woolen goods by hand fulling-mills, coloring the same to suit their fancy in the old-fashioned dye-tubs.

The first movement to establish fulling-mills in town for the dressing of woolen cloth came up for consideration in town-meeting in 1674, when favorable action was taken upon a letter addressed to the towns of New London, Norwich, and Stonington, by Roger Playsted, of Rhode Island, which, with the answer of the town, is as follows, viz.:

"This may certify, the towns or the inhabitants of the township of New London, Stonington and Norwich that in answer to ye request of John Lamb, concerning building of a fulling mill at or about the head of the River, for ye milling of the cloth that shall be made in those towns. Now if those towns shall please to engage certainly that they will bring all the cloth they shall have occasion to have milled to this mill mentioned, without suffering others to be built within those townships, or sending their cloth unto other places, so long as this mill can answer, or in case this cannot, that one may be erected in some other convenient place allowed and freely granted with what accommodation is requisite for the carrying along of such a design by any of the aforesaid towns from time to time and at all times need shall require.

"Now this may certainly inform you that if God shall spare my life and afford me strength to go on with this design, that I will build a substantial fulling mill with fixtures to dry your cloth which shall be under one yard and half in breadth, unto what size of thickness yourselves shall direct, you paying me for doing, three pence for each yard, so milled and dried, in money or pay equivalent, brought home to the said mill or some other convenient place not withholding my pay above six months after the work is done, and it be concluded on in some short time, I doubt not but in eighteen months after the mill may be finished and ready to go, and if after this is done, any shall desire to have their cloth sheared and dried, I shall join my son to that work provided those that have it so done shall pay what in reason such work is worth, and to conclude if what above said be granted, I to the performance of what is written have subscribed my hand this 18th of June 1674.

"ROGER PLAYSTED.

"Stonington."

"Stonington answer to Mr. Playsted's petition, that they are freely willing that Mr. Playsted should go on about erecting a fulling mill in these parts and to manifest their liking of the petitions made by the said Playsted unto them and their acceptance of the same; this was agreed upon and manifested by a vote at a public town meeting and ordered to be recorded by the selectmen, &c.

"December 29, 1674."

The towns of New London and Norwich did not accept of his proposition, so the whole matter failed.

John Shaw built the first fulling-mill in town on Stony Brook, west of the present residence of Mr. and Mrs. Burnside Coon, and on land owned by them. The date of its erection is not certainly known. The location of the dam and the margin of the pond can now be traced. It is more than a hundred years since it went out of use.

"Weave-shops" were introduced and in use as early as fulling-mills. The one manufactured the cloth and the other dressed it. The wool was carded and spun by hand; the flax was pulled, rotted, broke, swingled, hetcheled, spun, wove, and bleached by hand. Later on these "weave-shops" became a sort of manufacturing establishment for the production of first-class goods. As early as 1760 the basement of the dwelling-house of Richard Wheeler was used by him for a weave-shop. He was also engaged in tanning leather, using vats made of chestnut logs, dug out and imbedded in the ground near Stony Brook. Apprentices for this trade were regularly indentured and served for a given time, and then set up business for themselves.

A mill for the manufacture of potash, saltpetre, and powder, before and during the Revolutionary war, stood near Stony Brook, on land now owned by Nelson H. Wheeler, occupied by Arthur G. Wheeler, owned and operated by the Shaws. During the Revolutionary war the blockade of our seacoast by the British was so close and effective that sugar and molasses became so scarce that it was well-nigh impossible to get any for use. So a sugar-mill was erected on lands of Deacon Joseph Denison and operated by horse-power, in which sweet-corn stalks were ground up and the juice pressed out and boiled down for molasses and sugar.

Before the Revolution a grist-mill was erected on Stony Brook, and known for a time as the Fellows' Mill. Afterwards it became the property of Dr. William Lord, who held it until he left town, when it was purchased by the late Capt. Charles H. Smith, who erected a new dam, increasing the area of the pondage, and built a new mill below the old one, with a powerful water-fall, which made it one of the best grist-mills in the State. After the death of Capt. Smith the property was sold to Frank

Sylvia, who in turn sold it to the New York, Providence and Boston Railroad Company for a reservoir.

Mechanics and artisans are important persons in any community, more especially in a new settlement, where a large share of the capital is used in new buildings. Carpenters, masons, and blacksmiths are indispensable in a new settlement. William Chesebrough, our first planter, was a blacksmith and gunsmith, but did not follow either branch of his trade after he came here to reside. James Babcock, of Westerly, was a blacksmith, and continued the business as long as he lived. John Frink was our first carpenter, and resided on Taugwonk. In 1673 there were blacksmiths in New London and Westerly, but none in Stonington. At a town-meeting in 1671, two twelve-acre lots were given to Jeremie Burch, if he would come here and do the town's smithery, which, however, he declined. Whereupon the town ordered the lots given to him to be attached and restored to the town, which was done July 24, 1674. The town did not procure a blacksmith for a year or more, nor until James Dean of Taunton, Plymouth Colony, came here and entered into an arrangement with the town, which was adopted at a town-meeting as follows:

"At a public town meeting Legally warned and held on February the 28th, 1676.

"For encouragement of James Dean in order to his settlement in our town, Sundry inhabitants do engage themselves to pay unto the said Dean a certain sum, which, for and in consideration the said Dean promiseth to repay all such persons in smithery work as each person shall have occasion for, and that these presents shall reciprocally be binding each to the other.

"The first, Mr. Stanton Sen. promiseth five pounds, Mr. Amos Richardson & his son Stephen five pounds, Nehemiah Palmer twenty shillings, Nathaniel Chesebrough twenty shillings, Thomas Stanton Jun, twenty shillings, Ephraim Miner twenty shillings, Joseph Miner twenty shillings, Goodman Reynolds and his son Thomas four shillings, Thomas Bell twenty shillings, Henry Stephens twenty shillings, Edmund Fanning twenty shillings, Joshua Holmes twenty shillings, Ezekial Main twenty shillings, Samuel Minor twenty shillings, Adam Gallup twenty shillings, Mr. James Noyes ten shillings, Goodman Searles twenty shillings.

"The sum above mentioned is to be payed to James Dean at some place in Stonington where he may or shall dwell, in either pork, butter or wheat at or before the last of November next ensuing after the date hereof; the species mentioned are to be paid at price currant.

"The same day was granted to James Dean twenty-four acres of upland which was formerly reserved by the town for the accommodation of a smith, which grant is to him and his heirs or assigns, provided he doth the towns iron work for and during the full term of three years, but if the said Dean shall decease in our town within the term, then the said grant shall properly appertain to the heirs of the said Dean without molestation by or from the town, and this grant obligeth no further, but that for the future each person payeth honestly for what work they have done."

"At a Town meeting legally warned, Sept. 6, 1677, it was voted for the smith's encouragement, Mr. Richardson promiseth to cart the thatch to cover his house, and to allow him ten days work more.

"Adam Gallup, Thomas Edwards, and Thomas Fanning promiseth to cut the thatch for his house.

"Lieutenant Mason and Gershom Palmer each of them one day's work in carting.

"Mr. Wheeler promiseth him two hundred of laths.

"At the same day James Dean had granted him one hundred acres of land where he can find it upon the commons, provided it intrench not upon any former grant i. e.: all former grants being first satisfied.

"The selectmen vide."

"At a legal town meeting held June 1st, 1682, it was passed by vote that James Dean hath performed his condition made with the town.

"February the 26th, 1676."

The two twenty-four acre lots, or double lots, as they were sometimes called, set apart and designed for the use of a blacksmith, were situated a little way easterly of the quarry ledge at Quiambaug.

Here Mr. James Dean erected his home and shop, and commenced business in 1676. Subsequently he received other grants of land, and became a prominent man in the affairs of the town. He continued to reside in Stonington until 1698, when he and several other of the planters of Stonington went up and joined the new settlement of Plainfield, Conn., and was chosen town clerk there in 1699.

His son, James Dean, Jr., remained and built what in our early days was known as the "Old Dean House," at Dean's Mills, about the year 1700, which was destroyed by fire in 1848. James Dean, Jr., did not confine himself to blacksmithing, but learned the business of fulling and dressing woolen cloth, and for that purpose erected a fulling-mill on Mistuxet Brook, afterwards known as Dean's Brook, about one-third of the way from the old post road down to the Dean's Mills. There he continued both branches of business until his son, John Dean, reached manhood, when he and his father built a new dam and erected another fulling-mill near his dwelling-house, where the dam now crosses the brook. After this arrangement was effected they devoted their time and attention to cloth-dressing until 1807, when the fulling-mill was enlarged into a factory building, with a grist-mill, new machinery for cloth-dressing, wool-carding, and for the manufacture of cotton and woolen goods were obtained. These were introduced by Mr. James Dean, the son of John Dean, with whom he had been engaged in business from his early manhood. Mr. James Dean continued in business until 1830, when he retired. The property was subsequently purchased by Capt. Charles H. Smith, who improved the premises by raising the dam, increasing the pondage, and deepening the raceway, and leasing it to parties for cloth-dressing, wool-carding, and for manufacturing purposes generally.

Samuel Gallup built a saw-mill and dam and mill-house, about 1765. The site of this saw-mill is now overflowed by the pond of the Mystic Valley Water Power Company. Farther up this brook and west of the residence of Uriah D. Harvey, Mr. Amos Denison built a saw-mill more than one hundred years ago, which for a while commanded a good share of business, but after his death, ran down and was discontinued. Still farther up the stream the late Samuel Wheeler erected a saw-mill in 1845, which was run successfully for several years, and after his death became the property of his son, Samuel P. Wheeler, who kept it in use while he lived, but after his death it ran down, and has since been abandoned. Previous to the year 1800 a grist-mill was erected on Mystic Brook, above the village of Mystic, which from its location and its water-power was considered very valuable property.

In 1814 the General Assembly of this State incorporated the Mystic Manufacturing Company "for the purpose of manufacturing cloths and other fabrics of cotton and of wool, and of cotton and wool together; and of brass, iron, and wood into tools, engines, and machines for mechanical uses; and also of grain into flour and meal in the most advantageous manner," with a capital stock not to exceed two hundred thousand dollars. This company organized immediately and commenced business, leasing the grist-mill property above the village, and the erection of two factories at the north end of the village, which were successfully managed and finally purchased by the late Hon. John Hyde. The south factory has been destroyed by fire. The north one is still standing, though abandoned.

In 1850 another Mystic Manufacturing Company was organized as a joint-stock corporation "for the manufacture of cotton or woolen goods, or both," with the late Henry Harding, Esq., as president. Capital stock, fifteen thousand dollars. The company built the factory at the south end of the village, which, with steam-power and apparatus, was transferred to A. B. Taylor in 1864, who ran it successfully for about ten years. Afterwards it became the property of the Groton Savings Bank, which sold it to the Messrs. Rawitser & Bros.

The firm of George Greenman and Co. built a factory in 1849, at Greenmanville, which was owned and operated as corporate property under the management of Messrs. Crandall & Barber for seven years, since which the factory has been enlarged and run by various parties down to 1873, when it was purchased by W. F. Prosser and George W. Greenman, and they, in company with George Greenman & Co. run it until it was sold by them and others interested therein to James H. Bidwell and Dwight Loomis March 5, 1888. During the late Rebellion a large amount of capital was invested in an establishment for the manufacture of machinery, and located at Pistol Point in the village of Mystic, Stonington side. After the close of the war it was changed so as to manufacture cotton and woolen goods. After several changes as to ownership and management it was destroyed by fire in 1875. Hitherto a planing-mill, in connection with a sash and blind business, was established at Mystic, Stonington side, but after several business changes and structural alterations and introduction of new machinery, it is now known and operated as the Lantern Hill Silex Works.

The Allen Spool and Printing Company, organized as a joint stock corporation in Norwich, Conn., October 31st, 1879, and removed to Stonington January 28th, 1889, and located their plant near Pistol Point at Mystic, where they have prosecuted a successful business, employing the requisite number of persons necessary for its success. Edwin Allen, President; George Dimock, Secretary.

The Mystic Valley Water Company was incorporated under and by virtue of a resolution of the General Assembly of the State of Connecticut, April 13th, 1887, the object and purpose of which was to furnish pure fresh water for the inhabitants of Stonington Borough, the Mystics and Noank. The company was organized agreeably to its charter, elected its officers and commenced operations during the summer of 1887, selecting its water from the Mistuxet Brook in Stonington, purchasing the necessary real estate for its dam flowage, pumping station and reservoir, laying its pipes to the villages aforesaid; furnishing water to its customers agreeably to the provisions of its charter, successfully operating its plant with increasing demand for its water supply. The officers of the company for 1897 were: Thomas E. Packer, Mystic, President; George E. Grinnell, Mystic, Secretary; William Wheeler, Boston, Treasurer. Directors: Lucius H. Fuller, Putnam; Edward E. Fuller, Putnam; Edward Mullan, Putnam; Thomas E. Packer, Mystic; Henry B. Noyes, Mystic; William Wheeler, Boston; D. B. Spalding, Stonington.

The Mystic Industrial Company was organized under the laws of this State as a joint stock corporation, Feb. 5th, 1894, for the manufacture of velvet goods. The plant thereof is located at Greenmanville, near Mystic, on the Stonington side. The officers are Benj. F. Williams, President; John S. Heath, Vice-President; C. H. Latham, Secretary and Treasurer;. Directors: H. B. Noyes, B. F. Williams, Wm. N. Latham, Elias Williams, C. L. Allen, J. S. Heath, D. F. Packer, R. D. Hiersch and Ferd. Avery.

It is not certainly known when the mill dam below Pawcatuck Bridge was built, but probably before 1760. If that dam or any of the up stream dams on Pawcatuck River below the Ashaway junction had been built before that time, the Connecticut General Assembly would have been called upon to enact a law before 1760, which is the date of the first law of Connecticut compelling the owners of dams on that river to open them during the spring season for shad and alewives to pass up to make their annual deposits. Connecticut passed similar laws for other rivers, some before 1760, and others later.

Formerly a grist-mill stood on the Connecticut side, a short distance below the bridge, which has been supplemented by the saw and planing-mills of the Messrs. Maxsons, in aid of their extensive and successful building operations, and other buildings for manufacturing purposes have been erected between them and the bridge. The steam mill on Mechanic street, at Pawcatuck, in Stonington, which was operated by the Moss Manufacturing Company in making cotton goods until 1888, when it changed owners and became the property of the Crefeld Mills Company, organized and existing under and by virtue of the laws of the State of Connecticut, has been enlarged and successfully operated.

Messrs. Cottrell & Babcock commenced business at Pawcatuck in 1855, employing a large number of men in manufacturing machinery of all kinds. Later on they confined their operations principally to the construction of printing presses. In 1880 Mr. Cottrell bought out the interest of his partner therein and organized another partnership known as C. B. Cottrell & Sons, who enlarged and successfully operated said plant until his death, after which his sons continued the business of the partnership in making printing presses of up-to-date inventions, employing a large number of men in their successful business.

At the village of Stillmanville there was built a dam and saw mill on the Connecticut side of the river, when, it is not known. It was owned and operated at one time by Mr. John Congdon, who added an oil mill, and after a while he sold his entire premises to Mr. John Schofield, an Englishman, who introduced carding, spinning, weaving, fulling and dressing of woolen goods. Mr. O. M. Stillman bought this property in 1831, and by industry and various important inventions, added largely to his wealth and to the beauty of the village of Stillmanville. Mr. Stillman built a bridge across the river at that village, which is now public property. The O. M. Stillman factory is now owned and operated by the Messrs. Arnold Brothers, in connection with their mills on the Rhode Island side of Pawcatuck river, under the firm name of the Westerly Woolen Company.

In 1891 the Clark Thread Mill Company purchased of the Messrs. C. B. Cottrell Company a tract of land on the old historic Paul Babcock farm, and erected thereon a large brick establishment with surrounding buildings thereto attached, which plant is now successfully operated by the Thread Mill Company, employing a large number of persons.

Five granite quarries have been opened and worked in Stonington, one at Quiambaug, one at Taugwonk, one at Pequotsepos, and two on the farm of the late Thomas Hinckley.

MILLS AND MANUFACTURING.

A wind-mill at Stonington Point was erected before the Revolutionary war, and as such was used in grinding corn and other grains for several years, but could not compete with the water power mills in town, and so was given up.

John F. Trumbull, Esq., in 1851, built a stone factory in Stonington Borough, which was first used for the manufacture of horse shoe nails. In 1861 the Joslyn Firearms Company was formed, under the joint stock corporation laws of Connecticut, which leased this factory for their business. The close of the war of the Rebellion ended the demand for their goods and the company went out of business in 1864.

The Standard Braid Company was organized in 1866, with a capital of $100,000 and purchased this building and went forward with their business, but the great reduction in the price of their goods and heavy losses compelled them to suspend. Nothing was done in this factory for some time, nor until the Atwood Machine Company purchased the factory and commenced making machinery therein for the manufacture of silk goods. Under the skillful management of this company their business has increased to such an extent that they have been compelled to enlarge the factory, and have their hands full to fill their orders. They give constant and remunerative employment to about one hundred and fifty men.

A company for the manufacture of textile goods was organized in the Borough which did not succeed to the satisfaction of its stockholders, and soon went out of business.

The Stonington Manufacturing Company was organized in 1869, with a capital of $10,000, for the purpose of making household furniture; commenced and carried on their business for a short time and then closed out the same.

The Stonington Jewelry Company was formed in 1873, and subsequently its capital was increased, and after about two years went out of business.

The Stonington Steamboat Company was organized in 1867, with a capital of $500,000. In order to make a satisfactory terminus for its new line of boats in Providence, they changed their base and organized the company as a Rhode Island corporation.

The Stonington Building Company organized as a joint stock corporation, Dec. 19th, 1891, with a capital of $21,500, which was invested in a building now known as the Silk Velvet Factory, which is occupied and operated by the American Velvet Company. Charles A. Wimpheimer, of 131 Spring street, New York city, superintendent. Business operations have been so successful as to require an enlargement of the plant, which was accomplished by adding to its capital $14,500, aggregating $36,000. Officers: Samuel H. Chesebrough, President; F. B. Noyes, Secretary and Treasurer; Directors: Samuel H. Chesebrough, James Pendleton, Edward E. Bradley, D. Burrows Spalding.

BANKING.

The first effort of the citizens of Stonington to obtain banking facilities was in the year 1805. A few prominent men associated themselves under written articles, which, when approved and adopted by the Legislature, were designed to become the fundamental articles of the constitution of the bank, as follows:

"Articles of Agreement between the subscribers to the Washington Bank, to be established in Stonington, Connecticut, are as follows:

"Article 1st.—The capital stock of the bank shall consist of not less than fifty thousand, nor more than one hundred thousand dollars, and shall consist of one thousand shares of fifty dollars each.

"Article 2d.—The subscription shall be payable in four equal payments, the first to be made on the 1st day of March next, when the subscription shall be closed, the second on the 1st day of May, the third at the distance of three calendar months from the second, and the fourth at the distance of three calendar months from the third, unless the directors shall think best to suspend or postpone the payment of the fourth payment to such time or times as the directors may think proper, in which case the directors shall give reasonable notice to the stockholders. The payment to be made in silver or gold coin current in the United States. If there shall be any failure of the first payment on any share, the subscription for such share shall be void. If there be any failure of the second payment, the first shall be forfeited to the bank, and the subscription shall be void; and in case of any failure of the third and fourth payment of any shares, the money paid in previously to such failure on said shares shall be forfeited to said bank and the subscription be void.

"3d.—The capital of the company shall not be employed otherways than in the ordinary course of banking business, and shall not trade in anything except bills of exchange, gold, negotiable notes, or silver bullion, or in sale of goods pledged for money lent and not redeemed in due time, or in lands taken for debts previously contracted, nor shall the corporation take more than at the rate of six per cent. for or upon its loans.

"4th.—The stock of said corporation shall be assignable or transferable only at the bank by the stockholder owning such stock, or by his agent or atttorney duly authorized for that purpose, in such way, manner, and under such regulations as may be instituted by the laws of the said corporation.

"5th.—The affairs of the bank as to all matters not herein regulated shall be under the management of eight directors, and there shall annually, on the ——day of —— in each and every year, after the first meeting, be a choice of directors to serve for one year, and the directors, at their first meeting after their election, shall choose one of their number as president, and none but stockholders shall be eligible as directors.

"6th.—The number of votes to which each stockholder shall be entitled shall be according to the number of shares he may hold, one vote to each share to be given in by himself, or by any person by him legally authorized and appointed for that purpose.

"7th.—Any stockholder or more who hold sixty shares in said company may call a general meeting of the stockholders for purposes relative to the institution, giving at least one week more notice in the public Gazette, or by giving personal or actual notice under his or their hand to each stockholder, specifying the time, place, and object of said meeting.

"8th.—No director shall be entitled to any compensation for his attendance on the business of the bank, unless allowed him by the stockholders at a general meeting, and not less than three directors shall constitute a board for doing or transacting any business of the bank, and in case of death, resignation or removal from office of any director, his place may be filled by a new choice for the remainder of the year.

"9th.—Dividends of the profits of the bank shall be made once in every six months or so much thereof as shall appear to the directors advisable, and the state of the bank shall be made known by the directors at a general meeting of the stockholders whenever they are thereto required.

"10th.—Every cashier, treasurer, or clerk employed in the bank shall, before entering on the duties of his office, give bond with two or more sureties, to the satisfaction of the directors, in such sum as the directors shall order, conditioned for the faithful discharge of his trust.

"In witness whereof we have hereunto set our hands this 12th day of October, 1805.

"WILLIAM WILLIAMS,
"CODDINGTON BILLINGS,
"JOHN DENISON, JR.
"THOMAS SWAN, JR.
"STILES PHELPS,
"JONATHAN PHELPS,
"WILLIAM LORD,
"ELISHA DENISON."

For reasons not now fully understood the Legislature did not charter the bank provided for in the foregoing articles of association, nor was there any bank chartered and established in this town until 1822, when the Stonington Bank was chartered and located at Stonington Borough. Col. William Randall was in the Senate that year, and it was mainly through his influence that the charter for the bank was obtained. He was elected its first president, and held the office until his health compelled

BANKING.

him to resign. He was succeeded in the presidency by Gen. William Williams, who in turn was succeeded by the Hon. Ephraim Williams, followed by Francis Amy, Esq. The bank commenced and carried on business successfully until after the close of the Rebellion, when heavy losses compelled it to suspend, and its affairs soon wound up by receivers, paying forty per cent. on the dollar of the original stock.

Old Mystic National Bank.—This bank was chartered by the General Assembly in June, 1833, with a capital of fifty thousand dollars. The stock was assigned, and the officers elected were as follows, viz.: Elias Brown, Elisha Faxon, Elisha Haley, John Hyde, Asa Fish, Latham Hull, Nathan Daboll, Stephen Haley, Silas Beebe, George W. Noyes (2), Elias Hewitt, and William H. Woodbridge, directors, who elected Elias Brown, president, and George W. Noyes (2), cashier. In 1865 this bank was changed into a national institution, under the laws of Congress. It continued in business until July 7th, 1887, when by a vote of the stockholders thereof it went into voluntary liquidation, paying 115\frac{1}{8}$ per $100 of the capital stock.

The officers of the bank at the close of its business were Nehemiah M. Gallup, Allen P. Williams, Jabez Watrous, Jr., John L. Manning, John Forsyth, directors; Nehemiah M. Gallup, president; Jabez Watrous, Jr., cashier.

Pawcatuck National Bank.—This institution was chartered by the Legislature in July, 1849, with a capital of seventy-five thousand dollars. The bank was organized and elected its officers as follows, viz.: O. M. Stillman, John Brown, Thomas Hinckley, Jonathan Maxson, Jr., Francis Sheffield, D. C. Pendleton and Asa Fish, directors; O. M. Stillman, president; John A. Morgan, cashier.

In 1866 this bank was changed under a law of Congress into a national institution, with a capital of eighty-five thousand dollars. The present board of directors are Peleg Clark, Peleg S. Barber, Charles H. Hinckley, J. Daniel Davis, E. H. Knowles; Peleg Clark, president; Peleg S. Barber, vice-president; J. A. Brown, cashier.

First National Bank of Stonington.—This bank was chartered by the Legislature of 1851 as the Ocean Bank, with a capital of one hundred thousand dollars. The bank was duly organized under its charter, and the stock regularly assigned.

The first board of directors were Charles P. Williams, Gurdon Trumbull, William Hyde, Jr., Stiles Stanton, A. S. Matthews, Latham Hull, Jr., and F. C. Walker; Charles P. Williams, president; W. J. H. Pollard, cashier. This bank was nationalized Feb. 1st, 1865, and its capital increased to two hundred thousand dollars, and the board of directors were reduced from seven to five persons; and at present are as follows: William J. H. Pollard, Moses A. Pendleton, Frank B. Noyes, N. A. Pendleton, Samuel C. Langworthy; William J. H. Pollard, president; Moses A. Pendleton, vice-president; N. A. Pendleton, cashier.

National Bank of Mystic Bridge.—This bank was organized Feb. 8th, 1864, by articles of association bearing that date, with a capital of one hundred thousand dollars, which was increased to one hundred and fifty thousand dollars, with which business was commenced. The first board of directors were Charles Mallory, Charles H. Mallory, David D. Mallory, George W. Mallory and Benjamin E. Mallory; Charles Mallory, president; Elias P. Randall, cashier. The bank continued in business until May 21st, 1894, when by a unanimous vote and consent of its stockholders went into voluntary liquidation, and closed its business operations at that date, except in liquidation. The officers of the bank at the close of its business were Francis M. Manning, George H. Greenman, Henry B. Noyes, J. Alden Rathbun, Elias P. Randall, directors; Francis M. Manning, president; Elias P. Randall, cashier.

Stonington Savings Bank.—This bank was chartered in 1850, incorporating Charles P. Williams, Gurdon Trumbull, William Hyde, Jr., Ephraim Williams, John F. Trumbull, Stiles Stanton, Hiram Shaw, Oliver B. Grant, Jesse N. Brown, Benjamin Pomeroy, Francis Pendleton, Joseph E. Smith and Horace L. Niles, under the name and style of the Stonington Savings Bank. The present board of directors are: Richard A. Wheeler, William J. H. Pollard, Daniel B. Spalding, Moses A. Pendleton, Oscar F. Pendleton, George H. Robinson, Horace N. Pendleton; Richard A. Wheeler, president; William J. H. Pollard, vice-president; Daniel B. Spalding, secretary and treasurer.

The People's Saving Bank.—This bank was chartered in 1886, incorporating Peleg S. Barber, C. B. Cottrell, Charles Perrin, Stanton Hazard, Charles H. Hinckley, Charles Richmond,

Benjamin G. Richmond, Charles H. Browning, Calvin Davis, John McDonald, William F. Watrous, A. R. Stillman, and their successors, under the name and style of the People's Savings Bank. Said corporation to be located in the village of Pawcatuck, in the town of Stonington, County of New London. The present board of trustees are: Peleg S. Barber, C. B. Cottrell, Peleg Clark, C. H. Browning, E. H. Knowles, D. M. Newell, and C. G. Stanton; Peleg S. Barber, president; C. B. Cottrell, vice-president; J. A. Brown, secretary and treasurer.

RAILROADS.

The first railroad in Stonington was incorporated in May, 1832, under the name of the "New York and Stonington Railroad Company," with the following named persons as corporators, viz.: Charles H. Phelps, Gurdon Trumbull, Peter Crary, William H. Woodbridge, William W. Rodman, George E. Palmer, Charles H. Smith, William C. Denison, Courtlandt Palmer, N. A. Norton, Joseph Goddard, and their associates, successors and assigns. The first board of directors were John S. Crary, S. F. Denison, Charles H. Phelps, Gurdon Trumbull, Courtlandt Palmer, F. A. Norton, and Joseph Goddard. The May session of the General Assembly of this State, in 1833, passed a resolution merging the New York and Stonington Railroad Company in the New York, Providence and Boston Railroad Company, a corporation previously chartered by the State of Rhode Island, to take effect on the 1st day of July, 1833, on condition that the Legislature of that State would before that time pass a similar act or merger of their company with ours; which when accepted and adopted by such aforesaid corporations, the railroad from Stonington to Providence should be known and operated under the name and title of the "New York, Providence and Boston Railroad Company." The State of Rhode Island passed such an act, and both corporations accepted and adopted the merging acts of both States, and the railroad has been so known and operated ever since.

The next and only other railroad company in Stonington was chartered in 1852, under the name of the "New London and Stonington Railroad Company," embodying as corporators Charles P. Williams, Thomas Fitch (2), Charles Mallory, Asa Fish, Frederick R. Griffin, Henry L. Champlain, Nathan G. Fish, Charles C. Griswold, Belton A. Kopp, E. E. Morgan, B. C. Baxter, Henry Hotchkiss, William P. Burrall, N. S. Perkins, Jr., F. W. Lawrence, J. Hammond Trumbull, Benjamin

F. Palmer, Isaac Randall, Louis Bristol, Matthew Morgan, John W. Hull, John P. C. Mather, and Ralph D. Smith, et al. This road was to extend from the river Thames easterly to a junction with the track of the New York, Providence and Boston Railroad in Stonington. It was not built for several years, nor was it finished until it was consolidated and merged with the New Haven and New London Railroad Company in 1856, under the name of the New Haven, New London and Stonington Railroad Company, with authority as such to establish a ferry across the river Thames. This consolidation resulted in the completion of the road from Stonington to New London. This extension road, as it was called, though furnishing the last link of railway communication between Boston and New York, did not prove successful. It became embarrassed, and in the year 1858 the Legislature authorized the New York, Providence and Boston Railroad Company to lease this road from New London to Stonington for a term of two years, provided such a lease would be acceptable to such corporation.

The next year the General Assembly authorized and empowered these railroads to extend their lease or contract for twenty years, provided it was acceptable to both corporations. The leasing operations did not result in a financial success to the new road, nor were they able to pay the interest on their bonded indebtedness. So the bondholders petitioned for a foreclosure of their mortgages, and while they were pending the aid of the Legislature was invoked to enable the trustees of the bondholders to run, lease or sell the road for their benefit.

The Legislature finally, in 1864, reorganized the New Haven, New London and Stonington Railroad Company, under the name of the Shore Line Railway, extending from New Haven to New London. The Legislature the same year also reorganized the old New London and Stonington Railroad Company, embracing the railroad between New London and Stonington, by associating themselves corporators to form a new company and buy out the bondholders, and authorizing the trustees to sell or lease their interest in the road; dissolving the connection between the old New Haven and New London, and the old New London and Stonington Railroad Companies, formed by the merging act of 1856. The New York, Providence and Boston Railroad Company purchased this railroad, ferry property and franchises on the 1st day of December, 1864, and has operated it ever since.

In 1875 the Legislature amended the charter of the New York, Providence and Boston Railroad Company, so as to enable them to form a connection between their tracts west of the Borough of Stonington, and as so arranged it is now in successful operation.

The New York, Providence and Boston Railroad Company, acting under its amended charter of 1875, formed the aforesaid connections, and so as arranged, the road was ably and successfully operated by its officers, who in order to make a connection with the New York, New Haven, and Hartford Railroad Company tracks at New London, in 1882 in response to a petition of the new Providence and Boston Railroad Company, the General Assembly of Connnecticut authorized this company to construct and maintain a railroad bridge with suitable openings across the Thames river, not below Winthrop's Point, with approaches to connect with other railroads in the towns of New London or Waterford. In 1885 the General Assembly of Connecticut passed resolutions providing for a union depot at New London, to be constructed, maintained and used as a union passenger station in the city of New London, by the New York, New Haven and Hartford Railroad, the New London Northern Railroad Company and the New York, Providence and Boston Railroad Company.

The construction of the railroad bridge over the Thames River, as provided for in the year 1882 by the Connecticut General Assembly, was not commenced until June 1st, 1888, and was formally opened for business October 10th, 1889. This bridge is double tracked, 1,423 feet in length, with a swing draw of 503 feet long, two spans 310 feet each, and two spans of 150 feet each. This bridge and the necessary approaches cost the New York, Providence and Boston Railroad Company over $1,600,000. The New York, New Haven and Hartford Railroad Company took the road of the New York, Providence and Boston Railroad Company under a lease of April 1st, 1892, and by February, 1893, had purchased every share of its stock, when the company was merged and consolidated with the New York, New Haven and Hartford Railroad Company, which with all of its railroad purchases is now known and operated successfully as the New York, New Haven and Hartford Railroad Company, by the following directors and officers thereof: Officers: Charles P. Clark, president, New Haven, Conn.; John M. Hall, vice-president, New Haven, Conn.; C. S. Meller, second vice-president, New Haven, Conn.; J. R. Kendrick, third vice-president, New Haven, Conn.; W. D. Bishop, Jr., secretary, Bridgeport, Conn.; Wm. L. Squires, treasurer, New Haven, Conn. Directors: William D. Bishop, Bridgeport, Conn.; Henry C. Robinson, Hartford, Conn.; Charles P. Clark, New Haven, Conn.; Joseph Park, New York, N. Y.; Chauncey M. Depew, New York, N. Y.; Henry S. Lee, Springfield, Mass.; William Rockefeller, New York, N. Y.; Leverett Brainard, Hartford, Conn.; J. Pierpont Morgan, New York, N. Y.; George MacCulloch Miller, New York, N. Y.; John M. Hall, New Haven, Conn.; Charles F. Choate, Boston, Mass.; Nathaniel Thayer, Boston, Mass.; Royal C. Taft, Providence, R. I.; Charles F. Brocker, Farmington, Conn.; Carlos French, Seymour, Conn.; L. De Ver Warner, Bridgeport, Conn.; Arthur D. Osborn, New Haven, Conn.

THE PRESS.

In 1798, Mr. Samuel Trumbull, son of John Trumbull, printer of Norwich, Conn., came to this village, known then as Stonington Port, and on October 2nd issued the first number of a newspaper entitled "The Journal of the Times." The motto of the paper was:

> "Pliant as reeds where streams of freedom glide,
> Firm as the hills to stern oppression's tide."

The first twelve numbers were printed on small sized paper, but in January, 1799, paper of demi-folio size was used. The next year the title of the paper was changed to "The Impartial Journal." Mr. Trumbull conducted his paper with as much ability as the editors of cotemporary papers. His paper was discontinued in 1805, the editor becoming a merchant.

Mr. John Munson, of New Haven, came to Stonington, and on July 6th issued the first number of a newspaper entitled "America's Friend." It is not known how long this paper continued, probably not more than two or three years.

In March, 1824, Mr. Samuel A. Seabury came here from Long Island and commenced the publication of a newspaper entitled "The Stonington Chronicle." Only one number was issued. The editor died suddenly before another number was issued.

In July, 1824, Mr. William Storer, Jr. (who had previously published a newspaper at Caldwell, situated at the head of Lake George, Warren county, New York), came here, and on July 28th was issued the first number of a newspaper entitled "The Yankee," and took for its motto:

> "Where liberty dwells, there is my country."

After three years its title was changed to "The Stonington Telegraph," under which name the paper existed till July 22nd, 1829, when it was discontinued. Mr. Storer was an able editor, but the enterprise was a financial failure.

The next adventurers in the newspaper line were Charles W. Denison, a native of Stonington, and William H. Burleigh. They were both good writers, and many excellent articles appeared in the "Stonington Phenix" and "Stonington Chronicle." The first number appeared in May, 1832, and the last in May, 1834, but the enterprise was a failure financially. After this, despite the ill success of so many editors, Mr. Thomas H. Peabody, of North Stonington, came here and published a paper styled "The Stonington Spectator," which had for its motto:

"We are the advocates of no party."

He was assisted at first by David Austin Woodworth of North Stonington, and later by Marcus B. Young of Norwich. He was forced by ill health to discontinue the paper after it had existed six months from May, 1834. After him a few other attempts were made at publishing, when Mr. Jerome S. Anderson (who had many years before when a very young man attempted to publish a paper here), commenced the publication of the "Stonington Mirror," Nov. 27th, 1869. This paper has been continued without intermission for thirty years, and its circulation is becoming more extensive every year.

CIVIL OFFICERS.

The following is a list of the judges of the County Court, sheriffs, probate judges, assistants, senators, representatives, selectmen, and town clerks of Stonington, etc.

JUDGE OF THE COUNTY COURT.
Benjamin Pomeroy.

ASSOCIATE JUDGE.
William Randall, for sixteen years.

SHERIFF.
Richard A. Wheeler was elected sheriff in 1860, and re-elected in 1863, 1866, and 1869, holding the office for twelve years; then declined.

ASSISTANTS UNDER THE OLD CHARTER.
1683-87, Samuel Mason; 1818, Enoch Burrows.

SENATORS UNDER THE CONSTITUTION.
1819-21, Enoch Burrows; 1822, William Randall; 1831, Jesse Dean; 1832, Samuel F. Denison; 1838, Asa Fish; 1840, Asa Fish; 1843, William Hyde, M. D.; 1847, Ephraim Williams, Sr.; 1848, Ephraim Williams; 1849, Asa Fish; 1854, Clark Greenman; 1857, Franklin A. Palmer; 1861, Elisha D. Wightman; 1865, Charles H. Mallory; 1867, Ephraim Williams; 1870, Amos B. Taylor; 1876-77, Alexander S. Palmer; 1884-6, Stiles Stanton; 1898, James Pendleton.

The probate district of Stonington was established in 1767, including the present towns of Stonington, North Stonington, Groton and Ledyard.

1767.—Charles Phelps, M. D., judge; Paul Wheeler, clerk.
1770.—June 26th, Elnathan Rossiter, clerk.
1785.—January 4th, Charles Phelps, Jr., clerk.
1785.—August, William Phelps, clerk.
1786.—August 1st, John Denison (4), clerk.
1787.—November 6th, John Denison (3), clerk.
1800.—September 1st, Stiles Phelps, clerk.
1806.—Latham Hull, Esq., judge; Coddington Billings, clerk.
1806.—August 5th, Wm. Lord, M. D., clerk.
1806.—Coddington Billings, clerk.
1807.—December, Edward Smith, clerk.
1810.—Edward Smith, appointed special judge; Alexander G. Smith, clerk.
1811.—Coddington Billings, judge; Edward Smith, clerk.

CIVIL OFFICERS.

1811.—June 4th, Alexander G. Smith, clerk.
1814.—Ralph Hurlburt, judge; Alexander G. Smith, clerk.
1818.—March 17th, Erastus T. Smith, clerk.
1819.—Wm. Williams, Esq., judge; George Hubbard, clerk.
1831.—Asa Fish, Esq., judge; Nathan Daboll, clerk.
1835.—The town of North Stonington was set off by an act of the General Assembly, and established as an independent district.
1836.—Stephen Haley, judge; John D. Noyes, clerk.
1837.—The town of Ledyard was set off by an act of the General Assembly, and established as an independent district.
1838.—Asa Fish, Esq., judge; John D. Noyes, clerk.
1839.—The town of Groton was set off by an act of the General Assembly, and established as an independent district.
1846.—Ephraim Williams, Esq., judge; William H. Woodbridge, clerk.
1847.—Asa Fish, Esq., judge; John D. Noyes, clerk.
1860.—Stiles Stanton, Esq., judge; John D. Noyes, clerk.
1863.—Elias P. Randall, Esq., judge; John D. Noyes, clerk.
1864.—Richard A. Wheeler, judge; John D. Noyes, clerk.
1873.—Moses A. Pendleton, clerk.
1887.—Ephraim Williams, judge; Moses A. Pendleton, clerk.
1892.—Elias B. Hinckley, judge; William R. Palmer, clerk; John Ryan, clerk.

STONINGTON REPRESENTATIVES.

Under the charter of King Charles II. representatives were elected semi-annually.

1664.—William Chesebrough.
1665.—Thomas Miner, Samuel Chesebrough, John Gallup.
1666.—Thomas Stanton, Samuel Chesebrough.
1667.—Thomas Stanton, John Gallup, John Miner.
1668.—Thomas Stanton, Nehemiah Palmer.
1669.—Thomas Stanton, Nehemiah Palmer, Elisha Chesebrough.
1670.—Thomas Stanton, Samuel Chesebrough, Thomas Miner.
1671.—Thomas Stanton, Samuel Chesebrough, George Denison.
1672.—Thomas Stanton, Samuel Chesebrough, Thomas Miner.
1673.—Thomas Stanton, Samuel Chesebrough, Thomas Wheeler.
1674.—Thomas Stanton, Nehemiah Palmer, George Denison.
1675.—George Denison, John Gilbert.
1676.—Nehemiah Palmer, Amos Richardson, Ephraim Miner.
1677.—Thomas Miner, Amos Richardson, Ephraim Miner.
1678.—George Denison, Samuel Mason.
1679.—Thomas Miner, Amos Richardson, Samuel Mason.
1680.—Amos Richardson, Thomas Miner, Samuel Mason, Ezekiel Maine.
1681.—Samuel Mason, Nehemiah Palmer, Amos Richardson, Ephraim Miner.
1682.—George Denison, Samuel Mason.
1683.—George Denison, Thomas Stanton.
1684.—George Denison, Daniel Mason.
1685.—George Denison, Nehemiah Palmer, John Gallup.

1686.—George Denison, Nehemiah Palmer, James Avery, for New London and Stonington.
1687.—George Denison, Steven Richardson.
1688.—No sessions were held.
1689.—Nehemiah Palmer, Thomas Miner.
1690.—Ephraim Miner, John Stanton.
1691.—Nehemiah Palmer.
1692.—Isaac Wheeler.
1693.—George Denison, Nehemiah Palmer.
1694.—George Denison, Nehemiah Palmer, John Denison.
1695.—John Holborn, Nehemiah Palmer, John Denison, Nathaniel Chesebrough.
1696.—John Gallup, Joseph Miner, Ezekiel Maine.
1697.—John Gallup.
1698.—Manasseh Miner, Robert Denison, John Gallup.
1699.—Nehemiah Palmer, Ephraim Miner, Henry Stephens.
1700.—Nehemiah Palmer, Manasseh Miner, Henry Stephens.
1701.—Ephraim Miner, Henry Stephens
1702.—Manasseh Miner, Henry Stephens.
1703.—William Gallup, Nehemiah Palmer.
1704.—Ephraim Miner, Samuel Stanton.
1705.—Nehemiah Palmer, Manasseh Miner, Nathaniel Chesebrough, Elnathan Miner.
1706.—Joseph Miner, Gershom Palmer, Ephraim Miner, Jr., Henurie Hopkins.
1707.—Ephraim Miner, Henurie Hopkins, Manasseh Miner, Ichabod Palmer.
1708.—Ephraim Miner, Samuel Stanton.
1709.—Daniel Eldredge, William Gallup, Ephraim Miner.
1710.—Nathaniel Chesebrough, Manasseh Miner, William Gallup.
1711.—Ephraim Miner, Manasseh Miner, Jr.
1712.—Manasseh Miner, William Gallup, Daniel Palmer.
1713.—William Gallup, Thomas Noyes, Joseph Miner.
1714.—Ephraim Miner, Daniel Palmer, Samuel Chesebrough, Francis West.
1715.—William Gallup, Ebenezer Searles, Nathaniel Chesebrough, Nathaniel Miner.
1716.—Nathaniel Chesebrough, William Gallup, Manasseh Miner, Samuel Stanton.
1717.—Manasseh Miner, William Gallup, Thomas Noyes.
1718.—Manasseh Miner, Thomas Noyes, John Noyes.
1719.—Daniel Palmer, Stephen Richardson, William Gallup, Joseph Stanton.
1720.—Joseph Stanton, John Noyes.
1721.—Joseph Stanton, Ebenezer Billings, John Noyes, Samuel Prentise.
1722.—John Mason, Ebenezer Billings, Ephraim Miner.
1723.—William Gallup, Samuel Chesebrough, Daniel Palmer, Ephraim Miner.
1724.—John Mason, Samuel Prentise, Daniel Palmer, Ephraim Miner.
1725.—Thomas Noyes, Ebenezer Searles, James Miner, William Gallup.
1726.—James Miner, William Gallup.
1727.—John Williams, Increase Billings, Thomas Noyes.
1728.—Daniel Palmer, Increase Billings, Ephraim Miner, John Noyes.
1729.—John Noyes, Theophilus Baldwin, Thomas Noyes, Increase Billings.

CIVIL OFFICERS. 161

1730.—John Noyes, Theophilus Baldwin, Daniel Palmer, Increase Billings.
1731.—John Noyes, Theophilus Baldwin, Joseph Miner.
1732.—John Noyes, Increase Billings, Daniel Palmer, Theophilus Baldwin.
1733.—Thomas Noyes, Increase Billings, John Noyes.
1734.—John Noyes, Increase Billings.
1735.—Daniel Palmer, Israel Hewitt, Theophilus Baldwin, John Breed.
1736.—Joseph Palmer, Theophilus Baldwin.
1737.—Daniel Palmer, Theophilus Baldwin, Increase Billings, John Noyes.
1738.—Joseph Palmer, Increase Billings, Joseph Denison.
1739.—Joseph Palmer, John Williams, Amos Chesebrough, Simeon Miner.
1741.—John Breed, Simeon Miner, Amos Chesebrough, Joseph Denison.
1741.—John Breed, Simeon Miner, Amos Chesebrough, Joseph Denison
1742.—Joseph Palmer, Increase Billings, John Whiting, Joseph Denison.
1743.—Joseph Denison, Simeon Miner.
1744.—Joseph Denison, Simeon Miner.
1745.—Israel Hewitt, Amos Chesebrough, Joseph Denison, Rufus Miner.
1746.—Simeon Miner, John Breed, John Noyes, Joseph Denison.
1747.—Joseph Denison, Rufus Miner, Jonas Prentice.
1748.—John Williams, Rufus Miner, Joseph Denison, Nehemiah Palmer.
1749.—Simeon Miner, Joseph Denison, Samuel Prentice, Nehemiah Palmer.
1750.—Joseph Denison, Amos Chesebrough, Samuel Prentice.
1751.—Rufus Miner, Josiah Prentice, Simeon Miner.
1752.—Simeon Miner, Joseph Prentice, Jonas Prentice.
1753.—John Williams, Simeon Miner, Samuel Prentice.
1754.—Simeon Miner, John Williams, Jonah Prentice.
1755.—Simeon Miner, Joseph Denison, John Williams.
1756.—Simeon Miner, Joseph Prentice, Amos Chesebrough.
1757.—Simeon Miner, John Williams, Samuel Prentice, Amos Chesebrough.
1758.—Simeon Miner, Phineas Munson, Joseph Denison.
1759.—John Williams, John Baldwin, Simeon Miner, Amos Chesebrough.
1760.—Simeon Miner, Amos Chesebrough, John Denison.
1761.—Simeon Miner, John Williams, Amos Chesebrough, Phineas Stanton.
1762.—Simeon Miner, Joseph Denison, Jonas Prentice, Charles Phelps.
1763.—Joseph Denison, Simeon Miner.
1764.—Joseph Denison, Charles Phelps, Jonas Prentice, Paul Wheeler.
1765.—Joseph Denison, Charles Phelps, Paul Wheeler.
1766.—Amos Chesebrough, Paul Wheeler, Henry Babcock, Charles Phelps
1767.—Paul Wheeler, Charles Phelps, Joseph Denison.
1768.—Amos Chesebrough, Paul Wheeler, Charles Phelps, Phineas Stanton.
1769.—Charles Phelps, Paul Wheeler, Henry Babcock.
1770.—Charles Phelps, Phineas Stanton, Benjamin Clark.
1771.—Charles Phelps, John Williams, Daniel Fish.
1772.—Charles Phelps, Daniel Fish.
1773.—Charles Phelps, Benjamin Clark, Daniel Fish.
1774.—John Dean, Nathaniel Miner, Charles Phelps, Samuel Prentice.
1775.—Charles Phelps, Nathaniel Miner, William Williams.
1776.—John Dean, Charles Phelps, Daniel Fish, Joshua Prentice.
1777.—Charles Phelps, Nathaniel Miner, Paul Wheeler.

1778.—John Williams, Peleg Chesebrough, Paul Wheeler, John Swan.
1779.—Jonathan Palmer, Oliver Smith, Phineas Stanton, Benjamin Clark.
1780.—Charles Phelps, Oliver Smith, Henry Babcock.
1781.—Gilbert Fanning, Sanford Billings, Paul Wheeler, Henry Miner.
1782.—Paul Wheeler, Oliver Smith, Henry Miner.
1783.—Charles Phelps, Gilbert Fanning, Samuel Prentice, John Randall.
1784.—Charles Phelps, William Williams.
1785.—William Williams, Nathaniel Miner, Jonathan Palmer.
1786.—Jonathan Palmer, Jr., Joshua Prentice, Elisha Denison, John Randall.
1787.—Jonathan Palmer, Jr., Charles Phelps, Elisha Denison.
1788.—Latham Hull, Jonathan Palmer, Jr., Charles Phelps, Sanford Billings.
1789.—Jonathan Palmer, Jr., Latham Hull, Thomas Swan.
1790.—Charles Phelps, Jonathan Palmer, Elias S. Palmer.
1791.—Charles Phelps, Jonathan Palmer, Latham Hull.
1792.—Charles Phelps, Amos Palmer, Edward Swan, Isaac Williams.
1793.—Charles Phelps, Latham Hull, Daniel Denison.
1794.—Latham Hull, Charles Phelps, Elias S. Palmer.
1795.—Latham Hull, Sanford Billings, Amos Palmer, Isaac Williams (2).
1796.—Amos Palmer, Charles Phelps, Latham Hull, Elias S. Palmer.
1797.—Latham Hull, Amos Palmer, Edward Swan, Elisha Swan.
1798.—Latham Hull, Elisha Denison, Thomas Swan, Isaac Williams (2).
1799.—Latham Hull, Elisha Denison, Stephen Avery (2), Elias S. Palmer.
1800.—Latham Hull, Elisha Denison, Edward Smith, Coddington Billings
1801.—Latham Hull, Edward Smith, Amos Palmer, Sands Cole.
1802.—Amos Palmer, Latham Hull, William Williams, Nathaniel Pendleton.
1803.—Latham Hull, Nathaniel Pendleton.
1804.—Latham Hull, Amos Palmer, Nathan Pendleton.
1805.—Nathan Pendleton, Amos Gallup, Latham Hull, Edward Smith.
1806.—Latham Hull, Nathaniel Pendleton, Amos Gallup.
1807.—Latham Hull, Nathan Pendleton, Amos Gallup, Amos Palmer.
1808.—Coddington Billings, Amos Gallup.
1809.—Amos Palmer, Coddington Billings, Nathaniel Palmer, Jr.
1810.—Coddington Billings, Nathaniel Palmer, Amos Palmer, Enoch Burrows.
1811.—Coddington Billings, Enoch Burrows, Jesse Dean, Amos Palmer.
1812.—Jesse Dean, William Randall, Peleg Denison.
1813.—William Randall, Peleg Denison, Amos Denison, Amos Gallup.
1814.—Amos Gallup, Amos Denison, Enoch Burrows, John Hallam.
1815.—Enoch Burrows, John Hallam, Jesse Dean.
1816.—William Randall, Amos Denison, Enoch Burrows, Jesse Dean.
1817.—Jesse D. Noyes, Enoch Burrows, George Hubbard.
1818.—George Hubbard, William Randall, Samuel F. Denison, Amos Williams.

Under the constitution representatives were elected annually in May.

1819.—Samuel F. Denison, Amos William.
1820.—Giles R. Hallam, Asa Fish.
1821.—Giles R. Hallam, Asa Fish.

CIVIL OFFICERS. 163

1822.—Elisha Faxon, Amos Gallup.
1823.—Elisha Faxon, Jesse Dean.
1824.—Jesse Dean, Jesse D. Noyes.
1825.—Jesse D. Noyes, William Randall.
1826.—Jesse Dean, William Williams.
1827.—Jesss Dean, William Williams.
1828.—William Williams, John Hyde.
1829.—John Hyde, Elisha Faxon, Jr.
1830.—Ephraim Williams, Jesse Dean.
1831.—Asa Fish, George E. Palmer.
1832.—Samuel Chesebrough, Elias Brown.
1833.—Elias Brown, Gilbert Collins.
1834.—Gilbert Collins, John D. Noyes.
1835.—John D. Noyes, Charles H. Smith.
1836.—Thomas Hinckley, Samuel Chesebro.
1837.—Eleazer Williams, Jesse D. Noyes.
1838.—Jesse D. Noyes, John F. Trumbull.
1839.—George Sheffield, John F. Trumbull.
1840.—Gurdon Trumbull, George Sheffield.
1841.—Jeremiah Holmes, Stiles Stanton.
1842.—Henry Harding, Ezra Chesebro.
1843.—Asa Fish, Charles T. Stanton.
1844.—Jesse D. Noyes, Elias B. Brown.
1845.—Benjamin F. Palmer, Oliver B. Grant.
1846.—Benjamin F. Palmer, Charles H. Allyn.
1847.—Charles H. Allyn, Joseph Noyes, Jr.
1848.—Joseph Noyes, Jr., Gurdon Trumbull.
1849.—William Hyde, Jr., Noyes Palmer.
1850.—William Hyde, Jr., Noyes Palmer.
1851.—Gurdon Trumbull, Richard A. Wheeler.
1852.—Jeremiah Holmes, Ossemus M. Stillman.
1853.—Erastus Wentworth, Benjamin F. Langworthy.
1854.—Benjamin F. Langworthy, John Holdridge
1855.—Franklin A. Palmer, Daniel W. Denison.
1856.—John F. Trumbull, Thomas W. Russell.
1857.—Alexander S. Palmer, Joseph Wheeler.
1858.—George E. Palmer, Alexander S. Palmer.
1859.—John F. Trumbull, Elias P. Randall.
1860.—Joseph Cottrell, Horace N. Trumbull.
1861.—Charles Grinnell, Joseph E. Smith.
1862.—Horace N. Trumbull, Jesse D. Noyes (2).
1863.—Horace R. Hall, George E. Lanphere.
1864.—Charles H. Mallory, John F. Trumbull.
1865.—Jonathan Maxon, Amos B. Taylor.
1866.—Thomas S. Greenman, Gurdon S. Crandall.
1867.—George Sheffield, Joseph O. Cottrell.
1868.—Giles Babcock, Asa Fish.
1869.—David D. Mallory, Benjamin B. Hewitt.

1870.—Benjamin F. Stanton (2), George S. Brewster.
1871.—Henry B. Noyes, De Witt C. Pendleton
1872.—Alexander G. Frink, Nathan S. Noyes.
1873.—Giles Babcock, Benjamin F. Stanton (2).
1874.—Samuel H. Chesebro, John Forsyth.
1875.—Alexander S. Palmer, Charles Perrin.
1876.—Joseph S. Williams, George W. Bliven.
1877.—Benjamin F. Lewis, Joseph E. Smith.
1878.—Ephraim Williams, George W. Bliven.
1879.—Joseph E. Smith, Elijah A. Morgan.
1880.—Alexander G. Frink, Elias Williams.
1881.—Elijah A. Morgan, Stiles T. Stanton.
1882.—Stiles T. Stanton, Alexander S. Palmer, Jr.
1883.—Ebenzer P. Couch, Alexander S. Palmer, Jr.
1884.—Ebenezer P. Couch, Peleg S. Barber.
1885.—Louis Lambert Palmer, Minthorn D. Tompkins.
1886.—George W. Tingley, Joseph W. Chesebro.
1887.—George W. Tingley, Joseph W. Chesebro.
1888.—Warren W. Chase, Silas B. Wheeler.
1890.—Silas B. Wheeler, Warren W. Chase.
1892.—George R. McKenna, Arthur G. Wheeler.
1894.—James Pendleton, Henry B. Noyes, Jr.
1896.—James Pendleton, Elias Williams.
1898.—Frank H. Hinckley, George H. Maxson.

TOWN CLERKS.

Southertown.

In 1658, Capt. George Denison was elected town clerk, and held the office up to 1660.

In 1660, Thomas Miner was elected town clerk, and held the office up to 1662.

In 1662, Capt. John Stanton was elected town clerk, and held the office up to 1664.

Mystic.

In 1665, Capt. John Stanton was elected town clerk, and held the office for one year.

Stonington.

In 1666, Capt. John Stanton was elected town clerk, and held the office up to 1669.

In 1669, Thomas Miner was elected town clerk, and held the office up to 1674.

In 1674, Capt. John Stanton was again elected town clerk and held the office up to 1699.

In 1699, Deacon Nehemiah Palmer was chosen town clerk, and held the office up to 1702.

In 1702, Elnathan Miner was chosen town clerk, and held the office up to 1729.

In 1729, Joseph Palmer was chosen town clerk, and held the office up to 1742.

In 1742, Samuel Prentiss was chosen town clerk, and held the office up to 1773.

CIVIL OFFICERS.

In 1773, Peleg Chesebrough was chosen town clerk, and held the office until 1791.

In 1791, Stephen Avery (2) was chosen town clerk, and held the office until the division of the town in 1807.

In 1807, Jesse Dean was chosen town clerk, and held the office up to 1831.

In 1831, John D. Noyes was chosen town clerk, and held the office up to 1873.

In 1873, Moses A. Pendleton was chosen town clerk, and held the office up to 1890.

In 1890, Elias B. Hinckley was elected town clerk, and holds the office to the present time, 1899.

SELECTMEN OF SOUTHERTOWN.

1658.—Capt. George Denison, Robert Park, William Chesebrough, Thomas Stanton, Walter Palmer, Thomas Miner.

1659.—Capt. George Denison, Thomas Park, Thomas Miner, Thomas Stanton, Samuel Chesebrough.

1660.—William Chesebrough, Walter Palmer, Thomas Stanton, Thomas Miner, Elihu Palmer.

1661.—William Chesebrough, Walter Palmer, Thomas Stanton, Thomas Miner, Elihu Palmer.

1662.—Capt. George Denison, William Chesebrough, Thomas Stanton, Samuel Chesebrough, Elihu Palmer.

1663.—Capt. George Denison, William Chesebrough, Thomas Stanton, Thomas Miner, Elihu Palmer.

1664.—William Chesebrough, Samuel Chesebrough, Elihu Palmer, John Gallup, Sr., Thomas Stanton, Sr.

In 1665 the General Court enacted as follows: Southertown is by this court named Mystic, in memory of that victory God was pleased to give this people of Connecticut over the Pequot Indians.

1665.—William Chesebrough, Thomas Stanton, Sr., Samuel Chesebrough, John Gallup, Sr., Elihu Palmer.

In 1666, the General Assembly enacted as follows: The Town of Mystic is by this court named Stonington.

1666.—William Chesebrough, Thomas Stanton, Sr., Thomas Miner, John Gallup, Samuel Chesebrough, Amos Richardson and Nehemiah Palmer.

1667.—William Chesebrough, Thomas Stanton, Sr., Goodman Gallup, Nehemiah Palmer, Thomas Stanton, Jr.

1668.—Thomas Stanton, Thomas Wheeler, Samuel Chesebrough, Nehemiah Palmer, John Gallup.

1669.—Thomas Stanton, Sr., Thomas Wheeler, Samuel Chesebrough, Nehemiah Palmer, Thomas Miner.

1670.—Thomas Stanton, Sr., Samuel Chesebrough, John Gallup, Sr., Nehemiah Palmer, Thomas Miner.

1671.—Thomas Stanton, Sr., Samuel Chesebrough, John Gallup, Sr., Nehemiah Palmer, Thomas Miner.

1672.—Thomas Stanton, Sr., Capt. George Denison, Samuel Chesebrough, Nehemiah Palmer, Amos Richardson.

1673.—Thomas Stanton, Sr., Samuel Chesebrough, John Gallup, Sr., Samuel Mason, Nehemiah Palmer.

1674.—Thomas Stanton, Sr., Nathaniel Chesebrough, George Denison, Sr., Samuel Mason, John Denison.

1675.—Nehemiah Palmer, Samuel Mason, Nathaniel Chesebrough, Thomas Stanton, Jr., Ephraim Miner.

1676.—Nehemiah Palmer, Samuel Mason, Nathaniel Chesebrough, Thomas Stanton, Jr., Ephraim Miner.

1677.—James Pendleton, Nehemiah Palmer, Tobias Sanders, Ephraim Miner, Capt. George Denison.

1678.—James Pendleton, Amos Richardson, Samuel Mason, Nehemiah Palmer, Ephraim Miner.

1679.—James Pendleton, Amos Richardson, Samuel Mason, Nehemiah Palmer, Ephraim Miner.

1680.—Samuel Mason, Capt. George Denison, Nehemiah Palmer, John Denison, Ephraim Miner.

1681.—John Baldwin, Thomas Stanton, Ephraim Miner, Nehemiah Palmer, John Gallup.

1682.—Samuel Mason, Thomas Miner, Ephraim Miner, Nehemiah Palmer, John Denison.

1683.—Samuel Mason, Nehemiah Palmer, Ephraim Miner, John Denison, Thomas Stanton.

1684.—Samuel Mason, Nehemiah Palmer, Ephraim Miner, Thomas Stanton, John Denison

1685.—Samuel Mason, Nehemiah Palmer, Ephraim Miner, Thomas Stanton, John Denison

1686.—Samuel Mason, Nehemiah Palmer, Ephraim Miner, Thomas Stanton, John Denison.

1687.—Samuel Mason, Nehemiah Palmer, Ephraim Miner, Thomas Stanton, John Denison.

1688.—Samuel Mason, Nehemiah Palmer, Ephraim Miner, Thomas Stanton, John Denison.

1689.—Samuel Mason, Nehemiah Palmer, Ephraim Miner, Thomas Stanton, John Denison.

1690.—Nehemiah Palmer, Ephraim Miner, John Denison, Moses Palmer, John Gallup.

1691.—Fergus McDowell, Daniel Mason, Gershom Palmer, Robert Stanton, James Dean.

1692.—Capt. George Denison, Nehemiah Palmer, William Billings, Sr., Ephraim Miner, John Gallup.

1693.—Capt. George Denison, Nehemiah Palmer, William Billings, Sr., Ephraim Miner, John Gallup.

1694.—Deacon Nehemiah Palmer, Thomas Stanton, Sr., Joseph Miner, John Denison, Isaac Wheeler.

CIVIL OFFICERS.

1695.—Deacon Nehemiah Palmer, Joseph Miner, Isaac Wheeler, John Gallup, Nathaniel Chesebrough.
1696.—Deacon Nehemiah Palmer, Joseph Miner, Joseph Saxton, Henry Stevens, Benadam Gallup.
1697.—Deacon Nehemiah Palmer, Joseph Miner, Joseph Saxton, Henry Stevens, Benadam Gallup.
1698.—Deacon Nehemiah Palmer, Joseph Saxton, Joseph Miner, Henry Stevens, Benadam Gallup.
1699.—Ephraim Miner, Sr., Henry Stevens, Joseph Saxton, Manasseh Miner, Nathaniel Chesebrough.
1700.—Ephraim Miner, Joseph Saxton, Gershom Palmer, William Denison, Nathaniel Chesebrough.
1701.—Ephraim Miner, Sr., Gershom Palmer, Joseph Saxton, Nathaniel Chesebrough, Manasseh Miner.
1702.—Nehemiah Palmer, Ephraim Miner, Henry Stevens, Nathaniel Chesebrough, Joseph Saxton.
1703.—Samuel Mason, Nehemiah Palmer, Ephraim Miner, Henry Stevens, Nathaniel Chesebrough
1704.—Ephraim Miner, Sr., Nathaniel Chesebrough, Joseph Miner, Sr., Henry Stephens, Banadam Gallup, Gershom Palmer, William Bennet.
1705.—Nathaniel Chesebrough, Ephraim Miner, Robert Denison, Daniel Palmer, Ebenezer Searle, Ebenezer Billings, William Bennet.
1706.—Nathaniel Chesebrough, Daniel Mason, John Gallup, Isaac Wheeler, Ebenezer Searle, Samuel Richardson, Ebenezer Billings.
1707.—Nehemiah Palmer, Henry Stephens, Joseph Saxton, Benadam Gallup, Benjamin Hewitt.
1708.—Nehemiah Palmer, Daniel Eldredge, Nathaniel Chesebrough, Deacon Manasseh Miner, Benjamin Hewitt.
1709.—Nathaniel Chesebrough, Joseph Miner, Sr., William Gallup, Samuel Frink, Ichabod Palmer, Benjamin Hewitt, William Bennet.
1710.—Nathaniel Chesebrough, Joseph Miner, Sr., Robert Denison, Ephraim Miner, Joshua Holmes, William Gallup, Benjamin Hewitt.
1711.—Manasseh Miner, John Gallup, Thomas Noyes, Benjamin Hewitt, Samuel Stanton, Sr., Samuel Frink, Joshua Holmes.
1712.—Nathaniel Chesebrough, Deacon Manasseh Miner, Ephraim Miner, Daniel Palmer, William Gallup, Benjamin Hewitt, Joshua Holmes.
1713.—Ephraim Miner, Daniel Palmer, Benjamin Hewitt, Joseph Miner, Ichabod Palmer, William Bennet, Sr., Samuel Chesebrough, Sr.
1714.—Capt. Nathaniel Chesebrough, Lieut. William Gallup, Thomas Noyes, David Hillard, Isaac Wheeler, Ichabod Palmer, Josiah Grant.
1715.—Capt. Nathaniel Chesebrough, William Gallup, Thomas Noyes, David Hillard, Isaac Wheeler, James Miner, Moses Palmer.
1716.—Capt. Nathaniel Chesebrough, William Gallup, Thomas Noyes, Isaac Wheeler, Benjamin Hewitt, James Miner, Moses Palmer.
1717.—Capt. Nathaniel Chesebrough, William Gallup, Thomas Noyes, Daniel Denison, Stephen Richardson, Samuel Prentis, Benjamin Hewitt.
1718.—Capt. Nathaniel Chesebrough, Manasseh Miner, John Gallup, Stephen Richardson, Daniel Denison, Samuel Prentis, William Bennet.

1719.—Ichabod Palmer, Benjamin Hewitt, Adam Gallup, Joseph Denison, James Miner, Samuel Chesebrough, Sr., Joshua Holmes.
1720.—Deacon Manasseh Miner, Joseph Stanton, Stephen Richardson, John Noyes, Samuel Prentis.
1721.—Ichabod Palmer, Elihu Chesebrough, Joseph Denison, James Miner.
1722.—Capt. John Mason, Thomas Noyes, James Miner, Samuel Prentis, Joshua Holmes.
1723.—John Mason, Thomas Noyes, James Miner, Daniel Denison, Elihu Chesebrough.
1724.—Capt. Nathaniel Chesebrough, Capt. Thomas Noyes, Daniel Palmer, James Miner, Samuel Prentis.
1725.—Capt. Nathaniel Chesebrough, Ephraim Miner, Thomas Noyes, Isaac Wheeler, John Frink.
1726.—Capt. Nathaniel Chesebrough, Daniel Denison, Thomas Noyes, Israel Hewitt, Samuel Prentis.
1727.—Capt. Daniel Denison, Joseph Stanton, Ephraim Miner, Samuel Prentis, Israel Hewitt.
1728.—Capt. Nathaniel Chesebrough, Joseph Stanton, Daniel Denison, Daniel Palmer, Israel Hewitt.
1729.—Daniel Palmer, Joseph Miner, Deacon John Noyes, Israel Hewitt, Increase Billings.
1730.—Joseph Miner, Daniel Palmer, John Noyes, Israel Hewitt, I. Billings.
1731.—Joseph Miner, Ichabod Palmer, Daniel Palmer, John Noyes, Israel Hewitt, Increase Billings, Mathew Randall.
1732.—Joseph Miner, Ichabod Palmer, Daniel Palmer, John Noyes, Israel Hewitt, Increase Billings, Mathew Randall.
1733.—Daniel Palmer, Joseph Miner, John Noyes, Samuel Hinckley, Israel Hewitt, Increase Billings, John Williams.
1734.—Daniel Palmer, Joseph Miner, John Noyes, Israel Hewitt, Samuel Hinckley, Increase Billings, Thomas Miner.
1735.—Daniel Palmer, Jr., John Noyes, Capt. Israel Hewitt, Samuel Hinckley, Increase Billings, Daniel Brown, Silas Greenman.
1736.—Daniel Palmer, Jr., John Noyes, Capt. Israel Hewitt, Samuel Hinckley, Increase Billings, Daniel Brown, Silas Greenman.
1737.—Daniel Palmer, Daniel Denison, Israel Hewitt, Samuel Hinckley, Increase Billings, John Denison, Silas Greenman.
1738.—John Noyes, Israel Hewitt, Capt. John Williams, Increase Billings, Nathan Chesebrough, Simeon Miner, John Denison.
1739.—John Noyes, Israel Hewitt, John Williams, Increase Billings, Nathan Chesebrough, Simeon Miner, John Denison.
1740.—John Noyes, Israel Hewitt, Increase Billings, Nathan Chesebrough, John Breed, George Denison, Simeon Miner.
1741.—John Noyes, Israel Hewitt, Increase Billings, Nathan Chesebrough, John Breed, George Denison, Simeon Miner.
1742.—Capt. Israel Hewitt, Nathan Chesebrough, George Denison, Thomas Wheeler, John Whiting, Nehemiah Palmer, Daniel Brown.
1743.—Israel Hewitt, Nathan Chesebrough, John Williams, Increase Billings, Joseph Denison, Simeon Miner, Nehemiah Palmer.

CIVIL OFFICERS. 169

1744.—Israel Hewitt, John Williams, Nathan Chesebrough, Thomas Wheeler, Joseph Denison, Simeon Miner, John Holmes.
1745.—Israel Hewitt, John Williams, Nathan Chesebrough, Thomas Wheeler, Joseph Denison, Simeon Miner, Clement Miner.
1746.—Capt. John Williams, Nathan Chesebrough, Rufus Miner, Nehemiah Palmer, Daniel Brown, William Denison, John Holmes.
1747.—John Williams, Nathan Chesebrough, Rufus Miner, Nehemiah Palmer, Daniel Brown, William Denison, John Holmes.
1748.—John Williams, Nathan Chesebrough, Rufus Miner, Daniel Brown, John Palmer, William Denison, John Holmes.
1749.—John Williams, Nathan Chesebrough, Joseph Denison, William Denison, Nehemiah Palmer, John Holmes, John Randall.
1750.—Israel Hewitt, Nathan Chesebrough, Rufus Miner, John Palmer, Daniel Brown, Joseph Hewitt, Jonas Prentice.
1751.—Israel Hewitt, Nathan Chesebrough, Rufus Miner, John Palmer, Daniel Brown, Jonas Prentice, Joseph Stanton.
1752.—Israel Hewitt, Nathan Chesebrough, Rufus Miner, John Palmer, Daniel Brown, Jonas Prentice, John Hallam.
1753.—Israel Hewitt, Nathan Chesebrough, Rufus Miner, John Palmer, Jonas Prentice, Daniel Brown, John Hallam.
1754.—Maj. Israel Hewitt, John Williams, Nathan Chesebrough, Thomas Wheeler, John Palmer, Daniel Brown, Jonas Prentice.
1755.—Israel Hewitt, John Williams, Nathan Chesebrough, Daniel Brown, John Palmer, Jonas Prentice, John Hallam.
1756.—Israel Hewitt, John Williams, Nathan Chesebrough, John Palmer, Daniel Brown, John Hallam, Jonas Prentice.
1757.—Israel Hewitt, John Williams, Nathan Chesebrough, John Palmer, Daniel Brown, Jonas Prentice, John Hallam.
1758.—Israel Hewitt, John Williams, Nathan Chesebrough, Daniel Brown, John Palmer, Jonas Prentice, Phineas Stanton.
1759.—Israel Hewitt, John Williams, Nathan Chesebrough, Daniel Brown, Jonas Prentice, Phineas Stanton, John Denison.
1760.—Maj. Israel Hewitt, Nathan Chesebrough, Jonas Prentice, Phineas Stanton, Benjamin Clark, Robert Stanton, John Williams.
1761.—Maj. Israel Hewitt, Nathan Chesebrough, Jonas Prentice, Phineas Stanton, Benjamin Clark, John Williams, James Noyes.
1762.—Jonas Prentice, Benjamin Clark, John Williams, James Noyes, Samuel Miner, Amos Denison, Capt. Samuel Hubbard Burdick.
1763.—Jonas Prentice, John Williams, James Noyes, John Breed, Amos Denison, Paul Wheeler, Daniel Brown.
1764.—Jonas Prentice, John Williams, James Noyes, John Breed, Paul Wheeler, Daniel Brown, John Dean.
1765.—Simeon Miner, Paul Wheeler, Henry Babcock, Samuel Hubbard Burdick, George Denison, Thomas Prentice, Edward Hancox.
1766.—Paul Wheeler, John Denison (2), Thomas Prentice, Samuel Hubbard Burdick, Edward Hancox, Joseph Page, Joseph Palmer.
1767.—Paul Wheeler, John Denison (2), Thomas Prentice, Samuel Hubbard, Burdick, Edward Hancox, Daniel Denison, Joseph Palmer.

170   HISTORY OF STONINGTON.

1768.—Paul Wheeler, John Denison (2), Thomas Prentice, Samuel Hubbard Burdick, Edward Hancox, Joseph Palmer, Daniel Denison.
1769.—Charles Phelps, Thomas Prentice, Samuel Hubbard Burdick, Joseph Palmer, William Williams, Nathaniel Miner, Simon Rhodes .
1770.—Charles Phelps, Thomas Prentice, Samuel Hubbard Burdick, Joseph Palmer, William Williams, Nathaniel Miner, Elnathan. Rosseter.
1771.—Charles Phelps, Thomas Prentice, Samuel Hubbard Burdick, Joseph Palmer, William Williams, Nathaniel Miner, Elnathan Rosseter.
1772.—Charles Phelps, Thomas Prentice, Samuel Hubbard Burdick, Joseph Palmer, William Williams, Nathaniel Miner, Elnathan Rosseter.
1773.—Charles Phelps, Avery Denison, Cyrus Wheeler, Joseph Palmer, William Williams, Nathaniel Miner, John Breed.
1774.—Charles Phelps, Avery Denison, Cyrus Wheeler, Nathaniel Miner, Joseph Palmer, Elnathan Rosseter, John Breed.
1775.—Charles Phelps, Cyrus Wheeler, Joseph Palmer, Nathaniel Miner, John Breed, Jr., Elnathan Rosseter, Joshua Prentice.
1776.—Charles Phelps, Joseph Palmer, Nathaniel Miner, John Breed, Jr., Elnathan Rosseter, Joshua Prentice, Samuel Mason.
1777.—Charles Phelps, Paul Wheeler, John Williams, Peleg Chesebrough, Jonathan Palmer, Christopher Brown, Joseph Smith.
1778.—Charles Phelps, Paul Wheeler, John Williams, Peleg Chesebrough, John Denison (3), Joshua Prentice, Jonathan Palmer.
1779.—Charles Phelps, Jonathan Palmer, Christopher Brown, Paul Wheeler, James Rhodes, Henry Miner, John Davis (2).
1780.—Charles Phelps, Paul Wheeler, Henry Miner, James Rhodes, John Davis, Joshua Prentice, Gilbert Fanning.
1781.—Charles Phelps, Paul Wheeler, Henry Miner, James Rhodes, Joshua Prentice, Gilbert Fanning, Elisha Denison (2).
1782.—Charles Phelps, Paul Wheeler, Henry Miner, James Rhodes, Joshua Prentice, Gilbert Fanning, Elisha Denison (2).
1783.—Charles Phelps, John Randall, William Williams, Christopher Brown, John Swan, Joseph Denison, Joshua Prentice.
1784.—John Randall, William Williams, Paul Wheeler, Joseph Denison, John Swan, Joshua Prentice, Christopher Brown.
1785.—John Randall, Jonathan Palmer, Joshua Prentice, Nehemiah Mason, Christopher Brown, Sanford Billings, John Holmes.
1786.—John Randall, Jonathan Palmer, Joshua Prentice, Nehemiah Mason, Christopher Brown, Sanford Billings, John Holmes.
1787.—John Randall, Jonathan Palmer, Joshua Prentice, Nehemiah Mason, Christopher Brown, Sanford Billings, John Holmes.
1788.—Charles Phelps, Jonathan Palmer, Latham Hull, Thomas Swan, John Holmes, William Woodbridge, William Chesebrough.
1789.—Latham Hull, John Palmer, William Woodbridge, John Holmes, Christopher Brown, Thomas Swan, Ichabod Eclestone, Jr.
1790.—Latham Hull, Jonathan Palmer, Samuel Stanton, John Holmes, William Woodbridge, Thomas Swan, Charles Phelps, Jr.
1791.—Latham Hull, Daniel Denison, William Woodbridge, Elias S. Palmer, Rufus Wheeler, Daniel Main, Amos Palmer.

CIVIL OFFICERS.

1792.—Latham Hull, Daniel Denison, Amos Palmer, Rufus Wheeler, Elias S. Palmer, Daniel Main, James Dean.
1793.—Latham Hull, Daniel Denison, Amos Palmer, Elias S. Palmer, Daniel Main, James Deane, Samuel Palmer.
1794.—Latham Hull, Esq., Daniel Denison, Capt. Amos Palmer, Elias S. Palmer, Daniel Main, James Deane, Capt. Thomas Noyes.
1795.—Latham Hull, Elias S. Palmer (2), Edward Swan, Nathan Brown, William Woodbridge, Joshua Swan, Elisha Denison.
1796.—Latham Hull, Elisha Denison, Noyes Palmer, Edward Swan, Elias S. Palmer, Stephen Hull, Edward Smith.
1797.—Latham Hull, Elisha Denison, Edward Swan, Edward Smith, Stephen Avery, Stephen Hull, Elias S. Palmer.
1798.—Latham Hull, Elisha Denison, Edward Smith, Edward Swan, Stephen Hall, Gabriel Rogers, Nathan Pendleton.
1799.—Latham Hull, Elisha Denison, Edward Smith, Edward Swan, Stephen Hall, Nathan Pendleton, Luther Avery.
1800.—Latham Hull, Elisha Denison, Nathan Pendleton, Edward Smith, Luther Avery, Chester Smith, Gershom Palmer.
1801.—Latham Hull, Elisha Denison, Nathan Pendleton, Luther Avery, William Williams, Chester Smith, Gershom Palmer.
1802.—Latham Hull, Elisha Denison, Nathan Pendleton, Luther Avery, William Williams, Chester Smith, Gershom Palmer.
1803.—Latham Hull, Nathan Pendleton, William Williams, Chester Smith, Gershom Palmer, Coddington Billings, William Stanton.
1804.—Latham Hull, Nathan Pendleton, Chester Smith, Oliver York, Amos Gallup, Jeremiah York, John Davis.
1805.—Latham Hull, Nathan Pendleton, Chester Smith, Amos Gallup, John Davis, Jeremiah York, Coddington Billings.
1806.—Latham Hull, Nathan Pendleton, Chester Smith, Amos Gallup, John Davis, Coddington Billings, David Coats.
1807.—Latham Hull, Nathan Pendleton, Chester Smith, Amos Gallup, John Davis, Jeremiah York, Coddington Billings.
1808.—Coddington Billings, Amos Gallup, Enoch Burrows, William Randall, Amos Denison, Adam States, Richard Wheeler.
1809.—Coddington Billings, Amos Gallup, William Randall, Elisha Faxon, Amos Denison, Nathaniel Clift, Adam States.
1810.—Coddington Billings, Amos Gallup, William Randall, Elisha Faxon, Amos Denison, Nathaniel Clift, Adam States.
1811.—Coddington Billings, Amos Gallup, William Randall, Amos Denison, Nathaniel Clift, Adam States, Lodowick Niles.
1812.—Coddington Billings, Amos Gallup, William Randall, Amos Denison, John Brown, Nathaniel Clift, Adam States.
1813.—Amos Gallup, William Randall, Amos Denison, Enoch Burrows, Adam States, George Haley, Jesse Breed.
1814.—Amos Gallup, William Randall, Amos Denison, Enoch Burrows, Jesse Breed, Adam States, Jeremiah Holmes.
1815.—Amos Gallup, William Randall, Amos Denison, Enoch Burrows, Adam States, Jesse Breed, Joseph D. Mason.

1816.—Amos Gallup, William Randall, Amos Denison, Enoch Burrows, George Hubbard, Joseph D. Mason, Elias Chesebrough.

1817.—William Randall, Amos Denison, George Hubbard, Elias Chesebrough, Samuel Stanton (2), Amos Williams, Alexander Bradford.

1818.—William Randall, Amos Denison, Giles R. Hallam, Elias Chesebrough, Samuel Stanton (2),, Amos Williams, Alexander Bradford.

1819.—William Randall, Amos Denison, Giles R. Hallam, Elias Chesebrough, Amos Williams, Alexander Bradford, Thomas Palmer.

1820.—William Randall, Amos Denison, Giles R. Hallam, Elias Chesebrough, Amos Williams, Thomas Palmer, John Davis.

1821.—William Randall, Amos Denison, Giles R. Hallam, Elias Chesebrough, Asa Fish, Thomas Palmer, John Davis.

1822.—William Randall, Amos Denison, Giles R. Hallam, Elias Chesebrough, Jesse D. Noyes, Thomas Palmer, Asa Fish.

1823.—William Randall, Amos Denison, Giles R. Hallam, Elias Chesebrough, Henry Harding, Thomas Palmer, Asa Fish.

1824.—William Randall, Amos Denison, Giles R. Hallam, Thomas Palmer, Elias Chesebrough, John Davis, Henry Harding.

1825.—William Williams, Elisha Faxon, Jasper Latham, Nathaniel Clift, David C. Smith, Denison Palmer, Thomas Hinckley.

1826.—William Williams, Elisha Faxon, Jasper Latham, Nathaniel Clift, David C. Smith, Denison Palmer, Thomas Hinckley, Jr.

1827.—William Williams, Reuben Chesebrough, Jasper Latham, John D. Noyes, David C. Smith, Denison Palmer, Nathaniel Clift.

1828.—William Williams, Elias Chesebrough, Benjamin F. Babcock, Jasper Latham, John D. Noyes, Thomas Hinckley, Jr., John Davis.

1829.—William Williams, George E. Palmer, Joseph D. Mason, John Davis, Thomas Hinckley, Jr.

1830.—Elias Brown, George E. Palmer, Joseph D. Mason, George Sheffield, Denison Palmer.

1831.—Elias Brown, George E. Palmer, Joseph D. Mason, Mason Manning, Thomas Hinckley.

1832.—Jesse Dean, Mason Manning, Thomas Hinckley, Gilbert Collins, Jesse York.

1833.—William Randall, Mason Manning, Gilbert Collins, Thomas Hinckley, Denison Palmer.

1834.—William Randall, Mason Manning, Thomas Hinckley, Eleazer Williams, Charles Bennet.

1835.—Thomas Hinckley, Eleazer Williams, Charles Bennet, Samuel Chesebrough, Daniel Bentley.

1836.—Thomas Hinckley, Eleazer Williams, Charles Bennet, Samuel Chesebrough, Daniel Bentley.

1837.—Asa Fish, J. D. Noyes, C. H. Smith, W. C. Moss, Gilbert Collins.

1838.—Asa Fish, Jesse D. Noyes, Charles H. Smith, William C. Moss, George W. Noyes.

1839.—Asa Fish, Jesse D. Noyes, Charles H. Smith, George W. Noyes, Daniel Bentley.

CIVIL OFFICERS. 173

1840.—Asa Fish, Jesse D. Noyes, Charles H. Smith, George W. Noyes, Daniel Bentley.
1841.—Charles T. Stanton, George W. Noyes, Daniel Bentley, Benjamin F. Langworthy, Elias B. Brown.
1842.—Charles T. Stanton, Elias B. Brown, Benjamin F. Langworthy, Francis Sheffield, John Davis.
1843.—Ephraim Williams, Elias B. Brown, Benjamin F. Langworthy, John Davis, Henry Noyes, Oliver B. Grant.
1844.—Ephraim Williams, Elias B. Brown, John Davis, Oliver B. Grant, Henry Sheffield, Ezra Miner.
1845.—Elias B. Brown, Oliver B. Grant, Benjamin F. Palmer, Henry Sheffield, Richard A. Wheeler.
1846.—Ephraim Williams, Benjamin F. Palmer, Henry Sheffield, Richard A. Wheeler, Hiram Shaw, Perez Wheeler, Giles C. Smith.
1847.—Benjamin F. Palmer, Hiram Shaw, Perez Wheeler, Giles C. Smith, John W. Hull, Francis Sheffield, Samuel Copp.
1848.—Hiram Shaw, Giles C. Smith, John W. Hull, Samuel Copp, Elias P. Randall, Pitts D. Frink, Henry Harding.
1849.—Giles C. Smith, Elias P. Randall, Pitts D. Frink, Peleg Noyes, Daniel P. Collins, David N. Prentice, George D. Hyde.
1850.—Giles C. Smith, Pitts D. Frink, Peleg Noyes, David N. Prentice, Ezra Chesebro.
1851.—Giles C. Smith, Pitts D. Frink, Peleg Noyes, David N. Prentice, Ezra Chesebro.
1852.—Giles C. Smith, Pitts D. Frink, Peleg Noyes, David N. Prentice, Ezra Chesebro.
1853.—John W. Hull, Elisha D. Wightman, Ezra Chesebro.
1854.—John W. Hull, Clark Greenman, Henry Sheffield.
1855.—Henry Sheffield, Harris Pendleton, Mason C. Hill.
1856.—Henry Sheffield, Harris Pendleton, Jr., Mason C. Hill.
1857-58.—Alexander S. Palmer, William C. Moss, Leonard C. Williams.
1859-60.—Horace R. Hall, William S. Noyes, Franklin Williams, Leonard C. Williams, Benjamin B. Hewitt.
1861.—Horace R. Hall, William S. Noyes, Leonard C. Williams, Benjamin B. Hewitt, Harris Pendleton, Jr.
1862.—Horace R. Hall, William S. Noyes, Leonard C. Williams, Benjamin B. Hewitt, Thomas E. Swan.
1863.—Horace R. Hall, William S. Noyes, Benjamin B. Hewitt, Thomas E. Swan, Benjamin F. Stanton (2).
1864-65.—Horace R. Hall, Benjamin B. Hewitt, Benjamin F. Stanton (2), Gurdon S. Crandall, Charles H. Denison.
1866.—Horace R. Hall, Benjamin B. Hewitt, Benjamin F. Stanton (2), Gurdon S. Crandall, Charles Grinnell.
1867.—Benjamin F. Stanton (2), Gurdon S. Crandall, Charles Grinnell, Nathan G. Wheeler, Charles H. Rhodes.
1868.—Horace R. Hall, Benjamin F. Stanton (2), Charles Grinnell, George S. Brewster, Nathan G. Wheeler.
1869.—Horace R. Hall, Benjamin F. Stanton (2), Charles Grinnell, George S. Brewster, Nathan G. Wheeler.

HISTORY OF STONINGTON.

1870.—George S. Brewster, Charles Burch, Joseph S. Williams, Sr., Charles S. Bennet.
1871.—Leonard C. Williams, Benjamin F. Stanton (2), Charles Grinnell, Amos B. Taylor, Samuel H. Chesebrough.
1872.—Benjamin F. Stanton (2), Charles H. Rhodes, Joseph S. Williams, Nathan G. Wheeler, William E. Brewster.
1873.—Benjamin F. Stanton (2), Charles H. Rhodes, Joseph S. Williams, Nathan G. Wheeler, William E. Brewster.
1874.—Benjamin F. Stanton (2), Charles H. Rhodes, Joseph S. Williams, Nathan G. Wheeler, William E. Brewster.
1875.—Benjamin F. Stanton (2), Charles H. Rhodes, Joseph S. Williams, William E. Brewster, Leonard C. Williams.
1876.—John Forsyth, Samuel H. Chesebrough, Abel H. Hinckley, George W. Bliven.
1877.—Elijah A. Morgan, Charles Grinnell, Samuel H. Chesebrough, John Forsyth, George W. Bliven.
1878.—Elias Babcock, Joseph S. Williams, Jr., Elijah A. Morgan, Charles Grinnell, George W. Bliven.
1879.—Elias Babcock, Alexander G. Frink, Joseph S. Williams, Jr., Joseph E. Smith, Benjamin F. Stanton (2).
1880.—Elijah A. Morgan, Benjamin F. Stanton (2), Elias Babcock, Joseph S. Williams, Jr., Laughlin Harty.
1881.—Elijah A. Morgan, George S. Brewster, Laughlin Harty, Benjamin F. Stanton (2), Joseph S. Williams, Jr.
1882.—Samuel S. Brown, Samuel L. Dickens, William C. Harris, George E. Tripp, Albigence Hyde.
1883.—Charles H. Cottrell, Samuel L. Dickens, George D. Stanton.
1884.—Charles H. Cottrell, Samuel L. Dickens, George D. Stanton.
1885.—Charles H. Cottrell, Benjamin F. Stanton (2), George D. Stanton, George W. Bliven, William H. Weems.
1886.—George D. Stanton, Joseph W. Chesebro, William H. Weems, Charles H. Cottrell, Samuel L. Dickens.
1887.—Charles H. Cottrell, James Pendleton, George D. Stanton, Eugene O'Neil, George W. Tingley.
1888.—George D. Stanton, Eugene O'Neil, George W. Tingley, James Pendleton, Samuel L. Dickens.
1889.—George D. Stanton, Eugene O'Neil, George W. Tingley, James Pendleton, Benjamin F. Stanton (2).
1890.—George D. Stanton, Bernard Halpin, Benjamin F. Williams.
1891.—George D. Stanton, Bernard Halpin, Benjamin F. Williams.
1892.—Benjamin F. Williams, James Purtell, George D. Stanton.
1893.—George D. Stanton, James Purtell, Benjamin F. Williams.
1894.—Benjamin F. Williams, Eugene O'Neil, Henry M. Stillman.
1895.—George D. Stanton, Benjamin F. Williams, Henry M. Stillman.
1896.—Benjamin F. Williams, Henry M. Stillman, George D. Stanton.
1897.—Benjamin F. Williams, George D. Stanton, Henry M. Stillman.
1898.—Benjamin F. Williams, Henry M. Stillman, James Purtell.
1899.—George D. Stanton, M. D., Henry M. Stillman, Benjamin F. Williams.

PEQUOT INDIANS.

The Pequots were doubtless a branch of the great Mohegan natives, whose principal seat or central place of residence was on the east bank of the Hudson River nearly opposite Fort Orange, now the city of Albany, New York. In their efforts to enlarge their dominions they crossed the Hudson River and attempted to invade the tribal land of the Mohawk Indians, which resulted in war, and after an exhaustive struggle they were driven back across the Hudson and away from their tribal homes and lands in a southeasterly direction, until they reached the territory now known as the State of Connecticut. During their war with the Mohawks, a powerful sachem by the name of Pequoat greatly distinguished himself, and his followers assumed for him the name of Pequot, and in their eastern progress they gave him the name of Wopigwooit, alias Wapyquart, signifying a powerful leader.

After the defeat and dispersion of the Mohegan tribe by the Mohawks, they emigrated easterly and became divided into small tribes, under, and sometimes hostile, chiefs. The Pequots were the most powerful clan of the great Mohegan tribe and lorded it over the smaller clans with a high hand, and in their progress they crossed the Connecticut River and invaded the tribal lands of the Niantic Indians, which bordered on the seashore between the Narragansett and Connecticut Rivers.

The Pequots succeeded in dividing the Niantic tribe into two clans, leaving one clan to occupy Niantic in Rhode Island, and the other clan to occupy Niantic in Connecticut, taking possession of and holding all the lands between the divided clans of the Niantic Indians.

After establishing their authority over the central tribal lands of the Niantic Indians, they commenced and built for themselves two wigwam villages, one on each side of the River Thames, now known as the city of New London and Groton

Bank, which the Pequots occupied when Governor John Endicott, in 1636, came with ninety men to chastise them for murdering Capt. John Oldham and others. Elated with their success in dividing the Niantic Indians, and in being able to hold their central tribal lands in defiance of their power and authority, yet, while so doing they were apprehensive of an invasion by the eastern Niantics and the powerful Narragansett tribe of Indians, who might dispossess them of their seashore dominions and restore the entire Niantic tribal lands to them. So they built two forts to protect themselves from any invasion of the eastern Niantics and Narragansetts, on or near what is now known as Fort Hill in the town of Groton, and the other farther east on Mystic Hill in said town, which they regarded as an all sufficient defense against their eastern enemies.

Thus protected, they felt able to extend their dominions to the north and west, and after arming themselves with their rude munitions of war, they invaded the tribal lands of the Sequeen Indians, which lay on both sides of the Connecticut River in the present county of Hartford, Conn., which was doubtless one of the clans of the original Mohegan tribe, and after three hand to hand conflicts with them compelled the Sequeens to acknowledge their power and authority and became tributary to them.

According to the Dutch account the successful invasion of the tribal lands of the Sequeens by the Pequots was after the discovery of our seacoast by the Dutch in 1614, but no exact date of the time has been preserved.

From Broadhead's Dutch history of New York, vol. i, page 238, we learn that the Dutch projected a trading-house to be located on the Connecticut River, in 1623, but it was not built till 1633, when the Dutch General Van Twiller dispatched John Van Culer, one of his commissaries, with six others, to finish the long projected fort on the Connecticut River and to obtain a formal deed of the tract of land previously selected by the Dutch for a fort and trading-house. One clan of the Mohegan tribe of Indians that migrated to Connecticut from the Hudson River adhered to the original tribal name of Mohegan, and at the time of the first settlement of this State was under the sachemdom of a powerful leader, known as Uncas, who repeatedly revolted against the power of the Pequot sachems,

Wopigwooit and his son Sassacus, but could not release himself and clan from their authority.

His tribal lands were situated in what is now Montville, Conn., where his central wigwam village was located, the site of which still exists. The site of the fort purchased by Van Culer of the sachem of the Pequots, by the general consent of the Sequeen clan, was situated on the west bank of the Connecticut River, within the present limits of the city of Hartford, Conn., adjoining Little River on the north and the Connecticut River on the east. There was a condition in the agreement with the Pequots in the purchase of the land for the fort and trading-house, which appears in the deed of the same as follows: "That the said purchase was made with the free will and consent of the inhabitants there; that the ceded territory, Sicajoock, should always be a central ground, where all the Indian tribes might resort for purposes of trade, and where no war should ever be waged." With the consent of the Pequot sachem and Magasitinne, chief of "Sloops Bay," it was also arranged that the chief of the Sequeens should thereafter live with the Dutch. This land was bought of the Pequots, as conquerors, with the good will and assent of the Sequeens. This deed was dated June 8th, 1633, and the trading-house and fort erected thereon was called "Good Hope."

Previous to the erection of the fort and trading-house, and as early as 1631, an Indian sachem visited the governors of Massachusetts and Plymouth Colonies in the guise of a suppliant, calling himself Waquimacut, and described his tribal lands as a rich and beautiful valley occupied by his and kindred tribes, abounding in corn and game of all kinds and divided by a river called Connecticut. The governors gave him a courteous reception, but declined to enter into any arrangement with him relative to his assumed dominions. This sachem was doubtless a Tunxis Indian, who belonged to one of the clans of the original tribe of the Mohegans, and before the invasion of the Pequots occupied the territory now known as Windsor, Conn., from which he had been driven by the Pequots.

Whether the governors of Massachusetts and Plymouth Colonies were aware of the successful invasions of the Connecticut River valley by the Pequots does not appear. Be that as it may, Governor Winslow of the Plymouth Colony became interested in the story of the Tunxis sachem and sent some men to explore the Connecticut River region to learn the condition of the alluvial deposits on each side of the river, which are now known to be some of the richest meadows in New England. Governor Winslow was so well pleased with their explorations of the Connecticut valley that under the sanction of his Colonial magistrates, he decided to establish and build a trading-house near the mouth of the Tunxis River, in what is now known as Windsor, Conn., in defiance of the Dutch at Fort "Good Hope," some six miles below the site of the contemplated Plymouth trading-house.

In October, 1633, Gov. Winslow selected William Holmes to build the Plymouth trading-house at Windsor. So with the frame of this trading-house and all the requisite materials for its erection and with his commission in his pocket, Holmes set sail for the Connecticut River, which he entered and ascended without meeting with any opposition until he arrived at the Dutch fort at Hartford, when he was threatened with dire vengeance by them, which he disregarded and sailed on to his destination, where he erected his trading-house and palisaded it.

The Tunxis sachem, who had visited Massachusetts and Plymouth with some of the chiefs of the river clans, had been driven away from their tribal lands by the Pequots. It appears that Holmes had brought back to Windsor with him in his vessel some of the chiefs of these river clans, of whom he purchased such land as he found requisite for carrying out his plans. This aggravated and enraged the Pequot sachems, inciting them to acts of violence against the English traders.

Capt. Stone, one of the fur traders on our New England coast, on his way from Boston to Virginia in 1634, entered the mouth of the Connecticut River, for the purpose of trading at the Dutch fort, and while on his way up the river was treacherously murdered by the Pequots.

The massacre of Capt. Stone and his comrades was followed soon afterward by the killing of some friendly Sequeen Indians, who had come to the Dutch fort to trade, relying on the conditional covenants of the Pequot deed of the Dutch Good Hope trading fort.

This massacre was ordered done by Wopigwooit, the chief sachem of the Pequots at the time. Commissary Van Culer with his soldiers punished the treacherous savages by slaying the old Sachem Wopigwooit, alias Wapyquart, and several of his associate assassins.

This excited and angered the Pequots to such an extent that they commenced and prosecuted an unrelenting war with the Dutch, and all pale faces that they caught in their assumed dominions.

At first they sought an alliance with the English of the Massachusetts Colony, for the purpose of diverting all the fur trade of the New England coast from the Dutch and giving it to the English traders. To effect their purpose they negotiated a treaty with the Governor and Magistrates of Massachusetts, by which the Pequots agreed to surrender the murderers of Capt. Stone and his party, giving them also all of their right and title in the Connecticut River and adjoining valley, on condition that they would give all their trade to the Pequots. This treaty was in direct contravention with the claims of the Dutch, derived from their assumed discoveries and conveyances from the Pequots. To recover which, the Dutch sent a strong force to dislodge Capt. Holmes and his men from their trading-house at Windsor, Conn.

Meeting with unexpected resistance, the Dutch force did not attempt to reduce the palisaded fort there, and thus ended all of their efforts to hold by force any trading place on the Connecticut River.

But Capt. Holmes soon found difficulties beginning to thicken around him. The sachems of the river tribes, who had been driven away from their territories by the Pequots, and had been brought by him in his vessel and of whom he had purchased such land as he found requisite for carrying out his enterprise, enraged the Pequots, who claimed that such sachems and their clans were tributary to them and were being restored by the English to their former tribal lands on the Connecticut River, which incited them to acts of violence against the English traders. The Massachusetts and Plymouth Colonies generally regarded the treaty with the Pequots as opening up the rich and fertile valley of the Connecticut alluvial lands to their migration and settlement there. Some of the colonists, however, doubted the validity of their title and appealed to the English courts for a solution of the matter.

Pending the consideration thereof, the Pequots, doubtless apprehending the motives of the English and treacherously disregarding their treaty obligations with the colonists, commenced the massacre of the English and Dutch indiscriminately, and when reminded of their treaty obligations responded by saying that they could not tell the difference between the Dutch and English, as they were all pale faces.

During the years of 1634 and 1635, the Pequots sought every available opportunity to murder every Englishman whom they could find alone or so situated as to be unable to defend himself.

In 1635 the migration overland of the English colonists from Dorchester, Mass., to Windsor, Conn., took place. The towns of Hartford and Wethersfield were settled about the same time.

The atrocious and inhuman murder of the English by the Pequots aroused the Massachusetts and Plymouth authorities to a sense of their duty, as well as their own safety, to put a stop by force to such atrocities and inflict if possible adequate punishment upon the assassins.

So in 1636, they sent General Endicott with ninety men with full power and authority to deal with the Pequots as their treacherous and inhuman conduct demanded. Endicott's expedition resulted in the destruction of a good deal of the property of the Indians, but no decisive results as to the protection of the English from the murderous assaults of the Pequots was attained or secured thereby. The settlement of Windsor, Hartford and Wethersfield, with a General Court organized and acting independent of Massachusetts authority, with deputies thereto elected by said towns, and so terrible and ferocious had the Pequots become and the victims of their atrocities so numerous that the Connecticut General Court when assembled in May, 1637, declared war against the Pequots, and passed an act to raise ninety men, forty-two from Hartford, thirty from Windsor and eighteen from Wethersfield, and appointed Capt. John Mason, of Windsor, commander of the expedition.

The soldiers were enlisted, equipped and provisioned in ten days, and sailed from Hartford May 10th, 1637, accompanied by Uncas and seventy friendly Mohegan Indians. The fleet consisted of three vessels and the English being unacquainted with the navigation of the river ran their vessel aground several times, and after five days they reached Saybrook fort. Capt. Underhill with his detachment of Massachusetts soldiers then at the fort, tendered his services with nineteen men for the expedition, on condition that Capt. Lyon Gardner, the commander of the fort, would consent, which was readily granted.

Capt. Mason then sent back twenty of his men to guard the well nigh defenseless settlements during his absence. After some delay, caused by adverse winds, and after a council of war, Capt. Mason says: "On Friday morning we set sail for Narragansett Bay, and on Saturday towards evening we arrived at our desired port; then we kept the Sabbath. On the Monday following the wind blew so hard at the northwest that we could not go on shore, so also on Tuesday until sunset," at which time Mason landed and marched up to the place of the chief sachem's residence and told him that "we had not an opportunity to acquaint him with our coming around into his country sooner, yet not doubting but it would be well accepted by him, there being love between himself and us, well knowing also that the Pequots and themselves were enemies, and that he could not be acquainted with those intolerable wrongs and injuries that the Pequots had lately done unto the English, and that we were now come, God assisting us, to avenge ourselves upon them, and that we did only desire free passage through his country." He returned us this answer, "That he did accept of our coming and did approve of our design, only he thought our numbers were too weak to deal with the enemy, who were great captains and men skilled in war, thus he spoke somewhat slightingly of us."

Canonicus' wigwam was situated near Wickford harbor or landing place in Rhode Island, and he was the chief sachem of the Narragansett Indians at the time. This was the opinion of the late Hon. Elisha R. Potter, who in his day was the best informed Indian historian of Rhode Island. Mason was undoubtedly piloted to or as near Canonicus' residence as he could go with his fleet by Uncas, with whom Mason desired an interview to explain his coming with armed men into his dominions, as it might be regarded by him as a cause for war, unexplained.

Mason adds to his history of the Pequot war the following: "On Wednesday morning we marched from Canonicus' residence to a place called Niantic, it being about eighteen or twenty miles distant, where another of these Narragansett sachems lived in a fort, it being a frontier of the Pequots. They did not carry themselves very friendly towards us, not permitting any of us to come into their fort. We beholding their carriage, and the falsehood of Indians, and fearing lest they might discover us to the enemy, especially they having many times some of their near relations among their greatest foes, we therefore caused a strong guard to be set about their fort, giving charge that no Indian should be suffered to pass in or out. We also informed the Indians that none of them should stir out of the fort, upon peril of their lives, so as we would not suffer any of them to go out of the fort." Continuing, Capt. Mason says: "That we quartered that night, the Indians not offering to stir out all the while. In the morning there came to us several of Miantonomo's men, who told us they had come to assist us in our expedition, which encouraged diverse Indians of that place to engage also, who suddenly gathering into a ring one by one, making solemn protestations how gallantly they would demean themselves and how many men they would kill. On Thursday about eight of the clock in the morning, we marched thence towards Pequot, with about five hundred Indians. But, through the heat of the weather and want of provisions some of our men fainted, and having marched about twelve miles came to Pawcatuck River at a ford where our Indians told us the Pequots did usually fish; there making a halt we stayed some small time."

An affidavit on our old Stonington land records shows that Miantonomo and Ninigret, sachems of the Narragansett and Niantic tribes, were with Capt. Mason and his friendly Mohegans when they reached Wecapaug, five miles east of Pawcatuck River. But evidently these sachems with a large part of the Indian allies, left Capt. Mason before he reached Pawcatuck River. Uncas renewed his friendship and assurances of assistance to Capt. Mason, and faithfully kept his declarations. After Mason and his soldiers and friendly Indians had refreshed themselves with their rations, they marched to Westerly, about three miles, and came to a field which had lately been planted with Indian corn, where he made another halt and called his council of war, supposing that they drew near the enemy. Mason in his narrative says:

"And being informed by the Indians that the enemy had two

forts almost impregnable, but we were not at all discouraged, but rather animated in so much that we were resolved to assault both forts at once. But understanding that one of them was so remote that we could not come up with it before midnight, though we marched hard, whereat we were much grieved, chiefly because the greatest and bloodiest sachem there resided, whose name was Sassacus, we were constrained, being exceedingly spent in our march with extreme heat and want of necessaries, to accept the nearest." Continuing, Mason says:

"We then marching on in a silent manner, the Indians that remained fell all into the rear, who formerly kept the van (being possessed with great fear), we continued our march till about one hour in the night and coming to a little swamp between two hills, there we pitched our little camp, much wearied with hard travel, keeping great silence, supposing we were very near the fort, as our Indians informed us, which proved otherwise. The rocks (now known as 'Porter's Rocks') were our pillows, yet rest was pleasant, the night proved comfortable, being clear and moonlight. We appointed our guard and placed our sentinels at some distance, who heard the enemy singing at the fort, who continued that strain until midnight with great insulting and rejoicing as we were afterwards informed; they seeing our pinnaces sail by them some days before, concluded we were afraid of them, and durst not come near them, the burthen of their song tending to that purpose. In the morning, we awaking, and seeing it very light, supposing it had been day, and so we might have lost our opportunity, having purposed to make our assault before day, roused the men with all expedition and briefly commending ourselves and designs to God, thinking immediately to go to the assault, the Indians showing us a path, told us that it led directly to the fort. We held on our march about two miles, wondering that we came not to the fort, and fearing we might be deluded, but seeing corn newly planted at the foot of a great hill, supposing the fort was not far off, a champion country being round about us, there making a stand, gave the word for some of the Indians to come up.

"At length Uncas and one Wequash appeared. We demanded of them where was the fort? They answered: 'On the top of that hill.' Then we demanded: 'Where was the rest of the Indians?' They answered: 'Behind, exceedingly afraid.' We wished them to tell the rest of their fellows that they should by no means fly, but stand at what distance they pleased and see whether Englishmen would now fight or not.

"Then Capt. Underhill came up, who marched in the rear and commending ourselves to God, divided our men. There being two entrances into the fort, intending to enter both at once, Capt. Mason leading up to that on the northeast side, who, approaching within one rod, heard a dog bark and an Indian crying out 'Owanox,' Owanox,' which is Englishmen, Englishmen. We called up our forces with all expedition and gave fire upon them through the palisades, the Indians being in a dead, indeed their last sleep. Then wheeling off, fell upon the main entrance, which was blocked up with bushes about breast high, over which Capt. Mason passed, intending to make good the entrance, encouraging the rest to follow.

"Lieut. Seeley endeavored to enter, but being encumbered somewhat, stepped back and pulled out the bushes, and so entered with sixteen men. We had formerly concluded to destroy them by the sword and save the plunder, whereupon Capt, Mason, seeing no Indians, entered a wigwam, when he was beset with many Indians, watching an opportunity to lay hands on him, but could not prevail. At length William Hayden, espying the breach in the wigwam, supposing some English might be there, entered, but on his entrance fell over a dead Indian, but speedily recovering himself; some of the Indians fled, others crept under their beds. The captain, going out of the wigwam, saw some Indians in the lane or streets and he marching towards them they fled and were pursued to the end of the lane, where they were met by Edward Pattison, Thomas Barber and some others, when seven of them were slain as they said. The captain, facing about, marched at a slow pace up the lane. He came down feeling himself very much out of breath and coming to the other end, near the place where he first entered, saw two soldiers, standing close to the palisades with their swords pointing to the ground. The captain said that we should never kill them after that manner, but said we must burn them and immediately stepping into the wigwam, where he had been before, brought out a fire-brand and putting it into the mats with which the wigwams were covered set them on fire. Lieut. Thomas Bull and Nicholas Olmstead, beholding, came up and when it was thoroughly kindled the Indians ran as men most dreadfully amazed. And indeed such a dreadful terror did the Almighty let fall upon their spirits that they would fly from us and run into the very flames, where many of them perished, and when the fort was thoroughly fired, command was given that all should fall off and surround the fort, which was readily attended by all, only one, Arthur Smith, being so wounded that he could not move out of the place, but he was happily espied by Lieut. Bull and by him removed and rescued.

"The fire was kindled on the northeast side to windward, which did swiftly overrun the fort to the extreme amazement of the enemy and great enjoyment of ourselves, some of them climbing to the top of the palisades, others of them running into the very flames, many of them gathering to windward, lay pelting at us with their arrows, and we repaid them with small shot. Others of the stoutest issued forth as we did guess to the number of forty, who perished by the sword. What I have formerly said is according to my own knowledge, there being sufficient living testimony to every particular. But in reference to Capt. Underhill, and his party acting in the assault, I can only intimate as we were informed by some of themselves.

"Immediately after the fight, then they marching up to the entrance on the southwest side of the fort, there made some pause, a valiant, resolute gentleman, one Mr. Hedge, stepping towards the gate, saying, 'If we may not enter, whereupon came we here,' and immediately endeavored to enter, but was opposed by a sturdy Indian who did impede his entrance, but the Indian being slain by himself and Sergeant Davis, Mr. Hedge then entered the fort with some others, but the fort being on fire the smoke and flames were so violent that they were constrained to desert the fort."

Capt. Mason in his history of the fight says nothing of the size of the fort, which has been described by some others as containing from ten to fifteen acres of land. G. H. Hollister, in his history of Connecticut, estimates the area of the fort at twenty acres within the palisades surrounding it. This estimate is far too great, for the charcoal of the palisades that were burned, did not assimilate with the soil in which they stood, and when the site of the fort was plowed up and cultivated by the colonists, the charcoal appeared very plain, showing that the fort was round, and did not contain over one and one-half acres of land.

Mr. Hollister also says: "That the area of the fort was sufficient to afford room for a large Indian village with more than twenty houses with adequate lanes and streets." He and several other historians claim that the houses in the fort were the homes for all the women and children of the Indians who garrisoned it, all of whom perished in the conflagration that destroyed the fort. Mason does not say anything about women or children in the fort, nor is it probable, when we consider the size of the fort and the number of Indians that it contained and the purpose for which it was built, that any of their women and children made it their home, nor does Mason in his history thereof say anything about the houses it contained. He speaks of a wigwam which he entered at first and later to get a firebrand to burn their wigwams, which as he says was covered with mats. His object in burning their wigwams doubtless was to drive the Indians from their hiding places in and about their wigwams, so as to bring them out into a fair open hand to hand fight. Mr. Hollister in his history greatly overestimates the area of the fort and the number of the Indians there.

The Pequots had two wigwam villages, which were known to the New England colonists before the Pequot war. Their fort was not built for the purpose of enclosing and protecting an Indian wigwam village, nor was the Pequot fort on Groton hill, where Sassacus and some of his warriors bivouacked at the time when the fort on Mystic hill was destroyed, built for any such purpose. They were evidently built by the Pequots to enable them to resist and prevent the Narragansetts and Niantics from invading their tribal lands, from which the Pequots had previously driven them for the purpose of regaining possession thereof. The wigwams of which Mason speaks were mainly designed for barracks for the Indians to occupy when they occupied the fort for its defense. Mason also says in his history of the Pequot war, that the Pequots knew of his contemplated invasion of their tribal lands and had seen his vessels when they sailed by for Narragansett Bay, and felt assured that the English were afraid of them. Doubtless being apprehensive of an attack from the east, they gathered all of their warriors into their forts so as to resist and defeat the English if they attempted to attack them there, showing conclusively that these forts were built for war purposes and not for the protection of their wigwam villages. Wigwams for Indian families to occupy were not generally clustered into villages, but were more frequently erected near their cultivated lands for the convenience of their women, who did all the work of cultivation of all sorts, while the men were roaming on hunting excursions, or training and drilling as warriors for war purposes. Mason gives the casualties of the Pequot fight as follows: "There were two of his soldiers killed outright and about twenty wounded," adding that some fainted by reason of the sharpness of the weather and small comforts and necessaries as were needful in such a case, especially his surgeon was much needed, whom he had left with his bark in Narragansett Bay, who had orders there to remain until the night before the intended assault, adding that thereupon grew many difficulties: "Our provisions and munitions of war were spent, we were in the enemies' country, who did far exceed our numbers, being much enraged and nearly all of our Indians, except Uncas, deserting us; our pinnaces at a great distance from us and when they would come we were uncertain. But as we were consulting what course to take it pleased God to discover our vessels to us before a fair gale of wind, sailing into Pequot Harbor to our great rejoicing. We had no sooner discovered our vessels, but immediately came up the enemy from the other fort, three hundred or more as we conceived. The captain led a file or two of men to skirmish with them, chiefly to try what temper they were of, who put them to a standstill, we being much encouraged thereat, whereupon we presently prepared to march towards our vessels. Four or five of our men were so severely wounded that they had to be carried by our men, we being also faint, were constrained to put four of our men to each one of the four or five men who were dangerously wounded, so that we had not above forty men free. At length we hired several of our friendly Indians to carry our disabled wounded men, which eased us of that burthen and after marching about one quarter of a mile, the enemy coming up to the place where the fort was and beholding what was done there stamped and tore the hair from their heads and after a little space came mounting down the hill upon us in a full career as if they would run over us, but when they came within shot, the rear faced about, giving fire upon them, some of them being shot made the rest of them more wary, yet they kept on running to and fro and shooting their arrows at random. At the foot of the hill was a small brook, where we rested and refreshed ourselves, having by that time taught them a little more manners than to disturb us. We then marched on towards Pequot Harbor, and falling upon several wigwams, burnt them, the enemy still following us in the rear, which was to windward, though to little purpose, yet some of them lay in ambush behind rocks and trees, often shooting at us, yet through mercy touched not one of us, and as we came to any swamp or thicket we made some shot to clear the passage. Some of them fell with our shot and probably more might but for want of munitions. When any of them fell our Indians would give a great shout and thus would they take so much courage as to fetch their heads. And thus we continued until we came within two miles of Pequot Harbor, when the enemy gathered together and left us, we marching on to the top of a hill adjoining the harbor, with our colors flying, having left our drums at the place of our rendezvous the night before. We seeing our vessels there riding at anchor to our great rejoicing and came to the water side, we there sat down in quiet. Capt. Patrick, being arrived there with our vessels, who as we were informed was sent with forty men by the Massachusetts Colony upon some service against the Block Islanders, who coming to the shore in our shallop, with all of his company, as he said to rescue us, supposing that we were pursued, though there did not appear the least sign of such a thing. But we could not prevail with him by any means to put his men ashore, so that we might carry our wounded men aboard, although it was our own boat in which he was. We were very much troubled, but knew not how to help ourselves.

"At length we were fetched aboard to the great rejoicing of our friends. Shortly after our coming aboard, there fell out a great contest between Capt. Underhill and Capt. Patrick. Capt. Underhill claiming an interest in the bark where Capt. Patrick was, which indeed was Underhill's right. The contest grew to a great height. At length we propounded that if Patrick would ride with that bark in contention and secure the Narragansett Indians, it being also the place of rendezvous to those vessels that were expected from Massachusetts, until we transported our wounded men to Saybrook, five leagues distant, then we would immediately return our pink to convey the Narragansetts home, the which Capt. Patrick seemed very ready to accept.

"Capt. Underhill soon after set sail in one of our barks for Saybrook, but before he was out of sight signified by writing, that he could not attend that service, but he must wait for the Bay vessels at Saybrook, wishing us having the honor of that service to complete it, by securing the Narragansett Indians, which at first seemed very difficult, if not impossible, for our pink could not receive them, and to march by land was very dangerous, it being near twenty miles in the enemy's country, our numbers being much weakened, as we were then about twenty men, the rest we had sent home for fear of a Pequot invasion. But absolutely necessitated to march by land we hasted ashore with our Indians and small numbers. Capt. Patrick seeing what we intended came ashore also with his men, although in truth we did not desire or delight in his company and so we plainly told him; however, he would and did march along with us. About the midway between that and Saybrook we fell upon a people called Niantics, belonging to the Pequots, who fled to a swamp for refuge, they hearing or espying us fled. We pursued them a while by the track as long as they kept together, but being much spent with former travel and the Sabbath drawing on, it being about two or three of the clock on the Saturday in the afternoon, we leaving our pursuit hasted towards Saybrook and about sunset we arrived at Connecticut River side, being nobly entertained by Lieut. Gardner, with many great guns, and were forced there to quarter that night. On the morrow we were all fetched over to Saybrook, receiving many courtesies from Lieut. Gardner, and after we had taken order for the safe conduct of the Narragansett Indians, we repaired to the places of our abode, where we were entertaind with great triumph and rejoicing and praising God for His goodness to us, in succeeding our weak endeavors, in crowning us with success and restoring us with so little loss. Almost immediately after we left, the whole body of the remaining Pequots repaired to the fort, where Sassacus, the chief sachem, resided, charging him that he was the sole cause of all trouble that had befallen them, and therefore they would destroy both him and his, but by the entreaty of their counsellors, they spared his life and after consulting what course to take, concluded there was no abiding any longer in their country, and so resolved to fly into several places. The greatest body of them went towards Manhatance (now New York city). Passing over Connecticut River they met with three Englishmen in a shallop, going for Saybrook, whom they slew. The Englishmen fought very stoutly as they afterward confessed, wounding many of them."

Mason further says: "That about a fortnight after his return home, which was about one month after the fight at Mystic, there arrived in Mystic River several vessels from the Massachusetts Colony, Capt. Israel Stoughton being commander in chief, and with him about one hundred and twenty men, being sent by that colony to pursue the war against the Pequots, the enemy being all fled before they came, except some few stragglers, who were surprised by the Moheages and others of the Indians and by them delivered to the Massachusetts soldiers. Connecticut Colony being informed thereof, sent forthwith forty men, Capt. Mason being chief commander, with some other gentlemen to meet those of the Massachusetts to consider what was necessary to be attended respecting the future, who meeting with them of the Massachusettts in Pequot Harbor, after some time of consultation, concluded to pursue those Pequots that were fled towards Manhatance and forthwith marched after them, discovering several places where they had rendezvoused and lodged not far distant from their several removes, making but little haste by reason of their children and want of provisions, being forced to dig for clams and to procure such other things as the wilderness afforded, our vessels sailing along by the shore. In about the space of three days we all arrived at New Haven Harbor, then called Quinnypiag, and seeing a great smoke in the woods not far distant we, supposing that some of the Pequots, our enemies, might be there, hastened ashore, but quickly discovered them to be Connecticut Indians; then we returned aboard our vessels, where we stayed some short time, having sent a Pequot captive upon discovery; we named him Lux, who brought no tidings of the enemy, which proved true, so faithful was he to us, though against his own nation. Such was the terror of the English upon them that a Moheage Indian named Jack Eatow, going ashore at that time, met with three Pequots, took two of them and brought them aboard. We then hastened our march towards the place where the enemy was and coming into a corn field, several of the English espied some Indians, who fled from them and they pursued them, and coming to the top of a hill saw several wigwams just opposite, only a swamp intervening which was almost divided into two parts, Sergeant Palmer hastening with about twelve men, who were under his command, to surround the smaller part of the swamp, that he might prevent the Indians flying. Ensign Davenport and Sergeant Jeffries, entering the swamp, intended to have gone to the wigwams, were there set upon by several Indians, who in all probability were deterred by Sergt. Palmer. In this skirmish the English slew but few, two or three of themselves were wounded, the rest of the English coming up, the swamp was surrounded. Our council being called, and the question propounded, how we should proceed, Capt. Patrick advised that we should cut down the swamp, there being many Indian hatchets taken, Capt. Trask concurring with him, but was opposed by others; then they would have a hedge made like those of Gotham, all of which was judged by some almost impossible and to no purpose and that for several reasons and therefore strongly opposed, but some others advised to force the swamp, having time enough, it being about three of the clock in the afternoon, but that being opposed it was then propounded to draw up our men close to the swamp, which would have much lessened the circumference and withal to fill up the open passages with bushes, that so we might secure them until morning and then we might consider further about it.

"But neither of these would pass, so different were our apprehensions, which were very grievous to some of us, who concluded the Indians would make an escape in the night as easily they might and did. We keeping a great distance, what better could be expected. Yet Capt. Mason took order that the narrows in the swamp should be cut through, which did much shorten our leagues. It was resolutely performed by Sergeant Davis.

"We being loath to destroy women and children, as also the Indians belonging to that place, whereupon Mr. Thomas Stanton, a man well acquainted with Indian language and manners, offered his services to go into the swamp and treat with them, to which we were somewhat backward, by reason of some hazard and danger he might be exposed unto, but his importunity prevailed, who going to them did in a short time return to us with near two hundred old men, women and children, who delivered themselves to the mercy of the English. And so night drawing on, we beleaguered them as strongly as we could. About half an hour before day, the Indians that were in the swamp attempted to break through Capt. Patrick's quarters, but were beaten back several times, they making a great noise as their manner is at such times; it sounded round about our leaguer, whereupon Capt. Mason sent Sergeant Stears to enquire into the cause and also to assist if need require. Capt. Trask coming also to their assistance, but the tumult growing to a very great height we raised our siege and marching up to the place at a turning of the swamp, the Indians were forcing out upon us, but we sent them back by our small shot. We waiting a little for a second attempt, the Indians in the meantime facing about, pressed violently upon Capt. Patrick, breaking through his quarters and so escaped. They were about sixty or seventy as we were informed. We afterwards searched the swamp and found but few slain. The captives we took were about one hundred and eighty, whom we divided, intending to keep them as servants, but they could not endure the yoke, few of them continuing any considerable time with their masters. Sassacus, his brother Mononoto and several of his sachems did not surrender to the English, but fled to the Mohawks for protection and personal safety, but contrary to their expectations the Mohawks, remembering their old-time wars with the Pequots, put Sassacus and several of his refugee sachems to death, but his brother Mononoto escaped, though seriously wounded by them. After taking the life of Sassacus the Mohawks cut off his head and sent it by special messenger to the Connecticut authorities as a token of their friendship for the English."

In the foregoing history of the Pequot Indians, I have consulted Broadhead's Dutch history of New York, and have closely followed Capt. John Mason's history of the causes that resulted in the declaration of war by the Connecticut Colonial General Court against the Pequots and the successful progress and consummation, of the expedition that he conducted against them. After the close of the Pequot war, Uncas, Miantonomo and Ninigret, with the remaining captive Pequots, on the 21st day of Sept., 1637, met the magistrates of Connecticut at Hartford, and after mutual friendly intercourse, a treaty was entered into between the colony of Connecticut and the Mohegan, Narragansett and Niantic Indians, which by its terms established perpetual peace between the colony of Connecticut and the Mohegan, Narragansett and Niantic Indians, and then with imposing ceremonies the magistrates divided the remnant of the Pequots among the Mohegan, Narragansett and Niantic Indians as follows: They gave eighty to Uncas, to Miantonomo they gave eighty, and to Ninigret they gave twenty, upon condition that the Pequots were no longer to be known by their tribal name, and were debarred from ever again dwelling in their old homes or occupying their old hunting and planting grounds. This treaty stipulation did not control the Pequots, for as soon as those assigned to Miantonomo reached Rhode Island, they left him and were afterward joined by those who were assigned to Ninigret, and in disobedience of the terms of the treaty with the Connecticut magistrates, they located themselves at a place called Massatuxet in Westerly, R. I., about three and one-half miles north of Watch Hill, where they built a wigwam village and planted adjoining lands with Indian maze or corn.

In order to compel these Pequot Indians to live with Miantonomo and Ninigret according to their treaty obligations of 1637, the Connecticut authorities sent Capt. John Mason and forty men to break up their settlement at Massatuxet, and drive them back to the tribal homes of the Niantics and Narragansetts, but they refused to go, whereupon Mason burned their wigwams, seized and carried off in his vessel all of their canoes, corn and wigwam furniture, but all to no purpose; the Pequots would not leave their Massatuxet home. They rebuilt their wigwams and planted the adjoining land and lived peaceably with the neighboring Indian tribes, claiming that their place of abode was on some of the old Pequot tribal lands, where they continued to reside from 1637 to 1661, when a renegade Pequot captain, Sosoa, who lived with the Narragansetts, claimed that Massatuxet and nearly all of the present town of Westerly, which he called Misquamicut, belonged to him by virtue of a gift of the Narragansett sachems for his valiant services for them in their previous wars with the Pequots, before Mason overthrew them in 1637.

The original Indian title to Massatuxet, and in fact to Misquamicut, claimed by Sosoa as his property by virtue of a gift from the Narragansett sachems, never belonged to that tribe, but was the tribal lands of the Niantic Indians, before their original territory was seized and held by the Pequots and the Niantics suffered to live on the east and west ends thereof, which is now known as Niantic, Rhode Island, and Niantic in Connecticut. These Pequots remained at Massatuxet until 1660, when they were driven from their homes where they had lived for over twenty years (long enough to have acquired a title thereto by possession in any civilized community) over Pawcatuck River into Stonington, Conn., and occupied land at Causet Point, on the north side of Pawcatuck or Little Narragansett Bay, for a few years. Subsequently they occupied land at Taugwonk and Cosatuc Hill, then in Stonington, and finally on a reservation, now in North Stonington, provided for them by the Connecticut Colony in 1686, and there the remnants of Miantonomo and Ninigret, and Pequots resided, until nearly all of them found homes elsewhere or departed this life, subject to more or less annoyance by some of the surrounding English settlers and yielding a passive obedience to their overseer, appointed by the Connecticut General Court at first, and later by the Superior Court of Connecticut. The eighty Pequots who were assigned to Uncas by said magistrates would not live with him and his tribal clan at Mohegan, now Montville, Conn. To offset his enforced obedience to Sassacus, he lorded it over them with a high hand, which caused them to leave him and pitch their wigwam tents in the present town of Groton, where they continued to live until a reservation was provided for them by the Connecticut Colony at Mashantuxet, in the present town of Ledyard, Conn., which they reluctantly consented to accept in lieu of their Noank homes, reserving the right of fishing in Mystic River, Conn.

In this reservationary home they were more or less annoyed by the surrounding English neighbors and for relief repeatedly petitioned the General Assembly of Connecticut, which resulted in very little benefit to them.

Pending the French and Indian war and the American Revolutionary struggle, a number of them enlisted and served with our Connecticut soldiers, and during their absence from home their families were provided for by the towns and General Assembly. The Pequot reservation in Ledyard and North Stonington do not at the present time contain a single wigwam house, nor a residence of any Pequot descendants. A large part of the Ledyard reservation has been sold with the timber of the rest of it, and the avails thereof have been safely invested under the care and control of their overseers. The North Stonington reservation remains intact and is leased as pasture land and the yearly income of both reservations is applied by the overseers thereof for the benefit of the sick and feeble old men and women of both of the clans of the Pequots, wherever they may reside.

Genealogical Register

—OF—

STONINGTON FAMILIES.

AVERY FAMILY.

1. CHRISTOPHER AVERY, the emigrant ancestor and progenitor of the Avery family, was born in England about 1590. He was a weaver by trade, and came to this country and located at Gloucester, Mass., where he was selectman in 1646, 1652 and 1654. At a court in Salem he took the freeman's oath, June 29, 1692, and was chosen clerk of the band, constable, and clerk of the market. His wife did not come to this country. In 1658 he sold lands at Gloucester and removed to Boston, where on the 16th of March, 1658-9 he purchased land, a small lot, about twenty-six by forty-six feet. It was located in what is now the centre of the post-office building, facing on Devonshire street. The famous old spring, which gave the name to Spring Lane and which is now preserved under the post-office, was near. This Avery plot was a part of, or at least adjoined, the site of two notable resorts of later days—the well known restaurant whence first came the famous "Julien soup," and the "Stackpole House," not much less famous. The Winthrop estate was not far away, and near by, in after years, Benjamin Franklin was born. Christopher Avery did not long retain this property, for March 22, 1663, he sold land to Ambrose Dew, for forty pounds. There had evidently been no increase of value in the five years that he had held possession. After being owned by two or three different persons, it was bought by Mr. Stackpole about 1790. Christopher Avery now followed his son James to Connecticut, and August 8, 1665, purchased a house, orchard and lot of Robert Burrows in New London. Here he claimed exemption from watching and training, on account of age, in June, 1667, and was made freeman of the colony October, 1669. He died March 12, 1670, by Minor diary.

HAD SON:

2. Capt. James Avery, the only child of Christopher, was born in 1620. Came to America with his father, and lived at

Gloucester for several years. The Rev. Mr. Blinman, who had been the minister of Gloucester for eight years, was engaged to become the minister of the Pequot Plantation. A party of his friends proposed to move with him, and came on to make preparatory arrangements, Oct. 19, 1650. It appears that James Avery went back to Gloucester, sold his possession there to his father, and in 1651 returned to New London. In March of that year the principal body of these eastern families arrived. Capt. James acquired large tracts of land at what is now Poquonoc Bridge, Groton, east of New London. About 1636 he built the hive of the Avery's at the head of Poquonoc Plain, a mile and a half from the river Thames. In 1684, the old Blinman edifice, first church of New London, the unadorned church and water-tower of the wilderness, which had stood for thirty years, was sold to Capt. Avery for six pounds, with the condition that he should remove it in one month's time. According to tradition, the church was taken down, its materials carried across the river, and added to the house he had already built at Poquonoc. In spite of this analytic and synthetic process, the ancient dwelling seemed to have retained some of its sacred character, for a century later it was occupied until July 21, 1894, when a spark from a passing locomotive ignited its well-seasoned frame, and in a short time only the ancient chimney remained to mark the spot of this historic house of Eastern Connecticut. A few years later the chimney was taken down, the grounds graded, and a tasteful monument was erected by the descendants of James Avery. He was ensign, lieutenant and captain of the New London companies and served throughout King Philip's war in command of forty Indians from Stonington, New London and Lyme. In 1676 he was captain of one of the four companies which protected the frontier, and for twenty-three years an officer of the town, and twelve times deputy to the General Court, 1656-80; also assisting judge in the Prerogative Court, and was most prominent in matters relating to the church, as references to him in such connections are numerous. He m. 1st, Nov. 10, 1643, Joanna Greenslade, b. about 1622; she d. after 1693. He m. 2nd, Mrs. Abigail (Ingraham) Chesebrough, widow of Joshua Holmes, July 4, 1698, (No. 2) Holmes family. He d. April 18, 1700. His widow was living at late as 1714.

AVERY FAMILY.

CHILDREN:

3 HANNAH, b. at Gloucester, Oct. 11, 1644, m. Ephraim Miner, June 20, 1666, (No. 15) that family.
4 JAMES, b. at Gloucester, Dec. 15, 1646, m. Deborah Sterling, or Stallyon, Feb. 18, 1669.
5 MARY, b. Feb. 19, 1648, m. Joseph Miner, Oct. 28, 1668, (No. 16) that family.
6 THOMAS, b. May 6, 1651, m. Hannah Miner, Oct. 22, 1677.
7 JOHN, b. Feb. 10, 1654, m. Abigail Chesebrough.
8 REBECCA, b. Oct. 6, 1656, m. William Potts of New Castle, England, Aug. 5, 1678.
9 JONATHAN, b. Jan. 5, 1658, buried Sept. 15, 1681.
10 CHRISTOPHER, b. Apr. 30, 1661, d. Dec. 8, 1683.
11 SAMUEL, b. Aug. 14, 1664, m. Susannah Palmes, dau. of William Palmes and Ann Humphrey, Oct. 25, 1686, of Swanzey, Mass. He was a large farmer, and was chosen moderator upon the legal organization of the town of Groton in 1704, and its first townsman at the first town meeting in 1705, and held that office until his death, May 1, 1723. His farm was in what is now South Groton. He is buried about a mile northwest of Seth Williams' farm in Ledyard, on the farm of C. H. Stanton.
12 JOANNA, b. in 1669.

Lieut. James Avery, Jr., (No. 4) m. Deborah, daughter of Edward Sterling, or Stallyon, Feb. 18, 1669. Like his father he was an important man of affairs. Their names are first in the list of those who were in full communion in the church of Groton, in the old church record, begun by John Owen, pastor, before 1727. He was lieutenant in the Connecticut Colonial forces during the frontier wars. Mr. and Mrs. Avery are buried near the centre of the west burying ground at Pequonoc. He d. Aug. 22, 1748; she d. Mar. 27, 1729.

CHILDREN:

13 DEBORAH, b. Aug. 10, 1670, m. Robert Allyn, June 29, 1691.
14 JAMES, b. Apr. 20, 1673, m. Mary Griswold in 1696, d. Sept. 18, 1754.
15 MARGARET, b. Feb. 5, 1674, m. William Morgan, July 7, 1696.
16 EDWIN, b. Mar. 20, 1676, m. Susanna Rose, June 3, 1699, at Preston, Ct.
17 EBENEZER, b. May 1, 1678, m. Dorothy Park.
18 CHRISTOPHER, b. Jan. 23, 1679, m. 1st, Abigail Park; 2nd, Mrs. Prudence Wheeler; 3rd, Mrs. Esther Prentice; 4th, Susannah ———.
19 JONATHAN, b. Nov. 9, 1681, m. Elizabeth Waterman.
20 MARY, b. Aug. 4, 1683, d. y.
21 HANNAH, b. Mar. 24, 1685, m. Samuel Morgan.
22 SARAH, b. May 10, 1688, m. Mr. Luther.
23 JOSEPH, b. Aug. 9, 1691, m. Tabitha Gardiner.
24 BENJAMIN, b. 1693, m. Thankful Avery.
25 MARY, b. 1696, m. William Morgan, (No. 35) that family.

Thomas Avery (No. 6) m. Hannah Miner (No. 21) that family, Oct. 22, 1677; she d. 1692. Married 2nd, Mrs. Hannah Buckley, widow of Edward Buckley, M. D., Mar. 11, 1693. He was in King Philip's war and was a successful Indian interpreter. During the latter part of his life he removed to Montville, Conn. He d. Jan. 5, 1737; she d. 1692.

CHILDREN BY 1ST MARRIAGE:

26 THOMAS, b. Apr. 20, 1679, m. Ann Shapley.
27 SAMUEL, b. Nov. 15, 1680, m. Elizabeth Ransford in 1702.
28 a daughter, b. Oct. 2, 1682.
29 JONATHAN, b. 1683, m. Elizabeth Bill.
30 WILLIAM, b. 1683 (twin), buried 1684.
31 EPHRAIM, b. 1685, m. Abigail ———.
32 HANNAH, b. May 4, 1686, m. Thomas Miner, (No. 62) that family.
33 MARY, b. 1688, m. Benjamin Baker of Fairfield.
34 ABRAHAM, b. 1690, m. Jane Hill.
35 ELIZABETH, b. 1692, m. Sylvester Baldwin, (No. 20) that family; she d. July 17, 1728.

CHILDREN BY 2ND MARRIAGE:

36 JOSHUA, bapt. Aug. 25, 1695, m. Jerusha Rockwell.
37 Daughter, b. 1697.
38 Daughter, b. 1699.
39 ISAAC, b. 1702, m. Elizabeth Fox.
40 CHARLES, b. 1704, d. y.

John Avery (No. 7) m. Abigail Chesebrough, Nov. 29, 1675, (No. 15) that family. He owned land in Stonington, Groton, and Preston, and was in King Philip's war.

CHILDREN:

41 ABIGAIL, b. Jan. 15, 1677, d. y.
42 ABIGAIL, b. Jan. 18, 1679, m. James Packer.
43 MARY, b. Nov. 14, 1680, m. William Denison, (No. 53) that family. She m. 2nd, Daniel Palmer, (No. 23) that family.
44 JOHN, Jr., b. Apr. 1, 1683, m. Sarah Denison in 1705.
45 BENJAMIN, b. 1686, m. Sarah Denison, (No. 68.)
46 WILLIAM, b. 1687, m. Anne Richardson; 2nd, Sarah Walker.
47 ANNA, b. 1692, m. William Satterlee Sept. 6, 1711.
48 ELISHA, b. 1694, m. Elizabeth Babcock, (No. 34) that family.
49 DESIRE, b. (twin) 1694.
50 JOSIAH, b. 1697, m. Miss Edmund.
51 DANIEL, b. Nov. 5, 1699.
52 NATHANIEL, b. 1701, m. Abigail ———.
53 THOMAS, b. 1703.

AVERY FAMILY. 203

54. James Avery (No. 14) m. Mary, daughter of Mathew Griswold and Hannah Wolcott. Her father was the founder of the town of Lyme, and Governor of Connecticut in 1784-1786.

CHILDREN:

55 JAMES, b. May 27, 1698, m. Elizabeth Smith.
56 JOHN, b. Feb. 4, 1700, m. Elizabeth Morgan.
57 EBENEZER, b. Mar. 29, 1704, m. Lucy Latham.
58 ELIHU or ELISHA, b. July 29, 1708.
59 MARY, b. Feb. 23, 1710, m. William Morgan.
60 HANNAH, b. Apr. 7, 1712.
61 PRUDENCE, b. Mar. 21, 1715.
62 THOMAS, b. 1717.

Ebenezer Avery (No. 17) m. Dorothy Park, June 19, 1707. He d. July 19, 1752; she d. Nov. 6, 1732.

CHILDREN:

63 PARK, b. Dec. 9, 1710, m. Mary Latham.
64 MARY, b. Feb. 17, 1713, m. Mr. Latham.
65 DOROTHY, b. Jan. 10, 1716, m. Joseph Morgan.
66 LUCY, b. Oct. 14, 1718, d. y.
67 EBENEZER, b. Apr. 3, 1721, m. Lucy Davis; 2nd, Eunice Park.
68 AMY, b. Feb. 17, 1724, m. Jabez Smith.
69 EUNICE, b. Mar. 2, 1725, m. George Williams, (No. 180) that family.
70 SIMEON, b. Apr. 25, 1730, m. Sarah Niles; 2nd, Lucy Morgan.

Christopher Avery (No. 18) m. Abigail Park, Dec. 19, 1704; she d. Feb. 12, 1713. Married 2nd, Mrs. Prudence (Payson) Wheeler, widow of Richard Wheeler, (No. 10) that family. Married 3rd, Esther Prentice, widow of Samuel Prentice, (No. 11) Prentice family and dau. of Nathaniel Hammond of Newton, Mass. He m. 4th, Sussannah ———.

CHILDREN BY 1ST MARRIAGE:

71 JOHN, b. Oct. 26, 1705, m. Anna Stanton.
72 ABIGAIL, b. July 16, 1707, m. Robert Allyn, Jr.
73 CHRISTOPHER, b. Nov. 16, 1709, m. Eunice Prentice.
74 NATHAN, b. Mar. 12, 1712, m. Hannah Stoddard, Mar. 27, 1746.

CHILDREN BY 2ND MARRIAGE:

75 PRISCILLA, b. Apr. 29, 1715, m. Joseph Breed, (No. 11) that family.
76 ISAAC, b. May 26, 1717.
77 HANNAH, b. Feb. 10, 1719, m. Benadam Gallup, (No. 77) that family.
78 JACOB, b. Aug. 26, 1721, m. Elizabeth Avery; 2nd, Sylvia Eddy.
79 TEMPERANCE, b. Sept. 14, 1725, m. William Morgan, (No. 36) that family.

John Avery (No. 44) m. Sarah Denison, Aug. 23, 1705.

CHILDREN:

80 JOHN, b. May 14, 1706, m. Lydia Smith.
81 ANNA, b. June 13, 1711, d. 1720.
82 SARAH, b. Oct. 10, 1713.
83 ABIGAIL, b Dec. 25, 1715, m. John Denison (No. 120) that family.
84 THANKFUL, b. Apr. 15, 1718, m. Benjamin Avery.
85 WILLIAM, b. 1722, m. Phebe Denison, Dec. 4, 1746, (No. 123).
86 GEORGE, b. Sept. 2, 1724, m. Eunice Avery.

Benjamin Avery (No. 45) m. Sarah Denison in 1711, (No. 68) that family.

CHILDREN:

87 THANKFUL, b. 1712, d. 1814, aged 101 yrs.
88 SARAH, b. 1714, m. 1st, Beebe Denison, (No. 116); 2nd, Benadam Denison, (No. 160) that family.
89 BENJAMIN, b. 1715, m. Mary Morgan.
90 GEORGE, b 1716, m. Lydia Gardiner.
91 WILLIAM, b. 1717.
92 ABIGAIL, b. 1718, m. Jonathan Rathbone.
93 DAVID, b. 1719, m. Hannah Meach.
94 MARY, b. 1721, m. John Morgan.
95 LUCY, b. 1723, m. Peter Buckley.
96 DANIEL, b. 1725.
100 JOHN, b. 1727, m. Mary Hough.

William Avery (No. 46) m. 1st, Anna Richardson, Mar. 7, 1715-16; she d. July 5, 1729. He m. 2nd, Mrs. Sarah Walker, dau. of William and Eleanor (Pendleton) Walker. The title Mrs. used above indicated good social position, and not widowhood. Lieut. Wm. Avery lived and died on his farm near the centre of North Stonington. His original will is on file in the probate office, New London, Conn.

CHILDREN:

101 WILLIAM, JR., b. Feb. 6, 1716-17, d. 1717.
102 RICHARDSON, b. Jan. 25, 1717-18, m. Sarah Plumb, No. 3, 1740. He removed about 1770 to the Wyoming Valley in Pennsylvania. In the battles which preceded the massacre July 3, 1778, he with many others sought refuge in Forty Fort, where they were made prisoners and remained several days. After their release by the Tories and Indians they, with 200 others, returned to Connecticut, walking all the way, the whole distance being over two hundred miles.
103 WILLIAM, bapt. Apr. 5, 1724, m. Abigail Williams, Dec. 13, 1750.
104 ANNE, bapt. 1724, m. Oliver Babcock, (No. 74) that family.
105 JOHN, b. Apr. 29, 1727, m. Mary Dennis; m. 2nd, Anna Miner, 1761.

AVERY FAMILY.

CHILDREN BY 2ND MARRIAGE:

106 AMOS, b. Jan. 30, 1732-33, m. Patience Borodel.
107 CHRISTOPHER, b. Apr. 1, 1734.
108 ELIAS, b. July 5, 1736.
109 DAVID, b. Oct. 30, 1718.
110 DANIEL, b. Oct. 29, 1741.
111 BENONI, b. Jan. 29, 1744.
112 ABIGAIL, b. Apr. 25, 1746.
113 JAMES, b. Dec. 27, 1748, m. Martha Smith.
114 NATHANIEL, b. Aug. 28, 1751, m. Amy ―――.
115 ABRAHAM, b. May 20, 1754, m. Mercy Packer.

John Avery (No. 56) m. Mary Elizabeth Morgan in 1729. He d. July 11, 1759.

CHILDREN:

116 JOHN, b. 1730, d. y.
117 GRISWOLD, b. July 30, 1732.
118 ELIJAH, bapt. Sept. 15, 1734, m. Prudence Morgan.
119 AMOS, b. Apr. 18, 1736, d. y.
120 JOHN, b. Apr. 21, 1738.
121 ANN, b. (twin) Apr. 21, 1738.
122 CALEB, b. Apr. 12, 1740.
123 AMOS, b. Mar. 6, 1743, m. Prudence ―――.
124 AARON, b. 1750.

Elder Park Avery of Groton (No. 63) m. Mary Latham, about 1735. He d. Mar. 4, 1797; she d. June 11, 1773.

CHILDREN:

125 DOROTHY, b. 1736, m. John Morgan.
126 ABIGAIL, b. May 15, 1737, m. Capt. Robert Niles.
127 PARK, b. Mar. 22, 1741, m. Hannah Morgan, 1783. He was fearfully wounded at the massacre of Fort Griswold, Sept. 6, 1781. He lived forty years afterwards.
128 JASPER, b. in 1743, was killed Sept. 6, 1781, at Fort Griswold.
129 EUNICE, b. 1745, m. Elder Soloman Morgan.
130 EBENEZER, b. 1749. He also was wounded at the massacre at Fort Griswold; he d. Jan. 11, 1828.
131 STEPHEN, b. May 10, 1750, m. Mary Denison; m. 2nd, Fanny Barnes.
132 LIEUT. SIMEON, b. Oct. 20, 1753, m. Lucy Swan, July 25, 1777. He was a patriotic and successful officer in the army of the Revolution, and d. Aug. 1, 1809.
133 ELISHA, b. 1755, m. 2nd wife, Grace Denison, Dec. 10, 1778.

John Avery (No. 71) m. Anna Stanton, Feb. 19, 1732, (No. 131) of that family. Married 2nd, Mrs. Rachel Park in 1750; m. 3rd, Mrs. Phebe Burrows.

CHILDREN:

134 JOHN, b. Dec. 6, 1732, m. Mary Park.
135 ABIGAIL, b. Apr. 1, 1735, m. Dea. John Hurlbut.
136 AMOS, b. Apr. 16, 1737, m. Hannah Niles.
137 ANNA, b. May 28, 1739, m. Thomas Niles.
138 MARGARET, b. Apr. 19, 1741, m. Joshua Downer.
139 ISAAC, b. Mar. 24, 1743, m. Mercy Williams, Jan. 5, 1766.
140 JONAS, b. July 13, 1745, m. Mary Avery.
141 HANNAH, b. Oct. 9, 1747, m. ———— Brewster.

Christopher Avery (No. 73) m. Eunice Prentice (No. 20) that family, Sept. 10, 1735. He d. July 2, 1778; she d. Mar. 22, 1796.

CHILDREN:

142 ESTHER, b. Apr. 14, 1736, m. Daniel Williams.
143 CHRISTOPHER, b. Jan. 23, 1737-8, m. Dorothy Heath; m. 2nd, Mary Eldredge.
144 EUNICE, b. Dec. 11, 1740, m. George Avery.
145 LUCY, b. Dec. 10, 1742, m. ———— Allyn.
146 NATHAN, b. May 2, 1744, m. Rebecca Elderkin.
147 THOMAS, b. Feb. 10, 1746, m. Hannah Smith.
148 ANNA, b. Feb. 2, 1748, d. 1778.
149 SAMUEL, b. Nov. 15, 1752, m. Lucy Jane Foye.
150 PRENTICE, b. Feb. 10, 1755, d. June 10, 1778.
151 OLIVER, b. Feb. 8, 1757, m. Margaret Avery.
152 ABIGAIL, b. Feb. 22, 1759, m. Vine Stoddard.
153 SARAH, b. Aug. 7, 1761, m. Nathaniel Hewitt, (No. 119).
154 HANNAH, b. Jan. 20, 1763.

Rev. Nathan Avery (No. 74) came from Groton to Stonington, and purchased a farm south of and adjoining the village of now North Stonington, where he built him a dwelling-house, which stood where the present residence of Mrs. Dudley R. Stewart now stands. He became a member of the Separatist or strict Congregational Church, and subsequently was chosen and ordained pastor thereof, which he held until he departed this life. He enjoyed the respect and confidence of his parishioners, and was a devoted and able preacher. He m. Hannah Stoddard of Groton, Mar. 21, 1746. She d. Oct. 19, 1810; he d. Sept. 7, 1780.

CHILDREN:

155 ISAAC, b. Aug. 23, 1747, m. Lucy Swan.
156 NATHAN, b. Dec. 21, 1749, d. y.
157 HANNAH MARY, b. Feb. 28, 1752, m. Roswell Randall (No. 66); m. 2nd, John Randall (No. 65) that family.

AVERY FAMILY.   207

158 LUTHER, b. ————, m. Mary Wheeler.
159 STEPHEN, b. Jan. 13, 1756, m. Anna Wheeler, Elizabeth Morgan.
160 PHEBE, b. Jan. 10, 1758, m. Roswell Randall, (No. 66) that family.
161 WEALTHY, b. Oct. 5, 1772, m. Darius Hewitt, (No. 100) that family;
    2nd, Col. Wm. Randall, (No. 71) that family.

Elijah Avery (No. 118) m. Prudence Morgan, Mar. 10, 1770.

CHILDREN:

162 ELIZA, b. Dec. 1, 1771, m. William Eldridge, Jr.
163 CALEB, b. 1772.
164 JOHN, b. Mar. 17, 1776, m. Anna or Nancy Murdock.

Stephen Avery (No. 131) m. Mary Denison, (No. 212) that family; she d. Feb. 27, 1815. Married 2nd, Fanny Barnes, Apr. 26, 1818, and she d. Sept. 16, 1874. He d. July 15, 1827.

CHILDREN:

165 MARY, b. Feb. 19, 1819, d. Aug. 23, 1825.
166 ELIZA, b. Mar. 23, 1821, m. Eliza B. Brown, of Old Mystic, (No. 28)
    that family.
167 STEPHEN, b. Feb. 8, 1827, d. y.

John Avery (No. 134) m. Mary Park, Jan. 22, 1752. He d. July 23, 1794; she d. Jan. 14, 1752.

CHILDREN:

168 ELIZABETH, b. Aug. 22, 1752, d. y.
169 ZIPPORAH, b. Sept. 22, 1753, m. Thomas Williams; m. 2nd, Daniel
    Cook; m. 3rd, Elias ————.
170 JOHN, b. Dec. 14, 1755, m. Lucy Ayer.
171 ANNA, b. Dec. 3, 1757, d. Nov. 29, 1769.
172 SAMUEL, b. Jan. 3, 1760, m. Sarah Eldridge.
173 ROBERT, b. Sept. 28, 1762, drowned May 21, 1764.
174 WILLIAM, b. Mar. 22, 1765, m. Margaret Avery.
175 HANNAH, b. Dec. 17, 1767, m. David Avery.
176 ROBERT, b. Feb. 25, 1771, m. Sarah Crary.
177 NATHANIEL, b. May 14, 1773, m. Amy Denison (No. 322).
178 AMOS, b. Nov. 3, 1775, m. Dorothy Crary, May 10, 1804.

Christopher Avery (No. 143) m. Dorothy Heath, Dec. 16, 1763; she d. June 14, 1803. He m. 2nd, Mary Eldridge Nov. 7, 1803. He was a Separatist minister in Stonington for 33 years, and was ordained Nov. 20, 1785. He d. July 5, 1819. His last wife d. Dec. 7, 1848.

CHILDREN:

179 TIMOTHY, b. May 8, 1766, d. 1795.
180 CHRISTOPHER, b. Dec. 10, 1768, m. a Miss Ayer.
181 TEMPERANCE, b. June 14, 1773, m. Abel Avery.
182 JONATHAN, b. Mar. 5, 1775, m. Anna Hewitt.
183 HENRY, b. July 27, 1783, drowned June 30, 1799.

Isaac Avery (No. 155) m. Lucy Swan, June 11, 1771, (No. 59) Swan family.

CHILDREN:

184 LUCY, b. Jan. 18, 1773, m. a Mr. Daniels.
185 NATHAN, b. Sept. 21, 1775, m. Matilda Babcock, Dec. 16, 1802.
186 ISAAC, b. Jan. 14, 1777, m. Nabby (or Tabitha) Wheeler, April 27.
    (No. 179) Wheeler family.
187 MARY H., b. July 18, 1780, m. Elisha Avery.
188 PHEBE, b. Feb. 18, 1783, d. Sept. 12, 1795.
189 WEALTHY, b. Sept. 19, 1795, d. May 12, 1795.
190 CHRISTOPHER SWAN, b. Nov. 25, 1788, m. a Miss Brewster.
191 WILLIAM WHEELER, b. June 20, 1791, m. Nancy Smith, Mar. 29, 1812.

Luther Avery (No. 158) m. Mary Wheeler, Oct. 13, 1782, (No. 101) that family.

CHILDREN:

192 LUTHER, JR., b. June 27, 1784, d. Aug. 4, 1853; unmarried.
193 NATHAN, b. Dec. 19, 1786, d. Apr. 11, 1848; unmarried.
194 PAUL WHEELER, b. May 18, 1789.
195 POLLY, b. Mar. 14, 1792, m. Elisha Satterlee.
196 ALFRED, b. Dec. 1, 1794, m. Fanny S. Wheeler, Mar. 1, 1827 (No. 268).
197 PHEBE, b. May 7, 1797, m. Elisha Burnham, Nov. 1815.
198 MIRANDA, b. Feb. 7, 1800.
199 WILLIAM RANDALL, b. Mar. 18, 1802, m. Rhoda Emeline Avery, Feb. 28, 1832.
200 HANNAH, b. Nov. 8, 1808, d. Oct. 3, 1813.

Stephen Avery (No. 159) m. 1st, Anna Wheeler, Dec. 9, 1781, (No. 100) that family; m. 2nd, Elizabeth Morgan, Aug. 18, 1804, (No. 34) that family. Mrs. Anna d. Aug. 10, 1801; Mrs. Elizabeth d. Aug. 11, 1841. He was a prominent man in Stonington, and held various public offices of trust, particularly town clerk, which he held a number of years before and at the time when the town was divided and the town of North Stonington was established, 1807, again being elected town clerk of North Stonington, which he held until his death. He served in the Revolutionary war. He d. April 1, 1828.

AVERY FAMILY.

CHILDREN:

201 NANCY, b. Dec. 29, 1783, m. Isaac Williams, June 8, 1804, (No. 298) Williams family.
202 STEPHEN LYMAN, b. May 12, 1786, m. Mrs. Rebecca Wheeler, (No. 169) that family.
203 HANNAH MARY, b. June 18, 1789, m. Luther Miner.
204 ROSWELL RANDALL, b. Nov. 5, 1791, m. Mary Wheeler. Apr. 19, 1818, (No. 265) that family.
205 CHARLES GRANDISON, b. Apr. 9, 1796, m. Ede Wheeler, Nov. 4, 1823, (No. 266) that family.
206 CYRUS, b. Oct. 10, 1788, d. Oct. 12, 1884.

CHILDREN BY 2ND MARRIAGE:

207 ELIZA ADALINE, b. Nov. 17, 1805, m. Elisha Park, Mar. 20, 1823; she died Oct. 9, 1865.
208 WEALTHY ALMIRA, b. Sept. 29, 1807, m. Col. George Ayer, May 16, 1831; she died Nov. 30, 1835.
209 ROGER GRISWOLD, b. Sept. 4, 1809, d. Dec. 31, 1885; unmarried.
210 CALVIN GODDARD, b. Feb. 9, 1812, d. Mar. 30, 1833.
211 ALEXANDER HAMILTON, b. June 28, 1814, m. 1st, Mary Whittaker, Aug. 9, 1838; she d. Sept. 14, 1853. Married 2nd, Sarah H. Osgood, daughter of Dr. Samuel Osgood of Springfield, Mass., Nov. 30, 1854. He died June 27, 1872.
212 RALPH HURLBUT, b. Apr. 22, 1816, m. Martha Chesebrough Randall, (No. 106) that family, June 21, 1842. He d. May 16, 1889; she d. ——.
213 ERASTUS, b. Aug. 8, 1818, d. Nov. 16, 1861, unmarried.
214 FRANCES MARY, b. Sept. 20, 1821, m. Richard Anson Wheeler, Jan. 12, 1843, (No. 429) Wheeler family, d. Sept. 3, 1855.

John J. Avery (No. 164) m. Anna or Nancy Murdock, 1794; m. 2nd, Mrs. Margaret Taylor (nee Foote), 1820.

CHILDREN:

215 MARIA M., b. Jan. 26, 1796, d. July 13, 1867; **unmarried.**
216 ELIJAH MURDOCK, b. Mar. 17, 1798, d. 1834.
217 DEAN LAY, b. Feb. 14, 1800.
218 GEORGE ANSON, b. Jan. 28, 1802, m. Frances M. Stanton.
219 DELIA ANN, b. Mar. 6, 1804, m. S. B. Wheeler, Nov. 27, 1827, (No. 267) that family.
220 CARLETON M., b. Apr. 24, 1806, m. Mary J. Millard, Sept. 6, 1849.
221 COURTLAND, b. Dec. 8, 1807, m. Mary Ann Burlingame, Sept. 10, 1840.
222 ERASTUS, b. Dec. 8, 1809, m. Mary Elizabeth Denison, Mar. 21, 1844.
223 ALBERT L., b. July 12, 1811, m. Phebe B. E. Wheeler, Mar. 15, 1837, (No. 318); she died Aug. 9, 1837. He m. 2nd, her sister, Joanna B. Wheeler, Jan. 5, 1839, (No. 320) Wheeler family; she d. Mar. 5, 1866. He m. 3rd, Mrs. Abby J. Burrows (nee Jackson), of Norwich, Conn., Feb. 24, 1869.
224 OSCAR FITZALEN, b. Mar. 24, 1813, m. Phebe A. Ely, Nov. 21, 1842.

HISTORY OF STONINGTON.

225 AMANDA MALVINA, (twin) b. Mar. 24, 1813, m. Samuel P. Wheeler, (No. 505) that family.
226 SOLON CICERO, b. May 27, 1816, m. Susan Avery Cook, Aug. 11, 1845.

Robert Avery (No. 176) m. Sarah Crary, June 14, 1807; she d. Jan. 3, 1829. He married 2nd, Nancy Crary, June 8, 1829.

CHILDREN:

227 ROBERT S., b. May 1, 1808, m. Lydia Tyler, Oct. 16, 1861.
228 ULYSSES, b. July 17, 1809, m. Lucy Ann Williams, Nov. 13, 1848, (No. 65) Groton Williams family.
229 ISAAC, b. Mar. 31, 1811, m. Henrietta Billings, May 14, 1850.
230 EUNICE, b. Nov. 15, 1813, m. William Huntington; 2nd, Aaron E. Emmons.
231 MARY ANN, b. Sept. 8, 1815, d. Sept. 26, 1881; unmarried.
232 SARAH, b. Aug. 15, 1817, m. William Morse, Jan. 13, 1851.
233 REV. JOHN, b. Aug. 1819, m. Susan Mitson Champion, Nov. 6, 1851.
    He graduated from Yale College, 1843, and Yale Divinity School, 1847.
235 ERASMUS, b. May 6, 1822, m. Eunice Serviah Williams, Jan. 21, 1847, (No. 66) Groton Williams family.

Jonathan Avery (No. 182) m. Anna Hewitt, Feb. 2, 1802, (No. 115) Hewitt family.

CHILDREN:

236 ELIZABETH, b. Oct. 25, 1803, m. Gurdon S. Crandall (No. 315) Thomas Stanton family of Stonington, Ct.
237 MARY ANN, b. Feb. 20, 1807, d. unmarried.

Ebenezer Avery (No. 67) m. Eunice Park for his 2nd wife, Nov. 9, 1758; had son

238 EBENEZER, b. Oct. 10, 1760, m. Abigail Story, Dec. 11, 1783, had son
239 ASA, b. May 16, 1785, m. Desire Giddings, May 21, 1809; had son
240 ASA, b. Feb. 19, 1810, m. Abby Eliza Morgan, Sept. 23, 1832, and their son, Allen Avery, m. Alice B. Hinckley, Aug. 19, 1862, and lives in Mystic.

BABCOCK FAMILY.

1. JAMES BABCOCK, born in 1612, who was the progenitor of the Babcock family of Westerly and the region roundabout, first appears in Portsmouth, R I., in 1642. He held the office of Commissioner from 1656 to 1659 and was by occupation a blacksmith and gunsmith. He came to Westerly with his family soon after 1664, after having sold his house and land in Portsmouth to Thomas Fish. During the year 1670 he gave testimony, calling his age 58 years, his son James 29, and his son John 26. He m. 1st, Sarah ―――, and he d. June 12, 1679.

CHILDREN OF JAMES AND SARAH BABCOCK.

2 JAMES, b. in 1641, d. in 1698; m. Jane Brown, daughter of Nicholas Brown; she d. 1719.
3 JOHN, b. 1644.
4 JOB, b. in ―――.
5 MARY, b. in ―――, m. William Champlin. She d. 1747; he d. 1715.

Mrs. Sarah Babcock d. in 1665 and Mr. James Babcock m. for his second wife, Elizabeth ―――. After his death his widow m. 2nd, William Johnson, Sept. 22, 1679.

CHILDREN:

6 NATHANIEL, b. in 1666.
7 JOSEPH, b. in 1670.
8 ELIZABETH, b. in ―――, m. Benjamin Sumner, May 3, 1706.

James Babcock (No. 2) m. Jane, daughter of Nicholas Brown.

CHILDREN:

9 JAMES, b ―――.
10 SARAH, b. ―――, m. James Lewis.
11 JANE, b. ―――, m. Israel Lewis.
12 MARY, b. ―――, m. George Brown.
13 HANNAH, b. ―――, m. Roger Larkin.
14 ELIZABETH, b. ―――, m. David Lewis.

John Babcock (No. 3) m. Mary, daughter of George and Elizabeth (Hazard) Lawton. He d. in 1685 and his wife Mary d. Nov. 8th, 1711.

CHILDREN:

15 JAMES, b. ———.
16 ANN, b. ———.
17 MARY, b. ———.
18 JOHN, b. ———.
19 JOB, b. ———.
20 GEORGE, b. 1673, d. May 1st, 1756.
21 ELIHU, b. ———. Was an invalid and helpless.
22 ROBERT, b. ———.
23 JOSEPH, b. ———.
24 OLIVER, b. ———.

John Babcock (No. 3) d. either the last of December, 1684, or the very first of January, 1685, for on the 6th day of January, 1685, his eldest son, James Babcock, and his mother, Mrs. Mary Babcock, recognizing the English law of primogeniture as in force in Rhode Island, agreed that he might take all of the real estate of his father, which he assumed, and gave his mother one-half thereof by deed. Mrs. Mary Lawton Babcock afterwards m. Erasmus Babbitt, April 21st, 1698.

The oldest son and child, James Babcock, was appointed guardian to the four youngest children, viz.: Elihu, Robert, Joseph and Oliver, April 21, 1698.

Job Babcock (No. 4) m. Jane, daughter of John Crandall. He d. 1718 and she d. 1715.

CHILDREN:

25 JOB, b ———.
26 JOHN, b ———.
27 BENJAMIN, b ———.
28 JANE, b. ———, m. ——— Braman, ———.
29 SARAH, b. ———, m. ——— Hall, ———.
30 MARY, b. ———, m. ——— Tanner, ———.
31 ELIZABETH, b. ———, m. ——— Brand———.
32 HANNAH, b. ———. m.
33 MERCY, b. ———, m. ———.

Joseph Babcock (No. 7) m. 1st in 1696, April 3rd, Dorothy Key; she d. Dec. 14, 1727; and Mr. Joseph Babcock m. 2nd, Jan. 1st, 1729, Hannah Coates.

CHILD BY FIRST WIFE:

34 ELIZABETH, b. Jan. 29th, 1698, m. Elisha Avery, (No. 48) that family, Sept. 30, 1714.

BABCOCK FAMILY.

CHILDREN BY 2ND WIFE:
35 DOROTHY, b. Feb. 2, 1730.
36 ABIGAIL, b. Apr. 20, 1731.
37 JOSEPH, b. Oct. 15, 1733.
38 JOHN, b. Jan. 26, 1736.

James Babcock (No. 15) b. probably 1664, m. Elizabeth ————, probably 1687. His wife d. Mch. 3, 1731, and he m. 2nd, Content Maxson, July 9th, 1731. He made his will, Jan. 9, 1737, and d. Jan. 17, 1737.

NOTE.—"In Memory of Captain James Babcock, who died January 17, 1736-7. In ye ———— of his age,
 Having been in his life
One of righteousness, charity and benevolence,
And not altogether silent at his death."

CHILDREN BY FIRST WIFE, ELIZABETH:
39 JAMES, b. Dec. 23, 1688, m. Sarah Vose.
40 ELIZABETH, b. Feb. 5, 1691.
41 SAMUEL, b. Feb. 15, 1697.
42 DANIEL, b. April 11, 1699.
43 ANNA, b. Nov. 19, 1701.
44 SARAH, b. Dec. 3, 1704, d. Nov. 13, 1705.
45 JOSHUA, b. May 19, 1707, m. Hannah Stanton.

Mrs. Elizabeth Babcock d. Mch. 3, 1731, aged 68, and her husband m. Miss Content Maxson, July 9, 1731.

THEIR CHILDREN:
46 ANNE, b. Mch. 30, 1732, m. Capt. Simon Rhodes, (No. 1) that family, Dec. 15, 1756.
47 JAMES, b. Nov. 1, 1734.
48 JONATHAN, b. Oct. 11, 1736.

George Babcock (No. 20) m. Elizabeth Hall, Nov. 28th, 1694. His will was proved May 10, 1756. Elizabeth was daughter of Henry and Content Hall of Kingston, R. I.

CHILDREN:
49 MARY, b. 1695, m. Thomas Potter, Mch. 19, 1717.
50 GEORGE, b. 1699.
51 DAVID, b. 1700.
52 JOHN, b. 1702.
53 ABIGAIL, b. 1706, m ———— Hall.
54 RUTH, b. 1709.
55 EUNICE, b. 1712, m. Silas Greenman, (No. 11) that family, 1st, and 2nd, ————.
56 HEZEKIAH, b. 1715.
57 ELISHA, b. 1718, lived in Richmond, R. I.
58 ELIZABETH, b. ————, mentioned in will as the widow of Edward Sanders; other children are found on the Wickford records.

Oliver Babcock (No. 24) m. Susannah Clark in 1704. She was daughter of Joseph Clark and wife, Bethiah Hubbard, and was b. Aug. 31st, 1683; was a grand-daughter to Samuel Hubbard of Newport.

CHILDREN:

59 SUSANNAH, b. Sept. 20, 1705.
60 THOMAS, b. Mch. 3, 1710.
61 MARY, b. Feb. 8, 1713, m. Henry Cobb (No. 23) Cobb family.
62 NATHAN, b. Oct. 12, 1715.
63 SIMEON, b. Sept. 27, 1717.
64 JOHN, b. May 5, 1720.
65 OLIVER, b. Sept. 16, 1722.
66 JOSEPH, b. Oct. 18, 1726.

Joseph Babcock, Jr., (No. 37) m. Mary Bentley, Dec. 28, 1755.

CHILDREN:

67 MARY, b. Jan. 8, 1757.

James Babcock (No. 39) m. Sarah Vose, of Milton, Mass She was the daughter of Edward Vose, and was born Aug. 30, 1684, and m. June 12, 1706. He d. April 9, 1731.

CHILDREN:

68 JAMES, b. May 29, 1708.
69 NATHANIEL, b. March 6, 1710.
70 ELIAS, b. Feb. 20, 1712.
71 ELIZABETH, b. Aug. 25, 1715, m. John Davison, Feb. 5, 1736.
72 MARTHA, b. Mch. 18, 1717, d. April 18, 1717.
73 ISAIAH, b. Jan. 29, 1719.
74 OLIVER, b. July 27, 1720.
75 GRACE, b. Dec. 31, 1722, m. Samuel Plumb, Aug. 16, 1738.
76 TIMOTHY, b. Oct. 12, 1724.

Joshua Babcock (No. 45) m. Hannah Stanton, (No. 227) that family, Aug. 11th, 1735.

CHILDREN:

77 (COL.) HENRY, b. April 26, 1736.
78 LUKE, b. July 6, 1738.
79 ADAM, b. Sept. 27, 1740.
80 HANNAH, b. Jan. 22, 1742, m. John Brown of Newport, R. I.
81 FRANCES, b. May 11, 1745, m. Capt. Dudley Saltonstall.
82 PAUL, b. Dec. 5, 1748.
83 AMELIA, b. Apr. 19, 1751.
84 SALLY, b. Oct. 18, 1753.
85 HARRIET, b. May 18, 1756.

James Babcock (No. 47) was a physician in the Revolutionary war. He m. 1st, Sarah (No. 229), dau. of Joseph Stanton, Jr., and wife, Esther Gallup, Dec. 2, 1754. He m. 2nd, Joanna McDowell, Aug. 27, 1769; he d. Sept. 1781.

CHILDREN:

86 AMELIA, b. Nov. 4, 1756, m. Nathan Pendleton, (No. 31) Pendleton family, Jan. 22, 1775.
87 SIMON, b. ———.
88 SARAH, b. ———, m. Sylvester Gavitt, Sept. 30, 1781.
89 JAMES, b. ———.
90 EZRA, b. ———.
91 JOANNA, b. ———.
92 CHARLOTTE, b. ———.
93 ANNE, b. ———.

Jonathan Babcock (No. 48) m. Ether Hazard, dau. of Robert and Esther (Stanton) Hazard in 1758.

CHILDREN:

94 ESTHER, b. June 23, 1759, m. Nathan Brand of Stonington.
95 JONATHAN, b. May 30, 1761, m. Ruth Rodman, of South Kingston.
96 ROBERT, b. Dec. 13, 1763, m. Mary Hazard.
97 HANNAH, b. Feb. 11, 1766.

George Babcock (No. 50) m. Susannah, dau. of John and wife, Sarah (Wilson) Potter, Dec. 20, 1721.

CHILDREN:

98 ELIZABETH, b. Jan. 25, 1725, m. Beriah Brown, Dec. 11, 1771, and d. Sept. 24, 1815.
99 GEORGE, b. Dec. 9, 1727.
100 MARTHA, b. Dec. 8, 1729, m. 1st, Capt. Simon Rhodes, (No. 1) that family, Aug. 27, 1769, and 2nd, Col. James Rhodes, May 12, 1800.
101 SUSANNAH b. Mch. 16, 1731, m. Benjamin Clark.
102 CHRISTOPHER, b. Feb. 27, 1736, m. Martha Perry; d. 1801.
103 SAMUEL, b. May 30, 1739, m. Ruth Babcock, 1769, d. Dec. 15, 1817.
104 HEZEKIAH, b. May 30, 1739, m. Martha Hoxie, Dec. 12, 1769, d. Apr. 7, 1807.
105 ROUSE, b. Apr. 29, 1746, m. Ruth Maxson, Oct. 12, 1769, d. June 13, 1801.

David Babcock (No. 51) m. Dorcas, dau. of Daniel Brown and wife, Dorcas Gardiner, Feb. 24, 1730. They lived in South Kingston.

CHILDREN ON WESTERLY RECORDS:

106 DAVID, b. Apr. 10, 1734.
107 JONATHAN, b. Nov. 19, 1735.
108 BENEDICK, b. Oct. 21, 1737, but there was a daughter
108a MARY, b. in 1746, who m. Joseph Denison, (No. 174) that family, Oct. 10, 1765, and she d. Dec. 15, 1798, aged 52 years.

James Babcock (No. 68) m. Phebe Swan May 7th, 1730.

CHILDREN:

109 PHEBE, b. May 2, 1731.
110 SARAH, b. Feb. 12, 1733.
111 JAMES, b. Feb. 22, 1735.
112 ELIAS, b. Dec. 16, 1736.
113 ABEL, b. April 28, 1739.
114 MARTHA, b. Feb. 22, 1741.

Nathaniel Babcock (No. 69) m. Sarah Billings, of Preston Nov. 20, 1733.

CHILDREN:

115 NATHANIEL, b. Jan. 24, 1735.
116 JONAS, b. Feb. 24, 1737.

Elias Babcock (No. 70) m. Ann Plumb, Nov. 10, 1737.

CHILDREN:

117 ELIAS, b. July 5, 1738, d. July 15, 1738.
118 ELIJAH, b. Aug. 15, 1739.
119 ANNE, b. July 5, 1743.
120 NANCY, b. April 4, 1746.
121 LYDIA, b. Dec. 9, 1752.
122 RUFUS, b. April 22, 1758.

Isaiah Babcock (No. 73) m. Elizabeth Plumb, Dec. 25th, 1738.

CHILDREN:

123 ISAIAH, b. April 27, 1741.
124 ENOCH, b. Dec. 27, 1742.
125 ELIZABETH. b. June 9, 1745.
126 ELISHA, b. July 26, 1747.
127 GEORGE, b. July 27, 1749.
128 JOHN, b. Nov. 13, 1752.
129 PHEBE, b. Oct. 5, 1755.

Oliver Babcock (No. 74) m. Anna Avery, (No. 104) that family, Mch. 6, 1740.

CHILDREN:

130 OLIVER, b. Jan. 22, 1741.
131 JOSHUA, b. June 5, 1743.
132 ANNE, b. July 15, 1745.
133 WILLIAM, b. Mch. 19, 1747.
134 RUFUS, b. Nov. 10, 1748.
135 GERSHOM, b. Nov. 9, 1752.
136 ATTANA, b. Jan. 14, 1755.
137 CHRISTOPHER, b. Jan. 26, 1757.
138 ELIZABETH, b. Jan. 15, 1759.
139 DANIEL, b. Aug. 31, 1760.

BABCOCK FAMILY.

Timothy Babcock (No. 76) m. Lois Billings, (No. 68) that family, July 12th, 1745.

CHILDREN:
140 LOIS, b. April 18, 1746, m. Oliver Clark.
141 TIMOTHY, b. Aug. 22, 1747.
142 JESSE, b. Mch. 24, 1750.
143 GRACE, b. Sept. 4, 1753.
144 DESIRE, b. May 4, 1756.

Mrs. Lois Babcock d. Oct. 14, 1756, and Mr. Timothy Babcock m. 2nd, Thankful Read in Norwich, Ct., Oct. 20, 1757.

CHILDREN:
145 SARAH, b. Jan. 20, 1761, m. Stanton Campbell.
146 ANNE, b. Mch. 20, 1763. She was unmarried at the time of her father's death, 1795.
147 JOHN, b. July 26, 1766, m. Louisa Gilmore, dau. of Robert and Sarah Gilmore, of Keene, New Hampshire, Oct. 18, 1787; he d. April 24, 1806. His wife d. Mch. 21, 1844.

CHILDREN:
148 JOHN READ, b. Jan. 28, 1788, m. Eliza Ely, Nov. 1, 1815, and moved to Pennsylvania; he d. Oct. 15, 1836. They had ten children.
149 LOUISA M., b. Dec. 17, 1789 in North Stonington, m. Jesse Brown, Sept. 13, 1815; he d. in Hopkinton, R. I., July 27, 1869. His wife d. Sept. 17, 1870; had seven children.
150 ROBERT G., b. Feb. 29, 1792, in Pomfret, Ct., m. 1st, in Boston, Mass., Sally Otis, Aug. 3, 1817; she d. two months after and he m. Lucy Blackman April 22, 1822; she was of Dorchester, and they had eleven children.
151 JAMES, b. July 5, 1770; supposed to have gone to New York state.

Timothy Babcock, Jr., (No. 141) m. Esther Billings.

Col. Henry or Harry Babcock (No. 77) m. Mary Stanton, (No. 288) Stanton family, Dec. 2nd, 1764. She was dau. of Robert and Anna Stanton.

NOTE.—Colonel Henry Babcock, (No. 77), served in a Rhode Island Regiment in the French and Indian wars, 1755-59; captain under Sir William Johnson, after the battle of Fort George; major 1756-58; colonel Rhode Island Regiment at Ticonderoga, wounded there, 1759. Led his regiment at capture of Ticonderoga, and publicly thanked by Lord Amherst.

CHILDREN:
152 BENJAMIN F., b. Nov. 6, 1765, d. July 27, 1781.
153 PAUL, b. Mch. 13, 1768, d. Mch. 14, 1839.
154 DUDLEY, b. Jan. 7, 1770, m. Nancy Wright of Newport, R. I.
155 JOSHUA, b. Oct. 29, 1771, d. Mch. 1797.
156 HANNAH, b. Nov. 30, 1773, m. Joseph D. Phelps, (No. 36) Phelps family, Sept. 30, 1792.

Major Paul Babcock (No. 153) m. 1st, Nancy Bell, April 2nd, 1789; had six children.

CHILDREN:

157 BENJAMIN F., b. Feb. 3, 1790, m. Maria Eells, April 1813; he d. July 21, 1829.
158 MARY A., b. April 3, 1792, m. David Sherman, Oct. 6, 1813, d. Aug. 3, 1815.
159 DUDLEY, b. May 10, 1794, d. Nov. 17, 1794.
160 JOSHUA, b. May 11, 1796, d. Sept. 1, 1818.
161 HENRY, b. Oct. 4, 1798, m. Ann E. Smith, Dec. 3, 1828, d. May 15, 1834.
162 NANCY B., b. Mch. 5, 1802 m. William R. Palmer, (No. 391) that family, July 3, 1822, d. Dec. 22, 1845.

Mrs. Nancy Bell Babcock was b. Sept. 30, 1767, and d. Nov. 2, 1803, and April 15, 1804, Major Paul m. Lucy Bell, the cousin of his first wife; they had ten children.

CHILDREN:

163 COURTLAND, b. Mch. 25, 1806, m. Elizabeth Cany, May 3, 1834, d. Feb. 10, 1853.
164 GILES, b. Jan. 8, 1808, m. Anne Denison, (No. 552) that family, Oct. 1, 1832; d. Mch. 4, 1862.
165 ELIZA T., b. Feb. 13, 1810, m. Nathaniel B. Palmer, (No. 474) that family, Dec. 7, 1826; d. April 17, 1872.
166 ABBY E., b. Sept. 4, 1811, m. Jedediah Leeds, Nov. 13, 1833.
167 GEORGE W., b. Oct. 26, 1813, m. Louisa Boucher, Mch. 19, 1845, and d. Feb. 11, 1874.
168 LUCY B., b. Mch. 30, 1815, m. Giles F. Ward, Dec. 22, 1836.
169 ROBERT S., b. Feb. 8, 1818, m. Emily Hall, Sept. 11, 1850; d. Apr. 20, 1885.
170 MARY A., b. Apr. 1, 1821, m. John Breckenridge, Sept. 1, 1840.
171 DAVID S., b. Aug. 13, 1822, m. Charlotte A. Noyes, (No. 278) that family, May 28, 1850; d. Aug. 24, 1885.
172 HANNAH, b. June 6, 1825, d. Aug. 18, 1829.
    Mrs. Lucy Bell Babcock was b. Mch. 10, 1784, and d. Feb. 8, 1846.

George Babcock (No. 99), of South Kingston, m. Mehitable Wheeler, (No. 59) that family, June 26, 1751.

CHILDREN:

173 GEORGE, b. Sept. 22, 1753.
174 LUCY, b. Dec. 15, 1754.
175 CYRUS, b. Dec. 11, 1756.
176 EPHRAIM, b. May 19, 1758.
177 SUSANNAH, b. May 2, 1760.
178 MARY, b. Jan. 17, 1767.
179 FREDERICK, b. Sept. 10, 1771.
180 THOMAS WHEELER, b. Aug. 13, 1773.

BABCOCK FAMILY.

Rouse Babcock (No. 105) m. Ruth Maxson, Oct. 12, 1769.

CHILDREN:

181 RHODA, b. Dec. 17, 1769, m. Gen. William Williams, (No. 271) that family, June 15th, 1799; d. Aug. 29, 1801.
182 ROUSE, b. Feb. 27, 1771, d. Dec. 4, 1772.
183 ROUSE, b. May 12, 1773, m. Hannah Brown, Jan. 13, 1801; d. Apr. 2, 1841.
184 ELIZABETH, b. Mch. 14, 1775, m. Joseph Noyes, (No. 153) that family, Jan. 13, 1799; d. July 1, 1846.
185 MARTHA, b. May 2, 1777, d. June 15, 1778.
186 BENJAMIN, b. Sept. 2, 1779, m. Nancy Wilcox, Jan. 26 1806; d. July 10, 1815.
187 SALLY, b. April 6, 1782, m. Jeremiah Thurston; d. Feb. 27, 1841.
188 NANCY, or ANN, b. May 15, 1786, m. Gen. Wm. Williams, (No. 271) that family, Dec. 23, 1804; d. Oct. 23, 1855.

Rouse Babcock (No. 183) b. May 12, 1773, and m. Hannah Brown, Jan. 13, 1801. He d. April 21, 1841. She d. July 14, 1872, and was 86 years old, being b. Oct. 10, 1785.

CHILDREN:

189 ROUSE b. Oct. 19, 1801; d. May 4, 1802.
190 ROUSE, b. May 4, 1803, m. Mary Townsend, April 27, 1832; d. Mch. 6, 1872.
191 HANNAH B., b. Nov. 1805, m. Oliver D. Wells, Nov. 29, 1825, and d. July 30, 1874.
192 MARTHA, b. Sept. 1807, m. Thomas P. Stanton, (No. 419) that family, Oct. 25, 1827; d. Apr. 24, 1864.
193 HARRIET, b. Oct. 5, 1809, m. Horatio Campbell, Sept. 8, 1846, and d. Aug. 28, 1884.
194 SARAH A., b. Jan. 27, 1812, m. John G. Pierce, June 1, 1840; d. Jan. 10, 1881.
195 WILLIAM R., b. Mch. 28, 1814, m. Catharine Pearce, Oct. 6, 1840.
196 ALBERT, b. Sept. 6, 1816, d. young.
197 EDWIN, b. April 8, 1819, m. Olive S. Cady, April 21, 1845.
198 HORACE, b. Aug. 14, 1822, m. 1st, Abby Jane Cross, Sept. 11, 1843; she died at the expiration of sixteen years, and Mr. Horace Babcock m. for his 2nd wife, her sister, Harriet Cross, Dec. 18, 1861.

Daniel Babcock (No. 139) m. Content, dau. of George and Content (Maxson) Potter, April 8, 1784. He d. Sept. 18, 1846. She was b. May 25, 1765, and d. Sept. 14, 1850.

CHILDREN:

199 DANIEL, b. Dec. 16, 1784, d. Apr. 2, 1874.
200 BETSEY, b. Feb. 21, 1787, d. June 4, 1858.
201 JACOB, b. Jan. 20, 1789, d. June 17, 1867.

202 ANN, or NANCY, b. May 9, 1791, d. Nov. 20, 1868.
203 GEORGE P., b. Nov. 4, 1795, d. Sept. 29, 1825.
204 OLIVER, (twin) b. Dec. 12, 1797, d. Sept. 9, 1859.
205 LUCY, (twin) b. Dec. 12, 1797, d. Sept. 9, 1869.
206 MARY, b. Nov. 2, 1807, d. Jan. 18, 1883.
207 EMILY H., b. June 14, 1810, d. May 23, 1890.

Oliver Babcock (No. 204) m. Phebe, (No. 219) of that family, dau. of Stephen and Phebe (Burch) Babcock, Jan. 11, 1824. She was b. Mch. 5, 1802, d. Oct. 15, 1886.

CHILDREN:

208 NATHAN, b. Nov. 19, 1824.
209 PHEBE M., b. Feb. 20, 1826, d. May 18, 1833.
210 AMANDA, b. Oct. 20, 1827, d. July 15, 1887.
211 DANIEL, b. Dec. 4, 1828.
212 ANN E., b. Jan. 7, 1831, d. Apr. 2, 1859.
213 STEPHEN, b. Dec. 22, 1832.
214 LUCY A., b. Sept. 17, 1834.
215 MARTHA J., b. Dec. 9, 1836, d. Oct. 31, 1837.
216 PHEBE J., b. Sept. 30, 1838.
217 CYNTHIA C., b. May 28, 1841, d. Apr. 25, 1842.
218 JULIA M., b. Apr. 13, 1843.

The above said Stephen Babcock, father of Phebe, who m. Oliver Babcock (No. 204) is descended from John and Mary (Lawton) Babcock (according to the views of Mr. Stephen Babcock of New York.) Capt. John Babcock, fourth child of John and Mary (Lawton) Babcock, b. in Westerly, R. I., about 1669, d. in Westerly, Mch. 28, 1746. He m. about 1770, Mary Champlin, dau. of Wm. and Mary Babcock Champlin. William Babcock, fourth child of Capt. John and Mary Champlin Babcock, b. in Westerly, Apr. 15, 1708, d. there Jan. 15, 1752. He m. Aug. 11, 1730, Sarah Dennison, of Saybrook, Ct. Their third child, Christopher Babcock, b. Sept. 12, 1734, m. Mehitable Chaucer, of Saybrook. Their tenth child, Stephen Babcock, b. in Westerly, Feb. 27. 1772, m. Mch. 22, 1801, Phebe Burch, (No. 55) that family, dau. of Henry and Mary (Irish) Burch, b. in Stonington, Nov. 2nd, 1774, d. Nov. 10, 1837.

CHILDREN:

219 PHEBE, b. Mch. 5, 1802, d. Oct. 15, 1886; m. Oliver Babcock (No. 204) that family.
220 STEPHEN, b. May 10, 1804, d. Jan. 22, 1856.
221 ELIAS, b. Mch. 19, 1806, d. Mch. 19, 1881.
222 NATHAN, b. July 27, 1808, d. Dec. 11, 1814.
223 AMANDA, b. Nov. 29, 1810, d. Sept. 19, 1812.

BABCOCK FAMILY.

Robert Babcock (No. 22) m. Lydia ———, and their son
224. Ezekiel Babcock, b. in Westerly, R. I., June 23rd, 1716, m. Eunice Billings (No. 67) that family, Oct. 26, 1740. In 1794 the sons of this family went to New York State.

CHILDREN:

225 ELIHU, b. July 8, 1741, m. Elizabeth Jeffries, Aug. 28, 1766.
226 MARY, b. Dec. 18, 1744, m. Nathan Hinckley, Sept. 8, 1776, (No. 35) Hinckley family.
227 DAVID, b. 1745, m. Mary Hinckley, (No. 36) that family.
228 MARTHA, b. ———, m. Nath. Eells, Jr., Dec. 24, 1772, (No. 20) that family.
229 ROBERT, b. ———, m. Grace Hinckley, Feb. 27, 1780, (No. 40) of Hinckley family.

David Babcock (No. 227) m. Mary Hinckley, Mch. 12, 1769. He d. Nov. 16, 1820. She d. Mch. 5, 1838.

CHILDREN:

230 DANIEL, b. May 13, 1769, d. 1831.
231 DAVID, b. Feb. 28, 1770, d. 1801.
232 HENRY, b. July 29, 1771, d. 1824; m. Anna Bull.
233 ROBERT, b. July 6, 1773.
234 GURDON, b. Oct. 6, 1775.
235 POLLY, b. Apr. 22, 1778, m. Rev. Elisha Morgan.
236 DUDLEY, b. Apr. 29, 1780, d. 1846.
237 FREDERICK, b. June 16, 1782.
238 MERIT, b. Sept. 18, 1784.
239 FANNY, b. July 5, 1787, m. Amos Cell.
240 FRANKLIN, b. Dec. 18, 1789.

Benj. F. Babcock (No. 157) m. Maria Eells, Apr. 1813, (No. 42) of that family.

CHILDREN:

241 FRANK, b. ———, m. Phebe Swan, (No. 153) of the Swan family.
242 SAMUEL D., b. ———, m. ——— Crary, dau. of Peter Crary.
243 MARIA, b. ———, m. Rev. Mr. Moore.
244 PARTHENIA, b. ———, m. William Babcock.
245 CHARLES, b. ———, m. ——— Crary.

David S. Babcock (No. 171) m. Charlotte A. Noyes, (No. 278), on May 28th, 1850.

Elias Babcock (No. 221) m. Lucretia, dau. of Clark Davis.

CHILDREN:

246 MARIA, b. ———, m. Samuel H. Chesebrough.
247 ELIAS, b. ———, m. Miss Hancox.

Courtland Babcock (No. 163) m. Elizabeth Cany, May 3rd, 1834.

CHILDREN:

248 LOUISE, b. ———, m. Edmund Stanton; and 2nd, Edwin Tillinghast.
249 GEORGIA P., b. ———, m. Capt. Charles P. Williams (No. 297) Williams family.
250 COURTLAND C., b. ———, m. Mary B. Woodruff.
251 AMELIA C., b. ———, d. ———.
252 HENRY S., b. ———, m. Lena Denison.

BALDWIN FAMILY.

SYLVESTER BALDWIN, father of the family that settled in New Haven, Conn., in 1638, was b. in Aston-Clinton, Buckinghamshire, Eng., a little previous to the year 1600. His father, Sylvester Baldwin, and his mother, Jane Willis, were married in 1590, and he was their fifth son. His grandfather, Henry Baldwin, held the manor of Dundridge, in Aston-Clinton, which went from him to Richard, his oldest son, and from Richard to our Sylvester's brother Henry.

1 Sylvester Baldwin (son of Henry) was m. to Jane Wissis, in 1590. Had six sons, and d. previous to 1632.

CHILDREN:

2 HARRY, b. ———, buried in 1594.
3 JOHN, living in 1632.
4 HENRY, inherited Dundridge.
5 RICHARD, no record.
6 WILLIAM, no record.
7 SYLVESTER, b. ———, m. Sarah Bryan in 1620. These six sons were born between 1590 and 1600.

Sylvester Baldwin (No. 7), before coming to America, lived at St. Leonards in Aston-Clinton, near Dundridge, where he owned the "Chapel Farm." He m. Sarah Bryan, early in 1620. In 1638, Sylvester and his wife Sarah and six living children, sailed for America in the ship Martin. They belonged to the "New Haven Company." Sylvester d. on the passage, "in mid ocean," July 21, 1638. His will was admitted to probate, in Boston, where the ship Martin arrived. He left a large estate. His widow and six children settled with the rest of the emigrating company in New Haven. In 1643, "the Widow Baldwin" was recorded in New Haven as one of the wealthiest proprietors. In 1643 she m. Capt. John Astwood; they settled in Milford, Conn. Capt. Astwood d. in London in 1654. She d. in Milford in 1669.

CHILDREN BY 1ST MARRIAGE.

8 SARAH, b. or bapt. April 22, 1621, m. Benjamin Fenn.
9 RICHARD, b. or bapt. Aug. 25, 1622, m. Elizabeth Alsop.
10 MARY, b. or bapt. Feb. 28, 1624, d. in 1624.
11 MARY, b. or bapt. Feb. 19, 1625, m. Robert Plum of Milford.
12 MARTHA, b. or bapt. Apr. 20, 1628.
13 RUTH, b. or bapt. in 1630.
14 SAMUEL, b or bapt. Jan., 1632, d. 1632.
15 ELIZABETH, b. or bapt. Jan. 25, 1633, d. 1633.
16 JOHN, b. or bapt. in 1635, m. Mrs. Rebecca (Palmer) Chesebrough.

John Baldwin, of Stonington, (No. 16) m. first wife, name unknown. It is conjectured that she was a daughter of Capt. John Atwood, his mother's second husband, in 1656, and it appears in the records that "a house lot of an acre and half" was then assigned to him in Milford, Conn. His first wife d. in 1657, soon after the birth of her child. In 1664 he settled in New London, and July 24, 1672, he m. 2nd wife, Rebecca Palmer (No. 13) Palmer family, young widow of Elisha Chesebrough, and daughter of the first Walter Palmer, of Stonington. They settled permanently in Stonington, where they owned an extensive tract of land. He d. Aug. 19, 1683. She outlived him thirty years, and d. May 2, 1713.

CHILDREN:

17 JOHN, b. April 13, 1657, d. in England, 1676.
18 REBECCA, b. May 20, 1673, m. Elnathan Miner, Mar. 21, 1694, (No. 59) Miner family.
19 MARY, b. Feb. 24, 1675, m. John Randall, Nov. 25, 1706, (No. 2) Randall family.
20 SYLVESTER, b. Mar. 4, 1677, m. Lydia Miner; 2nd, Elizabeth Avery.
21 SARAH, b. ———, 1680, d. unmarried.
22 JANE, b. ———, 1681, d. previous to 1692.
23 THEOPHILUS, b. ———, 1683, m. Priscilla Mason.

Sylvester Baldwin, of Stonington, (No. 20) m. first, Lydia Miner, July 8, 1706, (No. 63) Miner family. She d. April 22, 1707. He m. 2d wife, Elizabeth Avery, of New London, May 19, 1724, (No. 35) that family. She d. July 17, 1728. He d. in 1732, leaving a large estate.

CHILDREN:

24 JOHN, b. and d. April 18, 1707.
25 ELIZABETH, b. July 6, 1725, m. Capt. Thomas Prentice, Feb. 1, 1744, (No. 21) Prentice family.
26 MARY, b. Sept. 14, 1726, m. Humphrey Avery of Preston, June 19, 1745.

BALDWIN FAMILY. 225

Theophilus Baldwin, of Stonington, (No. 23) m. 1st, Priscilla Mason, (No. 27) that family, May 25, 1710, dau. of Daniel Mason, and granddaughter of the famous Major John Mason; granddaughter also of Rev. Jeremiah Hobart, of Hingham, Mass., whose daughter Rebecca was Daniel Mason's second wife. Mrs. Priscilla (Mason) Baldwin d. soon after the birth of her son Sylvester. He m. May 1, 1724, Jemima Powers, who d. in 1733, and Oct. 18, 1733, m. Mrs. Elizabeth Hascall, of Norwich. He was the first deacon of the church organized in 1727, in what is now North Stonington. In many ways a man of mark in the town, having character, ability, wealth, and a remarkably sunny temper.

CHILDREN:

27 JOHN, b. July 12, 1711, m. Mary Clark; 2nd, Eunice Spaulding.
28 PRISCILLA, b. Nov. 17, 1713, m. Daniel Calkins of Norwich, Sept. 2, 1731, son of Hugh Calkins, a great great grandson of the first American John Calkins.
29 THEOPHILUS, b. Oct. 23, 1716, m. Sarah Lamb; 2nd, Elizabeth Billings.
30 SYLVESTER, b. Mar. 29, 1719, m. Anna ————; 2nd, Bridget Chesebrough.

John Baldwin, of Stonington, (No. 27) m. Mary Clark, Feb. 6, 1736. She d. Jan. 24, 1737, four weeks after the birth of a son. He m. 2nd, Eunice Spaulding, of Plainfield, Conn., July 3, 1740. He d. in 1762, having been known in Stonington as Capt. John Baldwin, and she was m. Nov. 1, 1764, to Elisha Williams, (No. 51) Williams family. He d. Sept. 22, 1788; she d. in Jan. 1819, aged 98 years and 6 months.

CHILDREN:

31 JOHN, b. Dec. 27, 1736, d. Jan. 8, 1737.
32 MARY, b. Feb. 9, 1741, m. Stephen Frink, Nov. 5, 1780, (No. 47) Frink family.
33 PRISCILLA, b. May 20, 1743, m. Hubbard Burroughs, Jr., Dec. 24, 1761, (No. 87) that family.
34 ELIZABETH, b. June 23, 1745, m. Jesse Swan, (No. 49) Swan family.
35 EUNICE, b. Oct. 25, 1747, d. Apr. 23, 1766.
36 THOMAS, b. Apr. 6, 1751, d. Apr. 10, 1751.
37 JOHN, b. May 12, 1752, m. Sarah Denison.
38 ZIBA, b. Feb. 16, 1755, m. Amy Brown.

Theophilus Baldwin (No. 29) m. 1st, Sarah Lamb, of Stonington, Feb. 5, 1738, who d. Aug. 20, 1764. He m. 2nd, Elizabeth Billings, Jan. 20, 1764. They lived in Stonington, Conn.

CHILDREN:

39 THANKFUL, b. Jan. 26, 1739, m. Ichabod Brown (No. 119) that family.
40 DAVID, b. Aug. 17, 1741, m. Phebe Billings.
41 ABIGAIL, b. May 17, 1744, d. unmarried.
42 SARAH, b. Oct. 6, 1746, m. John Davis.
43 THEOPHILUS, b. Feb. 26, 1749, d. young.
44 JOSEPH, b. Sept. 13, 1751, m. Sabra Billings.
45 NATHAN, b. May 17, 1754, d. young.
46 ASA, b. Dec. 17, 1756, m. Dolly Brown.
47 LUCY, b. Oct. 19, 1758, m. Randall Billings, (No. 139) Billings family.
48 REBECCA, b. Oct. 25, 1761, d. unmarried.

Sylvester Baldwin (No. 30) m. 1st, Anna ———; she d. childless, Oct. 1754; and Oct. 22, 1759, he m. 2nd, Bridget Chesebrough. He d. Oct. 12, 1795; his wife d. Sept. 14, 1818, all of Stonington.

CHILDREN:

49 THEOPHILUS, b. Nov. 13, 1762, d. in 1781.
50 SYLVESTER, b. Nov. 13, 1761; married.
51 WILLIAM, b. Dec. 2, 1763, d. Feb. 9, 1765.
52 JONATHAN, b. Dec. 24, 1765, m. Lucy Slack, 1788.
53 ANNA, b. June 27, 1768, m. Edward Chesebrough, (No. 232) Chesebrough family.
54 BRIDGET, b. June 27, 1768, m. John Leray, in 1791.
55 PRISCILLA, b. Oct. 7, 1770, d. in 1788.
56 AMOS, b. Jan. 2, 1773, m. Rebecca Palmer, Jan. 2, 1793.
57 THOMAS, b. Dec. 7, 1775, d. young.
58 PHEBE, b. Apr. 21, 1778.

John Baldwin (No. 37) m. Sarah Denison, Jan. 23, 1772, (No. 213) Denison family. They settled on the old homestead in Stonington, Conn. She d. June 19, 1813; he d. Aug. 3, 1814, leaving a large estate.

CHILDREN:

59 JOHN, b. Oct. 28, 1772, m. Abigail Boardman; 2nd, Mrs. Anner Rose.
60 EUNICE, b. Mar. 16, 1775, m. Stephen Tucker, Jan. 17, 1793.
61 DENISON b. Mar. 25, 1778, d. unm.
62 ANDREW, b. Dec. 15, 1780, m. Mary Boardman, Nov. 22, 1801.
63 DANIEL, b. May 21, 1783, m. Eunice Frink; 2nd. Lucy Boardman, Aug. 27, 1806; 3rd, Hannah, dau. of Nathaniel Stanton, Apr. 21, 1808, the mother of his nine children.
64 POLLY, b. Feb. 1, 1786, m. Stephen Frink in 1807.
65 GEORGE WASHINGTON, b. July 21, 1788, m. Mary C. Kinney, Nov. 16, 1809.
66 SARAH, b. Nov. 1790, m. Thomas Holmes.
67 NANCY, b. Oct. 1793, d. in 1834, unmarried.

BALDWIN FAMILY. 227

Ziba Baldwin (No. 38) m. Amy Brown of Preston, July 20, 1775, and settled in North Stonington, where he d. Sept. 27, 1803. His widow m. 2nd, Isaac Randall, Aug. 31, 1817.

CHILDREN:

68 THOMAS, b. May 3, 1777, m. Nancy, dau. of Dr. Asa Spalding, of Stonington, Apr. 16, 1801.
69 AMOS, b. June 4, 1779, m. Sally White of Hartford, May 2, 1807.
70 TURNER, b. July 6, 1781, m. Elizabeth Gray in 1805.
71 HEZEKIAH, b. Aug. 12, 1783, m. Amanda, dau. of Dr. Asa Spalding of Stonington, Mar. 22, 1812.
72 ELISHA, b. Aug. 11, 1786, m. Patty, dau. of Asa Spalding, in 1808.
73 ALANSON, b. Oct. 15, 1788, d. unmarried.
74 ASHER, b. Dec. 9, 1791, m. Polly Morgan, Nov. 13, 1814.
75 BILLINGS, b. Sept. 25, 1795, m. Orla O. Jones, Jan. 1, 1815.
76 NATHAN, b. Aug. 13, 1797, m. Betsey A. Bromley, Jan. 3, 1823.
77 AMY, b. Oct. 26, 1801, m. Ephraim Randall, only child of her mother's second husband, Mar. 8, 1818.

David Baldwin (No. 40) m. Phebe Billings, Dec. 1, 1763, both of Stonington, Conn.

CHILDREN:

78 PHEBE, b. ——, d. unmarried.
79 MARTHA, b. June 27, 1764, m. ——— Brown.
80 DAVID, b. Aug. 5, 1766, m. Susan Stewart.
81 THEOPHILUS, b. 1769, m. Philura Holmes, (No. 97) Holmes family.

Joseph Baldwin (No. 44) m. Sabra Billings in 1771.

CHILDREN:

82 ELIZABETH, b. ——, m. Thomas Holmes, (No. 59) that family, Nov. 19, 1789.
83 SALLY, b. 1774, m. Simeon Clark.
84 SABRA, b. 1777, m. Daniel Thurston.
85 BRIDGET, b. 1780, d. unmarried.
86 ANDREW, b. Jan. 2, 1788, m. Betsey Hutchins, Jan. 1, 1811.
87 HENRY, b. Mar. 8, 1790, m. Abigail Baldwin, Sept. 18, 1815.

David Baldwin (No. 80) m. Susan Stewart, May 29, 1793. He d. Oct. 14, 1805; she d. June 5, 1835.

CHILDREN:

89 SUSAN, b. Mar. 2, 1794, m. Capt. Samuel Prentice, (No. 85) that family.
90 STEWART, b. Mar. 6, 1796, m. Mary A. Baldwin.
91 DAVID, b. May 5, 1798, m. Mary Brown.
92 WOLCOTT, b. Oct. 20, 1801, m. in Troy, N. Y.
93 BENJAMIN, b. Sept. 20, 1805, d. Jan. 6, 1806.

David Baldwin (No. 91) m. Mary Brown, Feb. 13, 1823, and settled in Preston, Conn. He d. Apr. 17, 1848; she d. Jan. 2, 1865.

CHILDREN:

94 MARY, b. Apr. 12, 1824, d. infant.
95 DAVID D., (twin) b. Apr. 12, 1824, m. Belle F. Sturgis, of Providence, R. I.
96 SUSAN, b. May 5, 1828, m. Thomas S. Wheeler, (No. 284) Wheeler family.
97 LUCY, b. Mar. 17, 1830, m. Henry T. Loring, of St. Louis, Mo.
98 MARY ELLEN, b. Sept. 4, 1831, m. Samuel B. Wheeler, (No. 267) Wheeler family.
99 CHARLOTTE W., b. Aug. 28, 1854.

John Baldwin (No. 59), of Stonington, m. Abigail Boardman, of Griswold, Jan. 31, 1796. She d. July 30, 1814, aged 35, and he m. 2nd, Mrs. Anna Rose, who d. in 1864. He d. in 1858.

CHILDREN:

100 ABIGAIL, b. Mar. 21, 1797, m. Henry Baldwin.
101 JOHN ADAMS, b. May 26, 1799, d. 1805.
102 BETSEY MASON, b. Apr. 18, 1801, m. William S. Grant, of North Stonington, (No. 74) Grant family.
103 LUCY P., b. Nov. 13, 1803, m. Isaac Swan.
104 EUNICE, b. Sept. 26, 1806.
105 BENJAMIN, b. Jan. 15, 1809, d. infant.
106 EMILY A., b. Apr. 26, 1810, m. John Smith Hewitt; 2nd, Russell Griffin.
107 SALLY ANN, b. June 1, 1814, m. George N. Griffing.

BENNETT FAMILY.

1. JOHN BENNETT, the first of this name in Stonington, Conn., came here from New London, and m Oct. 22, 1691, but who, it is not known.

CHILDREN:
2 JOHN, b. in 1658, d. Feb. 11, 1660.
3 WILLIAM, b. Apr. 18, 1660.
4 JOHN, b. Feb. 19, 1666, m. Elizabeth Park.
5 ELIZABETH, b. Oct. 28, 1672.
6 JOSEPH, b. Mch. 20, 1681.

William Bennett (No. 3) m. Susannah Bright, Oct. 30, 1676. He served in King Philip's war.

CHILDREN:
7 REBECCA, b. Nov. 22, 1678.
8 JOHN, b. Aug. 11, 1683.
9 WILLIAM, b. Feb. 8, 1685.
10 HENRY, b. ———.

John Bennett (No. 4) m. Elizabeth Park, Mch. 8, 1687. He served in King Philip's war.

CHILDREN:
11 HANNAH, b. Apr. 2, 1688.
12 JOHN, b. Jan. 24, 1691.
13 SAMUEL, b. Sept. 7, 1694.
14 THOMAS, b. Nov. 14, 1697.
15 JOSEPH, b. Feb. 8, 1699.
16 ELIZABETH, b. July 31, 1702.
17 ISAAC, b. July 14, 1705.
18 NATHAN, b. July 14, 1709.

Joseph Bennett (No. 6) m. Sarah Bequess, Nov. 4, 1702.

CHILDREN:
19 JOSEPH, b. Oct. 16, 1703.
20 JERUSHA, b. Oct. 26, 1705.
21 STEPHEN, b. Apr. 8, 1707.
22 SARAH, b. Mch. 4, 1709.
23 HANNAH, b. Apr. 19, 1711.
24 PHEBE, b. May 19, 1713.
25 DANIEL, b. Aug. 19, 1715.
26 WILLIAM, b. Oct. 22, 1717.
27 JOSEPH, b. Feb. 20, 1724.

Joseph Bennett (No. 15) m. Joanna Williams, Nov. 14, 1724.
William Bennett (No. 9) m. Mary Church, Feb. 2, 1718.

CHILDREN:

28 SAMUEL, b. Apr. 3, 1719.
29 MARY, b. Jan. 3, 1722.
30 SARAH, b. Aug. 3, 1729.
31 ESTHER, b. Jan. 28, 1725.

Stephen Bennett (No. 21) m. Mehitable Stebbens, Sept. 23, 1736.

CHILDREN:

32 MEHITABLE, b. June 25, 1738.
33 STEPHEN, b. Apr. 22, 1740.
34 JESSE, b. Aug. 20, 1742.
35 NATHANIEL, b. Aug. 6, 1744.
36 NOAH, b. July 4, 1746.
37 AARON, b. Oct. 25, 1748.
38 MARY, b. Jan. 16, 1751.
39 ELISHA, b. May 18, 1753.
40 SAMUEL, b. July 18, 1755.
41 THANKFUL, b. Oct. 5, 1757.
42 DAVID, b. ———.
43 JOSEPH, b. ———.
44 CHARLES, b. ———.

Joseph Bennett (No. 27) m. Anna Wyllis, Oct. 27, 1743.

CHILDREN:

45 JERUSHA, b. May 1, 1744, d. y.
46 JOSEPH, b. Aug. 8, 1746.
47 JOANNA, b. Mch. 28, 1749.
48 JEDEDIAH, b. July 17, 1751.

Aaron Bennett (No. 37) m. Hannah Holdredge, Sept. 15, 1773.

CHILDREN:

49 AARON, b. Aug. 9, 1774.

Mrs. Hannah Bennett d. ———, and Mr. Bennett m. 2nd, Abigail Smith, Feb. 13, 1777.

CHILDREN:

50 HANNAH, b. Feb. 11, 1779, m. Jonathan Fish.
51 SALLY, b. Dec. 14, 1780, m. Mark Ethridge.
52 AMOS, b. June 28, 1783.
53 THANKFUL, b. Mch. 14, 1785, m. 1st, Jerry Burrows, and 2nd, Joseph Chapman.
54 MERRANDA, b. July 19, 1788, m. Samuel Hempstead.
55 CHARLES, b. Nov. 11, 1790.
56 OLIVER, b. Mch. 29, 1793.
57 DUDLEY, b. June 6, 1797, m. Mary Lamphere.
58 MARY ANN, b. Dec. 15, 1803.

BENNETT FAMILY.

Aaron Bennett (No. 49) m. Lucy Williams, dau. of Elisha Williams, April 19, 1796, (No. 133), that family.

CHILDREN:

59 AARON, b. May 25, 1797, d. y.
60 ELISHA WILLIAMS, b. June 7th, 1798.
61 SABRA, b. ———, d. at 18 years.
62 NATHAN DENISON, b. Dec. 20, 1802.
63 AARON, b. Dec. 1, 1800.
64 LUCY, b. Apr. 21, 1805.
65 JESSE, b. Oct. 3, 1807.
66 ESTHER, b. Mch. 29, 1810.
67 JOHN, b. May 15, 1812, d. Oct. 19, 1819.
68 JANE, b. ———.

Charles Bennett (No. 55) m. Martha Babcock, the dau. of Ichabod and wife Dorcas (Hoxie) Babcock, and granddaughter of Hezekiah, (No. 104) Babcock family, and Martha (Hoxie) Babcock, Nov. 11, 1810.

CHILDREN:

69 CAROLINE, b. Aug. 29, 1811, m. Henry Bennett, Sept. 21, 1828.
70 MARY ANN, b. Jan. 5, 1813, m. Thomas Franklin, June 24, 1830.
71 CHARLES S., b. Dec. 17, 1815, m. Wealthy Ann Frink, Jan. 2, 1842.
72 EMILY, b. Mch. 6, 1818, m. Elder Cyrus Miner, Nov. 7, 1834.
73 AMANDA, b. July 7, 1820, m. William Miner, Apr. 25, 1844.
74 JOHN, b. June 7, 1822, m. Mercy Topliff, Feb. 13, 1845.
75 PERRY, b. Mch. 1, 1824, m. Amanda Morgan, Oct. 18, 1846.
76 BENJAMIN F., b. Apr. 18, 1826, m. Mary Graves, Oct. 27, 1852.
77 MARTHA, b. Mch. 10, 1828, m. Samuel Culver, Sept. 29, 1847.
78 ELIZA, b. Feb. 7, 1830, m. James Miner, Aug. 25, 1847.
79 JAMES C., b. Mch. 6, 1832, m. a Miss Berry, Dec. 26, 1866.
80 ALONZO, b. Aug. 7, 1834, m. a Miss Berry, Dec. 25, 1866.
81 ELLEN, b. Apr. 9, 1837, m. Walter Coan, Nov. 11, 1858.

Dea. Elisha Bennett (No. 39) m. Esther Davis about 1774.

CHILDREN:

82 ELISHA, JR., b. in 1776, m. Eunice Smith.
83 ESTHER, b. in 1778.
84 HENRY, b. in 1780.
85 PHEBE, b. in 1782, m. a Smith.
86 JOHN, b. in 1785, m. Sarah Williams.
87 ERASTUS, b. in 1787.
88 MARY, b. in 1790, m. a Frink.
89 CYNTHIA, b. in 1793.
90 EPHRAIM T., b. in 1797, m. Abby White.

Oliver Bennett (No. 56) m. Fanny, dau. of Ramsford Hempstead.

CHILDREN:
91 OLIVER, b. ———.
92 WILLIAM, b. ———.
93 FANNY, b. ———.
94 MELINDA, b. ———.
95 RAMSFORD, b. ———.
96 and 97 (twins) ALLEN and ABBY. Allen d. young, but Abby m. John Eldredge.

Elisha Williams Bennett (No 60) m. 1st, Huldah Lewis, June 18, 1820.

CHILDREN:
98 JOHN, b. ———, m. Sarah Williams.
99 SUSAN, b. ———, m. ——— Burch.
100 SALLY ANN, b. ———, m. ——— Potter.
101 REUBEN, b. ———, m. ——— Champlin.

Mrs. Huldah Bennett d. and Mr. Bennett m. 2nd, Mrs. Harriet H. Stanton, (No. 201) that family.

CHILDREN:
102 WILLIAM, b. Jan. 13, 1846, m. 1st, a ——— Peckham, of Ledyard, and 2nd, Ella, dau. of Albert Brown.
103 JOHN, b. ———, m. Sarah, dau. of James Williams.

BENTLEY FAMILY.

1. WILLIAM BENTLEY came to New England in the ship Arabella, Richard Sprague, master, which sailed from Gravesend May 27th, 1671, and he was resident of Narragansett, R. I., Jan. 29, 1679. His will approved in 1720 at Kingston mentions wife, Sarah ———, and

CHILDREN:

2 WILLIAM, b. ———.
3 JAMES, b. ———.
4 THOMAS, b. ———.
5 BENJAMIN, b. ———.
6 JANE, b. ———, m. John Wightman, Jan. 6, 1700. They lived on the Great Plain, now Exeter, and are buried on a farm about a mile northwest of Slocumville, lately owned by John F. Gardiner. There is said to have been a son, Robert Bentley, who in 1709 purchased land southeast of Exeter Hill, but no mention is made of him in his will.

William Bentley (No. 2) m. Apr. 21, 1703, Mary Eliot, (No. 3) York family, dau. of Henry Eliot and wife, Deborah (York), of Stonington, Ct. He d. 1760.

CHILDREN:

7 JOHN, b. ———.
8 GEORGE, b. ———.
9 CALEB, b. ———.
10 EZEKIEL, b. ———.
11 ELIZABETH, b. ———, m. Nathaniel Potter, May 12, 1727.
12 TABITHA, b. ———, m. Thomas Sweet, April 1728.
13 RUHAMA, b. ———, m. ——— James.
14 MARY, b. ———, m. ——— James.

Mrs. Mary Bentley d. ———, and he m. 2nd, Bathsheba, widow of Israel Lewis, Aug. 1, 1734.

CHILDREN:

15 WILLIAM, b. May 29, 1735.
16 THOMAS, b. 1737.
17 JAMES, b. June 6, 1739.
18 GREEN, b. Mch. 23, 1741.
19 BENJAMIN, b. Jan. 11, 1744.

James Bentley (No. 3) m. Dorothy Albro, dau. of Samuel and wife, Isabel (Lawton) Albro; she d. and he m. 2nd, Hannah ————.

1ST WIFE'S CHILD:
20 HANNAH, b. Mch. 25, 1703.

2ND WIFE'S CHILD.
21 Daughter, b. Dec. 15, 1718.

Thomas Bentley (No. 4) m. Elizabeth Chamberlin, June 6th, 1706.

Benjamin Bentley (No. 5) m. ———— Rathbone, dau. of Thomas and wife, Mary (Dickens) Rathbone.

CHILD:
22 WILLIAM, b. ————.

John Bentley (No. 7) m. Elizabeth Gardner, May 30, 1727.

George Bentley (No. 8) m. Ruth Barber, dau. of Moses and wife, Susannah (Wiat) Barber, of Kingston, R. I., Mch. 4, 1724. She was b. Jan. 23, 1705. Their son

23. George Bentley, of Westerly, R. I., called junior, b. 1730, and d. Oct. 28, 1814; m. Amy Carter, June 27, 1751.

CHILDREN:
24 MARY, b. Sept. 25, 1752.
25 GEORGE, b. June 26, 1756.
26 SARAH, b. April 25, 1761.
27 ROBERT, b. Aug. 6, 1765.
28 ANNE, b. July 9, 1769.

George Bentley (No. 25) m. Lucy Gardiner. He d. May 3, 1831. She was b. 1756, d. June 7, 1844, aged 88.

CHILDREN:
29 JONATHAN, b. ————, m. Nancy Bly, d. Aug. 22, 1848.
30 LUCY, b. ————, never m.; d. May 1, 1854.
31 GEORGE, b. ————.
32 DANIEL, b. Mch. 27, 1789.
33 RUSSEL, b. Oct. 12, 1791, d. Sept. 25, 1852.
34 HENRY, b. ————, d. Apr. 15, 1833.
35 IRA, b. ————, d. July 9, 1838.

Daniel Bentley (No. 32) m. Esther Wheeler (No. 272) of the Wheeler family, Apr. 29, 1819.

CHILDREN:
36 Infant daughter, b. and d. May 23, 1822.
37 Infant son, b. and d. Oct. 24, 1823.
38 ANNA ESTHER, b. July 14, 1825.

39 DANIEL E., b. Feb. 15, 1827, d. young.
40 DANIEL EDWIN, b. May 30, 1828, d. young.
41 REV. EDWIN, b. Oct. 29, 1829.
42 COURTLAND W., b. Nov. 5, 1831.
43 Infant son, b. and d. May 8, 1834.
44 ADONIRAM JUDSON, b. May 16, 1836, d. young.
45 SAMUEL HORTON, b. Aug. 14, 1837.
46 SARAH, b. Aug. 14, 1837.

Russel Bentley (No. 33) m. Oct. 22, 1822, Susan Stanton, (No. 93) daughter of Amos and wife, Amelia (Babcock) Stanton. She was b. Aug. 17, 1798, and d. Nov. 20, 1844.

CHILDREN:

47 HARRIET D., b. Jan. 1, 1824, m. 1st, John D. Babcock, Jan. 5, 1843, m. 2nd, David N. Gallup, Jan. 25, 1859, and m. 3rd, Henry D. Hungerford, Apr. 9, 1869; d. Jan. 31, 1889.
48 MARTHA E., b. Apr. 8, 1825, m. John H. Crary, Nov. 12, 1845.
49 SUSAN E., b. Sept. 24, 1827, d. Dec. 22, 1844.
50 Infant daughter, b. and d. May, 1831.
51 LUCY G., b. July 17, 1829, m. Richard Wheeler, (No. 501) of that family, Oct. 20, 1850.
52 MARY J., b. Sept. 10, 1832, m. Henry L. Miner, son of (No. 298) Miner family, Jan. 5, 1858.
53 EMELINE N., b. May 4, 1835, m. Charles H. Kenyon, June 25, 1861.

BILLINGS FAMILY.

1. WILLIAM BILLINGS, the progenitor of the Billings family of Stonington, Conn., came from Taunton, Eng., and first appears in this country at Dorchester and Braintree, Mass., as we learn from Mr. Somersby, a distinguished genealogist of Massachusetts. He m. Mary ———— (family name and birth date not given), at Dorchester, Mass., Feb. 5, 1658. The time of his coming to Stonington is not certainly known, but his name appears here among the planters of Stonington. He built him a dwelling-house on Cosatuc Hill, where the site may still be seen. He became by grants and purchases a large land owner. Our records do not contain a list of his children, with their births. What is known of them is by his will. He d. in 1713.

CHILDREN:

2 WILLIAM, b. in 1660, m. Hannah Sterry, 1689. He d. 1738.
3 LYDIA, b. ———.
4 MARGARET, b. ———, m. Edmund Fanning, (No. 2) that family.
5 MARY, b. ———.
6 ABIGAIL, b. ———.
7 DOROTHY, b. ———.
8 PATIENCE, b. ———.
9 EBENEZER, b. ———, m. Anna Comstock.

William Billings (No. 2) m. Hannah Sterry in 1689, (No. 4) Hewitt family, both of Stonington, Conn. He was in the early Colonial wars, and d. 1738.

CHILDREN:

10 MARY, b. 1689, m. John Boardman, 1713.
11 JOSEPH, b. June 28, 1692, m. Comfort Denison; 2nd, Sarah ————.
12 PRUDENCE, b. June 12, 1694.
13 REV. WILLIAM, b. Feb. 16, 1697, m. Bethiah Otis; d. 1733.
14 SAMUEL, b. Aug. 18, 1699, m. Hannah Williams.
15 DOROTHY, b. Feb. 5, 1702, m. Thomas Edwards in 1720.
16 RACHEL, b. Mar. 25, 1704, m. ———— Kennedy.
17 SARAH, b. Sept. 10, 1705.
17a HANNAH, b. 1706, m. Eleazar Putnam, of Preston, 1730-1.
18 ROGER, b. Mar. 19, 1708, m. Abigail Denison.
19 ICHABOD, b. Sept. 5, 1710.
20 ELIZABETH, b. Jan. 5, 1713, m. Theophilus Avery, son of Edward and Joanna (Rose) Avery, of Groton, Conn.

BILLINGS FAMILY.

Ebenezer Billings (No. 9) m. Anna Comstock, March 1, 1680. He was in the Colonial wars.

CHILDREN:

21 ANNA, b. Oct. 7, 1681, m. Soloman Hakes, Jan. 16, 1718.
22 EBENEZER, b. Jan. 1, 1684, m. Phebe Denison.
23 WILLIAM, b. Apr. 4, 1686.
24 JAMES, b. Oct. 4, 1688, m. Mary Hewitt.
25 MARGARET, b. 1690, m. Jeremiah Burch, Feb. 8, 1717, (No. 10) that family.
26 ZIPPORAH, b. Apr. 4, 1693.
27 JEMIMA, b. Apr. 15, 1695.
28 INCREASE, b. May 13, 1697, m. Hannah Hewitt.
29 THANKFUL, b. Feb. 8, 1699, m. Daniel Smith, Mar. 18, 1725, (No. 13) that family.
30 BENJAMIN, b. Sept. 15, 1703, m. Mary Denison.

Joseph Billings (No. 11) m. Comfort Denison in 1711; both of Stonington, Conn. Married 2nd, Sarah ————.

CHILDREN:

31 ANNA, b. Dec. 18, 1712.
32 SARAH, b. Dec. 27, 1714.
33 JOSEPH, b. Dec. 17, 1716, m. Thankful Denison.

Samuel Billings (No. 14) m. Hannah Williams, Jan. 6, 1726. He d. Sept. 21, 1733; both of Stonington, Conn. She d. 1727.

CHILD:

34 HANNAH, b. Jan. 6, 1727.

Capt. Roger Billings (No. 18) m. Abigail Denison, (No. 107) that family, July 3, 1729.

CHILDREN:

35 ABIGAIL, b. Feb. 21, 1730, m. Benjamin Coit, 1753. She d. 1760.
36 JOHN, b. Dec. 15, 1732, m. Eunice Gallup.
37 CAPT. WILLIAM, b. May 8, 1734, d. 1774; m. Mrs. Mary (Leffingwell) Richards, 1757.
38 PELEG, b. June 26, 1738, m. Mary Stanton.
39 DOROTHY, b. Apr. 16, 1741.
40 BENJAMIN, b. Oct. 10, 1743.
41 CAPT. HENRY, b. Apr. 19, 1746, d. 1797; m. Lucretia Leffingwell, 1770, sister of William's wife.
42 SABRA, b. Jan. 21, 1747, m. Elias Brown.
43 MARY, b. May 24, 1755, m. Darius Denison, (No. 293) that family.

Lieut. Ebenezer Billings, b. 1684, (No. 22), ensign 1721, lieutenant 1731, at Stonington, Conn.; m. Phebe Denison, Apr. 2, 1706, (No. 58) that family.

HISTORY OF STONINGTON.

CHILDREN:
44 ABIGAIL, b. Mar. 1, 1707, m. Dea. Samuel Prentice, (No. 13) that family.
45 JOHN, b. Dec. 8, 1708, d. young.
46 EBENEZER, b. Mar. 20, 1711, m. Mary Noyes, Mrs. Sarah Chesebrough Geer.
47 PHEBE, b. Apr. 4, 1714, m. Dr. Nathan Palmer, (No. 99) that family.
48 GRACE, b. May 27, 1716, m. James Noyes, (No. 114) that family.
49 ANN, b. Jan. 21, 1718, m. Col. Samuel Prentice, (No. 38) that family.
50 JOHN, b. Sept. 29, 1720, m. Elizabeth Page, (No. 14) that family.
51 CHRISTOPHER, b. Feb. 10, 1723, m. Anna Fanning, Abigail Babcock.
52 DANIEL, b. Feb. 10, 1725, m. Katherine Geer.
53 NATHAN, b. Apr. 9, 1727, m. Anna Bell.
54 ANN BORODEL, b. Apr. 18, 1732, m. Oliver Grant, (No. 24) that family.

William Billings (No. 23) m. ———.
CHILDREN:
55 BENAJAH, b. Apr. 12, 1711.
56 THANKFUL, b. Feb. 28, 1716.
57 ICHABOD, b. June 15, 1721.
58 MOSES, b. Dec. 25, 1723.
59 DOROTHY, b. May 16, 1727.
60 SAMUEL, b. Apr. 11, 1729, m. Patience Billings.
61 PRUDENCE, b. Jan. 26, 1732.
62 MARY, b. Jan. 1, 1734, m. Daniel Prentice, (No. 40) that family.
63 ESTHER, b. June 1, 1735.
64 WILLIAM, b. Aug. 25, 1736.

James Billings (No. 24) m. Mary Hewitt, Mar. 17, 1715, (No. 10) that family.
CHILDREN:
65 ZIPPORAH, b. Oct. 22, 1715, m. Dr. Joseph Palmer, (No. 148) Palmer family.
66 JAMES, b. Sept. 20, 1719, m. Margaret ———.
67 EUNICE, b. Aug. 17, 1721, m. Ezekiel Babcock, (No. 224) that family.
68 LOIS, b. Jan. 6, 1724, m. Timothy Babcock (No. 76) Babcock family.
69 AMOS, b. May 9, 1728, m. Bethia Miner.
70 DAVID, b. Sept. 6, 1730.
71 JESSE, b. Apr. 18, 1737.

Increase Billlings (No. 28) m. Hannah Hewitt, Dec. 29, 1720, (No. 13) that family.
CHILDREN:
72 ANDREW, b. Feb. 22, 1721.
73 STEPHEN, b. Mar. 23, 1723, d. young.
74 INCREASE, b. Feb. 15, 1725.
75 ABIGAIL, b. Oct. 27, 1726.
76 LUCY, b. Aug. 12, 1728.
77 JEMIMA, b. July 30, 1732.
78 STEPHEN, b. May 18, 1734, m. Bridget Grant.
79 JARED, b. Dec. 30, 1735.

BILLINGS FAMILY. 239

Benjamin Billings (No. 30) m. Mary Denison, June 22, 1724, (No. 128) that family.
CHILDREN:
80 DESIRE, b. June 5, 1726.
81 BENJAMIN, b. Dec. 12, 1728, m. Abby Brown, (No. 62) that family.

John Billings (No. 36) of Preston, Conn., m. Eunice Gallup of Groton (No. 93) that family, June 19, 1751.
CHILDREN:
82 JOSEPH, b. Apr. 6, 1759, m. Sarah Belcher.
83 ROGER, b. Apr. 6, 1759 (twin).
84 JOHN, b. Oct. 4, 1761, m. Elizabeth Page.
85 RUFUS, b. Dec. 18, 1763
86 ABIGAIL, b. July 26, 1764.
87 BENJAMIN, b. Nov. 11, 1766.
88 EUNICE, b. Sept. 1, 1771.
89 WILLIAM, b. June 22, 1774.
90 CHARLES, b. Mar. 21, 1780.

Peleg Billings (No. 38) m. Mary Stanton in 1771.
CHILDREN:
91 THEOPHILUS, b. May 11, 1773, m. Ethridge Whipple.
92 SUSANNAH, b. Jan. 19, 1775.
93 LUCY, b. July 26, 1778.
94 PELEG, b. Dec. 4, 1780.

Ebenezer Billings (No. 46) m. Mary Noyes, Nov. 20, 1733, (No. 113) that family. He m. 2nd, Mrs. Sarah (Chesebrough) Geer, (No. 73) Chesebrough family.
CHILDREN:
95 ELIZABETH or ABIGAIL, b. Aug. 6, 1734, m. Capt. Nathan Stanton, (No. 342) that family.
96 SANFORD, b. Apr. 20, 1736, m. Lucy Geer.
97 PHEBE, b. Mar. 21, 1738.
98 EBENEZER, b. Feb. 26, 1740.
99 REBECCA, b. Apr. 5, 1742.
100 GILBERT, b. Sept. 15, 1744.
101 MARY, b. Apr. 5, 1747.
102 ELISHA, b. Aug. 6, 1750.

John Billings (No. 50) m. Elizabeth Page, Apr. 7, 1743 (No. 14) Page family.
CHILDREN:
103 ANDREW, b. Nov. 24, 1743.
104 PHEBE, b. Feb. 17, 1745.
105 JOHN, b. Jan. 27, 1747, d. young.
106 DANIEL, b. May 19, 1749.
107 JOHN, b. Aug. 1, 1750.
108 SABRA, b. June 16, 1752, m. Elias Brown, (No. 17) that family.

Christopher Billings (No. 51) m. Anna Fanning, Nov. 14, 1743; she d. Nov. 16, 1758. He m. 2nd, Abigail Babcock.

CHILDREN:
109 MERCY, b. Nov. 28, 1745.
110 CHRISTOPHER, b. Nov. 5, 1748.
111 NATHAN, b. May 15, 1750.
112 MARGARET, b. Apr. 1, 1752.
113 LYDIA, b. Dec. 18, 1755.

CHILDREN BY 2ND MARRIAGE:
114 ANNA, b. Aug. 26, 1759.
115 JOHN, b. Apr. 8, 1761.
116 JOSEPH, b Apr. 18, 1763.
117 JONAS, b. Feb. 15, 1765.

Daniel Billings (No. 52) m. Katharine Geer, of Groton, Mar. 21, 1779.

CHILD:
118 NANCY, b. Dec. 19, 1779.

Nathan Billings (No. 53) m. Anna Bell, daughter of John Bell, Apr. 21, 1757, of Stonington, Conn.

CHILDREN:
119 NATHAN, b. May 6, 1758.
120 POLLY, b. 1762, m. Eleazer Williams (No. 461) that family.
121 GRACE, b. Jan. 23, 1774, m. Gilbert Williams, (No. 462) that family. He d. Apr. 15, 1799. She m. 2nd, John Denison Smith, about 1800.

Joseph Billings (No. 33) m. Thankful Denison, Nov. 10, 1737, (No. 110) that family.

CHILDREN:
122 COMFORT, b. Sept. 24, 1740.
123 SARAH, b. Jan. 15, 1746.
124 NATHAN, b. Jan. 9, 1748.

Amos Billings (No. 69) m. Bethia Miner, Jan. 10, 1750.

CHILD:
125 MARY, b. Aug. 21, 1750.

Stephen Billings (No. 78) m. Bridget Grant, Dec. 4, 1746, (No. 23) Grant family; she d. Aug. 15, 1762. He m. 2nd, Mary Ledyard, Dec. 12, 1765; she d. Mar. 7, 1787. He m. 3rd, Martha Denison, Apr. 9, 1789.

CHILDREN:
126 HANNAH, b. July 3, 1748.
127 STEPHEN, b. July 3, 1748, m. Cynthia Hewitt; 2nd, Ann Raymond.
128 BRIDGET, b. Feb. 16, 1754.
129 KATHARINE, b. May 5, 1758.
130 ANDREW, b. Aug. 3, 1760. He was killed at the massacre of Fort Griswold, Sept. 6, 1781.
131 EUNICE, b. Aug. 6, 1763, d. Aug. 28, 1764.

BILLINGS FAMILY.

CHILD BY 2ND MARRIAGE.
132 ELIZABETH, b. Aug. 14, 1766.

James Billings (No. 66) m. Margaret ———— in 1740; she d. Mar. 27, 1752.
CHILDREN:
133 JONAS, b. Feb. 6, 1742.
134 BENJAMIN, b. Nov. 5, 1744, m. Rahama Palmer.
135 ALPHEUS, b. Oct. 27, 1746.
136 AMOS, b. Jan. 16, 1749.
137 JAMES, b. Oct. 11, 1751.

Samuel Billings (No. 60) m. Patience Billings, Aug. 22, 1749.
CHILDREN:
138 THANKFUL, b. June 24, 1751.
139 RANDALL, b. Jan. 25, 1753, m. Lucy Baldwin, (No. 47) that family.
140 ANNA, b. Aug. 15, 1755.
141 SAMUEL, b. Aug. 31, 1757.
142 BENAJAH, b. Oct. 20, 1759, m. Lucy Smith, Jan. 25, 1771.
143 WILLIAM, b. Jan. 19, 1761.
144 ELI, b. Mar. 23, 1764.
145 ADAM, b. Mar. 27, 1765.
146 PATIENCE, b. no date given.

Joseph Billings (No. 82) m. Sarah Belcher, Nov. 15, 1781.
CHILD:
147 BETSEY, b. May 8, 1783.

Stephen Billings (No. 127) m. Cynthia Hewitt, Oct. 6, 1774, (No. 93) that family; she d. May 13, 1786. He m. 2nd, Anna Raymond, May 24, 1787. He d. Aug. 15, 1850.
CHILDREN:
148 ISAAC, b. Nov. 6, 1775.
149 Infant daughter, b. and d. young.
150 HENRY, b. Sept. 5, 1779.
151 STEPHEN, b. Sept. 25, 1781, m. Martha Allyn.
CHILDREN BY 2ND MARRIAGE:
152 BETSEY, b. Apr. 16, 1788.
153 Infant, b. Jan. 6, 1790.
154 ANDREW, b. Dec. 31, 1790.
155 NANCY, b. Dec. 23, 1792.
156 EUNICE, b Nov. 22, 1794.
157 FRANCES, b. Oct. 3, 1797.

Theophilus Billings (No. 91) m. Ethridge Whipple, Jan. 1, 1799.
CHILDREN:
158 PELEG, b. Sept. 24, 1800.
159 DANIEL, b. Mar. 17, 1804.
160 GEORGE, b. Jan. 16, 1807.
161 CODDINGTON, b. May 15, 1810.

242 HISTORY OF STONINGTON.

Sanford Billings (No. 96) m. Lucy Geer, of Groton, Jan. 24, 1760. He d. Apr. 25, 1806; she d. Apr. 19, 1810.

CHILDREN:

162 EBENEZER, b. Jan. 21, 1761, d. Apr. 7, 1787.
163 SANFORD, b. Apr. 15, 1763, d. Feb. 22, 1787.
164 ROBERT, b. Dec. 15, 1764, d. Feb. 15, 1796.
165 Son, b. Apr. 7, and d. Apr. 30, 1767.
166 GILBERT, b. Nov. 25, 1768, m. Lucy Swan.
167 CODDINGTON, b. Oct. 25, 1770, m. Mrs. Eunice (Williams) Wheeler; 2nd, Ann (Wilcox) Babcock.
168 NOYES, b. Mar. 20, 1773, d. Oct. 17, 1797.
169 LUCY, b. June 20, 1775, m. Stephen Meech, Mar. 20, 1796.
170 JAMES GEER, b. Oct. 4, 1777, d. July 2, 1798.
171 SARAH, b. July 17, 1781, d. Jan. 8, 1800.
172 WASHINGTON, b. Dec. 21, 1783, d. Sept. 9, 1799.

Benjamin Billings (No. 134) m. Rahama Palmer, Nov. 7, 1766.

CHILDREN:

173 PEREZ, b. in 1767.
174 EZRA, b. Oct. 5, 1768.
175 LYDIA, b. Aug. 5, 1770.

Stephen Billings (No. 151) m. Martha Allyn, (No. 191) Stanton family, Apr. 9, 1809. She d. Feb. 24, 1861.

CHILDREN:

176 CYNTHIA, b. Jan. 11, 1800, m. Col. William Morgan (No. 36) that family.
177 HANNAH ADELIA, b. June 12, 1812, m. Alexander Palmer, (No. 350) that family.
178 ANNA S., b. Sept. 1, 1814, m. Christopher M. Gallup, (No. 180) that family.
179 POLLY, b. Apr. 18, 1817, m. Jonah Witter.
180 STEPHEN, b. Nov. 23, 1818, d. Dec. 25, 1840, aged 22 years.
181 JAMES ALLYN, b. Feb. 24, 1821, m. Margaret J. Allyn, Dec. 28, 1852.
182 HENRIETTA, b. Oct. 25, 1824, m. Isaac Avery, (No. 229) that family.

Gilbert Billings (No. 166) m. Lucy Swan in 1792, (No. 73) Swan family. He d. May 4, 1856; she d. Dec. 16, 1854, aged 84.

CHILDREN:

183 SANFORD, b. June 21, 1793, d. Sept. 22, 1820.
184 LUCY, b. June 30, 1798, m. Asher Coates, (No. 26) that family.
185 ROBERT, b. May 23, 1800, m. Calista Keeney.
186 JAMES, b. Jan. 2, 1802.
187 GEORGE, W., b. Dec. 9, 1803, d. Feb. 14, 1873.
188 HORATIO NELSON, b. Nov. 26, 1805, m. Mary Ann Fish.
189 Child, b. Sept. 19, 1807.
190 JOHN S., b. Mar. 4, 1809, d. Aug. 28, 1812.
191 BENJAMIN F., b. Jan. 15, 1811, m. Mrs. Abby Jane Starkweather, widow of Denison Stewart (No. 51) Stewart family.
192 MARY P., b. Jan. 24, 1813, d. Mar. 20, 1856.

BILLINGS FAMILY.

Coddington Billings (No. 167) m. Mrs. Eunice (Williams) Wheeler, widow of Rufus Wheeler, Sept. 13, 1797, (No. 272) Williams family. He m. 2nd, Mrs. Ann (Wilcox) Babcock, July 18, 1819. He d. Feb. 6, 1845.

CHILDREN BY 1ST MARRIAGE:

193 CODDINGTON, b. in Stonington, Sept. 3, 1798, d. Jan. 19, 1801.
194 HON. NOYES, b. in Stonington, Mar. 31, 1800, was graduated from Yale College in 1819, and Lieutenant Governor of Connecticut in 1846. He m. Isabella Stewart, Oct. 1826.
195 HON. WILLIAM WILLIAMS, b. in Stonington, Feb. 16, 1802, a graduate of Yale in 1821, and was one of the most prominent and successful business men of New London. He m. Louise Trott, Apr. 6, 1828.
196 EUNICE W., b. in Stonington, June 15, 1804, m. Dr. Ralph Farnsworth, who was an eminent and successful physician of Norwich, Conn.

CHILDREN BY 2ND MARRIAGE:

197 ANN, b. May 14, 1821, m. Calvin G. Williams, (No. 351) that family.
198 HARRIET, b. Jan. 13, 1832, m. Theo. D. Palmer, (No. 483) that family.
199 CODDINGTON, b. Feb. 8, 1834, m. Mary B. Williams, Nov. 15, 1855, (No. 388) that family.

Robert Billings (No. 185) m. Calista, daughter of Lot Keeney.

CHILD:

200 GILBERT, b. ———, m. Mary Ann Hewitt, (No. 258) that family.

Horatio N. Billings (No. 188) m. Mary Ann Fish, Jan. 30, 1838. He was a sea-faring man. He went to California and was never heard from.

CHILDREN:

201 LUCY H., b. ———, m. John L. Spalding.
202 SANFORD N., b. ———, m. Lucy E. Main, Oct. 28, 1867.
203 EDWARD E., b. ———, m. twice.
204 MARY A., b. ———, m. Charles D. Thompson.

BREED FAMILY.

1. ALLEN BREED, the progenitor of the Breed family, appears first in Lynn, Mass., in 1630. He was b. in England in 1601. The name of his wife is unknown. He d. Mar. 17, 1692, and had five children.

THEIR SON

2. Allen Breed, b. 1626, m. Mary ———, and had six children.

THEIR SON

3. John Breed, b. Jan. 18, 1663, m. 1st, Mary Kirtland, Apr. 28, 1686. He m. 2nd, Mercy Palmer, June 8, 1690, (No. 31) Palmer family. He resided in Lynn until after the death of his first wife and daughter, and then removed to Stonington, Conn., where he purchased land of Gershom Palmer, the father of his second wife. They were both buried at Wequetequock burial ground, and they were members of the First Congregational Church of Stonington, Conn. He d. in 1761; his wife d. Jan. 28, 1752.

CHILDREN:

4 SARAH, b. July 15, 1687, d. Jan. 28, 1688.

CHILDREN BY 2ND MARRIAGE:

5 ANNA, b. Nov. 8, 1693, m. Israel Hewitt, (No. 8) that family.
6 MARY, b. Jan. 8, 1697, m. Daniel Brown, June 21, 1721, (No. 24) that family.
7 JOHN, b. Jan. 26, 1700, m. Mary Prentice.
8 ELIZABETH, b. Jan. 28, 1702, m. John Hinckley (No. 18) that family.
9 SARAH, b. Feb. 1, 1704, m. James Miner, (No. 74) that family.
10 ZERVIAH, b. Aug. 27, 1706, m. Samuel Hinckley, (No. 20) that family.
11 JOSEPH, b. Oct. 4, 1708, m. Priscilla Avery.
12 BETHIA, b. Dec. 30, 1710.
13 ALLEN, b. Aug. 29, 1714, m. Ann Cole; 2nd, Hannah Dewey.
14 GERSHOM, b. Nov. 15, 1715, m. Dorothy McLaren, May 10, 1747.

John Breed (No. 7) m. Mary Prentice, (No. 16) that family, Oct. 14, 1725.

CHILDREN:

15 MERCY, b. Aug. 3, 1727, m. John Noyes, (No. 123) that family.
16 JOHN, b. Sept. 5, 1729, m. Silence Grant.

BREED FAMILY.   245

17 NATHAN, b. Dec. 13, 1731, m. Lucy Babcock.
18 MARY, b. Dec. 25, 1733.
19 SARAH, b. Dec. 28, 1737, m. Joshua Grant, (No. 26) that family.
20 EUNICE, b. Feb. 23, 1738, m. Wyatt Hinckley, (No. 31) that family.
21 GRACE, b. June 2, 1740.
22 ANN, b. June 2, 1742, m. Jesse York, (No. 36) that family.
23 AMOS, b. Dec. 23, 1744, m. Lucy Randall.
24 LUCY, b. Dec. 18, 1746.

Joseph Breed (No. 11) m. Priscilla Avery, (No. 75) that family, June 2, 1737.

CHILDREN:

25 JOSEPH, b. April, 1708, m. a Miss Avery.
26 AVERY, b. Nov. 21, 1739.

John Breed (No. 16) m. Silence Grant, May 19, 1750, (No. 25) that family.

CHILDREN:

27 MARY, b. Feb. 9, 1751.
28 JOHN, b. Nov. 15, 1752.
29 SARAH, b. Dec. 16, 1754.
30 OLIVER, b. Feb. 6, 1757, m. Grace Green, Mar. 11, 1779.
31 REUBEN, b. Sept. 23, 1758.
32 PRENTICE, b. Jan. 1, 1761, m. Mary Stanton.
33 EUNICE, b. Feb. 25, 1763.
34 SAMUEL, b. Mar. 23, 1765, m. Eunice Allyn.
35 MARCY, b. Feb. 6, 1769.

Allen Breed (No. 13) m. Ann Cole, Feb. 2, 1737; m. 2nd, Hannah Dewey, July 5, 1752.

CHILDREN (ALL BORN IN STONINGTON):

36 ANN, b. July 11, 1739.
37 ABIGAIL, b. Jan. 30, 1740.
38 ZERVIAH, b. Oct. 23, 1741.
39 MARY, b. Jan. 3, 1744.
40 WILLIAM, b. Sept. 20, 1745, m. Prudence Palmer, (No. 274) that family.
41 ALLEN, b. Nov. 14, 1747.
42 SUSANNAH, b. June 3, 1750, m. Joshua Stanton, (No. 48) that family.

CHILDREN BY 2ND MARRIAGE:

43 REV. GERSHOM, b. Apr. 29, 1756, m. Hannah Palmer.
44 JABISH, b. Feb. 24, 1758, m. Sarah Chapman.
45 ESTHER, b. Aug. 5, 1759.
46 CHRISTOPHER, b. July 25, 1761.
47 JOSEPH, b. Feb. 21, 1763, m. Rhoda Greene.
48 HANNAH, b. July 29, 1765.

Gershom Breed (No. 14) m. Dorothy McLaren, May 10, 1747.

CHILDREN:

49 JOHN McLAREN, b. April 28, 1748, in Stonington, Conn. He graduated from Yale College in 1768. He was a merchant at Norwich, Conn., and Mayor of the city. Married Mary Devotion, Nov. 14, 1771.
50 SUSANNAH B., b. Nov. 19, 1749, m. Rev. David Brewer.
51 GERSHOM, b. Oct. 2, 1751, d. young.
52 GERSHOM, b. Sept. 5, 1753, d. young.
53 DAVID, b. June 6, 1755, m. Elizabeth Clement.
54 ALLEN, b. Sept. 6, 1757, d. young.
55 SHUBAL, b. April 20, 1759, m. Lydia Perkins.
56 JESSE, b. May 21, 1761, m. Cynthia Buckley.
57 SIMEON, b. July 17, 1763, d. unmarried.
58 ANNA, b. May 14, 1767, m. Rev. Salmon Cone.

Dea. Nathan Breed (No. 17) m. Lucy Babcock in 1751.

CHILDREN:

59 NATHAN, b. March 30, 1752.
60 LUCY, b. May 10, 1754, m. William Slack, March 4, 1779.
61 JOSEPH, b. July 9, 1759, m. Mercy Holmes.
62 STEPHEN, b. March 15, 1760, m. Esther Wheeler.
62a ESTHER, b. ———, 1762, m. William Witter, (No. 58) that family.
63 ANNA, b. ——— 1764, m. Gilbert Grant, (No. 49) that family.
64 PRUDENCE, b. ——— 1766, m. Nathaniel Wheeler, (No. 361) that family.
65 GRACE, b. ——— 1768, m. Jesse Billings.
66 THOMAS, b. ——— 1770.
67 JOSHUA, b. ——— 1771.

Amos Breed (No. 23) m. Lucy Randall, Jan. 25, 1768, (No. 63) that family, both of Stonington, Conn. He d. Mar. 20, 1885. She m. 2nd, Elias Sanford Palmer, (No. 238) Palmer famliy.

CHILDREN:

68 AMOS, b. May 5, 1769, m. three times.
69 JESSE, b. June 12, 1771, m. Hannah Randall.
70 JEDEDIAH, b. Aug. 15, 1773, m. Nancy ———.
71 LUCY, b. Feb. 10, 1776, m. Samuel Peabody.
72 JONAS, b. April 23, 1779, m. Betsey Niles, July 14, 1803.
73 DEA. ELIAS, b. March 12, 1782, m. Betsey Randall, (No. 84) that family. Settled near Norwich, N. Y., and became wealthy.

Oliver Breed (No. 30) m. Grace Green, Mar. 11, 1779.

CHILDREN:

74 HENRY, b. March 10, 1781, m. Eleanor Fish, June 10, 1801.
75 JOHN, b. March 15, 1782, m. Catherine Fish, April 11, 1805.
76 REUBEN, b. July 4, 1783, m. Martha Everett.
77 NANCY, b. ———, m. John York.
78 LUCY, b. ———, m. Mr. Williams.
79 ADIN, b. Feb. 2, 1787, m. Nancy ———.

BREED FAMILY.   247

80 OLIVER, b. ――――, 1789.
81 CYRUS, b. ――――, 1792, m. Susan Ward.
82 EUNICE, b. ――――, m. a Mr. Frink.
83 MARTHA, b. ――――.
84 GRACE, b. ――――, m. a Mr. York.

Prentice Breed (No. 32) m. Mary Stanton, Dec. 1, 1780, (No. 300) that family. He d. Oct. 7, 1816. She d. Jan. 20, 1844.
CHILDREN:
85 POLLY, b. Aug. 20, 1781.
86 SOPHIA, b. Oct. 8, 1784.
87 FANNY, b. March 27, 1787.
88 BETSEY, b. Feb. 21, 1789.
89 JOHN P., b. March 21, 1798.

Samuel Breed (No. 34) m. Eunice, daughter of Thomas and Lucy (Avery) Allyn.
CHILDREN:
90 JULIA, b. Oct. 14, 1788, d. May 12, 1867.
91 SAMUEL, b. Aug. 19, 1790, m. Eliza P. Williams.
92 THOMAS, b. Aug. 25, 1792.
93 JOHN, b. Sept. 18, 1794, m. Prudence Hancox; 2d, Polly Sheffield.

Jabish Breed (No. 44) m. Sarah Chapman, Jan. 30, 1782, (No. 18) that family.
CHILDREN:
94 SALLY, b. March 22, 1783, m. William Pendleton, (No. 89) Pendleton family.
95 HANNAH, b. Dec. 18, 1784, m. Reuben York, (No. 84) that family.
96 POLLY, b. April 7, 1788.
97 ANDREW, b. Jan. 25, 1790.
98 PATTY, b. Aug. 19, 1791, m. Nathan York, (No. 81), that family.
99 ALLYN, b. May 10, 1793.
100 GERSHOM, b. Feb. 10, 1795.
101 LUCY, b. March 21, 1797, m. ―――― Ray.
102 WILLIAM, b. Jan. 10, 1799.
103 ANNA, b. Jan. 26, 1801, m. Jonathan Wheeler, (No. 403) that family.

Joseph Breed (No. 61) m. Mercy Holmes, (No. 67a) that family, Jan. 25, 1781.
CHILDREN:
104 JOSEPH, b. July 23, 1781.
105a CHARLES, b. March 17, 1785, m. Polly Hancox, (No. 20) that family.
105b MERCY, b. Feb. 17, 1795, m. Amos Hancox, (No. 26) that family.
106 LUCY, b. May 20, 1787, m. Gilbert Collins, (No. 12) that family.
107 NATHAN, b. Jan. 26, 1789.
108 ANNA, b. Jan. 6, 1791.
109 JOHN, b. Nov. 8, 1792.
110 PRUDENCE, b. Nov. 17, 1794, m. a Mr. Lines.
111 NANCY, b. ――――, m. a Mr. Beeler.
112 ABIGAIL, b. ――――, m. a Mr. Greason.

Stephen Breed (No. 62) m. Esther, daughter of Richard Wheeler, (No. 360) that family.

CHILDREN:

114 ESTHER, b. ———, m. Oliver Grant in 1801, (No. 54) that family.
115 STEPHEN, b. July 1, 1785, m. Sophia Geer.
116 SILENCE, b. Dec. 1, 1791, m. Stephen Chalker, March 2, 1813.
117 HANNAH, b. ———, m. ——— York.
118 ALICE, b. ———, m. ——— Coon; 2d, ——— Williams.
119 FREDERICK WILLIAM, b. July 4, 1809, m. Ann Holbrook.

Jesse Breed (No. 69) m. Hannah Randall, (No. 89) that family, Apr. 12, 1794, at Stonington. She d. June 12, 1824. He m. 2nd, Hannah Randall, (No. 83) that family, July 9, 1825. He d. at Homer, N. Y., Jan. 20, 1831. She d. May 2, 1838.

CHILDREN (ALL BORN IN STONINGTON):

120 HANNAH T., b. March 5, 1795, m. Joseph Frink, (No. 98) that family.
121 JESSE BILLINGS, b. July 15, 1798, m. Freelove Breed, (No. 135).
122 BENJAMIN FRANKLIN, b. Feb. 3, 1801, m. Mary Ann Breed, (No. 134).
123 JOSHUA RANDALL, b. May 27, 1803.
124 AMOS PALMER, b. May 13, 1805, d. at Stonington, Nov. 4, 1826.
125 CALVIN G., b. Aug. 22, 1808, d. at Stonington, Oct., 1872.
126 PRUDENCE MARY, b. Aug. 22, 1811.
127 LUCY PENDLETON, b. Jan. 27, 1814.
128 RHODA ANGELINE, b. March 10, 1816.
129 AMANDA, b. June 8, 1818, d. at Stonington, July 3, 1818.

Samuel Breed (No. 91) m. Eliza P. Williams, (No. 355) that family, Nov. 21, 1822. He d. Feb. 9, 1826.

CHILDREN:

130 SAMUEL EDWIN, b. ———, d. in infancy.
131 LUCY PALMER, b. ———, d. in infancy.
132 ANN ELIZABETH, b. ———, m. John Hart.

John Breed (No. 93) m. Prudence Hancox (No. 22) that family; m. 2nd, Polly Sheffield, daughter of Isaac Sheffield. He d. Sept. 14, 1860.

CHILDREN BY SECOND MARRIAGE.

133 EUNICE, b. Nov. 26, 1799.
134 MARY ANN, b. Feb. 21, 1802, m. Benjamin F. Breed, (No. 122).
135 FREELOVE, b. May 7, 1803, m. Jesse B. Breed, (No. 121) Nov. 25, 1837.
136 ISAAC SHEFFIELD, b. Dec. 19, 1804, m. Phebe P. Hewitt, (No. 241) that family.
137 HARRIET, b. Dec. 24, 1806.
138 Twins, b. and d. at birth.

BREWSTER FAMILY.

1. ELDER WILLIAM BREWSTER, son of William Brewster, was b. in 1560, a graduate of Cambridge College, England, afterward the confident friend of William Davison, Queen Elizabeth's ambassador to Scotland, then joining the independent church, he entertained their meetings at his house, fled with them to Amsterdam and Leyden, was appointed their elder, sailed in the Mayflower and landed on Plymouth Rock, Dec. 20, 1620. He drafted in the cabin of the Mayflower the first written constitution. He served in the early Indian wars under Capt. Myles Standish. The Plymouth Church Records say of him that with the most submissive patience he bore the novel and trying hardships to which his old age was subjected; lived abstemiously, and after having been in his youth the companion of ministers of state, the representative of his sovereign familiar with the magnificence of court, and the possessor of a fortune, sufficient not only for the comfort but for the exigencies of life, this humble Pilgrim labored steadily with his own hands in the field for daily subsistence; yet he possessed that happy electricity of mind which could accommodate himself with cheerfulness to all circumstances; destitute of meat, of fish, and bread, even with his single meal of clams would he return thanks to the Lord, that he could suck of the abundance of the seas and treasures hid in the sand. He enjoyed a healthy old age and was sick but one day, when he d. Apr. 16, 1644. He m. Mary ———, before 1592, who came to this country with him, and d. Apr. 17, 1627.

CHILDREN:

2 JONATHAN, b. at Scrooby in Nottinghamshire, Aug. 12, 1593, m. Lucretia Oldham of Darby, April 10, 1624. He d. in Connecticut, Aug. 7, 1659; she d. March 4, 1678-9.
3 PATIENCE, b. in England, m. Gov. Thomas Prence, Aug. 5, 1624, and d. 1634.
4 FEAR, b. in England, m. Isaac Allerton, 1626, d. 1633-4.
5 LOVE, b. in England about 1636, m. Sarah Colliers March 15, 1634.
6 WRESTLING, b. in England, m. Emla Story in 1630.

Jonathan Brewster (No. 2) m. Lucretia Oldham. Their son

7 BENJAMIN, b. Nov. 17, 1633, m. Anna Dart, Feb., 1659. He died Sept. 14, 1710; she d. May 9, 1709. Their son

8 DANIEL, b. March 1, 1666-7, m. Hannah, dau. of John Gager, Dec. 23, 1686; m. 2d Dorothy Witter, Dec. 19, 1727, probably widow of Ebenezer Witter, and dau. of Lieut. Joseph and Dorothy (Park) Morgan. He d. May 7, 1735. Their son

8 CAPT. JOHN, b. July 18, 1695, m. Dorothy Treat, Sept. 20, 1725. He d. Aug. 29, 1776. Their son

9 DANIEL, b. ———, m. Phebe Williams, May 31, 1753; 2d Elizabeth Swan of Stonington, Conn, (No. 53) that family, Oct. 4, 1764.

Benjamin Brewster (No. 7) m. Anna Dart. Their son

10 JONATHAN, b. Nov., 1664, m. Judeth Stevens of Norwich, Dec. 18, 1690. He d. Nov. 20, 1704. His widow m. 2d, Christopher Huntington, Oct. 1706. Their son

11 JOSEPH, b. Aug. 13, 1695, m. Dorothy Witter, March 17, 1723. He d. Oct. 15, 1770. Their son.

12 ELIJAH, b. Sept. 3, 1724, m. Elizabeth Fitch, Jan. 25, 1749. Their daughter

13 ELIZABETH, b. March 15, 1757, m. Israel Morgan, (No. 39) that family, July 22, 1777. He d. June 4, 1816; she d. Sept. 15, 1826. Their daughter

14 ELIZABETH MORGAN, who married Stephen Avery, (No. 159) that family, had daughter Frances Mary Avery, who married Richard A. Wheeler, (No. 429). that family.

REV. CHAD BROWN FAMILY.

1. REV. CHAD BROWN, not related so far as known to the three Brown Brothers, of Lynn, Mass., came as we learn from his deposition to New England with his wife Elizabeth ————, and their son John, in the good ship Martin, and landed in Boston, Mass., in the year 1638. He located himself and family in Salem, Mass., where he did not long reside. Entertaining religious and political sentiment in sympathy with Roger Williams, he went to reside with him in Providence, R. I. Mr. Brown soon rose to prominence in Providence Plantation, where he merited and enjoyed the confidence of his fellow townsmen to an unlimited extent, receiving some of the highest positions of honor and trust in their power to bestow upon him. Having previously studied for the ministry, he was called to the pastorate of the First Baptist Church of Providence, where he was ordained in 1642 as the first settled minister of that church, (a disputed point by some, who claim that Roger Williams was the first minister of that church). Be that as it may, it is very evident that their labors with and for the church were harmonious and their ministry may have been an ideal, dual, coadjuting pastorate.

CHILDREN OF ELDER CHAD BROWN AND WIFE ELIZABETH.
2 PHEBE, b. ————, in England, m. Thomas Lee; 2d, Greenfield Larrabee.
3 JOHN, b. ————, 1630, in England.
4 JAMES, b. ————, in England, d. 1683.
5 JEREMIAH, b. ————, in England, d. 1690.
6 CHAD, alias Judah, b. ————, place unknown, d. unmarried May 10, 1663.
7 DANIEL, b., probably in New England.

John Brown (No. 3) m. Mary Holmes, dau. of Obadiah and Catharine Holmes, in 1659; d. 1706.

CHILDREN:
8 SARAH, b. ————.
9 JOHN, b. ————.
10 JAMES, b. ————.
11 OBADIAH, b. ————.
12 MARTHA, b. ————.
13 MARY, b. ————.
14 DEBORAH, b. ————.

James Brown (No. 4) and Elizabeth Carr were m., date and place unknown. She m. 2nd, Samuel Gardiner.

CHILDREN:
15 JOHN, b. in the year 1671.
16 JAMES, b., date unknown.
17 ESECK, b. March 8, 1679.
18 CLARK, b. ———.

Jeremiah Brown (No. 5) m. Mary Gardiner; and 2nd, Mary Cook.

CHILDREN:
19 JAMES BROWN, b. ———.
20 SAMUEL, b. in 1680, m. 1st Mary ———; 2d, Mary Carr, d. 1762.
21 DANIEL, b. ———, d. in 1726.
22 WILLIAM, b. in 1676, m. Elizabeth Robinson; d. 1756.

Daniel Brown (No. 7) m. Alice Hearndon, Dec. 25, 1669.

CHILDREN:
23 JUDAH, b. ———, m. Hannah ———, d. Jan. 13, 1734.
24 JABEZ, b. ———, m. Anne ———.
25 SARAH, b. Oct. 10, 1677, m. Thomas Angell, April 4, 1700.
26 JEREMIAH, b. ———, m. Sarah Tinker, Feb. 8, 1715.
27 HALLELUJAH, b. ———, m. James Olney, Aug. 31, 1702.
28 HOSANNAH, b. ———, m. Mary Hawkins.
29 JONATHAN, b. ———, no record than that he sold by consent of his brothers, Judah and Daniel, certain real estate, May 21, 1713.
30 DANIEL, b. ———, m. Mary Sprague. He was a cooper by trade.

John Brown (No. 15) m. Elizabeth Cranston, dau. of John and wife, Mary (Clarke) Cranston. He d. Oct. 20, 1731.

CHILDREN:
31 JEREMIAH, b. Sept. 30, 1693.
32 JOHN, b. Dec. 26, 1696, m. Jane Lucas, d. Jan. 2, 1764.
33 JAMES, b. ———.
34 WILLIAM, b. ———.
35 ROBERT, b. ———.
36 PELEG, b. in 1709, d. Feb. 21, 1756. m. Sarah Freebody, Feb. 20, 1746.
37 ELIZABETH, b. ———, m. John Gridley.

James Brown (No. 16) m. 1st, Ann Clarke, and 2nd, Catharine Greene, April 27th, 1740. He d. in 1756.

CHILDREN ALL BY FIRST WIFE:
38 JAMES, b. in 1700, m. Ann Noyes, (No. 103). He d. 1765; she d. in Norwich in 1754.
39 JOHN, b. in 1702, m. Dorothy Noyes, (No. 107), July 4, 1728.
40 CLARKE, b. in 1704.
41 HOPE, b. in 1706, m. Nathaniel Coddington, March 20, 1720.
42 THOMAS, b. in 1708, m. Almey Greene, April 3, 1746.

REV. CHAD BROWN FAMILY.

Eseck Brown (No. 17) m. Mercy Carr, Nov. 29, 1705, d. Dec. 10, 1772.

CHILDREN:

43 MARY, b. March 28, 1707, d. young.
44 ELIZABETH, b. Oct. 10, 1708.
45 DEBORAH, b. June 10, 1711, d. young.
46 ESEK, b. Aug. 13, 1712.
47 ROBY, b. March 10, 1715.
48 DEBORAH, b. Oct. 13, 1716.
49 MARY, b. Jan. 18, 1718.
50 JAMES, b. Nov. 12, 1719.
51 BENJAMIN, b. July 17, 1721.
52 JEREMIAH, b. July 17, 1723.

Daniel Brown (No. 21) m. Frances Watson, daughter of John and wife, Dorcas Gardiner Watson. They both d. in 1726.

CHILDREN:

53 ELIZABETH, b. March 13, 1704.
54 MARY, b. Aug. 3, 1706.
55 BENJAMIN, b. March 16, 1708.
56 DANIEL, b. Nov. 15, 1709.
57 ELISHA, b. Jan. 20, 1711.
58 DORCAS, b. May 22, 1713.
59 JOHN, b. Feb. 18, 1714.
60 DESIRE, b. Jan. 8, 1722.
61 FRANCES, b. ——.

John Brown (No. 39) b. at Newport, R. I., m. Dorothy Noyes, (No. 107) that family. They made Stonington their home for life.

CHILDREN:

62 ABBY, b. ——, m. Benjamin Billings, (No. 81) that family, Nov. 22, 1750.
63 ANNA, b. ——, m. Caleb Arnold.
64 JONATHAN, b. ——, d. young.
65 JOHN, b. ——, m. Mary Holmes.
66 NOYES, b. ——, d. at sea.
67 SANFORD, b. ——, m. Lucy Peabody.
68 PELEG BROWN, b. ——, m. Mercy Denison, (No. 242).
69 DOLLY, b. ——, m. Samuel Copp, Dec. 10, 1769, (No. 32) Copp family.
70 MARY, b. ——, m. Ebenezer Cobb, Jan. 26, 1776, (No. 30) Cobb family.
71 HOPE, b. ——, d. young.
72 ABIGAIL, b. ——, m. Elkanah Cobb, April 18, 1773, (No. 32).
73 BRIDGET, b. ——, m. Jonathan Crarey, June 16, 1781.

Benjamin Brown (No. 55) m. Abigail, dau. of John and wife, Anne Maccoon, of Westerly, R. I.

CHILDREN:
74 BENJAMIN, b. March 7, 1731.
75 DESIRE, b. June 18, 1733, d. young.
76 FRANCES, b. March 12, 1735.
77 JAMES, b. March 13, 1737.
78 JOHN, b. April 13, 1739.
79 JEREMIAH, b. April 4, 1741.
80 DESIRE, b. March 18, 1743.
81 JESSE, b. April 1, 1745.
82 ELIJAH, b. June 10, 1747.
83 ABIJAH, b. Nov. 3, 1749.

John Brown (No. 65) b. July 25, 1735, and m. Mary Holmes, July 2, 1767.
CHILDREN:
84 JOHN, b. Oct. 30, 1768, d. young.
85 (Rev.) CLARK, b. Jan. 25, 1771.
86 MARY, OR MOLLY, b. May 9, 1773, d. young.
87 NOYES, b. Mch. 13, 1775, m. Polly Palmer.
88 SANFORD, b. May 2, 1777.

Peleg Brown (No. 68) m. 1st, Mary or Mercy Denison (No. 242) that family, April 14th, 1776.
CHILDREN:
89 MERCY, b. Feb. 22, 1777, m. Nathaniel Palmer, (No. 357) that family, on Mch. 18, 1798.
90 BETSEY OR ELIZABETH D., b. Jan. 29, 1781, m. Stiles Phelps, (No. 40).
91 PELEG, b. Mch. 16, 1779, d. young.

Capt. Peleg Brown m. 2nd, Nancy Ingraham, Oct. 24, 1782.
CHILDREN:
92 ABIGAIL, b. Aug. 6, 1783, d. young.
93 PELEG, b. Aug. 14, 1784, d. young.
94 ANN OR NANCY, b. July 16, 1785, m. Jonathan Phelps (No. 39).
95 PELEG, b. April 5, 1787.
96 POLLY or MARY, b. April 30, 1789.

Jesse Brown (No. 81) m. Jan. 1774, Mary Palmer.
CHILDREN:
97 JESSE, b. Sept. 2, 1774, m. Sally Adams.
98 MARY, b. March 23, 1776, m. Richard Jerome.
99 DAVID P., b. Oct. 11, d. unm.
100 LUCY P., b. Dec. 12, 1784, d. unm.
101 BENJAMIN, b. Nov. 17, 1789, d. young.

Noyes Brown (No. 87) m. Apr. 18, 1793, Polly Palmer, (No. 361) that family.
CHILDREN:
102 JOHN NOYES, b. May 2, 1799.

REV. CHAD BROWN FAMILY.

103 EDGAR M., b. Feb. 24, 1801, m. Jane Bergh.
104 NATHANIEL, b. Jan. 4, 1803.
105 HENRY A., b. June 5, 1809.
106 WILLIAM A., b. May 5, 1811.
107 MARY, b. Nov. 14, 1813, d. young.
108 DANIEL, b. Sept. 12, 1815.
109 MARY, b. ———.

Jesse Brown (No. 97) m. Sally Adams, dau. of Nathan and Elizabeth (Comstock) Adams, Jan. 1794.

CHILDREN:

110 BENJAMIN, b. June 13, 1797, m. Mary A. Middleton.
111 WILLIAM N., b. Sept. 16, 1798.
112 FREDERICK F., b. Mch. 1, 1801, d. young.
113 MARY P., b. Oct. 23, 1803.
114 JESSE, b. Apr. 4, 1805.
115 ORLANDO, b. Aug. 4, 1807. These two last were drowned in Middle Race, Aug. 13, 1825, and bodies never found.
116 ROBERT D., b. Oct. 8, 1809.
117 PARDON TAYLOR, b. Nov. 17, 1811.
118 WELLINGTON, b. Jan. 2, 1816.

Pardon Taylor Brown (No. 117) m. 1st, Prudence Spicer, and 2nd, Eunice M. Avery, Jan. 30, 1854.

EDWARD BROWN FAMILY.

The descendants of Edward Brown of Ipswich and Wenham:

1. EDWARD BROWN, of Ipswich, made his will Feb. 9, 1659, and it was proved 27th, 1 mo., 1660, in which he mentions wife, Faith ———, sons

    2 THOMAS, d. who had an Aunt Watson in Old England.
    3 JOSEPH.
    4 JOHN, and daughters, but no names mentioned; also brother Bartholomew of whom he purchased land.

John Brown (No. 4) m. Elizabeth ———, and d. Sept. 13, 1677; had first son

    5 NATHANIEL, b. ———, and m. Judith Perkins in Ipswich, Mass., Dec. 16, 1673, and settled on the north side of Mile River in Hamilton, and were original members of the church in that part of Ipswich, called the Hamlet, organized in 1714. Nathaniel Brown d. Sept. 13, 1717. They had son
    6 JOHN, b. 1675. He was a cordwainer of Wenham, Mass. He m. Elizabeth ———. They sold land Mch. 25, 1701, to Samuel Kemball; also on Mch. 30, 1702, sold a dwelling house, shop and barn to John Gilbert, and on Dec. 26, 1702, John Brown, of Preston, Conn., (with consent of his wife Elizabeth) sold to John Frost, of Salem, 11¼ acres of upland in Ipswich. So it seems that he resided close to the line between Ipswich and Wenham and his lands were both sides of the line. John Brown purchased land in Preston, Conn., May 29, 1702.

John Brown d. Feb. 17, 1767, and his wife Elizabeth d. Jan. 19, 1739.

CHILDREN:

    7 NATHANIEL, b. Jan. 22, 1704.
    8 JOHN, b. July 19, 1706.
    9 ELIZABETH, b. Nov. 7, 1708.
    10 JACOB, b. July 6, 1711.

EDWARD BROWN FAMILY. 257

Capt. John Brown (No. 8) and Amie Fellows were m. Dec. 16, 1731, and he d. March 17, 1776.

CHILDREN:
11 AMIE, b. Oct. 4, 1732.
12 JUDITH, b. Aug. 19, 1734.
13 JOHN, b. Nov. 16, 1737.
14 ELIZABETH, b. Nov. 4, 1738.
15 RACHEL, b. Feb. 10, 1740.
16 HANNAH, b. Mch. 15, 1743.
17 ELIAS, b. Feb. 24, 1745.
18 EUNICE, b. July 15, 1747.

Elias Brown (No. 17) and Sabra Billings, (No. 108) that family, were m. Nov. 22, 1769. He d. Sept. 15, 1801, and his wife Sabra d. Nov. 22, 1820.

CHILDREN:
19 JOHN, b. June 18, 1770, d. at sea Sept. 1804, left widow but no children.
20 JOSIAH, b. Mch. 19, 1777, d. unmarried Mch. 30, 1842.
21 BETSEY, b. April 26, 1779, d. April 17, 1802.
22 SABRA, b. Dec. 18, 1782, and d. in infancy.
23 BILLINGS, b. Sept. 17, 1790. From other records are
24 ZERUAH, b. Aug. 17, 1772, d. in infancy.
25 ELIAS, b. Jan. 28, 1786.
26 ROGER, b. July 28, 1774, d. in infancy.
27 WILLIAM HENRY, b. Mch. 17, 1789, drowned when 4 years old.

Elias Brown (No. 25) was a graduate of Brown University, and member of the New London County Bar. He m. in Mystic, Mary Louisa Burrows (No. 138) daughter of Enoch and Esther (Denison) Burrows. He d. in Brooklyn, N. Y., May 8, 1861, and his wife d. there July 12, 1868.

CHILDREN:
28 ELIAS BILLINGS, b. July 3, 1817, m. Eliza Avery (No. 166) that family, May 10, 1838. She d. Feb. 20, 1893. He d. Oct. 28, 1887.
29 WILLIAM HENRY, b. July 17, 1819, d. Jan. 28, 1838.
30 MARY LOUISA, b. Aug. 26, 1821, d. Mch. 8, 1825.
31 JOSEPH W., b. April 20, 1824, d. Dec. 13, 1824.
32 MARY ELIZABETH, b. Mch. 17, 1826, m. James E. Southworth July 20, 1859.
33 CHARLES WOLCOTT, b. June 28, 1828, d. Nov. 24, 1851.
34 ESTHER B., b. Feb. 12, 1831, d. April 7, 1852.
35 ENOCH BURROWS, b. June 26, 1833, m. Helen Agalice Hyde (No. 43) that family, Sept. 17, 1862.
36 ROGER, b. June 7, 1835, d. Sept. 11, 1835.

Billings Brown (No. 23) m. Mary Tyler, daughter of John Brown Tyler, of Griswold, Conn., Feb. 24, 1825. She was b. Oct. 15, 1804 and d. Oct. 10, 1853. He was again m. Nov. 7,

1855, to Mrs. Abby Ann Goodwin, daughter of Nathan Whiting. They had one child, John Herbert Brown, b. April 8, 1862, and d. April 22, 1864. Billings Brown d. at Groton, Conn., April 6, 1883.

    CHILDREN OF BILLINGS BROWN AND MARY TYLER:
37 JOHN T., b. Nov. 22, 1825, d. July 18, 1851.
38 EDWARD A., b. June 24, 1832, d. Sept. 15, 1832.
39 HENRY B., b. Mch. 2, 1836.
40 MARY S., b. May 12, 1836, d. May 2, 1851.

Henry B. Brown (No. 39) graduate of Yale College, settled in Detroit, Mich., where he m. July 13, 1864, Caroline, daughter of Samuel Pitts of Detroit. He was appointed judge of the United States court for Michigan in 1875, which position he held until Jan. 1, 1891, when he was appointed by President Harrison a justice of the Supreme Court of the United States.

LYNN BROWN FAMILY.

The greater number of the Brown families of Stonington, descend from three brothers, Thomas, John and Eleazer Brown, sons of Thomas Brown of Lynn, Mass. The names of the parents of his father has not as yet been ascertained. Thomas Brown, senior, of Lynn, Mass., married Mary Newhall, the youngest child of Thomas and Mary Newhall of Lynn, date not preserved. Thomas Brown and wife were doubtless both of English origin, but the place of their nativity is unknown.

1. THOMAS BROWN, senior, was born in the year 1628, and his wife, Mary Newhall, was born in the year 1637.

THEIR CHILDREN WERE:

2 THOMAS, Jr., b. in Lynn, Mass., and m. there Hannah Collins, Feb. 8, 1677, and soon after removed to Stonington.
3 MARY, b. Feb. 10, 1655, and d. there May 18, 1662.
4 SARAH, b. Aug. 20, 1657, d. Aug. 1, 1658.
5 JOSEPH, b. Feb. 16, 1658, and m. Sarah Jones, Jan. 22, 1680.
6 SARAH, b. Sept. 13, 1660, and d. April 2, 1662.
7 JONATHAN, b. and d. April 12, 1662.
8 JOHN, b. date unknown, and when a young man removed to Stonington, Conn.
9 MARY, b. July 26, 1666, and m. Thomas Norwood, Aug. 24, 1685.
10 JONATHAN, b. Feb. 11, 1668.
11 ELEAZER, b. Aug. 4, 1670, and came to Stonington at maturity.
12 EBENEZER, b. March 16, 1672, and d. in the year 1700.
13 DANIEL, b. April 24, 1673, and d. young.
14 ANN and
15 GRACE (twins), b. Feb. 4, 1674, and both d. Feb. 7, 1674.
16 DANIEL, b. Feb. 1, 1676; bought out the rights of his three brothers, who came to Stonington and lived and died on the old Brown homestead in Lynn, Mass.

Thomas Brown (No. 2), m. Hannah Collins, Feb. 8, 1677; he d. Dec. 27, 1723.

CHILDREN:

17 SAMUEL, b. Dec. 8, 1678.
18 HANNAH, b. Dec. 5, 1680.
19 MARY, b. May 26, 1683, m. Thomas York (No. 7), York family.
20 JERUSHA, b. Dec. 25, 1688.
21 SARAH, b. July 11, 1689.

22 THOMAS, b. Feb. 14, 1692.
23 ELIZABETH, b. May 9, 1694.
24 DANIEL, b. Oct. 9, 1696.
25 PRISCILLAH, b. Jan. 30, 1699.
26 HUMPHREY, b. Sept. 16, 1701.

John Brown (No. 8) and Elizabeth Miner (No. 42), daughter of Ephraim and Hannah (Avery) Miner, were m. in the year 1692.

CHILDREN:

27 JOHN, Jr., b. in July, 1693, d. in April, 1694.
28 JONATHAN, b. March 15, 1695.
29 ELIZABETH, b. in 1699.
30 HEBSIBAH, b. ———.
31 Son, b. and d. unnamed in 1701.
32 ICHABOD, b. March 12, 1704.
33 PRUDENCE, b. April 28, 1707.
34 JEDEDIAH, b. April 28, 1709.
35 MEHITABLE, b. in Aug., 1712.
36 MARY, b. in Aug., 1716.

Eleazer Brown (No. 11) and Ann Pendleton (No. 10), daughter of Capt. James Pendleton, of Westerly, R. I., were m. Oct. 18, 1693. He d. Nov. 30, 1734.

CHILDREN:

37 JONATHAN, b. July 12, 1694.
38 JAMES, b. June 1, 1696.
39 ELEAZER, b. May 4, 1698, m. Temperance Holmes.
40 ANNAH, b. Feb. 1, 1700, m. Dea. Thomas Main (No. 18).
41 EBENEZER, b. June 28, 1702.
42 MARY, b. Nov. 28, 1703, m. Elder Wait Palmer (No. 145).
43 HANNAH, b. Dec. 12, 1705, m. William Wilcox (No. 35).
44 PATIENCE, b. Dec. 28, 1707.
45 ABIGAIL, b. June 3, 1712.
46 RUTH, b. June 30, 1714.

Thomas Brown (No. 22) and Deborah Holdredge were m. Oct. 4th, 1715.

CHILDREN:

47 THOMAS, b. April 5, 1717.
48 WILLIAM, b. July 9, 1719.
49 DEBORAH, b. May 30, 1721.
50 DOROTHY, b. Feb. 20, 1724.
51 JESSE, b. Aug. 18, 1731.
52 SAMUEL b. July 14, 1734.
53 LOIS, b. Sept. 1, 1736, m. Israel Palmer (No. 249).

Daniel Brown (No. 24) and Mary Breed (No. 6), **daughter of** John and Mary (Palmer) Breed, were m. June 21st, **1721,** by Rev. Hezekiah Lord, pastor of the church in Preston, Conn.

CHILDREN:
54 SAMUEL, b. Oct. 14, 1722.
55 DANIEL, b. March 20, 1725.
56 WALTER, b. Feb. 1, 1728.
57 AMOS, b. Oct. 28, 1730.
58 DESIRE, b. July 5, 1733.
59 CHRISTOPHER, b. March 12, 1736.
60 NATHAN, b. June 20, 1738.
61 NEHEMIAH, b. July 11, 1740.

Jonathan Brown (No. 28) and Hannah Richardson were m. Oct. 5, 1718.

CHILDREN:
62 NATHANIEL, b. Aug. 28, 1719.
63 JONATHAN, b. Aug. 14, 1721.
64 STEPHEN, b. Sept. 5, 1723, and d. Aug. 1, 1725.
65 HEPZABETH, b. May 8, 1726.
66 JAMES, b. Jan. 28, 1728.
67 ELIZABETH, b. Feb. 16, 1730.
68 JONATHAN, b. June 14, 1732.

James Brown (No. 38) and Elizabeth Randall (No. 6) were m. May 5, 1718.

CHILDREN:
69 JAMES, Jr., b. Jan. 29, 1719, and d. Dec. 24, 1741.
70 Daughter (twin), b. and d. Oct. 22, 1720.
71 THANKFUL (twin), b. Oct. 22, 1720, m. Jeremiah Main (No. 23).
72 SIMEON, b. Jan. 31, 1723, m. Dorothy Hearn, March 1, 1743.
73 ANN, b. March 23, 1728.
74 ZEBULON, b. Nov. 20, 1730, m. Anne Main (No. 33).
75 ELIZABETH, b. July 31, 1732, m. Timothy Main (No. 31).
76 ABIGAIL, b. April 23, 1737.
77 JOSHUA, b. April 8, 1740.

Ebenezer Brown (No. 41) and Elizabeth Main (No. 20) were m. April 5, 1723. He d. March 4, 1725.

CHILDREN:
78 DAVID, b. Feb. 23, 1724.

Jedediah Brown (No. 34) and Abigail Holmes (No. 21) were m. Nov. 27, 1728. He d. Jan. 15, 1732, and she d. June 6, 1732.

CHILDREN:
79 JEDEDIAH, Jr., b. March 14, 1729.
80 LUCIEN, b. Oct. 20, 1730.

Humphrey Brown (No. 26) and Tabitha Holdredge were m. July 22, 1724.

CHILDREN:
81 HUMPHREY, b. Aug. 13, 1725.
82 TABITHA, b. Nov. 23, 1727.

83 GERSHOM, b. Aug. 29, 1729.
84 MARY, b. Sept. 14, 1731.
85 CONTENT, b. Aug. 20, 1733.
86 EUNICE, b. July 26, 1736.
87 REUBEN, b. Aug. 20, 1738.

Thomas Brown (No. 22) and Deborah Holdredge were m. April 27, 1737.

CHILDREN:

88 COLLINS, b. June 13, 1743.
89 BENONI, b. Nov. 16, 1746.

Mrs. Deborah Brown (nee Holdredge) d. date unknown, and her husband m. for his second wife Sarah Randall, March 29, 1753.

CHILDREN:

90 WEALTHY, b. Oct. 19, 1753.
91 LUCY, b. March 9, 1755, m. John Randall (No. 42).
92 SAMUEL, b. Nov. 16, 1757.
93 SARAH, b. Oct. 1, 1758.
94 PEREZ, b. Oct. 2, 1760.
95 ABEL, b. Aug. 7, 1762.

Nathaniel Brown (No. 62) and Elizabeth Brown were m. in the year 1742.

CHILDREN:

96 ANNA, b. in the year 1743, and d. May 31, 1755.
97 RUFUS, b. in the year 1745.
98 HANNAH, b. in the year 1747.
99 HENRY, b. May 3, 1750.
100 NATHANIEL, b. Feb. 7, 1754.
101 CHARLES, b. July 15, 1757.
102 ESTHER, b. Aug. 18, 1760.
103 CYRUS, b. Jan. 13, 1765.

Christopher Brown (No. 59) and Margaret Holmes (No. 48) that family, were m. Dec. 25, 1763.

CHILDREN:

104 MOLLY, b. Aug. 29, 1766, m. David Coates (No. 24).
105 LOIS, b. July 1, 1768.
106 PEGGY, b. March 4, 1772.
107 CHRISTOPHER, b. Jan. 1, 1774.
108 PHEBE, b. June 16, 1776.
109 PATTY, b. June 28, 1778.
110 EUNICE, b. June 2, 1780.
111 BETSEY, b. Aug. 9, 1782.

Nehemiah Brown (No. 61) of Stonington and Rebecca Lewis of Westerly, R. I., were m. May 11, 1766.

LYNN BROWN FAMILY.

CHILDREN:
- 112 REBECCA, b. March 12, 1767.
- 113 NEHEMIAH, b. July 1, 1768.
- 114 MARY, b. Jan. 2, 1770.
- 115 PRUDENCE, b. May 14, 1772.
- 116 KETURAH, b. Jan. 28, 1774.
- 117 ESTHER, b. Nov. 22, 1777.
- 118 LEWIS, b. Oct. 9, 1778.

Ichabod Brown (No. 32) and Sarah Chapman (No. 2), both of Stonington, were m. May 30, 1731.

CHILDREN:
- 119 ICHABOD, b. Feb. 4, 1732.
- 120 ELIAS, b. Feb. 1, 1734.
- 121 STEPHEN, b. June 22, 1736.
- 122 SARAH, b. July 27, 1738.
- 123 ASA, b. July 29, 1740.
- 124 JONAS, b. Dec. 23, 1742.
- 125 MICAH, b. May 12, 1746.
- 126 ANDREW, b. Nov. 22, 1748.
- 127 KETURAH, b. Aug. 30, 1752.

Asa Brown (No. 123) and Deborah Grant, both of Stonington, were m. Feb. 12, 1761.

CHILDREN:
- 128 ASA, b. July 13, 1765.
- 129 OLIVER, b. Dec. 17, 1769.
- 130 DEBORAH, b. Jan. 26, 1772.
- 131 EUNICE, b. Nov. 6, 1774.
- 132 GRANT, b. May 15, 1777.
- 133 MINER, b. Feb. 4, 1781.
- 134 ASA, b. Feb. 9, 1783.
- 135 MARTHA, b. Feb. 20, 1786.
- 136 NATHAN, b. Dec. 10, 1788.

Eleazer Brown (No. 39) and Temperance Holmes, both of Stonington, were m. in 1723.

CHILDREN:
- 137 NATHAN, b. July 17, 1724.
- 138 MARY, b. Jan. 26, 1726.
- 139 ELEAZER, b. June 1, 1728, m. Anne Greene.
- 140 TEMPERANCE, b. May 15, 1731.
- 141 JOANNAH, b. May 12, 1733.
- 142 REBECCA, b. Jan. 19, 1735.
- 143 PHEBE, b. July 4, 1737.
- 144 TIMOTHY, b. June 7, 1739.
- 145 JOHN, b. Aug. 10, 1741.
- 146 PELEG, b. Sept. 26, 1749.
- 147 RUTH, b. June 27, 1746.

Eleazer Brown (No. 139) and Anne Green of Hopkinton, R. I., were m. Oct. 16th, 1755.

CHILDREN:

148 ELEAZER, b. July 4, 1757.
149 ANNE, b. Feb. 6, 1759.
150 REBECCA, b. April 8, 1761.
151 JOHN, b. Jan. 31, 1763.
152 BENJAMIN, b. Feb. 20, 1765.
153 LUTHER, b. Dec. 11, 1766.
154 HULDAH, b. March 3, 1769.
155 Mary, b. Feb. 29, 1771, m. Laban Main (No. 56).

John Brown (No. 145) and Mary Holmes, both of Stonington, were m. July 2, 1767.

CHILDREN:

156 JOHN, b. Oct. 30, 1768.
157 CLARK, b. May 25, 1771.
158 NOYES, b. March 13, 1775.
159 SANFORD, b. May 2, 1777.
160 MOLLY, b. Jan. 9, 1773, and d. Oct. 8, 1777.

Andrew Brown (No. 126) and Sarah Cobb (No. 34), both of Stonington, were m. Feb. 14, 1771.

CHILDREN:

161 EDWARD, b. Nov. 30, 1771.
162 STANTON, b. April 17, 1774.
163 SARAH, b. Feb. 19, 1776.
164 ALLEN, b. April 19, 1778.
165 HENRY, b. Jan. 9, 1781.
166 EZRA, b. Jan. 16, 1785, and d. March 7, 1785.
167 PAUL, b. Jan. 5, 1787.

Jedediah Brown (No. 79) and Mrs. Annah Holmes were m. Dec. 19th, 1751. He d. Oct. 31, 1791.

CHILDREN:

168 JEDEDIAH, b. Dec. 17, 1752.
169 LUCY, b. Oct. 28, 1754.
170 SHUBAEL, b. Oct. 5, 1758.
171 ROSWELL, b. Aug. 27, 1760.
172 TALOO, b. Oct. 13, 1762.
173 ABIGAIL, b. July 31, 1764.
174 MARTHA, b. Aug. 3, 1766.
175 THATCHER, b. in 1768; m.
176 EPHRIAM, b. Aug. 28, 1770.
177 DESIRE, b. July 26, 1772.

Daniel Brown of Stonington (No. 55) and Theody Park of Groton were m. Mch. 22d, 1750.

CHILDREN:

178 DANIEL, Jr., b. Feb. 5, 1751.

Mrs. Theody Brown (nee Park) d. Feb. 11, 1753, and her husband m. Abigail Brown for his second wife in the year 1753.

CHILDREN:

179 ABIGAIL, b. Feb. 11, 1754.
180 DESIRE, b. July 21, 1755.
181 EUNICE, b. March 21, 1757.
182 SUSANNAH, b. Sept. 3, 1760.
183 TEMPERANCE, b. April 12, 1763.

Samuel Brown (No. 54) of Stonington and Phebe Wilbur of Little Compton, R. I., were m. May 12, 1743.

CHILDREN:

184 MARY, b. Jan. 11, 1749.
185 PHEBE, b. Jan. 16,1751; m. Amos Palmer (No. 286).
186 SAMUEL, b. June 8, 1753.
187 ANNE, b. April 21, 1757.
188 DAVID, b. March 18, 1762.
189 EDITH, b. April 30, 1766.

Stephen Brown (No. 121) and Abigail Palmer, both of Stonington, were m. Nov. 2d, 1758.

CHILDREN:

190 ABIGAIL, b. June 30, 1759, and d. Oct. 1, 175..
191 STEPHEN, b. Aug. 10, 1760.
192 ABIGAIL, b. Jan. 22, 1762.
193 LUCY, b. Sept. 29, 1763.
194 LUTHUR, b. Aug. 21, 1765.
195 SARAH, b. Aug. 28, 1767.
196 ABEL, b. Oct. 3, 1769.
197 KETURAH, b. June 28, 1771.
198 JEDEDIAH, b. May 21, 1773.
199 ROSWELL, b. Dec. 19, 1774.

Nathan Brown (No. 60) and Lydia Dewey were m. Sept. 17th, 1761.

CHILDREN:

200 LYDIA, b. March 8, 1762.
201 NATHAN, b. June 18, 1765.
202 CHARLES, b. Feb. 6, 1767.
203 ESTHER, b. May 1, 1771.
204 DEBORAH, b. Aug. 14,1773.
205 DUDLEY, b. Dec. 16, 1774.
206 JOSEPH, b. March 16, 1778.
207 AVERY, b. May 28, 1780.
208 THEODA, b. April 16, 1786; m. Col. George Denison (No. 300).
209 POLLY, b. Feb. 7, 1789.

Amos Brown (No. 57) and Eunice Brown were m. June 5th, 1757.

CHILDREN:
210 AMOS, b. May 23, 1758.
211 ANNE, b. Oct. 7, 1759.
212 DAUGHTER, b. March 19, 1761.
213 DESIRE, b. April 23, 1763.
214 EUNICE, b. May 30, 1765.
215 SARAH, b. May 31, 1767.

Jedediah Brown (No. 168) and Sally Wheeler (No. 86), both of Stonington, were m. June 30, 1778.
CHILDREN:
216 JEDEDIAH, b. April 20, 1778.
217 WHEELER, b. Dec. 5, 1779.
218 RUSSELL, b. Jan. 29, 1782.
219 ROWLAND, b. Feb. 7, 1784.
220 SALLY, b. March 31, 1787.
221 SHEPARD, b. April 21, 1790.
222 CODDINGTON, b. April 24. 1792.
223 PATTY, b. Feb. 19, 1794.
224 NANCY, b. Sept. 2, 1799.

Shubael Brown (No. 170) and Lydia Palmer were m. in 1785. She was the dau. of Ichabod Palmer (No. 234) of Palmer family.
CHILDREN:
225 PHILURA H. b. Aug. 23, 1787, m. ——— Grant.
226 NANCY, b. Aug. 14, 1790.
227 POLLY, b. June 11, 1794.
228 ROXANNA, b. June 17, 1798, m. John Burrows (No. 39).
229 SHUBAEL, b. March 4, 1799.
230 BETSEY, b. June 30, 1801.

Roswell Brown (No. 171) and Esther Williams (No. 276), daughter of John and Keturah (Randall) Williams, were m. September 6th, 1786.
CHILDREN:
231 CYRUS WILLIAMS, b Nov. 30, 1788.
232 ROSWELL, b. March 13, 1790.
233 WILLIAM, b. June 5, 1792.
234 ELIAS W., b. Aug. 18, 1794.
235 ESTHER, b. June 15, 1796.

Roswell Brown (No. 171) d. and his widow m. for her second husband, Thatcher Brown, his brother (No. 175), Aug. 15, 1800.
CHILDREN:
236 THATCHER, b. Aug. 31, 1801, m. ——— Spalding.
237 RHODA, b. Jan. 15, 1803.
238 JEDEDIAH, b. Jan. 31, 1805.
239 KETURAH, b. Oct. 18, 1807, m. Charles Pendleton (No. 116).

Roswell Brown (No. 232) and Nancy Brown (No. 226) were m. April 7, 1814.

CHILDREN:

240 LUCY MARY, b. ——, m. Wm. Burrows, and 2d ———Hull.
241 LYDIA ESTHER, b.——, m. Simeon Haley, Jr. (No. 42), Haley family.
242 ROSWELL, b. ——.
243 SHUBAEL, b. ——

Mrs. Nancy Brown (No. 226), wife of Roswell Brown (No. 232), d. July 24, 1818, and after her death her husband m. for his second wife her sister, Betsey Brown (No. 230), Jan. 26, 1820. She d. July 26, 1839.

CHILDREN:

244 THOMAS W., b. ——, m. Mary A. Clarke.

Elias W. Brown (No. 234) and Martha Miner (No. 342), daughter of Elder Asher Miner, were m. Jan. 5, 1815.

CHILDREN:

245 ELIAS F., b. May 10, 1816.
246 ELIZA ANN, b. Mch. 22, 1818, m. Daniel Rodman, of South Kingston, R. I.
247 MARTHA ESTHER, b. May 1, 1821.
248 LUCY M., b. Sept. 15, 1822.
249 ABBY SMITH, b. Sept. 20, 1825.
250 ASHER MINER, b. Feb. 14, 1827.
251 MARY HOXIE, b. June 16, 1830.
252 JOSEPH PAGE, b. March 4, 1832.

Cyrus Williams Brown (No. 231) and Theoda Brown, daughter of Nathan Brown, were m. date not known.

CHILDREN:

253 DEA. CYRUS WILLIAM, b. March 11, 1806.
254 ESTHER, b. March 11, 1808.
255 LYDIA, b. May 24, 1814.
256 POLLY, b. March 25, 1817.
257 BENADAM, b. Jan. 12, 1819, and d. in the year 1820.
258 LUCY P., b. Feb. 26, 1822.

Dea. Cyrus W. Brown (No. 253) m. Elizabeth Stewart Babcock Dec. 12, 1826.

CHILDREN:

259 EMILY E., b. Jan. 16, 1828, m. Thomas W. Wheeler (No. 476) of Wheeler family.
260 CYRUS H., b. Nov. 24, 1829.
261 LOUISA A., b. March 21, 1832.
262 GIDEON P., b. Aug. 3, 1834.
263 BENADAM W., b. April 4, 1836.
264 THOMAS S., b. June 28, 1838.
265 JOHN B., b. Feb. 3, 1841.
266 SARAH E., b. May 23, 1843.
267 WILLIAM, b. July 11, 1845.
268 JAMES S., b. March 2, 1848.

HISTORY OF STONINGTON.

Roswell Brown (No. 242) and Catharine Chesebrough, both of Groton, at the time, were m. Mch. 17, 1844. She d. Mch. 28, 1897; he d. Oct. 20, 1896.

Elder Simeon Brown (No. 72) of Stonington, Conn., and Dorothy Hearn of Westerly, R. I., were m. Mch 1st, 1743.

CHILDREN:

275 SIMEON, Jr., b. Dec. 4, 1746.
276 JAMES, b. Dec. 5, 1752.
277 DOROTHY, b. Aug. 2, 1755.
278 JEPTHA, b. July 20, 1758.
279 JOSIAH, b. May 30, 1761.
280 ELIZABETH, b. Aug. 5, 1766.
281 MARTHA, b. April 14, 1769.

Joshua Brown (No. 77) and Joanna Rogers were m. Dec. 24th, 1761.

CHILDREN:

282 JOSHUA, b. Oct. 4, 1764.
283 ROGERS, b. July 11, 1766.
284 JOANNA, b. June 23, 1768.
285 MARTHA, b. Sept. 20, 1770.
286 ADAMS, b. Oct. 26, 1772.
286a PRUDENCE, b. June 10, 1776, m. James Dean (No. 24), that family.
287 ANNA, b. July 9, 1778.
288 MARGARET, b. Dec. 25, 1780.
289 RANDALL, b. June 20, 1783, m. Sally Palmer.
290 DELIA, b. April 9, 1786.

Mrs. Joanna Brown (nee Rogers) d. not known, and her husband m. for his second wife Mrs. Lydia Hewitt Stanton, a widow, Dec. 14, 1816. No children by this marriage.

Joshua Brown, Jr. (No. 282), and Eunice Palmer, both of Stonington, were m. April 9, 1785.

CHILDREN:

291 EUNICE, b. Sept. 27, 1786.
292 ESTHER, b. Aug. 19, 1788.
293 JOSHUA, b. Feb. 4, 1791.
294 SYLVIA, b. July 14, 1793.
295 JOANNA, b. Feb. 18, 1796.
296 CHARLES, b. Jan. 27, 1799.
297 GILES, b. Feb. 8, 1802.
298 DOLLY, b. Sept. 21, 1804.
299 HOSEA, b. May 7, 1807.

Josiah Brown (No. 279) and Deborah Griffin were m. Feb. 23d, 1786.

LYNN BROWN FAMILY. 269

CHILDREN:
300 DEBORAH, b. Oct. 9, 1786, and d. young.
301 NANCY, b. Dec. 8, 1789.
302 JOSIAH, b. April 15, 1793, and d. young.
303 SIMEON, b. March 8, 1795.
304 JOSIAH, b. Sept. 17, 1799.
305 DEBORAH, b. Sept. 12, 1802.

Ichabod Brown (No. 119) and Thankful Baldwin (No. 39), that family, were m. March 17, 1757.

CHILDREN:
306 SARAH, b. July 13, 1758.
307 PRISCILLA, b. Sept. 17, 1760.
308 THANKFUL, b. Nov. 25, 1762.
309 ICHABOD, b. Dec. 10, 1764.
310 EUNICE, b. Feb. 15, 1767.
311 CYNTHIA, b. Feb. 25, 1769.
312 POLLY, b. July 15, 1771.
313 BETSEY, b. Nov. 7, 1772.
314 JOHN, b. Dec. 5, 1774.
315 JOSEPH, b. Aug. 13, 1776.
316 BENJAMIN, b. Dec. 25, 1778.

Ichabod Brown (No. 309) and Lucy Palmer (No. 383) were m. June 8, 1788.

CHILDREN:
317 ICHABOD, b. Sept. 4, 1789.
318 LUCY, b. Jan. 19, 1791.
319 PALMER, b. Oct. 4, 1792.
320 NELLY, b. April 15, 1794.
321 SALLY, b. Sept. 17, 1795.
322 MARTHA, b. May 30, 1797.
323 NELSON, b. Feb. 13, 1799.
324 PRUDENCE, b. Oct. 9, 1800.
325 STILES, b. Sept. 13, 1802.
326 EDWARD, b. May 17, 1804.
327 SMITH, b. Nov. 25, 1805.
328 ERASTUS, b. April 23, 1807.
329 FRANCIS, b. Nov. 28, 1810.
330 ALMIRA, b. March 5, 1812, m. John A. Morgan.

Nelson Brown (No. 323) and Anne York were m. May 23, 1843.

CHILDREN:
331 HELANNA, b. July 27, 1844.
332 DEA. NELSON A., b. Feb. 16, 1847, m. Levisa Crary Feb. 19, 1871.
333 WELCOME P., b. March 8, 1849.
334 CALIFA, b. Sept. 8, 1851.
335 ELLEN, b. Sept. 7, 1854.
336 HERMAN, b. April 11, 1857.
337 CHARLES P., b. July 21, 1861.

Jesse Brown (No. 51) of Stonington and Hannah Leeds of Groton were m. Feb. 12th, 1652.

CHILDREN:

338 JESSE, b. Jan. 16, 1753, d. young.
339 ISRAEL, b. Sept. 28, 1754.
340 MARY, b. Aug. 30, 1757.
341 NATHAN, b. March 3, 1759.
342 ELISHA, b. May 25, 1761.

Mrs. Hannah Brown (nee Leeds) d., after which her husband m. for his second wife Lydia Brown in the year 1764.

CHILDREN:

343 ABIGAIL, b. Oct. 25, 1766.
344 ANNE, b. July 3, 1768.
345 JABEZ, b. Dec. 5, 1769.
346 LYDIA, b. May 23, 1772.
347 JESSE, b. Nov. 14, 1773.
348 POLLY, b. Feb. 1, 1776.
349 JOHN, b. Jan. 1, 1778.
350 SANFORD, b. April 9, 1780.
351 BETSEY, b. Sept. 26, 1782.
352 PHEBE, b. Sept. 17, 1784.
353 EUNICE, b. March 4, 1787.

David Brown (No. 188) and Lydia Miner were m. Jan. 8, 1786.

CHILDREN:

354 ABIGAIL, b. Sept. 22, 1786.
355 ELIJAH, b. March 14, 1789.
356 ELISHA, b. Jan. 20, 1791.
357 BETSEY, b. Aug. 15, 1793.
358 MARY, b. March 22, 1796.
359 DELIA, b. Jan. 22, 1801.
360 REBECCA, b. Jan. 4, 1803, m. Joshua Haley (No. 38).

Elijah Brown (No. 355) and Mary Saunders were m. July 16, 1826.

CHILDREN:

361 DAVID F., b. Jan. 3, 1827.
362 BETSEY, b. Sept. 13, 1828.
363 CHARLES H., b. July 14, 1834.
364 GEORGE W.,
365 JOHN M., } Triplets, b. Jan 4, 1839.
366 WILLIAM J.,
367 LYDIA, b. ———.
368 Edward, b. ———.

Elisha Brown (No. 356) and Desire Miner, both of Stonington, were m. Feb. 14, 1816.

LYNN BROWN FAMILY.

CHILDREN:

369 LYDIA M., b. Aug. 7, 1817, d. Nov. 15, 1830.
370 JOHN J., b. June 20, 1823.
371 ABBY D., b. Sept. 4, 1825.
372 WILLIAM M., b. Jan. 20, 1828.

Dea. Zebulon Brown (No. 74) and Ann Main were m. Dec. 24, 1749.

CHILDREN:

373 ANNE, b. May 3, 1751.
374 ELIZABETH, b. Sept. 15, 1752.
375 MARVIN, b. July 4, 1754.
376 ZEBULON, b. May 20, 1756.
377 JAMES, b. March 19, 1758.
378 OLIVER, b. Feb. 9, 1760.
379 HANNAH, b. June 15, 1761.
380 NABBE, b. Dec. 11, 1762.
381 THOMAS, b. Nov. 26, 1764.
382 MATHEW, b. in 1766.

Mathew Brown (No. 382) and Elizabeth Brown were m. May 25, 1788.

CHILDREN:

383 BETSEY, b. April 10, 1789.
384 MATILDA, b. March 10, 1791.
385 MATHEW, b. Sept. 5, 1793.

Mathew Brown (No. 385) and Lucy Ann Denison (No. 389), that family, were m. July 4, 1816.

CHILDREN:

386 DANIEL, b. May 23, 1817.
387 ANDREW, b. Sept. 24, 1818.
388 LUCY E., b. May 16, 1823.
389 HERMAN E., b. Sept. 7, 1830.

Josiah Brown (No. 304) and Rebecca Bliven were m. March 6th, 1823, and he d. Jan. 1st, 1841. Rebecca Bliven was daughter of Joshua Bliven and Rhoda Brown, daughter of Elder Eleazer Brown.

CHILDREN:

390 IRA, b. Sept. 21, 1823, and d. Sept. 21, 1861.
391 JERUSHA ANN, b. Jan. 16, 1826, m. Daniel Brown and d. Dec. 29, 1871.
392 ANGELINE, b. Dec. 31, 1828, m. Charles W. Vincent (No. 36), that family.

Randall Brown (No. 289) m. Sally Palmer (No. 344) about 1805.

CHILDREN:

393 RANDALL, b. March 28, 1807, m. Mary Ann Holmes, Jan. 1, 1832 (No. 106), that family.

394 SALLY A., b. in 1809.
395 PRUDENCE D., b. June 24, 1810, m. George W. Noyes (No. 267) that family, for his second wife.
396 JOSHUA ROGERS, b. June, 1812, m. Susan Almira Brown of New Haven. He d. July, 1858.
397 NOYES P., b. March 27, 1816, m. Martha Denison Noyes (No. 372), that family.
398 Infant son, d. young.
399 Infant son, d. young.
400 JOANNA, b. 1818, d. Oct. 10, 1845.

BROWNING FAMILY.

1. NATHANIEL BROWNING, the progenitor of the Browning family of Stonington, Conn., and other parts of the country, appears first at Portsmouth, R. I. Afterwards removed to Kingston, R. I., m. Sarah Freeborn, b. in 1632, daughter of William and Mary Freeborn.

CHILDREN:
2 WILLIAM, b. ———.
3 JANE, b. and d. in 17.
4 SARAH, b. Oct. 10, 1677.
5 JEREMIAH, b. ———.
6 HALL, b. ———.
7 HANNAH, b. ———.
8 JONATHAN, b. ———.
9 DANIEL, b. ———.

William Browning (No. 2) m. Rebecca, daughter of Samuel and Hannah (Porter) Wilbor, and 2d Sarah ———.

CHILDREN:
10 SAMUEL, b. Feb. 10, 1688.
11 HANNAH, b. July 16, 1691.
12 WILLIAM, b. Sept. 29, 1693, m. Mary Freelove.
13 SARAH, b. April —, 1695.
14 JOHN, b. March 4, 1697, m. Ann Hazard.
15 REBECCA, b. ———.

William Browning (No. 12) m. Mary Freelove, Dec. 7, 1721.

CHILDREN:
16 WILLIAM, b. Nov. 28, 1724.

After the death of his first wife William Browning m. 2d, Mary Wilkinson, Aug. 5, 1728.

CHILDREN:
17 WILKINSON, b. July 14, 1731, m. Susannah Hazzard, Feb. 4, 1753.
18 JOHN, b. July 26, 1733, m. Ann Browning (No. 31), Jan. 31, 1754.
19 MARY, b. June 10, 1735, m. Thomas Browning (No. 24).
20 DINAH, b. Sept. 10, 1736.
21 JOSEPH, b. ———, m. Mary Champlin, Feb. 12, 1761.
22 RUTH, b. ———, m. Jeremiah Browning (No. 25).
23 TABITHA, b. ———.

John Browning (No. 14) m. Ann Hazzard April 21, 1721.

CHILDREN:
24 THOMAS, b. ———, m. Mary Browning.

25 JEREMIAH, b. ——, m. Ruth Browning.
26 HANNAH, b. ——, m. Jedediah Frink of Preston, Conn., Sept. 7, 1748.
27 SARAH, b. ——, m. Samuel Stanton in 1755.
28 JOHN, b. Nov. 15, 1742, m. Mary Davis, Eunice Williams and Elizabeth Boss.
29 EPHRAIM, b. Sept. 20, 1776, m. Susannah Davis.
30 MARTHA, b. ——, m. Samuel Powers.
31 ANN, b. ——, m. John Browning, Jan. 31, 1754 (No. 18).
32 MARY, b. ——, m. Robert Champlin.
33 EUNICE, b. ——, m. Gideon Clark.

Thomas Browning (No. 24) m. his cousin, Mary Browning (No. 19) in 1755.

CHILDREN:

34 ROBERT, b. in 1757, m. Mary Allyn.
35 THOMAS, b. ——, m. Betsey Kenyon Pettis; 2d, Mary Morey.
36 WILLIAM, b. ——, m. Catharine Morey.
37 Mary, b. ——, m. Thomas Hoxey.
38 ANNE, b. ——, m. Samuel Powers.

Jeremiah Browning (No. 25) m. Ruth Browning (No. 22), his cousin, May 4, 1755. He was made freeman of South Kingston, R. I., in May, 1744; removed to Block Island in 1756, where he had purchased 110 acres of land for £5,500, old tenor, where he resided four years, or more, and came from there to Stonington, Conn., where he purchased large tracts of land. He d. of sunstroke in 1811; she d. Sept. 10, 1828.

CHILDREN:

39 JEREMIAH, b. Sept. 7, 1758, m. —— Morey.
40 RUTH, b. April 14, 1768, m. Robert Morey.
41 SAMUEL, b. March 16, 1770, m. Elizabeth Morey.
42 JOHN, b. July 22, 1777, m. Abigail (Lucy) Swan.
43 EUNICE, b. ——, m. Ephraim Browning.
44 SANDS, b. ——, m. —— Sheffield.
45 MARY, b. ——, m. Noah Grant (No. 87), Grant family.

William Browning (No. 36), known later in life as William Thomas, m. Catharine Mowry; came from South Kingston, R. I., to Stonington, Conn., in the later part of the last century, and lived upon a farm recently owned by Andrew J. Avery, now in North Stonington.

CHILDREN:

46 CATHARINE, b. Jan. 25, 1786, m. Rufus Williams (No. 287), Williams family.
47 MARY, b. Feb. 4, 1788, d. unmarried.
48 THOMAS, b. April 21, 1790, m. Amy Prentice.
49 ELIZABETH, b. Jan. 11, 1792, m. Latham Hull (No. 15), that family.
50 SARAH, b. Aug. 9, 1794, m. Daniel Averill.

BROWNING FAMILY.

51 ANNA, b. Aug. 9, 1794 (twin), m. Asa Prentice, Feb. 15, 1818 (No. 84).
52 WILLIAM, b. Aug. 25, 1746, m. Eliza Ann Averill.
53 JOSEPH M., b. June 21, 1798.
54 JOHN H., b. July 28, 1801, m. Eliza S. Hull Sept. 21, 1829 (No. 35).
55 LATHAM H., b. April 3, 1804, m. Emeline Wheeler (No. 161) that family.
56 ORRIN T., b. March 31, 1806, m. Elenora Fogel.
57 BENJAMIN, b. Feb. 18, 1808, m. Eunice Hull (No. 36), that family.
58 SUSAN, b. Nov. 8, 1810, m. Jonathan Slocomb.

Thomas (No. 48) m. Amy Smith Prentice, Nov. 22, 1812 (No. 83), that family.

CHILDREN:

59 WILLIAM T., b. Feb. 2, 1814, m. Nancy Avery.
60 MARY P., b. Dec. 28, 1816, m. Denison Hewitt (No. 195), that family.
61 MASON B., b. May 26, 1816, m. Anna Brower.
62 SARAH A., b. Oct. 10, 1817, m. Oliver Hewitt (No. 190), that family.
63 JOSHUA P., b. June 2, 1819.
64 ADELINE, b. July 21, 1820, m. William C. Osgood.
65 CATHARINE (twin), b. July 21, 1820, d. unmarried.
66 ELIZABETH H., b. Feb. 11, 1824, m. Rev. George H. Bryan.
67 FRANCES H., b. Dec. 25, 1825, d. unmarried.
68 HARRIET H., b. Feb. 4, 1828, d. unmarried.

John Browning (No. 42) m. Abigail or Lucy Swan (No. 96), Swan family (some give one Christian name and some the other, perhaps both were combined), Feb. 10, 1799. They lived about a mile north of the village of North Stonington. He was an intelligent and successful farmer. His wife d. June 20, 1852; he d. Sept. 2, 1852.

CHILDREN:

69 LUCY, b. Dec. 16, 1799, m. Cyrus Wheeler March 26, 1822 (No. 193), Wheeler family; d. Dec. 16, 1799.
70 CHARLES PHELPS, b. March 22, 1802, m. Mary Geer; he d. March 20, 1862.
71 SALLY MARIA, b. March 8, 1805, m. Major Dudley R. Wheeler (No. 191) that family.
72 CYRUS SWAN, b. June 7, 1807, m. Fanny Alice Wheeler, July 13, 1831; he d. Nov. 6, 1845 (No. 162), Wheeler family.
73 BENJAMIN FRANKLIN, b. April 13, 1819, m. Angeline C. Harris of Norwich, N. Y., Sept. 18, 1844, d. April 9, 1858; accidentally shot at Norwich, N. Y.

BURCH FAMILY.

Owing to the neglect of many of the progenitors of this family to place on Church, Probate, Town or Family records a correct statement of their marriages and birth dates of their children, it makes it very difficult, if not well nigh impossible, to write and compile a full and correct genealogy of the family. The first knowledge we have of the Burch family in this country is found in Savage's Genealogical Dictionary, Vol. 1st, Page 300, thus:

1. GEORGE BURCH appears in the town of Salem, Mass., where he m. Elizabeth ─────.

THEIR CHILDREN WERE:

2 MARY, b. June 30, 1659, d. young.
3 ELIZABETH, b. June 4, 1662.
4 JOHN, b. May 24, 1664.
5 MARY, b. Sept. 26, 1667.
6 ABIGAIL, b. Aug. 16, 1669.
7 GEORGE, b. April 27, 1671, d. Oct. 1, 1672.

Savage's Dictionary also tells us of a Joseph Burch of Dorchester, Mass., but the history of Dorchester, published in 1859, makes no mention of the Burch family.

8. Jeremiah Burch, the first of the family that appears in Stonington, Conn., came here before 1670, and had a grant of land east of the present village of Clarke's Falls. What relation he sustained to George Burch (No. 1) of Salem, Mass., the records fail to tell us. When and to whom he was married is to us unknown.

HIS SONS:

9 THOMAS, b. May 25, 1671.
10 JEREMIAH, b. July 14, 1673.
11 JOSEPH, b. July 14, 1673, d. July 20, 1673.
12 JONATHAN, b. ─────.

Jonathan Burch (No. 12) m. Mary Rathbone Aug. 22, 1706.

CHILDREN:

13 JONATHAN, b. Aug. 1, 1707.
14 JANE, b. Dec. 3, 1708.
15 JOHN, b. June 4, 1711.
16 ZURVIAH, b. June 4, 1713.
17 JEREMIAH, b. July 8, 1715.
18 MARCY, b. Aug. 18, 1717.
19 DAVID, b. June 23, 1719.
20 JOSHUA, b. Nov. 11, 1721, m. Abigail Udall Feb. 16, 1749.

BURCH FAMILY.

Jeremiah Burch (No. 10) and Margaret Billings (No. 25), Billings family, were m. Feb. 5th, 1717.

CHILDREN:

21 JOSEPH, b. Dec. 26, 1717.
22 THOMAS, b. Nov. 9, 1719.
23 ISAIAH, b. Feb. 11, 1720.
24 MARY, b. Jan. 19, 1722.
25 JEREMIAH, b. May 26, 1724, m. Sarah Downer Oct. 24, 1744.
26 MARTHA, b. July 14, 1726.
27 JONATHAN, b. Jan. 10, 1730.
28 INCREASE, b. Oct. 25, 1728.
29 BENJAMIN, b. March 15, 1731, m. Mrs. Anna Udall Nov. 8, 1750. They had son,
30 BENJAMIN, b. Nov. 4, 1751.

Jonathan Burch (No. 13) and Mary Rathbone of Lyme, were m. Jan. 15, 1736.

CHILDREN:

31 JANE, b. March 10, 1738.
32 JONATHAN, b. Sept. 16, 1740.
33 WILLIAM, b. June 24, 1742.

John Burch (No. 15) and Mary Bessey were m. June 23, 1737.

CHILDREN:

34 JOHN, b. Dec. 13, 1738.
35 JOSHUA, b. Jan. 26, 1741.

Thomas Burch (No. 22) and Martha Davis of Westerly were m. Oct. 10, 1740, and he was drowned in Pawcatuck River.

CHILDREN:

36 THOMAS, b. ———, m. Desire Elliott.
37 SAMUEL, b. ———.
38 POLLY or MARY, b. ———, m. Peleg Palmer (No. 224).
39 BILLINGS, b. ———, m. Susan Bentley, and 2d, Ellen J. Clark.
40 HENRY, b. June 6, 1744, m. Mary Irish.

Thomas Burch (No. 36) m. Desire Elliott. He was taken prisoner in the war of 1812 and d. in Halifax prison.

CHILDREN:

41 THOMAS, b. ———, m. Mary Burdick Nov. 27, 1806.

CHILDREN:

42 THOMAS, b. ———, m. Harriett Miner.
43 MARY, b. ———, never m.
44 HARRIETT, b. ———, m. Benjamin F. States.
45 DESIRE, b. ———, m. Hiram Shaw.
46 FREDERICK, b. ———, m. Mary Ann Thompson.
47 PAUL, b.———, m. Abby Thompson.

Samuel Burtch (No. 37) m. Record not known.

CHILDREN:

48 MARTHA, b. ———, m. John Dean

49 MARION, b. ———, m. ——— Wilcox.
50 SALLY, b. ———, m. ——— Chapman.
51 ELLEN, b. ———, lived in Newport.
52 STANTON, b. ———, lived in Newport.
53 BILLINGS, b. ———, lived in Newport.

Henry Burtch (No. 40) m. Mary Irish June 9, 1772. She was b. Dec. 8, 1750, d. June 16, 1838. He d. April 6, 1813.

CHILDREN:

54 RHODA, b. July 13, 1773, m. George Sheffield (No. 30), Sheffield family, Jan. 3, 1802; she d. Feb. 1, 1850.
55 PHEBE, b. Nov. 22, 1774, m. Stephen Babcock (No. 10) of John and Mary Babcock, March 22, 1801; d. 1837.
56 THOMAS, b. June 17, 1776, d. Nov., 1868; m. Susan Pendleton.
57 SALLY, b. Dec. 6, 1777, d. June 23, 1866; unmarried.
58 NATHAN, b. Jan. 6, 1781, d. June, 1858.
59 HENRY, b. July 7, 1784, d. April 8, 1834, m. Elizabeth Daboll.
60 POLLY, b. Nov. 22, 1786, d. Sept. 10, 1824, never m.
61 LYDIA, b. Jan. 8, 1787, d. April 28, 1864, m. Ransom Smith.
62 BETSEY, b. Nov. 23, 1793, m. Henry Adams.

Billings Burtch (No. 39) m. Susan, dau. of John Bentley of Richmond, R. I., Nov. 13, 1770; was afterwards m. to Ellen J. Clark. He was a Revolutionary soldier, having been a member of a regiment from Hopkinton, R. I. He was a pensioner, and is buried in the Warren Palmer burying ground.

CHILDREN BY FIRST MARRIAGE.

63 SAMUEL, b. ———, m. Polly Sloan.
64 SUSAN, b. ———, m. Archibald Merritt.
65 BETSEY or ELIZABETH or ELIZA, b. ———, m. Joshua Burdick, and m. 2d, a Carr.
66 BILLINGS,, b. ———.
67 KATY, b. ———, m. ——— Chipman.
68 THOMAS, b. ———.
69 MARTHA, b. ———.

Samuel Burtch (No. 63) m. Polly Sloan, March 7th, 1811. He d. March 21st, 1861, and she d. May 28, 1828.

CHILDREN:

70 SAMUEL, b. May 23, 1812, d. March 28, 1815.
71 WILLIAM HENRY, b. Feb. 12, 1814, m. Rhoda Thompson, and lived at Hanover, Conn., and had four children.
72 SAMUEL JAMES, b. March 8, 1816, m. Susan Bennett; had four children.
73 GEORGE C., b. Sept. 27, 1820, m. Mary Esther Holmes, Oct. 26, 1843, and had seven children. He d. Aug. 14, 1893.
74 BILLINGS, b. Oct. 19, 1818, now living at Stonington, Conn. He m. Nancy Maria Chesebrough (No. 415), March 10, 1847; have had six children.
75 MARY, b. Sept. 20, 1822, m. Capt. William E. Brewster; no children.
76 CHARLES, b. Sept. 20, 1825, d. in 1893, m. Harriet Newhall States; had two children, but they are both dead.

BURROWS FAMILY.

1. ROBERT BURROWS probably came from Boston, Mass., or vicinity, and settled first at Wethersfield, Ct., where he owned land in 1641. He m. Mary, widow of Samuel Ireland, prior to 1642, moved to New London about 1650, and soon settled at Poquonnock, and was one of the earliest settlers on the west side of Mystic River. He was by appointment the first ferryman on Mystic River; he d. 1682, and his wife d. Oct. 2, 1672.

CHILDREN:
2 JOHN, b. 1642.
3 SAMUEL, b. ———.

John Burrows (No. 2) m. Hannah, b. April 11, 1651, dau. of Edward and wife Ann Culver, Dec. 14, 1670. He d. in Groton, Conn., Feb. 12, 1716.

CHILDREN:
4 JOHN, b. 1671.
5 MARY, b. ——— .
6 MARGARET, b. ———.
7 SAMUEL, b. ———, m. Mary Chester Nov. 21, 1706.
8 ROBERT, b. ———.
9 JEREMIAH, b. ———.
10 ISAAC, b. ———.

John Burrows (No. 4) m. Lydia Hubbard, dau. of Hugh and Jane (Latham) Hubbard, Oct. 14, 1700; d. in Groton, 1752.

CHILDREN:
11 JOHN, b. Nov. 14, 1701.
12 LYDIA, b. April 19, 1703, m. William Pendleton (No. 18), March 10, 1726, d. in Westerly Aug. 18, 1750.
13 MARY, b. Nov. 4, 1704, m. Nathan Fish, d. May 11, 1732,
14 HUBBARD, b. Feb. 10, 1707, m. Mercy Denison (No. 155).
15 HANNAH, b. Jan. 23, 1709, m. William Denison Jan. 30, 1733 (No. 106).
16 SILAS, b. Oct. 4, 1710, m. Hannah Gore (No. 36), Gore family.
17 ABIGAIL, b. July 19, 1712, m. ——— Latham.
18 AMOS, b. Aug. 6, 1714, m. Mary Rathbun, d. 1773.

John Burrows (No. 11) m. Desire Packer.

CHILDREN:
19 MARY, b. June 17, 1732, m. Samuel Ahorn, d. 1797.
20 LYDIA, b. ———, m. John A. Ahorn.
21 PHEBE, b. ———, m. William Holdredge May 27, 1770.
22 LUCRETIA, b. ———, m. William Burrows Nov. 19, 1767.
23 WAITY, b. ———, m. Dea. Jabez Smith.

280   HISTORY OF STONINGTON.

24 DESIRE, b. ———, m. Joseph Elliot.
25 NABBY, b. ———, m. Uriah Wilbur.
26 JOHN, b. ———, m. Hannah Wilbur Sept. 13, 1761.
27 NATHAN, b. 1744, m. 1st,Amy Williams, and 2d, Sarah Williams, 1788.
28 DANIEL, b. ———, m. Kezia Rhodes and 2d, Abigail E. Park.
29 JAMES, b. ———, d. young.
30 THOMAS, b. ———, d. young .
31 Son, b. ———, d. young.

John Burrows (No. 26) m. Hannah Wilbur Sept. 13, 1761.
CHILDREN:
32 MARY, b. ———, m. Nathan Niles.
33 PHEBE, b. ———, m. William Thornton.
34 LYDIA, b. ———, m. Thomas Eldredge.
35 HANNAH, b. ———, m. George Eldredge.
36 ELEANOR, b. ———, m. Zebulon Williams.
37 ELAM, b. Sept. 6, 1773, m. Sarah Denison Oct. 15, 1797, d. Jan. 8, 1840.
38 DELIGHT, b. ———, m. Daniel Deboise.

Elam Burrows (No. 37) m. Sarah Denison (No. 401), that family, Oct. 15, 1797. She was b. April 9, 1778; d. Oct. 13, 1835.
CHILDREN:
39 JOHN, b. Oct. 28, 1798.
40 EUNICE, b. March 29, 1801, m. Elam Eldredge Aug. 12, 1821.
41 DENISON, b. Oct. 7, 1804.
42 HANNAH, b. June 15, 1806.
43 PHEBE, b. Feb. 19, 1809, m. Isaac D. Miner May 10, 1832 (No. 278).
44 SALLY, b. May 22, 1811, m. Nathan Noyes March 18, 1830 (No. 337).

John Burrows (No. 39) m. Roxanna Brown (No. 228), Aug. 23, 1821.
CHILDREN:
45 EUNICE E., b. April 3, 1823, m. Isaac W. Denison (No. 566).
46 FRANCES E., b. May 23, 1825, m. Horace H. Clift Oct. 25, 1848 (No. 45).
47 MARY E., b. April 29, 1827, d. young.
48 MARY E., b. July 12, 1828, m. John L. Denison May 10, 1853 (No. 570).
49 LYDIA E., b. June 20, 1831, m. Daniel Morgan Dec. 25, 1861.
50 SARAH J., b. April 15, 1834, m. Samuel Buckley Nov. 26, 1860.
51 JOHN, b. July 21, 1836, d. young.

Nathan Burrows (No. 27) m. 1st, Amy Williams, June 2, 1765; d. in 1808.
CHILDREN:
52 JOSEPH, b. July 18, 1765, m. 1st, Sarah Rice, March 30, 1788; m. 2d, Henrietta Rice, Sept. 25, 1803, and 3d, Frances Packer Jan. 10. 1808.
53 WAITY, b. ———, m. Latham Fitch.
54 GEORGE, b. ———, m. Sarah Fitch.
55 BETSEY, b. ———, m. Benjamin Ashby.
56 AMY, b. ———, m. Mason Packer.
57 ABIGAIL, m. ———, m. Samuel Rathbun.

BURROWS FAMILY.

58 JAMES, b. ——, m. Polly Brown.
59 NANCY, b. ——, m. Beriah Grant.
60 EXPERIENCE, b. ——, m. John Woodward.
61 LYDIA, b. ——, m. ——.
62 DESIRE, b. ——.

Mr. Nathan Burrows m. 2d, Sarah Williams in 1788.
CHILDREN:
63 BENJAMIN, b. Oct. 20, 1789.
64 JESSE, b. 1791.
65 NATHAN, b. 1793.
66 SIMEON, b. ——.
67 BETSEY, b. ——.
68 EDWARD, b. ——, d. young.
69 EDWARD, b. June, 1806.

Mrs. Sarah Burrows (nee Williams) d. May 1st, 1820.

Benjamin Burrows (No. 63) m. 1st, Rebecca Thompson March 17, 1808; m. 2d Lucy Perkins, Nov. 10, 1844; m. 3d —— Williams, and m. 4th, Sarah R. Holdredge, Nov. 22, 1864.
CHILDREN BY REBECCA THOMPSON:
70 NATHAN, b. July 12, 1809.
71 WILLIAM T., b. Dec. 26, 1810, m. Almira W. Smith July 4, 1833.
72 HANNAH, b. April 1, 1813, m. Franklin Gallup (No. 206); she d. Jan. 1, 1843.
73 BENJAMIN, b. Feb. 6, 1815, m. 1st, Sarah Hammond July 25, 1838, and m. 2d, Ann M. Avery Oct. 23, 1854, and m. 3d, Frances L. Denison March 26, 1867 (No. 574), Denison family.
74 CALVIN, b. March 22, 1817, m. 1st, Mary A. Niles; m. 2d, Catharine Gates.
75 EDWIN S., b. April 19, 1819.
76 ROSWELL S., twin, b. Dec. 2, 1820, m. Clarissa Edgecomb.
77 RUFUS S., twin, b. Dec. 2, 1820, d. young.
78 SARAH, b. Feb. 19, 1823, m. Franklin Gallup (No. 206), her sister's husband.
79 SIMEON S., b. July 9, 1825, m. Frances Lewis.
80 MARY A., b. May 2, 1827, m. G. W. Morgan Feb. 18, 1849.
81 GEORGE, b. Feb. 17, 1829, m. Maria Burdick, and 2d, Anna ——.
82 JOSEPH, b. Feb. 3, 1831.
CHILDREN BY LUCY PERKINS:
83 LORENZO, b. June 24, 1845.
84 DANIEL, b. April 3, 1847. These both died in the army.

Hubbard Burrows (No. 14) m. Mercy Denison (No. 185), oldest dau. of William and Mercy (Gallup) Denison, May 28, 1730.
CHILDREN:
85 ESTHER, b. Nov. 21, 1731, m. —— Packer.
86 HANNAH, b. Nov. 21, 1733, m. Daniel Packer.
87 HUBBRAD, Jr., b. June 26, 1739, m. Priscilla Baldwin (No. 33) Dec. 24, 1761.

88 ELISHA, b. Nov. 27, 1744, d. young.
89 SARAH, b. Aug. 6, 1747, m. Elisha Niles.
90 MARY, b. Oct. 7, 1749, m. Benjamin Avery.
91 MERCY, b. ——, m. Nathan Avery.
92 JONATHAN, b. May 3, 1752, m. Lucy Avery.
93 ANNA, b. ——, m. Nathan Whiting.

Capt. Hubbard Burrows, Jr. (No. 87) m. 1st Priscilla Baldwin (No. 33), dau. of Capt. John and wife Eunice (Spalding) Baldwin, and he was killed at Fort Griswold Sept. 6, 1781.

CHILDREN:

94 HUBBARD, b. ——, m. Mary Dickenson.
95 JOHN B., b. ——, m. Betsey Haley (No. 35). John was born Feb. 2, 1768.
96 VYIBY, b. ——, unm.
97 SETH, b. ——, d. young from smallpox.

Capt. Hubbard Burrows m. 2d, Sarah Avery.

CHILDREN:

98 SARAH, b. July 2, 1770, m. Caleb Haley (No. 32), that family.
99 ELISHA, b. ——, m. Rebecca Turner.
100 PERCY, twin, b. ——, m. Deborah Wightman.
101 PRISCILLA, twin, b. ——, m. Daniel Morgan.
102 BENJAMIN, b. ——, scalded to death when two years old.
103 SOLOMON, b. ——.
104 DANIEL, b. ——, d. young.
105 DENISON, b. ——, m. Nancy Burrows.

Silas Burrows (No. 16) m. Hannah Gore (No. 36), Gore family, June 17, 1740, and died in Groton April 19, 1741.

CHILD:

106 SILENCE, b. July 1, 1741, nearly three months after her father's death, and she m. Richard Wheeler, Dec. 24, 1761. See Wheeler family. No. 343). Mrs. Hannah Gore Burrows m. 2d, Nathaniel Gallup, and had several children. See Gallup family.

Amos Burrows (No. 18) m. Elizabeth or Mary Rathbun of Colchester, Conn. She d. Jan. 25, 1808, aged 87 yrs.

CHILDREN:

107 AMOS, b. ——; went to New York State.
108 SILAS, b. Aug. 8, 1741, d. in Groton, Aug. 8, 1818.
109 JOSHUA, b. ——, m. Jane Fish, dau. of John Fish, of Groton.
110 ELISHA, b. ——, m. Susan, dau. of John Fish, and m. 2d, a Fish.
111 PAUL, b. ——, m. Catharine Haley, d. Feb. 28, 1834.
112 NATHAN, b. ——, m. Ann Smith, July 24, 1774.
113 JOSEPH, b. ——, m. Abby Chipman, d. in Pennsylvania.
114 ELIZABETH, b. ——, m. 1st, Richard Mitchell of Block Island Nov. 16, 1769, and 2d, Sylvester Havens.
115 ANNA, b. ——, m. Asa Franklin Jan. 5, 1769, and 2d, Daniel Lewis.
116 EUNICE, b. ——, m. Solomon Tift.

Rev. Silas Burrows (No. 108) m. 1st, Mary, dau. of Isaac and Esther Smith, April 7, 1764; she was b. Nov. 15, 1743, and d. Oct. 26, 1816, aged 72 yrs and 11 mos. He m. 2d; widow Phebe Smith, Feb. 8, 1818. He was the first pastor of the Fort Hill Baptist Church and held the position till his death, a period of 53 years.

CHILDREN:

117 SILAS, b. March 14, 1765, d. Dec. 22, 1781.
118 DANIEL, b. Oct. 28, 1766, m. Mary Avery Dec. 16, 1787, d. Jan. 23, 1858, aged 91 years. He was a Methodist minister and had 10 children.
119 ROSWELL, b. Sept. 2, 1768, m. Jerusha Avery, Jan. 28, 1790, d. May 28, 1836; his wife d. Nov. 3, 1838, aged 67 years. He was pastor of the Second Baptist Church in Groton.
120 ENOCH, b. July 28, 1770, d. Dec. 5, 1852, aged 82 years.
121 JABEZ, b. April 13, 1772, m. Betsey Bell, d. March 13, 1855.
122 GILBERT, b. May 10, 1774, d. Oct., 1775.
123 JOSHUA, b. Jan. 10, 1779, d. in Spain, Jan. 28, 1809.
124 MARY, b. May 9, 1782, m. Jedediah Randall (No. 132), May 19, 1799, d. May 25, 1871.
125 ELIZABETH, b. Aug. 9, 1784, d. Dec. 9, 1785.
126 LUCY, b. Dec. 5, 1786, d. Jan. 28, 1809.

Roswell Burrows (No. 119) m. Jerusha Avery, dau. of Latham and Jerusha Avery, Jan. 28, 1790.

CHILDREN:

127 LATHAM AVERY, b. Aug. 30, 1792, m. Sarah Lester, d. 1855.
128 JERUSHA AVERY, b. June 24, 1795, d. Oct. 12, 1814.
129 ROSWELL S., b. Feb. 22, 1798.
130 LUCY L., b. Jan. 19, 1801, m. Alexander Stewart Feb. 22, 1821.
131 LORENZO, b. April 7, 1809, d. Oct. 7, 1814.
132 MARY E., b. April 7, 1809, d. Oct. 7, 1814.
133 JULIA A., b. Aug. 20, 1811, m. Albert G. Smith May 13, 1830.

Roswell Burrows (No. 129) m. Mary Ann Randall (No. 133), dau. of Jedediah and wife Mary Randall, Jan. 19, 1822.

CHILDREN:

134 CHARLES R., b. Aug. 26, 1826.
135 WILLIAM, b. July 11, 1828, d. 1859.
136 MARY E., b. July 11, 1830, m. Alexander Stewart May 25, 1852.

Enoch Burrows (No. 120) m. 1st, Esther, dau, of George and wife Jane (Smith) Denison (No. 310), D. family, Aug. 28, 1791; m. 2d, Mrs. Caroline Hyde King, Dec. 28, 1826, and he d. Dec. 5, 1852, aged 82 yrs. They had one child, Randall King, bapt. Aug. 1, 1830.

CHILDREN:

137 LUCY, b. Jan 8, 1791, m. John Hyde Feb. 21, 1808 (No. 14), Hyde family.
138 MARY, b. in 1793, m. Esquire Elias Brown (No. 25), Brown family.
139 SILAS ENOCH, b. Oct. 29, 1794.

Silas E. Burrows (No. 139) m. 1st, Mary Van Buskirk, Nov. 20, 1820, by whom he had 4 children.

CHILDREN:

140 ENOCH, b. June 7, 1822, d. young.
141 SILAS E., b. March 28, 1824, m. Mary W. Trowbridge, Feb. 21, 1860.
142 MARY J., b. June 2, 1826, m. Charles A. Greene Feb. 12, 1850.
143 OGDEN HOFFMAN, b. July 22, 1828, m. Sarah E. Maynard June 3, 1863.

Mrs. Mary Burrows d. Jan. 30, 1831, and Mr. Burrows m. 2d, Mary D. Russ, May 19, 1834.

CHILDREN:

144 MARY RUSS, b. Dec. 14, d. April 23, 1857.
145 JOHN RUSS, b. Sept. 13, 1838, d. Aug. 11, 1871, unmarried.
146 WILLIAM H., b. Dec. 21, 1840, d. Aug., 1841.

Mr. Silas E. Burrows d. Oct. 12, 1870, and his last wife d. March 22, 1841.

John B. Burrows (No. 95) m. Betsey Haley (No. 35), Haley family, Nov. 25, 1788. Betsey was born Sept. 14, 1767.

CHILDREN:

147 BETSEY, b. May 2, 1790, m. Coddington Burch.
148 SETH, b. Oct. 13, 1791, m. Charlotte Stark.
149 HUBBARD, b. Oct. 10, 1793, m. 1st, Amy Newton, and 2d, Mary E. Wheeler (No. 438).
150 PRUDENCE, b. Sept. 12, 1795, never m.
151 CALEB, b. Nov. 5, 1797, m. Julia Leeds.
152 JOHN, b. March 7, 1800, m. Sylvia A. Wells.
153 WAITY, b. Oct. 21, 1801, never m.
154 STEPHEN, b. Sept. 14, 1803, never m.
155 CHARLES, b. Oct. 29, 1805, m. Emily A. Wheeler (No. 440).
156 PRISCILLA, b. Nov. 12, 1809, m. Capt. Simeon Haley (No. 31).
157 MARY, b. Jan. 31, 1812, m. Henry Haley.

CHAPMAN FAMILY.

1. JOHN CHAPMAN, the progenitor of the Chapman family of this region round about, was of English origin, the son of John Chapman and wife, Joanna Sumner, who resided about fifty miles from London. Tradition has it that he was forced into the British Navy, by a press-gang, and after a while, the ship visited Boston, New England, when he availed himself of the opportunity to assume the liberty of which he had been deprived. He fled and found succor in the abode of Samuel Allen, in what is now called Wakefield, in Rhode Island. He was a weaver, having become proficient therein by several years service. He came to Stonington, now North Stonington, where he worked at his trade the remainder of his life. He m. Sarah Brown, Feb. 16, 1710, and d. in 1760.

CHILDREN:

2 SARAH, b. Nov. 25, 1710, m. Ichabod Brown (No. 32).
3 JONAH, b. Sept. 2, 1712.
4 JOHN, b. Sept. 9, 1714, m. Mary Boardman, April 28, 1742.
5 WILLIAM, b. Dec. 19, 1716, m. Abigail Plumb, Jan. 31, 1740.
6 ANDREW, b. March 3, 1719, m. Hannah Smith.
7 THOMAS, b. about 1721, m. Mary ———.
8 SUMNER, b. about 1723, m. Elizabeth Herrick.
9 EUNICE, b. ———.

Andrew Chapman (No. 6) m. Hannah, daughter of Benomi Smith and Ruth Pendleton, Oct. 15, 1745. He lived in North Stonington, Conn.

CHILDREN:

10 ANDREW, b. Jan. 27, 1748, d. Dec. 19, 1752.
11 JOSEPH, b. June 2, 1749, m. Prudence Lewis; 2d, Mary Main.
12 RUTH, b. March 20, 1751.
13 HANNAH, b. Dec. 10, 1752.
14 ANDREW, b. May 10, 1754, m. Ann York.
15 NAHUM, b. Nov. 6, 1757, m. Mary Stewart.
16 NATHAN, b. Oct. 7, 1760, m. Abigail Peabody.
17 AMOS, b. Sept. 7, 1763, m. Abigail Burdick.
18 SARAH, b. Sept. 4, 1766, m. Jabez Breed (No. 44), Breed family.
19 JONAS, b. Aug. 25, 1768, m. Susannah Peabody (No. 40).

Sumner Chapman (No. 8) m. Elizabeth Herrick, Feb. 23, 1756. He resided in Westerly, R. I.

CHILDREN:

20 JOHN, b. ———, d. unmarried.
21 SUMNER, b. ———, m. a Miss Greenman.

HISTORY OF STONINGTON.

22 ELIZABETH, b. ——, m. John Taylor.
23 TIMOTHY, b. May 28, 1760, m. Nancy Pendleton.
24 JOSEPH, b. 1767, m. Elizabeth Kenyon; 2d, Eunice Clark.
25 ISRAEL, b. 1769, m. Mary Kenyon; 2d, Nancy Kenyon
26 CASE, b. 1171, m. Mary Pendleton (No. 70).

Joseph Chapman (No. 11) m. Prudence Lewis, April 18, 1771; 2d, Mary Main Nov., 1780. Resided in Bolton, Conn.

CHILDREN:

27 SYBIL, b. Jan. 7, 1775.
28 HANNAH, b. Nov. 28, 1776, m. Thomas Main (No. 66), that family.
29 SARAH, b. Feb. 24, 1779.

CHILDREN BY SECOND MARRIAGE:

30 LEWIS, b. June 10, 1782.
31 STEPHEN, b. Oct. 1, 1785, m. Keturah Palmer Sept. 27, 1801.
32 GIDEON, b. ——, m. Hannah Wheeler Sept. 4, 1808 (No. 180), that family.

Andrew Chapman (No. 14) m. Ann York (No. 78), that family, March 30, 1780, both of Stonington, Conn.

CHILDREN:

33 ANNA, b. July 3, 1781.
34 LOUIS, b. July 6, 1783.
35 ANDREW, b. Nov. 27, 1785.
36 LUCY, b. Oct. 23, 1787.
37 JESSE, b. Nov. 20, 1789.
38 KETURAH, b. Dec. 28, 1791.

Nahum Chapman (No. 15) m. Mary Stewart Dec. 11, 1783 (No. 23), that family, both of North Stonington, Conn.

CHILDREN:

39 CHARLES, b. Dec. 24, 1785.
40 EZRA, b. June 22, 1787.
41 ELIAS, b. Feb. 20, 1790.
42 SANFORD, b. March 10, 1792.
43 PALMER, b. June 18, 1794.
44 SILAS, b. March 8, 1796.
45 STEWART, b. May 15, 1797.
46 ELISHA, b. Aug. 9, 1801.
47 BETSEY, b. Feb.24, 1803.

Nathan Chapman (No. 16) m. Abigail Peabody in 1785. He was for many years deacon of the First Baptist Church of North Stonington, and d. Feb. 14, 1824.

CHILDREN:

48 NATHAN, b. March 17, 1786.
49 NABBY, b. Oct. 19, 1787.
50 SAMUEL, b. Sept. 15, 1789.
51 THOMAS, b. Sept. 12, 1791.
52 LYDIA, b. Jan. 21, 1795.
53 POLLY, b. March 4, 1796.
54 SMITH, b. Feb. 9, 1796, m. Eunice Miner Dec. 11, 1823.

CHAPMAN FAMILY. 287

Amos Chapman (No. 17) m. Abigail Burdick, Nov. 20, 1783. They lived in North Stonington, Conn.

CHILDREN:

55 AMOS, b. July 23, 1784.
56 BETSEY, b. Nov. 24, 1785, m. Zebulon T. York (No. 105), that family.
57 JOHN, b. July 29, 1787.
58 LUCY, b. May 26, 1789.
59 SARAH, b. Nov. 2, 1791.
60 ABEL, b. Oct. 3, 1793.
61 ADAM, b. Feb. 12, 1796.
62 HANNAH, b. Jan. 17, 1798.

Jonas Chapman (No. 19) m. Hannah Peabody April 28, 1792. He removed from Stonington to Knox, Albany County, N. Y. Seven of his children are recorded on Stonington records. The other six are supposed to have been born after his removal

CHILDREN:

63 SALLY, b. July 3, 1792.
64 JONAS, b. May 20, 1795.
65 CYRUS, b. March, 1797.
66 THOMAS P., b. May 24, 1798.
67 CLARISSA, b. May 17, 1799.
68 LAVINIA, b. May 28, 1801.
69 ROXANNA, b. Aug. 15, 1802.
70 ERASTUS, b. ———.
71 ELDRIDGE, b. ———.
72 ALBERT, b. ———.
73 DANIEL, b. ———.
74 THADDEUS, b. ———.
75 CORDELIA, b. ———.

Capt. Timothy Chapman (No. 23) m. Nancy, daughter of Maj. Joseph Pendleton of Westerly, R. I. (No. 63), that family. He d. at Franklin, Conn., in 1827; she d. there in 1831.

CHILDREN:

76 NANCY, b. about 1784, m. Samuel H. Hinckley (No. 68), that family.
77 BETSEY, b. 1787, m. Samuel Copp (No. 69), that family.
78 JOSEPH P., b. ———, d. in 1825, and left one son.
79 DEMARIOUS, b. 1793, m. David Leeds of Stonington.
80 OLIVER, b. ———, d. in the last war with Great Britain.
81 SUMNER, b. ———, d. at 8 years of age.
82 JOHN, b. ———, d. at Natchez, Miss.; unmarried.
83 ENOCH C., b. 1802, m. Elizabeth Demarest of New York, 1826.
84 FREEMAN C., b. 1804, m. Fanny Hide of Franklin, Conn.
85 WILLIAM P., b. 1806, m. Eliza Pendleton of New London; removed to Sandusky, Ohio.
86 DUDLEY B., b. 1810, m. Mary Setchel of Norwich, Conn.

WILLIAM CHESEBROUGH FAMILY.

WILLIAM CHESEBROUGH, the first white man who made what is now Stonington, in Connecticut, his permanent place of abode, was born in Boston, Lincolnshire, England, in the year 1594, where he m. Anna Stevenson, December 6th, 1620. He was a gunsmith, and worked at his trade in England, and in this country, until he came to Stonington in 1649, when he changed his occupation to that of farming and stock raising, occupying and improving the large grants of land given him by the town of Pequot, now New London.

In the early part of the year 1630 he joined a large party of immigrants who came with John Winthrop, Esq., to this country. Mr. Chesebrough located himself in Boston, Mass., and soon after became a member of the first church. He was admitted a freeman of the Massachusetts Colony in May, 1631, and afterwards took an active part in public affairs. In 1632, Mr. Chesebrough was elected as "one of two" from Boston to unite with two from every plantation to confer with the court about raising a public stock, and "Prince" in his "Annals" says that this seems to pave the way for a house of representation in the General Court.

In 1634, Mr. Chesebrough was elected constable of Boston, where he continued to reside for several years. Previous to 1640 he removed to Braintree, and that year was elected deputy to the Massachusetts General Court. Soon after which he removed his residence to Rehoboth, Plymouth Colony, where in 1643 his list was returned at £450. The next year lots were drawn for a division of the woodland near the town, and Mr. Chesebrough received lot No. 4. During this year the planters of Rehoboth drew up and signed a compact by which they agreed to be governed by nine persons, "according to law and equity until we shall subject ourselves jointly to some other government." Mr. Chesebrough was a party to that transaction, which was participated in by thirty of the planters of the new settlement. He had taken an active and prominent part in organizing the town of

Rehoboth, and at a public meeting held July 12, 1644, his services were recognized by the town in ordering that he "should have division in all lands of Seakunk, for one hundred and fifty three pounds, besides what he is to have for his own proportion, and that in way of consideration for the pains and charges he hath been at for setting off this plantation." He was propounded for freeman at the General Court in Plymouth in 1645, but was not admitted till 1648. Notwithstanding the prominent part he acted in establishing the plantation of Rehoboth, and the recognition of his services by the new town, he was not treated with much favor by the General Court of that colony, which ordered him to be arrested for an affray with an Indian by the name of Vassamequine, and harshly treated him in other respects. This led him to look further for a permanent place of abode. About this time Mr. John Winthrop, Jr., acting under a commission from the Massachusetts General Court, commenced a settlement at Nameaug, afterward called Pequot, and then New London. Mr. Chesebrough visited the place in 1645 for the purpose of making it his future home. He was kindly treated by Mr. Winthrop, and urged to settle there; but finding the place in several respects unsuitable to his expectations, he concluded not to stay. Subsequently he examined the Pawcatuck region, and finally concluded to settle at the head of Wequetequock Cove. He shared the friendship of Roger Williams, and was encouraged and assisted by him in removing his habitation to Pawcatuck. He did not, however, immediately remove his family there, and not until he had provided for them a comfortable place of abode. It was during the summer of 1849 that his family came to Wequetequock and occupied their new house in the wilderness. The marsh land bordering on Wequetequock Cove furnished hay for his stock in abundance.

He brought his entire family with him, which consisted of his wife and four sons, namely, Samuel, Nathaniel, John and Elisha. The two eldest and the youngest subsequently married and had families, and after the death of each, their widows married again. John died single in 1660.

Mr. Chesebrough, like most of the early planters, traded more or less with the Indians, and was also engaged in trade with people of Long Island and elsewhere. The first act of the General Assembly of Connecticut was an order prohibiting all persons from selling firearms and ammunition to the Indians; another act was passed in 1642 "forbidding smiths from doing any work for the Indians, or selling them any instruments or matter made of iron or steel without a license from two magistrates." Various other acts were passed regulating and in some cases prohibiting trade with the Indians. Mr. Chesebrough while living at Rehoboth, had incurred the displeasure of certain parties in the Plymouth Colony, and no sooner was he located here, than they informed the General Court of Connecticut that he had removed here for the purpose of selling firearms to the Indians; whereupon the Court, in November, 1649, issued a warrant "to the constable of Pequot to repair forthwith to Chesebrough of Long Island (where he was trading at the time), and to let him understand that the government of Connecticut doth dislike and distaste the way he is in and trade he doth drive among the Indians, and that they do require him to desist therefrom immediately; and that he should repair to Capt. Mason of Seabrook or some of the Magistrates upon the river (Connecticut) to give an account to him or them of what he hath done hitherto." Mr. Chesebrough at first disregarded this order, claiming that his new home was within the jurisdiction of Massachusetts, but subsequently, acting under the advice and assurance of Mr. Winthrop and other friends at Pequot, he so far yielded to the authorities of Connecticut as to engage to appear at the General Court at Hartford in March, 1651, some sixteen months after the issue of said order, and related to them the reason why he had taken up his abode at Wequetequock, and that he was not engaged in any unlawful trade with the Indians, and assured them that his religious opinions were orthodox, neither did he intend to remain alone in the wilderness, and was in hopes that in a short time he should be able to procure a competent company of desirable persons for the planting of the place. The court reluctantly permitted him to remain on condition that if he would give a bond of £300 not to prosecute any unlawful trade with the Indians, and that he would furnish them with the names of such persons as he could induce to settle at Pawcatuck before the next winter, they would not compel him to remove. While the planters of Pequot were friendly to Mr. Chesebrough, they preferred that he should become an inhabitant of that settlement, rather than to establish a new township. In September of the same year, Mr. Chesebrough again visited Hartford for the purpose of obtaining a legal title to the land he occupied. Mr. Winthrop and the deputies from Pequot engaged that if he would put himself on the footing of an inhabitant of Pequot he should have his lands confirmed to him by a grant of the town. To this he acceeded, but the bounds of Pequot did not include his lands, whereupon "on request" the court extended the bounds of the settlement to Pawcatuck River, and the town in November following gave him a house lot at Pequot, which he never occupied. In January, 1652, a large tract of land was given him by the town of Pequot, which was afterwards liberally enlarged until it embraced between two and three thousand acres, and was included within the following boundaries, namely, beginning at the harbor of Stonington, running northerly up the same, and Lambert's Cove, and Stony Brook to the old Post Road, thence following said road easterly to Anguilla Brook; thence down said brook and Wequetequock Cove and the Sound, to the place of beginning. Mr. Chesebrough succeeded in drawing around him a sufficient number of "acceptable persons" to satisfy the General Court; and the settlement of the town was begun, went on in a flourishing condition until 1654, when the planters here desired a separation for religious, as well as civil purposes. This measure was resisted by the planters at Pequot. Meantime, Massachusetts laid claim to the settlement, and the controversy went up to the court of the Commissioners of the United Colonies, and terminated in 1658 in awarding all the territory east of Mystic River to the Massachusetts Colony, under the name of Southertown, and so remained until 1662, when it was included in the new charter, and again became a part of the colony of Connecticut. In 1665, the name of Southertown was changed to that of Mystic, and in 1666, it was again changed to Stonington. Mr. Chesebrough was a man of more than ordinary ability, and held positions of trust not only in the Massachusetts Colony, but was prominent in the settlement of the town of Rehoboth, in Plymouth Colony. After his place at Wequetequock was included in the township of Pequot, he was elected deputy thereof to the General Court at Hartford in 1653-4-5-6, and on one occasion rate-maker or assessor.

When in 1658 the Massachusetts General Court asserted jurisdiction over this town, Mr. Chesebrough with others were appointed to manage the prudential affairs thereof, and one of the Commissioners to end small causes and deal in criminal matters. He held the office of Townsman (Selectman) until Southertown was annexed to Connecticut, and was the first man elected deputy after the reunion, 1653, '55, '57, '64, and succeeded in restoring amicable relations with the Court which had been seriously disturbed by the jurisdictional controversy. After his return he was elected first selectman of the town, and re-elected every year up to the time of his death, which took place June 9, 1667. His dwelling house stood on the west side of Wequetequock Cove, near the head of tide water.

I. WILLIAM CHESEBROUGH, b. in Boston, England, in 1594, m. Anna Stevenson, who was b. in England in 1598. They were m. in Boston, Eng., Dec. 6, 1620. He d. June 9, 1667.

CHILDREN:

2 MARIE, bapt. Boston, Eng., May 2, 1622, buried June 9, 1622.
3 MARTHA, bapt. Boston, Eng., Sept. 18, 1623, buried Sept. 28, 1623.
4 DAVID, bapt. Boston, Eng., Sept. 9, 1624, buried Sept. 9, 1624.
5 JONATHAN, bapt. Boston, Eng., Sept. 9, 1624 (twin), d. young.
6 SAMUEL, bapt. Boston, Eng., April 1, 1627, m. Abigail Ingraham.
7 ANDRONICUS, bapt. Boston, Eng., Feb. 6, 1629, d. Feb. 8, 1629.
8 JUNICE, bapt. Boston, Eng. (twin), Feb. 6, 1629, d. Feb. 6, 1629.
9 NATHANIEL, bapt. Boston, Eng., Jan. 28, 1630, m. Hannah Denison.
10 JOHN, bapt. Boston, Mass., Sept. 2, 1632, d. Stonington, Conn., 1660.
11 JABEZ, bapt. Boston, Mass., May 3, 1635, d. young.
12 ELISHA, bapt. Boston, Mass., June 4, 1637, m. Rebecca Palmer.
13 JOSEPH, b. at Braintree (now Quincy), Mass., July 18, 1640, d. young.

Samuel Chesebrough (No. 6) m. Abigail Ingraham, Nov. 30, 1655; he was buried July 31, 1673. His widow m. 2d, Joshua Holmes (No. 2), Holmes family; 3d husband, Capt. James Avery; for his 2d wife (No. 2), Avery family.

CHILDREN:

14 MARIA, b. Feb. 28, 1658, d. Sept. 30, 1669.
15 ABIGAIL, b. Sept. 30, 1656, m. John Avery (No. 7), Avery family.
16 SAMUEL, b. Nov. 20, 1660, m. Marie Ingraham.
17 WILLIAM, b. April 8, 1662, m. Mary McDowell.
18 SARAH, b. Dec. 24, 1663, m. John Bolton March 8, 1683.
19 ELISHA, b. Aug. 4, 1667, m. Mary Miner, Rebecca Mason.
20 ELIZABETH, b. Aug. 6, 1669, m. William Ingraham of Bristol, R. I.

Nathaniel Chesebrough (No. 9) m. Hannah Denison in 1659 (No. 38), that family, both of Stonington, Conn. He served in the Colonial Indian war.

CHILDREN:

21 ANNA, b. Oct. 12, 1660, m. Samuel Richardson, 1685.
22 SARAH, b. Jan. 30, 1662, m. William Gallup (No. 10), that family.

WILLIAM CHEESEBROUGH FAMILY.

23 NATHANIEL, b. April 14, 1666, m. Sarah Stanton.
24 BRIDGET, b. March 25, 1669, m. William Thompson, Dr. Joseph Miner (No. 16), Miner family.
25 HANNAH, b about 1671, m. Joseph Prentice.
26 SAMUEL, b. Feb. 14, 1674, m. Priscilla Alden.
27 MARGARET, b. about 1676, m. Joseph Stanton (No. 111), that family.
28 MARY, b. June 30, 1678.

The first six children were born previous to the organization of the church in the town of Stonington. Nathaniel Chesebrough was one of the first nine members of the church. He d. Nov. 22, 1678, and July 15, 1680, his widow, Mrs. Hannah Denison Chesebrough, m. Capt. Joseph Saxton, of Stonington, Conn. He was thirteen years younger than his wife. He was b. in Boston, Mass., May 9, 1656, and was the third son of Thomas Saxton, of Boston, and his 2d wife, Ann (Copp) Atwood. He settled in Stonington, and was largely engaged in the West India trade, by which he became very wealthy.

CHILDREN BY SECOND MARRIAGE:

29 MARY, bapt. Sept. 4, 1681, m. Benjamin Miner (No. 53), that family; m. 2d, Joseph Page, March 5, 1713; she d. Oct. 17, 1750.
30 JERUSHA, bapt. Dec. 2, 1683, m. Nehemiah Palmer (No. 24), Palmer family.
31 MERCY, bapt. May 30, 1686, m. Isaac Bailey of Roxbury, Mass., June 4, 1702; m. 2d, William Dewey of Lebanon, Conn.

Elisha Chesebrough (No. 12) m. Rebecca Palmer April 20, 1665 (No. 13), Palmer family. He d. Sept. 1, 1670; she m. 2d, John Baldwin (No. 16), Baldwin family. No children.

CHILD BY FIRST MARRIAGE:

32 ELIHU, b. Dec. 3, 1668, m. Hannah Miner.

Samuel Chesebrough (No. 16), m. Marie, daughter of William and Mary (Barstow) Ingraham in 1690, who was b. June 26, 1666; she d. Jan. 8, 1742

CHILDREN:

33 SAMUEL, b. Sept. 16, 1691, m. Mary Rossiter.
34 JEREMIAH, b. Aug. 27, 1692, d. young.
35 WILLIAM, b. Aug. 27, 1693, m.
36 JEREMIAH, b. Aug. 25, 1697, m. Susannah Rossiter.
37 JONATHAN, b. Feb. 13, 1700, m. Bridget Miner.
38 ANN, bapt. Oct. 9, 1706, m. John Palmer (No. 28), that family.
39 MARY, bapt. Sept. 10, 1710, m. Nathaniel Palmer (No. 139), that family.
40 JOSEPH, bapt. April 12, 1703, m. Thankful Thompson.

William Chesebrough (No. 17) m. Mary McDowell, daughter of Fergus McDowell, Dec. 13, 1698. He d. Jan. 2, 1739-40; she d. March 23, 1744.

CHILDREN:

41 WILLIAM, b. Oct. 20, 1669, d. Feb. 1, 1700.
42 WILLIAM, b. Feb. 1, 1701, m. Lucy Palmer.
43 DAVID, b. Feb. 1, 1702, m. Margaret ———.
44 ABIGAIL, bapt. May 14, 1700, m. Thomas Mumford.
45 THOMAS, b. ——— 1706, d. Jan. 26, 1763, unmarried.
46 MARY, bapt. Jan. 9, 1715.

Elisha Chesebrough (No. 19) m. Mary, daughter of Joseph Miner, Jan. 27, 1692 (No. 51), Miner family; she d. March 29, 1706. He m. 2d, Rebecca, daughter of Daniel Mason (No. 23), that family, Feb. 6, 1707. He d. Sept. 7, 1727.

CHILDREN BY FIRST MARRIAGE:

47 MARY, b. Dec. 15, 1692, m. Daniel Stanton (No. 333), that family.
48 ELISHA, b. Sept. 15, 1694, m. Hannah Chesebrough.
49 ELIHU, b. Sept. 15, 1694, m. Anna McDowell July 23, 1745.
50 JOHN, b. Sept. 25, 1696.
51 JAMES, b. May 20, 1699, m. Prudence Harris.
52 JABEZ, b. Jan. 10, 1701, m. Priscilla Chesebrough.
53 ZEBULON, b. July 6, 1704, d. 1704.

CHILDREN BY SECOND MARRIAGE:

54 REBECCA, b. Nov. 16, 1707, m. S. Turner; 2d, Andrew Denison (No. 92), Denison family, Jan. 29, 1724; 3d, William Austin.
55 JEDEDIAH, b. Oct. 12, 1710, m. Molly Hancock.
56 ZEBULON, b. June 13, 1712, m. Mary McDowell.
57 PRUDENCE, b. July 12, 1716, d. young.
58 ABIGAIL, b. Sept. 28, 1717, m. William Slack, March 5, 1739.
59 LUCY, b. July 3, 1721, m. Edward Hancox (No. 5), Hancox family, July 28, 1741.
60 NATHANIEL, b. Sept. 6, 1724, d. 1725.
61 ELISHA, b and d. in 1727.

Nathaniel Chesebrough (No. 23) m. Sarah Stanton (No. 14), that family, Jan. 13, 1692, both of Stonington, Conn. He d. Aug. 23, 1732.

CHILDREN:

62 SARAH, b. Jan. 3, 1693, d. Jan. 8, 1693.
63 SARAH, b. Sept. 25, 1694, d. Nov. 22, 1707.
64 HANNAH, b. July 27, 1699, d. May 27, 1707, 9 yrs, 10 mos.
65 NATHANIEL, b. May 11, 1700, d. Aug. 5, 1701.
66 THANKFUL, b. April 4, 1703, d. Nov. 6, 1704.
67 NATHAN, b. Aug. 2, 1707, m. Bridget Noyes.

Samuel Chesebrough (No. 26) m. Priscilla Alden, who was the great-granddaughter of John Alden, who m. Priscilla Mullins (and whose courtship has been immortalized by Longfellow) of Duxbury, Mass., Jan. 4, 1699-1700.

WILLIAM CHESEBROUGH FAMILY.

CHILDREN:

68 MARY, b. Sept. 21, 1702, m. Joseph Hewitt (No. 11), that family.
69 PRISCILLA, b. Nov. 6, 1704, m. Jabez Chesebrough (No. 52); 2d, Thomas Palmer (No. 106).
70 NATHANIEL, b. Aug. 9, 1706, d. April 22, 1709.
71 AMOS, b. Feb. 2, 1709, m. Desire Williams.
72 HANNAH, b. July 16, 1712, m. Richard Shaw, Dec. 24, 1730.
73 SARAH, b. Aug. 14, 1715, m. James Geer of Groton, Nov. 27, 1739; she m. 2d, Ebenezer Billings (No. 46), that family; she m. 3d, Capt. John Denison (No. 126), Denison family, March 3, 1762.
74 PRUDENCE, b. Feb. 28, 1722, m. Capt. John Stanton (No. 134), that family.

Elihu Chesebrough (No. 32) m. Hannah, daughter of Manassah Miner, July 4, 1698 (No. 61), that family, both of Stonington, Conn.

CHILDREN:

75 HANNAH, b. Feb. 25, 1699, m. Elisha Chesebrough (No. 48), Chesebrough family.
76 SARAH, b. Feb. 3, 1700, m. Zebediah Mix Feb. 17, 1725.
77 ELIHU, b. Nov. 30, 1704, m. Esther Dennis.
78 LYDIA, b. March 10, 1710, m. John Williams Dec. 23, 1736 (No. 173), Williams family.
79 REBECCA, b. March 16, 1712, m. Col. Joseph Champlin of Charlestown, R. I.
80 ELISHA, b. June 30, 1714, d. 1719.

Capt. Samuel Chesebrough (No. 33) m. Mary Rossiter, sister of Rev. Mr. Rossiter, April 4, 1726. They lived in Stonington, Conn.

CHILDREN:

81 ANN, b. Feb. 12, 1727.
82 PHEBE, b. Aug. 6, 1728.
83 JOHN, b. Jan. 26, 1731, d. Nov. 4, 1733.
84 EUNICE, b. Jan. 14, 1732, d. Jan. 25, 1733.
85 CHARLES, b. June 6, 1736, m. Bridget Chesebrough.
86 WILLIAM, b. Sept. 27, 1738, m. Dorothy Yeoman.

Rev. Jeremiah Chesebrough (No. 36), m. Susannah Rossiter, sister of the Rev. Ebenezer Rossiter, Oct. 16, 1728. They lived in Stonington, Conn.

CHILDREN:

87 JEREMIAH, b. Sept. 7, 1729, d. Oct. 21, 1753.
88 SUSANNAH, b. Feb. 7, 1731, d. Feb. 8, 1731.
89 SUSANNAH R., b. July 5, 1732, m. Amos Pendleton of Westerly, R. I., Feb. 1, 1753 (No. 22), that family.
90 JOHN, b. June 25, 1735, m. Rebecca Mix (No. 442), Chesebrough family.
91 ESTHER, b. Dec. 16, 1737, m. Moses Yeomans Nov. 22, 1761.
92 RUTH, b. Jan. 9, 1741, d. unmarried.
93 DAVID, b. Sept. 18, 1743, d. Oct. 1, 1763, aged 20 yrs.

Jonathan Chesebrough (No. 37) m. Bridget Miner, Nov. 5, 1730 (No. 58), that family.

CHILDREN:

94 BRIDGET, b. Sept. 14, 1731, d. July 23, 1733.
95 JONATHAN, b. Nov. 20, 1734, m. Esther Chesebrough.
96 BRIDGET, b. Dec. 21, 1737.
97 EUNICE, b. Feb. 19, 1740, m. Rufus Miner.
98 ANN, b. Jan. 6, 1743, m. William Griffin Dec. 22, 1762.
99 PHEBE, b. May 24, 1746, m. Jesse Palmer (No. 165), that family.
100 THOMAS, b. Jan. 19, 1755.

Joseph Chesebrough (No. 40) m. Mrs. Thankful (Hinckley) Thompson, Jan. 1, 1739, of Stonington, Conn.

CHILDREN:

101 JOSEPH, b. Jan. 13, 1740, m. Abigail Herrick.
102 MARY, b. Dec. 6, 1741, d. Jan. 10, 1742.
103 SAMUEL, b. March 25, 1743, m. Submit Palmer.
104 MARY, b. Feb. 3, 1745, m. Asa Phillips of Plainville, Conn.
105 ABIGAIL, b. Dec. 5, 1746, m. Capt. Nathaniel Dyer Nov. 12, 1775.
106 SARAH, b. Oct. 26, 1748, d. young.

William Chesebrough (No. 42) m. Lucy Palmer, Sept. 18, 1720 (No. 136), Palmer family. He d. Feb. 23, 1737, aged 36 years; she d. March 2, 1736.

CHILDREN:

107 NATHANIEL, b. March 28, 1723, d. March 4, 1724.
108 WILLIAM, b. Feb. 14, 1725, d. Jan. 17, 1727.
109 DANIEL, b. Oct. 21, 1727, d. Oct. 25, 1727.
110 LUCY, b. Aug. 15, 1729, m. Joseph Denison Dec. 8, 1746 (No. 150), Denison family.
111 HANNAH, b. July 12, 1732, m. James Palmer June 4, 1749 (No. 103), Palmer family.

David Chesebrough (No. 43) m. Margaret ————, about 1729, who d. April 1, 1738, aged 27 yrs; m. 2d, Abigail Rogers, June 12, 1749; m. 3d, Margaret ————; she d. in 1782, aged 62 yrs. He d. Feb. 27, 1782, aged 80 years.

CHILDREN:

112 MARY, b. April 6, 1730.
113 WILLIAM, b. Oct. 17, 1731.
114 ABIGAIL, b. May 16, 1734, m. Alexander Grant.

Elisha Chesebrough (No. 48) m. Hannah Chesebrough (No. 75), Jan. 4, 1721.

CHILDREN:

115 ELISHA, b. Nov. 21, 1723., m. Hannah Jamison.
116 HANNAH, b. Jan. 4, 1726, m. Joseph York May 10, 1744 (No. 21), York family.
117 SARAH, b. Sept. 6, 1728, m. Nathaniel Johnson of Westerly, R. I., Jan. 2, 1749.

WILLIAM CHESEBROUGH FAMILY. 297

118 MARY, b. Dec. 6, 1730.
119 CHRISTOPHER, b. July 28, 1732.
120 JOANNA, b. Dec. 17, 1737.
121 SYLVESTER, b. July 28, 1735, m. Hannah Carpenter.

James Chesebrough (No. 51) m. Prudence Harris of Middletown, Nov. 24, 1718.

CHILDREN:

122 PRUDENCE, b. Oct. 16, 1719.
123 JABEZ, b. July 21, 1721, d. young.
124 ELISHA, bapt. April 28, 1723.
125 REBECCA, bapt. Feb. 6, 1726, m. Abraham Lewis July 28, 1745.
126 SYBIL, b. Feb. 15, 1732.
127 JABEZ, bapt. Aug. 24, 1729.
128 JAMES, bapt. June 17, 1736.

Jabez Chesebrough (No. 52) m. Priscilla Chesebrough (No. 69), Dec. 26, 1723. She was descended from John Alden of the Mayflower fame; after his death his widow m. 2d, Thomas Palmer (No. 106), Palmer family.

CHILDREN BY FIRST MARRIAGE:

129 MARY, bapt. April 10, 1726.
130 JABEZ, bapt. July 20, 1727.
131 PRISCILLA, bapt. May 18, 1729, m. Thomas Leeds, Jr., son of Thomas Leeds, 1746.

Jedediah Chesebrough (No. 55), m. Molly Hancock in 1736. He d. July 12, 1760, aged 50 yrs.

CHILDREN:

132 JEDEDIAH, bapt. April 3, 1738, m. Rebecca Slack.
133 HEPSIBAH, bapt. Nov. 5, 1738.
134 EDWARD, bapt. June 15, 1740.
135 MARY, bapt. Aug. 15, 1742.
136 JOHN, bapt. Nov. 3, 1745.
137 BENJAMIN, b. April 24, 1748, m. Keturah Palmer.
138 ZEBULON, b. Nov. 25, 1750, m. Zerviah Hubbard or Hobart (No. 10).
139 REBECCA,, b. Oct. 13, 1754, m. Amos Chesebrough (No. 209).
140 JAMES, b. June 27, 1756, m. Abby Galloway, Nov. 14, 1783.
141 ANDREW, b. ———.

Zebulon Chesebrough (No. 56) m. Mary McDowell, daughter of John McDowell, March 29, 1739. He d. Feb. 21, 1750; she m. 2d, William Pendleton (No. 18), that family, April 25, 1751.

CHILDREN:

142 ZEBULON, b. Feb. 11, 1740, m. Lydia Pendleton.
143 ANDREW, b. April 13, 1742, drowned April 29, 1743.
144 PRUDENCE, b. Jan. 7, 1744, d. young.
145 MOLLY, b. June 11, 1747, m. Thomas Randall (No. 145), that family.
146 PRUDENCE, b. Aug. 28, 1749, m. Robert Randall.

Dea. Nathan Chesebrough (No. 67) m. Bridget Noyes (No. 106), that family, Nov. 23, 1727, both of Stonington, Conn. She d. Oct. 24, 1774.

CHILDREN:

147 NATHAN, b. Nov. 14, 1728, m. Anna Stanton.
148 SARAH, b. Jan. 2, 1731, m. Thomas Stanton (No. 281), that family.
149 NATHANIEL, b. Jan. 6, 1735, m. Hannah Wheeler; 2d, Mary Hallam.
150 PELEG, b. Jan. 16, 1737, m. Rebecca Barber.
151 ROBERT, b. Feb. 22, 1739, m. Hannah Chesebrough.
152 CODDINGTON, b. Feb. 11, 1741, d. Sept. 16, 1751.
153 BRIDGET, b. Sept. 23, 1742, m. Charles Chesebrough (No. 85), Chesebrough family, Feb. 2, 1766.
154 JAMES, b. Oct. 14, 1744, d. Nov. 17, 1745.
155 ANNA, b. Jan. 26, 1747, m. Elijah Palmer Sept. 27, 1767 (No. 166), Palmer family.
156 WILLIAM, b. Oct. 14, 1750, m. Mercy McDowell.
157 KETURAH, b. Sept. 24, 1752, m. John W. Witmore; 2d, Prosper Witmore.

Col. Amos Chesebrough (No. 71) m. Desire Williams, Dec. 2, 1729 (No. 202a), Williams family, both of Stonington, Conn.

CHILDREN:

158 AMOS, b. Dec. 31, 1730, m. Mary Christophers.
159 DESIRE, b. March 14, 1733, m. Ephraim Miner Dec. 30, 1751 (No. 110), that family.
160 LYDIA ESTHER, b. Dec. 1, 1735, m. Hempstead Miner (No. 152), that family.
161 PRISCILLA, b. June 11, 1738, m. William Pendleton.
162 MARY, b. Nov. 13, 1740, m. Nehemiah Palmer (No. 164), that family.
163 SAMUEL, b. April 3, 1743, m. Mary Slack.
164 HANNAH, b. Sept. 27, 1745, m. Joseph Stanton (No. 144), that family.
165 JOHN, b. April 4, 1748, m. widow Lois Hillard Oct. 25, 1777.
166 JOSHUA, b. Oct. 14, 1750, d. unmarried.
167 ELIZABETH, b. July 27, 1755, m. Oliver Hillard Dennis Aug. 26, 1781.

Elihu Chesebrough (No. 77) m. Esther Dennis, daughter of Ebenezer and Sarah Dennis, Feb. 18, 1740, both of Stonington, Conn. He d. Oct. 27, 1769; she d. Dec. 5, 1768, aged 58 yrs.

CHILDREN:

168 ESTHER, b. Nov. 27, 1740, m. Capt. Jonathan Chesebrough (No. 95), Chesebrough family.
169 ELIHU, b. June 9, 1743, m. Phebe Denison.
170 WILLIAM, b. Jan. 7, 1745, m. Esther Williams.
171 HANNAH, b. July 30, 1747, m. Robert Chesebrough (No. 151), Chesebrough family.
172 ELIZABETH, b. March 5, 1749, m. Thomas, son of Robert Stanton (No. 291), Stanton family.
173 NABOTH, b. April 1, 1751, m. Phebe Palmer.
174 REBECCA, b. Oct. 1, 1754, d. Feb. 8, 1760, aged 6 yrs.

Charles Chesebrough (No. 85) m. Bridget Chesebrough (No.

153), Chesebrough family, Feb. 2, 1766, both of Stonington, Conn.

CHILDREN:

175 DAVID, b. Sept. 16, 1766, d. 1792.
176 DANIEL, b. Jan. 21, 1768, m. Anna Denison (No. 390), that family.
177 MARY, b. May 1, 1770, m. William Packer Oct. 11, 1818.
178 BRIDGET, b. May 1, 1770, m. William Elmandorf.
179 PHEBE, b. March 9, 1772, m. Ransford Hempstead, Nov. 29, 1792.
180 ANNA, b. Sept. 7, 1774, m. Clement Miner Feb. 21, 1793 (No. 353), Miner family.
181 JOSHUA, b. Jan. 7, 1775, m. an English woman and d. in Cuba.
182 BENEDICT ARNOLD, b. Oct. 12, 1777, m. Elizabeth Denison (No. 201) that family.
182a NANCY, b. Sept. 4, 1800, m. Richard Chesebrough (No. 339), that family.

William Chesebrough (No. 86) m. Dorothy Yeomans, Dec. 3, 1765.

CHILDREN:

183 JONATHAN, b. Sept. 20, 1768, m. Eunice Miner.
184 LUCRETIA, b. May 23, 1771, m. Hempstead Chesebrough Miner March 6, 1791 (No. 255), that family.

John Chesebrough (No. 90) m. Rebecca, daughter of Zebediah Mix, July 22, 1760.

CHILDREN:

185 CHARLES, b. Dec. 5, 1760, m. Lydia Yeomans Feb. 13, 1791.
186 REBECCA, b. March 20, 1764, m. David Fanning of Groton May 13, 1782.
187 SARAH, b. Sept. 21, 1766, m. Thomas Payson Cottrell; m. 2d, ——— Eldridge.

Jonathan Chesebrough (No. 95) m. Esther Chesebrough (No. 168), Chesebrough family, June 20, 1762, both of Stonington, Conn. He d. at Antigua, Feb. 10, 1764, aged 30 yrs; she d. Oct. 13, 1803, aged 63 yrs.

CHILDREN:

188 ASA, b. Sept. 15, 1762, m. Sabra Palmer (No. 293), Palmer family; 2d, Abigail Stanton.
188a JONATHAN, b. Feb. 10, 1764.

Joseph Chesebrough (No. 101) m. Abigail Herrick Dec. 29, 1763. He d. and his widow m. 2d, Capt. Nathaniel Dyer, Nov. 12, 1775.

CHILDREN:

189 ABIGAIL, bapt. Sept. 21, 1766, m. Azariah Stanton (No. 45), that family.
190 KATE, bapt. Aug. 14, 1768, d. young.
191 ELIZABETH, bapt. Aug. 5, 1773, m. ——— Boardman.
192 PRUDENCE, b. ———, m. Henry Palmer Feb. 7, 1790 (No. 295), Palmer family.

CHILDREN BY SECOND MARRIAGE:

1 JOSEPH CHESEBROUGH, bapt. Feb. 11, 1781.
2 DORCAS, bapt. May 23, 1784.
3 NATHANIEL, b. Dec. 22, 1782.

Samuel Chesebrough (No. 103) m. Submit Palmer Jan. 10, 1765 (No. 167), Palmer family, both of Stonington, Conn. He d. Sept. 9, 1811; she d. Dec. 12, 1835.

CHILDREN:
193 JESSE, b. June 20, 1765, m. Martha Putnam.
194 THANKFUL, b. July 24, 1766, m. Zebulon Hancox.
195 ELIAS, b. April 13, 1768, m. Lucretia Palmer.
196 EZRA, b. Dec. 27, 1769, m. Sally Palmer.
197 SIMEON, b. Dec. 7, 1771, m. Abigail Slack.
198 REUBEN, b. April 30, 1773, m. Deborah Sheffield.
199 LOIS, b. June 14, 1775, m. Jedediah Putnam Jan. 11, 1795.
200 SARAH, b. Nov. 23, 1777, m. Charles Phillips of Plainfield Nov. 28, 1799.
201 SUBMIT, b. Jan. 10, 1780, m. Samuel Thompson Dec. 2, 1804.
202 JOSEPH, b. Jan. 21, 1782, m. Betsey Babcock Jan. 3, 1813.
203 RHODA, b. Oct. 27, 1783, d. aged 18 yrs.
204 MERCY, b. July 27, 1786, m. Thomas R. Chesebrough (No. 251), Jan. 27, 1805.
205 SAMUEL B., b. Nov. 25, 1788, m. Sally Robinson; he m. 2d, Harriet Pollard; 3d, widow Lydia Langworthy.

Elisha Chesebrough (No. 115) m. Hannah Jamison May 19, 1747.

CHILDREN:
206 ROBERT, b. ———.
207 ELISHA, b. Jan. 23, 1749.
208 HANNAH, Sept. 30, 1750.
209 AMOS, Aug. 25, 1752, m. Rebecca Chesebrough (No. 139), Chesebrough family.
210 CHRISTOPHER, b. Nov. 16, 1754, m. Abigail Williams (No. 72).
211 JABEZ, b. Nov. 14, 1756.
212 ELISHA, b. Oct. 1, 1759, m. Thankful Williams; m. 2d, Mary Palmer.

CHILDREN:
213 NEHEMIAH, b. ———.
214 MABRINA, b. ———.

Simeon Chesebrough (No. 197) m. Abigail Slack Oct. 23, 1800.

CHILDREN:
215 WILLIAM FRANKLIN, b. Oct. 9, 1801.
216 ALMIRA, b. July 5, 1803, m. Henry Sheffield.
217 PALMER, b. Nov. 10, 1805, m. Eunice Wheeler (No. 441), that family.
218 ALBERT S., b. Nov. 8, 1807, m. Emily Thompson.
219 EMILY R., b. Sept. 18, 1809, d. Oct. 2, 1830, unmarried.
220 LUCY A., b. Jan. 12, 1812, d. Sept. 22, 1830, unmarried.
221 SIMEON L., b. Aug. 19, 1814, d. April 7, 1846, unmarried.
222 REUBEN M., b. Feb. 17, 1817, m. Laurah A. Pierce Nov. 14, 1847.
223 WARREN, b. July 18, 1819, d. young.

Sylvester Chesebrough (No. 121) m. Hannah, daughter of Nathaniel Carpenter, Oct. 25, 1758.

CHILDREN:

224 ESTHER, b. ———.
225 ELISHA, b. ———.
226 OLIVER, b. March 9, 1764, lived at Adams, Mass.
227 SYLVESTER (twin), b. March 9, 1764.
228 NATHANIEL, b. Aug. 15, 1771, lived at Adams, Mass.
229 HANNAH, b. May 29, 1769.
229a SARAH, b. May 20, 1774.
230 POLLY, b. Aug. 15, 1776.

Jedediah Chesebrough (No. 132) m. Rebecca, daughter of William Slack, March 18, 1762.

CHILDREN:

231 JEDEDIAH, b. Nov. 20, 1762.
232 EDWARD, b. June 19, 1766, m. Anna Baldwin (No. 53), that family.
233 ABEL, b. April 1, 1768, m. Betsey Smith.
234 ABIGAIL, b. Sept. 21, 1769.
235 JOHN, b. Dec. 27, 1771, m. Betsey, daughter of Prentice Frink.
236 MARY, b. Feb. 21, 1773.
237 HEPSIBATH, b. Nov. 19, 1775.

Benjamin Chesebrough (No. 137) m. Keturah Palmer May 1, 1774.

CHILDREN:

238 BENJAMIN, b. Sept. 22, 1774.
239 WEALTHY, b. Dec. 26, 1776.
240 RUFUS, b. ———.

Zebulon Chesebrough (No. 138) m. Zerviah Hubbard or Hobart April 15, 1776 (No. 10), that family.

CHILDREN:

241 ZERVIAH, b. March 17, 1777, m. Jonathan Ward March 3, 1802; she d. Sept. 15, 1858. Had four children, all died in infancy, except Winthrop Ward, b. March 2, 1819; m. Lucy L. Spicer May 24, 1853; he d. at Mystic, Conn., Feb. 17, 1899.
241a ZEBULON, b. May 3, 1779, m. Hopestill Fellows.
242 ANDREW, b. ———, m. Deborah ———.
242a NANCY, b. ———, had a daughter Julia, who m. Edward Hallam.
243 AMOS, b. July 10, 1790, m. Mrs. Clarissa (Palmer) Denison, widow of Elam (No. 538), that family; he d. April 6, 1876.
244 ANNA, b. May 22, 1753, m. Robert Denison (No. 220) that family.

Zebulon Chesebrough (No. 142) m. Lydia Pendleton Dec. 10, 1761 (No. 27), that family. He d. Feb. 22, 1827, aged 87 yrs.

CHILDREN:

245 WILLIAM, b. Oct. 10, 1762.
246 LYDIA, b. Nov. 5, 1863, d. young.
247 ZEBULON, b. Feb. 6, 1766, m. Phebe Chesebrough (No. 318); 2d, Abigail Randall.
248 ISAAC, b. July 14, 1769, m. Sarah Chesebrough (No. 287).

249 LYDIA, b. July 10, 1770, m. Rev. Elihu Chesebrough (No. 316).
250 MOLLY, b. Dec. 25, 1774, d. unmarried.
251 THOMAS RANDALL, b. Dec. 24, 1776, m Mercy Chesebrough.
252 PRUDENCE, b. Feb. 24, 1780, m. Samuel Thompson.
253 AMELIA, b. March 20, 1784, m. Capt. Jonathan Stanton of Voluntown.

Nathan Chesebrough (No. 147) m. Anna Stanton (No. 283), that family, Dec. 6, 1752, both of Stonington, Conn. She d. March 20, 1805.

CHILDREN:

254 ANNA, b. May 22, 1753, m. Robert Denison (No. 220), that family.
255 NATHANIEL, b. July 30, 1775, m. Bridget Stanton (No. 298.)
256 ABIGAIL, b. July 20, 1757, m. Robert Williams (No. 227), that family.
257 NATHAN, b. Oct. 8, 1759.
258 PEREZ, b. March 2, 1762, m. Priscilla, daughter of Daniel Thompson.
259 BRIDGET, b. May 9, 1764, m. Hempstead Miner.
260 ELAM, b. Aug. 30, 1767, m. Sarah Hewitt (No. 228), that family.
261 THOMAS, b. July 27, 1770, m. Eunice, daughter of John Whitman.
262 DOROTHY, b. Feb. 7, 1773, d. Dec., 1798, unmarried, aged 25 yrs.
263 EDWARD, b. Feb. 4, 1775, m. Sophia Palmer, daughter of Jonathan Palmer.

Nathaniel Chesebrough (No. 149) m. Hannah Wheeler Feb. 22, 1759 (No. 65), that family. She d. July 5, 1762; married 2d, Mary, daughter of John Hallam, March 21, 1766 (No. 13), Hallam family; she d. Nov. 17, 1830.

CHILDREN BY FIRST MARRIAGE.

264 NATHANIEL, b. June 6, 1760, d. ———.
265 HANNAH, b. Nov. 17, 1761, m. Beebe Denison (No. 226), Denison family.

CHILDREN BY SECOND MARRIAGE.

266 NATHANIEL, b. Dec. 25, 1766, m. Mary Sanford May 29, 1799.
267 KETURAH, b. Oct. 13, 1768, d. Dec. 23, 1853, unmarried.
268 PRUDENCE, b. Jan. 21, 1770, d. Jan. 28, 1843, unmarried.
269 MARY, b. June 20, 1772, m. Nicholas Hallam (No. 19), Hallam family.
270 NATHAN, b. July 25, 1775, m. Cynthia Crary, daughter of Thomas Crary.
271 HALLAM, b. Aug. 1, 1779, lost at sea in 1811.
272 ENOCH STANTON, b. Oct. 23, 1781, m. Sally Sheffield.
273 CHARLES GRANDISON, b. April 15, 1785, d. April 6, 1855, unmarried; served in war of 1812.

Peleg Chesebrough (No. 150) m. Rebecca, daughter of John Barber, Feb. 27, 1772. He d. Oct. 30, 1793.

CHILDREN:

274 REBECCA, b. March 7, 1773, m. Hezekiah Whitman Feb. 11, 1797.
275 CLARISSA, b. Feb. 12, 1775, m. John R. Todd, 1798.
276 BETSEY, b. May 9, 1777, m. William Freeman in 1805; 2d, Henry Spencer April 5, 1821.
277 PELEG, b. Aug. 27, 1779, m. Sarah More in 1810.
278 BENJAMIN FRANKLIN, b. Oct. 1, 1781.
279 JABEZ, b. Nov. 23, 1783, d. at the West Indies in 1803.

WILLIAM CHESEBROUGH FAMILY. 303

280 SALLY, b. Feb. 26, 1786, m. Lewis Newman Sept. 16, 1840.
281 MARIA, b. April 9, 1788, m. Alanson Fox.
282 LUCY, b. Nov. 6, 1790, m. 2d, Mr. Alton.
283 NANCY, b. Dec. 9, 1792, d. in Albany, N. Y., 1799.

Robert Chesebrough (No. 151) m. Hannah Chesebrough (No. 171), Dec. 25, 1764, both of Stonington. He d. July 26, 1802; she d. Sept. 6, 1804.

CHILDREN:

284 ROBERT, b. April 9, 1766, m. Lucy Palmer (No. 294), Palmer family, Feb. 3, 1783; 2d, Content Rathbun, April 1, 1792.
285 CODDINGTON, b. April 9, 1769, d. Jan. 25, 1776.
286 HANNAH, b. May 29, 1771, d. Dec. 19, 1797.
287 SARAH, b. Jan. 26, 1774, m. Capt. Isaac Chesebrough (No. 248).
288 MINETTA, b. March 6, 1776, m. Dudley Palmer (No. 318), that family.
289 CODDINGTON, b. May 30, 1779, m .Sally Palmer, daughter Col. Jonathan Palmer.
290 ANDRONICUS, b. June 13, 1782, m. Margaret More.
291 EUNICE, b. Oct. 22, 1789, m. Phebe, daughter of Nathan Beebe.
292 ELIZA, b. Sept. 11, 1785, m. Aaron Rathbun, son of John.

William Chesebrough (No. 156) m. Mercy McDowell, daughter of Ebenezer of New London, Nov. 13, 1773.

CHILDREN:

293 MERCY, b. July 16, 1774, d. young.
294 HULDAH, b. Nov. 19, 1776, m. Rev. B. Howe, 1800.
295 EBENEZER, b. March 25, 1778.
296 SAXTON, b. Aug. 10, 1779, m. Mary Young, 1799.
297 NATHAN, b. Feb. 11, 1781, m., went to sea, never heard from.
298 OBED, b. Feb. 2, 1783, m. Margaret Conger.
299 BERIAH, b. March 2, 1785, m. Sarah Young.
300 MARY, b. Sept. 29, 1796.
301 NICHOLAS, b. July 9, 1788, m Clara Crippen.

Amos Chesebrough (No. 158) m. Mary, daughter of Richard Christophers.

CHILDREN:

302 MARY, b. ———, m. Gideon Babcock of South Kingston, R. I., June 27, 1776.
303 DESIRE, b. ———, m. Charles Congdon.
304 HENRY, b. Sept. 30, 1764.
305 LYDIA, b. Oct. 26, 1766, m. a Mr. Leavitt.
306 FRANCES, b. Aug. 27, 1768, m. Benedict Babcock.
307 RICHARD CHRISTOPHERS, b. and d. young.
308 ABIGAIL, b. ———, m. Hazzard Perry.

Samuel Chesebrough (No. 163) m. Mary, daughter of William Slack, April 26, 1772, both of Stonington, Conn. He d. Oct. 11, 1825; she d. Aug. 25, 1814.

CHILDREN:

309 AMOS, b. Dec. 14, 1773, m. Phebe Denison.
310 ABIGAIL, b. June 13, 1776, m. Nathan Langworthy.
311 DESIRE, b. Aug. 31, 1778, m. Robert Williams, son of Robert Williams.
312 ELIZABETH, b. Sept. 21, 1780, m. John Noyes (No. 171), that family.
313 MARY, b. Aug. 29, 1783, m. Elisha Fish; 2d, Rev. Elihu Chesebrough (No. 316), Chesebrough family.
314 PRISCILLA, b. March 26, 1786, m. John Noyes (No. 171).
315 GEORGE, b. Aug. 16, 1788, m. Elizabeth Bass.

Lieut. Elihu Chesebrough (No. 169) m. Phebe Denison May 19, 1768 (No. 219), Denison family. He d. Oct. 26, 1781; his widow m. Gilbert Smith Jan. 30, 1793, and after his death she m. Rev. Silas Burrows, and died April 8, 1833, aged 86 yrs; buried by her first husband at Wequetequock.

CHILDREN:

316 REV. ELIHU, b. Dec. 26, 1769, m. Lydia Chesebrough; m. 2d, widow Mary Fish Chesebrough.
317 DANIEL, b. Jan. 12, 1771, m. Fanny Williams (No. 467), that family, Jan. 6, 1793.
318 PHEBE DENISON, b. March 11, 1773, m. Zebulon Chesebrough (No. 247), Feb. 6, 1791.
319 HENRY, b Feb. 25, 1775, d. young.
320 HENRY, b. June 15, 1778, d. young.
321 NANCY, b. Oct. 5, 1780, m. Samuel Corwin of Long Island.

William Chesebrough (No. 170) m. Esther Williams (No. 212), Williams family, Feb. 3, 1774, both of Stonington, Conn. He d. Dec. 21, 1840; she d. June 2, 1814.

CHILDREN:

322 WILLIAM, b. Dec. 11, 1774, m. Fanny Page, Oct. 27, 1796 (No. 27), that family.
323 ESTHER, b. Aug. 26, 1776, m. Rev. Reuben Moss (No. 29), Moss family.
324 EPHRAIM, b. June 12, 1778, m. Hannah Pickett Latimer of Waterford.
325 MARTHA, b. July 7, 1780, m. Col. William Randall (No. 71), Randall family.
326 EUNICE, b. Dec. 27, 1781, m. Joseph Noyes (No. 167), that family.
327 LUKE, b. April 1, 1783, d. July 5, 1783.
328 HENRY, b. May 13, 1784, m. Sarah Williams (No. 301), that family, July, 1813; m. 2d, Martha Williams (No. 303), that family.
329 SILAS, b. Nov. 19, 1796, m. Phebe Esther Williams (No. 307), Williams family, Feb. 1, 1819.

Naboth Chesebrough (No. 173) m. Phebe, daughter of Capt. Andrew Palmer, Oct. 29, 1775 (No. 307), that family. He d. Jan. 27, 1804; she d. April 22, 1787.

CHILDREN:

330 NABOTH, b. in 1776, d. young.

WILLIAM CHESEBROUGH FAMILY.

331 FREDERICK, b. in 1778, m. Priscilla Miner (No. 276).
332 FANNY, b. in 1780, m. Adam States, Nov. 21, 1800.
333 MARY, b. in 1782, m. John Pendleton.
334 LUCY, b. in 1784, d. young.
335 PAUL S., b. in 1786, d. young.

Amos Chesebrough (No. 309) m. Phebe Denison (No. 394), Denison family, July 13, 1801, both of Stonington, Conn. He d. Aug. 3, 1846; she d. Oct. 9, 1846.

CHILDREN:
336 GRACE, b. July 13, 1803.
337 EDMUND D., b. Aug. 26, 1805, m. Nancy D. Clift (No. 36).
338 HENRY D., b. Dec. 5, 1807, m. Sophia Williams (No. 114), that family.
339 RICHARD C., b. March 14, 1810, m. Nancy Chesebrough (No. 182), that family.
340 SAMUEL, b. Oct. 8, 1814, d. unmarried.
341 AMOS, b. Dec. 22, 1816, m. Eunice Gates, Sept. 24, 1851.
342 GIDEON, b. Aug. 17, 1823, m. Anna Adelia Lasher Sept. 5, 1854.

Samuel B. Chesebrough (No. 205) m. Sally Robinson Dec. 25, 1814; she d. April 23, 1830. He m. 2d, Mrs. Harriet (Haskell) Pollard Dec. 5, 1830; she d. Dec. 11, 1855. He m. 3d, Mrs. Lydia (Fellows) Langworthy, March 19, 1857; she d. Aug. 24, 1882. He d. May 24, 1858.

CHILDREN BY FIRST MARRIAGE:
343 JOHN ROBINSON, b. Nov. 7, 1815, m. Almira F. Burdick Jan. 2, 1842.
344 DUDLEY R., b. May 28, 1818, m. Jane Tinker Sept. 24, 1843.
345 ANN ELIZABETH, Sept. 23, 1820, m. George W. Ashbey Oct. 11, 1838.
346 FRANCES MARY, b. Sept. 13, 1822, m. Ichabod Dickinson, Dec. 25, 1842.
347 SAMUEL, b. April 29, 1826, d. Sept. 9, 1830.
348 SARAH JANE, b. April 29, 1829, m. Marcus M. Swazey; 2d, Mr. Wolfe.

CHILDREN BY SECOND MARRIAGE.
349 HARRIET, b. Sept. 13, 1831, d. Sept. 29, 1831.
350 SAMUEL, b. Aug. 2, 1836, d. Sept. 22, 1836.
351 HARRIET, (twin), b. Aug. 2, 1836, d. Sept. 15, 1836.
352 SAMUEL HENRY, b. Dec. 8, 1838, m. Lucretia Maria Babcock (No. 246), Sept. 26, 1865.

Jesse Chesebrough (No. 193) m. Martha Putnam Dec. 26, 1790. He d. June 23, 1830. She d. Nov. 15, 1825. They removed to Manluis, N. Y., in 1798.

CHILDREN:
353 JESSE, b. Dec. 25, 1791.
354 GURDON, b. Aug. 20, 1793.
355 ELI, b. April 4, 1795.
356 JOHN P., b. April 22, 1795.
357 SAMUEL, b. March 13, 1799.
358 REUBEN, b. Nov. 6, 1800.
359 MARTHA, b. Oct. 27, 1802.

360 ABISHA, b. Feb. 21, 1805.
361 SUBMIT, b. Aug. 30, 1807.
362 ANNA, b. July 8, 1809.
363 JOSEPH, b. Oct. 8, 1811.
364 ELMANSON, b. May 29, 1813.
365 Infant, b. Aug. 25, 1815.

Elias Chesebrough (No. 195) m. Lucretia Palmer (No. 296), that family, Nov. 14, 1793. He d. Feb. 22, 1849; she d. May 23, 1841.

CHILDREN:

366 HULDAH, b. Aug. 16, 1794, d. young.
367 SALLY, b. April 26, 1796, d. April 10, 1836, unmarried.
368 MARVIN, b. Feb. 23, 1798, d. Jan. 26, 1872, unmarried.
369 ELIAS, b. Dec. 12, 1799, d. Jan. 21, 1800.
370 LUCRETIA P., b. Dec. 20, 1800, d. Nov. 5, 1864, unmarried.
371 DENISON P., b. Jan. 24, 1803, m. Sarah Jane Hancox Oct. 28, 1854.
372 RODMAN, b. Jan. 24, 1805, d. Oct. 17, 1806.
373 JOSEPH, b. March 3, 1807, m. Louisa S. Noyes Jan. 18, 1831 (No. 358), Noyes family.
374 SOPHIA, b. Jan. 31, 1809, m. Thomas J. Wheeler (No. 215), that family.
375 MARY ANN, b. Feb. 3, 1811, m. Fred D. Chesebrough (No. 403), Oct. 25, 1837.

Ezra Chesebrough (No. 196) m. Sarah Palmer Dec. 18, 1796 (No. 300), that family. He d. Feb. 13, 1838; she d. Aug. 24, 1828.

CHILDREN:

376 SABRA, b. Oct. 21, 1797, m. Nathaniel Robinson.
377 HULDA, b. June 9, 1799, d. July 5, 1801.
378 RHODA, b. Aug. 4, 1801, m. Cyrus Grant Nov. 18, 1820 (No. 72), Grant family.
379 EZRA, b. March 31, 1804, m. Nancy Deane Dec. 28, 1828 (No. 37), Deane family.
380 SALLY ANN, b. Nov. 18, 1806, d. April 15, 1849, unmarried.
381 ALBERT, b. Dec. 14, 1808, m. Phebe E. Cobb Dec. 20, 1832.
382 NANCY LORD, b. July 10, 1811, m. Richard B. Eldred Jan. 22, 1832.
383 EMMA, b. Aug. 24, 1815, m. Amos Allen Palmer Oct. 4, 1846 (No. 444).
384 HANNAH, b. June 26, 1818, m. Amos Allen Palmer in 1834 (No. 444), Palmer family.

Enoch Stanton Chesebrough (No. 272) m. Sally Sheffield, b. Nov. 23, 1793, dau. of Capt. Amos Sheffield, Jan. 1, 1811. He d. Sept. 25, 1859; she d. July 5, 1863.

CHILDREN:

385 FRANCES MARIA, b. Dec. 2, 1811, d. March 12, 1814.
386 AMOS SHEFFIELD, b. Aug. 22, 1813, m. Harriet, dau. of George H. Chapman, Nov. 16, 1841. She was b. April 15, 1819, d. June 14, 1897.
387 ELLSWORTH, b. July 10, 1816, m. Anna Louise Addison June 28, 1842; m. 2d, Anna Euphenia Kearney April 10, 1847. He d. Oct. 24, 1864.

WILLIAM CHESEBROUGH FAMILY.   307

388 ABBY SHEFFIELD, b. Aug. 23, 1818, m. Joseph Eells Smith, Feb. 16, 1841 (No. 112), Smith family; she d. Feb. 17, 1880; he d. March 15, 1893.
389 NICHOLAS HALLAM, b May 13, 1821, m. Henrietta Hatfield Nov. 21, 1848. He d. April 6, 1899; she d. Jan. 1, 1899.
389 DANIEL CAREW, b. Nov. 17, 1823, d. Aug. 24, 1826.

Thomas Randall Chesebrough (No. 251) m. Mercy Chesebrough (No. 204) Jan. 27, 1805. He d. Dec. 21, 1817; she d. Oct. 18, 1864.

CHILDREN:

390 MERCY SUBMIT, b. Oct. 20, 1805, d. Aug. 31, 1836.
391 THOMAS W., b. Feb. 11, 1807, m. Eliza Birdsell Feb. 3, 1835.
392 COURTLAND P., b. Feb. 6, 1809, m. Hannah Maria Hinckley Jan. 17, 1842.
393 THANKFUL C., b. Oct. 26, 1811, m. Peter Forsyth Sept. 28, 1831.
394 SABRINA N., b. Sept. 21, 1812, d. Oct. 4, 1836.
395 LYDIA C., b. Jan. 24, 1814, m. Charles Niles Dec. 17, 1835.
396 PRUDENCE MARY, b. May 16, 1816, m. Henry Hinckley Dec. 12, 1838 (No. 81), that family.

Rev. Elihu Chesebrough (No. 316) m. Lydia Chesebrough (No. 249) March 20, 1791. She d. May 31, 1841. He m. 2d, Mrs. Mary (Chesebrough) Fish Oct. 8, 1848 (No. 313), Chesebrough family. He d. April 29, 1868; she d. July 22, 1866.

CHILDREN:

397 ELIHU, b. Jan. 3, 1792, m. Nancy Pendleton.
398 DENISON, b. Jan. 16, 1794, m. Martha Denison.
399 LYDIA, b. March 28, 1796, d. young.
400 GILBERT S., b. Sept. 21, 1798, m. Prudence Miner, Lucy Stanton.
401 PRUDENCE, b. Oct. 5, 1800, m. Samuel Langworthy.
402 ETHAN ALLEN, b. Dec. 25, 1803, m. Eliza Ann Pendleton.
403 FREDERICK D., b. Oct. 20, 1805, m. Mary Chesebrough (No. 375), Oct. 25, 1837.
404 LYDIA, b. Aug. 1, 1807, m. Joseph Sewell Wright.
405 AMELIA, b. July 17, 1809, m. Thomas J. Wheeler (No. 315), that family.
406 MARY ANN, b. Sept. 29, 1811, m. William Chesebrough Stanton, son of Jonathan G. Stanton of Voluntown.

Zebulon Chesebrough (No. 241a) m. Hopestill, daughter of Nathaniel Fellows, she b. May 16, 1776, d. July 1, 1868. He d. Feb. 28, 1851.

CHILDREN:

407 ELDREDGE, b. Sept. 3, 1801, d. Feb., 1824.
407a SALLY, b. Sept. 13, 1803, m. William Murphy Aug. 23, 1829.
408 DUDLEY, b. Oct. 27, 1805, m. Celia Ann Sheffield Aug. 27, 1826.
409 ELIZA, b. Jan. 12, 1808, d. unmarried Feb. 8, 1876, aged 68 years.
410 ANDREW, b. Sept. 13, 1810, m. Betsey C. Lewis; 2d, Elizabeth Read. He d. July 31, 1864, aged 54 years.
411 EZRA D., b. May 7, 1813, d. March 29, 1878, unmarried .
411a LUCENA P., b. Sept. 8, 1815, m. Josiah Baylies, 1835; **they had seven children.**

Elihu Chesebrough (No. 397) m. Nancy Bell Pendleton Jan. 10, 1819 (No. 115), that family. She d. May 26, 1871; he d. Sept. 20, 1881.

CHILDREN:

412 ELIHU, b. Nov., 1819, m. Mary Ann Wilbur.
413 CHARLES H., b. Aug. 26, 1821, m. Prudence Potter Oct. 20, 1844.
414 ENOCH C., b. Nov. 20, 1823, m. Margaret Conant Dec. 3, 1855.
415 NANCY MARIA, b. Sept. 25, 1825, m. Billings Burch March 10, 1847 (No. 74), that family.
416 ANN ELIZABETH, b. Aug. 29, 1827, m. 1st, Warren Palmer (No. 414), that family; 2d, William E. D. Miller, Aug. 14, 1846.
417 FRANCES MARIAN, b. Aug. 17, 1829, unmarried.
418 ERASTUS S., b. May 13, 1832, m. Emeline Hancox Sept. 17, 1860.
419 PRUDENCE MARY, b. Oct. 22, 1834, d. unmarried.
420 HARRIET, b. Dec. 11, 1836, m. Oscar Miller.
421 DENISON ALLEN, b. Feb. 21, 1839, m. Jemima Giles Jan. 8, 1863.

Andrew Chesebrough (No. 242) m. Deborah Lewis, as given on her grave stone, but on record found Deborah Haley.

CHILDREN:

422 LUKE, b. in 1814, m. Mary E. Miner, (No. 311d), that family, d. Sept. 6, 1852.
423 MARY ANN, b. in 1816, m. Nathaniel Brand, d. Dec. 26, 1835.
424 ANDREW, b. Feb. 17, 1819, m. 1st, Nancy Wilcox April 4, 1847; 2d, Avis Wilcox, April 7, 1850.
425 GRACE M., b. May, 1822, m. Sanford Holdridge in 1857.
426 WILLIAM, b. in 1827, d. May 17, 1830.

William Chesebrough (No. 244) m. Eliza Noyes (No. 328), that family, Nov. 25, 1830. He d. Dec. 8, 1876; she d. Aug. 18, 1803.

CHILDREN:

427 NANCY, b. Sept. 5, 1832, m. John A. Fish; 2d, Dr. William C. Hussey.
428 WILLIAM F., b. April 1, 1837, m. Elizabeth Davis March 28, 1871.
429 ALMIRA, b. Oct. 8, 1839, d. unmarried March 10, 1862.

Zebulon Chesebrough (No. 247) m. Phebe Chesebrough (No. 318) Feb. 7, 1791; she d. June 21, 1815. He m. 2d, Abigail Randall, his cousin (No. 78), that family. He d. Dec. 15, 1828; she d. June 20, 1849.

CHILDREN:

430 PHEBE, b. ———, m. Joshua Lawton.
431 POLLY, b. ———, m. Acors Lawton Dec. 2, 1821.
432 EMMA, b. ———, m. Andrew Billings Holmes.
433 MARIA, b. ———.
434 ALEXANDER, b. ———, m. Harriet Wilcox.
435 JANE, b. ———.

Nathaniel Chesebrough (No. 266) m. Polly, dau. of Elisha and Priscilla (Noyes) Sanford, May 29, 1799.

WILLIAM CHESEBROUGH FAMILY. 309

CHILDREN:
436 ELIZA ANN, b. 1802, m. Simeon Palmer Feb. 26, 1824.
437 MARY ANN, b. ———.
438 FRANCIS, b. ———.
439 HALLAM, b. ———, m. Mary ———.

Denison Chesebrough (No. 398) m. Martha Denison (No. 537), that family, Nov. 15, 1818. He d. Aug. 31, 1834; she d. Dec. 4, 1863.

CHILDREN:
440 OLIVER D., b. Jan. 20, 1820, m. Frances, dau. of Benjamin F. Hancox, Jr., and wife Eunice Stevens, dau. of Stanton Stevens, and wife, Eunice (Hall) Short.
441 JAMES MONROE, b. Aug. 2, 1820, m. Frances Wilcox, daughter of Phineas and Mercy (Taylor) Wilcox.
*442 BENJAMIN F., b. Nov. 22, 1825, d. unmarried in California.
*NOTE.—Rebecca Chesebrough, which was (No. 442), will now be found as (No. 450).
443 EMILY, b. Oct. 18, 1831, m. Capt. John Brown.

Ethan Allen Chesebrough (No. 402) m. Eliza Ann Pendleton July 14, 1828. He was lost at sea Sept., 1833. She m. 2d, Denison Palmer.

CHILDREN BY FIRST HUSBAND:
444 ELIZA ANN, b. ———, m. William J. H. Pollard (No. 19), that family.
445 MARY, b. ———, m. James Miner, b. Jan. 27, 1825.

Sarah Chesebrough (No. 76) m. Zebediah Mix Feb. 17, 1725.

CHILDREN:
446 AMOS MIX, bapt. Feb. 6, 1726.
447 ZEBEDIAH, bapt. March 3, 1728, m. Olive Bell Dec. 2, 1751.
448 HANNAH, bapt. Jan. 11, 1730, m. Nathaniel Thompson (No. 10), that family.
449 SARAH, bapt. Nov. 3, 1734, m. Noyes Palmer (No. 127), that family.
450 REBECCA, bapt. ———, m. John Chesebrough July 27, 1760 (No. 90).

CLIFT FAMILY.

The first Clift in this country is given by "Savage" as

1. WILLIAM CLIFT, born in England and came to Scituate, Mass., in his youth, and later was of Marshfield, Mass., married Nov. 25, 1691, Lydia, dau. of Samuel Willis or Wills, who was the son of William Wills, the first of the name in Scituate, who lived on Wills Island and died in 1688. William Clift d. Oct. 17, 1722.

CHILDREN:

2 LYDIA, b. July 13, 1697.
3 WILLIAM, b. April 30, 1700, m. Judith ———, d. in Marshfield, Jan 23, 1750.
4 SAMUEL, b. Oct. 22, 1709.
5 JOSEPH, b. in 1712, d. in North Carolina in 1766, m. Mary Edgell.
6 MARY, b. July 6, 1714.

Samuel Clift (No. 4) m. before 1733 Lydia Dagget; he removed to Plainfield, Conn., about 1745, and d. in Griswold, Conn., Aug. 22, 1794.

CHILDREN:

7 RHODA, b. in Marshfield Aug. 29, 1733, d. Dec. 22, 1734.
8 RHODA, b. in Marshfield, Mass., April 29, 1735, d. Sept. 5, 1739.
9 AMOS, b. in Marshfield, Mass., Sept. 20, 1737.
10 MARY, b. in Marshfield, Mass., Oct. 7, 1738, m. Joseph Kimball and d. July 9, 1780.
11 LEMUEL, b. in Marshfield, Mass., April 20, 1740, d. Feb. 14, 1741.
12 WATERMAN, b. in Marshfield, Mass., Dec. 28, 1741, settled in Windham, Conn.
13 BETHIAH, b. in Marshfield, Mass., Feb. 21, 1744, m. Elian Woodward.
14 WILLS, b. in Marshfield, Mass., June 18, 1745, d. 1810.
15 DEBORAH, b. in Plainfield, Conn., June 6, 1749.
16 JOSEPH, b. in Plainfield, Conn., Sept. 13, 1750, d. May 9, 1827.
17 LEMUEL, b. in Plainfield, Conn., Oct. 10, 1755, m. Sarah Hall, d. Sept. 13, 1821.

Amos Clift (No. 9) m. Mary Coit, Feb. 12, 1761, and 2d, Anna Denison Avery, Sept. 2, 1798. He d. in Griswold, Conn., July 29, 1806.

CHILDREN:

18 HEZEKIAH, b. in Preston, Conn., Dec. 4, 1761, m. Lucy Walton, d. in Vermont Oct. 10, 1822.
19 WILLIAM, b. in Preston, Conn., Aug. 28, 1763, m. Nancy D. Avery June 5, 1813, d. Jan. 30, 1831; she d. Nov. 27, 1871.

They had two children, viz., William Clift, who was b. Sept. 12, 1817. He graduated from Amherst College in 1839, and from Union Theological Seminary, N. Y. city, in 1843. He was pastor of the Congregational Church at Stonington Borough for twenty years, and pastor of the Mystic Bridge Congregational Church for nine years. He m. Harriet A. Peters, dau. of Rev. Absolom and wife, Harriet Peters, of New York. They had three children. His brother, Samuel Clift, was b. June 4, 1820, and m. Mary J. Prentice, but had no children.

20 MARY, b. May 31, 1765, m. John Watson in 1784, d. March 10, 1840.
21 LYDIA, b. July 24, 1767, m. Nathan Coggswill, d. June 28, 1790.
22 AMOS, b. in Preston, Conn., May 27, 1769, d. in Mystic, Conn., Nov. 15, 1818.
23 BETSEY, b. Feb. 6, 1772, m. John Prentice, d. July 1, 1814.
24 ABIGAIL, b. Feb. 4, 1774, m. Nathan Prentice in 1794, d. July, 1859.
25 NATHANIEL, b. Oct. 29, 1775, d. in Stonington, Conn., Feb. 14, 1837.

Amos Clift (No. 22) m. Esther Williams (No. 132) R. Williams family, of Stonington, Conn., Sept. 28, 1791.

CHILDREN:

26 LYDIA, b. at Berne, New York, where her parents had moved Dec. 28, 1792, and she m. Jabish Holmes (No. 43), of that family, of Stonington, Conn., May 26, 1811.
27 DENISON, b. in Berne, N. Y., and d. there.
28 LEMUEL, b. April 22, 1798, m. Mary Fish in Feb., 1829; after her death he m. Almira Harris Dec. 25, 1844.

Mrs. Esther Williams Clift d. and Mr. Amos Clift m. 2d, Thankful Denison (No. 402), Denison family, Aug. 4, 1798. He d. Nov. 15, 1818.

CHILDREN:

29 ESTHER, b. Aug. 7, 1805.
30 MARGERY, b. July 4, 1802, d. young.
31 AMOS, b. Aug. 7, 1805, m. Charity Morgan Jan. 29, 1829.
32 JOHN C., b. May 2, 1807, m. Lydia P. Gillson Sept. 30, 1828.
33 WATERMAN, b. Sept. 17, 1809, m. Esther Hazard Aug. 31, 1835.
34 HORATIO, b. March 24, 1811, d. young.
35 FREDERICK D., b. Oct. 10, 1815, m. Prudence A. Welch July 11, 1837.
36 NANCY D., b. March 23, 1817, m. Edmund Chesebrough (No. 337), Sept. 30, 1840.

Nathaniel Clift (No. 25) m. Eunice (No. 403), Denison family, daughter of Isaac Denison and wife Eunice Williams, Aug. 5, 1801. He d. Feb. 14, 1837.

CHILDREN:

37 HIRAM, b. April 3, 1803, m. Mary E. Crary Jan. 1, 1852.
38 WILLIAM, b. April 20, 1805, m. Bridget Fish June 18, 1833 (No. 53).
39 NATHAN, b. May 20, 1807, d. young.

40 MARY C., b. Nov. 26, 1808, m. Capt. John Holdredge Jan. 14, 1829.
41 NATHANIEL, b. May 20, 1811, m. Martha Ann Denison (No. 604), **May** 11, 1837.
42 HARRIET, b. Feb. 10, 1816, m. Benjamin F. Hoxie Nov. 19, 1843.
43 IRA H., b. April 27, 1818, m. Frances A. Leeds April 22, 1846.
44 EUNICE, b. July 19, 1819, m. Charles H. Mallory July 25, 1841.
45 HORACE H., b. Feb. 8, 1821, m. Frances E. Burrows, Oct. 25, 1848 (No. 46).
46 ISAAC D., b. Oct. 14, 1822, m. Elizabeth I. Tift Oct. 5, 1853.

COATES FAMILY.

There were three men by this family name that settled in Stonington, Conn., now North Stonington, soon after the year 1700. They are supposed to be brothers, if not, they were doubtless near relatives. Their names were:

1 ROBERT, b. ———.
2 WILLIAM, b. ———.
3 JOSEPH, b. ———.

Robert Coates (No. 1) and Mary ——— were probably m. in 1705.

CHILDREN:

4 BARTHOLOMEW, b. Sept. 1, 1707.
5 MARY, b. April 8, 1713.
6 OBADIAH, b. March 26, 1715.
7 SUSANNAH, b. May 4, 1717.
8 DANIEL, b. Oct. 3, 1719.
9 MARTHA, b. Oct. 28, 1721.
10 VICTORIA, b. Oct. 17, 1723.
11 DAVID, b. Dec. 28, 1726.
12 THANKFUL, b. Feb. 23, 1728.

William Coates (No. 2) and Hannah Bill were m. by the Rev. Mr. Ephriam Woodbridge, pastor of the church of Groton, Conn., June 9, 1714.

CHILDREN:

13 EXPERIENCE, b. Aug. 7, 1717, d. Dec. 3, 1743.
14 MARY, b. Oct. 14, 1719.
15 WILLIAM, b. Nov. 31, 1721.
16 JOHN, b. July 8, 1723.

Joseph Coates (No. 3) and Hopestill Elliot were m. by the Rev. Mr. Hezekiah Lord of Preston, Conn., Nov. 7, 1723. No children recorded.

John Coates (No. 16) of Stonington and Anna Gray of Little Compton, R. I., were m. Dec. 14, 1749, by Rev. Jonathan Ellis.

CHILDREN:

17 THOMAS, b. Oct. 14, 1750, d. Feb. 28, 1753.
18 EDWARD, b. Jan. 15, 1753.
19 ASAHEL, b. Sept. 8, 1755.
20 ELIZABETH, b. Nov. 6, 1756.
21 REBECCA, b. May 28, 1759.
22 AMOS, b. Oct. 17, 1761.
23 RUBIE, b. March 18, 1764.
24 DAVID, b. Dec. 17, 1766.

David Coates (No. 24) and Molly Brown (No. 104), that family, both of Stonington, were m. by Elder Eleazer Brown June 29, 1788.

CHILDREN:

25 DAVID, b. Jan. 4, 1789, m. Susan Maine (No. 164), that family, Oct. 14, 1824.
26 ASHER, b. Oct. 16, 1790, m. for his 1st wife Lucy, dau. of Capt. John Holmes, March 27, 1817, and m. for 2d wife, Lucy, dau. of Gilbert Billings, April 18, 1826 (No. 184), that family.
27 ANSEL, b. March 4, 1794, m. Eunice Randall (No. 101), Randall family.
28 POLLY, b. Feb. 28, 1799, m. Cyrus Swan.
29 CLARISSA H., b. June 16, 1801.
30 LUCY P., b. July 22, 1806, m. Austin Wheeler Feb. 9, 1843.
31 JOHN C., b. Nov. 1, 1811, m. Mary E. Cates Sept. 3, 1854.

COBB FAMILY.

1. ELDER OR DEACON HENRY COBB came to this country from Southwark, Kent, England, in 1630, and located first at Plymouth, Mass., where he remained about seven years, afterwards moving to Scituate. He was deacon of the church and pastor of the church at Barnstable, Mass., in 1645, where he spent the remainder of his days. He was also deputy five terms. He married Patience, daughter of Dea. James and Catharine Hurst of Plymouth, Mass., in 1631, and had

CHILDREN:

2 JOHN, b. at Plymouth, Mass., June 7, 1632, m. Martha Nelson in 1658, dau. of William Nelson.
3 JAMES, b. at Plymouth Jan. 14, 1634, m. Sarah Lewis in 1663.
4 MARY, b. at Plymouth or Scituate March 24, 1637, m. Jonathan Dunham.
5 HANNAH, b. at Scituate Oct. 5, 1639, m. Edward Lewis.
6 PATIENCE, b. at Barnstable March 15, 1641, m. Robert Parker.
7 GERSHOM, b. at Barnstable Jan. 10, 1644, m. Hannah Davis.
8 ELEAZER, b. March 30, 1648.

Mrs. Patience Cobb was buried May 4, 1648, and on the 12th of Dec., 1649, Dea. Henry Cobb married Sarah (No. 5), dau. of Samuel Hinckley. Dea. Henry Cobb d. in 1679.

THEIR CHILDREN:

9 MEHITABLE, b. Sept. 1, 1651, at Barnstable, d. March 8, 1652.
10 SAMUEL, b. Oct. 12, 1654, at Barnstable, m. Elizabeth Taylor.
11 SARAH, b. Jan. 15, 1658, at Barnstable, d. Jan. 25, 1658.
12 JONATHAN, b. April 10, 1660, at Barnstable, m. Hope Hawkins in 1683.
13 SARAH, b. March 10, 1663.
14 HENRY, b. Sept. 3, 1665.
15 MEHITABLE, b. Feb. 15, 1669.
16 EXPERIENCE, b. March 11, 1671.

Henry Cobb (No. 14) inherited the paternal mansion at Barnstable, Mass., and was m. April 10, 1690, to Lois, dau. of Joseph and Elizabeth Hallet, who were m. in 1666. The Stonington church records say that Henry Cobb's dismission from the church at Barnstable was read Nov. 11, 1705. He d. Sept. 24, 1722.

CHILDREN BORN AT BARNSTABLE WERE:

17 GIDEON, b. April 11, 1691.
18 EUNICE, b. Sept. 18, 1693, m. Benadam Gallup (No. 36), Jan. 11, 1716.
19 LOIS, b. March 2, 1696, m. Samuel Stanton (No. 332a) of Stonington, Conn., March 19, 1718.
20 NATHAN, b. Jan. 1, 1701, d. Nov. 15, 1726.

In 1703 Henry Cobb and family came to Stonington to reside, and their children born here as follows. In 1725 they removed to Windham, Conn.

CHILDREN:

21 EBENEZER, b. Jan. 28, 1705, d. Nov. 17, 1726.
22 MARY, b. Feb. 7, 1707.
23 HENRY, b. April 15, 1710, m. Mary Babcock.
24 HALLET, b. May 2, 1719, m. Bridget Champlin in Feb. 3, 1748. There was also a Mary Cobb, who m. Joshua Thompson of Westerly, whose birth does not appear in the records, and also a Bridget Cobb, who married Hezekiah Monroe Aug. 12, 1752, and these may have been the children of these same parents.

Gideon Cobb (No. 17) m. Margaret Fish (No. 7) Sept. 25, 1717, dau. of John Fish, Jr., and wife Margaret. The daughter Margaret was sometimes called Margaret Cleveland, as her mother married Samuel Cleveland of Canterbury, Conn., after the death of her first husband, John Fish, Jr.

CHILDREN:

25 GIDEON, bapt. at Stonington, Conn., Oct. 19, 1718, and the same day his parents were admitted to the Stonington Church. They were dismissed from the church here June 12, 1726, and recommended to the church at Canada, but joined the church at Hampton, Conn. Gideon Cobb (No. 25) married Abigail Dyer of Canterbury, Conn., in 1726.

Henry Cobb (No. 23) m. Mary Babcock (No. 61) of the Babcock family, about 1732 or 1733. He m. 2d, Prudence Champlin, March 2, 1768.

THEIR CHILDREN WERE:

26 NATHAN, b. June 12, 1734, d. 1805.
27 SUSANNAH, b. Nov. 10, 1735, m. Azariah Stanton (No. 44), that family, Oct. 15, 1760, and m. 2d, Jeremiah Tenney in 1774.
28 LOIS, b. Oct. 24, 1737, m. Acors Sheffield Nov. 26, 1761.
29 MARY, b. Feb. 15, 1740, m. Thomas Noyes (No. 140), that family, Jan. 24, 1760, d. March, 1833.
30 EBENEZER, b. March 30, 1742.
31 OLIVER, b. March 13, 1744.
32 ELKANAH, b. March 6, 1746.
33 EUNICE, b. Aug. 3, 1748, m. Sylvester Pendleton April 11, 1773.
34 SARAH, b. Sept. 30, 1750, m. Andrew Brown Feb. 14, 1771 (No. 126), Lynn Brown family.
35 ANNE, b. Jan. 4, 1756, m. ———— Ward.

Ebenezer Cobb (No. 30) m. Mary Brown (No. 70), Rev. Chad Brown family, Jan. 16, 1766.

CHILDREN:

37 EBENEZER, b. Dec. 9, 1766.
38 MARY, b. Aug. 7, 1769, m. Henry Stanton Cobb of Norwich (No. 68).
39 OLIVER, b. Jan. 29, 1772.

COBB FAMILY.

40 HENRY, b. March 14, 1774, d. 1776.
41 NATHAN, b. March 28, 1777, d. young.
42 HENRY, b. Feb. 7, 1778.
43 NATHAN, b. Dec. 18, 1780.
44 SARAH, b. Dec. 27, 1783.
45 SANFORD, b. April 23, 1785.
46 JAMES NOYES, b. April 29, 1787.

Elkanah Cobb (No. 32) m. Abigail Brown (No. 72), Rev. Chad. Brown family, April 18, 1773.

CHILDREN:

47 NABBY, b. July 2, 1774.
48 NATHAN, b. Nov. 29, 1776, d. young.
49 JOHN, b. April 8, 1779.
50 ELKANAH, b. July 27, 1781.
51 NATHAN, b. Sept. 20, 1783.
52 HALLET, b. Nov. 2, 1766, d. young.
53 ABBY, b. Nov. 9, 1788.

Ebenezer Cobb (No. 37) m. Patty or Martha Stanton (No. 400), dau. of Enoch and wife Waity Dyer Stanton, Jan 12, 1794.

CHILDREN:

54 JOHN, b. ———.
55 EMELINE, b. ———.
56 ELIZA, b. ———.
57 ENOCH, b. ———.
58 EDWARD, b. ———.

Oliver Cobb (No. 39) m. Abigail Denison (No. 328), that family, Nov. 1, 1795.

CHILDREN:

59 JULIAN, b. Aug. 6, 1796, d. Aug. 6, 1797.
60 MARIAH, b. Jan. 24, 1798.
61 OLIVER E., b. Oct. 5, 1799, d. Sept. 24, 1801.
62 OLIVER E., b. March 6, 1802.
63 SAMUEL D., b. ———, and d. Sept. 3, 1805.
64 CHARLES D., b. Oct. 4, 1804.
65 SANFORD, b. Dec. 12, 1806.
66 ABBY D., b. Sept. 27, 1809.

The Henry Cobb who came to Stonington in 1703 lived in the southeastern part of the town, near the present residence of Mr. Daniel Brown.

Nathan Cobb (No. 26) m. Catharine Copp (No. 30) Dec. 28, 1757, and went to Norwich, Conn. She d. in 1793.

CHILDREN:

67 HENRY, b. Jan. 5, 1759, d. 1761.
68 HENRY S., b. 1761.
69 KATHARINE, b. in 1762.

70 JERUSHA, b. in 1764.
71 MARGARET, b. 1766.
72 MARY, b. 1768.

Henry Stanton Cobb (No. 68) m. Mary (No. 38) Cobb family, dau of Ebenezer and wife Mary (Brown) Cobb, of Stonington, in 1791.

CHILDREN:

73 FRANCES, b. in 1793.
74 CATHARINE, b. 1794, d. 1796.
75 HENRY HALLET, b. in 1796.
76 ALFRED, b. 1797.
77 CATHARINE, b. 1800, in Stonington, Conn.
78 MARY, b. in 1803 in Stonington.
79 NATHAN, b. in 1805 in Stonington, Conn.

COLLINS FAMILY.

1. DANIEL COLLINS, b. A. D. 1710, d. July 16, 1797. He was the son (or grandson) of James Collins, who, with his brothers John and Robert, came from Kent or Essex in England in 1669, and settled in Massachusetts. His birthplace is not known, but at the time of his marriage he dwelt in New London, and afterwards removed to Stonington. He m. Alice Pell of New London, Feb. 7, 1731, and had by her one son, Daniel Collins (No. 2). By the records of the first Congregational Church of Stonington it appears that Daniel Collins of New London married Rebecca Stanton of Stonington, July 7, 1754, widow of Samuel Stanton (No. 18), that family. She d. childless in 1755.

CHILD BY FIRST MARRIAGE.

2 DANIEL, b. March 10, 1732, d. April 6, 1819. He was born in New London, but made Stonington his abiding place and became the progenitor of a large family, one branch only of which, viz., that descended from his son Gilbert, remained here. He served in the Continental army from 1775, and was 1st Lieutenant in the 1st Regiment of the Connecticut line, formation of 1776. He was a man of prominence in the town. His farm was on the old Post Road, opposite the present meeting house of the First Congregational Society of Stonington. He m. 1st, Dorothy Wells, Dec. 26, 1756; 2d, Anne Potter (widow Hillard) of Stonington.

CHILDREN BY FIRST MARRIAGE:

3 WILLIAM, b. March, 1759, m. Polly Ross.
4 PELL, b. ———, d. unmarried.
5 HANNAH, b. ———.
6 DANIEL, b. ———, d. unmarried.
7 LYDIA, b. ———.
8 POLLY, b. ———.
9 ELEY, b. ———, d. young.
10 JOHN WELLS, b. Dec. 5, 1773, m. Mercy Langworthy.

The fact as to the marriage and descendants of the daughters have not been ascertained.

CHILDREN BY SECOND MARRIAGE:

11 ROBERT, b. April 14, 1788, m. Ruth Browning.
12 GILBERT, b. April 14, 1790, m. Prudence Frink; 2d, Lucy Breed.
13 REBECCA, b. ———, m. Henry Worden.
14 MARIA, b. ———, m. Justin Denison (No. 535), that family.
15 BETSEY, b. ———, d. young.
16 ANNE, b. ———, m. John D. Noyes (No. 217), Noyes family.

William Collins (No. 3) m. Polly Ross of Stonington and emigrated to Brownville, Jefferson County, New York. He d. in 1852.

CHILDREN:

17 POLLY, b. ———, m. Freeman Kilburn.
18 JOHN B., b. 1787, m. Clarissa Rhodes.
19 RACHEL, b. ———, m. Robert Smith.
20 TRACY, b. ———, m. Lawrence Kilby.
21 SOPHIA, b. ———, m. Moses Huse.
22 HANNAH, b. ———, m. William Rouse.
23 WILLIAM, b. 1791, m. Sally Crawford in 1816.
24 LYDIA, b. ———, m. Roswell Baxter.

John Wells Collins (No. 10) m. Mercy, dau. of Sanford and Anna (Babcock) Langworthy of Stonington, Jan., 1794; d. Dec., 1810; removed to Oneida County, New York.

CHILDREN:

25 NANCY, b. ———, m. Selah Bronson.
26 BETSEY, b. ———, m. Lewis Bailey.
27 DANIEL, b. ———, d. young.
28 JOHN WELLS, b. May 10, 1801, m. Amy Kinney; 2d, Sarah Peck.
29 POLLY, b. ———, m. Henry Greenleaf.
30 SANFORD LANGWORTHY, b. April 4, 1805, m. Harriet, dau. of Major Noah Ashley Whitney, Jan. 19, 1834.
31 MORGAN LEWIS, b. Feb. 8, 1807, m. Lucinda Lewis.
32 HARRIET, b. ———, m. Silas Penoyer.

Robert Collins (No. 11) m. Ruth Browning of Stonington Jan. 13, 1812, and removed to West Halifax, Vt.

CHILDREN:

33 SARAH, b. ———, d. unmarried.
34 ROBERT, b. March 15, 1815, m. Louisa Plumb; 2d, Mary Plumb.
35 LEWIS, b. Feb. 22, 1817, m. Mary E. Potter in 1848.
36 DANIEL, b. March 22, 1819, m. Eliza M. Carter.
37 SAMUEL B., b. Oct. 13, 1821, m. Elizabeth Steenbarger.
38 SMITH, b. Dec. 27, 1823, m. Mary E. Thurber; 2d, Arminta Sheridan.
39 GILBERT, b. ———, d. young.
40 ANN ELIZABETH, b. ———, d. young.
41 THOMAS G., b. July 24, 1831, m. Mary M. Carter.
42 SUSAN A., b. ———, m. her cousin, Thomas B. Collins.

Gilbert Collins (No. 12) m. Prudence Frink of Stonington (No. 103), that family, May 3, 1807. After her death he m. 2d, Lucy Breed (No. 106), that family, April 28, 1816. He m. for his 3d wife, Susan Wells (widow Dickens) of Stonington. He was a farmer by occupation, a highly respected citizen and for several terms represented the town in the State Legislature. He always lived in Stonington and d. March 24, 1865.

COLLINS FAMILY.

CHILDREN BY FIRST MARRIAGE:
43 BENJAMIN FRANKLIN, b. Sept. 10, 1808, m. Mary Denison.
44 ANNE, b. ———, m. John Robbins.
45 DANIEL PRENTICE, b. Aug. 21, 1813, m. Maria E. Stanton; 2d, Sarah R. Quinn.

CHILDREN BY SECOND MARRIAGE:
46 GILBERT WILLIAMS, b. Feb. 19, 1817, m. Mary Randall (No. 115), that family, of Stonington, April 1, 1845. He d. Jan. 19, 1865.
47 ETHAN ALLEN, b. Nov. 24, 1818, m. Lucy Grant of Stonington, Conn. He d. in 1896.
48 JOHN NOYES, b. ———, d. young.
49 THOMAS B., b. Feb. 10, 1823, m. Frances Morgan; 2d, Lucy Ann Morgan; 3d, Susan A. Collins, (No. 42).
50 FRANCES MARION, b. ———, d. young.
51 JOHN PIERCE, b. Oct. 21, 1827, m. Mary Margaret Palmer of Stonington, Aug. 19, 1850. He d. Feb. 28, 1857.

Benjamin Franklin Collins (No. 43), m. Mary Denison Oct. 12, 1835 (No. 630), that family, by whom he had nine children. He removed to Cleveland, Ohio.

CHILDREN WHO REACHED MAJORITY WERE:
52 CHARLES D., b. ———.
53 ELLA, b. ———, m. a Mr. Draper.
54 FRANK S., b. ———, d. unmarried.
55 JANE, b. ———, m. Eben Boalt.

Daniel Prentice Collins (No. 45) m. 1st, Maria E. Stanton, Feb. 1839 (No. 329), that family; m. 2d, Sarah, daughter of John and Clarissa (Wells) Quinn, Dec. 25, 1843.

CHILDREN BY FIRST MARRIAGE:
56 DANIEL WEBSTER, b. Dec. 13, 1839, d. Feb. 9, 1858, unmarried.
57 MARIA SMITH, b. Dec. 3, 1840, m. Lewis Neil, d. Jan. 5, 1868.
58 HANNAH ELIZABETH, b. ———, d. young.

SON BY SECOND MARRIAGE:
59 GILBERT, b. Aug. 26, 1846, m. June 2, 1870, Harriet Kingsbury Bush of Jersey City. He has been Mayor of Jersey City and is now a Justice of the Supreme Court of the State of New Jersey. He resides in Jersey City, N. J., but has his summer home in Stonington, Conn.

COPP FAMILY.

1. WILLIAM COPP came over to this country from England in the good ship Blessing in 1635. He located himself at Boston, Mass. He was 26 years of age at the time of his migration. He was by trade a shoemaker, was from London, England, and was admitted freeman of the Massachusetts Colony June 2, 1641. He m. Judith ———.

CHILDREN:

2 JOANNA, b. in England, ———.
3 ANN, b. in England, ———.
4 DAVID, b. in England, ———, m. Obedience Topliff.
5 NAOME, b. in Boston Aug. 5, 1638.
6 JONATHAN, b. Aug. 23, 1640.
7 REBECCA, b. May 6, 1641.
8 RUTH, b. Nov. 24, 1643.
9 LYDIA, b. July —, 1646.

David Copp (No. 4) m. Obedience Topliff Feb. 20, 1660.

CHILDREN:

10 DAVID, b. Dec. 8, 1661, d. young.
11 DAVID, b. March 2, 1663.
12 JONATHAN, b. Feb. 23, 1665, m. Catharine Laye.
13 WILLIAM, b. March 14, 1667.
14 SARAH, b. March 4, 1669.
15 SAMUEL, b. April 15, 1671.

Jonathan Copp (No. 12) m. Catharine Laye Aug. 18, 1690.

CHILDREN:

16 CATHERINE, b. July 7, 1692.
17 JONATHAN, b. June 12, 1694, m. Margaret Stanton, Sarah Hobart.
18 OBEDIENCE, b. Sept. 17, 1696.
19 MARY, b. Oct. 27, 1698.
20 SARAH, b. Sept. 24, 1700.
21 DAVID, b. Oct. 3, 1702.
22 SAMUEL, b. Jan. 24, 1705.
23 ANN, b. Sept. 24, 1707.
24 JOHN, b. Sept. 29, 1709.
25 SARAH, b. and d. Dec. 21, 1710.
26 SARAH, b. Dec. 3, 1712.

Jonathan Copp (No. 17) m. Margaret Stanton (No. 128) Dec. 28, 1721, Stanton family.

COPP FAMILY.

CHILDREN:

27 DOROTHY, b. Nov. 25, 1722.
28 JONATHAN, b. July 22, 1725.
29 MARGARET, b. May 29, 1727, m. her cousin, Hobart Mason (No. 65), Nov. 10, 1749.
30 CATHERINE, b. July 15, 1730, m. Nathan Cobb (No. 26), that family.
31 JOSEPH, b. Nov. 28, 1732, d. 1815, m. Rachel Denison.

Mrs. Margaret Copp (nee Stanton) d. Dec. 11, 1740. Her husband, Mr. Jonathan Copp, m. for his second wife Sarah Hobart of New London, June 30, 1742.

CHILDREN:

32 SAMUEL, b. April 20, 1743, m. Dolly Brown (No. 69), Rev. Chad Brown family.
33 JOHN, b. June 11, 1744.
34 MARY, b. Nov. 28, 1745.
35 EBENEZER, b. March 3, 1747.
36 DAVID, b. Sept. 18, 1748.

Joseph Copp (No. 31) m. Rachael Denison, daughter of Daniel Denison and Rachael Starr, Dec. 11, 1757.

CHILDREN:

37 JOSEPH, b. in January, 1760.
38 RACHAEL, b. in ———, 1762.
39 ELIZABETH, b. Nov. 11, 1768.
40 DANIEL, b. Aug. 4, 1770, m. Sarah Allyn.
41 CATHERINE, b. in ———, 1772.
42 MARGARET, b. Nov. 13, 1773.
43 JONATHAN, b. in ———, 1778.

Daniel Copp (No. 40) m. Sarah Allyn, daughter of Dea. Joseph Allyn of Groton, now Ledyard, date unknown.

CHILDREN:

44 BELTON ALLYN, b. May 22, 1796, m. Betsey Ann Barber.
45 DANIEL, b. in 1798.
46 SARAH, b. in 1801.
47 JOSEPH, b. in 1804.
48 MARY, b. in 1809.
49 WILLIAM, b. in 1811.
50 ELIZA, b. in 1815.
51 GEORGE, b. in 1819.

Belton Allyn Copp (No. 44) m. Betsey Ann, dau. of Noyes Barber, by his 1st wife, Catharine Burdick, Aug. 15, 1833.

CHILDREN:

52 ELLEN BARBER, b. July 20, 1834.
53 SARAH M., b. May 29, 1836.
54 DANIEL ROGERS, b. March 4, 1838.
55 JOHN JOSEPH, b. June 28, 1840.

56 CATHARINE B., b. Aug. 27, 1842.
57 GEORGE D., b. Nov. 17, 1845.
58 JULIA, b. Aug. 13, 1848.
59 WILLIAM, b. Feb. 2, 1851.
60 BELTON ALLYN, b. Jan. 8, 1854.

Dea. Samuel Copp (No. 32) m. 1st, Dolle Brown, Dec. 10, 1769 (No. 69), Rev. Chad Brown family.

CHILDREN:

61 SARAH, b. Oct. 9, 1770.
62 DOLLE, b. Feb. 12, 1772.
63 JONATHAN, b. Feb. 3, 1774.
64 BETTE, b. Dec. 2, 1775.
65 MOLLY, b. Aug. 30, 1777.
66 JOHN BROWN, b. Aug. 16, 1779.
67 ESTHER, b. Aug. 2, 1781.
68 NANCY, b. Jan. 4, 1785.
69 SAMUEL, b. April 28, 1787, m. Phebe Pheale, Betsey Chapman, Mrs. Mercy (Williams) Stanton.

Samuel Copp (No. 69) m. Phebe Pheale in New York city July 11, 1812; she was b. in Rye, New York, Oct. 17, 1795; m. 2d, Betsey Chapman, Nov. 12, 1844 (No. 77), that family; she d. July 15, 1859. He m. 3d, Mrs. Mercy (Williams) Stanton, Aug. 6, 1860 (No. 353), Williams family. He d. June 8, 1865; she d. Aug. 6, 1866, aged 66.

CHILDREN BY FIRST MARRIAGE:

70 PHEBE, b. Nov. 9, 1813, d. in New York Feb. 8, 1837.
71 SAMUEL, b. Feb. 16, 1816, m. Sarah Anna Chappell at St. Louis, Mo., Oct. 16, 1843.
72 JOHN HOWARD, b. in Sharon, Conn., July 18, 1818, m. 1st, Louise Barnes, Sept. 10, 1839; 2d, Anna Eliza Whiting, July 3, 1855.
73 MARY ELIZABETH, b. in Stonington, Conn., March 12, 1821, m. Leonard C. Williams (No. 500), that family, May 11, 1843.
74 DAVID HENRY, b. in Stonington, Conn., Oct. 10, 1823.

COTTRELL FAMILY.

1. NICHOLAS COTTRELL is first mentioned at Newport, R. I., in 1639, he died in 1680, left a widow, Martha ————, and a will in which he mentions eight children, viz.:

CHILDREN:
2 NICHOLAS, b. ————.
3 JOHN, b. ————.
4 GERSHOM, b. ————.
5 ELEAZER, b. ————.
6 MARY, b. ————.
7 HANNAH, b. ————.
8 JAMES, b. ————.
9 JABEZ, b. ————.

Nicholas Cottrell (No. 2) was admitted freeman at Westerly Oct. 28, 1668, and served in the Narragansett war of 1675. He was Constable, Fenceviewer, Deputy Councilman and Juryman. He married ————, and died in Westerly in Dec., 1715. He left a will, not signed, which the court refused to probate, and the records also state that there were five

CHILDREN:
10 NICHOLAS, b. about 1658.
11 JOHN, b. ————.
12 MARY, b. ————, m. Edward Larkin before 1701, his second wife.
13 ELIZABETH, b. ————.
14 DOROTHY, b. ————, and m. Samuel Cottrell, son of Nathaniel Cottrell.

THEIR CHILDREN WERE:
15 SAMUEL, b. ————.
16 NATHANIEL, b. ————.
16a AMEY, b. ————, m. Joseph Crumb.
17 ELIZABETH, b. ————, m. Sands Niles Sept. 4, 1745.

John Cottrell (No. 3) m. Elizabeth ————; he d. 1721.

CHILDREN:
18 HANNAH, b. 1679.
19 JOHN, b. ————, m. Elizabeth Gardiner.
20 SAMUEL, b. in 1687.
21 Daughter, b. ————.

Gershom Cottrell (No. 4) married Bethia Wilcox Feb. 15, 1677; he was in Norwich in 1678, in Westerly in 1679 and then in North Kingstown, where he died in 1711.

CHILDREN:

22 STEPHEN, b. ———.
23 GERSHOM, b. ———, d. young.
24 Daughter, b. ———.
25 MERCY, b. ———.
26 SARAH, b. ———.
27 RACHEL, b. ———.
28 ELIZABETH, b. ———.
29 SUSANNAH, b. ———.
30 JUDITH, b. ———.
31 MARY, b. ———.

Jabez Cottrell (No. 9) married Ann, dau. of John Peabody. Nicholas Cottrell (No. 10) married Dorothy Pendleton (No. 14) in March, 1706. She was dau. of Capt. James Pendleton and wife, Hannah Goodenow, bapt. at Stonington Oct. 3, 1686. She was admitted to membership in the same church July, 1709. He was in the early Colonial wars. Nicholas Cottrell died in 1727.

THEIR CHILDREN:

32 DOROTHY, bapt. July 31, 1709, m. John Randall (No. 8), Dec. 22, 1726.
33a MARY, bapt. Aug. 19, 1711, m. Nathan Randall (No. 12), Dec. 16, 1730; she d. Dec. 2, 1735.
33b AMEY, bapt. July 31, 1709, m. Josiah Smith (No. 16).
34 ELINNER, bapt. June 12, 1715, m. her sister's husband, Nathan Randall (No. 12), July 22, 1736.
35 NICHOLAS, b. July 7, 1717.
36 JOSEPH, b. Aug. 7, 1726.

Dorothy Cottrell, wife of Nicholas, was admitted to the First Church in Stonington July 24, 1709; also two children, Dorothy and Amie, were bapt. July 31st, 1709. They were called daughters of Gershom, but as no Gershom appears, it is supposed that they belonged to Nicholas Cottrell.

John Cottrell (No. 11) m. Penelope ————, and their son, called

37 MAJOR JOHN, b. ———, m. Lois Boardman of Preston, Conn; he d. in Westerly, R. I., in 1778. Their son
38 ELIAS, b. ———, m. Nov. 7, 1776, Phalley, daughter of Joseph and Thankful Gavitt, born May 13, 1752. Their son
39 LEBBEUS, b. Jan. 29, 1792, m. Lydia Maxson, and

Their son, Calvert B. Cottrell, was b. in Westerly Aug. 20, 1821, and m. Lydia W. Perkins, dau. of Elisha and wife, Nancy Russell Cottrell, May 4, 1849.

CHILDREN:

40 EDGAR H., b. ———.
41 HATTIE, b. ———.

42 CHARLES P., b. ———.
43 C. B. Jr., b. ———.
44 L. ANGIENETTE, b. ———.
45 ARTHUR M., b. ———.

Nathaniel Cottrell (No. 16) m. Mary Niles March 3, 1744-5.
CHILDREN:
46 DOROTHY, b. Jan. 22, 1746.

Nicholas Cottrell (No. 35) m. Rebecca Randall Oct. 3, 1735.

Joseph Cottrell (No. 36) m. Mary ———, and in 1750 were living in Stonington in the vicinity of Pendleton Hill.
CHILDREN:
47 PRUDENCE, b. March 25, 1746.
48 JOSEPH, b. Aug. 16, 1748.
49 MARY, b. Dec. 28, 1750.
50 ABIGAIL, b. April 15, 1775.
51 REUBEN, b. Aug. 15, 1758.
52 CHARLES, b. Aug. 17, 1769.
53 ROYZEL, b. Jan. 10, 1772.

Charles Cottrell (No. 52) m. Esther Denison (No. 400), that family, dau. of Isaac Denison, and wife, Eunice Williams, Oct. 18, 1795. They had one child

54 JOSEPH, b. in 1797, and he m. Fanny (No. 442), dau. of Capt. Jabez and wife Fanny Potter Stanton. She was b. in 1807 and d. on July 19, 1865, at Mystic, and her husband d. there April 19, 1865.

THEIR CHILDREN:
55 MARY A., m. Charles H. Denison May 24, 1848 (No. 633), Denison family.
56 HARRIET, m. George Harris.
57 JOSEPH OSCAR, m. 1st, Josephine Williams, Oct. 22, 1863 (No. 538), Robert Williams family; 2d, ———.
58 CHARLES H., m. Georgianna Crary.
59 IDA, d. unmarried.
60 FANNY E., m. Joseph Griswold of Coleraine, Mass.
61 EMMA.

DAVIS FAMILY.

1. JOHN DAVIS, the progenitor of the Davis family of Stonington, was b. in England in 1612. The family name of his wife is unknown, probably she was b. in England. She d. in East Hampton, L. I., Dec. 17, 1696; he d. there Dec. 22, 1705, aged 93 years.

Four children came with them to this country

2 JOHN, b. in England in 1767, m. Susanna Osborne; she d. July, 1704. He m. 2d, Puah, widow of Abraham Reeves, July 3, 1706.

3 HANNAH, b. in 1680, m. Jonathan Baker Jan. 6, 1701.

4 THOMAS, b. in 1686, m. Abigail Parsons.

5 MARYETTE, bapt. Sept. 16, 1704. "Under head of adult baptism."

Thomas Davis (No. 4) m. Abigail Parsons Jan. 11, 1722.

CHILDREN:

6 JOHN, b. at E. Hampton, L. I., March 4, 1723, m. Catharine Talmage; 2d, Mary Conklin.

7 ABIGAIL, b. at E. Hampton April 26, 1725, m. Daniel Conklin of E. Hampton, L. I., in Dec., 1746.

John Davis (No. 6) was a farmer at East Hampton, L. I., and carried on, in connection, an extensive business in manufacturing leather, and shoe making. In 1765 he hired a farm in Stonington, Conn., situated on the east bank of the Pawcatuck River, near Osbrook, which he afterwards purchased, and put his eldest son John, then only seventeen years of age, in charge of. He came to Stonington with his family in 1772 to reside, having purchased said farm from Robert Stanton. "The Old Mansion House," with its spacious fireplace in the dining room, and hand carved solid mahogany staircase, is still in good preservation; the farm having been handed down from father to son, and is now occupied by his great great-grandsons, John J. and Alphonso W. Davis. John Davis (No. 6) returned to East Hampton in April, 1784, that he might have better opportunity for educating his younger children, at Clinton Academy, which had been established about that time. He carried on the business of cordwainer and shoe making, in connection with his farming in Stonington. He m. 1st, Catharine Talmage, Dec. 31, 1744; she d. April 11, 1759. He m. 2d, Mary Conklin of East Hampton. He d. Dec. 15, 1798. Mrs. Davis returned to Stonington, Conn.,

DAVIS FAMILY.

and resided with her stepson, John Davis, until after his death in 1809, when she went to live with her stepson, Thomas Davis, in Preston, Conn., whose wife, Mary Conklin, was her neice, where she lived until her death, Jan. 18, 1814, in the 80th year of her age.

CHILDREN BY FIRST MARRIAGE:

8 CATHARINE, b. at East Hampton, L. I., March 13, 1746.
9 JOHN, b. at East Hampton Jan. 20, 1748, m. Abigail Baker.
10 BENJAMIN, b. at East Hampton Jan. 4, 1750, d. young.
11 THOMAS, b. at East Hampton Nov. 27, 1751, m. Mary Conklin.
12 BENJAMIN, b. at East Hampton May 15, 1754, d. young.
13 ENOS, b. at East Hampton Oct. 14, 1755, m. Phebe Mulford; m. 2d, Mrs. Lois (Palmer) Perkins.
14 CATHARINE, b. at East Hampton April 5, 1758, m. Capt. Amos Pendleton, Jr., of Westerly, R. I., Feb. 24, 1782 (No. 36), that family.
15 ABIGAIL, b. in East Hampton, L. I., April 5, 1758, d. in infancy.

CHILDREN BY SECOND MARRIAGE:

16 MARY, b. in East Hampton, L. I., April 27, 1763, d. unmarried April 6, 1852.
17 DR. SAMUEL, b. in East Hampton, L. I., Oct. 7, 1765, m. Mrs. Mary (Kirby) Dunham, Oct. 3, 1789.
18 ABIGAIL, b. Jan. 15, 1767, m. John Stratton Nov. 20, 1803.
19 REV. HENRY, b. Sept. 15, 1771, m. Hannah Phoenix Treadwell Sept. 22, 1801.
20 BENJAMIN, b. at Stonington, Conn., Feb. 6, 1774, m. Abigail Foster Sept. 30, 1804.

John Davis (No. 9) m. Abigail, daughter of Daniel Baker of East Hampton, Nov. 14, 1773. They lived in Stonington at the "Old Family Homstead." He d. March 31, 1809.

CHILDREN:

21 JOHN, b. Sept. 19, 1776, m. Sally Stanton.
22 ABIGAIL, b. Oct. 12, 1778, m. Lemuel Palmer (No. 204), that family.
23 DANIEL, b. March 6, 1783, m. Mary Robinson.
24 MARIA, b. Oct. 16, 1786, m. Benjamin Franklin Stanton (No. 44), Robert Stanton family.
25 NANCY, b. June 13, 1793, m. Elias Stanton Oct. 27, 1812 (No. 311), Thomas Stanton family.

Thomas Davis (No. 11) m. Mary Conklin Dec. 25, 1780. He lived in Stonington until in the spring of 1802, in company with his brother Enos. He purchased of Jonathan Brewster a farm on the left bank of the Thames River, about two miles below Chelsea Landing, now Norwich City, Thomas taking the north and Enos the south part. He was also engaged in the manufacture of leather and shoe making, in connection with farming. He d. Jan. 23, 1831, in the 80th year of his age.

HISTORY OF STONINGTON.

CHILDREN:

26 THOMAS, b. in Stonington, Conn., Sept. 21, 1781, m. Mary, daughter of Peleg and Lucretia Billings Shaw, of Westerly, R. I., April 4, 1813.
27 MARY, b. in Stonington, Conn., July 12, 1784.
28 HENRY, b. in Stonington, Conn., Aug. 26, 1788.
29 DUDLEY, b. in Stonington, Conn., March 18, 1795.
30 JULIA, b. in Stonington, Conn., Aug. 24, 1797.
31 CLARISSA, b. in Stonington, Conn., March 29, 1803.

Enos Davis (No. 13) m. Phebe Mulford in 1792; m. 2d, Mrs. Lois (Palmer) Perkins of Groton, Conn. He d. May 31, 1837.

CHILDREN:

32 PHEBE MULFORD, b. in Stonington, Conn., in 1793, m. Jason Rogers.
33 JEREMIAH, b. in Stonington, Conn., Oct. 1, 1795, m. Harriet Sydleman.
34 HULDAH, b. in Stonington, Conn., Aug. 15, 1799, m. George A. Sydleman.
35 FANNY, b. in Preston, Conn., Sept. 12, 1802, m. George A. Sydleman.

John Davis (No. 21) m. Sally Stanton Feb. 27, 1804 (No. 65), Thomas Stanton family, both of Stonington, Conn. He d. April 21, 1864; she d. Sept. 6, 1861.

CHILDREN:

36 CLARISSA, b. June 18, 1806, m. James Green of Westerly March 10, 1857.
37 JOHN, b. April 11, 1808, m. Phebe M., daughter of Jeremiah Davis (No. 33), Dec. 22, 1851.
38 ABIGAIL, b. April 6, 1810, m. Thomas W. Robinson Nov. 25, 1830.
39 SARAH, b. Dec. 15, 1813.
40 MARY, b. May 29, 1814, m. Oliver D. Cole of Hopkinton, R. I., Jan. 14, 1839.
41 THOMAS WILLIAM, b. June 11, 1818, m. Susan Davis March 14, 1842.

DEAN FAMILY.

1. JAMES DEAN, the first person of this family who came to Stonington to reside, was the son of Walter Dean and wife, Eleanor Cogoes Dean, of Somerset, South County, England, and the grandson of William Dean of said county, England.

Walter Dean, the father of Mr. James Dean, after he reached New England in 1638, lived for about one year in Dorchester, Mass., after which he moved with his family to Taunton, Plymouth County, Mass., where his son, James Dean, was born in 1647, and married Sarah Tisdale, daughter of John and Sarah (Walker) Tisdale, in 1693, and for a short time resided in Scituate, Mass. In 1675, James Dean came to Stonington and entered into an arrangement with the town by which it was agreed and made obligatory on both parties by a vote of the town, legally warned and held Feb. 28th, 1676, and publicly assented to by him. He was a blacksmith, and agreed to do the smith work of the inhabitants of the town in consideration of a grant of land and pledge, on the part of the most prominent persons then residing here, to assist him in money and material for building him a dwelling house and smith shop. In 1677 the town granted him another tract of land of one hundred acres. Mr. Dean continued to do the smithery of the town until 1682, when at a legal town meeting it was passed by a vote that Mr. Dean had performed all of the conditions of his agreement with the town.

Mr. James Dean erected him a dwelling house a short distance east of the Quarry Ledge at Quiambaug, with his shop nearby, and commenced business there in the latter part of the year 1676. Subsequently he received other grants of land from the town and individuals, and became a prominent man in the affairs of the town, until 1698, when, with several planters here, he went up and joined the settlement of the town of Plainfield, Conn., and was chosen town clerk there in 1699.

When Mr. James Dean had in contemplation his migration to Plainfield, he sold and turned over his smithing business to his son, James Dean, who was his oldest child.

HISTORY OF STONINGTON.

CHILDREN OF JAMES DEAN AND WIFE, SARAH DEAN:

2 JAMES, b. Oct. 31, 1674.
3 SARAH, b. Sept. 4, 1676.
4 JOHN, b. May 15, 1678, m. Lydia Thatcher, June 10, 1708.
5 MARY, b. March 28, 1680, m. Thomas Thatcher of Lebanon, Conn.
6 ONESIPHORES, b. March 28, 1680, twin, d. young.
7 FRANCIS, b. in 1682, d. Aug. 9, 1700.
8 WILLIAM, b. Sept. 24, 1684, d. Oct. 7, 1684.
9 HANNAH, b. in 1686.
10 WILLIAM, b. Sept. 12, 1689, m. Sarah ————, who d. in Plainfield, Dec. 21, 1746.
11 NATHAN, b. in 1693, m. Joannah Fisher at Dorchester, Mass., May 17, 1716.
12 JONATHAN, b. in 1694, m. at New London, Conn., Jan. 17, 1716, Sarah Douglass, and they became the parents of nine children.

Our Stonington records show that Mr. James Dean, Sr., conveyed by deed to his son, James Dean, Jr., two of his land grants in Stonington, Conn., and James Dean, Jr., remained in Stonington and built the old Dean House in the year 1700, which was destroyed by fire in 1848. Mr. James Dean, Jr., did not confine himself to the smithing business, but learned the business or trade of fulling and dressing woolen cloth, and for that purpose erected a dam and fulling mill on the Mistuxet brook, about one-half of the distance from the old Post road down to the dam of the Dean mill pond. There he continued his business until his son, John Dean, reached manhood, when he and his father built a new dam and erected another fulling mill near his dwelling house, where the dam now crosses the Mistuxet brook. Afterward they devoted their time and attention to cloth dressing until 1807, when the fulling mill was enlarged into what was known as a factory building, with a grist mill, with new and improved machinery, for cloth dressing, wool carding and for the manufacturing of cotton and woolen goods. The new deal was consummated mainly by James Dean, the son of John Dean, with whom he had been in business from his early manhood. Mr. James Dean continued in business until 1830, when he retired.

James Dean (No. 2) m. 1st, Sarah Packer June 2, 1697, and m. for his second wife Mrs. Jerusha (Saxton) Palmer (No. 24), Palmer family, Dec. 29, 1735. He d. Oct. 22, 1747.

CHILDREN:

13 JAMES, b. March 19, 1698.
14 SARAH, b. April 23, 1699.
15 FRANCIS, b. July 2, 1701.

DEAN FAMILY.

16 CHRISTOPHER, b. April 9, 1702.
17 ELIZABETH, b. Oct. 5, 1703, m. William Dean Dec. 25, 1735.
18 JABEZ, b. Feb. 16, 1705.
19 JOHN, b. April 14, 1707.
20 BENAJAH, b. March 6, 1710.
21 DAVID, b. April 30, d. Sept. 24, 1711.
22 SARAH, b. Dec. 20, 1712.
23 THANKFUL, b. Jan. 13, 1714.

John Dean (No. 19) of Stonington m. Martha Black of Groton, Oct. 17, 1750, by Ebenezer Rossiter.

CHILDREN:

24 JAMES, b. Sept. 9, 1751.
25 JOHN, b. Jan. 14, 1753.
26 SARAH, b. Oct. 13, 1754, and d. May 8, 1766.
27 CHRISTOPHER, b. Jan. 26, 1756.
28 WELTHIAN, b. June 17, 1757, m. Amos Gallup (No. 101), that family.
29 MARTHA, b. Nov. 24, 1758.
30 THANKFUL, b. July 26, 1760, m. Nathan Denison (No. 306), that family.
31 JABEZ, b. Jan. 2, 1762.
32 PRUDENCE, b. Dec. 29, 1763, d. young.
33 PHANNEE, b. Sept. 6, 1765.
34 JESSE, b. June 13, 1769.

James Dean (No. 24) m. Prudence Brown (No. 286), that family, Sept. 9, 1796, both of Stonington; she d. July 22, 1799.

CHILDREN:

35 PRUDENCE B., b. June 3, 1799, m. Judge Asa Fish (No. 46), that family.

Jesse Dean (No. 34) and Nancy Denison (No. 342), that family, both of Stonington, were m. Dec. 6, 1801.

CHILDREN:

36 JESSE, Jr., b. Oct. 22, 1802, never married.
37 NANCY, b. Oct. 2, 1803, m. Mr. Ezra Chesebrough (No. 379), that family.
38 FANNY, b. Nov. 23, 1806, m. Elias Gallup of Groton Sept. 28, 1828.

DENISON FAMILY.

The Denison family of New England was originally from Bishop's Stratford, Hertford shier, England. From the old Parish Register there, Stratford is spelled Stortford, and Denison is spelled in various ways, viz.: Denyson, Dennyson, Denizen, Denizon.

1. JOHN DENYSON, living at Stortford in 1567, d. there of plague, and was buried Dec. 4, 1582. He m. Agnes ———, who, after his death, m. May 3, 1584, John Gace, for by his will proved in 1602, he mentions George, Edward and William Denyson, children of my wife, also Elizabeth Crouch, a daughter of my wife.

CHILDREN OF JOHN AND AGNES DENYSON.
2 LUCE, bapt. 1567, buried at Stortford Dec. 9, 1582.
3 WILLIAM, bapt. at Stortford Feb. 3, 1571.
4 EDWARD, bapt. at Stortford April 6, 1575.
5 MARY, bapt. at Stortford April 28, 1577.
6 ELIZABETH, bapt. at Stortford Aug. 23, 1579.
7 GEORGE, bapt. at Stortford March 17, 1582.

William Denison (No. 3) m. Margaret (Chandler) Monck at Stortford, Eng., Nov. 7, 1603. He was very well seated in Stortford or Stratford, but hearing of the then famous transplantation to New England, unsettled himself and recalling his son Daniel from Cambridge, removed himself and family in the year 1631 to New England, and brought over with him his son Daniel, then aged about 19 years, and two younger brothers, Edward and George, leaving his oldest son, John, who had also been bred at Cambridge and was then a minister, married, with a good portion, and who lived about Pelham or in Hartford shier, not far from Stratford, where they were all born. He was Vicar of Standon, County Herts, 1660 to 1670. William Denison brought with him into New England a very good estate and settled himself at Roxbury, Mass., and there lived till Jan. 25, 1653, when he died, having buried his wife about 8 years before, viz., 1645.

CHILDREN OF WILLIAM AND MARGARET DENISON.
8 JOHN, bapt. at Stratford April 7, 1605, educated at Cambridge and became a minister, m. ———.

DENISON FAMILY. 335

9 WILLIAM, bapt. at Stratford Oct. 5, 1606, and at about the age of 18 years must needs go a soldier into Holland in the year 1624, at the famous siege of Breda, when it was taken by Spinola and Count Mansfield, who had an army out of England to raise the siege, but the army miscarried and this William was never heard of again.
10 GEORGE, bapt. at Stratford Oct. 15, 1609, buried there 1615.
11 DANIEL, bapt. at Stratford Oct. 18, 1612, graduated at Cambridge University and went to New England in 1631.
12 SARAH, bapt. 1615, and buried at Stratford 1615.
13 EDWARD, bapt. at Stratford Nov. 3, 1616, went to New England in 1631.
14 GEORGE, bapt. at Stratford Dec. 10, 1620, went to New England in 1631.

Edward Denison (No. 4) m. in the year 1631, removed himself and family into Ireland, where he died and left a son, called John Denison, who was a soldier and major of a regiment in the time of the wars, and Deputy Governor of Cork. He was living in Dublin in the year 1670.

EDWARD DENISON'S CHILDREN WERE:
15 ANNE, bapt. Feb. 19, 1603.
16 SUSAN, bapt. Nov. 24, 1605.
17 ELIZABETH, bapt. Sept. 18, 1608, buried Aug. 30, 1615.
18 JOHN, bapt. Sept. 13, 1612.

George Denison (No. 7) m. Constance, daughter of William Glascock, Esq., and widow of ———— Gooch.

THEIR CHILDREN:
19 GEORGE, said to have been living at Stortford in 1672, and m. Mary ————. They had two children, who both d. young. He d. Dec. 9, 1678, and Mary d. March 22, 1678.

Daniel Denison (No. 11) came with his father to New England in 1631.

The following is from the New England Historical and Genealogical Register of April, 1892, written by himself:

"I was the eldest of the three brothers that was brought to New England, and the next year after our arrival (viz.) in the year 1632, on the 18th day of October, on which day twenty years before I was bapt. at Stratford, and seven years before I was admitted into the University of Cambridge, I married Patience, the second daughter of Thomas Dudley, who was a principal undertaker of the Plantation of Massachusetts, and one of those first comers in the year 1630 that brought over the patent and settled the government. He came over Deputy Governor, and was afterwards at divers times Governor. Thomas Dudley then lived at Cambridge, but afterwards removed to Ipswich, where he stayed one year, settling himself at Roxbury, where he d. July 30,

1653, and his wife d. about 10 years before, the latter end of December, 1643.

"For myself, after I was married to Patience Dudley, I lived about 2 years at Cambridge, and in the year 1635 I removed to Ipswich, where we lived together without children till Jan. 16, 1640, when my son John was born, and two years and quarter after, Elizabeth was born, April 10, 1642; about nine years after another daughter, Mary, was born, and three years after Deborah, our last, was born.

CHILDREN OF DANIEL AND PATIENCE DENISON:
20 JOHN, b. Jan. 16, 1640.
21 ELIZABETH, b. April 1, 1642, m. 1660, John Rogers, having five children.
22 MARY, b. 1651, d. young.
23 DEBORAH, b. 1654, d. young.

Edward Denison (No. 13) was married about the beginning of the year 1641, and lived the rest of his days at Roxbury in the same house his father built, lived and died in. Edward m. March 20, 1641, Elizabeth, daughter of Joseph Weld. He departed this life in April, 1669, and left but one son, William, and five daughters, of all his large family.

CHILDREN OF EDWARD AND ELIZABETH DENISON:
24 ELIZABETH, b. Aug. 8, 1642.
25 JOHN, b. May 14, 1644, d. young.
26 EDWARD, who d. Oct. 6, 1646.
27 JEREMIAH, b. Dec. 6, 1647, d. young.
28 JOSEPH, bapt. April 8, 1649, d. young.
29 MARGARET, bapt. Dec. 19, 1650, m. Daniel Mason (No. 8), that family.
30 MARY, bapt. March 27, 1654.
31 HANNAH, bapt. Sept. 16, 1655.
32 SARAH, bapt. Dec. 6, 1657.
33 DEBORAH, bapt. Sept. 13, 1660, d. young.
34 Baby, b. and d. June 2, 1664.
35 WILLIAM, b. Sept. 18, 1664.
36 DEBORAH, b. Oct. 30, 1666, d. young.

Edward Denison d. April 26, 1668, and his widow d. Feb. 5, 1717.

George Denison (No. 14) m. about 1640 Bridget Thompson, b. Sept. 11, 1622 (No. 4), Thompson family; she was daughter of John Thompson and wife Alice, gentleman of Preston, of Northamptonshire, Eng. She d. 1643. They had two children.

37 SARAH, b. March 20, 1641, m. Thomas Stanton (No. 2), that family.
38 HANNAH, b. May 20, 1643, m. Nathaniel Chesebrough, 1659 (No. 9), that family. She m. 2d, Joseph Saxton July 15, 1680.

This Capt. George Denison having buried his wife in the year 1643, went back to England the same year, where, as we learn from a letter of his brother, Maj. Gen. Daniel Denison, published in the April number of the New England Historical and Genealogical Register of 1892, in which he says: "My brother George was a soldier there above a year, was at the battle of York, or Marston Moor, where he did good service, and was afterwards taken prisoner, but got free and married a second wife, Miss Ann Borodell, and with her returned to New England in the year 1645, and took up his abode again in Roxbury, Mass., where he continued to live until 1651, when he came with his family to Connecticut and located himself at New London, Conn., where he resided until 1654, when he came to Stonington with his family to live, and remained there until his death, which took place at Hartford, Conn., Oct. 24, 1694." We learn from the records of Massachusetts and Connecticut that Capt. George Denison was not only distinguished as a civilian, but became the most distinguished soldier of Connecticut in her early settlement, except Maj. John Mason. His military services are on record in our Colonial archives where his eminence is recognized and portrayed. Also, you will find his name in the History of New London and Stonington, where his services are acknowledged and described in full. There is no date of the marriage of Capt. George Denison and Ann Borodell, but he was doubtless married in England. Pending their courtship an agreement was made between them, which was afterwards ratified and confirmed at Hartford, Conn., May 3, 1662, as follows: "This witnesseth that I, George Denison, of Southertown, in Connecticut jurisdiction in New England, for and in consideration of a jointure due unto my now wife, Ann Borodell Denison, upon marriage and upon my former engagement, in consideration of the sum of three hundred pounds by me received of Mr. John Borodell, which he freely gave to my wife, his sister, Ann Borodell Denison, and I have had the use and improvement of and for, and in consideration of conjugal and dearer affection moving me, thereunto." This jointure agreement may be seen on the First Book of Connecticut State Records, in Hartford, Conn., page 274. This recorded instrument is proof positive of the marriage of Capt. George Denison and wife, Ann Borodell, to say nothing of the births of their children and his will in his own handwriting bequeathing to them his entire property.

CHILDREN OF CAPT. GEORGE DENISON AND ANN BORODELL.
39 JOHN B., b. July 14, 1646.
40 ANN, b. May 20, 1649, m. Gershom Palmer. See Palmer family (No. 12).
41 BORODELL, b. in 1651, m. Samuel Stanton. See Stanton family (No. 11).
42 GEORGE, b. in 1653.
43 WILLIAM, b. in 1655, m. widow Sarah Prentice (No. 10), of Stanton family.
44 MARGARET, b. in 1657, m. James Brown, Jr.
45 MARY, b. in 1659, d. March 10, 1671.

NOTE.—Capt. George Denison (No. 14) was captain of New London County forces in King Philip's war, with Capt. John Mason, Jr., under Maj. Robert Treat, in the great swamp fight Dec. 19, 1675. Also served the next year in command of the forces raised by him as Provo-Marshal, who pursued the remnant of the Narragansett and Wampanaug Indians, and succeeded in defeating them and capturing the Indian Chief Canonchet, who was brought to Stonington, and on his refusal to make peace with the English, was shot. He assisted as magistrate to enable the Pequot chiefs designated by the English to control the remnants of the Pequots. He was assistant and deputy from Stonington to the General Court for fifteen sessions.

The Town of New London granted Capt. George Denison 200 acres of land in the Pequot-se-pos valley at Mystic in 1652, upon which he subsequently built him a dwelling house (May 3, 1663, it was raised), wherein he and his family made their permanent, final home, known as the Oliver Denison house, and which stood a few feet west of the present residence of Mr. and Mrs. Reuben Ford (1899). He d. Oct. 24, 1694, and his widow d. Sept. 26, 1712, aged 97, by the gravestone, which may be found in the Elm Grove Cemetery at Mystic.

NOTE.—One of the ancestors of Admiral George Dewey was a Stonington man, viz., Capt. George Denison (No. 14), the distinguished Indian warrior of Connecticut, who came to New England with his parents and settled in Roxbury, Mass., where Capt. Denison was married to his first wife, Bridget Thompson, in 1640. Their daughter, Hannah, b. May 20, 1643, m. Nathaniel Chesebrough of Stonington in 1659. Her husband d. Nov. 22, 1678. She m. 2d, Capt. Joseph Saxton of Stonington, July 15, 1680; their daughter, Mercy Saxton, b. in 1686, married 1st, Isaac Bailey of Roxbury, Mass., Jan. 4, 1702. In 1707, Mr. and Mrs. Bailey moved with their family to Lebanon, Conn. Mr. Bailey died, date not preserved. His widow, Mrs. Mercy Bailey (nee Saxton) married 2d, William Dewey of Lebanon, great grandson of Thomas Dewey, the emigrant ancestor of the family, who came from Sandwich, England, soon after 1630, who settled first at Dorchester, Mass., but soon after migrated to Windsor, Conn., where he married Frances Clarke in 1635. Their son, Dea. Josiah Dewey, Sen., of Northampton, Mass., and Lebanon, Conn., b. at Windsor, Conn., Oct. 10, 1641, m. Hepzibah Lyman, Nov. 6, 1662; their son, Josiah Dewey, b.

DENISON FAMILY. 339

Dec. 24, 1666, m. Mehitable Miller, Jan. 15, 1691; their son, William Dewey, b. Jan., 1692, m. Mercey Bailey (nee Saxton), July 2, 1713; their son, Simeon Dewey, b. May 1, 1718, m. Anna Phelps, March 29, 1739; their son, William Dewey, b. Jan. 11, 1746, m. Rebecca Carrier, in 1768; their son, Capt. Simeon Dewey, b. Aug. 20, 1770, m. Prudence Yeomans, Feb. 27, 1794; their son, Dr. Julius Dewey, b. Aug. 28, 1801, m. Mary Perrin, June 9, 1825; their son, Admiral George Dewey, b. in 1837.

John Denison (No. 20) m. Martha, daughter of Dep. Gov. Symonds, Feb. 2, 1663, and lived at the farm at Ipswich the remainder of his days, he was married seven years and had three children.

46 JOHN, b. Sept. 22, 1665.
47 MARTHA, b. March 1, 1668, m. Matthew Whipple.
48 DANIEL, b. April 14, 1671.

John Denison (No. 20) was taken violently sick the first day, and died on the 9th day of Jan., 1670, aged not quite 31 years. "So early had he finished his course and done his work, and if his work had then to have been done (as he then said) he should have been miserable; but he had lived a Godly and exemplary life, being a constant seeker of God. His wife afterwards said he used to pray five times a day; he was a dutiful child, a loving husband and father, a loving friend, a good man in all his ways and he departed most Christian-like and comfortable, to the unspeakable grief and loss of all his friends." On the beginning of April, 1672, Mrs. Martha (Symonds) Denison m. for her second husband, Mr. Richard Martyn, and went to live at Portsmouth taking with them two children, Daniel and Martha, and leaving the son John with his grandparents.

John B. Denison (No. 39) m. Phebe, daughter of Robert Lay of Saybrook, Nov. 26, 1667. He served in the Colonial Indian war. She d. 1699, aged 49 yrs. He d. 1698.

CHILDREN:
49 PHEBE, b. 1667, d. young.
50 JOHN, b. Jan. 1, 1669.
51 GEORGE, b. March 28, 1671.
52 ROBERT, b. Sept. 17, 1673.
53 WILLIAM, b. April 7, 1677.
54 DANIEL, b. March 28, 1680.
55 SAMUEL, b. Feb. 23, 1683, d. young.
56 ANN, b. Oct. 3, 1684, m. 1st Samuel Minor (No. 45); 2d, Edward Denison (No. 59), of Westerly, R. I.
57 SARAH, b. July 29, 1692, m. Isaac Williams (No. 156).
58 PHEBE, b., probably, between Ann and Sarah. Phebe Denison (No. 58) m. Ebenezer Billings. See that family (No. 22).

George Denison (No. 42) m. Mercy Gorham, daughter of John Gorham, and wife Desire Howland, daughter of John Howland of the May Flower. John Gorham was son of Ralph Gorham of Plymouth, b. in England, baptized at Benefield, Northamptonshire, Jan. 28, 1621, and was captain in King Philip's war. Date of the m. of George Denison and Mercy Gorham is not known, but she d. Sept. 24, 1725, in the 67th year of her age, and he d. Dec. 27, 1711, in his 59th year.

CHILDREN:

59 EDWARD, bapt. in 1683.
60 JOSEPH, bapt. in 1683, m. Prudence Minor. See that family (No. 56).
61 MERCY, bapt. in 1683, m. Mordecai Dunbar.
62 SAMUEL, bapt. in 1686, m. Mrs. Mary Miner. See that family (No. 57).
63 ELIZABETH, bapt. in 1690, m. Christopher Champlin, Jr.
64 DESIRE, bapt. in 1693, m. John Williams. See that family (No. 156).
65 THANKFUL, bapt. in 1695, m. Thomas Stanton. See that family (No. 271).
66 GEORGE, bapt. in 1699.

Capt. William Denison (No. 43) m. Mrs. Sarah (Stanton) Prentice (No. 10), the widow of the second Thomas Prentice, and daughter of Thomas Stanton. William Denison d. March 2, 1715, and his wife d. Aug. 7, 1713. He served in King Philip's war.

CHILDREN:

67 WILLIAM, b. March 24, 1687.
68 SARAH, b. April 14, 1689, m. Benjamin Avery (No. 45), that family, and lived in Groton.
69 GEORGE, b. Feb. 28, 1692.

Rev. John Denison (No. 46), m. Elizabeth, dau. of Nathaniel Saltonstall of Ipswich, Mass.

CHILDREN:

70 RUTH, b. 1686, m. Joseph Kingsbury.
71 JOHN, b. 1688, m. Mary Leverett, 1719.
72 HANNAH, b. 1689, m. Nathaniel Kingsbury, 1710.

Rev. John Denison d. 1689, aged 24, and his widow m. Rev. Roland Cotton.

John Denison (No. 50) m. Ann (No. 19), daughter of Capt. John Mason, in 1690, and they lived in Saybrook, Conn., and d. there 1699.

CHILDREN:

73 JOHN, b. March 30, 1692, d. in 1732, unmarried.
74 DANIEL, b. Oct. 13, 1693, m. Mehitable Foster.
75 JAMES, b. Feb. 26, 1695, d. in 1717, unmarried.
76 ABIGAIL, b. Aug. 25, 1696, m. Dea. Ebenezer Pratt May 6, 1717.
77 JABEZ, b. Aug., 1698, m. Dorothy Cogswell.

DENISON FAMILY.   341

In March, 1701, Mrs. Ann (Mason) Denison m. Samuel Cogswell, her first husband having d. in 1699.

George Denison (No. 51) settled in New London and m. in 1694 Mrs. Mary (Wetherell) Harris. George Denison d. Jan. 22, 1720. His wife d. Aug. 22, 1711.

CHILDREN:
78 GRACE, b. March 4, 1695, m. Edward Hallam.
79 PHEBE, b. March 16, 1697, m. Gibson Harris.
80 HANNAH, b. March 28, 1699, m. John Hough.
81 BORODELL, b. May 17, 1701, m. Jonathan Latimer.
82 DANIEL, b. June 27, 1703, m. Rachel Starr.
83 WETHERELL, b. Aug. 24, 1705, m. Lydia Moore.
84 ANN, b. Aug. 15, 1707, m. twice.
85 SARAH, b. June 20, 1710, m. William Douglass.

Robert Denison (No. 52) m. in 1696 Joanna Stanton (No. 266), that family. He settled in what is now known as Montville; he d. in 1737.

CHILDREN:
86 ANN, b. in 1695, d. young.
87 ROBERT, b. in 1697; twice m.; d. in Nova Scotia.
88 JOHN, b. March 28, 1698, m. Patience Griswold.
89 JOANNA, b. in 1699, m. Thomas Morehouse.
90 MARY, b. ———, d. young.
91 NATHANIEL, b. in 1702, d. in 1722.
92 ANDREW, b. in 1704, m. Mrs. Rebecca (Chesebrough) Turner (No. 54), Chesebrough family.
93 SARAH, b. in 1706, d. in 1714.
94 ANN, b. in 1707, m. James Fitch in 1725.
95 THOMAS, b. Oct. 20, 1709, m. Elizabeth Bailey.
96 LUCY, b. in 1711, m. Samuel Rogers.
97 ELIZABETH, b. in 1712, d. young.
98 ABIGAIL, b. in 1714, m. William Wattles.
99 GEORGE, b. in 1715, d. young.

William Denison (No. 53) m. in 1698 Mary (No. 43), dau. of the first John Avery of Groton. They lived in North Stonington, Conn., he d. there Jan. 30, 1730. His widow, being 52 years old, was m. Jan. 12, 1732, to Daniel Palmer (No. 23), who was 59 years old. She outlived him and d. in 1762, aged 82 yrs.

WILLIAM DENISON AND MARY'S CHILDREN:
102 MARY, b. in 1699, d. in 1699.
103 MARY, twin, b. in 1701.
104 PHEBE, twin, b. in 1701.
105 ANN, b. in 1703, m. John Denison (No. 126), in 1720, and was drowned in a well in 1721.
106 WILLIAM, b. in 1705.

107 ABIGAIL, b. in 1708, m. Roger Billings. See Billings family (No. 18).
108 LUCY, b. in 1710, m. John Swan 2d. See Swan family (No. 21.)
109 AVERY, b. in 1712.
110 THANKFUL, b. in 1714, m. Joseph Billings. See Billings family (No. 33).
111 DESIRE, b. in 1716, m. John Stanton. See Stanton family (No. 116).
112 CHRISTOPHER, b. in 1719.
113 JOHN, b. Feb. 23, 1722, m. Martha Wheeler (No. 339), Wheeler family.

Daniel Denison (No. 54) m. 1st, Jan. 1, 1703, Mary (No. 269), dau. of Robert and Joanna (Gardner) Stanton, and she was the mother of 11 children. She d. Sept. 2, 1724, in the 38th year of her age. She was b. Feb. 3, 1687, and m. when not sixteen years old. He m. 2d, Jane Cogswell of Long Island, Oct. 27, 1726; and 3d, Nov. 17, 1737, Mrs. Abigail (Fish) Eldredge, who outlived him about 37 years, and d. June 17, 1784, aged 94 yrs. He d. Oct. 13, 1747, aged over 67 yrs. The children, all by the first wife, Mary Stanton, were:

CHILDREN:
114 MARY, b. Aug. 29, 1705, m. Nathan Smith.
115 DANIEL, b. Nov. 11, 1707, d. young.
116 BEEBE, b. Jan. 27, 1709, m. Sarah Avery (No. 88).
117 RACHEL, b. July 16, 1710.
118 ESTHER, b. March 22, 1712, m. Isaac Smith.
119 LUCY, b. Oct. 13, 1714, m. Jonas Prentice Nov. 29, 1733 (No. 17).
120 JOHN, b. May 21, 1716.
121 PRUDENCE, b. Jan. 27, 1718, m. William Denison. See Denison family (No. 158.)
122 DANIEL, b. March 22, 1720.
123 PHEBE, b. April 24, 1723, m. William Avery. See Avery family (No. 85).
124 SARAH, b. Aug. 25, 1724.

Edward Denison (No. 59) had two wives; first, Mercy ———, the mother of his children, living in 1715; the second wife was his cousin, Ann (No. 56), dau. of Capt. John Denison, and widow of Samuel Minor, to whom he was m. March 2, 1718. He was drowned Dec. 9, 1726.

CHILDREN:
125 EDWARD, b. in 1699, d. young.
126 JOHN, b. in 1701.
127 ELISHA, b. in 1703, d. young.
128 MARY, b. in 1705, m. Benjamin Billings. See Billings family (No. 30).
129 DESIRE, b. ———, m. Jabez Smith Nov. 11, 1730.
130 ABBY, b. ———, and m. Andrew Galloway.

Joseph Denison (No. 60) m. Feb. 17, 1707, Prudence (No. 56), dau. of Dr. Joseph Minor. He d. Feb. 18, 1725. His wife d. May 26, 1726, in her 68th year. He lived and d. in Stonington.

DENISON FAMILY.   343

CHILDREN:

131 JOSEPH, b. Sept. 24, 1707.
132 PRUDENCE, b. Nov. 28, 1709, m. Benjamin Sprague Jan. 20, 1726.
133 BORODELL, b. Feb. 14, 1712, m. Ezekiel Turner.
134 AMOS, b. Feb. 18, 1714.
135 NATHAN, b. Feb. 20, 1716.
136 ELIZABETH, b. Feb. 15, 1720, m. Samuel Minor. See that family (No. 73).
137 JOANNA, b. Jan. 28, 1718, m. Henry Hewitt. See Hewitt family (No. 14).
138 THANKFUL, bapt. April 7, 1723, m. Elisha Williams (No. 51). See that family.
139 ANNA, b. May 3, 1724, m. Amos Allen in 1739.

Samuel Denison (No. 62) m. Mrs. Mary (Lay) Minor, the widow of Christopher Minor (No. 57), Minor family, whom she m. March 9, 1704, and her maiden name was Lay. They lived in Stonington till July 4, 1716. when he bought a homestead on Oyster River, in Saybrook, Conn., and immediately occupied it. His first four children were b. in Stonington; the others in Saybrook.

CHILDREN:

140 SARAH, b. Jan. 6, 1710, m. William Babcock.
141 SAMUEL, b. Oct. 23, 1711.
142 MERCY, b. in 1713, m. Nathaniel Chapman.
143 ELIZABETH, bapt. June 6, 1714.
144 JOANNA, b. Dec. 13, 1716, m. Moses Tyler.
145 MARY, twin, b. Jan. 6, 1718.
146 GEORGE, twin, b. Jan. 6, 1718.
147 CHRISTOPHER, b. 1720.
148 GIDEON, b. in 1724, m. Elizabeth ——— in 1752.
149 STEPHEN, b. Feb. 6, 1725.

George Denison (No. 66) m. 1st, Sarah Miner (No. 81), Sept. 28, 1721. She was dau. of Dr. Joseph and Sarah (Tracey) Miner. She d. Sept. 27, 1724, in the 25th year of her age. He was m. 2d, to Joanna Hinckley (No. 21), May 10, 1727. She was dau. of Samuel and Martha (Lathrop) Hinckley. He lived on his father's farm at Westerly, R. I., and d. Jan. 16, 1737.

CHILDREN:

150 JOSEPH b. Jan. 26, 1723.
151 MARY, b. Sept. 24, 1724.
152 ELIJAH, b. July 6, 1728, d. young.
153 GEORGE, b. April 14, 1730, d. young.
154 SARAH, b. Sept. 7, 1733, m. Ezra Keeney.

William Denison (No. 67) m. Mercy Gallup (No. 35) May 10, 1710. They lived in Stonington, Conn. He d. Feb. 24, 1724, aged 37; she d. March 2, 1724, aged 35.

CHILDREN:

155 MERCY, b. June 25, 1711, m. Hubbard Burrows (No. 14), Burrows family.
156 SARAH, b. July 2, 1713, m. Elisha Niles.
157 ESTHER, b. Feb. 6, 1715, m. Jonathan Wheeler. See that family (No. 21).
158 WILLIAM, b. Dec. 9, 1716.
159 HANNAH, b. April 19, 1719, d. 1721.
160 BENADAM, b. Feb. 6, 1721.
161 JONATHAN, b. May 12, 1722, m. Martha Williams (No. 448) that family; no children.
162 NATHAN, b. Feb. 11, 1724.

George Denison (No. 69) m. Lucy Gallup (No. 39), Gallup family, June 6, 1717. They lived on the old homestead farm in Stonington.

CHILDREN:

163 ANN, b. Aug. 16, 1718, d. young.
164 Daughter, b. and d. in Sept., 1720.
165 LUCY, b. Oct. 13, 1721, d. young.
166 MARY, b. Nov. 27, 1723, d. young.
167 GEORGE, b. July 3, 1725.
168 WILLIAM, b. June 14, 1727.
169 MERCY, b. Feb. 24, 1729, m. Elisha Gallup. See that family (No. 90).
170 ESTHER, b. Sept. 16, 1732, d. in 1754.
171 SAMUEL, b. Feb. 18, 1735, d. Sept. 10, 1754.
172 DAVID, b. Jan. 29, 1736.

William Denison (No. 106) m. 1st, Jan. 30, 1732, Hannah Burrows (No. 15), who d. Jan. 1, 1737; he m. 2d, Hannah Tyler Jan. 20, 1738, who d. in 1797, aged 86. He d. Jan. 29, 1760.

CHILDREN:

173 WILLIAM, b. Dec. 31, 1733, d. young.
174 JOSEPH, b. Feb. 24, 1735.
175 HANNAH, b. Dec. 1, 1736, m. Dr. Charles Phelps (No. 27), Phelps family.
176 NATHAN, b. Feb. 24, 1739, d young.
177 DANIEL, b. July 20, 1740.
178 AMY, b. March 22, 1742, m. Thomas Swan (No. 34).
179 ANN, b. Sept. 12, 1744, m. George Palmer. See that family (No. 259).
180 ESTHER, b. April 23, 1746, m. John James.
181 SARAH, b. Feb. 7, 1748, m. John W. Geer.
182 JOHN, b. Nov. 5, 1749.
183 ELIJAH, b. Nov. 6, 1751, m. Mary Geer; no children.

Avery Denison (No. 109) m. Thankful Williams (No. 175) Jan. 31, 1734. They lived in North Stonington, Conn. He d. April 3, 1775; she d. May 2, 1767.

CHILDREN:

184 ELISHA, b. Nov. 3, 1734.
185 NATHAN, b. Aug. 12, 1736, d. young.
186 WILLIAM, b. March 22, 1738.

DENISON FAMILY.

187 DESIRE, b. June 5, 1739, m. Thomas Minor. See Minor family (No. 119).
188 MOLLY, b. Nov. 8, 1741, m. Jesse Denison (No. 234), that family, son of
189 PRUDENCE, b. Oct. 3, 1743, m. Joseph Noyes. See that family(No. 129).
190 MERCY, b. Nov. 7, 1745, m. Edward Eells (No. 22).
191 THANKFUL, b. July 17, 1747, m. Alexander Stewart.
192 ZERVIAH, b. July 13, 1751, d. unmarried.
193 REBECCA, b. March 24, 1754, d. unmarried.
194 AVERY, b. April 10, 1756.

Beebe Denison (No. 116) m. Sarah Avery (No. 88), dau. of Benjamin and Sarah (Denison) Avery, Jan. 27, 1709. He d. March 24, 1745, and she m. Benadam Denison Oct. 18, 1752 (No. 160), Denison family.

BEEBE DENISON'S CHILDREN:
195 MARY, b. Jan. 24, 1735, m. William Hilliard.
196 DANIEL, b. Feb. 9, 1737, d. young.
197 SARAH, b. Sept. 11, 1739, m. William Latham.
198 DANIEL, b. Nov. 9, 1742, m. Dorothy Denison (No. 303), daughter of George and Jane (Smith) Denison, in 1770. He d. Jan. 17, 1808, and she d. Feb. 22, 1803.

THEIR CHILDREN:
199 OLIVER, b. and d. unmarried in the war of 1812.
200 SAMUEL, b. and m. AliphWoodward, lived in Stonington, Conn.
201 BETSEY, b. and m. Arnold Chesebrough, and went to New York.
202 FANNY, b. and m. Robert Holmes; went to New York State.
203 DOROTHY, b. and m. Peleg Williams of Stonington (No. 78).
204 DANIEL, b. and d. unmarried.
205 JANE, b. and m. a Mr. Porter; went to New York State.
206 NANCY, b. and m. Daniel Gallup; went to New York State.

John Denison (No. 120) m. about 1738 Abigail Avery (No. 83) dau. of the second John Avery of Groton. They lived in Stonington, and had ten children.

CHILDREN:
207 ABIGAIL, b. and m. Zebulon Eliot.
208 DESIRE, b. and d. young.
209 AVERY, b. and d. young.
210 ANNA, b. and twice m.
211 LUCY, b. and d. unmarried.
212 MARY, b. 1750, and m. Stephen Avery (No. 131), no child.
213 SARAH, b. May 2, 1752, m. John Baldwin (No. 37), Jan. 23, 1772.
214 NATHAN, b. 1754, m. Betsey Conklin.
215 JULIA, b. 1758, m. Pierre Laroche.
216 ANDREW, b. Dec. 3, 1761, m. Sally Williams (No. 75).

Daniel Denison (No. 122) m. Esther Wheeler (No. 41) May 27, 1742; she was b. Feb. 15, 1722, and d. March 31, 1814. He d. in Stonington May 9, 1776.

THIRTEEN CHILDREN:

217 ESTHER, b. Oct. 11, 1743, and m. William Gardner.
218 DANIEL, b. Dec. 9, 1745, m. Elizabeth Andros.
219 PHEBE, b. Dec. 5, 1747, thrice m. (No. 169), Chesebrough family.
220 ROBERT, b. Dec. 12, 1749, m. Anna Chesebrough (No. 254).
221 ISAAC, b. Dec. 20, 1751, m. Eunice Williams (No. 82).
222 HENRY, b. Nov. 26, 1751, m. Mary Gallup (No. 125).
223 HANNAH, b. Feb. 13, 1755, d. young.
224 MARY, b. Nov. 6, 1757, twice m.; 1st, Jeremiah Holmes (No. 50); 2d, Jedediah Lee.
225 HANNAH, b. Oct. 16, 1759, m. John Gallup (No. 134).
226 BEEBE, b. Feb. 22, 1761, twice m.
227 FREDERICK, b. Sept. 21, 1762, m. Hannah Fish (No. 47), that family.
228 EUNICE, b. May 18, 1764, m. Reuben Hatch.
229 ANN B., or NANCY, b. Oct. 2, 1769, m. John Wheeler (No. 367).

John Denison (No. 126) m. Anna Denison (No. 105), daughter of William, of North Stonington, Conn., Nov. 9, 1720. She was drowned in a well Sept. 15, 1721, and he m. 2d, Mary Noyes (No. 104), daughter of Dr. James Noyes, and had these children:

CHILDREN:

230 ANN, child of 1st wife, b. and d. in 1721.
231 EDWARD, b. March 4, 1725, m. Lois Stanton (No. 340), that family, Dec. 19, 1750.
232 JOHN, b. Jan. 26, 1727, m. Eunice Stanton (No. 341), that family.
233 ANN (twin), bapt. Sept. 4, 1737, m. Nathaniel Minor (No. 151).
234 JESSE (twin), bapt. Sept. 4, 1737, m. Mary Denison (No. 188).
235 ELISHA, bapt. April 14, 1739, d. young.
236 MARY, bapt. Jan. 24, 1742, m. Oliver Smith.

The second wife d. June 14, 1742, and he m. Rebecca Noyes (No. 117), Noyes family, July 7, 1743. She was daughter of Capt. Thomas Noyes. They had

CHILDREN:

237 REBECCA, bapt. July 24, 1744, d. in infancy.
238 REBECCA, bapt. Nov. 3, 1745, d. young.
239 REBECCA, bapt. Aug. 2, 1747, m. Paul Crandall.
240 ELISHA, bapt. July 2, 1749, d. young.
241 ELISHA, bapt. Nov. 3, 1751, m. Elizabeth Noyes (No. 146).
242 MERCY, bapt. Feb. 24, 1754, m. Peleg Brown (No. 68), in the Chad Brown family.

The wife, Rebecca Noyes Denison, d. Sept. 11, 1754, and he m. for his fourth wife Sarah (Chesebrough) (No. 73), that family, who had been the wife of 1st, Capt. James Geer, second, the wife of Ebenezer Billings, and she became the wife of Capt. John Denison for her third husband, and for his fourth wife. He was also called Merchant John. The m. occurred March 3, 1762.

DENISON FAMILY. 347

She lies buried in the North Stonington Cemetery beside her Billings husband.

Joseph Denison, Jr. (No. 131) m. 1st, Jan. 16, 1733, Mrs. Content (Hewitt) Russell (No. 15), that family, widow of Ebenezer Russell. She d. childless, Sept. 20, 1749, and he m. 2d, Mrs. Bridget Wheeler, daughter of Thomas Noyes, April 23, 1751. Mrs. Bridget's first husband was Isaac Wheeler, who was drowned in Lantern Hill Pond. Mr. Joseph Denison, Jr., was made deason of the First Congregational Church in Stonington, Conn., July 21, 1748, and his name is signed to church records as late as March 30, 1789. He d. Feb. 15, 1795. His children, all by Mrs. Bridget (Noyes) Wheeler, were, viz.:

CHILDREN:

243 CONTENT, b. Jan. 29, 1752, m. John Williams (No. 206) of Robert Williams family.
244 PELEG, b. Nov. 24, 1753, d. young.
245 PELEG, b. July 6, 1755, m. Mary Gray.
246 AMOS, b. March 18, 1757, m. Hannah Williams (No. 217).
247 MARY, b. ———.
248 EZRA, b. May 5, 1759, d. young.
249 EPHRAIM (twin), b. May 5, 1761, d. young.
250 MANASSETH, (twin), b. May 5, 1761, d. young.
251 BRIDGET, b. March 23, 1763, m. Nehemiah Mason (No. 93), of Mason family, Nov. 6, 1782.
252 JOSEPH, bapt. April 23, 1765, d. young and unmarried Aug. 20, 1789.
253 ELIZABETH, bapt. April 26, 1767, d. young.

Amos Denison (No. 134) m. Martha Gallup (No. 88), Gallup family, May 20, 1742, and lived in Stonington; they had six children:

CHILDREN:

254 EUNICE, b. April 16, 1744, m. Gilbert Smith of Groton, Conn.
255 MARTHA, b. Dec. 30, 1746, m. Joshua Swan (No. 32), Dec. 1, 1763.
256 PRUDENCE, b. March 20, 1748, m. Stephen Babcock Aug. 21, 1766.
257 JOSEPH, b. March 20, 1750, m. Mary Smith of Norwich June 13, 1771.
258 AMOS, b. in 1752.
259 CYNTHIA, bapt. June 15, 1766, m. James Rogers of Richmond, R. I.

Nathan Denison (No. 135) m. Ann Carey in 1736; she was dau. of Eleazer Carey of Windham. Ann d. May 16, 1776, aged 60 yrs, and he m. 2d, Hannah Fuller, March 15, 1778, and about the year 1800 he went to Kingstown, Pa., where he d. March 10, 1803, aged 88 yrs. His children, all by the first wife:

CHILDREN:

260 JOSEPH, b. Nov. 2, 1738.
261 COL. NATHAN, b. Jan. 25, 1740.

262 ANN, b. Nov. 19, 1742, m. Solomon Huntington.
263 ELEAZER, b. Dec. 24, 1744, m. Susanna Elderkin.
264 LYDIA, b. April 27, 1747, m. Joshua Elderkin.
265 AMOS, b. May 31, 1749, d. young.

Joseph Denison (No. 150) m. Lucy Chesebrough (No. 110), Chesebrough family, in 1746. They lived in Stonington.

CHILDREN:

266 NATHANIEL, b. in 1748.
267 GEORGE, b. in 1750.
268 LUCY, b. in 1752.
269 SARAH, b. in 1754.
270 ANN, b. in 1756.
271 HANNAH, b. in 1758.
272 THANKFUL, b. in 1760.

Nathaniel Denison (No. 266) m. about 1767; he was a soldier of the Revolutionary war, and his grandson, Dudley F. Denison, had the gun he carried. He was lost at sea in 1795; his will is in the Stonington Probate Office.

CHILDREN:

273 BENADAM, b. in 1772.
274 BETSEY P., b. in 1782, m. Charles Palmer (No. 299).
275 HANNAH, b. and m. Henry Palmer (No. 295).
276 DESIRE, b. and m. Robert Bentley.
277 ETHER, b. and m. Joseph Davis.
278 MARY, b. and m. a Taylor.

Benadam Denison (No. 273) m. in 1794, Rhoda Randall (No. 88). They emigrated from Stonington to Halifax, Vt. His first five children were born in Stonington and the rest in Halifax.

CHILDREN:

279 BENADAM, b in 1795.
280 RHODA, b. in 1797.
281 PRUDENCE, b. in 1799.
282 ESTHER, b. in 1801.
283 BETSEY, b. in 1803.
284 CHARLES, b in 1805.
285 DUDLEY F., b. in 1808.
286 HANNAH, b. in 1810.
287 EUNICE, b. in 1812.
288 ANNIS, b. in 1815.

William Denison (No. 158) m. Prudence Denison (No. 121) June 23, 1737. They lived in Stonington, Conn.

CHILDREN:

289 WILLIAM, bapt. Oct. 15, 1738, d. young.
290 PRUDENCE, b. Nov. 27, 1740, m. James Minor (No. 332).

291 ANDREW, b. Nov. 30, 1742, d. young.
292 BEEBE, b. Jan. 1, 1744.
293 DARIUS, b. March 11, 1747, m. Mary Billings.
294 MERCY or MARY, b. July 19, 1749, m. Daniel Minor (No. 149).
295 ALICE, b. Nov. 27, 1753, m. Robert Denison (No. 299).

William Denison the 3d d. July 7, 1779, and his widow m. for her second husband Thomas Prentice, Dec. 9, 1779, and d. Feb. 11, 1812. This William Denison 3d was a very dissolute man up to about his 60th year, when he thought to experience religion, which so changed his life that he became a very prudent and exemplary man, and abandoned his drinking habits, and his property, which had been put into the hands of a conservator, was restored to him, and he became a very prudent, careful manager of it.

Benadam Denison (No. 160) m. Anna Swan (No. 28), Swan family, Nov. 3, 1742; lived in Stonington; m. 2d, Mrs. Sarah (Avery) Denison, widow of Beebe Denison (No. 88), Avery family.

CHILDREN:

296 LUCY, b. Jan. 8, 1744, m. William Gallup (No. 92).
297 JAMES, b. Aug. 25, 1745.
298 BENADAM, b. July 9, 1747, m. Dimis Reed in 1770, and lived in Norwich, Conn. They had eight children and he d. in 1811, and his wife d. in 1821.
299 ROBERT, b. Sept. 28, 1749.
300 GEORGE, b. Oct. 8, 1751.

George Denison (No. 167) m. Jane Smith, daughter of (No. 114) Mary Denison, and husband Nathan Smith. M. Feb. 23, 1748. They lived in Stonington on the old homestead and had

CHILDREN:

301 LUCY, b. Feb. 9, 1750; m. Elisha Williams. See that family (No. 79).
302 GEORGE, b. Sept. 16, 1753.
303 DOROTHY (twin), b. April 8, 1756, m. Daniel Denison (No. 198).
304 WILLIAM (twin), b. April 8, 1756.
305 OLIVER, b. March 2, 1758.
306 NATHAN, b. April 8, 1760.
307 GILBERT, b. Sept. 18, 1762.
308 ELISHA, b. Oct. 12, 1764, d. on the Jersey Prison ship in the Revolutionary war.
309 DUDLEY, b. July 25, 1767, m. Nancy Latimer in 1795, d. Oct. 1, 1797, aged 28 yrs; had no children.
310 ESTHER, b. Nov. 16, 1769, m. Enoch Burrows. See that family (No. 120).
311 JANE, b. Sept. 16, 1772, d. young.

William Denison (No. 168) m. Priscilla Fellows of Plainfield,

Conn.; had two children and d. Sept. 20, 1754. He was a physician.

CHILDREN:

312 MARY, b. Dec. 12, 1750; twice m.
313 PRISCILLA, b. Aug. 19, 1754, m. William Dixon of Rhode Island; she was brought up by her uncle and aunt, Mr. George Denison and wife, Jane (Smith) Denison. Their son, Nathan F. Dixon, was United States Senator from Rhode Island, and their grandson, Nathan F. Dixon, of Westerly, was a member of Congress from Rhode Island for six years. Priscilla Denison d. in Westerly, R. I., Sept. 24, 1842.

David Denison (No. 172) m. Keziah Smith of Groton, Conn., Dec. 30, 1756. They lived first in Stonington and then in New London. He served in the Revolutionary war as an officer. In 1785 he went to New Hampshire, and then to Guilford, Vt. He d. Jan. 24, 1808; his wife d. June 28, 1815.

CHILDREN:

314 SAMUEL, b. Aug. 25, 1757, d. young.
315 JABEZ, b. May 4, 1759, m. Mary Briggs.
316 DAVID, b. March 16, 1761, m. Mary Babcock.
317 SAMUEL, b. March 17, 1763, m. Eunice Houghton.
318 EDWARD, b. Oct. 4, 1765, m. Ruey Babcock.
319 WEALTHY, b. Nov. 29, 1767, d. young.
320 JOHN, b. 1771, m. Mary Avery.
321 DESIRE, b. in 1773, d. unmarried.
322 AMY, b. in 1775, m. Nathaniel Avery (No. 177), that family.
323 EMMA, b. in 1777, m. William Fox of New York.

Joseph Denison (No. 174) m. Mary Babcock (No. 108a) Oct. 10, 1765, and lived in Stonington. He d. Nov. 15, 1785, aged 50 yrs; she d. Dec. 15, 1798, aged 52 yrs.

CHILDREN:

324 MARY, b. April 16, 1767, m. Nathan Smith.
325 HANNAH, b. Oct. 6, 1768, m. Stephen Brown.
326 DORCAS, b. Aug. 9, 1770, m. Benjamin Eells (No. 33), that family.
327 AMY, b. Nov. 4, 1771, m. Paul Rhodes.
328 ABIGAIL, b. Feb. 18, 1776, m. Oliver Cobb (No. 39).
329 JOSEPH, b. Feb. 12, 1778.
330 BETSEY, b. June 19, 1780, m. Peter Crary.
331 SAMUEL F., b. Sept. 19, 1782.
332 CHARLES P., b. Feb. 16, 1785, m. Rebecca Shearwood; no child.
333 SARAH, b. Dec. 14, 1773, m. Thomas Butler.

Daniel Denison (No. 177) m. Martha Geer May 28, 1771. They lived in North Stonington, and about the year 1800 went to New York State.

CHILDREN.

334 HANNAH, b. Sept. 29, 1772, m. William Popple.
335 PRUDENCE, b. Dec. 15, 1775, m. Joseph Denison, Jr. (No. 329).

DENISON FAMILY.

336 WILLIAM, b. March 20, 1777, m. Betsey Ledyard.
337 MARTHA, b. June 2, 1779, m. Spaulding.
338 MARY, b. April 3, 1782, d. unmarried.
339 DANIEL, b. March 20, 1787, m. Betsey Hunt, went to New York State.

John Denison (No. 182) m. Sept. 6, 1772, Abigail Minor (No. 254), dau. of Nathaniel and Ann (Denison) Minor. They lived and d. in Stonington on the Rev. Ebenezer Rossiter's farm, which John Denison bought. John Denison d. July 12, 1801, and his wife d. May 25, 1795.

CHILDREN:

340 MOSES, b. Sept. 27, 1776, d. young.
341 NATHANIEL, b. Nov. 29, 1777, d. young.
342 NANCY, b. Nov. 18, 1780, m. Jesse Dean. See Dean family (No. 34).
343 LOIS, b. March 11, 1783, m. Elisha Williams. See that family (No. 135).
344 EDWARD, b. July 12, 1785, d. young.
345 ETHAN A., b. July 4, 1787.
346 HANNAH P., b. Dec. 17, 1789, m. Moses T. Geer.
347 FANNY P., b. Dec. 6, 1791, m. David Smith.
348 ABBY, b. in 1795, d. young.

Elisha Denison (No. 184) m. Keturah Minor (No. 120) Feb. 23, 1758. They lived in Stonington, Conn., and Ludlow, Vt. He d. May 6, 1809; his wife d. March 24, 1813. Children b. in Stonington.

CHILDREN:

349 SIMEON, b. Oct. 22, 1758, d. Dec. 9, 1776, in the Revolutionary war.
350 GRACE, b. Nov. 11, 1760, d. at 20 yrs.
351 DESIRE, b. Dec. 7, 1762, m. David Blossom.
352 EUNICE, b. Jan. 16, 1764, m. Arima Smith.
353 NATHAN, b. Feb. 3, 1766, twice m.; lived in New York State.
354 THANKFUL, b. Aug. 2, 1767, d. young.
355 ELISHA, b. Aug. 28, 1769, m. Ruth Robinson of New York State.
356 HANNAH, b. Sept. 18, 1771, d. young.
357 ZERVIAH, b. Oct. 23, 1773, d. young.
358 AVERY, b. Dec. 15, 1775, m. Eunice Williams.
359 ISAAC, b. April 23, 1778, m. Electa Newell.
360 LOIS, b. Aug. 14, 1780, m. J. Spaulding.
361 PRUDENCE, b. Oct. 26, 1782, m. George Fyler.

William Denison (No. 186) m. Susanna Swan (No. 54), Feb. 25, 1762, and lived in North Stonington till about 1788, when they moved to Vermont. He d. there June 3, 1799. His wife d. 1809.

CHILDREN:

362 LYMAN, b. Dec. 24, 1762, d. on the Jersey Prison ship.
363 MARY, b. May 19, 1764, m. Phillip Caverly.
364 ABIGAIL, b. Nov. 4, 1766, m. Rev. Abisha Colton.
365 THANKFUL, b. May 28, 1769, m. Daniel Colton.

366 MERCY, b. Oct. 12, 1771, d. in 1773.
367 REBECCA, b. Jan. 27, 1774, twice married.
368 BETSEY, b. May, 1776, m. Thomas Hurlburt
369 ASA A., b. Nov., 1778, m. Betsey Smith.
370 LUCY, b. April 12, 1781, m. Edmund McIntyre.
371 WILLIAM, b. 1783, m. Sally Brown.
372 ASAHEL, b. 1786, m. Bathsheba Blake.

Avery Denison (No. 194) m. Prudence Brown Aug. 17, 1778. They had no children, and he d. Aug. 23, 1800, and she d. in 1847, aged 91 yrs.

Samuel Denison (No. 200) m. to Aliphr Woodward about 1796, and he d. Sept. 20, 1843.   CHILDREN:

373 ALIPH, b. Aug., 1798.
374 SAMUEL, b. June 5, 1800, m. Mary Grinnell.
375 WILLIAM W., b. in 1802, m. Sally M. Howell.
376 JOHN I., b. in 1804, m. Laura O. Gilson.
377 SILAS, b. in 1812, m. Diana Burrows.
378 STEPHEN, b. in 1816, m. Ann E. Denison (No. 616).
379 DUDLEY, b. in 1818, d. in California.
380 DANIEL, b. in 1820, d. young.

Andrew Denison (No. 216) m. Sally Williams in 1782. They lived in Stonington, and afterwards in Vermont. He d. March 25, 1813. His wife d. in North Stonington Jan. 12, 1853, aged 92 yrs.
CHILDREN:
381 CHARLES H., b. March 1, 1784, d. young.
382 BENJAMIN F., b. June 1, 1785, m. Nancy Stark and lived in Vermont.
383 STEPHEN W., b. Feb. 16, 1787, d. young.
384 SALLY, b. June 10, 1789, m. John Brown.
385 ABIGAIL, b. May 12, 1791, d. young.
386 JOHN, b. June 4, 1793, m. Mary Chesebrough.
387 DESIRE, b. March, 1795, d. young.
388 SOPHIA, b. March 6, 1797, d. young.
389 LUCY A., b. Feb. 18, 1799, m. Matthew Brown (No. 385), that family.

Robert Denison (No. 220) m. Anna Chesebrough (No. 254) of Stonington March 17, 1774. About 1793 he went to Knox, New York.
CHILDREN:
390 ANNA, b. in 1775, m. Daniel Chesebrough (No. 176), that family.
391 ROBERT, b. in 1777, d. young.
392 CLARISSA, b. in 1779, m. Nicholas Vanderbogert.
393 NATHAN, b. March 2, 1781, m. Elizabeth Thompson.
394 PHEBE, b. Dec. 30, 1782, m. Amos Chesebro (No. 309).
395 RENSALLEAR, b. March 2, 1784, m. Mary Wood.
396 MARTHA, b. Aug. 26, 1787, m. Dr. John Wood.
397 ESTHER, b. Nov. 15, 1790, m. Alexander Thompson.
398 POLLY, b. 1792, m. William Vanderbogert.

DENISON FAMILY. 353

Isaac Denison (No. 221) m. Eunice Williams (No. 82), Nov. 10, 1773. They lived at Stonington; d. Feb. 14, 1817.
CHILDREN:
399 EBENEZER, b. July 10, 1774, twice married.
400 ESTHER, b. April 26, 1776, m. Charles Cottrell (No. 52), Oct. 18, 1795; had one child. He d. Dec. 11, 1803; she m. Isaac Miner (No. 179), Miner family, and had nine children.
401 SARAH, b. April 9, 1778, m. Elam Burrows (No. 37), Oct., 1797; had six children.
402 THANKFUL, b. May 20, 1780, m. Amos Clift (No. 22), Aug. 4, 1798; had eight children.
403 EUNICE, b. May 20, 1782, m. Nathaniel Clift (No. 25), Aug. 5, 1801. They lived at Mystic and had 10 children
404 ANN B., b. Sept. 22, 1784, m. Dec. 12, 1803, John D. Gallup (No. 305); had no children, and he d. and she m. 2d, Jeremiah Holmes (No. 98), Sept. 8, 1809; they had nine children.
405 MERCY, b. Feb. 9, 1787, m. Zebediah Gates June 7, 1820, and had five children.
406 ISAAC, b. Feb. 1, 1790.
407 DANIEL, b. April 26, 1791.
408 FREDERICK, b. Dec. 27, 1795, d. at 19 yrs.
409 ELISHA W., b. April 3, 1798.
410 HEZEKIAH, b. July 19, 1803, d. young.

Henry Denison (No. 222) m. Mary Gallup (No. 125) in 1778 in Stonington; he went to Knox, but did not stay there. He d. in Stonington 1836; his wife d. 1843.
CHILDREN:
411 SARAH, b. Dec. 9, 1780, d. unmarried.
412 HENRY, b. May 15, 1783, m. Deborah Pierce.
413 MARY, b. in 1785, d. young.
414 DANIEL, b. March 31, 1787, was a physician.
415 MARY, b. May 17, 1789, m. Amos Crary.
416 GIDEON, b. Feb. 4, 1793, d. unmarried.
417 LOIS, b. Jan. 21, 1796, m. John Freeman .
418 ESTHER, b. May 22, 1800, m. Anson Taylor.

Beebe Denison (No. 226) m. Hannah Chesebro (No. 265) Nov. 21, 1784; lived in Stonington, Conn.
CHILDREN:
419 HANNAH, b. in 1785, m. Moses Root.
420 KETURAH, b. Sept. 20, 1787, m. Dr. Enos Lewis.
421 NANCY, b. in 1790, m. Solomon White.
422 BEEBE, b. July 28, 1794, m. Harriet Thompson.
423 JEREMIAH, b. in 1796, d. young.
424 WILLIAM, b. in 1798, d. young.
425 JOHN, b. April 6, 1800, m. Jane Fairchild.

After his first wife d. he m. Phebe Hinckley March 10, 1805. They had two children.

CHILDREN:
426 WILLIAM H., b. Jan. 4, 1809, m. Caroline Turner.
427 GILBERT P., b. July 24, 1813, m. Betsey Andrews.

Frederick Denison (No. 227) m. Hannah Fish (No. 47) Aug. 19, 1789. They lived in Stonington, Conn.
CHILDREN:
428 FREDERICK, b. May 22, 1790, m. Desire Frink.
429 ERASTUS, b. Dec. 22, 1791, m. Prudence Spicer.
430 HANNAH, b. Oct. 10, 1795, d. unmarried.
431 NATHAN, b. Oct. 7, 1794, m. Mary Avery.
432 SALLY, b. July 10, 1797, d. young.
433 BETSEY, b. July 4, 1799, m. Henry Avery.
434 HANNAH, b. Nov. 24, 1801, d. young.
435 DELIA, b. Dec. 13, 1803, m. Daniel Latham.
436 ALFRED, b. Jan. 24, 1806, d. young.
437 CHARLES, b. Feb. 24, 1811, d. young.
438 DANIEL, b. June 19, 1813, m. Decha Gardner.

John Denison (No. 232) m. Eunice Stanton (No. 341), dau. of Samuel and Sarah (Gardiner) Stanton, Dec. 19, 1750.
CHILDREN:
442 EUNICE, bapt. Aug. 30, 1752, m. James Noyes. See that family (No. 144).
443 EDWARD, bapt. March 3, 1754, d. young.
444 LOIS, bapt. Dec. 27, 1755, m. Jonathan Waldron.
445 MARY, bapt. in May, 1757, d. in 1781.
446 JOHN, b. June 3, 1759.

Jesse Denison (No. 234) m. Mary Denison or Molly, daughter of Avery Denison (No. 188), Jan. 24, 1759.
CHILDREN:
447 MARY, b. Feb. 8, 1765, d. unmarried.
448 ELIZABETH, b. and m. a Mr. Drummond.

Elisha Denison (No. 241) m. Elizabeth Noyes (No. 146) April 26, 1772.
CHILDREN:
449 ELIZABETH, b. Nov. 29, 1773, m. Nathaniel Ledyard.
450 MEHITABLE, b. Sept. 5, 1776, m. Samuel Hurlburt.
451 PHEBE, b. April 22, 1782, m. W. J. Robinson.
452 ELISHA, b. May 2, 1779, d. young.

Peleg Denison (No. 245) m. Mary Gray March 9, 1780. They lived in Stonington. He d. March 21, 1800, and she d. in New York State July, 1837.
CHILDREN:
453 NOYES, b. Dec. 9, 1780, d. young.
454 MARY, b. Nov. 26, 1782, m. Nathan Stanton (No. 194), lived in New York State.
455 SAMUEL, b. June 15, 1784, d. young.
456 LEONARD, b. Jan. 1, 1792, m. Phebe Ely of New York State.

457 PELEG, b. May 15, 1786.
458 JOSEPH, b. March 11, 1788, d. in 1843.
459 ELIZABETH, b. June 13, 1790, d. in 1836.
460 SAMUEL, b. Oct. 7, 1796, d. 1862.
461 BRIDGET, b. May 28, 1794, m. Dea. Noyes Palmer. See that family (No. 345).

Amos Denison (No. 246) m. Hannah Williams (No. 217) Aug. 3, 1777. They lived in North Stonington, and he d. there Oct., 1835; she d. Aug. 19, 1829.

CHILDREN:

462 CHARLES W., b. June 26, 1778.
463 AMOS, b. Aug. 19, 1780, m. Lois Denison.
464 HANNAH, b. Aug. 23, 1782, d. young.
465 SARAH P., b. Sept. 3, 1785, m. Luke Palmer (No. 359), that family.
466 EDWARD, b. Nov. 30, d. young.
467 EZRA S., b. June 26, 1793, d. young.
468 MARTHA, b. March 17, 1796, m. Rev. Henry Sherman.
469 HANNAH E., b. June 11, 1799, m. Ephraim Williams (No. 295), that family.

Beebe Denison (No. 292) m. Prudence Holmes (No. 64) Oct. 13, 1774. They lived in Stonington, Conn., and he d. Feb. 10, 1823; and she d. Aug. 2, 1844.

CHILDREN:

470 MERCY, b. and d. in June, 1776.
471 CONTENT, b. June 4, 1777, m. Samuel Remington.
472 ABIGAIL, b. Oct. 9, 1779, d. young.
473 ANDREW, b. April 15, 1781, m. Mary Middleton, and 2d, widow Mary Ann Ecclestone.
474 PRENTICE, b. June 16, 1783.
475 BEEBE, b. March 13, 1785.
476 PRUDENCE, b. Nov. 25, 1787.
477 RUSSEL, b. June 16, 1789, d. young.
478 EUNICE, b. July 21, 1791, m. Illustrious Remington.
479 HENRY, b. April 8, 1793.
480 POLLY, b. Jan. 18, 1795.
481 NANCY, b. Aug. 17, 1798, m. David Kellogg.

Beebe Denison (No. 475) m. Eunice Parke Feb. 9, 1806, and had

CHILDREN:

482 MARY, b. Nov. 6, 1808, m. Elisha Wilcox (No. 77).
483 ABIGAIL, b. June 21, 1811.
484 ELIZA, b. Sept. 19, 1814.

Mrs. Eunice Denison d. in 1816, and he m. Fanny Allen Dec. 24, 1819, and had

CHILDREN:

485 RUSSELL, b. Jan. 6, 1822.
486 CHARLES H., b. March 14, 1824.

HISTORY OF STONINGTON.

Henry Denison (No. 479) m. Lucy Smith April 21, 1817. They lived at Old Mystic, and had

CHILDREN:
487 LUCY, b. Jan. 27, 1818, m. Amos Gay.
488 HANNAH, b. Sept. 27, 1820, m. Elias Wilcox (No. 81).
489 EUNICE, b. Oct. 30, 1822, m. James Standish.
490 JULIA, b. Feb. 22, 1825, m. Elnathan Wilcox (No. 79).
491 WILLIAM, b. Feb 18, 1828, m. Caroline Dow.
492 HARRIET D., b. Jan. 5, 1831, m. Aldredge Kenyon.
493 ROWLAND, b. Oct. 25, 1832, m. Eliza Bushnell.
494 EMILY, b. Jan. 16, 1836, m. Horace Spencer.
495 JEROME, b. Sept. 5, twin, m. Ann A. Williams, and 2d, Mary A. Gibson.
496 JANE, b. Sept. 5, twin, 1838, m. Charles Sabin; m. 2d, William Brown.

Darius Denison (No. 293) m. Mary Billings (No. 43), that family, 1771. They lived in Stonington, Conn. He d. Aug. 1, 1829, and she d. June 1, 1823.

CHILDREN:
497 PRUDENCE, b. March 21, 1772, m. Christopher Dean.
498 POLLY, b. Nov. 10, 1774, twice m. 1st, to Obediah Stanton, and 2d, to Henry Vanderpoel.
499 WILLIAM, b. Oct. 13, 1776, m. Phebe Irish.
500 MERCY, b. May 10, 1779, m. Amos Grinnell.
501 DARIUS, b. Dec. 28, 1783, m. Nancy Hyde (No. 21).
502 NANCY, b. Oct. 3, 1781, m. Joseph Lawton.
503 AMOS B., b. Feb. 21, 1786, d. young.
504 LODOWICK, b. July 27, 1790, m. Elizabeth Irish.
505 FANNY, b. Jan. 18, 1793, m. Hazard Holmes (No. 148), that family.

James Denison (No. 297) m. Eunice Stanton (No. 150), daughter of Joseph Stanton, Jr., Sept. 29, 1773. He d. April 26, 1813; she d. April 9, 1813.

CHILDREN:
506 JOSEPH A., b. Dec. 22, 1774, m. Rachel Chane of New Hampshire.
507 ANNA, b. Dec. 1, 1780, m. Nathan Geer.
508 DIMIS, b. Feb. 3, 1783, m. Stephen Paine.
509 EUNICE, b. June 19, 1785, m. Timothy Fay.
510 LUCY, b. Aug. 4, 1788, d. young.
511 JAMES, b. Oct. 24, 1791, twice m.
512 GEORGE, b. June 21, 1794, d. young.

Robert Denison (No. 299) m. 1st, Alice Denison (No. 295).

CHILDREN:
513 ROBERT, b. Sept. 2, 1774, m. Betsey Baker.
514 MARTHA, b. Sept. 2, 1777, m. Cary Ingraham.
515 BENADAM, b. April 1, 1783, m. Harriet Babcock.
516 JONATHAN, b. Feb. 2, 1780, m. Catharine Brown.
517 JAMES, b. July 1, 1785, m. Cynthia Babcock.
518 EDWARD, b. Feb. 6, 1788, d. young.
519 ELSIE, b. June 4, 1790, m. William Dewey.
520 ELIAS, b. June 15, 1794, d. young.

DENISON FAMILY. 357

Mrs. Alice Denison d. Sept. 2, 1794, and he m. for his 2d wife Deborah Dewey, Nov. 2, 1796.

CHILDREN:

521 DEBORAH, b. 1797, m. Dea. Charles Lewis.
522 JOSEPH S., b. March 8, 1798, m. 1st, Martha Gallup. In 1826 he m. 2d, Maria Babcock, and had three children.
523 LUCY A., b. 1800, m. 1st, Nathaniel Lewis, and 2d, Capt. Henry Crary.
524 WILLIAM, b. Oct. 7, 1802, m. Mary Allen.
525 NOYES P., b. in 1804, m. 1st, Harriet L. Smith, Dec. 8, 1830; she d. March 30, 1846, and m. 2d, Mary A. Minor Feb. 17, 1861.
526 ALLEN, b. in 1807, m. Eliza Parke.
527 GEORGE, b. in 1809, m. Almira Chesebro.
528 EMELINE, b. Oct. 13, 1811, m. Francis W. Miner (No. 38).
529 ELIZA A., b. May 8, 1815, m. Thomas Minor (No. 181).

Mr. Robert Denison d. Feb. 9, 1820, in Stonington, Conn.

George Denison (No. 300) m. Theody Brown (No. 208), Jan. 9, 1772, in Stonington, and after he removed to Hartland, Vt., where he was a prominent man and was called Col. George Denison. Had ten children.

George Denison (No. 302) m. widow Abigail Palmer (No. 243), Palmer family, in 1784, and d. in 1835.

CHILDREN:

530 GEORGE, b. 1785, m. Hannah Latham of Pennsylvania.
531 WILLIAM G., b. April 26, 1788, lived in Vermont.
532 HENRY, b. in 1784, d. in Kentucky.
533 JULIA, b. May 20, 1798, m. John Phillips of Somers, Conn.

William Denison (No. 304) m. Anna Slack. They went to Zanesville, Ohio. Had eight children, and he d. July 21, 1820, and she d. June 19, 1841.

Oliver Denison (No. 305) m. Martha Williams (No. 463), that family, Jan. 1, 1786. He d. Feb. 14, 1817, aged 59 yrs. His wife lived till Aug. 20, 1855, and d. at the ripe age of 93 yrs. They lived at the Old Denison Homestead.

CHILDREN:

534 OLIVER, b. Jan. 2, 1787.
535 JUSTIN W., b. in March, 1789.
536 MARCIA P., b. in 1791, m. Warren Palmer (No. 363).
537 MARTHA, b. in 1793, m. Denison Chesebro (No. 398), son of Elder Elihu, Nov. 15, 1818. They lived in Stonington.
538 ELAM, b. in 1794, m. Clarissa Palmer (No. 306).
539 GRACE B., b. Aug. 24, 1799, m. Joseph Noyes. See that family (No. 263).
540 LUKE P., b. in 1797, d. unmarried.
541 EUNICE W., b. Oct. 24, 1801, m. Thomas Noyes. See that family (No. 264).
542 THOMAS J., b. May 30, 1804, d. unmarried.

Nathan Denison (No. 306) m. Thankful Dean (No. 30) in 1787. They lived in Coleraine, Mass. He d. in 1803, and his wife d. in 1814.

CHILDREN:

544 NATHAN, b. in 1789, m. Ascah Hendee.
545 PRUDENCE, b. in 1791, m. John D. Gallup (No. 151).
546 THANKFUL, b. Aug. 1, 1794, m. Calvin Tyler of Norwich.

Joseph Denison (No. 329) m. his cousin, Prudence Denison (No. 335) Feb. 12, 1797. Lived in New York State; had five children, and they all died unmarried.

Samuel F. Denison (No. 331) m. Mary Cleveland Nov. 6, 1804. They lived in Stonington.

CHILDREN:

547 MARY E., b. Aug. 18, 1805, d. young.
548 CAROLINE G., b. Feb. 21, 1807, d. young.
549 WILLIAM C., b. Dec. 11, 1809, d. young.
550 REV. SAMUEL D., b. Oct. 7, 1810, m. Sarah F. Bleeker.
551 MARY C., b. July 11, 1812, m. William H. Plummer.
552 ANN E., b. 1814, m. Giles Babcock (No. 164).
553 JANE I., b. March 31, 1816, m. John A. Burnham.
554 HARRIET M., b. Aug. 20, 1818, m. Joseph Bennet.
555 HENRY C., b. Sept. 10, 1820.
556 EVELINA (twin), b. Sept. 14, 1822, m. Stephen D. Thatcher.
557 EDWARD C. (twin), b. Sept. 14, 1822, m. Elizabeth Lathrop.
558 PULASKI, b. Feb. 4, 1825, d. young.
559 FRANKLIN B., b. July 1, 1832, d. young.

Mr. Samuel F. Denison d. Jan. 28, 1855, and his wife d. Oct. 11, 1866.

Ethan A. Denison (No. 345) m. Eliza Williams (No. 483) of the Williams family, March 14, 1809. They lived in Stonington on the Rev. Mr. Rossiter's farm, inherited from his father.

CHILDREN:

560 NANCY, b. Jan. 24, 1810, m. Nathan Noyes (No. 268), of the Noyes family.
561 LOIS W., b. Oct. 4, 1811, m. Joseph Griswold. They lived in Griswoldville, Mass., m. Nov. 23, 1828.
562 ABBY C., b. March 14, 1813, d. young.

Mr. Ethan Denison d. Oct. 2, 1814.

Ebenezer Denison (No. 399) m. Jane (Branch) Williams Feb. 10, 1798 (No. 134) of Williams family.

CHILDREN:

563 DANIEL, b. May 15, 1800, d. young.
564 EBENEZER, b. May 30, 1802.
565 SARAH, b. July 22, 1805, d. young.

Mr. Ebenezer Denison's first wife d. March 19, 1806, and Sept. 12, 1816, he m. 2d, Phebe Smith, but had no children. He was a deacon, and Mrs. Phebe was one prominent in organizing Sunday Schools in Stonington. He d. Dec. 20, 1856, and she d. April 4, 1840.

Ebenezer Denison, Jr. (No. 564), m. Mary N. Hazard Nov. 5, 1831, and had five children, and his wife d. in 1846, and he m. Lydia S. Noyes (No. 341) of the Noyes family, April 9, 1849; they had five children.

Isaac Denison (No. 406) m. Levina Fish (No. 48) Feb. 18, 1817. He d. Aug. 28, 1855. Mrs. Levina Denison d.

CHILDREN:

566 ISAAC W., b. Nov. 20, 1817, m. Eunice E. Burrows (No. 45), May 10, 1843, and 2d, Mrs. Julia M. Wilbur; had nine children by first wife.
567 REV. FREDERICK, b. Sept. 28, 1819, m. Amy R. Manton Jan. 12, 1848, and had two children.
568 CHARLES C., b. Sept. 20, 1821, d. unmarried, 1847.
569 BRIDGET G., b. March 13, 1824, m. Cyrus W. Noyes (No. 305) of the Noyes family.
570 JOHN L., b. Sept. 19, 1826, m. Mary E. Burrows (No. 48), May 10, 1853, and 2d, Frances M. Breed, March 5, 1861; had five children by first wife.
571 DANIEL W., b. Sept. 5, 1828, m. Eleanor C. Harris Jan. 16, 1856, and had two children.
572 EMILY F., b. March 13, 1831, m. George W. Noyes (No. 267), of the Noyes family; had two children.
573 ELIZA F., b. Aug. 21, 1833, m. Dudley W. Stewart (No. 56), May 6, 1856. Had three children. See Stewart family.
574 FRANCES L., b. May 8, 1837, m. Benjamin Burrows, Jr., March 26, 1867 No. 73).

Elisha W. Denison (No. 409) m. Fanny Hicks June 5, 1820. They lived at Mystic and had

CHILDREN:

575 ELISHA A., b. April 8, 1821, m. Susan A. Dickenson Feb. 2, 1845.
576 FRANCES I., b. Aug. 25, 1823, m. Robert Greene.
577 PHEBE E., b. Sept. 22, 1825, m. John Prentice.
578 HIRAM C., b. Nov. 27, 1829, m. Eliza A. Minor.
579 ABBY C., b. Aug. 29, 1827, m. William B. Noyes.
580 EUNICE C., b. June 8, 1833, m. Henry P. Hewitt.
581 SARAH M., b. Dec. 8, 1835, m. Caleb Burdick.
582 ANN E., b. April 11, 1841, d. young.

John Denison (No. 446) m. Ede Brown, daughter of Samuel Brown of Stonington, Conn., Sept. 24, 1786.

CHILDREN:

583 MARY, b. Oct. 14, 1787, m. Isaac Champlin Nov. 8, 1807.
584 LOIS, b. Dec. 16, 1789, m. Amos Denison (No. 463), Nov., 1808.
585 EDWARD, b. Oct., 1793, m., no child; d. 1874.
586 JOHN, b. in 1795, m. Jane Mott, and 2d, Elizabeth Nitchie.
587 SAMUEL, b. in 1797. No record.

Peleg Denison (No. 457) m. Harriet Eldredge in 1809. He d. March 12, 1843.

CHILDREN:

588 HANNAH E., b. March 26, 1810, m. George W. Noyes. See Noyes family (No. 267).
589 HARRIET E., b. Dec. 13, 1811, d. young.
590 PELEG, b. Dec. 16, 1816, m. Martha A., Haverstraw, N. Y., Nov. 22, 1843.
591 MARY, b. April 13, 1814, m. Hiram DeW. Keyser.
592 BRIDGET, b. Nov. 7, 1818, m. Pardon T. Kinney.
593 DANIEL E., b. June 20, 1821, d. young.
594 CAROLINE E., b. Feb. 23, m. Rev. J. B. Gould.

Charles W. Denison (No. 462) m. Elizabeth Stanton (No. 404), daughter of Zebulon, Nov. 24, 1805. He d. Aug. 14, 1817; she d. Aug. 8, 1825.

CHILDREN:

595 ELIZA, b. Aug. 30, 1806, m. J. E. Culver.
596 REV. CHARLES W., b. in 1808, m. Mary Palmer; m. 2d, Mary A. Andrews
597 ELISHA, b. in 1810, d. young.
598 SARAH, b. in 1812, m. Nathan Storrs.
599 HARRIET, b. in 1814.

Amos Denison (No. 463) m. Lois Denison (No. 584), daughter of John and Ede (Brown) Denison. Lived in Stonington, and he d. there. His wife d. in Ohio, 1875.

CHILDREN:

600 HARRIET E., b. Aug. 27, 1809, m. Frederic Cogswell.
601 AMOS E. W., b. Sept. 20, 1811, m. Mary Dexter April 12, 1838.
602 MARY C., b. May 19, 1814, m. Samuel H. Greene.
603 CAROLINE EDITH, b. Nov. 11, 1816, m. William C. Moss (No. 42), that family.

Oliver Denison (No. 534) m. 1st, Nancy Graves March 3, 1811.

ONE CHILD:

604 MARTHA A., b. Dec. 21, 1811, m. Nathaniel Clift (No. 41), in Clift family.

Mrs. Nancy Graves Denison d. Feb. 24, 1825, and Mr. Oliver Denison m. 2d, Nancy D. Noyes (No. 336) of Noyes family. He d. Sept. 8, 1873, she d. June 1, 1870.

CHILDREN:

605 EMMA C., b. Oct. 24, 1828, m. Asa F. Kendrick.
606 OLIVER, b. April 18, 1825, m. Harriet N. Wilcox.
607 MARCIA P., b. April 8, 1830, m. Paul B. Stanton (No. 67) Robert Stanton family.
608 EDGAR, b. Jan. 20, 1833, m. Margaret E. Mandeville, and m. 2d, Phebe E. Green.
609 SARAH E., b. March 29, 1835, d. unmarried.
610 NATHAN N., b. Jan. 29, 1838, m. Sarah A. Green.
611 PHEBE M., b. May 30, 1840, m. Reuben Ford.

Justin W. Denison (No. 535) m. Maria Collins (No. 14) of the Collins family, March 11, 1811. He d. Oct., 1839, and his wife d. Aug. 2, 1839.

CHILDREN:

612 JUSTIN W., b. Jan. 1, 1815, d. unmarried.
613 OLIVER, b. Aug. 25, 1815, m. Charlotte Sawyer.
614 ELISHA P., b. July 31, 1817, m. Mary Dickenson.
615 MARIA, b. May 30, 1819, m. James Fish.
616 ANN E., b. Jan. 10, 1821, m. Stephen Denison (No. 378), of Denison family.
617 MERCY A., b. Feb. 2, 1825, m. Fred Funch.
618 THOMAS L., b. July 25, 1825, d. Aug. 13, 1837.
619 ELIAS W., b. June 18, 1827, m. Phebe A. Stoddard.
620 ANDREW L., b. Nov. 4, 1829, d. unmarried.

Elam Denison (No. 538) m. Clarissa Palmer (No. 306) of Palmer family. He d., and Mrs. Clarissa Denison m. 2d, Amos Chesebrough (No. 243).

CHILDREN:

621 CLARISSA, b. ———, m. John Green.
622 ELAM, b. in 1822, d. Jan. 21, 1824.

Gilbert Denison (No. 307) m. Huldah Palmer (No. 291), Dec. 26, 1784. They lived in Vermont.

CHILDREN:

623 GILBERT, b. in 1786, m. Sophia Culver.
624 HULDAH, b. in 1788, m. Phineas Stewart.
625 SOPHIA, b. in 1790, m. Henry Clark.
626 ELISHA, b. in 1792.
627 HENRY, b. ———, d. unmarried.

Gilbert Denison (No. 623) m. Sophia Culver in 1808.

CHILDREN:

628 GILBERT P., b. Oct. 31, 1810.
629 HENRY C., b. May 27, 1812.
630 MARY, b. April 2, 1814, m. Benjamin F. Collins (No. 43), of Collins family.
631 ANN MARIA, b. in 1818, m. Dr. Ezra Vincent (No. 28) of Vincent family.
632 CHARLES W., b. Sept. 20, 1818, d. young.
633 CHARLES H., b. in 1821, m. Mary A. Cottrell (No. 55) of Cottrell family.
634 JANE B., b. in 1823, m. Rev. Pliny S. Warner.
635 LOUISA, b. March 28, 1825, d. young.

Nathan F. Denison (No. 431) m. Mary E. Avery Dec. 25, 1823.

CHILDREN:

636 MARY E., b. June 18, 1825, m. Erastus Avery.
637 HANNAH F., b. Feb. 15, 1827, m. Hiram C. Holmes (No. 111) of Holmes family.
638 EMILY A., b. Nov. 14, 1828, m. Gurdon Bill.
639 LUCY C., b. June 30, 1831, m. Frederick Bill.

EELLS FAMILY.

1. JOHN EELLS, the progenitor of the Eells family, appears first on this side of the Atlantic Ocean at Dorchester, Mass. He was made freeman May 14, 1634. His son

2. Samuel Eells, bapt. May 3, 1640, removed to Newbury, Mass., in 1645; there he was called "Beehive Maker." He m. Ann, daughter of Rev. Robert Lenthall of Newport, Aug. 1, 1663.

CHILDREN:

3 SAMUEL, b. June 1, 1664, d. young.
4 JOHN, b. July 3, 1665, d. young.
5 SAMUEL, b. Sept. 2, 1666.
6 JOHN, b. ———, 1668.
7 MARY, b. Feb. 18, 1672.
8 ROBERT, b. Dec. 4, 1672, d. young.
9 ROBERT, b. Jan. 25, 1675.
10 NATHANIEL, b. Nov. 26, 1677, m. Hannah North.

Rev. Nathaniel Eells (No. 10), of Scituate, ordained June 14, 1704, m. Hannah North, of Hingham.

CHILDREN:

11 SARAH, b. Aug. 5, 1705.
12 SAMUEL, b. Feb. 23, 1707.
13 JOHN, b. Jan. 23, 1709.
14 NATHANIEL, b. Feb. 4, 1711, m. Mercy Cushing, Mrs. Mary Darrel.
15 EDWARD, b. Jan. 4, 1713.
16 HANNAH, b. Jan. 30, 1715.
17 MARY, b. May 13, 1716.
18 NORTH, b. Sept. 28, 1718.
19 ANN, b. Oct. 16, 1721.

Rev. Nathaniel Eells (No. 14) was the third ordained minister of Stonington, a graduate of Harvard College in 1728. After he was ordained in 1733, he pursued his labors with unremitting zeal and success. He lived on Hinckley Hill, and preached in the Center meeting house until 1762, when Mr. Rossiter d. in 1762. Then, upon the request of the east and west parishes in Stonington, he preached at the Centre and Agreement Hill or Road meeting house for a year or two, after which he preached at the Road in the morning, and in the old Academy at Stonington Point, in the afternoon, until the Centre meeting house was taken down, and re-erected in the village of Stonington. When the war of

EELLS FAMILY. 363

the Revolution broke out, and the news of the battle of Lexington set the patriotism of the country on fire, Putnam left his plough and Mr. Eells his pulpit, and rushed to Boston to defend with their lives if need be, the liberties of their country. Mr. Eells was a great favorite, especially among the young people, and an able devoted preacher of the Gospel. He m. 1st, Mercy Cushing Oct. 18, 1733; she d., then he m. 2d wife, Mrs. Mary Darrell, Oct. 10, 1753. He d. June 16, 1786, in the 76th year of his age, and the 53d year of his ministry.

CHILDREN BY FIRST MARRIAGE:

20 NATHANIEL, b. May 9, 1735, m. Martha Babcock (No. 228).
21 JOHN, b. March 8, 1737.
22 EDWARD, b. Jan. 9, 1739, m. Mercy Denison.
23 SARAH, b. and d. March 17, 1741.
24 MERCY, b. Jan. 4, 1743, m. Dr. Joshua Lathrop Nov. 5, 1761.
25 SARAH, b. March 10, 1745.
26 LUCRETIA, b. June 15, 1747.

CHILDREN BY SECOND MARRIAGE:

27 REBECCA, b. Aug. 8, 1754.
28 LYDIA, b. Dec. 3, 1755, m. Jedediah Parker of Boston Sept. 18, 1783.
29 SAMUEL, b. Sept. 27, 1757.
30 JOSEPH, b. March 13, 1759, m. Anna Stanton.
31 HANNAH, b. Sept. 14 1760, m. Samuel Palmer Nov. 9, 1780 (No. 212), that family.
32 ELIZABETH, b. July 25, 1762, m. William Sheffield May 29, 1783.
33 BENJAMIN, b. Sept. 6, 1763, m. Dorcas Denison.

Edward Eells (No. 22) m. Mercy Denison (No. 190), Denison family, May 10, 1764, by Rev. Joseph Fish, both of Stonington; moved to Preston, Conn.

CHILDREN:

34 LUCRETIA, b. May 8, 1766.
35 SAMUEL, b. Feb. 14, 1768.
36 CUSHING, b. Aug. 27, 1769.
37 EDWARD, b. Jan. 24, 1773.
38 REBECCA, b. April 28, 1774.

Joseph Eells (No. 30) m. Anna Stanton (No. 39), Feb. 2, 1785, Stanton family. He d. Dec. 19, 1791, aged 33 years. Anna then m. Dea. Sans Cole of Hopkinton, R. I., and d. Aug. 8, 1850. She was called Nancy Stanton.

CHILDREN:

39 NANCY, b. Sept. 11, 1786, m. Col. Joseph Smith Jr. (No. 105), son of Joseph and Hannah (Hewitt) Smith, m. Feb. 9, 1806.
40 BETSEY, b. Oct. 31, 1788, m. Russell Hall of Hopkinton, R. I., Jan. 20, 1811.
41 JOSEPH, b. July 19, 1791, d. young.

Benjamin Eells (No. 33) m. Dorcas Denison Dec. 20, 1789, (No. 326), Denison family.

CHILDREN:

42 MARIA, b. Sept. 22, 1790, m. B. F. Babcock April, 1813 (No. 157), that family.
43 LYDIA, b. Nov. 13, 1791, d. July 25, 1795.
44 CHARLOTTE, b. July 12, 1793, m. Nathan Smith Dec. 24, 1818 (No. 108).
45 BENJAMIN S., b. June 12, 1795, d. Sept. 5, 1796.
46 ELIZABETH, b. Dec. 30, 1798, m. Rev. Oliver Brown July 8, 1828.

FANNING FAMILY.

1. EDMUND FANNING, the emigrant ancestor of the Fanning family of this region round about, d. in Stonington, Conn., in Dec., 1683. He left a widow, Mrs. Ellen Fanning, five sons and one daughter.

He was doubtless of Irish origin, but his native place cannot be defined, for there are two storied traditions relative to it, which are so variant in their conditions and locality, that it is impossible to determine his nativity. One tradition speaks of him as escaping from Dublin in Ireland, in 1641, at the time of the great rebellion in which 100,000 Protestants fell victims to the fury of the Roman Catholics, which tradition followed him in his travels over the ocean and to America, where after a few years he located himself in that part of New London, now Groton, in 1652. Later on he removed to Stonington, Conn., where he lived the remainder of his life. The other tradition would make him a descendant of Dominicus Fanning, who was mayor of a city in Ireland under Charles the First, and was taken prisoner at the battle of Drogheda in 1649. All of the garrison except himself was put to the sword. He was beheaded by Cromwell, and his head was stuck on a pole at the principal gate of the city. His property was confiscated, because when Charles the First made a proclamation of peace, he was a member of the Irish Council. He advised not to accept, unless the British Government would secure to the Irish their religion, their property and their lives. His son Edmund, was born in Kilkenny, Ireland, and m. Catharine, daughter of Hugh Hayn, Earl of Connaught, and emigrated to this country with two sons, Thomas and William, and settled in Stonington, Conn. This tradition is taken from an old tombstone at Riverside, Long Island, and is claimed by many as the ancestral connecting line of Edmund Fanning, who d. in Dec., 1683, neither of which storied traditions are to be relied upon as correct, for they are so variant in their descriptions of his ancestry, marriages and names of his wives that places them beyond an intelligent belief.

CHILDREN OF EDMUND AND WIFE, ELLEN FANNING:
2 EDMUND, b. ———.
3 THOMAS, b. ———.
4 JOHN, b. ———.
5 WILLIAM, b. ———.
6 JAMES, b. ———.
7 MARY, b. ———, m. Benjamin Hewitt.

Edmund Fanning (No. 2) m. Margaret Billings (No. 3), that family, Aug. 31, 1678. He was in King Philip's war.

Thomas Fanning (No. 3) and Frances Ellis were m. Oct. 19, 1684. He served in King Philip's war.

HIS SON:

8 JAMES, m. Hannah Smith, time not known.

THEIR SON:

9 GILBERT, m. Huldah Palmer (No. 175), Palmer family, Dec. 25, 1753. They were both of Stonington.

CHILDREN:

10 NATHANIEL, b. May 31, 1755.
11 GILBERT, b. Jan. 30, 1757.
12 WILLIAM, b. July 19, 1758.
13 JAMES, b. April 10, 1760.
14 HULDAH, b. July 19, 1762, d. April 10, 1765.
15 THOMAS, b. May 17, 1765.
16 HULDAH, b. May 30, 1767.
17 EDMUND, b. July 16, 1769.
18 SAMUEL, b. April 21, 1771.
19 RICHARD, b. June 22, 1774.
20 HENRY, b. April 13, 1778.

Mary Fanning (No. 7), m. Benjamin Hewitt, Sept. 24, 1683. See Hewitt family (No. 3).

Capt. Nathaniel Fanning (No. 10) was a midshipman commanding the maintop of the ship called Good Man Richard, under Capt. John Paul Jones, in her famous fight with the English ship Serapis. He so distinguished himself in that action as to draw from Capt. Jones the following certificate: "I do hereby certify that Nathaniel Fanning of Stonington, State of Connecticut, has sailed with me in the station of midshipman eighteen months, while I commanded the Good Man Richard, until she was lost in the action with the Serapis, and in the "Alliance" and Ariel frigates. His bravery on board the first mentioned in the action with the Serapis, a King's ship of fifty guns, off Flamborough Head, while he had command of the maintop, will, I hope, recommend him to the notice of Congress in the line of promotion with his other merits. "JOHN PAUL JONES."

Dec. 17th, 1780.

He was promoted to a lieutenantcy in the United States Navy, and d. of the yellow fever while in command of the United States Naval Station at Charleston, South Carolina, Sept. 30, 1805.

FELLOWS FAMILY.

1. WILLIAM FELLOWS came to this country from England prior to 1641 and settled in Ipswich, Mass., and became an inhabitant of that town.

He was m. in the old country, but the name of his wife is not known. The following named children are mentioned in his will:

CHILDREN:
2 EPHRAIM, b. in England.
3 SAMUEL, b. in England.
4 JOSEPH, b. in England.
5 ISAAC, b. in England.
6 MARY, b. in England.
7 ELIZABETH, b. in New England.
8 ABIGAIL, b. in New England.
9 SARAH, b. in New England.

Isaac Fellows (No. 5) and Joannah Brown were m. Jan. 29, 1672.

CHILDREN:
10 ISAAC, b. Nov. 27, 1673.
11 SAMUEL, b. Feb. 8, 1676.
12 EPHRAIM, b. Sept. 3, 1679.
13 JONATHAN, b. Sept. 18, 1682.
14 JOANNA, b. Nov. 19, 1689.

Ephraim Fellows (No. 12) m. Hannah Warner, dau. of Nathaniel Warner, May 19, 1703.

CHILDREN:
15 EPHRAIM, b. in Massachusetts, and probably others.
16 SARAH, b. Jan. 3, 1711.
17 NATHANIEL, b. June 22, 1713.
18 NATHAN, b. ———, 1714.
19 ISAAC, b. Feb. 19, 1719.
20 JOHN, b. Oct. 8, 1722.
21 JOANNAH, b. April 4, 1724.
22 MARY, b. Aug. 16, 1726.

Mr. Ephraim Fellows d. March 12, 1726, and his wife, Hannah d. March 19, 1758.

Nathaniel Fellows (No. 17) and Hopestill Holdredge were m. March 2, 1737.

CHILDREN:
23 DEBORAH, b. April 4, 1738, d. April 11, 1738.
24 NATHANIEL, b. Feb. 4, 1739.
25 WARNER, b. Feb. 11, 1741.
26 WILLIAM, b. Jan. 19, 1743.
27 HOPESTILL, b. Feb. 8, 1745.

28 LYDIA, b. Feb. 20, 1747, m. Nathan Noyes (No. 142), that family.
29 MERCY, b. Aug. 1, 1749.
30 ELNATHAN, b. Aug. 13, 1751.
31 EPHRAIM, b. Nov. 19, 1753.
32 PRISCILLA, b. April 14, 1755.
33 MARY, b. and d. May 16, 1757.
34 JOSEPH, b. Sept. 29, 1759.
35 DAVID, b. March 16, 1760.

Ephraim Fellows (No. 15) and Prudence Plumb were m. May 13, 1731.

CHILDREN:

36 HANNAH, b. Dec. 28, 1731.
37 EPHRAIM, b. Oct. 2, 1733.
38 GEORGE, b. Aug. 15, 1735, and d. Dec. 1, 1736.
39 SAMUEL, b. Oct. 4, 1737.
40 WARNER, b. Oct. 13, 1739, d. Nov. 3, 1739.
41 JOHN, b. Nov. 7, 1740.
42 PRUDENCE, b. Nov. 2, 1742.
43 SARAH, b. Sept. 28, 1744.
44 JOSEPH, b. Oct. 7, 1746.

Warner Fellows (No. 25) and Eunice Hall, both of Stonington, Conn., were m. Nov. 22, 1762. No children on record.

Ephraim Fellows (No. 37) and Rhode Smith, both of Stonington, were m. April 24, 1766.

CHILDREN:

45 EPHRAIM, b. Jan. 27, 1767.
46 JEREMIAH, b. Feb. 24, 1769.
47 RHODA, b. Jan. 3, 1771.
48 ASA, b. March 15, 1773.
49 MARTHA, b. Feb. 2, 1775.
50 PRUDENCE, b. Oct. 17, 1777.
51 RHODA, b. Jan. 12, 1782, and d. young.

Samuel Fellows (No. 39) and Mary Udall, both of Stonington, were m. March 7, 1765.

CHILDREN:

52 MARY, b. March 27, 1766.
53 MARTHA, b. July 20, 1776.
54 SAMUEL, b. Feb. 4, 1770.
55 SARAH, b. July 20, 1776.
56 ABIGAIL, b. Jan. 31, 1779.

Dea. Jeremiah Fellows (No. 46) and Lois Miner (No. 339), that family, both of Stonington, were m. May 30, 1802.

CHILDREN:

57 LOIS FELLOWS LEE, daughter of Tully and Lois Lee, b. in Stonington May 5, 1805. and was an adopted child of Jeremiah Fellows and his wife, Lois Miner Fellows, and m. Dea. —— Potter Dec. 18, ——. He was a native of Middletown, Conn.

FISH FAMILY.

1. It has not yet been ascertained when Mr. John Fish, whose mature life and declining years were spent in Groton and Stonington, came to this country, or of what nationality he was. Miss Caulkins, in her History of New London, speaks of a John Fish of Lynn, Mass., as early as 1637, but the history of Lynn does not mention his name. Miss Caulkins gives no further account of him until 1655, when he appeared with his wife and children, John, Jonathan and Samuel Fish. She gives no account of Mr. Fish between 1637 and 1655, when she locates him and his family in New London, prior to 1655. A Mr. John Fish was living in the town of Stratford, Conn. How long he made that town his abiding place does not appear, nor when he was married to Miss Eland, whose ancestral home was Yorkshire, Eng. He sold out his home lot and about six acres of land in Stratford to John Willcockson, Sept. 29, 1655, the same year that Miss Caulkins locates him and family in New London. She was doubtless mistaken in saying that his son Samuel Fish was one of his family when he came to New London to live, for the epitaph on his gravestone shows that he was not born until 1656. How long Mr. Fish lived in New London is not certainly known, but his residence there was of short duration, for the Stonington records show that he had lived here long enough in 1668 to become an inhabitant of Stonington, which requires a two years' residence to obtain. The following biographical sketch of Mr. John Fish, written by Mr. John D. Fish, one of his descendants, was carefully prepared by him, and is doubtless correct:

"In 1654, and probably for several years previously, John Fish lived in the town of Stratford, Conn. He was a young man and impulsive. The family name of his wife was probably Eland, as Sarah Eland, his sister-in-law, was a young woman and a member of his household. The Elands were an ancient and knightly family of Yorkshire, Eng. John Fish's house lot of about six acres, where he lived, was at the northerly end of the present village of Stratford, and bounded on the west by Main street, on the north and east by Ferry road and on the south by land of

Daniel Titterson. The location of his house lot is shown on a map drawn by Rev. Benjamin L. Swan, and printed in the 'Hawley Record' at page 432, where it is marked as belonging to John Willcockson, the person to whom it was sold by Mr. Fish. In the autumn of 1654, a controversy commenced between John Fish and some young men in the town, growing out of unwarwanted accusations which he made against them. This trouble was carried into the courts and very probably was the cause of his selling all his property in Stratford a year later, to John Willcockson, and leaving town. The town records contain four different entries of separate parcels of land so sold. The date of the deeds of sale was Sept. 29, 1655, but the records were not made until 1662-1671. Miss Caulkins in her History of New London says that John Fish appeared there early in 1655 with wife and children, whose names she gives as John, Jonathan and Samuel. There are no records of the birth of these children in Stratford. I judge that Samuel was the second of John Fish's children who reached maturity, and as he d. Feb. 27, 1733, in the 77th year of his age, he appears to have been born soon after his father came to New London. The records of the Congregational Church of Stonington, under date of March 13, 1680, show the baptisms of Samuel, son of John Fish; Mary, daughter of John Fish, and John, son of John Fish. These were all adult persons at that time. Of John Fish's children, I have further records of only Samuel and John, Junior. At what date John became a resident of the town of Stonington, I cannot say, but in 1668, when a census was ordered by the colonial authorities to be taken of the inhabitants or heads of families in Stonington, John Fish was one of forty-three persons enumerated. A home lot was laid out to each of these inhabitants, upon condition that it should be built upon within six months and inhabited. A twelve-acre home lot was granted to John Fish, being allotment No. 5, and was retained by him through life. His son, Samuel Fish, under date of Dec. 26, 1710, conveyed this lot to James Dean, who afterwards, on Nov. 8, 1711, conveyed it to Ebenezer Searles, as is shown by the Stonington land records. The first wife of John Fish was doubtless the mother of all his children named above. Aug. 6, 1674, John Fish was acting town clerk at a town meeting held in Stonington. See town records."

In 1675 was the Narragansett war, or expedition against the

Indians under King Philip. The colony of Connecticut contributed about three hundred volunteers to this expedition from her white settlers, besides a large number of friendly Pequot Indians. Both John Fish and his son Samuel were among these volunteers, and about 1700, when the colony set apart the town of Voluntown to be allotted to the Indian war volunteers, there were grants made for each of them. As John Fish had then been dead several years his grant came into the possession of his son Samuel, who in his will, dated Aug. 7, 1730, bequeathed his own grant to his son Samuel, and divided his father's grant between his sons Moses and Aaron. Two of Samuel's grandsons settled on these lands in Voluntown, and their descendants are still owners thereof. Aug. 22, 1679, the same day Mr. John Fish was chosen and unanimously voted schoolmaster for the town of Stonington, to instruct children in reading, writing, arithmetic and grammar, such as shall be inclined. December 5, 1680, Mr. John Fish was admitted a member of the Congregational Church of Stonington, Aug. 25, 1681, Mr. John Fish and widow Hannah (Palmer) (No. 7) Hewitt Sterry were married. She was a daughter of Walter and Rebecca (Short) Palmer, and was married April 26, 1659, to Capt. Thomas Hewitt, who was a seafaring man. He sailed upon one of his voyages and was never heard of again. In 1670, Mrs. Hewitt petitioned the General Court for permission to marry again, which was granted, and on Dec. 27, 1671, she was married to Roger Sterry. Mr. Sterry died before 1680, and on Aug. 25, 1681, she became the third wife of John Fish. Mr. Fish seems not to have any children who survived except by the first wife. He was a land surveyor, and laid out some of the public grants as the Stonington records bear witness. His brother-in-law, Gershom Palmer, was associated with him in such work in 1680 and 1681. By grant and by purchase he himself became proprietor of considerable tracts of land in Groton and Stonington and other towns near by.

2. John Fish (No. 2), eldest son of John Fish, Sr., m. Margaret ———, family name and birth unknown. He was bapt. as an adult in the First Congregational Church of Stonington, April 18, 1680, but did not unite with the church until April 18, 1695, when his wife Margaret, joined the church, and their children bapt. John Fish probably died not very long after this. His widow, Margaret Fish, m. Samuel Cleveland of Canterbury,

Conn., and had two more children, Abigail and Timothy. From the fact that John Fish's widow went to Canterbury so soon after his death and m. again, it is thought that she may have come from that neighborhood, or have had relatives there.

CHILDREN:

3 SAMUEL, bapt. April 18, 1695.
4 MARY, bapt. same day.
6 DAVID, bapt. same day, m. Grace Palmer March 30, 1721.
7 MARGARET, bapt. same day, m. Gideon Cobb (No. 17), Cobb family.
8 JOHN, bapt. Nov. 8, 1696, m. Esther Johnson July 19, 1726, and spent his life in Canterbury, Conn., and had a large family of children, and d. July 4, 1782, in the 87th year of his age.

Samuel Fish (No. 3), b. in 1656, as we learn by his epitaph on his gravestone, m. Sarah ―――. He d. Feb. 27, 1733; his widow d. Dec. 11, 1722, aged 62 yrs; both buried in the old Packer burying ground in Groton; m. 2d, widow Dorothy (Wheeler) Smith.

CHILDREN:

9 SAMUEL, b. in 1684, m. Sarah ―――.
10 JOHN, b. in 1686.
11 MOSES, b. in 1688, m. Martha Williams.
12 ABIGAIL, b. in 1691, m. Capt. Daniel Eldridge; 2d, Dea. Daniel Denison.
13 AARON, b. in 1693, m. Irene Sprague.
14 NATHAN, b. Aug. 19, 1699, m. Abigail Havens; 2d, Mary Burrows.
15 SARAH, b. Aug. 2, 1702, m. Hezekiah Lord of Preston, Conn.

David Fish (No. 6) m. Grace Palmer, March 29, 1721; both of Stonington, Conn.

CHILDREN:

16 DAVID, b. Jan. 20, 1721-2.
17 GRACE, b. Feb. 11, 1724.
18 JASON, b. Sept. 26, 1726.
19 TITUS, b. March 13, 1728-9.
20 JOHN, b. March 3, 1730-1.
21 EUNICE, b. June 2, 1734.
22 AMBROS, b. Aug. 21, 1735.
23 ISAAC, b. Aug. 13, 1740.

Samuel Fish (No. 9) m. Sarah ―――. He d. Jan. 20, 1724.

CHILDREN:

24 CAPT. JOHN, b. about 1712, m. Lucretia Packer, d. in Groton Oct. 4, 1795.
25 CAPT. DANIEL, b. about 1714, m. Rebecca Palmer (No. 122), that family, Feb. 17, 1743; 2d, Sarah Hillard, daughter of John Hillard, and wife Hannah Rossiter (No. 10), Rossiter family. He gave to the First Congregational Church of Stonington the house and farm at Wequetequock, still in its possession.
26 SARAH, b. ―――, m. ――― Morse.
27 ELIZABETH, b. ―――, m. ――― Rose.

FISH FAMILY.   373

28 SAMUEL, b. ———.
29 JANE, b. ———, m. Rev. Timothy Wightman.

Nathan Fish (No. 14) m. 1st, Abigail Havens in 1726; 2d, Mary Burrows.
CHILDREN:
30 NATHAN, b. in 1727, m. Catharine Niles; 2d, Catharine Helms.
CHILDREN BY SECOND MARRIAGE:
31 ABIGAIL, b. in 1729, m. Jonathan Fish, d. Sept. 18, 1790.
32 ICHABOD, b. in 1732, d. Nov., 1737.

Nathan Fish (No. 30) m. Catharine Niles Oct. 13, 1748. Mrs. Fish d. Jan., 1759. He m. 2d, Catharine Helms, July 24, 1759, d. Aug. 22, 1818.
CHILDREN:
33 NATHAN, b. July 31, 1749, m. Phebe Packer, d. at Halifax Aug., 1806.
34 SAMUEL, b. July 17, 1751, m. Sarah Lamb, d. at Halifax Nov. 26, 1837.
35 CATHARINE, b. Aug. 24, 1753, m. Jesse Gallup March 16, 1775.
36 SIMEON, b. March 24, 1756, d. Feb. 4, 1757.
CHILDREN BY SECOND MARRIAGE:
37 ABIGAIL, b. May 21, 1760, m. Luke Perkins; 2d, John Wood.
38 SARAH, b. July 1, 1761, m. Josiah Gallup Nov. 4, 1787, d. Feb. 11, 1791.
39 SANDS, b. Oct. 18, 1762, m. Bridget Gallup.
40 MARY, b. Nov. 3, 1765, m. Christopher Lester, d. Oct. 10, 1848.
41 SILAS, b. Aug. 29, 1767, m. Cynthia Bliss, d. June 1, 1836.
42 ROSWELL, b. March 5, 1772, m. Isabell Phelps of Springfield, Mass.
43 CYNTHIA, b. Sept. 21, 1770, m. Benadam Gallup Oct. 14, 1792 (No. 157), Gallup family.
44 EDMUND, b. Feb. 5, 1772, d. Sept. 8, 1798.
45 ANNA, b. Aug. 6, 1776, d. Nov. 14, 1859.

Sands Fish (No. 39) m. Bridget, daughter of Dea. Benadam and Bridget (Palmer) Gallup, June 18, 1789 (No. 158), Gallup family. He d. Aug. 20, 1838; his wife d. March 24, 1842.
CHILDREN:
46 HON. ASA, b. July 17, 1790, m. Prudence B. Deane.
47 HANNAH, b. March 10, 1762, d. Sept. 8, 1815, m. Fred Denison (No. 227).
48 LEVINIA, b. Oct. 1, 1794, m. Isaac Denison (No. 406), that family, Feb. 18, 1817.
49 SIMEON, b. Jan. 17, 1797, m. Eliza Roe Randall.
50 CHARLES, b. Feb. 3, 1801, m. Esther B. Williams April 10, 1822.
51 NATHAN GALLUP, b. Sept. 7, 1804, m. Emeline Frances Miner (No. 293), Miner family.
52 ALDEN, b. Aug. 7, 1808, m. Sally Ann Beebe March 15, 1843.
53 BRIDGET, b. Aug. 21, 1811, m. Capt. William Clift June 18, 1833 (No. 38). Clift family.

Hon. Asa Fish (No. 46) m. Prudence B. Deane Sept. 30, 1818, by the Rev. Ira Hart (No. 35), Deane family. He was one of the most prominent men of Stonington, holding the offices of Selectman, Senator and Judge of Probate, up to the life limit. He d. April 20, 1761.

CHILDREN:

54 JAMES DEANE, b. Aug. 7, 1819, m. Mary Esther Blodget June 4, 1843. She d. July 17, 1868; m. 2d, Isabella Rogers March 18, 1872; she d. Dec. 20, 1879.

55 SANDS HELME, b. Sept. 19, 1821, m. Emeline Beebe March 14, 1850.

56 HANNAH, b. June 6, 1823, m. Elias P. Randall (No. 107), that family, March 15, 1843.

57 SILAS, b. Oct. 23, 1825, m. Mary Dorrance Stoddard April 10, 1851.

58 ASA, b. April 11, 1828, m. Eleanor Hoxie Peckham May 12, 1857.

59 PRUDENCE, b. Aug. 1, 1830, m. Uriah H. Dudley April 10, 1855.

60 BENJAMIN, b. Sept. 2, 1834.

61 JOHN D., b. Feb. 23, 1837, d. Aug. 29, 1838.

62 FANNY DEANE, b. Sept. 5, 1839, m. Caleb Smith Woodhull Jan. 1, 1861.

Simeon Fish (No. 49) m. Eliza Roe Randall Oct. 15, 1823 (No. 134), that family. She d. June 23, 1872; he d. April 25, 1863.

CHILDREN:

63 WILLIAM R., b. July 13, 1824, m. Lydia W. Williams Jan. 19, 1848 (No. 27)

64 NATHAN SANDS, b. April 11, 1828, m. Janette Morgan of Poquonock March 24, 1850.

65 JED RANDALL, b. Nov. 20, 1832, m. Myra Oltz Nov. 18, 1868; she d. Feb. 23, 1870; m. 2d, Josephine Oltz Sept. 18, 1871.

THOMAS FISH FAMILY.

1. REV. JOSEPH FISH, son of Thomas Fish of Duxbury, Mass., b. Jan. 28, 1705, was a graduate of Harvard College in 1728. Among his classmates was the Rev. Nathaniel Eells, long his neighbor and friend, as pastor at Stonington, settled in the ministry at almost the same time. These earnest men went on side by side through nearly the whole of their long lives. Mr. Fish was settled in Stonington, now North Stonington, second pastor of the Congregational Church in 1732. He m. Rebecca (No. 20), daughter of William Pabodie of Duxbury, Mass., and great-granddaughter of John Alden, of the Mayflower, Dec. 6, 1732. He d. May 26, 1781, in the 76th year of his age, and the 50th of his ministry. His wife d. at Fairfield Oct. 27, 1783, aged 80 yrs.

CHILDREN:

2 MARY, b. May 19, 1736, m. Rev. John Noyes in 1758 (No. 139), Noyes family; m. 2d, Gen. Gold S. Silliman in 1775; m. 3d, Dr. J. Dickinson in 1804; d. at Wallingford July 2, 1818, aged 83 yrs.
3 REBECCA, b. Jan. 11, 1739, m. Benjamin Douglas, d. and was buried at New Haven Feb. 8, 1766, aged 28 yrs.
4 JOSEPH, Jr., b. and d. April 13, 1743.

Nathaniel Fish, brother of the Rev. Joseph Fish, lived in Stonington, now North Stonington, Conn., m. Mary Pabodie (No. 24), that family, in 1736, sister of his brother's wife.

CHILDREN:

6 MILLER, b. Oct. 9, 1737.
7 WILLIAM, b. April 26, 1738.
8 ELIAKIM, b. Feb. 2, 1741.
9 JOSEPH, b. March 21, 1742.
10 NATHANIEL, b. Feb. 6, 1744.
11 LYDIA, b. March 1, 1746.

FRINK FAMILY.

1. JOHN FRINK came to Stonington, Conn., as early as 1666. He was the son of John and Mary Frink of Ipswich, Mass. He bought a tract of land on Taugwonk in Stonington, upon which he erected a dwelling house for himself and family. He was in King Philip's war. He was m. several years before he came to Stonington to live, having been united in m. to Grace Stevens of Taunton, Mass., in 1657. He brought with him to Stonington his wife and three daughters.

CHILDREN:

2 GRACE, b. in 1658, m. James Willet June, 1677.
3 HANNAH, b. in 1661, m. William Park (No. 26), that family, Dec. 30, 1684.
4 DEBORAH, b. in 1665, m. Gershom Lambert in 1686.
5 SAMUEL, b. Feb. 14, 1668, m. Hannah Miner.
6 JOHN, b. May 18, 1671, m. Hannah Prentice.
7 THOMAS, b. May 25, 1674, m. Sarah Noyes.
8 JUDITH, bapt. April 15, 1680.

Samuel Frink (No. 5), m. Hannah, daughter of Ephraim Miner (No. 40), Miner family, Jan. 6, 1692.

CHILDREN:

9 SAMUEL, b. Feb. 14, 1693, m. Margaret Wheeler.
10 ANDREW, b. Aug. 7, 1694.
11 GRACE, b. Dec. 18, 1695.
12 JAMES, b. Nov. 5, 1697.
13 HANNAH, bapt. March 17, 1700.
14 JEDEDIAH, bapt. June 7, 1702.
15 JERUSHA, bapt. May 24, 1704.
16 ELIAS, bapt. Dec. 22, 1706.
17 ABIGAIL, bapt. May 2, 1708, m. John Holmes.

John Frink (No. 6) m. Hannah Prentice Feb. 15, 1694. He d. March 2, 1718.

CHILDREN:

18 JOHN, b. Oct. 7, 1694.
19 NICHOLAS, b. Dec. 17, 1696, m. Deborah Pendleton.
20 THOMAS, b. Jan. 15, 1700.
21 HANNAH, b. Nov. 27, 1701.
22 ZACHARIAH, b. Nov. —, 1702, m. Elizabeth Gallup.
23 MARY, bapt. April 19, 1705.
24 JOSEPH, bapt. June 6, 1708, m. Judith Palmer June 12, 1732.
25 BENJAMIN, b. Jan. 25, 1710, m. Tacy Burdick.
26 WILLIAM, bapt. March 10, 1714.
27 THANKFUL, bapt. Feb. 8, 1716.
28 ESTHER, bapt. Jan. 23, 1717.

FRINK FAMILY. 377

Thomas Frink (No. 7) m. Sarah Noyes of Sudbury, Mass, date of marriage not preserved.
CHILDREN:
29 ABIGAIL, b. ———.
30 ABIGAIL, b. ———.
31 THOMAS, b. ———.

Samuel Frink (No. 9) m. Margaret Wheeler (No. 18), that family, May 26, 1714.
CHILDREN:
32 SAMUEL, b. Feb. 26, 1715, m. Mary Stanton.
33 ISAAC, b. Dec. 25, 1717, m. Anna Noyes.
34 DAVID, b. May 30, 1720, m. Eunice Gallup.
35 MARGARET, b. Sept. 2, 1722.
36 ANDREW, b. Feb. 23, 1724, m. Abigail Billings.
37 HANNAH, b. May 28, 1727, m. John Gallup April 9, 1747.
38 ABIGAIL, b. May 6, 1729, m. Rufus Hewitt (No. 53), that family.
39 JABEZ, b. Jan. 16, 1732, m. Elizabeth Hobart.
40 MARY, b. Nov. 10, 1734, m. Thomas Holmes, Jr., March 15, 1764.

Samuel Frink (No. 32) m. Mary Stanton Feb. 19, 1741.
CHILDREN:
41 SARAH, b. Feb. 10, 1742.
42 DESIRE, b. Feb. 14, 1744.
43 SAMUEL, b. Aug. 31, 1747, m. widow Joannah Hinckley.
44 HENRY, b. Feb. 14, 1749, m. Desire Palmer.
45 DANIEL, b. Feb. 23, 1752, m. Elizabeth Davis.

Andrew Frink (No. 36) m. Abigail Billings Aug. 6, 1746.
CHILDREN:
46 ANDREW, b. Nov. 8, 1746.
47 STEPHEN, b. Aug. 12, 1748, m. Mary Baldwin.
48 OLIVER, b. May 16, 1750.
49 LUCY, b. Dec. 9, 1752.
50 PHILURA, b. Jan. 21, 1755, m. William Searle (No. 22), that family.
51 LATHAM, b. Dec. 14, 1757.

Isaac Frink (No. 33) m. Anna Noyes (No. 119), Noyes family, Nov. 6, 1738; both of Stonington, Conn.
CHILDREN:
52 MARGARET, b. Aug. 28, 1739.
53 ISAAC, b. July 20, 1741, m. Margaret Stanton.
54 ANN, b. Aug. 19, 1743.
55 MARY, b. May 4, 1745.
56 ELIZABETH S., b. July 6, 1748, m. Jeremiah Holmes (No. 50), that family.

David Frink (No. 34) m. Eunice Gallup in 1744, both of Stonington, Conn.
CHILDREN:
57 EUNICE, b. Dec. 4, 1745.
58 LOIS, b. April 8, 1746.
59 ABIGAIL, b. Feb. 12, 1747.

60 HANNAH, b. Dec. 30, 1748.
61 DAVID, b. June 12, 1750.
62 MARY, b. Jan. 26, 1752, m. Peter Hobart (No. 8), that family.
63 ESTHER, b. Oct. 21, 1754.
64 ADAM, b. March 8, 1756.
65 NATHAN, b. April 8, 1759.
66 ISAAC, b. Feb. 4, 1761.

Nicholas Frink (No. 19) m. Deborah Pendleton Nov. 30, 1715 (No. 16), that family.

CHILDREN:

67 NATHAN, b. Oct. 12, 1716.
68 JOHN, b. March 7, 1718, d. young.
69 WILLIAM, b. Oct. 30, 1719.
70 DEBORAH, b. June 15, 1722.
71 SARAH, b. March 7, 1724.
72 OLIVER, b. Dec. 12, 1726.
73 EPHRAIM, b. Jan. 8, 1728.
74 WILLIAM, b. Jan. 20, 1731.

Zachariah Frink (No. 22) m. Elizabeth Gallup (No. 29), that family, daughter of John and Elizabeth (Harris) Gallup.

CHILDREN:

75 UZZIEL, b. in 1716.

Benjamin Frink (No. 25) m. Tacy Burdick of Westerly, R. I., Jan. 12, 1732.

CHILDREN:

76 JOHN, b. Oct. 26, 1732, m. Anna Pendleton.
77 SAMUEL, b. Oct. 24, 1734, m. Prudence Wilcox July 27, 1756.
78 AMOS, b. Jan. 18, 1737, m. Mary Fitch.
79 JOSEPH, b. June 20, 1739.
80 PRENTICE, b. July 31, 1741, m. Desire Frink.
81 PRUDENCE, b. March 18, 1744.
82 TRACY, b. Sept. 22, 1748.
83 ANN, b. Sept. 22, 1748.
83a OLIVER, b. Sept. 4, 1751.

Samuel Frink (No. 43) m. Mrs. Joannah (Rose) Hinckley, widow of John Hinckley, Nov. 29, 1764.

CHILDREN:

84 PRUDENCE, b. Jan. 19, 1764, m. Prentice Frink.
85 SAMUEL, b. Sept. 16, 1765.
86 JOANNAH, b. Jan. 26, 1769, m. William Vincent (No. 16), that family.
87 MARY, b. Sept. 23, 1770.

Henry Frink (No. 44) m. Desire Palmer (No. 184), that family, July 15, 1772.

CHILDREN:

88 SAMUEL, b. and d. Dec. 24, 1772.
89 SAMUEL, b. Jan. 16, 1773.

FRINK FAMILY. 379

90 HENRY (twin), b. Jan. 16, 1773.
91 Twins, b. Nov. 27, 1774, b. d. young.
92 POLLY, b. May 24, 1774.

Daniel Frink (No. 45) m. Elizabeth Davis in 1776.
CHILDREN:
93 BETSEY, b. Sept. 10, 1778.
94 DANIEL, b. April 21, 1781.
95 ELISHA, b. July 16, 1783.
96 DUDLEY, b. Sept. 23, 1785.
97 SAMUEL, b. March 23, 1788, d. unmarried.
98 JOSEPH, b. Dec. 3, 1790, m. Hannah Breed.

Stephen Frink (No. 47) m. Mary Baldwin (No. 32), that family, Nov. 8, 1780; both of Stonington, Conn.
CHILDREN:
99 STEPHEN, b. Oct. 20, 1781.
100 EDWIN, b. March 4, 1784.

Prudence Frink (No. 84) m. Prentice Frink March 4, 1784.
CHILDREN:
101 PRENTICE, b. Sept. 19, 1784.
102 JOSEPH, b. Dec. 20, 1786.
103 PRUDENCE, b. Oct. 6, 1788, m. Gilbert Collins (No. 12), that family.
104 NANCY, b. Dec. 20, 1790, m.

Isaac Frink (No. 53) m. Margaret Stanton (No. 145), that family, Jan. 23, 1762.
CHILDREN:
104a WILLIAM, b. Nov. 23, 1762, m. Wealthy Downer.
105 ISAAC, b. April 26, 1765.
106 ANNA, b. Oct. 24, 1767.
107 ELIAS, b. Feb. 9, 1770.
108 CYRUS, b. Jan. 5, 1772.
109 POLLY, b. Feb. 26, 1778.
110 DARIUS, b. Feb. 26, 1778, m. Ruby Armstrong of Franklin, Nov. 2, 1806.
111 EUNICE, b. Feb. 24, 1780.

Prentice Frink (No. 80) m. Desire Frink Nov. 13, 1763.
CHILDREN:
112 PRENTICE, Jr., b. June 26, 1764.
113 ROSWELL, b. April 9, 1766.
114 NATHAN, b. April 22, 1768.
115 RUFUS, b. April 21, 1770.
116 DESIRE, b. July 7, 1772.
117 STANTON, b. April 12, 1775.
118 LOIS, b. Aug. 20, 1777.

John Frink (No. 76) m. Anna Pendleton Nov. 22, 1750.
CHILDREN:
119 JOHN, b. Sept. 12, 1751.
120 GILES, b. May 12, 1753.
121 SARAH, b. Dec. 9, 1755.

Joseph Frink (No. 98) m. Hannah Breed (No. 120), daughter of Capt. Jesse Breed Oct. 31, 1823; she d. June 20, 1827; m. 2d, Mrs. Lucy (Billings) Coats, widow of Asher Coats.

CHILDREN:

122 HANNAH, b. ———, m. Thomas H. Baldwin May 24, 1847.
123 JOSEPH, b. ———.

CHILD BY SECOND MARRIAGE:

124 MARY, b. ———.

William Frink (No. 104a) m. Wealthy Downer Jan. 3, 1790.

CHILDREN:

125 WILLIAM, b. Dec. 7, 1790.
126 FANNY, b. Aug. 8, 1792.
127 BENJAMIN F., b. Aug. 12, 1794.
128 PITTS D., b. Oct. 12, 1796, m. Nancy Pendleton (No. 83).
129 MARY A., b. Oct. 12, 1798.
130 ISAPENA, b. Sept. 28, 1800.
131 ALEXANDER, b. ———, m. ——— Miner.

Amos Frink (No. 78) m. Mary Fitch Feb. 4, 1759.

CHILDREN:

132 AMOS, b. Nov. 18, 1760.
133 GILBERT, b. Dec. 12, 1762.

Jabez Frink (No. 39) m. Elizabeth Hobart Sept. 20, 1759.

CHILDREN:

134 JABISH, b. Aug. 4, 1760.
135 ELIZABETH, b. Nov. 13, 1761.
136 CHARLES, b. June 11, 1763.
137 PEREZ, b. Oct. 3, 1765.
138 MARY, b. April 3, 1767.
139 EZRA, b. April 2, 1769.
140 JONATHAN, b. Nov. 14, 1770.
141 DUDLEY, b. Jan. 11, 1773.

Samuel Frink (No. 77) m. Prudence Wilcox July 27, 1756.

CHILDREN:

142 JANIUS, b. Dec. 8, 1758.
143 LUCRETIA, b. ———.

GALLUP FAMILY.

The name is said to be derived from the German words "Gott" and Lobe"—God and Praise, as Godfrey comes from "Gott" and "Frende"—God and Peace. In the old English records the name is spelled in different ways, as Gollop, Gollopp, Golloppe, Golop. The present English family still retain Gollop. In the Boston records, we find almost as great a variety of spelling as the ancient England records, Gallup preponderating, however, by the large majority in this country.

1. JOHN GALLUP, the ancestor of most of the families of that name in this country, came to America from the Parish of Mosterne, County Dorset, England, in the year 1630. He was the son of John Gollop, who m. ──── Crabbe, who was the son of Thomas and Agnes (Watkins) Gollop, of North Bowood and Strode, and whose descendants still own and occupy the manors of Strode. He m. Christobel ────────, whose full name does not appear. He sailed from England March 20, 1630, in the ship Mary and John, arriving at Nantasket (the name was changed to Hull in 1646), May 30, 1630. He first went to Dorchester, but soon after he was a resident of Boston. The family being again united, they became members of the first church, the old South, in Boston. He became a landholder, owning land in the town, and an island of sixteen acres in Boston Bay, which still bears his name. He owned Mix's Mate or Monumental Island, as sometimes called, where he pastured sheep. He was a skillful mariner, well acquainted with the harbor around Boston. He achieved great distinction by piloting in the ship Griffin, a ship of three hundred tons, in Sept., 1633, through a new found channel, when she had on board the Rev. John Cotton, Rev. Thomas Hooker, Rev. Mr. Stone and other fathers of New England, among her two hundred passengers. Perhaps the most notable and interesting episode, if it may be so called, in the life of the sturdy captain, was his successful encounter with a boat load of Indians, whom he captured and destroyed off Block Island. They had murdered John Oldham, a man of ability, and they were having a hilarious time in his boat when they were overtaken by Capt. Gallup, and after a brief encounter, were captured. This has been

called the first naval battle on the Atlantic coast. He was accompanied by his two sons and a hired man. This battle gave the captain a colonial, and later a national reputation, and more than anything else made him famous. This incident and what is revealed of the purpose of the Indians was the beginning of the great Pequot war.

Mr. and Mrs. Gallup both died at Boston, he in 1649, as an inventory of his estate was made Dec. 26, 1649. She died July 27, 1655. An inventory of her estate was made Oct. 31, 1655. Their wills are the earliest on record. (See Appendix.)

CHILDREN:

2 JOHN, b. in England about 1615, m. Hannah Lake in 1634.
3 SAMUEL, b. in England; came to this country in 1633, m. Mary Phillips.
4 NATHANIEL, b. in England; came to this country in 1633, m. Margaret Eveley.
5 JOAN, b. in England; came to this country in 1633, m. Thomas Joy in 1627.

John Gallup (No. 2) came to this country with his mother, two brothers and sister Joan, in the ship Griffin, arriving at Boston on the 4th day of Sept., 1633. He married Hannah Lake, daughter of John and Margaret Lake, and sister of Elizabeth Read, who married John Winthrop, Jr., Governor of Connecticut. She also came to this country with her mother, in the ship Abigail, arriving Oct. 6, 1635, after a passage of ten weeks.

He left Boston in 1640, and went to Taunton, then a part of Plymouth Colony, where he remained until 1651, when he removed with his family to New London, where he lived until 1654, when he came to what is now Stonington, then a part of New London, and settled upon a grant of land given him by that town in 1653, in recognition of the distinguished services of himself, and father in the Pequot war.

His dwelling house where he resided, was situated near where there is now (1899) an old well, in an orchard, on the farm recently owned by the Messrs. Greenman brothers, under the improvement and management of Dea. Warren Lewis. Capt. John Gallup's land grant was bounded on the west by Mystic River, on the south by Capt. John Stanton's homestead place and Capt. George Denison's land, on the east by said Denison's land and the so-called town lots, and on the north by Thomas Park's land, which he purchased of the Rev. Richard Blinman. He represented the town at the General Court in 1665, 1667. He was also an Indian interpreter. When King Philip's war broke out, although he was over sixty, age had not quenched his martial ardor, New London County having raised seventy men under Capt. John Mason of Norwich, and Capt. George Denison of Stonington, Capt. Gallup joined with them at the head of the Mohegans. These troops forming a junction with those of the other colonies, were engaged in the fearful swamp fight at Narragansett, Dec. 19, 1676, within the limits of the present town of South Kingston. R. I. In storming the fort he led his men bravely forward, and was one of the six captains who fell in this memorable fight, and was buried with his fallen comrades in one grave, near the battle ground. A complete victory was gained over the savage foe, but with great loss of life on both sides. The General Court afterwards made several grants of land to his widow and children, in consideration of the great loss they had sustained by his death and for his public services.

CHILDREN:

6 HANNAH, b. at Boston Sept. 14, 1644, m. Stephen Gifford June 18, 1672.
7 JOHN, b. at Boston Sept., 1646, m. Elizabeth Harris.
8 ESTHER, b. at New London March 24, 1653, m. Henry Hodges Dec. 17, 1674.
9 BENADAM, b. at Stonington in 1655, m. Hester Prentiss.
10 WILLIAM, b. at Stonington in 1658, m. Sarah Chesebrough.
11 SAMUEL, b. at Stonington.
12 CHRISTOBEL, b. at Stonington, m. Peter Crary Dec. 31, 1677.
13 ELIZABETH, b. at Stonington, m. Henry Stevens of Stonington.
14 MARY, b. at Stonington, m. John Cole of Boston, Mass.
15 MARGARET, b. at Stonington, m. Joseph Colver of Groton, Conn.

Samuel Gallup (No. 3) m. Mary Phillips Nov. 20, 1650. He lived at Boston; was a sea captain and d. before 1670.

CHILDREN:

16 MARY, b. Dec. 4, 1651.
17 HANNAH, b. Sept. 3, 1654.
18 SAMUEL, b. Feb. 14, 1656.
19 MEHITABLE, b. April 5, 1659.
20 ABIGAIL, b. June 27, 1664.

Nathaniel Gallup (No. 4) m. Margaret Eveley at Boston April 11, 1652, and d. before 1670.

CHILDREN:

21 NATHANIEL, b. June 14, 1658.
22 JOSEPH, b. March 20, 1661, m. Hannah Sharp Nov. 1, 1694.
23 BENJAMIN, b. Jan. 3, 1664.
24 MARY, b. June 25, 1668.

John Gallup (No. 7) m. Elizabeth Harris of Ipswich, Mass.,

1675, daughter of Thomas and Martha Lake Harris, and granddaughter of Madame Margaret Lake; she d. Feb. 8, 1654. They lived in Stonington in the dwelling house where his parents resided, occupying and improving his father's grants of land. He represented the town in the General Court in 1665, 1666, 1667, 1668. He served with his father in King Philip's war, and was probably with him at the Narragansett swamp fight. He was on friendly terms with the Indians, and often acted as their interpreter. He d. April 14, 1735.

CHILDREN:

25 JOHN, b. in 1676, m. Elizabeth Wheeler.
26 THOMAS, bapt. ――――.
27 MARTHA, b. April 2, 1683, m. John Gifford of Norwich, Conn.
28 SAMUEL, bapt. Oct. 9, 1687, m. Mehitable Blunt.
29 ELIZABETH, bapt. July 14, 1689, m. Zachariah Frink (No. 22), that family.
30 NATHANIEL, b. July 4, 1692, m. Margaret Gallup.
31 WILLIAM, bapt. May 26, 1695, d. at Voluntown Aug. 18, 1735.
32 BENJAMIN, bapt. Nov. 1, 1696.

Benadam Gallup (No. 9) m. Hester Prentiss, daughter of John and Hester Prentiss, and granddaughter of Valentine and Alice Prentiss of New London, Conn. He and his nephew, John Gallup, who m. Elizabeth Wheeler, lived on the eastern part of his father's land grants, known as the Pe-quot-se-pos Valley. They jointly built and occupied the dwelling house, where an old chimney thereof now stands (1899) which with their lands, is now mainly owned by the heirs-at-law of Hiram W. Wheeler and Lodowick Wilcox. He served in the colonial wars. They both united with the First Congregational Church of Stonington. He d. Aug. 2, 1727; his wife d. May 17, 1751.

CHILDREN:

33 HANNAH, b. May 22, 1683, m. William Wheeler May 30, 1710 (No. 12), Wheeler family.
34 HESTER, b. Nov. 1, 1685, m. Joseph Stanton of Westerly, R. I. (No. 216), Stanton family.
35 MERCY, b. Aug., 1690, m. William Denison (No. 67), Denison family.
36 BENADAM, b. April 18, 1693, m. Eunice Cobb.
37 JOSEPH, b. Sept. 27, 1695, m. Eunice Williams.
38 MARGARET, b. May 11, 1698, m. Nathaniel Gallup (No. 30), June 4, 1717.
39 LUCY, b. Jan. 12, 1701, m. George Denison June 4, 1717 (No. 69), Denison family.

Lieut. William Gallup (No. 10) m. Sarah, (No. 22), daughter of Capt. Nathaniel Chesebrough, of that family, who was one of the early planters of Stonington, Jan. 4, 1684. He, too, built him a dwelling house on the northern portion of his father's land grants, which was situated on the White Hall plain, where Mr. Samuel H. Bentley now (1899) resides. He d. May 15, 1731; his wife d. Sept. 9, 1729. They are both buried in the White Hall burial place. He served in the colonial wars.

CHILDREN:

40 SARAH, b. Feb. 24, 1688, m. Andrew Stanton.
41 MARY, b. April 7, 1695, m. Dea. John Noyes (No. 34), Noyes family.
42 HANNAH, b. April 24, 1698, d. unmarried.
43 TEMPERANCE, b. May 25, 1701, m. Rev. William Worthington Sept. 20, 1726. He was the first minister (Cong.) of North Stonington, and a graduate of Yale College, 1716. His first wife, Elizabeth, was the grand-daughter of Maj. John Mason. She d. Feb. 24, 1724; he d. at Saybrook, after a long pastorate, Nov. 16, 1756.

CHILDREN:

44 ELIZABETH WORTHINGTON, b. Feb. 27, 1728.
45 SARAH WORTHINGTON, b. April 3, 1730.
46 TEMPERANCE WORTHINGTON, b. April 18, 1732, m. Rev. Cotton Mather Smith of Sharon, Conn. Their only son was the Hon. John Cotton Smith, one of the Governors of Connecticut. He was President of the American Bible Society from 1831 to 1845.
47 MEHITABLE WORTHINGTON, b. Sept. 11, 1736.
48 WILLIAM WORTHINGTON, b. Nov. 21, 1740.

Capt. John Gallup (No. 25) m. Elizabeth Wheeler of Stonington in 1709 (No. 13), Wheeler family. He removed to Voluntown about 1710, and was one of the early settlers of that town, taking up a large tract of land there. At the first town meeting held in the town June 20, 1721, he was chosen one of the selectmen, was active in securing religious privileges for the early settlers, giving three acres of land as a site for a meeting house and burial ground, and one of a committee to build a house of worship, and was chosen one of the ruling elders of the first church formed in the town, 1723, which was Presbyterian. He d. Dec. 29, 1755; his wife d. April 14, 1735. From his will it appears he m. again, but no record of it has been found.

CHILDREN:

49 WILLIAM, b. Sept. 2, 1710, d. Feb. 10, 1734.
50 ISAAC, b. Feb. 24, 1712.
51 ELIZABETH, b. April 9, 1714, m. Zachary Frink.
52 MARTHA, b. Sept. 3, 1716, m. Thomas Douglass Jan. 4, 1727.
53 HANNAH, b. Jan. 29, 1719, m. Manuel Kinne in 1741.
54 DOROTHY, b. March 22, 1721, m. John Read in 1744.
55 JOHN, b. June 9, 1724.

Thomas Gallup (No. 26) was bapt. at Stonington, Conn., April 30, 1682 (Voluntown Town Records). "Thomas Gallup and Hannah French were lawfully joined in marriage the 4th day of Jan., 1721-22, by Capt. Thomas Williams, justice of the peace." He probably came to Voluntown with his brother John, or soon after, and was a large land owner there. His name is appended to a call to the first minister of Voluntown, Rev. Samuel Dorrance, April 17, 1723. He also gave liberally for his support. He left no children.

Reliable, available evidence establishes the fact that there were two Thomas Gallups, born in Stonington, within a few years of each other. Thomas Gallup, the son of John Gallup and wife, Elizabeth Harris, was probably b. in 1681. The other Thomas Gallup was undoubtedly the son of Benadam Gallup and wife, Hester Prentiss, and was probably born between the birth date of their children, viz.: Marcy Gallup, b. Aug., 1687, and Benadam Gallup, Jr., b. April 18, 1693. For reasons not now fully understood the birth dates of their children, Marcy and Thomas, does not appear among their other children on our Stonington town records.

Thomas Gallup, the son of Benadam and Hester (Prentiss) Gallup, was reared to manhood in Stonington, and went with two of his cousins up to what is now Windham County, where they purchased and received large tracts of lands, the proposed boundaries of which overlapped the premises of the adjoining proprietors' lands, resulting in a controversy, which ended in reducing the area of the land purchased and received to such an extent before the deeds thereof were obtained, that the said Thomas Gallup, son of Benadam, retired from the land speculation and went to Gloucester, Mass., where he was engaged to build a breakwater for parties there. The location and construction of which were so ill advised that the breakwater received the name of Gallup's Folly, which it still retains, and so appears on the map of Babson's history of that town. After the completion of the breakwater, Thomas Gallup left Gloucester and went to Ipswich, Mass., where he had relatives, but did not remain there long, and went from Ipswich to Boxford, where he m. Love Curtis, widow of Zachariah Curtis, in 1719.

CHILDREN:

56 ABIGAIL, b. Dec. 9, 1720.
57 WILLIAM, b. Oct. 4, 1722.
58 SAMUEL, b. May 7, 1725.

GALLUP FAMILY. 387

59 GEORGE, b. Dec. 14, 1726.
60 JEREMIAH, b. in 1728.
61 SARAH, b. March 20, 1733.
62 MARY, b. Feb. 14, 1738.

Samuel Gallup of Stonington (No. 28) m. Mehitable Blunt May 11, 1727. He owned land at Voluntown, but it is not probable that he ever removed his family there to live, as he is mentioned in his father's will, as living with him and taking care of him. He and his wife united with the First Congregational Church in Stonington, May 11, 1729.

CHILDREN:
63 ELIZABETH, b. Dec. 26, 1728.
64 MEHITABLE, b. Feb. 21, 1733.
65 MARY, b. Jan. 28, 1737, m. Andrew Mason March 20, 1754 (No. 29), that family.
66 PRISCILLA, bapt. July 20, 1740.
67 MERCY (twin), bapt. June 2, 1745.
68 ANNA (twin), bapt. June 2, 1745.

Nathaniel Gallup of Stonington (No. 30) m. Margaret Gallup (No. 38) June 4, 1717. They lived on the Greenman farm, near the residence of Mr. Warren Lewis, and both united with the Congregational Church, Stonington, July 20, 1718. He d. April 3, 1739; his wife d. March 2, 1761.

CHILDREN:
69 NATHANIEL, b. April 29, 1718, m. Hannah Gore Burrows.
70 JOHN, b. Jan. 29, 1720, m. Bridget Palmer.
71 THOMAS, b. April 19, 1722, d. young.
72 MERCY, b. April 7, 1725, m. William Whipple Dec. 2, 1742.
73 THOMAS, b. Aug. 26, 1727, m. Hannah Dean; lived at Plainfield.
74 MARGARET, b. Oct. 12, 1730, m. Isaac Gallup March 29, 1749.
75 MARTHA, b. July 30, 1733.
76 BENJAMIN, b. July 26, 1736, m. Amy Kinne Jan. 20, 1763.

Benadam Gallup (No. 36) m. Eunice Cobb (No. 18), Cobb family, Jan. 11, 1716. He d. Sept. 30, 1755; his wife d. Feb. 1, 1759.

CHILDREN:
77 BENADAM, b. Oct. 26, 1716, m. Hannah Avery.
78 ESTHER, b. Feb. 24, 1718, m. ——— Miner.
79 EUNICE, b. March 29, 1721, m. ——— French.
80 LOIS (twin), b. March 29, 1721.
81 WILLIAM, b. July 4, 1723, m. Judith Reed of Norwich June 9, 1752.
82 HENRY, b. Oct. 5, 1725, m. Hannah Mason Oct. 4, 1750.
83 NATHAN, b. in 1727, m. Sarah Giddings of Norwich May 25, 1749.
84 EBENEZER, b. ———.
85 THOMAS, bapt. July 28, 1734, m. Prudence Allyn of Groton Jan. 20, 1729.
86 HANNAH, b. ———, m. Robert Allyn Jan. 26, 1755.
87 SARAH, b. ———.

Capt. Joseph Gallup of Stonington (No. 37) m. Eunice Williams (No. 161), Williams family, of Stonington, Feb. 24, 1720. They lived at Old Mystic, near the Lewis house; he d. Dec. 22, 1760; his wife d. Oct. 24, 1772.

CHILDREN:

88 MARTHA, b. Oct. 15, 1721, m. Amos Denison of Stonington (No. 134), that family.
89 JOSEPH, b. Feb. 21, 1725, m. Mary Gardner May 18, 1749.
90 ELISHA, b. April 21, 1727, m. Marcy Denison Jan. 25, 1747 (No. 169), that family.
91 OLIVER, b. March 28, 1729, m. Freelove ———.
92 WILLIAM, b. Jan. 19, 1735, m. Lucy Denison July 2, 1761 (No. 296), that family.
93 EUNICE, b. Oct. 11, 1738, m. John Billings of Preston (No. 36), that family.
94 PRUDENCE, b. Feb. 17, 1742.
95 LUCY, b. Jan. 5, 1747.

Nathaniel Gallup of Stonington (No. 69) m. Mrs. Hannah (Gore) Burrows Nov. 24, 1742 (No. 36), that family. He d. Jan. 11, 1786; she d. March 19, 1810.

CHILDREN:

96 NATHANIEL, b. June 4, 1744, drowned at sea, aged 20 yrs.
97 SAMUEL, b. Aug. 9, 1746, m. Jemima Enos.
98 SILAS, b. March 9, 1749, m. Sarah Gallup (No. 60), Jan. 13, 1774.
99 GEORGE, b. March 20, 1751, m. Freelove Packer of Groton June 19, 1776.
100 MARGARET, b. March 20, 1753.
101 AMOS, b. Aug. 1, 1755, m. Welthian Dean.
102 HANNAH, b. Aug. 22, 1757.
103 LEVI, b. March 26, 1760, m. Abigail Packer of Groton.
104 EZRA, b. March 13, 1763, m. Rebecca Hinckley, 1786 (No. 64), that family.

Capt. John Gallup (No. 70) m. Bridget Palmer (No. 113), that family, Nov. 5, 1747. He d. Nov. 1, 1801; she d. Sept. 2, 1809.

CHILDREN:

105 JERUSHA, b. 1748, d. 1841.
106 JOHN, b. 1750, m. Lydia Clark.
107 JONATHAN, b. 1752, m. Elizabeth Dow.
108 DAVID, b. 1754, m. Nancy Jacques.
109 MARGARET, b. ———, m. Samuel Frink.
110 ESTHER, b. ———, d. young.

Col. Benadam Gallup (No. 77) m. Hannah Avery of Groton (No. 77), that family, Aug. 11, 1740. He was a brave officer of the Revolution. He d. May 29, 1800; she d. July 28, 1799.

CHILDREN:

111 BENADAM, b. June 29, 1741, m. Bridget Palmer.
112 ISAAC, b. Dec. 22, 1742, m. Anna Smith.
113 HANNAH, b. Nov. 4, 1744, d. Jan. 10, 1771.

GALLUP FAMILY.

114 ESTHER, b. Dec. 9, 1746, m. Ralph Stoddard.
115 JAMES, b. May 1, 1749, d. Dec. 19, 1770.
116 JESSE, b. Feb. 2, 1751, m. Catharine Fish March 16, 1775.
117 JOHN, b. Jan. 13, 1753, d. Dec. 9, 1770.
118 PRUDENCE, b. Jan. 30, 1775, m. Timothy Allyn.
119 SUSAN, b. 1776, m. Nathan Lester.
120 JOSIAH, b. 1760, m. 1st, Sarah Fish; 2d, Mary Randall.
121 ABIGAIL, b. 1762, d. Nov. 24, 1770.

Col. Nathan Galllup (No. 83) m. Sarah Giddings, May 25, 1749. He was a brave soldier of the Revolution, who rose to colonel and d. Jan. 19, 1799.

CHILDREN:

122 SARAH, b. Dec. 29, 1751, m. Silas Gallup.
123 NATHAN, b. Nov. 14, 1754, d. Sept. 16, 1778.
124 EBENEZER, b. Feb. 8, 1757.
125 MARY, b. Jan. 31, 1759, m. Henry Denison in 1778 (No. 222), Denison family.
126 JACOB, b. July 26, 1761, m. Rebecca Morgan Jan. 11, 1784.
127 CHRISTOPHER, b. June 22, 1764, m. Mrs. Martha (Stanton) Prentice.
128 GIDEON, b. Aug. 17, 1766.
129 LOIS, b. Aug. 17, 1768, m. Jacob Morgan in 1787.
130 LODOWICK, b. Jan. 23, 1773, m. Margaret Phelps Feb. 28, 1779.

Capt. Joseph Gallup (No. 89) m. Mary Gardner, daughter of Joseph and Sarah Gardner, May 18, 1749; d. July 11, 1802.

CHILDREN:

131 JOSEPH, b. March 21, 1750, d. Feb. 11, 1753.
132 SARAH, b. Nov. 10, 1752.
133 JOSEPH, b. Sept. 26, 1754.
134 JOHN, b. July 17, 1758, m. Hannah Denison.
135 LUCRETIA, b. Aug. 15, 1760.
136 PHEBE, b. April 10, 1762, m. William Avery of Groton.
137 GARDNER, b. March 5, 1765.
138 JONATHAN, b. Nov. 23, 1766.
139 ESTHER, b. April 14, 1769.
140 GURDON, b. Dec. 18, 1771, m. Sibell Capron.

Samuel Gallup (No. 97) m. Jemima Enos of Stonington Jan. 1, 1769. Soon after the Revolution he with his four brothers, and several other families from Groton and Stonington, removed to New York State. He d. April 25, 1826; his wife d. Dec. 15, 1795; 2d wife, Sarah, d. Sept. 1, 1802.

CHILDREN:

141 JOSHUA, b. Aug. 4, 1760, m. Anne Hinckley (No. 66), that family.
142 NATHANIEL, b. Nov. 16, 1770, m. Lucy Latham.
143 SAMUEL, b. July 6, 1772, m. Fanny Morgan.
144 ANNA, b. Feb. 3, 1774, m. Richard Wheeler of Stonington Feb. 13, 1794 (No. 362), Wheeler family.

390 HISTORY OF STONINGTON.

145 HANNAH, b. Oct. 15, 1775, m. Moses Morgan March 29, 1794.
146 JOHN ENOS, b. July 17, 1777, m. Betsey Chipman; 2d, Mrs. Esther Denison.
147 JEMIMA, b. Sept. 27, 1780, m. Daniel Morgan in 1799.
148 LYDIA, b. Feb. 16, 1784, m. George Gallup.
149 NATHAN, b. May 3, 1786, m. Anna Elizabeth Weidman.

Amos Gallup of Stonington (No. 101), m. Welthean Deane of Stonington (No. 28), that family, Feb. 25, 1787. He d. Dec. 1, 1843; she d. Dec. 13, 1834.

CHILDREN:

150 AMOS, b. Dec. 9, 1787, d. May 5, 1870, unmarried.
151 JOHN DEANE, b. Sept. 26, 1789, m. Prudence Denison; 2d, Mary A. Crandall.
152 JABEZ, b. Feb. 22, 1791, m. Eunice Williams.
153 WEALTHEAN, b. July 15, 1793, d. Oct. 5, 1874, unmarried.
154 MARTHA, b. Jan. 22, 1796, d. Aug., 1882, unmarried.
155 NATHANIEL, b. Oct. 16, 1797, m. Sally McCollum; 2d, Maria D. Ford.
156 GEORGE, b. Jan. 22, 1801, d. Feb. 9, 1874, unmarried.

Col. Benadam Gallup (No. 111) m. Bridget Palmer of Stonington (No. 210), Palmer family, Jan. 30, 1766. He d. April 12, 1818; his wife d. Aug. 22, 1823.

CHILDREN:

157 BENADAM, b. Oct. 28, 1766, m. Cynthia Fish.
158 BRIDGET, b. Oct. 5, 1768, m. Sands Fish June 18, 1789 (No. 39), that family.
159 JAMES, b. May 27, 1771, d. May 11, 1834.
160 DESIRE, b. Nov. 20, 1773, m. Amos Worthington.
161 JOHN, b. May 27, 1776, m. Lucy Clark of Windham.
162 LUCY, b. June 23, 1779, m. Stephen Haley of Groton (No. 34), that family.
163 SIMEON, b. Sept. 29, 1781, d. April 13, 1836.

Isaac Gallup (No. 112) m. Anna Smith Oct. 5, 1786. He was captain in the Revolutionary war. He d. in Ledyard Aug. 3, 1814. Mrs. Anna (Smith) Gallup m. 2d, Seth Williams Jan. 30, 1825.

CHILDREN:

164 ANNA, b. Sept. 3, 1787, m. David Geer Jan. 11, 1810.
165 ISAAC, b. Jan. 21, 1789, m. Prudence Geer March 12, 1812.
166 RUSSEL, b. April 11, 1791, m. Hannah Morgan.
167 SARAH, b. Nov. 9, 1792, m. William McCall.
168 JABESH, b. Aug. 23, 1794, m. Lucy Meech; 2d, Louise Avery.
169 AVERY, b. April 6, 1796, m. Melinda Bailey; 2d, Mary Haley.
170 ELIAS, b. April 14, 1798, m. Fanny Dean Sept. 28, 1828.
171 ERASTUS, b. July 31, 1800, m. Eunice Williams (No. 52), that family; 2d, Frances Sheffield.
172 SHUBAEL, b. March 6, 1802, m. Sarah M. Isham; 2d, Mrs. Fanny S. Church.
173 ELIHU, b. Dec. 12, 1803, m. Emily Clark.

GALLUP FAMILY.

Christopher Gallup (No. 127) m. Mrs. Martha (Stanton) Prentice (No. 383), Stanton family, April 13, 1790. He d. July 30, 1849; his wife d. Feb. 12, 1818.

CHILDREN:

174 ASA, b. Dec. 17, 1792.
175 ELIZABETH, b. Jan. 21, 1795, m. Warren Williams Jan. 12, 1815 (No. 48), Williams family.
177 MARTHA, b. Sept. 26, 1796.
178 SARAH, b. Aug. 9, 1803.
179 JULIA, b. July 26, 1807, m. Joseph S. Williams Dec. 29, 1824 (No. 363), Williams family.
180 CHRISTOPHER M., b. Nov. 25, 1809, m. Anna S. Billings (No. 178), that family.

Henry Gallup (No. 82) m. Hannah Mason (No. 30), that family, Oct. 4, 1750. He d. Nov. 11, 1811; she d. Jan. 24, 1808.

CHILDREN:

181 NEHEMIAH, b. June 19, 1751, m. Elizabeth Brown.
182 EUNICE, b. Aug. 7, 1755, m. Samuel Dennis.
183 HENRY, b. Oct. 17, 1758, m. Desire Stanton.
184 ANDREW, b. Jan. 26, 1761, m. Nancy Welden.
185 JARED, b. Nov. 22, 1767, m. Mary Whipple.

Lodowick Gallup (No. 130) m. Margaret Phelps Feb. 28, 1779.

CHILDREN:

186 LUCY K., b. May 11, 1801.
187 NATHAN, b. Jan. 24, 1803.
188 CECELIA, b. Nov. 7, 1804, m. Giles Williams Dec. 6, 1869.
189 LOUISE, b. Jan. 21, 1807, d. March 6, 1891.
190 LODOWICK C., b. Feb. 11, 1809, m. Nancy White Sept. 22, 1834.
191 OLIVER E., b. April 24, 1811, d. Aug. 31, 1834, unmarried.
192 FANNIE M., b. March 2, 1814, m. Giles Williams Sept. 13, 1833.
193 LAWISTON, b. Nov. 16, 1816, d. Aug. 28, 1831.
194 ASA ORAN, b. Jan. 31, 1819, m. Wealthy P. Palmer July 4, 1849.
195 JOHN P., b. Dec. 14, 1821, d. Dec. 13, 1831.
196 DWIGHT, b. April 14, 1825, m. Lydia A. Wadhams Nov. 19, 1849.
197 MARGARET, b. Dec. 30, 1828.

Gurdon Gallup (No. 140) m. Sibell Capron of Preston, Feb. 15, 1795. He d. Dec. 17, 1847; his wife d. April 9, 1852. They are buried at Poquonock Bridge, in Ashbey burying ground.

CHILDREN:

198 LUCY, b. Nov. 5, 1796, m. Rev. Hector Bronson.
199 GURDON, b. May 16, 1798.
200 GRACE, b. Oct. 16, 1799.
201 FREDERICK, b. May 29, 1801.
202 JOSEPH, b. May 2, 1803, m. Abby Ann Denison Nov. 3, 1825.
203 GILES, b. May 7, 1805, m. Sarah O. Witter Jan. 20, 1833.
204 MARY A., b. Nov. 17, 1807.
205 SABRA, b. Nov. 11, 1809.
206 FRANKLIN, b. Aug. 18, 1812, m. 1st, Hannah Burrows (No. 72), that family, Aug. 18, 1834; 2d, Sarah E. Burrows (No. 78), sister of his first wife, April 9, 1843.

HISTORY OF STONINGTON.

Joshua Gallup (No. 141) b. in Stonington, Conn., Aug. 4, 1769, m. Anna Hinckley (No. 66), that family. He d. Jan. 4, 1837; his wife d. Jan. 16, 1843.

CHILDREN:

207 JOSHUA, b. March 2, 1790, m. Mary Gould in 1815.
208 ANNA, b. May 22, 1791, m. Oliver Forsyth of Mystic, Conn.
209 JEMIMA, b. Aug. 19, 1792, m. Levi Gallup.
210 SAMUEL, b. Jan. 27, 1794, m. Margaret Fisher March 17, 1816.
211 KETURAH, b. April 16, 1795, d. young.
212 ELIAS, b. Oct. 1, 1796, d. young.
213 SARAH, b. Feb. 23, 1798, m .Chester Willis.
214 MARY, b. Nov. 6, 1799, m. Samuel Morgan Nov. 25, 1827.
215 RHODA, b. April 11, 1803, m. Thomas Slade, whose first wife was her sister, Harriet.
216 HARRIET, b. Oct. 27, 1804.
217 LUKE, b. Sept. 26, 1806, m. Jemima Slade Sept. 26, 1830.

Nathaniel Gallup (No. 142), b. in Stonington, Conn., m. Lucy, daughter of Capt. William Latham and wife Eunice, of Groton, March 27, 1794. Capt. Latham was second in command at the massacre of Fort Griswold, and was severely wounded, but recovered. He d. Jan. 27, 1792, his wife d. March 5, 1799. Lucy Latham, afterwards Mrs. Gallup, was 12 years old at the time of the battle, and often related to her children the story of that memorable day. When the British appeared at Eastern Point, Lambo, the colored servant, gathered the family and drove them to the Avery house, two miles away, then hurried back to the fort with his gun. He fought at the side of his master, Capt. Latham, and fell. His own name is on the monument at Groton, as "Sambo," but it should be Lambo, as his name was Lambert. Samuel Gallup, father of Nathaniel, removed with his family to Albany County, New York, soon after the war of the Revolution. Nathaniel returned to Groton and was m. there. After his return to New York State he settled in Berne, Albany County, and d. April 20, 1834; his wife d. Feb. 1, 1862.

CHILDREN:

218 ALBERT, b. Jan. 30, 1796, m. Eunice Smith.
219 NATHANIEL, b. Oct. 2, 1798, m. Sally Walden Dec. 16, 1823.
220 EUNICE, b. Oct. 5, 1800, m. William Denison July 15, 1823.

John Dean Gallup of Stonington (No. 151) m. 1st, Prudence Denison (No. 545), Denison family. They had one child that d. in infancy. Married 2d, Mary A. Crandall. He was a farmer and wool manufacturer of Stonington, where he d. July 31, 1871. In

GALLUP FAMILY.

his will he gave $250 to the First Congregational Church of Stonington.

Jabez Gallup (No. 152) of Stonington m. Eunice Williams (No. 306), Williams family, Feb. 25, 1829.

CHILDREN:

221 MARTHA, b. Feb. 16, 1830, m. Dudley R. Hewitt (No. 265), that family, Oct. 11, 1854.
222 JOHN DEAN, b. Nov. 28, 1832.
223 HANNAH, b. April 17, 1834.

Nathaniel Gallup (No. 155) m. 1st, Sally McCollum, May 7, 1832; m. 2d, Maria D. Ford June 10, 1841, and d. April 8, 1877.

ONE CHILD:

224 ANN ELIZABETH, b. July 29, 1833, m. Franklin White Dec. 13, 1860.

Benadam Gallup (No. 157) m. Cynthia Fish Oct. 14, 1792 (No. 43), that family.

CHILDREN:

225 JAMES, b. Nov. 25, 1793, m. Abigail Spicer June 5, 1820.
226 AUSTIN, b. Feb. 24, 1796, d. young.
227 ROSWELL, b. March 11, 1798, d. July 24, 1817.
228 MARY, b. March 4, 1800, m. Nathaniel Smith March 13, 1875.
229 PALMER, b. June 14, 1802, m. Desire Ball.
230 BENADAM, b. June 3, 1804, m. Moselle Laura Moore March 15, 1828.
231 CYNTHIA, b. Aug. 14, 1806, m. Richard Wheeler of Stonington (No. 431), that family.
232 JOHN, b. March 6, 1809, m. Roxanna Fish Aug. 10, 1834.
233 SOPHIA, b. June 16, 1812, m. William E. Smith Aug. 10, 1834.
234 ROSWELL, b. July 24, 1817.

Isaac Gallup (No. 165) m. Prudence Geer March 12, 1812. He d. May 2, 1867; she d. July 6, 1871.

CHILDREN:

235 MARY ANN, b. Dec. 10, 1812, m. Elias B. Avery Jan. 1, 1835.
236 PRUDENCE ALMIRA, b. March 4, 1815, m. James L. Geer Nov. 19, 1834.
237 EMELINE, b. Feb. 27, 1818, m. Orlando Smith April 10, 1845.
238 ISAAC, b. Nov. 13, 1820, m. Maria T. Davis March 23, 1845.
239 JULIA, b. April 4, 1823, m. Jacob A. Geer Oct. 20, 1847.

Russell Gallup (No. 166) m. Hannah Morgan March 28, 1816. He d. Feb. 16, 1869; she d. April 29, 1868.

CHILDREN:

240 EDWIN R., b. Jan. 22, 1817, m. Eliza A. Leeds May 5, 1841.
241 RUFUS M., b. Sept. 24, 1818, m. Betsey Grey; 2d, Mrs. Eliza H. Randall.
242 SARAH, b. Sept. 10, 1821, m. William M. Grey Nov. 28, 1839.
243 JAMES, b. Nov. 18, 1823, m. Emily T. Hubbard; 2d, Charlotte R. Andrew.
245 NELSON, b. Jan. 8, 1827, m. Emily E. Miner Sept. 4, 1850.
246 ERASTUS, b. Sept. 8, 1828, d. on the way to California May 1, 1853.
247 FRANCIS E., b. Aug. 15, 1833.
248 JOSEPH A., b. July 8, 1835, m. Abby Cook Sept. 22, 1868.

Christopher Milton Gallup (No. 180) m. Anna S. Billings (No. 178), that family, June 5, 1833. He d. Feb. 19, 1874; his wife d. at St. Paul, Minn., Aug. 31, 1874.

CHILDREN:

249 MARTHA ANN, b. Sept. 7, 1834, m. Chauncey W. Griggs April 19, 1859.
250 CHRISTOPHER, b. May 31, 1836, m. Hannah Lamb May 13, 1868.
251 NATHAN, b. Oct. 13, 1848, m. P. Emma Geer March 18, 1874.
252 NOYES P., b. April 30, 1853, m. Cora E. Morgan Nov. 17, 1881.

Nehemiah Gallup (No. 181) m. Elizabeth Brown Jan. 28, 1783.

CHILDREN:

253 ELIZABETH, b. Nov. 10, 1783.
254 NEHEMIAH M., b. Feb. 12, 1785, m. Huldah Wheeler.
255 JOHN S., b. April 5, 1787.
256 ORINDA, b. March 8, 1790, m. Christopher Wheeler (No. 397), that family.
257 ELISHA, b. June 22, 1792, m. Content Wheeler of Stonington, 1816 (No. 447), Wheeler family.
258 LUKE, b. April 17, 1794, m. Melinda Williams (No. 14), Williams family.
259 SERVIAH, b. Oct. 16, 1796.
260 EBENEZER, b. April 27, 1800, m. Lavinia Stanton in 1822.

Henry Gallup (No. 183) m. Desire Stanton Nov. 17, 1757.

CHILDREN:

261 ALFRED, b. March 28, 1798, m. Eliza W. Hewitt (No. 223), that family.
262 ANNA, b. March 28, 1805.
263 DESIRE, b. March 26, 1808, m. Elisha J. Hewitt (No. 222), Hewitt family.

Hon. Albert Gallup (No. 218) m. Eunice Smith, daughter of Amos Smith and Priscilla (Mitchell) Smith of Groton. He d. at Albany, N. Y., Nov. 5, 1851; his wife d. Oct. 17, 1872.

CHILDREN:

264 CAROLINE, b. Aug. 5, 1821, m. Rev. Sylvanus Reed of Albany, N. Y.; in 1862 Mr. and Mrs. Reed removed to New York city. She had long in mind the idea of founding a school for the education of young ladies, and in 1864 the school, which has long borne her name, was begun. After twenty-five years of active life at the head of this school, Mrs. Reed resigned the supervision of it in 1890.
265 ALBERT SMITH, b. Sept. 20, 1823, m. Jane A. Balch, June 5, 1849.
266 PRISCILLA, b. June 21, 1828, m. George H. Whiting April 13, 1852.
267 LUCY, b. May 11, 1832, m. Henry Delavan Paine, M. D.
268 EDWIN C., b. March 21, 1835, m. Anna Colkett Jan. 5, 1870.
269 EUNICE IDA, b. April 14, 1840, m. Lieut. Commodore William H. Rhoades of the United States Navy.
270 FRANCES W., b. July 15, 1841, d. Sept. 17, 1842.

Palmer Gallup (No. 229) m. Desire Ball May 22, 1828. He d. at Mystic, Conn., Dec. 31, 1880; his wife d. Feb. 20, 1869.

CHILDREN:

271 MOZART, b. May 25, 1829, m. 1st, Mary Bagg Aug. 9, 1855; she d. July 13, 1857; he m. 2d, Hannah M. Gilbert July 29, 1862; she d. Nov. 28, 1882.

GALLUP FAMILY.

272 JOHN T., b. March 13, 1832, m. Jennie E. Young Nov. 1, 1858.
273 ADALINE M., b. May 6, 1834, m. Levi Watrous Dec. 27, 1859.
274 HORTENSE D., b. Sept. 29, 1836, m. William S. Fish Sept. 14, 1856.
275 LIBBIE M., b. Sept. 9, 1842, m. Samuel Edgcomb Oct. 17, 1863.
276 JAMES P., b. Jan. 21, 1845.

Nehemiah M. Gallup (No. 254) m. Huldah Wheeler of Stonington (No. 398), that family, April 26, 1812; d. Jan. 21, 1871.

CHILDREN:

277 ELIZA, b. Nov. 12, 1813, m. Lyman Gallup Dec. 9, 1840.
278 MARY A., b. April 17, 1815, m. William Fanning July 21, 1836.
279 NEHEMIAH M., b. Oct. 22, 1816, m. Laura, daughter of Judge William Williams of Ledyard, Oct. 21, 1841 (No. 21), Groton Williams family.
281 JOHN W., b. Nov. 6, 1818, m. Martha E. Richards Jan. 1, 1847.
282 HANNAH, b. Aug. 7, 1820, m. Eleazer W. Carter March 2, 1844.
283 EUNICE, b. May 11, 1822, m. Seth Peck Aug. 6, 1849.
284 PHEBE E., b. Feb. 8, 1824, d. May 30, 1842.
285 MASON, b. March 4, 1826, d. April 16, 1830.
286 WILLIAM R., b. May 19, 1828, m. Eliza Morgan May 3, 1864.
287 HARRIET A., b. Aug. 22, 1830, m. Frederick A. Button June 19, 1850.
288 BENJAMIN, b. June 19, 1832.
289 HENRY C., b. Nov. 6, 1834, m. Lucy Renard June 14, 1870.

Luke Gallup (No. 258) m. Melinda Williams Jan. 2, 1820 (No. 14), Groton Williams family.

CHILDREN:

290 OLIVE, b. Oct. 8, 1820.
291 LUKE W., b. Feb. 27, 1822.
292 OLIVE, b. Sept. 25, 1823.
293 PHEBE, b. Sept. 8, 1825, m. Warren S. Wheeler Feb. 8, 1847 (No. 510), that family.
294 AMOS, b. March 19, 1827.
295 JARED, b. April 17, 1829.
296 MELINDA, b. Nov. 2, 1831, m. Nelson H. Wheeler April 3, 1853 (No. 513), that family.
297 BRIDGET, b. Nov. 22, 1833, m. William B. Chapman April 19, 1865.

Alfred Gallup (No. 261) m. Eliza W. Hewitt Oct. 19, 1823 (No. 223), Hewitt family.

CHILDREN:

298 WILLIAM A., b. June 28, 1827, d. Aug. 31, 1843.
299 AUSTIN O., b. Dec. 27, 1828, m. Lucy A. Rathbun Jan. 22, 1855.
300 ELIZA A., b. Sept. 5, 1830, d. Sept. 2, 1832.
301 MARY A., b. June 3, 1832, d. Sept. 5, 1833.
302 HARRIET A., b. Oct. 1, 1836, m. Avery Morgan Dec. 25, 1853.
303 LAURA E., b. May 28, 1840, m. Sanford W. Havens Oct. 8, 1857.
304 LOUIS A., b. June 30, 1846, m. Ella Hitchcock June 7, 1866.

John Gallup (No. 134) m. Hannah Denison (No. 225), that family, Jan. 3, 1782. He d. Dec. 8, 1825; she d. Sept. 1, 1830.

CHILDREN:

305 JOHN GARDNER, b. Aug. 2, 1785, m. Anna B. Denison (No. 404), that family.
306 LUCRETIA, b. Aug. 22, 1784, m. Henry Gardner.
307 HANNAH, b. May 3, 1786, m. Nathan Crary.
308 DANIEL, b. Sept. 12, 1789.
309 JOSEPH, b. Dec. 9, 1791.
310 MARY, b. Jan. 23, 1794, d. March 11, 1880.
311 BEEBE D., b. April 22, 1796, d. unmarried Aug. 25, 1843.
312 GURDON, b. June 12, 1798.
313 ESTHER, b. July 19, 1800, m. Ebenezer Denison.
314 JOHN GARDNER, 2d, b. Sept. 15, 1805, d. unmarried Dec. 21, 1888.

GORE FAMILY.

1. JOHN GORE, b. in England, came from Waltham Abbey, Sussex, Eng., settled in Roxbury, as a freeman; was entered April 18, 1637; mentioned as a land owner in 1643, having 188 acres; a member of the artillery company in 1638; and for many years was town clerk and the records of Roxbury (now in the City Hall, Boston) are in the handwriting of himself and his son, John, who succeeded him. John Gore died in Roxbury, Mass., June 2, 1657; he married Rhoda ————.

CHILDREN:

2 MARY, b. in England; no trace of her existing.
3 JOHN, b. May 23, 1634, in England; d. in Roxbury June 26, 1705.
4 OBADIAH, b. June, 1636, in Roxbury, d. Sept., 1646.
5 ABIGAIL, b. Aug., 1641, d. young.
6 ABIGAIL, bapt. May 7, 1643, d. Oct. 31, 1671, unmarried.
7 HANNAH, b. May, 1645, d. July 1686, m. Ralph Bradhurst of Roxbury June 13, 1677; had four children.
8 OBADIAH, bapt. March 25, 1648, d. Sept. 3, 1653.
9 and 10 Twins, d. unbaptized June 11, 1651.
11 SAMUEL, b. in Roxbury, 1652, d. there July 26, 1692.
12 BENJAMIN, b. Nov., 1654, d. young.

After Mr. John Gore died his widow m. Lieut. John Remington.

John Gore (No. 3) m. May 31, 1683, Sarah, daughter of Peter Gardner.

CHILDREN:

13 JOHN, b. Feb. 27, 1684.
14 SARAH, b. Aug. 24, 1685.
15 HANNAH, b. Feb. 14, 1688.
16 EBENEZER, b. Nov. 7, 1689.
17 ABIGAIL, b. Feb. 15, 1692, d. young.
18 ABIGAIL, b. Oct. 26, 1693.
19 SAMUEL, b. Sept. 11, 1695, d. young.
20 SAMUEL, b. May 15, 1697, d. young.
21 SAMUEL, b. Sept. 1, 1699, d. young.

Samuel Gore (No. 11) m. Aug. 28, 1672, Elizabeth, daughter of John Weld of Roxbury; was a carpenter by trade, and for several years was a selectman of Roxbury.

CHILDREN:

22 ABIGAIL, b. May 29, 1673, d. young.
23 JOHN, bapt. Nov. 10, 1678, d. young.
24 SAMUEL, b. Oct. 20, 1681.
25 JOHN, b. June 22, 1683, d. at sea of smallpox Nov., 1720, m. Rebecca Smith May 12, 1713; no children.
26 THOMAS, b. Aug. 16, 1686, d. Oct. 17, 1689.
27 OBADIAH, b. July 13, 1688, d. Oct. 8, 1721, m. Sarah Kilby Oct. 26, 1710.
28 MARGARET, b. ———, m. ———, d. ———.

Samuel Gore (No. 24) d. at Norwich, Conn., May 27, 1756. He m. 1st, Hannah Draper, daughter of Moses Draper and wife Hannah, daughter of John Chandler, who were m. July 7, 1685. Mrs. Hannah (Chandler) Draper d. June 9, 1692. The daughter Hannah was b. April 8, 1686, and m. Samuel Gore; she d. in Norwich, Conn., July 11, 1741, and Mr. Gore m. 2d, Mrs. Dorcas Blunt May 13, 1742.

CHILDREN:

29 ELIZABETH, b. in Roxbury Jan. 12, 1704, m. Joseph Witter (No. 12), that family; had eight children and d. April 9, 1761.
30 SAMUEL, b. March 26, 1705, d. May 22, 1706.
31 SAMUEL, b. May 29, 1707, d. young.
32 MOSES, b. Sept. 23, 1709, d. ———.
33 JOHN, b. Oct. 11, 1711, d. at Norwich, Conn., Jan. 19, 1735.
34 OBADIAH, b. July 26, 1714, d. at Wyoming, Penn., Jan. 10, 1779, of small pox. This was the father of the sons killed in the massacre at Wyoming.
35 SAMUEL, b. Sept. 6, d. Oct. 4, 1719.
36 HANNAH, b. Dec. 20, 1720, d. March 19, 1810, m. first, July 17, 1740, to Silas Burrows (No. 16); that family, of Stonington; he d. April 19, 1741, and Mrs. Hannah Burrows m. 2d, Nathaniel Gallup (No. 69), that family, Nov. 24, 1742. By her first husband there was one child born a few months after its father died, named Silence, who m. Richard Wheeler, grandfather of the author of this book.
37 SARAH, b. Jan. 15, 1723, m. Eliphalet Hobart of Stonington, Conn., and d. July 28, 1743.

Obadiah Gore (No. 34), d. at Wyoming, Penn., Jan. 10, 1779, of smallpox; m. Hannah Parke of Preston, Conn., Nov. 4, 1742. She was b. July 3, 1721, and d. Aug. 14, 1804, at Sequin, Penn.

CHILDREN:

38 OBADIAH, b. April 7, 1744, d. in Pennsylvania March 22, 1821, m. Anna Avery March, 1764.
39 DANIEL, b. March 13, 1746, d. 1809.
40 SILAS, b. Dec. 23, 1747, m. Kessiah Yerrington, who was killed at Wyoming massacre.
41 ASA, b. Feb. 28, 1750, m. Elizabeth Avery; had one child, Asa A. Gore, and was killed at Wyoming massacre.
42 HANNAH, b. May 28, 1752, m. Timothy Pierce, who was killed at Wyoming massacre, and she m. 2d, Thomas Duane.

GORE FAMILY.

43 LUCY, b. May 28, 1754, d. Sept. 30, 1820, m. John Murphy, who was killed at Wyoming massacre; she was twice after m.
44 SARAH, b. Nov. 23, 1756, d. May, 1841, m. 1st, Lawrence Myers, and 2d, Rev. Benjamin Bidlack. She was in Forty Fort during the massacre.
45 GEORGE, b. Sept., 1759, slain in Wyoming massacre July 3, 1778.
46 SAMUEL, b. May 24, 1761, d. May 2, 1834, m. Sarah Brogan; had six children.
47 JOHN, b. Feb. 25, 1764, at Norwich, Conn., too young to go into the fight with his brothers.

John Gore (No. 47) went to Wilkesbarre with his father's family in 1769; was in the fort during the massacre, a lad of 14 yrs.; fled with the family; afterward returned, settled in Kingston, m. Elizabeth Ross, sister of Gen. William Ross; was b. Feb. 25, 1764, d. at Forty Fort Aug. 4, 1837.

CHILDREN:

48 ASA, b. 1794, d. June 3, 1855, not m.
49 JOHN, b. 1799, d. ———, m. Ruth Searles.
50 ELIZABETH, b. ———, d. March 3, 1808, aged 10 yrs and 7 mos.
51 MARY, b. 1802, d. 1861, m. Moses Woods; no children.
52 GEORGE, b. 1804, m. Harriet Smith, d. Nov. 16, 1841.
53 JEREMIAH, b. Nov. 6, 1808, d. not m.
54 SARAH, b. May 28, 1806, d. 1886, m. John B. Woods of Yorkshire, Eng.

GRANT FAMILY.

1. MATHEW GRANT, the progenitor and emigrant ancestor of the Grant family of New England, was b. in England on Tuesday, Oct. 27, 1601. He came to this country May 30, 1630, in the good "Ship Mary and John," with his family, and landed at Dorchester, Mass.

He was admitted a freeman in the Massachusetts Colony in 1631, but did not long remain in Dorchester, for as early as 1635, he took an active part in forming the company that migrated to Windsor, Conn., and went with them to that place, and was elected first town clerk thereof, which office he held for a good many years. He also held the position of town surveyor, and took a prominent part in the organization, and also in transplanting the Congregational Church there, which had been previously formed in Plymouth, England, and first transplanted in Dorchester, Conn. Mathew Grant and Priscilla ———, b. Feb. 27, 1600, m. Nov. 16, 1625; she d. April 27, 1644, aged 43 years. He m. 2d, Susannah (Chapen) Rockwell, widow of Dea. William Rockwell, May 29, 1645; she d. Nov. 14, 1666; he d. Dec. 16, 1681.

CHILDREN BY FIRST MARRIAGE:

2 PRISCILLA, b. Sept. 16, 1626, m. Michael Humprey Oct. 14, 1747.
3 SAMUEL, b. Nov. 12, 1631, m. Mary Porter May 27, 1658.
4 TAHAN, b. Feb. 3, 1633, m. Hannah Palmer Jan. 22, 1662.
5 JOHN, b. April 30, 1642, m. Mary Hull Aug. 2, 1666.

Samuel Grant (No. 3), b. at Dorchester, Mass., m. Mary Potter, May 27, 1658, at Windsor, Conn. She was b. about 1638, they lived at Windsor, Conn., and he was one of the petitioners May 13, 1680, for the new town of East Windsor, where he was a member of the church in 1700; he d. Sept. 10, 1718.

6 SAMUEL, b. at Windsor, Conn., April 20, 1659, m. Anna Filley Dec. 6, 1683; he m. 2d, Grace Miner April 11, 1688 (No. 26), that family; he d. April 16, 1753.
7 JOHN, b. April 24, 1664, m. Elizabeth Skinner June 5, 1690.
8 MATHEW, b. Sept. 22, 1666, m. Hannah Chapman Oct. 29, 1690.
9 JOSIAH, b. March 19, 1668, m. Rebecca Miner July 8, 1696.
10 NATHANIEL, b. April 14, 1672, m. Bethia Warner May 16, 1699.
11 MARY, b. Jan. 23, 1675, m. Dea. Joseph Skinner March 13, 1694.
12 SARAH, b. Jan. 19, 1677, d. 1680.

Josiah Grant (No. 9) came to Stonington, Conn., to reside, where he m. Rebecca Miner (No. 41), that family, July 8, 1696.

GRANT FAMILY.

They joined the First Congregational Church of Stonington Aug. 27, 1699; she d. Jan. 15, 1747; h. d. March 28, 1732.

CHILDREN:

13 JOSIAH, b. June 17, 1697, m. Grace Prentice Nov. 30, 1721.
14 JOHN, b. Oct. 19, 1698.
15 OLIVER, b. Sept. 30, 1703, m. twice.
16 NOAH, b. Jan. 13, 1706, m. Rachel ———; m. 2d, Harnah Miner Jan. 25, 1745.
17 MINER, b. Aug. 26, 1712.

Josiah Grant (No. 13) of Stonington, m. Grace Prentice (No. 15), that family, Nov. 30, 1721; he d. April 30, 1733.

CHILDREN:

18 REBECCA, b. June 20, 1723, m. Nathaniel Hewitt April 24, 1740 (No. 57), that family.
19 JOHN, b. March 4, 1726, d. Nov. 18, 1739.
20 LUCY, b. Dec. 12, 1728, d. ———.
21 LUCY, b. May 9, 1732, m. Caleb Green of Westerly, R. I., Nov. 9, 1750.
22 SARAH, b. May 9, 1732, d. young.

Oliver Grant of Stonington (No. 15) m. 1st Bridget Miner, May 26, 1726 (No. 69), Miner family. Mrs. Grant d.; he m. for 2d wife, Silence Williams May 18, 1729 (No. 45), Williams family. He d. May 7, 1757.

CHILDREN BY FIRST MARRIAGE:

23 BRIDGET, b. June 6, 1727, m. Stephen Billings (No. 78), that family.
24 OLIVER, b. July 18, 1729, m. Anna Borodel Billings May 23, 1749.

CHILDREN BY SECOND MARRIAGE:

25 SILENCE, b. Jan. 31, 1731, m. John Breed (No. 16), that family.
26 JOSHUA, b. Jan. 30, 1732, m. Sarah Breed.
27 EUNICE, b. Feb. 23, 1735, m. Collins York, May 29, 1755 (No. 23), York family.
28 MARY, b. July 9, 1737, m. Ichabod Palmer (No. 234).
29 SARAH, b. Sept. 24, 1739, m. William Walworth of Groton.

Noah Grant of Stonington (No. 16) m. Rachel ———, by her he had one son, Noah Grant, b. Oct. 9, 1730, d. young. He m. 2d wife, Hannah Miner (No. 72), that family, Jan. 25, 1745. He d. March 2, 1759.

CHILDREN BY SECOND MARRIAGE:

30 RACHEL, b. Nov. 2, 1745, m. Joseph Worden Dec. 6, 1770.
31 NOAH, b. Jan. 28, 1747, m. Mary Palmer Aug. 11, 1771.
32 JOSIAH, b. March 27, 1749, m. Sarah Miner; m. 2d, Mrs. Mary (Hewitt) Williams.
33 JOHN, b. July 7, 1754, m. Thankful Lewis Oct. 6, 1776.

Oliver Grant of Stonington (No. 24) m. Ann Borodel Billings May 23, 1749 (No. 54), Billings family. He d. March 22, 1798.

CHILDREN:

34 BRIDGET, b. Sept. 24, 1751, m. Hosea Wheeler Feb. 18, 1772 (No. 90), Wheeler family.
35 OLIVER, b. April 16, 1754, m. Hannah Fanning.
36 MINER, b. Feb. 28, 1756, m. Eunice Swift.

37 REBECCA, b. Dec. 12, 1759.
38 PHEBE, b. Feb. 13, 1762, m. James or (Oliver) Brown.
39 EPHRAIM, b. July 4, 1764, m. Olive Shepard.
40 LUCINDA, b. Oct. 3, 1766, m. Stanton Hewitt May 15, 1784 (No. 110),
41 WEALTHY, b. Oct. 5, 1768, m. Sanford Palmer, Feb. 10, 1788.
42 MARY, b. Aug. 8, 1770, m. Elijah Palmer.
43 DANIEL, b. in 1773, m. Mary Swan of Stonington.

Joshua Grant of North Stonington (No. 26) m. Sarah Breed Nov. 15, 1753 (No. 19), Breed family. He d. May 16, 1788.

CHILDREN:

44 JOSHUA, b. April 2, 1756, m. Lucy Green Jan. 1, 1778.
45 SILENCE, b. May 22, 1758, m. Benoni Gardner.
46 ESTHER, b. Sept. 3, 1760, m. Sands Cole June 13, 1784.
47 EUNICE, b. June 8, 1763, m. Allen York.
48 AMOS, b. Sept. 22, 1765, m. ――――― Edgecomb.
49 GILBERT, b. April 12, 1768, m. Anna Breed.
50 MARY, b. March 2, 1771, m. Edward Holmes Feb. 15, 1789 (No. 67), Holmes family.
51 DEBORAH, b. Aug. 21, 1773, m. Benajah Ladd; m. 2d, Judge ―――――
Pratt.
52 LUCY, b. June 7, 1776, m. Timothy Swan Wheeler Dec. 13, 1796 (No. 139), Wheeler family.
53 ELNATHAN, b. July 7, 1779, m. Betsey Fellows Nov. 12, 1801.

Oliver Grant of Stonington (No. 35) m. Hannah Fanning of Groton April 20, 1775.

CHILDREN:

54 OLIVER, b. in 1779, m. Esther Breed.
55 GEORGE, b. Aug. 7, 1782, d. unmarried.
56 WILLIAM, b. in 1784, d. unmarried.
57 HANNAH, b. in 1787, d. unmarried.
58 HOSEA, b. in 1789, m. Betsey Jaques.
59 WHEELER, b. in 1790.
60 REBECCA, b. in 1792, m. Elisha Keeney.
61 HENRY, b. in 1795, m. Polly Keeney.

Joshua Grant (No. 44) m. Lucy Green Jan. 1, 1778. He d. May 16, 1825; she d. May 15, 1836, both of Stonington, Conn.

CHILDREN:

62 JOSHUA, b. Nov. 7, 1778, m. Caroline Hinckley March 12, 1801.
63 LUCY, b. Dec. 24, 1781, m. Dudley Randall March 26, 1801 (No. 74), Randall family.
64 PRENTICE, b. Nov. 29, 1783, m. Lucy Brown Dec. 28, 1808; m. 2d, Mary Horton Bentley Dec. 10, 1824.
65 SARAH, b. Nov. 11, 1785, m. 1st, Daniel Farnham in 1809; he d. in 1815; m. 2d, her sister Lucy's husband, Dudley Randall, March 28, 1830.
66 CHARLES, b. Jan. 12, 1788, m. Lydia Barber.
67 HENRY, b. July 25, 1791, m. Fanny Bailey.
68 BETSEY, b. Oct. 2, 1794.
69 CALEB, b. June 19, 1797, m. Lura Peabody April 30, 1826.
70 ALMIRA, b. April 6, 1800, m. Noyes Weaver.

Gilbert Grant of Stonington (No. 49) m. Anna Breed (No. 63), Breed family, Feb. 21, 1790. He d. March 11, 1820.

GRANT FAMILY.

CHILDREN:
71 GILBERT, b. Dec. 8, 1793, m. Elizabeth Wells March 27, 1817.
72 CYRUS, b. Feb. 15, 1795, m. Rhoda Chesebrough Nov. 18, 1820 (No. 378), Chesebrough family.
73 JOHN, b. Feb. 3, 1798, m. Ann Wheeler Ayer Sept. 26, 1826.
74 WILLIAM SLACK, b. April 27, 1800, m. Betsey Mason Baldwin.
75 ANNA, b. July 27, 1802, m. Gilbert Dart.

Josiah Grant (No. 32) m. 1st, Sarah Miner Aug. 30, 1770; m. 2d, Mrs. Mary (Hewitt) Williams Feb. 8, 1784.

CHILDREN BY FIRST MARRIAGE:
76 JOSIAH, b. Aug. 18, 1771, m. Sybil Safford.
77 SARAH, b. March 28, 1774.
78 THOMAS, b. Sept. 12, 1775.
79 PRUDENCE, b. Sept. 24, 1777.
80 MARY, b. March 1, 1779.

CHILDREN BY SECOND MARRIAGE:
81 JOSEPH, b. Nov. 4, 1784, m. Matilda Marsh.
82 HANNAH, b. May 13, 1786, m. Jared Gardner Jan. 19, 1804.
83 CYNTHIA, b. April 24, 1788, m. Rev. John Warren.
84 NANCY, b. April 24, 1788.
85 DESIRE, b. Jan. 23, 1791.
86 WEALTHY, b. Sept. 30, 1793.

Noah Grant (No. 31) m. Mary Palmer Aug. 11, 1771. He d. April 8, 1801.

CHILDREN:
87 NOAH, b. in 1772, m. Polly Browning Nov. 25, 1789.
88 PATTY, b. Sept. 6, 1777.
89 ROSWELL, b. Nov. 17, 1779, m. Abigail Smith.
90 RUSSELL, b. Sept. 17, 1781.
91 MINER, b. July 28, 1787, m. Anna, daughter of Jesse Palmer.
92 LUCINDA, b. Oct. 31, 1791.

Oliver Grant of Stonington (No. 54) m. Esther Breed in 1801, daughter of Stephen Breed and Esther Wheeler (No. 114), Breed family. He d. May 23, 1813; she d. Oct. 9, 1861.

CHILDREN:
93 MARY ESTHER, b. Oct. 17, 1802, d. unmarried.
94 OLIVER BURROWS, b. Oct. 13, 1804, d. unmarried Oct. 1, 1891.
95 ANN MINER, b. June 29, 1807, m. Orrin Safford Dec. 29, 1830.
96 LUCY BREED, b. Oct. 13, 1810, m. Daniel Brown Spalding, May 10, 1832, son of Asa Spalding, M. D., and Lucy York.

William S. Grant (No. 74) m. Betsey Mason Baldwin May 16, 1827 (No. 102), Baldwin family. He d. June 15, 1860; lived in North Stonington.

CHILDREN:
97 NANCY ELIZABETH, b. Aug. 19, 1828.
98 WILLIAM FRANKLIN, b. Nov. 9, 1830, m. Harriet N. Williams (No. 68), Williams family, March 12, 1856.
99 MARY ANNA, b. Nov. 4, 1837, m. Thomas Lawton Reynolds, Nov. 23, 1858.
100 FRANCES JULIETTE, b. May 23, 1842.

Noah Grant (No. 87) m. Polly Browning Nov. 25, 1789 (No. 45), Browning family.

CHILDREN:

101 RUTH, b. Aug. 10, 1793, m. Jonathan Eccleston.
102 ANNA, b. June 2, 1795.
103 RUSSELL, b. May 14, 1797.
104 JOHN, b. July 11, 1800.
105 JUSTUS, b. Oct. 8, 1802.
106 DANIEL, b. Feb. 8, 1805.
107 MINER, b. April 2, 1806.
108 CYRUS, b. April 19, 1808.
109 POLLY, b. Sept. 23, 1812.
110 PATIENCE, b. March 3, 1813.
111 NOAH, b. July 15, 1815.

GREENMAN FAMILY.

The ancestor of the Greenman family about here is
1. JOHN GREENMAN of Newport, who m. ————.
    CHILDREN:
    2 DAVID, b. ————.
    3 EDWARD, b. ————.
    4 CONTENT, b. 1636, d. March 27, 1666, m. Walter Clarke, 1660.

Edward Greenman (No. 3) m. Mary ————, d. 1688.
    CHILDREN:
    5 EDWARD, b. 1663, d. 1749.
    6 WILLIAM, b. ————.
    7 JOHN, b. 1666, d. Sept. 30, 1727.
    8 THOMAS, b. 1669, d. 1728.
    9 MARY, b. ————, m. March 8, 1706, Adam Casey.

Edward Greenman (No. 5) m. Margaret ————.
    CHILDREN:
    10 ABIGAIL, b. ————.
    11 SILAS, b. about 1690.
    12 PHEBE, b. Jan. 29, 1692, m. Whiting.
    13 EDWARD, b. about 1694.
    14 NATHAN, b. ————.
    14a SARAH, d. aged 27 yrs.

William Greenman (No. 6) m. Ann Clark Westerly, 1706.

John Greenman (No. 7) m. Elizabeth ————; buried in Newport.

Thomas (No. 8) m. Mary Weeden, daughter of William and Sarah (Peckham) Weeden.

Silas Greenman (No. 11) m. Katharine Greenman in Kingstown Jan. 3, 1715, by Christopher Allen.
    CHILDREN:
    15 PHEBE, b. May 23, 1717.
    16 JOHN, b. Dec. 7, 1718, d. April 25, 1732.
    17 GARTHROT, b. Aug. 16, 1720, m. Thomas Edwards Nov. 1, 1742.
    18 EUNICE, b. Oct. 5, 1722.
    19 EDWARD, b. Oct. 9, 1724, d. Jan. 24, 1726.
    20 SARAH, b. Sept. 18, 1728, d. Sept. 22, 1728.

Mrs. Katharine d. April 17, 1730, aged 36 yrs, and Mr. Silas Greenman m. 2d, Anne Babcock March 23, 1731; she d. May 13, 1731, and after her death he m. Eunice Babcock (No. 55) of Babcock family, of South Kingstown, R. I., May 10, 1737.
    CHILDREN OF CAPT. SILAS AND EUNICE GREENMAN:
    21 KATHARINE, b. April 22, 1738.
    22 ABIGAIL, b. Aug. 15, 1740.
    23 ANNA, b. Jan. 30, 1742.
    24 ELIZABETH, b. Nov. 5, 1744.

Edward Greenman (No. 13), called Jr., of Westerly, m. Sarah Clarke of South Kingstown May 11, 1721.

CHILDREN:

25 SILAS, b. June 11, 1724.
26 MARGARET, b. Oct. 17, 1725.
27 ABIGAIL, b. Nov. 21, 1727.
28 EDWARD, b. March 9, 1731.
29 CATHARINE, b. Aug. 18, 1732.
30 MARY, b. April 12, 1735.
31 PRUDENCE, b. Oct. 28, 1736.
32 CHLOE, b. April 8, 1739.
33 NATHAN, b. Feb. 21, 1741.

Silas Greenman (No. 25) m. Sarah Peckham Oct. 27, 1751; they were both of Charlestown.

CHILDREN:

34 HANNAH, b. Aug. 4, 1753.
35 MARY, b. June 26, 1755.
36 TIMOTHY, b. March 22, 1757.
37 SARAH, b. Sept. 1, 1760.
(Probably other births during these ten years, which cannot be found.)
38 SILAS, b. Sept. 29, 1770.

Silas Greenman (No. 38) m. Mary or Polly, daughter of George and Esther Stillman, Oct. 17, 1793. He d. June 5, 1846, and Mrs. Mary Greenman d. April, 1846.

NOTE.—The Greenman family has been prominently identified with shipbuilding in Mystic. In 1827 George and Silas Greenman 3d, having learned shipbuilding from their father, went into partnership at Old Mystic (the head of the river), and remained there till 1835, when Silas removed to Westerly, R. I., and carried on the business there. His brother George carried on the shipbuilding alone for one year, when he took his two younger brothers, Clark and Thomas S., into partnership with him. In 1838, being solicited to build larger vessels than their yards would accommodate, they bought and removed their plant to Adams Point, near Mystic, and established the first shipyard in that place, and the list of vessels which they built is found under "Shipping" in this book. In 1849 the Greenman brothers organized the Greenmanville Manufacturing Co., which they established at Adams Point, giving the name of Greenmanville to the village, which had grown up there by their enterprising business capacity. They erected a large mill for the manufacture of fine woolen gooods, which was successfully operated and subsequently enlarged to its present size, and in 1863 they established a store there to supply their many employes and others. The Greenman brothers believed that in "union there is strength," and the perfect confidence between them and their strong opinions of right and justice have made them worthy of notice among their fellow men.

CHILDREN:

39 SARAH or SALLY, b. Oct. 22, 1794, m. Joseph Lanphear.
40 SILAS, b. Nov. 26, 1796.
41 MARY or POLLY, b. Dec. 1, 1798, m. Greene Champlin.
42 LUCY, b. Jan. 25, 1800, d. young.
43 CATHARINE, b. June 11, 1803, m. John Edmondson.
44 GEORGE C., b. at Westerly Aug. 27, 1805.
45 CLARK, b. at Hopkinton, June 23, 1808.
46 THOMAS S., b. at Westerly Oct. 5, 1810.
47 WILLIAM, d. young.

Silas Greenman (No. 40) m. Thankful, daughter of Samuel and wife Susan (Potter) Wells, b. Aug. 7, 1802, d. April 27, 1870; m. Dec. 20, 1821. He d. April 4, 1881; had seven children.

George Greenman (No. 44), b. at Westerly, R. I., Aug. 27, 1805, m. Feb. 10, 1828, Abby, daughter of Charles and wife Martha (Burch) Chipman, of Mystic.

Clark Greenman (No. 45) b. at Hopkinton, June 23, 1808, m. Jan. 4, 1841, Harriet, daughter of Peleg and wife Hannah (Amy) of Portsmouth, R. I.; she was b. July 30, 1812; he d. Aug. 26, 1877.

Thomas S. Greenman (No. 46) b. at Westerly, R. I., Oct. 5, 1810, m. Charlotte, daughter of David Rogers of Connecticut, Nov. 21, 1842. They had one child. Mrs. Greenman d. May 14, 1879.

HALEY FAMILY.

We do not know at what date the first Haley came from Devonshire, England, or whether he landed at Boston or Newport, but from what I have learned it is said that he came from Boston to Newport in 1738, and on the First Congregational Church records in Stonington is found this entry, "Dominie Haley and Ann Dorcas were married Oct. 29, 1739." Whether he was brother or not to the

1. JOHN HALEY of Groton is not known, but a John Haley and his wife, Mary Saunders, daughter of John and Silence Saunders, lived at Centre Groton in 1738 with their six children, viz.: John, Joshua, Jeremiah, Caleb, Martha and Elizabeth. John settled in Stonington, a mile or more north of the borough, near the present residence of John F. Chesebro. Caleb m. at Centre Groton, and Jeremiah settled at Mystic Bridge, Conn.

CHILDREN OF JOHN AND MARY:

2 JOHN, b. ———.
3 JOSHUA, b. Dec. 27, 1721.
4 JEREMIAH, b. ———.
5 CALEB, b. ———.
6 MARTHA, b. April 7, 1723.
7 ELIZABETH, b. Aug. 17, 1726.

John Haley (No. 2) m. Deborah, daughter of William and wife, Esther Fanning, March 28, 1745, by Rev. John Owen.

CHILDREN:

8 JOSHUA, b. June 30, 1746. He left no children.
9 ABIGAIL, b. Oct. 3, 1748, m. William Miner (No. 172), May 10, 1770.
10 MARY, b. Sept. 5, 1751, m. Thomas Leeds Feb. 11, 1773.
11 ZERVIAH, b. Nov. 26, 1753, m. Daniel Smith April 6, 1777.
12 HANNAH, b. April 15, 1756, m. Manassah Miner (No. 173).
13 MARTHA, b. June 3, 1758, m. John West.
14 PHEBE, b. Nov. 12, 1760, remained single.
15 EDMOND, b. April 4, 1763.
16 LUCY, b. April 15, 1765, m. Nathaniel Burdick of Charlestown, R. I., Jan. 22, 1754.
17 BELCHER, b. Feb. 20, 1767.
18 JOHN, b. ———.
19 DEBORAH, b. March 20, 1771, m. Elihu Hancock.
20 CONTENT, b. Aug. 8, 1773, m. Seth Burdick.

Jeremiah Haley (No. 4) m. Catharine Hilyard, daughter of Ambrose Hilyard, b. 1731, and wife Mary ———.

HALEY FAMILY.

CHILDREN:

21 KATHARINE, b. Jan. 4, 1759.
22 MARY, b. Aug. 8, 1760.
23 THOMAS, b. Aug. 28, 1762, and d. young.
24 RHODA, b. Nov. 1, 1764.
25 NATHAN, b. Oct. 31, 1766.
26 CHARLOTTE, b. Feb. 27, 1769.
27 JEREMIAH, b. June 30, 1771.
28 GEORGE, b. Sept. 9, 1773.
29 HANNAH, b. April 24, 1776.
30 NANCY, b. May 10, 1778.
31 SIMEON, b. Nov. 24, 1781.

All of the male members of this family, with the exception of Thomas, who d. young, were sea captains, and Nathan was appointed American Consul in Nantes, France, where he d. Jan. 3, 1841. He received the Cross of the Legion of Honor for important services rendered France under Bonaparte.

Caleb Haley (No. 5) m. Mary Helm, b. 1740, from Little Rest, Long Island. She was daughter of Rouse Helm, b. Feb. 11, 1713. He m. ——— Northrup.

CHILDREN:

32 CALEB, b. ———, m. Sally Burrows (No. 98), Burrows family.
33 ELISHA, b. and m. Nancy Crary. He was a member of Congress.
34 STEPHEN, b. and m. Lucy Gallup.
35 BETSEY, b. Sept. 14, 1767, m. John B. Burrows (No. 95); she d. June 13, 1847.

Stephen Haley (No. 34) m. Lucy Gallup (No. 62), Gallup family, and his son, Dudley Haley, m. Rebecca F. Voorhees, and their son, Albert Haley, m. Catharine Haley (No. 44).

Edmond Haley (No. 15) m. 1st, Polly Irish, and 2d, Sarah Miner Sept. 15, 1794.

CHILDREN:

36 JABEZ, b. April 6, 1796.
36a MARGARET, b. Jan. 12, 1799.

John Haley (No. 18) m. Priscilla Fellows, the widow of John Devol or Daboll, who she m. Dec. 1, 1771; she m. 2d, John Haley Oct. 4, 1792.

CHILDREN:

37 JOHN, b. ———.
38 JOSHUA, b. March 15, 1795.
39 ELIHU, b. May 2, 1797.

Simeon Haley (No. 31) m. March 15, 1803, Sarah, daughter of Daniel and wife Mary (Avery) Packer, who were among the early settlers of Groton, Conn. She was cousin of Judge Asa Packer, the eminent and distinguished millionaire of Mauch Chunk, Penn.

THEIR CHILDREN WERE:

40 CATHARINE, b. Dec. 28, 1805, m. Capt. Dudley Stark.
41 LUCY, b. March 15, 1807, m. Thomas Ash.
42 SIMEON, Jr., b. Aug. 20, 1812, m. Lydia Esther Brown (No. 241), Lynn Brown family.

Mrs. Sarah Haley d. Nov. 25, 1834, and on April 16, 1837, Capt. Simeon Haley m. Miss Priscilla Avery Burrows (No. 156), Burrows family, daughter of John and wife Betsey (Haley) Burrows.

THEIR CHILDREN:

43 NATHAN, b. Jan. 28, 1840, d. aged 26 yrs.
44 CATHARINE, b. Oct. 3, 1849, m. Albert Haley.

Joshua Haley (No. 38) m. Rebecca Brown (No. 360), Lynn Brown family, Nov. 29, 1821.

CHILDREN:

45 JOSHUA, b. Sept. 5, 1822, m. Matilda Williams.
46 REBECCA, b. June 1, 1824, m. Benadam Champlin Nov. 28, 1844.
47 MARY, b. Jan. 2, 1826, d. 1827.
48 MARY E., b. March 10, 1828, d. unmarried in 1831.
49 JANE, b. June 8, 1827, m. James Norman.
50 HARRIET, b. ———.
51 JOHN, b. ———.

HALLAM FAMILY.

1. MR. JOHN HALLAM, who was born in Barbadoes, West Indies, in the year 1662, came with his mother and younger brother, Nicholas Hallam, and his stepfather, Mr. John Liveen, of New London, Conn., in the year 1676, where he continued to reside, until he came to Stonington, soon after 1680, when and where he became acquainted with the family of Mr. Amos Richardson, one of the most prominent families in the town, whose daughter, Miss Prudence Richardson, he m. March 15, 1683. Mr. Hallam at once engaged in the mercantile business, which was the employment of his stepfather, in the West Indies, and at New London, after they had taken up their residence there. Mr. Hallam enlarged his business here and opened commercial relations with merchants at Barbadoes, which he very successfully prosecuted for several years. His mother, Mrs. Alice Hallam, when she m. John Liveen had an estate of about one thousand dollars, which she placed in her husband's hands, with the assurance from him that he would give the same, with its accumulations, to her two sons, the said John and Nicholas, after his death, which assurance he did not fulfill, but gave the same to the ministry of New London. This disposition of the property by Mr. Liveen was so at variance with his repeated promises, made to their mother before her marriage to him, and to her sons afterward, that they would receive their mother's property after his death, that they refused to abide by his will and appealed therefrom, which appeal after an extended controversy both here and in England, was disallowed, and the validity of Mr. Liveen's will was contested and finally confirmed by all the Courts having jurisdiction of the same.

Mr. Hallam, in prosecuting his commercial relations with Barbadoes and the West Indies, acted as super-cargo of the vessels conveying his goods to these islands, and in person superintended the sale thereof, and exchange of the same for goods of the islands, which he brought home and sold to the merchants in this region round about. During the year 1700 Mr. Hallam purchased and fitted out one of his vessels with the products of neighboring farms and went with the same to the West Indies as super-cargo. Somewhere on his return he caught the smallpox, with which he d. Nov. 20, 1700. Mr. Hallam, after his marriage with Miss Prudence Richardson, purchased a large and valuable tract of land of her brother, the Rev. John Richardson, whose father, Mr. Amos Richardson, had given him as a wedding present, on his marriage. The land embraced in said purchase, included the land lying between Stonington Harbor, Lambert's Cove and Stony Brook on the east, Fisher's Island Sound on the south and Quiambaug Cove on the west up to a point, from which a direct line easterly passing about thirty rods south of the residence of Mr. Henry M. Palmer to Stony Brook, constituted the north boundary line of said tract of land.

The protracted lawsuit, concerning Mr. Liveen's will, was not concluded until after Mr. Hallam's death. His brother Mr. Nicholas Hallam continued the litigation to its close, incurring a large amount of additional expense, which he charged to his brother's estate, which claim was considered exorbitant, and payment thereof refused. He then instituted legal proceedings which resulted in a recovery by him of a moiety of the entire expense of the litigation, concerning said will, which was so heavy that it required the sale of a large part of said purchase to liquidate the same, as related before. Mr. John Hallam (No. 1) m. Prudence Richardson, daughter of Amos Richardson, March 15, 1683.

CHILDREN:

2 JOHN, Jr., b. Jan. 24, 1684, and d. ———.
3 PRUDENCE, bapt. April 18, 1686, d. April 17, 1701.
4 JOHN, bapt. April 13, 1690, and d. Feb. 16, 1704, and was buried at Preston, Conn.
5 AMOS, bapt. July 6, 1696, and m. Phebe Greenman of Westerly, R. I., Dec. 8, 1716.

THEIR CHILDREN:

6 PRUDENCE, b. Sept. 22, 1717.
7 JOHN, b. Nov. 7, 1719.
8 PHEBE, b. Aug. 13, 1722.

Mr. Amos Hallam d. Dec. 11, 1728.

John Hallam (No. 7) m. Abigail Noyes (No. 118), that family, both of Stonington, Conn., Aug. 20, 1737.

CHILDREN:

9 AMOS, b. Aug. 26, 1738.
10 PHEBE, b. April 6, 1740, d. Sept. 13, 1748.
11 ABIGAIL, b. Feb. 1, 1742.
12 PRUDENCE, b. Jan. 18, 1744.
13 MARY, b. June 21, 1746, m. Nathaniel Chesebrough (No. 149), that family.
14 PHEBE, b. Nov. 18, 1748, d. June 18, 1749.

Amos Hallam (No. 9), m. Desire Stanton (No. 284), that family.

CHILDREN:

15 JOHN, b. June 8, 1759.
16 ABIGAIL, b. June 6, 1760.
17 AMOS, b. May 17, 1762.
18 THOMAS, b. July 26, 1764.
19 NICHOLAS, b. Jan. 7, 1767, m. Mary Chesebrough (No. 269), that family.
20 DESIRE, b. March 24, 1769.
21 EDWARD, b. April 3, 1771.
22 ALEXANDER, b. Nov. 11, 1774.
23 GILES RUSSELL, b. Feb. 19, 1776, and he m. Lucy Williams (No. 300), Robert Williams family, Feb. 2, 1806. She was daughter of Col. Isaac Williams.

THEIR CHILDREN:

24 GILES RUSSELL, b. ———.
25 ISAAC WILLIAMS, b. ———.
26 JOHN ALEXANDER, b. ———.
27 LUCY ELIZABETH, b. ———.
28 HARRIET RICHARDSON, b. ———.
29 EDWARD RICHARD, b. ———.
30 JOHN, b. ———.

HANCOX FAMILY.

There appears to be three distinct families of Hancox in early Stonington records, only one of which can be easily traced back to the first ancestor who came to New England.

1. JAMES HANCOX and wife Ann ———, whose children were:

    2 EDWARD, b. in Richmond, Yorkshire, Eng., Nov. 5, 1670.
    3 ANN, b. and m. Charles Mannel, and lived at Cheapside, London.

Edward Hancox (No. 2), m. Mary ———; he d. Dec. 9, 1755, aged 85 yrs.; she d. Aug. 21, 1768, aged 84 yrs. Children known are:

    4 ANN, b. and d. Feb. 5, 1760, aged 12 yrs.
    5 EDWARD, b. March 20, 1714, d. Sept. 17, 1803, aged 90 yrs.

Edward Hancox (No. 5) m. July 2, 1741, Lucy, daughter of Mr. Elisha Chesebrough; she was b. July 3, 1721, and d. May 17, 1797 (No. 59), that family.

CHILDREN:

    6 LUCY, b. Feb. 16, 1742, d. June 16, 1819, m. George Beebe Nov. 10, 1771.
    7 EDWARD, b. Nov. 16, 1744, d. Feb. 27, 1837.
    8 ANN, b. March 23, 1748, d. young.
    9 ZEBULON, b. Aug. 9, 1751, d. Aug. 23, 1805.
    10 NATHAN, bapt. Sept. 14, 1755, d. young.
    11 REBECCA, b. Aug. 6, 1755, m. Samuel Burdick; m. 2d, ——— Mason, March 7, 1773.
    12 NATHAN, b. Feb. 28, 1762, m. Phebe Palmer Dec. 1, 1784 (No. 427), of Palmer family.

Edward Hancox (No. 7) m. Sarah Sheffield April 29, 1771.

CHILDREN:

    13 EDWARD, b. June 3, 1772. Lost at Sag Harbor, 1824.
    14 ANNE, b. Nov. 6, 1774.
    15 SARAH, b. April 28, 1776, m. Roswell Breed; had two sons, William and Edward.
    16 ISAAC, b. Jan. 3, 1778, m. Rebecca Lewis May 18, 1799, d. 1819.
    17 LUCY, b. Sept. 26, 1779, m. Joseph Wright April 12, 1827.
    18 FREELOVE, b. July 6, 1783, m. Nathaniel Sheffield, d. 1829.
    19 MARTHA, b. Feb. 4, 1786.
    20 POLLY, b. April 1, 1789, m. Charles Breed and went West (No. 105a), Breed family.
    21 WILLIAM, b. Aug. 21, 1792. Lost at sea.
    22 PRUDENCE, b. April 21, 1794, m. John Breed (No. 13), son of Samuel Breed; d. 1882.
    23 JOHN, b. Apr. 10, 1798, d. 1827.

Zebulon Hancox (No. 9) m. Lydia Sheffield April 20, 1777; also m. 2d, Freelove Sheffield Feb. 21, 1790.

CHILDREN BY FIRST WIFE:
24 LYDIA, b. Nov. 14, 1777.
25 ZEBULON, b. Feb. 9, 1780, d. July 30, 1838.
26 AMOS, b. March 20, 1782.
27 BETSEY, b. Aug. 26, 1784.

Mrs. Lydia d. Aug. 14, 1786. Mr. Zebulon Hancox m. 3d, Thankful Chesebrough.

CHILDREN BY SECOND WIFE:
28 REUBEN, b. Dec. 26, 1793.
29 SAMUEL, b. May 22, 1796, m. Hannah Chesebrough Feb. 10, 1822.

Edward Hancox (No. 13) m. Nancy Minor Oct. 4, 1797.

CHILDREN:
30 SALLY ANN, b. Jan. 12, 1803.
31 EDWARD M., b. Oct. 12, 1800.
32 CLEMENT, b. Aug. 26, 1810.
33 JOSEPH W., b. July 4, 1813.
34 ETHAN A. D., b. July 30, 1815.
35 MARY ANN, b. Sept. 4, 1817.

Dea. Zebulon Hancox (No. 25) m. Feb. 15, 1807, Catharine Sheffield of Westerly, R. I. She was b. Sept. 14, 1788, d. June 13, 1840.

CHILDREN:
36 HARRIET, b. Nov. 21, 1807.
37 ZEBULON, b. Sept. 13, 1808, never married.
38 FRANKLIN, b. May 26, 1811, m. Miss Frances Emeline Noyes (No. 342), that family, May 21, 1843.
39 THOMAS S., b. April 7, 1813.
40 ALBERT, b. April 13, 1815.
41 CATHARINE, b. May 22, 1817.
42 ANN E., bapt. Sept., 1819.
43 JAMES, b. July 29, 1821.
44 WILLIAM, b. Jan. 29, 1823.
45 FRANCES M., b. Jan. 24, 1827.

Amos Hancox (No. 26) m. Mercy Breed Feb. 24, 1805 (No. 105), Breed family.

CHILDREN:
46 AMOS, b. Jan. 29, 1806.
47 MERCY, b. Sept. 16, 1807.

Reuben Hancox (No. 28) m. Sally Davison Jan. 1, 1824.

HART FAMILY.

1. REV. IRA HART, who was installed pastor of the First Congregational Church of Stonington Dec. 6, 1809, was b. at Farmington, Conn., Sept. 18, 1771, and graduated at Yale College in 1797.

He was lineal descendant of Dea. Stephen Hart of Braintree, Essex County, England, who was b. in 1605, emigrated to this country and d. at Farmington, Conn., in March, 1682. His son Capt. Thomas Hart in 1644, m. Ruth Hawkins of Windsor, Conn., and d. at Farmington, Conn., Aug. 27, 1726. Their son, Lieut. Hawkins Hart, b. at Farmington, Conn., in 1667, m. Sarah Royce of Wallingford, Conn., Sept. 7, 1701. Their son, Thomas Hart, b. at Farmington, Conn., Sept. 29, 1714, m. Hannah Coe March 23, 1743. Their son, Jonathan Hart, b. at Farmington March 22, 1746, m. Mary Coe, date not recorded. They became the parents of eight children. After the death of his first wife, he m. Lucie Clark, and became the parents of seven children. His son, Rev. Ira Hart, who was settled at Stonington in 1809, was the oldest child of his father's family, m. Maria Sherman at New Haven Dec. 3, 1798, and they became the parents of five children.

CHILDREN:

2 DAVID SHERMAN, M. D., b. at Middlebury, Conn., Sept. 26, 1799; lived and d. unmarried in Stonington, Conn.
3 CHARLES THEODORE, b. June 14, 1801, at New Haven, Conn.; lived and d. at Stonington unmarried.
4 HARRIET ELIZA, b. at Middlebury, Conn., March 12, 1803, m. Benjamin F. Palmer (No. 349), that family.
5 LOUISE MARIA, b. at Middlebury, April 11, 1805.
6 HENRY AUSTIN, b. at Middlebury Sept. 25, 1809.

The wife of the Rev. Ira Hart was a lineal descendant of Capt. John Sherman of Dedham, Essex County, England, b. in 1613, d. at Watertown, Mass., Jan. 25, 1691. He m. Martha Porter and became an inhabitant of Watertown, Mass., in 1634, where he became a prominent and useful citizen. His son, Joseph Sherman, b. at Watertown, Mass., May 14, 1650, m. Nov. 18, 1673, Elizabeth Winship of Cambridge, Mass., b. April 16, 1652. He became a prominent man, and held the responsible offices of that town. Their son, William Sherman, b. at Watertown, Mass., June 28, 1692, m. Rebecca Cutler of Charlestown, Mass., July 21, 1714. After her death he m. Mehitable Wellington Sept. 13, 1715. He resided at Canton and Newtown.

The Hon. Roger Sherman, son by his second wife, b. at Newtown, Mass., April 19, 1721. He resided at New Milford and New Haven, Conn., and d. at the latter place July 23, 1793. During his career he became one of the most prominent and eminent men of the United States. His name appears on the most important papers that made this country the land of freedom. The Articles of Federation and Declaration of Independence contained his signature, attached by him to those undying and immortal State papers. For his first wife he m. Elizabeth, oldest daughter of Dea. Joseph Hartwell Nov. 17, 1749. His 2d wife was Rebekah Prescott, whom he m. May 12, 1763. John Sherman, son of Roger and Elizabeth (Hartwell) Sherman, b. at New Milford, Conn., July 8, 1750, d. at Canton, Mass., Aug. 8, 1802. He m. 1st, Rebecca Austin at East Haven, Conn., Dec. 16, 1753. After her death he m. 2d Annie Tucker of Milton, Mass., in 1793. Mrs. Maria Sherman, daughter of John Sherman, and first wife, b. at New Haven, Conn., Sept. 30, 1774, d. at Stonington, Conn., Sept. 21, 1857. During the pastorate of Mr. Hart he devoted himself to his profession with earnest and untiring labors, not only for his church and society, but in a wider field of usefulness. He became prominent, particularly so in the organization of the Congregational Churches of New London County, which was formed at Preston, Conn., by pastor and delegate of the churches May 31, 1815. Mr. Hart represented this church as its pastor, with Mr. William Woodbridge as its delegate. After the organization of the consociation, Mr. Hart, acting in union with other prominent clergymen of the county, exerted a powerful influence in renovating their sister churches, which had felt the all-prevading declensions that followed the "New Light" revival of the previous century. Mr. Hart held the position of chaplain of Col. Randall's regiment at the battle of Stonington in Aug., 1814. He also held educational positions, and succeeded in promoting our common school system.

HEWITT FAMILY.

So far as is known from reliable sources, Thomas Hewitt, who was a seafaring man, was the first person of the Hewitt name that made Stonington his abiding place. The first we know of him is from the diary of Thomas Miner, Sr., who speaks of him as in command of his vessel in Mystic River in the year 1656, where he was receiving the surplus products of the early planters here, in exchange for Boston goods. In his business transactions he made the acquaintance of Walter Palmer, whose daughter, Hannah Palmer, he m. April 26, 1659. In order to make Stonington his abode for life he purchased a tract of land on the east side of Mystic River, which embraced the present site of the Elm Grove Cemetery in Stonington, Conn., on which he erected a dwelling house of primitive dimensions, pending which he continued his coasting trade, extending his business to the West Indies. During the year 1662 he purchased a cargo of neat stock, sheep and poultry, designed for the West Indies market, with which he set sail for that place, expecting a pleasant voyage and successful exchange of his cargo for goods in merchandise suitable for the inhabitants of this region round about. Months and years passed, and no glad tidings came of his safe arrival in the West Indies, nor any trace of him anywhere, which forced the conclusion upon his wife and friends, that amid some fearful storm, his vessel had foundered and all on board had found a grave in the cold, dark, heaving sea.

1. THOMAS HEWITT m. Hannah Palmer (No. 7), that family, April 26, 1659.

CHILDREN:

2 THOMAS, b. May 2, 1660, m. Lydia Utley.
3 BENJAMIN, b. 1662, m. Marie Fanning.

Thomas Hewitt (No. 1) was lost at sea in 1662.

Pending the session of the General Court of Connecticut in 1670, a hearing was had for the consideration of a petition of Mrs. Hannah Hewitt, the widow of Thomas Hewitt, for liberty to marry again, setting forth that she had not heard from her late husband for the space of eight years, and better, and her neighbors also testifying that the said Hewitt had so long been absent and that they had not heard of him, or the vessel or company he went with since their departure. "The court having considered the premises, declare that the said Hannah Hewitt is at liberty to marry again if she see cause." So on the 27th day of Dec., 1671, she was united in marriage with Roger Sterry. He d. before 1680; she m. 3d, John Fish Aug. 25, 1681, she being his 3d wife.

CHILDREN BY SECOND MARRIAGE:

4 HANNAH STERRY, b. Aug. 18, 1672, m. William Billings, 1689 (No. 2) that family.
5 SAMUEL STERRY, b. in 1674, m. Hannah Rose in 1703; m. 2d, Mehitable Starkweather.

Thomas Hewitt (No. 2) m. Lydia Utley in June, 1683. He d. June 3, 1686.

ONE CHILD:

6 THOMAS Hewitt, b. Feb. 3, 1685, m. Perces Cleveland.

Benjamin Hewitt (No. 3) m. Marie, daughter of Edmund and Ellen Fanning, Sept. 24, 1683 (No. 7), that family.

CHILDREN:

7 BENJAMIN, bapt. July 24, 1692, m. Ann Palmer.
8 ISRAEL, bapt. July 24, 1692, m. Anna Breed.
9 TABITHA, bapt. July 24, 1692.
10 MARY, bapt. Aug. 12, 1694, m. James Billings March 17, 1715 (No. 24), that family.
11 JOSEPH, bapt. Dec. 13, 1696, m. Mary Chesebrough.
12 ELKANA, bapt. May 7, 1699, m. Temperance Kenney.
13 HANNAH, bapt. June 29, 1701, m. Increase Billings (No. 28), that family.
14 HENRY, bapt. July 30, 1704, m. Joanna Denison.
15 CONTENT, bapt. April 3, 1708, m. 1st, Rev. Ebenezer Russell (No. 26), that family, June 14, 1727. He d. childless May 22, 1731. His widow m. 2d, Dea. Joseph Denison Jan. 16, 1733 (No. 131), Denison family.
16 HANNAH, bapt. June 3, 1711.

Samuel Sterry (No. 5) m. Hannah Rose Feb. 22, 1703; she d. July 19, 1724. He m. 2d, Mehitable Starkweather Feb. 8, 1725. He d. April 15, 1734.

CHILDREN BY FIRST MARRIAGE:

17 HANNAH, b. Feb. 22, 1705.
18 SAMUEL, b. April 4, 1706.
19 CYPRIAN, b. Dec. 18, 1707, m. Elizabeth Brown, daughter of John Brown of Preston.
20 ROBERT, b. June 5, 1711, m. 1st, Rosabillah ———, m. 2d, Lydia Olney.
21 ZERVIAH, b. May 27, 1713.

CHILDREN BY SECOND MARRIAGE:

22 SARAH CHESEBROUGH, b. Oct. 15, 1727, d. 1729.
23 ROGER CHESEBROUGH, b. Jan. 9, 1730, m. Temperance Holmes May 4, 1748 (No. 38), Holmes family.

CHILDREN:

24 SAMUEL, b April 15, 1749, d. 1751-2.
25 MARY, b. April 26, 1752, d. 1752.
26 MARY, b. Aug. 27, 1753, m. Daniel Kimball, 1773.
27 ARTHUR, b. Jan. 26, 1757, d. 1761.
28 MEHITABLE, b. Dec. 18, 1759.

29 CONSIDER, b. Oct. 5, 1761, m. 1st, Sabra Park; 2d, Mrs. Mary (Norman) Hazen.
30 ROGER, Jr., b. Sept. 14, 1764, m. Hurina ———.
31 REV. JOHN, b. Sept. 4, 1766, m. Rebecca Bromley in 1792.
32 ABIGAIL, b. Jan. 20, 1769, d. ———.

Thomas Hewitt (No. 6) m. Perces Cleveland of Canterbury, Conn., Oct. 24, 1706.

CHILDREN:

33 LYDIA, b. Nov. 4, 1707.
34 ELIZABETH, b. April 12, 1709, m. Dea. Thomas Main (No. 18), that family.
35 PRUDENCE, b. Sept. 26, 1711.
36 THOMAS, b. March 26, 1713.
37 JOHN, b. Jan. 24, 1715.
38 THANKFUL, b. Aug. 20, 1722.
39 EPHRAIM, b. Jan. 4, 1728.
The last two children were born after their parents moved to Windham, Ct.

Benjamin Hewitt (No. 7) m. Ann Palmer March 3, 1707 (No. 36), that family.

CHILDREN:

40 KESIAH, b. Aug. 13, 1708, m. Samuel Stockwell Nov. 18, 1735.
41 WALTER, b. March 20, 1710, m. Elizabeth Decthic.
42 NATHAN, b. June 11, 1712.
43 GERSHOM, b. Sept. 6, 1714.
44 BENJAMIN, b. March 7, 1717.
45 ABIAH, b. Jan. 13, 1719.
46 OLIVE, b. Dec. 13, 1720.
47 EDMUND, b. May 28, 1723.
48 JABISH, b. May 28, 1725.
49 CONTENT, b. March 26, 1727.

Israel Hewitt (No. 8) m. Anna Breed March 8, 1714 (No. 5), that family.

CHILDREN:

50 AMIE, b. Aug. 10, 1716, m. Nathaniel Williams (No. 50), that family.
51 ZERVIAH, b. May 3, 1719, d. young.
52 ISRAEL, b. Jan. 12, 1723, m. Tabitha Wheaton.
53 RUFUS, b. July 9, 1726, m. Abigail Frink.
54 CHARLES, b. Aug. 16, 1730, m. Hannah Stanton.
55 ANNA, b. Nov. 8, 1734, m. Simeon Miner Nov. 15, 1753 (No. 118), that family.

Joseph Hewitt (No. 11) m. Mary Chesebrough (No. 68), that family, Oct. 5, 1720.

CHILDREN:

56 NATHANIEL, b. Aug. 11, 1721, m. Rebecca Grant.
57 SAMUEL, b. May 11, 1723.
58 MARY, b. Jan. 20, 1725, m. Joseph Page, Jr., May 1, 1746 (No. 15) that family.
59 HANNAH, b. Dec. 22, 1728, m. Shepard Wheeler (No. 57), that family.
60 JOSEPH, b. May 2, 1731, m. Mrs. Mehitable (Brown) Swan (No. 24), Swan family.
61 ALDEN, b. Nov. 15, 1734.
62 PRISCILLA, b. May 28, 1737.
63 PRUDENCE, b. Oct. 10, 1742.
64 Infant daughter, b. May 26, 1744.
65 ANNA, b. May 26, 1746.

Elkanah Hewitt (No. 12) m. Temperance Keeney in 1722.
CHILDREN:
66 ELKANAH, b. May 10, 1723, m. Elizabeth Miner.
67 THANKFUL, b. Feb. 23, 1726.
68 SARAH, b. March 26, 1729.
69 HENRY, b. Aug. 7, 1730, m. Sarah Keeney, Phebe Prentice, Mrs. Content (Wheeler) Palmer.
70 ARTHUR, b. Aug. 8, 1732.
71 TABITHA, b. Dec. 7, 1735.
72 JONAS, b. Nov. 2, 1737, m. Temperance Holmes.
73 SIMEON, b. March 9, 1739, m. Rachael Geer.

Henry Hewitt (No. 14) m. Joanna Denison Dec. 25, 1735 (No. 137), Denison family.
CHILDREN:
74 AMOS, b. Feb. 20, 1737, m. Anna Miner.
75 HENRY, b. Jan. 7, 1739.
76 THOMAS, b. Nov. 2, 1740.
77 INCREASE, b. Nov. 2, 1742, m. Elizabeth Tyler.
78 JOANNAH, b. July 17, 1743, m. Uriah Cady.
79 ZERVIAH, b. Aug. 12, 1746.
80 CONTENT, b. May 1, 1748.
81 HANNAH, b. May 23, 1750.
82 STEPHEN, b. July 10, 1754, d. young.
83 STEPHEN, b. June 7, 1757, m. Olive Shepard.

Dea. Walter Hewitt (No. 41) m. Elizabeth Decthic Dec. 26, 1746.
CHILDREN:
84 DETHIC, b. in the year 1747, m. Elizabeth Searle.
85 RICHARD, b. in 1749.
86 GERSHOM, b. in 1753.
87 PALMER, b. March 6, 1757.
88 ASA, bapt. May 2, 1762.
89 HENRY, b. in 1763, m. Phebe Morgan.

Israel Hewitt (No. 52) m. Tabitha Wheaton of Little Compton, R. I., May 23, 1750.
CHILDREN:
90 MARY, b. Feb. 25, 1751, d. young.
91 ISRAEL, b. Sept. 15, 1753, d. young.
92 MARY, b. March 28, 1755.
93 CYNTHIA, b. May 18, 1757, m. Stephen Billings (No. 127), that family.
94 ISRAEL, b. Oct. 10, 1758, m. Sarah Williams.
95 NANCY, b. Jan. 5, 1760, m. George Williams (No. 230), that family.
96 WHEATON, b. Jan. 4, 1763.
97 DUDLEY, b. April 29, 1765.
98 GURDON, b. March 10, 1767.
99 RUSSELL, b. Feb. 1, 1769.
100 DARIUS, b. Oct. 28, 1771, m. Wealthy Avery.
101 DIADAMA, b. Oct. 28, 1771.

Rufus Hewitt (No. 53) m. Abigail Frink Nov. 5, 1746 (No. 38), Frink family, both of Stonington, Conn.
CHILDREN:
102 EUNICE, b. May 25, 1749.
103 ZERVIAH, b. June 23, 1753.

104 AMOS, b. Sept. 2, 1755.
105 LYDIA, b. Nov. 4, 1757, m. Peleg Stanton (No. 299), that family; m. 2d, Joshua Brown (No. 77), Lynn Brown family.
106 RUFUS, b. July 23, 1762, m. Martha Wheeler.
107 ELIAS, b. Aug. 27, 1764, m. Anna Hull.

Charles Hewitt (No. 54) m. Hannah Stanton (No. 143), that family, Oct. 28, 1756.

CHILDREN:

108 CHARLES, b. Aug. 16, 1757; was one of the men who assisted in taking the British General Prescott out of bed on the Island of Newport, during the Revolutionary war. Afterwards he engaged in privateering and d. at sea of the yellow fever.
109 HANNAH, b. Dec. 22, 1758, m. Col. Joseph Smith (No. 56), that family.
110 STANTON, b. Oct. 8, 1760, m. Lucinda Grant.
111 ISAAC, b. Jan. 28, 1762, m. Cynthia Swan.
112 ELI, b. July 31, 1764, m. Betsey Williams.
113 PEREZ, b. April 29, 1770, m. Nancy Williams.
114 PALMER, b. Jan. 14, 1777, m. Eunice Williams.
115 ANNA, b. Aug. 27, 1779, m. Jonathan Avery (No. 182), that family.
116 POLLY or MARY, b. Dec. 1, 1781, m. Richard Wheeler (No. 362), that family.

Nathaniel Hewitt (No. 56) m. Rebecca Grant April 24, 1740 (No. 18), Grant family.

CHILDREN:

117 JOSIAH GRANT, b. May 12, 1742, m. Mercy Williams Jan. 27, 1763.
118 GRACE, b. May 25, 1744.
119 NATHANIEL, b. Oct. 15, 1746, m. Anna Hobart, Sarah Avery.
120 MARY, b. July 6, 1751, d. young.
121 REBECCA, b. Feb. 22, 1754.
122 JOSEPH, b. May 10, 1756.
123 MARY, b. Jan. 25, 1759.

Elkanah Hewitt (No. 66) m. Elizabeth Miner (No. 166), that family, Oct. 11, 1749.

CHILDREN:

124 LYDIA, b. April 22, 1751.
125 THANKFUL, b. Sept. 2, 1753.
126 REBECCA, b. Jan. 19, 1756.
127 ELKANAH, b. March 19, 1759.
128 ROBERT, b. June 2, 1760.
129 ELIZABETH, b. March 2, 1763.
130 HANNAH, b. June 2, 1765.
131 ROGER, b. Dec. 18, 1767.
132 LOT, b. May 2, 1770.

Henry Hewitt (No. 69) m. Sarah Keeney Jan. 23, 1751; she d. He m. 2d, Phebe Prentice Jan. 2, 1772 (No. 30), that family; he m. 3d, Mrs. Content (Wheeler) Palmer March 30, 1784 (No. 348), Wheeler family.

CHILDREN:

133 JOSEPH, b. Aug. 8, 1774.
134 BENJAMIN, b. Aug. 8, 1774, m. Desire Babcock.
135 AMOS, b. Nov. 14, 1776.
136 PHEBE, b. Dec. 9, 1778.
137 PRENTICE, b. ———, m. Peggy Brown.

Jonas Hewitt (No. 72) m. Temperance Holmes, date of m. unknown, both of Stonington, Conn.

CHILDREN:

138 JONAS, b. Aug. 5, 1791.
139 EUNICE, b. Feb. 16, 1793.
140 THOMAS, b. Sept. 30, 1794.
141 BENJAMIN, b. Nov. 4, 1797.
142 DENISON, b. Nov. 4, 1797.

Simeon Hewitt (No. 73) m. Rachael Geer, date unknown.

CHILDREN:

143 SIMEON, b. ———.
144 ZEBRA, b. ———.
145 ISAAC, b. ———.
146 ABEL, b. ———.

Amos Hewitt (No. 74) m. Anna Miner in 1774 (No. 200), Miner family, both of Stonington, Conn. He was lost at sea, and his widow went to Cayuga, New York, to live with her son, but did not long remain there; she returned to Stonington, and lived with her husband's brother, Thomas Hewitt, until her death in 1838.

CHILD:

147 AMOS, b. Jan., 1775, m. ———.

Increase Hewitt (No. 77) m. Elizabeth, daughter of Daniel Tyler, and wife, Mehitable Shurtleff.

CHILDREN:

148 MEHITABLE, b. in 1664.
149 AMOS, b. in 1665.
150 DANIEL, b. June 13, 1768, d. 1801.
151 WILLIAM, b. in 1770, m. Abigail Hill.
152 INCREASE, b. in 1772.
153 THOMAS, b. in 1773.
154 BETSEY, b. in 1775, m. Elisha Bugbee, 1795.
155 ELIZABETH, b. in 1776.
156 MARY, b. in 1777, m. Abial Bugbee, Jr.
157 EUNICE, b. in 1780, d. unmarried.
158 HENRY, b. in 1782, m. Hannah Bugbee, 1802.
159 JAMES, b. in 1783, d. 1803.
160 JOSEPH, b. in 1787, d. ———.

Dethic Hewitt (No. 84) m. Elizabeth Searle July 11, 1773 (No. 25), Searle family.

CHILDREN:

161 ISAAC, b. ———.
162 DANIEL, b. ———.
163 ELIZABETH, b. ———.

Col. Henry Hewitt (No. 89) m. Phebe Morgan of Groton Nov. 26, 1786.

CHILDREN:

164 PHEBE, b. March 17, 1790.
165 ELIZABETH, b. April 28, 1792.
166 HENRY LEEDS, b. March 3, 1794.

167 ———— ————, b. June 17, 1796.
168 JAMES, b. Feb. 27, 1798.
169 CHARLES, b. Jan. 12, 1801.
170 SARAH, b. June 7, 1808.
This family moved to Genoa, New York.

Israel Hewitt (No. 94) m. Sarah Williams in 1781.
CHILDREN:
171 TABITHA, b. Aug. 25, 1782.
172 SARAH, b. May 10, 1784.
173 ISRAEL, b. Sept. 25, 1785.
174 POLLY, b. July 11, 1787.
175 FREEMAN, b. March 23, 1790.

Rufus Hewitt (No. 106) m. Martha Wheeler in 1788 (No. 114), Wheeler family.
CHILDREN:
176 NABBY, b. Jan. 8, 1789.
177 DESIRE, b. Feb. 14, 1791.
178 PATTY, b. July 30, 1795.
179 RUFUS, b. Nov. 27, 1798.
180 CYRUS, b. March 27, 1797.

Elias Hewitt (No. 107) m. Anna Hull (No. 13), Hull family, Jan. 27, 1791.
CHILDREN:
181 ELIAS, b. May 5, 1792, m. Polly Miner.
182 NANCY, b. June 23, 1793, m. Erastus Williams (No. 11), William Williams family.
183 EZRA, b. Oct. 16, 1794, m. Phebe Esther Randall (No. 102), that family.
184 LYDIA, b. May 7, 1797, m. Dudley R. Wheeler (No. 191), that family.
185 JOHN, b. April 6, 1799, d. unmarried.
186 GURDON, b. Sept. 1, 1800, d. unmarried.

Stanton Hewitt (No. 110) m. Lucinda Grant (No. 40), that family, May 15, 1784, both of Stonington, Conn.
CHILDREN:
187 CHARLES, b. July 13, 1786, m. Eunice Witter.
188 STANTON, b. July 11, 1788, m. Mary Avery Sept. 7, 1820.
189 WILLIAM, b. Jan. 23, 1792, m. Eliza Williams.
190 OLIVER, b. Oct. 15, 1795, m. Julia Punderson; m. 2d, Sarah A. Browning (No. 62), that family.
191 LUCINDA, b. April 17, 1797, m. Ezra Stanton in 1833 (No. 312), that family.
192 EPHRAIM, b. April 20, 1801, m. Eliza Prentice.
193 ELIZA, b. April 17, 1803, m. Henry Prentice Nov. 30, 1824 (No. 63), that family.
194 MARY, b. May 19, 1808, m. Asher Prentice (No. 75), Prentice family.
195 DENISON, b. Jan. 19, 1811, m. Mary Browning.

Isaac Hewitt (No. 111) m. Cynthia Swan in 1787 (No. 67), that family.
CHILDREN:
196 HANNAH, b. July 9, 1788, m. Robert Stanton (No. 172), that family.
197 POLLY, b. July 26, 1790, m. George P. Stewart Jan. 1, 1812 (No. 40), that family.

HEWITT FAMILY.

198 CYNTHIA, b. Dec. 19, 1791, m. Coddington Swan, Feb. 5, 1818 (No. 171), that family.
199 NANCY, b. June 8, 1795, m. Charles P. Wheeler (No. 146), that family.
200 SOPHIA, b. Nov. 17, 1798, m. Elias Smith Dec. 15, 1824.
201 HARRIET, b. Jan. 1, 1800, m. Joshua C. Stanton (No. 196), that family; 2d, E. Williams Bennet (No. 60), that family.
202 ISAAC, b. March 19, 1802, m. Caroline Allyn, Nov. 27, 1822.
203 CHARLES S., b. May 9, 1804, m. Cynthia Hewitt Sept. 4, 1825 (No. 217); 2d, Mary Gray, May 8, 1837.
204 AUSTIN D., b. 1806, m. Eunice Hewitt Dec. 9, 1828 (No. 218).
205 AMOS, b. 1808, m. Eunice Packer of Groton. He d. and his widow m. Charles Stanton.

Eli Hewitt (No. 112) m. Elizabeth or Betsey Williams April 24, 1796 (No. 283), that family.

CHILDREN:

206 GEORGE W., b. June 26, 1797, m. Bridget Wheeler (No. 256), that family.
207 BETSEY, b. Aug. 30, 1799.
208 CHARLES GRANDISON, b. Dec. 20, 1801, m. 1st, Lucy Randall. He m. 2d, Mary Wheeler.
209 HANNAH, b. Feb. 20, 1804, m. Rowland Stanton (No. 313), that family.
210 ELIZA, b. March 10, 1806.
211 BENADAM, b. April 30, 1808, m. Desire Wheeler Randall (No. 113), that family, Jan. 5, 1837; m. 2d, Phebe Wheeler.
212 ELI, b. Jan. 28, 1810, m. Mary Lamb.

Perez Hewitt (No. 113), m. Nancy Williams of Waterford (No. 311), that family, Feb. 12, 1797.

CHILDREN:

213 PEREZ, b. Feb. 24, 1798, m. Abby S. Crandall Nov. 13, 1823 (No. 315), Stanton family. After his death she m. Richard Main of North Stonington, Conn.
214 HANNAH, b. May 30, 1800, d. unmarried.
215 NANCY, b. May 30, 1800, d. unmarried.
216 HENRY, b. Sept. 7, 1802, m. Maria Williams July 9, 1837 (No. 113), that family.
217 CYNTHIA, b. June 10, 1804, m. Charles S. Hewitt (No. 203).
218 EUNICE A., b. Aug. 5, 1806, m. Austin D. Hewitt (No. 204).
219 MARY E., b. Oct. 16, 1808, m. William Comstock, Nov. 19, 1833.
220 GEORGE W., b. May 26, 1811, m. Louise Brown Oct. 17, 1841.
221 CHARLES G., b. Sept. 27, 1813, d. young.

Palmer Hewitt (No. 114) m. Eunice Williams Feb. 23, 1800 (No. 312), that family. She d. March 9, 1869; he d. April 11, 1850.

CHILDREN:

222 ELISHA JEFFERSON, b. Dec. 18, 1800, m. Desire Gallup Nov. 27, 1823 (No. 263), Gallup family.
223 ELIZA W., b. March 11, 1803, m. Alfred Gallup (No. 261), that family.
224 EMELINE S., b. July 24, 1806, m. Joseph Keeney Dec. 25, 1831.
225 EUNICE A., b. July 15, 1814, m. Edward Ashbey May 22, 1836.
226 AVERY P., b. July 15, 1814, m. Harriet Miner April 29, 1838.

Nathaniel Hewitt (No. 119), m. Anna Hobart of Stonington, Conn., Nov. 3, 1766. He m. 2d, Sarah Avery (No. 153), Avery family, in 1787.

CHILDREN BY FIRST MARRIAGE:
227 ELIPHALET, b. Aug. 7, 1767.
228 SARAH, b. June 30, 1770, m. Elam Chesebrough (No. 260), Chesebrough family.
229 NATHANIEL, b. March 12, 1774.
CHILDREN BY SECOND MARRIAGE:
230 REV. NATHANIEL, b. Aug. 25, 1788, m. Rebecca Hillhouse.
231 SARAH, b. 1790.
232 NANCY, b. 1792.
233 JOSEPH, b. 1794.
234 HENRY, b. 1797.
235 MARY, b. 1800.

Prentice Hewitt (No. 137) m. Peggy Brown Feb. 16, 1794. After her death he m. Eliza Prentice March 27, 1802.
CHILDREN:
236 PEGGY, b. March 27, 1795.
237 AMOS, b. April 6, 1797.

Benjamin Hewitt (No. 134) m. Desire Babcock Oct. 21, 1798.
CHILDREN:
238 DESIRE, b. Dec. 28, 1800, d. young.
239 SARAH, b. Jan. 17, 1802, m. Hezekiah Haskell.
240 DESIRE, b. Sept. 27, 1803, m. Ezra D. Miner Oct. 9, 1823 (No. 235), that family.
241 PHEBE, b. Aug. 24, 1806, m. Isaac P. Breed Nov. 25, 1837 (No. 136), that family.
242 EMMILLA, b. June 19, 1808, m. Joseph H. Robinson Dec. 25, 1827.
243 BENJAMIN BABCOCK, b. Oct. 11, 1811, m. Sally Brown Oct. 13, 1834; m. 2d, Rhoda (Pendleton) Richmond.
244 JOSEPH DENISON, b. Nov. 15, 1815, m. Emily L. Stanton March 14, 1839.
245 MARY LOUISE, b. April 13, 1818, m. William W. Maine of Windham Sept. 12, 1838.
246 FRANCES M., b. March 25, 1820, m. Charles Maine of Windham Sept. 12, 1838.

Stanton Hewitt (No. 188) m. Mary Avery Sept. 7, 1820.
CHILDREN:
247 MARY ANN, b. Sept. 10, 1821, d. Nov. 6, 1821.
248 WILLIAM S., b. March 23, 1823, d. unmarried.
249 MARY AUGUSTUS, b. April 1, 1825, d. March 29, 1835.
250 OLIVER A., b. April 3, 1827, d. Oct. 26, 1848.
251 MARGARET L., b. April 27, 1829, d. June 10, 1830.
252 MARGARET, b. April 28, 1831, d. young.
253 CHARLES EDWIN, b. Feb. 1, 1834, m. Eliza A. Hillard Feb. 22, 1860.
254 JANE ELIZA, b. July 13, 1836, m. Andrew J. Avery May 19, 1864.
255 MARIA LOUISE, b. March 30, 1841, d. young.

William Hewitt (No. 189) m. Eliza Williams (No. 51) William Williams family, March 6, 1814. He d. Jan. 25, 1869; she d. April 9, 1867.
CHILDREN:
256 FRANCES E., b. Sept. 6, 1816, m. George S. Browning; m. 2d, Roger W. Griswold.
257 ABBY LUCINDA, b. June 21, 1818, m. Russell B. Coates Sept. 27, 1838.
258 MARY ANN, b. Oct. 29, 1828, m. Gilbert Billings Aug. 24, 1852 (No. 200), Billings family.

Ephraim Hewitt (No. 192) m. Eliza Prentice Dec. 4, 1828, both of North Stonington, Conn. (No. 74), Prentice family.

CHILDREN:

259 ELIZABETH, b. ――――, m. Elisha Rood.
259 EPHRAIM, b. ――――, d. young.
260 HARRIET PRENTICE, b. ――――, m. Austin Maine.
261 MARY ESTHER, b. ――――, m. Daniel B. Morgan of Preston.
262 EMILY, b. ――――, m. Samuel O. Grant.
263 GILES, b. ――――, m. Harriet Eggleston.

Denison Hewitt (No. 195) m. Mary P. Browning (No. 60), that family.

CHILD:

264 THOMAS BROWNING, b. ――――, m. Amanda Brower. He is a prominent lawyer in New York; residence in Brooklyn, N. Y.

Charles Grandison Hewitt (No. 208) m. 1st, Lucy Randall Dec. 25, 1823. She d. April 19, 1839 (No. 108), that family. He m. 2d, Mary, daughter of Richard Wheeler, Jan. 18, 1843 (No. 428), Wheeler family.

CHILDREN BY FIRST MARRIAGE:

265 DUDLEY R., b. April 28, 1825, m. Martha Gallup (No. 221), that family.
266 LUCY ANN, b. Jan. 3, 1831.

Perez Hewitt (No. 213) m. Abby S. Crandall Nov. 13, 1823 (No. 315), Stanton family. After his death Mrs. Hewitt m. 2d Richard Maine of North Stonington.

CHILDREN:

267 ANN MARIA, b. ――――.
268 LYDIA, b. ――――, d. unmarried.
269 WARREN STANTON, b. ――――, m. ―――― Hewitt, daughter of Isaac Hewitt.

Rev. Nathaniel Hewitt (No. 230) m. Rebecca Hillhouse June, 1815.

CHILDREN:

270 REBECCA, b. Jan. 22, 1817.
271 JAMES, b. Jan. 14, 1819.
272 NATHANIEL, b. Nov. 24, 1820.
273 SARAH, b. April 13, 1823.
274 HENRY, b. Dec. 26, 1825.

Elias Hewitt (No. 181) m. Polly, daughter of Alpheus and Desire Miner (No. 215), Miner family, Feb. 6, 1817, by Stephen Avery, Esq.

CHILDREN:

277 ALPHEUS M., b. Sept. 16, 1818, m. Mary E. Manning Dec. 6, 1858.
278 ERASTUS W., b. Jan. 14, 1821, m. Ann Hull Aug. 13, 1851 (No. 39), that family.
279 NANCY MARY, b. Aug. 3, 1823, m. Charles G. Sisson June 21, 1840 (No. 54), that family.
280 DESIRE MATILDA, b. Nov. 24, 1825, m. John S. Schoonover May 13, 1851.
281 FRANCES ADELIA, b. Aug. 31, 1828, d in girlhood.
282 PHEBE ESTHER, b. March 23, 1831, m. Lathrop W. Hull Sept. 1, 1851 (No. 40), Hull family.

Darius Hewitt (No. 100) m. Wealthy Avery (No. 161) in 1793. He d. 1802.

ONE CHILD:

283 WEALTHY AVERY, b. Dec. 29, 1794, m. Hon. William Randall, Jr. (No. 92), that family, Dec. 23, 1813.

Charles Hewitt (No. 187) m. Eunice Witter Feb. 28, 1813.

CHILDREN:

284 CHARLES, b. Nov. 20, 1813.
285 STANTON, b. June 19, 1815.
286 FRANCINA E., b. July 5, 1817, d. Feb. 27, 1825.
287 ERASTUS F., b. Nov. 26, 1824.
288 JOSEPH H., b. May 30, 1827.
289 JOHN H., b. Aug. 8, 1835.

HINCKLEY FAMILY.

1. SAMUEL HINCKLEY, the first of the Hinckley family that appears in the early settlement of New England, came to this country with wife, Sarah ———, and four children, from Tenderden, in Kent, England, in the good ship Hercules of Sandwich in the year 1635, and settled in Scituate, Mass.

THEIR CHILDREN:

2 THOMAS, b. in England about 1618, m. 1st, Mary Richards, and 2d, Mary Glover, widow.
3 SUSANNAH, b. in England, m. John Smith in 1643.
4 MARY, b. in England.
5 SARAH, b. in England, m. Henry Cobb of Barnstable (No. 1), Cobb family.

Mrs. Sarah Hinckley joined the Scituate church Aug. 30, 1635, and had their child, Elizabeth, bapt. the next Sunday.

CHILDREN:

6 ELIZABETH, bapt. Sept. 6, 1635, m. Elisha Parker July 15, 1657.
7 SAMUEL, b. Feb. 4, 1638, d. young.
8 SAMUEL, b. Feb. 10, 1639, d. young.

Samuel Hinckley, Sr., and family, removed to Barnstable, Mass., in 1640, where the next children were born.

CHILDREN:

9 SAMUEL, b. July 24, 1642, m. Mary Goodspeed Dec. 14, 1662.
10 JOHN, b. May 26, 1644.

During the years 1640 and 1641 he had three other unbaptized children born and buried there. Mrs. Sarah Hinckley d. Aug. 18, 1656. Her husband m. for his second wife, Bridget Bodfish, and d. Oct. 31, 1662.

John Hinckley (No. 10) m. in 1668, Bethia, daughter of Thomas Lathrop, of Barnstable, Mass. He was a distinguished military man.

THEIR CHILDREN:

11 SARAH, b. in May, 1669.
12 SAMUEL, b. Feb. 20, 1671, m. Martha Lathrop.
13 BETHIA, b. in March, 1673.
14 HANNAH, b. in May, 1675.
15 JONATHAN, b. Feb. 15, 1678.
16 ICHABOD, b. Aug. 28, 1680.
17 GERSHOM, b. April 2, 1682.

Mrs. Bethia Hinckley d. July 10, 1694, and her husband m. 2d, Mary Goodspeed Nov. 24, 1697, and d. Dec. 7, 1709.

Samuel Hinckley (No. 12) m. Martha Lathrop Sept. 29, 1694,

and he and Henry Cobb, son of Dea. Henry Cobb of Barnstable, Mass., came to Stonington and bought a large tract of land, which they held and improved together until 1717, when they divided the same, Samuel Hinckley taking that part of their joint purchase that lay on Hinckley Hill, near Pawcatuck River, and Henry Cobb that part which lay on both sides of the road from Wequetequock to Pawcatuck Bridge. Samuel and Jonathan Hinckley (Nos. 12 and 15) joined the First Church at Stonington, 1708 and 1710.

CHILDREN OF SAMUEL AND MARTHA:

18 JOHN, b. in Barnstable July 25, 1700, bapt. Nov. 19, 1710, m. Elizabeth Breed.
19 MARTHA, b. in Barnstable March 8, 1702.
20 SAMUEL, b. in Barnstable March 4, 1706, m. Zerviah Breed; 2d, Mary Wyatt.
21 JOANNA, b. in Stonington March 29, 1708, m. George Denison (No. 66) of that family May 10, 1727, for his second wife.
22 MARY, b. Jan. 27, 1709, bapt. Nov. 19, 1710.
23 THANKFUL, b. March 22, 1712, bapt. June 4, 1712, m. Jedediah Thompson.
24 MERCY, bapt. Oct. 7, 1716, m. Walter Palmer Dec. 29, 1736 (No. 152).
25 NANCY, b. Jan. 17, 1717.

Mrs. Martha Hinckley d. June 21, 1737, in the 59th year of her age.

John Hinckley (No. 18) and Elizabeth (No. 8), Breed family, daughter of John and wife, Mercy (Palmer) Breed, of Breed family, were m. March 3, 1725, and they were admitted to the church Feb. 16, 1734-5.

CHILDREN:

26 JOHN, b. April 19, 1727, bapt. Oct. 26, 1729, m. Johanna Rose.
27 GERSHOM, b. Sept. 4, 1730, m. Catharine ———.
28 ELIZABETH, b. May 12, 1735.

Samuel Hinckley (No. 20) and Zerviah (No. 10), Breed family, daughter of John and wife, Mercy (Palmer) Breed, were m. Jan. 22, 1730.

CHILDREN:

29 ZERVIAH, b. April 11, 1731, m. Thaddeus Cook of Preston, Conn., Jan. 30, 1754.

Mrs. Zerviah Hinckley d. June 14, 1731, and Mr. Samuel Hinckley m. for his second wife, Mary Wyatt, Dec. 30, 1736.

CHILDREN:

30 SAMUEL, b. Aug. 22, 1737, d. Aug., 1757.
31 WYATT, b. Jan. 18, 1739, m. Eunice Breed, and 2d, Mrs. Lucy Frink.
32 DAVID, b. Jan. 28, 1741, d. Oct. 31, 1742.
33 ABEL, b. April 10, 1743, m. Sarah Hubbard.
34 ELIJAH, b. July 15, 1745.
35 NATHAN, b. Feb. 23, 1748, m. Mary Babcock Sept. 8, 1776 (No. 226), Babcock family.

HINCKLEY FAMILY.

36 MARY, b. July 8, 1750, m. David Babcock March 17, 1769 (No. 227), Babcock family.
37 GERSHOM, b. April 5, 1753, d. April, 1753.
38 VOSE, b. Aug. 28, 1754, m. Mary Miner Oct. 10, 1776 (No. 185), Miner family.
39 MARTHA, b. June 5, 1758.
40 GRACE, b. Sept. 14, 1760, m. Robert Babcock Feb. 27, 1780, (No. 229), Babcock family.

Mrs. Mary Wyatt Hinckley d., and Mr. Hinckley m. for his third wife Mary Bacon, Dec. 13, 1761, and he d. Nov. 9, 1763.

John Hinckley (No. 26) m. Johanna Rose Dec. 23, 1746, and after Mr. Hinckley's death she m. Samuel Frink (No. 43), Frink family, Nov. 24, 1764.

CHILDREN:

41 JOHN, b. July 15, 1747, d. Oct. 26, 1753.
42 DAVID, b. Aug. 4, 1749.
43 THOMAS, b. April 28, 1751, m. Eliphal Slack.
44 PAUL, b. Oct. 31, 1753, m. Mary ———.

Gershom Hinckley (No. 27) m. Catharine ———.

CHILDREN:

45 ANNE, b. Nov. 8, 1757.
46 PRUDENCE, b. June 4, 1759.
47 ELIZABETH, b. March 16, 1761.
48 GERSHOM, b. July 27, 1763.
49 DANIEL, b. Aug. 30, 1765.
50 JOHN, b. Jan. 22, 1768.

Wyatt Hinckley (No. 31) m. Eunice Breed (No. 20), Breed family, July 31, 1760.

CHILDREN:

51 SAMUEL, b. April 22, 1761.
52 WYATT, Jr., b. July 26, 1763.
53 EUNICE, b. Dec. 13, 1766.
54 MARCY, b. Dec. 19, 1768.
55 LUCY, b. Sept. 3, 1770, m. Frederick Pendleton (No. 42), Pendelton family; m. 2d, Jonathan Pendleton (No. 43), Pendleton family.

Wyatt Hinckley (No. 31) m. 2d, widow Lucy Frink of Stonington, Dec. 3, 1774.

CHILDREN:

56 ESTHER, b. Aug. 19, 1775.
57 DENCY, b. Dec. 9, 1776.
58 HARRY, b. Aug. 7, 1778.
59 CHARLES, b. June 5, 1780.
60 LUTHER, b. May 26, 1782.
61 EUNICE, b. May 15, 1784.
62 DAVID, b. March 23, 1786.

Abel Hinckley (No. 33) m. Sarah Hubbard or Hobart, 1764. She d. Oct. 16, 1806, and he d. March 20, 1818.

CHILDREN:

63 SARAH, b. March 11, 1765, m. George Fish.
64 REBECCA, b. Oct. 6, 1766, m. Ezra Gallup (No. 104), that family.
65 MARY, b. Feb. 23, 1768, m. Theophilus Morgan (No. 33), that family.
66 ANNE, b. Aug. 16, 1769, m. Joshua Gallup (No. 141), that family.

67 ABEL, b. May 13, 1771.
68 SAMUEL H., b. Dec. 26, 1772, m. Abigail Helms; 2d, Nancy Chapman.
69 ESTHER, b. Nov. 25, 1777, d. unmarried.

Thomas Hinckley (No. 43) m. Eliphal Slack Feb. 20, 1780.
CHILDREN:
70 ELIPHAL, b. Nov. 16, 1780.
71 CAROLINE, b. Aug. 16, 1782.
72 ABIGAIL, b. March 13, 1786.
73 THOMAS, b. Dec. 11, 1787, m. Mary Scholfield.

Paul Hinckley (No. 44) m. Mary ―――――.
CHILDREN:
74 PAUL, b. March 22, 1775.
75 MARY, b. Feb. 15, 1773.

Samuel Hobart Hinckley (No. 68) m. Abigail Helms April 13, 1800. She was daughter of Oliver Helms and Katharine Greenman.
CHILDREN:
76 SAMUEL, b. Jan. 11, 1801.
77 ABBY, b. Sept. 4, 1802.
78 ABEL, b. Nov. 3, 1803, m. Abbie Babcock.
79 ELIAS B., b. June 26, 1805, m. Catharine Barnes.
80 FRANK P., b. April 10, 1807, d. unmarried in 1833.
81 HENRY, b. July 15, 1809, m. Prudence M. Chesebrough (No. 396), Chesebrough family.
82 MARY E., b. April 11, 1811, m. Charles M. Davis.

Mrs. Abigail H. Hinckley d. May 31, 1813, and on the 9th day of March, 1815, Mr. Samuel H. Hinckley m. 2d, Mrs. Nancy Chapman Clarke (No. 76), Chapman family, widow of William Clarke.

Thomas Hinckley (No. 73) m. Mary Scholfield Dec. 9, 1810. She was b. Feb. 3, 1787, and d. May 23, 1882. Mr. Thomas Hinckley d. Dec. 11, 1876.

HOBART FAMILY.

1. DANIEL HOBART and Zerviah Miner, daughter of James and Abigail (Eldredge) Miner, were m. Dec. 4, 1729.

CHILDREN:

2 MARGARET, b. July 26, 1731, m. William Thompson March 21, 1751 (No. 9), Thompson family.
3 HANNAH, b. Oct. 11, 1733, m. John Hinks Jan. 22, 1756.
4 SUSANNAH, b. March 24, 1736, m. Nathaniel Hall Nov. 26, 1761.
5 JOHN, b. April 15, 1739.
6 DANIEL, b. Aug. 31, 1741, m. Hannah Shaw Sept. 21, 1760.
7 SAMUEL, b. May 24, 1744, m. Rebecca Shaw Sept. 8, 1768.
8 PETER, b. March 2, 1750.
9 ELIPHALET, b. June 20, 1752.
10 ZERVIAH, b. Nov. 12, 1755, m. Zebulon Chesebrough (No. 138) of the Chesebrough family, April 25, 1776.

Peter Hobart (No. 8) and Mary or Mercy Frink (No. 62), daughter of David Frink and Eunice (Gallup) Frink, were m. May 20, 1781.

CHILDREN:

11 MERCY, b. June 22, 1782, m. Christopher Leeds March 7, 1819.
12 NANCY, b. Feb. 16, 1784, never m.
13 RUSSELL, b. June 30, 1785, never m.
14 RILLA, b. Feb. 7, 1787.
15 HENRY, b. March 3, 1789, m. Jane Skinner.
16 FANNA, b. Sept. 20, 1790, never m.
17 WILLIAM, b. ———, never m.

Eliphalet Hobart (No. 9) m. Mrs. Hannah (Page) Chesebrough (No. 19), of the Page family. Her former husband was ——— Chesebrough, date of m. thereof not known; but five children are given, viz.:

CHILDREN:

1 PRISCILLA CHESEBROUGH, b. ———, m. Roswell Breed for his 2d wife. They had Roswell Breed, Jr., Thomas and Sally Ann.
2 DAVID CHESEBROUGH, b. ———, m. ———.
3 HANNAH CHESEBROUGH, b. ———, m. Benjamin Hancox, son of Benjamin, who m. Eunice, daughter of Stanton Stevens, and wife, Mrs. Eunice (Hall) Short. Hannah d. in 1861, aged 82 yrs.
4 POLLY CHESEBROUGH, b. ———, m. Henry Lewis, d. 1865, aged 84 yrs.
5 ELISHA CHESEBROUGH, b. ———, m. Lucy Chapman.

Children of Eliphalet Hobart and Hannah Page Chesebrough Hobart, who were m. before 1777.

CHILDREN:

18 DANIEL, b. Oct. 23, 1777, m. Fanny Slack.
19 JOSEPH, b. 1785, d. 1860, never m.

20 HANNAH, b. ———, m. 1st, Capt. John Sterrett, and had one child, Mary Ann Sterrett, who m. Capt. Joshua Stevens. After Capt. Sterrett's death, Mrs. Sterrett m. 2d, Capt. John Barnum; they had one child, Edward P. Barnum.

Daniel Hobart (No. 18) m. Fanny Slack, daughter of William Slack, and Lucy (Breed) Slack (No. 60), Breed family. She was b. Jan. 23, 1784, and m. Dec. 25, 1814.

CHILDREN:

21 ELAM W., b. Nov. 23, 1815, m. Julia A. Grinnell Oct. 21, 1846.
22 FRANCES M., b. May 18, 1817, m. Nelson Forsyth.
23 LUCY S., b. June 1, 1819, d. young.
24 WILLIAM S., b. Sept. 26, 1821, m. Caroline Bottum.
25 HANNAH T., b. March 7, 1824, d. young.
26 NANCY N., b. March 30, 1828, d. young.
27 EMMA P., b. Dec. 16, 1830, d. young.
28 PHEBE D., b. Sept. 14, 1834, d. young.

HOLMES FAMILY.

1. ROBERT HOLMES, the progenitor of the Stonington Holmes family, came to this town before the town was named Stonington, and purchased large tracts of land, and made this his permanent place of abode. He was registered here as an inhabitant Dec. 25, 1670, which implied previous residence, besides being a land holder and taxpayer. He served in the Colonial Indian wars. Where he resided is not certainly known, nor who he m., nor her family name and m. date. He had one child, whose name was:

2. Joshua Holmes, whose birth date does not appear in town or church records. He was doubtless b. before his father settled in Stonington. He did not long remain here after his m. with the widow Abigail (Ingraham) Chesebrough, widow of Samuel Chesebrough (No. 6), that family, June 5, 1675. He purchased land in Westerly, R. I., upon which he built him a dwelling house, which he occupied during his life, and by his will gave it, with all his land, to his widow, children and son-in-law. He served in King Phillip's war. After his death his widow m. Capt. James Avery, for his second wife, and her third husband (No. 2), Avery family.

CHILDREN:
3 MARY b. date not recorded, m. Isaac Thompson.
4 JOSHUA, b. Aug. 20, 1678, m. Fear Sturges.

Mary Holmes (No. 2) m. Isaac Thompson of Westerly, R. I., in 1696.

CHILDREN:
5 MARY, b. July 1, 1697.
6 ISAAC, b. Sept. 26, 1698.
7 SAMUEL, b. July 29, 1700.
8 ABIGAIL, b. Jan. 1, 1701.
9 SARAH, b. March 3, 1703.
10 WILLIAM, b. April 11, 1704.
11 NATHANIEL, b. Dec. 31, 1705.
12 ANNA (twin), b. Dec. 31, 1705.
13 ELIAS, b. Nov. 14, 1708.
14 MARY, b. March 18, 1710.
15 ABIGAIL, b. Oct. 14, 1711.
16 SUSANNAH, b. Nov. 25, 1713, m. Joseph Babcock Dec. 9, 1730.
17 JOSHUA, b. Aug. 13, 1714.
18 PRUDENCE, b. March 11, 1716.

Joshua Holmes (No. 4) lived with his father's family in Westerly. During his youth and young manhood, and before he reached his majority, he became acquainted with Miss Fear Sturges of Yarmouth, Cape Cod, Mass., whose house he often visited with increasing pleasure, until they were m. Nov. 21, 1698. Miss Sturges was the daughter of Edward Sturges, who came to this country from England to Charlestown, Mass., in 1634, and settled in Yarmouth. He was the son of Phillip Sturges of Hamington County, Northampton, and a descendant of Roger Sturges of Clifton County, Northampton, England, who was a resident there in 1530. He bought and received large tracts of land in Stonington, now North Stonington, which is intersected by the highway from Pawcatuck Bridge to Voluntown, at, above and below the junction of the highway leading therefrom to the Wyassup Reservoir, upon which he built him a dwelling house, which he occupied during life.

CHILDREN:

19 JOSHUA, b. Aug. 14, 1700, m. Mary Richardson.
20 JOHN, b. June 10, 1702, m. Abigail Frink; m. 2d, Mary Smith; m. 3d, Hannah Halsey.
21 ABIGAIL, b. Feb. 28, 1703, m. Jedediah Brown (No. 34), that family.
22 TEMPERANCE, b. Jan. 29, 1707, m. John Smith May 10, 1727; she m. 2d, James Treadway.
23 THANKFUL, b. Nov. 12, 1708, m. William Swan (No. 23), that family.
24 THOMAS, b. Jan. 19, 1711, m. Margaret Frink.
25 MARY, b. March 19, 1713, m. Elias Palmer (No. 141); 2d, Capt. John Randall (No. 8), that family.
26 BETHIA, b. July 29, 1715
27 MARVIN, b. Nov. 17, 1717, m. Asa Swan (No. 25), that family.

Joshua Holmes (No. 19) m. Mary Richardson, daughter of Stephen and Lydia (Gilbert) Richardson, Dec. 6, 1721.

CHILDREN:

28 FEAR, b. July 8, 1722, m. Andrew Main (No. 30), that family.
29 PRUDENCE, b. Feb. 27, 1724, m. Jonathan Palmer (No. 95), that family.
30 MARY, b. May 6, 1726.
31 JOSHUA, b. Dec. 28, 1726, m. Mrs. Prudence Wheeler.
32 SARAH, b. March 9, 1729, m. ——— Wallworth.
33 JAMES, b. April 17, 1731, m. Surviah Mason.
34 ANNA, b. June 24, 1733, m. Jedediah Brown (No. 79).
35 THANKFUL, b. Oct. 7, 1735.
36 ABIGAIL, b. Oct. 18, 1741, m. Rossel Smith.
37 JOSEPH, b. 1743, m. Martha Wheeler.

John Holmes (No. 20) m. Abigail Frink (No. 17), that family. Mrs. Frink d., and he m. 2d, Mary Smith of Groton April 2, 1738. She d. childless, Jan. 26, 1744. He m. 3d, Hannah Halsey of Southampton, Long Island, Oct. 31, 1744.

HOLMES FAMILY.

CHILDREN BY FIRST MARRIAGE:
38 TEMPERANCE, b. Jan. 27, 1728, m. Roger Sterry (No. 23), Hewitt family.

CHILDREN BY THIRD MARRIAGE:
39 MARY, b. Aug. 9, 1745, m. Peter Hobart May 20, 1781.
40 EUNICE, b. June 28, 1747, m. Charles Miner, Jr. (No. 145), that family.
41 JOHN, b. March 9, 1749, m. Martha Stanton.
42 JEDEDIAH, b. Nov. 12, 1761, m. Elizabeth Frink.
43 JABISH, b. May 2, 1753, m. Lydia Clift.
44 SILAS, b. June 5, 1755, m. Louisa Fox.
45 ELIAS, b. Feb. 2, 1757, d. young.
46 LUCRETIA, b. Jan. 14, 1759, m. Dr. Samuel Prentice (No. 44), that family.
47 LUCY, b. May 25, 1765, m. Amos Wheeler (No. 88), that family.

Thomas Holmes (No. 24) m. Margaret Frink Nov. 12, 1740. He d. April 9, 1796.

CHILDREN:
48 MARGARET, b. April 14, 1742, m. Christopher Brown (No. 59), that family
49 THOMAS, b. April 28, 1744, m. Mary Frink.
50 JEREMIAH, b. Oct. 4, 1745, m. twice.
51 BETHIAH, b. Nov. 17, 1747.
52 SAMUEL, b. Dec. 19, 1749.
53 JOSHUA, b. April 5, 1752, m. Lucretia Lamphere.
54 NATHAN, b. April 20, 1754.
55 MOLLY, b. June 17, 1756.
56 LUCY, b. April 4, 1760.
57 ABIGAIL, b. April 19, 1763.
58 MARVIN, b. March 6, 1765.

Thomas Holmes (No. 49) m. Mary Frink March 15, 1764 (No. 40), Frink family. Mrs. Holmes d. He m. for his second wife, Temperance Smith of Groton, Conn., Nov. 24, 1767.

CHILDREN BY SECOND MARRIAGE:
59 THOMAS, b. Aug. 6, 1768, m. Elizabeth Baldwin (No. 82), that family.
60 SHUBAEL, b. Aug. 2, 1769, m. Lois Brown.
61 NATHAN, b. Nov. 22, 1771, m. Mary Holmes.

Joshua Holmes, Jr. (No. 31), m. Mrs. Prudence, daughter of Jonathan and Esther Wheeler, Dec. 18, 1751 (No. 341), Wheeler family. He d. Nov. 21, 1799.

CHILDREN:
63 JOSHUA, b. March 3, 1754.
64 PRUDENCE, b. Nov. 2, 1755, m. Beebe Denison Oct. 13, 1774 (No. 292), Denison family.
65 ESTHER, b. Oct. 5, 1757.
66 MARY, b. Oct. 3, 1759, d. unmarried.
67 EDWARD, b. in 1763, m. Mary Grant.
67a MERCY, b. ———, m. Joseph Breed (No. 61), that family.
68 THANKFUL, b. July 18, 1766.
69 SARAH, b. March 27, 1768.
70 JONATHAN, b. Feb. 25, 1770, d. unmarried.
71 ABIGAIL, b. June 17, 1772, d. young.
72 RICHARD, b. March 22, 1774, d. unmarried.
73 WILLIAM, b. Sept. 13, 1776, m. Hannah Wheeler.
74 AMOS, b. Dec. 14, 1778.

438   HISTORY OF STONINGTON.

James Holmes (No. 33) m. Serviah Mason of Westerly, R. I., Feb. 5, 1755; lived in Stonington, Conn.

CHILDREN:
75 JAMES, b. April 22, 1755, m. Esther Babcock Jan. 18, 1776.
76 JARED, b. April 1, 1757, m. Martha Wheeler.
77 ZERVIAH, b. Dec. 28, 1758.
78 GILBERT, b. Sept. 22, 1760.
79 MARY, b. Dec. 11, 1762.
80 Son, b. March 2, 1765, d. May 7, 1765.
81 ROSWELL, b. Feb. 10, 1766.
82 CHARLES, b. April 29, 1768.
83 NEHEMIAH, b. Feb. 23, 1771, d. young.
84 EPHRAIM, b. July 2, 1772.
85 HENRY, b. March 20, 1774.

Joseph Holmes (No. 37) m. Martha Wheeler Nov. 19, 1767 (No. 78), Wheeler family. After the death of Mr. Holmes his widow m. a Mr. Williams; she m. for her third husband, Thomas Hammond in 1788.

CHILDREN:
86 JOSEPH, b. Nov. 14, 1768.
87 MARTHA, b. Dec. 11, 1770.
88 MERCY, b. March 1, 1773.
89 POLLY, b. Jan. 25, 1775.
90 ROSWELL, b. Jan. 14, 1777.
91 ABIGAIL, b. March 20, 1779, m. Benjamin Peabody (No. 41), that family.

CHILDREN BY SECOND MARRIAGE:
92 JOHN WILLIAMS, b. ———.

CHILDREN BY THIRD MARRIAGE:
93 THOMAS HAMMOND, b. June 15, 1789.
94 REBECCA HAMMOND, b. 1791.
95 EUNICE HAMMOND, b. 1794.

Jeremiah Holmes of Stonington (No. 50) m. Elizabeth Sanford Frink Dec. 10, 1772. She d. Feb. 18, 1789. For his second wife he m. Mary, daughter of Daniel and Esther (Wheeler) Denison, Jan., 1778 (No. 224), Denison family. He d. March 8, 1790. His widow, Mrs. Mary Holmes (nee Denison), m. for her second husband, Jedediah Lee, in 1797, and went with him to Stanstead, Canada, where he d. in Oct., 1824. His widow d. there April 29, 1828.

CHILDREN BY FIRST MARRIAGE:
96 MARY, b. Oct. 8, 1778, m. Thomas Crary, Jr.
97 PHILURA, b. Sept. 14, 1780, m. Capt. Theophilus Baldwin (No. 81), that family.
98 JEREMIAH, b. Sept. 6, 1792, m. Mrs. Ann B. (Denison) Gallup.
99 ESTHER, b. March 27, 1785, m. Joel Marsh, March 2, 1803; m. 2d, Joshua Blodgett, Jan. 20, 1819.
100 DANIEL D., b. Sept. 17, 1787, m. Melindia Lee March 23, 1791.
101 FREDERICK, b. Feb. 19, 1789, m. ——— Pittis.

NOTE.—Mary Holmes (No. 96) m. Thomas Crary, Jr., Feb. 2, 1797, son of Thomas Crary and Mehitable Mason, and grandson of Nathan Crary, and wife Dorothy Wheeler (No. 40), that family, and great-grandson of Peter Crary and wife, Christobel Gallup (No. 12), that family.

HOLMES FAMILY.

CHILDREN BY SECOND MARRIAGE:
102 ERASTUS LEE, b. in 1798, d. in Stanstead March 21, 1866.
103 LUCY, b. Jan. 1, 1801, m. Benjamin Pomeroy in 1824.

Jeremiah Holmes (No. 98) m. Mrs. Ann B. Denison (No. 404), Denison family, widow of John D. Gallup, Sept. 8, 1809. No children by first marriage.

CHILDREN:
104 JEREMIAH, b. Sept. 10, 1811, d. Sept. 19, 1811.
105 ISAAC D., b. Nov. 12, 1812, m. Ellen Kempt Aug. 8, 1837.
106 MARY ANN, b. Nov. 14, 1815, m. Randall Brown (No. 393), that family.
107 ESTHER C., b. March 23, 1816, m. Benjamin Latham.
108 JEREMIAH, b. Aug. 15, 1819, d. March 16, 1823.
109 BENJAMIN F., b. Jan. 8, 1822, m. Lucy M. Lewis Sept. 20, 1848.
110 JOSEPH WARREN, b. April 1, 1824, m. Mary O. Denison of Stillwater, N. Y., Sept. 4, 1847; m. 2d, Mrs. Palmer.
111 HIRAM C., b. Jan. 22, 1826, m. Hannah F. Denison (No. 637), that family, Jan. 30, 1850.
112 ERASTUS, b. April 7, 1830, d. April 30, 1832.

Jabish Holmes (No. 43) b. May 2, 1753, m. Lydia Clift of Groton, Conn., May 26, 1811, and d. Aug. 23, 1831 (No. 26), Clift family.

CHILDREN:
113 JABISH, b. Oct. 20, 1812, m. Emeline Williams Oct. 23, 1855 (No. 382), Williams family.
114 SILAS, b. July 21, 1816.
115 AMOS CLIFT, b. Feb. 27, 1818.

Dr. Silas Holmes of Stonington, Conn (No. 44), m. Louisa Fox of Montville in 1779. Dr. Holmes lived in what is now Stonington Borough, and had extensive practice as a physician in all the region round about, Sept. 12, 1790. He was summoned to visit a sick man on Block Island, who sent for him in his boat, which took and bore him safely over to the island, and after he had visited his patient and diagnosed his physical condition, he started with the boatman and craft to return to his home in Stonington, but unfortunately a terrible thunder storm arose with a rushing cyclone of wind, which lashed the ocean into fearful waving foam, which capsized their boat and filled it with water, which, in spite of all the efforts of the doctor and the boatman, sunk, and they were both drowned. Dr. Holmes widow m. for her second husband, Elijah Palmer, Esq., of Stonington, Conn., and they became the parents of one child.

CHILDREN BY FIRST MARRIAGE:
116 LOVISA, b. Nov. 8, 1780.
117 SILAS, b. May 27, 1782.
118 LUCRETIA, b. Aug. 4, 1783.
119 SILAS, b. May 30, 1785.
120 FRANCES, b. March 18, 1788.
121 JABISH, b. June 18, 1789.

CHILD BY SECOND MARRIAGE:
122 ABBY PALMER.

Dr. Joshua Holmes (No. 53) m. Lucretia Lamphere Sept. 16, 1790, both of Stonington, Conn.

CHILDREN:
123 SARAH, b. Feb. 21, 1791.
124 LUCY, b. April 8, 1793.
125 JOSHUA, b. Oct. 15, 1794.
126 SAMUEL, b. March 17, 1796.
127 PATTY, b. April 9, 1798.
128 POLLY, b. Nov. 30, 1799.

Shubael Holmes (No. 60) m. Lois Brown Jan. 22, 1792, both of Stonington.

CHILDREN:
129 SHUBAEL, b. Nov. 19, 1793.
130 POLLY, b. Jan. 22, 1796.
131 ASHER, b. Sept. 11, 1800.
132 CHRISTOPHER, b. Nov. 9, 1804.

Nathan Holmes (No. 61), m. Mary Holmes Sept. 28, 1791, both of Stonington.

CHILDREN:
133 NATHAN, b. Aug. 23, 1792.
134 TEMPERANCE, b. Aug. 23, 1794.

William Holmes (No. 73) m. Hannah Wheeler March 17, 1803 (No. 365), Wheeler family, both of Stonington, Conn. He d. Sept. 5, 1863; she d. Sept. 20, 1863.

CHILDREN:
135 HANNAH W., b. Feb. 24, 1804.
136 PRUDENCE, b. Dec. 16, 1805.
137 WILLIAM B., b. July 27, 1808.
138 SILENCE W., b. Oct. 23, 1813. Soon after the birth of their youngest child, the whole family moved to Halifax, Windham Co., Vermont.

John Holmes (No. 41) m. Martha Stanton Dec. 22, 1774 (No. 151), Stanton family, both of Stonington, Conn.

CHILDREN:
139 HANNAH, b. in 1775, m. Isaac Wheeler in 1808 (No. 134), Wheeler family.
140 JOHN, b. in 1777, m. Nancy Wheeler; m. 2d, Ruth Wheeler.

Jedediah Holmes (No. 42) m. Elizabeth S. Frink Dec. 10, 1772, both of Stonington Conn. She d. Feb. 18, 1789.

CHILDREN:
141 ELIZABETH, b. May 8, 1775.
142 JEDEDIAH, Jr., b. May 30, 1779.

James Holmes (No. 75) m. Esther Babcock Jan. 18, 1776.

CHILDREN:
143 EPHRAIM, b. in 1778.
144 NANCY, b. in 1780.
145 ROBERT, b. in 1782.

HOLMES FAMILY.

146 ESTHER and EUNICE, b. in 1784, d. in infancy.
147 NEHEMIAH, b. in 1786.
148 HAZZARD, b. in 1788, m. Fanny Denison (No. 505), that family.
149 ESTHER, b. in 1790.
150 JAMES, b. in 1792.
151 NOYES, b. in 1793.

John Holmes (No. 140) m. Nancy Wheeler (No. 176), that family, Dec. 22, 1798; m. 2d, Ruth Wheeler (No. 142), that family, in 1820.

CHILDREN BY FIRST MARRIAGE:

152 JOHN, b. Oct. 15, 1799, m. Nancy Angeline Williams; m. 2d, Eunice, daughter of Andrew Chapman.
153 CYRUS W., b. Nov. 24, 1801, m. Martha Reynolds.
154 PATTY, b. July 3, 1804, d. young.
155 B. FRANKLIN, b. Dec. 22, 1807, d. in Iowa.
156 NATHAN WHEELER, b. March 28, 1809, d. young.

CHILDREN BY SECOND MARRIAGE:

157 NANCY E., b. March 1, 1821.
158 LUCY, b. March 4, 1822.

Edward Holmes (No. 67) m. Mary Grant Feb. 15, 1789 (No. 50), that family. He d. in 1810; she d. in 1817.

CHILDREN:

159 PRENTICE, b. Feb. 10, 1793, d. unmarried.
160 JOSHUA,, b. March 12, 1796, d. unmarried.
161 RUSSELL, b. March 12, 1796, m. Martha Holmes, daughter of Jared and Martha (Wheeler) Holmes (No. 76).
162 HOSEA WHEELER, b. May 18, 1800, m. Sophronia Wilbur in 1824.
163 SILAS, b. July 17, 1803, m. Surviah Wheeler April 2, 1825 (No. 451), that family.
164 MARY, b. April, 1805.
165 EUNICE, b. April 12, 1808, m. Lester Tucker in 1847.
166 EDWARD, b. Jan. 5, 1811, m. Malissa Ann Wheeler May 11, 1858 (No. 453), that family.

HOXIE FAMILY.

The name of this family is spelled in many different ways. Hawksie, Hoxsey, Hoxsie, Hoxie, etc.

1. LODOWICK HAWKSIE came to America probably soon after 1650. He lived on the south side of Spring Hill, near Sandwich, Mass.; m. Mary, daughter of John Presbury, June, 1664.

CHILDREN:

2 BETHSHEBA, b. 1665, m. Samuel Allen.
3 JOSEPH, b. March 15, 1667, m. Sarah Tucker.
4 GIDEON, b. ——, m. Grace ——.
5 HEZEKIAH, b. ——.
6 JOHN, b. ——, m. Mary Hull.
7 SOLOMAN, b. ——.
8 CONTENT, b. ——.

Joseph Hoxie (No. 3) m. Sarah, daughter of Henry and wife, Martha Tucker. Their son:

9 JOSEPH, b. Nov. 25, 1701, m. Mary ——. Their son
10 GIDEON, b. Dec. 14, 1729, m. Dorcas Congdon, d. June 13, 1805. Their son
11 JOSEPH, b. in 1767, m. Mary Congdon. He d. Oct. 8, 1829, his widow d. April 8, 1851. Their son
12 WELCOME ARNOLD, b. in 1792, m. Mary A. (Fellows) Hoxie, widow of his brother John, in 1826. He d. at Westerly Dec. 10, 1875. They had a daughter, Mrs. Stephen Wilcox, and a son, William Hoxie, b. March 1, 1840, who is town clerk at Westerly, R. I.

Gideon Hoxie (No. 10) m. Dorcas Congdon. Their son:

13 LODOWICK, b. ——, m. Ruth ——; they had son, Benjamin Franklin, who was a prominent business man at Mystic, Conn., m. Harriet W. Clift Nov. 19, 1843, (No. 42) Clift family, where they lived and died.

John Hoxie (No. 6) b. April 25, 1669, m. Mary, daughter of Joseph and wife, Experience (Harper) Hull. Their son:

14 STEPHEN, b. Nov. 28, 1713, m. Elizabeth, daughter of John and Elizabeth Kenyon, Feb. 27, 1735. Their daughter
15 RUTH, b. in 1749, m. John Foster in 1836. Their son
16 ETHAN, b. in 1779, m. Temperance Bragg in 1801. Their son
17 ETHAN, b. in 1808, m. Anna Wilbur Oct. 24, 1837; had son, John Barclay Foster, b. in 1841, who resides in Westerly, R. I., where he is cashier of the Phenix National Bank. He also is descended from Solomon Hoxie, another son of John Hoxie (No. 6) and wife, Mary Hull, through his mother, as follows: Solomon, b. Sept. 17, 1711, m. Mary Davis, had son, Peter, b. Oct. 5, 1706, m. Mary ——; had daughter, Mary, b. Sept. 9, 1736, m. Thomas Wilbur, July 27, 1758; had son, John, b. July 17, 1774, m. Lydia Collins, Oct. 17, 1793; had daughter, Anna Wilbur, b. April 20, 1813, m. Ethan Foster Oct. 24, 1837.

HULL FAMILY.

This family was not among the first families who settled in Stonington. Their ancestors had previously lived in Massachusetts and Rhode Island, a large number of whom were Friend Quakers.

1. STEPHEN HULL, who lived near Point Judith, R. I., was b. in 1715, and was an industrious, enterprising man and successful farmer, who m. Martha Mory, both of Kingston, R. I., April 27, 1737.

CHILDREN:

2 JOSEPH, b. March 22, 1739.
3 ELIZABETH, May 15, 1741.
4 STEPHEN, b. Sept. 17, 1743.
5 SAMUEL (twin), b. Jan. 20, 1748.
6 ELIAS (twin), b. Jan. 20, 1748.
7 LATHAM, b. Feb. 9, 1749.
8 SARAH, b. July 1, 1752.
9 HANNAH, b. Aug. 22, 1754.

Latham Hull (No. 7) came to Stonington, Conn., before the American Revolution and m. first, Anna Wheeler, daughter of Jeremiah and Anna (Pellet) Wheeler. See Wheeler family (No. 84), date unknown.

CHILDREN:

10 JEREMIAH, b. ———.
11 AMOS, b. ———.
12 BRIDGET, b. ———.
13 ANNA, b. ———, m. Elias Hewitt (No. 107).

After Mrs. Anna Wheeler Hull died, Mr. Hull m. Desire Williams in Feb., 1782 (No. 216), that family.

CHILDREN:

14 JOSEPH, b. ———.
15 LATHAM, b. Dec. 19, 1782.
16 JOHN W., b. Jan. 5, 1789, d. Feb. 28, 1878.
17 MARTHA, b. ———.
18 EUNICE, b. ———.
19 ALMIRA, b. ———.

Latham Hull (No. 7) took a prominent part in the public affairs of Stonington, holding the office of selectman for a number of years in succession, besides representing the town in the General Assembly of the State for several sessions, and he d. Dec. 18, 1807.

Jeremiah Hull (No. 10) m. Keturah Williams (No. 280), Robert Williams family, March 20, 1796.

CHILDREN:

20 WILLIAM P., b. Jan. 30, 1797.
21 CHARLES, b. Dec. 3, 1799.
22 ANNA W., b. Jan. 6, 1801.
23 CYRUS W., b. Feb. 7, 1803.
24 ELISHA, b. April 19, 1805.
25 JOHN W., b. July 5, 1807.
26 KETURAH R., b. July 2, 1810.
27 BENADAM W., b. Dec. 5, 1812.
28 DESIRE, b. May 1, 1815.
29 MARTHA E., b. June 5, 1817.

Amos Hull (No. 11) m. Esther Wheeler in 1803 (No. 197), that family.

CHILDREN:

30 THOMAS L., b. March 11, 1804.
31 ESTHER, b. Sept. 13, 1807, m. Russell Wheeler Oct. 1, 1827. See Wheeler family (No. 171).
32 MARTHA W., b. March 22, 1811.

After the death of his first wife Mr. Hull m. Zerviah Wheeler (No. 187), that family.

Latham Hull (No. 15) m. Elizabeth Browning (No. 49), that family, Aug. 15, 1811.

CHILDREN:

33 LATHAM, b. Oct. 28, 1812, m. twice.
34 WILLIAM B., b. Nov. 7, 1815, m. Susan Wattles.

John W. Hull (No. 16) m. Miss Elizabeth Smith May 16, 1811. She was daughter of Charles S. Smith and wife, Hannah (Williams) Smith, and was b. Oct. 6, 1795, and d. May 18, 1819.

CHILDREN:

35 ELIZA S., b. May 22, 1812, m. John H. Browning. See that family (No. 54).
36 EUNICE B., b. July 17, 1814, m. Benjamin Browning (No. 57), that family.
37 JOHN P., b. May 10, 1816.

Mrs. Elizabeth or Betsey (Smith) Hull d. May 18, 1819, and Col. John W. Hull m. 2d, Miss Nancy York of Stonington, Conn., Feb. 6, 1821. See York family (No. 166).

CHILDREN:

38 JESSE Y., b. June 10, 1822, m. Emma, daughter of Isaac D. Miner of North Stonington, Conn. See Miner family (No. 278).
39 NANCY or ANN, b. April 30, 1824, m. 1st, Erastus Hewitt (No. 278), and 2d, Latham Stewart.
40 LATHROP W., b. Jan. 26, 1826, m. Phebe E. Hewitt (No. 282), that family.
41 CHARLES S., b. Oct. 30, 1830, m. Mary Hall, daughter of William and wife, Charlotte (Stanton) Hall, Stanton family (No. 206), Nov. 15, 1860.
42 MARTHA ALMIRA, b. Jan. 8, 1833, m. ———— Argall.

Latham W. Hull (No. 33) m. Hannah T. Argall March 30, 1836.

William B. Hull (No. 34) m. Susan M. Wattles, daughter of Dr. Thomas P. Wattles and wife, Lucy Wheeler, Aug. 6, 1851.

HYDE FAMILY.

1. WILLIAM HYDE, the progenitor of the Hyde family, appears first at Hartford, Conn., in 1636. His name is on the monument in the old cemetery at that place, as one of the original settlers, and he had lands assigned him there; he owned land in Hartford as late as 1639. He probably went to Saybrook soon after that, and his daughter was m. there in 1652. No information has been obtained as to the family name of his wife. Norwich was settled in 1660, and his name was among the 35 original proprietors of that town. He d. at Norwich Jan. 6, 1681.

CHILDREN:

2 SAMUEL, b. about 1637, at Hartford, m. Jane Lord.
3 HESTER, b. in England, m. John Post.

Samuel Hyde (No. 2) m. Jane, daughter of Thomas Lord, June 1659; he d. in 1677, at the age of 40 years.

CHILDREN:

4 ELIZABETH, b. Aug., 1660. She was the first white child born in Norwich; m. Lieut. Richard Lord, son of William Lord, May, 1677.
5 PHEBE, b. Jan., 1663, m. Mathew Griswold May 21, 1683.
6 SAMUEL, b. May, 1665, m. Elizabeth Calkins Dec. 10, 1690.
7 JOHN, b. Dec., 1667, m. Experience Abel, March 3, 1698.
8 WILLIAM, b. Jan., 1670, m. Anne Bushnell Jan. 6, 1695.
9 THOMAS, b. July, 1672, m. Mary Backus Dec., 1697.
10 SARAH, b. Feb., 1675, d. the same year.
11 JABEZ, b. May, 1677, m. Elizabeth Bushnell.

Jabez (No. 11) m. Elizabeth Bushnell Dec. 29, 1709, a sister of his brother William's wife. He d. Sept. 5, 1762; had son:

12 PHINEAS, b. Feb. 20, 1720, m. Anne Rogers April 5, 1744; had son,
13 DR. PHINEAS, b. at Norwich, Conn., Nov. 15, 1749, m. Esther Holdridge, daughter of William Holdridge, and Prudence Gavitt of Groton, Sept., 1782. He was a physician, and they settled at Poquetanuck, Conn., and removed to Mystic about 1796. He was in the service of the United States as a surgeon in the navy, in the war of the Revolution. She d. July 6, 1810, at Mystic, where he d. Sept. 5, 1820.

CHILDREN:

14 JOHN, b. June 16, 1783, m. Lucy Ann Burrows.
15 THEOPHILUS ROGERS, b. June 18, 1786, m. Agalice Conrotte.
16 BENJAMIN F., b. July 12, 1798, d. July 15, 1798.
17 WILLIAM FRANKLIN, b. Dec. 19, 1799, m. Jane Van Buskirk April 7, 1831.
18 ENOCH BURROWS, b. Oct. 16, 1801, d. Feb. 17, 1833.
19 ELISHA BURROWS, b. Nov. 5, 1805, m. Anne M. Brown.
20 JOSEPH ADDISON PHINEAS, b. Sept. 16, 1807, d. June 19, 1837.
21 ANNE or NANCY, b. Oct. 3, 1784, m. Darius Denison (No. 501), Denison family.
22 PRUDENCE, b. Oct. 16, 1786, d. unmarried.
23 HARRIET, b. Oct. 13, 1788, d. Sept. 2, 1819, unmarried.
24 LAURA, b. Dec. 12, 1790, d. Dec. 12, 1850, unmarried.

25 ELIZABETH, b. May 27, 1792, d. May 1, 1810, unmarried.
26 SARAH, b. Aug. 14, 1794, d. Sept. 20, 1795.
27 CAROLINE ESTHER, b. June 23, 1803, m. George W. Moss April 30, 1831 (No. 40), Moss family.
28 FRANCES ELIZA, b. July 1, 1810, d. Oct. 1, 1810.

John Hyde (No. 14) m. Lucy Ann Burrows Feb. 21, 1808 (No. 137), Burrows family. He d. in 1861.

CHILDREN:

29 JOSHUA, b. June 29, 1809, m. Anna Maria Bamman Oct. 4, 1836.
30 JOHN, b. Feb. 15, 1811.
31 ENOCH BURROWS, b. Jan. 20, 1815, d. May 4, 1835.
32 SILAS, b. Sept. 27, 1816, d. Aug. 7, 1843.
33 JAMES WILLIAMS, b. May 18, 1818, d. March 29, 1820.
34 GEORGE DENISON, b. April 13, 1822.
35 THEOPHILUS ROGERS, b. May 20, 1824, m. Fanny Hazard Brown of Stillmanville, Conn., April 30, 1850.
36 REV. CHARLES CARROLL, b. Feb. 1, 1826.
37 WILLIAM PENN, b. Feb. 15, 1828, m. Seraphine L. Carr.
38 JOSEPH AUGUSTUS, b. Sept. 26, 1829, d. Oct. 31, 1831.
39 REV. EDWARD LAWRENCE, b. May 21, 1835.
40 LUCY ESTHER, b. Dec. 26, 1812, m. Rev. James M. McDonald.
41 HARRIET ELIZABETH, b. March 27, 1820, m. Lucien B. Hanks.
42 A daughter, b. Sept. 30, 1831, d. Oct. 2, 1831.
43 HELEN AGALICE, b. Dec. 19, 1832, m. E. Burrows Brown Sept. 17, 1862 (No. 35), Edward Brown family.

William Hyde (No. 8), b. Jan., 1670, m. Anne Bushnell Jan. 2, 1695; had son, Capt. William Hyde, b. May 1, 1702, m. Anna Basset, April 24, 1722; had son, William Hyde, b. Sept. 22, 1731, m. Abigail Langrel, March, 1754; had son, William Hyde, b. Jan. 16, 1756, m. his third cousin, Zerviah F. Hyde, Aug. 23, 1778. They settled in Ellington, Conn.

CHILDREN:

44 JOSEPH FANGREL, b. 1781, d. Aug. 29, 1822, unmarried.
45 WILLIAM, b. July 21, 1783, m. Rhoda Palmer March 23, 1808 (No. 321), Palmer family. He was a physician in Stonington, where he had a very extensive practice for many years.
46 SARAH, b. 1779, d. young and unmarried.

Dr. William Hyde (No. 45) m. Rhoda Palmer, daughter of Elijah Palmer (No. 321), that family, March 23, 1806.

CHILDREN:

47 WILLIAM, b. Dec. 21, 1806, d. Nov. 16, 1808.
48 WILLIAM, b. Oct. 27, 1808, m. Hepzibah Williams (No. 374), that family; she d. May 6, 1841; m. 2d, Ellen Williams, youngest daughter of Maj. Gen. Williams (No. 352), that family. He was the leading physician in Stonington for many years.
49 JAMES, b. June 24, 1835, m. Marian L. Darrow.
50 GURDON, b. Dec. 5, 1812, d. Sept. 23, 1814.
51 HARRIET C., b. July 31, 1817, d. Nov. 21, 1822.
52 DANIEL C., b. Feb. 13, 1820, m. Elizabeth Fordham Dec. 20, 1847.
53 HARRIET ANN, b. Oct. 6, 1822, m. Edwin A. Palmer.
54 HENRY P., b. March 13, 1825, d. Feb. 1, 1826.
55 BENJAMIN P., b. March 22, 1827, d. Aug. 14, 1828.
56 CAROLINE, b. May 22, 1829, d. unmarried.

KELLOGG FAMILY.

The Kellogg family originated in Scotland, in the British Empire, and came to New England not long after 1630. The earliest resident of the family in Connecticut was Nathaniel Kellogg, who appears in Hartford, Conn., in 1639, and afterwards removed to Farmington, Conn., where Lieut. Joseph Kellogg lived, who joined the church there Oct. 9, 1653.

There was also a Samuel Kellogg, supposed to have been a brother of Joseph Kellogg, and also a Daniel Kellogg of Norwalk, Conn., in 1655, but the exact relationship of these various branches is not known.

The first that is known of the family of Kelloggs who made Stonington their permanent place of abode is:

1. DAVID KELLOGG, of whose birth we have no record. (Tradition says that he m. Eunice Brown.) His home was on the west bank of the Mystic River, at a place called "The Narrows." He died at the siege of Boston, in 1776, and was buried at Dorchester Heights. He left a wife and two

CHILDREN:
2 DAVID, b. ———.
3 MARY, b. ———.

David Kellogg (No. 2) m. Bridget Newton of Stonington April 29, 1793.

CHILDREN:
4 DAVID, b. March 31, 1799, m. Lydia Smith Bennett.
5 JOSEPH, b. July 27, 1801, m. Angeline Pitcher.
6 MARY or POLLY, b. Nov. 17, 1803, m. Thomas Lamb.
7 ELIZA, b. Nov. 22, 1805, m. John Hillard.
8 AUSTIN, b. Oct. 19, 1807, m. Maria Moore.
9 DANIEL, b. Feb. 15, 1809, lost at sea, unmarried.
10 LAURA, b. July 19, 1811, m. Thomas Leeds.
11 EUNICE, b. Dec. 1, 1815, m. Frederick Johnson.
12 EMILY, b. July 3, 1817, m. Austin Henshaw.
13 CYRUS L., b. April 18, 1821, lost at sea, unmarried.
14 FRANK N., b. ———, no record save that he died when about 16 yrs. old.
15 HIRAM, b. ———, no record save that he died when a small child.

David Kellogg (No. 4) m. Lydia Smith Bennett July 17, 1825.

CHILDREN:
16 LYDIA ESTHER, b. Nov. 16, 1826, m. Francis E. Moore.
17 WILLIAM WILLIAMS, b. March 8, 1829, m. Lucy Ann Stanton.
18 HENRY BENNETT, b. Oct. 26, 1830.
19 LUCY ANN, b. Jan. 15, 1841.
20 MARY ELLEN, b. Oct. 22, 1843.
21 CYRUS, b. Feb. 1, 1846, m. Ella Dewey.

MAIN FAMILY.

1. EZEKIEL MAIN, the first person of that name who came to Stonington, Ct., to reside permanently, is not otherwise identified in this country. He came here in 1670 and in 1672 he received a grant of land from the town. He subsequently purchased other lands, and in 1680 received another town grant of land, all of which extended from the old goldsmith shop of Mr. David Main, nearly to the residence of Mr. Nathaniel M. Crary, in what is now North Stonington, Conn., bounded nearly all the way by Shunnock River on the south, and on the north in part by lands of Mr. Joshua Holmes.

This Mr. Ezekiel Main m. Mary ———. It is not known whether he m. before or after he came to this town to reside, probably a short time before, as Mrs. Ezekiel Main was a partaker at the ordination of Mr. James Noyes, the pastor of the first church in Stonington in 1674. Ezekiel Main was admitted to the church Sept. 3, 1676, and he d. June 19, 1714.

CHILDREN OF EZEKIEL AND MARY MAIN:

2 EZEKIEL, b. ———.
3 MARY, b. ———, bapt. July 1, 1677, d. young.
4 JEREMIAH, b. ———.
5 THOMAS, b. ———, bapt. Sept. 22, 1679, d. young.
6 PHEBE, b. ———, bapt. Aug. 7, 1681, m. ——— Kingsbury.
7 HANNAH, b. ———.

Ezekiel Main (No. 2) was admitted to the church in 1695, and he m. Mary, daughter of Thomas and wife, Naomi Wells, Jan. 14, 1689; he d. Oct. 20, 1715.

CHILDREN:

8 EZEKIEL, b. and d. Dec. 24, 1691.

Mrs. Mary Main d. Jan. 12, 1693, and Oct. 22, 1695, Mr. Ezekiel Main m. 2d, Hannah Rose.

CHILDREN:

9 HANNAH, b. Sept. 23, 1698.
10 MARY, b. June 14, 1700.
11 EZEKIEL, b. Dec. 10, 1701, d. Aug. 5, 1702.
12 ALLIS, b. March, 1704, d. young.
13 PATIENCE, b. Feb. 22, 1704-5.
14 JEREMIAH, b. Sept. 9, 1707.
15 PHEEBY, b. April 9, 1708.
16 ICHABOD, b. Aug. 3, 1710.
17 MERRIAM b. Nov. 4, 1712, d. Oct. 20, 1729.

MAIN FAMILY.

Jeremiah Main (No. 4) m. widow Ruth Brown. It is not certainly known whose daughter she was, but she with her daughter, Ruth, were admitted to the first church of Stonington and baptized July 16, 1699. Mr. Jeremiah Main was admitted May 18, 1712, and he d. Nov. 11, 1727. They were m. Oct. 11, 1699.

CHILDREN:

18 THOMAS, b. July 19, 1700.
19 HANNAH, bapt. May 17, 1702.
20 ELIZABETH, b. Feb. 22, 1702-3, m. Ebenezer Brown (No. 41), Brown family.
21 LYDIA, b. April 19, 1705.
22 SARAH, b. May 19, 1706.
23 JEREMIAH, b. April 10, 1708, m. Jan. 25, 1726-7, Abigail Worden.
24 HEPZIBAH, b. March 24, 1710, m. Oct. 31, 1727, Joseph Brown.
25 NATHANIEL, b. Aug. 4, 1714, m. Jan. 10, 1737-8, Anna Spaulding, and m. 2d, Johanna Parkhurst.
26 ANNA, b. Aug. 21, 1715.
27 JOHN, b. May 20, 1716, m. Nov. 8, 1738, Sarah Morgan.
28 PETER, b. Aug. 5, 1718, m. Sept. 17, 1740, Mary Egglestone.

On Feb. 22, 1727, a church was formed in North Stonington, Conn., and among others, Mr. Jeremiah Main and wife Ruth, were dismissed by request, in order to be embodied in church estate in North Stonington, in which society they were inhabitants. Mrs. Ruth Main's daughter, Ruth Brown, m. John Butler Oct. 10, 1714, and after her death he m. 2d, Mary Brown Feb. 11, 1747.

Dea. Thomas Main (No. 18) m. 1st, April 20, 1720, Ann (No. 40), daughter of Eleazer and wife, Ann (Pendleton) Brown. He was the son of Thomas Brown and wife, Mary Newhall of Lynn, Mass. She was b. Feb. 1, 1699-1700; d. March 11, 1766, and Mr. Main m. 2d, Elizabeth Hewitt (No. 34), May 14, 1766. He d. in 1771.

CHILDREN:

29 THOMAS, b. Feb. 13, 1720, m. Mary Pendleton Feb. 3, 1742.
30 ANDREW, b. Aug. 5, 1723, m. Fear Holmes Jan. 5, 1743 (No. 28), Holmes family.
31 TIMOTHY, b. April 8, 1727, m. Elizabeth Brown Jan. 27, 1749 (No. 75), Brown family.
32 JOSHUA, b. April, 1729, m. Rachel Peckham Nov. 2, 1752.
33 ANNE, b. July 31, 1733, m. Zebulon Brown Dec. 20, 1749 (No. 74), Brown family.
34 JONAS, b. Feb. 7, 1735.
35 ELIZABETH, b. and d. young.
36 EZEKIEL, b. July 8, 1742, m. Deborah Meacham Nov. 25, 1763.
37 PHEBE, b. Nov. 16, 1747, m. Samuel Meacham March 31, 1763.

Jeremiah Main (No. 23) m. Abigail Wordin, daughter of Thomas Wordin and wife, Sarah Butler, Jan. 4, 1727.

CHILDREN:
38 THANKFUL, b. Sept. 14, 1727.
39 RUTH, b. Dec. 12, 1729, m. Bell York (No. 24), of York family.
40 JEREMIAH, b. April 13, 1732.
41 AMOS, b. Sept. 2, 1735.
42 ABIGAIL, b. Sept. 21, 1740.

Mrs. Abigail Main d. Nov. 13, 1741, and Mr. Jeremiah Main m. 2d, Miss Thankful Brown (No. 71), that family, April 26, 1742. She was b. Oct. 22, 1720, the daughter of James Brown and wife, Elizabeth Randall, who were m. May 5, 1718.

CHILDREN:
43 JAMES, b. Jan. 27, 1743.
44 LYDIA, b. April 11, 1745.
45 THANKFUL, b. Jan. 14, 1748, m. Edward Thurston, Oct., 1764.
46 BRIDGET, b. June 14, 1749.
47 DAVID, b. Aug. 26, 1752.
48 NATHAN or NATHANIEL, b. ———.
49 DANIEL, b. Jan. 26, 1761.

Timothy Main (No. 31) m. Elizabeth, daughter of James Brown and wife, Elizabeth Randall, Jan. 27, 1750.

CHILDREN:
50 ELIZABETH, b. Nov. 2, 1750.
51 TIMOTHY, b. April 7, 1752.
52 NATHANIEL, b. July 12, 1754.
53 LYDIA, b. Aug. 31, 1756.
54 RUFUS, b. Nov. 15, 1758.
55 GRACE, b. April 22, 1761.
56 LABAN, b. Jan. 27, 1764.
57 LUTHER, b. April 18, 1766.
58 LUCY, b. Dec. 9, 1768.

Jonas Main (No. 34) m. 1st, Patience Peckham June 3, 1756. She d. July 23, 1758, and he m. 2d, April 14, 1760, Content, daughter of William and wife, Elizabeth (Dewey) Bromley. She d. Aug., 1825, aged 80 yrs.; he d. Jan. 24, 1804.

CHILDREN:
59 SABIUS, b. March 23, 1757.
60 CONTENT, b. Feb. 7, 1761, m. a Hakes.
61 REUBEN PECKHAM, b. Jan. 3, 1763, m. Sally Burdick.
62 PATIENCE, b. March 7, 1765, m. in 1784 Thomas H. Peckham.
63 LYMAN, b. March 14, 1767, m. Fanny Burdick.
64 DEWEY, b. Sept. 14, 1770, m. Lucinda Colsgrove.
65 JONAS M., b. May 14, 1722.
66 THOMAS, b. ———, and m. Hannah Chapman (No. 28), that family.
67 JABISH, b. June 1, 1776.
68 NANCY, b. ———, m. John Gray.
69 PAUL, b. ———, m. Lydia Miner.

John Main (No. 27) m. Sarah Morgan Nov. 8, 1738.

CHILDREN:
70 JUDITH, b. July 31, 1739.
71 JOHN, b. Feb. 12, 1741.
72 JONATHAN, b. Feb. 12, 1743.
73 CALEB, b. April 18, 1745.
74 SARAH, b. Oct. 5, 1750.

MAIN FAMILY.

Peter Main (No. 28) m. Mary Egglestone Sept. 17, 1740.
CHILDREN:
75 PETER, b. July 9, 1741, d. young.
76 PETER, b. July 9, 1742.
77 JOSEPH, b. Feb. 14, 1744, d. young.
78 MARY, b. Jan. 16, 1746.
79 ASA, b. June 17, 1748.
80 LUCY, b. Nov. 4, 1745, d. young.
81 JOSEPH, b. April 4, 1753.
82 SANDS, b. Feb. 5, 1756.
83 DAVID, b. Aug. 21, 1761.
84 LUCY, b. March 18, 1764.
85 PRUDENCE, b. March 7, 1768.

Thomas Main (No. 29) m. Mary Pendleton Feb. 3, 1742.
CHILDREN:
86 MARY, b. April 19, 1743.
87 SARAH, b. Aug. 19, 1745.
88 THOMAS, b. Aug. 8, 1747.
89 BENAJAH, b. Sept. 5, 1749.

Andrew Main (No. 30) m. Fear Holmes Jan. 5, 1744.
CHILDREN:
90 BETHIAH, b. April 6, 1745.
91 FEAR, b. Aug. 13, 1747.
92 ANNE, b. Nov. 18, 1748.
93 ANDREW, b. July 6, 1749.
94 RUTH, b. Sept. 23, 1750.
95 RACHEL, b. Jan. 8, 1753.
96 MOLLY, b. Aug. 6, 1755.
97 JOSHUA, b. Oct. 3, 1757.
98 ELIAS, b. Oct. 6, 1760.
99 REUBEN, b. Jan. 22, 1762.
100 EUNICE, b. March 17, 1764.

Ezekiel Main (No. 36) m. Deborah Meacham Nov. 25, 1761.
CHILDREN:
101 EZEKIEL, b. Aug. 17, 1762; and probably others.

Amos Main (No. 41) m. Abigail Brown May 19, 1756.
CHILDREN:
102 NABOE, b. Aug. 8, 1757.
103 ESTHER, b. July 1, 1759.
104 KETURAH, b. Jan. 23, 1762.
105 THANKFUL, b. Aug. 12, 1764.
106 TRYPHENIA, b. May 8, 1767.
107 ANNE, b. Aug. 11, 1769.
108 DESIRE, b. March 31, 1772, m. Gilbert Sisson (No. 38).
109 BETSEY, b. May 3, 1777.
110 AMOS, b. July 3, 1779.

James Main (No. 43) m. Hannah Wallace March 4, 1763.
CHILDREN:
111 HANNAH, b. Dec. 12, 1763.
112 JAMES, b. April 3, 1766.
113 GILBERT, b. Jan. 10, 1768.
114 LUCINDA, b. July 28, 1770.

David Main (No. 47) m. Hannah Wordin April 26, 1772.

CHILDREN:

115 THANKFUL, b. Feb. 27, 1775.
116 PATTY, b. Feb. 10, 1778.

Mrs. Hannah Main d. Nov. 29, 1779, and April 29, 1781, Mr. Main m. 2d, Judah Palmer

THEIR CHILDREN:

117 DAVID, b. July 26, 1781.
118 ROBERT, b. Jan. 19, 1783.

Mrs. Judah Main d. Nov. 16, 1783, and Mr. Main m. 3d, Esther the widow of Dr. Asher Palmer, and daughter of the Rev. Seth Dean, Jan. 8, 1787.

CHILDREN:

119 RIAL, b. May 29, 1788.
120 CHANDLER, b. Jan. 28, 1790.
121 FENNER, b. Oct. 29, 1791.
122 RHODA, b. May 16, 1794.
123 SAXTON, b. Aug. 27, 1796.

Daniel Main (No. 49) m. Grace, daughter of Timothy Main (No. 55), that family, July 21, 1779.

Reuben Peckham Main (No. 61) m. Sally Burdick.

CHILDREN:

124 PEREZ.
125 JONAS.
126 LEWIS.
127 JOHN.
128 FRANKLIN.
129 ASHER.
130 ADAM.
131 FANNY.
132 SOPHIA.

Lyman Main (No. 63) m. Fanny Burdick Dec. 14, 1789.

CHILD:

133 ISAAC, b. Oct. 17, 1793.

Dewey Main (No. 64) m. Lucinda Colsgrove Aug. 18, 1793.

CHILDREN:

134 LUCINDA, b. Dec. 22, 1795.
135 SHEFFIELD, b. March 22, 1798.
136 SUSAN, b. Feb. 17, 1800.
137 MILTON, b. March 4, 1802.
138 SEBIUS, b. ———.
139 PRENTICE, b. ———.
140 SILAS, b. ———.
141 NANCY, b. ———.
142 JULIA, b. ———.
143 LEVANTIA, b. ———.

Thomas Main (No. 66) m. Hannah Chapman (No. 28), Chapman family.

MAIN FAMILY.   453

CHILDREN:

144 THOMAS.
145 AARON.
146 FLEET.
147 JOSEPH.
148 POLLY.
148a HANNAH.
148b CONTENT.
149 NANCY.
150 SOPHIA.

Laban Main (No. 56) m. Mary or Polly Brown (No. 155), Brown family, daughter of Rev. Eleazer Brown and wife, Anna Greene, Oct. 19, 1794.

Jabish Main (No. 67) m. March 15, 1798, Freelove Edwards, who was b. in Stonington, Conn., Sept. 6, 1775. She d. April 10, 1856, and Mr. Main d. Oct. 30, 1856.

CHILDREN:

151 JABISH, b. ———, m. Lydia Edwards.
152 COLLINS, b. ———, m. Susan Peabody.
153 JONAS, b. ———, m. Melinda Turner.
154 IRA, b. ———, m. Electa Randolph.
155 SEBIUS, b. ———, m. Julia Stevens.
156 HIRAM, b. ———.
157 SIDNEY, b. ———, m. Eliza Wentworth.
158 FREELOVE, b. ———, d. young.
159 ZERVIAH, b. ———, m. Franklin Main.
160 CYNTHIA, b. ———, m. Alfred Turner.
161 CLARINDA, b. ———, m. Elias Sprague, and 2d, William Hunt.
162 MARY or FANNY, b. ———, d. young.
163 DIANTHUS, b. ———, m. Joseph Rood.

Amos Main (No. 110) m. Susan, daughter of Hosea Wheeler, March 29, 1804 (No. 168), that family.

CHILDREN:

164 SUSAN, b. May 24, 1806, m. Capt. David Coates (No. 25), Coates family, Oct. 14, 1824.
165 EPHRAIM, b. Oct. 31, 1812, m. Catharine Thompson.
166 BRIDGET, b. July 25, 1807, m. Leland D. Miner (No. 298).
167 NANCY, b. ———, m. Nathan York, Jr. (No. 167), York family.
168 RALPH, b. April 13, 1816, m. Elizabeth Irving.
169 CYRUS, b. ———, m. Julia Edgecomb.
170 AMOS, d. young.

Peter Main (No. 76) m. Patience Egglestone.

CHILDREN:

171 PETER, b. Dec. 4, 1765.
172 AGNES, b. Aug. 4, 1767.
173 JOSEPH, b. Sept. 21, 1769.
174 POLLY, b. May 9, 1774.
175 AMOS, b. Aug. 16, 1776, m. Abigail Slocom.
176 JARED, b. Jan. 22, 1778, m. ——— Egglestone.
177 JOHN, b. April 6, 1780.
178 DEBORAH, b. May 6, 1782.
179 DAVID, b. Aug. 20, 1784.

David Main (No. 179) m. for 2d wife, Dorcas Palmer, Nov. 21, 1811.

CHILDREN:

180 ROBERT, b. ———, m. Phebe Edwards.
181 MATILDA, b. ———, m. Nathan Edwards.
182 LUCY, b. ———, m. Isaac Edwards.
183 ISAAC, b. ———, m. Lucy Miner.
184 DAVID, b. ———, m. Sarah Palmer.
185 SANDS, b. ———, m. Maria Perry.
186 DORCAS, b. ———, m. 1st, William Main, and 2d, Frank Main.
187 ELIJAH, b. ———, never married.

Rufus Main (No. 54) m. Sarah York (No. 65), York family, about 1780.

CHILDREN:

188 RUFUS, b. ———.
189 LEWIS, b. in the year 1783, in Preston, Conn, d. in North Stonington Nov. 20, 1870.
190 STEPHEN, b. ———.
191 SANFORD, b. ———.
192 RUTH, b. ———, m. Joseph Chapman. There were also three other children, Edith, Prudence and Polly.

Rufus Main (No. 188) m. Sabra Wells.

CHILDREN:

193 RUFUS, b. ———, m. ——— Miner.
194 STEPHEN, b. ———, m. 1st, Susan Chapman; m. 2d, Lydia York, and 3d, Elizabeth Stewart (No. 65), that family.
195 THOMAS, b. ———, m. went West.
196 WILLIAM, b. ———, m. Elizabeth Williamson.
197 TIMOTHY, b. ———, never married.
198 REUBEN, b. ———, m. Mattie Niel.
199 EDE, b. ———, m. Randall Kenyon.
200 NANCY, b. ———, m. Porteous Park.
201 PHEBE, b. ———, m. James Wilson.
202 SARAH, b. ———, m. Abel Palmer.
203 MARY, b. ———, m. Charles Coates, lived in New York.
204 ABBY, b. ———, m. James Rider.

Lewis Main (No. 189) m. Hannah, daughter of Gershom Ray, Oct. 17, 1803. She was b. in Voluntown, Conn., and d. there July 30, 1848, aged 64 yrs. and 6 mos.

CHILDREN:

205 LEWIS, Jr., b. June 9, 1804, m. Cynthia Stewart (No. 57), of Stewart family.
206 CHARLES b. ———, m. Almira Egglestone, daughter of William and Lucy Geer Egglestone, Dec. 18, 1833, and had six children, Charles, Irtis, Alonzo, Louise, Mary and Emeline.
206a AVERY, b. Aug. 29, 1806.
207 GERSHOM, b. ———, m. Susan A. Billings.
208 JESSE, b. ———, m. Abby Benjamin.
209 ESTHER, b. ———, m. William Chapman.
210 MARY, b. ———, m. Stanton Main.
211 HANNAH, b. ———, never married.

MALLORY FAMILY.

There is perhaps no one family more worthy of notice than that of Charles Mallory, son of David and Amy (Crocker) Mallory, born in Waterford, Conn., Feb. 24, 1796. His father was a native of Milford, Conn. When but 16, David Mallory was in the Continental army and served three years under Washington, being in several engagements. Afterwards he shipped from New London as sailor on a privateer. He was a prisoner three times on prison ships, and each time exchanged. He m. when about 20 years old, Amy Crocker, and had ten children: Frances Mallory, Sally, who m. Nathan Beebe; Rebecca, who m. a Mr. West, and went out West; David, and Amy, who m. John Rogers; Richard, Amos, Charles, Benajah and Nathan, who d. young. Mr. David Mallory d. at the age of 79, and his wife lived to be 93, and she was cared for by her son, Charles, who inherited a strong constitution and persistency of purpose, which enabled him to rise to a true type of a successful Christian man. When but 14 years old he was indentured to his brother-in-law, Nathan Beebe, for seven years, to learn the sailmaking trade. He remained there till the expiration of his time, and at 18 he was foreman of the establishment. On Christmas morning, 1816, he came to Mystic and engaged to work on a vessel, and Jan. 1, 1817, he commenced his remarkable business career in Mystic, first as a sailmaker, which he continued until he was about 40 years old. During this time he became interested in numerous vessels, and at one time he owned ten whalers, which were all successful. About 1848 he purchased the lease of the Mystic shipyard and begun shipbuilding. He built 50 steamers and many sailing vessels. When the Mystic River Bank was organized he was made its president; he also founded the First National Bank of Mystic Bridge, and owned the entire stock of $100,000. From the time he came to Mystic he has been identified with its best growth. On Feb. 22, 1818, he m. Eliza Rogers, daughter of John and Hannah Rogers, of New London, and for 63 years this worthy couple walked hand in hand in the enjoyment of life, until the sudden death of Mrs. Mallory, Sept. 4, 1886. They were members of the Mystic Congregational Church, and ever helpful in all good causes. Their children were: Charles Henry, David D., George W., Franklin O., Benjamin E., and Anna M. Mallory. These children were all b. in Mystic, and spent the greater part of their lives there, with the exception of Charles Henry, who was b. Sept. 30, 1818, spent his childhood in Mystic, where he secured a common school education, also one year's tuition at the private school of John Kirby, one of the best teachers of his day. He was early taught the sailmakers' trade, and worked with his father till he was fifteen, when he went to sea, and before he was of age he became master of a brig. His life was passed on the water from 1833 to 1846, when his father's business needing a competent manager in New York, he was selected for the position and proved himself satisfactory in every particular. In 1865 the firm of C. H. Mallory & Co., a shipping and commission firm, was established in New York, and continued till 1870, when Mr. Mallory's two sons, Charles and Henry, were admitted members, and the firm has been very successful. It also runs and owns several steamship lines. Mr. Charles Henry Mallory m. Eunice Denison Clift (No. 44), daughter of Nathaniel and wife, Eunice (Denison) Clift, and they had five children. Although his life has been full of business activities, he has borne a conspicuous part in all works of morality, education and religion. His wife was a true help meet, full of good deeds and works, generous and benevolent. She made many of her friends and townspeople comfortable and happy during their lives, and the cemetery, near her old home at Mystic, bears testimony of her love for them in the grand arched gateway at the entrance to the silent city.

MANNING FAMILY.

1. WILLIAM MANNING, the emigrant ancestor of the Manning family of Stonington, and wife, Susannah Manning, came to New England with its early planters and settled in Cambridge, Mass., where he purchased valuable real estate in 1638. The residence of this family in England is not certainly known, nor is it known how many children they became the parents of in the old country, or how many in this country. Only one child, viz.:

> 2 WILLIAM, Jr., is known to have survived them, who was b. in England in 1614, and came with his parents to Massachusetts, and after their decease inherited their mansion place in Cambridge. He engaged in and pursued the mercantile business and became a prominent and successful merchant.

William Manning (No. 2) m. Dorothy ———, family name unknown. She d. July 26, 1692, aged 80 yrs. He d. March 14, 1690, aged 76 yrs.

CHILDREN:

3 HANNAH, b. July 21, 1642.
4 SAMUEL, b. July 21, 1644.
5 SARAH, b. June 28, 1646.
6 ABIGAIL, b. June 15, 1648, d. young.
7 JOHN, b. March 30, 1649.

Samuel Manning (No. 4) removed to Billerica, where he subsequently rose to prominence in business, social and political circles, representing the town of his adopted home in the Massachusetts General Court in 1695 and 1696, and held other positions of public trust.

Samuel Manning (No. 4) m. 1st, Elizabeth Stearns of Watertown, Mass., April 13, 1664.

CHILDREN:

8 SAMUEL, b. ———.
9 JOHN, b. Aug. 30, 1667.

After the death of Mrs. Elizabeth (Stearns) Manning, her husband m. for his second wife, Miss Abia Wright, May 6, 1673. They had twelve children.

Samuel Manning (No. 8) came back in early life to Cambridge, Mass., to live, when his father in 1698 gave him a deed of the real estate which his great-grandfather purchased there in 1638. For reasons not now fully understood he did not enjoy the ancestral home in Cambridge as well as he anticipated, which unrest caused him to seek a home for himself and family where they could enlarge their possessions and live more agreeably to their taste and comfort. So, in order to consummate his plans, he sold nearly all of his real estate in Cambridge, Mass., between the years of 1720 and 1724, and during this interval he removed his family to that part of the town of Windham known now as Scotland, Conn., where he spent the remainder of his life, dying Feb. 24, 1755. His wife departed this life before him, dying June 30, 1723.

Samuel Manning (No. 8) m. Deborah ———, unknown. They had eight children.

10 SAMUEL, b. in Cambridge Jan. 14, 1691, and m. there April 27, 1719, Irena Ripley. He came with his father to Windham and remained there during his life.

CHILDREN:

11 JOSIAH, b. March 18, 1720.
12 HEZEKIAH, b. Aug. 8, 1721.
13 ABIGAIL, b. Nov. 25, 1722.
14 SARAH, b. Feb. 22, 1724.
15 SAMUEL, b. Oct. 22, 1725.
16 DAVID, b. Jan. 14, 1727.

Hezekiah Manning (No. 12) m. Mary Webb Sept. 22, 1745.

CHILDREN:

17 CALVIN, b. March 4, 1746.
18 LUTHER, b. Sept. 5, 1748.
19 JERUSHA, b. Dec. 14, 1750.
20 LUCY, b. July 1, 1753.
21 ELIZABETH, b. July 7, 1755.

Luther Manning (No. 18) studied medicine and practiced as a physician successfully in Norwich Town, Conn. (now known as the town of Lisbon, and in the region round about). During the Revolutionary war he held the position of assistant surgeon and was stationed at New London, Conn., before the close of the war. After the incorporation of the town of Lisbon, in May, 1786, he was elected one of the selectmen thereof and represented the new town in the Legislature for several years. He participated in the organization of the State and County Medical Societies.

Dr. Luther Manning (No. 18) m. Sarah Smith.

CHILDREN:

22 OLIVE, b. ———.
23 LUTHER, b. ———.
24 LUCIUS, b. ———.
25 MASON, b. Aug. 27, 1796, m. Mary Hovey of the town of Windham, Conn., Nov. 20, 1821.

CHILDREN:

26 FRANCIS M., b. ———.

After the death of Mrs. Mary (Hovey) Manning her husband married for his second wife Miss Harriet (Chesebrough) Leeds of Stonington, Conn., Jan. 26, 1829. No children by this marriage.

ANDREW S. MATHEWS.

The history of this town would be incomplete without a sketch of the life of Andrew S. Mathews, who was so long and closely identified with the construction and management of the Providence and Stonington Railroad. He was b. at Elk Ridge, Anne Arundel Co., Md., Sept. 1, 1814. His father, Dr. William P. Mathews was a native of Ireland, and was educated and graduated at the University of Dublin, and shortly after came to America. He m. Eliza Sterritt of Maryland and had seven children, of whom Andrew was the sixth, his parents dying when he was but 7 years old. He early commenced to look out for himself. He left school when 12 years old and went to work with his brother, Charles, who was a railroad constructor. At 16 he was assistant engineer in the service of the Baltimore & Ohio Railroad Co. He was next superintendent of a gang of men on the Hudson Railroad, also in the same capacity on the Paterson & Hudson Railroad. Afterward he went to Boston and was civil engineer for the Boston & Providence Railroad Co., for three years. Also civil engineer for the Taunton Branch Railroad Co. As he grew older he filled even more responsible positions. In 1836 Mr. Mathews entered the service of the New York, Providence & Boston Railroad. In 1837 the road was finished to Stonington, and he was chosen chief engineer and road master, and at the same time was assistant engineer on the Boston & Albany Railroad. From 1840 to 1848 he was acting superintendent and master of transportation on the same road. In 1848 he was appointed general superintendent, which he held till on account of ill health, he resigned in 1878. He was immediately after appointed chief engineer, which office he held till his death, which occurred Feb. 8, 1884. Mr. Mathews m. Eliza A. Smith of Marlboro, Mass., in 1836, and came to Stonington to live in 1837, and was a resident here for nearly half a century, and none stood higher than he in the estimation of the community. It has been said, "If there was any blemish or fault in his personal or official life it was never discovered."

MAJOR JOHN MASON FAMILY.

1. MAJ. JOHN MASON was born in England in the year 1600, was bred a soldier and served in the English army, and after his election as lieutenant, served under Sir Thomas Fairfax. He emigrated to America in 1632 and settled first in Dorchester, Mass., and represented that town in the General Court. In 1635 he removed to Windsor, Conn., in company with the Rev. John Warham, Henry Wolcott and others, prominent settlers of that town, where he was elected an assistant or magistrate of the Connecticut Colony in 1642. In May, 1637, he commanded the successful expedition against the Pequot Indians, when he and his famous ninety men immortalized themselves in overthrowing and destroying the prestige and power of the Pequots and their fort near Mystic River, on Groton side, which event is commemorated by a boulder monument on Mystic Hill upon the pedestal of which is a life size statue of Maj. Mason drawing his sword, when he heard the war-whoop of "Owanux," "Owanux," by the Indians in their fort. In 1647 he removed his family to Saybrook, where he continued to live until 1660, when he united with a number of distinguished families in the settlement of Norwich, Conn., where he was Deputy Governor and Major General of the forces of Connecticut, and held other prominent official positions. After a life of great usefulness and eminence, he d. Jan. 30, 1672. His widow d. shortly afterwards. Unfortunately, the first wife of Maj. John Mason is not known, but she did not live long, but was the mother of one daughter.

CHILDREN:

2 JUDITH, b. ———, m. John Bissel of Windsor, Conn., June 17, 1658, d. 1665.

After the death of his first wife he m. 2d, Miss Anna Peck in July, 1640.

THEIR CHILDREN WERE:

3 PRISCILLA, b. Oct., 1641, at Windsor, and m. Rev. James Fitch, the first settled minister of Norwich, Conn.; she d. 1714.
4 SAMUEL, b. at Windsor in July, 1644.
5 JOHN, b. at Windsor in Aug., 1646.
6 RACHAEL, b. in Saybrook, Conn., in 1648, and m. Charles Hill of New London, Conn., 1678; d. 1679.

7 ANNE, b. in Saybrook in June, 1650, and m. Capt. John Brown of Swansey, Mass.
8 DANIEL, b. in Saybrook in April, 1652.
9 ELIZABETH, b. in Stonington, Conn., in Aug., 1654, m. Jan., 1676, Maj. James Fitch, oldest son of Rev. James Fitch, the first settled minister of Norwich, Conn., by his first wife, Abigail Whitfield.

Maj. Samuel Mason (No. 4) m. 1st, June, 1670, Miss Judith Smith, daughter of Capt. John Smith of Hingham, Mass., and 2d, Miss Elizabeth Peck of Rehoboth, Mass. He brought his first wife to Stonington, Conn., June 22, 1670.

CHILDREN:

10 and 11 Two unnamed daughters, b. and d. young.
12 JOHN, b. at Stonington Aug. 19, 1676, d. unmarried March 20, 1705.
13 ANNE, b. ———, m. her 1st cousin, Capt. John Mason, 3d.
14 SARAH, b. ———, m. her 1st cousin, Joseph Fitch.

Maj. Mason (No. 4) m. 2d, July 4, 1694, Elizabeth Peck of Rehoboth, Mass., and d. March 30, 1705, at Stonington. She survived him, and m. Gershom Palmer of Stonington (No. 12), Palmer family.

CHILDREN:

15 SAMUEL, b. at Stonington Aug. 26, 1695, d. Nov. 28, 1701.
16 ELIZABETH, b. May 6, 1697, m. Rev. William Worthington Oct. 13, 1720.
17 HANNAH, b. April 24, 1699, d. unmarried in Nov., 1724.

Maj. Mason (No. 4) held the office of major of the militia, and was an assistant of the colony, besides holding other positions of trust. He d. March 30, 1705, and was buried at Lebanon, Conn.

Capt. John Mason (No. 5) m. Abigail, daughter of the Rev. James Fitch of Norwich, Conn., and represented that town several times in the Colonial Legislature, and was one of the assistants of the colony. He commanded a company in King Phillip's war and was mortally wounded in the swamp fight at Narragansett, Dec. 19, 1675. He was carried to New London, where he lingered until Sept. 18, 1676, when he died.

CHILDREN:

18 JOHN, b. 1673.
19 ANNE, b. ———, m. Capt. John Denison in 1690 (No. 50), Denison family.

Daniel Mason (No. 8) m. Margaret (No. 29), daughter of Edward and Elizabeth (Weld) Denison, of Roxbury, Mass. She was b. Dec. 15, 1650, and d. May 13, 1678.

CHILDREN:

20 DANIEL, b. at Stonington Nov. 26, 1674.
21 HEZEKIAH, b. May 3, 1677, at Roxbury, Mass.

After Mrs. Margaret Denison's death Mr. Daniel Mason m. 2d, Oct. 10, 1679, Rebecca Hobart, daughter of Rev. Peter Hobart of Hingham, Mass. She d. April 8, 1727, and he d. Jan. 28, 1737.

THEIR CHILDREN WERE:

22 PETER, b. Nov. 9, 1680.
23 REBECCA, b. Feb. 10, 1682, m. Feb. 6, 1707, Elisha Chesebrough (No. 19), that family, of Stonington.
24 MARGARET, b. Dec. 21, 1683.
25 SAMUEL, b. Feb. 11, 1686.
26 ABIGAIL, b. Feb. 3, 1689.
27 PRISCILLA, b. Sept. 17, 1691, m. Theophilus Baldwin May 25, 1710 (No. 23), that family.
28 NEHEMIAH, b. Nov. 24, 1693, d. 1768.

Capt. John Mason (No. 18) m. his first cousin, Anne Mason (No. 13), that family, July 18, 1701. Settled first in Lebanon, but removed to Stonington about 1703, where she was received into the church Feb. 24, 1706.

CHILDREN:

29 JOHN, b. Sept. 13, 1702, at Lebanon.
30 RACHAEL, b. May 19, 1706, at Stonington.
31 SAMUEL, b. Aug. 30, 1707, at Stonington.
32 JEMIMA, b. Aug. 7, 1709, at Stonington.
33 JAMES, b. May 13, 1713, m. Sarah Denison (No. 22), 1738.
34 ELIJAH, b. June 12, 1715, m. his 2d cousin, Martha Brown.

After Mrs. Anne Mason's death Capt. John Mason (No. 18) m. 2d, Mrs. Anne Sanford Noyes, widow of Dr. James Noyes of Stonington, Conn. She was daughter of Gov. Peleg Sanford of Rhode Island, and granddaughter of Gov. William Coddington of Newport, R. I. Their m. was on July 15, 1719, and he d. Dec., 1736, at London, where he had gone with Mahomet, grandson of Owaneco, to obtain recognition by the Crown to the right of Mahomet to the sachemship of the Mohegans

CHILD BY LAST WIFE WAS:

35 PELEG SANFORD, b. April 6, 1720.

Daniel Mason (No. 20) m. April 19, 1704, Dorothy, third daughter of the Rev. Jeremiah Hobart of Topsfield, Mass. She was b. Aug. 21, 1679. They lived at Lebanon, where he d. May 7, 1705, and was buried at Stonington, Conn.

CHILD:

36 JEREMIAH, b. March 4, 1705, m. Mary Clark.

After the death of Daniel Mason (No. 20b) Mrs. Dorothy Mason m. Hon. Hezekiah Brainerd, one of the Colonial Council of George First, and her third son, David Brainerd, was the Indian missionary. She d. March 11, 1733.

Hezekiah Mason (No. 21) m. June 7, 1699, Anne Bingham, daughter of Thomas Bingham and Mary Rudd, of Windham, Conn.

MAJOR JOHN MASON FAMILY.

CHILDREN:
37 RACHEL, b. April 12, 1701, d. young.
38 HANNAH, b. June 14, 1702.
39 ANNE, b. in 1704, m. Thomas Dimmock.
40 MARY, b. ———, m. David Huntington.
41 RACHEL, b. Aug. 31, 1707, m. Charles Mudge.
42 DANIEL, b. ———.
43 JONATHAN, b. July 30, 1715.
44 LYDIA, b. ———.
45 ABIGAIL, b. ———, m. Jacob Lincoln.

After the death of Mrs. Anne Mason on Aug. 2, 1724, Mr. Hezekiah Mason m. 2d, Nov. 15, 1725, Sarah Robinson, and he d. Dec. 15, 1726.

Peter Mason (No. 22) m. July 8, 1703, Mary Hobart.

CHILDREN:
46 PETER, b. Aug. 25, 1704, d. young.
47 Daughter, b. Sept. 13, 1705.
48 DANIEL, b. March 25, 1707, m. Dec. 19, 1734, Hannah Chappell of New London. They settled in Stonington, where he d. Feb. 5, 1750.
49 JAPHET, b. Dec. 28, 1709, d. young.
50 MARY, b. May 31, 1711.
51 JAPHET, b. Sept. 30, 1713, m. Chappell ———.
52 ABIGAIL, b. Sept. 3, 1715, m. Samuel Lester Dec. 11, 1737.
53 PETER, b. Dec. 28, 1717, m. Margaret Fanning.
54 ALITHEA, b. Dec. 9, 1720.

Samuel Mason (No. 25) m. April 15, 1712, Elizabeth Fitch and settled at Stonington. She d. Feb. 8, 1715.

CHILDREN:
55 MEHITABLE, b. Sept. 15, 1713, d. young.

Mr. Samuel Mason m. Feb. 22, 1720, Rebecca Lippincott for his second wife; they settled at Stonington.

CHILDREN:
56 ELIZABETH, b. Oct. 16, 1720.
57 REBECCA, b. June 2, 1722, d. young.
58 REBECCA, b. March 21, 1724, d. young.
59 SAMUEL, b. May 25, 1726.
60 REBECCA, b. June 3, 1728.
61 PRUDENCE, b. April 2, 1730.
62 ELNATHAN, b. June 16, 1732.
63 and 64 Twins, Mehitable and Eunice, were b. June 1, 1734, at Stonington.

Nehemiah Mason (No. 28) m. Jan. 9, 1722, Zerviah Stanton (No. 129), of the Stanton family. He d. May 13, 1768; she d. Oct. 12, 1771.

CHILDREN:
65 HOBART, b. Oct. 6, 1722, m. Margaret Copp (No. 29), Copp family.
66 ANDREW, b. Oct. 12, 1724, d. young.
67 ANDREW, b. Feb. 30, 1730, m. Mary Gallup (No. 65), of that family.
68 HANNAH, b. June 13, 1731, m. Henry Gallup of Groton, Conn. (No. 82).
69 JARED, b. Feb. 29, 1733, m. Hannah Park.
70 ZERVIAH, b. Aug. 26, 1735, m. Holmes.

Peleg Sanford Mason (No. 35) m. Nov. 4, 1742, Mary Stanton of Charlestown, R. I. Settled at Stonington, but removed to Lebanon about 1745.

CHILDREN:

71 ANNE, b. Nov. 7, 1743.
72 PELEG S., b. May 5, 1746, d. unmarried.
73 ESTHER, b. Nov. 12, 1748.
74 MARY, b. March 22, 1751.
75 LUCY, b. Dec. 2, 1753.
76 ELIJAH, b. Sept. 26, 1756.
77 JAMES, b. April 7, 1759.

Peter Mason (No. 53) m. in 1741, Margaret Fanning, b. Nov. 23, 1724, at Groton, Conn. He d. about 1765; she d. Sept. 19, 1803.

CHILDREN:

78 ABIGAIL, b. Aug. 5, 1742, m. Rufus Branch.
79 RUFUS, b. in July, 1745.
80 ROBERT, b. in 1748, m. Chloe Case.
81 PETER, b. Aug. 1, 1752, m. ———— Farnum.
82 JOHN, b. Nov. 11, 1764, m. Sarah Woodward.

Hobart Mason (No. 65) m. Nov. 10, 1749, Margaret Copp, his cousin (No. 29), Copp family. Settled at Stonington, but afterwards removed to Groton.

CHILDREN:

83 MARGARET, b. June 17, 1750.
84 LOIS, b. April 29, 1752.
85 ELNATHAN, b. March 17, 1754, d. young.
86 HENRY, b. April 3, 1758.
87 ZERVIAH, b. Jan. 26, 1760.
88 ELIPHALET, b. Sept. 29, 1761, d. young.
89 HOBART, b. Nov. 15, 1764.
90 LUKE, b. May 7, 1767.

Hobart Mason's first wife d. and he m. again and had two children.

CHILDREN:

91 DUDLEY, b. Sept. 24, 1775.
92 NANCY, b. Feb. 22, 1778.

Andrew Mason (No. 67) m. Mary Gallup (No. 65b) of that family, on March 20, 1754. She d. May 13, 1797.

CHILDREN:

93 NEHEMIAH, b. April 10, 1754, and m. Bridget Denison (No. 251), Nov. 6, 1752; they settled at Stonington.

CHILDREN:

94 MARY, b. June 5, 1783, m. Amos Miner.
95 MEHITABLE, b. Sept. 19, 1784, m. Alexander Latham, d. April 2, 1806.
96 BRIDGET, b. April 9, 1786.
97 ANDREW, b. June 2, 1788.
98 JOSEPH, b. April 4, 1790.
99 DANIEL, b. July 23, 1792.
100 PELEG, b. Aug. 30, 1794.
101 NEHEMIAH, b. Nov. 4, 1800.

Daniel Mason (No. 99) m. Hannah Stanton Punderson Williams (No. 334b). Feb. 10, 1817. He d. Oct. 30, 1833.

CHILDREN:

102 HANNAH, b. Dec. 4, 1817, d. young.
103 DANIEL, b. April 22, 1819.
104 BRIDGET, b. Jan. 17, 1821.
105 MARY, b. Oct. 14, 1822, m. Alexander Young.
106 HANNAH, b. Nov. 23, 1825.
107 JOHN, b. Jan. 28, 1828.
108 ANDREW, b. Feb. 28, 1830.
109 ELIZABETH, b. April 17, 1832.

MINER FAMILY.

The surname of Miner originated in England during the reign of King Edward the Third, whose reign continued from 1327 to 1377. When preparing for war with France he took progress through Somersett, and coming to Mendippe Hill, where lived a man by the name of Bullman, whose extraordinary and successful efforts to aid the king in the munitions of war, with one hundred powerful men of volunteers in the service, so pleased the king that he granted him a coat-of-arms, with the name of Henry Miner thereon, in recognition of his loyalty and patriotic devotion to him and his cause.

I. This HENRY MINER died in the year 1359, leaving four sons, heirs-at-law of the realm.
    2.   HENRY, b. _____.
    3.   EDWARD, b. _____.
    4.   THOMAS, b. _____.
    5.   GEORGE, b. _____.

Henry Miner (No. 2) m. Henrietta Hicks. Their son:
    6.   WILLIAM, b. _____, m. a Miss Greeley. Their son:
    7.   LODOWICK, b. _____, m. Anna Dyer. Their son:
    8.   THOMAS, b. _____, m. Bridget Hervie. Their son:
    9.   WILLIAM, b. _____, m. Isabella Harcope. Their son:
    10. CLEMENT, b. _____, m. Sarah Pope. Their son:
    11. THOMAS, b. April 23, 1608, m. Grace Palmer, daughter of Walter Palmer, in Charlestown, Mass., April 23, 1634 (No. 2), Palmer family. Lieut. Thomas Miner served in the Colonial Indian wars.

NOTE. – General and President Ulysses S. Grant was a lineal descendant of Thomas Miner and wife, Grace Palmer, daughter of Walter Palmer, who were among the most prominent early planters of Stonington, as follows: Their Son, John Miner, b. 1636, m. Elizabeth Booth, Oct. 14, 1658; their daughter, Grace Miner, b. Sept. 20, 1669, m. Samuel Grant (No. 6), that family, April 11, 1688; their son, Noah Grant, b. Dec. 16, 1693, m. Martha Huntington, June 12, 1717; their son, Noah Grant, Jr., b. July 12, 1718, m. Susannah Delano, Nov. 5, 1746; their son, Noah Grant, 3d, b. June 20, 1748, m. Rachel Kelly, March 4, 1792; their son, Jesse Grant, b. Jan 23, 1794, m. Hannah Simpson, June 24, 1821; their son, General Ulysses S. Grant, b. April 27, 1822, m. Julia B. Dent Aug. 22, 1848. He d. July 23, 1885.

CHILDREN:
    12 JOHN, b. in Charlestown, Mass., in 1636; m. Elizabeth Booth.
    13 CLEMENT, bapt. in Hingham, Mass., March 4, 1638; m. Mrs Frances Winley (widow); 2d, Martha Wellman.
    14 THOMAS, bapt. in Hingham, Mass., May 10, 1640; d. unmarried at Narragansett, R. I., April, 1662.
    15 EPHRAIM, bapt. in Hingham, Mass., May 1, 1642, m. Hannah Avery Jan. 20, 1666.
    16. JOSEPH, bapt. in Hingham, Mass., Aug. 25, 1644, m. Mary Avery; 2d, Mrs. Bridget (Chesebrough) Thompson.

MINER FAMILY.

Mr. Thomas Miner (No. 11) removed his family from Hingham, Mass., to New London, Conn., during the year 1646, where the remainder of his children were born.

CHILDREN:
17 MANASSEH, b. April 23 1647, m. Lydia Moore.
18 ANN, b. April 28, 1649, d. Aug. 13, 1652.
19 MARIA, b. ____, 1650, d. in Stonington Jan. 24, 1666.
20 SAMUEL, b. March 4, 1652, served in King Phillip's war, d. 1682, m. Marie Lord, Dec. 15, 1681. Mrs. Marie Miner m. 2d, Joseph Pemberton March 19, 1683.
21 HANNAH, b. in Stonington Sept. 15, 1655, m. Thomas Avery Oct. 22, 1672 (No. 6), Avery family.

John Miner (No. 12) m. Elizabeth Booth, daughter of Richard Booth Oct. 14, 1658, lived at Fairfield, Conn. He d. Sept. 17, 1719, aged 85 yrs; wife d. Oct. 24, 1732, aged 98.

CHILDREN:
22 JOHN, b. Sept. 9, 1659.
23 THOMAS, b. May 29, 1662.
24 HANNAH, b. Aug. 2, 1664.
25 ELIZABETH, b. Jan. 16, 1666.
26 GRACE, b. Sept. 20, 1669, m. Samuel Grant (No. 6), that family.
27 JOSEPH, b. March 4, 1673.
28 EPHRAIM, b. Oct. 24, 1675.
29 SARAH, b. June 19, 1678.
30 ABAGAIL, b. Feb. 6, 1680.
31 JOANNA, b. July, 1685.

Clement Miner (No. 13) m. Frances Willey, relict of Isaac R. Willey, Jr., in 1662. She d. Jan. 6, 1673. He m. 2d, Martha, daughter of William Wellman. She d. 1700. He m. 3d, Joanna _____. He served in the Colonial Indian wars.

CHILDREN:
32 MARY, b. June 19, 1665.
33 JOSEPH, b. Aug. 6, 1666.
34 CLEMENT, b. Oct. 6, 1668.
35 WILLIAM, b. Nov. 6, 1670.
36 ANN, b. Nov. 30, 1672.

CHILD BY SECOND MARRIAGE:
37 PHEBE, b. April 13, 1679.

Ephraim Miner (No. 15) m. Hannah Avery June 20, 1666 (No. 3), that family. He was buried at Taugwonk. He served in King Phillip's war.

CHILDREN:
38 EPHRAIM, b. June 22, 1668, m. Mary Stephens.
39 THOMAS, b. Dec. 17, 1669, d. 1688.
40 HANNAH, b. April 21, 1671, m. Samuel Frink (No. 5), that family.
41 REBECCA, b. Sept., 1672, m. Josiah Grant (No. 9), that family.
42 ELIZABETH, b. April, 1674, m. John Brown (No. 8), that family.
43 SAMUEL, b. Dec., 1676, d. young.
44 DEBORAH, b. April 15, 1677, m. Joseph Pendleton (No. 8), that family.

45   SAMUEL, b. Aug., 1681, m. Anna Denison, April, 1702 (No. 56), that family.
46   JAMES, b. Nov., 1682, m. Abigail Eldredge.
47   GRACE, b. Sept., 1683, m. William Palmer (No. 34), that family.
48   JOHN, b. April 19, 1685, m. Mary Eldredge.
49   Twins, son and daughter, b. March 21, 1687, both d. same day.

Dr. Joseph Miner (No. 16) m. Mary Avery Oct. 23, 1668 (No. 5), that family. She d. Feb. 2, 1798. He m. 2d, Mrs. Bridget (Chesebrough) Thompson (No. 24), Chesebrough family, relict of William Thompson, Dec. 7, 1709. He served in King Phillip's war. He was buried at Taugwonk.

CHILDREN:

50   JOSEPH, b. Sept. 19, 1669, m. Sarah Tracy.
51   MARY, b. Sept. 17, 1672, m. Elisha Chesebrough (No. 19), that family.
52   MARCIE, b. Aug. 21, 1673, m. Francis West (No. 6), that family.
53   BENJAMIN, b. June 25, 1676, m. Mary Saxton.
54   JOANNA, b. March 30, 1681.
55   SARAH, bapt. March 30, 1679.
56   PRUDENCE, bapt. May 6, 1668, m. Joseph Denison Feb. 17, 1705 (No. 60), that family.
57   CHRISTOPHER, bapt. July 13, 1684, m. Mary Lay March 9, 1704; she m. 2d, Samuel Denison (No. 62), that family.

CHILD BY SECOND MARRIAGE:

58   BRIDGET, b. Jan. 31, 1711, m. Jonathan Chesebrough (No. 37), that family.

Dea. Manasseh Miner (No. 17) b. in New London 1647, being the first male child born in that town. He m. Lydia Moore Sept. 26, 1670, lived at the old Homestead at Quiambaug, and was buried at Wequetequock. He served in King Phillip's war.

CHILDREN:

59   ELNATHAN, b. Dec. 28, 1673, m. 1st Rebecca Baldwin; 2d, Mrs. Prudence (Richardson) Hallam; 3d, Tamzen Wilcox.
60   SAMUEL, b. Sept. 20, 1675.
61   HANNAH, b. Dec. 8, 1676, m. Elihu Chesebrough (No. 32), that family.
62   THOMAS, b. Sept. 20, 1683, m. Hannah Avery.
63   LYDIA, b. _____, m. Sylvester Baldwin (No. 20), that family.

Ephraim Miner (No. 38) m. Mary, daughter of Richard and Mary Linken Stevens of Taunton, Mass., May 24, 1694.

CHILDREN:

64   EPHRAIM, b. March 11, 1695, d. Sept. 10, 1728.
65   THOMAS, b. June 21, 1697.
66   MARY, b. Aug. 4, 1699, m. Thomas Wheeler (No. 19), that family.
67   HENRY, b. Aug. 5, 1701.
68   RUFUS, b. Aug. 21, 1703, m. Mary Miner.
69   BRIDGET, b. Oct. 7, 1705, m. Oliver Grant (No 15), that family.
70   SIMEON, b. May 14, 1708, m. Hannah Wheeler.
71   STEPHEN, b. Dec. 3, 1710, m. Hannah Page.
72   HANNAH, b. Nov. 13, 1712, m. Noah Grant (No. 16), that family.
73   SAMUEL, b. Jan. 1, 1713, m. Elizabeth Denison, Esther Gallup.

James Miner (No. 46) m. Abigail Eldredge Feb. 22, 1705.

MINER FAMILY.

CHILDREN:
74 JAMES, b. Oct. 28, 1708, m. Sarah Breed.
75 CHARLES, b. Nov. 14, 1709, m. Mrs. Mary Wheeler.
76 ZERVIAH, b. Oct. 8, 1711.
77 DANIEL, b. Jan. 24, 1713.
78 ABIGAIL, b. Aug. 18, 1715.

John Miner (No. 48) m. Mary Eldredge May 5, 1709.

CHILDREN:
79 ZERVIAH, b. Oct. 8, 1711.
80 JOHN, b. April 15, 1714.

Joseph Miner (No. 50) m. Sarah Tracey June 18, 1700.

CHILDREN:
81 SARAH, b. Feb. 23, 1702, m. George Denison (No. 66), that family.
82 JERUSHA, b. Jan. 27, 1703.
83 MARY, b. March 15, 1705, m. Rufus Miner (No. 68), that family.
84 GRACE, b. Nov. 20, 1707.
85 CHRISTOPHER, b. March 11, 1711.
86 JOSEPH, b. Feb. 26, 1712.
87 JABEZ, b. March 30, 1714.
88 THANKFUL, b. May 27, 1717.

Benjamin Miner (No. 53) m. Mary, daughter of Capt. Joseph and Hannah (Denison) Chesebrough Saxton, Dec. 15, 1697 (No. 29), Chesebrough family.

CHILDREN:
89 MARY, b. July 31, 1699.
90 MARCY, b. May 20, 1702.
91 BENJAMIN, b. June 22, 1704.
92 CLEMENT, b. Oct. 1, 1706, m. Abigail Hempstead.
93a SARAH, b. June 10, 1710.

Elnathan Miner (No. 59) m. Rebecca Baldwin March 21, 1694 (No. 18), that family; she d. March 12, 1700. He m. 2d, Mrs. Prudence (Richardson) Hallam March 17, 1702; she d. Aug. 6, 1716. He m. 3d, Tamzen Wilcox Oct. 14, 1718.

CHILDREN:
93 SAMUEL, b. Dec. 12, 1694, m. Elizabeth Brown.
94 MANASSEH, b. Dec. 1, 1695, m. Keziah Geer July 9, 1726.
95 ELNATHAN, b. June 24, 1697.
96 REBECCA, b. Feb. 13, 1699.

CHILD BY SECOND MARRIAGE:
97 RICHARDSON, b. Nov. 24, 1704.

Dea. Thomas Miner (No. 62) m. Hannah Avery Dec. 26, 1706 (No. 32), that family.

CHILDREN:
98 THOMAS, b. Oct. 4, 1707, m. Sarah Watson.
99 SYLVANUS, b. March 3, 1709.
100 HANNAH, b. Nov. 23, 1710.
101 JONATHAN, b. Feb. 25, 1714, m. Anna Avery.
102 LYDIA, b. Jan. 12, 1717, d. young.
103 PRUDENCE, b. Dec. 6, 1719, m. John Avery March 27, 1745.
104 MANASSEH, b. Feb. 25, 1724.
105 EPHRAIM (twin), b. Feb. 25, 1724.
106 LYDIA, b. April 26, 1727.

470 HISTORY OF STONINGTON.

Rufus Miner (No. 68) m. Mary Miner (No. 83), April 19, 1725.

CHILDREN:
107 SARAH, b. March 20, 1726, d. young.
108 SARAH, b. May 1, 1727.
109 JOSEPH, b. March 17, 1729, m. Philarner Wadsworth.
110 EPHRAIM, b. July 10, 1731, m. Desire Chesebrough.
111 MARY, b. July 5, 1733, d. young.
112 MARY, b. Aug. 30, 1738, m. John Wheeler Dec. 22, 1763.
113 PRUDENCE, b. Aug. 19, 1739.
114 JOHN, b. Sept. 18, 1741.
115 ANN, b. April 8, 1745.
116 JOSHUA, b. Aug. 6, 1747.

Simeon Miner (No. 70) m. Hannah Wheeler March 10, 1731 (No. 36), that family.

CHILDREN:
117 HANNAH, b. Dec. 8, 1731, m. Constant Searle (No. 14), that family.
118 SIMEON, b. Dec. 3, 1733, m. Anna Hewitt, Mary Owen.
119 THOMAS, b. June 14, 1736, m. Desire Denison (No. 187), that family.
120 KETURAH, b. March 4, 1738, m. Elisha Denison Feb. 23, 1750 (No. 184), that family.
121 ISAAC, b. July 5, 1740, m. Lydia Peabody.
122 EUNICE, b. Jan. 11, 1743.
123 LOIS, b. Jan. 30, 1745.
124 LUCY, b. April 6, 1747.
125 GRACE, b. Feb. 22, 1752, d. young.
126 WILLIAM, b. Jan. 10, 1754, d. young.

Stephen Miner (No. 71) m. Hannah Page Dec. 29, 1731 (No. 13), that family.

CHILDREN:
127 HENRY, b. Dec. 9, 1732, m. Desire Brown.
128 STEPHEN, b. Nov. 24, 1734, m. Lucy Palmer.
129 PHINEAS, b. Jan 6, 1737.
130 ASA, b. Sept. 12, 1741.
131 ALPHEUS, b. June 3, 1744, m. Desire Wheeler.
132 HANNAH, b. June 24, 1746.
133 DESIRE, b. Jan. 12, 1750.
134 KATHARINE, b. Aug. 11, 1753.
135 BRIDGET, b. Aug. 31, 1756.
136 SUSANNAH, b. Feb. 4, 1759.
136a HENRY, b. _____, m. Desire Brown Feb. 20, 1755.

Samuel Miner (No. 73) m. Elizabeth Denison April 29, 1739 (No. 136), that family. She d. Feb. 7, 1743. He m. 2d, Esther Gallup Oct. 22, 1743.

CHILDREN:
137 GEORGE, b. Aug. 26, 1744, d. young.
138 GEORGE, b. Nov. 24, 1745.
139 AMOS, b. April 17, 1747.
140 ESTHER, b. Feb. 13, 1751.
141 ADAM, b. Aug. 28, 1753.
142 ABEL, b. June 17, 1755.
143 PELEG, b. Jan 7, 1757.
144 EPHRAIM, b. Dec. 2, 1758.

MINER FAMILY.

Charles Miner (No. 75) m. Mrs. Mary Wheeler, widow of Isaac Wheeler, and sister of Paul Wheeler, Sr., Dec. 9, 1740 (No. 53), Wheeler family.

CHILDREN:
145 CHARLES, b. Oct. 3, 1741, m. Eunice Holmes.
146 THOMAS, b. March 11, 1743, m. Mary Page (No. 18), Lydia York (No.43).
147 CHRISTOPHER, b. March 16, 1745, m. Mary Randall.
148 MARY, b. Aug. 1, 1746, m. John Wheeler, (No. 346), that family.
149 DANIEL, b. June 21, 1749, m. Mary Denison.
150 ABIGAIL, b. Nov. 8, 1756, m. David Wheeler (No. 347), that family.

Clement Miner (No. 92) m. Abigail, daughter of Joshua Hempstead of New London, and granddaughter of Joshua Hempstead and wife, Elizabeth Larabee, and great-granddaughter of Robert Hempstead, Sept. 1, 1731.

CHILDREN:
151 NATHANIEL, b. April 30, 1732, m. Ann Denison; 2d, Mrs. Lois Denison.
152 HEMPSTEAD, b. Aug. 4, 1734, m. Lydia Chesebrough.
153 WILLIAM ROE, b. March 7, 1736.
154 CLEMENT, b. May 21, 1738, m. Mary Wheeler.
155 ABIGAIL, b. April 3 1740, m. John Denison Sept. 6, 1772.
156 BENJAMIN, b. June 17, 1742, m. Ann Champlin Dec. 24, 1766.
157 MARY, b. June 5, 1744.
158 EUNICE, b. Feb. 6, 1746.
159 PHEBE, b. April 27, 1749.

Samuel Miner (No. 93) m. Elizabeth Brown Dec. 3, 1719.

CHILDREN:
160 ELIZABETH, b. Aug. 18, 1720.
161 REBECCA (twin), b. Aug. 18, 1720.
162 SAMUEL, b. March 14, 1723, m. Mrs. Abigail Miner.
163 NATHAN, b. July 16, 1724, m. Sarah Smith.
164 DAVID, b. Sept. 26, 1726, m. Mrs. Bethia Billings.
165 JOHN, b. Dec. 22, 1728.
166 ELIZABETH, b. Nov. 24, 1730, m. Elkanah Hewitt (No. 66), that family.
167 JOHATHAN, b. Feb. 18, 1733.
168 ANNA, b. June 26, 1735.

Dea. Thomas Miner (No. 98) m. Sarah, daughter of William Watson of Nantucket, Jan. 3, 1745. He d. Nov. 22, 1760. His widow m. a Fellows, and d. May 12, 1803.

CHILDREN:
169 THOMAS, b. Feb. 24, 1746, d. young.
170 SARAH, b. June 27, 1747.
171 THOMAS, b. June 16, 1749.
172 WILLIAM, b. Dec. 18, 1751, m. Abigail Haley (No. 9), that family.
173 MANASSEH, b. June 13, 1755, m. Hannah Haley.
174 PRUDENCE, b. April 24, 1753.

Jonathan Miner (No. 101) m. Anna Avery April 22, 1739.

CHILDREN:
175 JONATHAN, b. Feb. 25, 1740.
176 ELIZABETH, b. Nov. 14, 1741.
177 CHRISTOPHER, b. Jan. 11, 1744.

Manasseh Miner (No. 94) m. Keziah Geer July 9, 1726.

CHILDREN:

177a KEZIAH, b. March 6, 1727.
177b LUCRETIA, b. in Voluntown Feb. 16, 1733, m. Amos York (No. 32), that family.

Manasseh Miner (No. 173) m. Hannah Haley Feb. 14, 1779 (No. 12), that family.

CHILDREN:

178 AMOS, b. July 25, 1781, m. Mary Mason.
179 ISAAC, b. March 21, 1783, m. Esther Cottrell.
180 MANASSEH, b. Jan. 29, 1785.
181 THOMAS, b. _____, m. Eliza Denison (No. 529), that family.
182 JOHN, b. _____.

Joseph Miner (No. 109) m. Philarner Wardsworth Dec. 13, 1750.

CHILDREN:

183 SARAH, b. Sept. 16, 1752.
184 PHILARNER, b. Jan. 30, 1754.
185 MARY, b. Dec. 25, 1755, m. Vose Hinckley (No. 38), that family
186 JOSEPH, b. March 3, 1758, d. young.
187 JERUSHA, b. Feb. 17, 1760.
188 JOSEPH, b. Nov. 13, 1763.

Ephraim Miner (No. 110) m. Desire Chesebrough Dec. 30, 1751 (No. 159), that family.

CHILDREN:

189 EPHRAIM, b. Oct. 26, 1753, d. July 15, 1759.
190 DESIRE, b. _____, m. David Frink.

Simeon Miner (No. 118) m. Anna Hewitt Nov. 15, 1753 (No. 55), that family. She d. Sept. 12, 1754; buried at Taugwonk in Stonington. Her husband m. 2d, Mary Owen, daughter of Rev. John Owen of Groton, Conn., Feb. 1, 1759.

CHILD BY FIRST MARRIAGE:

200 ANNA, b. July 22, 1754, m. Amos Hewitt in 1774 (No. 74), that family.

CHILDREN BY SECOND MARRIAGE:

201 SIMEON, b. Jan. 9, 1760.
202 JOHN OWEN, b. Jan. 9, 1762, m. Elizabeth Avery.
203 ELISHA, b. June 6, 1765.
204 FREDERICK, b. Sept. 28, 1768.
205a MARY, b. July 27, 1770.
206b WILLIAM, b. Feb. 14, 1773.
207c HANNAH, b. Dec. 14, 1776.

Isaac Miner (No. 121) m. Lydia Peabody May 17, 1761. He d. Dec. 13, 1763.

ONE CHILD:

205 LODOWICK, b. June 15, 1762.

Henry Miner (No. 127) m. Desire Brown Feb. 20, 1755.

MINER FAMILY.

CHILDREN:
206 MARY, b. Sept. 19, 1756.
207 HENRY, b. Sept. 9, 1758.
208 DANIEL, b. March 20, 1761.
209 LUKE, b. Aug. 25, 1764.
210 HANNAH, b. March 12, 1767.
211 SAXTON, b. June 2, 1769, m. Content York (No. 95), that family.

Stephen Miner (No. 128) m. Lucy Palmer March 7, 1757.

CHILDREN:
212 LUCY, b. Nov. 28, 1757.
213 SABRA, b. Feb. 11, 1759.
214 STEPHEN, b. Nov. 22, 1761.

Alpheus Miner (No. 131) m. Desire Wheeler Feb. 5, 1797.

CHILDREN:
215 POLLY, b. May 9, 1798, m. Elias Hewitt (No. 181), that family.

Charles Miner (No. 145) m. Eunice Holmes Jan. 10, 1765 (No. 40), that family.

CHILDREN:
216 CYNTHIA, b. Dec. 10, 1765, m. Jesse York (No. 80), that family.
217 HANNAH, b. Oct. 3, 1767, m. Perry Barber.
218 EUNICE, b. March 30, 1770, m. Adam Thurston.
219 MOLLY, b. Sept. 14, 1772, m. Clark Davis.
220 LUCRETIA, b. Jan. 29, 1775, m. Henry Niles.
221 LUCY, b. March 10, 1777, m. Joseph Brown.
222 CHARLES, b. April 12, 1779, m. Lucy Slack.
223 MARTHA, b. Feb. 7, 1782, m. Jesse Niles.
224 JOHN, b. April 17, 1786, m. Nancy Brown.

Thomas Miner (No. 146) m. Mary Page Sept. 8, 1765 (No. 18), Page family; m. 2d, Lydia York (No 48), that family, both of Stonington, Conn.

CHILDREN:
225 PERIS, b. Dec. 29, 1766.
226 PRISCILLA, b. April 26, 1768.
227 REV. ASHER, b. Jan. 30, 1772, m. Lucy Spalding.
228 ADAM, b. July 5, 1774, m. _____ Frink.
229 ROSWELL, b. Aug. 29, 1776, m. Betsey Smith.
230 SALLY, b. May 6, 1779.
231 PHEBE, b. Nov. 5, 1781.
232 BETSEY, b. Aug. 23, 1783.

CHILDREN BY SECOND MARRIAGE:
233 OLIVER, b. Dec. 14, 1791, m. _____ Park.
234 RALPH R., b. Aug. 16, 1793, m. Polly Randall.
235 DEA. EZRA D., b. 1795, m. Desire Hewitt (No. 240), that family.
236 LYDIA, b. 1797.
237 ABBY, b. 1800, d. unmarried.
238 LAURA, b. 1803, d. unmarried.

Christopher Miner (No. 147) m. Mary Randall Aug. 11, 1765 (No. 48), that family.

CHILDREN:
239 CHRISTOPHER, b. Dec. 10, 1765.
240 MARY, b. March 26, 1767, m. Robert Miner.
241 SABRA, b. Feb. 2, 1769.

242 ISAAC, b. March 2, 1773, m. Keturah Brown.
243 ELIAS, b. March 4, 1775, m. Elizabeth Brown; 2d, Betsey Brown.
244 CYRUS, b. May 4, 1777.
245 RANDALL, b. March 2, 1786.

Daniel Miner (No. 149) m. Mary or Mercy Denison Feb. 19, 1769 (No. 294), that family.

CHILDREN:

246 MARY, b. Jan. 31, 1771.
247 MARTHA, b. Sept. 26, 1776.
248 PRUDENCE, b. Oct. 18, 1778.
249 DANIEL, b. Oct. 18, 1780.
250 WHEELER, b. Jan. 30, 1782.
251 DARIUS, b. July 1, 1785.
252 LUTHER, b. March 27, 1788, m. Hannah Avery.
253 ANNA, b. Sept. 20, 1790.

Nathaniel Miner (No. 151) m. Ann Denison Feb. 20, 1754 (No. 233), that family. She d. April 19, 1769. He m. 2d, Mrs. Lois (Stanton) Denison, widow of Edward Denison.

CHILDREN:

254 ABIGAIL, b. _____, m. John Denison (No. 182), that family, Sept. 6, 1772.

Hempstead Miner (No. 152) m. Lydia Chesebrough Feb. 20, 1755 (No. 160), that family.

CHILDREN:

255 HEMPSTEAD CHESEBROUGH, b. March 21, 1771, m. Lucretia Chesebrough March 6, 1791 (No. 184), that family.

Samuel Miner (No. 162) m. Mrs. Abigail Miner July 14, 1752.

CHILDREN:

256 JONATHAN, b. Aug. 27, 1754.
257 ELNATHAN, b. April 5, 1756.
258 REBECCA, b. May 27, 1759.
259 PEREZ, b. July 25, 1760.
260 ABIGAIL, b. Aug. 16, 1766.

Nathan Miner (No. 163) m. Sarah Smith March 7, 1751.

CHILDREN:

261 DEBORAH, b. Dec. 24, 1751.
262 RICHARDSON, b. Sept. 10, 1753, m. Katharine Holmes.
263 SARAH, b. Dec. 7, 1755.
264 ELIZABETH, b. July 15, 1759.
265 ROBERT, b. Nov. 13, 1763, m. Marcy or Mary Miner.
266 NATHAN, b. Sept. 23, 1764.

David Miner (No. 164) m. Mrs. Bethia Billings, widow of _____ (No. 69), Billings family, Nov. 14, 1753.

CHILDREN:

267 AMOS, b. Aug. 30, 1754.
268 DAVID, b. March 9, 1757.
269 ELIAS, b. Oct. 31, 1759.
270 ANNA, b. Aug. 30, 1761.
271 JESSE, b. Aug. 10, 1767, m. Hannah Hillard.

Dea. Thomas Miner (No. 171) m. Lucretia Safford Oct. 10, 1771. She d. Jan. 6, 1781. He m. 2d, Prudence Williams Nov. 25, 1784.

CHILDREN:
272 LUCRETIA, b. April 19, 1773.
273 HENRIETTA, b. Jan. 29, 1775.
274 THOMAS, b. April 16, 1777.
275 ASA, b. Sept. 19, 1778, m. Hannah Harrington.
276 PRISCILLA, b. July 5, 1780, m. Frederick Chesebrough (No. 331), Chesebrough family.

Amos Miner (No. 178) m. Mary Mason Nov. 13, 1806.

CHILD:
277 AMOS, b. Aug. 20, 1807.

Isaac Miner (No. 179) m. Mrs. Esther (Denison) Cottrell, widow of Charles Cottrell, Dec. 11, 1803 (No. 400), Denison family.

CHILDREN:
278 ISAAC D., b. Nov. 26, 1804, m. Phebe Burrows (No. 43), that family.
279 HANNAH, b. Oct. 5, 1806, m. David Thompson of Coleraine, Mass.
280 LYDIA, b. Feb. 7, 1809, d. April 5, 1812.
281 EUNICE, b. March 12, 1811, m.
282 LYDIA, b. April 7, 1813, m. Charles Johnson.
283 FREDERICK D., b. Sept. 18, 1815, d. Jan. 28, 1841, unmarried.
284 MANASSEH, b. Aug. 5, 1818, m. Fanny Hooper.
285 ESTHER, b. Feb. 22, 1821, m. Gurdon Gates.

Dr. John Owen Miner (No. 202) m. Elizabeth, daughter of Col. Ebenezer and Phebe (Denison) Avery, and granddaughter of Ebenezer Avery (No. 57), that family, July 2, 1785. He d. April 27, 1851.

CHILDREN:
286 BETSEY, b. June 18, 1789, m. Asa Lord Avery Nov. 27, 1806.
287 MARY, b. June 15, 1791, m. Dr. John Smith Oct. 14, 1811.
288 NANCY, b. Oct. 13, 1793, m. Elisha Avery Nov. 18, 1810.
289 JOHN OWEN, b. Oct. 16, 1795, m. Adeline Avery Sept. 9, 1819.
290 LUCY A., b. March 16, 1798, m. Albert Morgan.
291 JULIA ANN, b. July 28, 1800, m. Dr. Benjamain Stoddard Nov. 27, 1817.
292 PHEBE DENISON, b. Aug. 1, 1802, m. Dr. William Miner July 4, 1844.
293 EMELINE FRANCES, b. Nov. 18, 1805, m. Capt. Nathan Fish Jan. 9, 1833 (No. 51).
294 HANNAH ADELINE, b. Sept., 1809, m. Isaac Randall (No. 136), that family.

Saxton Miner (No. 211) m. Content York Jan. 17, 1799 (No. 95), that family.

CHILDREN:
295 MARY, b. in 1800, m. Alex. G. Frink.
296 NANCY, b. in 1802, m. Henry Crandall, d. Aug. 5, 1849.
297 HENRY S., b. in 1804, d. May 2, 1828.
298 LELAND D., b. in 1806, m. Bridget W. Maine April 15, 1829 (No. 166), that family; m. 2d, Hannah M. Allyn April 1, 1840.

299 REV. BRADLEY, b. July 18, 1808, m. Phebe Esther Pendleton; 2d, Louisa Tucker.
300 LUCY P., b. in 1810, m. Robert Wheeler (No. 200), that family.
301 DESIRE B., b. in 1812, m. Solomon S. Wheeler (No. 201), that family.
302 HARRIET, b. in 1814, d. Jan. 20, 1826.
303 FRANKLIN H., b. in 1821, m. Harriet Wheeler (No. 205), that family.

Roswell Miner (No. 229) m. Betsey Smith Oct. 23, 1803.

CHILDREN:

304 COGGSWELL, b. Feb. 17, 1804.

Isaac Miner (No. 242) m. Keturah Brown March 3, 1795.

CHILDREN:

305 KETURAH, b. Sept. 28, 1797.
306 ISAAC W., b. in 1799, m. Eliza Green March 29, 1829.
307 ZEBULON, b. Jan. 13, 1801, m. _____ York.
308a ANNA, b. Dec. 11, 1803, m. _____ York.
309b PALMER, b. July 29, 1805, m. _____ York.
310c DENISON, b. _____, m. _____ York.
311d MARY E., b. _____, m. Luke Chesebrough (No. 422), that family.

Richardson Miner (No. 262) m. Katharine Holmes in 1775.

CHILDREN:

308 SAMUEL, b. March 21, 1776, m. Nancy Avery.
309 MARY, b. April 9, 1779.
310 MARTHA, b. Dec. 8, 1781.
311 KATHARINE, b. March 1, 1785.
312 SARAH, b. April 18, 1787.

Robert Miner (No. 265) m. Mary Miner (No. 240) Feb. 10, 1788.

CHILDREN:

313 ROBERT, b. March 7, 1789.
314 GILBERT, b. Dec. 26, 1791, m. Mary Ann Frink.
315 BETSEY, b. Feb. 18, 1795.
316 WILLIAM, b. Jan. 12, 1803.

Asa Miner (No. 275) m. Hannah Harrington Dec. 17, 1802. They lived in Quiambaug, in Stonington, Conn. He m. 2d, _____ Prosser.

CHILDREN:

317 PRUDENCE, b. April 15, 1803.
318 THOMAS, b. Sept. 24, 1806, m. Mary Green.
319 NANCY, b. Oct. 22, 1804.
320 MARY, b. Oct. 8, 1808, d. unmarried.
321 HENRY, b. Sept. 30, 1810.
322 ASA, b. Nov. 29, 1812, m. Eliza Lewis.
323 LUCRETIA, b. Aug. 25, 1815.
324 HARRIET, b. Jan. 8, 1818, m. Capt. Thomas Burch (No. 42), that family.
325 THERESA, b. Jan. 23, 1820, m. _____ Dibble.

James Miner (No. 74) m. Sarah Breed Aug. 20, 1724 (No. 9), that family.

CHILDREN:

326 SARAH, b. July 19, 1725.
327 EUNICE, b. Sept. 16, 1727, d. young.

MINER FAMILY. 477

328 EUNICE, b. Jan. 11, 1729.
329 BERTHA, b. March 10, 1731.
330 ABIGAIL, b. April 1, 1733, d. young.
331 ABIGAIL, b. Aug. 9, 1735.
332 JAMES, b. Nov. 30, 1737, m. Prudence Denison.
333 MARY, b. Nov. 7, 1739.
334 ASA, b. July 24, 1742.

James Miner (No. 332) m. Prudence Denison April 6, 1761 (No. 290), that family, both of North Stonington.

CHILDREN:

335 PHEBE, b. May 30, 1762.
336 JAMES, b. Oct. 4, 1764.
337 ANDREW, b. Sept. 8, 1766.
338 PRUDENCE, b. July 8, 1768.
339 LOIS, b. March 30, 1772, m. Dea. Jeremiah Fellows (N. 46), that family.
340 EUNICE, b. Feb. 18, 1775.
341 DENISON, b. Aug. 28, 1777.

Rev. Asher Miner (No. 227) m. Lucy Spalding Nov. 28, 1790.

CHILDREN:

342 MARTHA, b. Feb. 12, 1795, m. Elias Brown (No. 234), that family.
343 ANNA, b. June 4, 1797.
344 ASHER, b. Sept. 19, 1799, d. unmarried.
345 LUCY, b. Nov. 7, 1804.
346 JEDEDIAH, b. Sept. 23, 1806.
347 JOHN, b. Nov. 18, 1808.
348 ASA, b. March 8, 1811.
349 HANNAH, b. July 3, 1813.
350 EUNICE, b. Oct. 5, 1815, m. Benjamin Noyes (No. 236), that family.

Clement Miner (No. 154) m. Mary Wheeler Dec. 24, 1761 (No. 72), that family.

CHILDREN:

351 ZERVIAH, b. Sept. 10, 1762.
352 WILLIAM, b. Jan. 1, 1766.
353 CLEMENT, b. Sept. 22, 1769, m. Anna Cheseborough (No. 180), that family.
354 NATHANIEL, b. Oct. 26, 1771.
355 JESSE, b. July 25, 1778.
356 NANCY, b. Dec. 17, 1782.

Jesse Miner (No. 271) m. Hannah Hillard Feb. 24, 1803, of Stonington, Conn.

CHILDREN:

357 SALLY, b. Sept. 15, 1804.
358 ELIZA, b. Oct. 25, 1806.
359 JESSE, b. Feb. 10, 1809.
360 JAMES, b. March 7, 1812.
361 BERTHA, b. Aug. 20, 1815.

Elias Miner (No. 243) m. Phebe Brown; 2d, Betsey Brown.

CHILDREN:

362 CHRISTOPHER, b. _____.
363 THOMAS, b. _____.
364 MARY, b. _____, m. Benjamin Spalding.
365 PHEBE, b. _____, m. James Wheeler; 2d, Clark Davis.
366 ALFRED, b. March 14, 1810, m. Minerva Niles.
367 LATHAM, b. March 4, 1814, m. Lydia Dodge; 2d, Maria Johnson.

368 ALMIRA, b. _____, m. Rev. I. B. Maryott.
369 ELLIAS, b. _____, m. Clarissa Miner.
370 ERASTUS, b. _____, Jane Breed.
371 MARTHA, b. _____, m. Noyes Chapman.

Ralph Randall Miner (No. 234) m. Polly Randall Sept. 1818 (No. 98), that family. He d. at Groton, July 7, 1867; she d. June 14, 1825.

ONE CHILD:
372 HARRIET HULL, b. Aug. 2, 1819, m. Rev. William Harrison Randall Nov. 30, 1837 (No. 126), that family.

William Miner (No. 172) m. Abigail Haley (No. 9), that family, May 10, 1770. He was in the Revolutionary war, and d. Feb. 25, 1833. She d. June 5, 1818.

CHILDREN:
373 ABSALOM, b. Oct. 10, 1771, m. Susannah Wilcox.
374 SARAH, b. Nov. 13, 1773, d. in 1848, unmarried.
375 SABRINA, b. March 17, 1776, m. William Lewis.
376 GEORGE, b. April 6, 1778, lost at sea, aged 19 yrs.
377 WILLIAM, b. July 19, 1779, d. young.
378 ABIGAIL, b. Nov. 25, 1780, m. Joseph McCabe.
379 JOSEPH, b. March 5, 1783.
380 ENOCH, b. March 20, 1785, d. June 19, 1803.
381 ELIHU, b. Dec. 17, 1787.
382 DESIRE, b. Dec. 17, 1787, m. Elisha Brown.
383 REBECCA, b. July 2, 1790, m. Capt. Jesse Wilcox, Jr.
384 MARTHA, b. Nov. 2, 1793, m. J_____ Allen.

Joseph Miner (No. 379) m. Nancy (No. 70), daughter of William West and wife, Nancy Babcock, March 3, 1807. He d. March 4, 1860; she d. March 12, 1872.

CHILDREN:
385 JOSEPH, b. Aug. 26, 1808, m. Sabra Avery.
386 FRANCIS W., b. Oct. 1810, m. Emeline Denison.
387 MARY, b. Oct. 5, 1812, m. Jesse Miner Nov. 20, 1830.
388 WILLIAM, b. _____, d. Nov. 15, 1826.
389 ELIZABETH, b. _____, d. Nov. 9, 1826.
390 ABBY, b. Oct. 6, 1821, m. John Moredock.
391 GEORGE, b. Sept., 1825, d. young.

Francis West Miner (No. 386) m. Emeline Denison (No. 528), of that family, June 7, 1835.

CHILDREN:
392 FRANCIS E., b. July 15, 1837, d. young.
393 FRANCIS W., b. May 23, 1843.
394 CHARLES A., b. Aug. 31, 1847.
395 EMELINE, b. Feb. 23, 1844, m. Samuel B. Allen Sept. 3, 1874.
396 WILLIAM E., b. March 5, 1846.
397 ALONZO S., b. June 25, 1849, d. unmarried.

Thomas Miner (No. 181) m. Eliza A. Denison Aug. 25, 1835 (No. 529), that family.

CHILDREN:
398 GEORGE W., b. June 16, 1836, d. unmarried.
399 CHARLES H., b. July 1, 1837, d. young.
400 ELIZA, b. July 21, 1841, m. Hiram C. Denison (No. 578), that family.

MORGAN FAMILY.

1. JAMES MORGAN, the emigrant ancestor and progenitor of the Morgan family, was born in Wales in 1607. He m. Margery Hill of Roxbury, Mass., Aug. 6, 1640. He was made freeman there, May 10, 1645. Early in 1650 he had lands granted him in Pequot, now New London, as New London records show, which was soon occupied by him as a homestead, "on the path to New street or Cape Ann street," as it was called in honor of the Cape Ann Company, who chiefly settled there. On the 25th day of December, 1656, he sold his homestead and removed soon after, with several others, across the river, upon large tracts of land previously granted them by the town. The spot where he built his first house in Groton in 1657, and where he ever resided and died, is a few rods southeast of the dwelling of Elijah S. Morgan, about three miles from Groton ferry, on the road to Poquonock Bridge. He was one of the townsmen or selectmen of New London for several years, and one of the first "Deputys sent from New London Plantation" to the General Court at Hartford, May session, 1657, and was nine times afterwards chosen member of the assembly, the last in 1670, and he was also an active and useful member of Rev. Richard Blinman's church, as his name is prominent in every important movement or proceeding. He also served in the early Colonial wars. He d. in 1685, aged 78 years.

CHILDREN:

2 HANNAH, b. May 18, 1642, m. Nehemiah Royce Nov. 20, 1660.
3 JAMES, b. March 3, 1644, m. Mary Vine of England Nov., 1666.
4 JOHN, b. March 30, 1645, m. 1st, Rachael Dymond; 2d, wife, widow Elizabeth Williams, daughter of Lieut. Gov. William Jones of New Haven, and granddaughter of Gov. Theophilus Eaton.
5 JOSEPH, b. Nov. 29, 1646, m. Dorothy, daughter of Dea. Thomas Park, April, 1670 (No. 26), Park family.
6 ABRAHAM, b. Sept. 3, 1648, d. Aug., 1649.
7 A daughter, b. Nov. 17, 1650, d. young.

Capt. James Morgan (No. 3) m. Mary Vine Nov. 3, 1666. Had son

8 JAMES, b. Feb. 6, 1667, m. Hannah ———, who died about 1720. His son
9 JAMES, b. in 1693, m. daughter of John Morgan in 1729. His son
10 JAMES, b. in 1730, m. Catharine Street in 1758. His son

11 NICHOLAS, b. in 1762, m. Phebe Avery, March 17, 1790. They had twelve children. One settled in Mystic and two in Stonington, Conn. Had daughter
12 PHEBE, b. Sept. 23, 1792, m. Henry Harding Dec. 1, 1816, lived in Old Mystic. Also
13 LYDIA, b. Feb. 10, 1805, m. Horatio N. Fish Aug. 29, 1824, lived at Mystic. Also
14 JOHN, b. March 15, 1809, m. 1st, Almira, daughter of Ichabod and Lucy Brown of North Stonington. She d. March 30, 1839; he m. 2d, Susan Amelia, daughter of Gen. Nathan Pendleton of North Stonington. He resided at Pawcatuck, and was the cashier of the Pawcatuck National Bank from its organization in 1849 until his death.

Capt. James Morgan (No. 3) m. Mary Vine. Had son

15 WILLIAM, b. March 4, 1669, m. Margaret Avery July 17, 1696. His son
16 SOLOMAN, b. Oct. 5, 1708, m. Mary Walworth July 1, 1742. His son
17 NATHAN, b. Jan. 2, 1752, m. Hannah Perkins Sept. 8, 1774. His son
18 ELIJAH, b. March 1, 1809, m. Mary Ann Perkins March 6, 1832. His son
19 ELIJAH A., b. Aug. 11, 1836, m. 1st, Mary F. Davis Sept. 29, 1858; 2d, Sadie Lawton, all of Old Mystic.

James Morgan (No. 10) m. Catharine Street in 1758. Had son:

20 MOSES, b. March 14, 1769, m. Hannah Gallup March 29, 1794. His son
21 SAMUEL, b. March 29, 1801, m. Mary Gallup Nov. 25, 1827. Their daughter
22 MARY EMMA, b. April 27, 1843, m. Seth Noyes Williams (No. 67), William Williams family.

John Morgan (No. 4) m. Rachael Dymond Nov. 16, 1665. Had son

23 JOHN, b. June 10, 1667, m. Ruth Shapley. His son
24 JOHN, b. Jan. 4, 1700, m. Sarah Cobb, April 17, 1728. His son
25 JOHN, b. July 28, 1729, m. Prudence Morgan Feb. 1, 1750. His son
26 STEPHEN, b. April 19, 1762, m. Parthenia Park April 13, 1787. They lived in Groton, where all their ten children are recorded. Their son
27 JOHN, b. Jan. 1, 1799, m. Mary Allen Dec. 31, 1820. They lived in Ledyard and had thirteen children. A daughter
28 HANNAH MARIA, b. March 25, 1825, m. Frank Noyes (No. 339), Noyes family, and lived in Stonington, Conn. Also
29 LUTHER, b. Oct. 26, 1836, m. ———— Prentice, and lives in Mystic.

Stephen Morgan (No. 26) m. Parthenia Park. Had son

30 STEPHEN, b. June 20, 1808, m. Eliza M. D. Noyes June 17, 1830 (No. 338), that family.

John Morgan (No. 4) m. 1st, Rachael Dymond. Had son

31 SAMUEL, b. Sept. 9, 1669, m. Hannah Avery Dec. 30, 1709. His son
32 TIMOTHY, b. about 1723, m. Deborah ————. His son
33 THEOPHILUS, b. Oct. 12, 1759, m. Mary Hinckley (No. 65), that family, May 10, 1795. Had daughter
34 MARY or POLLY, b. March 10, 1796, m. Cyrus Allyn, Jan. 5, 1815, and their son, John Hobart Allyn, m. Flora Allyn, Sept. 15, 1858, who lives at Mystic, Conn.

John Morgan (No. 4) m. for his 2d wife, Mrs. Elizabeth Williams. Had son

MORGAN FAMILY.

35 WILLIAM, b. in 1693, m. Mary Avery (No. 25), that family. Their son
36 WILLIAM AVERY, b. June 17, 1723, m. Temperance Avery, July 4, 1744 (No. 79), that family. Their son, William Morgan, m. Lydia Smith; their son, Dea. Jasper Morgan, m. Catharine Avery (nee Copp), widow of Jasper Avery of Groton, July 8, 1805, where he resided and commenced business, principally farming, and receiving a good common school and academical education, taught school during the winter season in Groton and Stonington. While teaching in the seventh school district of Stonington he boarded round, as was the custom of his time, with the families comprising the district, making the residence of Richard Wheeler his welcome home, when children Esther, Nathaniel, Richard, Silas and Hannah attended his school. His son was Gov. Edwin Denison Morgan, b. Feb. 8, 1811, m. Eliza Matilda Waterman, Aug. 19, 1833. Gov. Morgan was a native of Massachusetts. In 1858 he was elected Governor of New York, and was a man of prominence, accumulating a princely fortune. He lived in New York city many years, where he died.

William Avery Morgan (No. 36), who m. Temperance Avery (No. 79), had son

37 CHRISTOPHER, b. Oct. 27, 1747, m. Martha Gates April 3, 1808. Their son
38 WILLIAM, b. March 28, 1809, m. Cynthia Billings (No. 176), that family. Their son, Christopher Morgan, m. Edith Noyes and lives at Mystic.

William Avery Morgan (No. 36), who m. Temperance Avery (No. 79), had son

39 ISRAEL, b. July 22, 1757, m. Elizabeth Brewster July 22, 1777 (No. 13), that family. He served in the army of the Revolution, and d. June 4, 1816.

CHILDREN:

40 ELIZABETH, b. Jan. 7, 1779, m. Stephen Avery (No. 159), that family, Aug. 18, 1804. Their daughter, Frances Mary Avery, m. Richard A. Wheeler (No. 429), that family.
41 SYBIL, b. Aug. 27, 1780, m. Edward Swan, Jr., of Stonington Dec., 1804 (No. 98), that family.
42 DOLLY, b. Nov. 23, 1781, d. unmarried July 25, 1867.
43 MARY (twin), b. Nov. 23, 1781, d. Jan. 11, 1782, aged 2 months.
44 TEMPERANCE, b. April 27, 1783, m. Guy Fitch Adams July 7, 1811.
45 POLLY, b. Feb. 27, 1785, m. John Brewster Feb. 5, 1806. Their son John Brewster, Jr., m. Mary E. Williams April 2, 1840 (No. 528), Robert Williams family. They live on the old Israel Morgan farm, Poquetanock, Conn.
46 AMY, b. Feb. 27, 1785 (twin), m. Amos Chapman of Preston. Their son, Francis Morgan Chapman, m. Lucy Freeman, and had three children. (1) William Chapman of Norwich, m. Lucy Perry; (2) Emma Chapman, m. Andrew Green; (3) Abby Prudence Temperance, m. Senator Nelson Aldrich of Providence, R. I.
47 HANNAH, b. May 18, 1787, m. Jonathan Stoddard Dec. 26, 1812.
48 PRUDENCE, b. May 18, 1790, m. Eldridge Havens June 2, 1831.
49 ISRAEL FITCH, b. Dec. 11, 1792, m. Lucy Stoddard Dec. 25, 1813.
50 BELA, b. Dec. 22, 1794, m. Charlotte Stoddard April 20, 1817.
51 WEALTHA, b. Jan. 11, 1798, m. Amos Turner Dec. 5, 1824.

MOSS FAMILY.

1. JOHN MOSS, the ancestor of the Moss family of Stonington, Conn., was born in England about 1619. Emigrated and settled at New Haven in 1639, and removed to Wallingford, Conn., 1670. The family name of his wife and the date of marriage is unknown.

CHILDREN:

2 MERCY, b. ——— .
3 JOHN, b. Oct. 12, 1650.
4 JOSEPH, b. Oct., 1651.
5 Daughter, b. ———, m. Thomas Kent of Upper Wallop, Eng.
6 HESTER, b. Jan. 2, 1653-4.
7 JOHN, b. ———, m. and lived in Newton Co., Wilts, Eng.

John Moss (No. 3) m. Martha Lathrop Dec. 12, 1677, d. Sept. 21, 1719.

CHILDREN:

8 ESTHER, b. Jan. 5, 1678-9.
9 DEA. SAMUEL, b. Nov. 10, 1680.
10 JOHN, b. Nov. 10, 1682.
11 MARTHA, b. Dec. 22, 1684.
12 SOLOMAN, b. July 9, 1690.
13 ISAAC, b. July 9, 1692.
14 MARY, b. July 23, 1694.
15 ISRAEL, b. Dec. 21, 1696.
16 BENJAMIN, b. Feb. 10, 1702.

Isaac Moss (No. 13) m. Hannah Royse May 2, 1717, d. March 1, 1736, at Cheshire; m. 2d wife, Keziah Bowers Oct. 14, 1736, d. Nov. 19, 1770.

CHILDREN:

17 HEMAN, b. July 21, 1718.
18 HANNAH, b. May 7, 1722.
19 ISAAC, b. Nov. 5, 1724.
20 HEMAN, b. Jan. 12, 1727.
21 JESSE, b. March 10, 1729.
22 ELIHU, b. May 25, 1731.
23 MEHITABLE, b. May 7, 1735.
24 EBENEZER, b. at Cheshire.
25 JABEZ, b. Jan. 23, 1741.

Capt. Jesse Moss (No. 21) m. Mary Moss Jan. 25, 1753. Inherited the farm cleared by his father on Ten-mile River in war, and was present with his company at the evacuation of Boston by British troops, 1776. He d. March 20, 1793; his wife d. Aug. 19, 1819, at Cheshire.

CHILDREN:

26 HANNAH, b. Jan. 19, 1754.
27 JOEL, b. Dec. 17, 1755.
28 JESSE, b. Sept. 10, 1757.

MOSS FAMILY.

29 REUBEN, b. June 11, 1759, m. Esther Chesebrough, of that family.
30 JOB, b. Sept. 26, 1761.
31 MARY, b. Feb. 25, 1763-4.
32 ISAAC, b. March 16, 1765.
33 LOTHROP, b. Feb. 8, 1768.
34 CLARINA, b. April 13, 1770.
35 RUFUS, b. July 1, 1772.
36 EMANUEL, b. June 2, 1774.
37 MARY CLARINA, b. April 4, 1777.

Rev. Reuben Moss (No. 29) m. Esther Chesebrough of Stonington, Conn, Aug. 15, 1795 (No. 323), Chesebrough family. At the age of 16 years he entered the American army as waiter with his father, and subsequently enlisted during the war. But on receiving his discharge in 1783, he commenced a regular course of studies, overtook scholars in advanced standing and graduated with honor from Yale College in 1787. He was ordained in 1792, over the Congregational Church of Ware, Mass., and was their pastor for over sixteen years. After his death his widow, with seven children, returned to her girlhood home in Stonington, Conn., the place now occupied by Col. James F. Brown.

CHILDREN:

38 LAZARUS, b. Feb. 9, 1797, afterward Ephraim C., d. at Westerly, R. I., Jan., 1843.
39 MARY ESTHER, b. Nov. 4, 1798, d. unmarried.
40 GEORGE WASHINGTON, b. April 21, 1800, m. Caroline E., daughter of Dr. Phineas Hyde of Old Mystic, April 30, 1821 (No. 27), Hyde family. He was a merchant at New Orleans.
41 TIRZAH, b. March 16, 1802, m. Henry C. Tyler of Griswold, Conn., March 25, 1828.
42 WILLIAM CHESEBROUGH, b. Dec. 9, 1803, m. Caroline Edith Denison Nov. 12, 1832 (No. 603), that family.
43 JESSE LATHROP, b. Oct. 23, 1805, m. Fanny S. Dixon, daughter of Hon. Nathan Fellows Dixon. Mrs. Moss died Dec. 11, 1850. He m. 2d, his wife's sister, Sally Rhodes Dixon, March 26, 1873. He d. July 20, 1884.
44 REUBEN E., b. Sept. 1, 1807, m. Harriet N. Randall Sept. 23, 1841 (No. 105), Randall family. He d. in Elmira, N. Y., Oct. 26, 1896, in his 90th year.

NOYES FAMILY.

Rev. William Noyes, ancestor of the Stonington family of this name, was born in England in 1568. He was instituted rector of Cholderton in 1602, and continued so for about 20 years. He m. Anne Parker about 1595, who was b. in 1575, and buried at Cholderton, England, March 7, 1657, aged 82 years. William Noyes departed this life about 1616, and his son, Nathan Noyes, succeeded him to the rectorship and continued so for 32 years, dying in 1651, Sept. 6, aged 54 years.

NOTE.—It seems the statement that the family name of Noyes in England was originally Noye is a mistake. From all that has been ascertained, the name originated in Normandy and the family name there was Des Noyers, the latter word meaning "Walnut Tree." The tendency being always to shorten rather than lengthen family names. The Doomsday book has recorded as one of the followers of William the Conqueror "William Des Noyers," William of the Walnut Tree.

It has been supposed and currently stated that Rev. William Noyes, rector of Cholderton, was related to the William Noyes who was Attorney General to Charles the First, but I have never seen proof of it, and I find that Prof. James Atkins Noyes and Col. Henry E. Noyes, who have made an exhaustive study of the Noyes family, are of the same opinion.

1. REV. WILLIAM NOYES and Anne Parker, sister of Rev. Robert Parker, were m. about 1595.

CHILDREN:

2 EPHRAIM, b. in 1596, m. a Parnell, buried at Cholderton Oct. 28, 1659.
3 NATHAN, b. in 1597, m. Mary ———, d. Sept. 6, 1651.
4 JAMES, b. in Cholderton, Eng., in 1608.
5 Daughter, b ———, m. Thomas Kent of Upper Wallop, Eng.
6 NICHOLAS, b. in 1614, m. Mary Cutting.
7 JOHN, b. ———, m. and lived in Newton Co., Wilts, Eng.

James Noyes (No. 4) and Nicholas Noyes (No. 6) came to New England, and from them sprung the line of Noyes' whose descendants are found nearly all over the United States.

James Noyes (No. 4) m. in 1634 Sarah, eldest daughter of Mr. Joseph Brown of Southampton, Eng., and in March of that year embarked for New England, in company with his brother Nicholas and his cousin, Thomas Parker, in the "Mary and John" of London. He preached for a short time at Medford, and then for a while at the Watertown church, but in 1635 went to Newbury, Mass., and preached there till his death, Oct. 22, 1656. Mrs. Sarah Brown Noyes d. Sept. 13, 1691. Mr. James Noyes was very much loved and honored in Newbury, and it was said of him that "He was of so loving and compassionate and humble carriage that there never was any one acquainted with him, but did desire the continuance of his society and acquaintance." He had a fine voice, and with his cousin Thomas Parker spent much time in singing and praising God, both at home and at divine worship. He had a long and tedious sickness, which he bore patiently and cheerfully, and d. joyfully in the 48th year of his age. He left six sons and two daughters, all of whom lived to be m. and have children. His will, dated Oct. 17, 1656, which was six days before his death, is preserved, and his inventory showed a good estate.

CHILDREN:

8 JOSEPH, b. Oct. 15, 1637, m. 1st, Mary Darrell in 1662; had eight children; after her death he m. 2d, Mary Willard, d. in Newbury, 1717.
9 JAMES, b. March 11, 1640, m. Dorothy Stanton.
10 SARAH, b. Aug. 12, 1641, d. young.
11 MOSES, b. Dec. 6, 1643, m. Ruth Picket.
12 JOHN, b. June 3, 1645.
13 THOMAS, b. Aug. 10, 1648, m. Martha Pierce.
14 REBECCA, b. April 1, 1651.
15 WILLIAM, b. Sept. 22, 1653, m. Sarah Cogswell.
16 SARAH, b. March 25, 1656, m. Rev. John Hale, March 31, 1684, and d. May 20, 1695, leaving four children.

Nicholas Noyes (No. 6) m. Mary, daughter of Capt. John Cutting. He was associated with Mr. James Noyes and Mr. Thomas Parker of Newbury, Mass., and the friendship was continued till death.

CHILDREN:

17 MARY, b. Oct. 15, 1641, m. John French.
18 HANNAH, b. Oct. 30, 1643, m. Peter Cheney March 14, 1663; m. 2d, John Atkinson.
19 JOHN, b. Jan. 20, 1646.
20 NICHOLAS, b. Dec. 22, 1647, d. Dec. 13, 1717.
21 CUTTING, b. Sept. 23, 1649.
22 SARAH, b. Sept. 13, 1651, d. young.
23 SARAH, b. Aug. 22, 1653, m. Matthew Pettingill Sept. 15, 1674.
24 TIMOTHY, b. June 23, 1655.
25 JAMES, b. May 16, 1657.
26 ABIGAIL, b. April 11, 1659, m. Simon French May 3, 1707.
27 RACHEL, b. May 10, 1661, m. James Jackman.
28 THOMAS, b. June 20, 1663.
29 REBECCA, b. May 18, 1665, d. Dec. 21, 1683.

Nicholas Noyes (No. 6) d. Nov. 23, 1701.

Rev. James Noyes (No. 9) came to Stonington to preach on an invitation of the town in 1664. The meeting house in which he preached was a short distance southwesterly of the present residence of Mr. Henry M. Palmer, west of Montauk avenue. Traditionally, we learn that he resided in the family of Thomas Stanton, Sr., until he was ordained Sept. 11, 1674, and the next day he was married to Miss Dorothy Stanton (No. 8), of Stanton family, daughter of Thomas and Ann (Lord) Stanton. He made his permanent place of abode upon a large tract of land in Stonington, Conn., which he purchased of Samuel Willis of Hartford, Conn., where he erected him a dwelling house on the site of the present first house, south of Anguilla on the highway from there to Wequetequock, which became the first parsonage of the First Congregational Church of Stonington, where he lived the remainder of his life, dying Dec. 30, 1719. For the first ten years of his ministry he preached as a licentiate, and the last 45 years as an ordained clergyman. He was chaplain with Capt. George Denison's expedition that captured Canonchet, chief sachem of the Narragansett Indians, April, 1676.

CHILDREN:
30 DOROTHY, b. June 20, 1675, m. Rev. Salmon Treat.
31 DR. JAMES, b. Aug. 2, 1677, m. Anna Sanford.
32 THOMAS, b. Aug. 15, 1679, m. Elizabeth Sanford.
33 ANN, b. April 16, 1682, d. young.
34 JOHN, b. Jan. 13, 1685, m. Mary Gallup.
35 JOSEPH, b. Oct. 18, 1688, m. Abigail Pierpont.
36 MOSES, b. March 19, 1692, d. young.

Mrs. Dorothy Noyes d. Jan. 19, 1743, in her 91st year.

Moses Noyes (No. 11) m. Ruth, daughter of John Picket, of New London, Conn. He was the first minister of Lyme, Conn., where he preached for 50 years, and d. Nov. 10, 1726.

Thomas Noyes (No. 13) m. Martha Pierce Dec. 28, 1669.

CHILDREN:
37 SARAH, b. Sept. 14, 1670.
38 MARTHA, b. Feb. 24, 1673.
39 DANIEL, b. Aug. 3, 1674.

Mrs. Martha Noyes d. ———, and Mr. Thomas Noyes m. for his second wife, Elizabeth, daughter of Stephen Greenleaf, Sept. 24, 1677.

CHILDREN:
40 JAMES, b. July 3, 1678.
41 THOMAS, b. Oct. 2, 1679.
42 PARKER, b. Oct. 29, 1681.
43 ELIZABETH, b. Feb. 29, 1684.
44 JOSEPH, b. Aug. 5, 1688.
45 MOSES, b. Jan. 29, 1692.
46 REBECCA, b. April 19, 1700.
47 JUDITH, b. April 17, 1702.

William Noyes (No. 15) m. Sarah Cogswell Nov. 6, 1685.

CHILDREN:
48 JOHN, b. July 27, 1688.
49 WILLIAM, b. Sept. 11, 1689.

NOYES FAMILY. 487

50 SARAH, b. May 10, 1691, d. young.
51 MOSES, b. Jan. 27, 1694, d. young.
52 SUSANNAH, b. Feb. 25, 1696.
53 MARY, b. May 24, 1699, d. young.
54 SARAH, b. June 5, 1703, d. young.
55 PARKER, b. Jan. 17, 1705.

John Noyes (No. 19) m. Mary, daughter of John Poor, Nov. 23, 1668.

CHILDREN:

56 NICHOLAS, b. May 18, 1671.
57 DANIEL, b. Oct. 23, 1673.
58 MARY, b. Dec. 10, 1675.
59 JOHN, b. Feb. 15, 1678.
60 MARTHA, b. Dec. 24, 1679, d. young.
61 MARTHA, b. Dec. 19, 1680.
62 NATHANIEL, b. Oct. 28, 1691.
63 ELIZABETH, b. Nov. 15, 1694.
64 MOSES, b. May 22, 1688.
65 SAMUEL, b. Dec. 9, 1692.

Cutting Noyes (No. 21) m. Elizabeth, daughter of John Knight Feb. 25, 1674.

CHILDREN:

66 JOHN, b. Dec., 1674.
67 CUTTING, b. Jan. 28, 1677.
68 ELIZABETH, b. Jan. 2, 1679.
69 NICHOLAS, b. May 22, 1681, d. young.
70 JOSEPH, b. Jan. 21, 1682.
71 MARY, b. March 27, 1683.

Timothy Noyes (No. 24) m. Mary, daughter of John Knight, Jan. 13, 1681.

CHILDREN:

72 JAMES, b. March 12, 1684.
73 ABIGAIL, b. Feb. 28, 1685.
74 MARY, b. Dec. 28, 1686.
75 SARAH, b. March 26, 1689.
76 TIMOTHY, b. Jan. 25, 1691.
77 RACHEL, b. Feb. 6, 1694.
78 JOHN, b. Feb. 19, 1696.
79 MARTHA, b. March 14, 1697.
80 NICHOLAS, b. March 7, 1701.

Mr. Timothy Noyes d. in 1718.

James Noyes (No. 25) m. Hannah, daughter of John Knight, March 31, 1684.

CHILDREN:

81 REBECCA, b. Jan. 12, 1685.
82 JOSEPH, b. Sept. 20, 1686.
83 HANNAH, b. March 13, 1688.
84 NICHOLAS, b. Feb. 9, 1690.
85 NATHAN, b. Feb. 5, 1692.
86 EPHRAIM, b. Nov. 20, 1694, d. young.
87 LYDIA, b. Nov. 30, 1695.
88 EPHRAIM, b. Dec. 25, 1698.

89 BENJAMIN, b. Feb. 22, 1701.
90 MARY, b. March 12, 1703.
91 JAMES, b. Aug. 19, 1705.

Thomas Noyes (No. 28) m. Sarah ———.

CHILDREN:

92 BETHIA, b. Oct. 20, 1691.
93 REBECCA, b. Jan. 20, 1694, d. young.

Dorothy Noyes (No. 30) m. Rev. Salmon Treat April 12, 1698. He was son of James and Rebecca (Lattimer) Treat of Wethersfield, Conn. Dorothy d. at Preston, Conn., Dec. 8, 1714, and Rev. Salmon Treat m. Mrs. Parks, widow of Capt. John Parks. He d. at Preston Jan. 5, 1762, aged 90 years. His second m. was Nov. 6, 1716.

CHILDREN:

94 ANNA TREAT, b. Aug. 26, 1699.
95 JAMES TREAT, b. Nov. 29, 1700.
96 DOROTHY TREAT, b. Feb. 9, 1702.
97 JERUSHA TREAT, b. Feb. 21, 1704.
98 PRUDENCE TREAT, b. Nov. 23, 1706.
99 SARAH TREAT, b. Sept. 19, 1708.
100 REBECCA TREAT, b. June 29, 1710.
101 SAMUEL (REV.) TREAT, b. July 21, 1712.
102 JEMIMA TREAT, b. Nov. 27, 1714.

Dr. James Noyes (No. 31) m. Anna, daughter of Gov. Peleg Sanford of Rhode Island. They lived at Noyes's Beach, R. I., on land bought of Harmon Garret, a Niantic chief. Ann Sanford was also granddaughter of Gov. William Coddington of Rhode Island. Dr. James Noyes d. in 1718, and his widow m. Capt. John Mason, son of Maj. John Mason July 15, 1719 (No. 18) of Mason family.

CHILDREN:

103 ANN, bapt. June 19, 1704, m. James Brown, Jr., of Newport, R. I. See Chad Brown family (No. 38).
104 MARY, b. in 1706, m. John Denison (No. 126), Denison family.
105 JAMES, b. May 2, 1708.
106 BRIDGET, bapt. July 30, 1710, m. Nathan Chesebrough (No. 67), that family.
107 DOROTHY, bapt. Dec. 22, 1712, m. John Brown (No. 39), in Chad Brown family.
108 SARAH, b. April 2, 1715, m. Rev. Jonathan Barber Nov. 2, 1740.
109 ELIPHAL, bapt. June 23, 1717, m. Rev. Oliver Prentice (No. 19), that family.

Capt. Thomas Noyes (No. 32) was captain of the Stonington Train Band, 1723. He m. Elizabeth Sanford, sister of Ann Sanford, who m. Dr. James Noyes. They were of Newport, R. I., and were m. Sept. 3, 1705. He d. June 26, 1755.

NOTE.—Capt. Thomas Noyes, the third child of Rev. James and wife, Dorothy (Stanton) Noyes, and his son, James Noyes, were Colonial officers. Also Col. Joseph Noyes, son of Capt. Thomas Noyes and Elizabeth Sanford, his wife, with three of his sons, Thomas, Joseph and Sanford, were Revolutionary soldiers.

NOYES FAMILY.

CHILDREN:
110 ELIZABETH, bapt. Dec. 22, 1706, m. Ichabod Palmer (No. 137), Palmer family.
111 DOROTHY, bapt. June 23, 1706, m. John Palmer (No. 28), Palmer family.
112 THOMAS, bapt. April 16, 1710.
113 MARY, bapt. Jan. 26, 1711, m. Ebenezer Billings (No. 46), Billings family.
114 JAMES, b. March 30, 1713, m. Grace Billings.
115 SANFORD, b. Nov. 29, 1715, d. young.
116 SANFORD, b. Feb. 12, 1717, m. Mary Lawton Nov. 24, 1738.
117 REBEKAH, b. March 15, 1719, m. Capt. John Denison (No. 126), Denison family.
118 ABIGAIL, b. May 12, 1721, m. John Hallam (No. 7), Hallam family.
119 ANN, b. June 10, 1723, m. Isaac Frink (No. 33), Frink family.
120 BRIDGET, b. July 16, 1725, m. Isaac Wheeler (No. 55); he was drowned in Indian Town Pond in 1749, and Mrs. Bridget Wheeler m. 2d, Dea. Joseph Denison April 23, 1751 (No. 131), Denison family.
121 JOSEPH, b. Oct. 9, 1727.

Dea. John Noyes (No. 34) m. Mary Gallup (No. 41) of Gallup family, March 16, 1714-5.

CHILDREN:
122 WILLIAM, b. March 18, 1715-16.
123 JOHN, b. May 22, 1718.
124 JOSEPH, b. April 1, 1721, d. young.
125 JAMES, b. April 14, 1723.
126 MARY, b. Aug. 14, 1725, m. Joseph Champlin of Westerly, R. I.
127 SARAH, b. Feb. 10, 1728, m. Andrew Stanton (No. 339), Stanton family.
128 ANNA, b. April 23, 1729, m. John Palmer (No. 125), Palmer family.
129 JOSEPH, b. Feb. 29, 1730, m. Prudence Denison.

Mary, wife of Dea. John Noyes, d. May 13, 1736, and Dea. John m. for his second wife Mrs. Elizabeth Whiting of Montville, Conn., March 13, 1739. He d. Sept. 17, 1751.

CHILDREN:
130 DOROTHY, b. March 24, 1740. No further record.

Dea. John Noyes's second wife, Mrs. Elizabeth Whiting's name in girlhood was Elizabeth Bradford, b. Dec. 15, 1697. She d. May 10, 1777. She was great-granddaughter of Gov. William Bradford, second governor of Plymouth Colony. Her husband was Lieut. Charles Whiting, b. July 1, 1692, and d. at Montville, March 7, 1738. He was son of Lieut. Col. William Whiting.

Rev. Joseph Noyes (No. 35) graduated at Yale College in 1709, and was ordained pastor of the First Church of New Haven, Conn., July 4, 1716, and he remained there until his death, June 14, 1761. He m. Abigail Pierpont, eldest daughter of Rev. James Pierpont Nov. 6, 1716.

CHILDREN:
131 JOSEPH, b. Aug. 6, 1718, d. young.
132 SARAH, b. March 19, 1722, d. young.
133 ABIGAIL, b. March 20, 1724, m. Thomas Darling of New Haven, Conn., d. in 1797.

134 JOSEPH, b. Sept. 25, 1726, d. young.
135 JOSEPH, b. Feb. 29, 1728, d. young.
136 DOROTHY, b. Jan. 3, 1730, d. young.
137 ANNA, b. Nov. 14, 1731, d. young.
138 JAMES, b. Dec. 13, 1733, d. young.
139 JOHN, b. Dec. 15, 1735.

Thomas Noyes (No. 112) m. Mary Thompson, daughter of Isaac and Mary (Holmes) Thompson, of Westerly, R. I., May 1, 1731.

CHILDREN:

140 THOMAS, b. ———.
141 WILLIAM, b. July 16, 1739.
142 NATHAN, b. ———.

The record of these children are obtained from the will of their grandfather, Capt. Thomas Noyes, dated 1755.

James Noyes (No. 114) m. Grace Billings (No. 48), that family, June 22, 1739. He d. April 19, 1793; she d. June 22, 1792.

CHILDREN:

143 PELEG, b. May 29, 1741.
144 JAMES, b. July 15, 1744.
145 GRACE, b. Dec. 20, 1746, m. Nathaniel Palmer Aug. 18, 1765. See Palmer family (No. 242).
146 ELIZABETH PALMER,, b. Nov. 4, 1750, m. Elisha Denison April 4, 1772. See Denison family (No. 241).
147 THOMAS, b. July 16, 1755.
148 PHEBE, b. Feb. 6, 1753. No record.
149 REBECCA, b. March 23, 1759. Never married.
150 BRIDGET, b. Feb. 6, 1763. Never married.

Col. Joseph Noyes (No. 121) m. Barbery Wells July 31, 1753. She was daughter of James Wells and Mary Barker. He d. March 13, 1802.

NOTE.—Col. Joseph Noyes (No. 121) and Joshua Babcock of Westerly, R. I., were members of the House of Representatives of Rhode Island in 1776 and voted for the "Act to repeal an act for the maintenance of the King's authority in Rhode Island." This act was passed several years before the "Declaration of Independence" was signed in Philadelphia, July 4, 1776.

CHILDREN:

151 THOMAS, b. Oct. 5, 1754, d. Sept. 19, 1759.
152 SANFORD, b. Oct. 20, 1756, d. Sept. 30, 1759.
153 JOSEPH, b. May 9, 1758, d. in 1847.
154 SANFORD, b. Jan. 18, 1761, d. Aug. 8, 1843.
155 POLLY, b. Oct. 11, 1763, m. Thomas Noyes (No. 147).
156 DR. JAMES, b. Feb. 8, 1768, d. Nov. 6, 1856.
157 ELIZABETH, b. July 30, 1770, never m., d. Sept. 15, 1845.
158 JOSHUA, b. Dec. 5, 1772, d. Oct. 13, 1856.
159 BARKER, b. March 13, 1775, d. in 1864.

James Noyes (No. 125) m. Margaret Woodburn Aug. 12, 1756, and afterwards removed from Stonington.

CHILDREN:

160 MARGARET, b. July 9, 1757, d. July 5, 1777.
161 ESTHER, b. June 26, 1759, m. Adam States April 11, 1778, d. Feb. 2, 1787.

162 MARY, b. April 26, 1761, m. 1st, John Pendleton Feb. 4, 1784, and 2d, Adam States, her sister's husband.
163 SARAH, b. July 22, 1763.
164 ELIZABETH, b. April 3, 1766.

Joseph Noyes (No. 129) m. Prudence Denison (No. 189), Jan. 27, 1763.

CHILDREN:

165 PRUDENCE, b. March 5, 1764, m. Henry Thorn of Westerly Jan. 20, 1785.
166 SARAH, b. Feb. 18, 1766, m. ——— Burdick.
167 JOSEPH, b. Sept. 30, 1768.
168 AVERY, b. Feb. 13, 1771.
169 THANKFUL, b. Oct. 29, 1773, m. Thomas Stanton Feb. 28, 1793. See Stanton family (No. 303).
170 ZERVIAH, b. Oct. 5, 1775, m. Rev. William Stillman of Westerly.
171 JOHN, b. Aug. 9, 1777, d. April 20, 1866.
172 ANNA, b. Jan. 13, 1780, m. Elijah Darrow Feb. 20, 1798.
173 REBECCA, b. March 6, 1782, m. Edward Stewart (No. 36), of Stewart family.
174 POLLY or MARY, b. March 8, 1784, m. Samuel Stanton (No. 358), Stanton family.
175 DENISON, b. March 8, 1788, m. Hannah Russell Stanton (No. 392), the Stanton family.

John Noyes (No. 139) m. Mary (No. 2), daughter of Rev. Joseph Fish of Stonington, Conn., Nov. 16, 1759. They had six children, but three d. young.

CHILDREN:

176 JOSEPH, b. Feb. 14, 1761, m. Amelia Burr; 2d, Lucy Morton.
177 JOHN, b. Aug. 27, 1763, m. Mrs. Fanny (Palmer) Swan (No. 385) of the Palmer family.
178 REV. JAMES, b. Aug. 4, 1764.

Mr. John Noyes d. in 1767, and his widow m. Gold Selleck Silliman.

CHILDREN:

179 GOLD SELLECK SILLIMAN, b. Oct. 26, 1777, at Fairfield, Conn.
180 BENJAMIN, b. Aug. 8, 1779, at North Stratford, Conn.

Thomas Noyes (No. 140) married Mary Cobb (No. 29) of the Cobb family, Jan. 24, 1760. He died in 1831, aged 92 years, and she died March, 1833, aged 94 years.

CHILDREN:

181 OLIVER, b. in 1768, at Stonington, Conn., d. near Rochester, N. Y., about 1838. He m. at Charlotte, Vt., about 1795, and his wife d. at the same place about 1805, at which place their only son, Oliver J. Noyes, was b. in 1802.
182 NATHAN, b. ———, m. Nancy Chapel.
183 NATHANIEL, b. in 1771, d. Nov. 27, 1854, m. Mary Saunders.
183a ERASTUS, b. ———.
184 GEORGE, b. ———.
185 HENRY, b. ———.
186 CAPT. BENJAMIN, b. in 1780, and d. a bachelor at Staten Island Dec. 7, 1847, aged 67 years. He commanded a ship running between New York and Italy for more than twelve years.
187 SUSANNAH, b. ———, d. young.

188 SUSANNAH, b. and m. Henry Harvey April 15, 1784. The date of her birth is not known, but she was probably one of the oldest children.
189 POLLY, b. ——, m. Capt. Richard Burnett of Burnett's Corners, near Mystic, Conn.
190 BETSEY, b. ——, d. Sept. 7, 1860; m. 1st, —— Haggett, has descendants in Lebanon; m. 2d, John Hale of Boston, Sept. 26, 1813.

William Noyes (No. 141) m. Sarah Fanning, daughter of John and wife Abigail (Minor) Fanning, Aug. 14, 1763.

CHILDREN:

191 SARAH, b. April 25, 1764, m. a —— Greene in Charlestown, R. I.
192 WILLIAM, b. May 17, 1766, d. at New London, Conn.
193 FREDERICK, b. May 30, 1768, went to Pennsylvania, and it is supposed d. there, as nothing is known about his family.
194 ROBERT F., b. ——, went to South Kingston, R. I., when a young man, m. Sarah, daughter of Samuel and Mary (Nichols) Arnold, and d. there aged over 70 years. He had eight sons and four daughters, viz.: Azel, who m. the youngest daughter of Arnold Sherman, named Sarah, had four children; d. May, 1879; Mary Noyes, m. Jeremiah C. Peckham; Arnold, Alfred, Elizabeth and Robert, who all d. in infancy. Sarah Noyes m. William Tisdale, d. in 1877. Susan Noyes never m., d. 1877. Edwin Noyes m. and lived in Maine. James Noyes was a physician in Detroit, Mich. Thomas Noyes m. and had three sons, viz.: Robert, who is a physician in Providence; also Lucien and George Noyes.
195 JOSHUA, b. Aug. 4, 1772, m., had children, d. Nov. 1, 1845. Mrs. William Noyes (nee Fanning) was b. at Groton, Conn., March 18, 1743, and was the daughter of John and wife, Abigail (Minor) Fanning. After her husband, William Noyes, was lost at sea she m. 2d, Maj. Ebenezer Adams. He d. at South Kingston, R. I., about 1797. By Maj. Adams she had five children, viz.: John, Hattie, Samuel, Nathan and Ethan Adams.

Nathan Noyes (No. 142) m. Lydia, daughter of Nathaniel and wife, Hopestill (Holdredge) Fellows, Sept. 23, 1770. See Fellows family (No. 28).

CHILDREN:

196 NATHAN, b. Jan. 16, 1775.
197 JOHN, b. ——.
198 LYDIA, b. ——, m. James Clark.
199 PRUDENCE, b. ——, m. John Gibbs.
200 DANIEL, b. ——, d. aged 22 years.

Col. Peleg Noyes (No. 143) m. Prudence Williams June 1, 1763. See Williams family (No. 204).

CHILDREN:

201 PELEG, b. Feb. 4, 1764.
202 JOHN, b. Sept. 27, 1765, m. Elizabeth Stanton.
203 ELIHU, b. Dec. 3, 1767.
204 DESIRE, b. Jan. 30, 1770.
205 LYDIA, b. Dec. 28, 1771, d. May 27, 1772.
206 Daughter, b. Aug. 9, d. Aug. 10, 1774.
207 EBENEZER, b. Aug. 9, 1775.
208 NATHANIEL, b. April 22, 1778, m. 1st, —— Slack, and 2d, Ruby West (No. 81), Dec. 31, 1826.
209 LYDIA, b. Jan. 4, 1781, d. Jan. 20, 1781.
210 GRACE, b. Jan. 4, 1781 (twin), m. Joshua Noyes (No. 158).
211 HANNAH, b. Oct. 17, 1784.

James Noyes (No. 144) m. Eunice Denison (No. 442), Dec. 2, 1772. She d. April 25, 1801, and he d. Aug. 5, 1731.

CHILDREN:

212 EDWARD D., b. Sept. 2, 1773, m. Sally Avery.
213 LOIS, b. May 1, 1776, m. John Slack.
214 JAMES, b. March 29, 1779, m. Lewis Stanton.
215 JESSE D., b. March 14, 1781, never m.
216 NATHANIEL M., b. Nov. 15, 1783, m. Mary Slack.
217 JOHN D., b. April 19, 1786; m. 1st, Ann Collins (No. 16), that family, and 2d, Hannah Sutton.
218 CHARLES P., b. Sept. 27, 1789, m. Sophia Palmer (No. 305) of Palmer family.

Thomas Noyes (No. 147) m. his cousin, Mary or Polly Noyes (No. 155), April 14, 1799, d. March 17, 1844.

CHILDREN:

219 GEORGE W., b. Jan. 15, 1800, d. March 6, 1849, m. Martha B. Noyes (No. 242), Noyes family, July 7, 1845.
220 PHEBE, b. Nov. 29, 1801.
221 THOMAS, b. April 14, 1804.
222 HENRY, b. Jan. 10, 1807.

Thomas Noyes (No. 151) m. Lydia Rogers Jan. 31, 1781.

CHILDREN:

222 SARAH, b. Dec. 6, 1781, d. young.
223 WILLIAM R., b. March 19, 1783, m. Eliza Dalton, Jan., 1813; had five children and lived in Rhode Island.
224 JAMES W., b. Dec. 22, 1784.
225 THOMAS, b. Nov. 22, 1786, m. Hannah Phelps (No. 46), Phelps family, Feb. 28, 1813.
226 JOSEPH, b. Nov. 29, 1788, m. 1st, Martha C. Thompson March 30, 1814; m. 2d, Prudence Cory.
227 MARTHA, b. April 25, 1791, m. Dr. Richard Noyes of Lyme, 1814.
228 DANIEL, b. Oct. 22, 1793, m. Phebe C. Lord May 16, 1827.
229 ABIGAIL, b. Sept. 29, 1795, m. Henry Perkins of Salem, Conn., March 19, 1820.
230 SANFORD, b. Nov. 4, 1797, d. young.

Joseph Noyes (No. 153) m. Elizabeth Babcock (No. 184), daughter of Rowse and wife, Ruth (Maxson) Babcock, Jan. 13, 1799.

CHILDREN:

231 ELIZA, b. July 2, 1800, m. Sylvester Robinson, d. Sept. 19, 1885.
232 RHODA A., b. Jan. 4, 1802, d. young.
233 RHODA A., b. Jan. 3, 1803, never m., d. Sept., 1827.
234 ROWSE B., b. Feb. 2, 1805, never m., d. Sept. 1, 1829.
235 CHARLES, b. Feb. 11, 1807, never m., d. Aug. 17, 1879.
236 BENJAMIN, b. June 14, 1811, m. Eunice Miner (No. 350), of Miner family, and d. Sept. 20, 1843.
237 RUTH, b. March 19, 1809, m. Edwin Allen, d. Aug. 19, 1861.
238 COURTLANDT, b. Dec. 6, 1813, m. Susan King, d. April 16, 1886.

Sanford Noyes (No. 154) m. Martha Babcock Feb. 2, 1800. She was daughter of Hezekiah and Martha (Hoxie) Babcock (No. 104) of Hopkinton, Rhode Island.

CHILDREN:

239 ANN M., b. July 6, 1801, m. Capt. Robert Brown.
240 DEA. SANFORD, b. Jan. 9, 1802, m. Eunice Witter Dec. 19, 1836.
241 LYDIA R., b. Sept. 1, 1804, m. Dr. Joseph D. Kenyon Oct. 11, 1829.
242 MARTHA B., b. March 11, 1806, m. George W .Noyes July 7, 1845 (No. 219).
243 SUSAN, b. Dec. 6, 1808, m. Peleg Kenyon.
244 LUKE B., b. April 20, 1810, m. Mary Ann Noyes.
245 GIDEON H., b. Oct. 4, 1814, m. Lois B. Dickens.
246 ELIZA, b. Oct. 4, 1814 (twin), m. Albert Witter.

Dr. James Noyes (No. 156) m. 1st, Fanny Wells and 2d, Nancy Wells, and 3d, Rebecca Clark, Dec. 19, 1872.

CHILDREN:

247 FRANCES, b. Oct. 20, 1805, she m. Dr. Joseph D. Kenyon and d. Dec. 20, 1825.

Joshua Noyes (No. 158) m. Grace Noyes (No. 210) May 6, 1810.

CHILDREN:

248 GRACE, b. Sept. 19, 1811, d. unmarried.
249 JOSHUA, b. June 6, 1814, m. Hannah W. Palmer (No. 487), March 8, 1848, and he d. March 27, 1888.
250 PELEG, b. June 18, 1816, m. Catharine Hazard Nov. 30, 1848, and d. Jan. 11, 1894.
251 BARBERY, b. Feb. 16, 1819, d. Sept. 23, 1861, unmarried.
252 FANNY, b. Feb. 7, 1822.

Barker Noyes (No. 159) m. Margaret Champlin March 18, 1810.

CHILDREN:

253 WILLIAM C., b. March 22, 1813, d. Sept. 20, 1874.
254 JOSEPH B., b. Nov. 25, 1814.
255 MARGARET D., b. Nov. 2, 1816.
256 JOHN D., b. Nov. 15, 1818, d. Feb. 3, 1823.
257 ROBERT B., b. March 6, 1821.
258 JOHN D., b. Sept. 26, 1823.
259 DAVID M., b. Dec. 20, 1826.
260 MARY E., b. Nov. 13, 1828, d. Feb. 14, 1829.
261 MARY E., b. Jan. 2, 1832.

Joseph Noyes (No. 167) m. Zerviah, daughter of Paul and wife Lucy (Swan) Wheeler (No. 104), on Nov. 30, 1790. He d. Aug. 24, 1852. She d. Aug. 6, 1806.

CHILDREN:

262 WILLIAM, b. Aug. 30, 1791, d. young.
263 JOSEPH, b. Feb. 25, 1793.
264 THOMAS, b. April 5, 1795.
265 PAUL W., b. March 5, 1797.
266 CYRUS, b. April 11, 1799, d. young.
267 GEORGE, b. Sept. 30, 1801.
268 NATHAN S., b. Jan. 7, 1804.
269 LUCY A., b. Nov. 4, 1805, m. Seth Williams (No. 53), William Williams family.

NOYES FAMILY. 495

Joseph Noyes m. for his second wife, Eunice, daughter of William and Esther Chesebrough (No. 326), on Jan. 29, 1811. She was b. Dec. 27, 1781, and d. Nov. 4, 1844.

CHILDREN:

270 ELISHA D., b. Oct. 28, 1811, d. young.
271 WILLIAM C., b. March 28, 1813.
272 EPHRAIM W., b. Nov. 19, 1814, d. unmarried.
273 SILAS C., b. Oct. 18, 1816, d. 1898, unmarried.
274 GURDON W., b. Aug. 13, 1818.
275 EUNICE E., b. March 12, 1820, never married.
276 NANCY L., b. March 13, 1822, m. John Starr Barber Sept. 2, 1841. After Mr. Barber's death she m. 2d, Benjamin F. Hillard in 1852. He d. March, 1866, and Mrs. Nancy Hillard m. 3d, Robert S. Taylor March 15, 1866.
277 T. EMILY, b. Nov. 3, 1823, and m. Charles G. Beebe Sept. 28, 1843.
278 CHARLOTTE A., b. April 3, 1826, m. David S. Babcock (No. 171).

William Noyes (No. 122) m. Sybil Whiting, daughter of his father's last wife, by a former husband, Lieut. Charles Whiting. She was b. in July, 1722, and d. April 27, 1790.

CHILDREN:

279 WILLIAM, b. April 24, 1742, m. Elizabeth Gillett, and their son, George, m. Martha Curtis, and their son, William Curtis Noyes, m. Julia Talmadge of Litchfield, Conn. This Mr. Noyes was the eminent and distinguished lawyer of New York, who rose to the highest eminence in his profession.
280 SYBIL, b. Nov. 19, 1745, m. Samuel Avery.
281 JOHN, b. in 1750, m. Mehitable Wright.
282 MARY, b. July 22, 1754, m. Elihu Plinney.
283 TEMPERANCE, b. in 1755, m. William Allen.
284 NATHAN, b. ———, m. Luba Baldwin.
285 LUCY, b. ———, m. Joseph Hancox of Stonington Borough, and were the parents of Peleg Hancox, who m. Betsey Burdick, who was the daughter of Betsey or Elizabeth Burch (No. 65), and Joshua Burch, who was the daughter of Billings Burch and wife, Susannah Bentley. The children of Peleg Hancox and wife, Betsey Burdick, were Lucy, d. young; John, Joseph, Peleg, Betsey, Lucy and Nathaniel Hancox.
286 ELIZABETH, b. in 1762, m. William Lewis. He was a sailor on board the vessel that captured the English ship Hannah.
287 SAMUEL A., b. ———, m. Abigail Harding.
288 CHARLES N., b. ———, m. Mrs. Samuel Noyes (his brother's widow).
289 NATHANIEL, b. ———, m. Temperance Champlin.

John Noyes (No. 123) m. Marcy or Mary Breed (No. 15), of the Breed family, on May 31, 1744. This family went to Vermont and from thence some of them went to New York State.

CHILDREN:

290 JOHN, b. Aug., 1745, m. Elizabeth Rogers.
291 MARCY, b. Jan. 7, 1748, m. William Sisson (No. 27), that family.
292 GERSHOM, b. in 1751, m. Mary Stanton Feb. 2, 1790.
293 JESSE, b. ———.
294 OLIVER, b. May 9, 1755, m. 1st, Thankful Clark, and 2d, Eunice Babcock.
295 AMOS, b. March 18, 1758, m. Eunice Walworth, went to New York State.
296 ANNE, b. March 7, 1761.

Avery Noyes (No. 168) m. Polly Slack Feb. 13, 1799.

CHILDREN:

297 POLLY, b. Nov. 6, 1799, m. Abel Crandall.
298 FANNY, b. April 20, 1801, m. John S. Moxley.
299 PRUDENCE, b. June 5, 1803, d. unmarried.
300 GRACE, b. March 13, 1805, d. young.
301 ANNA, b. Dec. 11, 1806, d. young.
302 AVERY D., b. Oct. 1, 1808.
303 WILLIAM, b. Jan. 2, 1811, m. Louisa Lamb Nov. 16, 1836.
304 ANNA or NANCY, b. July 18, 1813, m. Jonathan B. Stewart.
305 CYRUS, b. Feb. 20, 1816, m. Bridget C. Denison (No. 569), May 11, 1843.
306 SALLY, b. Nov. 7, 1818, m. Joseph Bishop.
307 CAROLINE A., b. Jan. 8, 1823, m. James Newcomb in 1845.

John Noyes (No. 171) m. Elizabeth Chesebrough (No. 312), that family, on Dec. 25, 1800.

CHILDREN:

308 DR. SAMUEL C., b. Oct. 11, 1801, m. Julia Cole.
309 JESSE D., b. Jan. 30, 1804, m. 1st, Eliza Crandall; m. 2d, Mary Gavitt, and m. 3d, Mary Noyes (No. 373). He d. Dec. 1, 1884.
310 JOHN, b. July 2, 1806, d. Oct. 11, 1840, unmarried.
311 WILLIAM, b. March 11, 1811, m. Susan Allen, d. Nov. 14, 1878.
312 ELIZA M., b. Oct., 1812.
313 ALBERT, b. 1816, m. 1st, Lydia Hibbard, and m. 2d, Mary Carter. He d. Dec. 28, 1861.
314 AMOS, b. 1817, d. Aug. 11, 1837, unmarried.
315 MARTHA A., b. in 1817 (twin), d. Feb. 1, 1825.

Mrs. Elizabeth (Chesebrough) Noyes d., and Mr. John Noyes m. 2d, Miss Priscilla Chesebrough, sister of Elizabeth. All children by 1st wife.

William Noyes (No. 311) m. Susan, daughter of Noel and wife Hannah (Dunham) Allen of Fall River, Mass.

CHILDREN:

316 SUSAN, b. in 1835, d. 1851.
317 URSULA, b. Dec., 1837, m. 1st, Joseph A. Starkweather, and 2d, Ichabod M. Cox.; she d July 30, 1882.
318 JOHN, b. in 1846, d. April 18, 1851.
319 BELLE V., b. Dec. 14, 1848, d. Nov. 16, 1868.
320 JOHN, b. ———, d. young.
321 CHARLES W., b. in 1855, d. Oct. 31, 1895, m. Lilian Hill.

Denison Noyes (No. 175), m. Hannah Russell Stanton (No. 392), on March 22, 1815. She was daughter of Hannah Russell and Samuel Stanton, son of Nathan and Elizabeth (Billings) Stanton, and granddaughter of Col. Giles Russell and Mrs. Prudence (Stanton) Coleman.

CHILDREN:

322 MARY R., b. Jan. 17, 1816, m. Daniel Cocks April, 1837, d. April, 1860.
323 BETSEY D., b. April 19, 1818, m. Frances Sheffield (No. 37), in Oct., 1824.
324 MARTHA W., b. Sept. 21, 1820, m. Lyman Paine Feb., 1846, d. Sept., 1848.
325 HARRIET S., b. Feb. 16, 1825, d. March, 1848.
326 MARIA H., b. Feb. 16, 1825, d. Aug., 1845.

NOYES FAMILY. 497

John Noyes (No. 177) m. 1st, Eunice Shearman March 8, 1786, and 2d, Mrs. Fanny Swan. She was formerly Fanny Palmer (No. 385), daughter of Amos and 1st wife, Phebe (Brown) Palmer, Oct. 16, 1827. He d. in 1846; left nine children.

James Noyes (No. 178) m. Anne Holbrook Jan. 22, 1789. He d. in 1844. He had fourteen children.

Nathaniel Noyes (No. 183) m. Mary Saunders Feb. 18, 1800.

CHILDREN:

327 WILLIAM, b. Nov. 30, 1801, d. Dec. 29, 1872, m. Clementina Noyes (No. 340), Noyes family, Feb. 14, 1843.
328 ELIZA, b. Aug. 18, 1803, m. William Chesebro (No. 244), Nov. 25, 1830.
329 FRANKLIN, b. Nov. 2, 1805, d. April 15, 1892, m. Susan, daughter of Capt. Paul and wife, Sabra Pendleton, of Westerly, R. I., June 14, 1829.
330 MARY, b. July 3, 1808, m. Anderson Burdick, d. Dec. 2, 1834.
331 SALLY, b. April 9, 1810, m. Joseph Wilbur.
332 FANNY, b. Aug. 31, 1812, d. Aug. 4, 1851.
333 MATILDA, b. Sept. 27, 1814, m. William Walton, d. May 18, 1893.
334 MELINDA, b. Sept. 27, 1814, m. Denison Woodmansee.

Nathan Noyes (No. 196) m. Sally Spargo or Sparger; she was sometimes called Sarah Belcher, as she lived with her uncle and aunt, Mr. and Mrs. John Belcher. She was daughter of Edward Sparger and Katharine Belcher, who were m. Dec. 26, 1769, by Rev. Gardiner Thurston, pastor of the Second Baptist Church of Newport, Rhode Island. It is said that Mr. and Mrs. Nathan Noyes, father and mother of this Nathan Noyes, were people of consumptive habits, and tradition says that they both d. the same day, comparatively young. Nathan Noyes (No. 196) m. Sally Spargo on Nov. 5, 1797.

CHILDREN:

335 MARY, b. March 27, 1799, m. George Green March 20, 1823.
336 NANCY, b. Aug. 7, 1801, m. Oliver Denison (No. 534), on Nov. 24, 1825.
337 NATHAN, b. April 15, 1804, m. 1st, Sarah Burrows (No. 44), and m. 2d, Esther Gallup, May 27, 1875.
338 ELIZA M. D., b. Aug. 31, 1807, m. Stephen Morgan (No. 30), on June 17, 1830.
339 FRANCIS B., b. Sept. 9, 1810, m. Maria Morgan (No. 28), on April 6, 1848.
340 CLEMENTINA, b. June 16, 1813, m. William Noyes Feb. 19, 1843 (No. 327).
341 LYDIA S., b. Oct. 20, 1816, m. Ebenezer Denison April 9, 1849 (No. 564).
342 FRANCES EMELINE, b. April 12, 1819, m. Benjamin Franklin Hancox (No. 38) of Hancox family on May 21, 1843.
343 JAMES S., b. Jan. 6, 1823, m. 1st, Jessie B. Page in 1867, and m. 2d, Mrs. Elizabeth S. Thresher Dec. 15, 1885.

John Noyes (No. 197) m. Susan Berry ———.

CHILDREN:

344 SAMUEL, b. ———.

John Noyes (No. 202) m. Elizabeth Stanton (No. 355), Stanton family.
CHILDREN:
345 LYDIA, b. ——.
346 ELIZABETH, b. ——, m. Asa Babcock, whose daughter Clara m. Amos Westcott; their son, Edward Noyes Westcott, was the author of "David Harum."
347 SAMUEL A., b. —— (twin).
348 EDWARD A., b. —— (twin).
349 MARY S., b. April 17, 1796, m. Moses B. Butterfield.
350 PRUDENCE, b. ——.
351 FANNY, b. ——.
352 PHEBE, b. ——.
353 LOIS, b. ——.
354 JOHN, b. May 8, 1812, d. Jan. 22, 1876.

Edward Noyes (No. 212) m. Sally Avery, ——.
CHILDREN:
355 JAMES A., b. ——, m. Eliza, daughter of Darius (No. 50) and Nancy (Hyde) Denison, Dec. 24, 1837.
356 EDWARD, b. ——, d. unmarried.
357 EUNICE, b. Aug. 16, 1806, m. Paul Noyes (No. 265), Noyes family.

James Noyes (No. 214) m. Lois, daughter of William and wife Eunice (Palmer) Stanton (No. 426), in 1804. He was lost at sea Sept. 15, 1810. She d. March 3, 1857.
CHILDREN:
358 LOUISA S., b. May 22, 1808, m. Joseph Chesebrough (No. 373), on Jan. 18, 1831.

John D. Noyes (No. 217) m. 1st, Ann Collins (No. 8); had three children, and m. 2d, Hannah E. Sutton Oct. 31, 1852; had two daughters.

James Noyes (No. 224) m. Nancy Phelps (No. 49) on Jan. 10, 1821.
CHILDREN:
359 THOMAS, b.——.
360 FRANKLIN, b. ——, m. Hattie Thompson; 2d, Mrs. Harriet (Wilder) Palmer.

Joseph Noyes (No. 263) m. Grace Billings Denison (No. 539), of Denison family. He d. June 12, 1872. She d. June 29, 1888.
CHILDREN:
361 PHEBE W., b. April 24, 1820, d. young.
362 CYRUS W., b. Jan. 27, 1822, m. Jane Harding, Dec. 13, 1848, d. July 2, 1853.
363 DENISON, b. Jan. 4, 1824, m. Mary Kemp Sept. 1, 1847, d. Dec. 13, 1859.
364 EDMUND S., b. Jan. 9, 1826, d. young.
365 LUCY A., b. Dec. 21, 1827, m. Richard A. Wheeler Nov. 5, 1856 (No. 429).
366 HANNAH D., b. Dec. 31, 1829, d. Sept. 16, 1873.
367 IRA HART, b. Jan. 9, 1832, d. Sept. 25, 1872.
368 CHARLES S., b. April 5, 1834, m. Henrietta D. Wheeler Jan. 24, 1877.
369 EDMUND S., b. May 24, 1836, m. Eliza P. Brown Feb. 5, 1867, d. May 31, 1877.
370 JOSEPH, b. July 3, 1839, d. at Columbus, Ohio, July 17, 1858, aged 19 yrs.
371 AVERY W. D., b. April 27, 1842, d. March 31, 1894.

NOYES FAMILY. 499

Thomas Noyes (No. 264) m. Eunice Denison (No. 541), Oct. 24, 1801. She d. Sept. 2, 1883.

CHILDREN:

372 MARTHA, b. Feb. 11, 1821, m. Noyes P. Brown (No. 397).
373 MARY, b. Nov. 4, 1828, m. Jesse D. Noyes (No. 309), Noyes family.
374 THOMAS W., b. Sept. 23, 1830, m. Phebe J. Kemp.
375 PHEBE, b. May 6, 1834, m. Enoch Chapman, son of (No. 83), Chapman family.
376 WILLIAM, b. May 6, 1836, m. Hannah Palmer.
377 ELIZA P., b. May 7, 1839, m. Seth Williams (No. 67), Groton Williams family.
378 JANE B., b. Feb. 3.

Paul W. Noyes (No. 265) m. Eunice Noyes (No. 357) on Feb. 27, 1834, by Rev. Joseph Ayer, Jr. He d. Feb. 2, 1879. She d. April 23, 1881.

CHILDREN:

379 PAUL A., b. ———, m. Susan York (No. 156), that family.
380 EUNICE, b. ———, m. Alden Palmer (No 507), that family.
381 ANNA, b. ———.
382 MARY A., b. ———, d.

George W. Noyes (No. 267) m. Hannah F. Denison on Sept. 2, 1827; she d. Sept. 5, 1829.

CHILDREN:

383 GEORGE D., b. March 23, 1829, d. March 4, 1854.

George W. Noyes (No. 267) m. 2d, Prudence D. Brown (No. 395), Lynn Brown family.

CHILDREN:

384 SARAH E., b. Nov. 24, 1835, d. March 5, 1836.
385 HENRY B., b. Jan. 15, 1837, m. Ellen Holmes, Jan. 10, 1870.
386 JOSEPH B., b. Nov. 26, 1838, d. July 30, 1869.
387 WILLIAM H., b. April 4, 1841, d. Sept. 24, 1858.
388 ELLEN E., b. July 27, 1846, m. John Gallup Oct. 5, 1870, son of (No. 232), Gallup family.
389 THEODORE, b. Aug. 25, 1847, d. Oct. 27, 1848.
390 EDWIN B., b. Jan. 27, 1849 m. Eliza Tift.

Mrs. Prudence Noyes d. Jan. 22, 1854, and Mr. George Noyes m. 3d, Emily F. Denison (No. 572) on Jan. 16, 1856.

CHILD:

391 G. FREDERICK, b. July 20, 1858.

Nathan S. Noyes (No. 268) m. Nancy Denison (No. 560) on Nov. 23, 1828. He d. Aug. 27, 1898. She d. Nov. 28, 1893.

CHILDREN:

392 Son, b. and d. Sept., 1829.
393 Son, b. and d. Feb. 7, 1831.
394 NATHAN D., b. Jan. 20, 1832, m. Adelia M. Randall (No. 141), on Aug. 4, 1857.
395 WILLIAM H., b. March 19, 1834, d. Sept. 5, 1837.
396 ELISHA E., b. Feb. 7, 1836, d. Sept. 2, 1837.

397 Daughter, b. and d. in 1838.
398 HARRIET E., b. Oct. 11, 1839.
399 A. LOUISA, b. March 19, 1842, m. B. F. Williams (No. 72).
400 FANNY S., b. May 11, 1844, m. David L. Gallup, son of (No. 240), Gallup family.
401 HENRY C., b. March 19, 1848, m. Sarah M. Heath.

William C. Noyes (No. 271) m. Jane Russell Keown Jan. 20, 1836.

CHILDREN:

402 WILLIAM RUSSELL, b. Oct. 20, 1836.
403 FRANCIS L., b. July 10, 1838.
404 ALFRED C., b. Aug. 25, 1840.
405 JANE C., b. Sept. 23, 1842.
406 JAMES W., b. in June, 1844.
407 CHARLES R., b. in June, 1846.
408 EDWARD H., b. Nov., 1848.
409 FREDERICK, b. Feb., 1853.

Gurdon W. Noyes (No. 274) m. Agnes McArthur Aug. 13, 1850.

CHILDREN:

410 LOUISE K., b. Oct. 22, 1851.
411 JAMES H., b. Oct. 14, 1853.
412 M. REGINE, b. June 24, 1879.
413 CARRIE C., b. Aug. 30, 1856.
414 EDWARD M., b. Oct. 12, 1858, m. July 3, 1884, Mary C. Simpson; she d. July 30, 1892.
415 FREDERICK F., b. Sept. 3, 1860, d. Aug. 12, 1862.
416 HERBERT L., b. Nov. 28, 1863, d. Nov. 9, 1888.
417 AGNES F., b. July 3, 1868.
418 ERNEST C., b. March 5, 1877.

Nathan Noyes (No. 182) m. Nancy Chapel in 1796.

CHILDREN:

419 NATHAN, b. ———, m. Elizabeth ———.
420 JAMES, b. ———, m. Mary Chapel.
421 BENJAMIN, b. ———.
422 THOMAS, b. ———.
423 ERASTUS, b. ———, m. Martha Gould.
424 ALEXANDER, b. ———, m. Susan Bennett.
425 AMANDA, b. in 1818, m. David Crowell in 1830, d. 1894.

Gershom Noyes (No. 292) m. Mary Stanton Feb. 2, 1790.

CHILDREN:

426 POLLY, b. Sept. 22, 1791.
427 GERSHOM, b. May 13, 1792.

Oliver Noyes (No. 294) m. 1st, Thankful Clark. The descendants are nearly all located in Vermont.

CHILDREN:

428 OLIVER, b. ———, 1779.
429 BREED, b. 1786.
430 REBEKAH, b. Dec. 3, 1784.
431 DAVID, b. Feb. 4, 1790.
432 JOSEPH C., b. Oct. 9, 1794.

NOYES FAMILY.

Mr. Oliver Noyes m. 2d, Eunice Babcock.

CHILDREN:

433 JESSE B., b. in Massachusetts, March 3, 1797.
434 GILBERT, b. Aug. 21, 1798, d. at Vermont May 2, 1851.
435 EUNICE, b. Aug. 17, 1800.

Avery D. Noyes (No. 302) m. Bathsheba Dickens, daughter of Capt. Jesse and wife, Bathsheba (Sheffield) Dickens. They were m. in Westerly, R. I., on Nov. 24, 1830, and lived in New London, Conn., about 40 years, and afterward in Pawcatuck, Conn., where he d. May 21, 1885.

CHILDREN:

436 JAMES D., b. Sept. 4, 1831, d. Sept. 18, 1831.
437 URSULA C., b. March 9, 1833, d. June 24, 1840.
438 AVERY D., b. Aug. 23, 1835, d. Jan. 10, 1837.
439 JAMES A., b. May 1, 1843, d. July 18, 1846.
440 CAROLINE A., b. Dec. 15, 1846, m. Jan. 16, 1868, Paul H. Hillard, son of William and wife, Lucy Morella (Dewey) Hillard.

PAGE FAMILY.

The emigrant ancestor of the Page family was John Page, who came in the fleet with Winthrop, was admitted freeman in Boston May, 1631. He was from Dedham, Essex County, England. His wife was Phebe Paine, who d. Sept. 25, 1677, in her 87th year. He d. Dec., 1676, aged 90 years.

CHILDREN:

2 JOHN, brought from England.
3 SAMUEL, b. Aug. 20, 1633.
4 DANIEL, b. Aug. 10, 1634, d. young.
5 ELIZABETH.
6 MARY.
7 PHEBE, one of which was b. in England.

John Page (No. 2) married Faith Dunster, May 12th, 1664. Removed to Groton, Mass.

CHILDREN:

8 JOHN, b. Dec. 10, 1669.
9 SAMUEL, b. June 4, 1672.
10 MARY, b. June 9, 1675.
11 JONATHAN, b. June 24, 1677.
12 JOSEPH, b. Feb. ye last day, 1679-80.

On the Stonington town records is found this entry: "Joseph Page, son of John Page of Watertown, was born Feb. ye last day, 1679-80, at said Watertown. The above writing was entered into record att ye desire of sd. Joseph Page, this 7th day of Aug., 1707, by me, Elnathan Minor, T. Clerk."

Joseph Page (No. 12) m. widow Mary Minor, March 5, 1712. She was formerly Mary Saxton, daughter of Capt. Joseph Saxton, and she m. Benjamin Minor Nov. 15, 1697. Mrs. Mary d. Oct. 17, 1750, aged 70 years. Mr. Joseph Page m. 2d, Catharine Ranger, April 3, 1751.

CHILDREN OF JOSEPH AND WIFE, MARY PAGE:

13 HANNAH, b. Dec. 24, 1713, m. Stephen Minor (No. 71), that family.
14 ELIZABETH, b. Aug. 8, 1717, m. John Billings (No. 50), that family.
15 JOSEPH, b. Sept. 25, 1720.
16 PHEBE, b. May 4, 1724.

Joseph Page, Jr. (No. 15), m. Mary Hewitt (No. 58), of the Hewitt family, May 1, 1746, by Joseph Fish, pastor.

PAGE FAMILY.

CHILDREN:

17 JOSEPH, b. Jan. 31, 1747, m. Patience Wheeler. No children. (No. 350.)
18 MARY, b. Jan. 30, 1749, m. Thomas Minor (No. 146).
19 HANNAH, b. July 11, 1751; m. 1st, ———— Chesebrough; m. 2d, Eliphalet Hobart (No. 9), that family.

Mrs. Mary Page d., and Joseph Page, Jr., and Lucy Wheeler (No. 61), both of Stonington, Conn., were m. May 9, 1756. Joseph Page d. Nov. 21, 1810.

CHILDREN:

20 LUCY, b. Dec. 12, 1756.
21 PHEBE, b. July 30, 1758.
22 KATHARINE, b. March 23, 1760, m. Daniel Stanton (No. 368) Jan. 4, 1781.
23 BRIDGET, b. May 30, 1764.
24 ABIGAIL, b. June 30, 1766.
25 MARTHA, b. Aug. 31, 1768, m. Edward Stanton (No. 370), Jan. 14, 1798.
26 CYRUS, b. Feb. 3, 1771.
27 FANNY, b. June 18, 1773, m. William Chesebrough (No. 322).
28 PAUL, b. July 18, 1775.
29 SAXTON, b. Sept. 16, 1777, d. Sept. 5, 1778.
30 ISAAC, b. April 23, 1780.
31 THOMAS, b. Feb. 28, 1782, d. Aug. 21, 1807.

PALMER FAMILY.

1. WALTER PALMER, the progenitor of the family of his name, who first settled in Stonington, Conn., came to New England as early as 1628, with his brother, Abraham Palmer, a merchant of London, England, and nine associates. They went from Salem, Mass., through a pathless wilderness to a place called by the Indians Mishawam, where they found a man by the name of Thomas Walford, a smith. Here they remained until the next year, when they were joined by nearly one hundred people, who came with Thomas Graves, from Salem and laid the foundation of the town, which they named Charlestown, in honor of King Charles the First, June 24, 1629. It is claimed that Walter Palmer built the first dwelling house in Charlestown after it was organized as a township, on the two acres of land that were assigned and set to him by the authority of the new town. Walter Palmer's inclinations tended to stock raising and farming, but he soon found his land was inadequate to his business, notwithstanding which he continued to reside in Charlestown until 1643. During his residence there he purchased additional real estate, which he improved in his line of business as best he could. While thus engaged he became acquainted with William Chesebrough, who lived at the time in Boston and Braintree, whose business pursuits were similar to those of Mr. Palmer, and after repeated interviews and consultations, they both decided to remove to the Plymouth Colony, and did so remove their families and with others, joined in the organization of the town of Rehoboth, as an independent township, which was continued as such until they should subject themselves to some other government. Such an organization, largely composed of strangers and situated in a remote part of the colony, was not very well calculated to secure their approval. It does not appear that they intended to establish this new township wholly as an independent organization, for as soon as the preliminary steps necessary for its formation were taken, and after its organization was effected, they elected deputies to the General Court of Plymouth. Walter Palmer was a prominent man when he lived in Massachusetts, and was admit-

ted a freeman there May 18, 1631, and held several local offices in that colony, and such was the estimation in which he was held by the first planters of Rehoboth and the confidence that they reposed in him, that his fellow townsmen elected him as their first representative to the General Court of Plymouth, and subsequently re-elected him to that office and also conferred upon him repeatedly the office of selectman and other local offices. His friend Chesebrough, not relishing the way and manner in which he was treated by the General Court of the Plymouth Colony decided to look farther westward for a permanent place of abode. He visited the then new settlement of New London, by the advice of Mr. John Winthrop, which after a thorough examination thereof, it did not answer his expectations, so he concluded to return homeward, and on his way came through the town of Stonington, Conn., where he visited the beautiful valley of Wequetequock, with which he was so well pleased that he decided to make it his future place of abode. When he reached home and described to his wife and family the situation and advantages of this valley, they all approved of it as a desirable place for their home. Mr. Chesebrough and sons immediately commenced operations for the erection of a dwelling house, fixing its site on the west bank of Wequetequock Cove. The salt marsh lands adjoining the cove furnished hay for the stock, and Mr. Chesebrough and Palmer and all the early settlers until they could clear up land and reduce it to cultivation by English grasses for their cattle. Mr. Chesebrough so far finished his house that he occupied it with his family during the year 1649, and so became the pioneer English planter of the new town now called Stonington.

The Connecticut General Court were not satisfied with his locating himself in the wilderness so far away from any English settlement, so they ordered him to report his proceedings to Maj. John Mason, which resulted in a compromise later on between him and said court, wherein and by which he was to remain in his new habitation on condition that he would induce a reasonable number of creditable persons to unite with him in organizing a new township as hereinbefore stated more at large.

Thomas Stanton, the interpreter general of New England, was the first to join Mr. Chesebrough in the new settlement, and obtained a grant from the General Court in March, 1650, of six acres of planting ground on Pawcatuck River, with liberty to erect a trading house thereon, with feed and mowing of marsh land, according to his present occasions, giving him the exclusive trade of the river for three years next ensuing. Mr. Stanton located his six-acre grant on the west bank of Pawcatuck River, around a place known as Pawcatuck rock, upon which grant he erected his trading house; and subsequently built him a dwelling house thereon, to which he moved his family in 1651, establishing it as his permanent place of abode, where he lived the remainder of his days. (For further particulars see Stanton family). William Chesebrough, in pursuance of his arrangement with the General Court, invited his friend Walter Palmer, then living in Rehoboth, to come and join him here in the organization of another new township. While Mr. Palmer was considering this proposition, Thomas Miner, who had married his daughter Grace, and was then a resident of New London, was also invited to join the new settlement, which he did, by obtaining a limited grant of land of the town of New London, which he located on the east bank of Wequetequock Cove, and built him a dwelling house thereon, to which he moved his family in the year 1652. The town of New London at the time claimed jurisdiction of the town of Stonington and had granted large tracts of land to William Chesebrough and Thomas Miner, and being anxious to assist Mr. Chesebrough in his efforts to induce a suitable number of prominent men to unite with him in settling a new township here, induced Gov. Haynes to accept of a grant of land of three hundred acres, for a farm lying east and southeast of Chesebrough's land, on the east side of Wequetequock Cove. This grant bore date April 5, 1652. Walter Palmer, who was then prospecting for a tract of land suitable for farming, with salt marsh grass land for his stock, ascertained that Gov. Haynes's grant covered the land he wished to obtain, and so visited the governor, with his son-in-law, Thomas Miner, and his eldest son, John Miner, who had previously learned that the Haynes grant of land embraced in its boundaries his son-in-law's land. But after a friendly interview with the governor, Walter Palmer purchased his grant of land in Stonington, by a contract deed which was witnessed by Thomas and John Miner, agreeing to pay the governor one hundred pounds for the place, with such cattle as Mr. Haynes should select out of Walter Palmer's stock. If any disagreement should arise, as to the price of the stock, it should be decided by indifferent persons. Their contract recognized the title to the house and lands occupied by Mr. Miner, and was dated July 15, 1653. Thomas Miner, Sr., was selected to put Mr. Palmer in possession of the land purchased of Gov. Haynes, and did so by a written instrument, embodying therein a conveyance of his own land, and dwelling house, included in the boundaries of the Haynes land (to Mr. Palmer), reserving the right, however, to occupy his said house until he could build another at Mistuxet, now known as Quiambaug, in Stonington. So 1653 marks the time when Walter Palmer came to Stonington to reside. He and his friend Chesebrough lived within a stone's throw of each other, and after life's fitful fever was ended, departed this life, and both lie buried in the old Wequetequock burial place, with Thomas Stanton, the interpreter general of New England. Walter Palmer was a man well advanced in life when he came to Stonington to reside with his family. He was born in London, England, as early as 1585, and at the time of his settlement here had reached the rugged steep of life's decline. The rough exposure of pioneer life, with its deprivations, seriously affected his health, which was so much impaired that as the chill November days had come, "the saddest of the year," he was gathered not to his fathers, but laid to rest in the old Wequetequock burial place, dying Nov. 10, 1661. Of his family, it may be said that he married in England, long before he came to this country. The name of his first wife has never been recorded. He m. 2d, Rebecca Short, who came to this country in 1632. They were joined in marriage June 1, 1633.

CHILDREN BY FIRST MARRIAGE:

2 GRACE, b. in England, of whom it is traditionally said that she was ot the same age as her husband, Thomas Miner, born in 1608 (No. 11), Miner family.

3 WILLIAM, b. in England; the eldest son came with his father's family to New England, and lived with them in Charlestown, Mass. He remained with his brother John, in Charlestown, after his father removed to Plymouth, and continued to reside there until after his father's death. Soon after he sold the land his father gave him in Rehoboth, and came to Stonington, and stayed with his brother-in-law, Thomas Miner, nearly a year, when he left here and went to Killingworth, Conn., where he lived the remainder of his days. The time of his death in not known. His brother, Gershom Palmer, under date of March 27, 1697, entered on record the following instrument: "Know all men by these presents, that, whereas, my brother, William, now deceased, did give and bequeath unto me his house, and all his lands in Killingworth, forever, I settling one of my sons thereon, and in compliance with my deceased brother's will, I do order my eldest

son, Gershom Palmer, Jr., to settle in said house upon said land. I, the said Gershom Palmer, Senior, do give and bequeath the aforesaid house and lot, with all its privileges and appurtenances thereto belonging, to my eldest son, Gershom Palmer, to him forever, according to the tenor of the will of my brother, William Palmer, deceased." This will renders it certain that he left no wife or children.

4 JOHN, b. in England in 1615; came to this country in 1628. He was admitted a freeman of Massachusetts Colony in 1639, and d. Aug. 24, 1677, aged 62 yrs. He left a will, giving the bulk of his property to his brother, Jonah and sister Elizabeth. He was never married.

5 JONAH, b. in England, m. Elizabeth Grissell.

6 ELIZABETH, b. in England, m. Thomas Sloan before 1663. He d. soon after, leaving no children of record. She m. for her 2d husband, William Chapman, Oct. 26, 1677. No children of record.

CHILDREN BY SECOND MARRIAGE:

7 HANNAH, b. in Charlestown, June 15, 1634. She came with her parents to Stonington, and m. 1st, Thomas Hewitt April 26, 1659 (No. 1), that family; m. 2d, Roger Sterry Dec. 27, 1671; m. 3d, John Fish, Aug. 25, 1681 (No. 1), Fish family. An interesting jointure between them is preserved in our old Stonington records.

8 ELIHU, bapt. (Charlestown church records), Jan. 25, 1636, and came to Stonington with his parents, via Rehoboth, and d. here Sept. 5, 1665. It is not probable that he ever married, for no children can be traced to him. He left a will in which he gave his property to his nephews. His will was lost in the burning of New London, Sept. 6, 1781, and the only knowledge we have of it, is from a deed on the Stonington records, where was set to his executor and vested in his nephews certain real estate in Stonington. If he had surviving children at the time of his death they would have been the subject of his bounty, but dying at the age of 29 years, and leaving such a will is proof positive that he had no offspring of his own.

9 NEHEMIAH, b. Nov. 2, 1637, m. Hannah Lord Stanton.

10 MOSES, b. April 6, 1640, m. Dorothy Gilbert.

11 BENJAMIN, b. May 30, 1642, in Charlestown, Mass., and came to Stonington via Rehoboth with his father and family and joined the church and subsequently became a large land holder. He m. and brought his wife home Aug. 10, 1681. All that is now known about his marriage we learn from Thomas Miner's Diary. He does not give her name, nor where she lived, nor is there any known record of his children, if any there were. He d. April 10, 1716, aged 74 yrs. In February before he died, he gave a deed of all his lands to two of his nephews, on condition that they should take good care of him during life and give him a Christian burial with headstones at his decease which care was administered, and the headstones mark his last resting place in the old Wequetequock burial ground.

12 GERSHOM, b. in Rehoboth, m. Ann Denison; 2d, Mrs. Elizabeth Mason.

13 REBECCA, b. in Stonington, m. Elisha Chesebrough (No. 12), that family; 2d, John Baldwin (No. 16), Baldwin family.

Jonah Palmer (No. 5) came with his father to this country in 1628; lived in Charlestown until 1657, when he m. Elizabeth Grissell, May 3, 1655, and moved soon after to Rehoboth, where he remained the rest of his life. He m. 2d, Abigail Titus.

CHILDREN ALL BY FIRST MARRIAGE:

14 HANNAH, b. Nov. 8, 1658.
15 SAMUEL, b. Nov. 22, 1659, m. Elizabeth Kingsbury.

16 JONAH, b. March 29, 1662, m. Elizabeth Kendrick.
17 MARY, b. Feb. 23, 1664.
18 MARTHA, b. July 6, 1666.
19 GRACE, b. Oct. 1, 1668.

Nehemiah Palmer (No. 9) came to Stonington with his parents from Charlestown, Mass., via Rehoboth, and m. Hannah Lord Stanton, Nov. 20, 1662 (No. 5), that family. He was a prominent man in the church, town and the State, and was of the Governor's Council, of the Connecticut Colony for several years. He d. Feb. 17, 1717. She d. Oct. 17, 1727.

CHILDREN:

20 JOSEPH, b. Oct. 3, 1663, m. Frances Prentice.
21 ELIHU, b. March 12, 1666, d. young.
22 JONATHAN, b. Aug. 7, 1668, m. Mary Manwarring.
23 DANIEL, b. Nov. 12, 1672, m. Margaret Smith; 2d, Mrs. Mary (Avery) Denison.
24 NEHEMIAH, bapt. July 18, 1677, m. Jerusha Saxton.
25 HANNAH, bapt. April 11, 1680, m. Ichabod Palmer (No. 33).

Moses Palmer (No. 10) b. in Charlestown, Mass., came to Stonington via Rehoboth, with his father's family, and m. Dorothy, daughter of John and Amy (Lord) Gilbert, a direct descendant of William the Conqueror, in 1672.

CHILDREN:

26 MOSES, bapt. Nov. 15, 1674, m. Abigail Allen.
27 DOROTHY, b. Nov. 7, 1675, m. William Wilcox (No. 8), that family.
28 JOHN, b. Dec. 2, 1677, m. Ann Chesebrough; 2d, Dorothy Noyes.
29 AMIE or ANNIE, b. April 23, 1680, m. Ebenezer Allen Oct. 4, 1704. Her daughter Annie, b. Aug. 22, 1705, and Mrs. Amie or Annie, d. Sept. 24, 1705.
30 REBECCA, b. April 30, 1682.

Dea. Gershom Palmer (No. 12) came to Stonington with his father and family. He served in early Colonial wars. He m. 1st, Ann, daughter of Capt. George Denison and wife, Ann (Borodell) Denison, Nov. 28, 1667 (No. 40), that family. She d. in 1694. He m. 2d, Mrs. Elizabeth (Peck) Mason, widow of Maj. Samuel Mason, Nov. 11, 1707 (No. 4), that family. The preliminaries of this union must have been interesting, not only in their reciprocal affections, but in their mutual financial interests, as appears by a jointure, bearing the date of their marriage. (See Appendix.) Soon after his last marriage he fixed his permanent place of abode on the eastern slope of Taugwonk, here in Stonington, placing his dwelling house on the site of the residence of Elias H. Miner, occupying and improving large tracts thereabouts, which after his death descended to his children by operation of the law, except what thereof had been transferred to them when in life. Subsequent to his marriage with Mrs. Elizabeth Mason, Dea. Gershom Palmer, as a condition precedent to a transfer of real estate to two of his sons, viz., George and Walter Palmer, had bound and obliged them, in consideration of said transfers, to pay to his then wife, the twenty pounds mentioned in the original jointure to be paid to her by his executor or administrator from his estate. When Mrs. Mason married the deacon she had two minor children, viz., Elizabeth and Hannah Mason, who went with their mother to reside in Dea. Palmer's family, where they were kindly entertained and treated with distinguished consideration by all, in recognition of their father's and grandfather's eminent services in the settlement of the State of Connecticut and also in consideration of the support and education of her daughters, their mother entered into a supplemental jointer with the deacon, by which she released and discharged his sons Walter and George Palmer from their liability to her for one-half of the twenty pounds mentioned in their first jointure. During the year 1719, Dea. Gershom Palmer departed this life, and in December of that year, in consideration of the affection and kindness to her daughters, and without any additional payment or favor of any kind to her from his heirs-at-law, she released his sons Walter and George Palmer from any and all liability to her, for the full consideration of the stipulations of the original jointure between her and Dea. Palmer. Miss Elizabeth Mason, who went with her mother to live with Dea. Palmer, after her mother's marriage to him, was at the time in her eleventh year. She was rarely endowed by nature, with pleasing accomplishments, which made her the idol of her social circle, and in her 23d year she became the wife of the Rev. William Worthington, Oct. 13, 1720. Her sister, Hannah Mason, was less than nine years old, in delicate health, with which she grew up to womanhood, afflicted with incipient consumption, until Nov., 1724, when she departed this life. (No. 17), Mason family.

CHILDREN ALL BY FIRST MARRIAGE:

31 MERCY, b. in 1668, m. John Breed (No. 3), Breed family.
32 GERSHOM, bapt. Sept. 2, 1677, m. Sarah Fenner.
33 ICHABOD, bapt. Sept. 2, 1677 (twin), m. Hannah Palmer (No. 25).
34 WILLIAM, bapt. April 25, 1678, m. Grace Miner.
35 GEORGE, b. May 29, 1681, m. Hannah Palmer (No. 84).
36 ANN, bapt. May 20, 1683, m. Benjamin Hewitt (No. 7), that family.
37 WALTER, bapt. June 7, 1685, m. Grace Vose.
38 ELIHU, bapt. May 6, 1688, d. young.
39 MARY, bapt. June 6, 1690, m. Joseph Palmer (No. 82), that family.
40 REBECCA, b. July 1, 1694, m. Benjamin Palmer (No. 85), that family.

PALMER FAMILY. 511

Samuel Palmer (No. 15) m. Elizabeth Kingsbury in 1681. Removed from Rehoboth, Mass., to that part of Windham County now known as Scotland, Conn.

CHILDREN:

41 JOHN, b. March 25, 1682.
42 SAMUEL, b. Jan. 4, 1684.
43 MEHITABLE, b. April 11, 1686.
44 NEHEMIAH, b. March 11, 1688.
45 BENONI, b. July 7, 1690.
46 MARY, b. Dec. 17, 1691.
47 SETH, b. April 11, 1694, m. Elizabeth Cary; 2d, Mary Mosely.
48 ELIZABETH, b. Feb. 6, 1696.
49 EBENEZER, b. Oct. 21, 1699.
50 MARY, b. Jan. 17, 1701.
51 ELEAZER, b. June 10, 1702.

Jonah Palmer (No. 16) m. Elizabeth Kendrick Jan. 20, 1689, and removed from Rehoboth, Mass., to Windham, Conn., where he purchased large tracts of land, and spent the remainder of his days in the improvement thereof.

CHILDREN:

52 REBECCA, b. Feb. 29, 1690.
53 ELIZABETH, b. Sept. 14, 1691.
54 JONATHAN, b. March 20, 1693.
55 GERSHOM, b. Nov. 14, 1694, m. Hannah Spencer.
56 HANNAH, b. April 28, 1696.
57 RUTH, b. March 27, 1698.
58 ELIHU, b. Jan. 19, 1700.

Seth Palmer (No. 47), m. Elizabeth Cary April 19, 1720; m. 2d, Mary Mosely June 14, 1739.

CHILDREN:

59 ELIZABETH, b. Aug. 15, 1721.
60 MARY, b. Oct. 17, 1725.
61 ABIGAIL, b. Jan. 9, 1727.
62 HANNAH, b. March 1, 1728.
63 ESTHER, b. June 1, 1730.
64 JEHOADAM, b. April 20, 1733.
65 SETH, b. May 14, 1734.
66 JOSEPH, b. June 22, 1737.

Gershom Palmer (No. 55) m. Hannah Spencer June 28, 1715.

CHILDREN:

67 JONAH, b. July 18, 1716, m. Abiel Robinson.
68 PHEBE, b. Nov. 20, 1718.
69 SHUBEL, b. Jan. 14, 1720.
70 HANNAH, b. May 16, 1726.

Jonah Palmer (No. 67) m. Abial Robinson Oct. 31, 1754.

CHILDREN:

71 JONAH, b. Nov. 18, 1755.
72 NAMIAH, b. Feb. 27, 1758.
73 WILLIAM, b. Oct. 15, 1759.
74 DESIRE, b. Nov. 5, 1761.
75 WEALTHIA, b. Nov. 4, 1763.

76 ABIGAIL, b. Jan. 25, 1765, d. young.
77 ABIGAIL, b. Jan. 6, 1768.
78 ABIAH, b. Oct. 11, 1769.
79 ELI, b. April 4, 1772.

Joseph Palmer (No. 20) m. Frances, daughter of Thomas and Rebecca (Jackson) Prentice, Nov. 12, 1687.

CHILDREN:

80 Son, b. July 8, 1688, d. young.
81 Son, b. Sept. 12, 1689, d. young.
82 JOSEPH, b. Nov. 14, 1690, m. Mary Palmer (No. 39).
83 Daughter, b. Sept. 23, 1692, d. young.
84 HANNAH, b. May 31, 1695, m. George Palmer (No. 35).
85 BENJAMIN, b. March 18, 1696, m. Rebecca Palmer (No. 40).
86 SARAH, b. April 28, 1698.
87 JONATHAN, b. May 2, 1703.

Jonathan Palmer (No. 22) m. Mary or Marcy Manwarring Dec. 1, 1706.

CHILDREN:

88 JUDITH, b. Jan. 6, 1708.
89 MARY, b. Feb. 27, 1709.
90 HANNAH, b. Dec. 12, 1711, m. William York (No. 16), that family.
91 ANNA, b. May 15, 1715.
92 IRENE, b. ———, m. Henry Rowland.
93 LOVE, b. March 3, 1717, m. Jonathan Shepard.
94 PRUDENCE, b. March 31, 1719, m. Thomas Shaw, Jr.
95 JONATHAN, b. Dec. 23, 1720, m. Prudence Holmes.

Daniel Palmer (No. 23) m. 1st, Margaret Smith of Groton, March 25, 1700. She d. June 4, 1727; m. 2d, Mrs. Mary (Avery) Denison, widow of William Denison (No. 53), that family, Jan. 12, 1732. He d. Feb. 30, 1762.

CHILDREN:

96 NEHEMIAH, b. April 9, 1702, m. Submit Palmer.
97 DANIEL, b. June 10, 1704, m. Mary Palmer Jan. 6, 1731.
98 SAMUEL, b. April 1, 1707, m., had a son, Samuel, of Thompson, Conn.
99 NATHAN, b. Oct. 24, 1711, m. Phebe Billings.
100 RUFUS, b. Oct. 7, 1713, m. Phebe Babcock Feb. 15, 1749.
101 HULDAH, b. Nov. 15, 1715, d. aged 12 yrs.
102 LYDIA, b. Aug. 16, 1718, d. aged 9 yrs.
103 JAMES, b. July 13, 1720, m. Hannah Chesebrough.
104 REBECCA, b. Sept. 13, 1726, m. Capt. Daniel Fish of Preston, Conn., Feb. 17, 1743; she d. July 12, 1786; he d. April 11, 1788.

Nehemiah Palmer (No. 24), m. Jerusha, daughter of Capt. Joseph and Mrs. Hannah (Denison) Chesebrough Saxton, Jan. 17, 1700 (No. 30), Chesebrough family. He d. She m. 2d, James Deane (No. 2), that family, and had another husband, but no children.

CHILDREN:

105 SAXTON, b. Nov. 29, 1701, m. Sarah Richardson.
106 THOMAS, b. Jan. 7, 1703, m. Mrs. Priscilla (Chesebrough) Chesebrough.
107 JERUSHA, b. April 30, 1705, m. John Thompson (No. 5), that family.
108 NEHEMIAH, b. Feb. 4, 1707, m. Mary Eldridge.
109 STEPHEN, b. May 1, 1709, m. Elizabeth Quimby.

PALMER FAMILY. 513

110 ABIJAH, b. Sept. 29, 1712, m. Dorothy Palmer.
111 THANKFUL, b. April 14, 1714.
112 DAVID, b. Dec. 22, 1717.
113 BRIDGET, b. April 3, 1721, m. John Gallup (No. 70), that family.

Moses Palmer (No. 26) m. Abigail, daughter of Daniel and Mary (Sherman) Allen, and granddaughter of Rev. John Sherman, April 1, 1703.

CHILDREN:

114 JOHN, b. June 14, 1705.
115 AMIE, b. Dec. 3, 1706, m. Jonathan Tracy Feb. 19, 1724.
116 Daughter, b. Aug. 28, 1708, d. young.
117 ABIGAIL, b. Sept. 16, 1709, m. Nathaniel Tracy July 7, 1731.
118 DOROTHY, b. Nov. 20, 1711, m. Abijah Palmer (No. 110).
119 MARY, b. June 28, 1713.
120 MOSES, b. July 18, 1715, d. young.
121 SUBMIT, b. May 3, 1718, m. Nehemiah Palmer (No. 96).
122 REBECCA, b. April 5, 1720, m. Capt. Daniel Fish.
123 LOIS, b. March 3, 1722.
124 MOSES, b. April 3, 1726, m. Prudence Turner.

John Palmer (No. 28) m. Ann Chesebrough Jan. 18, 1727 (No. 38), that family. She d. March 3, 1727. He m. 2d, Dorothy Noyes, Dec. 26, 1728 (No. 111), that family.

CHILDREN:

125 JOHN, b. March 21, 1729, m. Anna Noyes (No. 128), that family.
126 MOSES, b. Oct. 29, 1730.
127 NOYES, b. Aug. 20, 1732, m. Sarah Mix June 20, 1754.
128 GILBERT, b. Aug. 30, 1734, d. Oct. 17, 1734.
129 ABIGAIL, b. May 11, 1736.
130 DOLLE, b. Jan. 13, 1741.
131 GILBERT, b. June 8, 1743.

Amie Palmer (No. 115) m. Jonathan Tracy of Norwich Feb. 19, 1724.

CHILD:

132 MOSES, b. Feb. 26, 1733.

Gershom Palmer (No. 32) m. Sarah Fenner, date not given.

CHILDREN:

133 GERSHOM, b. ———.
134 JOHN, b. ———.
135 ANN, b. ———.

Ichabod Palmer (No. 33) m. his first cousin, Hannah Palmer (No. 25), in the year 1697.

CHILDREN:

136 LUCY, b. May 28, 1699, m. William Chesebrough (No. 42), that family.
137 ICHABOD, b. Oct. 25, 1702, m. Elizabeth Noyes (No. 110), that family.
138 PRUDENCE, b. May 29, 1706.
139 NATHANIEL, b. Oct. 11, 1707, m. Mary Chesebrough.
140 DANIEL, b. Dec. 1, 1709.
141 ELIAS, b. May 15, 1715, m. Mary Holmes.

William Palmer (No. 34) m. Grace Miner Jan. 10, 1701 (No. 47), that family. They lived in Taugwonk and later on moved to Pun-hun-gue-nuck Hill, North Stonington, Conn.

CHILDREN:
142 GRACE, bapt. June 27, 1703.
143 WILLIAM, bapt. March 10, 1705.
144 ELIHU, bapt. Dec. 6, 1706, m. Deborah Reynolds Jan. 19, 1721.
145 ELDER WAIT, bapt. May 27, 1711, m. Mary Brown.

George Palmer (No. 35) m. Hannah Palmer (No. 84) March 24, 1711.

CHILDREN:
146 CHRISTOPHER, b. Feb. 13, 1712, m. Esther Prentice.
147 ZEBULON, b. Feb. 4, 1714.
148 JOSEPH, b. Aug. 16, 1717, m. Zipporah Billings.
149 GEORGE, b. Sept. 6, 1719.
150 GERSHOM, b. Oct. 13, 1723, m. Dorothy Brown.

Walter Palmer (No. 37) m. Grace Vose, daughter of Edward and Waitstill Vose of Milton, Mass., Aug. 7, 1712.

CHILDREN:
151 GRACE, b. ———.
152 WALTER, Jr., b. July 29, 1717, m. Mercy Hinckley (No. 24), that family.

Joseph Palmer (No. 82) m. Mary Palmer (No. 39) April 2, 1711.

CHILDREN:
153 SARAH, b. Jan. 17, 1712.
154 MARY, b. March 21, 1714.
155 PHEBE, b. Nov. 24, 1717.
156 FRANCES, b. Oct. 27, 1721.
157 JOSEPH, b. Oct. 30, 1719, m. Katharine Coats.
158 AMOS, b. April 11, 1724.
159 MOSES, b. April 13, 1726.
160 HANNAH, b. Aug. 2, 1727.
161 JONATHAN, b. March 18, 1730.
162 ANN, b. Dec. 23, 1732.
163 ASENATH, b. March 26, 1735.

Nehemiah Palmer (No. 96) m. Submit Palmer (No. 121) April 29, 1736, both of Stonington, Conn. He d. July 25, 1762; she d. Jan. 29, 1793.

CHILDREN:
164 NEHEMIAH, b. May 1, 1738, m. Mary Chesebrough (No. 162), that family.
165 JESSE, b. June 30, 1740, m. Phebe Chesebrough (No. 99), that family.
166 ELIJAH, b. Sept. 12, 1742, m. Anna Chesebrough; 2d, widow Louise Holmes.
167 SUBMIT, b. Jan. 12, 1745, m. Samuel Chesebrough (No. 103), that family.
168 ABEL, b. Dec. 4, 1746, d. young.
169 DANIEL, b. June 17, 1749.
170 LOIS, b. Sept. 7, 1751.
171 REUBEN, b. Aug. 2, 1753.
172 ABEL, b. April 4, 1756.
173 ELI, b. July 8, 1766.

Dr. Nathan Palmer (No. 99) m. Phebe Billings April 21, 1735 (No. 47), that family. He d. March 28, 1795.

CHILDREN:
174 DENISON, b. Dec. 17, 1735, m. Marvin Palmer; 2d, Mrs. Sarah White.
175 HULDAH, b. Jan. 23, 1736, m. Gilbert Fanning (No. 9), that family.
176 ANDREW, b. Oct. 21, 1738, m. Lucy Palmer; 2d, Hannah Palmer.

PALMER FAMILY.   515

177 NATHAN, b. Sept. 5, 1740.
178 ASA, b. June 11, 1742.
179 LEMUEL, b. Aug. 8, 1743.
180 EBENEZER, b. Feb. 16, 1745.
181 PHEBE, b. Dec. 4, 1746, m. John C. Rossiter (No. 9), that family.
182 SABRA, b. Nov. 24, 1748.
183 LUCRETIA, b. Oct. 16, 1751.
184 DESIRE, b. Aug. 12, 1753, m. Henry Frink (No. 44), that family.
185 EDWARD, b. Jan. 21, 1756.
186 ELI MINER, b. March 17, 1759.

James Palmer (No. 103) m. Hannah Chesebrough Jan. 4, 1749 (No. 111), that family. He d. June 20, 1794; she d. Oct. 4, 1814.

CHILDREN:

197 EUNICE, b. Feb. 4, 1750, m. William Stanton (No. 351), that family.
198 HANNAH, b. Nov. 4, 1755, m. Capt. Andrew Palmer (No. 176).
199 BRIDGET, b. Nov. 12, 1755, d. Dec. 4, 1852, aged 97 yrs, unmarried.
200 SAMUEL, b. June 15, 1758.
201 MARGARET, b. Aug. 17, 1762, m. George Palmer (No. 310).
202 WILLIAM, b. Nov. 10, 1764, m. Mary Palmer (No. 308).
203 DESIRE, b. Aug. 1, 1766, m. Roswell Salstonstall Palmer (No. 311).
204 LEMUEL, b. Nov. 16, 1767, m. Abigail Davis.

Saxton Palmer (No. 105) m. Sarah Richardson May 13, 1722.

CHILDREN:

205 SAXTON, b. May 1, 1723.
206 PEREZ, b. Feb. 17, 1725.

Thomas Palmer (No. 106) m. Mrs. Priscilla Chesebrough, daughter of Samuel Chesebrough and wife, Priscilla Alden, and granddaughter of David Alden and wife, Mary Southworth of Duxbury, Plymouth Colony, and great-granddaughter of John Alden and Priscilla Mullines of Mayflower fame. They were m. in 1733 (No. 69), Chesebrough family.

CHILDREN:

207 LUCY, b. Dec. 23, 1734, m. Charles Thompson (No. 14), that family.
208 THOMAS, b. Feb. 9, 1737, m. Mary Rossiter.
209 JABEZ, b. Jan. 24, 1741.
210 BRIDGET, b. April 5, 1743, m. Benedam Gallup (No. 111), that family.
211 DESIRE, b. July 19, 1746, m. Elihu Thompson (No. 16), that family.
212 SAMUEL, b. June 11, 1749, m. Hannah Eells.

Nehemiah Palmer (No. 108) m. Mary Eldridge March 14, 1727.

CHILDREN:

213 MARY, b. Feb. 5, 1729.
214 SUSANNAH, b. June 15, 1731.
215 JABISH, b. Aug. 28, 1733.

Stephen Palmer (No. 109) m. Elizabeth Quimby July 16, 1730.

CHILDREN:

216 JOSHUA, b. April 4, 1731.
217 ELIZABETH, b. Feb. 13, 1733.

Abijah Palmer (No. 110) m. Dorothy Palmer (No. 118) Dec. 2, 1733. She d. March 10, 1741. He m. 2d, Bridget Stanton April 10, 1742. He d. March 7, 1793.

CHILDREN:

218 JERUSHA, b. May 16, 1734, m. Benjamin Adams May 9, 1757.
219 LYDIA, b. July 24, 1736.
220 SAXTON, b. June 22, 1738.
221 DOROTHY, b. March 2, 1740.

CHILDREN BY SECOND MARRIAGE:

222 ROBERT, b. Jan. 7, 1743, d. Dec., 1750.
223 SIMEON, b. Oct. 4, 1744, m. Sarah Stanton (No. 296), that family.
224 PELEG, b. Jan. 24, 1754, m. Mary Burch.
225 ROBERT, b. Aug. 6, 1756, d. Aug. 6, 1756.

Noyes Palmer (No. 127) m. Sarah Mix (No. 449), Chesebrough family, June 20, 1754.

CHILDREN:

226 NOYES, b. Oct. 19, 1755, m. Dorothy Stanton.
227 JOHN, b. Jan. 11, 1757.
228 ALLEN, b. Feb. 17, 1759.
229 AMOS, b. June 30, 1761, m. Betsey Stanton.
230 ZEBEDIAH, b. May 22, 1764.

Ichabod Palmer (No. 137) m. Elizabeth Noyes April 29, 1723 (No. 110), that family.

CHILDREN:

231 PRUDENCE, b. Feb. 29, 1724.
232 THOMAS, b. Jan. 27, 1726.
233 ELIZABETH, b. March 25, 1728.
234 ICHABOD, b. Aug. 8, 1730, m. Mary Grant (No. 28), that family.
235 HANNAH, b. Dec. 20, 1733.
236 MARY, b. July 6, 1736.
237 LUCY, b. June 26, 1739.
238 ELIAS SANFORD, b. March 14, 1742, m. Phebe Palmer; 2d, Mrs. Lucy (Randall) Breed.

Nathaniel Palmer (No. 139) m. Mary Chesebrough June 9, 1731 (No. 39), that family.

CHILDREN:

239 ANNA, b. March 12, 1732.
240 LUCRETIA, b. Aug. 31, 1734, m. Amos Whiting Jan. 8, 1752.
241 LUCY, b. Sept. 23, 1737, m. Andrew Palmer (No. 176).
242 NATHANIEL, b. April 17, 1740, m. Grace Noyes.
243 DAVID, b. June 9, 1742, m. Abigail Gardiner Nov. 15, 1773.
244 MARY, b. April 30, 1745, m. Wait Rathbun Feb. 18, 1778.

Elias Palmer (No. 141) m. Mary Holmes Feb. 26, 1734 (No. 25), that family. He d., and she m. 2d, Lieut. John Randall (No. 8), that family, and had ten children (see that family).

CHILDREN BY FIRST HUSBAND:

245 ELIAS, b. March 5, 1735, m. Esther Randall.
246 MARVIN, b. Feb. 18, 1739, m. Denison Palmer (No. 174).

Elder Wait Palmer (No. 145) m. Mary Brown, daughter of Eleazer and Ann (Pendleton) Brown, in the year 1727 (No. 42), that family.

CHILDREN:

247 WAIT, b. May 5, 1728, m. Mary Safford.

248 AMOS, b. Aug. 27, 1729, m. Mary York Nov. 15, 1749.
249 ISRAEL, b. Jan. 16, 1731, m. Lois Brown (No. 53), that family.
250 ISAAC, b. Feb. 15, 1732.
251 MARY, b. May 14, 1735.
252 CONTENT, b. Jan. 27, 1737.
253 EBENEZER, b. Jan. 21, 1739, m. Hannah Palmer.
254 ELIHU, b. March 10, 1741.

Christopher Palmer (No. 146) m. Esther Prentice Oct. 27, 1731 (No. 18), that family.

CHILDREN:

255 EUNICE, b. May 18, 1732.
256 ESTHER, b. March 25, 1734.
257 CHRISTOPHER, b. Oct. 10, 1735.
258 ABEL, b. Jan. 16, 1737.
259 GEORGE, b. Dec. 20, 1738, m. Ann Denison (No. 179), that family.
260 SARAH, b. Nov. 22, 1740.
261 OTHNID, b. Feb. 13, 1743.
262 LUCY, b. Sept. 18, 1745.
263 MICHAEL, b. Nov. 10, 1752.

Dr. Joseph Palmer (No. 148) m. Zipporah Billings July 10, 1737 (No. 65), that family. They lived at Pendleton Hill. After the death of his first wife he m. 2d, Elizabeth ———. He d. April 12, 1791.

CHILDREN:

264 DAVID, b. Aug. 30, 1739, m. Grace Plumb in 1760. He d. in 1821. They had eleven children and his descendants are a large proportion of the inhabitants of the State of Vermont. Their son, James, b. March 6, 1764, in Stonington, m. Agnes Boland of Voluntown. They had twelve children, and their son, David, b. 1789, m. Lavinia Bigelow, daughter of Judge Edmund Bigelow of Middletown, Vt.; he d. in 1840. He was a physician, and their eldest son, Benjamin Rush Palmer, M. D., m. in 1836, Araminta Graves, daughter of Rev. Increase Graves, b. in Bridgeport, Vt, in 1811. She d. in 1884 ,and he d. in 1865. They had an only son, Edmund Rush Palmer, M. D. This line of Palmers embrace men of reputation as physicians, surgeons and brilliant orators.
265 ETHEL, b. Jan. 25, 1740.
266 PHEBE, b. Sept. 5, 1742, m. Elias Sanford Palmer (No. 238).
267 JOSEPH, b. Feb. 1, 1745.
268 ZIPPORAH, b. March 31, 1747, m. ——— Coates.
269 CONTENT, b. Aug. 8, 1749.
270 GERSHOM, b. ———, m. Zerviah Palmer (No. 276).
271 JEMIMA, b. ———, m. ——— Phillips.
272 EUNICE, b. ———.
273 SABRA, b. ———.

Gershom Palmer (No. 150) m. Dorothy Brown of Preston, Conn., Nov. 5, 1747. They lived in Stonington, Conn.

CHILDREN:

274 PRUDENCE, b. Aug. 18, 1748, m. William Breed (No. 40), that family; 2d, James Thompson.
275 DOROTHY, b .———, m. Nathan Randall (No. 53), that family.
276 ZERVIAH, b. ———, m. Gershom Palmer (No. 270).
277 REUBEN, b. ———, m. Lucretia Tyler.
278 NAOMIE, b. ———, m. Stephen Ray.

279 LOIS, b. ——, m. Abel Palmer.
280 ESTHER, b. ——, m. Jonathan Palmer.
281 LUCRETIA, b. ——, m. Elijah Palmer.
282 KETURAH, b. ——, m. Jacob Button.
283 AMY, b. ——, m. Daniel Budlong.

Joseph Palmer (No. 157) m. Katharine Coates Nov. 7, 1741.
CHILDREN:
284 JOSEPH, b. July 24, 1742.
285 WILLIAM, b. Jan. 22, 1744.
286 AMOS, b. March 11, 1747, m. Phebe Brown (No. 185), that family.
287 PHEBE, b. April 18, 1749, m. Amos Randall (No. 55), that family.
288 HANNAH, b. ——, m. Peleg Randall (No. 59), that family.

Denison Palmer (No. 174) m. Marvin Palmer (No. 246) July 10, 1759. She d. Feb. 25, 1784. He m. 2d, Sarah, the widow of Dr. White of Long Island, 1786.
CHILDREN:
290 REBECCA, b. Sept. 15, 1760.
291 HULDIA, b. March 3, 1762, m. Gilbert Denison (No. 307), that family.
292 NATHAN, b. Nov. 15, 1763, d. June 18, 1801.
293 SABRA, b. Aug. 4, 1765, m. Asa Chesebrough, Nov. 8, 1785 (No. 188), that family.
294 LUCY, b. Dec. 7, 1767, m. Robert Chesebrough (No. 284), that family.
295 HENRY, b. Sept. 24, 1768, m. Prudence Chesebrough Feb. 7, 1790 (No. 192), that family; m. 2d, Hannah Denison Sept. 2, 1798 (No. 275), that family.
296 LUCRETIA, b. Oct. 29, 1770, m. Elias Chesebrough (No. 195), that family.
297 RICHARD, b. Aug. 3, 1772, m. Hannah Stanton (No. 306), that family.
298 ASA, b. June 3, 1774.
299 CHARLES, b. Sept., 1775, m. Betsey Denison (No. 274), that family.
300 SARAH or SALLY, b. Sept., 1777, m. Ezra Chesebrough (No. 196), that family.
301 WEALTHIAN, b. March 31, 1779, m. Nehemiah Palmer (No. 317).
302 DENISON, b. Oct. 10, 1781, m. Hannah Slack; 2d, Eliza, widow of Allen Chesebrough.

CHILDREN BY SECOND MARRIAGE:
303 PHEBE, b. in 1787, d. June 23, 1797.
304 MARVIN, b. in 1789, m. Samuel Helms.
305 SOPHIA, b. April 19, 1793, m. Charles Phelps Noyes March 20, 1814 (No. 218), Noyes family .
306 CLARISSA, b. Dec. 27, 1813, m. Elam Denison (No. 538), that family; m. 2d, Amos Chesebrough (No. 243), that family.

Capt. Andrew Palmer (No. 176) m. Lucy Palmer (No. 241) in 1760. He m. 2d, Hannah Palmer (No. 198), Dec. 14, 1778. He was lost at sea.
CHILDREN:
307 PHEBE, b. 1761, m. Naboth Chesebrough (No. 173), that family.
308 MARY, b. ——, m. William Palmer Dec. 17, 1750 (No. 202). Went to Goshen, Conn.
309 PRUDENCE, b. ——, m. John Williams.
310 GEORGE, b. ——, m. Margaret Palmer Dec. 22, 1785 (No. 201).
311 ROSWELL SALSTONSTALL, b. Aug. 1, 1766, m. Desire Palmer (No. 203). Went to Stockbridge, Mass.
312 ROBERT, b. ——; served in the Revolutionary war; was taken prisoner and confined on a prison ship; was released; came home and died, unmarried.

PALMER FAMILY.

CHILDREN BY SECOND MARRIAGE:

313 ROBERT, b. ———; settled in Goshen, Conn., and had nine children.
314 ANDREW, b. ———, d. unmarried.

Elijah Palmer (No. 166) m. Anna Chesebrough Sept. 27, 1767 (No. 155), that family. She d. Oct. 10, 1802; 2d, widow Louise (Fox) Holmes, widow of Dr. Silas Holmes.

CHILDREN:

315 ELIJAH, b. May, 1768. He was lost at sea Dec. 20, 1788, aged 20 yrs.
316 ANNA, b. ———, m. James Smith of Groton Nov. 25, 1795.
317 NEHEMIAH, b. ———, m. Welthian Palmer (No. 301).
318 DUDLEY, b. Aug. 17, 1774, m. Minetta Chesebrough (No. 288), that family.
319 GURDON, b. ———, m. ——— Holmes.
320 ABIGAIL, b. March, 1784, d. June 11, 1786.
321 RHODA, b. 1786, m. Dr. William Hyde (No. 45), that family.
322 DELIA, b. 1789, d. Aug. 21, 1791.

Thomas Palmer (No. 208) m. Mary Rossiter March 23, 1767 (No. 7), that family.

CHILDREN:

323 HANNAH, b. Oct. 23, 1767, m. Samuel Stanton (No. 382), that family.
324 THOMAS W., b. Jan. 1, 1770; m. Lucy Prentice Wheeler.

Samuel Palmer (No. 212) m. Hannah Eells Nov. 9, 1780 (No. 31), that family.

CHILDREN:

325 LUCY, b. Oct. 25, 1783.
326 SAMUEL, b. Aug. 20, 1785.
327 JOSEPH, b. Aug. 24, 1787.
328 BENJAMIN, b. Aug. 24, 1789.
329 FREDERICK, b. March 22, 1792.
330 BETSEY, b. May 8, 1794.
331 JAMES, b. Feb. 5, 1797.
332 MARIA, b. Sept. 21, 1799, m. Rowland Stanton (No. 313), that family.
333 CORNELIA, b. April 13, 1803.

Peleg Palmer (No. 224) m. Mary or Molly Burch (No. 38), Burch family, March 1, 1779.

CHILDREN:

334 LYDIA, b. Nov. 14, 1779, d. Sept. 11, 1872, aged 92 yrs.
335 PELEG, b. ———; lost at sea; a young man.
336 ADAM, b. March 27, 1784.
337 DESIRE, b. Aug. 3, 1786, m. James Stanton.
338 DEBORAH, b. May 26, 1788.
339 HULDAH, b. March 8, 1789, m. Asa Lee.
340 NANCY, b. Oct. 14, 1791, m. Capt. Samuel Bottom.
341 SUSAN, b. ———, 1796, m. Nathaniel Waldron.
342 DEA. SIMEON, b. Aug. 5, 1799, m. 1st, Ann Eliza Chesebrough (No. 428), that family; 2d, Caroline Tiffany, Aug. 5, 1828.

Noyes Palmer (No. 226) m. Dorothy Stanton May 22, 1784 (No. 153), that family.

CHILDREN:

343 ALLEN, b. Sept. 12, 1785, m. Elizabeth Palmer.
344 SARAH, b. Jan. 26, 1787, m. Randall Brown (No. 289), that family.

HISTORY OF STONINGTON.

345 DEA. NOYES, b. April 20, 1790, m. Bridget Denison; Mary Rossiter; Harriet Wheeler.
346 DOROTHY, b. March 13, 1795, d. April 15, 1888.
349 BENJAMIN FRANKLIN, b. Oct. 15, 1797, m. Eliza H. Hart; Susan Mary Smith.
350 ALEXANDER, b. Aug. 30, 1800, m. Hannah Adelia Billings.

Amos Palmer (No. 229) m. Betsey Stanton (No. 401), that family, Jan. 12, 1794. After Mr. Palmer's death she m. ——— a Brewster.

CHILDREN:

351 AMOS, b. ———, d. June 10, 1788.
352 JOHN, b. ———.
353 ZEBA D., b. May 30, 1790, m. Mary Palmer (No. 418).
354 ELIZABETH, b. ———, m. Allen Palmer (No. 343).
355 LUCY ANN, b. ———, m. John R. Cullum, and moved to Texas.

Nathaniel Palmer (No. 242) m. Grace Noyes Aug. 18, 1765 (No. 145), that family.

CHILDREN:

356 PAUL, b. May 24, 1766, d. young.
357 NATHANIEL, b. Dec. 15, 1768, m. Nancy or Ann Phelps (No. 37), that family; 2d, Mercy Brown (No. 89), that family.
358 GRACE, b. May 25, 1772, m. ——— Durfee.
359 LUKE, b. Feb. 14, 1775, m. Sally Potter Denison (No. 465), that family.
360 MARY, b. May 3, 1777, d. young.
361 POLLY, b. Jan. 21, 1780, m. Noyes Brown (No. 87), that family.
362 BETSEY, b. Sept. 8, 1785, m. David Chesebrough Smith.
363 WARREN, b. March 3, 1788, m. Marcia Denison (No. 536), that family.

David Palmer (No. 243) m. Abigail Gardiner of Westerly, R. I., Nov. 15, 1775. He was killed at the massacre at Fort Griswold Sept. 6, 1781. His widow m. 2d, George Denison Oct. 3, 1784 (No. 302), Denison family.

CHILDREN:

364 DAVID H., b. ———.
365 MARTHA, b. ———.

Elias Palmer (No. 245) m. Esther Randall April 28, 1757 (No. 44), that family.

CHILDREN:

366 MARY, b. Jan. 21, 1758.
367 WEALTHY, b. Nov. 26, 1759.
368 ELIAS, b. Jan. 4, 1762.
369 ESTHER, b. Dec. 9, 1763.
370 JOHN, b. March 6, 1766.
371 MARVIN, b. May 24, 1768.
372 PAUL, b. Sept. 23, 1770.

Wait Palmer (No. 247) m. Mary Safford of Coventry April 4, 1751. She d. Oct. 18, 1785.

CHILDREN:

373 WAIT, b. Aug. 24, 1754.
374 EDITH, b. Jan. 7, 1756.
375 STUCKLEY, b. Jan. 25, 1758.

PALMER FAMILY.

376 CHARLES, b. June 25, 1760.
377 ASA, b. Sept. 7, 1763.
378 ROWLAND, b. Oct. 31, 1766.
379 MARY, b. Aug. 24, 1770.

Israel Palmer (No. 249) m. Lois Brown Oct. 28, 1753 (No. 53), that family.

CHILDREN:

380 JESSE, b. July 20, 1754.
381 MARGARET, b. April 2, 1756.

Ebenezer Palmer (No. 253) m. Hannah Palmer Nov. 22, 1758.

CHILDREN:

382 HANNAH, b. Oct. 14, 1759.
383 LUCY, b. Sept. 7, 1761, m. Ichabod Brown (No. 309), that family.
384 MARTHA, b. July 26, 1764.

Amos Palmer (No. 286) m. Phebe, daughter of Samuel Brown of Stonington and Phebe Wilbur of Little Compton, R. I., Oct. 5, 1775 (No. 185), that family. She d. April 9, 1781. He m. 2d, Sally, daughter of Col. James Rhodes, Oct. 16, 1785.

CHILDREN BY FIRST MARRIAGE.

385 FANNY, b. July 9, 1776, m. Thomas Swan (No. 90), that family; 2d, Rev. John Noyes (No. 177), that family.
386 BETSEY, b. Aug. 16, 1778, m. Hon. Nathan F. Dixon Jan. 14, 1804.

CHILDREN BY SECOND MARRIAGE:

387 PHEBE, b. July 18, 1786, m. James Hammond.
388 AMOS, b. May 26, 1788, m. Sarah Foster.
389 HARRIET F., b. Aug. 20, 1790, m. Rev. Roswell Swan (No. 104), that family.
390 BENJAMIN F., b. July 10, 1793, m. a Miss Marshall, neice of Hon. Henry Clay.
391 WILLIAM RHODES, b. Oct. 18, 1795, m. Nancy Babcock July 3, 1822 (No. 162).
392 EMMA, b. Jan. 2, 1798, m. Dea. Thomas Wells of Kingston, R. I.
393 COURTLANDT, b. Nov. 11, 1800, m. Eliza Thurston of Hopkinton, R. I., m. 2d, Mary Ann Swayham of New York.
394 DR. GEORGE EDWIN, b. April 15, 1803, m. Emma Woodbridge May 23, 1826 (No. 34), that family; he m. 2d, Catharine J. McNeill of New York, March 23, 1840.

Gershom Palmer (No. 270) m. Zerviah Palmer Jan. 1, 1778 (No. 276) that family.

CHILDREN:

395 GERSHOM, b. Dec. 31, 1778.
396 JARIUS, b. Feb. 22, 1781, m. Abby York (No. 115), that family.
397 JULIUS, b. Sept. 11, 1784.
398 ZERVIAH, b. March 31, 1787.
399 JEMIMA, b. July 17, 1789.
400 SYLVIA, b. June 4, 1792.

Charles Palmer (No. 299) m. Betsey Denison Jan. 10, 1802 (No. 274), that family. He d. Oct. 15, 1837; she d. Aug. 6, 1834.

CHILDREN:

401 ELIZA H., b. Aug. 16, 1802, m. Clark Davis, Jr., Dec. 14, 1824.
402 EDWARD, b. March 19, 1805, m. Betsey Barnes, Jan. 31, 1827.
403 JEANNETTE, b. Sept. 21, 1809, m. Thomas Clark; Richard D. Simmons.

404 FRANCES, b. Dec. 9, 1812, m. Peter Durland.
405 CHARLES L., b. June 27, 1815, m. 1st, Maria Miller; m. 2d, Caroline S. Tinker; 3d, Mary Trickep.
406 PHEBE, b. Oct. 22, 1817, m. Peter Durland.
407 LUCY C., b. July 15, 1819.
408 LUCRETIA CRARY, b. June 3, 1821, m. Peter Durland Oct. 12, 1843.

Denison Palmer (No. 302) m. Hannah Slack Dec. 4, 1803; m. 2d, Eliza, widow of Allen Chesebrough.

CHILDREN:

409 DENISON, b. July 4, 1805.
410 WILLIAM, b. June 24, 1807.
411 CODDINGTON B., b. Feb. 8, 1810.
412 EPHRAIM W., b. May 4, 1812.
413 NATHANIEL N., b. March 23, 1815.
414 WARREN S., b. May 1, 1818, m. Ann Elizabeth Chesebrough (No. 416), that family. He d. aged 27 yrs.
415 NATHAN B., b. July 5, 1821.
416 HANNAH ELIZA, b. Feb. 1, 1823.

Lemuel Palmer (No. 204) m. Abigail Davis in 1797 (No. 22), that family. He d. May 14, 1850. She d. Jan. 22, 1832.

CHILDREN:

417 ABBY D., b. Sept. 13, 1797, m. Henry Smith (No. 106), that family.
418 MARY, b. Oct. 27, 1800, m. Zeba D. Palmer (No. 353).
419 JOHN D., b. Aug., 1802, m. Mary Smith Nov. 29, 1829 (No. 110), that family.
420 HANNAH EELLS, b. Dec. 6, 1804, m. Paul Smith Palmer (No. 536).
421 BRIDGET MATILDA, b. March 30, 1807, m. Henry Rhodes (No. 13), that family.
422 NANCY D., b. Feb. 22, 1810, m. Alden Palmer (No. 439).
423 JAMES W., b. Feb. 3, 1814, d. July 22, 1822.
424 HARRIET J., b. June 9, 1822, d. April 20, 1832.

Elias Sanford Palmer (No. 238) m. Phebe Palmer March 15, 1761 (No. 266). He m. 2d, Mrs. Lucy (Randall) Breed March 23, 1794 (No. 63), Randall family.

CHILDREN:

425 SANFORD, b. Aug. 4, 1763, m. Wealthy Grant Feb. 10, 1788.
426 BORODEL, b. March 5, 1765.
427 PHEBE, b. Aug. 9, 1766, m. Nathan Hancox (No. 12), that family.
428 ELIZABETH, b. March 14, 1768, m. Ziba Swan (No. 118), that family.
429 ROSWELL, b. Oct. 23, 1769.
430 NOYES, b. April 20, 1771.
431 DAVID, b. Jan. 17, 1773.
432 LUTHER, b. Nov. 25, 1774, m. Sarah Kenyon; 2d, Sarah Wells.
433 PRISCILLA, b. May 20, 1778.
434 CHARLES, b. Feb. 20, 1780.
435 REBECCA, b. Nov. 26, 1782.

Thomas W. Palmer (No. 324) m. Lucy Prentice Wheeler Nov. 15, 1795 (No. 126), that family.

CHILDREN:

436 LUCY, b. Nov. 9, 1796, m. John J. Stanton (No. 201), that family.
437 THOMAS W., b. Sept. 21, 1798, d. Oct. 10, 1801.
438 MARY ROSSITER, b. Aug. 10, 1800, m. Dea. Noyes Palmer (No. 345).
439 ALDEN, b. July 17, 1802, m. Nancy D. Palmer (No. 422).

PALMER FAMILY.   523

440 EUGENE, b. March 26, 1806, m. Jane ———.
441 HANNAH, b. Feb. 4, 1807, d. young.
442 LYDIA EMELINE, b. Feb. 19, 1813, m. Joseph Warren Stanton (No. 418), that family.
443 THOMAS W., b. July 20, 1716, m. Lucy Browning, daughter of Latham H. Browning (No. 55), that family.

Allen Palmer (No. 343) m. Elizabeth Palmer (No. 354) Jan. 14, 1810. He d. March 25, 1866.

CHILDREN:

444 AMOS ALLEN, b. ———, m. Hannah Chesebrough (No. 384), that family; m. 2d, sister of his first wife, Emma Chesebrough (No. 383).
445 JOHN D., b. ———.
446 NOYES, b. ———.
447 BRIDGET, b. ———.
448 ELIZA, b. ———.

Dea. Noyes Palmer (No. 345) was a prominent citizen of the town, and universally respected, a devoted and consistent member of the First Congregational Church, of which he was a lifelong member. He m. 1st, Bridget Denison, Jan. 4, 1816 (No. 461), that family; she d. June 6, 1818. He m. 2d, Mary Rossiter Palmer, Sept. 27, 1824 (No. 438); she d. April 7, 1831. He m. 3d, Harriet Wheeler, March 28, 1844 (No. 159), that family; she d. Oct. 17, 1853. He d. Feb. 18, 1869.

CHILD BY FIRST MARRIAGE:

449 NOYES, b. Nov. 12, 1817, d. Feb. 13, 1818.

CHILDREN BY SECOND MARRIAGE:

450 NOYES STANTON, b. March 29, 1826, m. Emeline Palmer (No. 510), Oct. 15, 1874.
451 HENRY MARTYN, b. Feb. 19, 1829, m. Mary Rossiter Palmer (No. 505), Nov. 3, 1863.

CHILD BY THIRD MARRIAGE.

452 FRANKLIN WHEELER, b. March 19, 1845, m. Eliza Babcock Palmer (No. 511), Sept. 12, 1883.

Benjamin Franklin Palmer (No. 349) m. Eliza H. Hart, daughter of Rev. Ira Hart and wife, Maria Sherman, Dec. 31, 1823 (No. 4), that family; m. 2d, Susan Smith (No. 117), that family.

CHILDREN:

453 FRANKLIN A., b. April 23, 1825, m. Arabella Stoddard.
454 CHARLES T. H., b. Jan. 23, 1827, m. Hattie Day.
455 MARIA S., b. Nov. 16, 1829, m. Selden S. Walkley.
456 HARRIET E., b. Dec. 2, 1832, m. Thomas W. Russell.
457 IRA HART, b. April 18, 1836, m. Harriet Trumbull (No 60), that family.
458 HENRY A., b. Dec. 23, 1842, m. Jennie Day.

CHILD BY SECOND MARRIAGE.

459 EDWIN TRUMBULL, b. ———.

Alexander Palmer (No. 350), m. Hannah Adelia Billings Jan. 26, 1831 (No. 177), that family.

CHILDREN:

460 EDWIN A., b. Sept. 27, 1833, m. Jane Grant June 3, 1863.
461 STEPHEN BILLINGS, b. April 20, 1836, m. Julia Newbury Nov. 18, 1868.
462 Infant, b. and d. March 28, 1839.
463 WILLIAM H., b. Aug. 17, 1840, m. Frances Collins of Hartford, Conn., Dec. 13, 1870.
464 JAMES A., b. June 7, 1842, d. unmarried.
465 JOHN S., b. Feb. 8, 1845.
466 NOYES, b. June 28, 1847, d. Nov. 25, 1851.
467 CHARLES FRANKLIN, b. May 30, 1849, d. Oct. 19, 1851.
468 ADELIA, b. Aug. 16, 1854 d. May 30, 1855.

NOTE.—William Henry Palmer (No. 463), son of Alexander and wife, Adelia (Billings) Palmer, was born in Stonington, Conn., Aug. 17, 1840. He graduated from Yale College and some years succeeding he spent in Cleveland, Ohio, and afterwards in New York city, where he engaged in the study of medicine. He was valedictorian of the class of 1866 at the College of Physicians and Surgeons in New York city. Returning to Cleveland, he commenced the practice of his profession there. Was Professor of Ophthalmology in Cleveland Medical College and visiting physician in Cleveland City Hospital. He died at Hartford, Conn., June 19th, 1871, of consumption. He married at Hartford six months before his death Miss Frances Collins Dec. 13, 1870.

A classmate, Mr. G. S. Merriam, has kindly furnished the following brief obituary:

"Remembrances of all his classmates as to Palmer will substantially agree, I think, differing only as some knew him more fully than others, but to all he was the same faithful, kindly, manly fellow. He was known at first as a very industrious student, who earned high rank by hard work. I remember the general surprise when this quiet scholar distinguished himself by a particularly audacious and successful raid against the Sophomores. He was as hearty in his enjoyment of a joke or a frolic as in his devotion to a hard lesson. He worked his way steadily upward in the scholarship list and took a Philosophical at commencement. His pleasant face, his big brown eyes, his pleasant smile and hearty laugh will come vividly back to all, telling their story of the man he was. Class of '64."

Zeba D. Palmer (No. 353) m. Mary Palmer (No. 418), Dec. 23, 1816; he m. 2d, Harriet Eliza Palmer (No. 539).

CHILDREN:

469 ZEBA D., b. Dec. 8, 1817, d. Oct. 12, 1819.
470 EDMUND L., b. Oct. 21, 1819, m. Adelaide E. Brackett, Oct. 19, 1847.
471 MARY T., b. Feb. 20, 1822, d. young.
472 MARY ABIGAIL, b. Aug. 17, 1824, m. Nathan Newton Tiffany April 5, 1855.

CHILD BY SECOND MARRIAGE:

473 HARRIET, b. ———, m. ——— Hawkins.

Nathaniel Palmer (No. 357) m. Nancy or Ann Phelps Nov. 11, 1790 (No. 37), that family; she d. in 1791. He m. 2d, Mercy Brown March 18, 1798 (No. 89), that family.

CHILDREN:

474 NATHANIEL, b. Aug. 8, 1799, m. Eliza T. Babcock, Dec. 7, 1826 (No. 165), that family.
475 ANN ADELAIDE, b. Nov. 26, 1800, m. Charles T. Stanton (No. 417), that family.
476 GRACE NOYES, b. Oct. 18, 1802, m. J. Warren Stanton (No. 418), that family.
477 LOUIS LAMBERT, b. Feb. 8, 1804, d. unmarried.
478 ALEXANDER S., b. Jan. 26, 1806, m. Priscilla Dixon June 19, 1837.

PALMER FAMILY.

479 JULIET, b. Feb. 25, 1808, m. Capt. William A. Fanning May 31, 1822.
480 MERCY, b. Aug. 8, 1811.
481 WILLIAM L., b. Nov. 13, 1813, m. Sarah Potter Williams (No. 378), that family.
482 NANCY, b. Nov. 13, 1813, m. Capt. Charles T. Stanton (No. 417), that family.
483 THEODORE DWIGHT, b. Aug. 29, 1816, m. Harriet Billings (No. 198), that family.

Luke Palmer (No. 359) m. Sally Potter Denison March 11, 1804 (No. 465), that family. He d. Dec. 25, 1822; she d. July 9, 1862.
CHILDREN:
484 SALLY MARIA, b. Jan. 7, 1805, d. Nov. 3, 1874, unmarried.
485 BETSEY DENISON, b. Nov. 29, 1806, m. William Weed, Nov. 6, 1836, d. in Stonington, July 12, 1843.
486 LUKE, b. Oct. 19, 1808, m. Mary E. Holbrook, Jan. 8, 1851.
487 HANNAH WILLIAMS, b. Aug. 4, 1810, m. Joshua Noyes, March 8, 1848 (No. 249), that family.
488 GRACE BILLINGS, b. Aug. 28, 1812, m. Daniel Carew June 21, 1830. He d. at sea Aug. 19, 1837; his widow m. 2d, Nathaniel Wilgus April 5, 1852.
489 HARRIET NEWELL, b. Aug. 31, 1814, m. Theodore Butler April 24, 1837.

Luther Palmer (No. 432) m. Sarah, daughter of Joshua and Mary Cross Kenyon of Westerly, R. I., Dec. 12, 1799; she d. July 3, 1815. He m. 2d, Sarah, daughter of Thomas and Mary (Robinson) Palmer Wells of Hopkinton, R. I.; she d. in 1859, aged 67 years; he d. Feb. 22, 1864, aged 89 years.
CHILDREN:
490 ELIAS SANFORD, b. May 27, 1801, m. Marian Olcott Oct., 1818.
491 MARY, b. March 1, 1803, m. Robert S. Potter Dec., 1821.
492 SARAH, b. Feb. 25, 1805, m. Paul Greene.
493 LUTHER AVERILL, b. Nov. 25, 1807, m. Rhoda Babcock Jan. 28, 1845.
494 PHEBE, b. Jan. 27, 1809, d. Nov. 4, 1894.
495 ALBERT GALLATIN, b. May 11, 1813, m. Sarah Amelia Langworthy; 2d, Amelia Wells, May 1, 1845.
496 ANNE POTTER, b. July 31, 1815, m. Benjamin Franklin Billings of Griswold.
CHILDREN BY SECOND MARRIAGE:
497 THOMAS ROBINSON, b. Sept. 29, 1819, m. Lucy H. Gay April, 1847; m. 2d, Mrs. Sarah Pendleton of Westerly, R. I.
498 LUCIOUS NOYES, b. July 2, 1821, m. Anne Culbert July 12, 1855.
499 JULIA WELLS, b. July 24, 1824.
500 ELIZABETH MARIA, b. April 3, 1826.
501 HARRIET CLARINDA, b. May 1, 1828, m. Hiram York.
502 ROBERT POTTER, b. July 6, 1830, m. Harriet Thompson Jan. 17, 1867.

Phebe Palmer (No. 387) m. James Hammond of Newport, R. I., in 1804.
ONE CHILD:
503 ANN R. HAMMOND, b. ———, m. Charles H. Phelps (No. 47), that family.

Major Alden Palmer (No. 439) m. Nancy D. Palmer (No. 422), Oct. 10, 1831.
CHILDREN:
504 HARRIET J., b. July 28, 1832, d. June 4, 1884, unmarried.
505 MARY ROSSITER, b. March 16, 1834, m. Henry Martyn Palmer (No. 451).

506 THOMAS, b. Aug. 13, 1835, m. Minnie Pond.
507 ALDEN, b. Sept. 14, 1837, m. Eunice Noyes (No. 380), that family.
508 LUCY W., b. Dec. 28, 1839, d. unmarried.
509 EUGENE, b. Nov. 29, 1841, m. Mary Chesebrough, daughter of Gideon P. Chesebrough (No. 342), that family.
510 EMELINE, b. March 3, 1846, m. Noyes S. Palmer (No. 450).
511 ELIZA BABCOCK, b. June 11, 1849, m. Frank W. Palmer (No. 452).

Jarius Palmer (No. 396) m. Abby York March 17, 1811 (No. 115), that family.   CHILDREN:
512 JARIUS, b. Dec. 2, 1813.
513 ABBY, b. April 9, 1816.
514 ELECTA J., b. Dec. 22, 1819.
515 JAMES E., b. March 9, 1822.
516 AMOS D., b. Aug. 6, 1825.
517 ABEL F., b. July 8, 1828.

George Palmer (No. 310) m. Margaret Palmer (No. 201), Dec. 22, 1783.
CHILDREN:
518 GEORGE, b. in 1784, d. March 4, 1866, unmarried.
519 LUCY, bapt. in 1787, m. ——— West, d. in 1807, in New York State.
520 LEMUEL, bapt. 1789, d. aged 18 years.
521 EUNICE, bapt. in 1794, d. unmarried.
522 FREDERICK, b. Jan. 4, 1792, m. Lucy Ann Burdick, b. May 25, 1804.
523 BRIDGET, b. in 1796, m. Nathan Franklin.
524 THOMAS, b. in 1798, m. Lydia Austin.
525 LOUIS, b. ———, m. Hannah Stanton, moved to New York State.
526 HANNAH, b. ———.
527 LUCRETIA, b. ———, d. unmarried.
528 SAMUEL, b. ———, d. young.

Jonathan Palmer (No. 95) m. Prudence Holmes (No. 29), that family, Sept. 12, 1745. He d. July 5, 1803; she d. Nov. 27, 1799.
CHILDREN:
529 COL. JONATHAN, b. 1747, m. Lucinda ———.
530 PRUDENCE, b. 1752, m. Joseph Wheeler (No. 354), that family.
531 CAPT ROBERT, b. 1763, m. Martha Williams.
532 ASHER, b. ———, m. ———. His widow m. David Main.

Roswell Saltonstall Palmer (No. 311) m. Desire Palmer (No. 203).
CHILDREN:
533 HANNAH, b. ———.
534 REBECCA, b. ———.
535 DESIRE, b. ———.
536 PAUL SMITH, b. Nov. 11, 1796, m. Hannah Eells Palmer (No. 420), Feb. 15. 1824.
537 MATILDA, b. ———.
538 WILLIAM PITT, b. Feb. 22, 1805. (The poet.)
539 HARRIET ELIZA, b. ———, m. Zeba D. Palmer (No. 353).
540 HENRY DWIGHT, b. ———.
541 HANNAH, b. ———.

Moses Palmer (No. 124), m. Prudence Turner, May 8, 1753.
CHILDREN:
542 MOSES, b. Nov. 23, 1755.
543 ABIGAIL, b. March 2, 1757, m. Andrew Pendleton (No. 37), that family.
544 GILBERT, b. May 21, 1760.

PARK FAMILY.

1. ROBERT PARK, the first of the name who appeared in this country, came from Preston, Lancashire, England; sailed from Cowes, Isle of Wight, in the ship Arabella, March 29, 1630, and landed at Salem, Mass., June 12, and at Boston June 17, 1630, with seventy-six passengers all told. He settled with his son, Thomas, in Wethersfield, Conn., in 1640, and was Deputy to the General Court in 1641-2. He removed to Pequot, now New London, in 1649, where he resided six years, and his new barn which stood on the corner of Hempstead and Granite streets, was used as the first house of worship in the new town, and the call to service was by the beat of drum. He finally settled at Mystic in Stonington, as he was one of the men appointed by the General Court of Massachusetts to an official position, in the organization of the town of Southertown in 1658. He died, and his will was probated in March, 1665, and son, Dea. William Park of Roxbury, Mass., was his executor. He served in the early Colonial wars. He m. 1st, Martha, daughter of Capt. Robert Chapen, in Edmundsbury, England; m. 2d, Mrs. Alice Thompson; they were doubtless m. in Roxbury, and soon after removed to Wethersfield, Conn. We cannot say which marriage took place first, whether it was that of Robert Park with the mother, or his son Thomas, with the daughter Dorothy. His wife d. before 1660.

CHILDREN:

2 WILLIAM, b. in England in 1604, m. Martha Holgrave.
3 SAMUEL, b. ―― in England, m. Hannah ――.
4 THOMAS, b. in England, m. Dorothy Thompson.
5 ANN, b. ――, m. Edward Payson, Aug. 10, 1640; she d. Sept. 10, 1641; he m. 2d, Mary, daughter of Bennet Elliot of Nazing, Eng., and sister of the Apostle Elliot.

Dea. William Park of Roxbury, Mass., (No. 2) m. Martha daughter of John Holgrave of Salem, Mass., in 1636. He was one of the wealthiest citizens of Roxbury, and for more than thirty years a member of the General Court. He d. May 11, 1685; she d. Aug. 25, 1708.

CHILDREN:

6 THEODA, b. May 2, 1637, m. Samuel Williams (No. 5), Robert Williams family.
7 HANNAH, b. Nov. 28, 1639, d. young.
8 MARTHA, b. March 2, 1641, m. Isaac Williams (No. 6), Robert Williams family.
9 SARAH, b. Dec. 2, 1643, d. young.
10 JOHN, bapt. July 6, 1645, d. young.
11 DEBORAH, bapt. Jan. 16, 1647, d. young.
12 JOHN, bapt. May 13, 1649, d. young.
13 DEBORAH, bapt. March 26, 1657, d. young.
14 Two unbaptized children, buried June 1, 1658.
15 WILLIAM, bapt. Oct. 8, 1654, d. young.
16 HANNAH, bapt. Sept. 28, 1658.

Samuel Park (No. 3) m. Hannah ———

CHILDREN:

17 ROBERT, b. ———.
18 WILLIAM, b. ———.

Thomas Park (No. 4) owned lands in Stonington (which he purchased of his brother-in-law, Rev. Richard Blinman), situated on the east bank of Mystic river, between the old Post road on the north, the White Hall land on the south and the stone house farm on the east. He disposed of his land and removed to Preston, Conn., in 1680; was the first deacon of Rev. Mr. Treat's church, organized in that town in 1698; m. Dorothy Thompson (No. 5), that family. He served in the early Colonial wars, and d. July 30, 1709.

CHILDREN:

19 MARTHA, b. in 1646, m. Isaac Wheeler (No. 2), that family.
20 THOMAS, b. in 1648, m. Mary, daughter of Robert Allyn, Jan. 4, 1672.
21 ROBERT, b. in 1651, m. Rachael, daughter of Thomas Leffingwell, Nov. 24, 1681.
22 NATHANIEL, b. ———, m. Sarah Geer.
23 WILLIAM, b. ———, m. Hannah Frink Dec. 3, 1684 (No. 3), that family.
24 JOHN, b. ———, m. Mary ———. He d. in 1716; she m. 2d, Rev. Salman Treat Nov. 6, 1716.
25 DOROTHY, b. March 6, 1652, m. April, 1670, Lieut. Joseph Morgan (No. 5), that family.
26 ALICE, b. ———, m. Greenfield Larabee March 16, 1673.

PEABODY FAMILY.

The emigrant ancestor of this family was:

1. JOHN PEABODY, who came to this country from England in 1635, and brought with him four children, viz.:

2 THOMAS, b. ———.
3 FRANCIS, b. ———.
4 WILLIAM, b. in 1620.
5 AMIE, b. ———.

William Peabody (No. 4) m. Elizabeth Alden, daughter of John Alden of the Mayflower fame, Dec. 26, 1644, and d. Dec. 13, 1707, aged 87 yrs.

CHILDREN:

6 JOHN, b. Oct. 4, 1645, d. unmarried.
7 ELIZABETH, b. April 24, 1647, m. John Rogers in 1666.
8 MARY, b. Aug. 7, 1648, m. Edward Southworth in 1667.
9 MERCY, b. Jan. 2, 1650, m. John Simmons in 1671.
10 MARTHA, b. Feb. 24, 1651, m. Samuel Seabury in 1677.
11 PRISCILLA, b. Jan. 15, 1653, m. Rev. Ichabod Wiswall.
12 SARAH, b. Aug. 7, 1656, m. John Coe in 1680.
13 RUTH, b. June 27, 1658, m. Benjamin Bartlett in 1683.
14 REBECCA, b. Oct. 16, 1660, m. William Southworth.
15 HANNA, b. Oct. 15, 1662, m. Samuel Bartlett in 1683.
16 WILLIAM, b. Nov. 24, 1664, removed to Little Compton, R. I., and m. Judith ———, who d. July 20, 1714; he m. 2d, Elizabeth ———, who d. Dec. 14, 1717, and for his third wife, he m. Mary ———, the family names of his three wives are unknown.

CHILDREN BY FIRST WIFE.

17 ELIZABETH, b. April 10, 1698.
18 JOHN, b. Feb. 7, 1700.
19 WILLIAM, b. Feb. 21, 1702.
20 REBECCA, b. Feb. 29, 1704, and m. Rev. Joseph Fish (No. 1), that family, the pastor of the Congregational Church of North Stonington, Ct.
21 PRISCILLA, b. March 4, 1706.
22 JUDITH, b. Jan. 23, 1708.
23 JOSEPH, b. July 26, 1710.
24 MARY, b. April 4, 1712, and m. Nathaniel Fish (No. 5), brother of the Rev. Joseph Fish.

CHILDREN BY SECOND WIFE ELIZABETH.

25 BENJAMIN, b. Nov. 25, 1717.
No child by third wife.

William Peabody (No. 19) and Jerusha Starr were m. in Little Compton, R. I., and children b. there, viz.:

26 RACHEL, b. ———.
27 THOMAS, b. Nov. 30, 1727.
28 HANNAH, b. ———.
29 WILLIAM, b. ———.
30 LYDIA, b. ———.
31 SAMUEL, b. ———.

This Mr. William Peabody (No. 19) came to Stonington, now North Stonington, in 1744, and purchased a farm of 250 acres, upon which he spent the remainder of his life, dying Jan. 3, 1778. After he came to Stonington to reside a pair of twins were b. to them, which he named

    32 JAMES, b. Dec. 14, 1745, and
    33 MARY, b. Dec. 14, 1745.

After the death of Mr. William Peabody, his farm was equally divided between his sons Thomas and Samuel, who lived and d. in Stonington.

Thomas Peabody (No. 27) and Ruth Babcock, both of Stonington, were m. Aug. 16, 1761.

CHILDREN:

    34 RUTH, b. Feb. 7, 1762.
    35 JERUSHA, b. April 8, 1763.
    36 WILLIAM, b. July 22, 1764.
    37 LYDIA, b. Feb. 28, 1766.
    38 REBECCA, b. Jan. 29, 1768.
    39 THOMAS, b. April 12, 1769.
    40 SUSANNAH, b. April 12, 1770, m. Jonas Chapman (No. 19), Chapman family.
    41 BENJAMIN, b. April 29, 1772.
    42 AMY, b. Feb. 22, 1779, d. young.
    43 JOHN, b. Aug. 28, 1775.
    44 LUCY, b. June 26, 1777.
    45 LEMUEL, b. Dec. 20, 1778.
    46 JOSEPH, b. April 18, 1781.

Benjamin Peabody (No. 41) m. Abigail Holmes (No. 9), Holmes family, Nov. 13, 1796.

CHILDREN:

    47 BENJAMIN, b. June 15, 1797.
    48 GEORGE W., b. Jan. 25, 1799.
    49 ABIGAIL, b. Feb. 17, 1801.
    50 JOHN, b. May 24, 1803.
    51 WILLIAM PITT, b. July 24, 1805.
    52 GILES H., b. Sept. 25, 1807, d. young.
    53 REBECCA H., b. Sept. 6, 1809.

After the death of Mrs. Abigail Peabody, Mr. Peabody m. Martha Peckham March 5, 1812.

CHILDREN:

    54 THOMAS H., b. March 10, 1813.
    55 FRANCIS S., b. April 29, 1815.
    56 MARTHA E., b. April 24, 1819.
    57 MARY, b. May 2, 1822.
    58 FANNY A., b. June 29, 1825.
    59 NANCY, b. Sept. 5, 1828.
    60 JAMES A., b. May 30, 1831.

PENDLETON FAMILY.

1. MAJOR BRIAN PENDLETON was b. in 1599 in England. He is the progenitor of the Pendletons found in this vicinity. He first settled in Watertown, and was made freeman there Sept. 3, 1634, and was Deputy for six years to the General Court. He moved to Sudbury and helped settle that town, and was selectman for several years. From Sudbury he went to Ipswich. He was a member of the famous artillery company of Boston. He removed to Portsmouth, New Hampshire, about 1651, and was Deputy there five years. In 1653 he purchased 200 acres of land near Winter Harbor, Saco, Me., and after a few years he returned to Portsmouth, where he made his will, which was proved April 5, 1681. He was an eminent man in his day, and held the office of captain and major for many years, besides important civil and military offices. He m. Eleanor ———; d. in 1681, and left

TWO CHILDREN:

2 MARY, b. ———, m. Rev. Seth Fletcher, d. leaving an only child, Pendleton Fletcher, whom his grandfather adopted in 1670, when he was 13 years old. He was taken captive by the Indians four times; d. in 1750.
3 CAPT. JAMES, b. ———, the only son of Major Brian Pendleton; was first at Watertown, then at Sudbury, Mass., and came to Westerly, R. I., in 1669. He was in the early Colonial wars. He was admitted to the First Church ot Stonington, Conn., Nov. 7, 1680. He m. 1st, Mary ———.

CHILDREN:

4 JAMES, b. at Watertown, Nov., 1650.
5 MARY, b. ———.
6 HANNAH, b. ———.

Mary, the first wife, d. Nov. 7, 1655, and Capt. James m. 2d, Hannah, daughter of Edmund Goodenow, April 29, 1656, and had nine

CHILDREN:

7 BRIAN, b. Sept. 27, 1659.
8 JOSEPH, b. Dec. 29, 1661, m. Deborah Miner (No. 44), that family.
9 EDMUND, b. June 24, 1665.
10 ANN, b. Nov. 12, 1667, m. Eleazer Brown (No. 11), Brown family.
11 CALEB, b. in 1669.
12 SARAH, bapt. at Stonington April 18, 1675.
13 ELEANOR, bapt. July 22, 1679.
14 DOROTHY, bapt. Oct. 3, 1686, m. Nicholas Cottrell (No. 10), Cottrell family.
15 PATIENCE, b. ———.

Capt. James Pendleton d. Nov. 29, 1709. His will is dated Feb. 9, 1702, but does not mention his son James, by the first wife, nor daughters Sarah or Patience by the second wife. They probably d. young or without children.

Joseph Pendleton (No. 8) m. 1st, Deborah Miner (No. 44), daughter of Ephraim and Hannah (Avery) Miner, July 8, 1696. He was buried Sept. 20, 1706.

CHILDREN:

16 DEBORAH, b. Aug. 29, 1697, m. Nicholas Frink (No. 19), that family, Nov. 30, 1715. Mrs. Deborah Pendleton d. Sept. 8, 1697, and Joseph Pendleton m. 2d, Patience Potts, daughter of William Potts of New London, and cousin of his first wife, Dec. 11, 1700.

CHILDREN BY SECOND MARRIAGE:

17 JOSEPH, b. March 3, 1702.
18 WILLIAM, b. March 23, 1704.
19 JOSHUA, b. Feb. 22, 1706.

Joseph Pendleton (No. 17) m. Sarah Worden of Newport, R. I., Jan. 9, 1723.

CHILDREN:

20 JOSEPH, b. Oct. 26, 1724.

Col. William Pendleton (No. 18) m. Lydia Burrows (No. 12), Burrows family, March 10, 1726.

CHILDREN:

21 WILLIAM, Jr., b. Feb. 4, 1727, bapt. Aug. 13, 1727.
22 AMOS, b. June 24, 1728, bapt. Aug. 4, 1728.
23 FREELOVE, b. Oct. 31, 1731, bapt. Nov. 7, 1731.
24 PELEG, b. July 9, 1733.
25 JOHN, b. May 9, 1737.
26 BENJAMIN, b. Sept. 18, 1738.
27 LYDIA, b. ———, m. Zebulon Chesebrough Dec. 10, 1761 (No. 142).
28 JOSHUA, b. May 6, 1744.
29 EPHRAIM, b. July 14, 1746.

Mrs. Lydia Pendleton d. Aug. 18, 1750, and Col. William m. 2d, the widow Mary Chesebrough; her maiden name was McDowell, the daughter of John and Lucia (Stanton) McDowell; she m. Zebulon Chesebrough March 29, 1739, and he d. Feb. 21, 1750, and she m. Col. William Pendleton April 25, 1751.

CHILDREN:

30 LUCY, b. April 22, 1752, m. Robert Randall (No. 50), that family.
31 NATHAN, b. April 2, 1754, m. Amelia Babcock (No. 86), that family.
32 ISAAC, b. June 23, 1757.
33 KETURAH, b. Jan. 25, 1767, m. Sylvester Gavitt March 16, 1788.

Joseph Pendleton (No. 20) m. Anne Champlin, daughter of William and Sarah (Thompson) Champlin of Westerly.

CHILDREN:

34 JOSEPH, b. Jan. 17, 1747.
35 WILLIAM, b. July 15, 1749.

These children were orphans in 1750, both parents being dead.

PENDLETON FAMILY. 533

Amos Pendleton (No. 22) m. Susannah Rossiter Chesebrough (No. 89) Feb. 1, 1753, by Rev. Nathaniel Eells. He served in the Revolutionary war.

CHILDREN:

36 AMOS, Jr., b. Nov. 5, 1754, m. Catharine Davis (No. 14), Feb. 24, 1782.
37 ANDREW, b. July 7, 1756.
38 MOLLY, b. Aug. 4, 1758, m. Capt. Nathan Barber of Avondale.
39 ZEBULON, b. May 27, 1760, m. Thankful Wells Oct. 15, 1780.
40 CHARLES, b. April 24, 1762, m. Abigail Rhodes.
41 LYDIA, b. Oct. 7, 1764, d. in infancy.
42 FREDERICK, b. June 15, 1766, he m. Lucy Hinckley (No. 55), Hinckley family, b. Sept. 3, 1770, daughter of Wyatt Hinckley and wife, Eunice Breed. He was lost at sea Dec. 1, 1790. They had no children, and his widow m. his half brother, Jonathan Pendleton.

Mrs. Susannah Pendleton d. May 31, 1768, and Mr. Amos Pendleton m. for his 2d wife, Anna Foster of Westerly, R. I., in 1768; she was b. in 1743, daughter of Jonathan Foster of Watch Hill; she d. June 5, 1819.

CHILDREN:

43 JONATHAN, b. Sept. 19, 1769, m. Mrs. Lucy (Hinckley) Pendleton (No. 55), Hinckley family.
44 NANCY, b. July 22, 1771, m. Nathaniel Barnes of Long Island, 1791.
45 ACORS, b. July 28, 1773, d. Dec. 16, 1790.
46 WILLIAM, b. July 23, 1775.
47 ISAAC, b. Nov. 22, 1777.
48 OTIS, b. March 7, 1780, m. Betsey Kenyon.
49 GILBERT, b. Sept. 7, 1782, m. 1st, Margaret Rhodes and 2d, her cousin, Celia Rhodes.
50 HARRIS, b. Nov. 19, 1786.

Benjamin Pendleton (No. 26) m. Feb. 9, 1763, Lois Burdick. She was b. April 1, 1738, daughter of David and Mary (Thompson) Burdick of Pawcatuck. Their son, Benjamin, b. Feb. 7, 1764, m. Nov., 1786, Lucy Frink, b. Dec. 9, 1767. This Benjamin sailed from Stonington Nov. 10, 1810 ,and was never heard from afterward. They had ten children, and their oldest son

50a BENJAMIN, b. Feb. 16, 1788, m. Cassandra Sheffield, and their daughter, Cassandra Pendleton, m. Thomas E. Swan (No. 178), Swan family.

Nathan Pendleton (No. 31) m. Amelia Babcock (No. 86), that family, daughter of Col. James and first wife, Sarah (Stanton) Babcock of Westerly, Jan. 2, 1775. He m. 2d, Rhoda (Babcock) Gavitt Oct. 24, 1816.

CHILDREN:

51 AMELIA, b. Oct. 20, 1775.
52 SALLY, b. Aug. 1, 1777.
53 NATHAN, b. June 1, 1779.
54 ISAAC, b. Jan. 16, 1781.
55 KETURAH, b. Dec. 5, 1782.
56 CHARLOTTE, b. Oct. 24, 1784.
57 MOLLY, b. Dec. 16, 1786.

58 CATHARINE, b. July 22, 1789.
59 SIMON, b. Feb. 17, 1792, d. young.
60 SIMON, b. July 30, 1793.
61 WILLIAM, b. April 29, 1795.
62 PELEG, b. March 20, 1798.

Joseph Pendleton (No. 34) m. 1st, Damaris Crandall Jan. 19, 1766, of Westerly.

CHILDREN:

63 NANCY or ANNA, b. June 19, 1766, m. Timothy Chapman (No. 23), that family, March 14, 1782.
64 ABEL, b. Sept. 21, 1768, m.
65 JOSEPH, b. June 30, 1771, m. Hannah Stanton (No. 39), Robert Stanton family.
66 DAMARIS, b. Aug. 9, 1773.

The first wife d. and he m. 2d, ———.

CHILD:

67 EUNICE, b. ———.

The second wife d. and he m. 3d, Nancy, daughter of Benjamin and Alice (Kenyon) Crandall, March 23, 1777. He d. in Westerly, 1822.

CHILDREN:

68 AMELIA, b. July 4, 1779, m. Joshua Pendleton, a cousin.
69 ALICE, b. March 19, 1781.
70 MARY M., b. July 17, 1783, m. Case Chapman (No. 26), Chapman family.
71 MARTHA, b. April 28, 1785.
72 FANNY, b. Dec. 11, 1787.
73 ELIZABETH, b. April 8, 1790.
74 WILLIAM, b. July 3, 1792.
75 BENJAMIN C., b. Nov. 10, 1794. Descendants live in California.
76 GURDON, b. July 14, 1797. Lived in Norwich.
77 LUCY A., b. April 15, 1799, m. David Pendleton.
78 ELLET, b. May 4, 1801.
79 ROWLAND, b. Oct. 28, 1803.

Andrew Pendleton (No. 37) m. April 1, 1782, Abigail, daughter of Moses and Prudence (Turner) Palmer, b. 1757, (No. 543) Palmer family. He d. May 5, 1834; his wife d. Dec. 25, 1822.

CHILDREN:

80 DENEY, b. ———, never married.
81 MOSES, b. ———, d. of yellow fever.
82 FANNY, b. in 1795, and m. Jonathan Grey Stanton (No. 406), Stanton family, b. Feb. 8, 1791, for his second wife.
83 NANCY, b. ———, m. Pitts Downer Frink (No. 128). She d. April 30, 1844.

Charles Pendleton (No. 40) m. Abigail Rhodes, daughter of Col. James and second wife, Abigail Greenman, April 1, 1792.

CHILDREN:

84 ABIGAIL, b. Jan., 1794, d. Jan., 1869.
85 CHARLES, b. ———, murdered at sea.
85a MARIA, b. ———, d. young.
86 MARY ANN, b. Jan. 1, 1797, d. Dec. 5, 1865, never married.
87 CAROLINE, b. April 8, 1800, d. Oct. 16, 1876, m. Jonathan Pendleton (No. 88).

Jonathan Pendleton (No. 43) m. Lucy Pendleton, widow of his half brother, Frederick.
CHILDREN:
88 JONATHAN, b. Nov. 18, 1794, m. Caroline Pendleton (No. 87).
89 WILLIAM, b. Nov. 19, 1796, m. Sally Breed (No. 94).
90 FREDERICK, b. Nov. 4, 1798.
91 FRANCIS, b. Jan. 25, 1801, m. Sarah S. Trumbull May 1, 1828 (No. 38), Trumbull family.
92 LUCY A., b. March 18, 1803, m. ——— Robinson.
93 WAIT H., b. Sept. 17, 1805, d. Jan. 4, 1810.
94 EUNICE, b. 1807, m. Horace Niles.
95 MARIA, b. Jan. 23, 1813, m. Simon Merritt.
96 EMELINE, b. March 24, 1815, never married.

Harris Pendleton (No. 50) m. May 10, 1810, Martha, daughter of Joshua and Mary (Cross) Kenyon of Westerly; she was b. 1791; she d. Feb. 16, 1852, and he d. June 11, 1863.
CHILDREN:
97 HARRIS, b. Feb. 25, 1811, m. Sarah Chester, daughter of Josiah Chester of New London, d. April 15, 1890.
98 GURDON, b. July 27, 1813, m. Mary A., daughter of Samuel Bottom.
99 AVERILL, b. May 14, 1816, d. unmarried.
100 MOSES, b. July 8, 1818, m. Frances Forsyth.
101 B. FRANK, b. Sept. 3, 1823, m. Mary J., daughter of David Cook of Haddam, Conn.
102 JAMES, b. Jan. 16, 1828, d. unmarried.

Nathan Pendleton (No. 53) m. Phebe Cole, b. Feb., 1786, both of Stonington, Oct. 6, 1803. They lived on Pun-hun-gue-nuck Hill, now North Stonington; had twelve
CHILDREN:
103 NATHAN S., b. Jan. 11, 1805.
104 RICHARD C. H., b. Jan. 12, 1807.
105 ENOCH B., b. Sept. 5, 1808, m. Mary, daughter of Andrew Chapman (No. 35), that family, and wife Welthian Palmer, daughter of Joseph Palmer (No. 267), that family.
106 PHEBE E., b. Aug. 30, 1810.
107 DE WITT C., b. May 27, 1812.
108 WILLIAM P., b. April 5, 1814.
109 SALLY A., b. May 23, 1816.
110 SUSAN A., b. March 18, 1818.
111 NANCY M., b. March 1, 1820.
112 JAMES M., b. Jan. 10, 1822.
113 LYDIA E., b. April 4, 1824.
114 KETURAH C., b. May 13, 1827.

Abel Pendleton (No. 64) m. Abigail Stanton (No. 40), Robert Stanton family, Feb. 10, 1795.
CHILDREN:
115 NANCY, b. Jan. 8, 1796, m. Elihu Chesebrough (No. 397), Chesebrough family.
116 CHARLES, b. March 3, 1798, m. Keturah Brown (No. 239).
117 BENJAMIN FRANK, b. March 19, 1799, m. Phebe Williams (No. 492), Williams family, Feb. 11, 1830; had six children.
118 DEMARIS, b. March 5, 1800, m. Samuel White.
119 EMILY, b. March 19, 1801, m. Noyes Williams (No. 488).

120 JOHN B., b. March 9, 1804, m. Lucy Clark, March 20, 1845.
121 JOSEPH, b. in Dec., 1810, d. April 14, 1812.
122 MARY A., b. in 1814, d. Sept. 5, 1833.

Jonathan Pendleton (No. 88) m. his cousin, Caroline Pendleton, daughter of Charles and wife, Abigail (Rhodes) Pendleton, June 10, 1821.

CHILDREN:

123 LUCY A., b. ———, and m. Nathan G. Smith (No. 118).
124 CHARLES, b. ——— and d. at sea.
125 MARY J., b. ———, and m. Horace N. Trumbull (No. 55), Trumbull family.
126 EMMA, d. young.
127 CAROLINE, b. ———, and m. Frederick Moser.
128 SALLY, b. ———.
129 WILLIAM, b. ———; lost at sea.

PHELPS FAMILY.

We learn from the annals of Dorchester, Mass., that William Phelps, the emigrant ancestor of the Phelps family of New England, came to this country in the good ship "Mary and John" in 1630, with one hundred and forty passengers; most of them were constituent members of the church formed in Plymouth, England, in 1629. On reaching this country they transplated their church in Dorchester in 1630, where they continued to reside until 1635, when the Rev. John Warham and a large majority of the church migrated overland to the Connecticut River, and formed the town of Windsor, in Connecticut, and transplated their church there. Mr. Phelps and wife were prominently active, not only in reorganizing the church, but also in establishing a social centre for their new town. Later on Mr. Phelps rose to prominence and eminence, and was repeatedly chosen Deputy to the General Court, and held other important official positions. He m. 1st, in England, ―――――, name and date of marriage not recorded; she d. in Windsor, Conn. He m. his second wife in Windsor, Mary Dover, an Englishwoman, in 1638; she d. Nov. 27, 1675. He d. July 14, 1672.

CHILDREN BY FIRST MARRIAGE:
2 WILLIAM, b. ―――.
3 SAMUEL, b. ―――.
4 NATHANIEL, b. ―――.
5 JOSEPH, b. ―――.

CHILDREN BY SECOND MARRIAGE:
6 TIMOTHY, b. at Windsor, Conn., Sept. 1, 1639, m. Mary Griswold.
7 MARY, b. at Windsor, Conn., May 2, 1644.

Timothy Phelps (No. 6) m. Mary, daughter of Edward Griswold, May. 19, 1661. He d. in 1719.

CHILDREN:
8 TIMOTHY, b. Nov. 1, 1663, m. Martha Crow.
9 JOSEPH, b. Sept. 27, 1666.
10 WILLIAM, b. Feb. 4, 1668.
11 CORNELIUS, b. April 26, 1671.
12 MARY, b. Aug. 14, 1673.
13 SAMUEL, b. Jan. 29, 1675.
14 NATHANIEL, b. Jan. 7, 1677.
15 SARAH, b. Dec. 27, 1679.
16 ABIGAIL, b. June 5, 1682.
17 HANNAH, b. Aug. 4, 1684.
18 ANN, b. Oct. 2, 1686.
19 MARTHA, b. Nov. 12, 1668.

Timothy Phelps (No. 8) m. Martha Crow, Nov. 4, 1686. He removed from Windsor, Conn, to Hebron, Conn., in 1704.

CHILDREN:

20 MARTHA, b. Oct. 29, 1690.
21 TIMOTHY, b. Jan. 29, 1693.
22 NOAH, b. Jan. 23, 1694.
23 CORNELIUS, b. March 5, 1698.
24 CHARLES, b. July 6, 1702, m. Hepzibeth Stiles.

Charles Phelps (No. 24) m. Hepzibeth Stiles, cousin of President Stiles of Yale College in 1725.

CHILDREN:

26 ZERUIAH, b. April 3, 1729.
27 CHARLES, b. Sept. 22, 1732, m. Hannah Denison; 2d, Sally Swan.
28 ASHBEL, b. April 28, 1743.
29 BETHUEL, b. April 25, 1744.
30 JAMES, b. May 29, 1745.

Dr. Charles Phelps (No. 27) came from Hebron, Conn., and took up his abode in Stonington, now North Stonington, where he built him a residence, near the foot of Cosatuc Hill. He afterwards removed to Stonington, where he spent the remainder of his life. He was one of the leading physicians of his day and generation, holding the office of Judge of Probate of the town and other offices. He m. 1st, Hannah Denison (No. 175), that family, Nov. 10, 1757; she d. Sept. 10, 1795, aged 59 yrs. He m. 2d, Sally Swan (No. 93), that family, Feb. 14, 1795. He d. Jan. 11, 1808, aged 76 yrs. His wife survived him and m. 2d, George Hubbard, Esq., Sept. 7, 1809.

CHILDREN BY FIRST MARRIAGE:

31 WILLIAM, b. Sept. 26, 1758, d. June 10, 1786.
32 HANNAH, b. Dec. 15, 1760, m. Andrew Huntington in 1777.
33 CHARLES, b. Feb. 23, 1763, m. Elizabeth Smith.
34 HEPZIBAH, b. May 13, 1765, m. Ephraim Williams Dec. 23, 1787 (No. 218), that family.
35 MARTHA (Patty), b. ———, 1767, m. Frederick Allen, d. 1794.
36 JOSEPH D., b. May 16, 1769, m. Hannah Babcock.
37 NANCY or ANN, b. May 8, 1772, m. Nathaniel Palmer Nov. 11, 1790 (No. 357), that family; she d. 1791.
38 JOHN, b. July 8, 1774, d. Oct. 16, 1775.
39 JONATHAN, b. Oct. 30, 1779, m. Nancy or Ann Brown.
40 STILES, b. June 20, 1781, m. Elizabeth or Betsey Denison Brown.
41 POLLY, b. June 10, 1785, d. unmarried in 1847.

CHILDREN BY SECOND MARRIAGE:

42 SWAN WILLIAM, b. June 24, 1797, d. Feb. 7, 1799.
43 BENJAMIN FRANKLIN, b. Dec. 2, 1800, m. Ameabel Wallace.
44 SALLY, b. Oct. 26, 1802, d. 1820.
45 CHARLES E., b. ———, 1808, d. 1833.

Joseph D. Phelps (No. 36) m. Hannah Babcock (No. 156), that family, Sept. 30, 1792. She d. Aug. 9, 1809; he d. Nov. 2, 1842.

CHILDREN:

46 HANNAH, b. June, 1793, m. Thomas Noyes Jan. 28, 1813 (No. 225), that family.
47 CHARLES H., b. 1795, m. Ann R. Hammond.
48 MARTHA, b. 1797, d. Oct. 20, 1834.
49 NANCY, b. March 20, 1800, m. James W. Noyes (No. 224), that family.

PHELPS FAMILY.

Charles Phelps (No. 33) m. Elizabeth Smith. He d. Dec. 2, 1791.

CHILDREN:

50 ELIZABETH, b. ———.
51 ANNE, b. ———.
52 ANN, b. ———.

Jonathan Phelps (No. 39) m. Nancy or Ann Brown Jan. 26, 1804 (No. 94), Rev. Chad Brown family.

CHILDREN:

53 PELEG B., b. Jan. 23, 1805, m. ——— Broadhead.
54 CHARLES T., b. Dec. 4, 1806, d. 1832.
55 GEORGE ALFRED, b. Oct. 14, 1808, d. unmarried.
56 FRANCIS R., b. Nov. 3, 1810, d. 1831.
57 JAMES H., b. Oct. 29, 1813.
58 JOSEPH D., b. Sept. 12, 1818.
59 WILLIAM WALLACE, b. Dec. 10, 1821.
60 NANCY B., b. June 14, 1824.
61 SARAH W., b. Feb. 18, 1827, m. Mortimer Williams.
62 EDMUND, b. Feb. 18, 1827.
63 MARTHA, b. Dec. 18, 1828, m. Gurdon Gates of Mystic, Conn.

Stiles Phelps (No. 40) m. Elizabeth or Betsey Denison Brown Jan. 29, 1781 (No. 90), Rev. Chad Brown family.

CHILDREN:

64 HORACE STILES, b. 1801.
65 WILLIAM BROWN, b. 1803.
66 ELIZABETH DENISON, b. 1805, m. William Woodbridge (No. 30), that family; he d. 1869.
67 CHARLES HENRY, b. 1807, d. 1808.
68 HARRIET BISHOP, b. 1813, m. Arthur Merritt; 2d, Charles Hill.

Charles H. Phelps (No. 47) m. Ann R. Hammond of Newport, R. I., July 28, 1824 (No. 503), Palmer family. He was lost on the burning steamer Lexington in Long Island Sound Jan. 13, 1840, by which the poor lost a friend and a liberal benefactor. His widow m. for her second husband Rev. Erskine Edwards, pastor of the Second Congregational Church, Stonington, Conn., and became the parents of two daughters.

CHILDREN BY FIRST MARRIAGE:

69 ANN HAMMOND, b. 1826, d. 1828.
70 SARAH, b. 1829, d. 1829.
71 MARTHA ELLEN, b. 1831, m. Eugene Edwards July 11, 1849.
72 CHARLES, b. in 1834, d. 1838.
73 EMILY, b. in 1836, d. 1838.
74 ERSKINE MASON, b. in 1839, m. Anna E. Wilder Oct. 26, 1864.

NOTE.—Hon. Erskine Phelps (No. 74), Phelps family, and Hon. Samuel D. Babcock (No. 215), Babcock family, whose ancestors were some of the most prominent planters of Stonington, Conn., feeling a deep interest in the happiness and welfare of the inhabitants of their native town, and realizing the importance of having a library building for the depository of a Public Library of books and magazines, that may be received from any one or purchased by contributions for that purpose, kindly and generously erected a building in 1899, costing twenty thousand dollars, on Wadawannuck square in Stonington borough, the grounds having been generously given by the descendants of Samuel F. Denison, for the library building.

POLLARD FAMILY.

The first of this family who resided here was Joseph Pollard.

1. JOSEPH POLLARD, m. Patience Holdredge, Aug. 4, 1731.

CHILDREN:

2 DEBORAH, b. Jan. 22, 1733.
3 LYDIA, b. June 30, 1735.
4 HANNAH, b. Aug. 30, 1738.
5 JOSEPH, b. March 24, 1740.
6 ABIGAIL, b. June 24, 1742.
7 BENJAMIN, b. April 9, 1744.
8 PHEBE, b. May 3, 1746.
9 ANN, b. Dec. 2, 1748.
10 JOHN, b. May 20, 1754.

This family left this town at the opening of the fertile West, and fixed their abode in places unknown to us, for the reason that no one of them or their descendants has compiled a genealogical record of the family.

11. In later years Mr. John Pollard of Preston, Conn., b. Nov. 20, 1765, m. Ann Elizabeth Sydleman of the State of New York April 20, 1788.

CHILDREN:

12 SAMUEL, b. in Preston, Conn., April 26, 1790, d. June 23, 1809.
13 JOHN, b. Feb. 3, 1792, d. June 4, 1795.
14 BETSEY (twin), b. Feb. 3, 1792, d. June 4, 1795.
15 WILLIAM, b. July 18, 1798, d. Nov. 6, 1824.
16 MARY ANN, b. Aug. 10, 1803.
17 ANN ELIZA, b. Oct. 8, 1804, d. Nov. 27, 1892.
18 JOHN, b. May 6, 1806, d. June 17, 1852.

William Pollard (No. 15) of Preston, Conn., and Harriet Haskell of the same town were m. Sept. 25, 1820, and their son (No 19), William John Henry Pollard, was b. at Preston, Conn., May 26, 1824, and came to Stonington, Conn., to reside, and m. Ann Eliza Chesebrough (No. 444), that family, Nov. 16, 1848. After a life of the most distinguished and eminent integrity and usefulness he d. Feb. 24, 1897, universally lamented by all who ever knew him, not only for his honesty, but also for his benevolence and liberal bestowal of the same without regard to sect or race. His father, Mr. William Pollard, d. on the island of Madagascar Nov. 26, 1824, and his widow subsequently m. Mr. Samuel Chesebrough of Stonington, Conn. (No. 205), of that family, Dec. 5, 1830, and d. Dec. 22, 1855. They became the parents of four children.

POMEROY FAMILY.

1. ELTWEED POMEROY, the emigrant ancestor of the family, with wife, Mary, family name unknown, came to this country from England in 1630, in the good ship "Mary and John," and after a voyage of 70 days and some detention at Nantasket, landed at Boston, Mass., but he did not long remain there, as the company with which he migrated to this country united in the settlement of Dorchester, Mass., which was so named after Dorchester in England, the home of a large number of the passengers of the good ship "Mary and John."

Mr. Eltweed Pomeroy became a leading citizen of Dorchester, Mass., and held various positions of trust. He purchased a tract of land with the evident intention of making it his permanent home. He held the position of first selectman in 1633, and about that time some of the planters of Dorchester became dissatisfied with the limited area of this new settlement and attracted by the favorable reports of the wonderful fertility of the land bordering on the Connecticut River, they decided in 1635 to leave their Dorchester home and migrate overland to Windsor, Conn. Mr. Eltweed Pomeroy was one of the party who settled in Windsor, Conn., with his family, but for reasons not now understood he removed again with his family to Northampton, Mass. They became the parents of eight children, the fourth was

2 DEACON MEDID, b. Aug. 16, 1638, and m. Experience, daughter of Henry Woodward, and d. June 5, 1686. They had twelve children, the sixth

3 JOSEPH, b. in 1672, and m. Nov. 29, 1692, to Hannah, daughter of Richard Seymour and wife, Hannah Woodruff. They lived in Suffield, Conn., and became the parents of nine children. The sixth

4 REV. BENJAMIN, b. in 1704, who m. Abigail, daughter of Ralph and Ruth (Huntington) Wheelock; she was b. March 3, 1717. They had thirteen children, and the twelfth

5 ELIHU, b. in 1755, and d. in 1834, who m. in 1776 Lydia, daughter of Capt. Stephen and Alice (Cass) Barber; she was b. July 20, 1757. They became the parents of seven children, the fourth

6 HON. BENJAMIN, b. in 1787, and d. in 1855, m. Jan. 1, 1818, Jerusha (No. 305), of Williams family, daughter of Col. Isaac and wife, Phebe Williams, and had

CHILDREN:

7 BENJAMIN, b. Nov. 2, 1818, d. Dec. 28, 1866, m. June 7, 1848, Mary J., daughter of Andrew and wife, Sally (Dimon) Bulkley, of Southport, Conn.

8 JERUSHA, b. May 24, 1820, d. Dec. 1, 1871, m. Nov. 26, 1844, William Woodbridge Rodman, M. D.
9 ISAAC, b. Feb. 16, 1823, m. June 9, 1852, Mary J., daughter of Charles and wife, Emily A. (Judd) Taylor; she d. April 7, 1880, and he m. 2d, May 14, 1888, Anna, daughter of James and wife, Joanna (Lyon) Bubeck, and widow of William W. Berry.
10 ELIHU, b. Feb. 16, 1823, d. Sept. 8, 1824.
11 LYDIA B., b. Aug. 4, 1825, d. Dec. 22, 1888, m. April 29, 1845, Thomas, son of Charles and wife, Rebecca (Williams) Wheeler (No. 319), that family.
12 PHEBE W., b. March 4, 1828, d. Nov. 15, 1846.
13 CYRUS, b. May 14, 1831, d. April 30, 1832.
14 CYRUS W., b. April 2, 1833, m. Jan. 24, 1861, Abby, daughter of Nathan and wife, Abigail (Graves) Cook, of Illinois.
15 REBEKAH W., b. Nov. 20, 1835, m. Feb. 12, 1862, Henry T., son of Jonathan and wife Miranda (Thorp) Bulkley of Southport, Conn.
16 FRANCES R., b. June 11, 1838, d. July 9, 1839.
17 ANNA G., b. Nov. 28, 1840, m. her sister's husband Dec. 26, 1872, William Woodbridge Rodman, M. D., son of William Woodbridge Rodman and wife, Lucy Sheldan (Woodbridge) Rodman of Stonington, Conn.

PRENTICE FAMILY.

1. CAPT. THOMAS PRENTICE, b. in England in 1621. The earliest record of his being in this country is the birth of his two children, Thomas and Elizabeth, twins, Jan. 22, 1650. He and his wife joined the church in Cambridge in 1652. They lived in the eastern part of Cambridge village, and later in Newton, Mass., where he d. from a fall from his horse July 6, 1710, aged 80 years. He was appointed captain of the troop of horse in the Indian war, June 24, 1675. He was a terrible enemy to the hostile Indians, but ever a friend to the Indian converts. He m. Grace ———, and brought her with him to this country with his eldest child. Mrs. Grace d. Oct. 9, 1692.

THEIR CHILDREN:

2 GRACE, bapt. in England in 1648, m. Capt. Thomas Oliver in 1667.
3 THOMAS, b. ———.
4 ELIZABETH, bapt. Jan. 22, 1650, m. Thomas Aldredge in 1675.
5 MARY, b. ———.
6 JOHN, bapt. in 1653, d. young.
7 JOHN, b. 1655, m. Elizabeth Jackson in 1677.
8 HANNAH, b. in 1661, d. April 25, 1738.

Thomas Prentice (No. 3) m. Sarah (No. 10), daughter of Capt. Thomas and wife Ann (Lord) Stanton, (who was the famous Indian interpreter), March 20, 1675. He d. April 19, 1665. Mrs. Prentice m. 2d, Capt. William Denison (No. 43), and d. 1713.

CHILDREN:

9 THOMAS, b. Jan. 13, 1676, m. Maria Russell Dec. 28, 1696, d. Dec. 7, 1709.
10 GRACE, b. in 1678.
11 SAMUEL, b. about 1680, m. Esther Hammond.
12 REV. JOHN, b. in 1682, m. 1st, widow Mary Gardner Dec. 4, 1705, and m. 2d, widow Prudence Swan.

Samuel Prentice (No. 11) m. Esther, daughter of Nathaniel Hammond, Sr., of Newton, Mass., before 1702. He owned a large tract of land in Stonington, Conn., before 1700, and came here to live about 1709. He d. April 24, 1728. She m. 2d, Christopher Avery (No. 18), that family.

CHILDREN:

13 SAMUEL, b. Nov. 25, 1702.
14 JOSEPH, b. Jan. 26, 1704, m. Mary Wheeler Nov. 10, 1725.
15 GRACE, b. Jan. 16, 1705, m. Josiah Grant (No. 13), that family.
16 MARY, b. April 12, 1708, m. John Breed (No. 7), that family.
17 JONAS, b. Sept. 28, 1710, in Stonington, Conn., m. Lucy Denison (No. 119), that family.
18 ESTHER, b. Dec. 12, 1713, m. Christopher Palmer (No. 146), that family.
19 OLIVER, b. Oct. 25, 1720, m. Eliphal Noyes (No. 109), April 7, 1743, d. Oct. 18, 1755.
20 EUNICE, b. Dec. 8, 1717, m. Christopher Avery Sept. 10, 1735 (No. 73), that family.

21 THOMAS, b. Oct. 25, 1719, m. Elizabeth Baldwin (No. 25). He d. March 3, 1783.
22 DOROTHY, b. Dec. 13, 1723.
23 LUCY, b. May 20, 1727.

Dea. Samuel Prentice (No. 13) m. Abigail, daughter of Ebenezer and wife, Phebe (Denison) Billings (No. 44), Billings family, before 1728. She d. Oct. 30, 1789, and Mr. Prentice d. Oct. 11, 1773.

CHILDREN:

24 DOROTHY, b. Jan. 7, 1728.
25 SAMUEL, b. Aug. 24, 1729, d. Jan. 15, 1734.
26 EBENEZER, b. Oct. 25, 1731.
27 JOHN, b. May 13, 1733.
28 ABIGAIL, b. Dec. 11, 1734, m. Eleazer Williams (No. 449), Robert Williams family, about 1754.
29 JOSHUA, b. July 2, 1737, m. Mrs. Elizabeth Stanton, and 2d, Mary Shepherd.
30 PHEBE, b. Feb. 22, 1738, m. Henry Hewitt Jan. 2, 1772 (No. 69), Hewitt family.
31 ASA, b. Sept. 7, 1740, d. young.
32 JONAS, b. Feb. 9, 1742.
33 JESSE, b. Jan. 24, 1743.
34 ESTHER, b. Jan. 31, 1745, d. young.
35 AMOS, b. April 24, 1748.
36 GRACE, b. Dec. 4, 1750, m. about 1769, ——— Shepherd.

Jonas Prentice (No. 17) m. Lucy Denison Nov. 29, 1733. He d. June 7, 1766.

CHILDREN:

37 MARY, b. Sept. 6, 1734, m. Capt. John Swan (No. 30), of Swan family.
38 SAMUEL, b. Oct. 4, 1736, m. Ann Billings.
39 ESTHER, b. Sept. 1, 1738.
40 DANIEL, b. May 4, 1740, m. Mary Billings.
41 THOMAS, b. April 7, 1743.
42 NATHAN, b. May 4, 1745.
43 LUCY, b. March 22, 1747, m. Capt. Thomas Wheeler (No. 74), of that family.

Col. Samuel Prentice (No. 38) m. Ann Billings (No. 49), of that family. He d. in Stonington July, 1807, and she d. Dec., 1829.

CHILDREN:

44 SAMUEL, b. 1759, surgeon, m. Lucretia Holmes (No. 46), of Holmes family.
45 LUCINDA, b. ———, and m. Dr. Elijah Herrick Jan. 19, 1786.
46 BETSEY, b. ———.
47 NANCY, b. ———.
48 SALLY, b. ———, m. David Moore.
49 REBECCA, b. 1765, d. young.
50 PHEBE, b. 1769, d. young.

Daniel Prentice (No. 40) m. Mary Billings (No. 62), that family, Jan. 10, 1765.

CHILDREN:

51 THOMAS, b. Feb. 5, 1766, m. Martha Stanton (No. 383), that family, about 1790. He d. a year after his marriage, and his widow m. Christopher Gallup (No. 127), that family, April 13, 1792.
52 MARY GALLUP, b. Sept. 2, 1769.

Thomas Prentice (No. 21) m. Elizabeth Baldwin (No. 25), that family, Feb. 1, 1743. She d. Dec. 21, 1777; he d. March 30, 1783.

PRENTICE FAMILY.

CHILDREN:
53 EUNICE, b. June 20, 1746, m. William Williams (No. 211), of that family.
54 REBECCA, b. Sept. 30, 1748, d. young.
55 ELIZABETH, b. July 25, 1751.
56 ESTHER, b. Jan. 14, 1754, d. young.
57 MARY, b. Sept. 30, 1756.
58 MARTHA, b. Oct. 4, 1759.
59 THOMAS, b. Aug. 25, 1765, m. Anna Downer April 17, 1789. He lived in North Stonington, Conn., and d. on the farm on which he was born.

CHILDREN:
60 SOPHIA, b. May 30, 1791, m. Samuel Browning Nov. 28, 1811.
61 THOMAS, b. July 2, 1793, m. Harriet Ayers, d. Nov. 22, 1847.
62 CHARLES, b. April 26, 1797, m. Phebe Ames, d. Aug., 1843.
63 HENRY, b. Sept. 7, 1802, m. Eliza Hewitt (No. 193), that family, Nov. 30, 1824.
64 ELIZA A., b. Nov. 6, 1804.
65 WILLIAM, b. May 21, 1807, m. 1st, Frances Avery and 2d, Sarah Hall.

John Prentice (No. 27) m. 1st, Dec. 1, 1757, Mary Haskell; she d. July 8, 1784. He m. 2d, Rebecca Haskell; she d. 1831. Mr. Prentice d. June 21, 1810.

CHILDREN BY FIRST WIFE:
66 SAMUEL, b. Oct. 8, 1758, d. in the Revolutionary war.
67 JOHN, b. June 22, 1761, m. Sarah Leonard July 7, 1787.
68 ASA, b. Sept. 5, 1763, m. Lucy Park in 1791.
69 ASHER, b. Jan. 29, 1769, m. Elizabeth Rix.

CHILDREN BY SECOND WIFE:
70 REBECCA, b. 1790, m. Samuel Wheeler (No. 387), of Wheeler family.
71 OLIVER, b. about 1793, d. 1825.
72 JOSHUA, b. in 1797.
73 PHEBE, b. in 1808.

Asher Prentice (No. 69) m. Elizabeth Rix in 1797.

CHILDREN:
74 ELIZA, b. Oct. 19, 1799, m. Ephraim Hewitt (No. 192), of Hewitt family.
75 ASHER, b. Jan. 1, 1802, m. Mary Hewitt (No. 194), of Hewitt family.

Joshua Prentice (No. 29) m. 1st, widow Elizabeth Stanton Hewitt, Jan. 14, 1776; she d. Dec. 10, 1776, and he m. 2d, Polly or Mary Shepherd April 25, 1787; she d. Aug. 27, 1840, and he d. Sept. 9, 1794.

CHILDREN:
76 SAMUEL, b. April 22, 1788, m. Amy Smith (No. 69), daughter of Chester and wife, Sally (Brewster) Smith, Dec. 21, 1810.

CHILDREN:
77 SAMUEL, b. Oct. 25, 1814, d. young.
78 CHESTER, b. Aug. 15, 1816, m. Lucy Crary Dec. 1, 1843.
79 CHARLES F., b. Aug. 8, 1820, d. young.
80 MARY E., b. Sept. 16, 1822.
81 WILLIAM, b. Aug. 26, 1825, m. Maria D. Meacham Feb. 4, 1850.
82 POLLY, b. April 24, 1791.
83 AMY, b. Sept. 10, 1792, m. Thomas Browning Nov. 22, 1812 (No. 48), Browning family.

Asa Prentice (No. 68) m. Lucy Park in 1791.

CHILDREN:
84 ASA, b. Feb. 13, 1792, m. Anna Browning (No. 51), of Browning family.
85 SAMUEL, b. May 31, 1794, m. Susan Baldwin (No. 89), of Baldwin family.
86 LUCY, b. Aug. 23, 1796, m. Dec. 11, 1814, John D. Wheeler (No. 433), of Wheeler family.

RANDALL FAMILY.

1. JOHN RANDALL, the progenitor of the Randall family of Westerly and Stonington, first appears at Newport, R. I., from which place he came to Westerly as early as 1667, where the remainder of his life was spent. He m. Elizabeth ———, whose family name and date of birth is not known. He d. in 1685; his wife d. in 1685.

CHILDREN:

2 JOHN, b. in 1666, m. Abigail ———; 2d, Mary Baldwin.
3 STEPHEN, b. in 1668, m. Abigail Sabin.
4 MATHEW, b. in 1671, m. Eleanor ———.
5 PETER, b. in 1704, m. Elizabeth Polly; 2d, Phebe Benjamin.

John Randall (No. 2) lived with his father in Westerly, on land purchased of Thomas Bell of Stonington, until he reached manhood, when he came to Stonington and bought large tracts of land, which was intersected by the society line, that divided the town of Stonington into two religious societies in 1721. Mr. Randall was a farmer by occupation, and as such reduced his land grants to cultivation, which he industriously and successfully improved during the remainder of his life. He m. 1st, at Stonington, Abigail ———, whose family name and birth date does not appear on record. He m. 2d, Mary Baldwin, granddaughter of the first Walter Palmer, Nov. 25, 1706 (No. 19), Baldwin family. He d. in Stonington in an honored old age.

CHILDREN BY FIRST MARRIAGE:

6 ELIZABETH, b. July 4, 1696, m. James Brown May 5, 1718, (No. 38), that family.
7 MARY, b. Dec. 16, 1698, m. Stephen Wilcox.
8 JOHN, b. Dec. 2, 1701, m. Dorothy Cottrell, Mrs. Mary (Holmes) Palmer.
9 DOROTHY, b. Dec. 7, 1703.
10 ABIGAIL, b. Dec. 4, 1705, m. John Brown, Oct. 16, 1729.

CHILDREN BY SECOND MARRIAGE:

11 SARAH, b. Nov. 10, 1707, d. at Stonington in 1812.
12 NATHAN, b. July 7, 1709, m. Mary Cottrell; 2d, Eleanor Cottrell.
13 ICHABOD, b. Oct. 21, 1711, d. at Havana, Cuba.
14 SARAH, b. March 12, 1714, d. Sept. 6, 1714.
15 JOSEPH, b. June 2, 1715, d. June 22, 1715.
16 BENJAMIN (twin), b. June 2, 1715, m. at Stonington in 1733, Ruth Brown. They settled at Colchester, Conn. He was admitted freeman there Dec. 6, 1763, but probably he was there several years before this date. He is represented as possessing great physical powers and endurance. He d. June 15, 1811.
17 REBECCA, b. July 31, 1717.
18 JOSEPH, b. July 17, 1720.

Stephen Randall (No. 3) m. Abigail, daughter of Joseph and Waitstill Sabin, Dec. 24, 1697. She was b. Aug. 16, 1678.

CHILDREN:
19 ABIGAIL, b. Dec. 10, 1698.
20 SAMUEL, b. May 19, 1701.
21 STEPHEN, b. March 13, 1705.
22 JONATHAN, b. March 7, 1707, m. Preserved ———.
23 ELIZABETH, b. Sept. 25, 1709, d. July 2, 1711.
24 PHEBE, b. Sept. 18, 1712.
25 WILLIAM, b. Feb. 26, 1716.
26 DAVID, b. May 4, 1719.

Mathew Randall (No. 4) m. Eleanor ——— about 1693.

CHILDREN:
27 ELEANOR, b. June 24, 1694.
28 MERCY, b. May 16, 1696.
29 MARY, b. April 21, 1700, m. Caleb Pendleton, Jr.
30 MATHEW, b. 1798.
31 BENJAMIN, b. 1702, m. Mary Babcock.
32 PATIENCE, b. ———.
33 THANKFUL, b. ———.
34 ELIZABETH, b. ———, m. Edwin Wells, Jan. 12, 1734.

Peter Randall (No. 5) m. Elizabeth Polly at Stonington, Conn., Nov. 27, 1706. He m. 2d, Phebe Benjamin at Preston, Conn., Sept., 1719.

CHILDREN BY FIRST MARRIAGE:
35 PRUDENCE, b. April 10, 1709.
36 PETER, b. Dec. 2, 1711, d. at Stonington in 1712.
37 PETER, b. May 31, 1713, m. Keturah Ellis Dec. 12, 1732, at Preston.

CHILDREN BY SECOND MARRIAGE:
38 ELIZABETH, b. June 20, 1720.
39 GREENFIELD, b. Oct. 2, 1722, m. Ann Bellows of Preston, Conn.
40 SAMUEL, b. April 13, 1736.

Lieut. John Randall (No. 8) m. Dorothy Cottrell Dec. 22, 1726 (No. 32), that family. He m. 2d, May 10, 1741, Mrs. Mary, widow of Elias Palmer (No. 141), and daughter of Joshua and Fear (Sturges) Holmes (No. 25), that family.

CHILDREN:
41 HANNAH, b. Jan. 13, 1726, m. Joshua Stanton (No. 26), that family.
42 JOHN, b. Aug. 4, 1730, m. Lucy Brown; 2d, Thankful Swan.
43 ABIGAIL, b. Jan. 13, 1734, m. Robert Swan (No. 46), that family.
44 ESTHER, b. June 17, 1735, m. Elias Palmer (No. 245), that family.
45 THOMAS, b. Dec. 13, 1741, m. Molly Chesebrough.
46 JOSHUA, b. March 3, 1743, m. Rhoda Chesebrough.
47 LUCY, b. March 23, 1745, m. Joseph Frink; 2d, Wait Hinckley.
48 MARY, b. July 13, 1746, m. Christopher, son of Charles and Mary (Wheeler) Miner, Aug. 11, 1765 (No. 147), that family; m. 2d, Samuel Brown, July 14, 1734.
49 KETURAH, b. Sept. 2, 1748, m. John Williams (No. 213), that family.
50 ROBERT, b. Oct. 25, 1751, m. Lucy, daughter of Col. William and Mrs. Mary (McDowell) Chesebrough Pendleton, May 6, 1773 (No. 30), that family. He d. at Courtland, N. Y. Nine of their children were born in Stonington, Conn., and the tenth born at Brookfield, N. Y.

Nathan Randall (No. 12), b. in Stonington, Conn., was admitted freeman of Westerly, R. I., May 4, 1736. He was a farmer in Westerly till about 1750-1, when he removed to Voluntown, where he bought 160 acres of land of Amos Kinney (3d Aug., 1750), for two thousand five hundred, money of ye "old tenor bills"; 20 acres of Andrew Elliott (6th April, 1755), for five hundred pounds in good and passable bills of credit, old tenor. He m. 1st, Mary Cottrell Dec. 16, 1730 (No. 33a), that family; she d. at Westerly, R. I., Dec. 2, 1735; m. 2d, Eleanor Cottrell July 22, 1736, sister of his first wife (No. 34).

CHILDREN:

51 NATHAN, b. Sept. 18, 1731, d. May 14, 1733.
52 JOSEPH, b. Sept. 8, 1733, m. at Voluntown, Content Palmer, Dec. 25, 1754.
53 NATHAN, b. Oct. 10, 1735, m. at Stonington Mrs. Borodell Palmer, Dec. 5, 1765; m. 2d, at Voluntown, Dolly Palmer (No. 275), Feb. 13, 1772. They removed to Paris, N. Y., after all their children were born at Stonington, Conn.
54 REUBEN, b. April 24, 1737, d. at Fort Edward, N. Y., Sept. 9, 1757.
55 AMOS, b. Oct. 11, 1749, m. Phebe Palmer (No. 287), that family, April 25, 1765.
56 DOROTHY, b. June 5, 1741.
57 ELEANOR, b. Feb. 24, 1743, m. Nathaniel Morgan at Voluntown Oct. 16, 1766.
58 AMY, b. Dec. 26, 1745.
59 PELEG, b. Oct. 19, 1748, m. Hannah Palmer (No. 288), that family, March 12, 1772, sister of Phebe, who m. Amos Randall. He was lieutenant in the army of the Revolution, and at the surrender of Burgoyne took command of the company after the captain was killed. In 1784 he united with the Baptist Church of Voluntown, and Jan. 18, 1789, was licensed to preach. He was ordained Oct. 25, 1792, and admitted elder of the First Baptist Church, Stonington, nearly twenty-three years.
60 LYDIA, b. June 3, 1751, m. John Gallup of Voluntown Nov. 28, 1777.
61 JONAS, b. Sept. 8, 1756.

John Randall (No. 42) m. 1st, Lucy Brown of Stonington May 6, 1750 (No. 91), Lynn Brown family; she d. Oct. 23, 1765; m. 2d, Thankful Swan Aug. 23, 1767 (No. 40), that family; she d. March 29, 1800.

CHILDREN:

63 LUCY, b. May 14, 1751, m. 1st, Amos Breed, Jan. 25, 1768 (No. 23), that family; he d. March 20, 1785; she m. 2d, Elias Sanford Palmer (No. 238), that family; she d. at Stonington Nov. 14, 1831.
64 ABIGAIL, b. Nov. 12, 1752, m. George Swan Sept. 4, 1774 (No. 37), that family.
65 JOHN, b. March 24, 1754, m. 1st, Mary Swan Nov. 7, 1775 (No. 68), that family; she d. at Norwich, N. Y., March 29, 1813; he m. 2d, Hannah Mary, widow of his brother Roswell Randall (No. 157), that family, May 3, 1816. By 1st m. they had thirteen children, first ten born in Stonington, Conn.

66 ROSWELL, b. July 18, 1756, m. 1st, Phebe Avery, March 4, 1779 (No. 160), that family; she d. Dec. 18, 1787; m. 2d, Hannah Mary Avery, sister of his first wife (No. 157). No children by either wife.
67 REV. JEDEDIAH, b. March 20, 1758, m. at Stonington, Patty York, Aug. 1, 1779. He was among the early settlers of Chenango county, Norwich, New York.
68 CHARLES, b. May 25, 1759, d. at Stonington July 30, 1759.
69 ESTHER, b. May 10, 1761, m. Thomas Wheeler in 1780 (No. 107), that family.
70 POLLY, b. Nov. 18, 1762, m. 1st, Collins York (No. 57), that family; m. 2d, John Crary of Preston in 1745.
71 WILLIAM, b. March 25, 1768, m. Eunice Wheeler, Mrs. Wealthy (Avery) Hewitt, Martha Chesebrough.
72 DESIRE, b. July 12, 1769, m. Perez Wheeler in 1787 (No. 102), that family; 2d, Christopher Palmer Nov. 1, 1823.
73 NANCY, b. Sept. 3, 1771, m. Benadam Williams, Jr., April 18, 1799 (No. 285a), that family.
74 DUDLEY, b. Dec. 7, 1772, m. Lucy Grant.

Thomas Randall (No. 45) m. Molly Chesebrough Sept. 26, 1765 (No. 145), that family; she d. in Stonington March 25, 1823; he d. at Norwich, N. Y., Jan. 28, 1831.

CHILDREN ALL BORN IN STONINGTON.

75 POLLY, b. Oct. 6, 1766, m. Josiah Gallup of Groton, Nov. 11, 1792.
76 THOMAS, b. May 1, 1769, m. Wealthy Ann Sheffield. Three children b. at Stonington and four in New York city.
77 PATTY, b. May 13, 1771, d. Sept. 19, 1862, unmarried.
78 ABBY, b. April 26, 1773, m. Zebulon Chesebrough (No. 247), that family.
79 KETURAH, b. Jan. 31, 1775, d. at Stonington June 20, 1809.
80 LYDIA, b. Oct. 31, 1776, d. at Litchfield, Conn., Jan., 1826.
81 ZEBULON CHESEBROUGH, b. April 1, 1778, d. at Wilmington, N. C., Feb. 15, 1800, unmarried.
82 PEYTON RANDOLPH, b. Feb. 10, 1780, m. Lucy Bradford; 2d, Adelia E. Wells.
83 HANNAH, b. Feb. 9, 1783, m. Jesse Breed, July 9, 1825 (No. 69), that family.
84 BETSEY, b. Aug. 17, 1784, m. Dea. Elias Breed (No. 73), that family, Jan. 22, 1807.
85 WILLIAM RHODES, b. April 26, 1786, m. Phebe McLane May 1, 1813.
86 CHARLES PHELPS, b. Feb. 22, 1790, m. Eunice Hotchkins Sept. 26, 1825.

Joshua Randall (No. 46) m. 1st, Rhoda Chesebrough in 1767; she d. in Stonington, Conn. He removed to Newport, R. I., where he m. 2d wife. In the fall of 1808 he sailed from that port, and was shortly after shipwrecked on No Man's Island, where he perished from cold and exposure, the date of which we have not been able to learn.

CHILDREN ALL BORN IN STONINGTON:

87 PRUDENCE, b. about 1770, d.
88 RHODA, b. about 1773, m. Adam Denison (No. 273), that family. He d. at Halifax, Vt., 1840.
89 HANNAH, b. about 1774, m. Jesse Breed (No. 69), that family.
90 JOSHUA, b. about 1775, m. Hulda Sisson at Stonington, 1796.
91 CHESEBROUGH, b. April 6, 1776, m. Prudence Miner of Stonington.

Hon. William Randall (No. 71) was lieutenant colonel commandant of the 30th regiment of Connecticut militia during the war of 1812 (that office corresponding with colonel in later organizations), and had command of his regiment when it was called out in 1813-14, for the defence of the State, notably at Stonington in August, 1814. In the General Assembly of Connecticut during six sessions, he was member of the Lower House, and in 1822 he had a seat in the Upper House, as one of the twelve Senators elected by the general ticket, of which that body was then composed. In 1818 he was a member of the convention which framed the Constitution of the State of Connecticut, as delegate from the town of Stonington. During sixteen consecutive years, from 1818 to 1833, inclusive, he held the position of associate judge of the county court of New London county, by annual appointment by the General Assembly of the State of Connecticut, by which authority he was also annually appointed a justice of the peace during twenty-eight years, and he held responsible offices in the town of Stonington. Was first president of the Stonington Bank, organized in 1822, and one of the directors thereof; he held the office for eight years. He m. 1st, Eunice Wheeler, March 8, 1787 (No. 103), that family; she d. Jan. 29, 1803; m. 2d, Mrs. Wealthy (Avery) Hewitt, widow of Darius Hewitt, June 30, 1803 (No. 161), Avery family; she d. Dec. 29, 1805; m. 3d, Martha Chesebrough March 30, 1809 (No. 325), that family; she d. Sept. 25, 1870. Col. William Randall d. June 17, 1841.

CHILDREN BY FIRST MARRIAGE:

92 WILLIAM, b. June 7, 1787, m. Wealthy Hewitt.
93 CYRUS, b. Sept. 8, 1789, d. Oct. 13, 1789.
94 EUNICE, b. July 18, 1790, d. Jan. 24, 1792.
95 RUSSELL, b. Oct. 2, 1792, d. April 11, 1793.
96 LUCY, b. March 3, 1794, m. Samuel Chapman Jan. 1, 1812, both of Stonington; she d. at Hartford, Conn., Oct. 30, 1838.
97 DESIRE, b. Dec. 3, 1795, m. Thomas Thompson Wells, M. D., son of Thomas and Betsey (Griffin) Wells, b. at Stonington, 1790; she m. Dec. 31, 1812, at Stonington.
98 POLLY, b. March 3, 1798, m. Ralph Randall Miner (No. 234), that family.
99 THANKFUL SWAN, b. March 17, 1800, m. George Wheeler Nov. 13, 1817 (No. 254), that family.
100 JEDEDIAH, b. Feb. 21, 1802, m. Philura Peckham Oct. 27, 1822.

CHILDREN BY SECOND MARRIAGE:

101 EUNICE, b. March 28, 1861, m. Ansel Coats, Jan. 18, 1826 (No. 27), that family.

CHILDREN BY THIRD MARRIAGE:

102 PHEBE ESTHER, b. Jan. 14, 1810, m. Ezra Hewitt Dec. 8, 1829 (No. 183), that family.
103 HANNAH AVERY, b. July, 1811, d. Aug. 8, 1812.

RANDALL FAMILY. 551

104 ROSWELL, b. Nov. 23, 1812, d. Sept. 25, 1833.
105 HARRIET NEWELL, b. Jan. 25, 1815, m. Reuben E. Moss Sept. 23, 1841 (No. 44), that family.
106 MARTHA CHESEBROUGH, b. April 4, 1817, m. Ralph H. Avery (No. 212), that family.
107 ELIAS PERKINS, b. July 4, 1821, m. Hannah Fish March 15, 1843 (No. 56), that family.

Dudley Randall (No. 74) m. Lucy Grant (No. 63), that family, March 26, 1801; she d. Aug. 22, 1829; he m. 2d, Mrs. Sally, widow of Daniel Farnham, sister of Lucy, March 28, 1830 (No. 65), that family; she d. May 15, 1851; he d. June 4, 1851.

CHILDREN:

108 LUCY, b. Jan. 13, 1802, m. Charles Grandison Hewitt (No. 208), that family.
109 NANCY WHEELER, b. Sept. 9, 1803, d. Jan. 28, 1842.
110 JOHN, b. Feb. 15, 1805, m. Eliza A., daughter of Charles S. Hewitt (No. 203), that family, Sept. 27, 1860.
111 ESTHER, b. Jan. 18, 1807, m. Allen B. Peabody, Jan. 14, 1830.
112 ELISHA, b. May 22, 1809, m. Eunice Pendleton Vincent, Feb. 27, 1843 (No. 35), that family.
113 DESIRE, b. Jan. 18, 1813, m. Benadam W. Hewitt Jan. 5, 1837 (No. 211), that family.
114 ALMIRA GRANT, b. Feb. 22, 1815, d. Feb. 4, 1835.
115 MARY, b. Aug. 1, 1817, m. Gilbert W. Collins, April 1, 1845 (No. 46), that family.
116 SALLY FARNHAM, b. Aug. 1, 1819, d. unmarried.

Peyton Randolph Randall (No. 82) m. Lucy Bradford Oct. 15, 1816; she d. Sept. 11, 1832. He m. 2d, Adeline E. Wells Nov. 26, 1836.

CHILDREN:

117 THOMAS ALEXANDER, b. March 4, 1822, d. Dec. 11, 1833.
118 WILLIAM ZEBULON, b. March 20, 1829, m. Catharine Hiscox Oct. 15, 1859.
119 CHARLES EDWARD, b. Dec. 5, 1831, m. Mary Ella Reynolds June 25, 1853.
120 DENISON CHESEBROUGH, b. Aug. 21, 1838, m. Harriet Sheffield March 2, 1859.
121 LUCY ESTHER, b. May 21, 1841, m. Frank Greenleaf Rice June 5, 1870.
122 HENRY CLAY, b. Sept. 2, 1843, m. Addie Hunting Nov. 8, 1874.
123 WARREN CLINTON, b. July 17, 1845.

Hon. William Randall, Jr. (No. 92), of North Stonington, Conn., was a delegate from the town of North Stonington to the convention which framed the constitution of the State of Connecticut in 1818. He was justice of the peace for the district of North Stonington in 1838-9, and county commissioner for New London County in 1839, 1840, 1841 and 1845. He m. Wealthy Hewitt Dec. 23, 1813 (No. 283), that family. He d. Sept. 22, 1871. She d. Sept. 24, 1869.

CHILDREN:

124 A son, b. and d. May 22, 1815.
125 HANNAH MARY, b. Aug. 31, 1816, m. Ezra Wheeler Nov. 25, 1840 (No. 285), Wheeler family.
126 REV. WILLIAM HARRISON, b. Aug. 11, 1818, m. Harriet Hull Miner Nov. 30, 1837 (No. 372), that family. He m. 2d, Helen Mar. Hutchinson Dec. 31, 1865. He d. in Florida March 7, 1874.
127 WEALTHY AVERY, b. Jan. 11, 1821, m. George L. Williams, Sept. 23, 1846.
128 DARIUS HEWITT, b. July 28, 1823, m. Abbie P. Frink Jan. 4, 1854.
129 REV. HENRY CLAY, b. Dec. 7, 1825, m. Mary L. Davis April 20, 1853.
130 EMILY MINER, b. Jan. 4, 1829, m. Albert W. Hillard Nov. 25, 1851.

Jonathan Randall (No. 22) m. Preserved ————,family name and date of marriage unknown. From the record of the distribution of his estate among his wife and children, in 1757, we learn that he lived in Groton, now Ledyard. His real estate was situated on the highway leading from Preston to New London ferry. After his death his widow m. 2d, Lemuel Darrow, son of Christopher and Elizabeth (Packer) Darrow, Sept. 19, 1751.

THEIR SON:

131 JONATHAN, b. March 30, 1745, m. Ann, daughter of Nathan and Dorothy (Wheeler) Crary, in Groton, March 5, 1769 (No. 40), Wheeler family.

THEIR SON:

132 JEDEDIAH HUNTINGTON, b. at Norwich, Conn., April 10, 1773, m. Mary, daughter of Elder Silas and Mary (Smith) Burrows (No. 124), that family, Fort Hill, Groton, May 19, 1799. He d. at Mystic Jan. 27, 1851, aged 77 yrs., 9 mos.; she d. May 25, 1871.

CHILDREN:

133 MARY ANN, b. at Groton Dec. 4, 1800, m. Mystic Jan. 19, 1822, Roswell Burrows (No. 129), of Burrows family.
134 ELIZA ROE, b. at North Stonington March 3, 1803, m. Simeon Fish Oct. 15, 1823 (No. 49), Fish family.
135 ERASTUS, b. North Stonington Nov. 7, 1805, d. young.
136 ISAAC, b. North Stonington Dec. 25, 1808, m. Hannah Adelia Miner.
137 WILLIAM PITT, b. Groton, Conn., Jan. 1, 1811, d. at Mystic, June 3, 1850, m. Maria L. Comstock Sept. 11, 1838, d. at the home of her son, Rev. William H. Randall, May 22, 1887.
138 SILAS BURROWS, b. July 4, 1814, m. Mary E. Tucker, Sept. 7, 1843; 2d, Emily F. Doane of Preston, Conn., May 27, 1847.
139 CHARLES, b. May 31, 1817, m. Mary Woolbright of Georgia April 27, 1842.
140 FRANCES E., b. April 1, 1818, m. William P. Smith Aug. 5, 1839.

Isaac Randall (No. 136) m. Hannah Adelia, daughter of Dr. John Owen and Elizabeth (Avery) Miner (No. 294) that family, Dec. 20, 1831, at Centre Groton. He d. at Mystic, March 9, 1881. His widow d. at the home of her daughter, Mrs. Adelia M. Noyes, at Newton Highlands, Mass., Aug. 19, 1893.

RANDALL FAMILY.

CHILDREN:
141 ADELIA MINER, b. Sept. 21, 1832, m. Nathan D. Noyes (No. 394), Noyes family, Aug. 4, 1857.
142 ELIZABETH FRANCES, b. March 3, 1834, d. Jan. 3, 1876.
143 JEDEDIAH, b. Sept. 13, 1835, d. June 9, 1863.
144 JULIA ANN, b. April 18, 1837, m. Samuel D. Davenport Aug. 9, 1862.
145 JOHN FREDERIC, b. April 13, 1839, m. Elizabeth F. Stark March 15, 1870.
146 NATHAN, b. March 11, 1841, d. Jan. 13, 1842.
147 GEORGE, b. June 28, 1844, d. March 23, 1845.
148 CHARLES ARTHUR, b. May 15, 1852, m. Victoria Frances Bourke.

RHODES FAMILY.

In the old town graveyard at Newport, R. I., is the heraldic tombstone of John Rhodes, Esq., who died March 31, 1746, aged 75 years, grandson of Sir Godfrey Rhodes of Rowden, in Yorkshire, Eng., and according to Burke's Extinct and Dormant Baronetcies, "Francis and Charles Rodes, grandsons of Sir Francis Rodes, Bart, a nephew of Sir Godfrey, went to America." As these are familiar names in the Rhodes family, which came to Stonington, Conn., we feel that this John Rhodes, Esq., may be the connecting link in the family between England and America, as he might have been the father of Capt. Simon Rhodes, who was born Jan. 24, 1716, and was of Newport, R. I., when he was married by Elder Joseph Park on Dec. 15, 1756, to Anne, who was the daughter of Capt. James and second wife, Content (Maxson) Babcock of Westerly, R. I. Tradition says that he had been married before and as he was 40 years old at the time he married Anne, this might have been so. The first mention of Capt. Simon Rhodes on the Stonington records is "A distribution of lands between Jonathan Babcock and his sister, Ann Rhodes, the wife of Capt. Simon Rhodes of Stonington, Oct. 24, 1759." Afterwards there are several deeds showing that he purchased large tracts of land. He built a house on the land owned by his wife, which is standing at the present time, and known as the Rhodes Mansion Place. It is situated not far from Westerly, R. I. Capt. Simon's wife, Anne Babcock (No. 46), Babcock family, was born March 30, 1732, and died Nov. 7, 1768, aged 37, and then Capt. Simon married Aug. 27, 1769, Martha Babcock (No. 100), Babcock family, who was born Dec. 8, 1729, daughter of George and Susannah (Potter) Babcock. Capt. Simon Rhodes died April 22, 1784, aged 68 years, and Mrs. Martha Babcock Rhodes married May 12, 1800, Col. James Rhodes, b. Aug. 5, 1730, (not known to be any relative of Capt. Simon Rhodes). He died June 21, 1806, and she died March 30, 1809, aged 80 years. Col. James Rhodes' first wife was Anna Crandall who he m. Dec. 14, 1752. After her death he married 2d, Abigail Greenman Feb. 21, 1768 (No. 22), of Greenman family. She died Dec. 17, 1799, aged 59 years.

Then for his third wife he married, as mentioned before, Mrs. Martha Babcock Rhodes. Some of the best people of Stonington have descended from Col. James Rhodes.

SIMON AND ANNE'S CHILDREN.

2 JAMES, b. Nov. 4, 1757, bapt. July 15, 1761, d. aged 4 yrs. 6 mos.
3 MARY, b. in Stonington Dec. 11, 1758, bapt. Aug. 9, 1761, and m. Lieut. Robert Rogers of Coventry, R. I., April 2, 1780, being Sunday.
4 SIMON, b. in Stonington June 22, 1760, bapt. Aug. 9, 1761.
5 HENRY, b. in Stonington April 25, 1762, bapt. Aug. 15, 1762. He was a sea captain, m. and settled at South Hampton, L. I., and d. Jan. 7, 1848. He had children. One son was a noted master ship builder, and was employed during his career in the naval departments of the Government of Great Britain and Turkey. His name was Foster Rhodes, suggesting to me that it might have been the family name of his mother.
6 ANNE, b. in Stonington Sept. 19, 1764, and m. Benjamin Hunting of Long Island Nov. 6, 1784, and d. Feb. 9, 1789.
7 ABIGAIL, b. Oct. 27, 1768, bapt. Aug. 21, 1769, m. Col. Job Greene of Warwick, R. I.; she d. April 18, 1845. Col. Greene was b. Nov. 19, 1759, and d. Aug. 23, 1808.

SIMON AND MARTHA'S CHILD:

8 GEORGE, b. July 30, 1771, d. May 3, 1776, aged 5 yrs.

Simon Rhodes (No. 4) m. Sarah Woodbridge (No. 29), Jan. 14, 1790. She was the daughter of Dr. Dudley Woodbridge and wife, Sarah (Sheldon) of Hartford, Conn. She was b. June 28, 1767, and d. Feb. 9, 1855, aged 88 years. Simon Rhodes d. Feb. 8, 1844, aged 84 years.

CHILDREN:

9 NANCY, b. Sept. 6, 1790, d. unmarried Feb. 8, 1871, aged 80 yrs.
10 DUDLEY, b. March 8, 1792.
11 LUCY, b. Jan. 12, 1794, d. unmarried March 7, 1871, aged 77 yrs.
12 SALLY, b. Aug. 8, and d. Aug. 28, 1801.
13 HENRY, b. Jan. 1, 1803, and d. Oct. 13, 1877.

Dudley Rhodes (No. 10) m. ———, was a physician and d. at Zanesville, Ohio, Oct. 18, 1840.

CHILDREN:

14 EMMA R., b. ———.
15 HENRY S., b. ———.
16 CHARLES, b. ———
17 DUDLEY W., b. ———
18 JOHN RATHBUN, b. ———.

Henry Rhodes (No. 13) m. Bridget M. Palmer (No. 421), of the Palmer family, Jan. 7, 1828, of Stonington, Conn.

CHILDREN:

19 DUDLEY W., b. Oct. 30, 1829.
20 ABBY P., b. in Trenton, N. Y., Sept. 6, 1832, d. Dec. 18, 1866.
21 EMMA M., b. July 23, 1834, and was twin to
22 CHARLES H., b. July 23, 1834; he d. April 17, 1878.
23 JOHN D. P., b. July 14, 1837.
24 JAMES L., b. Aug. 23, 1839, d. May 20, 1844.
25 MARY J., b. June 30, 1841, d. Aug. 24, 1854.
26 LUCY A., b. Dec. 4, 1843.

Dudley W. Rhodes (No. 17) m. Oct. 23, 1854, Lydia Sophia Stanton of Trenton, N. Y.

Charles H. Rhodes (No. 22) m. June 5, 1867, Harriet Hazard of Westerly, R. I.

John D. P. Rhodes (No. 23) m. Oct. 9, 1867, Sophia Jones of South Trenton.

CHILDREN OF COL. JAMES RHODES AND FIRST WIFE, ANNA CRANDALL:

1 WILLIAM, b. Sept. 13, 1753, m. Sarah ———, d.
2 NANCY, b. Oct. 20, 1755, m. ——— Foster; d. Aug. 10, 1835.
3 JOSEPH, b. Sept. 10, 1757.
4 CHRISTOPHER, b. ———.
5 SARAH, b. June 7, 1761, m. Capt. Amos Palmer, Oct. 16, 1785 (his second wife); she d. Dec. 29, 1832.
6 JAMES, b. Aug. 20, 1763.
7 ANNE, b. May 9, 1765.
8 PAUL, b. Sept. 20, 1767, m. Amy, daughter of Joseph and Mary (Babcock) Denison; he d. Jan. 21, 1817.

CHILDREN BY SECOND WIFE:

9 OLIVER, b. June 16, 1769, m. Eunice Pendleton Dec. 14, 1796.
10 ABIGAIL, b. Jan. 1, 1772, m. Charles Pendleton April 1, 1792, son of Amos and Susannah (Chesebrough) Pendleton.
11 HANNAH, b. ———, m. James Babcock May 6, 1802.

ROSSITER FAMILY.

1. REV. EBENEZER ROSSITER, b. Feb. 4, 1699, was the first of the name that came to Stonington, Conn. He was the seventeenth and youngest child of Josiah and Sarah (Sherman) Rossiter, and grandson of Dr. Benjamin and Elizabeth Rossiter, and great-grandson of Edward Rossiter of Plymouth, Eng., from which he came to this country in 1630, with the Rev. John Wareham and others, and settled in Dorchester, Mass. Rev. Ebenezer Rossiter was a graduate of Yale College in 1718. He was the second minister of the First Congregational Church, Stonington, and was ordained Dec. 19, 1722, which relation he sustained until his death, Oct. 11, 1762. He was a devoted, earnest and successful minister of the gospel. He m. Hannah White Oct. 7, 1723, daughter of the Rev. Ebenezer White of Long Island.

CHILDREN:

2 EBENEZER, b. June 17, 1724, d. young.
3 EBENEZER, b. Aug. 27, 1726, d. Jan. 9, 1750.
4 MEHITABLE, b. Dec. 29, 1728.
5 HANNAH, b. Dec. 22, 1730, m. John Hillard March 5, 1761.
6 SARAH, b. Nov. 19, 1732, d. Nov. 7, 1740.
7 MARY, b. Dec. 8, 1735, m. Thomas Palmer (No. 208), that family.
8 ELNATHAN, b. July 3, 1739, m. Mercy Coleman.
9 JOHN COTTON (twin), b. July 3, 1739, m. Phebe Palmer.

Hannah Rossiter (No. 5) m. John Hillard of Stonington, Conn., March 5, 1761. He gave by deed to the First Congregational Society of Stonington, Conn., the burial ground near the church. They had one

CHILD:

10 SARAH HILLARD, b. ———, and m. 1st, Daniel Fish of Preston and Stonington (No. 25), Fish family. She m. 2d, Thomas Stanton (No. 271), Stanton family; m. 3d, John Nichols of Preston, Conn. She lies at rest in the Road Church cemetery, the gift of her father to the Road Society.

Elnathan Rossiter (No. 8) m. Mercy Coleman (No. 293), Stanton family.

CHILDREN:

11 RUSSELL, b. ———.
12 WHITE, b. ———.
13 ROBERT, b. ———.
14 HETTIE, b. ———.
15 MOLLY, b. ———.
16 PRUDENCE, b. ———.

John Cotton Rossiter (No. 9) m. Phebe Palmer Oct. 20, 1765 (No. 181), that family, both of Stonington, Conn.

CHILDREN:

17 SARAH, b. July 30, 1766.
18 EBENEZER, b. Oct. 16, 1767.
19 MEHITABLE, b. Feb. 27, 1769, m. Elijah Williams (No. 77), that family.
20 ASA, b. Dec. 9, 1770.
21 JOHN COTTON, b. Oct. 4, 1772, d. ———.
22 HANNAH FISH, b. March 13, 1774.
23 WILLIAM, b. July 30, 1776.
24 JOHN COTTON, b. May 4, 1777.
25 PHEBE (twin), b. May 4, 1777.
26 ANDREW, b. Oct. 10, 1779.
27 WILLIAM LEDYARD, b. March 24, 1784.
28 GILBERT FANNING, b. May 22, 1786.
29 EDWARD, b. Aug. 12, 1787.
30 ELIAKIM (twin), b. Aug. 12, 1787.
31 REV. DUDLEY DENISON, b. May 25, 1789, m. Elizabeth Woodbridge Rogers Dec. 3, 1815.

RUSSELL FAMILY.

1. WILLIAM RUSSELL, son of James Russell, bapt. in England Oct. 11, 1612, settled in New Haven, Conn., and m. Sarah Davis, daughter of William Davis, in 1643.

CHILDREN:

2 SAMUEL, bapt. Feb. 16, 1645.
3 HANNAH, bapt. Aug. 4, 1650.
4 JOHN, bapt. Aug. 4, 1653.
5 NOADIAH, bapt. July 24, 1659.

Noadiah Russell (No. 5) and Mary Hamlin were m. in 1688.

CHILDREN:

6 WILLIAM, b. in 1690.
7 NOADIAH, b. in 1692.
8 GILES, b. in 1693.
9 MARY, b. in 1695.
10 JOHN, b. in 1697.
11 ESTHER, b. in 1699.
12 REV. DANIEL, b. in 1702.
13 MEHITABLE, b. in 1704.
14 HANNAH, b. in 1705.

Rev. Daniel Russell (No. 12) graduated at Yale College and was ordained as the first settled minister in that part of Wethersfield known as Stepney, now Rocky Hill, Conn., in July, 1726, which position he held until his death, which took place Sept. 6, 1764. He m. Lydia Stillman, daughter of George and Rebecca Stillman of Wethersfield, Conn., Nov. 13, 1728; she d. Sept. 3, 1750. Rev. Daniel m. 2d, Catharine Chauncey, daughter of Rev. Nathaniel and wife, Sarah Chauncey of Durham, Conn. No children by last wife.

CHILDREN:

15 GILES, b. Nov. 8, 1729.
16 LYDIA, b. Jan. 29, 1731, d. Nov. 30, 1735.
17 DANIEL, b. June 21, 1732, m. Rachel Stowe Oct. 16, 1755, d. Feb. 17, 1759.
18 JOHN, b. Feb. 8, 1734, d. Sept. 3, 1741.
19 BENJAMIN, b. Dec. 13, 1735, d. Jan. 31, 1758.
20 MARY, b. Aug. 15, 1737, m. John Robbins Nov. 25, 1784, d. Aug. 31, 1825.
21 LYDIA, b. Nov. 26, 1739, d. Sept. 24, 1841.
22 NATHANIEL, b. May 5, 1741, m. Elizabeth Willard d. Dec. 18, 1810.
23 JOHN, b. Dec. 26, 1742, d. Dec. 16, 1760.
24 HANNAH, b. May 31, 1746, d. Aug. 23, 1753.

Col. Giles Russell (No. 15) was graduated at Yale College and was admitted to the bar in Hartford, Conn., after which he came to Stonington about 1760. He commanded a company of Rhode Island and Connecticut men in the expedition against Havana in the early part of the year 1762, under Admiral Pococke and Lord Albemarle. The company of which he was the captain consisted of 55 men, of whom 37 were either killed or died of wounds and disease, so that only 18 reached home to die with friends.

After his safe return he was m. Dec. 8, 1762, to Prudence Stanton (No. 279), Stanton family, daughter of Thomas Stanton and wife, Thankful (Denison) Stanton. She had been previously m. to Juda Coleman March 4, 1747, and had two children, viz.: Mercy Coleman, b. July 18, 1748, and Robert Coleman, b. Oct. 26, 1749.

Capt. Russell purchased the John Denison house, now owned and occupied by Mrs. Eliza P. Noyes and son, Joseph Noyes. He built a lean-to on the east side of the house for an office, which was subsequently enlarged and was used as the town clerk and probate office by John D. Noyes during his service as town clerk, and until the office was removed to Stonington borough. Giles Russell was nominated and appointed a tavern keeper or inn keeper there as early as 1763, which position he held by subsequent yearly appointments at the old place until he entered the army of the American Revolution as lieutenant colonel in the third battalion, Wadsworth brigade, which was raised in June 1776, to reinforce Washington at New York; served there and on Long Island; suffered in the retreat from the city and engaged in batttle at White Plains. He re-entered the fourth regiment Connecticut line, Jan. 1, 1777, went into camp at Peekskill in the spring and in September ordered to Washington's army in Pennsylvania; engaged in battle of Germantown, was assigned later to Varnum's brigade and continued the brave defence of Fort Mifflin on the Delaware. At this time he is reported by Varnum as a "veteran of four campaigns in the French and Indian wars, in one of which he was wounded. Is now a sensible and excellent officer, but totally destitute of health, and had requested to be relieved, but was promoted to colonel of the Eighth regiment March 5, 1778, which was that winter at Valley Forge ,and the next June was at the batttle of Monmouth." Col. Russell d. at Danbury, Conn., Oct. 28, 1779, from effects of service, and is buried in Stonington in the cemetery near the Road Church.

RUSSELL FAMILY.

CHILDREN OF GILES AND PRUDENCE RUSSELL:

25 HANNAH, b. Jan. 20, 1764, m. Samuel Stanton (No. 358), son of Nathan and Elizabeth Billings Stanton, Dec. 15, 1782, and their only child, Hannah Russell Stanton (No. 392), m. Denison Noyes March 22, 1815 (No. 175), of the Noyes family. Few of the family can now be found in Stonington, but in Wayne county, New York and in Erie, Penn., are many of their descendants.

26 REV. EBENEZER, the first ordained pastor of the Congregational Church in North Stonington, Conn., Feb. 22, 1727, was not of the same line as Col. Giles Russell. He was b. May 4, 1703, graduated at Yale College in 1722. He m. Content (No. 15), daughter of Benjamin and Mary (Fanning) Hewitt, June 14, 1728, and d. May 22, 1731. He was the son of Rev. Samuel and wife, Abigail (Whiting) Russell, and grandson of the Rev. John and wife, Rebecca (Newbury) Russell, and great-grandson of Mr. John Russell, who came to this country from England in 1632.

SEARLE FAMILY.

1. JOHN SEARLE, the emigrant ancestor and progenitor of the Searle family, appears first, on this side of the Atlantic ocean in Boston, Mass. By his age at death, we learn that he was b. in 1629. Who his parents were has not been ascertained. In 1668 he came to Stonington with his family to reside. He was admitted a freeman of Connecticut for Stonington in 1673, and joined the First Congregational Church of Stonington, July 29, 1677. He bought and received from the town large tracts of land, which were all located in Stonington, became a useful citizen and d. Oct. 14, 1711, aged 82 years, and was buried in the Wequetequock burial place. He m. in Boston Katherine Warner Nov. 26, 1661, by Gov. John Endicott; she d. July 17, 1707.

CHILDREN:

2 ELIZABETH, b. in Boston Oct., 1662, d. July 8, 1664.
3 JOHN, b. in Boston Nov. 19, 1665, m. Mary Ruggles, Mary Feiler.
4 EBENEZER, b. in Boston March 6, 1666, m. Margaret Searle, probably of Roxbury, Mass., Jan. 14, 1697. They both joined the First Congregational Church of Stonington July 8, 1705, and became prominent and useful members thereof. He represented Stonington in the General Assembly of Connecticut in 1715, 1720, 1725, and served several years as selectman of the town. He d. Jan., 1740, leaving no children.

NOTE.—Ebenezer Searle (No. 4) left in his will £5 for the purpose of purchasing a Communion service for the First Congregational Church of Stonington, Conn., which is used at the present time.

John Searle (No. 3) went back to Massachusetts to live in early life, and took up his abode in Roxbury, where he m. Mary Ruggles June 6, 1682. No record appears of children. He m. 2d, Mary Feiler Oct. 2, 1713, and came to Stonington soon after to reside, and d. here Oct. 2, 1717. Two days after his death a son was born to him Oct. 4, 1717, which was named Benoni Searle, signifying a child of grief. The mother, Mrs. Mary Searle, united with the First Congregational Church of Stonington Nov. 17, 1723, at which time her son, Benoni Searle, was baptized. We have no date of her death. She was living here in 1740, as appears by her husband's brother, Ebenezer Searle's will.

CHILD:

5 BENONI, b. Oct. 4, 1717, m. Content Holdredge Nov. 29, 1738, by Rev. Ebenezer Rossiter.

CHILDREN:

6 EBENEZER, b. March 11, 1740.
7 JAMES, b. Aug. 10, 1742.
8 JOHN RUGGLES, b. Aug. 17, 1744, m. Mary, daughter of Napley Brown, Jan. 24, 1772. No record of children.
9 MARGARET, b. April 22, 1747, d. Jan. 13, 1750.
10 MARY, b. May 10, 1749, d. young.
11 MARY, b. April 10, 1750, m. David Fanning Feb. 3, 1772.
12 CONTENT, b. July 30, 1762.

ROBERT SEARLE FAMILY.

Constant Searle, no known relative of the family of John Searle, Sr., came to Stonington from Little Compton, R. I., and descended from Robert Searle of Dorchester, Mass, as follows:

1. Robert Searle and Deborah ———, were m. in 1660. He. d. Feb. 17, 1717; she d. March 2, 1714.

CHILDREN:

2 NATHANIEL, b. June 9, 1662.
3 SALTER, b. June 26, 1664.
4 EDNA, b. Feb. 24, 1669, d. young.
5 ROBERT, b. July 2, 1671.
6 EDNA, b. March 18, 1674.
7 DEBORAH, b. April 4, 1677.
8 JABEZ, b. March 16, 1679.

Nathaniel Searle (No. 2) m. Sarah Rogers, 1694.

NOTE.—Nathaniel Searle (No. 2), Robert Searle family, m. Sarah, daughter of John Rogers and Elizabeth Pebodie, granddaughter of John Rogers and Ann Churchman, and great-granddaughter of Thomas Rogers of the Mayflower. Elizabeth Pebodie was the daughter of William Pebodie (No. 4), that family, and wife Elizabeth Alden, and granddaughter of John and wife, Isabel ——— Pebodie. Elizabeth Alden was the daughter of John Alden of Mayflower fame, and the first white woman born in New England in 1622.

CHILDREN:

9 DEBORAH, b. Nov. 16, 1695.
10 JOHN, b. March 12, 1698.
11 SARAH, b. April 2, 1700.
12 NATHANIEL, b. April 26, 1703, m. Elizabeth Kinnecutt in Dec., 1725, and settled in Little Compton, R. I.

CHILDREN.

13 JOHN, b. Aug. 24, 1726.
14 CONSTANT, b. June 17, 1728.
15 DANIEL, b. Sept. 5, 1730.
16 BETSEY, b. June 3, 1732.
17 SARAH, b. Jan. 28, 1733.
18 NATHANIEL, b. Dec. 25, 1735.
19 JAMES, b. Oct. 5, 1739.
20 RUTH, b. Sept. 12, 1740.
21 COMFORT, b. Sept. 17, 1742.

Constant Searle (No. 14), who came to Stonington from Little Compton, R. I., m. Hannah, daughter of Simeon Miner and wife, Hannah Wheeler, May 16, 1751 (No. 117), Miner family.

CHILDREN:

22 WILLIAM, b. Dec. 2, 1751, m. Philura Frink Oct. 17, 1773 (No. 50), Frink family.
23 HANNAH, b. Jan. 25, 1754, m. Nathan Daton Miner.
24 CONSTANT, b. March 17, 1756, d. young.
25 ELIZABETH, b. March 4, 1757, m. Capt. Dethic Hewitt July 13, 1773 (No. 84), Hewitt family. The above children all born in Stonington.
26 CONSTANT, b. in Little Compton, R. I., in 1759.
27 REV. ROGER, b. in Preston, Conn., Aug. 13, 1762.
28 RUTH, b. in Preston, Conn., March 1, 1765, m. Nathan Crary of Groton, Conn.

NOTE.—Ruth Searles (No. 28) m. Nathan Crary, son of Peter Crary, and wife, Christobel Gallup (No. 12), that family of Groton, in 1788. She was b. in Preston, Conn., where her parents were living at the time, in the year 1755. Her father removed with his family in 1773 to Wyoming, Pa., where he and his son-in-law, Capt. Dethic Hewitt, were both killed in the battle and massacre of Wyoming, July 3, 1778. Ruth's brother swam the river to get away the next morning. Ruth and her sister, Sarah or Sally, as she was called, came away from Wyoming with some of the Gallup friends, and after reaching Groton, Ruth taught school for a while and was in the family of Nathan Crary before the death of his wife. At the time of his marriage to Ruth Searles he was over 70 years old, and she was a little more than 20. They were married in 1788. Their son, Jesse Crary, b. April 1, 1789, m. Catharine Burrows, Nov. 29, 1812; their son, Capt. George B. Crary, m. Catharine Latham; their daughter, Georgiana Crary, m. Charles Cottrell (No. 58), that family.

29 SARAH, b. in Stonington, Sept. 30, 1768, m. Jared Collins of Groton.
30 JAMES, b. in Stonington Aug. 4, 1769, m. Abigail Thurston in Providence, R. I., Aug. 25, 1793.

Rev. Rogers Searle (No. 27) of Preston, Conn., m. Catharine Scott. He d. June 19, 1813. Their son, Leonard Searle, b. Nov. 7, 1808, in Pittston, Pa., m. Lydia Dimock Oct. 23, 1832. He d. Dec. 31, 1880.

CHILDREN:

31 DAVIS DIMOCK, b. March 25, 1836, unmarried.
32 KATHARINE ELIZABETH, b. May 17, 1838, m. Gen. William H. McCartney of Wilkesbarre, Pa.
33 JOSEPHINE, b. Nov. 4, 1840, m. Benjamin S. Bentley.
34 KITTIE, b. Sept. 4, 1848, m. Leonard Searle, b. Nov. 6, 1850.

SHEFFIELD FAMILY.

1. JOSEPH SHEFFIELD was the first of this name in this country in 1640.
CHILDREN:
2 ICHABOD, probably also Edmund and Frederick.

Ichabod Sheffield (No. 2), b. 1626 and d. Feb. 4, 1712, m. Mary, daughter of George Parker, at Portsmouth; they were published in 1660.
CHILDREN:
3 JOSEPH, b. Aug. 22, 1661, d. in 1706.
4 MARY, b. April 30, 1664.
5 NATHANIEL, b. Nov. 8, 1667, d. Nov. 12, 1729, m. 1st, Mary ———, and 2d, Catharine Gould. Had five children.
6 ICHABOD, b. March 6, 1670, d. in 1736, m. Elizabeth Manchester Dec. 27, 1694.
7 AMOS, b. Jan. 25, 1673, d. 1710; m. 1st, Annie Pearce March 5, 1696, and m. 2d, Sarah Davis, Dec. 22, 1708.

Joseph Sheffield (No. 3) m. Feb. 12, 1685, Mary, daughter of Thomas and wife, Martha Sheriff, who d. in 1706.
CHILDREN:
8 JOSEPH, b. Nov. 2, 1685.
9 MARY, b. Nov. 2, 1687.
10 ELIZABETH, b. Feb. 15, 1688, d. young.
11 BENJAMIN, b. June 18, 1691.
12 EDMUND, b. April 5, 1694.
13 WILLIAM, b. Nov. 30, 1696.
14 ELIZABETH, b. June 1, 1698.

Joseph Sheffield (No. 8) m. Mary Earl Jan. 27, 1708.
CHILDREN:
15 JOSEPH, b. April, 1711, at South Kingston, R. I.
16 MARY, b. in 1712.
17 NATHANIEL, b. in 1714.
18 ELIZABETH, b. ———.
19 GEORGE, b. July 12, 1718.
20 MARTHA, b. Sept. 29, 1719.

Nathaniel Sheffield (No. 17) m. Feb. 6, 1740, Rebecca Stanton (No. 231), who d. Sept. 25, 1775, aged 61 years. He d. July 7, 1790.
CHILDREN:
21 THOMAS, b. Nov. 25, 1740.
22 JOSEPH, b. Aug. 11, 1742, d. April 20, 1776.
23 MARY, b. Jan. 9, 1745.

SHEFFIELD FAMILY. 567

Thomas Sheffield (No. 21) m. Weltha Pendleton, who was b. Feb. 14, 1744.

CHILDREN:

24 JOSEPH, b. Oct. 14, 1763, drowned June 3, 1789.
25 AMOS, b. Feb. 12, 1766, drowned June 3, 1789.
26 SAMUEL, b. June 27, 1768, d. Jan. 22, 1841, m. Susanna Daniels.
27 DORCAS, b. April 11, 1771, d. Feb. 16, 1856.
28 JAMES, b. Aug. 27, 1773.
29 THOMAS, b. Jan. 9, 1776.
30 GEORGE, b. June 27, 1778, d. June 18, 1847.
31 NANCY, b. Aug. 30, 1780, d. April, 1858.
32 NATHANIEL, b. Dec. 9, 1782, d. March 4, 1864.
33 ABEL, b. April 27, 1786.
34 CATHARINE, b. Sept. 14, 1788.

George Sheffield (No. 30) m. Rhoda (No. 54), Burch family, daughter of Henry and wife Mary (Irish) Burch, Jan. 3, 1802. She was b. July 13, 1773, d. Feb. 1, 1850. She was sister of Phebe Burch, who m. Stephen Babcock.

CHILDREN:

35 HENRY, b. Jan. 2, 1803, d. Oct. 18, 1858.
36 FRANCIS, b. Dec. 20, 1805, d. July 11, 1807.
37 FRANCIS, b. June 29, 1808, d. Nov. 13, 1881.
38 Twins to Francis, b. June 29, 1808, d. in infancy.

Francis Sheffield (No. 37) m. Betsey D. Noyes (No. 323), that family, Oct. 22, 1835. They had four children: Thomas; Hannah m. George Tapley of Springfield, Mass.; Maria, and William who d. in young manhood.

SISSON FAMILY.

1. RICHARD SISSON, b. 1608, was of Portsmouth, R. I., and Dartmouth, Mass., where he was a freeman May 17, 1653. He d. 1684. He m. Mary ———, who d. 1692.

CHILDREN:

2 GEORGE, b. 1644, d. Sept. 7, 1718.
3 ELIZABETH, b. April 8, 1650, m. Caleb Allen April 8, 1670.
4 James, b. ——— and d. 1734, m. Elizabeth Hathaway.
5 JOHN, b. ———, d. 1687, m. Mary ———.
6 ANNE, b. ———, d. 1713, m. Peleg Tripp.
7 MARY, b. ———, d. 1674, m. Isaac Lawton.

George Sisson (No. 2) m. Sarah Lawton, daughter of Thomas Lawton; she d. July 5, 1718. He went to Dartmouth with his father, but later returned to Portsmouth, where he was constable, deputy and justice of the peace.

CHILDREN:

8 ELIZABETH, b. Aug. 18, 1669, d. 1752, m. Jeremiah Clark.
9 MARY, b. Oct. 18, 1670, d. 1718.
10 ANN, b. Dec. 17, 1672, m. Philip Weeden.
11 HOPE, b. Dec. 24, 1674, m. William Sanford.
12 RICHARD, b. Sept. 10, 1676, d. 1752, m. Ann Card.
13 RUTH, b. May 5, 1680, m. Richard Tew.
14 GEORGE, b. March 23, 1683, m. 1st, Mercy ———; m. 2d, Lydia Cole.
15 ABIGAIL, b. March 23, 1685, d. Aug. 30, 1723, m. William Tew.
16 THOMAS, b. Sept. 10, 1686, d. 1775.
17 JOHN, b. June 26, 1688, d. 1784, m. Rebecca ———.
18 JAMES, b. July 26, 1690, m. Deborah Cook.

Thomas Sisson (No. 16) m. Jane ———, d. 1758.

CHILDREN:

19 GILES, b. ———.
20 WILLIAM, b. ———.
21 THOMAS, b. ———.
22 PELEG, b. ———.
23 REBECCA, b. ———.

William Sisson (No. 20) m.

CHILDREN:

24 OLIVER, b. March 30, 1738.
25 NATHAN, b. April 14, 1740.
26 HANNAH, b. June 17, 1742.
27 WILLIAM, b. July 12, 1744, d. Oct. 15, 1798.
28 BENAJAH, b. Sept. 17, 1746.
29 JAMES, b. Aug. 25, 1748.
30 ABIGAIL, b. Oct. 24, 1750.
31 JONATHAN, b. May 2, 1753.
32 HANNAH, b. June 17, 1755.
33 THOMAS, b. April 4, 1758, d. Oct. 2, 1841.

SISSON FAMILY.

Oliver Sisson (No. 24) and Mary Park of Preston were m. June 17, 1762.

CHILDREN:

34 JOSEPH, b. June 12, 1762.
35 EUNICE, b. Dec. 8, 1764.
36 MARY, b. Sept. 5, 1767.
37 REBECCA, b. July 3, 1771.

William Sisson (No. 27) m. Mary or Marcy Noyes (No. 291), of that family of Stonington, Conn., April 10, 1766.

CHILDREN:

38 GILBERT, b. March 13, 1769, d. Sept. 11, 1840.
39 MARCY, b. April 15, 1771.
40 LUCY, b. Jan. 28, 1773.
41 ABIGAIL, b. July 11, 1775.
42 HULDAH, b. Feb. 28, 1778.
43 NANCY, b. July 9, 1780.
44 WILLIAM, b. April 29, 1784.
45 POLLY, b. May 20, 1787.
46 HANNAH, b. Aug. 25, 1792.

Gilbert Sisson (No. 38) m. Desire Maine (No. 108), that family, March 22, 1791. She was b. March 31, 1772, d. Nov. 17, 1842.

CHILDREN:

47 POLLY, b. Nov. 17, 1791, d. Aug. 17, 1794.
48 ESTHER, b. Dec. 8, 1793, d. Feb. 18, 1875, m. William Lewis.
49 BETSEY, b. Sept. 19, 1796, d. April 11, 1869, m. Clark D. Thompson.
50 NOYES, b. Sept. 21, 1798, d. Aug. 7, 1872, m. 1st, Eliza Browning and 2d, Rachel Avery.
51 GILBERT, b. Sept. 1, 1800, d. July 27, 1876, m. Elizabeth Lewis.
52 WILLIAM, b. Sept. 6, 1802, d. April 6, 1875, m. Abbie Browning.
53 LUCY A., b. ———, d. Nov. 26, 1890, m. Henry Bliven.
54 CHARLES G., b. April 15, 1807, d. Aug. 21, 1874, m. 1st, Martha Wheeler (No. 269), that family; 2d, Nancy Mary Hewitt (No. 279), that family; 3d, Elizabeth Gasabrandt.
55 EMILY, b. June 7, 1809, d. Feb. 19, 1855, m. Robert A. Bliven.
56 BENJAMIN F., b. April 20, 1811, d. Sept. 8, 1885.
57 CYRUS S., b. March 5, 1813, d. March 22, 1813.
58 OLIVER A., b. May 1, 1816, d. 1885, m. 1st, Mary M. Segar; 2d, Sarah M. Perry.

Benjamin F. Sisson (No. 56) m. 1st, Manita York (No. 170), of that family; she was b. Sept. 26, 1815, d. Aug. 23, 1866.

CHILDREN:

59 MARTHA, b. May 26, 1839, d. April 11, 1842.
60 MARY E., b. March 20, 1845, m. James R. Welden.
61 CHARLES F., b. July 24, 1846, m. Annie Cary.
62 WILLIAM W., b. Oct. 15, 1849, m. Ida Bronson.
63 JULIA A., b. Nov. 16, 1854, d. June 1, 1860.
64 BENJAMIN F., b. Dec. 22, 1860, m. Harriet Frazier.

Benjamin F. Sisson (No. 56) m. 2d, Margaret Hillard of North Stonington, Conn.

JOHN SMITH FAMILY OF STONINGTON, CONN.

1. DANIEL SMITH of Watertown, Mass. (probably son of John and wife, Isabel), m. Elizabeth Rogers of Watertown, Mass., (daughter of Roger and Grace Porter by her former husband, Thomas Rogers), for her will mentions grandson Daniel Smith. He d. July 14, 1660, which is the date of his will and he makes wife, Elizabeth, executrix, and names son Daniel and brother Abraham, who, with Rev. John Sherman, he makes overseers. The town records show Daniel was the only

CHILD OF DANIEL AND ELIZABETH SMITH.

2 DANIEL, b. Sept. 27, 1642, m. Mary, daughter of Christopher and wife, Sarah ——— Grant of Watertown, Mass., Feb. 22, 1668. He d. Jan 7, 1681, and in his will (see Appendix) made eight days before his death, he mentions wife and three sons, "My two eldest sons, Daniel and John, and my third son, Joseph." The will of Daniel Smith speaks of his three sons as being under age at the time of the date of his will, and as his son John was born July 13, 1672, it corresponds with the age recorded on the gravestone of John Smith, buried in North Stonington, Conn., east of the farm owned by Mr. Nathan Stewart, proving conclusively that this Stonington John Smith is the son of Daniel Smith of Watertown, Mass. The gravestones of both John and wife, Susannah Smith, bear the following inscriptions: "Mr. John Smith departed this life May the 8th, A. D. 1739, in the 67th year of his age." Also by the side of this grave is another stone of "Susannah Smith, who died Sept. 28th, 1746, in the 78th year of her age." Here are also found the stones of their son, Daniel Smith and wife Thankful, who died in the years 1740 and 1741. The original will of John Smith is found at New London. (See Appendix.) The maiden name of his wife Susannah is not known, but a Susannah Chesley and John Smith were m. in Massachusetts in 1694, which would be about the time of the m. of this John Smith to Susannah ———, as their first child was born May 8, 1695.

CHILDREN OF DANIEL SMITH AND WIFE, MARY GRANT SMITH.

3 DANIEL, b. March 15, 1669, m. Hannah Coolidge.
4 GRACE, b. Jan. 13, 1671, m. Richard Oler in 1714.
5 JOHN, b. July 13, 1672.
6 ELIZABETH, b. Jan. 15, 1674, m. John Pierce.
7 SARAH, b. Dec. 27, 1675.
8 ABIGAIL, b. Dec. 3, 1678.
9 JOSEPH, b. June 8, 1680.
10 SUSANNAH, b. ———.

JOHN SMITH FAMILY OF STONINGTON, CONN.

John Smith (No. 5), m. Susannah ——— before 1695. They came to Preston, Conn., about 1709, as a deed is on record (and herewith appended) conveying land from William Denison and wife, Mary of Stonington, Conn., to John Smith of Preston, May 3, 1709, which land is bounded south and west by lands of Samuel Prentice. In 1715 the earmark of the cattle of John Smith of Stonington is on record, and in 1718, more land is purchased of William Denison by John Smith of Stonington, Conn. At that time Stonington's north line extended to the south line of Preston, Conn.

CHILDREN OF JOHN SMITH AND WIFE, SUSANNAH SMITH.

11 JERUSHA, b. May 8, 1695.
12 MARGARET, b. July 29, 1698.
13 DANIEL, b. Aug. 1, 1700.
14 ESTHER, b. July 20, 1703.
15 EPHRAIM, b. Oct. 5, 1704.
16 JOSIAH, b. May 27, 1707.
17 SILAS, b. ———, and drowned at Upper Falls, Mass., in 1729.
18 LUCY, b. ———.
19 SUSANNAH, b. ———, m. Ebenezer Brewster Aug. 27, 1735; she d. April 25, 1779, and he d. Oct. 4, 1740.

Daniel Smith (No. 13) m. Thankful (No. 29), of Billings family, daughter of Ebenezer and wife Ann (Comstock) Billings, March 18, 1724-5.

CHILDREN:

20 MARY, b. Dec. 24, 1725.
21 ANNA, b. Oct. 23, 1727, m. William Swan April 14, 1743.
22 JOSEPH, b. Dec. 22, 1729.
23 JOHN, b. April 3, 1733.
24 THANKFUL, b. April 4, 1735.
25 EPHRAIM, b. Oct. 25, 1737.

Daniel Smith (No. 13) d. Aug. 26, 1741, in his 41st year, and his wife Thankful d. July 20, 1740, in her 42d year.

Ephraim Smith (No. 15) m. Hannah Witter (No. 16), that family of Preston, Nov. 23, 1726.

CHILDREN:

26 JERUSHA, b. April 20, 1728, m. John Starkweather March 24, 1746; she d. May 9, 1751, and he d. Dec. 19, 1761.
27 GRACE, b. May 8, 1730.
28 SETH, b. May 6, 1733.
29 ZIPPORAH, b. July 10, 1735.
30 SUSANNAH, b. Oct. 11, 1737.
31 HANNAH, b. May 5, 1740.

Mrs. Hannah Smith d. April 31, 1743, aged 38 years, and Jan. 3, 1744, Mr. Ephraim Smith m. 2d, Mrs. Lucy Stevens, b. in 1717, the child of Henry Stevens and wife, Elizabeth, the daughter of Ephraim Fellows of Plainfield, who were m. March 2, 1708-9. Mrs. Lucy d. May, 1805, aged 95 years, her mother having lived to be 105. Ephraim Smith d. March 24, 1774.

CHILDREN:

32 ANNE, b. Oct. 20, 1744.
33 LUCY, b. Aug. 4, 1746.
34 THANKFUL, b. Sept. 20, 1748.
35 ELIPHAL, b. April 7, 1752; she m. Nathan Morgan, d. 1791, he d. 1790.
36 GILBERT, b. Jan. 7, 1756.
37 SANFORD, b. Feb. 27, 1760, a physician in New York State.

Josiah Smith (No. 16) m. Amie (No. 33b), the daughter of Gershom, or as given otherwise, Nicholas Cottrell, Nov. 4, 1729. She was baptized in the First Congregational Church July 31, 1709. After her death, July 13, 1746, Josiah Smith m. 2d, Elizabeth, the daughter of Peter Robinson. He moved from Preston to Windham, Conn. He d. 1781 or 1782. She d. 1798.

CHILDREN:

38 OLIVER, b. Feb. 8, 1730.
39 NATHANIEL, b. Nov. 20, 1731.
40 BENJAMIN, b. Oct. 22, 1733.
41 JONAH, b. Jan. 1735-6.
42 AMY, b. Sept. 23, 1737.
43 MARY, b. Nov. 19, 1739.
44 LYDIA, b. Jan. 18, 1742.
45 DANIEL or DAVID, b. Feb. 2, 1744.
46 PHEBE, b. Jan. 31, 1746.

CHILDREN BY SECOND WIFE:

47 JOSIAH, b. Dec. 13, 1747.
48 EPHRAIM, b. May 28, 1749.
49 ELIAS, b. June 17, 1750.
50 COTTERILL, b. June 22, 1751.
51 ELIZABETH, b. March 28, 1753.
52 SARAH, b. Feb. 9, 1755.
53 MARTHA, b. Sept. 4, 1757.
54 JAMES, b. July 1, 1759.

Joseph Smith (No. 22) m. Zipporah, daughter of Thomas and Zıpporah (Kinne) Branch, Nov. 20, 1751, and as this Joseph Smith is the immediate ancestor of the Smiths of Stonington at the present time I give a somewhat more particular account of the Branch family.

The ancestor of the Branch family was 1st, Peter Branch, b. in Holden, Kent county, England, and came to America in 1638. The son, John Branch, came with his father, and d. at Marshfield, Mass., in 1711. He m. Mary Speed, Dec. 6, 1652, and had son, Peter Branch, b. May 28, 1659, who d. at Preston, Conn., Dec. 27, 1713. He m. Hannah Lincoln at Taunton, Mass., about 1684, and d. in Preston, Jan. 16, 1731-2. Their son, Thomas Branch, b. Dec. 25, 1698, in Preston, and d. Nov. 1, 1778, m. Zipporah Kinne, Nov. 9, 1726, at Preston. She was the daughter of Joseph and Keziah or Casiah (Peabody) Keeney or Kinne of Salem, Mass. She was b. March 27, 1708. The children of Thomas and wife, Zipporah Kinne Branch, were two daughters, Casiah and Zipporah. The latter was b. Feb. 25, 1730, and bapt. Feb. 28, 1731, admitted to the church in Preston May 4, 1755, and d. Oct. 19, 1783, aged 53 years. She m. Joseph Smith Nov. 20, 1751, who d. Jan. 9, 1784, aged 54 years.

THEIR CHILDREN WERE:

55 DANIEL, b. Oct. 7, 1753, bapt. May 10, 1755.
56 JOSEPH, b. July 6, 1755, bapt. May 30, 1756.
57 WALTER, b. Nov. 28, 1757, bapt. Aug. 17, 1758.
58 LEMUEL, b. May 4, 1760, bapt. Aug. 17, 1760.
59 AMEY or AMIE, b. Jan. 27, 1762, bapt. Sept. 27, 1762, m. ——— Palmer.
60 SUSANNAH, b. Nov. 17, 1764, bapt. June 16, 1765, d. unmarried.
61 THOMAS, b. Nov. 18, 1767, bapt. July 3, 1768.
62 ZIPPORAH, b. Dec. 12, 1771, bapt. Sept. 19, 1772, m. ——— Crary.
63 POLLY or MARY, b. Dec. 9, 1774, bapt. Oct. 27, 1776; m. Capt. John Downer of Canaan, N. Y., and d. Feb. 8, 1798.

John Smith (No. 23) m. Hannah Tyler of Preston, Conn., Oct. 28, 1756.

CHILDREN:

64 RICHARD, b. May 1, 1759.

Seth Smith (No. 28) m. Sarah Tyler of Preston April 17, 1755. He d. March 16, 1804, and Sarah, his wife, d. March 26, 1827, aged 89 years.

CHILDREN:

65 MOSES, b. Jan. 9, 1756, and d. Jan. 17, 1777, of smallpox.
66 PARKER, b. Nov. 2, 1758.
67 SABRA, b. March 18, 1762.
68 CHESTER, b. June 24, 1764.
69 SHUBAL, b. March 17, 1769.

Gilbert Smith (No. 36) m. Delilah Bundy, daughter of Peter and wife, Priscilla Prentice, daughter of Joseph Prentice of Preston, who were m. July 4, 1746.

CHILDREN:

70 CAPT. ELISHA S., b. in New York State Oct. 19, 1785, and m. Elizabeth Birdsall, who was born Jan. 13, 1784.

CHILDREN:

71 GILBERT.
72 ANTENETA.
73 EJESTA.
74 DELIA.
75 MARY.
76 URSULA.
77 SQUIER.
78 MELANIA.
79 MELVINA.
80 ARCHALEUS.

Sanford Smith (No. 37) m. Priscilla Whippo; he was a physician in Cambridge, N. Y.

CHILDREN:

81 DR. JAMES W., b. ———, d. in Rochester, N. Y.
82 LAWRENCE, b. ———, lived in New York State.
83 CHARLOTTE.
84 MARIA.
85 LUCY.
86 KEZIA D.
87 HARRIET B.
88 CATHARINE.
89 PRISCILLA.

Oliver Smith (No. 38) m. Zeruiah Bingham before 1767 in Vermont.

CHILDREN:

90 OLIVER, b. Dec. 25, 1767, m. Patience Bibbin and had eight children.
91 ELIAS, b. ———.
92 JEDEDIAH.
93 ZERUIAH.
94 PHEBE.
95 ANNA.
96 LUCINDA.
97 FIDELIA.

Daniel Smith (No. 55) m. Ruth Pebodie April 19, 1781.

CHILDREN:

98 RUTH, b. Feb. 13, 1782.
99 DANIEL, b. Dec. 24, 1784.

Lemuel Smith (No. 58) m. Elizabeth Coates (No. 20), Coates family, Aug. 13, 1780. Mrs. Smith d. March 3, 1795.

CHILDREN:

100 LEMUEL, b. June 27, 1781.
101 BETTY or ELIZABETH, b. Sept. 28, 1783.
102 REBEKER, b. May 6, 1786.
103 JOHN, b. Nov. 9, 1789.
104 ERASTUS, b. Aug. 1, 1792.

JOHN SMITH FAMILY OF STONINGTON.

Col. Joseph Smith (No. 56) m. Hannah (No. 109), daughter of Charles and Hannah (Stanton) Hewitt, Jan. 26, 1783.

CHILDREN:

105 JOSEPH, b. April 30, 1784, m. Nancy Eells.
106 HENRY, b. May 25, 1788, m. Abby D. Palmer, Dec. 8, 1824 (No. 417), that family.
107 CHARLES H., b. May 8, 1790, m. Emma A. (No. 62), Robert Stanton family, daughter of Benjamin F. and Maria (Davis) Stanton, Jan. 18, 1832; she d. March 17, 1833, and he m. Maria (No. 322), daughter of Elias and wife, Nancy (Davis) Stanton, Feb. 28, 1837.
108 NATHAN, b. April 5, 1792, m. Charlotte D. (No. 44), daughter of Rev. Benjamin and wife, Dorcas Denison Eells, Dec. 24, 1818.
108a NANCY, b. March 19, 1794, m. Alexander G. Smith, a descendant of Rev. Nehemiah Smith, Sept. 4, 1819, d. Aug. 5, 1820.
109 GILES CRARY, b. Dec. 2, 1797, m. Hannah S. (No. 427), daughter of Richard and wife, Mary (Hewitt) Wheeler, Jan. 21, 1836.
110 POLLY or MARY, b. Feb. 14, 1800, m. John D. Palmer Nov. 29, 1829 (No. 419).

Chester Smith (No. 68) m. Sally or Sarah (Brewster) of Preston, Conn., Dec. 7, 1788, and their daughter (No. 69), Amy, m. Dec. 23, 1810, Samuel Prentice, and their son, Chester S. Prentice, b. Aug. 15, 1816, m. Lucy Crary, Dec. 13, 1843. She d. Jan. 17, 1900, and he d. ———. Their son, Samuel O. Prentice, is judge of the Superior Court at Hartford, Conn.

Joseph Smith (No. 105) m. Nancy (No. 39), daughter of Joseph and wife, Anna (Stanton) Eells, Feb. 19, 1806.

CHILDREN:

111 BETSEY E., b. Oct. 24, 1806, d. Nov. 26, 1806.
112 JOSEPH, b. Feb. 27, 1808, m. Abby L. Chesebrough (No. 388), that family.
113 ANNE ELIZA, b. Nov. 22, 1809, m. John F. Trumbull (No. 32), that family, for his second wife.
114 MARIA S., b. Nov. 24, 1811, m. 1st, Dudley Woodbridge (No. 31), and 2d, Elisha Faxon.
115 CHARLES H., b. July 19, 1813, m. Ann Sheffield, daughter of John and wife Elizabeth (Rogers) French, Oct. 3, 1844.
116 CHARLOTTE R., b. Oct. 31, 1816, m. Oliver York (No. 195).
117 SUSAN M., b. Sept. 13, 1818, m. Benjamin F. Palmer as his second wife (No. 349).
118 NATHAN G., b. Sept. 28, 1820, m. Lucy A. Pendleton (No. 123).
119 SAMUEL R., b. July 20, 1823.
120 BENJAMIN E., b. March 1, 1826, m. Catharine Roberts May 24, 1849.
121 EDWARD, b. Sept. 1, 1828, m. a Mrs. Boyden.

THOMAS STANTON FAMILY.

1. THOMAS STANTON, who became distinguished among the first planters of Stonington, Conn., was in early manhood in England designed and educated for a cadet, but, not liking the profession of arms, and taking a deep interest in the religious principles of the migrating Puritans, he left his native land, embarking on board of the good ship "Bonaventure," in 1635, and landed in Virginia, but left there almost immediately for Boston, mingling with the natives on the way, and rapidly acquired a knowledge of their language and customs. On arrival in Boston he was recognized by Winthrop and his associates as a valuable man, worthy of the most unlimited confidence, for the very next year he was selected by the Boston authorities to accompany Mr. Fenwick and Hugh Peters, as interpreter on a mission to Saybrook, Conn., to hold a conference with the Pequot Indians relative to the murder of Capt. Stone and Newton. After the close of the conference Mr. Stanton went up to Hartford, and there fixed his permanent abode in 1637. Mr. Stanton's accurate knowledge of the language and character of the Indians soon gave him prominence in the new settlements of Connecticut, for the very first year that he came to Hartford, the General Court gave him ten pounds for the service he had already done for the country, and declared that he should be a public officer, to attend the court upon all occasions, either general or particular, at the meetings of the magistrates, to interpret between them and the Indians, at a salary of ten pounds per annum. Mr. Stanton did not always agree with the policy of Capt. Mason and the court relative to the treatment of the Indians, and drew upon himself their displeasure; but being a man accustomed to speak his own mind and act upon his own convictions, maintained his position, though they discontinued his salary for two years, alleging long absence as the cause, and appointed Mr. Gilbert to take his place, but in 1648 they restored him to the place with its compensation. He became the intimate and especial friend of

Gov. Winthrop of Connecticut, acting as his interpreter in all of his intercourse with the Indians. It was while thus employed, in an interview with Ninigret in the Narragansett country that Mr. Stanton became acquainted with the Pawcatuck Valley, and selected it for his future residence. He was the first white man who joined Mr. William Chesebrough in his new settlement. He petitioned the General Court of Connecticut for liberty to erect a trading house there, which was granted in February, 1650. In the spring following he came to Pawcatuck and erected his trading house on the west bank of Pawcatuck river, in Stonington, in 1651, near a place ever since known as Pawcatuck Rock, for the reason that the deep water channel in the river touched the east side of said rock, where vessels trading with him could easily receive and discharge their cargoes without any expense for the erection of a wharf. Mr. Stanton did not remove his family to Pawcatuck in Stonington until 1657, where he had previously erected a dwelling house. The precise site of this house cannot now be ascertained, but no doubt it was conveniently near his trading house on Pawcatuck River. The object of building the trading house was to open trade with the coasting vessels which were cruising along our New England shores, gathering furs from the Indians and purchasing the surplus products of the planters, and selling the same either in Boston or in the West Indies. After the articles of confederation between the New England colonies had been established in 1643, among all of the distinguished interpreters of New England, Mr. Stanton was selected as interpreter general, to be consulted and relied upon in all emergencies. In this capacity and in their behalf he acted as interpreter, especially between the ministers employed by the Commissioners of the United Colonies, acting as agents of the London Missionary Society, and the Indians, to whom they preached. He also aided the Rev. Abraham Pierson in the translation of his catechism into the Indian tongue, certifying to the same in his official capacity. After Mr. Stanton became an inhabitant of Pawcatuck in Stonington he took an active part in town affairs, he became prominent, and was elected to almost every position of public trust in the new settlement. In 1658, when Pawcatuck was included in the town of Southertown, under the jurisdiction of Massachusetts, he was appointed selectman and magistrate. After Pawcatuck was set off to the Connecticut Colony by the charter of 1662, Mr. Stanton was appointed magistrate and commissioner, and re-appointed every year up to the time of his death. He was elected deputy or representative to the General Court of Connecticut in 1666 and re-elected every year up to 1675.

When courts were first established in New London County in 1666, Major Mason, Thomas Stanton, and Lieut. Pratt of Saybrook, were appointed judges. Thus it appears that Mr. Stanton took a prominent part in town, county and State affairs from 1636, when he acted as interpreter at Saybrook, until near the close of his life. His name is connected with the leading measures of the colony, and with almost every Indian transaction on record. In 1670, Uncas, the Mohegan sachem, went from Mohegan to Pawcatuck for Mr. Stanton to write his will, taking with him a train of his noblest warriors to witness the same, giving to the occasion all the pomp and pageantry of savage royalty. He d. Dec. 2, 1677, aged 68 years. His will was probated in June, 1678. His widow survived him about eleven years, making her home with her daughter, Mrs. Dorothy Noyes, at Anguilla in Stonington, Conn. He m. Anna, daughter of Thomas and Dorothy Lord, in 1637.

CHILDREN:

2 THOMAS, JR., b. in 1638, m. Sarah Denison in 1658.
3 JOHN, b. in 1641, m. Hannah Thompson.
4 MARY, b. in 1643, m. Samuel Rogers, Nov. 17, 1662.
5 HANNAH, b. in 1644, m. Nehemiah Palmer (No. 9), that family.
6 JOSEPH, b. in 1646, d. in 1714; m. Hannah Mead; 2d, Hannah Lord.
7 DANIEL, b. in 1648, lived in Barbadoes, d. in 1687.
8 DOROTHY, b. in 1651, m. Rev. James Noyes (No. 6), that family.
9 ROBERT, b. in 1653, m. Joanna Gardiner, Nov. 12, 1677.
10 SARAH, b. in 1655, m. 1st, Thomas Prentice (No. 3); 2d, William Denison (No. 43), that family.
11 SAMUEL, b. in 1657, m. Borodell Denison June 16, 1680.

Thomas Stanton (No. 2) m. Sarah Denison in 1658 (No. 37), Denison family, both of Stonington, Conn. She d. Dec. 19, 1701; he d. April 11, 1718.

CHILDREN:

12 MARY, b. in 1660, m. Robert Lay, Jr., Jan. 22, 1679.
13 THOMAS, b. in 1665, d. May 20, 1683, aged 18.
14 SARAH, bapt. Dec. 14, 1674, m. Nathaniel Chesebrough, Jr. (No. 23), that family.
15 ANNA, bapt. June 30, 1675, m. Thomas Stanton (No. 112), that family.
16 WILLIAM, b. May 6, 1677, m. Anna Stanton.
17 DOROTHY, b. April 24, 1682, m. Nicholas Lynde; m. 2d, John Trevice.
18 SAMUEL, b. May 21, 1682, twice married.

THOMAS STANTON FAMILY.

William Stanton (No. 16) m. Anna Stanton (No. 268), Stanton family, May 7, 1701. They lived in Stonington.

CHILDREN:

19 ANNA, b. Sept. 5, 1702.
20 WILLIAM, b. Jan. 26, 1705, m. Lucy Briggs, Sept. 10, 1745.
21 SARAH, b. Nov. 11, 1708.
22 PRUDENCE, b. April 8, 1711.
23 THOMAS, b. July 11, 1713, m. Elizabeth Bell.
24 ROBERT, b. July 14, 1715, d. young.
25 JOANNA, b. April 24, 1717.
25a BRIDGET, b. Feb. 19, 1719.
26 JOSHUA, b. June 26, 1721, m. Hannah Randall.
27 LUCY, b. May 10, 1724.

Dorothy Stanton (No. 17) m. Nicholas Lynde of Charlestown, Mass., May 9, 1696.

CHILDREN:

28 SARAH LYNDE, b. Feb. 26, 1699.
29 JOSEPH LYNDE, b. Jan. 7, 1703, m. Mary Lemmon.
Mr. Nicholas Lynde d. at Jamaica, West Indies, in Oct., 1703. His widow Mrs. Dorothy Lynde, m. for her second husband Mr. John Trerice, Jan. 22, 1708.

Samuel Stanton (No. 18) m. Mabel Treat, daughter of James and Rebecca (Latimer) Treat of Wethersfield, Conn., May 24, 1716. They lived in Hartford, Conn., and the wife died childless. His second wife was Rebecca Worden of Stonington, to whom he was m. Jan. 25, 1729. They lived in Stonington. He d. 1751, and in 1754 she m. 2d, Daniel Collins (No. 1), that family, and was living in 1770.

CHILDREN:

30 SARAH, b. July 9, 1730, m. Benjamin Stevens Feb. 11, 1759.
31 SAMUEL, b. Jan. 7, 1732, d. young man, Jan. 19, 1770.
32 MARY, b. Sept. 18, 1737.
33 JOHN, b. May 13, 1736, m. Susanna Champlin.
34 AMOS, b. Feb. 26, 1739, d. young.

Thomas Stanton (No. 23) m. Elizabeth, daughter of William and Anna (Quimby) Bell, May 5, 1746. She was bapt. March 31, 1738, and d. Feb. 10, 1818. He d. Jan. 24, 1784.

CHILDREN:

35 THOMAS, b. Nov. 22, 1747.
36 WILLIAM, b. Nov. 11, 1750, m. Sarah Breed.
37 ELI, b. June 4, 1754, m. Susan Dodge.
38 LUCY, b. July 15, 1757.
39 ANNA, b. May 8, 1760, m. 1st, Joseph Eells (No. 30), that family; 2d, Dea. Sands Cole.
40 JESSE, b. June 17, 1764.
41 ELIZABETH, b. Sept. 27, 1767, m. Lodowick Niles, 1797.
42 RHODA, b. Aug. 5, 1770, m. Staunton Frink July 14, 1798.
43 NATHAN, b. June 20, 1773, m. Prudence Stanton (No. 424), Jan. 16, 1797.

Bridget Stanton (No. 25a).   No record of marriage.

SON:

44 AZARIAH STANTON, bapt. Jan. 29, 1738, m. Susanna Cobb (No. 27), that family, in 1760. He d. aged 30 years; she m. 2d, Jeremiah Tenney May 29, 1774.

CHILD BY FIRST MARRIAGE:

45 AZARIAH, b. Jan. 28, 1761, m. Abigail Chesebrough (No. 189), that family.

CHILDREN BY SECOND MARRIAGE:

46 JEREMIAH TENNEY, JR., b. Oct. 29, 1775.
47 EBENEZER TENNEY, b. March 31, 1780.

Joshua Stanton (No. 26), m. Hannah Randall, 1746, both of Stonington, Conn. (No. 41), Randall family; m. for his 2d wife, Mary Davis, 1753. He d. Oct. 25, 1819.

CHILDREN:

48 JOSHUA, JR., b. 1747, m. Susanna Breed.
49 WILLIAM, b. 1749, m. a Loomis.
50 REV. ROBERT, b. 1751, m. Elizabeth Palmer.
52 JOHN, b. 1753, m. 1st, Elizabeth Fish; 2d, Martha Maine.
53 HENRY, b. 1756, m. Martha Davis.
54 LUCRETIA, b. 1759, m. Elisha Billings Oct. 4, 1778.
55 HANNAH, b. 1761, m. ——— Loomis.
56 ANN, b. 1764, m. ——— Gillett.
57 DENSEY, b. 1768, m. Rev. Elkanah Babcock.
58 LODOWICK, b. Dec. 12, 1775, m. Nabby Read Dec. 6, 1801.

John Stanton of Stonington (No. 33) m. Susannah Champlin, daughter of Stephen and Mary (Hazard) Champlin June 9, 1763. They lived in Stonington, where he d. 1819. He was a soldier of the French and Revolutionary war.

CHILDREN:

59 REBECCA, b. Feb. 14, 1764, m. David Wilcox (No. 98), that family.
60 JOHN, b. March 21, 1766, m. Lucy Peckham.
61 SUSANNA, b. May 25, 1768, m. William Hiscox.
62 AMOS (twin), b. May 25, 1768, m. Amelia Babcock.
63 BRIDGET, b. July 27, 1770, m. Jared Wilcox (No. 100), that family.
64 SAMUEL, b. April 10, 1778, m. Martha Wilcox (No. 102), that family.

William Stanton (No. 36) m. Sarah Breed Nov. 12, 1775.

CHILDREN:

65 SARAH or SALLY, b. in 1776, m. John Davis in 1804 (No. 21), that family.
66 MARY B., b. in 1786, m. Capt. William Dodge.
67 THOMAS B., b. in 1792, m. Experience Barber. He was killed in Stonington Feb. 23, 1815, aged 23.

CHILD:

68 SARAH, b. Dec., 1814, m. Rev. Thomas Barber of Westerly, R. I.

Joshua Stanton (No. 48) m. Susanna Breed (No. 42), that family, both of Stonington. He used to preach some, but was never ordained. He was a Baptist and d. in 1834.

THOMAS STANTON FAMILY.

CHILDREN:
69 SUSANNA, b. Oct. 6, 1775, m. Timothy Lull.
70 ANNA N., b. Aug. 13, 1778, m. Nathaniel Pease.
71 JOSHUA, b. Aug. 6, 1782, m. Roxana Day in 1812.
72 HANNAH, b. May 21, 1785, m. ——— Green.
73 JOHN, b. June 14, 1789, d. unmarried.
74 JAMES, b. Nov. 23, 1794, m. Lucia Stebbins in 1829.

Rev. Robert Stanton, Baptist minister (No. 50) m. Elizabeth Palmer April 10, 1775, both of Stonington, Conn. He d. May 1, 1811; she d. Aug. 19, 1821.

CHILDREN:
75 BETSEY, b. Feb. 16, 1776, m. Calvin Bugbee.
76 PATTY, b. July 22, 1778, m. Uriah Underwood.
77 OLIVER, b. Oct. 16, 1780, m. Cynthia Underwood; 2d, Rhoda Underwood.
78 ROBERT, b. Oct. 22, 1782, m. Marsena Upham.
79 RANDALL, b. May 24, 1785, m. Clarissa Spicer.
80 PALMER, b. July 22, 1787, m. Eunice Spicer, 2d wife.
81 KETURAH, b. Jan. 26, 1790, m. Josiah Willis.
82 MARY, b. 1793, m. William Glading.
83 NANCY, b. 1796, m. Minor Smith.
84 ROSWELL, b. 1797, unmarried.
85 JOHN MORSE, b. March 29, 1799, m. Elvira Martin, in 1827.
86 ADAMS, b. Feb. 6, 1801, m. Elmira Perrin in 1827.

Dea. John Stanton (No. 52) m. Elizabeth Fish; she d. April 1, 1833. He m. for 2d wife, Mrs. Martha Maine Dec. 16, 1799. He d. in North Stonington in 1851. He was a Revolutionary soldier.

CHILDREN BY FIRST MARRIAGE:
87 WILLIAM, b. and d. young man.
88 HANNAH, b. ———, m. Lodowick B. Stanton (No. 92).
89 LYDIA G., b. Dec. 21, 1799, m. Eldridge Spicer May 31, 1821.
90 JOANNA, b. ———, m. Ebenezer Fish.

Amos Stanton (No. 62) m. Amelia Babcock, b. Mar. 5, 1779, daughter of Elkanah and Esther Babcock. She d. Jan. 7, 1844; he d. June 8, 1841.

CHILDREN:
91 AMELIA, b. Nov. 2, 1792, m. Samuel Hiscox, her cousin.
92 LODOWICK B., b. Jan. 28, 1795, m. Hannah Stanton (No. 88).
93 SUSAN, b. Aug. 17, 1798, m. Russell Bentley of North Stonington (No. 33), that family.
94 SOPHRONIA, b. June, 1801, m. Saxton Maine of Stonington.
96 AMOS, b. July 22, 1804, m. Triphena Brown.
97 AVERY, b. Sept. 21, 1806, d. unmarried.
98 CAROLINE, b. Oct. 19, 1808, m. Samuel H. Babcock.
99 HOSEA, b. Dec. 5, 1815, m. Mary E. Thompson.

John Stanton, Jr. (No. 60) m. Lucy Peckham of Ledyard, Conn. He d. Nov. 16, 1838; she d. Oct. 19, 1862.

CHILDREN:
100 LUCY ANN, b. July 30, 1804, m. Jonathan Gray Stanton (No. 406).
101 CELIA, b. ———, d. 1806.
102 SAMUEL, b. Oct. 15, 1807, m. Nancy Lord Wheeler (No. 214), that family.
103 JOHN, b. Oct. 5, 1809, m. Lydia Waterman; 2d, Jane E. Barber.

582   HISTORY OF STONINGTON.

104 HENRY FRANKLIN, b. 1802, m. Ann James.
105 REBECCA W., b. Aug. 24, 1815, m. John Brewer.
106 ALFRED B., b. May 26, 1817, m. Marjory Lewis.
107 CHARLES C., b. Dec. 30, 1823, drowned Nov. 16, 1857, in Pawcatuck river.
108 MARTHA W., b. Nov. 27, 1825, m. James D. Smith of New London.
109 DAVID W., b. July 21, 1828, d. unmarried.

Capt. John Stanton (No. 3) m. Hannah Thompson in 1664, sister of Rev. William Thompson, Jr., of Braintree, Mass. In 1654 he and John Minor, son of Thomas, were selected by the Court of Commissioners to be educated for teachers of the gospel to the Indians. Both young men, however, ultimately left their studies and devoted themselves to other pursuits. He commanded one of the companies that was raised to participate in King Philip's war, and was present at the Narragansett swamp fight, Dec. 19, 1675. Subsequently, he and Capt. George Denison, with their companies, successfully pursued and overpowered the remnants of King Philip's tribe, and brought the war to a close. His homestead farm in Stonington, which descended to him from his father, was on the east bank of the Mystic River, adjoining lands of John Gallup on the north and George Denison on the south and east. It has never passed out of the possession of the family. His wife d. Oct. 3rd, 1813.

CHILDREN:

110 JOHN, b. May 22, 1665, m. Mary ———.
111 JOSEPH, b. Jan. 22, 1668, m. Margaret Chesebrough.
112 THOMAS, b. April, 1670, m. his cousin, Anna Stanton (No. 15).
113 ANN, b. Oct. 1, 1673, d. March 23, 1680.
114 THEOPHILUS, b. June 16, 1676, m. Elizabeth Rogers June 5, 1696.
115 DOROTHY, b. ———, 1680, d. April 28, 1699.

John Stanton (No. 110) m. Mary ———. He lived in Preston on lands given him by his father.

CHILDREN:

116 JOHN, b. Nov. 13, 1706, m. Desire Denison (No. 111), that family.
117 DANIEL, b. June 8, 1708, m. Dinah Starke.
118 JOSEPH, b. Feb. 11, 1710, m. Abigail Freeman.
119 LYDIA, b. July 15, 1712, m. Daniel Leonard.
120 ROBERT, b. Feb. 20, 1714, m. Mary Lester.
121 HULDA, b. June 3, 1716.
122 JABEZ, b. Dec. 19, 1718, m. Sarah Morse.
123 DAVID, b. Oct. 22, 1720, m. Sarah Kimball.
124 MARY, b. Sept. 11, 1722.
125 SARAH, b. Jan. 20, 1724.
126 SAMUEL, b. June 20, 1726, m. Mary Palmer.

Joseph Stanton of Stonington (No. 111) m. Margaret Chesebrough (No. 27), that family, July 18, 1696. They lived on the Stanton homestead farm, which he inherited from his father.

THOMAS STANTON FAMILY. 583

CHILDREN:
127 HANNAH, b. Dec. 15, 1698, m. William Morgan, Jr.
128 MARGARET, b. Oct. 7, 1701, m. Jonathan Copp (No. 17), that family.
129 ZERVIAH, b. Sept. 24, 1704, m. Nehemiah Mason (No. 28), that family.
130 SARAH, b. Sept. 24, 1706, m. William Halsey.
131 ANNA, b. Feb. 22, 1708, m. John Avery (No. 71), Avery family.
132 DOROTHY, b. and d. July, 1710.
133 JOSEPH, b. May 1, 1712, m. Anna Wheeler.
134 JOHN, b. Sept. 29, 1714, m. Prudence Chesebrough.
135 NATHANIEL, b. July 29, 1716, m. Mary Coit, 1738.

Hannah Stanton (No. 127) m. William Morgan of Groton Sept. 21, 1721. He d. May 14, 1778; his wife d. June 26, 1747.

CHILDREN:
136 MARGARET MORGAN, b. Sept., 1723, d. Sept., 1745.
137 HANNAH MORGAN, b. July 18, 1725, d. young.
138 ABIGAIL MORGAN, b. Aug. 5, 1727, d. in 1746.
139 ANN MORGAN, b. June 26, 1736, d. young.

Sarah Stanton (No. 130) m. William Halsey June 19, 1738. They lived in Stonington, Conn.

CHILDREN:
140 WILLIAM HALSEY, b. Sept. 20, 1739.
141 SARAH HALSEY, bapt. June 20, 1742.
142 JEREMIAH HALSEY, bapt. June 10, 1744, a lawyer, lived in Preston.

Lieut. Joseph Stanton (No. 133) m. Anna Wheeler (No. 38), that family, Nov. 6, 1735, both of Stonington, Conn. He d. March 14, 1773.

CHILDREN:
143 HANNAH, b. Aug. 8, 1736, m. Charles Hewitt Oct. 28, 1756 (No. 54), Hewitt family.
144 JOSEPH, b. May 31, 1739, m. Hannah Chesebrough.
145 MARGARET, b. Nov. 3, 1741, m. Isaac Frink (No. 53), that family.
146 ISAAC W., b. Jan. 14, 1743, m. Ruth Ayer, Sept. 19, 1765.
147 WILLIAM, b. March 5, 1745, m. Hannah Williams.
148 ANNA, b. Feb. 23, 1747, m. James Allyn, Jr., of Groton, Dec. 14, 1768.
149 NATHAN, b. Dec. 15, 1749, m. Anna Stanton.
150 EUNICE, b. Nov. 12, 1751, m. James Denison Sept. 29, 1773 (No. 297), Denison family.
151 MARTHA, b. Nov. 19, 1753, m. John Holmes, Jr., Dec. 22, 1774 (No. 41), Holmes family.
152 MARY, b. Aug. 28, 1756, m. David Geer, May 17, 1781.
153 DOROTHY, b. Jan. 21, 1760, m. Noyes Palmer May 22, 1785 (No. 226), Palmer family.

John Stanton of Stonington (No. 134) m. Prudence Chesebrough of Stonington, Feb. 27, 1737 (No. 74) Chesebrough family. They lived in Groton.

CHILDREN:
154 SARAH, b. July 31, 1739.
155 ZERVIAH, b. Sept. 17, 1742.
156 JOHN, b. May 17, 1745, m. Betsey Maples.
157 SAMUEL, b. Nov. 11, 1747.
158 AMOS, b. Nov. 29, 1750; killed in Fort Griswold, Sept. 6, 1781.

159 ROBERT, b. 1752, d. unmarried.
160 PRUDENCE, b. Nov. 7, 1754.
161 JAMES, b. Dec. 28, 1756.
162 CASINDA, b. 1762, m. Robert Geer, son of Amos and Mary (Wright) Geer.

Joseph Stanton (No. 144), b. in Stonington May 31, 1739, m. Hannah Chesebrough April 22, 1767 (No. 164), Chesebrough family. They lived in Groton. He d. in 1832; she d. in 1835.

CHILDREN:
163 JOHN, b. July 25, 1767, m. Polly Palmer.
164 JOSEPH, b. May 11, 1769, m. Polly Dennis.
164a ANNA, b. Aug. 13, 1771, d. April 3, 1779.
165 AMOS, b. June 10, 1773, m. Sabra Palmer Dec. 13, 1795.
166 DESIRE, b. June 10, 1775, m. Henry Gallup.
167 JOSHUA, b. April 1, 1777, d. March 28, 1779.
168 ANNA, b. May 2, 1779, d. unmarried.
169 JOSHUA C., b. June 1, 1781, m. Harriet Hewitt (No. 201), that family.
170 HANNAH, b. May 22, 1783, m. Samuel H. Palmer.
171 MARY, b. July 4, 1785, d. unmarried.
172 ROBERT, b. May 6, 1787, m. Hannah Hewitt Feb. 27, 1812 (No. 196), that family.

Capt. William Stanton (No. 147) m. Hannah Williams Nov. 10, 1773. She d. and he m. for his second wife, Hannah Foster. He d. at North Stonington July 12, 1828.

CHILDREN:
173 THANKFUL, b. July 22, 1774, m. Elias Williams Nov. 24, 1794 (No. 279). Williams family.

Isaac Wheeler Stanton, b. in Stonington Jan. 14, 1743 (No. 146), m. Ruth Ayer, daughter of John and Abby (Cook) Ayer, Sept. 19, 1765. He lived in Preston until eight of his children were born, and then removed to Vermont. He d. in 1829, aged 86 years; his wife d. aged 75 years.

CHILDREN:
174 ABIGAIL, b. Jan. 7, 1767, m. Levi Collins, about 1810.
175 ANNA, b. Nov. 4, 1768, m. David Blair.
176 HENRY, b. Dec. 7, 1770, m. Ann Harriman.
177 POLLY, b. Sept. 26, 1773, m. Joseph Phillips.
178 HANNAH, b. June 25, 1776, m. Robert Cox, Sept. 22, 1798.
179 ERASTUS, b. Sept. 9, 1778, m. Elizabeth Shepard in 1803.
180 ISAAC WHEELER, b. April 10, 1781, m. Martha Blunt in 1809.
181 WILLIAM JERVAISE, b. Aug. 27, 1783, d. at sea in 1803.
182 JOHN AYER, b. Dec. 7, 1785, m. Tamson Stevens in 1811.
183 JOSEPH, b. March 15, 1789, m. Lodicia Barron.
184 RUTH, b. Aug. 19, 1790, d. unmarried.

Anna Stanton (No. 148) m. James Allyn of Groton Dec. 14, 1768. They lived in Stonington, Conn.

CHILDREN:
185 JAMES ALLYN, b. Oct. 22, 1769.
186 ANNA ALLYN, b. Nov. 9, 1771.
187 JOSEPH ALLYN, b. Jan. 22, 1774.

THOMAS STANTON FAMILY. 585

188 ALTHEA ALLYN, b. Aug. 6, 1776.
189 JABEZ ALLYN, b. Jan. 12, 1779, d. Sept. 21, 1781.
190 CHARLES ALLYN, b. Sept. 28, 1781.
191 MARTHA ALLYN, b. April 17, 1784, m. Stephen Billings (No. 151), that family.
192 HANNAH ALLYN, b. July 7, 1787, d. Sept. 3, 1787.
193 ROSWELL ALLYN, b. July 11, 1789.

Nathan Stanton (No. 149) m. Anna Stanton (No. 381), Stanton family, Dec. 25, 1777, both of Stonington, Conn., until 1793, when they moved to Florida, N. Y., where she d. Sept. 27, 1825. He d. at Syracuse, N. Y., Sept. 26, 1835.

CHILDREN:

194 NATHAN, b. July 4, 1779, m. Mary Denison (No. 454), Denison family.
195 ANNA, b. May 8, 1780, d. young.
196 DANIEL, b. May 17, 1781, d. Aug. 27, 1783.
197 AMOS, b. Feb. 11, 1783, d. Aug. 23, 1793.
198 ANNA, b. Dec. 7, 1784, m. Asa Cady Jan. 23, 1802.
199 BENJAMIN FRANKLIN, b. Feb. 12, 1789, m. Martha Rogers; 2d, Charlotte Jenkins.
200 ELIZABETH, b. April 26, 1791, d. Oct. 2, 1791.
201 JOHN JAY, b. June 7, 1793, m. Lucy Palmer Sept. 26, 1816 (No. 436), Palmer family.
202 HIRAM, b. Feb. 26, 1796, d. March 9, 1797.
203 SOPHIA, b. Nov. 23, 1798, m. Robert Geer Oct. 25, 1820.

Eli Stanton (No. 37) m. Susan Dodge, both of Stonington, Conn.

CHILDREN:

204 JESSE, b. in 1809.
205 LUCY, b. in 1811.
206 CHARLOTTE, b. in 1812, m. William Hall.
207 MARY, b. in 1813.
208 JOHN, b. and d. in 1830, unmarried.
209 LUCRETIA, b. ———, was living in 1888.

Charlotte Stanton (No. 206) m. William Hall, date not recorded. She d. Oct. 25, 1839, aged 27 years, and left two children.

CHILDREN:

210 A son, who went to California.
211 MARY HALL, who was adopted by Henry and Abby (Palmer) Smith of Stonington, she m. Charles S. Hull of Stonington Nov. 18, 1860 (No. 41), Hull family.

Elizabeth, called Betsey, Stanton (No. 41) m. Capt. Lodowick Niles, both of Stonington, Conn., Nov. 5, 1797.

CHILDREN:

212 CHARLOTTE NILES, b. date unknown. She was killed while sitting between her two sisters in the old school house, by a stroke of lightning.
213 ELIZA MARY NILES, b. in 1798, m. John F. Trumbull (No. 32), that family for his first wife; she d. Feb. 29, 1828, leaving one son, Horace N. Trumbull.
214 MARIA NILES, b. in 1803, m. John D. Smith Feb. 7, 1822.
215 HORACE E. NILES, b. in 1806, m. Eunice Pendleton Nov. 1, 1830.

Joseph Stanton (No. 6), b. in Hartford, 1646. He was bapt. there March 21, 1646, and came to Stonington, Conn., with his parents in 1657. He m. June 19, 1673, Hannah Mead, daughter of William Mead of Roxbury, Mass., and settled upon a tract of land which his father, Mr. Thomas Stanton, had purchased of an Indian chief, "Cassawshett," alias Harmon Garret, Jan. 14, 1659. The consideration mentioned in the deed of land is as follows: "For good reasons leading me hereunto, have and do give a neck of land to Thomas Stanton called Quanccontaug, &c." Thomas Stanton took immediate possession of the land purchased of Harmon Garrett and built him a house thereon. Subsequently he ascertained that his title to the land so purchased was imperfect; that Harmon was not a sachem, invested with power to sell the tribal lands of the Niantic Indians, and on consulting with the Commissioners of the United Colonies, he found that the land in question had been previously purchased by the Maj. Humphrey Atherton Land Company (of which Thomas Stanton was an associate member), of Ninegret, Suncquash and Scuttup, three Niantic sachems, on conditions, introduced by the purchasers, that no associate member of said Atherton Company should sell out his share thereof until he had given the company an opportunity to buy it. Mr. Stanton assured them that he should hold possession of the land in question for himself and the company, with the result that they should regard it favorably to have his share of said company's land include his Harmon Garrett purchase, which was subsequently assented to by the company, and Mr. Stanton retained the possession thereof and gave it to his son, Joseph Stanton, in and by his last will and testament, who after his marriage took possession thereof, and occupied the same during the rest of his life. His first wife died and he married for his second wife, Hannah Lord, his cousin, of Hartford, Aug. 13, 1677, who was b. in 1656. Mrs. Hannah Stanton d. April 6, 1681. He m. a third wife, whose name, date of their marriage and the birth of their children has not been preserved. His third wife was admitted to the Stonington First Congregational Church March 16, 1683. He d. in 1714.

CHILDREN BY FIRST WIFE:

216 JOSEPH, b. in 1674, m. Hester Gallup.
217 HANNAH, b. in 1676, m. Dr. James York of Westerly, R. I., Nov. 13, 1695.

THOMAS STANTON FAMILY.

CHILDREN BY SECOND MARRIAGE:
218 THOMAS, b. Dec. 16, 1677, d. young.
219 REBECCA, b. April, 1678, m. Joseph Babcock.
The record of children baptisms in the Stonington church is as sons of Joseph Stanton of Westerly, and reads thus:
220 THOMAS, bapt. April 5, 1691, m. Esther Babcock.
221 DANIEL, b. April 1, 1694, m. Mercy Babcock.
223 SAMUEL, bapt. July 17, 1698, d. young man, unmarried.
By the Diary of Manasseh Miner we learn that Joseph Stanton's wife d. March 12, 1704.

Joseph Stanton (No. 216) m. Hester Gallup of Stonington Jan. 3, 1705 (No. 34), Gallup family.

CHILDREN:
224 JOSEPH, b. April 23, 1707.
225 ESTHER, b. 1708, m. Robert Hazard.
226 MARY, b. 1711, m. Peleg Sanford Mason Nov. 4, 1742 (No. 35), Mason family.
227 HANNAH, b. 1714, m. Dr. Joshua Babcock Aug. 11, 1735 (No 45), that family.
228 NANCY, b. 1716, d. unmarried.
229 SARAH, b. 1719, m. Dr. James Babcock (No. 47), that family.
230 LUCY, b. 1720, m. Christopher Champlin Aug. 19, 1756.

Thomas Stanton (No. 220) m. Esther Babcock, daughter of Job Babcock of Westerly, R. I.

CHILDREN:
231 REBECCA, b. ———, m. Nathaniel Sheffield Feb. 6, 1740 (No. 17), that family.
232 SARAH, b. ———, m. Benjamin Hoxie Nov. 19, 1756.
233 ISABEL, b. ———, m. Nathan Teft, Sept. 16, 1742.
234 A son, b. and was drowned when young.

Daniel Stanton (No. 221) m. 1st, Mercy, daughter of Job Babcock of Westerly R. I. She d.; he m. 2d wife, Elizabeth, daughter of George and Charity Brown of Westerly, R. I.

CHILDREN BY FIRST MARRIAGE:
235 DANIEL, b. ———, m. Mary Wilcox, daughter of Stephen and Mary (Randall) Wilcox.

CHILDREN BY SECOND MARRIAGE:
236 SAMUEL, b. ———, m. Sarah Browning.
237 JOHN, b. ———, m. Dorothy Richardson, daughter of Jonathan Richardson and Anne Treat, and granddaughter of Dorothy (Noyes) Treat.
238 JOSEPH, b. ———, m. Abigail Sheffield March 6, 1748.
239 GEORGE, b. ———, d. unmarried.
240 MARY, b. ———, m. Thomas Richardson.
241 ELIZABETH, b. ———, m. Joseph Champlin.

Col. Joseph Stanton (No. 224) m. Mary Champlin, daughter of William Champlin of Westerly, R. I., Aug. 9, 1738. She was b. July 13, 1722, and was admitted to the Stonington church July 11, 1842, and d. 1750. He was an officer in the French and Indian war.

CHILDREN:

242 JOSEPH, b. July 19, 1739, m. Thankful Babcock July 14, 1762, and after repeated promotions was elected Senator in Congress from Rhode Island.
243 ESTHER, b. Nov. 23, 1741, m. Ichabod Babcock March 17, 1756.
244 MARY, b. June 18, 1743, m. Elias Thompson.
245 AUGUSTUS, b. March 22, 1745, m. Eunice Crandall Feb. 6, 1765.
246 HANNAH, b. Feb. 24, 1746, m. Daniel Wells.
247 LODOWICK, b. May 27, 1749, m. Nancy ———.
248 GARDINER, b. ———, d. unmarried.
249 MALBOROUGH, b. ———, d. unmarried.
250 HENRY, b. ———, m. Cynthia Lewis.
251 ABIGAIL, b. ———, m. Rev. William Gardner.

Samuel Stanton (No. 236) m. Sarah, daughter of John and Ann (Hazard) Browning of Kingston, R. I., (No. 27) Browning family.

CHILDREN:

252 SARAH, b. ———, m. Dea. William Browning.
253 ELIZABETH, bapt. Jan. 6, 1760, d. unmarried.
254 EUNICE, bapt. Feb. 19, 1764, m. Daniel Sherman.
255 SAMUEL, bapt. April 10, 1771, m. Elizabeth Reynolds.

Samuel Stanton (No. 255) m. Elizabeth Reynolds of South Kingston, R. I., April 11, 1799. She d. in Charlestown, R. I., May 3, 1826, and he d. in Stonington, Conn., Jan. 23, 1855, aged 84 years.

CHILDREN:

256 SAMUEL, b. Oct. 27, 1803, m. Matilda K. Clark.
257 SARAH ANN, b. Nov. 23, 1805, m. George C. Brown and lived in Stonington.
258 ELIZABETH, b. Oct. 23, 1808, m. John T. Knowles.
259 JOHN, b. July 21, 1810, m. Celia Knowles May 26, 1833.
260 MARY, b. Nov. 6, 1814, m. James H. Kenyon Aug. 22, 1858.

The farm on which Samuel Stanton (No. 255) lived in Charlestown, R. I., was in 1858 the only remaining portion of the tract of land originally conveyed by Harmon Garret to Thomas Stanton in 1659. It had never been owned outside of this Stanton family, having been transmitted from father to son. Maj. Samuel Stanton (No. 256), that family, and Matilda Clark, both of Charlestown, R. I., were m. Jan. 6, 1838. She d. Sept. 13, 1866; he d. July 5, 1879. Mr. Stanton came here and bought a farm at Wequetequock in Stonington, where he spent the remnant of his days.

CHILDREN:

261 DR. GEORGE D., b. April 13, 1839, m. 1st, Maria Louise Pendleton Oct. 23, 1867; m. 2d, Anna W. Palmer, all of Stonington, Conn.
262 SARAH ELIZABETH, b. July 25, 1840, d. in infancy.
263 SAMUEL M., b. Feb. 10, 1845, m. Lucretia Noyes Chesebro.
264 JOHN R., b. Nov. 20, 1850, m. Mary E. Clark.

Daniel Stanton (No. 7), b. in 1648, m. and lived in Barbadoes, West Indies. He had one child

265 RICHARD.

This is the child mentioned in Mrs. Ann (Lord) Stanton's will, made in 1688, as the "fatherless child in Barbadoes," which indicates that Daniel Stanton was dead when that will was made. He d. in 1687. There is no further record of this child, Richard, except that he came to Stonington and sold his right to certain ancestral estate.

After the death of Thomas Stanton, Sr., his sons decided to enlarge their business through their trading house, and arranged with their brother, Daniel Stanton, to take up his residence on the island of Barbadoes, so as to dispose of their goods, furs and farm products in the West Indies in exchange for an equivalent in goods and groceries requisite for the needs of the New England planters. Before Mr. Daniel Stanton left for the West Indies to reside, and to enlarge his business there, he sold a portion of his real estate here in Stonington to his brother, Thomas Stanton, in 1681, describing it in the deed thereof as land willed to him by his father, Thomas Stanton, the interpreter general, which he failed to acknowledge before a magistrate. This omission subsequently led to a good deal of trouble. An effort was first made to correct it by an affidavit of two of the witnesses of said deed under date of Feb. 9, 1699, which did not prove satisfactory to the grantee of the deed. So, in 1715, Oct. 8th, Nicholas Cottrell made oath before a magistrate in Westerly, R. I., saying therein that he saw Daniel Stanton the grantor in the deed sign and seal the same, and that he, together with Mr. John Stanton, Mr. Samuel Stanton and Mrs. Anna Stanton, set their hands thereto as witnesses thereof. The proceedings was followed in a few days, to wit, Oct. 12, 1715, by an affidavit of Mr. Robert Stanton, before Nathaniel Chesebrough, a justice of the peace of Connecticut, testifying to his brother Daniel's handwriting, affixed to the deed, and to the possession of the land embraced therein by his brother, Thomas Stanton. These proceedings were doubtless instituted for the purpose of being used as evidence before the General Assembly of Connecticut in support of an application of Thomas Stanton the said grantee, praying for the confirmation of his said deed by the assembly, which application was presented thereto and considered at its October session of 1715, as follows:

"Upon application made by Thomas Stanton, representing that Mr. Daniel Stanton, sometime of Stonington, deceased, having signed and sealed a deed bearing date in the year of our Lord 1681, conveying to him, the said Thomas Stanton, a certain tract of land containing sixty acres in quantity, lying in the limits of the town of Stonington aforesaid, bounded on the north by a small run of water adjoining to the land belonging to the said Thomas Stanton, on the east by Pawcatuck River, on the south by a small brook called the Hot House brook, and on the west bounded all along by the west side of the swamp out of which the northermost brook runneth; and that the said deed was lawfully witnessed. The said Daniel Stanton died before a lawful acknowledgement of it, prayed an act of the Assembly to supply that defect. It appearing to this Court that Mr. Samuel Stanton and Nicholas Cottrell made oath before Samuel Mason, assistant, Feb. 9, 1699, that they signed as witnesses thereto, and further the said Nicholas Cottrell made oath before Thomas Hiscox, Justice of Peace in Westerly, in the Colony of Rhode Island, Aug. 1, 1715, that he did verily believe that he saw Daniel Stanton, the subscriber to the aforesaid deed, sign and seal the same, and that he, together with Mr. John Stanton, Mr. Samuel Stanton and Mrs. Anna Stanton, set their hands thereto as witnesses, which was ordered to be endorsed and signed by the secretary. HEZEKIAH WYLLYS, Secretary."

"Be it thereupon enacted by the Governor, Council and Representattives in General Court assembled, and by the authority of the same, that the said deed be taken as good and effectual to all intents and purposes in the law as it might or could have been if the said deed had been acknowledged by the grantor as the law directs, and this act be indorsed upon the said deed, and shall be signed by the secretary and received as a good, sufficient testimonial of the authentication of the said deed."

"HEZEKIAH WYLLYS, Secretary."

Notwithstanding the pains taken by the grantees to authenticate this deed, it all failed to perfect the title thereof, for the reason that none of the parties in interest, either grantees or grantors, had the authenticated provisions of the local authorities or those of the General Assembly recorded in the Stonington land records, so the original deed of said premises did not vest the title of the land embraced therein in the grantee thereof, and the failure to have said proceeding regularly recorded in our land records for twenty years after the original deed, left the title thereof remaining in Daniel Stanton, and in case of his death in his heirs-at-law. All that is known of this family is that he had a son, Richard Stanton, Jr., who, with him, claimed the land his grandfather, Daniel Stanton, sold to Thomas Stanton, his brother, in 1681, on account of his said grandfather's, Daniel Stanton, failure to acknowledge the deed thereof to his brother, Thomas Stanton, and his failure to have all of the authenticated proceedings in confirmation of said property recorded. After an extended and exhaustive correspondence between Richard Stanton and his son, Richard Stanton, Jr., of Barbadoes, party of the first part, and

Samuel Stanton, the son of the said Thomas Stanton of Pawcatuck, Conn., deceased, who lived upon and claimed the land in question at the time, of the second part, it was finally arranged between them that Samuel Stanton should give the said Richard Stanton, Sr., £46 for a quit-claim deed of all his interest in said tract of land. So, giving his son, Richard Stanton, Jr., a full and adequate power of attorney to transfer his title in said land to his cousin, Samuel Stanton, the said Richard Stanton, Jr., came to Stonington Feb. 12, 1736, and by virtue of said power conveyed the disputed premises to Samuel Stanton, fifty-five years after the execution of the original deed thereof to the said Thomas Stanton, by his brother, the said Daniel Stanton, who had other lands in Stonington given him by his honored father, in and by his last will and testament. One tract of 200 acres he sold to Capt. George Denison of Stonington, by a deed thereof executed in Barbadoes in 1682. Before Mr. Stanton went to the island of Barbadoes to reside he united with Mr. Alexander Pygan and Samuel Rogers of New London, and they together employed Mr. Joseph Wells, then of Westerly, but later on of the Mystic Valley, on the Groton side, to build them a vessel in 1681, called the "Alexander and Martha." The dimensions, but not the tonnage, stated in the contract are as follows: "The length to be 40 and one foot by the keel from the after part of the post to the breaking afore at the guardboard, 12 foot rake forward under her load mark, at least 16 foot wide upon the midship beam, to have 11 flat timbers and 9 foot floor, and the swoop at the cuttock 9 foot, and by transom 12 foot, the main deck to have a fall by the mainmast, with a cabin, and also a cook room with a forecastle." For payment the builder was to receive one-eighth of the vessel and £165, of which £16 was to be in silver money and the rest in merchantable goods, the spikes, nails and iron work were to be at the charge of the owners. After the vessel was launched, rigged and fitted for sea Daniel Stanton bought the builder's share thereof, as per the stipulations of the contract and annex. When the vessel had received her cargo, Mr. Stanton and his family embarked on board and went to Barbadoes in the vessel, where he continued to reside the remainder of his life. He opened a store there for the transaction of the Stanton Brothers' business which he successfully prosecuted. The said vessel continued to run between the West Indies and the trading store on

Pawcatuck River, doing a successful business for several years. But the West Indies' climate did not agree with Mr. Stanton's health, which so impaired it that he did not live but a few years, dying before 1688, which fact we learn from his mother's will.

Robert Stanton (No. 9) m. Joanna Gardiner Sept. 12, 1677, daughter of Thomas and Lucy (Smith) Gardiner of Roxbury, Mass. He lived in Pawcatuck, Stonington, Conn., and d. Oct. 24, 1724.

NOTE.—Robert Stanton was a soldier in King Philip's war, as was his older brothers, Capt. John and Joseph Stanton. In 1676, Capt. George Denison, with a large company of subordinate officers and men, who were raised in New London county, went in pursuit of the remnant of King Philip's army, and while a portion of them, under the command of Canonchet, the last of the Royal Narragansett Sachems, were encamped on the banks of the Pawcatuck River in Rhode Island, they were attacked by the English, under Capt. George Denison, accompanied by some of the friendly Pequot and Mohegan Indians, when most of the Narragansett and Wampanaog Indians fled, leaving Canonchet almost entirely alone. As soon as he realized his situation, he too sought safety in flight. The Indian allies of the English and a few of the fleetest whites pursued him, and as he saw his pursuers were gaining on him he threw off his blanket, then his silver-laced coat and belt of peage, and ran with all possible speed, to escape from his enemies, and as he crossed the rivers ford he fell and wet his gun, which so embarrassed him in his flight that he was soon overtaken and surrendered to Robert Stanton, son of the Interpreter General Thomas Stanton, then not 22 years old. Being questioned by the young man, whom he personally knew, about a treaty of peace, between the English and Indians, and not wishing to recognize the authority of his youthful inquisitor, he looked upon him with lofty and defiant contempt, and said you are a child, you cannot understand matters of war; let your brother, Capt. John Stanton, or your chief, Capt. George Denison, come, then I will answer. But when the officers whom he had requested to see came up, he refused to enter into any negotiations with them, so he was brought a prisoner to Stonington, where a council of war was held, which he declined to recognize, and after his absolute refusal to enter into and abide by a treaty of peace with the English, who, after considering their defenseless conditions and his ferocious temper, he was condemned and ordered to be shot, and when told of his fate he said that "he liked it well, and should die before his heart had grown soft or he had said anything unworthy of himself," and so he was shot near Anguilla in Stonington.

CHILDREN:

266 JOANNA, b. June 5, 1677, m. Robert Denison (No. 52), Denison family.
267 LUCY, b. Sept. 16, 1681, d. Sept., 1687.
268 ANNA, b. Oct. 26, 1684, m. William Stanton (No. 16).
269 MARY, b. Feb. 3, 1687, m. Daniel Denison (No. 54), Denison family.
270 REV. ROBERT, b. Dec. 7, 1689. He was graduated at Harvard College in 1712, and was ordained pastor of the East Church in Salem, Mass., Rev. Cotton Mather, D. D., preaching the ordination sermon. This celebrated minister married him to Katherine Simpkins of Boston May 5, 1719. He d. in Salem, Mass., May 3, 1727, and May 5 would have been his eighth wedding anniversary.
271 THOMAS, b. June 9, 1693, m. Thankful Denison.
272 LUCY, b. May 3, 1696, m. James McDowell May 7, 1715.
273 GARDINER, b. May 27, 1701, d. Feb., 1704.

THOMAS STANTON FAMILY. 593

Thomas Stanton (No. 271) m. Thankful Denison Dec. 30, 1713 (No. 65), Denison family, both of Stonington; m. 2d, Mrs. Sarah (Hillard) Fish (No. 10) Rossiter family.

CHILDREN:

274 ROBERT, b. Nov. 14, 1716, m. Anna Stanton.
275 THANKFUL, b. July 21, 1718, m. Col. Elias Thompson March 24, 1736.
276 MARY, b. May 21, 1720, m. Nathan Babcock .
277 ELIZABETH, b. June 10, 1722, m. Phineas Stanton (No. 347).
278 MERCY, b. June 14, 1724, m. Ebenezer Goddard of Groton March 3, 1751.
279 PRUDENCE, b. April 22, 1726, m. 1st, Juda Coleman; m. 2d, Col. Giles Russell (No. 15), that family.
280 NATHAN, b. June 19, 1728, d. in infancy.
281 THOMAS, b. Dec. 20, 1729, m. Sarah Chesebrough.
282 REBECCA, b. in 1731.
283 ANNA, b. March 22, 1732, m. Nathan Chesebrough (No. 147), Chesebrough family.
284 DESIRE, b. April 22, 1734, m. Amos Hallam Oct. 18, 1758 (No. 9), Hallam family.
285 HANNAH, b. Sept. 29, 1736, m. Robert Potter, Esq., Aug. 28, 1754.

Robert Stanton (No. 274) m. Anna Stanton May 26, 1736 (No. 348), that family. They lived in Stonington, Conn.

CHILDREN:

286 CYNTHIA, b. Oct. 16, 1737, d. unmarried.
287 ROBERT, b. March 16, 1739, m. Sabra Palmer Dec. 2, 1764.
288 MARY, b. Nov. 8, 1741, m. Col. Henry Babcock Dec. 2, 1764 (No. 77).
289 ANNA, b. Aug. 25, 1745.
290 ABIGAIL, b. May 1, 1748, m. Samuel Hazard Nov. 23, 1766, son of Esther Stanton Hazard (No. 225).
291 THOMAS, b. in 1750, m. Elizabeth Chesebrough April 25, 1771 (No. 172), Chesebrough family.
292 THANKFUL, b. in 1752, m. Lodowick Stanton Aug. 20, 1772.

Prudence Stanton (No. 279), m. 1st, Juda Coleman March 4, 1747. After the death of Mr. Coleman she m. for her 2d husband, Col. Giles Russell (No. 15), that family, Dec. 8, 1762.

CHILDREN BY FIRST MARRIAGE:

293 MERCY COLEMAN, b. July 18, 1748, m. Capt. Elnathan Rossiter (No. 8), that family.
294 ROBERT COLEMAN, b. Oct. 26, 1749.

CHILD BY SECOND MARRIAGE:

295 HANNAH RUSSELL, b. Jan. 20, 1764, m. Samuel Stanton (No. 358).

Thomas Stanton (No. 281) m. Sarah Chesebrough Jan. 10, 1751 (No. 148), Chesebrough family. She d. June 9, 1789. He d. July 30, 1799. They lived in Stonington, Conn.

CHILDREN:

296 SARAH, b. Nov. 12, 1751, m. Simeon Palmer Dec. 19, 1773 (No. 223), Palmer family.
297 PELEG, b. Nov. 10, 1752, d. young.
298 BRIDGET, b. Jan. 18, 1756, m. Nathaniel Chesebrough Oct. 14, 1787 (No. 255), Chesebrough family.

299 PELEG, b. March 13, 1758, m. Lydia Hewitt.
300 MERCY, b. July 6, 1760, m. Prentice Breed Dec. 7, 1780 (No. 32), Breed family.
301 ROWLAND, b. Aug. 10, 1762, d. young.
302 THANKFUL, b. Jan. 27, 1764, m. Chesebro Miner Oct. 29, 1797.
303 THOMAS, b. June 1, 1766, m. Thankful Noyes Feb. 28, 1793 (No. 169), Noyes family.
304 NATHAN, b. Oct. 15, 1768, killed Jan. 6, 1804, by falling from a haymow in a barn on the farm now owned by Sanford N. Billings of Stonington.
305 ROBERT, b. June 7, 1771, d. in infancy.
306 HANNAH, b. Oct. 17, 1772, m. Richard Palmer Feb. 16, 1794 (No. 297), Palmer family.

Lieut. Peleg Stanton (No. 299) m. Lydia Hewitt (No. 105), that family, of Stonington, Conn, June 10, 1781. He d. April 28, 1799, and his widow m. Capt. Joshua Brown (No. 77), Brown family.

CHILDREN:

307 LYDIA, b. in 1782, m. Gurdon Crandall in 1799, and d. in 1800, aged 18 years. No children.
308 SOPHIA, b. in 1784, m. Enoch Crandall, third wife.
309 BRIDGET, b. in 1786, m. Isaac Pendleton in 1808.
310 ABBY, b. in 1787, m. Enoch Crandall, second wife.
311 ELIAS, b. May 2, 1787, m. Nancy Davis (No. 25), that family.
312 EZRA, b. 1791, m. Lucinda Hewitt (No. 191), Hewitt family.
313 ROWLAND, b. 1793, m. 1st, Maria Palmer; 2d wife, Hannah Hewitt.
314 ISAAC, b. in 1799, m. Nancy H. Smith May 18, 1831; 2d, Anna Stark Sept. 29, 1832.

Abby Stanton (No. 310) m. Enoch Crandall, his second wife.

CHILD:

315 ABBY S., b. ———, m. 1st, Perez Hewitt (No. 213), that family; 2d, Richard H. Maine of North Stonington.

Sophia Stanton (No. 308) m. Enoch, son of Enoch and Mercy (Pendleton) Crandall of Charlestown, R. I. His first wife was Abby Gardner, who d. childless. His second wife was Abby (No. 310); and Sophia (No. 308) was his third wife.

CHILDREN:

316 GURDON S. CRANDALL, b. June 26, 1808, m. Elizabeth W. Avery Dec. 2, 1828 (No. 236), that family.
317 JAMES, b. about 1810, m. Betsey Hewitt.
318 CHARLOTTE, b. ———, m. Sept. 20, 1835, her cousin, Lewis Crandall, son of Lewis and Bathsheba (Crandall) Crandall. Bathsheba Crandall was the third child of Enoch and Mercy (Pendleton) Crandall.
319 FRANK, b. ———, d. aged 20 years.

Elias Stanton (No. 311) m. Nancy Davis Nov. 27, 1812 (No. 25), that family.

CHILDREN:

320 NANCY B., b. Dec. 20, 1813, m. Warren D. Rowley Oct. 20, 1835.
321 HARRIET, b. Oct. 20, 1815, d. Oct. 4, 1816.
322 MARIA, b. May 21, 1817, m. Charles H. Smith (No. 107), that family.

THOMAS STANTON FAMILY. 595

323 ELIAS, b. Aug. 5, 1819, m. Catherine C. Savage Feb. 28, 1843.
324 ABBY E., b. Aug. 15, 1822, m. Orrin Curry Oct. 18, 1842.
325 JANE C., b. Dec. 12, 1825, m. N. Curtiss White July 30, 1850.
326 LYDIA SOPHIA, b. April 30, 1830, m. Dudley W. Rhodes Oct. 3, 1854.
327 MARY, b. June 2, 1832, d. Oct. 31, 1850, unmarried.
328 WARREN J., b. April 8, 1836, m. Maria E. Merrill March 18, 1856.

Rowland Stanton (No. 313) m. Maria Palmer (No. 332), that family; m. 2d, Hannah Hewitt (No. 209), that family.

CHILD BY FIRST MARRIAGE:

329 MARIA E., b. ———, m. Daniel P. Collins (No. 45), that family.

CHILDREN BY SECOND MARRIAGE:

330 HANNAH, b. ———.
331 JOHN, b. ———.
332 SOPHIA, b. ———.

Samuel Stanton (No. 11) m. Borodel Denison June 16, 1680 (No. 41), that family. He lived in Stonington on that portion of the Stanton ancestral estate now known as Osbrook, extending southward to Pawcatuck Bay with Pawcatuck River on the east. He served in the early Colonial wars. She d. Jan. 11, 1702.

CHILDREN:

332a SAMUEL, b. June 16, 1683, m. Sarah Gardner; 2d, Lois Cobb (No. 19), that family.
333 DANIEL, b. Nov. 4, 1695, m. Mary Chesebrough.
334 ANNA, b. July 2, 1688, m. Lieut. Thomas Jackson.

Samuel Stanton (No. 332a) m. Sarah Gardner, daughter of Capt. Thomas Gardner of Brookline, Mass., May 20, 1711. They lived in Stonington, Conn. She d. Nov. 11, 1716. Samuel m. for his second wife Lois Cobb (No. 19), that family, March 19, 1718.

CHILDREN BY FIRST MARRIAGE:

235 BORODEL, b. March 28, 1712, m. Simeon Sparhawk Oct. 22, 1730.
336 SARAH, b. Oct. 10, 1714, m. Joshua Thompson of Charlestown, R. I.
337 MARY, b. Nov. 5, 1716, m. Samuel Frink, Jr., Feb. 19, 1741.

CHILDREN BY SECOND MARRIAGE:

338 SAMUEL, b. March 14, 1719, m. Susanna Champlin Nov. 5, 1742.
339 ANDREW, b. July 4, 1721, m. Sarah Noyes, June 24, 1747 (No. 127), Noyes family.
340 LOIS, b. April 9, 1725, m. Edward Denison Dec. 19, 1750 (No. 231), Denison family; m. 2d, Nathaniel Miner April 19, 1769; she d. without children.
341 EUNICE, b. July 1, 1728, m. John Denison, Jr., Dec. 19, 1750 (No. 232), Denison family.
342 NATHAN, b. April 3, 1732, m. Elizabeth Billings.

Lieut. Daniel Stanton (No. 333) m. Mary Chesebrough in 1712 (No. 47), Chesebrough family. They lived in Stonington, Conn. He d. Jan. 31, 1769; she d. Sept. 4, 1783, aged 91 years.

CHILDREN:

343 MARY, b. Dec. 30, 1713, d. young.
344 MARY, b. Aug. 24, 1715, m. Samuel Mason Jan. 9, 1738.
345 DANIEL, b. Sept. 4, 1716, m. Mary Eldridge.
346 A daughter, b. and d. in 1718.
347 PHINEAS, b. Oct. 28, 1719, m. Elizabeth Stanton.
348 ANNA, b. ———, m. Robert Stanton (No. 274).
349 AMARIAH, b. Jan. 19, 1724, m. Delight Champlin Dec. 17, 1750.

Samuel Stanton of Stonington (No. 338) m. Susanna Champlin Nov. 14, 1719, daughter of William and Mary (Clark) Champlin of Westerly, R. I. He served in the French war as a commissioned officer, and was buried in 1756, with military honors, at Fort Edward, between Lake George and the Hudson. His home was in Stonington.

CHILDREN:

350 SAMUEL, b. June 24, 1743. He and his uncle Edward Denison were drowned in sight of home while returning from New London.
351 WILLIAM, b. Sept. 19, 1744, m. Eunice Palmer Dec. 8, 1768.
352 ANDREW, b. March 15, 1750.
353 EUNICE, b. Dec. 5, 1752, m. Nathaniel Tripp Nov. 24, 1774.

Capt. Nathan Stanton (No. 342) m. Elizabeth, daughter of Ebenezer and Mary Noyes Billings (No. 95), Billings family, date not recorded. He was lost at sea.

CHILDREN:

354 LOIS, bapt. Nov. 5, 1758, m. Capt. Asa Palmer March 10, 1776.
355 ELIZABETH, b. ———, m. John Noyes (No. 202), Noyes family.
356 MARY, b. Nov. 5, 1758, m. ——— Denison; went to New York State.
357 EBENEZER, bapt. Nov. 5, 1758, m. Mary Smith Nov. 7, 1781.
358 SAMUEL, b. in 1760, m. twice.
359 EDWARD, b. July 3, 1763.
360 ANDREW, b. Aug. 26, 1764.

Daniel Stanton (No. 345) m. Mary Eldridge Oct. 6, 1740, both of Stonington, Conn. He d. Aug. 2, 1791.

CHILDREN:

361 MARY, b. June 1, 1742, m. Edward Williams in 1759 (No. 181), that family.
362 DANIEL, b. Feb. 12, 1743, d. young.
363 JAMES, b. Feb. 17, 1745, m. James Stanton.
364 ABIGAIL, b. March 6, 1748, d. young.
365 DANIEL, b. July 30, 1750, d. 1750.
366 PHEBE, b. July 25, 1751, d. young.
367 PHEBE, b. March 9, 1754, d. Jan. 15, 1844.
368 DANIEL, b. Dec. 20, 1757, m. Catherine Page Jan. 4, 1781 (No. 22), that family.
369 ANNA, b. Jan 5, 1759, m. Wareham Williams (No. 200), that family.
370 EDWARD, b. June 10, 1761, d. July 27, 1832, m. Martha Page (No. 25), that family.
371 DAVID, b. May 6, 1764, d. young.
372 LUCY, b. ———, m. Daniel Eldridge Nov. 12, 1780.

THOMAS STANTON FAMILY.

Phineas Stanton (No. 347) m. Elizabeth Stanton (No. 277) Jan. 7, 1740, both of Stonington, Conn. She d. March 9, 1814, aged 92 years. He d. Feb. 3, 1790, aged 71 years. Capt. Phineas served as captain in the Cape Breton campaign of the war with the French in 1745. From 1760 to 1771 he was a deputy from Stonington, Conn.

CHILDREN:

373 PHINEAS, b. Aug. 9, 1741, m. Zerviah Eldredge; 2d, Esther Gallup.
374 ELIZABETH, b. Sept. 10, 1743, m. ―――― Eldredge.
375 ENOCH, b. Sept. 15, 1745, m. Waity Dyer.
376 JABEZ, b. Oct. 7, 1747, d. Aug., 1777, unmarried.
377 ZEBULON, b. March 3, 1750, d. Nov. 12, 1752.
378 ZEBULON, b. June 10, 1753, m. Esther Gray.
379 A daughter, b. and d. in 1752.
380 DANIEL, b. Nov. 14, 1755, killed at Fort Griswold Sept. 6, 1781, unm.
381 ANNA, b. Sept. 5, 1758, m. Nathan Stanton (No. 149).
382 SAMUEL, b. April 16, 1760, m. Hannah Palmer.
383 MARTHA E., b. June 17, 1766, m. Thomas Prentice (No. 51), that family; 2d, Christopher Gallup (No. 127), that family.
384 ASA, b. March 11, 1770, d. Feb. 4, 1849, unmarried.

Amariah Stanton (No. 349) m. Delight Champlin Dec. 17, 1750. He d. Jan. 11, 1754.

CHILDREN:

385 AMARIAH, b. July 14, 1751, m. Dorothy Whipple Oct. 13, 1774.
386 DELIGHT, b. Feb. 19, 1753, d. young.
387 JONATHAN, b. ――――, m. Amelia Chesebrough (No. 253), that family.

Capt. Ebenezer Stanton (No. 357) m. Mary Smith March 1, 1781.

CHILDREN:

388 NATHAN S., b. Aug. 1, 1782, m. Eliza Smith; 2d, Mary Brown.
389 MARY, b. Jan. 11, 1788, m. Frank Richards.
390 EBENEZER, b. July 15, 1791.
391 EDWARD, b. May 10, 1793, d. young.

Samuel Stanton (No. 358) m. Hannah Russell (No. 25), Russell family (No. 295), Stanton family, Dec. 15, 1782. She d. about 1799. He m. 2d, Mary Noyes (No. 174), Noyes family, who d. May 4, 1849. He d. March 9, 1823.

CHILD BY FIRST MARRIAGE:

392 HANNAH R., b. in 1792, m. Denison Noyes (No. 175), Noyes family.

CHILDREN BY SECOND MARRIAGE:

393 STILES, b. March 27, 1803, m. Abby W. Lee June 2, 1828, d. 1881.
394 SAMUEL B., b. ――――, m. Lydia Conrad.
395 MARY, b. March 27, 1807, m. Franklin Williams July 20, 1835 (No. 349), Williams family.
396 HARRIET, b. ――――, d. April 3, 1870, unmarried.
397 BETSEY, b. ――――, d. Feb. 22, 1840, unmarried.
398 EDMUND, b. 1805, d. Oct. 5, 1825.

Lieut Enoch Stanton (No. 375) was killed in the massacre at First Griswold Sept. 6, 1781. He m. Waity Dyer of Newport,

R. I. Date of m. and date of the births of their seven children, at the time of his death, do not appear on record, only the names of three of their children are known.

CHILDREN:

399 LODOWICK, b. ———.
400 MARTHA, b. 1771, m. Ebenezer Cobb Jan. 12, 1794 (No. 37), that family.
401 BETSEY, b. ———, m. Amos Palmer Jan. 12, 1786 (No. 229).

Zebulon Stanton (No. 378) m. Esther Gray Feb. 5, 1778, who d. April 30, 1837. He d. July 18, 1828. They lived at Stonington, Conn.

CHILDREN:

402 JABEZ, b. in 1779, m. Fanny Potter.
403 HENRY, b. 1781, lost at sea, March, 1798.
404 ELIZABETH, b. 1783, m. Charles W. Denison (No. 462), Denison family.
405 ZEBULON, b. 1788, d. Sept. 25, 1819.
406 JONATHAN GRAY, b. 1791, m. Ruth Gardiner; 2d, Fanny Pendleton (No. 82), that family; 3d, Lucy A. Stanton (No. 100).
407 BENJAMIN F., b. 1792, d. young.
408 NATHAN, b. 1794, drowned off Nantucket, unmarried.
409 MARY M., b. 1795, m. Charles W. Smith Oct. 10, 1813.
410 ESTHER C., b. 1797, d. March 27, 1827, unmarried.
411 GEORGE W., b. 1800, d. in New Orleans Sept. 3, 1830, unmarried.
412 A child, b. and d. in 1802.
413 SAMUEL GRAY, b. April 24, 1804, m. Mary G. Hillman Sept. 2, 1833.

Samuel Stanton (No. 382) m. Hannah Palmer Feb. 20, 1788 (No. 323), Palmer family. He d. Feb. 4, 1838. She d. June 30, 1843, both of Stonington, Conn.

CHILDREN:

414 SAMUEL, b. Aug. 16, 1789, d. Feb. 27, 1861, unmarried.
415 MARY ROSSITER, b. May 2, 1791, m. Jedediah Leeds Nov. 15, 1821.
416 PHINEAS, b. Dec. 17, 1795, m. Fanny, daughter of Dudley Babcock, April 6, 1826.
417 CHARLES THOMPSON, b. Dec. 8, 1797, m. Ann A. Palmer Oct. 4, 1827 (No. 475). She d. May 3, 1833. He m. 2d, Nancy L. Palmer, sister of his first wife, Oct. 17, 1836 (No. 482), Palmer family. He was a prosperous shipmaster. He served in the war of 1812, and d. April 21, 1880.
418 JOSEPH WARREN, b. Oct. 18, 1800, m. Grace N. Palmer (No. 476), that family, Nov. 1, 1821; m. 2d, Emeline Palmer Dec. 27, 1871 (No. 442), that family. He d. at Washington, D. C., Jan. 19, 1879.
419 THOMAS PALMER, b. April 30, 1803, m. Martha Babcock (No. 192), that family.
420 HORATIO NELSON, b. 1803, d. unmarried in New Orleans Sept., 1839.
421 ALEXANDER HAMILTON, b. 1808, d. unmarried Nov. 8, 1842.
422 BENJAMIN FRANKLIN, b. ———, m. Sarah Wheeler (No. 486), Wheeler family.

William Stanton (No. 351) m. Eunice Palmer Dec. 8, 1768 (No. 197), that family. He d. Feb. 23, 1811, aged 67. She d. Feb. 10, 1835, aged 85.

THOMAS STANTON FAMILY. 599

CHILDREN:
423 POLLY or MARY, b. Sept. 8, 1770, m. Capt. Thomas Ash.
424 PRUDENCE, b. Aug. 21, 1774, m. Nathan Stanton (No. 43).
425 SAMUEL, b. Jan. 17, 1776, was drowned June 27, 1792.
426 LOIS, b. Sept. 3, 1778, m. James Noyes, Jr. (No. 214), Noyes family.
427 JAMES, b. Feb. 22, 1782, m. Desire Palmer Aug. 2, 1805.
428 EUNICE, b. Aug. 1, 1786, d. in 1873, unmarried.
429 ANDREW, b. Aug. 9, 1790, m. Elizabeth Chapman.

Phineas Stanton (No. 373), b. in Stonington, Conn., Aug. 9, 1741, m. Zerviah Eldridge Jan. 24, 1764, both then being residents of Groton. She d. March 13, 1766. He m. 2d, Esther Gallup April 2, 1768. They lived in Stonington, and removed to New York State.

CHILD BY FIRST MARRIAGE:
430 ZERVIAH, b. Nov. 27, 1765, m. Reuben Palmer May 17, 1785.

CHILDREN BY SECOND MARRIAGE:
431 ELDREDGE, b. Dec. 31, 1769, was killed Dec. 31, 1813, in the battle at Black Rock, near Buffalo, N. Y., and was buried at Wyoming, N. Y.
432 PHINEAS, b. Dec. 27, 1771, d. Jan. 30, 1776.
433 ESTHER, b. May 14, 1773.
434 POLLY, b. Dec. 13, 1775, d. Sept. 17, 1776.
435 POLLY, b. Oct. 18, 1777, d. Aug., 1840.
436 PHINEAS, b. May 21, 1780, m. Polly Thomas.
437 DANIEL, b. March 22, 1783.
438 ELIZABETH, b. Sept. 8, 1785.
439 MERCY, b. May 3, 1788.
440 ZERVIAH, b. Aug. 23, 1791.
441 EUNICE, b. Nov. 5, 1795, d. July 25, 1829.

Capt. Jabez Stanton (No. 402) m. Fanny Potter in 1806. He d. April 5, 1816. She d. Oct. 27, 1846. He was a sea captain.

CHILDREN:
442 FANNY, b. in 1807, m. Joseph Cottrell (No. 54), that family.
443 MARY, b. Nov. 24, 1808, d. Nov. 24, 1825.
444 JABEZ OSCAR, b. 1810, d. Sept. 9, 1811.
445 JABEZ OSCAR, b. 1811, d. Oct. 14, 1831, aged 20 years.
445a ROBERT H., b. 180—, d. Feb. 20, 1815.

General Phineas Stanton (No. 436) removed to Vermont, and at Woodstock, he m. Polly Thomas, a descendant of Arad Thomas, who was a Welshman. He was a soldier in the Revolutionary war, and fought at the battle of Saratoga. He served in the war of 1812 as major of the staff of Gen. Peter Porter; he served in eleven fights. During the engagement at Black Rock his brother Eldredge was killed while fighting under his command. At Queenstown Heights, while going to the aid of Lieut. Col. Winfield Scott, Phineas Stanton was severely wounded, and at Lundy's Lane he was captured and held a prisoner for eleven months. During the war he was a major on the staff of Gen.

Scott, and after the war he was placed in command of all the troops of the State militia in Western New York, with the rank of Major General. He d. March 21, 1842.

CHILDREN:

446 MARIA, b. Aug. 2, 1804, m. David Scott Feb. 5, 1822.
447 ESTHER, b. Sept. 1, 1806, m. Col. Wales Cheney.
448 ELIAS T., b. April 28, 1809, m. Julia M. Collar.
449 ABIGAIL T., b. Oct. 11, 1812, d. unmarried.
450 PERSIS T., b. Feb. 10, 1815, m. Edward Peck.
451 PHINEAS, b. Sept. 23, 1817, m. Emily E. Ingham.
452 ELIZA ANN, b. May 9, 1820, m. Merrick.
453 MARY JANE, b. Dec. 2, 1822, m. Rev. R. H. Dexter.
454 GEORGE, b. July 31, 1828, unmarried.
455 AMELIA, b. Nov. 27, 1828, m. Julius A. Hayes April 20, 1852.

Daniel Stanton (No. 368) m. Catherine Page (No. 22); that family, Jan. 4, 1781. No children. His brother, Edward Stanton (No. 370) m. Martha Page (No. 25), that family, sister of Catharine, Jan. 14, 1798. They were both desperately wounded in the Fort Griswold massacre Sept. 6, 1781.

CHILDREN OF EDWARD AND MARTHA STANTON.

456 EDWARD, b. June 10, 1799, d. Feb., 1804.
457 ELISHA, b. 1800, d. in 1800.
458 MARTHA, b. 1801, d. Sept. 1, 1861, unmarried.
459 DAVID, b. 1804, m. Mrs. Mary (Whiting) Parks.
460 LUCY, b. Dec. 19, 1806, m. Joseph Wheeler (No. 383), Wheeler family.
461 EDWARD, b. ———, 1810, d. unmarried Dec. 18, 1883.

ROBERT STANTON FAMILY.

Among the early settlers of New England were Robert Stanton and Thomas Stanton, supposed by some genealogists to have been brothers, but no proof of such relation exists.

1. ROBERT STANTON was b. in England in the year 1599, and came to this country and settled in Newport, R. I., in 1638, where he continued to reside until his death, which took place Aug. 5, 1672. He m. Avis ———, family name and date of m. not of record.

CHILDREN:

2 ROBERT, b. in 1640, m. Henry Tibbetts.
3 MARY, b. in 1642. No other record.
4 JOHN, b. Aug., 1645, m. Mary Harndel in 1667, m. 2d, Mrs. Mary Cranston, widow of Gov. John Cranston, and daughter of Gov. Jeremiah Clark. He d. in 1783, aged 83.

CHILDREN:

5 MARY, b. June 4, 1668.
6 HANNAH, b. Nov. 7, 1670.
7 PATIENCE, b. Sept. 10, 1672.
8 JOHN, b. April 22, 1674, m. Elizabeth Clark; 2d, Susanna Lamphere.
9 CONTENT, b. Dec. 20, 1675.
10 ROBERT, b. May 4, 1677.
11 BENJAMIN, b. March 13, 1684.

CHILD BY SECOND MARRIAGE:

12 HENRY, b. May 22, 1688; was the ancestor of the Hon. Edwin M. Stanton, Secretary of War, under President Lincoln.

John Stanton (No. 8) commenced business life as a merchant, but did not succeed as such. He continued to reside in Newport until 1733, when he removed his family to Westerly, R. I., now the town of Richmond, and settled on what is known as the Stanton purchase. Previous to this he purchased land in Stonington, Conn., of John Breed and others, situated on the northern slope of Cosatuc Hill. It is supposed that he had in contemplation a change of residence to Stonington when he purchased this land. If so, he abandoned it soon after, for in less than a month he sold it to Francis Robertson of Kingston, R. I. He m. Elizabeth, daughter of Latham Clark of Portsmouth, R. I., Feb. 9,

1698. Mrs. Stanton d. at Newport Sept. 10, 1730, aged 50 years. In 1734, in his 61st year he m. Susanna Lamphere, aged 19 years. He d. at Richmond, Jan. 22, 1762, aged 89 years. His wife survived him and m. Peter Ross, whom she survived. She d. at Richmond Sept. 25, 1807, in her 92d year.

CHILDREN BY FIRST MARRIAGE:

12a HANNAH, b. Oct. 4, 1698, m. ——— Easton, d. March 30, 1729.
13 JOHN, b. July 7, 1700, d. Feb., 1741.
14 ROBERT, b. Dec. 27, 1701, d. young.
15 MARY, b. Dec. 12, 1703, d. young.
16 JOSEPH, b. Dec. 12, 1705, d. July 8, 1707.
17 SAMUEL, b. March 25, 1708, d. on passage from Surinam in 1743.
18 DANIEL, b. May 5, 1710, d. July 13, 1717.
19 LATHAM, b. Aug. 12, 1712, d. in Jamaica, 1749.
20 ELIZABETH, b. Sept. 18, 1714, m. ——— Taylor; d. June 21, 1742.
21 JOSEPH, b. June 6, 1717, d. June 7, 1718.
22 JONATHAN, b. May 5, 1719, d. June 6, 1745.
23 DAVID, b. Dec. 22, 1721.

CHILDREN BY SECOND MARRIAGE:

24 ROBERT, b. at Westerly Aug. 18, 1735. He was a reputable farmer and judge of the Court of Common Pleas; d. in 1802.
25 JOB, b. Feb. 3, 1737, m. Elizabeth Belcher; 2d, Mrs. Amy Bell.
26 SUSANNAH, b. at Westerly Aug. 10, 1738, m. Samuel Clark.
27 BENJAMIN, b. at Charlestown July 4, 1740, d. Oct. 20, 1776.
28 HANNAH, b. at Charlestown July, 1742, d. young.
29 ELIZABETH, b. at Charlestown 1743, m. Peleg Kenyon.
30 SAMUEL, b. at Charlestown Oct. 10, 1745, d. in South Kingston.
31 JOHN, b. May 4, 1749, moved to New York State.
32 MARY, b. Jan. 11, 1750, d. young.
33 SABRA, b. Dec. 4, 1752, m. Jonathan Barber, d. aged 70 years.
34 MARY, b. Nov. 23, 1754, m. Samuel Peckham.
35 JOSEPH, b. March 26, 1757.
36 HANNAH, b. in 1759, m. Joseph Lewis.

Job Stanton (No. 25) m. 1st, Elizabeth Belcher Nov. 11, 1764. He located at Stonington, Conn. His wife d. Dec. 29, 1773. He m. 2d, Mrs. Amy Bell, June 2, 1774, the widow of John Bell and daughter of Nathaniel and Amy (Hewitt) Williams (No. 69), Williams family. He d. March 2, 1708. Mrs. Amy d. Aug. 11, 1833.

CHILDREN BY FIRST MARRIAGE:

37 CHRISTOPHER, b. Nov. 29, 1766, m. Anna Yeomans Jan. 9, 1791, d. 1811.
38 ELIZABETH, b. March 16, 1769, d. March 29, 1774.
39 HANNAH, b. July 17, 1771, m. Joseph Pendleton (No. 65), Pendleton family.

CHILDREN BY SECOND MARRIAGE:

40 ABIGAIL, b. Feb. 20, 1775, m. Abel Pendleton, d. July 26, 1844 (No. 64), Pendleton family.
41 JOHN BELL, b. April 23, 1776, m. Hannah Crandall, d. March 25, 1835.
42 NATHANIEL, b. April 22, 1778, m. Katharine Pendleton.
43 CHARLES, b. May 14, 1780, d. April 1, 1782.
44 BENJAMIN F., b. Feb. 25, 1782, m. Maria Davis.

ROBERT STANTON FAMILY. 603

John Bell Stanton (No. 41) m. Hannah Crandall, daughter of Enoch and Mercy Crandall of Charlestown, R. I., Nov. 9, 1800. She d. Nov. 19, 1865. He d. March 25, 1835.

CHILDREN:

45 BATHSHEBA, b. Dec. 21, 1801, d. Dec. 29, 1827.
46 GRACE, b. May 14, 1803, d. unmarried in 1899.
47 ENOCH, b. Oct. 24, 1804, m. Lucy Jane Shepard Feb. 16, 1829.
48 HANNAH, b. April 26, 1806, d. Aug. 11, 1881.
49 CHARLES, b. Aug. 16, 1808, m. Frances Mason in Norway, N. Y., May 28, 1834.
50 JOHN BELL, b. Aug. 27, 1812, d. Aug. 9, 1814.
51 WILLIAM FRANKLIN, b. May 27, 1814, m. Abbie Fosdick Billings June 7, 1846, Trenton, N. Y.
52 HENRY SHEPARD, b. in 1816, m. Mary Feller Sept. 28, 1853.
53 FANNY, b. June 21, 1818.
54 OLIVER WOLCOTT, b. Oct. 4, 1820, m. Emma M. Gregory Sept. 27, 1855.
55 JANE, b. Sept. 26, 1823.
56 JOHN BELL, b. Sept. 29, 1825.

Nathaniel Stanton (No. 42) m. Katharine Pendleton, daughter of Capt. Amos Pendleton, Jr., (No. 36), of that family, and Katharine Davis of Westerly, R. I. She d. April 7, 1840. He d. at Trinidad March 15, 1807.

CHILDREN:

57 AMOS, b. Dec. 27, 1802, m. Olivia White Aug. 6, 1829.
58 MARIA S., b. May 13, 1804, m. Oregon Perkins March 9, 1829.
59 NATHANIEL, b. Dec. 9, 1806, m. Mary Hall Sutton July 10, 1851.

Benjamin F. Stanton (No. 44) m. Maria Davis (No. 24), Davis family, Sept., 1808. He commenced life in Stonington. In the spring of 1819 he removed to Fishers Island, N. Y., where he carried on an extensive farming business until 1823, when he returned to Stonington and occupied a farm which he had previously purchased, where he resided until his death, Dec. 13, 1836. Besides farming he was largely engaged in other pursuits, by which he accumulated a competency. He was highly esteemed as a man and neighbor.

CHILDREN:

60 JOHN DAVIS, b. March 25, 1809, d. Sept. 19, 1882.
61 ABBY JANE, b. Jan. 11, 1811, m. Giles Williams March 23, 1831 (No. 489), Williams family. Mrs. Williams was drowned in the burning of the steamer Erie on Lake Erie, Aug. 9, 1841. He d. April 3, 1888.
62 EMMA ANN, b. Aug. 10, 1813, m. Charles Hewitt Smith (No. 107), Smith family, Jan. 18, 1832. She d. April 16, 1833. He m. 2d, Maria Stanton (No. 322), Thomas Stanton family.
63 DANIEL DAVIS, b. Sept. 9, 1815, d. April 23, 1887.
64 BENJAMIN FRANKLIN, b. Oct. 28, 1817, d. Sept. 25, 1891.
65 MARIA, b. Dec. 30, 1819, d. Dec. 5, 1880.
66 FANNY, b. July 12, 1822, d. Sept. 18, 1863.

67 PAUL, b. Nov. 28, 1824, m. Marcia Palmer Denison May 25, 1864. (No. 607), Denison family. He d. July 8, 1884.
68 MASON M., b. Dec. 7, 1826, d. Aug. 26, 1894.

STANTON BROTHERS.

NOTE.—John D., Daniel D., Benjamin F., 2d., Paul B. and Mason M., children of Benjamin F., and Maria (Davis) Stanton of Stonington after the death of their father associated themselves in a business partnership under the firm name of the Stanton Brothers, and as such became the proprietors of five large productive farms, which they jointly cultivated successfully through life, establishing a reputation for honorable dealing in all of their business intercourse with their fellow citizens, characterized with the strictest integrity and economical industry.

Their sister, Miss Maria, was so constituted as to be a controlling force in society. She was from early life a person of honest purpose and strong convictions, a Christian by profession, and, in fact, from the commencement of the Sunday school at the Road Church, she was a member, and continued so till her death. She was also an earnest and enthusiastic teacher for many years, and unfailing in her desire to serve in any capacity. The library, the church building and grounds about the church all bear witness to her love and zeal. She was deeply interested in missionary and temperance work, not only at home, but in the world at large. Her life was full of good works, the memory of which are an inspiration to go and do likewise.

STEWART OR STEWARD FAMILY.

There are so many sources from which the Stonington Stewarts may have sprung, that it is difficult to tell who was the emigrant ancestor of

1. WILLIAM STEWARD, who was bapt. in the First Congregational Church as an adult by the Rev. James Noyes, Feb. 13, 1710. He m. Sarah Church May 5, 1713. She d. March 2, 1745.

CHILDREN:

2 WILLIAM, JR., b. Dec. 26, 1714.
3 NATHAN, b. Jan. 8, 1717.
4 OLIVER, b. Feb. 12, 1719, m. Rebecca Pendleton Aug. 20, 1741.
5 PHINEAS, b. May 16, 1721.
6 LEMUEL, b. May 3, 1723, d. Feb. last, 1727.
7 SARAH, b. Jan. 10, 1725-6.
8 CONTENT, b. Dec. 24, 1727.
9 ELIPHALET, b. Nov. 10, 1729.
10 LEMUEL, b. Jan. 31, 1732, m. Elizabeth ———.

Lieut William Stewart (No. 1) m. 2d, Mary Bellows March 16, 1747. In 1728 he purchased of Richard and Henry Stevens lands containing Asoupsuck Pond, north of Stewart Hill, now in North Stonington.

William Stewart, Jr. (No. 2), m. Elizabeth Stevens Dec. 4, 1740. He was a pattern farmer of his day. He purchased of the Elliots what is now called Stewart Hill, and d. aged about 46 years, leaving a widow and nine children; she afterwards m. Joseph Palmer, a widower with nine children, and they had one daughter Sabra, making a family of nineteen children.

CHILDREN:

11 LUCRETIA, b. July 3, 1741, m. Dr. John Bartlett of Lebanon.
12 LUCY, b. July 30, 1743, m. ——— Stephens.
13 NATHAN, b. June 22, 1745.
14 ELIZABETH, b. Oct. 7, 1747, m. John Coates.
15 MARY, b. Nov. 28, 1749, m. Oliver Wilcox.
16 WILLIAM, b. Jan. 16, 1752.
17 CONTENT, b. June 6, 1754, m. Timothy Coates.
18 ELISHA, b. June 29, 1757; went West.
19 ELIPHALET, b. Aug. 14, 1759; went west.

Phineas Stewart (No. 5) m. Remember Babcock, Jan. 11, 1745. After her death he m. Hannah Barnaby.

CHILDREN BY FIRST WIFE:
20 PHINEAS, b. Aug. 17, 1748.
21 SARAH, b. Aug. 13, 1750.
22 WEALTHY, b. May 12, 1756.

CHILDREN BY LAST WIFE:
23 MERCY, b. in 1762, m. Naham Chapman (No. 15), that family.
24 LYDIA, b. in 1767, m. Amos Barber.
25 GILBERT, b. Dec. 4, 1772.
26 ESTHER, b. ———.

Lemuel Stewart (No. 10) m. ——— before 1757, Elizabeth ———.

CHILDREN:
27 SARAH, b. June 27, 1757.
28 LEMUEL, b. April 6, 1759.
29 MARGARET, b. Jan. 15, 1761.
30 ELIPHALET, b. Jan. 1, 1763.
31 DEBORAH, b. Nov. 23, 1764.
32 MARTHA, b. Nov. 6, 1766.
33 EPHRAIM, b. Sept. 15, 1768.

Nathan Stewart (No. 13) m. Barbary Palmer, daughter of William Palmer, May 1, 1768.

CHILDREN:
34 NATHAN, b. Feb. 20, 1769, m. ——— Brown.
35 BARBARY, b. July 5, 1771, m. Nehemiah Brown.
36 EDWARD, b. Dec. 8, 1774.
37 PRISCILLA, b. March 20, 1778, m. Noyes Wheeler (No. 137), that family.
38 BETSEY, b. Sept. 14, 1780, m. Col. Denison Randall, son of John Randall.
39 RUSSELL, b. April 6, 1783, m. ——— Lord.
40 GEORGE P., b. April 6, 1786, d. May 1, 1851.
41 PHEBE, b. May 12, 1789, m. Oliver Swan, son of Nathan (No. 135), of that family.
42 CYRUS b. Feb. 14, 1792.
43 APPHIA, b. March 19, 1795, d. young.

Nathan Stewart (No. 13) bought out the family rights in the old homestead and built a house, which was afterward occupied by his son Edward, and then by Denison Stewart. He was a man of great resolution, and his wife was a noble woman. He lived to see nearly all of his children married.

William Stewart (No. 16) m. Anna Coates Sept. 25, 1774, and m. 2d, Amanda Darrow. He was a master mechanic, built saw mills and grist mills. He d. at 92 years of age. He was in the Revolutionary war.

CHILDREN BY FIRST WIFE:
44 WILLIAM, b. May 10, 1775.
45 JOHN, b. March 23, 1782.
46 ANNA, b. Sept. 24, 1777.
47 Daughter, b. ———, d. ———.

STEWART OR STEWARD FAMILY.

CHILD BY LAST WIFE:
48 RUSSELL DARROW, b. Feb. 1, 1805; he d.; left no children.

Edward Stewart (No. 36) m. Rebecca Noyes (No. 173) of the Noyes family, Feb. 15, 1801. He d. April 29, 1837, and she d. Sept. 30, 1842. He was a farmer by occupation, and all who knew him loved him.

CHILDREN:
49 REBECCA, b. Nov. 8, 1801, m. Nathaniel M. Crary July 13, 1824.
50 BETSEY R., b. Nov. 24, 1803, m. Frederick Swan (No. 166), Swan family, Jan. 14, 1828, d. Feb. 26, 1849.
51 DENISON, b. Aug. 26, 1807, m. Abby J. Starkweather.
52 EMELINE, b. Jan. 6, 1810, m. William R. Wheeler (No. 195), of that family, Dec. 16, 1830; she d. Oct. 31, 1879, and he d. Feb. 15, 1851.
53 NANCY, b. Jan. 2, 1813, d. young.
54 CYRUS, b. Dec. 20, 1815, d. young.
55 EDWARD, b. Jan. 3, 1818, d. young.
56 DUDLEY, b. Dec. 17, 1820, m. Eliza Denison (No. 573) of the Denison family, May 6, 1856.

George P. Stewart (No. 40) m. Polly or Mary Hewitt (No. 197) of Hewitt family in Preston, Conn., Jan. 1, 1812. He d. May 1, 1851, and she d. March 15, 1870.

CHILDREN:
57 CYNTHIA, b. Oct. 10, 1812, m. Lewis Maine (No. 205), of Maine family, son of Lewis.
58 GEORGE W., b. March 31, 1816.
59 PHEBE E., b. May 31, 1819, m. Oliver S. Ecclestone.
60 HARRIET H., b. Dec. 9, 1821, d. April 25, 1828.
61 MARY A., b. Nov. 9, 1823, m. Peter C. Gadbois.
62 EMILY, b. June 25, 1825, m. Luther Yerrington, and m. 2d, John I. Plummer.
63 ELIZABETH, b. April 25, 1830; m.
64 JULIA A., b. Dec. 19, 1835, m. Henry A. Tomlinson.

George P. Stewart and wife were settled in New York State, but wolves and fevers and ague were such disastrous neighbors that they returned to Connecticut and spent the remainder of their days at North Stonington, Conn.

George W. Stewart (No. 58) m. Phebe E. Palmer, daughter of Cyrus Palmer, March 28, 1841. He d. May 21, 1861, and she d. March 15, 1870. His desire to own the land formerly belonging to his great-grandfather, William, that was purchased of the Elliots was accomplished. He settled on Stewart Hill, was a farmer and a most ingenious man, constructing tools and all things needful.

CHILDREN:
65 ELIZABETH, b. Jan. 9, 1842.
66 NATHAN W., b. March 26, 1843.
67 SARAH L., b. May 29, 1844.

68 CHARLES E., b. April 25, 1846, d. Nov. 25, 1867.
69 GEORGE P., b. June 14, 1848.
70 CYRUS H., b. Sept. 9, 1849.
71 ISABEL, b. May 19, 1855, d. Feb. 11, 1868.
72 WILLIAM E., b. Sept. 8, 1859.

Denison Stewart (No. 51) m. Abby Jane Starkweather, daughter of John Starkweather of Preston, April 18, 1844. He was a farmer and settled on Stewart Hill. He d. Jan. 19, 1867, and his widow m. the Hon. B. F. Billings of Griswold, Conn. (No. 191), Billings family.

CHILDREN:

73 EDWARD D., b. May 18, 1845.
74 WILLIAM L., b. April, 1847.
75 ELLA W., b. Feb. 1852, d. Dec. 11, 1861.

William and Edward settled in Kansas soon after their father's death, where William died.

SWAN FAMILY.

1. RICHARD SWAN, the emigrant ancestor and progenitor of the Swan family of Connecticut and Rhode Island, appears first on this side of the Atlantic Ocean in Boston, Mass., where he joined the church Jan. 6, 1639, and had one child, John, probably his youngest, baptized the Sunday after his admission. It is not certainly known when he came to New England, nor in what ship he came. His wife d. in England before he came to this country. Upon application he was dismissed with many others from the Boston church to join a church at Rowley, Mass. Soon after his dismission he removed his family to Rowley, where he remained during life, becoming a prominent citizen in that place, representing the town in the Massachusetts General Court in 1666, and many years after. He served in King Philip's war and expedition to Canada. He m. for his second wife Mrs. Ann Trumbull. She m. for her first husband Michael Hopkinson, who was buried Feb. 28, 1648; and for her second husband, John Trumbull in June, 1650, and for her third husband, Richard Swan March 1, 1658. Richard Swan d. May 14, 1678.

CHILDREN:

2 RICHARD, b. ———.
3 FRANCES, b. ———.
4 ROBERT, b. 1628, m. Elizabeth Acie.
5 JONATHAN, b. ———.
6 SUSAN, b. ———.
7 SARAH, b. ———.
8 JOHN, bapt. Nov. 24, 1638.

Robert Swan (No. 4) m. Elizabeth Acie. At the time of their marriage they both resided in Rowley, Mass. Soon after they went to Andover, Mass., to live, but did not remain there long, for as early as 1650 they were inhabitants of Haverhill, located in that part of the town which was subsequently set off, and incorporated as the town of Methuen, where many of his descendants have lived. He was a soldier at the great swamp fight, King Philip's war, Lieut. Benjamin Swett's company. His wife d. in 1689, and he m. for his second wife Hannah Russ, April 1, 1690. He d. Feb. 11, 1698.

CHILDREN BY FIRST MARRIAGE:

9 ELIZABETH, b. Sept. 30, 1653.
10 SARAH, b. Aug. 10, 1655.
11 ROBERT, b. May 30, 1657.
12 ANN, b. March 3, 1658.
13 RICHARD, b. Feb. 24, 1660.
14 TIMOTHY, b. March 12, 1663.
15 DOROTHY, b. Nov. 8, 1666.
16 JOHN, b. Aug. 1, 1668, m. Mrs. Susanna Wood.
17 SAMUEL, b. April 11, 1670, d. young.
18 SAMUEL, b. Oct. 24, 1672.
19 JOSHUA, b. Sept. 13, 1674.
20 CALEB, b. June 18, 1676, d. young.

John Swan (No. 16) m. Mrs. Susanna Wood Aug. 1, 1699, daughter of Philip Eastman and granddaughter of Roger Eastman. She m. Thomas Wood May 16, 1693. Thomas Wood and child, Susanna, were killed by the Indians March 15, 1697. They lived in Haverhill, Mass., until 1707, where three of their children were born. The following sketch of her heroism appears in the history of Haverhill, Mass.: "During the Indian war, when so many of the inhabitants of Haverhill were killed, the Indians attacked their house, which stood in the field now called White's lot, nearly opposite to the house of Capt. Emerson. Mr. Swan and his wife saw them approaching, and, determined, if possible, to save their own lives and the lives of their children from the knives of the ruthless butchers. They immediately placed themselves against the door, which was so narrow that two could scarcely enter abreast. The Indians rushed against it, but finding that it could not be easily opened, they commenced their operations more systematically. One of them placed his back to the door so that he could make his whole strength bear upon it, while others pushed against him. The strength of the besiegers was greater than that of the besieged, and Mr. Swan, being rather a timid man, almost despaired of saving himself and family and told his wife that he thought it would be better to let them in, but this resolute and courageous woman had no such idea. The Indians had now succeeded in partly opening the door, and one of them was crowding himself in, while the other was pushing lustily after. The heroic wife saw that there was no time for parleying; she seized her bake spit, which was nearly three feet in length, and a deadly weapon in the hands of the woman, as it proved, and collecting all the strength she possessed, drove it through the body of the foremost. This was too warm a reception for the besiegers; it was resistance from a source, and with a weapon they little expected, and, surely, who else could ever think of spitting a man? The two Indians thus repulsed immediately retreated and did not molest them again. Thus, by the fortitude and heroic courage of a wife and mother, this family was probably saved from a bloody grave."

Mr. Swan and his family came to Stonington in the year 1707, locating himself on what is now known as Swan Town Hill, North Stonington, where the rest of his children were born. He d. May 1, 1743, aged 75; she d. Dec. 20, 1772, in the hundredth year of her age.

CHILDREN:

21 JOHN, b. at Haverhill Dec. 28, 1700, m. Lucy Denison
22 RUTH, b. at Haverhill Dec. 31, 1703, m. Rev. Jabez Wight of Preston, Conn., Feb. 8, 1726.
23 WILLIAM, b. at Haverhill June 24, 1706, m. Thankful Holmes.
24 NATHANIEL, b. at Stonington April 13, 1709, m. Mehitable Brown.
25 ASA, b. at Stonington June 4, 1712, m. Marvin Holmes.
26 ELIZABETH, b. at Stonington May 14, 1715, m. Tebadiah Andros Dec. 19, 1737.
27 TIMOTHY, b. Sept. 2, 1721, m. Mary Smith.

John Swan (No. 21) m. Lucy Denison March 5, 1726 (No. 108), Denison family, both of Stonington, Conn.

CHILDREN:

28 ANNE, b. March 10, 1727, m. Benedam Denison Nov. 3, 1742 (No. 160), Denison family.
29 LUCY, b. Nov. 30, 1729, m. Paul Wheeler (No. 58), Wheeler family.
30 JOHN, b. Sept. 24, 1731, m. Mary Prentice, b. Sept. 6, 1734.
31 JOSEPH, b. March 12, 1734, m. Elizabeth Smith; 2d, Mary Miner.
32 JOSHUA, b. Nov. 15, 1736, m. Martha Denison.
33 PEREZ, b. Oct. 3. 1739.
34 THOMAS, b. March 18, 1742, m. Amy Denison.
35 EUNICE, b. Sept. 14, 1744.
36 EDWARD, b. Nov. 12, 1746, m. Mehitable Brown.
37 GEORGE, b. Aug. 26, 1750, m. Abigail Randall.

William Swan (No. 23) m. Thankful Holmes Jan. 20, 1726 (No. 23), that family; she d. Sept. 7, 1742. He m. 2d, Anna Smith of Groton, April 14, 1743.

CHILDREN BY FIRST MARRIAGE:

38 MARY, b. Jan. 1, 1731, m. John Cavalry March 15, 1753.
39 ABIGAIL, b. Aug. 6, 1733, m. Dea. Benjamin Blodget March 30, 1755.
40 THANKFUL, b. Sept. 30, 1734, m. John Randall (No. 42), that family; 2d wife.
41 WILLIAM, b. April 7, 1737.
42 DESIRE, b. July 22, 1739.
43 RUTH, b. Sept. 27, 1741, d. young.

CHILDREN BY SECOND MARRIAGE:
44 ANNA, b. Sept. 25, 1743.
45 CHARLES, b. May 24, 1746, m. Eunice Barnes.

Nathaniel Swan (No. 24) m. Mehitable Brown June 13, 1731, both of Stonington, Conn. She m. 2d, Joseph Hewitt June 4, 1755 (No. 60), that family.

CHILDREN:
46 ROBERT, b. Dec. 14, 1731, m. Abigail Randall.
47 NATHANIEL, b. Oct. 11, 1733.
48 JEDEDIAH, b. Aug. 5, 1735.
49 JESSE, b. Dec. 29, 1737, m. Elizabeth Baldwin.
50 LOIS, b. Oct. 14, 1741.
51 RUTH, b. Jan. 3, 1743.
52 AMOS, b. Jan. 23, 1745.

Asa Swan (No. 25) and his brother John lived on adjoining farms in North Stonington, vested in them equally after their father's decease. He m. Marvin Holmes, sister of his brother William's wife, Nov. 19, 1740 (No. 27), that family.

CHILDREN:
53 ELIZABETH, b. Dec. 8, 1741, m. Daniel Brewster (No. 9), that family.
54 SUSANNAH, b. Aug. 17, 1744, m. William Denison (No. 186), that family.
55 ASA, b. Sept. 12, 1747.
56 JABEZ, b. May 21, 1751, m. Mehitable Wheeler; he m. 2d, widow Lucy Wheeler.

Timothy Swan of Stonington (No. 27) m. Mary Smith of Groton Dec. 28, 1743.

CHILDREN:
57 MARY, b. Nov. 5, 1744, m. William Wheeler (No. 64), that family; she m. 2d, Capt. Thomas Wheeler (No. 54), that family; no children by either marriage.
58 RUTH, b. June 5, 1747, m. Isaac Wheeler (No. 82), that family.
59 LUCY, b. Jan. 17, 1750, m. Isaac Avery (No. 155), that family.
60 TIMOTHY, b. July 15, 1752, m. Ruama Ayer.
61 NATHAN, b. Jan. 23, 1755, m. Esther Avery.
62 ELISHA, b. Dec. 26, 1755, m. Experience Smith.
63 ELIAS, b. Jan. 31, 1758.
64 EUNICE, b. Aug. 20, 17—, m. John Wheeler (No. 99), that family.
65 OLIVER, b. Sept. 23, 17—.
66 ELIZABETH, b. July 25, 17—.
67 CYNTHIA, b. 1770, m. Isaac Hewitt (No. 111), that family.

John Swan (No. 30) m. Mary Prentice May 17, 1753 (No. 37), that family.

CHILDREN:
68 MARY, b. Nov. 29, 1757, m. John Randall (No. 65), that family.
69 JOHN, b. July 29, 1760.
70 PRISCILLA, b. July 4, 1763, m. Eliakin Palmer Dec. 13, 1781.
71 SAMUEL, b. May 11, 1765.
72 PEREZ, b. May 18, 1767.
73 LUCY, b. Jan. 5, 1770, m. Gilbert Billings (No. 166), that family.
74 JONAS, b. Feb. 25, 1772.
75 FANNY, b. March 3, 1774.

SWAN FAMILY. 613

Joseph Swan (No. 31) m. 1st, Elizabeth Smith of Groton Oct. 17, 1756. He m. 2d, Mary Miner Jan. 28, 1762.

CHILDREN BY FIRST MARRIAGE:
76 ELIZABETH, b. April 17, 1757.
77 JOSEPH, b. Dec. 8, 1758.
78 LUCY AVERY, b. March 30, 1760.

CHILDREN BY SECOND MARRIAGE:
79 ADIN, b. May 13, 1764.
80 ELIZABETH, b. Oct. 11, 1766.
81 LOIS, b. Nov. 8, 1770.
82 EUNICE, b. Oct. 6, 1772.

Joshua Swan (No. 32) m. Martha Denison (No. 255) that family Dec. 1, 1763.

CHILDREN:
83 AMOS, b. May 13, 1764.
84 JOSHUA, b. June 8, 1766, m. Esther Smith.
85 ADAM, b. June 29, 1768.
86 PELEG, b. July 20, 1770.
87 GILBERT, b. June 15, 1777.
88 ISAAC, b. July 10, 1779.

Thomas Swan (No. 34) m. his cousin, Amy Denison, Feb. 22, 1762 (No. 178), that family. Dea. Thomas died Dec. 27, 1830; she d. March 23, 1829. CHILDREN:

89 REBECCA, b. March 27, 1765, m. Oliver York (No. 58), that family.
90 THOMAS, JR., b. Oct. 17, 1767, m. Fanny Palmer.
91 CYRUS, b. Oct. 1, 1768, m. ——— Gould; 2d, ——— Sharon.
92 DANIEL, b. Sept. 1, 1770, m. Hannah Hawkins.
93 SALLY, b. Oct. 5, 1772, m. Dr. Charles Phelps (No. 27), that family; after his death she m. George Hubbard Sept. 7, 1809; she d. April 5, 1841.
94 AMY, b. Oct. 25, 1766, m. Charles Wheeler Williams (No. 281), that family.
95 HENRY, b. 1778, d. March 24, 1800, aged 22 years.
96 ABIGAIL or ABBY, b. June 6, 1779, m. John Browning (No. 42), that family.
97 JOHN, b. 1788, d. March 23, 1818, aged 30 years.

Edward Swan (No. 36) m. Mehitable Brown Feb. 16, 1775; she d. Sept. 27, 1790. He m. 2d, Hannah ———, name and date of m. not on record.

CHILDREN BY FIRST MARRIAGE:
98 EDWARD, JR., b. April 10, 1776, m. Sybil Morgan Dec., 1804 (No. 41), that family.
99 JOHN, b. April 12, 1778.

CHILDREN BY SECOND MARRIAGE:
100 MEHITABLE, b. Dec. 30, 1792.
101 MOSES, b. Oct. 1, 1795.
102 HANNAH, b. July 23, 1798.

George Swan (No. 37) m. Abigail Randall Sept. 4, 1774 (No. 64), Randall family, both of Stonington, Conn. He d. Jan. 3, 1798; she d. April 22, 1797.

CHILDREN:

103 GEORGE, b. May 24, 1776, d. April 30, 1802.
104 ROSWELL, b. June 16, 1778, m. Harriet F. Palmer.
105 LUCY, b. Sept. 16, 1781.
106 ANNA, b. Sept. 14, 1783.
107 ADAM, b. May 31, 1788, m. Angeline Betts.
108 GILES, b. April 29, 1793.

Robert Swan (No. 46) m. Abigail Randall Jan. 21, 1754 (No. 43), Randall family, both of Stonington, Conn.

CHILDREN:

109 ROBERT, b. Jan. 3, 1755.
110 GILBERT, b. May 18, 1756.
111 LOIS, b. Sept. 27, 1758.
112 PELEG, b. March 5, 1761, d. Jan. 31, 1767.
113 LUCY, b. Nov. 12, 1763.
114 ESTHER, b. March 16, 1766.
115 JEDEDIAH, b. March 23, 1769.
116 MINER, b. March 3, 1772.

Jesse Swan (No. 49) m. Elizabeth Baldwin Nov. 24, 1764 (No. 34), Baldwin family, both of Stonington, Conn.

CHILDREN:

117 LUCINDA, b. Nov. 16, 1765.
118 ZIBA, b. Nov. 17, 1767, m. Elizabeth Palmer.
119 EUNICE, b. March 22, 1770.
120 JESSE, b. Aug. 11, 1772.
121 POLLY, b. April 30, 1775.
122 NATHANIEL, b. Jan. 9, 1778.
123 JOHN, b. Jan. 9, 1778.
124 ELIZABETH, b. March 12, 1780.
125 PRISCILLA, b. May 30, 1787.
126 MARY, b. May 30, 1787.

Timothy Swan (No. 60) m. Ruama Ayer Feb. 18, 1773, both of Stonington, Conn.

CHILDREN:

127 RUSSELL, b. March 6, 1764.
128 JOSEPH, b. July 13, 1766.
129 OLIVER, b. July 6, 1768.
130 LAVINIA, b. Sept. 16, 1780.
131 ELISHA, b. April 26, 1783.

Nathan Swan (No. 61) m. Esther Avery March 10, 1776, both of Stonington, Conn.

CHILDREN:

132 AVERY, b. July 21, 1776.
133 ROBERT, b. Oct. 22, 1778.
134 ASA, b. Oct. 17, 1780, m. Fanny Wheeler.
135 OLIVER, b. Dec. 21, 1782, m. Phebe Stewart (No. 41), that family.
136 DESIRE, b. April 28, 1785.

Elisha Swan of Stonington (No. 62) m. Experience Smith of Norwich May 24, 1778.

SWAN FAMILY. 615

CHILDREN:

137 MARTHA, b. April 25, 1779.
138 MARY, b. July 17, 1780.
139 ELIZABETH, b. June 9, 1782.
140 FANNY, b. July 5, 1784.

Joshua Swan (No. 84) m. Esther Smith March 16, 1789; lived in Stonington.

CHILDREN ALL BORN IN STONINGTON.

141 ESTHER, b. Nov. 17, 1789, d. Sept. 7, 1790.
142 ESTHER, b. 1791, d. Jan. 23, 1793.
143 JOSHUA, b. Oct. 19, 1793, m. Nancy Swan Nov. 27, 1823.
144 BETSEY, b. Dec. 9, 1795.
145 JOSEPH, b. Feb. 20, 1798, m. Oct. 17, 1832.
146 JABEZ SMITH, b. Feb. 23, 1800, m. Laura Griffin of East Haddam, Conn. He was familiarly known as Elder Swan, a famous Baptist preacher.
147 WILLIAM HENRY, b. May 2, 1802, d. young.
148 WILLIAM HENRY, b. Nov. 5, 1804, d. at sea.
149 CHARLES, b. April 12, 1807, d. at sea.
150 LUCY, b. May 15, 1810.
151 MARY ESTHER, b. Aug. 4, 1813.

Thomas Swan of Stonington (No. 90) m. Fanny Palmer April 22, 1798 (No. 385), Palmer family. After his death she m. Rev. John Noyes of Weston, Conn., Oct. 16, 1827 (No. 177), Noyes family.

CHILD:

152 SARAH ANN, b. Feb. 23, 1799, m. Gurdon Trumbull (No. 30), Trumbull family.

Rev. Roswell Swan (No. 104), son of George and wife, Abigail (Randall) Swan, who were living in Stonington at time of his birth, June 16, 1778, at the place now known as the "Highland farm" of Charles P. Williams, on Taugwonk. He enjoyed the benefit of a good common school education, until he commenced his studies with the Rev. Hezekiah N. Woodruff, the pastor of the First Congregational Church of Stonington, who fitted him for a liberal education, after which he entered Yale College, graduated 1802, with a class who subsequently became eminent and distinguished men. He m. Harriet F. Palmer May 14, 1807 (No. 389), Palmer family. He d. March 22, 1819; his widow survived him and lived to a good old age, a comfort and blessing to her children and grandchildren, dying July 10, 1874, aged 84 years.

CHILDREN:

153 HARRIET P., b. Oct. 21, 1810, d. Oct. 8, 1814.
154 ROSWELL R., b. Oct. 12, 1812, d. Oct., 1836.

HISTORY OF STONINGTON.

155 PHEBE ANN, b. Jan. 12, 1814, m. Benjamin F. Babcock of Stonington (No. 214), Babcock family, d. Sept., 1841.
156 HARRIET P., b. March 20, 1816, m. Hon. Nathan F. Dixon of Westerly, R. I., June 28, 1843.

NOTE.—Hon. Nathan F. Dixon, who m. Harriet P. Swan (No. 156), became one of the most prominent and influential men of Rhode Island. He was a member of the Rhode Island bar, and by honorable dealing in his professional career rose to eminence in his profession. He represented his native town in the General Assembly of Rhode Island for a good many years, establishing a reputation of commanding influence. He was elected a member of Congress and served with distinguished ability in the House of Representatives at Washington, D. C., for several terms. His son, Non. Nathan F. Dixon, became a member of the Rhode Island bar and was distingushed for his ability and courtesy in all of the relations of life. He shared the confidence of his fellow citizens and was repeatedly elected to the Legislature of his native state, which to express their regard for him elected him a Senator of Congress, which position he held for a full term of six years with distinguished ability and commanding influence. He married Grace McClure. He d. 1898, sincerely mourned by all.

157 COURTLAND P., b. July 7, 1818, d. Jan. 24, 1819.

Adam Swan of Stonington (No. 107) m. Angelina Betts.
CHILDREN:
158 GEORGE M., b. May 24, 1813, m. Jane Gardner Knight, March 26, 1834; m. 2d, Mary Ann Compston in 1841.
159 LUCRETIA G., b. Dec. 25, 1815, m. George Hubbard, Jr., Aug. 11, 1834.
160 WILLIAM B., b. Sept. 17, 1820, m. Antoinette Lamb.
161 HENRY R., b. Oct. 14, 1822, lost at sea.
162 ANGELINE, b. Aug. 7, 1825, m. Albert Hancox June 4, 1847.

Ziba Swan (No. 118) m. Elizabeth Palmer Jan. 31, 1790 (No. 428), Palmer family.
CHILD:
163 BETSEY, b. July 11, 1790.

Charles Swan (No. 45) m. Eunice Barnes March 21, 1779.
CHILDREN:
164 AMOS, b. Sept. 12, 1780, m. Betsey Palmer.
165 CHARLES, b. April 3, 1782, m. Cynthia Brewster Dec. 25, 1803.
166 FREDERICK, b. July 18, 1784, m. Betsey Stewart Jan. 14, 1828 (No. 50), that family.
167 LOUISA, b. Feb. 6, 1786, d. March 18, 1786.
168 CHRISTOPHER, b. March 30, 1787, d. young.
169 SABRA, b. July 24, 1789, m. James Bailey.
170 DENISON, b. Nov. 6, 1791, m. Caroline Bailey Aug. 4, 1832.
171 CODDINGTON, b. Jan. 15, 1784, m. Cynthia Hewitt April 5, 1818 (No. 198), that family.
172 EUNICE, b. Sept. 13, 1796, m. John Meech of Norwich.
173 WILLIAM, b. Feb. 24, 1799, m. Deborah Ann Brown April 20, 1825.
174 EPHRAIM, b. Aug. 2, 1802, m. Julia A. Grinnell Nov. 29, 1831.
175 CHRISTOPHER, b. April 16, 1816, lost at sea.

Daniel Swan (No. 92) m. Hannah Hawkins April 3, 1803.
CHILDREN:
176 ABIGAIL, b. March 19, 1803.
177 HENRY T., b. July 28, 1806.
178 THOMAS E., b. April 8, 1809, m. Cassandra, daughter of Benjamin Pendleton (No. 50a), that family.
179 HARRIET Y., b. Dec. 20, 1812.

Asa A. Swan (No. 134) m. Fanny Wheeler Feb. 16, 1809.

CHILDREN:

180 MARY ANN, b. Dec. 13, 1810.
181 CLARISSA, b. July 22, 1812.
182 LUCY S., b. April 9, 1814.

Jabez Swan (No. 56) m. 1st, Mehitable Wheeler June 17, 1772 (No. 79), that family; m. 2d, widow Lucy Wheeler (No. 97), that family.

CHILDREN BY FIRST MARRIAGE:

183 JAMES, b. ———, m. Prudence ———.
184 HURLBURT, b. ———, m. ——— Easterbrooks.
185 THOMAS WHEELER, b. ———, m. Lina Emmons.
186 ASA, b. ———, m. Serviah Ely.
187 RUFUS, b. ———, m. Lucy ———.
188 BETSEY, b. ———, m. Nehemiah Spencer.
189 MEHITABLE, b. ———, m. ——— Cone, from Hartford.
190 POLLY, b. ———, m. ——— Lord.
191 CYNTHIA, b. ———, m. ——— King.

CHILDREN BY SECOND MARRIAGE:

192 WILLIAM, b. ———.
193 CYRUS, b. ———.

THOMPSON FAMILY.

From reliable information we learn that one of the many John Thompsons who were among the early planters of New England m. Hannah Brewster, daughter of Jonathan Brewster and granddaughter of Elder William Brewster of the Mayflower. She m. 2d, Samuel Starr Dec. 15, 1664.

CHILD BY 1ST MARRIAGE.

2 WILLIAM, b. ———.

William Thompson (No. 2) came to Stonington, Conn., and m. Bridget, daughter of Nathaniel Chesebrough (No. 24) of that family, and wife Hannah Denison Chesebrough, Dec. 7, 1692. They took up their abode on the Chesebrough grant of land in Stonington, where Mr. Eugene Palmer now lives.

CHILDREN:

3 WILLIAM, b. July 23, 1695, m. Katharine Richardson.
4 NATHANIEL, b. Dec. 30, 1697.
5 JOHN, b. Oct. 8, 1699, m. Jerusha Palmer.
6 SAMUEL, b. Oct. 27, 1701.
7 JEDEDIAH, b. July 10, 1704.

William Thompson d. in 1705, and his widow m. Dr. Joseph Miner of Stonington (No. 16), of that family Dec. 7, 1709.

William Thompson (No. 3) m. Katharine Richardson April 25, 1721.

CHILDREN:

8 BRIDGET, b. Jan. 26, 1722.
9 WILLIAM, b. May 31, 1723, m. Margaret Hobart (No. 2).
10 NATHANIEL, b. June 4, 1725, m. Hannah Mix Jan. 28, 1754 (No. 448), Chesebrough family.
11 DAVID, b. May, 1728.
12 JONATHAN, b. April 3, 1729.
13 CATHARINE, b. June 14, 1731.
14 CHARLES, b. April 18, 1734, m. Lucy Palmer.
15 JOSEPH, b. Jan. 24, 1736.
16 ELIHU, b. Sept. 5, 1741, m. Desire Palmer.

John Thompson (No. 5) and Jerusha Palmer (No. 107) of that family were m. Dec. 4, 1721.

THOMPSON FAMILY.

CHILDREN:

17 EUNICE, b. Feb. 14, 1722.
18 JOHN, b. Aug. 1, 1724, d. young.
19 NATHAN, b. Feb. 14, 1726.
20 AMOS, b. Sept. 14, 1727.
21 ZERVIAH, b. Oct. 22, 1729.
22 JOHN, b. Aug. 12, 1731.
23 JAMES, b. Nov. 4, 1733.

Elihu Thompson (No. 16) and Desire Palmer (No. 211) of that family were m. Jan. 14, 1767.

CHILDREN:

24 DESIRE, b. Jan. 29, 1769.
25 MARY, b. Feb. 22, 1770, m. Silas Wheeler (No. 363), that family.
26 JOSEPH, b. Oct. 5, 1771.
27 SARAH, b. Jan. 15, 1774.

Charles Thompson (No. 14) m. Lucy Palmer (No. 207), Palmer family, Sept. 19, 1765. No children.

THOMPSON FAMILY NO. 2.

1. JOHN THOMPSON, in the year 1626, was living at "Little Preston," in the Parish of Preston Capes, Northamptonshire, England, with his wife Alice, and children. On the sixth day of November in that year, 1626, John Thompson made his will, signing his name to that form; both forms of spelling, with and without the "h" are, however, used indiscriminately in the body of the will, and on the parish register. When the eleventh of April 1627, came around, John Tompson was dead, and at that date his will was probated in the Prerogative Court of Canterbury. Alice was probably the second wife of John Thompson. The son Thomas, who is mentioned in his will, was, doubtless, a child of the first wife, and the eldest son, by reason of a better inheritance than the others received. Thomas probably remained in England. We do not know what date the widow with her children came to America, but previous to 1640 she was living at Roxbury, Mass. Probably it was there that the daughter Mary was m. to Rev. Richard Blinman of Gloucester, Mass. The Tompson family in their English home held a high position, their social status being next to that of the county families. Mistress Alice must have been a lady of character and refinement. Her success in bringing her children through all their troubles and so well preparing them for the duties of life which they assumed, testifies to this. She m. 2d, Robert Park (No. 1), that family.

CHILDREN OF JOHN THOMPSON AND WIFE ALICE:

2 MARY, b. Nov. 14, 1619, m. Rev. Richard Blinman.
3 DOROTHY, b. July 2, 1621, d. Oct. 19, 1621.
4 BRIDGET, b. Sept. 11, 1622, m. George Denison in 1640 (No. 14), Denison family, d. 1643.
5 DOROTHY, b. July 5, 1624, m. Thomas Park (No. 4), that family.
6 NATHANIEL, b. Oct. 15, 1625.
7 MARTHA, b. Dec. 17, 1626.

TRUMBULL FAMILY.

1. JOHN TRUMBULL, b. about 1606, came to this country from Newcastle-on-Tyne, Northumberland, England; settled first in Cambridge, Mass., where he resided until May, 1655, when he changed his residence to Charlestown, Mass., where he spent the remainder of his life. He was a seafaring man, and commanded the good ship "Mary" on the voyage from England to Barbadoes, and also the good ship "Blossom" in 1662. He m. Elizabeth ———; she d. Aug. 15, 1696. He d. and was buried July 18, 1657.

CHILDREN:

2 ELIZABETH, b. 1638, m. Richard Martin.
3 JOHN, b. Aug. 4, 1641, m. Mary Jones.
4 HANNAH, b. 1642, m. John Baxter.
5 MARY, b. 1644, m. ——— Blackmore.
6 JAMES, b. 1647.

John Trumbull (No. 3) m. Mary Jones Sept. 26, 1665. She was b. in 1636, and she d. Dec. 27, 1721. He d. in 1731.

CHILDREN:

7 JOHN, b. May 21, 1677, d. aged 16 years.
8 JAMES, b. March 31, 1681.
9 SAMUEL, b. June 3, 1683, m. Hannah Fowle.

Samuel Trumbull (No. 9) m. Hannah Fowle Dec. 25, 1705. He d. Sept. 24, 1759.

CHILDREN:

10 SAMUEL, b. Dec. 1, 1706, d. young.
11 MARY, b. April 11, 1708, d. young.
12 SAMUEL, b. April 5, 1709, d. 1721.
13 JAMES, b. April 7, 1711, d. young.
14 JAMES, b. June 3, 1713.
15 JOHN, b. July 17, 1715, m. Mercy Jiggles; 2d, Ruth Wyer.
16 WILLIAM, bapt. June 30, 1717, d. young.
17 TIMOTHY, b. May 5, 1720.
18 MARY, bapt. Aug. 4, 1723, m. Timothy Austin.

John Trumbull (No. 15) m. June 17, 1742, Mercy Jiggles. She

d. July 24, 1754. He m. 2d, Ruth Wyer Aug. 27, 1760; she d. Jan. 31, 1763. He d. Oct. 12, 1791.

CHILDREN:

19 SAMUEL, b. ———.
20 MARY, b. ———.
21 JOHN, b. 1752, m. Lucy Springer.
22 NATHANIEL, bapt. Sept. 12, 1762.

John Trumbull (No. 21) came from Charlestown, Mass., to Norwich, Conn., and m. Dec. 25, 1776, Lucy Springer. He d. Aug. 14, 1802. She d. Aug. 23, 1813.

CHILDREN:

23 MARY, b. at Norwich, Sept. 21, 1777, d. Oct. 9, 1777.
24 SAMUEL, b. Oct. 1, 1778, m. Lucinda Palmer.
25 JOHN, b. April 7, 1780, d. young.
26 HENRY, b. Nov. 16, 1781, d. Aug. 14, 1842.
27 CHARLES E., b. Feb. 16, 1783, lost at sea March, 1804.
28 TIMOTHY, b. Aug. 23, 1784, d. Dec. 18, 1794.
29 LUCY, b. ———.
30 GURDON, b. Jan. 21, 1790, m. Sarah Ann Swan.
31 WILLIAM, b. May 15, 1795, d. Oct. 8, 1795.
32 JOHN F., b. July 21, 1796, m. Eliza Mary Niles; 2d, Ann E. Smith (No. 113).

Samuel Trumbull (No. 24) came to Stonington from Norwich in 1798, and m. Lucinda, daughter of Jonathan Palmer of Stonington (No. 529), that family. He d. in Stonington July 7, 1826.

CHILDREN:

33 SAMUEL, b. March 16, 1800, d. April 12, 1801.
34 LUCINDA, b. March 6, 1801, m. Thomas B. Stokes.
35 JOHN JEFFERSON, b. Jan. 26, 1803, d. Feb. 20, 1804.
36 JOHN, b. Feb. 25, 1805.
37 CHARLES HENRY, b. Dec. 18, 1807, d. Jan. 9, 1808.
38 SALLY SOPHIA, b. Dec. 20, 1808, m. Francis Pendleton (No. 91), Pendleton family.
39 ELIZABETH FRANCES, b. Aug. 13, 1811.
40 THOMAS JEFFERSON, b. in New York, March 4, 1814, d. March 20, 1814.
41 JAMES MADISON (twin), b. in New York, March 4, 1814, d. March 26, 1814.
42 MARIA LOUISE, b. April 25, 1815.
43 LUCY, b. June 29, 1817.
44 ANDREW JACKSON, b. Sept. 6, 1819.
45 SAMUEL FRANKLIN, b. Sept. 16, 1822, d. in Stonington.

Gurdon Trumbull (No. 30) m. Sarah Ann Swan May 1, 1817 (No. 152), that family, both of Stonington, Conn.

CHILDREN:

46 GURDON SWAN, b. May 28, d. young.
46a FRANCES, b. Feb. 6, 1820, d. young.
47 JAMES HAMMOND, b. Dec. 20, 1821, m. Sarah A. Robinson.
48 WILLIAM PALMER, b. May 3, 1825, d. young.

TRUMBULL FAMILY.

49 MARY, b. Aug. 5, 1827, m. William C. Prime.
50 HENRY CLAY, b. June 8, 1830, m. Alice C. Gallaudet.
51 CHARLES EDWARD, b. Oct. 31, 1832, d. March 17, 1856.
52 THOMAS SWAN, b. Feb. 15, 1835, d. March 30, 1865.
53 ANNA, b. May 18, 1838, m. Edward Slossom.
54 GURDON, b. May 5, 1841, m. Anna F. Niles.

John F. Trumbull (No. 32) m. Eliza Mary Niles (No. 213), Stanton family, Nov. 25, 1822; she d. Feb. 29, 1828. He m. 2d, Ann Eliza Smith Sept. 21, 1829 (No. 113), that family. She d. April 1, 1896. He d. Oct. 28, 1874.

CHILDREN BY FIRST MARRIAGE:

55 HORACE N., b. Feb. 20, 1825, m. Mary Jane Pendleton Oct. 21, 1847 (No. 125), that family.
56 ELIZA M., b. Feb. 11, 1828, d. young.

CHILDREN BY SECOND MARRIAGE—SIX OF WHICH D. IN INFANCY:

57 EDWIN B., b. June 5, 1830, m. Ellen P. Hakes, May 17, 1864.
58 JOHN F., b. Nov. 21, 1831.
59 ELIZA NILES, b. July 15, 1833, m. Hon. Henry C. Robinson of Hartford, Conn.
60 HARRIET, b. March 25, 1838, m. Ira H. Palmer (No. 457), that family.
61 LUCY, b. Dec. 13, 1841, m. D. W. Hakes of Colchester, Conn.
62 STILES STANTON, b. Dec. 30, 1843.
63 JAMES VAN ALEN, b. Sept. 13, 1848, m. Belle Burch, daughter of Billings Burch (No. 74), that family March 24, 1880.
64 MARIA BABCOCK, b. ———.

VINCENT FAMILY.

The Vincent family were natives of Amesbury, Wiltshire, England, and

1. WILLIAM VINCENT, the emigrant ancestor, came to New England and m. in Providence, R. I., Priscilla Carpenter, daughter of William and wife, Elizabeth (Arnold) Carpenter, May 31, 1670, and he d. in 1695.

THEIR CHILDREN WERE:

2 THOMAS, b. ———.
3 NICHOLAS, b. ———.
4 WILLIAM, b. ———.

Thomas and William Vincent remained in Providence, but Nicholas Vincent came to Westerly, R. I. The three brothers were cordwainers.

Nicholas Vincent (No. 3) m. Elizabeth, daughter of John Reynolds, and d. in 1749.

THEIR CHILDREN:

5 NICHOLAS, b. ———.
6 JEMIMA, b. ———.
7 WILLIAM, b. ———.
8 MARY, b. ———, m. Ephraim Bacon Feb. 25, 1754; she m. 2d, Samuel Hinckley.
9 MERCY, b. ———, m. Elisha Freeman.
10 JOSEPH, b. ———.
11 ELIZABETH, b. ———.
12 DEBORAH, b. ———.
13 HANNAH, b. ———.
14 JOSHUA, b. ———, d. young.

William Vincent (No. 7) was a physician and m. Zeriah Rudd of Norwich, Conn.

THEIR CHILDREN:

15 SUSANNAH, b. Nov. 11, 1760, m. Nathan Brand, and 2d, Benjamin Gardiner.
16 WILLIAM, b. March 31, 1764.
16a SURVIAH, b. ———.
17 SALLY, b. March 7, 1770, m. Elijah Hinckley, and after her death he m. her sister Serviah, whose birth is not given.
18 JOSEPH, b. April 19, 1772, m. at Stonington Phalla Hinckley, Jan. 2, 1824; she was b. in 1780, and d. Aug. 29, 1821. He m. 2d, Lois Bradford, who was b. in 1786, d. Sept. 23, 1848.
19 ELIZABETH, b. June 10, 1774, m. John Hubbart or Hobart.
20 THOMAS, b. July 28, 1781, m. Polly Crumb.

VINCENT FAMILY.

William Vincent (No. 16) of Westerly, R. I., m. Joannah (No. 86), Frink family, daughter of Samuel Frink of Stonington, Conn. She was b. March 26, 1769, and d. April 3, 1846, and he d. at North Stonington, Conn., March 16, 1854.

THEIR CHILDREN:

21 WILLIAM, b. Dec. 8, 1787.
22 THOMAS, b. Dec. 3, 1789.
23 HENRY or HARRY, b. May 12, 1792, m. Martha Scholfield, daughter of John; she was b. 1793, d. Jan. 27, 1878, at Montville; he d. there Aug. 19, 1878.
24 JOHN, b. July 26, 1794, m. Sept. 29, 1846, Sarah York; he d. Oct. 27, 1864.
25 ASA, b. Feb. 4, 1797, m. Nancy, daughter of Jarius and wife Polly Frink, March 18, 1821; she was b. in 1802, d. March 23, 1862. He m. 2d, Maria King of Plainfield, Conn. He d. in Rhode Island Feb. 28, 1884. No children.
26 IRA, b. March 7, 1799, m. Sarah, granddaughter of Daniel and Sarah Baker of Montville. She was b. March, 1802, d. Oct. 10, 1885. He d. Nov. 26, 1833.
27 JOANNA, b. Oct. 31, 1800.
28 DR. EZRA, b. Jan. 11, 1803.
29 MARY, b. June 5, 1805.
30 SAMUEL, b. June 19, 1807, m. Martha, daughter of Daniel and Sarah Baker of Montville. He d. Aug. 7, 1837.
31 CHARLES, b. Feb. 19, 1809.
32 FRANK, b. Feb. 29, 1812.
33 ALBERT, b. Jan. 8, 1814.
34 BENJAMIN, b. Sept. 16, 1815.

William Vincent (No. 21) m. Freelove, daughter of John and Susannah (Colgrove) Pendleton, Feb. 28, 1813. She was b. Feb. 20, 1796, and d. Oct. 12, 1853. He m. 2d, Eleanor J. Tracey, daughter of Robert and Mary (Charles) Tracey of New York. He d. at North Stonington, Conn., Feb. 8, 1874.

CHILDREN:

35 EUNICE, b. Sept. 4, 1814, m. Elisha D. Randall (No. 112).
36 CHARLES W., b. June 12, 1816, m. Angeline Brown (No. 392), of the Brown family.
37 MARTHA M., b. Jan. 22, 1813.

Dr. Ezra Vincent (No. 28) m. Ann Maria Denison (No. 631), Denison family, May 11, 1841; she was b. in 1816, and d. Oct. 27, 1848. He d. July 7, 1850.

CHILDREN:

38 WALTER B., b. Aug. 6, 1845.

FRANCIS WEST FAMILY.

1. FRANCIS WEST of Salisbury, Eng., was invited to America by a Mr. Thomas of Marshfield, Mass., and he married Margery Reeves Feb. 27, 1639. He was at Duxbury, Mass., in 1641. He moved from there and purchased land at Mill Brook in 1642, and was one of the first proprietors of Bridgewater in 1645. He returned to Duxbury in 1655. He held various public offices. Was surveyor in 1657 and constable in 1660. In 1671 was appointed by the court to have oversight of the ordinances, and in 1672 was one of the proprietors who received lots of land of five shares each. He d. Jan. 2, 1692, aged 86 years.

CHILDREN:

2 SAMUEL, b. in 1643.
3 PETER, b. ——, m. Patience ———.
4 PELATIAH, b. ——, came to Connecticut.
5 RICHARD, b. ——.

These children are found elsewhere as Samuel, Thomas, Peter, Mary and Ruth.

Samuel West (No. 2) m. Triphosa Partridge Sept. 26, 1668. She d. Nov. 1, 1701, and he d. May 8, 1689, aged 46 years.

CHILDREN:

6 FRANCIS, b. Nov. 13, 1669.
7 JEUEN, b. Sept. 8, 1671, d. Dec. 29, 1671.
8 SAMUEL, b. Dec. 23, 1672, m. Martha Delano.
9 PELATIAH, b. March 8, 1674, m. Elizabeth Chandler July 12, 1722, d. Dec. 7, 1756.
10 EBENEZER, b. July 22, 1676.
11 JOHN, b. March 6, 1679.
12 ABIGAIL, b. Sept. 26, 1682, m. Nathaniel Cole, 1714.
13 BATHSHEBA, b. ——.

Peter West (No. 3) m. Patience ———.

CHILDREN:

14 MARY, b. Oct. 3, 1675, d. young.
15 MARGERY, b. March 12, 1678.
16 ESTHER, b. Sept. 20, 1680.
17 ANNE, b. Feb. 16, 1682, m. Elisha Curtis, May 17, 1705.
18 WILLIAM, b. May 4, 1683.
19 MARY, b. Dec. 7, 1685.
20 BENJAMIN, b. July 7, 1688.
21 ELISHA, b. March 2, 1693.
22 SAMUEL, b. April 4, 1697.

FRANCIS WEST FAMILY.

Francis West (No. 6) is found at Preston, Conn., in the year 1696, where his marriage is recorded thus: "This may sartyfy all persons whome it may consern that franses west and marcy minor were Lawfully joyned in marage the 20 of December, 1696, by me, Samuel mason Assist" also ———

CHILDREN:

23 MERCY, b. Oct. 30, 1697.
On Nov. 1, 1702, Francis West and Mercy, his wife, were dismissed from Preston Church unto the First Congregational Church in Stonington (Road), and the baptisms of their children are recorded here all but Samuel.
24 SAMUEL, b. about 1699; not recorded at Stonington, but found probably in Preston, Conn., records.
25 JOSEPH, bapt. Nov. 30, 1701, m. Sarah Delano.
26 AMMASSA, b. March 27, 1704, m. Amy Hatch.
27 ZEBULON, b. March 16, 1707, m. Mary Delano.
28 CHRISTOPHER, b. June 19, 1709, m. Amy Delano.
29 PELATIAH, b. Sept. 30, 1711, m. Elizabeth Lathrop.

This Francis West owned large tracts of land in Stonington, where he lived till about 1720. His wife, Marcie Minor (No. 52), was daughter of Joseph Minor and wife, Marie Avery, who was daughter of Capt. James and wife, Joanna (Greenslade) Avery; she was b. Aug. 21, 1673. Her father, Joseph Minor, was son of Thomas Minor and wife, Grace Palmer, daughter of Walter and first wife, ——— Palmer. About 1720, Francis West moved with his family to Tolland, Conn., where he was one of the early settlers and the first deacon of that church. He d. May 12, 1764, aged 62. He owned over 700 acres of land there, lying in the southeast corner of the town.

Samuel West (poet) (No. 8) m. Martha Delano June 20, 1709; removed to Pembroke in 1749.

CHILDREN:

30 AMOS, b. May 29, 1710.
31 NATHAN, b. Aug. 18, 1711.
32 SARAH, b. Nov. 8, 1712.
33 MOSES, b. March 4, 1716.

Samuel West (No. 24) m. Sarah, daughter of Jonathan Delano, Nov. 4, 1724; she d. in 1752. He m. 2d, Abigail Lathrop Nov. 26, 1754. He d. Feb. 3, 1779.

CHILDREN BY FIRST WIFE:

33 PRUDENCE, b. Sept. 5, 1726.
34 SARAH, b. March 21, 1729.
35 SAMUEL, b. March 30, 1732, m. Sarah Lathrop.
36 ABIGAIL, b. July 22, 1734, d. 1750.
37 ABNER, b. May 1, 1737, m. Mary Hatch July 3, 1760.
38 JOANNA, b. Dec. 2, 1739.
39 ELISHA, b. Sept. 19, 1742.
40 ANNE, b. Sept. 10, 1745.

CHILDREN BY SECOND WIFE:

41 ANN, b. Sept. 12, 1756.
42 RUTH, b. Dec. 21, 1759.

Joseph West (No. 25) m. Joanna, daughter of Jonathan Delano, May 19, 1725. He d. Jan. 27, 1764.

CHILDREN:

43 MERCY, b. April 20, 1726.
44 JOSEPH, b. Nov. 2, 1728, m. Lois Strong March 10, 1752.
45 JOANNA, b. Aug. 21, 1732.
46 RUFUS, b. Oct. 1, 1735, m. Sarah Nye Nov. 22, 1764.
47 DEBORAH, b. Jan. 30, 1738.
48 BATHSHEBA, b. July 9, 1741.
49 EPHRAIM, b. Dec. 5, 1747, d. young.
50 JABEZ, b. Jan. 30, 1751.

Ammassa West (No. 26) m. Amy, daughter of Joseph Hatch, in 1730.

CHILDREN:

51 FRANCIS, b. Nov. 1, 1731, m. Abigail Strong in 1751.
52 OLIVER, b. Oct. 3, 1733, m. Thankful Nye in 1757.
53 PHEBE, b. Sept. 2, 1735.
54 LUCIA, b. Aug. 9, 1738.
55 REBECCA, b. Nov. 26, 1742, d. 1774.
56 AMY, b. Dec. 8, 1741, d. 1756.
57 MARCY, b. Sept. 16, 1744.
58 MEHITABLE, b. Feb. 7, 1747, d. 1755.
59 AMMASSA, b. May 4, 1749, m. Bathsheba Gibbs in 1767.
60 SUSAN, b. March 4, 1754, d. 1755.

Zebulon West (No. 27) m. Mary Delano of Barnstable, Mass., Oct. 7, 1731, by whom he had five children, and after Mrs. West's death in 1743, he m. 2d, Mrs. Mary Sluman, formerly Sarah Avery of Groton, who outlived him and married twice afterwards. They had six children and he d. Dec. 4, 1770. He was a man highly distinguished for integrity and benevolence and much respected in Tolland where he lived. He held public office from the time he was 29 years old till the day of his death. He was selectman for seventeen years, town clerk for thirty-four years. He was the first man who represented the town in the General Assembly and was elected for forty-three regular sessions, and was Speaker of the House for several sessions. Was judge of probate for eleven years. He was also one of the judges of the Hartford County Court, and one of the members of the Governor's Council. It used to be said that Zebulon West never did but one wrong thing, and that was when he succeeded in having the meeting house placed south of the centre of the town, against nearly a majority of the wishes of the inhabitants of the town. He educated three sons at Yale College. Stephen, who became a clergyman, settled at Stockbridge, Mass., and became one of the most distinguished theological writers of New England. Jeremiah, the youngest son, settled as a physician in Tolland.

CHILDREN BY FIRST WIFE:

61 MARY, b. Sept. 17, 1732, m. Ephraim Grant, Jr., in 1748.
62 STEPHEN, b. Nov. 2, 1735, m. Elizabeth, daughter of Col. Ephraim Williams, and m. 2d, Eleanor West of Sheffield.
63 ANN, b. March 19, 1738, and d. 1775.
64 THANKFUL, b. July 14, 1740.
65 ELIJAH, b. April 6, 1743.

CHILDREN BY SECOND WIFE:

66 SARAH, b. Jan. 27, 1745, d. 1750.
67 PRUDENCE F., b. Feb. 1, 1747, d. 1748.
68 NATHANIEL, b. Sept. 5, 1748, went to Vermont, m. Lucretia Woodbridge, 1771.
69 JEREMIAH, b. July 20, 1753, m. Amelia Ely; 2d, Martha Williams, and 3d, a Mrs. Baker.
70 DESIRE, b. Aug. 18, 1755, m. ——— Shepherd.
71 SARAH, b. May 27, 1758.

Christopher West (No. 28) m. Amy, daughter of Jonathan Delano, Oct. 25, 1732.

CHILDREN:

72 PRISCILLA, b. Aug. 26, 1734.
73 FRANCIS, b. Oct. 30, 1735.
74 JONATHAN, b. Dec. 30, 1737.
75 JERUSHA F., b. April 27, 1740.
76 MINER, b. Jan. 9, 1743.
77 LOIS, b. in Coventry.
78 MARY, b. May 25, 1750.

Pelatiah West (No. 29) m. Elizabeth Lathrop Dec. 5, 1734.

CHILDREN:

79 ELIZABETH, b. Sept. 17, 1735.
80 SUSANNAH, b. March 28, 1737.
81 ELEAZER, b. Nov. 9, 1738, m. Olive Redington in 1761.
82 HANNAH, b. March 28, 1741.
83 ZERVIAH, b. Aug. 2, 1743.
84 EUNICE, b. April 30, 1745.
85 ELIJAH, b. March 7, 1747.
86 DANIEL, b. July 22, 1749.
87 PRUDENCE, b. June 1, 1751.
88 MARY, b. June 28, 1753.

MATTHEW WEST FAMILY.

From the New England Historical and Genealogical Register we find that the family of Wests as early as 1587 were at the village of Wherwell in Hants, three and one-half miles from Andover, near the trouting stream of "The Test" in Hampshire, England.

The Vicar of the parish of Wherwell having died, William West, Lord Lawarr or De La Warr (as it was later called) presented the place to Stephen Bachiler.

Later on in 1687, the will of William West of Eaton in Bucks County, mentions son Thomas West, with his son and daughter Thomas and Anna; also mentions his son, William West, deceased, who lived in Virginia and left son William and daughters, Margaret and Mary. His will also mentions brother, Francis West, with his sons Edward and William .

A Thomas West, Lord De La Warr, was the First Lord Governor and Captain General of Virginia in 1610.

A Francis West was Admiral of New England after 1607, and on Dec. 20, 1627, he was appointed Governor General to succeed Sir George Yeardly.

The name of Richard West, Lord Chancellor of Ireland, and the friend of free suffrage in America, should not be forgotten. He was appointed King's Counsel in 1717, and sat in Parliament in 1721. He m. Elizabeth, daughter of Bishop Burnet, and sister of Gov. Burnet of New York and Massachusetts. He lived in Dublin and d. Dec. 3, 1726, much lamented.

In 1633 Thomas West came to New England in the ship "Mary and John," and two years later John West, aged eleven years, Nathaniel West, aged fifteen, Thomas West, aged seventeen, and Twiford West, aged nineteen, came to New England, and may have been the sons of Thomas West, who came in 1633.

Also in 1635 Richard and John West came to Virginia from Gravesend. The similarity of names in all these families, Francis, William, Richard and John, show that they were the ancestors

MATTHEW WEST FAMILY.

(though not here fully explained) of the families whose descendants came later to Stonington, viz.: Francis West, who m. Margery Reeves in 1639, and was at Duxbury in 1641, came to Preston and then to Stonington, and after removed to Tolland and many of the descendants went to Stockbridge, Mass.; also Matthew West, who was probably brother or cousin to Francis, as he was at Lynn in 1636 and at Newport in 1646. This Matthew West is the ancestor of the West family whose descendants lived in Stonington and Quiambaug.

1. MATTHEW WEST, b. ———, m. ———.

CHILDREN:

2 NATHANIEL, b. ———, and m. before 1648, when he and his wife were members of the First Baptist Church in Newport.
3 JOHN, b. ———, no record, except he was freeman at Newport in 1655.
4 ROBERT, b. ———, freeman of Providence in 1655; in Portsmouth in 1663; Monmouth, New Jersey, in 1667; m. Elizabeth ———, and had children, Joseph, John and Robert. He d. before 1697.
5 BARTHOLOMEW, b. in Portsmouth and m. Catharine Almy, d. before 1703.
6 FRANCIS, b. ———, of Kingstown, R. I., where he was taxed with his sons, Francis, Jr., and Richard, in 1687.
7 JOAN, b. ———, m. Joshua Coggeshall, b. in England Dec. 22, 1652; she d. April 24, 1676, aged 41 years.

Francis West (No. 6) m. ———, not known, d. Jan. 2, 1692.

CHILDREN:

8 FRANCIS, JR., b. ———.
9 RICHARD, b. ———; no account given.
10 THOMAS, b. ———, m. Elizabeth Dungan, were members of the Seventh Day Baptist Church in Newport in 1692; also Peter and his wife.
11 PETER, b. ———, m. Ruth ———.
12 MARTHA, b. ———, m. 1st, James Card and 2d, Jeremiah Fones of Kingstown.

Francis West (No. 8) m. Susan ———.

CHILDREN:

13 WILLIAM, b. in 1681.
14 THOMAS, b. in 1684.
15 SUSANNAH, b. ———, m. John Tanner of Kingstown in 1723.
16 MARY, b. June 29, 1711.

This Francis West (No. 8) probably had a second wife Mary and child.

17 SAMUEL, b. Feb. 2, 1732, recorded in Westerly and is the Samuel who m. Anna (Hall), widow of Nathan Maccoon in 1757.

Thomas West (No. 10) m. Elizabeth, daughter of Thomas Dungan of Newport (whose wife was Elizabeth Weaver, daughter of Clement and Mary).

CHILDREN:

18 ELDER THOMAS, b. ———, m. 1st, Elizabeth Gladding, and 2d, Amey ———.
19 JAMES, b. ———, m. Susannah Pullman.
20 FRANCIS, b. ———, m. Mary Lawton.
21 TIMOTHY, b. ———, m. 1st, ———; 2d, Content Lamphere.
22 JOHN, b. ———, m. Amey Wilcox.

Elder Thomas West (No. 18) m. Elizabeth Gladding Feb. 28, 1752, and m. 2d, Amey ————, and with her was received into the Seventh Day Baptist Church at Newport Sept. 13, 1756. Among the list of patriots at Hopkinton who signed a document binding them to fight for the united colonies was this Elder Thomas West of Hopkinton, with his son, Jonathan, and Francis West, the brother of Elder Thomas West.

CHILDREN:

23 JONATHAN, b. Nov. 28, 1754, m. 1st, Martha Haley (No. 13), of Haley family, and m. 2d, Prudence Allen of Stonington, Conn., July 27, 1780.
24 SUSANNAH b. June 3, 1756, m. Nathan Tanner Oct. 19, 1775.
25 MICHAEL, b. Dec. 15, 1759.
26 THOMAS, b. Feb. 21, 1762.
27 FRANCIS, b. April 15, 1764.
28 SAMUEL (Rev.), b. Oct. 6, 1766, m. Jerusha Stanton.
29 JOSEPH, b. Oct. 4, 1771.
30 AMIE, b. April 3, 1774.
31 ABIGAIL, b. July 31, 1776.

James West (No. 19) m. Susanna Pullman Dec. 18, 1751.

CHILDREN:

32 JAMES, b. Aug. 11, 1752.
33 MARY, b. July 12, 1754.
34 SUSANNA, b. April 9, 1756, m. Cornelius Stetson July 10, 1777.
35 ROBERT, b. March 25, 1758, d. Aug. 2, 1759.
36 LYDIA, b. July 6, 1760, m. Gardiner Champlin, son of William, Aug. 31, 1791.
37 ARNOLD, b. Sept. 10, 1762, m. Hannah Babcock, daughter of Joseph Babcock, Nov. 19, 1796. She was b. June 2, 1767.
38 ROBERT, b. Nov. 11, 1765.

Francis West (No. 20) m. Mary Lawton Feb. 17, 1757.

CHILDREN:

39 SARAH, b. June 5, 1758.
40 WILLIAM, b. Sept. 7, 1760.

Timothy West (No. 21) m. 1st, ————, not known, and m. 2d, Content Lamphere Dec. 3, 1755. He d. before 1767, and is buried near Mystic, and his widow m. Peleg Sisson, Sr., for his second wife, Feb. 26, 1767.

MATTHEW WEST FAMILY.

CHILDREN BY FIRST WIFE:

41 TIMOTHY, b. ———, m. Mary ———, had son Frederick, b. March 10, 1767.
42 WILLIAM, b. about 1745, m. Anna or Nancy, Susannah Babcock.
43 ESTHER, b. ———, m. Peleg Sisson, Jr., Feb. 10, 1777, had son Joshua, who was b. Feb. 14, 1780, and m. Alice or Elsie Crumb and their daughter Caroline m. Noyes Sisson (No. 7).
44 SIMEON b. ———, m. Nancy Thompson Oct. 31, 1784.

CHILDREN OF PELEG SISSON, SR., AND MRS. CONTENT (WEST) SISSON.

1 JOSEPH SISSON, b. ———, m. Lucy Chapman Feb. 4, 1798.
2 SANFORD SISSON, b. ———, m. Elizabeth Chapman.
3 BARNABAS SISSON, b. ———, m. Cynthia Lamphere.

Sanford Sisson (No. 2) m. Elizabeth Chapman on March 3, 1799. She was the daughter of William Chapman, Jr., and wife, Bridget Johnson, who were m. March 14, 1773, and their daughter Elizabeth was b. Sept. 17, 1778.

THEIR CHILDREN:

4 ELIZABETH SISSON, b. July 20, 1800, m. Barnabas Sisson.
5 SOPHIA SISSON, b. Jan. 30, 1802, m. James Sisson.
6 DAMARIUS SISSON, b. Aug. 13, 1804, m. William West (No. 78).
7 SANFORD NOYES SISSON, b. ———, m. Caroline Sisson.
8 BRIDGET SISSON, b. ———, m. Jacob Kenyon.
9 LYDIA SISSON, b. ———, m. William Saunders.
10 HANNAH SISSON, b. ———, m. Warren Main.
11 EUNICE SISSON, b. ———, m. Robinson Dunham Aug. 18, 1844, and m. 2d, a Crumb.

John West (No. 22) m. Amey Wilcox (No. 54a) of that family Dec. 29, 1765.

CHILDREN:

45 HENRY, b. May 24, 1767, m. Hannah Saunders.
46 HANNAH, b. Sept. 12, 1769, never m., d. Aug. 15, 1850.
47 ELISHA, b. Jan. 6, 1771, m. Lydia Lamphere Nov. 23, 1794.
48 ABIGAIL b. July 30, 1773, m. ——— Crandall, went West.
49 THOMAS, b. April 13, 1776.
50 ESTHER, b. Jan. 26, 1780, never m., d. Nov. 30, 1871.
51 PELEG, b. Sept. 15, 1782, m. Mary Gavitt.
52 MARY, b. March 4, 1787, m. Samuel Crumb.

Samuel West (No. 17) m. Anna Maccoon, widow of Nathan Maccoon, and daughter of James and Rachel (Maccoon) Hall of Westerly March 17, 1757. She had five children by first husband, viz.: Mary, b. in 1744; Nathan, b. in 1746; Isabel, b. in 1748; Timothy, b. in 1750; Abram, b. in 1753. By her second husband, Samuel West, they had

CHILDREN:

53 SAMUEL, b. in 1757.
54 ANNA, b. in 1759.
55 AMEY, b. in 1760.

Rev. Samuel West (No. 28) m. Jerusha, daughter of David and wife, Sarah (Kimball) Stanton, March 10, 1785. She d. Feb. 24, 1816, at Norwich, Conn., and he d. Nov. 1, 1836, at North Madison, Conn. He was pastor of the New London First Baptist Church for ten years.

CHILDREN:

56 DAVID S., b. Aug. 24, 1787, m. Keziah Stanton.
57 THOMAS, b. Nov. 26, 1785, m. Abby Weeks.
58 SALLY, b. Aug. 26, 1789, m. Ezekiel Glover.
59 MICHAEL, b. Jan. 21, 1792, m. Rebecca Mallory.
60 LEVI, b. April 19, 1796, d. young.
61 SAMUEL, b. Feb. 25, 1798, m. Harriet Bailey.
62 NANCY, b. Jan. 19, 1800, m. Edmund Doane, Jr.
63 ANNIE, b. March 17, 1802, d. young.

William West (No. 42) m. Anna, Nancy or Susannah Babcock, daughter of Joseph and wife, Susannah (Thompson) Babcock, who were m. Dec. 9, 1730. Susannah Thompson (No. 16) was daughter of Isaac and Mary (Holmes) Thompson of Stonington, who were m. Nov. 25, 1713.

William West and Anna Babcock were m. Nov. 1, 1772. He d. at sea Oct. 18, 1800, aged 55 years, and she d. March 4, 1833, aged 78 years. (This is the date on her gravestone, while the records give her birth as June 18, 1749.)

CHILDREN:

64 SARAH, b. March 11, 1773, m. Luke Calvin Davis.
65 CAPT TIMOTHY, b. June 22, 1774, m. Betsey ———.
66 PRUDENCE, b. Aug. 19, 1775.
67 JESSE, b. May 21, 1799, d. young.
68 JOSEPH, b. May 8, 1781, m. Polly Wilcox, daughter of (No. 85), Wilcox family.
69 JESSE B., b. Oct. 9, 1783.
70 NANCY, b. May 4, 1785, m. Joseph P. Miner (No. 379), that family.
71 WILLIAM, b. Feb. 24, 1787.
72 GEORGE, b. Feb. 18, 1789.
73 ASA, b. Feb. 18, 1789.
74 LYDIA, b. ———, m. ——— Gardiner.
75 CAPT. FRANCIS, b. ———, m. ———, lived in Essex, had two children.

Henry West (No. 45) m. Hannah Saunders about 1790. She was of Newport, R. I.

CHILDREN:

76 PRUDENCE, b. ———, never married.
77 ABBY, b. ———, m. Welcome Carpenter, an Englishman.
78 WILLIAM, b. ———, m. Demarius Sisson.
79 HENRY, b. ———, m. Betsey Chapman.
80 AMEY, b. ———, m. James Kenyon.
81 RUBY, b. ———, m. Nathaniel Noyes (No. 208), as second wife, Dec. 31, 1826.

MATTHEW WEST FAMILY.

Elisha West (No. 47) m. Lydia Lamphere Nov. 23, 1794.

CHILDREN:

82 LYDIA, b. ———, m. Barney Sisson Nov. 23, 1794.
83 ELISHA, b. ———, m. Catharine Sisson.
84 JOHN, b. ———, m. ——— Gavitt.
85 AMEY, b. ———, m. ———.
86 JOSEPH, b. ———, m. Mrs. Caroline (West) O'Connor, the widow of James O'Connor.
87 DANIEL, b. ———, drowned.
88 ESTHER, b. ———, never married.
89 MARY, b. ———, m. ——— Hooper.
90 ABBY, b. ———, never married.

Peleg West (No. 51) m. Mary Gavitt.

CHILDREN:

91 FRANK, b. ———, m. Mrs. Gillette of New London.
92 DANIEL, b. ———, drowned with his father in Pawcatuck River.
93 SALOME, b. ———, never married.
94 JASON LEE, b. ———, m. Susan Thompson May 14, 1837.
95 AMOS, b. ———, m. ———.
96 CELIA, b. ———, m. Noel Lawrence of Newport, R. I.
97 PELEG, b. ———, m. ———, went West.

Joseph West (No. 68) m. Polly, daughter of John and Polly (Packer) Wilcox, Jan. 22, 1802.

CHILDREN:

98 LUCRETIA, b. Dec. 18, 1802, m. Nathan Crandall.
99 JESSE, b. Jan. 24, 1805, never m.
100 CAROLINE, b. Feb. 20, 1807, m. 1st, James O'Connor, and 2d, Joseph West (No. 86).
101 JOHN, b. Feb. 2, 1810.
102 CAPT. TIMOTHY, b. Jan. 18, 1812, drowned.
103 SALLY, b. April 30, 1814, m. Varnum Burdick.
104 WILLIAM, b. Jan. 26, 1816.
105 CAPT. ALFRED, b. about 1818, m. 1st, Frances, daughter of Ephraim Miner; m. 2d, Ann E. Lewis and went to California.

William West (No. 78) m. Damarius Sisson (No. 6).

CHILDREN:

106 WILLIAM ROBINSON, b. ———, m. Mary Knight.
107 LUCY A., b. ———, m. Nelson B. Vars.
108 ALFRED, b. ———, d. in the war of the Rebellion.
109 EMILY, b. ———, m. John Johnson.
110 ELIZABETH, b. ———, m. Henry Barber.
111 EDWIN, b. ———, m. Sarah A. Yerrington March 18, 1855.

Henry West (No. 79) m. Betsey, daughter of Lewis Chapman.

CHILDREN:

112 THOMAS, b. ———.
113 WASHINGTON, b. ———.
114 WILLIAM, b. ———.
115 FRANCES, b. ———.
116 MARTHA, b. ———.

WHEELER FAMILY.

1. THOMAS WHEELER, the ancestor of the Wheeler family of Stonington, Conn., and region round about, was doubtless of English origin, but the place of his birth and nationality are not certainly known, nor has the time of his migration to this country been ascertained, so as to associate him with any of the passengers of the early emigrant ships. The first knowledge that we have of him in this country is when he appears as a resident of the town of Lynn, Mass., in 1635, when and where he was elected constable, and held other official positions later on. In 1642 he was admitted to the privilege of a freeman of the commonwealth of Massachusetts, purchasing large tracts of land there, including a mill site, upon which he built and operated a saw and grist mill. During his residence in Lynn he m. Mary ————, a young lady of his acquaintance, whose family name is unknown, but our family traditions represent her as a woman of pleasing and attractive accomplishments, and in every way worthy of her liege lord; she graced her domestic duties with cheerful loveliness, filling his home with light and love. They were m. in 1645, and became the parents of three children.

CHILDREN:

2 ISAAC, b. in 1646, m. Martha Park.
3 ELIZABETH, b. in 1648, m. Josiah Witter (No. 2), Witter family.
4 SARAH, b. in 1650, m. June 1, 1671. This record is taken from the Diary of Thomas Miner, without the name of her husband, but it is believed for various reasons that her husband was Daniel Stanton (No. 7) of the Thomas Stanton family.

What induced our ancestor, Thomas Wheeler to leave Lynn, Mass., and sell out his business and real estate there, and take up his abode in the town of Stonington in 1667, is not fully understood, but whatever motive actuated him in coming this way it is plainly evident that he intended to make Stonington his final home. He was an intimate friend of Rev. James Noyes, who came to Stonington the same year that he did, and it has been supposed that the friendship between them was the cause of his coming. Be that as it may, there were men of his name that lived in the English home of the Noyes family, and crossed the ocean about the same year that he did. Thomas Wheeler was made freeman in the Connecticut Colony in the year 1669, and was nominated and elected one of the Stonington representatives to the Connecticut General Court in the year 1673. The next year his name appears among the immortal nine who organized the First Congregational Church of Stonington, June 3, 1674, and his wife, Mary Wheeler, was one of the partakers with the church in their first communion service. Soon after Thomas Wheeler and his wife came to Stonington to live, he and his son Isaac built them a residence in North Stonington, where Col. James F. Brown now resides, where they lived and died. Thomas Wheeler left a will, which was lost by being burned when the infamous Arnold burned the city of New London, Sept. 6, 1781. The existence of his will is proved by his descendants referring to it in later instruments conveying the real estate that belonged to him and given to them in his will. They are both buried in the old Whitehall burial place, situated on the east bank of the Mystic river. He d. March 6, 1686, aged 84 years, consequently he was b. 1602.

Isaac Wheeler (No. 2) m. Martha, daughter of Thomas and Dorothy (Thompson) Park, Jan. 10, 1667, by Thomas Stanton (No. 19), Park family. He served in the Colonial Indian wars. He d. June 5, 1712, aged 66 years; buried in Whitehall cemetery. She d. Feb. 14, 1717.

CHILDREN:

5 MARY, b. Nov. 22, 1668, m. Ebenezer Williams (No. 38), of that family.
6 MARTHA, b. Feb. 6, 1670, m. John Williams (No. 25), that family.
7 THOMAS, b. Dec. 1, 1671, d. at the age of 20 years. He was murdered by the Indians, under the supposed leadership of a chief known as the black sachem. Mr. Wheeler was away from home, out on a hunting excursion, traversing the forests of the town of Preston, and when near Quinebaug River he met a squad of Indians, who were hunting in the same region, who ordered him to clear out and leave the game to them, as they were the original owners of it. He refused to obey their orders, when they told him if he did not leave the game of the forest to them they would kill and scalp him on the spot. He bid defiance to their threats, when they attacked him with their tomahawks and scalping knives. He defended himself as best he could, and a terrible struggle ensued which resulted in his death, and that of five of the Indians.
8 ISAAC, b. Aug. 6, 1676, m. Mary Shepard.
9 ANNA, b. Aug. 20, 1675, m. John Tongue, son of George and grandson of George Tongue, Nov. 21, 1702.
10 RICHARD, b. March 10, 1677, m. Prudence Payson.
11 DOROTHY, b. Dec. 6, 1679, m. Nehemiah Smith April 22, 1696; 2d, Samuel Fish.
12 WILLIAM, b. Sept. 9, 1681, m. Hannah Gallup.

13 ELIZABETH, b. May 22, 1683, m. John Gallup in 1709 (No. 25), that family.
14 EXPERIENCE, b. May 21, 1685, m. Rev. Joseph Coit, first minister of Plainfield, Conn.

Elizabeth Wheeler (No. 3) m. Josiah Witter in Lynn, Mass., Feb. 25, 1662. She d. Aug. 5, 1672.

CHILDREN:
15 ELIZABETH WITTER, b. March 15, 1663.
16 MARY WITTER, b. Feb. 25, 1665.
17 EBENEZER WITTER, b. March 25, 1668.

Isaac Wheeler (No. 8) m. Mary Shepard, b. 1679, daughter of Rev. Jeremiah Shepard, first pastor of Lynn, Mass., and wife, Mary Wainwright, and granddaughter of the Rev. Thomas Shepard, first pastor of Cambridge, Mass., and third wife, Margaret Borodel, Sept. 8, 1647, sister of Ann Borodel, who m. Capt. George Denison, for his second wife. Isaac Wheeler erected him a house in Stonington, on lands given him by his grandfather, Thomas Wheeler, where he brought his bride on their wedding tour, and commenced life at farming. But his wife aspired to a more active business life, and to gratify her wishes he changed and enlarged his house, making it two stories on the south, and one on the north, with show windows on the west, which were utilized for a variety store, by Madam Wheeler, who became the leading merchant of the town, buying all of the surplus farm products of the region round about, which she sent to Boston and the West Indies for a market, exchanging the same for goods necessary for the planters of the town. She made equestrian trips to Boston alone, where she purchased her dry goods. She was not only the leading merchant of the town, but her mansion house was the centre of all the neighborhood families. Her store was not only a place of business, but a political center, where slates were made for all the offices of the town. She became wealthy, and at her death was the richest woman of the county. They both united with the First Congregational Church in 1771, and were active and useful members. He d. June 25, 1737; his widow d. Sept. 20, 1761, aged 83 years. They are buried in the graveyard west of Frank Mattison's present residence.

CHILDREN:
18 MARGARET, b. Sept. 16, 1698, m. Samuel Frink (No. 9), that family.
19 THOMAS, b. Feb. 15, 1700, m. Mary Miner.

Richard Wheeler (No. 10) m. Prudence, daughter of Dea. John

WHEELER FAMILY.

Payson and wife, Bathsheba Tilestone Payson, of Roxbury, Mass., and granddaughter of Edward Payson, and Mary Elliott, sister of the apostle Elliott, and daughter of Bennet Elliott of Nazing, Eng., Dec. 12, 1702. He d. April 12, 1712. His widow m. 2d, Christopher Avery of Groton (No. 18), that family.

CHILDREN:

20 JOHN, b. Jan. 31, 1706, m. Zerviah Fanning.
21 JONATHAN, b. Feb. 7, 1708, m. Esther Denison.
22 RICHARD, b. July 23, 1710, m. Anne Pellet.
23 PRUDENCE, b. Sept. 28, 1712, m. Ebenezer Geer of Groton Jan. 2, 1735. She d. June 2, 1797. He d. Aug. 26, 1763; had ten children.

Dorothy Wheeler (No. 11) m. Nehemiah Smith April 22, 1696. She d. May 25, 1736; he d. Nov. 21, 1724.

CHILDREN:

24 DOROTHY SMITH, b. Aug. 26, 1697.
25 HANNAH SMITH, b. Feb. 20, 1699.
26 ELIZABETH SMITH, b. Nov. 17, 1700.
27 NATHAN SMITH, b. Sept. 16, 1702.
28 JOHN SMITH, b. June 14, 1704, m. Temperance Holmes, May 10, 1727 (No. 22), Holmes family.
29 WILLIAM SMITH, b. May 15, 1706.
30 ISAAC SMITH, b. May 29, 1707.
31 MARY SMITH, b. Nov. 16, 1709.
32 LYDIA SMITH, b. June 24, 1713.
33 JABEZ SMITH, b. Feb. 17, 1714.
34 ANNA SMITH, b. Nov. 1, 1717.
35 SARAH SMITH, b. July 14, 1719.

William Wheeler (No. 12) m. Hannah Gallup May 30, 1710 (No. 33), Gallup family. She d. Aug. 17, 1754; he d. Aug. 11, 1747.

CHILDREN:

36 HANNAH, b. Jan. 12, 1712, m. Simeon Miner March 19, 1731 (No. 70), that family.
37 ISAAC, b. Jan. 24, 1714, m. Mary Wheeler.
38 ANNA, b. Dec. 23, 1715, m. Joseph Stanton (No. 133), that family.
39 MARTHA, b. April 23, 1717, m. William Williams (No. 174), that family.
40 DOROTHY, b. March 15, 1721, m. Nathan Crary Nov. 2, 1742.
41 ESTHER, b. Feb. 15, 1722, m. Daniel Denison (No. 122), that family.
42 EUNICE, b. July 3, 1727, m. Joseph Williams of Norwich Feb. 20, 1746.

Experience Wheeler (No. 14) m. Rev. Joseph Coit of Plainfield, Conn., May 26, 1704. He was the first minister of Plainfield and son of Joseph Coit and Martha Harris of New London, and grandson of John and Mary Coit, who came to New London in 1651, from Gloucester, Mass. She d. Jan. 8, 1759. He d. July 1, 1750, aged 77 years.

CHILDREN:

43 ELIZABETH COIT, b. Feb. 17, 1706, d. young.
44 SAMUEL COIT, b. 1708.
45 JOSEPH COIT, b. 1711.
46 MARTHA C. COIT, b. 1713.
47 ISAAC COIT, b. Dec. 26, 1714.
48 ABIGAIL COIT, b. 1716.
49 MARY COIT, b. 1718.
50 WILLIAM COIT, b. Nov. 27, 1720.
51 EXPERIENCE COIT, b. 1722.
52 DANIEL COIT, b. 1731.

Thomas Wheeler (No. 19) m. Mary Miner Nov. 25, 1718 (No. 66), Miner family. He was one of the most prominent and wealthiest men of the town in his day and generation. His inventory will be found in the Appendix. He and his wife are buried in the old burial place west from the present residence of Frank Mattison. He d. Oct. 23, 1755, aged 56 years; she d. July 28, 1750.

CHILDREN:

53 MARY, b. July 19, 1720, m. Isaac Wheeler (No. 37); 2d, Charles Miner (No. 75), Miner family.
54 THOMAS, b. March 16, 1722, m. Mercy Williams.
55 ISAAC, b. Feb. 12, 1724, m. Bridget Noyes.
56 JEREMIAH, b. July 31, 1725, m. Susannah Babcock; 2d, Mrs. Anna Pellet Wheeler.
57 SHEPARD, b. Feb. 12, 1726, m. Hannah Hewitt.
58 PAUL, b. Sept. 11, 1728, m. Lucy Swan.
59 MEHITABLE, b. Sept. 5, 1731, m. George Babcock of Rhode Island (No. 99), that family.
60 CHARLES, b. 1736, m. Martha Williams.
61 LUCY, b. June 14, 1737, m. Joseph Page (No. 15), that family.
62 CYRUS, b. Sept. 11, 1739, d. unmarried.
63 EPHRAIM, b. Dec. 16, 1740, m. Lucy Lamb.

Isaac Wheeler (No. 37) m. Mary Wheeler (No. 53), daughter of Thomas Wheeler, June 2, 1737. They lived a short distance north of the present residence of Col. James Brown, North Stonington, Conn. He d. Jan. 5, 1740. His widow m. for her second husband, Charles Miner (No. 75), that family, Dec. 9, 1741.

CHILDREN BY FIRST MARRIAGE:

64 WILLIAM, b. Jan. 18, 1738, m. Mary Swan Dec. 9, 1761 (No. 57), Swan family.
65 HANNAH, b. Sept. 1, 1739, m. Nathaniel Chesebrough (No. 149), Chesebrough family.

Six children by second marriage, in Miner family.

Thomas Wheeler (No. 54) m. Mercy Williams Feb. 7, 1739 (No. 176), Williams family, both of Stonington, Conn.

CHILDREN:

72 MARY, b. April 22, 1741, m. Clement Miner (No. 154), Miner family.
73 MERCY, b. Jan. 22, 1742, m. Christopher Gardiner Jan. 25, 1760.

WHEELER FAMILY. 641

74 THOMAS, b. Oct. 12, 1745, m. Lucy Prentice; 2d, Mrs. Mary (Swan) Wheeler.
75 THANKFUL, b. May 20, 1747.
76 DESIRE, b. Nov. 25, 1748; m. John Watson Oct. 17, 1764, of South Kingston.
77 PRUDENCE, b. April 24, 1751.
78 MARTHA, b. Oct. 14, 1752, m. Joseph Holmes (No. 37), that family; 2d, Mr. Williams; 3d, Thomas Hammond, in 1788.
79 MEHITABLE, b. May 10, 1754, m. Jabez Swan (No. 56), Swan family.
80 RUFUS, b. Dec. 15, 1755, m. Eunice Williams (No. 272), that family; she m. 2d, Coddington Billings (No. 167), Billings family.
81 JOHN, b. March 23, 1760.

Isaac Wheeler (No. 55) m. Bridget Noyes April 9, 1746 (No. 120), that family. He was drowned in Indian Town Pond while washing sheep, May 26, 1747. His widow m. Joseph Denison, Apr. 23, 1751.

CHILD:

82 ISAAC, b. Dec. 26, 1746, m. Ruth Swan (No. 58), that family.

Jeremiah Wheeler (No. 56) m. 1st, Susannah Babcock, April 20, 1749; she d. Dec. 26, 1750. He m. 2d, Mrs. Anna Pellet Wheeler, widow of Richard Wheeler, March 11, 1752 (No. 22), that family. She d. April 30, 1772. He d. Aug. 10, 1770.

CHILD BY FIRST MARRIAGE:

83 SUSANNAH (BABCOCK), b. Feb. 10, 1750.

CHILDREN BY SECOND MARRIAGE:

84 ANNA, b. Sept. 26, 1752, m. Latham Hull (No. 7), Hull family.
85 LYDIA, b. March 8, 1754, m. David Moore March 15, 1783.
86 SARAH, b. Oct. 26, 1755, m. Jedediah Brown Jan. 13, 1778 (No. 168), Brown family.
87 JEREMIAH, b. Oct. 6, 1758.
88 AMOS, b. Oct. 15, 1759, m. Lucy Holmes.
89 BRIDGET, b. Oct. 20, 1761, m. Robert Wheeler (No. 111), that family.
90 HOSEA, b. ———, m. Bridget Grant.

Shepard Wheeler (No. 57) m. Hannah Hewitt Oct. 18, 1751 (No. 59), that family, both of Stonington, Conn.

CHILDREN:

91 MARY, b. Oct. 7, 1754, m. Paul Wheeler (No. 96).
92 SHEPARD, b. Dec. 5, 1756, m. Lucy Wheeler.
93 DESIRE, b. in 1768.

Paul Wheeler (No. 58) m. Lucy Swan May 1, 1751 (No. 29), Swan family, both of Stonington, Conn. He d. Oct. 25, 1787; she d. Nov. 11, 1781.

CHILDREN:

94 EUNICE, b. Dec. 26, 1751, d. y.
95 THOMAS, b. Oct. 25, 1753.
96 PAUL, b. Dec. 26, 1755, m. Mary Wheeler.
97 LUCY, b. Sept. 27, 1757, m. Shepard Wheeler (No. 92); 2d, Jabish Swan (No. 56), that family.

98 EUNICE, b. and d. Oct. 7, 1759.
99 JOHN, b. May 24, 1762, m. Eunice Swan.
100 ANNA, b. June 30, 1764, m. Stephen Avery (No. 159), that family.
101 MARY, b. Nov. 6, 1765, m. Luther Avery (No. 158), that family.
102 PEREZ, b. Nov. 20, 1767, m. Desire Randall.
103 EUNICE, b. Dec. 3, 1769, m. Col. William Randall (No. 71), that family.
104 ZERVIAH, b. Nov. 19, 1771, m. Joseph Noyes (No. 167), that family.

Charles Wheeler (No. 60) m. Martha Williams (No. 210), that family, Feb. 26, 1756, both of Stonington, Conn. He d. Nov. 23, 1787; she d. Jan. 18, 1788.

CHILDREN:

105 CHARLES, b. and d. in infancy.
106 WILLIAM, b. Dec. 5, 1758, d. in the Revolutionary army.
107 THOMAS, b. in 1760, m. Esther Randall.
108 ISAAC, b. Nov. 23, 1764, d. in Florida.
109 CYRUS, b. and d. same year, 1766.
110 GEORGE, b. March 30, 1770, d. in West Indies.
111 ROBERT, b. June 17, 1772, m. Bridget Wheeler; 2d, Sophia Smead.
112 DESIRE, b. in 1774, m. Col. Nathan Wheeler (No. 163).
113 MARTHA, b. ———, d. in infancy.
114 MARTHA, b. ———, m. Rufus Hewitt (No. 106), that family.
115 ELIZABETH, b. ———, m. Abel Hinckley.
116 HANNAH, b. ———. m. Russel Avery.
117 ABIGAIL, b. ———, m. Isaac Avery.

Ephraim Wheeler (No. 63) m. Lucy Lamb, Dec. 2, 1762, both of Stonington, Conn. Went west.

CHILDREN:

118 EPHRAIM, b. March 17, 1764, d. young.
119 WEALTHY, b. Feb. 1, 1766.
120 REBECCA, b. Feb. 8, 1768.
121 SUSANNA, b. Jan. 24, 1770.
122 MEHITABLE, b. Jan. 11, 1772.

Thomas Wheeler (No. 74) m. Lucy Prentice (No. 43), that family, Jan. 17, 1765, both of Stonington, Conn. She d. in 1792, aged 45. He m. 2d, Mrs. Mary (Swan) Wheeler, Aug. 14, 1794 (No. 57), Swan family, and widow of William Wheeler (No. 64).

CHILDREN:

123 MERCY, b. Aug. 13, 1767, m. William Williams (No. 271), that family.
124 THOMAS, b. Nov. 12, 1769, d. young.
125 Twins, b. and d. 1771.
126 LUCY P., b. May 7, 1774, m. Thomas W. Palmer (No. 324), Palmer family.
127 CYNTHIA, b. June, 1776, d. young.
128 Unnamed child, b. in 1777.
129 LYDIA, b. July 2, 1778, m. William Williams (No. 278), of that family.
130 Twins, b. 1780.
131 THOMAS, b. Oct. 15, 1781, m. Rebecca Wheeler.
132 Child, b. and d. 1782.

Isaac Wheeler (No. 82) m. Ruth Swan Dec. 31, 1766 (No. 58),

WHEELER FAMILY.   643

Swan family, both of Stonington, Conn. He d. Dec. 31, 1831; she d. Dec. 6, 1834.

CHILDREN:

133 MARY, b. Sept. 16, 1767, m. Jesse Hakes; she d. Dec. 11, 1862.
134 ISAAC, b. June 6, 1769, m. Hannah Holmes (No. 139), that family; 2d, Olive Burdick.
135 BRIDGET, b. March 26, 1770, d. young.
136 LODOWICK, b. Feb. 19, 1771, m. Mary Brown; 2d, Betsey Brown.
137 NOYES, b. Dec. 17, 1772, m. Priscilla Stewart (No. 37), that family.
138 PELEG, b. Feb. 18, 1775, m. Eunice Utter.
139 TIMOTHY S., b. March 17, 1777, m. Lucy Grant.
140 BRIDGET, b. June 25, 1779, m. Benjamin Green.
141 WILLIAM, b. Oct. 7, 1781, m. Saraphina Haley.
142 RUTH, b. Feb. 2, 1784, m. John Holmes (No. 140), that family.
143 OLIVER, b. March 22, 1786.
144 MATILDA, b. Dec. 6, 1788, d. unmarried.
145 BETSEY, b. Jan. 26, 1792, m. James Pitman.
146 CHARLES PHELPS, b. July 1, 1795, m. Nancy Hewitt (No. 199), that family.

Mercy Wheeler (No. 73) m. Christopher Gardiner of South Kingston, R. I., Jan. 23, 1760.

CHILD:

147 MERCY GARDINER, b. ———, m. Hosea Wheeler, Jr. (No. 165).

Desire Wheeler (No. 76) m. John Watson of South Kingston, R. I., Oct. 17, 1764.

CHILDREN:

148 JOHN WATSON, b. ———.
148a ELISHA WATSON, b. ———.
149 MARY WATSON, b. ———.
149a WALTER WATSON, b. ———.
150 JOB WATSON, b. ———.
150a BRIDGET, b. ———.
150b ISABELLA, b. ———.

Amos Wheeler (No. 88) m. Lucy Holmes Dec. 21, 1783 (No. 47), Holmes family. He d. Oct. 8, 1843, aged 84 years; she d. Nov. 30, 1832, aged 67 years.

CHILDREN:

151 AMOS, b. June 27, 1784, m. Ann Charles, d. June 9, 1822.
152 NANCY, b. June 7, 1786, m. James Lord Lester Nov. 22, 1810, d. Feb. 10, 1819.
153 JEREMIAH HALSEY, b. Dec. 7, 1787, d. unmarried June 30, 1844.
154 GURDON, b. July 21, 1789, d. unmarried Dec. 20, 1845.
155 LUCY, b. Nov. 10, 1791, m. James Lord Lester Sept. 5, 1820, d. Sept. 22, 1868.
156 POLLY or MARY, b. Feb. 26, 1793, d. unmarried May 18, 1817.
157 SILAS HOLMES, b. Oct. 2, 1796, d. unmarried March 23, 1827.
158 ELIZA P., b. June 9, 1799, d. unmarried Jan. 9, 1823.
159 HARRIET, b. June 17, 1801, m. Dea. Noyes Palmer (No. 345), that family.
160 FRANCIS H., b. July 9, 1803, m. Nancy W. Avery June 3, 1846 d. April, 1880.

161 EMELINE, b. July 4, 1807, m. Latham Hull Browning Nov. 18, 1830 (No. 55), that family; d. Jan. 4, 1858.
162 FANNY A., b. Feb. 4, 1809, m. Cyrus Browning July 13, 1831 (No. 72), that family, d. March 2, 1877.

Hosea Wheeler (No. 90) m. Bridget Grant Feb. 18, 1772 (No. 34), that family. She d. Sept. 8, 1819, aged 68 years. He d. July 13, 1829; m. widow.

CHILDREN:

163 NATHAN, b. Dec. 29, 1772, m. Desire Wheeler.
164 ASA, b. Sept. 22, 1774, m. Polly Brown.
165 HOSEA, b. Oct. 21, 1776, m. Nancy Brown; Mercy Gardiner.
166 BRIDGET, b. Feb. 17, 1779, m. Robert Wheeler (No. 111).
167 DOROTHY, b. April 28, 1781.
168 SUSANNAH, b. May 14, 1783, m. Amos C. Main March 29, 1804 (No. 110), that family.
169 REBECCA, b. Feb. 28, 1785, m. Thomas Wheeler (No. 131); 2d, Stephen L. Avery (No. 202), that family.
170 EPHRAIM, b. Dec. 29, 1788, m. 1st, Bridget Slack; 2d, Bridget Ayer; 3d, Hannah Elizabeth Miner.
171 RUSSELL, b. Aug. 20, 1796, m. Esther Wheeler Hull.

Shepard Wheeler (No. 92) m. Lucy Wheeler (No. 97) Feb., 1780. He d. Dec. 9, 1798.

CHILDREN:

172 SHEPARD, b. March 11, 1781.
173 PHINEAS, b. April 3, 1784.
174 CYRUS, b. Nov. 13, 1792.
175 RUFUS, b. Oct. 2, 1795.

Paul Wheeler (No. 96) m. Mary Wheeler (No. 91) April 6, 1776.

CHILDREN:

176 NANCY, b. July 1, 1777, m. John Holmes (No. 140), that family.
177 PAUL, b. May 24, 1778, m. Nancy Prentice Oct. 23, 1799.
178 LUCINDA, b. Aug. 7, 1784, m. Col. Gideon Chapman; 2d wife.
179 NABBY or TABITHA, b. April 2, 1786, m. Isaac Avery, Jr., April 27, 1800 (No. 186), that family.
180 HANNAH, b. Nov. 18, 1788, m. Gideon Chapman Sept. 4, 1808 (No. 32), that family.

John Wheeler (No. 99) m. Eunice Swan May 9, 1784 (No. 64), that family.

CHILDREN:

181 LUCY, b. Sept. 20, 1785.
182 JOHN, b. Sept. 9, 1787.
183 FANNY, b. Jan. 29, 1790.
184 ELIAS, b. March 25, 1793.
185 LUKE, b. Oct. 29, 1795.
186 ANN, b. 1804, m. Pierpont Keeney.

Perez Wheeler (No. 102) m. Desire Randall Sept. 27, 1787 (No. 72), Randall family. He d. Feb. 12, 1808. His wife m. 2d, Christopher Palmer Nov. 1, 1823. She d. Sept. 8, 1855.

WHEELER FAMILY.

CHILDREN:
187 ZERVIAH, b. Feb. 29, 1788, m. Amos Hull (No. 11), that family.
188 PEREZ, b. Sept. 17, 1789, m. Desire Wheeler (No. 253).
189 POLLY, b. July 17, 1791.
190 EUNICE, b. Jan. 4, 1794.
191 DUDLEY R., b. Sept. 14, 1796, m. Lydia Hewitt; 2d, Sally Maria Browning
192 JEDEDIAH R., b. Jan. 9, 1799, m. Delia B. Wheeler.
193 CYRUS, b. March 9, 1801, m. Lucy S. Browning; 2d, Eliza Dow.
194 LUCY ANN, b. Jan. 30, 1803.
195 WILLIAM R., b. Aug. 29, 1805, m. Emeline Stewart.
196 FANNY, b. April 17, 1808, d. June 29, 1809.

Col. Thomas Wheeler (No. 107) m. Esther Randall in 1780 (No. 69), that family. She d. Apr. 22, 1791; he d. Aug. 26, 1824.

CHILDREN:
197 ESTHER, b. in 1781, m. Amos Hull in 1803 (No. 11), that family.
198 MARTHA, b. March 17, 1787, m. Cyrus Williams (No. 299), that family.
199 DEA. CHARLES, b. Sept. 20, 1789, m. Rebecca Williams (No. 302), that family.

Robert Wheeler (No. 111) m. Bridget, daughter of Hosea Wheeler, Nov. 13, 1796 (No. 89), Wheeler family. Mrs. Wheeler d. Feb. 15, 1814. He m. 2d, Sophia Smead of Greenfield, Mass., Jan. 8, 1815. He d. Jan. 18, 1863. Mrs. Sophia d. Apr. 1, 1843.

CHILDREN:
200 ROBERT, b. Nov. 13, 1802, m. Lucy Palmer Miner March 24, 1831 (No. 300), that family.

CHILDREN BY SECOND MARRIAGE:
201 SOLOMAN S., b. Oct. 31, 1815, m. Desire B. Miner (No. 301), that family, Sept. 10, 1840.
202 BRIDGET, b. July 10, 1818, m. David Allen Aug. 18, 1840.
203 SOPHIA T., b. July 31, 1821; she perished on the steamer Lexington, burned on Long Island Sound Jan. 13, 1840, aged 18 years.
204 CLARISSA, b. Oct. 2, 1823, m. John T. Morton April 28, 1842.
205 HARRIET, b. March 2, 1826, m. Franklin H. Miner; 2d, Edward Barney.

Thomas Wheeler (No. 131), m. Rebecca Wheeler (No. 169), Wheeler family Mar. 14, 1805; she m. 2d, Stephen L. Avery Dec. 1, 1815 (No. 202), that family.

CHILD:
206 LUCY P., b. Jan. 25, 1806, m. Dr. Thomas P. Wattles.

Isaac Wheeler (No. 134) m. Hannah Holmes (No. 139), that family, March 20, 1790; she d. in 1808. He m. 2d, Olive Burdick March, 1810; he d. May 11, 1856; 2d wife d. Dec. 8, 1873.

CHILDREN:
207 HANNAH, b. June 4, 1791, m. William Wright.
208 ISAAC, b. Sept. 25, 1793, d. unmarried.
209 JOHN HOLMES, b. Nov. 6, 1795, m. Esther H. Buddington Nov. 22, 1821.
210 GEORGE WASHINGTON, b. Jan. 23, 1798, m. Eliza Baldwin.

211 PITTS D., b. April 7, 1802, m. Rebecca Roberts.
212 HOMER HOLMES, b. Nov. 27, 1803, m. 1st, Mary Ann Roberts; 2d, Luretta Jeffereys; 3d, Augusta Miner; 4th, Frances S. Wheeler (No. 245).
213 MARTHA ANN, b. Oct. 1, 1805, m. Henry Stanton Burdick April 4, 1828.

CHILDREN BY SECOND MARRIAGE:

214 NANCY LORD, b. Jan. 3, 1811, m. Samuel Stanton (No. 102), that family.
215 THOMAS JEFFERSON, b. Jan. 9, 1812, m. Amelia Chesebrough, Oct. 9, 1843 (No. 405), that family; m. 2d, Sophia P. Chesebrough July 11, 1856 (No. 374), that family; m. 3d, Almira Phillips March 2, 1879; m. 4th, Mary (Denison) Collins June 8, 1813.
216 ELIZABETH DENISON, b. Oct. 20, 1813.
217 STILES DENISON, b. March 13, 1815, m. Sarah Elizabeth Briggs March 12, 1846.
218 CALVIN, b. Oct. 21, 1816, d. young.
219 HARRIET SOPHIA, b. Sept. 12, 1817, d. June 18, 1834.
220 WILLIAM NELSON, b. March 11, 1819, m. Susan Wilcox Oct. 31, 1843.
221 MARY ANN, b. Nov. 19, 1820.
222 EMILY M., b. Sept. 2, 1822.
223 SARAH MARIA, b. April 3, 1824.
224 FRANCES ALMIRA, b. Feb. 28, 1826, m. Robert R. Mattison Jan. 1, 1846.

Peleg Wheeler (No. 138) m. Eunice Utter; he d. in 1858.

CHILDREN:

225 PELEG, b. ———.
226 ROSWELL, b. ———.
227 PRENTICE, b. ———, d. young.
228 PRENTICE, b. ———.
229 ALBERT, b. ———.
230 CYNTHIA, b. ———.
231 GILBERT, b. ———.
232 JERUSHA, b. ———.
233 LEONARD, b. ———.

Timothy S. Wheeler (No. 139) m. Lucy Grant Dec. 12, 1796 (No. 52), that family.

CHILDREN:

234 SALLY, b. June 26, 1798, m. Benjamin M. Carr Nov. 13, 1817.
235 LUCY A., b. July 29, 1800, d. in Oct., 1800.
236 EUNICE G., b. Aug. 23, 1801, m. Noyes Wells Kenyon May 16, 1817.
237 ESTHER COLE, b. May 15, 1804, d. Aug. 12, 1887.
238 JOSEPH SWAN, b. Sept. 23, 1807, m. Hannah Burdick, 1830.
239 LUCY GRANT, b. Feb. 20, 1811.
240 ADELINE, b. Oct. 28, 1814, m. Welcome C. Burdick in 1836.
241 NOYES DENISON, b. Jan. 31, 1818, m. Susan S. Wilbur Nov. 23, 1844.
242 MARY ELIZA, b. July 17, 1822, m. John Segar Champlin, 1817.

Charles P. Wheeler (No. 146) m. Nancy Hewitt June 8, 1795 (No. 199), that family. He d. June 9, 1888; she d. Aug. 20, 1874.

CHILDREN:

243 CHARLES P., b. Dec. 19, 1818, d. March 4, 1840.
244 ANN E., b. May 31, 1821, m. Joseph P. Aylesworth.
245 FRANCES S., b. July 20, 1823, m. Homer Wheeler Oct. 5, 1856, (No. 212).
246 ISAAC A., b. Dec. 7, 1825, d. Jan. 15, 1833.
247 JAMES P., b. Jan. 8, 1827, m. Sarah J. Keeney May 30, 1860.
248 OLIVER W., b. March 26, 1830, m. Antoinette Norton.

WHEELER FAMILY.

249 CAROLINE M., b. May 21, 1832.
250 IRVING A., b. June 19, 1835, m. Frances Julia Edgecomb Dec. 15, 1857.
251 ARTHUR J., b. June 30, 1837, d. April 24, 1842.
252 WARREN A., b. July 16, 1841.

Col. Nathan Wheeler (No. 163) m. Desire Wheeler (No. 112), Nov. 20, 1791, both of North Stonington, Conn. He d. July 15, 1829, aged 56 years; she d. Nov., 1839.

CHILDREN:

253 DESIRE, b. Oct. 8, 1792, m. Perez Wheeler (No. 188).
254 GEORGE, b. March 2, 1795, m. Thankful Randall.
255 NATHAN, b. May 14, 1797, m. Lydia Sheffield.
256 BRIDGET, b. May 9, 1799, m. George Hewitt (No. 206), that family.
257 GILES, b. May 9, 1801, m. Hannah A. Avery.
258 DELIA B., b. Aug. 28, 1803, m. Jedediah Wheeler (No. 192).
259 CHARLES, b. Sept. 3, 1805, d. aged 20 years.
260 EMMA, b. Jan. 4, 1807, d. unmarried.
261 REBECCA, b. Feb. 17, 1809, m. Henry Clinton Brown, M. D.
262 CALVIN, b. Jan. 22, 1812, d. unmarried.
263 BILLINGS, b. April 4, 1815, m. Anna Williams (No. 350), that family. He m. 2d wife, Harriet Rogers of Brooklyn, New York.

Asa Wheeler (No. 164) m. Polly Brown in 1796.

CHILDREN:

264 LUKE, b. March 16, 1797, d. April 11, 1855.
265 MARY, b. June 27, 1800, m. Roswell R. Avery (No. 204), that family.
266 EDE DENISON, b. Oct. 22, 1803, m. Charles G. Avery (No. 205), that family.
267 SAMUEL B., b. Dec. 23, 1805, m. Delia Avery; 2d, Mary Ellen Baldwin.
268 FANNY S., b. Aug. 4, 1807, m. Alfred Avery (No. 196), that family.
269 MARTHA, b. 1810, m. Charles G. Sisson May 11, 1829 (No. 54).
270 LYDIA, b. Oct. 29, 1813, m. William Johnson Jan. 8, 1829.
271 LUCINDA, b. Oct. 23, 1817, m. Sanford Brown.

Hosea Wheeler (No. 165) m. Nancy or Anna Brown Oct. 31, 1799, (No. 287), Lynn Brown family; m. 2d, Mercy Gardiner (No. 147), Wheeler family.

CHILDREN:

272 ESTHER, b. Oct. 20, 1800, m. Daniel Bentley (No. 32), that family.
273 SMITH, b. Sept. 1, 1802.
274 RANDALL, b. Aug. 18, 1804.
275 NANCY, b. Sept. 23, 1809, m. Ezra Langworthy, Sept. 12, 1835.
276 HOSEA, b. June 17, 1812.

Ephraim Wheeler (No. 170) m. Sabra Slack Jan. 15, 1815; m. 2d, Bridget Ayer, Oct. 8, 1829; m. 3d, Hannah Miner Nov. 22, 1835.

CHILD BY SECOND MARRIAGE:

277 EPHRAIM, b. Jan. 3, 1831, m. Elizabeth Coates Dec. 29, 1852.

CHILD BY THIRD MARRIAGE:

278 ELLEN, b. ———, m. George Frink.

Russell Wheeler (No. 171) m. Esther Hull Oct. 1, 1827 (No. 31), Hull family. He d. July 8, 1856; she d. March 7, 1858.

CHILDREN:

279 RUSSEL L., b. June 23, 1830, m. Mary M. Conklin; 2d, Florence D. Thomas.
280 MARTHA, b. Aug. 4, 1840, m. Jacob Best Murray June 20, 1855.
281 ANN ELIZABETH, b. August 4, 1840, d. Oct. 26, 1842.

Perez Wheeler (No. 188) m. Desire Wheeler (No. 253) Feb. 10, 1811. They lived in Stonington, Conn. He d. Oct. 8, 1867; she d. Jan. 26, 1870.

CHILDREN:

282 ROBERT, b. Dec. 24, 1811, d. July 29, 1839, unmarried.
283 MARY ANN, b. Aug. 7, 1814, m. John Denison Brown.
284 THOMAS SPENCER, b. Oct. 15, 1815, m. Susan Baldwin (No. 96), that family.
285 EZRA, b. March 11, 1818, m. Mary Hannah Randall (No. 125), that family.
286 EDWIN P., b. March 9, 1820, d. March 15, 1828.
287 CYRUS, b. Oct. 15, 1822, m. Marian E. Adams Nov. 8, 1844.
288 HARRIET ATWOOD, b. June 19, 1825, m. John Pitts Williams (No. 411), that family.
289 JANE MARIA, b. June 5, 1828, d. Dec. 3, 1828.
290 NATHAN G., b. Sept. 18 1829 m. Mary Elizabeth Wheeler June 18, 1872.
291 LUCY, b. July 13, 1832.
292 REBECCA JANE, b. Sept. 1, 1836, d. March 31, 1842.

Maj. Dudley R. Wheeler (No. 191) m. 1st, Lydia Hewitt, Dec. 1, 1818 (No. 184), Hewitt family. Mrs. Wheeler d. Sept. 27, 1826. He m. 2d, Sally Maria Browning March 4, 1828 (No. 71), Browning family. He d. June 19, 1888, aged 92 years.

NOTE.—Major Dudley R. Wheeler (No. 191) was one of the most prominent and successful merchants of North Stonington, accumulating a large fortune from which he gave liberally for his town and the church. His memory will ever be perpetuated through the benevolence of his children, Edgar, Jennie and Dwight Wheeler, in the fine and substantial granite library and school building now in process of erection in their native village of North Stonington, Conn.

CHILDREN:

293 LOUISE, b. Oct. 19, 1819.
294 DUDLEY, b. March 4, 1821.
295 CHAUNCEY, b. Nov. 30, 1823.
296 LYDIA ANN, b. Sept. 26, 1825, m. Warren Newton in 1851.

CHILDREN BY SECOND MARRIAGE:

297 HENRY DWIGHT, b. June 22, 1830.
298 CHARLES H., b. April 27, 1832.
299 EDWARD E., b. Feb. 20, 1836, d. Jan. 29, 1837.
300 SARAH JANE, b. Nov. 5, 1839.
301 MARIA, b. Aug. 22, 1842, d. Nov. 27, 1842.
302 EDGAR HOWARD, b. May 25, 1844.

Jedediah R. Wheeler (No. 192) m. Delia B. Wheeler (No. 258) March 15, 1821. He d. Sept. 22, 1888; she d. July 28, 1884.

CHILDREN:

303 DELIA, b. July 13, 1822, m. John A. Randall March 9, 1843.
304 JEDEDIAH R., b. Aug. 26, 1824, m. Theresa H. Wheeler (No. 329).
305 EMMA SURVIAH, b. March 2, 1828.

WHEELER FAMILY. 649

306 NATHAN P., b. Jan. 22, 1830, d. in Brooklyn, N. Y., April 24, 1884.
307 PEREZ, b. July 15, 1833, d. March 5, 1852, aged 18 years.
308 BILLINGS, b. Sept. 8, 1835.
309 HENRY, b. April 30, 1838.
310 ANN ELIZABETH, b. July 30, 1840, d. June 7, 1841.
311 CALVIN, b. Sept. 30, 1842, d. Feb. 16, 1845.
312 ELLEN, b. Dec., 1846, m. James Case.

Cyrus Wheeler (No. 193) m. Lucy S. Browning March 24, 1822 (No. 69), that family; m. 2d, Eliza Dow Dec. 17, 1833. He d. in Ohio Oct. 5, 1884.

CHILDREN BY FIRST MARRIAGE:

313 LUCY ANN, b. Dec. 27, 1822, m. James Squires June 22, 1852.
314 CYRUS TRUMAN, b. Sept. 24, 1824, d. unmarried in California Jan. 17, 1892.
315a SARAH PHELPS, b. Sept. 30, 1826, m. Horace C. Starr July 5, 1849.

CHILDREN BY SECOND MARRIAGE:

315b MARY MELINDA, b. at Norwich, N. Y., Aug. 5, 1835, d. 1836.
315c ELIZA DOW, b. Dec. 15, 1836, m. John Leavitt Dec. 15, 1864; she m. 2d, John Mansfield in 1883.
315d ANNETTE ESTELLE, b. Feb. 2, 1839, m. Carlos M. Fisher Oct. 10, 1883.
315e ANDALUCIA RHODES, b. at Norwich, N. Y., May 11, 1841.

William R. Wheeler (No. 195) m. Emeline Stewart Dec. 16, 1830 (No. 52), that family. He d. Feb. 15, 1851.

ONE DAUGHTER:

316 SARAH E., b. Aug. 20, 1832, m. Thomas Clark June 20, 1855.

Dea. Charles Wheeler (No. 199) m. Rebecca Williams Jan. 26, 1812 (No. 302), that family.

CHILDREN:

317 MARTHA, b. Oct. 18, 1812, d. unmarried March 17, 1880.
318 PHEBE, b. July 5, 1815, m. Albert Avery (No. 223), that family.
319 THOMAS, b. May 29, 1817, m. Lydia B. Pomeroy (No. 11), that family.
320 JOANNA BROWN, b. March 29, 1819, m. Albert L. Avery (No. 223), that family.
321 CHARLES THEODORE, b. Aug. 17, 1822, m. Lydia Cooley Dec. 9, 1859.

Robert Wheeler (No. 200) m. Lucy Palmer Miner March 24, 1831 (No. 300), that family.

CHILDREN:

322 JAMES EVERETT, b. ———, d. in 1862 in the Civil war.
323 PHEBE ESTHER, b. ———, d. in 1862, unmarried.
323a EDWIN ———, b. June 17, 1844, m. Ella Marian Welch of New Haven, Conn.

Joseph Swan Wheeler (No. 238) m. Hannah Burdick in 1830.

CHILDREN:

324 MARY J., b. June, 1832.
324a ALBERT G., b. July, 1834.
325 LUCY A., b. April, 1836.
326 ANN E., b. Oct., 1838.
327 HENRY J., b. April, 1840.
328 JAMES S., b. Sept., 1843.

Giles Wheeler (No. 257) m. Hannah A. Avery, daughter of Peter Avery of Groton Dec. 26, 1825. They lived in North Stonington.

CHILDREN:

329 THERESA H., b. ———, m. Jedediah R. Wheeler, Jr. (No. 304).
330 CHARLES N., b. ———, m. Eleanor Tracy.
331 ADELINE, b. ———, m. Benjamin Gage Berry.
332 HENRY, b. ———, d. young.
333 EUNICE, b. ———.

Dea. Samuel B. Wheeler (No. 267) m. 1st, Delia Avery (No. 219), that family, Nov. 27, 1827; m. 2d, Mary Ellen Baldwin of Preston, Conn., Feb. 11, 1879 (No. 98), that family.

CHILDREN BY FIRST MARRIAGE:

334 DEAN AVERY, b. Feb. 20, 1835, d. young.
335 GEORGE ANSON, b. April 17, 1831, d. March 7, 1850, at Jacksonville, Fla.

George Wheeler (No. 254) m. Nov. 13, 1817, Thankful S. Randall (No. 99), Randall family. He d. Dec. 6, 1869; she d. April 19, 1863.

CHILDREN:

336 GEORGE F. b. July 8, 1819, d. unmarried.
337 HORACE C., b. Aug. 20, 1821, m. Ann Maria Allen.
338 EUNICE R., b. Jan. 4, 1825, m. Russell Burdick.

John Wheeler (No. 20) m. Zerviah Fanning Oct. 28, 1727. She d. Feb. 26, 1791, aged 85 years.

CHILD:

339 MARTHA, b. Dec. 31, 1728, m. John Denison (No. 113), that family; 2d, Stephen Billings.

Jonathan Wheeler (No. 21) m. Esther Denison (No. 157), that family, March 1, 1732, both of Stonington, Conn. He d. Oct. 8, 1790; she d. Mar. 18, 1790.

CHILDREN:

340 ESTHER, b. Dec. 27, 1732, m. Elisha Williams (No. 51), that family.
341 PRUDENCE, b. Dec. 20, 1734, m. Joshua Holmes (No. 31), that family.
342 JONATHAN, b. Jan. 20, 1737, m. Priscilla Lester April 29, 1756.
343 RICHARD, b. July 16, 1739, m. Silence Burrows.
344 THANKFUL, b. Jan. 1, 1742, d. Oct. 23, 1775.
346 JOHN, b. Aug. 6, 1744, m. Mary Miner.
347 DAVID, b. June 13, 1747, m. Abigail Miner.
348 CONTENT, b. Aug. 30, 1749, m. Joseph Palmer; m. 2d, Henry Hewitt (No. 69), that family.
349 ZERVIAH, b. Oct. 3, 1752, m. Allen York (No. 40), that family.
350 PATIENCE, b. Feb. 6, 1756, m. Joseph Page in 1779 (No. 17), that family.
351 JOSHUA, b. Dec. 13, 1763, m. Molly Turner June 7, 1789.

Richard Wheeler (No. 22) m. Anna Pellet of Canterbury, Conn, Aug. 25, 1734. He d. April 10, 1749.

WHEELER FAMILY.

CHILDREN:
352 PATIENCE, b. April 8, 1745, m. William Swan.
353 ASA, b. May 12, 1746, m. Susan Hull.
354 JOSEPH, b. Jan. 23, 1747, m. Prudence Palmer.

Jonathan Wheeler (No. 342) m. Priscilla Lester (No. 444), Williams family, April 29, 1756, both of Stonington, Conn. He d. Jan. 28, 1807; she d. Dec. 20, 1803.

CHILDREN:
355 LESTER, b. July 24, 1757, m. Eunice Bailey.
356 JONATHAN, b. Aug. 19, 1760, m. Martha Stanton.
357 ELISHA, b. June 3, 1764, m. Lois York (No. 79), that family.
358 ELEAZER, b. Nov. 16, 1771, m. Cynthia Ingraham.
359 MARTHA, b. Oct. 29, 1774, m. John York (No. 85), that family.

Richard Wheeler (No. 343) m. Silence Burrows Dec. 24, 1760 (No. 106), that family. They lived in Stonington, Conn. He d. Aug. 30, 1799; she d. Dec. 18, 1820.

CHILDREN:
360 ESTHER, b. May 23, 1761, m. Stephen Breed (No. 62), that family.
361 NATHANIEL, b. Jan. 20, 1763, m. Prudence Breed.
362 RICHARD, b. April 30, 1769, m. Anna Gallup; 2d, Mary Hewitt.
363 SILAS, b. Dec. 29, 1771, m. Mary Thompson.
364 JESSE, b. Jan. 21, 1775, d. young.
365 HANNAH, b. Aug. 6, 1778, m. William Holmes (No. 73), that family.

John Wheeler (No. 346) m. Mary Miner Dec. 22, 1763 (No. 148), that family, both of Stonington, Conn.

CHILDREN:
366 HANNAH, b. Aug. 20, 1764.
367 JOHN, b. March 20, 1765, m. Ann Borodel Denison.
368 PRUDENCE, b. Oct. 16, 1767, d. unmarried.
369 ELIAS, b. Jan. 1, 1772.
370 JAMES, b. Aug. 16, 1777, m. ———.

David Wheeler (No. 347) m. Abigail Miner July 11, 1769 (No. 150), that family, both of Stonington, Conn.

CHILDREN:
371 DAVID, b. Jan. 11, 1770.
372 MINER, b. July 5, 1771.
373 DENISON, b. Jan. 26, 1774.

Joshua Wheeler (No. 351) m. Molly Turner June 7, 1787.

CHILDREN:
374 ESTHER, b. March 30, 1783, m. Jonathan Knapp; 2d wife.
375 JOSHUA, b. March 30, 1791, d. unmarried.
376 HANNAH, b. 1792, m. Jonathan Knapp.
377 JOHN T., b. Oct. 8, 1793, m. Martha H. Lewis.
378 BENJAMIN, b. in 1795.
379 ERASTUS, b. in 1799, d. young.
380 IRA, b. ———, m. Amelia A. Williams Jan. 9, 1825.
381 STEPHEN AVERY, b. May 2, 1806, m. Lucy Bailey May 18, 1831.

Joseph Wheeler (No. 354) m. Prudence Palmer Sept. 18, 1774 (No. 530), that family. She d. March 6, 1790, aged 38 yrs.

CHILDREN:

382 PRUDENCE, b. April 18, 1775, m. David Swan.
383 JOSEPH, b. Dec. 29, 1776, m. Sarah Mabbet; 2d, Lucy Stanton (No. 460), Stanton family.
384 FANNY, b. June 25, 1778.
385 ASHER, b. Dec. 22, 1779, m. Eunice Williams.
386 EDWARD, b. April 7, 1782, m. Martha Mabbet, sister of Sarah.
387 SAMUEL, b. Sept. 14, 1784, m. Rebecca Prentice (No. 70), of Prentice family.
388 SANFORD, b. Jan. 17, 1787, m. Jerushy Denison.
389 CODDINGTON, b. Aug. 6, 1789, d. unmarried.

Lester Wheeler (No. 355) m. Eunice Bailey, daughter of David Bailey and Eunice Brown, Feb. 9, 1774. They lived in Stonington, Conn. He d. May 15, 1835; she d. June 29, 1837.

CHILDREN:

390 PRISCILLA, b. Aug. 23, 1774.
391 DAVID, b. April 4, 1776, m. Zerviah York (No. 94), that family.
392 EUNICE, b. July 17, 1778, m. Lodowick Lewis Dec. 28, 1793.
393 JONATHAN, b. Nov. 11, 1779, m. Nancy Thompson.
394 WILLIAM, b. Jan. 21, 1782, m. Wealthy Turner.
395 PHINEAS, b. April 24, 1784, m. Wealthy Maxon.
396 JESSE, b. May 28, 1786, m. Nancy Peckham.
397 CHRISTOPHER, b. July 10, 1788, m. Orinda Gallup.
398 HULDAH, b. April 2, 1791, m. Nehemiah M. Gallup (No. 254), that family.
399 MATILDA, b. Aug. 17, 1794, m. William Bailey, Apr. 28, 1812.
400 ANNA, b. Aug. 23, 1798, m. Horatio G. Lewis Nov. 19, 1820.

Jonathan Wheeler (No. 356) m. Martha Stanton Dec. 29, 1789, both of Stonington, Conn. He d. Feb. 9, 1841; she d. Sept. 17, 1807.

CHILDREN:

401 PATIENCE, b. Oct. 19, 1790, d. unmarried.
402 ZERVIAH, b. June 1, 1792, d. unmarried.
403 JONATHAN, b. June 1, 1794, m. Anna Breed.
404 MERCY, b. July 26, 1796, d. unmarried.
405 STANTON, b. April 1, 1798, d. unmarried.
406 GILBERT, b. July 25, 1799, m. Esther Ann Potter; 2d, Angelina Byron Wood.
407 LOIS, b. 1803, d. unmarried.
408 MARTHA, b. March 31, 1807, m. Thomas York (No. 190), that family; 2d, Baxter Grey.

Elisha Wheeler (No. 357) m. Lois York March 30, 1786 (No. 79), York family.

CHILDREN:

409 REUBEN, b. June 15, 1788, m. ——— Lewis.
410 ALLEN, b. May 25, 1793, m. Jemima Wheeler (No. 422), Wheeler family.

Eleazer Wheeler (No. 358) m. Cynthia Ingraham Dec. 12, 1790.

WHEELER FAMILY. 653

CHILDREN:
411 CYNTHIA, b. Dec. 21, 1792.
412 ELEAZER, b. Jan. 27, 1794, m. Lucinda Morgan Aug. 1, 1830.
413 PATTY, b. Feb. 7, 1796.
414 DUDLEY D., b. Feb. 25, 1798, m. Nancy Wheeler Sept. 3, 1820.
415 PRISCILLA, b. Jan. 25, 1800.
416 LUCY, b. Feb. 4, 1802.
417 BRIDGET, b. Dec. 1, 1805.

Nathaniel Wheeler (No. 361) m. Prudence Breed Jan. 31, 1790 (No. 64), Breed family, both of Stonington, Conn.

CHILDREN:
419 JESSE, b. Sept. 2, 1792.
420 SILAS, b. Oct. 30, 1798.

Richard Wheeler (No. 362) m. 1st, Anna Gallup Feb. 13, 1794 (No. 144), that family. She d. Jan. 22, 1810; m. 2d, Mary Hewitt May 25, 1811 (No. 116), that family. They lived in Stonington, Conn. He d. Feb. 7, 1847; she d. Jan. 22, 1850.

CHILDREN BY FIRST MARRIAGE:
421 ELAM, b. Oct. 3, 1795, d. March 27, 1804.
422 JEMIMA, b. March 17, 1800, m. Allen Wheeler (No. 410), Feb. 28, 1821.
423 HANNAH, b. Aug. 30, 1804, d. April 8, 1805.
424 LYDIA ESTHER, b. April 10, 1806, d. May 23, 1834.
425 RICHARD EDMUND, b. Feb. 29, 1808, d. Oct. 17, 1808.

CHILDREN BY SECOND MARRIAGE:
427 HANNAH S., b. July 26, 1812, m. Giles C. Smith Jan. 21, 1836 (No. 109), that family.
428 MARY, b. March 27, 1814, m. Charles G. Hewitt Jan. 18, 1843 (No. 208), Hewitt family.
429 RICHARD A., b. Jan. 29, 1817, m. Frances Mary Avery Jan. 12, 1843 (No. 214), Avery family. Mrs. Wheeler d. Sept. 3, 1855. He m. 2d, Lucy Ann Noyes Nov. 5, 1856 (No. 365), Noyes family.

Silas Wheeler (No. 363) m. Mary Thompson (No. 25), that family, Nov. 12, 1799, both of Stonington, Conn.

CHILDREN:
431 RICHARD, b. June 12, 1800, m. Cynthia Gallup (No. 23), that family.
432 HIRAM, b. Feb. 9, 1805, m. Mary Wheeler (No. 506), Wheeler family.

John Wheeler (No. 367) m. Ann Borodel Denison July 8, 1790 (No. 229), that family, both of Stonington, Conn.

CHILDREN:
433 JOHN D., b. June 10, 1791, m. Lucy Prentice Dec. 11, 1814 (No. 86).
434 DANIEL, b. July 14, 1793, m. Margaret Hewitt.
435 ERASTUS, b. Oct. 16, 1795, d. Sept. 27, 1881, unmarried.
436 NANCY, b. March 27, 1798, m. Russell Williams (No. 477), that family.
437 PRUDENCE, b. June 18, 1800, d. Sept. 3, 1867, unmarried.
438 MARY ESTHER, b. Nov. 20, 1802, m. Hubbard Burrows Feb. 17, 1829 (No. 149), that family.
439 ELIAS H., b. April 30, 1807, m. Mary Leeds; 2d, Mary Bein.

440 EMILY A., b. Feb. 26, 1814, m. Charles Burrows (No. 155); 2d. Dea. Albert Edgcomb Oct. 20, 1867.
441 EUNICE H., b. Aug. 8, 1816, m. Palmer Chesebrough Feb. 17, 1841 (No. 217),Chesebrough family.

John T. Wheeler (No. 377) m. Martha H. Lewis Dec. 25, 1817.

CHILDREN:

442 JOHN D., b. Dec. 29, 1820, m. Wealthy A. Packer July 2, 1849.
443 MARTHA E., b. April 15, 1823, m. Dr. Alfred Coates.

Stephen A. Wheeler (No. 381) m. Lucy Bailey May 18, 1831.

CHILDREN:

444 MARY, b. March 13, 1833, m. Edward Hewitt.
445 CHARLES A., b. Oct. 4, 1836, m. Sarah Riley.
446 MARGARET, b. Feb. 17, 1838, m. Mason Crary Hill.

David Wheeler (No. 391) m. Zerviah York June 19, 1796 (No. 94), York family, both of Stonington, Conn. He d. Aug. 29, 1862; she d. July 7, 1865.

CHILDREN:

447 CONTENT, b. Sept. 30, 1797, m. Elisha Gallup March 21, 1816 (No. 257), Gallup family.
448 DAVID L., b. Feb. 11, 1800.
449 EUNICE, b. Nov. 12, 1801, d. unmarried.
450 SAXTON M., b. March 14, 1804, m. Nancy Lanphere; 2d Rebecca Lanphere.
451 ZERVIAH, b. May 6, 1806, m. Silas Holmes (No. 163), that family.
452 RUSSELL A., b. Nov. 6, 1808, m. Cornelia Clow May 17, 1849.
453 MELISSA, b. Feb. 14, 1811, m. Edward Holmes (No. 166), that family.
454 ELAM B. b. Nov. 21, 1813, m. Mary Clark Feb. 13, 1843; Josephine West.
455 EMELINE, b. March 19, 1816, d. young.
456 WILLIAM F., b. Oct. 19, 1819, m. Theresa M. Brown Jan. 1, 1868.

Jonathan Wheeler (No. 393) m. Nancy Thompson in 1801; m. 2d, Mrs. Mary Murphy, 1828.

CHILDREN:

457 NANCY, b. May 17, 1802, m. Dudley D. Wheeler (No. 414).
458 WILLIAM LESTER, b. Jan. 28, 1804, m. Mary Hallam Sept. 28, 1826.
459 CELIA, b. March 7, 1805.
460 EDWIN B., b. Aug. 9, 1806, m. Mary Ann Lewis Sept. 3, 1826.
461 ADELINE, b. March 27, 1808.
462 ELIZA, b. Dec. 17, 1809.
463 MAY, b. Oct. 22, 1811.
464 JOHN L. THOMPSON, b. Aug. 24, 1813.
465 ALEXANDER F., b. Sept. 24, 1815.
466 ISABELLE, b. May 16, 1817.
467 JAMES H., b. March 19, 1819.
468 JONATHAN J., b. Feb. 18, 1822.
469 ASA, b. and d. in infancy.

William Wheeler (No. 394) m. Wealthy Turner in 1800.

CHILDREN:

470 ELIZA ANN, b. in 1802, m. Benjamin F. Williams Sept. 26, 1828 (No. 118), Williams family.
471 WILLIAM E., b. June 16, 1807, m. Pedee Heath Aug. 24, 1831.

WHEELER FAMILY.

Phineas Wheeler (No. 385) m. Wealthy Maxon Feb. 24, 1810. He d. Aug. 15, 1831; she d. Jan. 1, 1851.

CHILD:

472 PHINEAS M., b. July 15, 1817, m. Harriet Swan; 2d, Sarah Woodmancy.

Jesse Wheeler (No. 396) m. Nancy Peckham May 30, 1811. He d. Jan. 16, 1852; she d. March 9, 1885.

CHILDREN:

473 STEPHEN HAZARD, b. March 6, 1812, m. Harriet Newell Williams.
474 ELISHA PACKER, b. Dec. 15, 1815, m. Emeline E. Clark.
475 JOHN OWEN, b. June 5, 1818.
476 THOMAS WILLIAM, b. Oct. 20, 1822, m. Emily Elizabeth Brown.

Christopher Wheeler (No. 397) m. Orinda Gallup March 19, 1812 (No. 256), that family.

CHILDREN:

477 EMELINE, b. Dec. 29, 1812, d. young.
478 CHRISTOPHER P., b. May 2, 1814, m. Mary C. Collins Jan. 20, 1840.
479 ELIZA ORINDA, b. Nov. 8, 1815.
480 CHARLES DENISON, b. Nov. 18, 1817, m. Mary Elizabeth Guild.
481 EMELINE ANN, b. Feb. 3, 1820.
482 WILLIAM COLLINS, b. Feb. 10, 1822.
483 ELIZABETH HARRIET, b. Nov. 22, 1823.
484 MARY ANN, b. Nov. 28, 1825.
485 DAVID MINER, b. Jan. 2, 1828.

Jonathan Wheeler (No. 403) m. Anna Breed June 21, 1819 (No. 103), that family. They lived in Stonington, Conn.

CHILDREN:

486 SARAH ANN, b. Jan. 3, 1821, m. Benjamin F. Stanton (No. 422), Stanton family.
487 JONATHAN ANDREW, b. Aug. 1, 1823, m. Lydia Larkham.
488 ESTHER D., b. Sept. 19, 1825.
489 OLIVER W., b. Oct. 23, 1827, m.
490 FANNY W., b. Feb. 1, 1830, m. Joseph F. Rindge April 10, 1854.
491 JAMES, b. May 27, 1832, d. young.
492 BENJAMIN S., b. May 20, 1833, m. Delia A. Fredenburg Nov. 12, 1858; 2d, Anna E. Major Jan. 22, 1870.
493 EMMA JANE, b. Sept. 4, 1835, m. John S. Heath.
494 HENRY EDWIN, b. March 17, 1838, m. Mary A. McFall Dec. 31, 1865.
495 HARRIET NEWELL, b. Aug. 31, 1840, d. unmarried.
496 ALBERT, b. Aug. 13, 1842.
497 MARTHA ELLA, b. April 14, 1845, d. unmarried.

Allen Wheeler (No. 410) m. Jemima A. Wheeler (No. 422), Feb. 28, 1821.

CHILDREN:

498 ANNA, b. June 24, 1822, m. J. Burrows Palmer July 4, 1843.
499 ALLEN, b. Aug. 8, 1823, m. Mary A. Coates Dec. 15, 1846.
500 ELISHA, b. Jan. 15, 1827, m. Mary J. Gallup Nov. 2, 1856.
501 RICHARD, b. Feb. 16, 1829, m. Lucy G. Bentley Oct. 29, 1850 (No. 51), that family.
502 HARRIET, b. Feb. 1, 1831, m. Edgar R. Palmer in 1857.
503 ELLEN C., b. April 13, 1833, m. Dr. Edwin C. Maine June 13, 1852; went west.
504 FRANCES ABBY, b. April 14, 1839, m. John S. Maine March 18, 1860.

Samuel Wheeler (No. 387) m. Rebecca Prentice (No. 70), in 1809; m. 2d, Mrs. Hannah (Heath) Havens. He d. March 24, 1852. Mrs. Rebecca d. Dec. 9, 1842.

CHILDREN:

505 SAMUEL PRENTICE, b. Sept. 12, 1810, m. Amanda M. Avery Nov. 22, 1838 (No. 225), that family.
506 MARY, b. June 1, 1812, m. Hiram Wheeler (No. 432).
507 REBECCA, b. Sept. 17, 1813, m. Joseph Davis Nov. 15, 1832.
508 JOSEPH, b. Oct. 20, 1815, m. Mary M. Swan May 23, 1843, daughter of Thomas W. Swan (No. 185), that family.
509 PHEBE, b. Dec. 8, 1817, m. Clark N. Whitford Sept. 9, 1843.
510 WARREN S., b. July 13, 1819, m. Phebe Gallup (No. 293), that family.
511 CODDINGTON, b. March 23, 1823, d. young.
512 PRUDENCE, b. Jan. 18, 1823, m. Giles Haley.
513 NELSON H., b. March 28, 1827, m. Melinda Gallup (No. 296), that family.

CHILD BY SECOND MARRIAGE:

514 HANNAH E., b. Feb. 3, 1846, m. George Wilcox.

Hiram Wheeler (No. 432) m. Mary Wheeler (No. 506), Feb. 17, 1832, both of Stonington, Conn.

CHILDREN:

515 HIRAM W., JR., b. ———, d. young man; unmarried.
516 SAMUEL A., b. ———, m. Martha Emma Green Sept. 30, 1862.
517 RALPH, b. May 14, 1843, m. Mrs. Helen M. Graves Feb. 28, 1884.
518 SILAS B., b. June 25, 1845, m. Mary A. Cooper Sept. 30, 1872.
519 MARY AUGUSTA, b. ———.

Thomas W. Wheeler (No. 476) m. Emily Elizabeth Brown (No. 259) that family, Nov. 7, 1844, daughter of Dea. Cyrus Brown. They lived in North Stonington.

CHILD:

520 NANCY MARY, b. Sept. 2, 1847, m. William Horace Hillard Dec. 3, 1878.

Gilbert Wheeler (No. 406) m. Esther Ann Potter Feb., 1829. He m. 2d, Angelina Byron Wood March 15, 1840.

CHILDREN BY FIRST MARRIAGE:

521 HARRIET ELIZABETH, b. Nov. 18, 1829.
522 HORACE NILES, b. Feb. 1, 1831, m. Margaret A. Havens June 21, 1853.
523 CAROLINE ARABELLA, b. Nov. 18, 1832, m. John F. Larkham April 10, 1854.
524 SARAH ELIZABETH, b. Oct. 5, 1834, m. William A. Green July 25, 1854.
525 ANNA AUGUSTA, b. Feb. 14, 1837, m. Charles A. Geer Feb. 8, 1856.

CHILDREN BY SECOND MARRIAGE:

526 CLINTON GILBERT, b. March 28, 1841, m. Fannie M. Beebe Nov. 26, 1866.
527 ADA ANGELINA, b. June 16, 1844, m. Albert P. Pendleton Sept. 20, 1870.
528 ADRIAN LORENZO, b. March 8, 1846.

Richard Wheeler (No. 431) m. Cynthia Gallup, Nov. 25, 1824. He d. Oct. 28, 1868.

WHEELER FAMILY.

CHILDREN:

529 LUCY M., b. Sept. 3, 1825.
530 CYNTHIA, b. Aug. 9, 1827, d. young.
531 NANCY I., b. Aug. 17, 1828, d. young.
532 DESIRE, b. Oct. 12, 1830, d. young.
533 EMILY, b. Oct. 27, 1832.
534 CHARLES T., b. Nov. 21, 1834.
535 JOHN G., b. June 10, 1837.
536 ELLEN I., b. Apr. 27, 1840.
537 HANNAH E., b. Aug. 1, 1842, d. young.
538 DELIA D., b. June 4, 1845.
539 ERASTUS D., b. Apr. 5, 1848.
540 JENNIE L., b. Oct. 8, 1851.

Dudley D. Wheeler (No. 414) m. Nancy Wheeler (No. 457), Sept. 3, 1820.

CHILDREN:

541 DUDLEY D., b. Apr. 29, 1821.
542 MARTHA A., b. May 3, 1822.
543 SALLY H., b. Oct. 5, 1823.
544 LUCY O., b. May 8, 1825.
545 WILLIAM L., b. Mar. 8, 1827.
546 MARY E., b. (twin).
547 PHEBE J., b. May 24, 1829.
548 CELIA M., b. Feb. 11, 1831.
549 LYDIA E., b. Dec. 21, 1832.
550 JOHN A., b. July 3, 1836.
551 LOUISA S., b. June 3, 1838.
552 CHAUNCEY P., b. July 3, 1840.

WILCOX FAMILY.

1. In 1638 the name of Edward Wilcox is found among the list of inhabitants of the Island of Aquidneck; he also had land at Manhattan. It is not known who he married, but there may have been a son,

>2 JOHN, and surely Daniel and Stephen, who had grants of land at Portsmouth, and Stephen was a freeman there in 1658.
>3 STEPHEN, b. about 1633, d. in 1690.
>4 DANIEL, b. ———, and m. Elizabeth Cook Nov. 28, 1661.

Stephen Wilcox (No. 3) m. in 1657 Hannah, daughter of Thomas and wife, Martha Hazard. Some time before 1669 he came to Westerly. He left six sons and one daughter when he died.

>5 EDWARD, b. about 1662 in Westerly, R. I., d. Nov. 5, 1715.
>6 THOMAS, b. at North Kingston, d. 1728.
>7 DANIEL, b. in Kingston.
>8 WILLIAM, b. ———.
>9 STEPHEN, b. ———.
>10 JEREMIAH, b. ———.
>11 HANNAH, b. ———, m. Samuel Clarke, son of Jeremiah, Jr., of Newport.

Edward Wilcox (No. 5) m. 1st, ——— Hazard, daughter of Robert and wife, Mary (Brownell) Hazard; was the ancestor of the Westerly and Charlestown, R. I., Wilcoxes.

>CHILDREN:
>12 MARY, b. ———, m. Joseph Lewis.
>13 HANNAH, b. ———, m. Ezekiel Gavitt.
>14 STEPHEN, b. ———. The ancestor of the Stephen Wilcox who has been the most liberal benefactor Westerly has ever had.
>15 EDWARD, b. ———.

Edward Wilcox (No. 5) m. 2d, May 1, 1698, Thomasin, daughter of Richard Stevens of Taunton. She was b. July 3, 1677.

>THEIR CHILDREN:
>16 SARAH, b. May 30, 1700.
>17 THOMAS, b. Feb. 18, 1702.
>18 HEZEKIAH, b. April 4, 1704.
>19 ELISHA, b. July 9, 1706.
>20 AMEY, b. Oct. 18, 1709.
>21 SUSANNAH, b. April 4, 1712.

Thomas Wilcox (No. 6) m. Martha, daughter of Robert and wife, Mary (Brownell) Hazard; she d. 1753.

WILCOX FAMILY.

CHILDREN:

22 ROBERT, b. ―――.
23 STEPHEN, b. ―――.
24 JEFFREY, b. ―――.
25 THOMAS, b. Oct. 24, 1693.
26 ABRAHAM, b. ―――.
27 GEORGE, b. ―――.
28 EDWARD, b. ―――.
29 HANNAH, b. ―――.

Daniel Wilcox (No. 7) m. in 1697 Mary Wordell, and in 1717 they were residents of Stonington, Conn. Dec. 8, 1727, he m. 2d, Mary Robeson.

CHILDREN:

30 STEPHEN, b. ―――.
31 DANIEL, b. ―――.
32 HEZEKIAH, b. ―――.

William Wilcox (No. 8) m. Jan. 25, 1698, Dorothy (No. 27), daughter of Moses and wife, Dorothy Gilbert Palmer, and granddaughter of Walter Palmer.

This family is the ancestor of the North Stonington Wilcox family. After the death of Mrs. Dorothy Palmer he m. 2d, Mrs. Abigail Palmer of Stonington April 1, 1754. He d. Dec. 27, 1757.

CHILDREN:

33 DOROTHY, b. Oct. 28, 1698.
34 ANNA, b. June 14, 1700.
35 WILLIAM, b. June 3, 1703, d. Dec. 27, 1757.
36 JEMIMA, b. July 21, 1705.
37 MARY, b. Dec. 1, 1709.
38 AMEY, b. July 7, 1711.
39 SARAH, b. Aug. 29, 1713.
40 NATHAN, b. Dec. 3, 1716.

Stephen Wilcox (No. 9) m. Elizabeth, daughter of John and wife, Elizabeth (Gorton) Crandall, in 1704.

CHILDREN:

41 STEPHEN, b. ―――.
42 ROBERT, b. ―――.
43 JOHN, b. ―――.

Jeremiah Wilcox (No. 10) m. Mary, daughter of Thomas and wife, Mary Mallett, of Newport, R. I.

Elisha Wilcox (No. 19) m., not known.

THEIR CHILDREN WERE:

44 EDWARD, b. Aug. 12, 1726.
45 ELISHA, b. July 11, 1728.
46 HEZEKIAH, b. Dec. 25, 1731.
47 THOMAS, b. July 9, 1733.
  Also two or three daughters.

William Wilcox (No. 35) m. Hannah Brown (No. 43), Brown family, March 24, 1725; she was b. Dec. 12, 1705.

CHILD:

48 HANNAH, b. Dec. 24, 1726, and d. young.

Mrs. Hannah Wilcox d. Jan. 4, 1727, and Mr. Wilcox m. 2d, Elizabeth Brown June 5, 1727.

CHILDREN:

49 PRUDENCE, b. March 6, 1728, m. Samuel Frink July 27, 1756 (No. 77), that family.
50 NATHAN, b. April 4, 1730.
51 WILLIAM, b. March 20, 1732.
52 JOHN, b. July 16, 1734.
53 DOROTHY, b. Sept. 16, 1736.
54 HANNAH, b. Nov. 12, 1738, m. Oliver Bentley March 16, 1758.

Hezekiah Wilcox (No. 46) m. Hannah Parker before 1758. He d. in 1819, buried at Watch Hill.

CHILDREN:

54a AMEY, b. ———, m. Capt. John West, 1765 (No. 22).
55 HEZEKIAH, b. in 1758, m. Patty or Martha Whittlesey.
56 MARTHA, b. in 1760, m. Tristam Dickens.
57 JESSE, b. Dec. 29, 1762.
58 PELEG, b. ———, m. Lucy Whittlesey.
59 DANIEL, b. ———, m. Prudy Wilcox.
60 SUSANNAH, b. ———, m. Braddock Hall.
61 SYLVESTER, b. ———, m. Marvel Burtch.
62 THOMAS, b. ———, m. Abby Pendleton.
63 ASA, b. ———, m. Abby Dunbar.
64 SAMUEL, b. ———, m. Prudy Grant.
65 ABIGAIL, b. ———, d. young.

Stephen Wilcox (No. 30) m. Susannah, daughter of Caleb Pendleton.

CHILDREN:

66 ELIZABETH, b. July 23, 1725.
67 CALEB, b. June 8, 1727.
68 MARY, b. Jan. 21, 1729.

Capt. Jesse Wilcox (No. 57) of Westerly, R. I., m. Nancy or Ann Pendleton Dec. 9, 1784.

CHILDREN:

69 SUSANNAH, b. Dec. 16, 1785, m. Absalom Miner, son of William Miner.
70 NANCY, b. March 15, 1787, m. 1st, Joseph Sheffield; 2d, Samuel Taylor.
71 JESSE JR., b. Nov. 23, 1788, m. 1st, Sally Arden; 2d, Rebecca Miner Dec. 22, 1822.
72 ABIGAIL, b. Sept. 12, 1790, m. Lyman Hall, lived at Lotteryville.
73 PHINEAS, b. Nov. 22, 1792, m. Mercy Taylor.
74 LODOWICK, b. Sept. 18, 1794, m. Fanny Cottrell.

Mrs. Nancy Wilcox d. Sept. 2, 1796, aged 35 yrs, and May 6, 1798, Mr. Jesse Wilcox m. Mehitable, daughter of Ebenezer and wife, Iantha (Mason) Wilcox.

WILCOX FAMILY 661

CHILDREN:
75 IANTHA, b. Nov. 3, 1799, m. Moses Sawyer.
76 EBENEZER, b. June 30, 1801, m. Caroline Cottrell.
77 ELISHA, b. Nov. 13, 1803, m. Mary Denison (No. 482), that family.
78 MASON, b. Nov. 13, 1806, m. Louisa Brown.
79 ELNATHAN F., b. April 2, 1808, m. 1st, Mehitable Wilcox; 2d, Julia Denison (No. 490), that family.
80 SILAS, b. Dec. 29, 1811, m. Emma Haskel, lives in Griswold.
81 ELIAS, b. April 3, 1815, m. Hannah Denison (No. 488), lives in Quiambaug Capt. Jesse Wilcox and his son. Jesse Wilcox, Jr., were drowned July 5, 1828, in a thunder squall on their way from Stonington to Quiambaug.

Edward Wilcox (No. 44) m. Eleanor Rathbone.
CHILDREN:
82 EBENEZER, b. ———, m. Iantha Mason.
83 ELISHA, b. ———, m. Molly Gates.
84 JOSHUA, b. ———, m. Jane Ashcraft.
85 JOHN, b. ———, m. Polly Packer.
86 PRUDY, b. ———, m. Daniel Wilcox.
87 SARAH, b. ———, m. Nathan Austin.
This Sarah Wilcox's mother may have been a second wife.

Sylvester Wilcox (No. 61) m. Marvel Burtch Sept. 27, 1800.
CHILDREN:
88 SYLVESTER, JR., b. Sept. 25, 1802.
89 ALLEN P., b. July 4, 1804.
90 MARY A., b. March 2, 1807.
91 WILLIAM, b. Jan. 9, 1810.
92 FRANCIS, b. Sept. 30, 1812.

Nathan Wilcox (No. 50) m. Tabitha Prosser Jan. 25, 1753.
CHILDREN:
93 NATHAN, b. Nov. 15, 1753.
94 WILLIAM, b. Jan. 4, 1755.
95 TABITHA, b. March 15, 1757, m. ——— Burdick.
96 LUCY, b. in 1759, m. Benjamin Peckham and d. in 1847.
97 PRUDENCE, b. March 30, 1761, m. ——— Williams.
98 DAVID, b. in 1764, m. Rebecca Stanton (No. 59), that family.
99 JOHN, b. ———.
100 JARED, b. in 1770, m. Bridget Stanton (No. 63), that family.
101 DESIAH, b. ———, m. ——— Denison.
102 MARTHA, b. in 1775, m. Samuel Stanton (No. 64), that family.

ROBERT WILLIAMS FAMILY.

The planters of Stonington by the name of Williams were Ebenezer and John Williams, first cousins, sons of Samuel and Isaac Williams of Roxbury, Massachusetts, and grandsons of

1. ROBERT WILLIAMS, son of Stephen and Margaret Cook Williams, b. 1598, bapt. in Great Yarmouth, England, under date of Dec. 11, 1608, m. Elizabeth Stalham of Great Yarmouth, and sailed for America in the ship "Rose" from Great Yarmouth, landing in New England in the year 1635. His wife d. July 28, 1674, aged 80 years. He m. again, it is supposed, to Martha Strong, who d. Dec. 22, 1704. He was a member of the Ancient and Honorable Artillery Company of Boston, 1644. He d. at Roxbury, Mass., Sept. 1, 1693.

CHILDREN:

2 ELIZABETH, b. in England, m. Richard Cutter in 1644, he d. June 16, 1693; she d. at Cambridge March 5, 1662.
3 DEBORAH, b. in England, m. John Turner in 1648, he d. in 1705; his wife d. in 1675.
4 JOHN, b. in England, d. Oct. 6, 1658, unmarried.
5 SAMUEL, b. in England in 1632, m. Theoda Park.
6 ISAAC, b. at Roxbury Sept. 1, 1638, m. Martha Park.
7 STEPHEN, b. at Roxbury, Nov. 8, 1640, m. Sarah, daughter of Joseph and Mary (Thomson) Wise, in 1666; she d. in 1728, and he d. Feb. 15, 1720.
8 THOMAS, b. and d. young.

Dea. Samuel Williams of Roxbury, Mass. (No. 5) m. March 2, 1654, Theoda, daughter of Dea. William and wife Martha (Holgrave) Park (No. 6), that family, and sister of Martha, who married his brother, Isaac Williams. He d. Sept. 28, 1698.

CHILDREN:

9 ELIZABETH, b. Feb. 1, 1655, d. March 10, 1655.
10 SAMUEL, b. April 27, 1656, m. Sarah May Feb. 24, 1680; she d. Dec. 29, 1712; he d. Aug. 8, 1735.
11 MARTHA, b. April 29, 1657, d. Feb. 6, 1661.
12 ELIZABETH, b. Feb. 11, 1660, m. Stephen Paine.
13 THEODA, b. July 27, 1662, d. Feb. 8, 1679.
14 JOHN, b. Dec. 10, 1664, m. Eunice Mather July 21, 1687, first minister of Deerfield, Mass., in 1686.
15 EBENEZER, b. Dec. 6, 1666, lived in Stonington.

ROBERT WILLIAMS FAMILY.

16 DEBORAH, b. Nov. 20, 1668, m. Joseph Warren of Boston, Mass. She was the grandmother of Gen. Joseph Warren, who fell at Bunker Hill June 17, 1775, nobly defending the liberties of this country.
17 MARTHA, b. May 19, 1671, m. Jonathan Hunt.
18 ABIGAIL, b. July 12, 1674, m. May 26, 1698, Experience Porter.
19 PARK, b. Jan. 11, 1677, m. Priscilla Payson.
20 Unnamed infant, b. and d. April, 1680.

Isaac Williams (No. 6) m. Martha Park (No. 8), that family, in 1660; she d. Oct. 24, 1674. He m. 2d, Judith, daughter of Peter and Elizabeth (Smith) Hunt, widow of Nathaniel Cooper; she d. 1724; her husband d. Feb. 11, 1707.

CHILDREN:
21 ISAAC, b. and d. March 7, 1661.
22 ISAAC, b. Dec. 11, 1661, m. Elizabeth Hyde, who d. June 26, 1699; m. 2d, Mary, widow of Nathaniel Hammond, who is said to have been sister of his first wife; m. 3d, Hannah ———; he d. in 1739.
23 MARTHA, b. Dec. 27, 1663, m. John Hunt.
24 WILLIAM, b. Feb. 2, 1665, m. Elizabeth Cotton.
25 JOHN, b. Oct. 31, 1667, settled in Stonington, Conn., m. Martha Wheeler.
26 ELEAZER, b. Oct. 22, 1669, settled in Stonington, Conn., m. Mary (Rediat) Hyde.
27 HANNAH, b. Oct. 8, 1671, m. John Hyde of Newton, Mass.
28 ELIZABETH (twin), b. Oct. 8, 1671, m. Jonathan Hyde.
29 THOMAS, b. Dec. 23, 1673.

CHILDREN BY SECOND MARRIAGE:
30 PETER, b. Aug. 31, 1680, d. unmarried in 1732.
31 SARAH, b. Oct. 2, 1699, m. John March; 2d, Samuel Gray.
32 MARY (twin), b. Oct. 2, 1699, m. Joseph Hyde.
33 EPHRAIM, b. Oct. 21, 1691, m. Elizabeth Jackson Aug. 8, ———; 2d, he m. Abigail Jones May 21, 1719.

CHILDREN:
34 EPHRAIM, b. Feb. 23, 1715; killed in the French and Indian war in battle near Lake George. N. Y., Sept. 8, 1755. He left his fortune, by will, to found a free school at Williamstown, Mass., incorporated in 1685; afterwards became a college, which was called after his name; d. unmarried.
35 THOMAS, b. April 1, 1718. He was a surgeon and was in the army with his brother when he was killed. He m. Anna Childs; m. 2d, Esther Williams, daughter of Rev. William Williams (No. 53).

CHILDREN:
36 EPHRAIM, b. in 1760, m. Emily Trowbridge, their son,
37 REV. JOHN, Senior Bishop of the Episcopal Church of the United States, was b. Aug. 30, 1817.

Ebenezer Williams (No. 15) came to Stonington about 1685, m. Mary Wheeler, daughter of Isaac and Martha (Park) Wheeler (No. 5), Wheeler family, Jan. 24, 1687. She d. Nov. 3, 1709. He m. 2d, July 12, 1711, Sarah, daughter of Nathaniel and Mary (French) Hammond of Newton; she d. Sept. 5, 1751. He d. Feb. 13, 1747. He settled on lands which he purchased of the Winthrops, just north of what is now Old Mystic, near the junction of the Lantern Hill road with the turnpike.

CHILDREN:

39 THEODA, b. Oct. 29, 1687, d. Jan. 19, 1694.
40 Unnamed child, b. Sept. 17, 1691.
41 MARY, b. Jan. 7, 1694, d. Jan. 10, 1704.
42 SAMUEL, b. Feb. 4, 1696, m. Jemima Sheldon; 2d, **Mary Williams**.
43 EBENEZER, bapt. June 23, 1699, d. young.
44 THEODA, bapt. Jan. 3, 1701, never married.
45 SILENCE, bapt. Dec. 8, 1703, m. Oliver Grant (No. 15), that family.
46 EBENEZER, bapt. Oct. 21, 1705, m. Deborah Smith; 2d, Prudence **Fellows**.
47 ELIZABETH (twin), bapt. Oct. 21, 1705, m. Jonathan Smith June 8, **1732.**
48 MARTHA, bapt. April 3, 1708, m. Jeremiah Smith Dec. 16, 1730.

CHILDREN BY SECOND MARRIAGE:

49 Unnamed child, b. June 10, 1713.
49a Unnamed child, b. May 27, 1714.
50 NATHANIEL, b. July 24, 1715, m. Amy Hewitt; 2d, Abigail Eldridge.
51 ELISHA, b. Jan. 12, 1719, m. Thankful Denison; 2d, Eunice Williams; 3d, Esther Wheeler; 4th, Mrs. Eunice (Spaulding) Baldwin.

Rev. William Williams (No. 24) graduated from Harvard, 1683, settled at Hatfield, Mass., in 1685, m. Elizabeth, daughter of Rev. Dr. Cotton, July 8, 1686; m. 2d, Christain, daughter of Rev. Soloman and Esther (Warham) Mather Stoddard, Aug. 9, 1699; he d. Aug. 31, 1741.

CHILDREN:

52 WILLIAM, b. April 30, 1687, d. May 5, 1687.
53 REV. WILLIAM, b. May 11, 1688, m. Hannah Stoddard; 2d, Sarah, widow of Rev. James Stone.
54 MARTHA, b. Oct. 8, 1690, m. Edward Partridge.
55 REV. ELISHA, b. Aug. 26, 1694, m. Eunice Chester. He graduated from Harvard 1711, ordained at Newington, Conn., Oct. 22, 1722; he was chosen President of Yale College 1726, and served thirteen years and resigned on account of ill health July 25, 1755.
55a JOHN, b. March 7, 1698, d. July 29, 1699.

CHILDREN BY SECOND MARRIAGE:

56 REV. SOLOMAN, b. Jan. 4, 1701, minister of Lebanon, Conn., a graduate of Harvard 1719 m. Mary Porter, who were the parents of Hon. William Williams, signer of the Declaration of Independence; he m. **Mary** Trumbull, daughter of Governor Trumbull of Connecticut.
57 ELIZABETH, b. June 7, 1707, m. Samuel Barnard.
58 ISRAEL, b. Nov. 30, 1709, m. Sarah Chester; he d. in 1789.
59 DOROTHY, b. June 20, 1713, m. Rev. Jonathan Ashley.

Samuel Williams (No. 42) of Stonington, m. 1st, Jemima Sheldon of North Hampton, Mass.; she d. Sept. 21, 1724; he m. 2d, Mary Williams (No. 440) of Stonington April 26, 1725; she d. Jan. 28, 1776; he d. Sept. 18, 1780.

CHILDREN:

60 MARY, b. Jan. 22, 1738.
61 JEMIMA, b. Nov. 12, 1730.
62 SAMUEL, b. Jan. 12, 1734, m. Lois Allyn.
63 CAROLINE, b. July 3, 1735, d. Oct. 24, 1738.
64 JESSE, b. Jan. 13, 1742.
65 EBENEZER, b. May 25, 1743.

ROBERT WILLIAMS FAMILY.

Nathaniel Williams (No. 50) m. Amy Hewitt July 1, 1759 (see Hewitt family) (No. 50), both of Stonington. Mrs. Amy Williams d. March 16, 1756; he m. 2d, Abigail Eldridge of Groton, Conn., Sept. 19, 1756. He d. Dec. 19, 1793; his wife, Abigail, d. July 13, 1818. Mr. Williams and both of his wives are buried at Old Mystic, in the burying ground on the Elias Brown farm.

CHILDREN:
66 Daughter, b. and d. same day.
67 SARAH, b. Oct. 4, 1742, d. Oct. 6, 1744.
68 ANNA, b. Oct. 2, 1744, m. Col. William Ledyard.
69 AMIE, b. Jan. 14, 1746, m. John Bell; 2d, Job Stanton.
70 ISRAEL, b. Aug. 4, 1749.

CHILDREN BY SECOND WIFE:
71 NATHANIEL, b. Aug. 3, 1757.
72 ABIGAIL, b. Aug. 25, 1768, m. Christopher Chesebrough (No. 210), Chesebrough family.
74 EBENEZER, b. Dec. 24, 1759.
75 SARAH, b. June 3, 1761, m. Andrew Denison (No. 216), of that family.
76 THOMAS, b. ———, m. Abigail Hempstead.
77 ELIJAH, b. ———, m. Mehitable Rossiter.
78 PELEG, b. 1768, m. Dorothy Denison.

Elisha Williams (No. 51) m. Nov. 5, 1740, Thankful Denison (No. 138), Denison family; she d. Dec. 15, 1740. He m. 2d, Eunice Williams (No. 447) Nov. 24, 1743; she d. July 26, 1753; he m. 3d, Esther Wheeler (No. 340), Wheeler family, April 25, 1754; he m. for his fourth wife, Mrs. Eunice (Spaulding) Baldwin Nov. 1, 1765. He d. Sept. 22, 1788. Mr. Williams and his wives are buried at Old Mystic in the graveyard on the Elias Brown farm.

CHILDREN BY SECOND MARRIAGE:
79 ELISHA, b. Dec. 14, 1744, m. Lucy Denison.
80 EBENEZER, b. Feb. 26, 1748, d. young.
81 THANKFUL, b. July 26, 1750, d. Oct. 13, 1751.

CHILDREN BY THIRD MARRIAGE:
82 EUNICE, b. Aug. 3, 1755, m. Isaac Denison Nov. 19, 1773, (No. 221), that family.

Samuel Williams (No. 62) m. Lois Allyn of Groton June 26, 1757.

CHILDREN:
83 LOIS, b. Nov. 4, 1757, m. Gershom York (No. 51), that family.
84 JAMES, b. Dec. 16, 1759.
85 ADIN, b. Nov. 27, 1761.
86 SIMEON, b. Dec. 18, 1763.
87 DEBORAH, b. July 16, 1766.
88 ALLYN, b. Jan. 22, 1769.
89 DUDLEY, b. July 26, 1771.
90 ELIZABETH, b. Dec. 28, 1773.
91 ALTHEA, b. May 18, 1777.

Anna Williams of Stonington (No. 68) m. Col. William Ledyard of Groton b. Dec. 6, 1761, the brave defender of Fort Griswold in the assault and capture of that fort by the British Sept. 6, 1781, when he lost his life.

CHILDREN:

92 MARY LEDYARD, b. Feb. 16, 1763, d. March 9, 1782.
93 SARAH LEDYARD, b. May 6, 1765, d. July 25, 1781.
94 WILLIAM LEDYARD, b. Dec. 30, 1766, d. Sept. 14, 1777.
95 DEBORAH LEDYARD, b. Jan. 27, 1769, m. ———— Smith Nov. 28, 1786, d. Dec. 20, 1791.
96 JOHN YARBOROUGH LEDYARD, b. June 24, 1773, d. Jan. 22, 1792.
97 PETER VANWORT LEDYARD, b. Sept. 2, 1775, m. Sept. 22, 1796, Maria Van Tuyl.
98 WILLIAM LEDYARD, b. Sept. 1, 1777, d. Sept. 9, 1795.
99 HENRY YOUNG LEDYARD, b. Jan. 6, 1780, d. May 23, 1782.
100 CHARLES GROVER LEDYARD, b. Aug. 27, 1781, d. Feb. 20, 1790.

Amy Williams of Stonington (No. 69) m. John Bell July 6, 1766. He d. July 17, 1769. She m. 2d, Job Stanton June 2, 1774 (No. 25) of the Robert Stanton family.

CHILDREN BY FIRST MARRIAGE.

101 NANCY BELL, b. Sept. 30, 1767, m. Paul Babcock.
102 AMY BELL, b. July 14, 1769.

CHILDREN BY SECOND MARRIAGE:

103 ABIGAIL STANTON, b. Feb. 29, 1775.
104 NATHANIEL STANTON, b. April 22, 1778, d. at Trinidad March 15, 1808.
105 CHARLES STANTON, b. May 14, 1780, d. April 1, 1782.
106 BENJAMIN F., b. Feb. 25, 1782, m. Maria Davis.

Thomas E. Williams (No. 76) m. Abigail, daughter of Christopher and Mary Hempstead May 7, 1787, both of Stonington, Conn.

CHILDREN:

107 ELDRIDGE, b. Dec. 25, 1787.
108 NANCY, b. Jan. 4, 1790, m. Nathan Whiting, 1807.
109 SALLY A., b. Dec. 19, 1793, unmarried, d. July 22, 1868.
110 THOMAS, b. Nov. 6, 1795, m. Lucretia Dudley.
111 EMMA, b. Aug. 19, 1797, m. George Wolf Oct. 11, 1818.
112 ABBY, b. Feb. 20, 1799, d. March 21, 1897, unmarried.
113 MARIA, b. Nov. 20, 1801, m. Henry Hewitt July 9, 1837 (No. 216) Hewitt family.
114 SOPHIA, b. Dec. 9, 1803, m. Henry D. Chesebrough Nov. 10, 1831. See Chesebrough family (No. 338).
115 DANIEL, b. Jan. 26, 1806, m. Matilda Appelman Aug., 1832.
116 GILES, b. Sept. 22, 1808, m. Ann Brown Aug. 5, 1855; 2d, Mary Ann Rogers, Jan. 11, 1882; he d. April 3 1887.

Elijah Williams (No. 77) m. Mehitable Rossiter (No. 19), that family, in 1796, both of Stonington, Conn. They are buried in the graveyard on the Elias Brown farm, Old Mystic.

ROBERT WILLIAMS FAMILY.

CHILDREN:
117 PHEBE, b. Feb. 12, 1797.
118 BENJAMIN F., b. Nov. 27, 1798, m. Eliza Ann Wheeler Oct. 12, 1825. See Wheeler family (No. 470).
119 SALLY, b. Aug. 30, 1800.

Peleg Williams (No. 78) m. Dorothy Denison (see No. 203, Denison family), both of Stonington, Conn. He d. Aug. 29, 1849; his wife d. Feb. 27, 1836.

CHILDREN:
120 MARY ANN, b. ———, m. John Harris.
121 ELIAKIM, b. May 22, 1799, m. Sarah Ann Wightman.
122 ERASTUS, b. ———, m. Mercy Wightman.
123 DUDLEY, b. ———, m. Lydia Harris.
124 CHARLES D., b. ———, m. Aurelia Gore.
125 JANE D., b. ———, m. Barton Saunders.
126 BETSEY, b. ———, m. Capt. Thomas Eldridge.
127 NANCY, b. ———, m. Nathan Saunders.
128 CLARK, b. ———, unmarried.
129 FANNY, b. ———.

Elisha Williams (No. 79) m. Lucy Denison (No. 301), Denison family, Dec. 22, 1767, both of Stonington, Conn.

CHILDREN:
130 THANKFUL, b. Nov. 12, 1768.
131 EUNICE, b. June 20, 1770.
132 ESTHER, b. April 15, 1772, d. in 1798, m. Amos Clift (No. 22), of that family.
133 LUCY, b. Nov. 25, 1773, m. Aaron Bennet April 16, 1796 (No. 49).
134 JANE B., b. July 10, 1775, d. March 19, 1806, m. Ebenezer Denison (No. 399).
135 ELISHA b. Aug. 26, 1777, m. Lois Denison.
136 SARAH or SALLY, b. Sept. 16, 1779.
137 EBENEZER, b. Oct. 30, 1781, d. June 11, 1786.
138 JESSE, b. Jan. 26, 1784.
139 DENISON, b. May 7, 1788.

Eliakim Williams of Stonington (No. 121) m. Sarah Ann Wightman Dec. 3, 1823, of Groton.

CHILDREN:
140 MARY ANN, b. March 9, 1825, m. M. C. Hill March 10, 1842.
141 JAMES, b. Dec. 17, 1837, d. June, 1852, unmarried.
142 PELEG, b. July 16, 1830, m. 1st, Eliza C. Strickland Oct. 13, 1856; she d. Oct. 3, 1869; he m. 2d, Elizabeth T. Tate June 3, 1872.
143 SARAH, b. July 31, 1832, m. Dr. Charles Sweet Dec. 3, 1860.
144 MATILDA, b. June 4, 1835, m. Henry Troupe of Lebanon.
145 JOHN, b. Nov. 20, 1837, unmarried.
146 GEORGE, b. April 12, 1840, d. Dec., 1892, m. Catherine Rogers May 14, 1872.
147 MERCY C., b. July 2, 1842, m. Elisha M. Miner Nov. 6, 1872.
148 ERASTUS, b. Oct. 1, 1844, m. Emma C. Mallory Nov. 18, 1875.

Thomas Williams of Stonington (No. 110) m. Lucretia Dudley Nov., 1826. He d. May 30, 1849.

CHILDREN:

149 ELLEN, b. ———.
150 DUDLEY, b. ———.
151 ALBERT, b. ———.
152 MARIA, b. ———.
153 LUCRETIA, b. ———.

Elisha Williams (No. 135) m. Lois Denison (No. 343), Denison family, March 28, 1807, both of Stonington, Conn.

CHILD:

154 HANNAH, b. Aug. 22, 1808, d. May 8, 1827.
    After the death of Mrs. Lois Williams, her husband m. 2d, Mrs. Rebecca Mumford May 5, 1815. No children.

John Williams (No. 25) of Roxbury, Mass., moved to Stonington, Conn., about 1685, m. Martha Wheeler of the Wheeler family (No. 6), Jan. 24, 1687, the same day his cousin, Ebenezer Williams (No. 15) m. Mary Wheeler, sister of his wife, Martha. The following inscription is on the gravestone at Whitehall burying ground, which was erected by General William Williams (No. 342):

    "To the memory of John Williams, who came from Roxbury, Massachusetts, settled at Stonington, and married Martha, daughter of Isaac Wheeler, one of the ancient proprietors of this town, died Nov. 15, 1702, aged 33 years. His father, Capt. Isaac Williams, died in Massachusetts Feb. 11, 1707, aged 69 years. His grandfather, Robert Williams, came from Norwich, England, and died in Roxbury in 1693, aged 86 years."

CHILDREN:

155 ISAAC, b. April 10, 1689, m. Sarah Denison.
156 COL. JOHN, b. Oct. 31, 1692, m. Desire Denison.
157 MARTHA, b. Aug. 5, 1693, m. Moses Fish of Groton.
158 DEBORAH, b. April 2, 1695, m. Nehemiah Williams (No. 438), Williams family.
159 WILLIAM, b. March 29, 1697.
160 NATHAN, b. Dec. 11, 1698.
161 EUNICE, bapt. Aug. 16, 1702, m. Joseph Gallup Feb. 24, 1720 (No. 37), Gallup family.
162 BENAJAH, bapt. Aug. 28, 1700, m. Deborah Fanning.
    After the death of John Williams (No. 25) his wife, Martha, m. Thomas Atwood June 1, 1714.

Isaac Williams (No. 155) m. Nov. 7, 1711, Sarah Denison (No. 57), Denison family, both of Stonington, Conn.

CHILDREN:

163 SARAH, b. March 12, 1712, m. Joshua Culver.
164 MARTHA, bapt. ———, 1716.
165 ISAAC, bapt. March 11, 1717.
166 NATHAN, bapt. July 22, 1720, m. Elizabeth Haley.
167 ATWOOD, bapt. April 16, 1723, m. Elizabeth Gallup.
168 WARHAM, bapt. April 9, 1727, m. Rebecca Satterly.
169 PHEBE, bapt. March 8, 1731, m. Daniel Brewster.
170 EUNICE, bapt. Dec. 25, 1733, m. Richard Williams.

ROBERT WILLIAMS FAMILY. 669

Col. John Williams (No. 156) m. Desire Denison (No. 64), Denison family, Feb. 19, 1711, both of Stonington; she d. Aug. 13, 1737. He m. 2d, Mary Helms of Kingston, R. I.; she d. Dec. 20, 1740. He m. for his third wife, Prudence Potter of Portsmouth, R. I., Nov. 21, 1761. He d. Dec. 30, 1761; his last wife d. Sept. 17, 1792.

CHILDREN BY FIRST MARRIAGE:
172 DESIRE, b. Aug. 25, 1712.
173 JOHN, b. May 14, 1714, m. Lydia Chesebrough.
174 WILLIAM, b. May 1, 1716, m. Martha Wheeler.
175 THANKFUL, b. Feb. 8, 1718, m. Avery Denison Jan. 31, 1734. (No. 109), Denison family.
176 MERCY, b. Nov. 7, 1719, m. Thomas Wheeler (No. 54), Wheeler family.
177 THOMAS, b. Sept. 20, 1721, m. Marcy Raymond.
178 ROBERT, b. March 8, 1723, m. Rebecca Mumford.
179 PRUDENCE, b. Jan. 17, 1725, d. Jan. 25, 1725.
180 GEORGE, b. July 8, 1726, m. Eunice Avery.

CHILDREN BY SECOND MARRIAGE:
181 EDWARD, b. July 27, 1740, m. Mary Stanton.
182 MARY, bapt. after her mother's death, Jan. 25, 1741.

Benajah Williams (No. 162) of Stonington m. May 14, 1722, Deborah Fanning of Groton (widow).

CHILDREN:
183 JOSEPH, b. Dec. 5, 1725.
184 JABEZ, b. July 2, 1727.
185 PRUDENCE, b. Feb. 20, 1729-30.
186 DESIRE, b. Feb. 16, 1732-3.
187 BENAJAH, b. Sept. 3, 1735.

Nathan Williams (No. 166) of Stonington m. Elizabeth Haley in 1744.

CHILDREN:
188 PRUDENCE, b. Dec. 18, 1745.
189 LUCY, b. March 11, 1746.
190 JOSHUA, b. July 18, 1749, m. three times.
191 CALEB, b. July 18, 1749, m. Freelove Fanning.
192 ISAAC, b. June 10, 1751, m. Phebe Hurlbert Aug. 14, 1783.
193 JOHN, b. June 10, 1751.
194 MARTHA, b. July 10, 1754.
195 ELIZABETH, b. July 7, 1756.
196 CATY or CATHERINE, b. Feb. 27, 1758.
197 MOLLY or MARY, b. Feb. 27, 1758.

Atwood Williams (No. 167) m. Aug. 3, 1749, Elizabeth Gallup, both of Stonington, Conn.

CHILDREN:
198 PRISCILLA, b. June 27, 1751.
199 SAMUEL, b. March 19, 1754.

Warham Williams (No. 168) m. May 14, 1758, Rebecca Satterly, both of Stonington, Conn.

HISTORY OF STONINGTON.

CHILDREN:

200 WARHAM, b. Feb. 19, 1759, m. Anna Stanton.
200a CHARLES, b. July 6, 1760.
201 PHEBE, b. Dec. 1, 1761, m. Col. Isaac Williams (No. 219).
201a ASA, b. Aug. 13, 1763.
202 LUKE, b. Oct. 26, 1765.

John Williams (No. 173) m. Dec. 25, 1736, Lydia Chesebrough (No. 78), Chesebrough family, both of Stonington, Conn.

CHILDREN:

202a DESIRE, b. July 10, 1737, m. Amos Chesebrough (No. 71), Chesebrough family.
203 LYDIA, b. March 30, 1739, d. July 29, 1762.
204 PRUDENCE, b. Dec. 11, 1741, m. Peleg Noyes (No. 143), Noyes family.
205 HANNAH, b. Jan. 16, 1744.
206 JOHN, b. July 1, 1746, m. Content Denison (No. 243), that family.
207 ELIHU, b. July 29, 1748.
208 ISRAEL, b. April 4, 1755.
209 ZERVIAH, b. April 19, 1757, m. William Woodbridge (No. 21), that family.

William Williams (No. 174) m. Feb. 15, 1737, Martha Wheeler (No. 39), Wheeler family, both of Stonington. He m. 2d, Mrs. Mary Jewett of New London, March 17, 1785; d. July 27, 1801.

CHILDREN:

210 MARTHA, b. Sept. 26, 1738, m. Charles Wheeler (No. 60), Wheeler family.
211 WILLIAM, b. July 14, 1740, m. Eunice Prentice (No. 53), Prentice family.
212 ESTHER, b. Jan. 8, 1743, m. William Chesebrough (No. 170), Chesebrough family.
213 JOHN, b. Dec. 23, 1744, m. Keturah Randall.
214 BENADAM, b. March 21, 1747, m. Hannah Lathrop.
215 HANNAH, b. May 24, 1749, d. Nov. 17, 1762.
216 DESIRE, b. Jan. 24, 1751, m. Feb., 1782, Latham Hull (No. 7), Hull family.
217 HANNAH, b. June 17, 1753, m. July 3, 1777, Amos Denison (No. 246), Denison family.
218 EPHRAIM, b. May 16, 1756, m. Sarah Potter; 2d, Hepsibeth Phelps.
219 ISAAC, b. March 20, 1758, m. Phebe Williams.

Thomas Williams of Stonington (No. 177) m. Oct. 11, 1742, Mercy Raymond of New London. He was killed at the massacre at Groton Heights Sept. 6, 1781. Buried at the Whitehall burial place in Stonington.

CHILDREN:

220 JOHN, b. July 27, 1743.
221 MARCY, b. Jan. 24, 1745.
222 ELIZABETH, b. Jan. 25, 1748.
223 LUCY, b. Feb. 5, 1752.

Robert Williams of Stonington (No. 178) m. Oct. 29, 1747, Rebecca Mumford of Fishers Island.

CHILDREN:

224 ABIGAIL, b. Dec. 15, 1748.
225 ROBINSON, b. Dec. 29, 1750.

226 MARY, b. Dec. 8, 1752.
227 ROBERT, b. May 15, 1755, m. Abigail Chesebrough Feb. 11, 1781 (No. 256), Chesebrough family.
228 REBECCA, b. Nov. 17, 1757.

George Williams of Stonington (No. 180) m. Nov. 3, 1748, Eunice Avery of Groton, Conn (No. 69), Avery family.

CHILDREN:

229 PRUDENCE, b. July 25, 1749.
230 GEORGE, b. Nov. 2, 1751, m. Nancy Hewitt.
231 SOLOMAN, b. Sept. 19, 1756.
232 WELTHEA, b. Sept. 6, 1758.
233 AMOS, b. Aug. 23, 1760.
234 DESIRE, b. Oct. 23, 1763.
235 DUDLEY, b. Sept. 30, 1765.
236 ROBERT, b. Jan. 30, 1768.

Edward Williams (No. 181) m. Feb. 15, 1759, Mary Stanton (No. 361), Stanton family, both of Stonington, Conn.; he d. Aug. 4, 1777. From his gravestone, where he is buried at Newport: "Edward Williams, a Revolutionary soldier, d. on board a British prison ship, Aug. 1777."

CHILDREN:

237 DYER E., b. Nov. 2, 1762, m. Clarissa Hempstead Dec. 26, 1821.
238 EDWARD, b. March 30, 1765.
239 AMARIAH, b. Oct. 9, 1767, m. Thankful Packer.
240 NICHOLAS, b. June 30, 1770, m. Lucretia Hempstead Sept. 4, 1794.
241 EARL, b. April 10, 1773, m. Mercy Hempstead.
242 ROBERT, b. July 13, 1776.

Joshua Williams (No. 190 of Stonington, m. 1st, July 22, 1773, Dorothy Edgecomb; he m. 2d, Priscilla Ruff May 27, 1787; she d. April 23, 1838. He m. 3d, Hannah Hurlbert March 10, 1789; she d. Sept. 10, 1842.

CHILDREN BY FIRST MARRIAGE:

243 NATHAN, b. June 27, 1776, unmarried.
244 JOSHUA, b. Nov. 6, 1778, m. and d. in Glastonbury.

CHILDREN BY SECOND MARRIAGE:

245 JABEZ, b. Feb. 21, 1788, m. Ann Tuthill.

CHILDREN BY THIRD MARRIAGE:

246 OLIVER, b. Dec. 31, 1789, d. 1793.
247 AVERY, b. Sept. 20, 1791, d. Nov. 21, 1808 (drowned).
248 HANNAH, b. March 21, 1794, m. Robert Fellows of Pawcatuck, R. I.
249 HENRY, b. Oct. 13, 1796, m. twice, Martha and Julia Niles, sisters.
250 SARAH, b. Aug. 5, 1799, m. Elisha Daboll Oct. 30, 1825.
251 HARRIETTA, b. Nov. 15, 1801, m. Henry Finch.
252 FREELOVE, b. Dec. 9, 1804, m. William H. Starr.
253 MARY, b. April 16, 1811.

Caleb Williams of Stonington (No. 191) m. Freelove Fanning of Groton.

CHILDREN:
254 JESSE, b. June 28, 1774, m. Elizabeth Avery.
255 ALFRED, b. ———.
256 CALEB, b. ———.
257 MINER, b. ———.
258 EDMUND, b. ———.

Warham Williams (No. 200) m. Anna Stanton (No. 369) of Stanton family, April 5, 1789, both of Stonington, Conn.

CHILDREN:
259 ANNA, b. Aug. 22, 1790, m. George Bentley.
260 POLLY, b. Feb. 17, 1792, m. Appleton Woodward, Dec. 3, 1815.
261 PHEBE, b. Feb. 15, 1794, m. John Bentley.

John Williams (No. 206) m. Jan. 18, 1770, Content Denison (No. 243), Denison family, both of Stonington.

CHILDREN:
262 JOHN, b. Nov. 20, 1771.
263 ELIHU, b. Oct. 8, 1772.
264 LYDIA, b. May 23, 1774.
265 JOSEPH, b. March 27, 1776.
266 BRIDGET, b. Jan. 10, 1778.
267 DESIRE, b. July 18, 1780.
268 WILLIAM, b. May 5, 1782.
269 STANTON (twin), b. May 5, 1782.
270 GEORGE, b. Oct. 3, 1784.

William Williams of Stonington (No. 211), was a seafaring man, acting as supercargo. He m. Eunice Prentice (No. 53), that family, Nov. 25, 1764, both of Stonington, Conn. He d. at sea and was buried in the ocean Oct. 25, 1770; she d. Oct. 23, 1770, aged 24 years.

CHILDREN:
271 WILLIAM, b. June 30, 1765, m. three times.
272 EUNICE, b. Jan. 30, 1767, m. first, Rufus Wheeler, April 2, 1787 (No. 80), that family; m. 2d, Coddington Billings of New London Sept. 13, 1797 (No. 167), that family.
273 GURDON, b. March 24, 1769, d. Nov. 13, 1769.

John Williams (No. 213) m. Keturah Randall Sept. 29, 1765, both of Stonington, Conn. (No. 49), Randall family.

CHILDREN:
274 JOHN, b. Dec. 22, 1766.
275 MARTHA, b. Feb. 25, 1767.
276 ESTHER, b. Dec. 10, 1768, m. 1st, Roswell Brown (No. 171), that family; m. 2d, his brother, Thatcher Brown (No. 175) that family.
277 BENADAM, b. Dec. 26, 1769.
278 WILLIAM, b. Feb. 2, 1772, m. Lydia Wheeler.
279 ELIAS, b. Sept. 3, 1773, m. Thankful Stanton.
280 KETURAH, b. May 4, 1777, m. Jeremiah Hull (No. 10), that family.
281 CHARLES W., b. Dec. 5, 1778, m. Amy Swan.
282 RANDALL, b. Oct. 28, 1781.

Benadam Williams (No. 214) of Stonington m. Oct. 17, 1771, Hannah Lathrop of Chelsea.

ROBERT WILLIAMS FAMILY.

CHILDREN:
283 ELIZABETH or BETSEY, b. Aug. 11, 1772, m. Eli Hewitt April 24, 1796 (No. 112), Hewitt family.
284 HANNAH, b. in 1775, m. Charles S. Smith Jan. 26, 1792; she m. 2d, Elisha Way, and d. March 26, 1860, aged 85 years.
285a BENADAM, JR., b. April 4, 1776, m. Nancy Randall April 18, 1799 (No. 73), that family.
285 GEORGE, b. July 13, 1779.
286 LATHROP, b. Aug. 2, 1781.
287 RUFUS, b. Jan. 6, 1784, m. Catherine Browning Nov. 11, 1810 (No. 46), Browning family, both of Stonington.

CHILDREN:
288 BENADAM, b. Nov. 6, 1812.
289 WILLIAM, b. April 18, 1813.
290 JOSEPH, b. ———.
291 RUFUS, b. Jan., 1815.
292 AVERY, b. May 11, 1819.
293 ASA, b. Jan. 14, 1821.
294 CATIE, b. ———.

Ephraim Williams of Stonington (No. 218) m. Sarah Potter, daughter of John Potter, Esq., of South Kingston, R. I., March 15, 1781. She d. May 9, 1787. He m. 2d, Hepsibeth Phelps (No. 34), that family, Dec. 23, 1787. He d. July 6, 1804.

CHILDREN:
295 EPHRAIM, b. July 3, 1791, m. Hannah Eliza Denison.
296 SARAH POTTER, b. July 15, 1802, d. July 24, 1824, unmarried.
297 CHARLES PHELPS, b. June 11, 1804, m. Betsey Smith; 2d, Georgia P. Babcock.

Isaac Williams of Stonington (No. 219) m. Phebe Williams (No. 201), Dec. 13, 1780. He d. Oct. 10, 1844; his wife d. Aug. 12, 1822; m. 2d, Miss Nancy Browning of Waterford.

CHILDREN:
298 ISAAC, b. Aug. 23, 1781, m. Nancy Avery; 2d, Susan Burnham.
299 CYRUS, b. Nov. 23, 1783, m. Martha Wheeler.
300 LUCY, b. Sept. 29 1785, m. Giles R. Hallam Feb. 2, 1806 (No. 23), Hallam family. She d. April 4, 1862.
301 SALLY POTTER, b. Aug. 18, 1787, m. Henry Chesebrough (No. 328), Chesebrough family.
302 REBECCA, b. Sept. 16, 1789, m. Charles Wheeler Jan. 26, 1812 (No. 199), Wheeler family.
303 MARTHA, b. July 27, 1791, m. Henry Chesebrough Jan. 27, 1812 (No. 328), Chesebrough family.
304 JOHN PITTS, b. Aug. 12, 1793, m. Cynthia York Nov. 28, 1816.
305 JERUSHA, b. Aug. 16, 1795, m. Benjamin Pomeroy Jan. 1, 1818 (No. 6), that family.
306 EUNICE, b. July 25, 1797, m. Jabez Gallup Feb. 25, 1829 (No. 152), that family.
307 PHEBE ESTHER b. Nov. 16, 1799, m. Silas Chesebrough Jan. 31, 1819 (No. 329), that family.
308 FANNY ROGERS, b. Oct. 30, 1801, d. Oct. 29, 1869.
309 EMILY WATSON, b. Oct. 25, 1805, m. William Stanton Williams Oct. 19, 1826 (No. 362), that family.

ONE CHILD:
310 EMILY AUGUSTA, b. ———.

George Williams of Waterford, Conn. (No. 230), m. Nancy Hewitt (No. 95), that family, daughter of Capt. Israel Hewitt and wife, Tabitha Wheaton, of Little Compton, R. I., Dec. 3, 1798. They lived and died in Stonington, now North Stonington.

CHILDREN:

311 NANCY, b. Sept. 13, 1779, m. Perez Hewitt Feb. 12, 1797 (No. 113), Hewitt family.
312 EUNICE, b. March 11, 1781, m. Palmer Hewitt Feb. 23, 1800 (No. 114), Hewitt family.
313 CYNTHIA, b. Sept. 26, 1782, m. Joseph S. Allen of Groton.
314 THANKFUL, b. Feb. 18, 1785, m. Moses Benjamin of New London.
315 FRANCES, b. June 20, 1787, m. Robert Bowser.
316 CHARLOTTE, b. March 20, 1789, m. Edward R. Warner.
317 DIADAMA, b. April 19, 1791, m. Jeremiah Comstock; 2d, Charles Worthington.
318 CLARISSA, b. May 25, 1794, m. Benjamin E. Champlin.
319 GEORGE, b. Aug. 28, 1796, and lived fourteen days.
320 ELIZABETH, b. May 22, 1798, d. Oct. 19, 1819.

Dyer E. Williams (No. 237) m. Clarissa Hempstead Dec. 26, 1821.

CHILDREN:

321 MARY ESTHER, b. May 7, 1822, m. Leander F. Smith.
322 MERCY ANN, b. Jan. 5, 1824, m. Charles O. Braymah.
323 NANCY, b. Nov. 6, 1825, m. Joseph Lewis.
324 WILLIAM EDWARD, b. Nov. 18, 1827, m. Elizabeth Niser.
325 ALBERT DAVIS, b. April 20, 1830, m. Ellen Richmond.
326 ROBERT LESTER, b. Feb. 3, 1832, m. Elizabeth Packer.
327 CHARLES HENRY, b. Sept. 28, 1834, d. April 17, 1835.
328 OSCAR FITCZLAND, b. May 18, 1837, m. Hannah L. Brown.
329 CHARLES HENRY, b. Nov. 18, 1839, d. in the Civil war.
330 HORACE ORVILLE, b. July 26, 1843, m. Ellen L. Steverson June 20, 1861.

Amariah Williams (No. 239) m. Thankful Packer.

CHILD:

331 MARIA, b. ———, m. William Pierce.

Nicholas Williams (No. 240) m. Lucretia Hempstead Sept. 4, 1794.

CHILDREN:

332 GRACE, b. March 13, 1795.
333 LUCY H., b. Sept. 11, 1796.
334 MARY, b. March 7, 1798.
335 AMELIA, b. Feb. 24, 1800.

Jesse Williams (No. 254) m. Elizabeth Avery Oct. 13, 1802.

CHILDREN:

336 ELIZA, b. Dec. 22, 1803.
337 CALEB MINER, b. March 30, 1806, m. Sabra Gallup.
338 ALONZA, b. June 26, 1808.
339 EBENEZER, b. June 6, 1811.
340 LYDIA, b. May 1, 1813.
341 FREDERICK, b. May 11, 1816.

ROBERT WILLIAMS FAMILY.

William Williams of Stonington (No. 271) became Major General of the militia of Connecticut, and served at the battle at Stonington, 1814. He m. Mercy Wheeler Sept. 27, 1787 (No. 123), Wheeler family; she d. June 17, 1797. He m. 2d, Rhoda Babcock (No. 181), Babcock family, Jan. 6, 1799; she d. Aug. 28, 1801. He m. for his 3d wife, Nancy or Ann Babcock Dec., 1804, (No. 188), Babcock family. He d. at Stonington May 15, 1838.

CHILDREN BY FIRST MARRIAGE:

342 WILLIAM, b. March 12, 1788, m. Harriet Peck.
343 THOMAS WHEELER, b. Sept. 28, 1789, m. Lucretia W. Perkins.
344 GURDON, b. Feb. 17, 1792, d. March 26, 1795.
345 EUNICE, b. June 4, 1794, d. Feb. 26, 1796.
346 RUFUS, b. Jan. 23, 1795, d. Jan. 3, 1797.

CHILDREN BY SECOND MARRIAGE:

347 ROUSE BABCOCK, b. Nov. 28, 1799, d. Aug. 19, 1800.
348 RHODA ANN, b. May 31, 1801, d. Oct. 11, 1801.

CHILDREN BY THIRD MARRIAGE:

349 FRANKLIN, b. June 19, 1806, m. Mary Stanton.
350 ANN ELIZABETH, b. Oct. 10, 1814, m. Billings Wheeler (No. 263), that family.
351 CALVIN GODDARD, b. June 2, 1818, m. Ann Billings.
352 ELLEN, b. Feb. 11, 1820, m. Dr. William Hyde Sept. 11, 1843 (No. 48), Hyde family.

William Williams of Stonington (No. 278) m. Lydia Wheeler Oct. 16, 1796 (No. 129), Wheeler family.

CHILDREN:

353 MERCY, b. Oct. 9, 1797, m. 1st, Azariah Stanton Jan. 1, 1818; m. 2d, Samuel Copp (No. 69), that family.
354 JOHN W., b. Aug. 26, 1799, d. young.
355 ELIZA P., b. Jan. 18, 1801, m. 1st, Samuel Breed Nov. 21, 1822 (No. 91), that family; 2d, Erastus Edgcomb.
356 THOMAS WHEELER, b. July 4, 1802, m. Lucy Ann Fairfield, 1826.
357 RHODA ANN, b. Feb. 15, 1804, d. at 20, unmarried.
358 JAMES STEPHENSON, b. Oct. 2, 1806, d. at 20, unmarried.
359 LUCY CAROLINE b. July 22, 1809, m. Deacon Charles Butler Sept. 4, 1833.

Elias Williams of Stonington (No. 279) m. Thankful Stanton (No. 173), that family, Nov. 27, 1794, of Stonington, Conn. He d. Jan. 31, 1809; she d. Sept. 8, 1861.

CHILDREN:

360 HANNAH PUNDERSON, b. March 6, 1796, m. Daniel Mason Feb. 10, 1817 (No. 99), Mason family.
361 HARRIET Z., b. Feb. 7, 1798, m. Noyes Ladd May 14, 1821.
362 WILLIAM STANTON, b. Jan. 23, 1800, m. Emily Watson Williams (No. 309) of the Williams family.
363 JOSEPH STANTON, b. March 19, 1802, m. Julia Ann Gallup (No. 179), that family, of Ledyard, Dec. 9, 1824; he d. Feb. 19, 1889.

676 HISTORY OF STONINGTON.

CHILDREN:
364 JOSEPH STANTON, b. Dec. 11, 1825, d. Sept. 11, 1834.
365 WILLIAM, b. Dec. 19, 1828, m. Lydia H. Clift May 3, 1853.
366 **ELIAS**, b. Jan. 19, 1830, m. Sarah Brown.
367 JULIA ANN, b. June 29, 1832, m. Salmon C. Foote Oct. 16, 1851.
368 JOSEPH STANTON, b. Aug. 12, 1834, m. Elizabeth C. Foote.
369 CHARLES, b. March 28, 1837, m. Julia A. Lewis Nov. 23, 1859.
370 WARREN, b. June 16, 1844, d. Nov. 9, 1869.
371 MARTHA E., b. Jan. 26, 1847, d. Oct. 15, 1857.

Charles W. Williams of Stonington (No. 281) m. Amy Swan in 1802 (No. 94), that family.

CHILDREN:
372 CAROLINE, b. ———, d. in infancy.
373 EMMA, b. in 1805, m. Grandison Phillips Nov. 5, 1826.

Ephraim Williams of Stonington (No. 295) m. Hannah Eliza, daughter of Amos Denison (No. 469), that family, April 13, 1815, both of Stonington, Conn.

CHILDREN:
374 HEPZIBAH P., b. Feb. 9, 1816, m. Dr. William Hyde March 2, 1836 (No. 48), that family.
375 HANNAH ELIZABETH, b. Nov. 16, 1817, m. Courtland P. Dixon Sept. 9, 1841.
376 MARTHA D., b. March 15, 1820, d. Nov. 28, 1820.
377 EPHRAIM, b. Jan. 25, 1822, d. Oct. 27, 1822.
378 SARAH POTTER, b. May 1, 1825, m. William L. Palmer (No. 481), Palmer family; she d. May 18, 1877.
379 EPHRAIM, b. Dec. 1, 1826, m. 1st, Pauline Denison Oct. 19, 1849; 2d, Mary D. Babcock July 3, 1873.
380 EDWARD, b. April 21, 1830, d. Sept. 11, 1830.
381 CHARLES P., b. Sept. 28, 1828, d. May 16, 1832.
382 EMELINE PENDLETON, b. May 18, 1832, m. Jabish Holmes Oct. 23, 1855 (No. 113), that family.
383 AMOS DENISON, b. June 30, 1834, m. Elizabeth Fitch Dec. 24, 1860.
384 JOSEPH PHELPS, b. Aug. 8, 1836, m. Elizabeth Town Oct. 24, 1866.
385 MARTHA JANE, b. July 27, 1838, m. John H. Hunter Sept. 9, 1868.
386 CHARLES P., b. Aug. 19, 1840, m. Fannie Mallory Oct. 18, 1868.

NOTE.—Hon. Ephraim Williams and his brother, Charles P. Williams, were very prominent and successful business men of Stonington. They accumulated large fortunes, which they liberally bestowed in generous benefactions to their relatives and friends.

Charles P. Williams (No. 297) m. Betsey Smith, April 23, 1837. She d. Sept. 12, 1860. He m. for his second wife, Georgia P. Babcock (No. 249), Babcock family, June 11, 1862, all of Stonington, Conn.

CHILDREN BY FIRST MARRIAGE:
387 BESSIE S., b. Sept. 9, 1833, m. Oct. 20, 1862, E. Sherman.
388 MARY B., b. Sept. 20, 1835, m. Nov. 15 1855, Coddington Billings (No. 199), that family.
389 CHARLES P., b. Nov. 6, 1841, d. Nov. 30, 1861.

CHILDREN BY SECOND MARRIAGE:
390 GEORGIA, b. ———, m. ———.
391 CHARLES P., b. ———, m. ———.

ROBERT WILLIAMS FAMILY. 677

Isaac Williams of Stonington (No. 298) m. Nancy Avery (No. 201), that family, Aug. 18, 1804, both of Stonington; m. 2d, Susan Burnham, June 14, 1827.

CHILDREN:

392 NANCY A., b. Nov. 19, 1804, m. John Holmes, Jr.
393 STEPHEN A., b. Sept. 22, 1806, d. April 21, 1807.
394 HANNAH A., b. Feb. 21, 1808, d. Dec. 29, 1860.
395 MARY A., b. March 17, 1810.
396 ISAAC A., b. May 30, 1813, d. Aug. 26, 1834.
397 LUCY HALLAM, b. April 22, 1816.
398 JOEL BENEDICT, b. Dec. 22, 1818, m. Elizabeth A. Niles.
399 AUGUSTUS POMEROY, b. Aug. 12, 1821, d. Sept. 22, 1857.

CHILDREN BY SECOND MARRIAGE:

400 SUSAN, b. ——.
401 ABIGAIL POWERS, b. ——.
402 PHEBE, b. ——.
403 JOSHUA PERKINS, b. ——.

Cyrus Williams of Stonington (No. 299) m. Martha Wheeler Aug. 31, 1806 (No. 198), Wheeler family. He d. Oct. 30, 1863; she d. Dec. 27, 1857.

CHILDREN:

404 JOANNA, b. ——.
405 THOMAS WHEELER, b. ——.
406 MARTHA ESTHER, b. ——.
407 SARAH, b. ——.
408 TIRZAH MOSS, b. ——.

John Pitts Williams (No. 304) m. Cynthia York (No. 165), of that family, Nov. 28, 1816, both of Stonington, Conn.; he d. May 13, 1872; his wife d. Feb. 27, 1875.

CHILDREN:

409 PHEBE, b. Jan. 29, 1818, m. Noyes Ladd.
410 NANCY, b. Feb. 20, 1820.
411 JOHN PITTS, b. Jan. 5, 1822, m. Harriet Wheeler (No. 288), Wheeler family.
412 EMILY, b. April 13, 1824.
413 HARRIET, b. Aug. 30, 1826.
414 ELIZABETH, b. Jan. 31, 1827, m. Andrew Chapman.
415 ANN, b. April 17, 1831, m. ——, Mr. Sampson.
416 CYNTHIA, b. April 4, 1835.
417 MARTHA, b. Nov. 26, 1837.

Gen. William Williams, Jr., of Norwich (No. (342), m. Harriet, daughter of Capt. Bela Peck, —— 11, 1812. He was one of the founders of the Norwich Free Academy and d. Oct. 28, 1870.

CHILDREN:

418 THOMAS WHEELER, b. July 14, 1815.
419 BELA PECK, b. April 12, 1817, d. July 6, 1831.

Major Thomas Wheeler Williams (No. 343) of New London was in the whaling and sealing business, one of the incorporators of the New London Northern R. R. Co., and its first president. He was elected to Congress in 1838, and served two terms; m. Lucretia Woodbridge Perkins May 15, 1817.

CHILDREN:

420 LUCRETIA SHAW, b. Feb. 12, 1818.
422 WILLIAM PERKINS, b. Aug. 17, 1819.
423 HARRIET, b. May 28, 1821.
424 THOMAS SHAW, b. Jan. 16, 1823.
425 RICHARD LAW, b. Nov. 17, 1824.
426 MARY, b. April 12, 1826.
427 ELLEN PERKINS, b. Feb. 12, 1828.
428 CHARLES AUGUSTUS, b. March 15, 1829, m. Elizabeth Hoyt, Aug. 28, 1861.

CHILDREN:

429 WILLIAM, b. June 2, 1862 (now Major U. S. V.)
430 MARY HOYT, b. April 28, 1864.

Franklin Williams (No. 349) m. Mary Stanton, July 20, 1835 (No. 395), Stanton family. He was postmaster at Stonington for many years. He d. Dec. 28, 1885.

CHILDREN:

431 HORACE THURSTON, b. Aug. 22, 1837, d. Feb. 9, 1856.
432 MARY STANTON, b. Aug. 28, 1843, d. March 11, 1844.
433 WILLIAM, b. Jan. 10, 1845, m. Emily F. Breed Jan. 21, 1874; she d. Dec. 30, 1876. He m. 2d, Mrs. Parmenus Avery.

Calvin Goddard Williams (No. 351) m. Ann Billings Oct. 25, 1841 (No. 197), that family.

CHILDREN:

434 THOMAS WHEELER, b. ———, m. Ella E. Crosby June 23, 1878.
435 CALVIN GODDARD, b. ———, m. Louise M. Potts Jan. 16, 1873.

Thomas Wheeler Williams (No. 356) m. Lucy Ann Fairfield, 1826.

CHILDREN:

436 LYDIA, b. Jan. 2, 1827.
437 JAMES, b. Sept. 13, 1828.

Eleazer Williams (No. 26) of Roxbury, Mass., m. Mary (Rediat) Hyde of Newton, Mass., in 1695. Went first to Lebanon, Conn., from whence he removed to Stonington, Conn., in 1712, where he purchased a large tract of land on Quaugutaug Hill, built him a house, where he lived the remainder of his days. He d. May 19, 1725.

CHILDREN:

438 NEHEMIAH, b. Feb. 4, 1695, m. Deborah Williams; 2d, Hannah Stoddard.
439 MARTHA, b. March 11, 1700, d. 1703.
440 MARY, b. Jan. 18, 1704, m. (2nd wife) to Samuel Williams (No. 42).
441 HANNAH, b. ———, m. Ephraim Woodbridge.
442 ELIZABETH, b. ———, m. Jonathan Smith June, 1732.
443 PRISCILLA, b. ———, m. David Lester May 17, 1738.

ROBERT WILLIAMS FAMILY. 679

CHILD:

444 PRISCILLA WILLIAMS LESTER, m. Jonathan Wheeler April 29, 1756 (No. 342), that family.

Nehemiah Williams (No. 438) m. Deborah Williams (No. 158) June 16, 1719, both of Stonington, Conn. He d. Aug. 25, 1778; she d. Jan. 31, 1756; m. 2d, Hannah Stoddard March 2, 1757, who d. Aug. 7, 1818, aged 77 years.

CHILDREN:

445 DEBORAH, b. Aug. 25, 1720.
446 NEHEMIAH, b. Jan. 20, 1723, m. Abigail Allen.
447 EUNICE, b. Sept. 20, 1726, m. Elisha Williams (No. 51).
448 MARTHA, b. May 23, 1728, m. Jonathan Denison (No. 161), Denison family.
449 ELEAZER, b. Aug. 1, 1730, m. Abigail Prentice.
450 LUCRETIA, b. April 21, 1733, m. Titus Smith.
451 PRUDENCE, b. July 17, 1738, d. Sept. 14, 1744.

Nehemiah Williams of Stonington (No. 446) m. Abigail Allen of Groton April 29, 1747. He d. Aug. 19, 1797; his wife d. June 23, 1767. He m. 2d, Mrs. Bethia Wilber of Stonington, Conn.

CHILDREN BY FIRST MARRIAGE:

452 NEHEMIAH, b. Sept. 26, 1749, m. Mary Noyes.
453 CHRISTOPHER, b. July 5, 1751, d. in the West Indies.
454 EUNICE, b. July 25, 1753.
455 PARK, b. July 25, 1755, m. Deborah Williams (No. 460).
456 DANIEL, b. April 6, 1758.
457 ABIGAIL, b. Aug. 5, 1760, m. Seth Williams of Groton (No. 39), Robert Williams family.

CHILDREN BY SECOND MARRIAGE:

458 ELAM, b. Nov. 4, 1769.

Dea. Eleazer Williams of Stonington (No. 449) m. Abigail Prentice (No. 28), that family, March 14, 1754; she d. Aug. 18, 1786.

CHILDREN:

459 MARTHA, b. Oct. 26, 1755, d. Aug. 18, 1756.
460 DEBORAH, b. July 24, 1757, m. Park Williams (No. 455).
461 ELEAZER, b. June 27, 1759, m. Mary or Polly Billings (No. 120), that family.
462 GILBERT, b. April 16, 1761, m. Grace Billings April 15, 1799 (No. 121), that family.
463 MARTHA, b. Dec. 15, 1762, m. Oliver Denison (No. 305), Denison family.
464 AMOS, b. Dec. 31, 1764.
465 DANIEL, b. Jan. 28, 1767, m. Eunice Smith.
466 PRENTICE, b. April 15, 1769.
467 FANNY, b. Feb. 8, 1771, m. Daniel Chesebrough Jan. 6, 1793 (No. 317), Chesebrough family.
468 ELAM, b. July 14, 1773, m. 1st, in the spring 1797, Katharine Bogart; 2d, m. Abbie Weed, ———; 3d, m. Eliza Ten Eyck; 4th, m. Deborah Vanderpool.
469 HANNAH, b. June 16, 1775, m. Amos Hallam.

Nehemiah Williams, 3d, of Stonington (No. 452) m. Mary Noyes. He d. at sea, aged 29 years. His wife m. again, Joseph Culver of Groton.

CHILDREN:

470 NEHEMIAH, b. ———.
471 POLLY, b. ———.

Park Williams of Stonington (No. 455) m. Deborah Williams (No. 460) of Stonington, in 1779. He d. Dec. 9, 1833; his wife d. June 20, 1846.

CHILDREN:

472 AMOS, b. April 9, 1780, m. Lucy Coats.
473 BETSEY, b. Feb. 14, 1782, d. in infancy.
474 ABIGAIL, b. Nov. 20, 1783, d. Sept. 20, 1819.
475 PARK, b. June 26, 1786, m. Sarah B. Avery.
476 ALLEN, b. Oct. 30, 1788, d. in infancy.
477 RUSSELL, b. Aug. 19, 1790, m. Nancy Wheeler.
478 Son, b. ———, d. May 6, 1793.
479 FANNY, b. Feb. 6, 1795, d. June 30, 1818.
480 PRENTICE, b. July 22, 1798, m. Roxanna Williams (No. 46), Groton Williams family.
481 SANFORD, b. Aug. 27, 1800, m. twice.

Eleazer Williams of Stonington (No. 461) m. Mary Billings (No. 120), that family, Nov. 5, 1786, of Stonington. He d. March 20, 1814.

CHILDREN:

482 MARY, b. March 28, 1788, m. Charles Crary.
483 ELIZA, b. Oct. 28, 1789, m. Ethan Denison (No. 345), Denison family.
484 ELEAZER, b. July 30, 1791, m. Nancy S. Avery of Groton.
485 DENISON, b. March 2, 1793, m. Hannah Avery of Groton.
486 MATILDA, b. Jan. 29, 1797, m. 1st, James Avery; 2d, Rev. Ira Stewart.
487 FRANK, b. March 4, 1797, m. Nancy Hutcherson.
488 NOYES, b. March 28, 1799, m. Emily Pendleton (No. 119), that family.
489 GILES, b. March 26, 1801, m. 1st, Abbie Stanton; 2d, Mary Vanderpool.
490 AUSTIN, b. March 19, 1803, m. Mary Avery of Groton.
491 ALFRED, b. July 16, 1805, m. Frances Phelps.
492 PHEBE, b. Dec. 16, 1808, m. Frank Pendleton Feb. 11, 1830 (No. 117).
493 IRA, b. ———, m. Eliza Sanger of Syracuse, N. Y.

Daniel Williams of Stonington (No. 465) m. Eunice Smith April 1, 1792.

CHILDREN:

494 EUNICE, b. Dec. 25, 1792, d. Oct. 12, 1801.
495 CHARLES SMITH, b. Nov. 25, 1796, d. Jan. 17, 1797.
496 MARY SMITH, b. March 5, 1804, d. unmarried.
497 CHARLES SMITH, b. March 25, 1806, m. Lucy R. Swan Jan. 6, 1850.

Amos Williams of Stonington (No. 472) m. Lucy Coats Sept. 27, 1807.

ROBERT WILLIAMS FAMILY. 681

CHILDREN:

498 CYNTHIA C., b. March 20, 1809, m. Henry Williams.
499 CALVIN, b. Nov. 17, 1819, d. June 1, 1882.
500 LEONARD, b. Nov. 24, 1812, m. Mary Copp May 11, 1843 (No. 73), Copp family; he d. May 30, 1876.
501 EDWARD, b. Aug. 21, 1819, d. Dec. 21, 1819.
502 MARY ELLEN, b. June 18, 1825.

Park Williams of Stonington (No. 475) m. Sarah Belton Avery of Groton, Jan. 13, 1811; he d. in Vermont in 1875.

CHILDREN:

503 ELIZABETH, b. May 7, 1812, d. May 24, 1812.
504 PERRY ALLEN, b. Sept. 10, 1813, d. June 3, 1814.
506 PARK AVERY, b. March 10, 1815.
507 ALFRED GRISWOLD, b. Dec. 19, 1817.
508 JAMES AUGUSTUS, b. Nov. 29, 1819, d. Nov. 15, 1835.
509 COURTLAND AURELIUS, b. Oct. 14, 1821, d. Aug. 12, 1822.
510 SARAH ELIZABETH, b. May 23, 1823.
511 DEBORAH, b. Feb. 15, 1825.
512 MARY, b. Dec. 23, 1826.
513 FRANCES ANN, b. Sept. 3, 1829, d. June 3, 1892.

Russell Williams of Stonington (No. 477) m. Nancy Wheeler (No. 436), Wheeler family, Jan. 30, 1817. He d. April 14, 1852; she d. June 10, 1877.

CHILDREN:

514 FRANCES E., b. Feb. 4, 1818, m. Appleton A. Woodward Aug. 12, 1840.
515 ABBY, b. Jan. 19, 1820, m. Oliver H. Perry Aug. 10, 1842.
516 ESTHER D., b. Aug. 11, 1829, m. Rev. William Turkington Oct. 11, 1852.
517 NANCY B., b. Aug. 28, 1831, m. Samuel Gladding May 11, 1854.

Prentice Williams of Stonington (No. 480) m. Roxanna (No. 46), of the William Williams family, May 28, 1820. He d. March 14, 1869; his wife d. July 2, 1872.

CHILD:

518 ALLEN PRENTICE, b. March 27, 1821, m. Delia Avery of Groton, Conn., Oct. 13, 1863; he d. May 9, 1894.

Sanford Williams of Stonington (No. 481) m. 1st, Sally Prentice, who d. May 2, 1827. He m. 2d, Betsey Williams (No. 520) Dec. 31, 1829. He d. Aug. 16, 1847.

CHILD BY FIRST MARRIAGE:

519 BETSEY, b. ——, m. —— Cook.

Isaac Williams of Stonington (No. 192) m. Phebe Hurlbert of Groton Aug. 14, 1783.

CHILDREN:

520 BETSEY, b. Oct. 13, 1790, m. Sanford Williams (No. 481).
521 POLLY, b. July 17, 1793.
522 ISAAC, b. May 9, 1797.
523 JOHN, b. April 29, 1801.

Eleazer Williams of Stonington (No. 484) m. Nancy S. Avery of Groton Nov. 30, 1815.

CHILDREN:

524 ELEAZER, b. Dec. 7, 1816, m. Eliza Ann Bradley Dec. 10, 1849.
525 YOUNGS, b. Oct. 4, 1819, d. July 23, 1830.
526 ANN ELIZABETH, b. Dec. 17, 1827, m. Dr. Francis M. Manning Dec. 8, 1847.
527 MARY ABBY, b. June 24, 1829, m. Abel N. Simmons Nov. 20, 1850.

Denison Williams of Stonington (No. 485) m. Hannah Avery of Groton.

CHILDREN:

528 MARY ESTHER, b. March 13, 1818, m. John Brewster April 2, 1840.
529 CELIA, b. July 9, 1822, m. Welcome Browning Aug. 24, 1857.
530 DENISON, b. June 30, 1819, d. Feb. 28, 1867.
531 LUKE L., b. Jan. 12, 1824, d. Feb. 16, 1859.
532 PARK AVERY, b. Feb. 28, 1826, d. Aug. 31, 1892.
533 YOUNGS AVERY, b. May 25, 1833, d. Aug. 24, 1865.
534 ELAM V., b. July 1, 1837, d. March 9, 1849.
535 EUNICE, b. March 1, 1828, m. Richard A. Roberts July 24, 1866.
536 FRANK, b. April 26, 1830, m. Mary Clark Sept. 8, 1858.

Giles Williams (No. 489) m. 1st, Abby Jane Stanton (No. 61), Robert Stanton family, March 23, 1831. She was drowned by the burning of the steamer Erie on Lake Erie. Mr. Williams m. 2d, Mary Elizabeth Vanderpool Dec. 12, 1848. He d. Apr. 3, 1888; his widow d. May —, 1900.

CHILDREN BY FIRST MARRIAGE:

537 ABBY JANE, b. Aug. 10, 1832, m. Charles A. Jones June 5, 1878.
538 JOSEPHINE, b. Nov., 1839, m. Joseph Oscar Cottrell Oct. 22, 1863 (No. 57), that family.

WILLIAM WILLIAMS FAMILY.

1. Descendants of WILLIAM WILLIAMS, b. in Wales, a part of the British dominions. He came to this country in 1662 and settled in New London, now Ledyard, in 1663. He served in King Philip's war. He m. Arabella Thompson, date not given.

CHILDREN:

2 RICHARD, b. ———.
3 WILLIAM, b. ———, m. Margaret Cooke.
4 HENRY, b. ———, m., name of wife unknown.
5 STEPHEN, b. ———.
6 MARY, b. ———.

William Williams (No. 3) m. Margaret Cooke.

CHILDREN:

7 WILLIAM, b. Jan. 26, 1709, m. Margaret Morgan. He d. in 1795. Their son,
8 LIEUT. WILLIAM, b. Feb. 17, 1741. He was in the military and Naval Service during the war of the Revolution, from 1775 to 1783. (Groton Town Records.) He m. Mrs. Prudence (Stanton) Fanning.

CHILDREN:

9 WILLIAM, b. Oct. 13, 1780, m. Amy Stanton.
10 JAMES, b. June 4, 1783, d. unmarried.
11 ERASTUS, b. Sept. 16, 1785, m. Nancy Hewitt (No. 182), Hewitt family.
12 SALINA, b. April 24, 1788, m. Mr. Packer.
13 SARAH, b. Nov. 6, 1790, m. Elisha Ayer.
14 MELINDA, b. Sept. 8, 1793, m. Luke Gallup (No. 258), Gallup family.
15 AMANDA, b. April 7, 1798, m Baxter Gray.

Judge William Williams (No. 9) was appointed by the General Assembly in 1819, Judge of the Probate District of Stonington, which then included the towns of Stonington, Groton, Ledyard and North Stonington, which office he held twelve years. He m. Amy Stanton, daughter of Amos Stanton (No. 158), that family.

CHILDREN:

16 WILLIAM, b. ———, d. unmarried.
17 JEFFERSON, b. ———, d. unmarried.
18 JAMES, b. ———, m. Sabra Gray.
19 MARY LOUISA, b. ———, m. Rufus Leeds Fanning.
20 JENNETTE, b. ———, m. John D. Williams.
21 LAURA, b. Oct. 23, 1817, m. Nehemiah M. Gallup Oct. 27, 1841 (No. 279), that family.

Erastus Williams (No. 11) m. Nancy Hewitt Feb. 15, 1818 (No. 182), that family. He served in the war of 1812, and was at the bombardment at Stonington, Aug. 10, 1814. He lived at the Williams homestead in Ledyard, on Cider Hill.

CHILDREN:

22 ELIAS H., b. July 23, 1819, m. Hannah Larrabee April 23, 1849.
23 PRUDENCE A., b. Sept. 11, 1821, m. Gustavus A. Appelman Oct. 28,1841.
24 WILLIAM, b. May 21, 1823, m. Mary Allen April 26, 1848; m. 2d, Mary E. Williams May 14, 1855.
25 DUDLEY R., b. April 16, 1825, m. Mrs. Alice Otis March 1, 1883.
26 JOHN, b. Jan. 31, 1827.
27 LYDIA W., b. March 21, 1829, m. William R. Fish Jan. 19, 1848 (No. 63), Fish family.
28 JOHN HEWITT, b. Oct. 1, 1831, d. Sept. 21, 1850.
29 HANNAH MARIA, b. Dec. 12, 1834, d. June 5, 1854.
30 SARAH LOUISE, b. Feb. 25, 1837, d. Sept. 21, 1850.

Henry Williams (No. 4), m., name of wife and date of marriage unknown. Their son,

31 HENRY, b. June 13, 1716, m. Mary Boardman in 1743. She was b. March 14, 1725.

CHILDREN:

32 JOHN, b. Sept. 5, 1744.
33 JOSEPH, b. Aug. 7, 1747, m. Hopestill Elliott.
34 LIEUT. HENRY, b. Dec. 14, 1749, m. Eunice ———; he was killed in the massacre at Fort Griswold Sept. 6, 1781.
35 A daughter, b. and d. Feb. 28, 1752.
36 PELEG, b. March 20, 1753.
37 ABIGAIL, b. March 17, 1756.
38 AMOS, b. July 13, 1758.
39 SETH, b. Jan. 21, 1761, m. Abigail Williams; 2d, Anna Smith Gallup.
40 ROGER, b. Dec. 24, 1763.
41 RUSSELL, b. June 26, 1769.

Joseph Williams (No. 33) m. Hopestill Elliott. Their son,

42 JOSEPH, b. ———, m. Sarah, daughter of Stephen and Phebe Hurlbert, Feb. 4, 1780.

CHILDREN:

43 STEPHEN, b. ———.
44 SALLY, b. ———.
45 PRUDENCE, b. ———, m. 1st, Ambrose Fish; 2d, Nathan Barnes.
46 ROXANNA, b. ———, m. Prentice Williams May 28, 1820 (No. 480), Robert Williams family.

Seth Williams (No. 39) m. Abigail Williams (No. 457), Robert Williams family, Jan. 11, 1787. He m. 2d, Mrs. Anna Smith Gallup Jan. 30, 1825. He d. May 21, 1843.

CHILDREN:

47 BETHIA, b. Nov. 11, 1787, m. John Sands Avery in 1812.
48 WARREN, b. April 15, 1789, m. Elizabeth Gallup (No. 175), Gallup family.
49 GURDON, b. March 28, 1791, d. at Detroit, Mich., July 20, 1854, aged 63.
50 ABIGAIL, b. Sept. 24, 1792, m. John Avery of Griswold Dec. 9, 1812.
51 ELIZA, b. Sept. 18, 1794, m. William Hewitt (No. 189), that family.
52 EUNICE, b. Dec. 20, 1797, m. Dea. Erastus Gallup (No. 171), that family.
53 SETH, b. Jan. 25, 1802, m. Lucy Ann Noyes (No. 269), that family.
54 ASENETH, b. Jan. 25, 1804, m. Col. Isaac W. Geer Jan. 9, 1825.

WILLIAM WILLIAMS FAMILY.

Warren Williams (No. 48) m. Elizabeth Gallup Jan. 12, 1815 (No. 175), that family.

CHILDREN:

55 HENRY WARREN, b. Jan. 20, 1816, m. Lucy J. Stone May 20, 1846.
56 GURDON OSMOND, b. Nov. 14, 1817, m. Frances C. Griggs July 17, 1847.
57 ELIZABETH MARTHA, b. Feb. 2, 1820, m. John Pattern Feb. 3, 1846.
58 HEZEKIAH UFFORD, b. Aug. 10, 1822, m. Cynthia A. K. Niles Sept. 8, 1850.
59 JULIA ANN, b. Feb. 11, 1825, m. Edward P. Hayward April 20, 1854.
60 ASENETH GEER, b. May 13, 1827, d. Jan. 9, 1890.
61 CHARITY MORGAN, b. May 2, 1829, m. C. K. Robinson July 3, 1861.
62 SARAH GALLUP, b. Aug. 6, 1831.
63 NATHAN GALLUP, b. June 28, 1833, m. 1st, Helen C. Dunham April 14, 1859; 2d, Julia Hanna Dec. 14, 1870.
64 JANE EMERETTE, b. Dec. 25, 1838, m. John P. Derby March 18, 1863.

Seth Williams (No. 53) m. Lucy Ann Noyes Feb. 23, 1827 (No. 269), Noyes family. He d. June 20, 1854. She d. at Mystic, June 8, 1890, in the 85th year of her age.

CHILDREN:

65 LUCY ANN, b. Jan. 31, 1823, m. Ulysses Avery (No. 228), that family.
66 EUNICE ZERVIAH, b. March 19, 1829, m. Erasmus Avery (No. 235), that family.
67 SETH NOYES, b. April 23, 1831, m. Eliza P. Noyes Nov. 26, 1857, (No. 377), that family; she d. May 20, 1870. He m. 2d, Mary Emma Morgan June 28, 1871 (No. 22), that family. He d. April 7, 1889.
68 HARRIET NEWELL, b. Nov. 22, 1823, m. Frank Grant (No. 98), that family.
69 GURDON, b. Nov. 6, 1834, m. Eliza Cook, daughter of Rev. Nehemiah Cook.
70 JOSEPH WARREN, b. Aug. 27, 1837, m. Emma M. Pine, Oct. 4, 1865.
71 WILLIAM HENRY, b. Oct. 22, 1839, m. Susan Hunter.
72 BENJAMIN FRANKLIN, b. Sept. 7, 1841, m. Anna Louisa Noyes (No. 399), Noyes family.
73 ABBIE ELIZA, b. July 7, 1843.
74 ORIN MERWIN, b. Nov. 17, 1845, d.

WITTER FAMILY.

WILLIAM WITTER, the first of this family of whom we have any certain knowledge, was evidently one of the early settlers of Lynn, Mass. He appears there in court in April, 1657. In his depositions he said that he was a farmer in Swampscot, Mass., which was a short distance from Nahant, Mass. The court proceedings to which he was a party at this time related to the title of the land upon which he had erected his then dwelling house. The contention was between him and an Indian, called Duke William, who claimed that his house site was the ground where his wigwam formerly stood. After a conference and compromise the affair was settled satisfactorily to both parties.

    1 WILLIAM, b. in the year 1584, and died in the year 1659, as his will is dated May 6, 1659, he was, therefore, 75 years old. He m. Annis ———, doubtless before he came to this country, and they became the parents of two children, viz.:
    2 JOSIAH, b. ———.
    3 HANNAH, b. ———, m. Robert Burdick, and 2d, Edmund Chamberlain, and she d. in 1696. Her father, William Witter, left a will which gave one-half of his estate to his wife and the other half to his son, Josiah Witter, simply giving his daughter Hannah an ewe and lamb, in one year after his death.

Josiah Witter (No. 2) m. for his first wife, Elizabeth (No. 3), daughter of Thomas and Mary Wheeler, in Lynn, Mass., Feb. 25, 1662, and soon after came to Stonington, Conn., to reside. He purchased large tracts of land and built him a dwelling house thereon, situated a short distance from the residence of Thomas Wheeler, his father-in-law, where he lived the remainder of his life, and where all of his children were born. The house was situated in what is now North Stonington, a short distance north of the present residence of Col. James T. Brown, which occupies the homestead site of Thomas Wheeler, born in 1602. The house was more recently occupied by James Irish, and before that owned by Jeremy Wheeler. Mrs. Elizabeth (Wheeler) Witter d. Aug. 5, 1672, and Mr. Josiah Witter m. 2d, Sarah Crandall, daughter of Elder John Crandall of Rhode Island, date not known. He d. before 1690, and his widow m. for her second husband Peter Button, and had four children, viz.: Peter, Mary,

Matthias and Eliphal Button. Josiah Witter's two sons, Ebenezer and John, after their father's death, relinquished all their right, title and interest in and to their late father's estate, by giving to the administrator thereof a receipt in full discharge in the year 1689. The son John Witter, also by his receipt, relinquished all right, title and claim against his mother, Mrs. Sarah Crandall Button, and her husband, Peter Button. After the death of his father, Mr. Ebenezer Witter moved to the town of Preston, Conn., where he became a prominent and useful citizen.

CHILDREN OF JOSIAH WITTER AND MARY WHEELER WITTER.
4 ELIZABETH, b. March 15, 1663.
5 MARY, b. Feb. 20, 1665.
6 EBENEZER, b. March 25, 1668.

CHILDREN OF JOSIAH WITTER AND SECOND WIFE SARAH CRANDALL:
7 JOHN, b. March 11, 1677, m. Sarah Tefft, and 2d, Mary ———.
8 SARAH, b. Feb. 9, 1679.
9 HANNAH, b. March 17, 1681, m. Thomas Parke Nov. 5, 1703.

Ebenezer Witter (No. 6) m. Dorothy Morgan, daughter of Joseph (No. 5), Morgan family, and Dorothy (Park) Morgan, May 5th, 1693; she was b. Feb. 29, 1675. She was then of New London, which was later Groton, Conn. Ebenezer Witter d. Jan. 31, 1712, and his widow m. Daniel Brewster (No. 8), of that family, Dec. 19, 1727, and she d. March 9, 1759.

CHILDREN:
10 ELIZABETH, b. March 3, 1694, m. Benjamin Brewster Oct. 16, 1714.
11 MARY, b. March 2, 1696, m. Jeremiah Tracey Oct. 13, 1713.
12 JOSEPH (twin), b. June 12, 1698, m. Elizabeth Gore.
13 JOSIAH (twin), b. June 12, 1698, d. Sept. 20, 1698.
14 EBENEZER, b. Nov. 30, 1700, m. Elizabeth Brown March 26, 1726.
15 DOROTHY, b. Dec. 11, 1702.
16 HANNAH, b. Nov. 26, 1705, m. Ephraim Smith (No. 15), Smith family.
17 WILLIAM, b. May 24, 1707.
18 ABIGAIL, b. and d. Jan. 31, 1712.

John Witter (No. 7) m. 1st, Sarah Tefft, daughter of Samuel Tefft of South Kingston, R. I. She d. some time before March 16, 1725, and m. 2d, Mary ———, who probably died very soon after Dec. 22, 1743. He was admitted a freeman in Westerly Jan. 29, 1702, and became a prominent man and a large landholder, some of which remains in the possession of his descendants now. It is not surely known just how many children he had.

CHILDREN:
19 SARAH, b. ———.
20 JOHN, JR., b. ———, m. Sept. 7, 1740, Annie Davis.
21 JOSEPH, b. April 4, 1716, m. Dec. 9, 1736, Sarah Steward.
22 MARTHA, b. ———, m. Oct. 18, 1747, Stephen Lewis.

Joseph Witter (No. 12) m. Elizabeth Gore (No. 29), of that family, Aug. 13, 1722.

CHILDREN:

23 SAMUEL, b. May 28, 1723.
24 JOSEPH, b. Dec. 15, 1724.
25 EZRA, b. Jan. 22, 1729.
26 HANNAH, b. Oct. 3, 1730.
27 EBENEZER, b. Sept. 11, 1732.
28 ELIJAH, b. April 7, 1735.
29 EUNICE, b. Dec. 8, 1740.

Ebenezer Witter (No. 14) m. Elizabeth Brown, daughter of John Brown, March 26, 1729. She d. Aug. 27, 1754, and he m. 2d, Mrs. Mary Avery of Groton.

CHILDREN:

30 JOSIAH, b. and d. Nov. 17, 1729.
31 NATHAN, b. Nov. 15, 1731.
32 JOHN, b. and d. Sept. 17, 1733.
33 MARY, b. July 11, 1735.
34 JACOB, b. May 6, 1737.
35 ELIZABETH, b. Jan. 2, 1739.
36 JOHN, b. and d. Sept. 10, 1742.
37 EZRA, b. Oct. ———.
38 JAMES, b. and d. Sept. 30, 1746.
39 ESTHER, b. May 12, 1753.

Capt. William Witter (No. 17) m. 1st, Mary Douglass, and she d. Nov. 30, 1734, and Capt. Witter m. 2d, Zerviah Smith of Canterbury, Conn., Jan. 1, 1735. She d. Jan. 30, 1737, and Capt. Witter m. 3d, Hannah Freeman Nov. 6, 1738. She d. April 19, 1759, and Capt. Witter m. for his fourth and last wife, Elizabeth ———; she d. Aug. 9, 1798, aged 81 years, and Capt. Witter d. Sept. 9, 1798, aged 91 years.

CHILDREN BY THIRD WIFE, HANNAH FREEMAN:

40 MARY, b. May 12, 1740.
41 JOSIAH, b. Feb. 19, 1741.
42 WILLIAM, b. Jan. 31, 1744, d. 1759.
43 ZERVIAH, b. and d. March 19, 1746.
44 DANIEL, b. May 9, 1748.
45 HANNAH, b. May 15, 1750, m. Jonathan Smith Nov. 23, 1769, and she d. May 29, 1823.
46 FREDERICK, b. Aug. 13, 1752.
47 ELISHA, b. April 27, 1755.

John Witter, Jr. (No. 20) m. Annie Davis Sept. 7, 1740. He d. Nov., 1793.

CHILDREN:

48 SAMUEL, b. June 29, 1745, m. Tacy Porter Jan. 3, 1769.
49 SARAH, b. ———, m. David Dewey Jan. 12, 1768.
50 JOHN, b. ———, m. Meriam Worden April 7, 1763.
51 HANNAH, b. ———, m. Nathan Porter Nov. 29, 1764.

WITTER FAMILY.   689

Joseph Witter (No. 21) m. Sarah Steward Dec. 9, 1736. She was b. May 23, 1715, and d. March 23, 1802. He d. Jan. 12, 1799.

CHILDREN:

52 JOSEPH, JR., b. ———, never married, d. Feb., 1831.
53 JOSIAH, b. Jan. 25, 1739, m. Tacy Reynolds Feb. 2, 1764.
54 WILLIAM, b. ———, m. Martha Cole Nov. 1, 1764.

Ezra Witter (No. 25) and Anna Morgan, both of the town of Preston, Conn., were m. Feb. 1, 1752.

CHILDREN:

55 ANNA, b. April 30, 1753.
56 EZRA, b. Jan. 4, 1755.
57 ISAAC, b. Jan. 10, 1757.
58 WILLIAM, b. March 16, 1759, m. Esther Breed (No. 62a), daughter of Dea. Nathan and Lucy (Babcock) Breed, date unknown, and moved with his family to Eastern New York State.

Ezra Witter (No. 25) while in a state of mental aberration, conceived the idea that his wife and children were alienated from him, which alienated him from them, in consequence of which he determined to end their existence and his own, and before his friends and neighbors suspected his purpose he succeeded in taking the lives of his wife and three oldest children, but before he consummated his determination to take the life of his youngest child, William Witter, and his own life, he was seized and bound by his friends, which had been attracted to the awful scene by the heartrending screams of his wife and children. Almost immediately after the consummation of this awful tragedy he became a raving maniac, followed by idiocy. During the remnant of his life his friends made an enclosure of timber in one of the rooms of his dwelling house, in which he was kept confined, until death ended all of his besetting horrors. His uncle, Joseph Witter (No. 24), was appointed guardian of the surviving son, William Witter (No. 58), who took him to Stonington, Conn., and by a proper business indenture bound him to Richard Wheeler in 1760, to live with him until he became 21 years of age, and to learn the farmers' occupation and weavers' trade, which he faithfully performed, growing up to manhood a model young man and subsequently becoming a prominent and useful citizen. He m., as told above, Esther Breed.

Samuel Witter (No. 48) m. Tacy Porter Jan. 5, 1769.

CHILDREN:

59 MARY, b. Dec. 10, 1769.
60 HULDAH, b. March 1, 1772.
61 DAVIS, b. May 4, 1774, d. Nov. 1, 1775.

62 SAMUEL, JR., b. Jan. 17, 1776, m. Mary Popple Nov. 12, 1796.
63 TACY, b. Feb. 14, 1779.
64 JOHN, b. March 31, 1781.
65 HANNAH, b. July 27, 1784.
66 PAUL, b. Sept. 19, 1787.
67 ANNIE, b. Nov. 9, 1789.

John Witter (No. 50) m. Merriam Worden, daughter of James Worden of Stonington, April 7, 1763. He d. before March 5, 1790.

CHILDREN:

68 ANNE, b. May 9, 1766.
69 JOHN, b. Dec. 19, 1768.
70 HOLLY, b. July 14, 1772.

Josiah Witter (No. 53) m. Tacy Reynolds Feb. 2, 1764. She was b. March 19, 1743.

CHILDREN:

71 WEEDEN, b. April 30, 1765.
72 SUSANNAH, b. May 7, 1767, m. Amos Langworthy Jan. 21, 1802.
73 LOIS, b. Oct. 1, 1768, never married.
74 HANNAH, b. Aug. 12, 1771.
75 JOSEPH F., b. March 28, 1773.
76 EUNICE F., b. Oct. 31, 1775.
77 JOSIAH, b. March 28, 1777.
78 SARAH, b. Feb. 6, 1779.

William Witter (No. 54) m. Nov. 1, 1764, Martha Cole.

CHILDREN:

79 SARAH, b. Nov. 12, 1765, d. Dec. 6, 1765.
80 SARAH, b. Dec. 3, 1766.
81 MARTHA F., b. April 27, 1769.
82 ELIZABETH, b. Aug. 4, 1771.
83 MARY, b. Nov. 6, 1773.
84 WEALTHY, b. Feb. 17, 1776.
85 WILLIAM, b. Aug. 26, 1778, m. Lucy Crandall Jan. 2, 1800.
86 ANNE F., b. Aug. 24, 1780.
87 JOSEPH, b. Dec. 13, 1782.
88 PHEBE, b. ———.

Susannah Witter (No. 72) m. March 21, 1802, Amos Langworthy, Jr., son of Amos Langworthy and wife, Sarah Babcock. She d. July 29, 1859, aged 92 years. Their daughter, Susan Langworthy, b. Dec. 8, 1810, m. Benjamin F. Chester, who was b. Sept. 13, 1816, and d. Jan. 23, 1889. She d. March 26, 1880. Their son, Albert L. Chester of Westerly, R. I., has contributed to the families of Witter and York.

WOODBRIDGE FAMILY.

Rev. John Woodbridge, a follower of Wickliffe, b. not far from 1492, and his descendants by the name of John to the fifth generation, braved the dangers of the same faith. The fifth in succession was the Rev. John Woodbridge, pastor of a Puritan church in Stanton, Wilts, England. He was the father of the first

1. REV. JOHN WOODBRIDGE in America. The family on this side of the water has also been illustrious by a long line of ministers.

Rev. John Woodbridge (No. 1), b. 1613, bred at Oxford, but left the university and was brought to New England by his uncle, Rev. Thomas Parker, in company with his cousin, Rev. James Noyes, in 1634, and were some of the first at Newbury, Mass. He seems to have had but little tendency to preach, for in 1637, the same year his father died in England, he was made Surveyor of the Arms and Representative to the General Court. Afterwards he taught school in Boston. He was living in Newbury when his father-in-law, Gov. Thomas Dudley, stirred him up to seek advancement as a minister, and on Oct. 24, 1645, he was ordained as first minister at the new town of Andover. In 1647, he went to England and remained there sixteen years. He was employed while there as a minister and teacher, but returned to Boston July 27, 1663, and was engaged with his uncle Parker in the ministry for a few years, until some dissension arose in the church, when he was dismissed before 1670. He d. March 17, 1695. He m. in 1639, Mercy, daughter of Gov. Thomas Dudley, who was the son of Capt. Roger Dudley, b. in England in 1576, came to New England in 1630, was several years Governor of Massachusetts Colony, and d. at Roxbury July 31, 1653, aged 77 years. His first wife, or the one who came with him, d. in 1643. He m. again before 1645, and had five more children, four by the first wife, of which Mercy, the wife of Rev. John Woodbridge, was one; she was b. Sept. 27, 1621, and d. July 1, 1691, aged 70. Her sister, Patience, m. Maj. Gen. Daniel Denison, and so this family is connected and related to both Denison and Noyes, as the mother of this Rev. John was daughter of Rev. Robert Parker and sister of the wife of Rev. William Noyes of Choulderton, Eng. Through this name of Dudley comes the favorite baptismal name into the Woodbridge family.

CHILDREN OF REV. JOHN AND MERCY WOODBRIDGE:

2 SARAH, b. June 7, 1640.
3 LUCIA, b. March 13, 1642, m. Rev. Simon Bradstreet of New London, and 2d, Capt. Daniel Epps Oct. 2, 1667.
4 DOROTHY, b. ———.
5 ANNE, b. ———.
6 JOHN, b. 1644.
7 THOMAS, b. 1649, m. June 12, 1671, Mary Jones, daughter of Mrs. Ann, second wife of Capt. Paul White, by a former husband, d. March 30, 1681, aged 33 years. In Judge Sewall's diary is the following: "Thomas Woodbridge, so burnt, in his own fire, that he dieth of insupportable torment, in about twelve hours' time."
8 MARY, b. 1652.
9 MARTHA, b. ———.
10 TIMOTHY, b. 1656, in England; was sixth minister of Hartford; m. Mehitable, daughter of Samuel Wyllis, widow of Rev. Isaac Foster, and she had first been widow of Daniel Russell of Charlestown. He m. 2d, Abigail, daughter of the rich widow of Phineas Wilson of Hartford, by her third husband, John Warren of Boston. He m. 3d, Mary, daughter of Hon. William Pitkin, widow of a minister. Only one child, Theodore, b. June 23, 1717.
11 JOSEPH, b. ———, m. Martha, eldest child of Ezekiel Rogers of Ipswich, May 20, 1688.
12 BENJAMIN, b. ———, m. Mary, daughter of Rev. John Ward of Haverhill, June 13, 1672; he d. Jan. 15, 1710.

Three of these sons, viz., John, Timothy and Benjamin, were ministers, and two of the daughters were ministers' wives.

John Woodbridge (No. 6), b. probably at Andover, 1644, began to preach there 1666, at Windsor in 1668, and he was ordained April 7, 1669, at Kenilworth, Conn., as it was called before modern barbarity inflicted the present name of Killingworth, and the government of the colony made him a grant of 250 acres of land the next year for good conduct. In 1679 he was settled at Wethersfield. He m. Oct. 26, 1671, Abigail, eldest daughter of Gov. William Leete. He d. 1690.

CHILDREN OF JOHN AND ABIGAIL:

13 JOHN, b. in Killingworth, 1678, settled in West Springfield in 1698, and m. Nov. 14, 1699, Jemima Elliot. He d. June 10, 1718.
14 EPHRAIM, b. 1680, graduated at Harvard College 1701; m. Hannah Morgan May 4, 1704. He was the first minister of Groton, and was ordained Nov., 1704. He continued pastor of this church till 1724, and d. in December of the following year, 1725.

WOODBRIDGE FAMILY.

CHILDREN:

15 DUDLEY, b. April 21, 1705.
16 PAUL, b. March 12, 1708. He was father of Rev. Ephraim of New London.
17 AUGUSTUS, b. Oct. 29, 1710.
18 HANNAH, b. Feb. 9, 1714.
19 MARY, b. Oct. 27, 1719.
20 OLIVER, b. Dec. 3, 1723.

Dr. Dudley Woodbridge, physician at Stonington (No. 15), graduated at Harvard College 1724, m. Sarah Sheldon 1739. She was daughter of Dea. Isaac and wife, Elizabeth (Pratt) Sheldon, of Hartford, Conn.; he d. Oct. 4, 1790. She d. Nov. 11, 1796.

CHILDREN:

21 WILLIAM, b. July 18, 1745, m. Zerviah Williams (No. 209), Aug. 7, 1775. No children.
22 DUDLEY, b. Oct. 9, 1747, in Stonington, moved to Norwich and m. April, 1774, Lucy, daughter of Elijah and Lucy (Griswold) Bachus; they went to Marietta, Ohio, 1788, and he d. there Aug. 6, 1823. Four children survived him. His wife d. Oct. 6, 1817. He was a judge in Ohio.

HIS CHILDREN WERE:

1 LUCY, b. 1775, d. 1816 in Ohio, m. 1795, Dr. J. G. Petit.
2 SARAH, b. 1777, d. 1828, m. John Mathews of New Britain, Mass.
3 DUDLEY, b. Nov. 10, 1778, m. 1st, Jane R. Gilman in 1807, and 2d, Maria Morgan. He d. 1853.
4 WILLIAM, b. Aug. 20, 1780. He m. June 29, 1806, Julianna, daughter of Hon. John Trumbull, LL. D. He d. Oct. 20, 1861. He was member of the Legislature of Ohio, delegate to Congress, judge of the Superior Court, Governor of the State of Michigan and U. S. Senator two terms. He d. 1861.
5 DAVID, b. and d. young.
6 JOHN, b. Nov. 25, 1785, m. Jan. 22, 1816, Elizabeth, daughter of Henry Buchanan; they had 16 children. He d. May, 1863, aged 78 years. She d. Aug. 15, 1861.
23 JOSEPH, b. Jan. 1, 1749, d. 1809, m. 1st, Elizabeth Sheldon, and 2d, Lucy Sheldon, and had ten children.
24 ELIZABETH or BETSEY, b. May 13, 1752, d. 1793, m. Daniel Rodman June 9, 1774; six children.
25 SAMUEL, b. Oct. 31, 1757, m. Elizabeth, daughter of Col. Zabdiel and wife, Elizabeth (Tracy) Rogers, 1778; had nine children; she d. 1800.
26 BENJAMIN, b. Dec. 15, 1758, d. unmarried.
27 LUCY, b. May 4, 1760, d. unmarried.
28 CHARLOTTE, b. Dec. 28, 1761, m. Giles Mumford Dec. 23, 1779; 2d, Dr. Simon Wolcott of New London.
29 SARAH or SALLY, b. June 28, 1767, m. Simon Rhodes (No. 4), June 14, 1790.

Dr. Dudley Woodbridge (No. 15) was born at Poquonock, now Centre Groton, studied medicine, graduated and commenced practice in Old Mystic, Conn., and built the house, now owned and occupied by Mrs. Lucy (Stanton) Wheeler. After a few years at that place he bought the "Whitehall" farm in Stonington and erected the present mansion house now owned by Mr. Samuel Bentley, and he remained there till his death.

Joseph Woodbridge (No. 23) m. Elizabeth Sheldon, and, 2nd, Lucy Sheldon. Had ten children.

30 WILLIAM, b. ——, and m. Eliza D. Phelps (No. 66), of the Phelps family, Jan. 18, 1831.
31 DUDLEY, b. ——, and m. Maria Smith (No. 114), that family.
32 CHARLOTTE, b. ——, and m. —— White.
33 LUCY, b. ——, and m. William W. Rodman Jan. 10, 1816.
34 EMMA, b. ——, and m. Dr. George E. Palmer May 23, 1826 (No. 394), that family.
35 JULIA, b. ——, and m. a Mr. Eddy.

YORK FAMILY.

June 20, 1635, there embarked on board the good ship "Philip," Richard Morgan, master, forty-two passengers, who were to be transported from England to Virginia, in America. They had been previously examined by the minister of Gravesend as to their conformity to the orders and discipline of the Church of England and had taken the oath of allegiance.

1. JAMES YORK, SR., was one of the passengers of the good ship "Philip" in 1635, rated therein at the age of 21 years, consequently he was born in the year 1614. It is not known at what place in Virginia Capt. Morgan landed his passengers, or whether he landed them in that colony at all. If they were landed there, our James York did not remain there long. He doubtless soon after his arrival in this country, came north, whether by land or water, we do not know, but the first record we have of him is in Braintree, Mass.

James York, Sr., came to Stonington, Conn., in the year 1660, when this town was under the jurisdiction of Massachusetts, and called by the name of Southertown, and settled on grants of land which then included the present farm of Gideon P. Chesebrough, east of Anguilla or Wequetequock brook, also the farm of Erastus D. Miner and the Simon Rhodes place, now owned by Clark Chapman, and there he built him a dwelling house on the north side of the then Indian path, now known as the old Post road, where he lived the remainder of his life, dying in 1683, aged 69 years. His widow died in 1685.

James York (No. 1) m. Joannah ———— the family name of his wife is not known, neither the place of their marriage, but the date thereof must have been about 1637.

CHILDREN:

2 ABIGAIL, b. about 1638 or 1639; she m. John Beebe of New London, Conn; she d. March 9, 1725, aged 86 or 87 years. Their children were John, Benjamin and Rebecca Beebe. Rebecca Beebe married Richard Shaw of Easthampton.

3 JAMES, JR., b. June 14, 1648. He doubtless came to Stonington, Conn., with his father, when under age, for his name is mentioned in the town records several times before the date 1672, when Savage says, "He sold his estate in Boston, Mass., where he was engaged in business, and came to Stonington," for on the Stonington town records, under date of Jan. 15, 1667, "100 acres of land layed out to James York, Jr.," and he was also one of the men who received land grants for service in Indian wars. He was made a freeman in Connecticut in 1673, and died Oct. 26, 1676, and his widow m. for her second husband Henry Elliot, March 12, 1679.

James York, Jr., (No. 3) m. in Stonington, Conn., Jan. 19, 1669, Deborah Bell, daughter of Thomas and Anna Bell.

CHILDREN:

4 DEBORAH BELL, b. Jan. 8, 1670, d. Feb. 21, 1672.
5 JAMES, b. Dec. 17, 1672.
6 WILLIAM, b. July 24, 1674, m. Mary Alley Dec. 18, 1695.
7 THOMAS, b. Oct. 14, 1676, m. Mary Brown Jan. 9, 1704 (No. 19), of Lynn Brown family. A Mary York m. Beriah Brooks April 8, 1698, who was probably daughter of this James York, Jr., and wife, Deborah Bell. The children of Mrs. Deborah Bell York and second husband, Henry Elliot, were:

1 DEBORAH ELLIOT, b. April 11, 1680.
1a ANNA ELLIOT, b. Nov. 28, 1681.
2 HOPESTILL ELLIOT, b. Aug. 18, 1684.
3 MARY ELLIOT, b. May 22, 1687, m. William Bentley (No. 2).
4 DOROTHY ELLIOT, b. April 15, 1688.
5 ELIZABETH ELLIOT, b. Aug. 3, 1690.
6 HENRY ELLIOT, b. April 16, 1693.
7 JOSEPH ELLIOT, b. Oct. 21, 1694.

James York (No. 5) m. Hannah Stanton, daughter of Joseph and wife, Hannah (Meade) Stanton, of Quonacontaug, Westerly, R. I., Nov. 13, 1695, and he d. in 1759.

CHILDREN:

8 HANNAH, b. March 28, 1697.
9 JOANNAH, b. Dec. 31, 1699.
10 JAMES, b. Sept. 6, 1702, m. Elizabeth Case.
11 ANNA, b. Jan. 21, 1704.
12 EDWARD, b. June 21, 1706.
13 STANTON, b. March 14, 1708, m. Jemima Shaw April 30, 1730.
14 THANKFUL, b. Feb. 26, 1710.

William York (No. 6) m. Mary Alley Dec. 18, 1695, and he was drowned June 17, 1697.

CHILDREN:

15 DEBORAH, b. Oct. 6, 1696.

Thomas York (No. 7) m. Mary Brown (No. 19) of Lynn Brown family, daughter of Thomas and wife, Hannah (Collins) Brown, Jan. 9, 1704.

YORK FAMILY.

CHILDREN:
16 WILLIAM, b. Oct. 3, 1705.
17 MARY, b. Oct. 17, 1710.
18 THANKFUL, b. April 23, 1712.
19 THOMAS, b. Jan. 24, 1714.
20 JOHN, b. March 16, 1716.
21 JOSEPH, b. Jan. 22, 1718.
22 DEBORAH, b. Jan. 13, 1720.
23 COLLINS, b. in 1722.
24 BELL, b. in 1725.

James York (No. 10) m. Elizabeth Case Jan. 11, 1728. She was of South Kingston, R. I., and b. in Charlestown, R. I.; she d. in South Kingston March 27, 1784, in her 78th year. He was admitted freeman in Westerly March 1, 1727, and chosen constable June 5, 1738.

CHILDREN:
25 EDWARD, b. April 18, 1730.
26 ELIZABETH, b. Feb. 11, 1732.
27 STEPHEN, b. May 24, 1735.
28 HANNAH, b. Feb. 28, 1738.
29 JAMES, b. Nov. 25, 1740.
30 WILLIAM, b. Jan. 20, 1742.

William York (No. 16) m. Comfort Burdick May 18, 1727.

CHILDREN:
31 WILLIAM, b. Feb. 22, 1728.

Mrs. Comfort York d. July 22, 1728, and her husband m. 2nd, Hannah Palmer (No. 90) that family, Feb. 22, 1730.

CHILDREN:
32 AMOS, b. Oct. 15, 1730, m. Lucretia Miner.
33 MARY, b. April 30, 1732.
34 JONATHAN, b. Aug. 29, 1735.

Thomas York (No. 19) m. Deborah Brown Nov. 10, 1737.

CHILDREN:
35 THOMAS, b. July 28, 1738.
36 JESSE, b. Aug. 1, 1740.
37 DEBORAH, b. Feb. 5, 1742.
38 SAMUEL, b. May 22, 1745.
39 JABISH, b. July 25, 1748.
40 ALLEN, b. Jan. 1, 1754; was pensioner under the act of 1832 in New London, Conn.
41 DOROTHY, b. June 16, 1758.
42 HANNAH, b. May 15, 1760.
43 CHARLOTTE, b. Aug. 13, 1764.

John York (No. 20) and Anna Brown, both of Stonington, Conn., were m. July 30, 1743.

CHILDREN:
44 JOHN, b. July 30, 1744.
45 ANNA, b. May 26, 1746, d. young.

46 ANNA, b. July 17, 1755.
47 LUCY, b. Aug. 31, 1758, m. Asa Spalding, M. D.
48 LYDIA, b. Dec. 28, 1760, m. Thomas Miner (No. 146), that family.
49 MARTHA, b. April 17, 1762.

Joseph York (No. 21) and Hannah Chesebrough, both of Stonington, Conn. (No. 116) were m. May 10, 1744. This Mrs. Hannah York died soon after her marriage, and Mr. Joseph York m. 2d, Esther Jamison Aug. 25, 1748.

CHILDREN:

50 CHRISTOPHER, b. July 10, 1749.
51 GERSHOM, b. April 7, 1753, m. Lois Williams (No. 83), Feb. 3, 1785, and went to Randolph, Vt.
52 JOSEPH, b. Sept. 6, 1756.
53 ESTHER, b. Aug. 16, 1759.
54 ROBERT, b. Oct. 17, 1761.
55 HANNAH, b. March 11, 1764.

Collins York (No. 23) and Eunice Grant (No. 27), both of Stonington, Conn., were married May 29, 1755.

CHILDREN:

56 EUNICE, b. April 16, 1756.
57 COLLINS, b. Sept. 25, 1758.
58 OLIVER, b. March 15, 1762, m. Rebecca Swan (No. 89), that family.

Mrs. Eunice (Grant) York died, and her husband m. 2d, Freelove Palmer, Dec. 11, 1766.

Bell York (No. 24) and Ruth Main (No. 39), of Main family, both of Stonington, were m. Feb. 18, 1747.

CHILDREN:

59 RUTH, b. May 14, 1748.
60 BELL, b. Feb. 16, 1750.
61 JAMES, b. Oct. 9, 1752, d. young.
62 MARY, b. May 15, d. young.
63 JAMES, b. Sept. 11, 1756.
64 THEDE, b. Oct. 4, 1758.
65 SARAH, b. Jan. 22, 1761, m. Rufus Maine (No. 54), Maine family.
66 PHEBE, b. Nov. 30, 1762.
67 JEREMIAH, b. Jan. 3, 1765, m. Thankful Thurston, daughter of (No. 45) in the Main family, April 18, 1793, and d. May 26, 1853.
68 MARY, b. Feb. 15, 1767.
69 YEOMANS, b. March 4, 1773.

William York (No. 30) m. Anna Peckham, daughter of Daniel and Mary Peckham, on Nov. 15, 1766. She was b. Sept. 20, 1742. He d. Feb. 29, 1834. He was a soldier in the Revolution, and for two years a sergeant in Capt. Congdon's company, Col. Noyes regiment of Massachusetts troops, for which he received a pension.

YORK FAMILY.

CHILDREN:

70 BENJAMIN, b. Sept. 25, 1767.
71 HANNAH, b. Nov. 15, 1770, never married.
72 JAMES, b. Feb. 6, 1772, m. Martha Saunders.
73 ISAAC, b. April 4, 1776.
74 AUGUSTUS, b. July 28, 1778, never married.
75 WILLIAM, b. Oct. 15, 1780, never married.
76 ELIZABETH, b. March 5, 1785, m. John Wilde July 24, 1804.
77 ANNA, b. Aug. 24, 1788, m. ——— Thurston.

Jesse York (No. 36) m. Anna Breed (No. 22) Jan. 7, 1762. He d. Dec. 13, 1808.

CHILDREN:

78 ANNA, b. Dec. 5, 1762, m. Andrew Chapman (No. 14).
79 LOIS, b. Sept. 14, 1765, m. Elisha Wheeler (No. 357), March 30, 1786.
80 JESSE, b. April 15, 1768.
81 NATHAN, b. Sept. 8, 1771.
82 DEBORAH, b. Aug. 15, 1774, m. Bell York (No. 60).
83 WILLIAM, b. Jan. 1, 1777.
84 REUBEN, b. Oct. 2, 1780.

John York (No. 44) m. Keturah Brown. She was b. May 24, 1770.

CHILDREN:

85 JOHN, b. March 17, 1771, m. Martha Wheeler (No. 359).
86 THOMAS, b. Feb. 24, 1773.
87 KETURAH, b. June 1, 1775.
88 ICHABOD, b. June 27, 1777.
89 PALTSEY, b. Feb. 23, 1780.
90 ANNA, b. Jan. 16, 1782.
91 LUCINDA, b. Feb. 24, 1785.
92 SARAH, b. Oct. 20, 1787.
93 LUCY, b. July 15, 1794.

Allen York (No. 40) m. Zerviah Wheeler (No. 349), Jan. 18, 1776.

CHILDREN:

94 ZERVIAH, b. Dec. 14, 1776, m. David Wheeler (No. 391).
95 CONTENT, b. Oct. 28, 1781, m. Saxton Miner (No. 211), that family.

Collins York (No. 57) m. Polly Randall (No. 70) May 3, 1781.

CHILDREN:

96 COLLINS, b. June 15, 1784.
97 POLLY, b. June 21, 1787.
98 CHARLES, b. July 22, 1793, went to Chenango, New York State.

Bell York (No. 60) m. Anna Brown, Dec. 28, 1770. She d. May 6, 1795.

CHILDREN:

99 BELL, b. April 10, 1771.
100 ANNA, b. Feb. 15, 1773.
101 SARAH, b. Nov. 23, 1774.
102 ESTHER, b. Oct. 27, 1776.
103 MARTHA, b. Dec. 16, 1780.
104 MARVIN, b. Nov. 7, 1784.
105 ZEBULON, b. Oct. 20, 1783.
106 RUTH, b. March 20, 1786.

After Mrs. Anna (Brown) York died, her husband m. 2d, Deborah York (No. 82), in 1808.

CHILDREN:
107 ISAAC, b. July 13, 1810.
108 DANIEL, b. Sept. 29, 1812, m. Esther Babcock Jan. 28, 1838. He d. Jan. 22, 1866.

THEIR CHILDREN WERE:
109 SAMUEL A., b. May 25, 1839, m. Helen E. Osborn Nov. 1, 1865.
110 JOHN L., b. July 22, 1845, m. Emma Edgecomb Sept. 13, 1882.

James York (No. 63) m. Lucy Palmer March 11, 1781.

CHILDREN:
111 LUCY, b. Jan. 29, 1782.
112 HANNAH, b. March 24, 1783.
113 MARTHA, b. June 14, 1784.
114 SUSANNA, b. Oct. 20, 1786.
115 NABBY or ABBY, b. May 22, 1790, m. Jarius Palmer March 17, 1811 (No. 396), of Palmer family.

Jeremiah York (No. 67) m. Thankful Thurston April 18, 1793.

CHILDREN:
116 JEREMIAH, b. Sept. 25, 1794.
117 FANNIE, b. Jan. 7, 1796.
118 EDWARD, b. Aug. 20, 1797.
119 MARTIN, b. July 31, 1799.
120 ELECTA, b. July 30, 1802. Also
121 RANDALL, b. ———.
122 THANKFUL, b. ———.
123 HIRAM, b. ———.
124 RUTH, b. ———.
125 CAROLINE, b. ———.
126 LYDIA, b. ———.

Yeomans York (No. 69) m. Prudence Chapman June 9, 1791; Mrs. York d. May 9, 1792, and he m. 2d, ———.

Benjamin York (No. 70) m. 1st, Nov. 4, 1790, Zilpha Crandall, daughter of Caleb and Patience Crandall of Charlestown, R. I. She d. Aug. 8, 1794, aged 27 years.

They had two children, but both died young, and Mr. York m. 2d, Jan. 21, 1801, Desire Saunders, daughter of Joshua Saunders of Charlestown. She d. Nov. 29, 1863, aged 85 yrs. He d. June 7, 1850.

CHILDREN:
127 SAUNDERS, b. Oct. 30, 1801.
128 ISAAC, b. June 24, 1804.
129 WELCOME, b. Feb. 6, 1807, d. young.
130 MARY ANN, b. Oct. 21, 1808, m. Emerson Bibber.
131 ASENATH, b. March 1, 1812, m. Malborn Saunders.
132 CODDINGTON, b. ———, drowned.
133 BENJAMIN, b. Sept. 20, 1819, m. Jan. 9, 1842, Prudence Bliven.

Benjamin York, Jr. (No. 133) m. Jan. 9, 1842, Prudence Bliven,

YORK FAMILY.

daughter of Capt. Nathan Bliven of Westerly, R. I. She d. Jan. 14, 1892. He d. April 27, 1899.

CHILDREN:

134 ISAAC F., b. Feb. 8, 1843, d. in Andersonville prison.
135 WALBERT G., b. May 17, 1844, m. Jane Larkin.
136 COURTLAND D., b. and CAROLINE D., b., twins, April 17, 1846, d. young.
137 ELIZABETH R., b. Nov. 22, 1848, m. Albert L. Chester.
138 MARY ANN, b. ———, and m. Edward C. Brown.
139 FRANCIS, b. twins, Nov. 20, 1851, m. Lillian Hawkins.
140 ALICE M., b. Sept. 11, 1855, m. George F. Wells.

James York (No. 72) m. Martha Saunders, daughter of Joshua Saunders, and sister of Desire, who m. Capt. Benjamin York.

CHILDREN:

141 JAMES, b. ———, m. Betsey Nash.
142 WILLIAM, b. June 13, 1809, m. Mary Barber.
143 MARTHA, b. ———, m. Benjamin Barnes.

James York (No. 141) m. Betsey Nash, ———.

CHILDREN:

144 JOSEPH C., b. ———, m. Elizabeth Potter March 6, 1851.
145 JONATHAN W., b. ———, m. Susan S. Potter Aug. 6, 1850.
146 FRANCES, b. ———, m. Otis Prentice.
147 JOSHUA, b. ———, m. Hannah Hammond.
148 MARTHA (twin), b. ———, m. John Chappell.
149 ELIZABETH (twin), b. ———, m. Orrin Lester.
150 JANE, b. ———, m. William D. Potter.
151 JAMES, b. ———, m. Sarah Smith.
152 LYDIA, b. ———, m. Alfred H. Hartley.
153 NATHAN, b. ———, m. Almira C. Bentley; two other children, d. young.

William York (No. 142) m. Mary Barber Jan. 29, 1832. He d. Feb. 2, 1888. She was b. Oct. 29, 1808, and d. Sept. 3, 1880.

CHILDREN:

154 MARY C., b. April 2, 1833, d. Feb. 7, 1873.
155 WILLIAM, JR., b. April 15, 1835, m. Mary Sophia Wheeler, daughter of (No. 454), Wheeler family, Nov. 20, 1863.
156 SUSAN, b. Feb. 10, 1837, m. Paul A. Noyes (No. 379), of Noyes family.
157 ALBERT D., b. May 30, 1838, d. young.
158 NANCY B., b. Oct. 27, 1839.
159 EDWIN, b. May 7, 1842.
160 MARTHA B., b. May 1, 1844, d. young.
161 CAROLINE, b. June 9, 1845.
162 HARRIET, b. April 25, 1847.
163 ALBERT, b. May 9, 1849, d. young.
164 HERBERT, b. Oct. 7, 1852, d. young.

Jesse York (No. 80) and Cynthia Miner (No. 216), that family, were m. in 1794.

CHILDREN:

165 CYNTHIA, b. Oct. 21, 1795, m. John P. Williams Nov. 28, 1816 (No. 304).
166 NANCY, b. July 4, 1801, m. John W. Hull (No. 16), that family.

Nathan York (No. 81) m. Martha or Patty Breed (No. 98a), Breed family.

CHILDREN:

167 NATHAN, b. Sept. 16, 1811, m. Nancy Main (No. 167).
168 MARY A., b. Sept. 12, 1812, d. young.
169 MARTHA, b. June 7, 1814.
170 MANITA, b. Sept. 26, 1815, m. B. F. Sisson (No. 56), that family.
171 ELISHA W., b. Oct. 9, 1817, d. young.
172 REUBEN, b. Jan. 22, 1819.
173 SARAH E., b. Jan. 25, 1821.
174 ELIZA, b. July 31, 1822, d. young.
175 SAMUEL B., b. Feb. 8, 1824, d. young.
176 ABEL B., b. Aug. 2, 1825, d. young.
177 EUNICE, b. Sept. 30, 1827, d. young.
178 HORACE F., b. Nov. 14, 1828.
179 CALVIN, b. Aug. 13, 1830, d. young.
180 EMELINE, b. March 15, 1833, d. young.
181 WILLIAM O., b. Jan. 23, 1836.

William York (No. 83) m. Naomi Ray at Preston, Conn., Feb. 17, 1802.

CHILDREN:

182 NAOMI, b. Dec. 12, 1803.
183 SPEDA, b. Feb. 4, 1806.
184 JESSE, b. April 19, 1809.
185 STEPHEN, b. Aug. 3, 1811.
186 MARYETTA, b. April 1, 1814.
187 ANNIE, b. June 14, 1817.
188 RAY, b. Feb. 14, 1820.
189 DEBORAH F., b. June 22, 1824.

Reuben York (No. 84) and Hannah Breed (No. 95) of that family were m. Jan. 1, 1804.

CHILDREN:

190 THOMAS J., b. Feb. 5, 1806, d. Jan. 5, 1834, m. Martha Wheeler (No. 408).
191 LOIS, b. Oct. 25, 1807, d. Nov. 22, 1878.
192 JABISH B., b. June 25, 1811, d. Feb. 2, 1871.
193 MARY E., b. June 27, 1813, d. Aug. 9, 1870.

Thomas York (No. 35) m. Abigail Main March 9, 1758.

SON:

194 THOMAS, b. Jan. 5, 1759.

Oliver York (No. 58) m. Rebecca Swan (No. 89) of the Swan family Nov. 4, 1784. He kept a hotel, which was situated on the southeast corner of the Wadawanuck square, in Stonington borough.

CHILDREN:

195 OLIVER, b. ———, m. Charlotte Smith (No. 116), Smith family. No children.
196 EUNICE, b. ———, m. Rev. William R. Gould Sept. 18, 1805.
197 EMMA, bapt. Oct. 1, 1809.
198 REBECCA, bapt. March 25, 1810.

YORK FAMILY.

199 HARRIET, bapt. March 25, 1810.
200 ELIZA, bapt. Sept. 11, 1814.
201 STILES, bapt. Sept. 11, 1814.

Zebulon T. York (No. 105) m. Betsey Chapman (No. 56), that family, of Voluntown, March 17, 1803.

CHILDREN:

202 AVERY, b. Feb. 28, 1806, d. Oct. 12, 1847.
203 ABBY, b. July 9, 1807, d. April 18, 1848.
204 JOHN C., b. April 8, 1812, d. March 25, 1848.
205 EUNICE E., b. May 16, 1815, d. Dec. 24, 1833.
206 ZEBULON T., b. July 19, 1817, d. Feb. 10, 1899.
207 AMOS C., b. May 24, 1826, d. Jan. 22, 1834.
208 ECMINA, b. April 4, 1809, m. Aaron Thompson and d. March 14, 1822.

Amos York (No. 32) m. Lucretia Miner (No. 177b) of the Miner family Oct. 15, 1752. She d. Oct. 3, 1821, and he d. Oct. 30, 1778.

CHILDREN:

209 WEALTHY ANN, b. Nov. 6, 1752, d. 1753.
210 ESTHER M., b. Nov. 15, 1754, m. Aaron Smith.
211 LUCINDA, b. April 21, 1757, m. Ahobiah Buck.
212 WEALTHY ANN, b. Nov. 3, 1759, m. Benjamin Smith.
213 KEZIAH, b. Jan. 1, 1762, m. Lot Turrell.
214 SARAH, b. May 4, 1764, m. Robert Carr.
215 TEMPERANCE, b. May 6, 1766, m. Daniel Turrell.
216 MANASSAH, b. Oct. 11, 1768, m. Betsey Arnold.
217 BRINTHIA, b. Sept. 27, 1770, m. William Sherman Buck.
218 HANNAH, b. April 22, 1772, m. Stephen Beckwith.
219 AMOS, b. July 1, 1775, d. young.
220 AMOS, b. June 21, 1777, d. young.

APPENDIX.

APPENDIX.

COPY OF AGREEMENT BETWEEN JAMES BABCOCK AND HIS MOTHER.

To all persons whom these presents may concern, Greeting:

Know Ye, That I James Babcock, son to John Babcock of the Town of Westerly in the Colony of Rhode Island and Providence Plantations, and King's Province & Deceased, who died Intestate. I being the rightful heir by law unto all my Father's inheritance, consisting of lands, doe by these presents declare that for and in consideration of the premises hereafter to be expressed, I doe covenant and agree with my loving, natural mother Mary Babcock to except of the one-half of the Farm that we are now dwelling on, my part to begin at the west end of the farme and go to extend eastward untill the complement be made by upon an equal division.

And also the value of a double portion of the moveable estate to be divided among my brothers, and the new dwelling house now standing upon the farme, I say, I doe except of what is abovesd, in full satisfaction for my parte, or portion of my deceased father's estate. And doe further declare by these presents that I doe freely surrender up to my loving mother my whole right, title and interest unto all the rest of the lands, belonging to my deceased father, with all the privileges and appurtenances thereunto belonging, or any wise appertaining, to have and enjoy and dispose of as she shall see it meet during the term of her life or after her decease, provided, that she shall see it meet during the time of her life or after her decease, provided she shall dispose of it unto my father's male children, I say, given, granted and surrendered by me, James Babcock, from me, my heirs, assigns, forever, upon the condition abovesd. In witness whereof we have hereunto set our hands and seals.

        JAMES BABCOCK,   (Seal.)
           Mark
        MARY 111 BABCOCK.   (Seal.)
           Her

Signed and sealed in the presence of
 TOBIAS SAUNDERS,
 JEFFRES CHAMPION
  his mark.
This present day of June, 1685.

This is a true copy compared with the original and entered by Joseph L. Clark, Clerk of the Towne, this 28th day of Jan. 1685.

DISTRIBUTION OF ESTATE OF JOHN BABCOCK BY TOWN COUNCIL.

These are to certify all persons whom it may concern, that whereas John Babcock of the Town of Westerly, deceased without a will, whereby the care of the widow and orphans respecting the settlement of the deceased man's estate is by law commanded to the cognizance of the Town Council.

We, therefore, who are the Commissioners appointed by the Towne, according to trust committed unto us, having taken an inventory of the deceased's persons estate and likewise finding a settled agreement between the widow and the eldest son, James Babcock, the son of John Babcock, respecting his own portion out of his deceased's father's estate, judge it meet to make no alteration of the said agreement. and likewise finding the remaining part of the moveable estate to amount to the sum of 790 pounds, 3 S. 0 Pence, we do order and appoint unto the widow of the deceased John Babcock, the sum of 263 pounds, seven shillings and 8 pence for her part of the abovesd. sum, it being one-third part; and whereas there are nine children more, to wit: Ann Babcock, Mary Babcock, John babcock, Job Babcock, George Babcock, Elihu Babcock, Robert Babcock, Joseph babcock, Oliver babcock, we doe order and appoint to the several children the sum of sixty seven pounds, two shillings and four pence for each child, out of the remaining parte of the aforesd. sum as they come of age.

And furthermore we doe by these presents, order, constitute and appoint, Mary Babcock, the widow of the deceased John Babcock, executrix of all the orphan's estate consisting of lands or catttle or houses or monies and whatsoever else valuable according to Inventory. And likewise to charge care of the orphans, drawing their monies, and in case any one or more of the orphans die before they come of age, then his or their portion to be equally divided among those that survive; we doe hereby also order and appoint that the widow shall pay or cause to be paid the several legacies unto the children as is before expressed in the meantime To give in bonds to the Council for the performance thereof.

TOBIAS SAUNDERS,
WILLIAM W. CHAMPION.

This is a true copy of the original, compared and entered by Joseph Clark, Clerk to the Town, this 7th of Feb., 1685.

EDWARD V. LARKIN,

A LIST OF STONINGTON MEN WHO SERVED IN THE COLONIAL INDIAN WARS OF NEW ENGLAND.

1. Capt. George Denison,
2. John Frink,
3. John Avery,
4. Thomas Avery,
5. Samuel Yeomans,
6. John Fish,
7. George Denison, Jr.,
8. William Denison,
9. Nathaniel Beebe,
10. Henry Stephens,
11. Edmund Fanning,
12. John Bennet,
13. William Bennet,
14. Ezekiel Mayn.
15. William Wheeler,
16. Gershom Palmer,
17. Thomas Stanton,
18. Thomas Stanton, Jr.,
19. Samuel Stanton,
20. Robert Stanton,
21. Daniel Stanton,
22. Manasseth Miner,
23. James Millit,
24. Rev. James Noyes,
25. Capt. John Stanton,
26. Joseph Stanton,
27. James York,
28. Thomas Bell,
29. Lieut. Thomas Miner,
30. Robert Park.
31. Thomas Park,
32. Henry Elliott,
33. Isaac Wheeler,
34. John Gallup,
35. Benadam Gallup,
36. William Gallup,
37. Nathaniel Chesebrough,
38. Ephraim Miner,
39. Joseph Miner,
40. Samuel Miner,
41. John Ashcraft,
42. Joshua Holmes,
43. Edmund Fanning, Jr.,
44. John Denison,
45. Henry Bennet,
46. Henry Hall,
47. Capt. James Pendleton,
48. Daniel Crumb,
49. Nicholas Cottrell.
50. Clement Miner,
51. William Randall,
52. Thomas Williams,
53. Robert Holmes,
54. Joseph Ingraham,
55. William Billings,
56. John Shaw,
57. Stephen Richardson,
58. Ebenezer Billings,
59. Jonathan Burch,
60. Samuel Richardson,

WILL OF NICHOLAS COTTRELL, SR.

Last will and testament of Nicholas Cottrell, Sen., living by Taunton River, taken ——— day of Feb. 1680, as followeth:———as Cottrell having my perfect memory and understanding, but being weak in body———my body to the grave and my soule to God that gave it, and I give unto my eldest son, Nicholas Cottrell, five shillings hee having received a sufficient portion of me before. I give and bequeath unto my son John Cottrell, one hundred acres of land which he now liveth upon, at Skonomicutt by Narragansett. I give and bequeath unto my son Gershom Cottrell, one hundred acres at Skonomicutt, that he now liveth upon. I give unto my son Eleazer five shillings. I give unto my daughter Mary two pounds, ten shillings. I give unto my grand-child Hannah Crowe two pound, to be payed att her day of marriage. I give unto my daughter Hannah eight pound, which her husband owed me upon bond, and my warming pan. I give and bequeath unto my grand-child Nicholas Osborne an hundred acres of land upon the lott I now live on by Taunton River, beginning at the path that is now the roadway to Rhode Island and to begin at that side of the lot next to Job Winslows lott, and so to run half the breadth of my lott and soe into the woods until it extends to an hundred acres from the path before mentioned, he is not to receive this land until after the decease of his father and mother. I give and bequeath unto my wife Martha Cottrell an hundred acres of land, beginning att that side of my lott next to John Hathaway, Jr., his lott and soe to run to that land in breadth that I give my grand-child above mentioned and from the said path above mentioned until it extends to one hundred acres. This land to bee my wife's only during her life, and after her decease to fall to my son James Cottrell, hee paying to her agents or assigns what rationall men shall judge for what the land may be better by what she shall doe upon it in her life by building or renting or breaking up. I likewise give my wife three cows, one mare and one breeding sow and one pot and kettle and one bed and bedding belonging to it, and if please God to take me away now, then my wife to have so much provision as will serve her own spending until the next harvest ensuing the date thereof. I likewise will, that my wife shall have libertie to cutt so much grass of my meddow as will winter her three cows, two years next insuing. I give and bequeath unto my son James, all the rest of my land that I now dwell upon and meddow or whatsoever other land or meddow that belongeth unto me with all the rest of my catttle and hoggs and horse-kind and all the rest of my household stuff that is not above mentioned or disposed of in my will and doe make and appoint my son Jabez my whole and sole executor to see this my will performed, this was done in the presence of us,

JOHN HATHAWAY, SR.   The mark of I rf NICHOLAS COTTRELL, SR.

The mark of M of MARTHA COTTRELL.
The mark of / rf RICHARD OSBORNE.
HANNAH OSBORNE.

Martha Cottrell aged 36 yrs. testifyeth and saith that this was the last will of her husband Nicholas Cottrell, she hath taken her oath the first day of July 1681. Taken before me,

GEORGE LAWTON, assistant.

Att the court of his Majtt. held at Plymouth the 29th of October, 1682, John Hathaway of Taunton made oath to the truth of the above written will before the Court.

WILL OF WILLIAM CHESEBROUGH.

Stonington, May ye 23rd, 1667.

The last Will and Testament of William Chesebrough, aged 73 years, as followeth: First, I Give unto my son Samuel all lands formerly granted to him and taken in by him farm; Nextly, I give unto my sons Nathaniel and Elisha, ye neck of land called Waddawonnet, which was formerly granted to them, bounded by ye fence yt crosses ye aforesaid neck called Waddawonnet, with their broken up lands which they now have in possession, all other lands which is in my management, broken up or meadow, and two or three acres my son Elisha improveth this year.

I give to my loving wife, the Commons, answering to it, during ye time of her life, and after her decease, I give unto my son, Samuel, Two acres—next to ye said Samuel's Dwelling-house, and ye remainder of my broken up lands and meadow to be divided equally between my two sons, Nathaniel and Elisha, The Little Island, I give to my son Nathaniel, and ye piece of meadow land by Goodman York's, I give to my son Elisha, and all other lands that I had from New London, I give to my three sons, every one of them, an equal share. And if these do want advice about ye dividing of it, I do ordain my trusty and well-beloved friends, Mr. James Noyes and Mr. Amos Richardson, to be helpful to them about ye Dividing of it. And ye farm of land and meadow, three hundred and fifty acres, more or less, near to a place, Cowsatuck, I give to my son Samuel's second son William. For all my housing I give to my loving wife, to be wholly at her Disposing, to keep or sell, or dispose of as she shall please, and likewise ye pasture by ye house, only a piece to my son Elisha, from ye place where his house joyneth to mine, throughout ye pastore to ye stone wall next to ye highway, and for my son Samuel's eldest son Samuel and his youngest daughter Sarah and what his wife is now with child with, I give five pounds a piece, and likewise my son Nathaniel their children, five pounds a piece, which is to paid within six years, all ye rest of my goods and chattels, my debts being paid, I give to my loving wife, whom I make full and Lawful Executrix.

WILLIAM CHESEBROUGH.

Witness:
GERSHOM PALMER,
THOMAS BELL.

WILL OF MRS. ANNA CHESEBROUGH.

The Last will and Testament of Anna Chesebrough aged 75 years, or thereabouts:

Imp. I give to my two sons Samuel and Nathaniel yt land which was given to me by my husband upon his will yt my son Elisha should have had if he had outlived me. I give to my son Nathaniel, my barn. I give to my son Samuell my yard, between my barns and his orchard.

I give to William Chesebrough, my son Samuel's second son, my dwelling-house with ye pastor to ye yard.

I give to my son Samuell, my fifteen acres of land on ye east side of Pawcatuck river. I give to my son Nathaniel, one of ye mares yt my son Elisha leased or hired of me, and ye other mare I give to my son Samuell's son William. My bay horse I give to my Son Nathaniel. My black horse I give to my son Samuell. I give to my son Samuell a feather-bed. I give to my daughters Abigail and Hannah my cloathes and linnen. The rest of my estate (my debts being paid) I give to my two sons, an equal share, whom I make my full and lawful Executors.

Dated in Stonington, this 19th of March 1672-3.

ANNA A. CHESEBROUGH.
her mark and seal.

Signed and sealed d. and D. D. in presence of us,
THOMAS STANTON, SEN.
JAMES NOYES.

Mr. James Noyes appearing before me, this fifth of September, 1673, made oath yt ye was ye will of Anna Chesebrough, Deceased, and yt his hand is twice to it as a witness.

THOMAS STANTON, Commissioner.

JOINTURE OF CAPT. GEORGE DENISON.

During the courtship of Capt. George Denison and wife Ann Borodell, he made a jointure which became a part of their marriage vows; their agreement in after years was fulfilled by Capt. Denison, as follows:

[Extract from 1st Book State Records, Vol. 1, Pages 273 and 274.]

This witnesseth that I, George Denison of Southerton, in Quenecticut Jurisdiction, in New England, for and in consideration of an Jointure due unto my now wife Ann Denison, upon marriage, and upon my former engagement, in consideration of the sum of three hundred pounds by me received, of Mr. John Borodell, which he freely gave to my wife, his sister Ann Denison, and I have had the use and improvement of, and for and in consideration of conjugal and dearer affection moving me thereto, have for the reasons above said, and for the only use and benefit of my said wife Ann Denison, her heirs, and assigns, and by these presents do fully and absolutely give, grant, alien, make over and confirm unto my brother Edward Denison, all that my farm, which, I now dwell upon, consisting of five hundred acres, more or less, as it lyeth at Mystick in Southerton upon the East side of Mystick River, together with all the housing that at present are, or hereafter may be raised upon the said farm, with the household furniture, together with all the fencing privileges, and appurtenances belonging to it, with all the stock upon that farm aforesaid, reserving only to myself there, my bald faced mare and all my goats, and the present use and improvement of the said farm, housing household stuff, lands, stock, fencing, and privileges according to my pleasure during my natural life, to have and to hold the said farm, housing, lands, furniture, stock, and fences, with all the privileges and appurtenances for the only use of the said Ann Denison, under him the said Edward Denison his heirs and assigns forever, to his and their own proper use and behoof for the only benefit of the said Ann Denison, and the said George Denison, for himself, his heirs, executors and administrators, doth further covenant and grant to and with the said Edward Denison, his heirs and assigns, that he, the said George Denison, his heirs and executors, shall at all times forever hereafter warrant the said bargained premises, against all persons whatsoever claiming any right thereunto by from or under me. In witness hereof, I have hereunto set my hand and seal. Dated according to a former deed of the same to my wife, May the third, One thousand six hundred and sixty-two. GEORGE DENISON, (Seal.

Read, sealed, and delivered in the presence of
THOMAS MICHELL,
ELIZABETH DENISON,

This is a true copy of the Original examined and compared therewith this 17th of March, 1667-8.
From me, JOHN ALLEN, Secretary.

THE WILL OF CAPT. GEORGE DENISON.

Stonington, Nov. 20, 1693.

I, George Denison of Stonington, in the county of New London and Colony of Connecticut in New England, being aged and crazy in body, but sound in mind and memory, and being desirous to make preparation for death, and to set my house in order before I die, I do, therefore, as it becometh a Christian, first, freely and from my heart, resign my soul, through Christ, into the hands of God who gave it to me, and my body to the earth from whence it came, and to be buried in decent manner by my executor and friends, in the hope of a joyful and glorious resurrection, through the perfect merits and mediation of Jesus Christ, my strong Redeemer.

And as concerning my outward estate, which the Lord hath still entrusted me with after all my just debts are paid, I give and dispose of as followeth: First, I give and bequeath unto my dear and loving wife, Ann Denison, my new mansion place, to wit, the house we live in, the barns and buildings, the orchards, and the whole tract of land and improvements thereon, as far as Mistuxet eastward, and it is bounded upon record, south, west, and north, except only thirty acres given to my son, John Denison, which is to lie on the south side next to Capt. Mason's, east of our field, and also one hundred pounds in stock, prised at the county price, all which is and hath been under our son William Denison's improvement and management for these several years to mutual comfort and content, which I do will and bequeath unto my said wife for her comfortable supply during her natural life.

And I give unto my said wife, all the household stuff that was and is properly belonging unto us, before my son William took the charge of the family, to be wholly at her disposal, to bequeath to whom she pleaseth at her death.

Unto my eldest son, John Denison, I have already given his portion, and secured to him by a deed of deeds, and I do also give unto him, his heirs or assigns, forever, a county grant of two hundred acres of land or two hundred pounds in silver money, which grant may be found on the General Court Records.

Also I give unto him, my great sword and the gauntlet which I wore in the wars of England, and a silver spoon of ten shillings, marked G. & A. Unto my son, George Denison, I have formerly given a farm, lying and being at the northwest angle of Stonington bounds, and adjoining the ten mile tree of the said bounds, which farm contained one hundred and fifty acres, more or less, as also, the one half of a thousand acres of land, lying to the northward or northwest of Norwich, given to me as a legacy by Joshua the son of Uncas, the same time Mohegan sachem, the same land to be divided as may more fully appear in the deed, which I then gave him of both those tracts in one deed, signed and sealed with both my own and my wife's hand, and delivered to him and witnessed, and I have several times tendered to him to acknowledge it before authority, that so it might have been recorded according to the formality of law, the which he had wholly neglected or refused, and will not comply with me therein, and yet hath sold both those parcels of land and received pay for them; what his motive may be I cannot certainly divine, but have it to fear they are not good, nor tending to peace after my decease. Wherefore, to prevent further trouble, I see cause herein to acknowledge said deed, and to confirm those said parcels of land unto him, according to the date of said deed, and the conditions therein expressed, but do hereby renounce any other deed not herein expressed, the which two tracts of land before mentioned, with two Indian servants, to wit, an Indian youth or young man, and a woman, together with a considerable stock of neat cattle, horses, sheep and swine I then give him, and permitted him to have and carry with him, I do now confirm to him, the which was and is to be, the whole of his portion, I either have or do see cause to give him, and I give unto him twenty shillings in silver, or a cutlas or rapier, the which I leave to the discretion of my executors, to choose which of them to do.

Unto my son William Denison, I have formerly given him one hundred and thirty acres of land, be it more or less, to wit, all of the land to the eastward of Mistuxet brook which did originally belong unto my new mansion place, and is part of three hundred acres granted unto me by New London, as may appear upon record, and three hundres acres of land, lying and cutting upon the North boundary of Stonington, as may more fully appear in record in Stonington, and the native right thereof, with some addition, confirmed to me by Oneco (as may more fully appear by a deed under his hand and seal, acknowledged before Capt. Mason, and recorded in Stonington. Also, I then gave him two Indian servants, viz., John whom I bought of the county, and his son Job, which was born in our house, together with one third part of stock which we have together, all which as aforesaid we formerly give unto my son William Denison by a former deed, unto our hands and seals, and I see just reason to confirm the same unto my son William in this my last will, that so I may take off all scruple or doubt respecting the said deed. Moreover I give

APPENDIX. 713

unto my son William Denison, fifty acres of land, as it was laid out and bounded unto me by Stonington surveyors, and joins upon the before-mentioned three hundred acres, on south side thereof, cuts also upon lands belonging to my son John Denison, to be to him my said son William Denison, and his heirs forever. Also, I give unto my son William Denison, and his heirs forever, the one half of my allotment at Windham, to wit., five hundred acres of land, which is a part of a legacy given me by Joshua, the son of Uncas, the same time sachem of Mohegan, as may more fully appear upon the Court Records at New London, as also, upon that former experience we have had of his great industry and child-like duty in the management of all our concern, for our comfort and comfortable supply &c., it is therefore my will, and in confidence of his love, duty and wonted care of his loving mother, my dear wife, after my decease, I say, I do still continue him in the possession and improvement of my new mansion place, with the stock mentioned herein in my deed to my loving wife, he taking care of his said mother for her comfortable supply, with what may be neccessary for her comfort during her natural life, and do, or cause to be paid to his said mother, forty shillings in silver money yearly, or half-yearly, while she shall live, and at her decease, I fully and absolutely give and bequeath that my aforesaid mansion place, together with the stock mentioned before, unto my said son, William Denison and his heirs forever.

Also, I give unto my son, William Denison, my rapier, and broad buff belt, and tin cartridge box, which I used in the Indian wars, together with my long carbine, which belt and sword I used in the same service.

Unto my eldest daughter Sarah Stanton, as I have given her formerly her portion as I was then able, so I do now give her ten pounds out of the stock as pay, and one silver spoon of ten shillings price, marked G. & A. Unto my daughter Hannah Saxton, as I have given unto her also, her portion as I was then able, so I do now give unto her ten pounds out of the stock, as pay.

Unto my daughter Ann Palmer, besides that I have formerly given her, I do now give her ten pounds out of the stock as pay.

Unto my daughter Margaret Brown, I have given already her portion, and give ten pounds out of the stock as pay.

Unto my daughter Borrodel Stanton, I have formerly given, and do now give her five pounds out of the stock as pay, and command it to my beloved wife, that at or before her death, she would give her silver cup, which was sent us from England, with brother Borrodel's name, J. B., under the head, to her.

Unto my grandson, George Denison, the son of my oldest son John Denison, I give my black-fringed shoulder belt, and twenty shillings in silver money, toward the purchase of a handsome rapier to wear with it.

Unto my grandson, George Palmer, I give the grant of one hundred acres of land, which was granted unto me by the town of Stonington, not yet laid out, or forty shillings out of my stock, as pay, at the discretion of my executor to choose which. And whereas there is considerable rent due me for a house of my wife in Cork, in Ireland, which was given unto her as a legacy by her father, John Borrodell, at his death, and no doubt may appear upon record in Cork, the which house stands upon lands which they call Bishop's land, and was built by our said father, he to have lived in the same, whereof my said wife was next to himself, as may also appear there upon record; and whereas I have a right to land in the Narragansett country, which is mine by deed of the native right from the true proprietors thereof, as may appear upon record in Boston, and in the records of Stonington, the which, my rights, have been and are under the possession and improvement of those who have no just right to them, to which by reason of the many troubles, woes and difficulties which have arisen, together with our remoteness, we have not been able to vindicate our just rights, but have been great sufferers thereby; but if it please God to send peaceable times, and our rights be recordable in law, I do by this my last will, give and bequeath my said right unto my sons John Denison and George Denison, to be equally divided betwixt them, provided that they each one bear their equal share in the trouble and recovery of the same. Provided, also, that my son George Denison, do relinquish and deliver up any right he may pretend unto by a former deed which I gave him of the one half of Achagromeconsist, according as I formerly obliged him to do in a deed I gave him of the other farm, and gave him upon that consideration. And in reference with Nathaniel Beebe, who hath been a retainer and boarder in our family between thirty and forty years, and for his board at our last reckoning, which was March 20th, 1680, he was indebted to me forty-six pounds six shillings and three pence, I say £46, 6s. & 3d. as may appear under his hand to said account in my book, since which time he hath boarded in the family near upon fourteen years, which at four shillings and sixpence the week, amounts to one hundred and sixty three pounds, sixteen shillings, out of which I do give unto Nathaniel Beebe, fifty pounds, in way of gratification and satisfaction for his love to me and my children and officers of love shown unto myself and any of them, in mine or their sickness or weakness, which fifty pounds must be deducted from the one hundred and sixty three pounds, sixteen shillings, and the remainder will be one hundred and thirteen pounds, which one hundred and thirteen pounds, sixteen shillings, together with the forty-six pounds, six shillings and three pence due upon book, under his hand, at our last reckoning as aforesaid, being added unto one hundred and thirteen pounds and sixteen shillings, the whole will be £160, 2s. 3d. the which I give unto my son William Denison, and his heirs forever, for him or them or any of them, or if they cause to demand, receive and improve as their own proper estate.

Also, I give unto my son William Denison, all and singular, whatsover that belongeth unto me, not already disposed of, to be to him and his heirs forever, whom also I do hereby constitute, appoint and make my sole executor, to pay all just debts, if any shall appear of which I know not any, and to receive all dues which either are or shall be due to me,, and to pay all legacies according to this my will, within twelve months after my wife's decease, and to take care for my decent burial. But in case my son William Denison shall decease before he hath performed this my will, or before his children are of age, then my will is that the whole estate be under the improvement of his wife, our daughter-in-law Sarah Denison, during the time of her widowhood, for her comfortable supply, and the well educating and bringing up their children in religion and good learning; all which she shall do by the advice of the Revererd and my loving friend Mr. James Noyes, my son John Denison and my son-in-law, Gershom Palmer, them or any two of them, if three cannot be obtained; but without advice she may not act, which three my dear friends, I do earnestly desire and hereby appoint as overseers for the children, and to take effectual care that this my will may be performed according to the true intent thereof; but if my said daughter-in-law shall marry again, then this whole estate do fall into the hands of my overseers, and by them to be secured for my son William Denison's children, to wit, William Denison, George Denison and Sarah Denison, and by those overseers to be improved for their well bringing up as aforesaid, and faithfully to be delivered unto the children as they shall come of age, to wit: the males at twenty-one years of age, and the females at eighteen; and if any of the said children should die before they come of age, the survivors shall inherit the same, and if they should all die before of age, (the which God forbid, but we are all mortal), then it is my declared mind and true intent of this my will that my grandson George Denison, the son of my eldest son John Denison, shall be the sole heir of that estate, out of which he shall pay unto his four brothers, to wit., John Denison, Robert Denison, William Denison, and Daniel Denison, ten pounds apiece in current pay, and also ten pounds in current pay unto his cousin, Edward Denison, the son of my son George Denison; and in token that this is my last will and testament, I have hereunto set my hand and seal this 24th day of January, in the year of our Lord, one thousand six hundred and ninety three-four.

GEORGE DENISON. (Seal.)

APPENDIX.

DEED.

To all People to whom these presents shall come, William Denison, Jr., of Stonington, in ye County of New London, in ye Collony of Connecticut, sendeth Greeting: Know ye, that I William Denison abovesd. with the consent of Mary, my wife, for and in consideration of ye sd. full and just sum of thirty pounds of current money (silver) of New England to me in hand well and truly payed by John Smith of Preston, in ye County and Collony abovesd. the reason whereof I acknowledge myself fully satisfied, contented and paid and of every part and parcel thereof, do exonerate and acquit and discharge him the abovesd. John Smith, his heirs, executors, administrators and assigns forever, I ye sd. William Denison do therefore by these presents do fully, freely, clearly and absolutely give, grant, bargain, sell, alienate, enfee of, make over and confirm from me, my heirs and assigns forever unto ye sd. Smith, his heirs, executors and assigns forever a certain parcell of upland and swamp land in estimation, three score acres, scituate and lying within ye Township of Stonington as it is butted and bounded, beginning at the southeast corner at an ash tree, by a brook and from thence running northerly fifty-four rods to a horn beam tree marked on four sides standing by sd. brook, thence running east to a white oak tree marked and keeping the same course until it comes to Elihu Chesebrough's line, thence running south 54 rods to a white oak tree marked on four sides, thence running west 8 score rods to ye tree first mentioned. To Have and To Hold, possess and enjoy all and singular every part and parcell thereof to ye only provision, benefit and behoof of him, ye sd. John Smith, his heirs, executors and assigns forever, with all the rights, privileges, appurtenances hereunto belonging or any wise appertaining thereunto belonging or any wise appertaining of wood, timber, stones, rocks, mines, minerals, herbage and water and water courses, and that I ye sd. William Denison, on ye day of ye date hereof have full power and lawful authority to give, grant, bargain, sell, alienate, enfeoff and confirm all ye above bargained premiess in manner and form as above mentioned, to ye sd. John Smith, his heirs and assigns forever, so that he and they shall and may forever hereafter peaceably and quietly possess and enjoy the same free and clear and freely and clearly acquitted and discharged of and from all and all manner of gifts, grants, bargains, sale, lease, mortgage, executions, dowries, jointures, entails, entanglements or all other acts of incumbrances whatsoever had made or done or suffered ─── by me ye sd. William Denison or any other person, or persons, ─── and I ye said William Denison do by these presents bind myself───executors, administrators or assigns for us to defend ye above bargained premises against all manner of person or persons whatsoever lawfully claiming ye sd. lands.

In witness whereof I have set my hand and affix my seal this the 23rd day of May, one thousand seven hundred and nine, 1709.

WILLIAM DENISON.

Signed, sealed and delivered in presence of us,
JONATHAN TRACEY,
DAVID TRACEY.

It is always to be understood that ye land in ye above written deed is bounded south and west upon the land of Samuel Prentice, of Stonington. This was entered before signing and sealing the within written deed. It is also always to be understood that there is a highway allowed through ye sd. land.

July 8th, 1709, Mr. William Denison of Stonington personally appeared and acknowledged the within written instrument to be his free act and deed before me, JONATHAN TRACEY, Justice of the Peace.

This within deed recorded in Preston in ye 2nd Book of Deeds, following 24th of July, 1709.

Signed   JONATHAN TRACEY, Recorder.

JOHN SMITH,
WILLIAM DENISON.

WILL OF MAJOR ISRAEL HEWITT.

In the name of God, AMEN. The 18th day of March, A. D. 1776. I, ISRAEL HEWITT, of Stonington, in the Co. of New London and Colony of Conn. in New England, being in a measure of health, and of sound mind and memory, and in the free exercise of my reason, Knowing that it is appointed unto man once to die, and calling to mind my own mortality, do make and ordain this my last Will and Testament. That is to say, principally and first of all, I give and recommend my soul to God, that gave it and my body I submit to the earth, to receive a christian burial, at the discretion of my executors, hereinafter mentioned, hoping to receive the same again through the merits of Christ at the resurrection of the just, And touching such worldly estate as it has pleased God to bless me with, I give and dispose of the same, after my just debts are paid, out of my moveable estate by my executors in form and manner following: Imprimis, I give and bequeath to my beloved son, Israel Hewitt, the farm and buildings, and all the appurtenances thereof, where I now live, viz., all that land that was given to me by my honored father, Benjamin Hewitt, deceased, as by deed on record appears, also all that land and the appurtenances thereof that I bought of my brother, Henry Hewitt, as by deed on record may appear. Also, ten acres of the land which I bought of Mr. Henry Stevens, being the north part of the land that was formerly Mr. Thomas Hewitt's, deceased, said ten acres are bounded, beginning at the northwest corner of said land which was the dividing line between said Thomas Hewitt and Benjamin Hewitt, deceased, and is at the southwest corner of a small orchard, thence running southerly as the fence now stands, so far as to include ten acres, thence easterly to lands that was formerly Samuel Utley's, thence northerly, to the north east corner of Thomas Hewitt's land, and is the south east corner of Walter Hewitt's land, thence westerly to the bounds first mentioned, holding the same width at the east end as at the west. Only reserving ten acres of the land which my said father gave me, which he bought of Mr. Thomas Rose, lying at the west end of said tract, and on the west side of an old rye field, being woodland, to be laid out in a handsome form with a convenient cart-way to said wood-land, which ten acres reserved as above, I give and bequeath to my son, Charles Hewitt, To him and to his heirs forever, with egrees and regress, and reserving one half acre of land westward of my house where I now dwell, in the orchard and where my late wife, Ann Hewitt, and my brother, Benjamin Hewitt, and his wife, Ann Hewitt, deceased, were buried, which half acre reserved as above I give and bequeath for a burying place, for the family of the Hewitt's, so long as any of the name remain. Item—I give to my said son, the one half part of my house, and land in the Neck which I bought of Col. Amos Chesebrough, deceased, and the one half of all the appurtenances thereof to be divided by judicious free-holders, according to quantity and quality and also the one half of a bed and furniture in said house, and also my silver sword and belt, all the above I give my said son, Israel Hewitt, to him and his heirs forever, except the ten acres of land and the half acre above reserved, and is to be the whole of his portion of my estate.

Item.—I give to my beloved son Rufus Hewitt and to his heirs forever, the farm, buildings and all the appurtenances thereof where he now lives, namely, all the land and appurtenances thereof, which I bought of Joseph Ayers of said Stonington, as by deed from him on record may appear; adso all the land and appurtenances thereof which I bought of Richardson Avery, of said Stonington, as by two certain deeds from him on record may appear, and also my clock, and this to be the whole of his portion of my estate. I give and bequeath to beloved son, Charles Hewitt, to him and his heirs forever, the farm and buildings and all the appurtenances thereof, where he now lives, viz., which I bought of Capt. Joseph Hewitt, as by deed from his on record appears, also all the land and appurtenances thereof, which I bought of Henry Stevens, Jr., as per deed from his on record appears; also the remainder of the land which I bought of Henry Stevens, and also all the land which I bought of John Frink and Nicholas Frink and Samuel Utley, late of said Stonington, deceased, bounded as by deed from each of them may appear; also I give to my said son, Charles Hewitt, and to his heirs forever, the other half part of my house and the land in the Neck, and the one half of all the appurtenances thereof according to quantity and quality which I bought of Col. Amos Chesebrough deceased, to be divided by judicious free holders as before, setting to Charles the south part and also one half the bed and furniture that is now in said house; also I give to my son Charles, and to his heirs forever, the land in the Neck, which I took a deed of from Mr. Nathaniel Palmer, containing about ten acres more or less, bounded as it has been divided by my sons Israel and Charles; also I give to my son, Charles, my best saddle and my gun or firelock, and my shot mould, this to be the whole of his portion of my estate. Item.—I give and bequeath to my beloved granddaughter, Ann Hewitt, ten pounds of lawful money, to be paid to her by my son, Israel Hewitt, within three months of my decease and also ten pounds lawful money to be paid by my son, Israel Hewitt in horses, cattle sheep or swine as she shall choose within three months after my decease which ten pounds of lawful money and ten pounds in live stock as above, when paid shall be considered and allowed as so much paid on a certain note of hand, which I have upon my son Israel, said live stock shall be appraised by indifferent judicious men; also I give to my said Granddaughter Ann, all of my household goods or indoor moveables that are not already disposed of exceping four silver spoons, together with her grandmother's and her own natural mother's wearing apparel, this to be the whole of her portion of my estate. Item.—I give to my two granddaughters, Ann Ledyard, wife of Col. William Ledyard of Groton, and Amy Stanton, wife of Job Stanton of Stonington, a certain house lot or piece of land which I bought of Mr. John Hallam, lying on the west side of Stonington harbor and near to Capt. Israel Wordin's house, and lot containing one quarter of an acre, be it more or less, as by a deed of record may appear, said lot of land or the money which it shall be sold for to be equally divided between my two said granddaughters, Ann and Amy. I also give to my said granddaughters Ann and Amy four silver spoons, reserved as above to be equally divided between them, and is to be the whole of their portion of my estate.

I give to my beloved wife, Mary Hewitt ten pounds of lawful money, to be paid her by my son Israel Hewitt, in one month after my decease, also I give her my negro man servant, named Cato, or the money which he shall be sold for, if she sees cause to sell him, and she the said Mary, is to occupy and improve the west lower room in my now dwelling house and the north west bedroom, adjoining to the said west lower room and the east great chamber, together with such privileges in the kitchen as she shall need. All the above rooms to be improved by said Mary, for twelve months after my decease, if she sees cause to tarry so long; and I order my executors hereafter mentioned to provide and supply the said Mary Hewitt with a sufficiency of all kinds of provisions for her table, suitable for a person of her estate and condition, and to keep her riding beast well, both provision and keeping said beast as above to continue for twelve months after my decease or for so much of that time as she shall choose to tarry in my house. All of which I give to my said wife Mary Hewitt above and besides what she is to receive out of my estate, by virtue of a jointure or covenant made between me and the said Mary Hewitt dated Dec. 8th, 1773, which jointure or covenant is to be paid or fulfilled by my son Israel Hewitt, out of that part of my estate which I have as above ordered and given to him. Item.—Notwithstanding what is above mentioned particularly with respect to my household goods or indoor moveables, my will is that all my wearing apparel shall be to my two sons, Rufus and Charles Hewitt, to be equally divided between them, and also it is my will that my pew in the meeting house where the Rev. Mr. Joseph Fish officiates shall be to my two sons, Rufus and Charles Hewitt, to each an equal privilege. Finally,—I do hereby nominate, constitute and appoint my three beloved sons, Israel Hewitt,

Rufus Hewitt and Charles Hewitt, to be my executors to this my last will and Testament, utterly revoking and disannulling all other and former wills by me made, hereby ratifying and confirming this and no others to be my last Will and Testament.

In witness whereof I do hereby set my hand and seal.

              ISRAEL HEWITT. (Seal.

Witnesses:
MINER GRANT,
WILLIAM PHELPS,
HANNAH PHELPS,

ABSTRACT OF THE WILL OF MRS. ANNE PARKER NOYES.

Abstract of the will of Mrs. Anne (Parker) Noyes, widow of Rev. William Noyes of Cholderton, England:

"Ann Noyes of Cholderton, Wilts, widow, 18, March 1655, proved 21, April 1658. I give and bequeath to James and Nicholas Noyes, my two sons, now in New England, twelve pence apiece and to such children as they have living twelve pence apiece. To my son-in-law Thomas Kent of Upper Wallop twelve pence, to his wife five shillings and to their children twelve pence apiece. To Robert Read of Cholderton in the Co. of Southampton, Genl. all the rest and residue & and I do make the said Robert Read sole Executor.

            "Signed ANNE NOYES."

WILL OF THE REV. JAMES NOYES.

To all Christian people, Greeting: Know ye that I being sensible that days are upon me, and that in duty I am concerned to justly settle my estate upon my deare wife and children for their support and comfort when I shall die, which great change I have no reason to be preparing for, I being at this time in good health, and perfect understanding, Doe first will and believing I bequeath my Soul to God, that gave it, and humbly and firmly relying upon my Lord and Saviour, Jesus Christ, for Life, righteousness and Eternal Salvation, and also hereby order my body to be decently buried in a lively hope of a glorious resurrection at the last day, by my Executrix or Executors without any great expense; unto my deare and loving wife I have and doe hereby will and bequeath a third part of the profits of the farm I now live on, and the keeping winter and summer six cows, she shall choose out of my stock and their calves they shall have yearly, untill their calves they shall have yearly be a year old, and two mares and their colts, until their colts shall be a year old. And I give and bequeath unto my loving wife, One half of the house, I now live in, with one of the cellars and one of the ovens, and two beds and their furniture, as bed-steads, and curtains, And all the household stuff and utensels, belonging to the house, except Seven pounds of household stuff within doors which I give my loving son, Thomas. Also I give my wife my sheep, and son Thomas must winter fourteen sheep yearly for my wife, and she must have three or four Swine to run on the farm, for her use. Also I give to my loving wife my bees, only I give one Stock of bees to my son Thomas if there be two, and my wife must have a garden, of some rod square, Sufficient, for a garden near the house, where she shall choose. Also I give my wife, after my debts are payed, my stock of neat cattle, not particularly disposed of. And son Thomas shall find my wife fire-wood and a boy if need be to goe to mill and on errands for her. The moveables above given, I give my wife, forever, the other profits and privileges I only gave my wife during her natural life. If my wife marrie I only give her the third of the profits of the farm whilst she lives, I now live on, and two beds and furniture and a third of the household stuff left to her and six cows, the other estate is to be divided amongst my children to help those that have least, by this will. It is to be understood I dispose not of those horse-kind and cattle, my wife calls her own, which are known to some of the children, but have them as her own proper estate to be disposed of by her as she sees cause. Also some cattle which are Anna Treat's, I dispose not of. Moreover, I give to my beloved wife and loving son, Joseph Noyes (my Executor as after mentioned), all estate I have not mentioned in this will. Unto my loving son James Noyes, I give and bequeath the farm he now lives on, with all appurtenances thereof called Muxquita Neck, to be his and his heirs forever, lawfully begotten of his body, together with what I have already given him of stock and other things, which farme I give to son James with this provision, that my son James pay three hundred and fiftie pounds, and the use thereof which is yet due to Mr. John Gardner or his heirs or assigns according to the tenour of a mortgage I have given to Mr. Gardner, as was just I should to get money to pay to James Noyes, his honest debts, which were of justice and necessity to be payed, I having with son James this knowledge and consent mortgaged one half of the farm to J. Gardner, I having full power so to do, I having never given him, sd James Noyes, a deed of his farme, and it being done with sd James his consent and to pay his just debts. Also I having been forced to sell a hundred and fiftie pounds' worth of land in money and twenty pounds worth of Land unto Mr. John Chandler of Woodstock, which lands on the north of them, I allotted to be my son Joseph Noyes', his or part of his portion from me, I having paid son James' debts, faithfully putting myself to considerable charge and trouble, to pay sd James his debts, as appears on a paper of account what I payed and upon receipt from the Creditors I am necessitated to oblige and doe hereby oblige firmly son James Noyes to pay to my son, Joseph Noyes, one hundred and seventy pounds in New England silver money, at fifteen penniweight or bils of credit, I say I hereby oblige my son James Noyes, him, his heirs or assigns, to pay as above said, a hundred and seventy pounds to Joseph Noyes, his heirs and assigns, or otherwise if son James Noyes faile of the above said, I doe hereby order my son James Noyes, his heirs or assigns, to set out as much of the land as will pay said Joseph Noyes, a hundred and seventie pounds as above sd. the land to be prized and set out by indifferent men. mutually chosen if they do not otherwise agree themselves, and this to be done within two years of the date thereof, if it be not done before that time. Also my son James Noyes owing two debts more that I have reason to take care that they should be payed out of son James, his estate, viz., About ninety six pounds, to her that was Mrs. Heath, I hear now Mrs. Burroughs, and to Mrs. Mary Cole of Newport, about thirty pounds and some use, as appears on a bond as I am informed, I doe hereby order my Executrix, Executors or Executor to see that those debts be honestly payed out of my son James, his estate, Or if need be out of the land of Muxquita Neck; unto my loving son Thomas Noyes, I give and bequeath, the farm I now live on with all the housing thereon the condition abovesd. viz., All my land on the East of the mill brooke and west of the brook according to the true boundaries thereof, viz., the land I bought of Mr. Willis, the land I bought of Mr. Samuel Richardson and the land I bought of Mr. Samuel and Elisha Chesebrough to be his and his heirs lawfully begotten of his body, After my wife's death and before my wife's death so far as will stand with what I have above given my deare wife.

Also my son Thomas is to have, if he hath it not, a bed and bedding, his share of stock he hath already given him, And my son, is to have the use of the house, sellars, ovens, not given to my wife above, whilst my wife lives, but if she marrie or die, son Thomas is to have the housing and appurtenances and all the utensils aforesaid, as the cart, plows, chaines, axes, hoes or any other utensile whatsoever of that nature and one hive of bees at least. Unto my son John, I give and bequeath my land at the wares, upland and meadow, the house and all the appurtenances thereof, the whole farm according to the true boundaries thereof, and my piece of meadow lying by the upland, a small creek compassing it southward, and a great creek northward, according to the boundaries on record. And my four acres of Salt meadow at the point according to the true boundaries on record.

Also I doe give and hereby bequeath to my son John and his heirs a piece of swamp meadow lying on a brook northward of Joshua Holm's house, according to the boundaries appearing on the Record, he hath a bed and bedding and Stock already.

Unto my son Joseph Noyes, I give and bequeath all my books at home (except English Bibles and small English books which are of common use in the familie) which I leave to my loving wife to dispose of as she pleaseth.

Also I give son Joseph, all my books at Lyme in my brother Moses custody, Also I give unto my son Joseph and bequeath seventie acres of land layed out to the Volunteers whether it be upland or meadow, to be sd Joseph Noyes, his, his heirs forever. The records will show the bounds thereof at New London. I leave my wearing clothes unto my son Treat and give two cows amongst my son Treat's children. Also it is always provided, that notwithstanding I have given son James, Maxquita Neck, Thomas the farm I live on, and son John his farm, that they shall not sell the farmes they live on without the consent of my Executrix or Executors, whilst they live.

And I doe hereby make my deare and loving wife my Executrix, and Capt. Nathan Chesebrough, my son Joseph Noyes, joynt Executors with my wife, to execute and fulfill faithfully this my last will and Testament, making void any former wills or Testaments.

Witness my hand and seale affixed November 12th, 1716. The word (settle) in the second line, and in the eleventh line, the words (until their calves) are so cancelled; and in the sixteenth line the word (winter) interlined. In the three and fortieth line the words (worth of land) interlined, and in the three and fiftieth line the word (Order) interlined. In the six and hundredth line, some words are blotted out. JAMES NOYES, (Seal)

Witnesses:
EBENEZER SEARLE,
MARY M. DENISON.
  her mark.
JOHN MACDOWELL.

Recorded in the Fourth Book of Wills for the County of New London Folio 146,147, January 29th, 1719-20.   J. C. CHRISTOPHERS, Clerk.

Mr. Ebenezer Searle, Mr. John Macdowell and Mrs. Mary M. Denison of Stonington, all of them personally appeared before me and made oath that they saw the Reverend Mr. James Noyes signe and seal ye will written on ye other part of this sheet of paper, and declared it to be his last will and Testament, and that at the time of his signing and sealing of it was in perfect mind and memory, and they all of them at the same time signed to it as witnesses in the presence of the Testator.

Stonington, January 22nd day 1719-20.
Test.   DANIEL PALMER, Justice of the peace.

Endorsed, The last Will and Testament of the Revd. Mr. James Noyes. Jan. 27th, 1719-20.

WILL OF CAPT. THOMAS NOYES.

In the name of God, Amen, The tenth day of Feb. in the Twenty-eighth year of the reign of George the 2nd, King of Great Britain, Anno que Domini, 1755. I, Thomas Noyes, of Stonington in the County of New London, in the Colony of Connecticut in New England yeoman, Being of perfect mind and memory, thanks be given to God, and calling to mind the mortality of my body, knowing it is appointed for all men to die, Do make and ordain this my last will and Testament in the following manner, and form. That is to say, I resign my soul to God, that gave it, when it shall please him to call for it, to be redeemed, by his Son Jesus Christ, to be sanctified by his Spirit and made meet for Heaven, and my body I recommend to the earth to be therein buried in Christian decent burial at the discretion of my Executors, nothing doubting but it will be raised again at the Resurrection of the just, being glorified by the mighty power of God. And as touching my worldly estate, wherewith it hath pleased God, of his goodness to bless me in this life, I give, demise and dispose of the same in the manner and form following:

Imp. I give to my dearly beloved wife, Elizabeth, the use of all my household stuff during her life, and my slave called Peter, and the profit of one-third part of my real estate, and also the one half of my dwelling house, and cellar which half she shall choose during her natural life. Item I give to Mary Noyes, the widow of my son Thomas Noyes, late deceased, one hundred pounds in bills of credit as they now pass, and I also give to the three sons of my sd. son Thomas Noyes, decd. namely, Thomas, William and Nathan, to each of them, one hundred pounds, in bills as aforesd. to be paid to them at one year's end after my decease, their sd. father having had the estate that came by his mother.

Item. I give and bequeath to my son James Noyes, and to his heirs and assigns forever, all the lands I have lying in Stonington, aforesaid, except the little pasture lying north of ye country road adjoining to Capt. John Denison's land. He my son James paying three thousand pounds in bills of credit as it now passes in old tenor, to my Executors in one year after my decease. I also give to my sd. son, James, the one half of my dwelling house, during the life of my sd. wife, and after her decease I give the whole of my sd. house to him, his heirs and assigns forever.

Item. I give to my beloved son, Sanford Noyes, during his natural life, the use of one half of my house and cellar and the use and improvements of one hundred and sixty acres of land, all lying in Westerly in the Colony of Rhode Island, to be set out to him, off of my farm, in sd. Westerly, in such manner as that it may be reckoned alike for quality of goodness with the rest of sd. farm, in proportion, and when my sd. son Sanford dies, if he leaves a child or children, begotten in wedlock, by a present or future wife, my will is that ye sd. one hundred and sixty acres of land shall be settled upon his sd. children or child in manner and form as the laws in that Colony do settle Intestate Estates, and if my said son Sanford, doth die leaving no lawful issue as aforesd. my will is that sd. one hundred and sixty acres of land shall be to my son Joseph Noyes, his heirs, administrators paying to each of his sisters that shall be then living the sum of one hundred pounds in money, or bills of credit as it now passes, and also paying the sum of one hundred pounds of like money to the children of each of his sisters that shall be then dead, to be equally divided among them.

Item. I give and bequeath to my beloved son, Joseph Noyes, to his heirs and assigns forever the other half of my house and cellar, in Westerly, aforesd. and all the residue of my land, lying in the sd. town of Westerly, the barn and other buildings now standing thereon being his own already.

Item. I give to be equally divided between my sons all my wearing apparel, and my utensils belonging to husbandry.

Item. My will is that my debts and funeral charges be paid out of my moveable estate by my Executors and when that is done, my will is, that two thirds of my moveable estate and two thirds of my money and two thirds of the debts due to me by book, bond or otherwise, shall be equally divided or distributed by my Executors to and among my beloved daughters or their children, viz., Elizabeth Palmer, Dorothy Palmer, Mary Billing, Rebecca Denison, Abigail Hallam, Ann Frink and Bridget Denison. That is to say, to divide or distribute among them or their children if they or any of them be dead, as that including what I have already given them at their marriage or at other times as may appear by my memorandum papers, and what I now give them by will, they may all be made equal.

Item. My will is and I hereby order my son James Noyes, at two years after my decease, to pay or distribute equally among all my daughters aforesd. and the children of them my sd. daughters that are or shall be then dead, the sum of one thousand pounds in bills of credit of the old tenor, as they now pass, or other money equivalent thereto, so that each daughter my be equal sharer in sd. thousand pounds.

Item. I give and bequeath to the children of my daughter, Rebecca Denison, decd. and to their heirs and assigns forever, a small pasture, being the northwest part of my farm in Stonington, aforesd., lying on the north side of the Country Rhoade, joyning to Capt. John Denison's land, this to be accounted towards making their mother equal with her sisters, as aforesd.

Lastly. I hereby constitute and ordain my beloved wife, Elizabeth Noyes, Executrix, and my sons James Noyes and Joseph Noyes, Executors, of this my last will and Testament, hereby disallowing and revoking and making voyde all other former wills by me in any wise made. Ratifying this and no other to be my last Will and Testament, and they only my Executors. In witness whereof, I have hereunto set my hand and seal the day, month and year first above written.

THOMAS NOYES. (Seal)

Signed, sealed, published and declared by the sd. Thomas Noyes, his last Will and Testament, in the presence of us, the subscribers.
SAMUEL CROSS.
NATHAN BILLING.
ELISHA BERRY.

New London, Aug. 6th, 1755, Approved.

G. SALTONSTALL, Judge Probate.

Stonington in New London County, July ye 3rd, 1755.

Personally appeared, Samuel Cross, Nathan Billing and Elisha Berry, ye witnesses to this foregoing Will and made oath that they saw ye aforesd. Thomas Noyes ye signer to ye foregoing Will sign and seal ye same and heard him pronounce and declare ye same to be his last Will and Testament, and that at ye same time he was of a sound, disposing mind and memory (To ye best of their judgment) and that they, at ye same time signed thereto as witnesses in ye presence of ye Testator.

Sworn before me,

SIMEON MINOR,
Justice of the Peace.

WILL OF BRIAN PENDLETON.

I, Brian Pendleton, sometime of Saco, in ye County of York, now resident, in Portsmh, on Pascataq River in N. E. doe make & ordain this to be my last Will & Testament, hereby revoking all former wills by me made.

1st. I give to my beloved wife Eleanor Pendleton, (besides which I have reserved for her in a deed of Gift to my Grandchild Pendleton Fletcher, all my household Goods, together with all that piece of land belonging to me, lying between my son James's & Mr. Deering's upon the Great Island, which I have excepted & reserved out of my Deed of Gift, of all to my son James.

2nd. Furthermore, I give to my wife all of my houseing & land at Cape-Porpus which Richard Palmer's wife hath the use of during her life, together with my six hundred & forty acres, more or lesse, lying on ye east side of Westbrook, near Saco Falls, which I bought of Jno West & Maj. Wm. Phillips as ye Deeds will appear, as also Timber Island at ye Little River, all which I give to my wife, absolutely to be at her disposal.

2nd. Unto my Grandchild, James Pendleton, Jun'r, I give my hundred acres upland & ten acres of meadow which I bought of Jno. Bush & lies within ye Township of Cape-Porpus, adjoining to Prince's Rock.

3rd. All my houseing and land at Wells, with all the privileges and appurtenances I give unto my two Grand-children Mary and Hannah Pendleton, which my son had by his ffmer wife, to bee equally divided between ym.

4th. I give to my wife all my wearing clothes to be disposed of as she shall see meet, desiring her to (remember some poor).

5th. Finally I make my wife my Executrix and joyn my beloved son James Pendleton, executor, together with his mother willing my Executrix to disburse what is needed for my Funerall charge, and my Executor to pay all my debts. And I request Mr. Joshua Moodey and Mr. Richard Martyn to bee overseers to this my last will and Testament.

In witness to all and singular yt p'misses I have set to my hand and seale this 9th August, 1677.

BRIAN PENDLETON. (Seal)

Witnesses:
JOSHUA MOODEY,
ANN MOODEY.

As a schedule to this my last will and testament, I give unto my beloved son, James Pendleton, all my land on the East of Westbrook, butting on the great river of Saco, six hundred acres, more or less, my house and lands lying at Cape-Porpus, in all three hundred acres in the occupation of Richard Palmer, all my several Islands in or near sd. Cape-Porpus the one half of my stock of cattle of what sort soever upon my farm at Winter Harbour found after mine and my wives decease with all my wearing apparel and one third of my household goods, except my utensils of Husbandry. And unto Mary and Hannah Pendleton, daughters of my sd. son James, all my lands in Wells being three plantations or lotts, bought of Mr. Fletcher Hammond, and were improved by Joseph Cross, and to each of them one third part of my household goods after mine and my wives decease.

Item. To Brian Pendleton, my Grandson, the remainder of my land on Great Island Pascataq, what is contayned herein is addition to my will, anything in sd. will notwithstanding.

BRIAN PENDLETON. (Seal.)

This schedule was signed and sealed in presenc of us,
JOSEPH DUDLEM,
JOSHUA MOODEY,

Joshua Moodey made oath yt ye writing on ye otherside was signed and sealed by maj. Brian Pendleton, and declared by him to be his last will and Testament, and yt. Mr. Joseph Dudley did write and sign to the schedule annexed at ye foot and annexed to ye foot of ye foregoing page.
This 3rd day of April, 1681,
Before us,
JOHN WINCOLL,
T———. S.———.

CHARLES FROST,
Justice of the Peace.

This will within ——— written ——— attest above, ———
———————. For Mr. ——— ——— 23, Ap. 1681. pd. Ed. Rishworth.

WILL OF WALTER PALMER.

Walter Palmer——Will——Vnto my sonne, John, a yoake of three yeare old steares and a horse; to my dau. Grace 20s. to all my Grand-Children 20s. apeece. To my sonne Jonas, halfe the planting lott at ye new meadow River, by Seaconcke, and ye Lott betweene John Butterwoths, according to the foure score pound estate, and the yse of halfe ye houseing and halfe of the whole farme for fower years. To my sonne William, the other halfe of saide farme at Seaconck forever, and to take Robert Martine or some other skill full man and to divide the houseing and the whole farme in two equall pts and to take his owne and dispose of it as he pleaseth. I give him also a Mare with her foale, two redd oxen, a paire of Steares of three years old a piece, fower Cowes and a Musket, with all such things as are his owne already. The other halfe of the farme at Seaconcke I give to my sonne Gershom forever after the ende terme of fower yeares. All the rest of my Land, goods and chattel vndesposed I Leave vnto my wife, whome with my sonne, Elihu, I make my full executor, to pay my debts, bring up my Children and pay them their portions as my lands and estate will beare; but in case my wife marry againe, before my children are brought up and their portions payed, then my three sonnes, Elihu, Nehemiah and Moses, to enter vpon the farme and Estate and pay vnto their mother 10 pounds pr annum dureing her life and ye land and estate duely valued to be equally distributed among my Children, Elyhu, Nehemia, Moses, Benjamin, Gershom, Hannah and Rebecca with Consideration of the tenn pound yearely to be payd to their mother out of my land. But if my wife pay their portions according to her discretion and my three sonnes, Elyhu, Nehemia and Moses, Possesses the land, they shall give 20 pounds a piece out of the land to my sonne Benjamine, besides his mother's portion in 3 years after they are possessed of the Farme.

WALTER PALMER.

In the p'nce of
WILLIAM CHESEBROUGH,
SAM'LL CHESEBROUGH,
NATHANIEL CHESEBROUGH.

Memorandum.—If Elyhu, Nehemia or Moses decease before they have any yeare, Benjamine is to succede in their pl. of ye farme, and give to my dau., Elizabeth, two Cowes. I give my Executor a yeare's time for payment of these Legacies.

Testified to by the three witnesses, on oath before George Denison Com. Approved by the Court on Petition of Lieut. Richard Cooke in behalfe of ye Widow Palmer, relict of Walter, and Elihu, their sonne, on the oathes of us, Samuell and Nathan Chesebrough, 11 May, 1662.

Inventory of the goods and chattels of Walter Palmer, now deceased, at Sothertowne in the Countie of Suffolke, as it was taken the last of Mch. 1662, by William Chesebroke and Thomas Stanton of the same towne.

Amt. 1644 pounds, 05s.

One Horse valued at 12 pounds added by Elihu Palmer as executor who deposed 13 May, 1662.

MARRIAGE CONTRACT.

Stonington, July the 9th, 1680.

This witnesseth, that upon contract of marriage betwixt Joseph Saxton and Hannah Chesebrough, widow and relict of Nathaniel Chesebrough, deceased, the said Saxton doth covenant and promise to and with the said widow Cheseebrough and with the overseers, Capt. George Denison and Mr. Nehemiah Palmer, to wit, that he the said Saxton upon the consideration of marriage with the aforesaid widow, shall and will take upon him the management of the whole estate, belonging unto the said relict and children and in consideration of the use and improvement of the said estate to bring up and maintain the children in a Christian and discreet manner and shall not charge them any way debtors for the same, but shall and will pay all and each of the children the full of their portions ordered them as they shall come of age, and

APPENDIX.   725

in land at the same right it was inventoried, always provided and it is to be understood that the thirds due unto the widow, during her natural life, is not to be paid until her decease, unless the said Saxton and widow shall see cause to do it of their own good will; it is also to be understood that the widow's third is not to be deducted out of any one or more of their portions, but out of each and every one of them, their just portions until her decease, at which time, they are each one to receive the full complement of their portions in case they have not received it before, as above expressed in the mean season and until all the children have received the whole of their portions assigned them, by the Court. It shall not be lawful for any one upon any pretense whatsoever to sell, mortgage, alienate or any way to alter the portion of any of the aforesaid house or land until as the children, shall receive each and their particular portion in land, being of full age, they shall see cause for their own comity to sell or alienate their own particular portions, but otherwise and until such time to be and to remain, in the same state as at this time present and for the reason aforesaid and for the true and faithful performance of all and each particular contained the said Saxton, doth bind himself, his heirs, executors, administrators and assigns firmly by these presents.

In confirmation whereof, he the said Saxton hath hereunto set his hand this 7th of July, one thousand six hundred and eighty.
JOSEPH N. SAXTON.

Witness to these Presents,
SAMUEL STANTON,
DANIEL STANTON.

The above written contract and obligation was entered in this Book the 27th of July, 1680.
JOHN STANTON, Recorder.

WILL OF DANIEL SMITH (No. 2 in Smith Family).

I, Daniel Smith of Watertowne, in ye Countie of Middlesex, being very sick and weake in my bodie and daily looking when my leaving shall be, yet through ye mercie and goodness of God I am in my understanding and memorie sound, and doe declare this to be my last will and testament as followeth: I return my spirit unto God yt gave it and my bodie to the earth from whence it was taken to be decently buried at ye discretion of my executor, hopeing at the last day to have a glorious resurrection both of bodie and soule through ye merits of ye Lord Jesus Christ.

I give unto my deare and loving wife, my whole ———— both houses and lands and moveables for her comfort and maintenance and ye bringing up of my children so long as she shall contenue a widdow after my decease, but if she shall see reason to marrie again, then my will is, she shall injoy the thirds of ye yearly income of my lands and that onely.

I give unto my two eldest sons, namely Daniell Smith and John Smith, after my wives deecase or marriage, my houseing, both dwelling house and barne with all my lands both meddow and upland equally to them and their heirs forever. They paieing out of them as is after expressed and if eighther of them die before they atttained to ye age of one and twentie years, then my will is that my third son, namely, Joseph Smith, shall injoy the part and proportion of him that dies as before and if all my three sone doe live, then my will is that my son Joseph, abovesaid, shall have an equall portion with his eldest brethren to be paid him out of my houses and lands, but not in house and land. I give unto my oldest son Daniell Smith abovesaid my horse and armes and furniture for ye horse with all my wearing cloath both linen and woolen. My will is that my moveable estate after my wives deecease or marriage be equalie divided among all my daughters and what my mother's will and mind was to bestow upon any of my daughters my will is yt it should be performed without any alteration.

And I doe nominate and appoint my deare and loving wife to be sole executrix to this my last will and testament and doe earnestly desire my good friends, John Bisco and William Bond, Sr., to be overseers of this my will to be helpfull to my wife in her desolate condition in ye performance of this my will and in looking after my children, and as a confirmation of this my will I have set to my hand this one and thirtieth of May, sixteen hundred eighty and one.

DANIELL SMITH,

21, 4 mo. sworn by the witnesses as attests.
JONATHAN REMINGTON, Clerk.

As witnesseth,
JOHN BISCO,
WILLIAM BOND.

WILL OF JOHN SMITH (No. 5 Smith Family).

In the name of God, Amen———the fourth day of March, 1729-30.

I, John Smith of North Stonington, in ye County of New London, being very weak of body but of perfect mind and memory, thanks be given to God for it. Therefore calling to mind the mortality of my body and that it is appointed for all men once to die, Doe make and ordain this my last will and Testament that is to say, First of all I Recommend my Soul unto the hands of God that is, and my body I Recommend to ye earth to be buried at ye discretion of my executors nothing doubting but at ye general Resurrection I shall receive the same again by ye mighty power of God. And as touching such worldly Estates wherewith it hath pleased God to Bless me with all here in this life, I give and dispose of ye same in ye following manner and form:

Imprimis.——I give and bequeath unto Susannah my dearly beloved wife ye east end of my dwelling house, half my barn and ye one half of all my housings, with all my moveables excepting sixty pounds thereof (and what my estate is in debt) during the time she continue my widow, but if she marries again then to have but one third part of ye moveables above sd. during her natural life and then to be divided equally amongst my three daughters or their heirs. I give unto my loving son Daniel my homestead with all the buildings thereupon excepting as above given, he paying unto my son Josiah, 80 pounds money within two years after my death and five shillings to my son Ephraim. I give unto my loving son Ephraim, 5 shillings money to be paid by my Executors which together with what I have formerly given him is to ye full of his portion. I give unto my loving son Josiah 80 pounds money to be paid by my Executors within two years after my death which together with what I have already given him is ye full of his portion out of my estate. My loving daughter Lucie deceased I gave formerly unto her ye full of her portion out of my estate. I give unto my loving daughter Margaret, one third part of my moveables given to my loving wife above after she has done with them as abovesd. with what I have formerly given her is ye full of her portion out of my estate.

I give unto my loving daughter Ester the value of thirty pounds, money, out of my moveable estate and one third part of moveables given to my loving wife after she hath done with them as abovesd.

I give unto my loving daughter Susannah the value of thirty pounds money out of my moveable estate and one third part of moveables given above to my loving wife after she hath done with them as abovesd.

I likewise make and ordain my dearly beloved wife Susannah my Executrix and my loving son Daniel, Executor of this my last will and Testament and I do hereby utterly revoke and disanul all and every other former Testament,

wills, and bequests by me in any way before named willed and bequeathed.
Ratifying and confirming this and no other to be my last Will and Testament.

In witness whereof I have hereunto set my hand and seal ye day and year above written.

JOHN SMITH.

Signed, sealed, published, pronounced and declared by ye sd John Smith to be his last will and testament in presence of us witnesses.

THEOPHILUS BALDWIN,
SAMUEL PRENTICE,
ABIGAIL PRENTICE.

New London, Co., Stonington, May ye 31st A. D. 1739.

Then Theophilus Bawldin, Esq., Samuel Prentice and Mrs. Abigail Prentice, personally appeared and made solemn oath that they saw John Smith ye subscriber to ye above and within written, sign and seal ye same and heard him publish and pronounce and declare ye same to be his last will and testament and that he was in a perfect, sound mind and memory when he executed the same and that we signed ye same as witnesses in ye presence of ye testator,

Before Me,

INCREASE BILLINGS, Justice of the Peace.

WILL OF JOSEPH SMITH, HUSBAND OF ZIPPORAH BRANCH (No. 22).

I, Joseph Smith of Stonington, in the County of New London, and State of Connnecticut, being sick and weak in body, but by the blessings of God, am sound in my understanding and mind and memory, calling to mind the mortality of my body and that it is appointed for all men once to die and considering my present weakness as a symptom of the close of my days, I do make and ordain this my last will and Testament. First, I recommend my soul to God, that gave it me, and my body to the dust to be buried in a decent and Christian manner, at the discretion of my Executor hereinafter named, and as to the worldly Interest it hath pleased God to bless me with, I give and dispose of it in the following manner.

First, My will is that all my just debts and funeral charges should first of all be paid by my Executor out of the legacy given him in this Will.

Item. I give to my well beloved son Daniel Smith, two hundred and twenty pounds, lawful money, to be paid him by my Executor hereafter named, one hundred and twenty pounds of sd. sum to be paid in fifteen months after my decease, and the other hundred in one year and ten months after my decease, the said Daniel Smith paying to Charles Phelps, esq., 10 ewe sheep and twelve lambs and also 18 lbs. of sheeps wool, and also pay and settle with Mr. Daniel Prentice a debt which I owe him by book, and the above legacy when paid is his full share in my estate.

Item. I give to my well beloved son Joseph Smith Jr., the farm on which I now live with all the buildings on the same belonging to him, his heirs and assigns forever, he the said Joseph Smith, Jr., complying with such divisions and provisions as are and shall be made in this will relating to him.

Item. I give unto my said son Walter Smith one third part of a right of land I own in the State of Vt., so called, to him, his heirs and assigns forever and also one half of my wearing apparel, except a fine holland shirt dress, I do give to my son Walter Smith, ten pounds lawful money to be paid him by my Executor hereafter named within twelve months after my decease which said land, clothing and money when paid, is in full of his share in my estate.

Item. I give to my well beloved son Lemuel Smith, one third part of a right I own in the State of Vt., so called, to him and his heirs and assigns forever, and also one half of my wearing apparel, except a fine holland shirt, the said land and clothing when paid is in full of his share in my estate.

Item. I give to my well beloved son Thomas Smith, the other third part of a right of land I own in the State of Vt., so called, to his heirs and assigns forever, the said one third part to be supported as to taxes and expenses by my Executor hereafter named, till my said son Thomas shall arrive to the age of 21 yrs., also I do give to my son Thomas, the holland shirt heretofore described in this will and also my silver knee buckles and forty silver dollars to be paid to him by my Executors hereafter named, when he shall arrive to the age of 21 yrs. which land, shirt, buckles and money when paid is in full of his share in my estate.

Item. I give to my well beloved daughter Amy Palmer, three pounds lawful money to be paid to her by my Executor hereafter named, within twelve months after my decease, which money when paid, with what she hath already had is her full share in my estate.

Item. I give to my well beloved daughter Susannah Smith, thirty pounds lawful money to be paid her by my Executor hereafter named, when she shall arrive to the age of twenty yrs., also I do give to my said daughter, Susannah one third part of my household stuff, which said money and household stuff when recd. is her full share in my estate.

Item. I give to my beloved daughter Zipporah Smith, thirty pounds lawful money, to be paid her by Executor hereafter named, when she shall arrive to the age of twenty yrs. also I do give to my sd. daughter Zipporah one third part of my household stuff which money and household stuff when recd. is her full share in my estate.

Item. I do give to my well beloved daughter Polly Smith, thirty pounds lawful money to be paid her by my Executor hereafter named, when she shall arrive to the age of eighteen years, and also I do give to my sd. dau. Polly, the other third part of my household stuff, which sd. money and household stuff when recd. is in full for her share in my estate.

Item. I do give to my said son Joseph Smith, Jr., all the rest and remnant of my estate both real and personal not especially disposed of in this will and I do appoint my said son Joseph, Guardian to my sd. son Thomas during his minority and further my will is that my said son Joseph should learn my sd. son Thomas to read, write and cipher as far as the rule of three and also to put him to a trade when he shall arrive to the age of seventeen yrs., and that he be kept to his said trade till he shall arrive to the age of 21 yrs., also I do appoint my sd. son Joseph, guardian to my daughters Zipporah and Polly during their minority, and my will is that he learn them to read and write, and I do make and ordain my sd. son Joseph Smith, Jr., Executor to this my last will and Testament, wholly revoking any will heretofore by me made, and declaring this only to be my last will. In witness whereof I have hereunto set my hand and seal this twenty-fourth day of December 1783.

Signed, Sealed, Published, pronounced and declared.

JOSEPH SMITH.

In presence of
JOSHUA PRENTICE,
JESSE PRENTICE,
PHEBE LANGFORD.

WILL OF ISAAC WHEELER, SR.

In the name of God, Amen. The last Will and Testament of Mr. Isaac Wheeler, Sr., of Stonington, in the County of New London and in the Colony of Connecticut, being in perfect mind and memory, blessed be God, which is as followeth, I give my soul to God, who gave it and my body to the earth to be buried in a decent and Christian manner by my Executor in the hope of a glorious resurrection, and that as a Christian I may further provide for my family, I order my temporal concerns as followeth:

Imprimis. I order and direct my Executors to pay my just debts and recover my just dues of my estate. I give to my loving wife Martha, the biggest room of my house and the leanto (or ell) and two of the best beds and bedclothes and curtains, such as she best like, and four cows and a score of sheep to be kept and provided for by my son William, and so much of the household stuff as she has occasion for, and to be honorably maintained and to be comfortably provided for, in all things she needs during her natural life, at the care and cost of my son William Wheeler.

I give and bequeath to my son Isaac Wheeler, beside what his grandfather Thomas Wheeler, has given him in Lynn, Mass., and besides one hundred and fifty acres of land given him by his grandfather and besides what I have given in buildings and stock, I do now give him three score acres of land in lieu of forty acres his grandfather gave to his brother Thomas, Deceased, lying to the west and south of his own field and he is to take it Westerly from an horn beam tree till he makes up the complement of three score acres and a straight line from the said horn beam tree to a black oak tree, which is the corner tree of his grandfather's land he now dwelleth upon, which tree standeth by a brook; also I give to my son Isaac, four score acres of land which I bought of Ebenezer Witter and from that black oak which is a bound tree of Nathaniel Chesebrough's land, and from thence a straight line to a great chestnut tree; also I give him one hundred acres which I bought of Nathaniel Chesebrough, and one hundred acres which I bought of John Reynolds, and fifty acres bought of Capt. James Pendleton, and also one other hundred acres bought of John Witter, also one hundred and twenty acres now at the north corner of my land, which hundred acres was his grandfather's, and also fifty acres as it is bounded which may appear upon record, which was a grant formerly purchased of Lieut. Mason.

I give to Richard's children that are males, that are or shall be begotten of his body the lands following, equally to be divided among them, and my Executors shall give them as they come of age out of the following land a just proportion for their settlement, provided my son Richard and his wife shall have the house and homestead they now live in and to it one hundred and fifty acres during their natural lives. I give fifty acres lying by Samuel Miner, which was part of a grant of land bought of Capt. John Stanton and fifty acres more bought of Capt. Samuel Mason, and also a sixteen-acre lot lying southerly of old Mr. Stanton's land, and westerly of land which I bought of Capt. Mason and also the remainder of 150 acres which was bought of father Park and James Fanning.

I give to my son Richard, a west line from the corner of the cow pasture, the south corner of a west line to the brook, which we ride over when we go to meeting, which brook runs out of the said cow-pasture and bounded by said brook to the end of Witter land to a white oak tree, which tree is a corner tree of James Miner's and Cornish's and mine.

I give to my son Richard's children from a black oak tree of Nathaniel Chesebrough's a straight line to a great chestnut tree which is a corner of land I bought of Capt. John Stanton, and from thence a straight line just leaving out the meadow, the brook being the bound, that lyeth in the said tract of land I bought of Capt. John Stanton and from thence to my fence only leaving out to William's land six rods in length and one rod and a half in breadth from the fence that runs along by my fence southward to a great rock, which rock stands very nigh the partition fence now betwixt us and so along by the same fence till it come to the end of the fence that heads my great pasture, and from thence a west line to the end of what land is mine, and so to the outside of my land eastward not given already.

I give to my son William my new dwelling house and housing and orchards, and all the several tracts of land undisposed of in Stonington to him and his heirs forever. I give to my daughters, Mary, Martha, Anna, Dorothy, Elizabeth and Experience to each of them, I give seventy pounds a piece to be paid out of the stock, money, household stuff, to each a proportion to be paid forthwith and to make it up seventy pounds apiece to be paid by my unwilled landed estate, or else my two sons Isaac and William are to make it up out of their own estates, they having four years time to do it in, and the seventy pounds which I give to my daughter Mary, John Williams' deceased wife, is to pay it to her children as they come of age to each an equal share or proportion. I give to my three sons my wearing clothes equally divided betwixt them, only William is to have my blue waist coat.

In witness whereof I have hereunto set my hand and seal January 3rd 1712.

ISAAC WHEELER.

Probated in New London, March 12th 1712.

Isaac and William, his sons, were appointed with their uncle John Park, executors of his will, who accepted the trust and executed the will.

His son Richard died soon after his father, and their youngest child, a daughter, was born some five months after his death and was named after her mother, Prudence. She grew up to womanhood and married Mr. Ebenezer Geer of Groton, and had a large family of children. Her mother married Mr. Christopher Avery of Groton and had five children by him. The youngest, Temperance Avery, was the great-grandmother of the late Governor Morgan of New York.

WILL OF THOMAS WHEELER.

In the Name of God, Amen.—June 24th, 1755.

I, Thomas Wheeler of Stonington, County of New London, Conn., being now in health and of sound mind and memory, I do make this my last Will and Testament. I give unto my son Thomas Wheeler, all my lands in the Town of Litchfield in County of Litchfield. I also give him one eighth part of other land, including the land I gave him, by deed, with the buildings, to him and heirs forever.

I also give him, my silver-hilted sword, my cane, my gold sleeve buttons, my silver ring, and my watch, and my largest silver tankard, and also one thousand, five hundred pounds, old tenor bills of credit.

I give unto my grandson Isaac Wheeler, one eighth part of my lands and buildings, where my honored father Isaac Wheeler dwelt. I also give him my negro boy, and five hundred pounds in old tenor bills to be set out to him, when he arrives to the age of twenty one years.

I give unto my son Jeremiah Wheeler, one eighth part of all my lands and buildings. I also give him my negro man Sam, and my silver Tankard.

I give unto my son Shepherd Wheeler, one eighth part of all my lands and buildings and my negro man Cippeo.

I give unto my son Paul Wheeler, one eighth of all my land and buildings and my negro man Cabb, and my third silver tankard, also my mulatto girl Elizabeth.

I give also to my son Cyrus Wheeler, one eighth part of all my lands and buildings and my negro boy Plato, and five hundred pounds, bills of credit.

I give unto my son Charles Wheeler, one eighth part of all my lands and buildings and also my mulatto boy Harry, and five hundred pounds of bills of credit.

I give unto my son Ephraim Wheeler, one eighth part of all my lands and buildings to be set out to him when he arrives at the age of 21 years, and also I give him one thousand pounds of old tenor bills, to be paid to him at 21 years old.

I give unto my daughter Mary Miner, my negro woman Hagar, also two thousand pounds old tenor, which with what I have heretofore given her is her portion.

APPENDIX. 731

I give unto my daughter Mehitable Babcock, my negro girl Joanna, and also two thousand pounds old tenor which, with what I have already given is her portion.

I give unto my daughter Lucy Wheeler, my negro girl Cloe, also four thousand pounds in old tenor bills, to be set out to her when she arrives at 21 years, or the day of her marriage, and I give her six best silver spoons.

I give unto my grandson Thomas Wheeler, one cow and ten sheep.

I give unto my grandson Thomas Miner, one cow and ten sheep.

I give unto my son Thomas, my right in common in Stonington, also the remainder of my moveable and personal estate that is left, not above or before been disposed of.

I give to my sons Thomas, Jeremiah, Shepherd, Paul, Cyrus, Charles, Ephraim and my grandson Isaac equally.

THOMAS WHEELER.

SIMEON MINER,
ISAAC SMITH,
EZEKIEL GALLOP,
Witnesses.

INVENTORY OF CAPT. THOMAS WHEELER.

An inventory of the Estate of Capt. Thomas Wheeler of Stonington, deceased, appraised, December 11th, 1755.

	£.	s.	d.
1 Suit of clothes, gray broadcloth, coat, breeches, and fustian jacket	3	6	8
1 suit serge, and leather breeches	3	6	8
1 suit, blue coat, lead colored jacket and breeches	2	18	4
1 striped Banayan and Holland jacket and breeches	2	4	8
1 scarlet broadcloth great coat	2	18	4
1 old cloth colored " "		8	4
3 periwigs	2	18	4
1 beaver hat, 30s.; to 2 do., 24s. 2d	2	14	2
3 fine Holland shirts	4	10	
2 do., 20s.; 2 do., 16s. 8d	1	16	8
4 neck bands, 5s.; 2 Holland caps, 2s. 1d		7	1
2 pair linen breeches, 4s. 2d.; 2 pair gaiters, 8d		4	10
1 pair linen stockings, 5s.; to 6 pair worsted stockings, £1 3s. 4d..	1	8	4
4 pair yarn stockings, 8s. 4d.; to pair gloves, 3s. 9d		12	1
2 handkerchiefs, 6s. 8d.; to 2 pair shoes, 7s. 1d		13	9
1 pair boots, 10s.; 2000 shingle nails, 6s. 6d		16	8
61 silver coat buttons	4	5	
38 jacket " " round	1	11	8
14 flat " "		11	8
1 sealed gold ring	2	10	
1 pair gold sleeve buttons	1	6	8
1 silver watch	5	8	4
1 silver headed cane		16	8
1 silver hilted sword	2	1	8
1 silver snuff box	1		
1 pair money scales, 2s. 6d.; to 1 pair saddle bags, 6s. 8d		9	2
1 large silver tankard	12	10	
1 do., £10; to 1 do., £8 15s	18	15	
1 large flowered silver cup	3	15	
1 plain silver cup	3	6	8
2 small " "	3	6	8
1 large silver porringer	3	6	8
1 silver porringer, 50s.; to 2 do., small, £4 3s. 4d	6	13	4
1 silver salt cellar	2	18	8

	£.	s.	d.
1 silver pepper box	1	13	4
38 silver spoons	18	6	8
1 bed and furniture	11	13	4
1 do., £11 13s. 4d.; to 1 do., £10 16s. 8d.	22	10	
1 do., £10 16s. 8d.; to 1 do., £9 3s. 4d.	20		
1 do., £8 6s. 8d.; to 1 do., £7 10s.; to 1 do., £6 13s. 4d.	22	10	
1 bed and furniture, 3s. 4d.; to 1 bed and furniture, £3 15s.	7	18	4
4 Holland sheets	2	13	4
14 cotton " £6, 5s.; to 25 linen sheets, £9	15	5	
6 pillow cases		6	8
5 diaper table cloths	2	1	8
3 tow do., 11s. 8d.; to 13 diaper napkins, £1 2s. 11d.	1	14	7
29 linen do., 40s.; to 24 yards tow cloth, 40s.	4		
1 broken hour clock	1	5	
1 desk, £2 1s. 8d.; to 1 do., £1 13s. 4d.	3	15	
1 case with drawers, £3 6s. 3d.; 1 do., 50s.	5	16	8
1 do., £3 6s. 8d.; to 1 do., £2 1s. 8d.	5	8	4
1 chest with drawers, 8s. 4d.; 1 chest drawers, 8s. 4d.		16	8
1 chest with drawers, 8s. 4d.; 1 chest drawers, 6s. 8d.; 1 chest, 3s. 4d.		18	4
1 Chest, 2s. 6d.; 1 Chest, 8s. 3d.; 1 Chest, 2s. 6d.		13	3
1 Trunk, 8s. 4d.; 1 Trunk, 6s. 8d.; 1 Trunk, 6s. 8d.	1	1	8
1 Looking glass, £2 18s. 4d.; 1 Looking glass, £1 14s. 4d.	4	12	8
1 Looking glass, 25s.; 1 Looking glass, 8s. 4d.; 1 do., 8s. 4d.	2	1	3
1 square table, 16s. 8d.; to 1 do., 5s. 10d.; to 1 do., 13s. 4d.	1	15	10
1 do., 3s. 4d.; 1 do., 6s. 8d.; 1 old square table, 1s.		11	
1 round table, 16s. 8d.; to 1 do., 7s. 8d.	1	4	2
1 do., 11s. 8d.; 1 do., 6s. 8d.; 1 do. double, 16s. 8d.	1	15	
1 do., 13s. 4d.; 1 do., 10s.; 1 do., 10s. 6d.	1	13	10
1 do., 13s. 4d.; 1 eight square do., 8s. 4d.	1	1	8
19 banister black chairs, £2 7s. 6d.; to 2 great do., 6s. 8d.	2	14	2
6 Turkey worked chairs, 30s.; to 1 great do., 2s.	1	12	11
17 chairs, £1 8s. 4d.; to 9 do., 11s. 3d.; to 6 do., 5s. 10d.	2	5	5
1 great chair, 2s. 1d.; to 2 do., 3s. 4d.		5	5
1 small trunk, 3s. 4d.; to 1 case with bottles, 12s. 6d.		15	10
1 warming pan, 8s. 4d.; to 1 do., 15s.	1	3	4
6 green chairs, 15s.; 1 great do., 6s. 8d.	1	1	8
12 pewter platters	3	1	3
6 do., 10s.; to 3 do., 12s. 6d.	1	2	6
6 basins, 17s. 6d.; to 50 plates, £2 19s. 2d.	3	16	8
10 porringers, 7s. 6d.; to 6 old plates, 5s.		12	6
Old pewter, 16s. 10d.; to brass candlesticks, 4s. 2d.	1	1	
1 large brass kettle, £3 6s. 8d.; 1 do., 16s. 8d.	4	3	4
2 old do., 30s.; to earthen ware, 17s. 1d.	2	7	1
3 pair of hand irons, 50s.; 2 pair do., 18s. 4d.	3	8	4
5 iron pots, 29s. 2d.; to 7 iron kettles, 26s. 8d.	2	15	10
2 iron spits and fender, and dripping pan		10	10
2 old chafin dishes, old gridiron and iron perth		5	
1 frying pan, 4s. 7d.; to 1 box iron waiter and grate, 6s. 8d.		11	3
7 iron trammels, 24s. 2d.; tongs and slices, 15s.	1	19	2
1 pair bellows, 1s. 8d.; to 2 pair steelyards, 7s. 11d.		9	7
2 iron kettles, 5s.; to 2 skimmers, 1s. 3d.		6	3
2 pewter candlesticks, 2s.; to iron pewter candlesticks, 1s. 8d.		3	8
41 trays, and six pails	1	13	4
3 coolers, 5s.; 2 wooden dishes, 8s. 4d.		13	4
1 large churn, 8s. 4d.; to 1 small churn, 2s. 1d.		10	5
1 runlet, 1s. 8d.; to 1 bucket and more wooden ware, 10s. 10d.		12	6
1 large cheese tub, 7s. 6d.; to 1 do., 3s. 4d.		10	10
2 wash tubs, 3s. 9d.; to 4 cheese tubs, 5s.		8	9
1 butter tub, 2s. 6d.; 1 small meat tub, 1s. 8d.		4	2

APPENDIX. 733

	£.	s.	d.
2 woolen wheels, 5s.; to 3 linen do., 15s............................	1		
Meat cask, 33s. 4d.; to old cedar tub, 4s. 2d........................	1	11	6
Meal chests, 6s. 3d.; to 3 meal bags, 7s. 6d........................		13	9
8 grain chests, 8s. 4d.; 2 brand irons, 5s. 5d.....................		13	9
2 padlocks, 3s. 4d.; 1 pair wool cards, 3s. 4d......................		6	8
1 hatchet, 5s. 10d.; to 3 cart ropes and 1 halter, 13s. 4d...........		19	2
1 gem, 25s.; 1 do., 20s.; 1 do., 8s. 4d.............................	2	13	4
1 old saddle and bridle, 8s. 4d.; to 1 pillion, 5s..................		13	4
13 old cider hhds., 43s. 4d.; to 10 barrels, 20s. 10d................	3	4	2
Old open cask, 8s. 4d.; 3 small casks, 4s. 2d......................		12	6
6 narrow axes, 5s.; to 2 broad do., 4s. 2d.........................	1	3	4
1 adz, 2 hammers, handsaw and hatchet...........................		8	
1 shaving knife, 2 augers, 1 chisel................................		5	10
2 pair hinges, 3s.; to sett harrow teeth, 25s......................	1	8	
5 chairs, 30s.; to 9 hoes, 7s. 6d.; 1 iron crow bar, 10s. 10d.........	2	8	4
4 yokes and irons, 10s.; pitch forks, 4s. 2d........................		14	2
5 plows and irons, 33s. 4d.; 1 sled, 8s. 4d.........................	2	1	8
1 cart and wheels, iron and ladder................................	3	6	8
4 scythes and tacklings, 20s.; to beatles and wedges, 7s. 6d.......	1	7	6
2 horse geers, 8s. 4d.; 1 grinding stone, 10s......................		18	4
4 cycles, 3s. 4d.; 4 pair sheep shears, 3s. 4d.; iron dog, 6d........		7	2
1 gimlet, 1s. 3d.; to old iron, 12s. 6d..............................		13	9
1 great gate, 2s. 6d.; to 2500 shingles, 25s........................	1	7	6
1 razor and hone, 2s. 3d.; to ease fleams (a lancet), 10s...........		12	3
1 small boll (a Scotch measure), 2s. 1d.; to 2 do., 3s.; to 3 hives bees, 31s..	1	15	1
398 bushels of Indian corn...	40	9	2
8 bushels wheat, 30s.; 15 bushels rye, 37s. 6d.....................	3	7	6
5 bushels beans, 16s. 8d.; 50 bushels salt, 6s. 5d.................	7	1	8
1½ bushels malt, 4s. 4d.; 27 lbs. tallow, 9s.........................		13	4
2574 pounds cheese, 3d. per lb....................................	31	6	13
187 bundles flax in ye swingle, 6d. per lb.........................	4	13	9
Flax in ye bundle not dressed.....................................	2	10	
Oats in ye straw...		4	
125 tons hay, 25s. a ton 105	15		
Leather, £7 10s.; to flax seed, 3s. 4d. half bushels; to flax seed, 1s. 3d..	7	14	4
350 pine boards, 17s. 6d.; to 80 square glass, 16s. 8d..............	1	14	2
Sundry books, 56s. 3d.; to 1 book of accounts, 6s. 8d.............	3	8	4
£12 7s. 6d. in Connecticut bills....................................	1	9	
£27 12s. 10d. in Old tenor bills.....................................	2	6	1
Notes and bonds on sundry persons............................3170	3	4	
Ye farm and buildings, with all ye lands adjoining where he dwelt 7000			
Ye farm and buildings where Mr. Thomas Wheeler now dwells....756			
A tract of land by Lanthorn Hill...................................166	13	4	
His riding horse, saddle & bridle..................................	16	13	4
1 old sorrel horse..	7	18	4
1 black " "	16	13	4
1 sorrel horse, swift nose...	11	5	
1 " " bald face..	12	5	
1 pied horse...	10		
1 small horse, swift nose..	6	13	4
1 sorrel stone horse, two years old................................	9	11	S
1 sorrel, year old horse, £4 11s. 8d.; 1 sorrel, year old, £4 11s. 8d..	9	3	4
1 old sorrel mare and mare colt...................................	2	18	4
1 old bay " " horse "	3	6	8
1 old black " " " "	8	6	9
1 black " white face, and mare colt........................	8	6	8

		£.	s.	d.
1	large sorrel mare, white face, horse colt	14	3	4
1	old sorrel mare, and a year old mare colt	1	6	8
1	old bay mare, £2 18s. 4d.; 1 sorrel two year old mare colt	7	1	8
1	sorrel mare, swift nose	10	8	4
1	black " " "	10	16	8
1	brown "	5	16	8
1	fat ox, £5 3s. 4d.; 2 speckled lean do., £11 13s. 4d.	17	7	8
2	brown pied oxen	10	8	4
2	do., £10 16s. 8d.; to 2 red pied do., £13	23	16	8
2	white pied oxen	8	15	
1	brown fat cow, £4 3s. 4d.; to 1 speckled cow, £3 3s. 4d.	7	6	8
23	fat cattle at £2 18s. 4d. per head	67	1	8
1	bull, £2 18s. 4d.; 32 cows, £77 8s. 4d.	79	6	3
25	two year old cattle	41	13	4
26	one " " "	30	6	8
25	calves	15	12	6
179	store sheep	26	2	1
5	sheep rams	1	5	
56	fat swine	65		
65	store swine	14	15	
1	negro man named Quash	2	10	
1	old negro woman named Juno		16	8
1	negro man named Cab	41	14	4
1	" " " Ceazar	37	30	
1	" " " Cipeo	45	16	8
1	" woman " Hager	37	10	
1	" " " Flora	31	13	
1	" " " Sarah	40		
1	" " " Jane	37	10	
1	" " " Cloe	37	10	
1	" girl " Phillis	15		
1	" boy " Pharaoh	8	8	
1	servant mulatto boy Harry	8	6	8
1	" " girl Elizabeth	5		
1	servant Indian woman Mary	1	13	4

Whole amount ....£12,669 9s. 5d.

                        Certified by us Appraisers,
                            SIMEON MINER,
                            ISAAC FRINK.

Capt. Thomas Wheeler, whose estate is here recorded, was the son of Isaac Wheeler and Mary (Shephard) Wheeler, and was born in the year 1700. He married Mary Miner, daughter of Ephraim and Mary Stevens Miner, who was a direct descendant in the thirteenth generation of Henry Miner, who died in the year 1357. Isaac Wheeler was the son of Isaac and Martha (Park) Wheeler, and grandson of Thomas and Mary Wheeler. Thomas Wheeler came to this country before 1637, and resided in Massachusetts until 1664, when he removed to Stonington. He died in 1686, aged 85 years.

WILL OF ROBERT WILLIAMS.

Last Will and Testament of me, Robert Williams of Roxbury, in the county of Suffolk in New England, being at present in bodily health, of perfect understanding, and of sound mind (through the merciful providence of God towards me) do ordain this my last will, hereby disannulling all former wills whatever, and do constitute this for the use and benefit of those that shall come after me.

In the first place and chiefly, I commit my soul into the hands of my merciful Redeemer, the Lord Jesus Christ, who hath undertaken for the same in the covenant of his grace, that where he is I might be also. And my body I commit unto the dust to be decently buried by my Executors hereafter named, trusting that at the day of his appearing I shall receive a glorious body. And for my temporal estate I dispose of it in the manner following:

Imprimis. I will, the true and faithful performance of the covenant between myself and my well beloved wife, in full and in specie according to the time mentioned in said covenant, and that my three sons, Samuel, Isaac and Stephen, shall pay the same by equal proportions.

Item. I give to my son Samuel, besides what I have already given him, and is in his possession, my middle lot between my swamp and my rocks lying before his door.

Item. All my swamp except fourscore and ten rods next my barn, which I reserve to the same.

Item. Ten acres of wood-land, more or less, at Walkhill.

Item. To my son Isaac, three acres of salt-marsh (purchased with my house), adjoining to Nathaniel Holmes, his marsh.

Item. All my ploughing land at Dorchester, being five acres, more or less.

Item. Six acres of wood-land behind the great lots.

Item. To my grandson Isaac, I give my piece of salt-marsh lying next to John Heminway's, formerly bought of Goodman Riggs.

Item. I give to my son Stephen, my dwelling house, orchards, barns, and other out houses and home lots thereto adjoining, with the fourscore and ten rods adjoining to my barn reserved out of the swamp.

Item. My part of Mr. Hews' meadows.

Item. Six acres of pasture land called the Rocks, adjoining to my lot, (given my son Samuel).

Item. Thirty-two acres of wood-land lying together near the fresh meadows.

Item. My horse distinct from the rest of my moveables.

Item. I will that the cause be equally maintained by my sons Samuel and Stephen. Inasmuch as I have in this my will given my son Stephen, somewhat more than the rest of my sons, I would not have them or others think hardly of me for so doing, for he lives under the same roof with me, and thereby hath been more helpful and comfortable unto me than the other sons have.

Item. I give to my brother Nicholas Williams, thirty shillings per annum, to be equally paid by my sons Samuel and Stephen.

Item. My wearing clothes woolen and linen.

Item. A pair of sheets and a blanket from off my maid's bed, and also a rug. Also four bushels of Indian corn. Also my will is, that my brother Nicholas have house room, washing and lodging, by my sons Samuel and Stephen.

Item. I give my grandchild Deborah Totman (or Tolman), forty shillings.

Item. To my grandchild Elizabeth Robinson, twenty shillings, both legacies to be paid out of my moveables within the space of twelve months after my decease, And the residue of them to be equally divided between my sons after my debts are discharged. And for the full performance of this my last will, I do depute my three sons Executors of the same, whom I intreat and of whom I expect that they will see the faithful performance of the same. And in witness of these premises I have hereunto subscribed my hand and affixed my seal this twenty-sixth of November, in the year of our Lord, 1685.

(Signed)

ROBERT WILLIAMS, and Seal.

Signed and sealed in the presence of
GILES PAYSON,
BENJAMIN TUCKER,
JOHN SMITH.
Date of Probate,
    29th of September, 1693.

Births.

Marriages.

Deaths.

HISTORICAL INDEX.

A.—Area of Stonington, 1; Association of Pawcatuck People, 11; Assembly Acts, 41 to 46.

B.—Bridges and Ferries: Mystic Bridge, 118; Pawcatuck Bridge, 122; first Blacksmith, 139; Banking, 147.

C.—Clergy: Wm. Thompson, 13; Zachariah Brigden, 13; Mr. Chauncey, 14; Mr. Fletcher, 14; Rev. James Noyes, 14; Rev. Joseph Noyes, 24; Rev. Mr. Rossiter, 30; Rev. Nathaniel Eells, 32.
Census of 1668, 18; Charter of Connecticut, 21; Chesebrough Wm. grant of land, 4; Connecticut first settlement, 3; Commissioners of United Colonies decision, 11; Commerce, 130; Civil Officers, 158; Judge of County Court, 158; Associate Judge, 158; Sheriffs, 158; Asistants, 158; Senators, 158-9; Representatives, 154-164; Town Clerks, 164-5; Selectmen, 165-174.

D.—Denison, Capt. George house, 5; Dean Old house, 140.

E.—Ecclesiastical history: First Congregational Church, 87-89; Second Congregational Church, 89-90; Baptist Church, Pung-hung-we-nuck Hill, 90; East Baptist Church, 90; Baptist Church at Long Point, 90; Methodist Episcopal Church at Old Mystic, 91; Third Congregational Church, 92; Methodist Episcopal Church at Mystic, 93; Pawcatuck Congregational Church, 93; Third Baptist Church at Stonington, 95; Greenmanville Seventh Day Baptist Church, 95; Calvary Episcopal Church, 95; Pawcatuck Catholic Church, 96; Mystic Congregational Church, 96; Advent Christian Association, 97; Mystic Catholic Church, 98; Quiambaug Chapel, 98; Wequetequock Chapel, 98; Stonington Catholic, 99.

F.—Fort Griswold victims, 59.

G.—Gallup Capt. John, 5; death, 22; Government, local, 13.

H.—Home lots assigned, 18; house dwelling of Mr. James Noyes, 18; Haynes, Gov. grant of land, 4; Heroine of Stonington, 79; Highways, 103, including Mail-stage route, 109; Turnpike road, 113; The 16 pole way of Major Mason, 115; County highways, 115.

I. Indians: Soche, 14; Oneko, 21; Canonchet, 22; King Philip, 21; Pequots, 175-195.

M.—Meeting house, located and erected, 13; Mystic named, 17; Meeting house at Agreement Hill, 18, 19, 20; Meeting house dimensions, 20; Miner, Thomas new house, 5; Meeting house another, 21; Meeting house at the Centre, 29, 30; Meeting house at Long Point, 32, 35; Mills and Manufacturing, 136; First mill, 138; Weave shops, 138; Mill for Powder, 138; Grist Mill, 138; Saw Mill, 141.

N.—Name first local, 5.

P.—Pequot plantation, 1; Palmer, Walter purchased land, 5; Park, Capt. Robert, 5; Palmer's land, 134; Press, 156.

R.—Regiment of Col. Randall, 62, 70, 71; Roll copies of 30th Regt., 71, 72; Railroad, 152.

S.—Stonington, settlement of, 3; Southertown named, 12; Services, first religious, 6; Stanton, Thomas trading house, 4; Swamp fight and Military expeditions, 21, 23; Society, organization of First Congregational, 26; Stonington, bombardment, 38; Soldiers of the Revolution, 46-48; Stonington Borough bombardment, 65-78; Stonington, Account of the Battle, 73-75; Schools, Common, 100, 102; Ship Building, 123; at Pawcatuck, 124; Old Mystic, 125; Adam's Point, 125; Mystic, 127, 128; Stonington Borough, 128-9.

T.—Town meetings, resolution of, 48-59; Town meeting, 60; Town, division of, 91.

V.—Vessels engaged in Sealing and Whaling, 132-5.

W.—War, soldiers of Narragansett, 22; War, Revolutionary, 36; War of 1812, 60; Officers in command, 70; War of 1861-5, Names of Infantry, Artillery, Cavalry, 81-85; War, Spanish-American, 86.

GENEALOGICAL INDEX.

AVERY.—Aaron, 205; Abigail, 202, 3, 4, 5, 6; Abraham, 202, 5; Albert, 209; Alexander, 209; Alfred, 208; Allen, 210; Amanda, 210; Amos, 205, 6, 7; Amy, 203; Ann, 205; Anna, 202, 4, 6, 7; Asa, 210; Benjamin, 201, 2, 4; Benoni, 205; Caleb, 205, 7; Calvin, 209; Carleton, 209; Charles, 202, 9; Christopher, 199, 201, 3, 5, 6, 7, 8; Courtland, 209; Cyrus, 209; Daniel, 202, 4, 5; David, 204, 5; Dean, 209; Deborah, 201; Delia, 209; Desire, 202; Dorothy, 203, 5; Ebenezer, 201, 3, 5, 10; Edwin, 201; Elias, 205; Elisha, 202, 3, 5; Elijah, 205, 9; Eliza, 207, 9; Elizabeth, 202, 7, 10; Ephraim, 202; Erasmus, 210; Erastus, 209; Esther, 206; Eunice, 203, 5, 6, 10; Frances, 209; George, 204, 9; Griswold, 205; Hannah, 201, 2, 3, 6, 7, 8, 9; Henry, 208; Isaac, 202, 3, 6, 8, 10; Jacob, 203; James, 199, 201, 3, 5; Jasper, 205; Joanna, 201; John, 201, 2, 3, 4, 5, 6, 7, 9, 10; Jonathan, 201, 2, 8, 10; Jonas, 206; Joseph, 201; Joshua, 202; Josiah, 202; Lucy, 203, 4, 6, 8; Luther, 207, 8; Margaret, 201, 6; Maria, 209; Marinda, 208; Mary, 201, 2, 3, 4, 7, 8, 9, 10; Nancy, 209; Nathan, 203, 6, 8; Nathaniel, 202, 5, 7; Oliver, 206; Oscar, 209; Park, 203, 5; Paul, 208; Phebe, 207, 8; Polly, 208; Prentice, 206; Priscilla, 203; Prudence, 203; Ralph, 209; Rebecca, 201; Robert, 207, 10; Roger Griswold, 209; Roswell, 209; Richardson, 204; Samuel, 201, 2, 6, 9; Sarah, 201, 4, 6, 10; Simeon, 203, 5; Solon, 210; Stephen, 205, 7, 8, 9; Temperance, 203, 8; Thankful, 204; Thomas, 201, 2 3, 5; Timothy, 208; Ulysses, 210; Wealthy, 207, 8, 9; William, 202, 4, 7, 8; Zipporah, 207.

BABCOCK.—Abby, 218; Abel, 216; Abigail, 213; Adam, 214; Albert, 219; Amanda, 220; Amelia, 214, 15, 22; Ann, 212, 19, 20; Anna, 213; Anne, 213, 15, 16, 17; Attana, 216; Benedict, 215; Benjamin, 212, 17, 18, 19, 21; Betsey, 219; Charles, 221; Charlotte, 215; Christopher, 215, 16, 20; Courtland, 218, 22; Cynthia, 220; Cyrus, 218; Daniel, 213; 16, 19, 20, 21; David, 213, 15, 18, 21; Desire, 217; Dorothy, 213; Dudley, 217, 18, 21; Edwin, 219; Elias, 214, 16, 20, 21; Elihu, 212, 21; Elijah, 216; Elisha, 213, 16; Eliza, 218; Elizabeth, 211, 12, 13, 14, 15, 16, 19; Emily, 220; Enoch, 216; Ephraim, 218; Esther, 215; Eunice, 213; Ezekiel, 221; Ezra, 215; Fanny, 221; Frances, 214; Frank, 221; Frederick, 218, 21; George, 212, 13, 15, 16, 18, 20; Georgia, 222; Gershom, 216; Giles, 218; Grace, 214, 17; Gurdon, 221; Hannah, 211, 12, 14, 15, 17, 18, 19; Harriet, 214, 19; Henry, 214, 17, 18, 21, 22; Hezekiah, 213, 15; Horace, 219; Isaiah, 214, 16; Jacob, 219; James, 211, 12, 13, 14, 15, 16, 17; Jane, 211, 12; Jesse, 217; Job, 211, 12; Joanna, 215; John, 211, 12, 13, 14, 16, 17, 20; Jonas, 216; Jonathan, 213, 15; Joseph, 211, 12, 13, 14; Joshua, 213, 14, 16, 17, 18; Julia, 220; Lois, 217; Louisa, 217; Louise, 222; Lucy, 218, 20; Luke, 214; Lydia, 216; Maria, 221; Mary, 211, 12, 13, 14, 15, 18, 20, 21; Martha, 214, 15, 16, 19, 20, 21; Mercy, 212; Merritt, 221; Nancy, 216, 18, 19, 20; Nathan, 214, 20, 26; Nathaniel, 211, 14, 16; Oliver, 212, 14, 16, 20; Parthenia 221; Paul 214, 17, 18; Phebe 216, 20; Polly, 221; Robert, 212, 15, 17, 18, 21; Rhoda, 219; Rouse, 215, 19; Rufus, 216; Ruth, 213; Sally, 214, 19; Samuel, 213, 15, 21; Sarah, 211, 12, 13, 15, 16, 17, 19; Simeon, 214; Simon, 215; Stephen, 220; Susannah, 214, 15, 18; Thomas, 214, 18; Timothy, 214, 17; William, 216, 19.

BALDWIN.—Abigail, 226, 28; Alanson, 227; Amos, 226, 27; Andrew, 226, 27; Anna, 226; Asa, 226; Asher, 227; Benjamin, 227, 28; Betsey, 228; Billings, 227; Bridget, 226, 27; Charlotte, 228; Daniel, 226; David, 226, 27, 28; Denison, 226; Elisha, 227; Elizabeth, 224, 25, 27; Emily, 228; Eunice, 225, 26, 28; George, 226; Henry, 223, 27; Hezekiah, 227; Jane, 224; John, 223, 24, 25, 26, 28; Jonathan, 226; Joseph, 226, 27; Lucy, 226, 28, 31; Martha, 224, 27; Mary, 224, 25, 28; Nancy, 226; Nathan, 227; Phebe, 226, 27; Polly, 226; Priscilla, 225, 26; Rebecca, 224, 26; Richard, 223, 24; Ruth, 224; Sabra, 227; Sally, 227, 28; Samuel, 224; Sarah, 224, 26; Steward, 227; Susan, 227, 28; Sylvester, 223, 24, 25, 26; Thankful, 226; Theophilus, 224, 25, 26, 27; Thomas, 225, 26, 27; Turner, 227; William, 223, 26; Wolcott, 227; Ziba, 225, 27.

BENNETT.—Aaron, 230, 31; Abby, 232; Allen, 232; Alonzo, 231; Amanda, 231; Amos, 230; Benjamin, 231; Caroline, 231; Charles, 230, 31; Cynthia, 231; Daniel, 229; David, 230; Dudley, 230; Elisha, 230, 31, 32; Ellen, 231; Eliza, 231; Elizabeth, 229; Emily, 231; Ephraim, 231; Erastus, 231; Esther, 230, 31; Fanny, 232; Hannah, 229, 30; Henry, 229, 31; Huldah, 232; Isaac, 229; James, 231; Jane, 231; Jedediah, 230; Jerusha, 229, 30; Jesse, 230, 31; Joanna, 230; John, 229, 31, 32; Joseph, 229, 30; Martha, 231; Mary, 230, 31; Mehitable, 230; Melinda, 232; Meranda, 230; Nathan, 229, 31; Nathaniel, 230; Noah, 230; Oliver, 230, 32; Perry, 231; Phebe, 229, 31; Ramsford, 232; Rebecca, 229; Reuben, 232; Sabra, 231; Sally, 230, 32; Samuel, 229, 30; Sarah, 229, 30; Stephen, 229, 30; Susan, 232; Thankful, 230; Thomas, 229; William, 229, 30, 32.

BENTLEY.—Adoniram, 235; Anna, 234; Anne, 234; Benjamin, 233, 34; Caleb, 233; Courtland, 235; Daniel, 234, 5; Edwin, 235; Elizabeth, 233; Emeline, 235; Ezekiel, 233; George, 233, 4; Green, 233; Hannah, 234; Harriet, 235; Henry, 234; Ira, 234; James, 233, 4; Jane, 233; John, 233, 4; Jonathan, 234; Lucy, 234, 5; Martha, 235; Mary, 233, 4, 5; Robert, 234; Ruhama, 233; Russel, 234, 5; Samuel, 235; Sarah, 234, 5; Susan, 235; Tabitha, 233; Thomas, 233, 4; William, 233, 4.

BILLINGS.—Abigail, 236, 7, 8, 9; Adam, 241; Alpheus, 241; Amos, 238, 40, 41; Andrew, 238, 9, 40, 41; Ann, 238, 43; Anna, 237, 40, 41, 42; Benajah, 238, 41; Benjamin, 237, 9, 41, 2; Betsey, 241; Bridget, 240; Charles, 239; Christopher, 238, 40; Coddington, 241, 2, 3; Comfort, 240; Cynthia, 242; Daniel, 238, 9, 40, 41; David, 238; Desire, 239; Dorothy, 236, 7, 8; Ebenezer, 236, 7, 8, 9, 42; Edward, 243; Eli, 241; Elisha, 239; Elizabeth, 236, 9, 241; Esther, 238; Eunice, 238, 9, 240, 1, 3; Ezra, 242; Frances, 241; George, 241, 2; Gilbert, 239, 42, 3; Grace, 238, 40; Hannah, 236, 7, 240, 2; Harriet, 243; Henrietta, 242; Henry, 237, 41; Horatio, 242, 3; Ichabod, 236; Increase, 237, 8; Isaac, 241, 8; James, 237, 8, 241, 2; Jared, 238; Jemima, 237, 8; Jesse, 238; John, 237, 8, 9, 240, 2; Jonas, 241; Joseph, 236, 7, 9, 40, 41; Katharine, 240; Lois, 238; Lucy, 238, 9, 42, 3; Lydia, 236, 40, 2; Margaret, 236, 7, 40; Mary, 236, 7, 8, 9, 40, 2, 3; Mercy, 240; Moses, 238; Nancy, 240, 1; Nathan, 238, 40; Noyes, 242, 3; Patience, 236, 41; Peleg, 237, 9, 41; Perez, 242; Phebe, 238, 9; Polly, 240, 2; Prudence, 236, 8; Rachel, 236; Randall, 241; Rebecca, 239; Robert, 242, 3; Roger, 236, 7, 9; Rufus, 239; Sabra, 237, 9; Samuel, 236, 7, 8, 41; Sanford, 239, 42, 3; Sarah, 236, 7, 40, 42; Stephen, 238, 40, 1, 2; Susannah, 239; Thankful, 237, 8, 41; Theophilus, 239, 41; Washington, 242; William, 236, 7, 8, 9, 41, 3; Zipporah, 237, 8.

BREED.—Abigail, 245, 7; Adin, 246; Alice, 248; Allen, 244, 5, 6; Allyn, 247; Amanda, 248; Amos, 245, 6, 8; Andrew, 247; Ann, 245, 8; Anna, 244, 6, 7; Avery, 245; Benjamin, 248; Bethiah, 244; Betsey, 247; Calvin, 248; Charles, 247; Christopher, 245; Cyrus, 247; David, 246; Elias, 246; Elizabeth, 244; Esther, 245, 6, 8; Eunice, 245, 7, 8; Fanny, 247; Freelove, 248; Frederick, 248; Gershom, 244, 5, 6, 7; Grace, 245, 6, 7; Hannah, 245, 7, 8; Harriet, 248; Henry, 246; Jabish, 245, 7; Jedediah, 246; Jesse, 246, 8; John, 244, 5, 6, 7, 8; Jonas, 246; Joseph, 244, 5, 6, 7; Joshua, 246, 8; Julia, 247; Lucy, 245, 6, 7, 8; Marcy, 245; Martha, 247; Mary, 244, 5, 8; Mercy, 244; 7; Nancy, 246, 7; Nathan, 245, 6, 7; Oliver, 245, 6, 7; Patty, 247; Polly, 247; Prentice, 245, 7; Prudence, 246, 7, 8; Reuben, 245, 6; Rhoda, 248; Sally, 247; Samuel, 245, 7, 8; Sarah, 244, 5; Shubael, 246; Silence, 248; Simeon, 246; Sophia, 247; Stephen, 246, 8; Susannah, 245, 6; Thomas, 246, 7; William, 245, 7; Zerviah, 244, 5.

BREWSTER.—Benjamin, 250; Daniel, 250; Elijah, 250; Elizabeth, 250; Fear, 244; John, 250; Jonathan 249, 50; Joseph, 250; Love, 249; Patience, 249; William, 249; Wrestling, 249.

CHAD BROWN.—Abby, 253; Abigail, 253; 4; Abijah, 254; Ann, 254; Anna, 253; Benjamin, 253, 4, 5; Bridget, 253, 4; Betsey, 254; Chad, 251; Clark, 252, 4; Daniel, 251, 2, 3, 5; David, 254; Desire, 253, 4; Deborah, 251, 3; Dolly, 253; Dorcas, 253; Edgar, 255; Elijah, 254; Elisha, 253; Elizabeth, 252, 3; Eseck, 252, 3; Frances, 253, 4; Frederick, 255; Hallelujah, 252; Henry, 255; Hope, 252, 3; Hosannah, 252; Jabez, 252; James, 251, 2, 3, 4; Jeremiah, 251, 2, 3, 4; Jesse, 254, 5; John, 251, 2, 3, 4; Jonathan, 252, 3; Judah, 252; Lucy, 254; Martha, 251; Mary, 251, 3, 4, 5; Mercy, 254; Nathaniel, 255; Noyes, 253, 4; Obediah, 251; Orlando, 255; Pardon, 255; Peleg, 252, 3, 4; Phebe, 251; Polly, 254; Robert, 252, 5; Roby, 253; Samuel, 252;

Sanford, 253, 4; Sarah, 251, 2; Thomas, 252; Wellington, 255; William, 252, 5.

EDWARD BROWN.—Amy, 257; Betsey, 257; Billings, 257; Charles, 257; Edward, 256, 8; Elias, 257; Elizabeth, 256, 7; Enoch, 257; Esther, 257; Eunice, 257; Hannah, 257; Henry, 258; Jacob, 256; John, 256, 7, 8; Joseph, 256, 7; Josiah, 257; Judith, 257; Mary, 257, 8; Nathaniel, 256; Rachel, 257; Roger, 257; Sabra, 257; Thomas, 256; William, 257; Zeruah, 257.

LYNN BROWN.—Abby, 267, 71; Abel, 262, 5; Abigail, 260, 1, 4, 5, 70; Adams, 268; Allen, 269; Almira, 269; Amos, 261, 5, 6; Andrew, 263, 4, 71; Angeline, 271; Ann, 259, 61; Anne, 264, 5, 6, 70, 1; Annah, 260, 2, 8; Asa, 263; Asher, 267; Avery, 265; Benadam, 267; Benoni, 262; Benjamin, 264, 9; Betsey, 262, 6, 9, 70, 1; Califa, 269; Charles, 262, 5, 8, 9, 70; Christopher, 261, 2; Clark, 264; Coddington, 266; Collins, 262; Content, 262; Cynthia, 269; Cyrus, 262, 6, 7; Daniel, 259, 60, 1, 4, 71; David, 261, 5, 70; Deborah, 260, 2, 3, 5, 9; Delia, 268, 70; Desire, 261, 4, 5, 6; Dolly, 268; Dorothy, 260, 8; Dudley, 265; Ebenezer, 259, 60, 1; Edith, 265; Edward, 264, 9, 70; Eleazer, 259, 60, 3, 4; Elias, 263, 6, 7; Elisha, 270; Elijah, 270; Ellen, 269; Eliza, 267; Elizabeth, 260, 1, 8, 71; Emily, 267; Ephraim, 264; Erastus, 269; Esther, 262, 3, 5, 6, 7, 8; Eunice, 262, 3, 5, 6, 8, 9, 70; Ezra, 264; Francis, 269; George, 270; Gideon, 267; Giles, 268; Grace, 259; Grant, 263; Gershom, 262; Hannah, 259, 60, 2, 70, 1; Helannah, 269; Hepsibah, 260, 1; Henry, 262; Herman, 269, 71; Hosea, 268; Huldah, 264; Humphrey, 260, 1; Ichabod, 260, 3, 9; Ira, 271; Israel, 270; Jabez, 270; James, 260, 1, 7, 8, 71; Jesse, 260, 70; Jedediah, 260, 1, 4, 5, 6; Jeptha, 268; Jerusha, 259, 71; Joannah, 263, 8, 72; John, 259, 60, 3, 4, 7, 9, 70, 1; Jonas, 263; Jonathan, 259, 60, 1; Joseph, 259, 65, 7, 9; Josiah, 268, 9, 71; Joshua, 261, 8, 72; Keturah, 263, 5, 6; Lewis, 263; Lois, 260, 2; Louisa, 267; Lucien, 261; Lucy, 262, 4, 5, 7, 9, 71; Luther, 264, 5; Lydia, 265, 7, 70, 1; Margaret, 268; Martha, 263, 4, 7, 8, 9; Mary, 259, 60, **2, 3, 4, 5, 7,** 70; Marvin, 271; Mathew, 271; Matilda, 271; Mehitable, 260; Micah, 263; Miner, 263; Molly, 262, 4; Nabbe, 271; Nancy, 266, 7, 9; Nathan, 261, 3, 5, 70; Nathaniel, 261, 2; Nehemiah, 261, 2, 3; Nelly, 269; Nelson, 269; Noyes, 264, 72; Oliver, 263, 71; Palmer, 269; Patty, 262, 6; Patience, 260; Paul, 264; Peggy, 262; Peleg, 263; **Perez, 262;** Phebe, 262, 3, 5, 70; Philura, 266; Polly, 265, 6, 7, 9, 70; Priscillah, 260, 9; Prudence, 260, 3, 8, 9, 72; Randall, 268; 71; Rebecca, 263, 4, 70; Reuben, 262; Rhoda, 266; Rogers, 268; Roswell, 264, 5, 6, 7, 8; Rowland, 266; Roxanna, 266; Rufus, 262; Russell, 266; Ruth, 260, 3; Sally, 266, 9, 72; Samuel, 259, 60, 1, 2, 5; Sanford, 269, 70; Sarah, 259, 62, 3, 4, 5, 6, 7, 9; Shepard, 266; Shubael, 264, 6, 7; Simeon, 261, 8, 9; Smith, 269; Stanton, 264; Stephen, 261, 3, 5; Stiles, 269; Susannah, 265; Sylvia, 268; Tabitha, 261; Taloo, 264; Thankful, 261, 9; Temperance, 263, 5; Thatcher, 264, 6; Theoda, 265; Theody, 265; Thomas, 259, 60, **2, 7,** 71; Timothy, 263; Walter, 261; Wealthy, 262; Welcome, 269; Wheeler, 266; William, 260, 6, 7, 70, 1; Zebulon, 261, 71.

BROWNING.—Adeline, 275; Ann, 274; Anna, 275; Anne, 274; Benjamin, 275; Catharine, 274, 5; Charles, 275; Cyrus, 275; Dinah, 273; Elizabeth, 274, 5; Ephraim, 274; Eunice, 274; Frances, 275; Hall, 273; Hannah, 273, 4; Harriet, 275; Jane, 273; Jeremiah, 273, 4; John, 273, 4, 5; Joseph, 273, 5; Joshua, 275; Latham, 275; Lucy, 275; Martha, 274; Mason, 275; Mary, 273, 4, 5; Nathaniel, 273; Orrin, 275; Rebecca, 273; Ruth, 273, 4; Sally, 275; Samuel, 274; Sands, 274; Sarah, 273, 4, 5; Susan, 275; Tabitha, 273; Thomas, 273, 4, 5; William, 273, 4, 5; Wilkinson, 273.

BURCH.—Abigail, 276; Benjamin, 277; Betsey, 278; Billings, 277, 8; Charles, 278; David, 276; Desire, 277; Elizabeth, 278; Ellen, 278; Frederick, 277; George, 276, 8; Harriet, 277; Henry, 277, 8; Increase, 277; Isaiah, 277; Jane, 276, 7; Jeremiah, 276, 7; John, 276, 7; Jonathan, 276, 7; Joseph, 276, 7; Joshua, 276, 7; Katy, 278; Lydia, 278; Marion, 278; Martha, 277, 8; Mary, 276, 7, 8; Mercy, 276; Nathan, 278; Paul, 277; Phebe, 278; Polly, 277, 8; Rhoda, 278; Sally, 278; Samuel, 277, 8; Stanton, 278; Susan, 278; Thomas, 276, 7, 8; William, 277, 8; Zurviah, 276.

BURROWS.—Abigail, 279, 80; Amos, 279, 82; Amy, 280; Anna, 282; Benjamin, 281, 2; Betsey, 280, 1, 4; Caleb, 284; Calvin, 281; Charles, 283, 4; Daniel, 280, 1, 2 3; Delight, 280; Denison, 280, 2; Desire, 280, 1; Edward, 281; Edwin, 281; Elam, 280; Eleanor, 280; Elisha, 282; Elizabeth, 282, 3; Enoch, 283, 4; Eunice, 280, 2; Experience, 281; Frances, 280; George, 280, 1; Gilbert, 283; Hannah, 279, 80, 1; Hubard, 279, 81, 2, 4; Isaac, 279; Jabez, 283;

INDEX. 741

James, 281; Jeremiah, 279; Jerusha, 283; Jesse, 281; John, 279, 80, 2, 4; Jonathan, 282; Joseph, 280, 1, 2; Joshua, 282, 3; Julia, 283; Latham, 283; Lorenzo, 281, 3; Lucretia, 279; Lucy, 283; Lydia, 279, 80, 1; Margaret, 279; Mary, 279, 80, 1, 2, 3, 4; Mercy, 282; Nabby, 280; Nancy, 281; Nathan, 280, 1, 2; Ogden, 284; Paul, 282; Percy, 282; Phebe, 279, 80; Priscilla, 282, 4; Prudence, 284; Robert, 279; Roswell, 281, 3; Rufus, 281; Sally, 280; Samuel, 279; Sarah, 280, 1, 2; Seth, 282, 4; Silas, 279, 82, 3, 4; Silence, 282; Simeon, 281; Solomon, 282; Stephen, 284; Thomas, 280; Vyiby, 282; Waity, 279, 80, 4; William, 281, 3, 4.

CHAPMAN.—Abel, 287; Adam, 287; Albert, 287; Amos, 285, 7; Andrew, 285, 6; Anna, 286; Betsey, 286, 7; Case, 286; Charles, 286; Clarissa, 287; Cordelia, 287; Cyrus, 287; Daniel, 287; Demarious, 287; Dudley, 287; Eldredge, 287; Elias, 286; Elisha, 286; Elizabeth, 286; Enoch, 287; Erastus, 287; Eunice, 285; Ezra, 286; Freeman, 287; Gideon, 286; Hannah, 285, 6, 7; Israel, 286 Jesse, 286; John, 285, 7; Jonas, 285, 7; Jonah, 285; Joseph, 285, 6, 7; Keturah, 286; Lewis, 286; Louis, 286; Levinia, 287; Lucy, 286, 7; Lydia, 286; Nabby, 286; Nahum, 285, 8; Nancy, 287; Nathan, 285, 8; Oliver, 287; Palmer, 286; Polly, 286; Roxanna, 287; Ruth, 285; Sally, 287; Samuel, 286; Sanford, 286; Sarah, 285, 6, 7; Silas, 286; Smith, 286; Stephen, 286; Stewart, 286; Sumner, 285, 7; Sybil, 286; Thaddeus, 287; Thomas, 285, 6, 7; Timothy, 286, 7; William, 285, 7.

CHESEBROUGH.—Abby, 307; Abigail, 292, 4, 6, 9, 301, 2, 3, 4; Abel, 301; Anna, 292, 8, 9, 301, 2, 6; Abisha, 306; Albert, 300, 6; Alexander, 308; Almira, 300, 8; Amelia, 302, 7; Amos, 295, 8, 300, 1, 3, 4, 5, 6, 9; Andronicus, 292, 303; Ann, 293, 5, 6, 305, 8; Andrew, 297, 301, 8; Asa, 299; Benedict, 299; Benjamin, 297, 301, 2, 9; Beriah, 303; Betsey, 302; Bridget, 293, 6, 8, 9, 302; Charles, 295, 8, 9, 302, 8; Christopher, 297, 300; Clarissa, 302; Coddington, 298, 303; Courtland, 307; Daniel, 296, 9, 304, 7; David, 292, 4, 5, 6, 9; Denison, 306, 7, 8, 9; Desire, 298, 303, 4; Dorcas, 299; Dorothy, 302; Dudley, 305, 7; Ebenezer, 303; Edmund, 305; Edward, 297, 301, 2; Elam, 302; Eldredge, 307; Eli, 305; Elias, 300, 6; Elihu, 293, 4, 5, 8, 304, 7, 8; Elsworth, 306; Elisha, 292, 3, 4, 5, 6, 7, 300; Elmanson, 306; Eliza, 303, 7, 9; Elizabeth, 292, 8, 9, 304; Emma, 206, 8; Emily, 300, 9; Enoch, 302, 6, 8; Ephraim, 304; Erastus, 308; Esther, 295, 8, 301, 4; Ethan, 307, 9; Eunice, 295, 6, 303, 4; Ezra, 300, 6; Fanny, 305; Frances, 303, 5, 6, 8; Francis, 309; Frederick, 305, 7; George, 304; Gideon, 305; Gilbert, 307; Grace, 305, 8; Gurdon, 305; Hallam, 302, 9; Hannah, 293, 4, 5, 6, 8, 300, 1, 2, 3, 6, 9; Harriet, 305, 8; Henry, 303, 4, 5; Hepsibah, 297, 301; Huldah, 303, 6; Isaac, 301; Jabez, 292, 4, 7, 300, 2; James, 294, 7, 8, 309; Jane, 308; Jedediah, 294, 7, 301; Jeremiah, 293, 5; Jerusha, 293; Jesse, 300, 5; Joanna, 297; John, 292, 3, 4, 5, 7, 8, 9, 301, 5; Jonathan, 292, 6, 9; Joseph, 292, 3, 6, 9, 300, 6; Joshua, 298, 9; Junice, 292; Kate, 299; Keturah, 298, 302; Lois, 300; Lucena, 307; Lucretia, 299, 306; Luke, 294, 8; Lucy, 294, 6, 300, 3, 5; Lydia, 295, 8, 301, 2, 3, 7; Mabrina, 300; Margaret, 293; Maria, 292, 303, 8; Marie, 292; Martha, 292, 304, 5; Marvin, 306; Mary, 293, 4, 5, 6, 7, 8, 9, 301, 2, 3, 4, 5, 6, 7, 8, 9; Mercy, 293, 300, 3, 7; Minetta, 303; Molly, 297, 302; Naboth, 298, 304; Nancy, 299, 301, 3, 4, 6, 8; Nathan, 294, 8, 302, 3; Nathaniel, 292, 3, 4, 5, 6, 8, 9, 301, 2, 8; Nehemiah, 300; Nicholas, 303, 7; Obed, 303; Oliver, 301, 9; Palmer, 300; Paul, 305; Peleg, 298, 302; Perez, 302; Phebe, 295, 6, 9, 304, 8; Polly, 301, 8; Priscilla, 295, 7, 8, 304; Prudence, 294, 5, 7, 9, 302, 7, 8; Rebecca, 294, 5, 7, 8, 9, 302, 9; Reuben, 300, 5; Rhoda, 300, 6; Richard, 303, 5; Robert, 298, 300, 3; Rodman, 306; Rufus, 301; Ruth, 295; Sabra, 306; Sabrina, 307; Sally, 303, 6, 7; Samuel 292, 3, 4, 5, 6, 8, 300, 3, 5; Sarah 292, 4, 5. 6, 8, 9, 300, 1, 3, 5, 9; Saxton, 303; Silas, 304; Simeon, 300; Sophia, 306; Sybil, 297; Sylvester, 297, 300, 1; Submit, 300, 6; Susannah, 295; Thankful, 294, 300, 7; Thomas, 294, 6, 302, 7; Warren, 300; Wealthy, 301; William, 288, 92, 3, 4, 5, 6, 8, 9, 300, 1, 3, 4, 8; Zebediah, 309; Zebulon, 294, 7, 301, 7, 8; Zerviah, 301.

CLIFT.—Abigail, 311; Amos, 310, 11; Bethiah, 310; Betsey, 311; Deborah, 310; Denison, 311; Esther, 311; Eunice, 312; Frederick, 311; Ira, 312; Isaac, 312; John, 311; Joseph, 310; Margery, 311; Mary, 310, 11, 12; Nancy, 311; Nathan, 311; Nathaniel, 311, 12; Rhoda, 310; Samuel, 310, 11; Waterman, 310, 11; William, 310, 11; Wills, 310.

COATES.—Amos, 313; Ansel, 314; Asahel, 313; Asher, 314; Bartholomew, 313; Clarissa, 314; Daniel, 313; David, 313, 14;

742 INDEX.

Edward, 313; Elizabeth, 313; Experience, 313; John, 313, 14; Joseph, 313; Lucy, 314; Martha, 313; Mary, 313; Obadiah, 313; Polly, 314; Rebecca, 313; Robert, 313; Rubee, 313; Susannah, 313; Thankful, 313; Thomas, 313; Victoria, 313; William, 313.

COBB.—Abby, 317; Alfred, 318; Anne, 316; Catharine, 318; Charles, 317; Bridget, 316; Ebenezer, 316, 17; Edward, 317; Eleazar, 315; Eliza, 317; Elkanah, 316, 17; Emeline, 317; Enoch, 317; Eunice, 315, 16; Experience, 315; Frances, 318; Gershom, 315; Gideon, 315, 16; Hallett, 316, 17; James, 315, 17; Jerusha, 318; John, 315, 17; Julian, 317; Katharine, 317; Lois, 315, 16; Margaret, 318; Mariah, 317; Mary, 315, 16, 18; Mehitable, 315; Nabby, 317; Nathan, 315, 16, 17, 18; Oliver, 316, 17; Patience, 315; Sanford, 317; Samuel, 317; Sarah, 316, 17; Susannah, 316.

COLLINS.—Ann, 320; Anne, 319, 21; Benjamin, 320; Betsey, 319, 20; Charles, 321; Daniel, 219, 20, 1; Ella, 321; Eley, 319; Ethan, 321; Frances, 321; Frank, 321; Gilbert, 319, 20, 21; Hannah, 319, 20, 21; Harriet, 320; James, 319; Jane, 321; John, 319, 20, 1; Lewis, 320; Lydia, 319, 20; Maria, 319, 21; Morgan, 320; Nancy, 320; Pell, 319; Polly, 319, 20; Rachel, 320; Rebecca, 319; Robert, 319, 20; Samuel, 320; Sanford, 320; Sarah, 320; Smith, 320; Sophia, 320; Susan, 320; Thomas, 320, 1; Tracy, 320; William, 329, 30.

COPP.—Ann, 322; Belton, 323, 4; Bette, 324; Catharine, 322, 3, 4; Daniel, 323; David, 322, 3, 4; Dolle, 324; Dorothy, 323; Ebenezer, 323; Elizabeth, 323; Eliza, 323; Ellen, 323; Esther, 324; George, 323, 4; Joanna, 322; John, 322, 3, 4; Jonathan, 322, 3, 4; Joseph, 323; Julia, 324; Lydia, 322; Margaret, 323; Mary, 322, 3, 4; Molly, 324; Naome, 322; Nancy, 324; Obedience, 322; Phebe, 324; Rachael, 323; Rebecca, 322; Ruth, 322; Samuel, 322, 3, 4; Sarah, 322, 3, 4; William, 322, 3, 4.

COTTRELL.—Abigail, 327; Amey, 325, 6; Angienette, 327; Arthur, 327; Calvert, 326; Charles, 327; Dorothy, 325, 6, 7; Edgar, 326; Eleazer, 325; Elias, 326; Elinner, 326; Elizabeth, 325, 6; Emma, 327; Fanny, 327; Gershom, 325, 6; Hannah, 325; Harriet, 327; Hattie, 326; Ida, 327; Jabez, 325, 6; James, 325; John, 325, 6; Joseph, 326, 7; Judith, 326; Lebbeus, 326; Mary, 325, 6, 7; Mercy, 326; Nathaniel, 325, 7; Nicholas, 325, 6, 7; Prudence, 327; Rachael, 326; Reuben, 327; Rozzel, 327; Russell, 326; Samuel, 325; Sarah, 326; Stephen, 326; Susannah, 326.

DAVIS.—Abigail, 328, 9, 30; Alphonso, 328; Benjamin, 329; Catharine, 329; Clarissa, 330; Daniel, 329; Dudley, 330; Enos, 329, 30; Fanny, 330; Hannah, 328; Henry, 329, 30; Huldah, 330; Jeremiah, 330; John, 328, 9, 30; Julia, 330; Maria, 329; Mary, 329, 30; Maryette, 328; Nancy, 329; Phebe, 330; Samuel, 329; Sarah, 330; Thomas, 328, 9, 30.

DEAN.—Benajah, 333; Christopher, 333; David, 333; Eleanor, 331; Elizabeth, 333; Fanny, 333; Francis, 332; Hannah, 332; Jabez, 333; James, 331, 2, 3; Jesse, 333; John, 332, 3; Jonathan, 332; Martha, 333; Mary, 332; Nancy, 333; Nathan, 332; Onesiphores, 332; Phannee, 333; Prudence, 333; Sarah, 332, 3; Thankful, 333; Walter, 331; Welthian, 333; William, 331, 2.

DENISON.—Abby, 342, 51, 8, 9; Abigail, 340, 1, 2, 5, 50, 1, 2, 5; Alfred, 354; Alice, 349, 56; Aliph, 352; Allen, 357; Amos, 343, 7, 8, 55, 6, 60; Amy, 344, 50; Andrew, 341, 5, 9, 52, 5, 61; Ann, 337, 8, 9, 41, 4, 6, 8, 53, 8, 9, 61; Anne, 335; Anna, 343, 5, 6, 52, 6; Annis, 348; Asahel, 352; Asa, 352; Avery, 342, 4, 5, 51, 2; Beebe, 342, 5, 6, 9, 53, 5; Betsey, 345, 8, 50, 2, 4; Benadam, 344, 8, 9, 56; Benjamin, 352; Borodell, 338, 41, 3; Bridget, 347, 55, 9, 60; Caroline, 358, 60; Charles, 348, 50, 2, 4, 5, 9, 60, 1; Christopher, 342, 3; Clarissa, 352; Content, 347, 55; Cynthia, 357; Daniel, 334, 5, 7, 9, 40, 1, 2, 4, 5, 6, 50, 1, 2, 3, 4, 8, 9, 60; Darius, 349, 56; David, 344, 50; Deborah, 336, 57; Delia, 354; Desire, 340, 2, 5, 8, 50, 1, 2; Dimis, 356; Dorcas, 350; Dorothy, 345, 9; Dudley, 348, 9, 52; Ebenezer, 353, 8, 9; Edgar, 360; Edward, 334, 5, 6, 40, 2, 6, 50, 1, 4, 5, 6, 8, 9; Elam, 357, 61; Eleazer, 348; Elijah, 343, 4; Elisha, 342, 4, 6, 9, 51, 3, 4, 9, 60, 1; Elias, 356, 61; Eliza, 355, 7, 9, 60; Elsie, 356; Elizabeth, 334, 5, 6, 40, 1, 3, 7, 54, 5; Emma, 350, 60; Emeline, 357; Emily 356, 9, 61; Ephraim, 347; Erastus, 354; Esther, 342, 4, 6, 8, 9, 52, 3; Ethan, 351, 8; Eunice, 346, 7, 8, 51, 3, 4, 5, 6, 7, 9; Evelina, 358; Ezra, 347, 55; Fanny, 345, 51, 6; Frances, 359; Franklin, 358; Frederick, 346, 53, 4, 9; George, 334, 5, 6, 7, 8, 9, 40, 1, 3, 4, 8, 9, 50, 6, 7; Gideon, 343, 53; Gilbert, 349, 54, 61; Grace, 341, 51, 7; Hannah, 336, 40, 1, 4, 6, 8, 50, 1, 3, 4, 5, 6, 60, 1; Harriet, 356, 8, 60; Henry,

346, 53, 5, 6, 7, 8, 61; Hezekiah, 353; Hiram, 359; Huldah, 361; Isaac, 346, 51, 3, 8; Jabez, 340, 50; James, 340, 9, 56; Jane, 345, 9, 56, 8, 61; Jeremiah, 336, 53; Jerome, 356; Jesse, 346, 54; Joanna, 341, 3; John, 334, 5, 6, 8, 9, 40, 1, 2, 4, 5, 6, 50, 1, 2, 3, 4, 9; Jonathan, 344, 56; Joseph, 336, 40, 2, 3, 4, 7, 8, 50, 5, 6, 7, 8; Julia, 345, 56, 7; Justin, 357, 61; Keturah, 353; Leonard, 354; Lodowick, 356; Lois, 351, 3, 4, 8, 9; Louisa, 361; Luce, 334; Lucy, 341, 2, 4, 5, 8, 9, 52, 6, 7, 61; Luke, 357; Lydia, 348; Lyman, 351; Manasseth, 347; Marcia, 357, 60; Maria, 361; Margaret, 334, 6, 8; Martha, 339, 47, 51, 2, 5, 6, 7, 60; Mary, 334, 6, 8, 41, 2, 3, 4, 5, 6, 7, 8, 9, 50, 1, 3, 4, 5, 8, 9, 60, 1; Mehitable, 354; Mercy, 340, 3, 4, 5, 6, 9, 52, 3, 5, 6, 61; Molly, 345; Moses, 351; Nancy, 345, 6, 51, 3, 4, 5, 6, 8, 60; Nathan, 343, 4, 5, 7, 9, 51, 2, 8, 60, 1; Nathaniel, 341, 8, 51; Noyes, 354, 7; Oliver, 345, 9, 57, 60, 1; Peleg, 347, 54, 5, 60; Phebe, 339, 41, 2, 6, 52, 4, 9, 60; Polly, 352, 5, 6; Prentice, 355; Priscilla, 350; Prudence, 342, 3, 5, 7, 8, 50, 1, 5, 6, 8; Pulaski, 358; Rachel, 342; Rebecca, 345, 6, 52; Rensaliear, 352; Rhoda, 348; Robert, 339, 41, 6, 9, 52, 6, 7; Rowland, 356; Russel, 355; Ruth, 340; Sally, 352, 4; Samuel, 339, 40, 3, 4, 5, 50, 2, 4, 5, 8, 9; Sarah, 335, 6, 9, 40, 1, 2, 3, 4, 5, 8, 50, 3, 5, 8, 9, 60; Silas, 352; Simeon, 351; Sophia, 352, 61; Stephen, 343, 52; Susan, 335; Thankful, 340, 2, 3, 5, 8, 51, 3, 8; Thomas, 341, 57, 61; Wealthy, 350; Wetherell, 341; William, 334, 5, 6, 8, 9, 40, 1, 3, 4, 6, 8, 9, 51, 2, 3, 4, 6, 7, 8; Zerviah, 345, 51.

EELLS.—Ann, 362; Benjamin, 363, 4; Betsey, 363; Charlotte, 364; Cushing, 363; Edward, 362, 3; Elizabeth, 363, 4; Hannah, 362, 3; John, 362, 3; Joseph, 363; Lucretia, 363; Lydia, 363, 4; Maria, 364; Mary, 362; Mercy, 363; Nancy, 363; Nathaniel, 362, 3; North, 362; Rebecca, 363; Robert, 362; Samuel, 362, 3; Sarah, 362, 3.

FANNING.—Edmund, 365, 6; Ellen, 365; Gilbert, 366; Henry, 366; James, 365, 6; John, 365; Mary, 365, 6; Nathaniel, 366; Richard, 366; Samuel, 366; Thomas, 365, 6; William, 365, 6.

FELLOWS.—Abigail, 367, 8; Asa, 368; David, 368; Deborah, 367; Elizabeth, 367; Elnathan, 368; Ephraim, 367, 8; George, 368; Hannah, 368; Hopestill, 367; Isaac, 367; Jeremiah, 368; Joanna, 367; John, 367, 8; Jonathan, 367; Joseph, 367, 8; Lois, 368; Lydia, 368; Martha, 368; Mary, 367, 8; Mercy, 368; Nathan, 367; Nathaniel, 367; Priscilla, 368; Prudence, 368; Rhoda, 368; Samuel, 367, 8; Sarah, 367, 8; Tully, 368; Warner, 367, 8; William, 367.

FISH.—Aaron, 371, 2; Abigail, 372, 3; Alden, 373; Ameros, 372; Anna, 373; Asa, 373, 4; Benjamin, 374; Bridget, 373; Catharine, 373; Charles, 373; Cynthia, 373; Daniel, 372; David, 372; Edmund, 373; Elias, 376; Eliakin, 375; Elizabeth, 372; Eunice, 372; Fanny, 374; Grace, 372; Hannah, 373, 4; Ichabod, 373; Isaac, 372; James, 374; Jane, 373; Jason, 372; Jed, 374; John, 369, 70, 1, 2, 4; Jonathan, 369; Joseph, 375; Levinia, 373; Lydia, 375; Margaret, 371, 2; Mary, 370, 3, 5; Miller, 375; Moses, 371, 2; Nathan, 372, 3, 4; Nathaniel, 375; Prudence, 374; Rebecca, 375; Roswell, 373; Samuel, 369, 70, 1, 2, 3; Sands, 373, 4; Sarah, 372, 3; Silas, 373, 4; Simeon, 373, 4; Thomas, 375; Timothy, 372; Titus, 372; William, 374, 5.

FRINK.—Abigail, 376, 7; Adam, 378; Alexander, 380; Amos, 378, 80; Andrew, 376, 7; Ann, 377, 8; Anna, 379; Betsey, 379; Benjamin, 376, 8, 80; Charles, 380; Cyrus, 379; Daniel, 377, 9; Darius, 379; David, 377, 8; Deborah, 376, 8; Desire, 377, 9; Dudley, 379, 80; Edwin, 379; Elias, 379; Elisha, 379; Elizabeth, 377, 80; Ephraim, 378; Esther, 376, 8; Eunice, 377, 9; Ezra, 380; Fanny, 380; Gilbert, 380; Giles, 379; Grace, 376; Hannah, 376, 7, 8, 80; Henry, 377, 8, 9; Isaac, 377, 8, 9; Isapena, 380; Jabez, 377, 80; James, 376; Jarius, 380; Joannah, 378; John, 376, 8, 9; Jonathan, 380; Jedediah, 376; Jerusha, 376; Joseph, 376, 8, 9, 80; Judith, 376; Latham, 377; Lois, 377, 9; Lucretia, 380; Lucy, 377; Margaret, 377; Mary, 376, 7, 8, 80; Nancy, 379; Nathan, 378, 9; Nicholas, 376, 8; Oliver, 377, 8; Perez, 380; Philura, 377; Pitts, 380; Polly, 379; Prentice, 378, 9; Prudence, 378, 9; Roswell, 379; Rufus, 379; Samuel, 376, 7, 8, 9, 80; Sarah, 377, 8, 9; Stanton, 379; Stephen, 377, 9; Thankful, 376; Thomas, 376, 7; Tracy, 378; Uzziel, 378; William, 376, 8, 9, 80; Zachariah, 376, 8.

GALLUP.—Abigail, 383, 6, 9; Adeline, 395; Albert, 392; Alfred, 394, 5; Amos, 388, 90, 5; Ann, 393; Andrew, 391; Anna, 387, 9, 90, 2, 4; Asa, 391; Austin, 393, 5; Avery, 390; Beebe, 396; Benadam, 383, 4, 6, 7, 8, 90, 3; Benjamin, 383, 4, 7, 95; Bridget, 390, 5; Caroline, 394; Cecelia,

391; Christobel, 383; Christopher, 389, 91, 4; Cynthia, 393; Daniel, 396; David, 388; Desire, 390, 4; Dorothy, 385; Dwight, 391; Ebenezer, 387, 9, 94; Edwin, 393, 4; Elias, 390, 2; Elihu, 390; Elisha, 388, 94; Eliza, 395; Elizabeth, 383, 4, 5, 7, 91, 4; Emeline, 393; Erastus, 390, 3; Esther, 383, 7, 8, 9, 96; Eunice, 387, 8, 91, 2, 4, 5; Ezra, 388; Fannie, 391; Frances, 394; Francis, 393; Franklin, 391; Frederick, 391; Gardner, 389; George, 387, 8, 90; Gideon, 389; Giles, 391; Grace, 391; Gurdon, 389, 91, 6; Hannah, 383, 4, 5, 7, 8, 90, 3, 5, 6; Harriet, 392, 5; Henry, 387, 91, 4, 5; Hester, 384; Hortense, 395; Isaac, 385, 8, 90, 3; Jabesh, 390; Jabez, 390, 3; Jacob, 389; James, 389, 90, 3; Jared, 391, 5; Jemima, 390, 2; Jeremiah, 387; Jerusha, 388; Jesse, 389; Joan, 382; John, 381, 2, 3, 4, 5, 6, 7, 8, 9, 90, 1, 2, 3, 4, 5, 6; Jonathan, 388, 9; Joshua, 389, 92; Joseph, 383, 4, 8, 9, 91, 3; Josiah, 389; Julia, 391, 3; Keturah, 392; Laura, 395; Lawiston, 391; Levi, 388; Libbie, 395; Lodowick, 389, 91; Lois, 387, 9; Louise, 391; Louis, 395; Lucretia, 389, 96; Lucy, 384, 8, 90, 1, 4; Luke, 392, 4, 5; Lydia, 390; Margaret, 383, 4, 7, 8, 91; Martha, 384, 5, 7, 8, 90, 1, 3, 4; Mary, 383, 5, 7, 9, 91, 2, 3, 5, 6; Mason, 395; Mehitable, 383, 5, 7; Melinda, 395; Mercy, 384, 6, 7; Mozart, 394; Nathan, 387, 9, 90, 1, 4; Nathaniel, 382, 3, 4, 7, 8, 9, 90, 2, 3; Nehemiah, 391, 4, 5; Nelson, 393; Noyes, 394; Olive, 395; Oliver, 388, 91; Orinda, 394; Palmer, 393, 4; Phebe, 389, 95; Priscilla, 387, 94; Prudence, 388, 9, 93; Rhoda, 392; Roswell, 393; Rufus, 393; Russell, 390, 3; Sabra, 391; Samuel, 382, 3, 4, 6, 7, 8, 9, 92; Sarah, 385, 7, 9, 90, 1, 2, 3; Serviah, 394; Shubael, 390; Silas, 388; Simeon, 390; Sophia, 393; Susan, 389; Temperance, 395; Thomas, 384, 5, 6, 7; Wealthean, 390; William, 383, 4, 5, 6, 7, 8, 95.

GORE.—Abigail, 397, 8; Asa, 398, 9; Benjamin, 397; Daniel, 398; Ebenezer, 397; Elizabeth, 398, 9; George, 399; Hannah, 397, 8; Jeremiah, 399; John, 397, 8, 9; Lucy, 399; Margaret, 398; Mary, 397, 9; Moses, 398; Obediah, 397, 8; Samuel, 397, 8, 9; Sarah, 397, 8, 9; Silas, 398; Thomas, 398.

GRANT.—Almira, 402; Amos, 402; Ann, 403; Anna, 403, 4; Betsey, 402; Bridget, 401; Caleb, 402; Charles, 402; Cynthia, 403; Cyrus, 403, 4; Daniel, 402, 4; Deborah, 402; Desire, 403; Elnathan, 402; Ephraim, 402; Esther, 402; Eunice, 401, 2; Frances, 403; George, 402; Gilbert, 402, 3; Hannah, 402, 3; Henry, 402; Hosea, 402; John, 400, 1, 3, 4; Joseph, 403; Joshua, 401; Josiah, 400, 1, 3; Justus, 404; Lucinda, 402, 3; Lucy, 401, 2, 3; Mathew, 400; Mary, 400, 1, 2, 3; Miner, 401, 3, 4; Nancy, 403; Nathaniel, 400; Noah, 401, 3, 4; Oliver, 401, 2, 3; Patty, 403; Patience, 404; Phebe, 402; Polly, 404; Prentice, 402; Priscilla, 400; Prudence, 403; Rachael, 401; Rebecca, 401, 2; Roswell, 403; Russell, 403, 4; Ruth, 404; Samuel, 400; Sarah, 400, 1, 2, 3; Silence, 401, 2; Tahan, 400; Thomas, 403; Wealthy, 402, 3; Wheeler, 402; William, 402, 3.

GREENMAN.—Abigail, 405, 6; Anna, 405; Catharine, 406; Chloe, 406; Clark, 406, 7; Content, 405; David, 405; Edward, 405, 6; Elizabeth, 405; Eunice, 405; Garthrot, 405; George, 406, 7; Hannah, 406; John, 405; Katharine, 405; Lucy, 406; Margaret, 406; Mary, 405, 6; Nathan, 405, 6; Phebe, 405; Prudence, 406; Sarah, 405, 6; Silas, 405, 6, 7; Thomas, 405, 6, 7; Timothy, 406; William, 405, 6.

HALEY.—Abigail, 408; Belcher, 408; Betsey, 409; Caleb, 408, 9; Catharine, 410; Charlotte, 409; Content, 408; Deborah, 408; Dominie, 408; Edmond, 408, 9; Elihu, 409; Elisha, 409; Elizabeth, 408; George, 409; Hannah, 408, 9; Harriet, 410; Jabez, 409; Jane, 410; Jeremiah, 408, 9; Joshua, 408, 9, 10; John, 408, 9, 10; Katharine, 409; Lucy, 408, 10; Margaret, 409; Martha, 408; Mary, 408, 9, 10; Nancy, 409; Nathan, 410; Phebe, 408; Rebecca, 410; Rhoda, 409; Sarah, 410; Simeon, 409, 10; Stephen, 409; Thomas, 409; Zerviah, 408.

HALLAM.—Abigail, 412, 13; Alice, 411; Alexander, 413; Amos, 412, 13; Desire, 413; Edward, 413; Giles, 413; Harriet, 413; Isaac, 413; John, 411, 12, 13; Lucy, 413; Mary, 412; Nicholas, 411, 12, 13; Phebe, 412; Prudence, 412; Thomas, 413.

HANCOX.—Albert, 415; Amos, 415; Ann, 414, 15; Anne, 414; Betsey, 415; Catharine, 415; Clement, 415; Edward, 414, 15; Ethan, 415; Frances, 415; Franklin, 415; Freelove, 414; Harriet, 415; Isaac, 414; James, 414, 15; John, 414; Joseph, 415; Lucy, 414; Lydia, 415; Martha, 414; Mary, 415; Mercy, 415; Nathan, 414; Polly, 414; Prudence, 414; Rebecca, 414; Reuben, 415; Sally, 415; Samuel, 415; Sarah, 414; Thomas, 415; William, 414, 15; Zebulon, 414, 15.

INDEX. 745

HART.—Charles, 416; David, 416; Harriet, 416; Hawkins, 416; Henry, 416; Ira, 416, 17; Jonathan, 416; Louise, 416; Stephen, 416; Thomas, 416.

HEWITT.—Abby, 426; Abel, 423; Abiah, 420; Abigail, 420; Alden, 420; Alpheus, 427; Amy, 420; Amos, 421, 2, 3, 5, 6; Anna, 420, 2; Ann, 427; Arthur, 419, 21; Austin, 425; Asa, 421; Avery, 425; Benadam, 425; Benjamin, 418, 19, 20, 2, 3, 6; Betsey, 423, 5; Charles, 420; 2, 4; Consider, 420; Content, 419, 20, 21; Cyprian, 419; Cyrus, 424; Cynthia, 421, 5; Daniel, 423; Darias, 421, 8; Denison, 423, 4, 7; Desire, 424, 6, 7; Dethic, 421, 3; Diadama, 421; Dudley, 421, 7; Edmond, 420; Eli, 422, 5; Eliphalet, 426; Elias, 422, 4, 7; Elisha, 425; Eliza, 424, 5; Elizabeth, 420, 2, 3, 7; Elkana, 419, 21, 2; Emeline, 425; Emmilla, 426; Emily, 427; Ephraim, 420, 4, 7; Erastus, 427, 8; Eunice, 421, 3, 5; Ezra, 424; Frances, 426, 7; Francina, 428; Freeman, 424; George, 425; Gershom, 420, 1; Giles, 427; Grace, 422; Gurdon, 421, 4; Hannah, 418, 19, 20, 1, 2, 4, 5; Harriet, 425, 7; Henry, 419, 21, 2, 3, 5, 6, 7; Increase, 421, 3; Isaac, 422, 3, 4; Israel, 419, 20, 1, 4; Jabish, 420; James, 423, 4, 7; Jane, 426; Joannah, 421; John, 420, 4, 8; Joseph, 419, 20, 2, 3; Jonas, 421, 3; Josiah, 422; Kesiah, 420; Lot, 422; Lucy, 427; Lucinda, 424; Lydia, 420, 2, 4, 7; Margaret, 426; Maria, 426; Mary, 419, 20, 1, 3, 4, 5, 6, 7; Mehitable, 419, 23; Nabby, 424; Nancy, 421, 2, 4, 5, 6, 7; Nathaniel, 420, 2, 5, 6; Nathan, 420; Olive, 420; Oliver, 424, 6; Palmer, 421, 2, 5; Patty, 424; Perez, 422, 5, 7; Peggy, 426; Phebe, 422, 3, 6, 7; Polly, 422, 4; Prentice, 422, 6; Priscilla, 420; Prudence, 420; Rebecca, 422, 7; Richard, 421; Robert, 419, 22; Roger, 419, 20, 2; Rufus, 420, 1, 2, 4; Russell, 421; Samuel, 419, 20; Sarah, 419, 21, 4, 6, 7; Simeon, 421, 3; Sophia, 425; Stanton, 422, 4, 6, 8; Stephen, 421; Tabitha, 419, 21, 4; Thankful, 420, 1, 2; Thomas, 418, 19, 20, 1, 3, 7; Walter, 420, 1; Warren, 427; Wealthy, 428; Wheaton, 421; William, 423, 4, 6; Zerviah, 419, 20, 1; Zebra, 423.

HINCKLEY.—Abby, 432; Abel, 430, 1, 2; Abigail, 432; Anne, 431; Bethia, 429; Caroline, 432; Charles, 431; Daniel, 431; David, 430, 1; Deney, 431; Elias, 432; Elijah, 430; Elizabeth, 429, 30, 1; Eliphal, 432; Esther, 431, 2; Eunice, 431; Frank, 432; Gershom, 429, 30, 1; Grace, 431; Hannah, 429; Harry, 431, 2; Ichabod, 429; Joanna, 430; Jonathan, 429, 30; John, 429, 30, 1; Lucy, 431; Luther, 431; Martha, 430, 1; Mary, 429, 30, 1, 2; Mercy, 430, 1; Nancy, 430; Nathan, 430; Paul, 431, 2; Prudence, 431; Rebecca, 431; Samuel, 429, 30, 1, 2; Sarah, 429, 31; Susanna, 429; Thankful, 430; Thomas, 429, 31, 2; Vose; 431; Wyatt, 430, 1; Zerviah, 430.

HOBART.—Daniel, 433, 4; David, 433; Elam, 434; Eliphalet, 433; Elisha, 433; Emma, 434; Fanna, 433; Frances, 434; Hannah, 433, 4; Henry, 433; John, 433; Joseph, 433; Lucy, 434; Margaret, 433; Mercy, 433; Nancy, 433, 4; Peter, 433; Phebe, 434; Polly, 433; Priscilla, 433; Rilla, 433; Russel, 433; Samuel, 433; Susanna, 433; William, 433, 4; Zerviah, 433.

HOLMES.—Abby, 440; Abigail, 435, 6, 7, 8; Anna, 435, 6; Amos, 437, 9; Asher, 440; Benjamin, 439; Bethia, 436, 7; Charles, 438; Christopher, 440; Cyrus, 441; Daniel, 438; Edward, 437, 41; Elias, 435, 7; Elizabeth, 440; Ephraim, 438, 40; Erastus, 439; Esther, 437, 8, 9, 41; Eunice, 437, 8, 41; Fear, 436; Frances, 439; Franklin, 441; Frederick, 438; Gilbert, 438; Hannah, 440; Hazzard, 441; Henry, 438; Hiram, 439; Hosea, 441; Isaac, 435, 9; Jabish, 437, 9; James, 436, 8, 40, 1; Jared, 438; Jedediah, 437, 40; Jeremiah, 437, 8, 9; John, 436, 7, 8, 40, 1; Jonathan, 437; Joseph, 436, 8, 9; Joshua, 435, 6, 7, 40, 1; Lovisa, 439; Lucy, 437, 9, 40, 1; Lucretia, 437, 9; Margaret, 437; Martha, 438; Mary, 435, 6, 7, 8, 9; Marvin, 436; Mercy, 437, 8; Molly, 437; Nancy, 440, 1; Nathaniel, 435; Nathan, 437, 40, 1; Nehemiah, 438, 41; Noyes, 441; Patty, 440, 1; Prentice, 441; Philura, 438; Polly, 438, 40; Prudence, 435, 6, 7, 40; Rebecca, 438; Richard, 437; Robert, 435, 40; Roswell, 438; Russell, 441; Samuel, 435, 7, 40; Sarah, 435, 6, 7, 40; Shubael, 437, 40; Silas, 437, 9, 41; Silence, 440; Susannah, 435; Temperance, 436, 7, 40; Thankful, 436, 7; Thomas, 436, 7, 8; William, 435, 7, 8; William, 435, 7, 40; Zerviah, 438.

HOXIE.—Bethsheba, 442; Content, 442; Ethan 442; Gideon, 442; Hezekiah, 442; John, 442; Joseph, 442; Lodowick, 442; Peter, 442; Ruth, 442; Soloman, 442; Stephen, 442; Welcome, 442.

HULL.—Almira, 443; Amos, 443, 4; Anna, 443, 4; Benadam, 444; Bridget, 443; Charles, 444; Cyrus, 444; Desire, 444;

Elias, 443; Elisha, 444; Eliza, 444; Elizabeth, 443, 4; Esther, 444; Eunice, 443, 4; Hannah, 443; Jeremiah, 443; Jesse, 444; John, 443, 4; Joseph, 443; Keturah, 444; Latham, 443, 4; Martha, 443, 4; Nancy, 444; Samuel, 443; Sarah, 443; Stephen, 443; Thomas, 444; William, 444.

HYDE.—Anne, 445; Benjamin, 445, 6; Caroline, 446; Charles, 446; Daniel, 446; Edward, 446; Elisha, 445; Elizabeth, 445, 6; Enoch, 445, 6; Frances, 446; George, 446; Gurdon, 446; Harriet, 445, 6; Helen, 446; Henry, 446; Hester, 445; Jabez, 445; James, 446; John, 445, 6; Joseph, 445, 6; Joshua, 446; Laura, 445; Lucy, 446; Nancy, 445; Phebe, 445; Phineas, 445; Prudence, 445; Samuel, 445; Sarah, 445, 6; Silas, 446; Theophilus, 445, 6; Thomas, 445; William, 445, 6.

KELLOGG.—Austin, 447; Cyrus, 447; Daniel, 447; David, 447; Eliza, 447; Emily, 447; Eunice, 447; Frank, 447; Henry, 447; Hiram, 447; Joseph, 447; Mary, 447; Nathaniel, 447; Samuel, 447; William, 447.

MAIN.—Aaron, 453; Abigail, 450;. Abby, 454; Adam, 452; Agnes, 453; Allis, 448; Amos, 450, 1, 3; Andrew, 449, 51; Anna, 449; Anne, 449, 51; Asa, 451; Asher, 452; Avery, 454; Benajah, 451; Bethiah, 451; Betsey, 451; Bridget, 450, 3; Caleb, 450; Chandler, 452; Charles, 454; Clarinda, 453; Collins, 453; Content, 450, 3; Cynthia, 453; Cyrus, 453; Daniel, 450, 2; David, 448, 50, 1, 2, 3; Deborah, 453; Desire, 451; Dewey, 450, 2; Dianthus, 453; Dorcas, 454; Ede, 454; Elias, 451; Elizabeth, 449, 50; Elijah, 454; Ephriam, 453; Esther, 451, 4; Ezekiel, 448, 9; Fanny, 452; Fear, 451; Fenner, 452; Fleet, 453; Franklin, 452; Freelove, 453; Greshom, 454; Gilbert, 451; Grace, 450; Hannah, 448, 9, 51, 2, 3, 4; Hepzibah, 449; Hiram, 453; Ichabod, 448; Ira, 453; Isaac, 452, 4; Jabish, 450, 3; James, 450, 1; Jared, 453; Jesse, 454; Jeremiah, 448, 9, 50; John, 449, 50, 2, 3; Jonas, 449, 50, 2, 3; Jonathan, 450; Joshua, 449, 51; Joseph, 451, 3; Judith, 450; Judah, 452; Julia, 452; Keturah, 451; Laban, 450, 3; Levantia, 452; Lewis, 452, 4; Lucy, 450, 1, 4; Lucinda, 451, 2; Luther, 450; Lydia, 449, 50; Lyman, 450, 2; Matilda, 454; Mary, 448, 51, 3, 4; Merriam, 448; Milton, 452; Molly, 451; Naboe, 451; Nancy, 450, 2, 3, 4; Nathan, 450; Nathaniel, 449, 50; Patty, 452; Patience, 448, 50; Paul, 450; Perez, 452; Peter, 449, 51, 3; Polly, 453; Phebe, 448, 9, 54; Prentice, 452; Prudence, 451; Rachel, 451; Ralph, 453; Reuben, 450, 1, 2, 4; Rhoda, 452; Rial, 452; Robert, 452, 4; Rufus, 450; Ruth, 449, 50, 1, 4; Sabius, 450, 2, 3; Sands, 451, 4; Sanford, 454; Sarah, 449, 50, 1, 4; Saxton, 452; Sheffield, 452; Sidney, 453; Silas, 452; Sophia, 452, 3; Stephen, 454; Susan, 452, 3; Thankful, 450, 1, 2; Thomas, 448, 9, 50, 1, 2, 3, 4; Timothy, 449, 50, 4; Tryphenia, 451; William, 454; Zerviah, 453.

MALLORY.—Amos, 455; Amy, 455; Anna, 456; Benjamin, 456; Benajah, 455; Charles, 455, 6; David, 455, 6; Frances, 455; Franklin, 456; George, 456; Henry, 456; Nathan, 455; Rebecca, 455; Richard, 455.

MANNING.—Abigail, 457, 8; Calvin, 458; David, 458; Elizabeth, 458; Francis, 458; Hannah, 457; Hezekiah, 458; Jerusha, 458; John, 457; Josiah, 458; Lucius, 458; Lucy, 458; Luther, 458; Mason, 458; Olive, 458; Samuel, 457, 8; William, 457.

MATHEWS.—Andrew, 459; William, 459.

MASON.—Abigail, 462, 3; Anne, 461, 2, 3, 4; Alethea, 463; Andrew, 463, 4, 5; Bridget, 464, 5; Daniel, 461, 2, 3, 4, 5; Dudley, 464; Elijah, 462, 4; Elnathan, 463, 4; Elizabeth, 461, 3, 5; Eliphalet, 464; Esther, 464; Eunice, 463; Hannah, 461, 3, 5; Henry, 464; Hezekiah, 461, 2; Hobart, 463, 4; James, 462, 4; Japhet, 463; Jared, 463; Jemima, 462; Jeremiah, 462; John, 460, 1, 2, 4, 5; Joseph, 464; Jonathan, 463; Judith, 460; Lois, 464; Lucy, 464; Luke, 464; Lydia, 463; Margaret, 462, 4; Mary, 463, 4, 5; Mehitable, 463, 4; Nancy, 464; Nehemiah, 462, 3, 4; Peleg, 462, 4; Peter, 462, 3; Priscilla, 460, 2; Prudence, 463; Rachel, 460, 2, 3; Rebecca, 462, 3; Robert, 464; Rufus, 464; Samuel, 460, 1, 2, 3; Sarah, 461; Zerviah, 463, 4.

MINER.—Abel, 470; Abby, 473, 8; Abigail, 467, 9, 71, 4, 7, 8; Absolom, 478; Adam, 470, 3; Almira, 478; Alpheus, 470, 3; Alonzo, 478; Alfred, 477; Amos, 470, 2, 4, 5; Andrew, 477; Ann, 467, 70; Anna, 471, 2, 4, 6, 7; Asa, 470, 5, 6, 7; Asher, 473, 7; Benjamin, 468, 9, 71; Bertha, 477; Betsey, 473, 5, 6; Bradley, 476; Bridget, 468, 70; Charles, 469, 71, 3, 8; Christopher, 468, 9, 71, 3, 7; Clement, 466, 7, 9, 71, 7; Cogswell, 476; Cynthia, 473; Cyrus, 474; Daniel, 469, 71, 3, 4; Darius, 474; David, 471 4; Deborah, 467, 74; Denison, 476, 7; Desire, 470, 2, 6, 8; Edward, 466;

INDEX. 747

Elias, 474, 7, 8; Elihu, 478; Elisha, 472; Elnathan, 468, 9, 74; Elizabeth, 467, 71, 84; Eliza, 477, 8; Emeline, 475, 8; Enoch, 478; Ephraim, 466, 7, 8, 9, 70; Erastus 478; Esther, 470, 5; Eunice, 470, 1, 3, 5, 6, 7; Ezra, 473; Francis, 478; Franklin, 476; Frederick, 472, 5;; George, 466, 70, 8; Gilbert, 476; Grace, 467, 8, 9, 70; Hannah, 467, 8, 9, 70, 2, 3, 5, 7; Harriet, 476, 8; Hempstead, 471, 4; Henry, 466, 8, 70, 2, 3, 5, 6; Henrietta, 475; Isaac, 470, 2, 4, 5, 6; Jabez, 469; James, 468, 9, 76, 7; Jedediah, 477; Jesse, 474, 7; Jerusha, 469, 72; John, 466, 7, 8, 9, 70, 1, 2, 3, 5, 6; Joanna, 467, 8; Jonathan, 469, 71, 4; Joshua, 470; Joseph, 466, 7, 8, 9, 70, 2, 8; Julia, 475; Katharine, 470, 6; Keturah, 470, 6; Keziah, 472; Latham, 477; Laura, 473; Leland, 475; Lodowick, 466, 72; Lois, 470, 7; Lucy, 470, 3, 5, 6, 7; Luther, 474; Lucretia, 472, 3, 5, 6; Luke, 473; Lydia, 468, 9, 73, 5; Manasseh, 467, 8, 9, 71, 2, 5; Marcie, 468, 9; Martha, 473, 6, 7, 8; Mary, 467, 8, 9, 70, 1, 2, 3, 4, 5, 6, 7, 8; Maria, 467; Molly, 473; Nancy, 475, 6, 7; Nathan, 471, 4; Nathaniel, 471, 4, 7; Oliver, 473; Palmer, 476; Peleg, 470; Perez, 473, 4; Phebe, 467, 71, 3, 5, 7; Phineas, 470; Philarner, 472; Polly, 473; Priscilla, 473, 5; Prudence, 468, 9, 70, 1, 4, 6, 7; Ralph, 473, 8; Randall, 474; Rebecca, 467, 9, 71, 4, 8; Richardson, 469, 74, 6; Robert, 474, 6; Roswell, 473, 6; Rufus, 468, 70; Sabra, 473; Sabrina, 478; Sally, 473, 7; Samuel, 467, 8, 9, 70, 1, 4, 6; Sarah, 467, 8, 9, 70, 1, 2, 4, 6, 8; Saxton, 473, 5; Simeon, 468, 70, 2; Stephen, 468, 70, 3; Susannah, 470; Sylvanus, 469; Thankful, 469; Theresa, 476; Thomas, 466, 7, 8, 9, 70, 1, 2, 3, 5, 6, 7, 8; Wheeler, 474, William, 466, 7, 70, 1, 2, 6, 7, 8; Zebulon, 476; Zerviah, 469, 77.

MORGAN.—Abraham, 479; Amy, 481, Bela, 481; Christopher, 481; Dolly, 481; Edwin, 481; Elizabeth, 481; Elijah, 480; Hannah, 479, 80, 81; Israel, 481; James, 479, 80; Jasper, 481; John, 479, 80; Joseph, 479; Luther, 480; Lydia, 480; Mary, 480, 1; Moses, 480; Nathan, 480; Nicholas, 480; Phebe, 480; Polly, 481; Prudence, 481; Samuel, 480; Soloman, 480; Stephen, 480; Sybil, 481; Temperance 481; Theophilus, 480; Timothy, 480; Wealtha, 481; William, 480, 1.

MOSS.—Benjamin, 482; Clarina, 483; Ebenezer, 482; Emanuel, 483; Elihu, 482; Esther, 482; George, 483; Hannah, 482; Hester, 482; Heman, 482; Isaac, 482, 3; Israel, 482; Jabez, 482; Jesse, 482, 3; Job, 483; Joel, 482; John, 482; Joseph, 482; Lazarus, 483; Lothrop, 483; Mary, 482, 3; Martha, 482; Mercy, 482; Mehitable, 482; Reuben, 483; Rufus, 483; Samuel, 482; Soloman, 482; Tirzah, 483; William, 483.

NOYES.—Abigail, 485, 7, 9, 93; Agnes, 500; Albert, 496; Alexander, 500; Alfred, 500; Amanda, 500; Amos, 495, 6; Ann, 486, 8, 9, 94; Anna, 489, 90, 1, 6, 9; Anne, 495; Avery, 491, 6, 8, 501; Barbery, 494; Barker, 490, 4; Betsey, 492, 6; Belle, 496; Bethia, 488; Benjamin, 488, 91, 3, 500; Breed, 500; Bridget, 488, 9, 90; Carrie 500; Caroline, 496, 501; Clementina, 497; Charles, 493, 5, 6, 8, 500; Charlotte, 495; Courtlandt, 493; Cutting, 485, 7; Cyrus, 494, 6, 8; Daniel, 486, 7, 92, 3; David, 484, 500; Desire, 492; Denison, 491, 6, 8; Dorothy, 486, 8, 9, 90; Ebenezer, 492; Edward, 493, 8, 500, Edmund, 498; Edwin, 499; Ellen, 499; Eliphal, 488; Elihu, 492; Elisha, 495, 9; Eliza, 493, 4, 6, 7, 9; Elizabeth, 486, 7, 9, 90, 1, 5, 6, 8; Emeline, 497; Ephraim, 484, 7, 95; Emily, 495; Ernest, 500; Erastus, 491, 500; Esther, 490; Eunice, 495, 8, 9, 501; Fanny, 494, 6, 7, 8, 500; Francis, 497, 500; Frances, 494, 7; Franklin, 497, 8; Frederick, 492, 9, 500; George, 491, 3, 4, 9; Gershom, 495, 500; Gideon, 494; Gilbert, 501; Grace, 490, 2, 4, 6; Gurdon, 495, 500; Hannah, 485, 7, 92, 8; Harriet, 496, 500; Henry, 491, 3, 9, 500; Herbert, 500; Ira, 498; James, 484, 5, 6, 7, 8, 9, 490, 1, 3, 4, 7, 8, 500, 1; Jane, 499, 500; Jesse 493 5, 6, 501; John, 484, 5, 6, 7, 9, 90, 1, 2, 3, 4, 5, 6, 7, 8; Joshua, 490, 2, 4; Joseph, 485, 6, 7, 9, 90, 1, 2, 3, 4, 5, 8, 9, 500; Judith, 496; Lois, 493, 8; Louisa,, 498, 500; Lucy, 494, 5, 8; Luke, 494; Lydia, 487, 92, 497, 8; Maria, 496; Margaret, 490, 4; Martha, 486, 7, 93, 4, 6, 7; Mary, 485, 7, 8, 9, 91, 4, 5, 6, 7, 8, 9; Marcy, 495; Matilda, 497; Melinda, 497; Moses, 485, 6, 7; Nancy, 495, 7; Nathaniel, 487, 91, 2, 3, 5, 7; Nathan, 484, 7, 90, 1, 2, 4, 5, 7, 9, 500; Nicholas, 484, 5, 7; Oliver, 491, 5, 500, 1; Parker, 486, 7; Paul, 494, 9; Peleg, 490, 2, 4; Phebe, 490, 3, 8, 9; Polly, 490, 1, 2, 6, 500; Prudence, 491, 2, 6, 8, 9; Rachel, 485, 7; Rebecca, 485, 6, 7, 8, 9, 90, 1, 500; Regine, 500; Rhoda, 493; Robert, 492, 4; Rouse, 493; Ruth, 493; Sally, 496, 7; Samuel, 487, 95, 6, 7, 8; Sarah, 485, 6, 7, 8, 9, 91, 2, 3, 9; Sanford, 489, 90, 3; Silas, 495; Susan, 494, 6; Susannah, 487, 91, 2; Sybil, 495; Temperance, 495; Thankful, 491, 5; Theodore, 499; Thomas, 485, 6, 8, 9, 90, 1, 3, 4, 8, 9, 500; Timothy, 485, 7; Ursula, 496, 501; William, 484, 5, 6, 9, 90, 2, 3, 4, 5, 6, 7, 9, 500; Zerviah, 491.

PAGE.—Abigail, 503; Bridget, 503; Cyrus, 503; Daniel, 502; Elizabeth, 502; Fanny, 503; Hannah, 502, 3; Isaac, 503; John, 502; Jonathan, 502; Joseph, 502, 3; Katharine, 502; Lucy, 503; Mary, 502, 3; Martha, 503; Paul, 503; Phebe, 502, 3; Samuel, 502; Saxton, 503; Thomas, 503.

PALMER.—Abel, 514, 17, 26; Abby, 522, 6; Abiah, 512; Abigail, 511, 12, 13, 19, 26; Abijah, 513, 15; Abraham, 504; Adelia, 524; Adam, 519; Allen, 516, 19, 23; Alden, 522, 5, 6; Albert,, 525; Alexander, 520, 3; Amos, 514, 16, 17, 18, 20, 1, 3, 6; Anna, 512, 16, 19; Anne, 525; Annie or Amie, 509, 13, 18; Ann, 510, 13, 14, 24, 5; Andrew, 514, 18, 19; Asenath, 514; Asa, 515, 18, 21; Asher, 526; Betsey, 519, 20, 1, 5; Benoni, 511; Benjamin, 508, 12, 19, 20, 1, 3; Borodel, 522; Bridget, 513, 15, 22, 3, 6; Charles, 518, 21, 2, 3; Christopher, 514, 17; Coddington, 522; Clarissa, 518; Content, 517; Cornelia, 519; Courtlandt, 521; Daniel, 509, 12, 13, 14; David, 513, 16, 20, 22; Deborah, 519; Delia, 519; Desire, 511, 15, 19, 26; Denison, 514, 18, 22; Dolle, 515; Dorothy, 509, 13, 16, 17; Ebenezer, 511, 15, 17, 21; Edith, 520; Edmund, 524; Edward, 515, 21; Edwin, 523, 4; Eleazer, 511; Eli, 512, 14, 15; Elias, 513, 16, 20, 2; Electa, 526; Elihu, 508, 9, 10, 11, 14, 17; Elijah, 514, 19; Eliza, 521, 3, 6; Elizabeth, 508, 11, 15, 16, 20, 2, 5; Emma, 521; Emeline, 523, 6; Ephraim, 522; Esther, 511, 17, 18, 20; Ethel, 517; Eugene, 523, 6; Eunice, 515, 17, 26; Fanny, 521; Frances, 514, 22; Franklin, 523; Frederick, 519, 26; Gershom, 507, 8, 9, 10, 11, 13, 14, 17, 21; George, 510, 14, 17, 18, 21, 6; Gilbert, 513, 26; Gurdon, 519; Hannah, 508, 9, 11, 12, 14, 15, 16, 18, 19, 21, 2, 3, 5, 6; Harriet, 521, 2, 3, 4, 5, 6; Henry, 518, 23, 6; Huldah, 512, 14, 18, 19; Ichabod, 510, 13, 16; Ira, 523; Irene, 512; Isaac, 517; Israel, 517, 21; Jabez, 515; James, 512, 15, 19, 22, 4, 6; Jarius, 521, 6; Jeannette, 521; Jemima, 517, 21; Jesse, 514, 21; Jerusha, 512, 16; Jehoadam, 511; John, 507, 8, 9, 11, 13, 16, 20, 2, 3, 4; Jonah, 508, 9, 11; Joseph, 503, 11, 12, 14, 17, 18, 19; Jonathan, 509, 11, 12, 14, 26; Joshua, 515; Judith, 512; Julius, 521; Julia, 525; Juliet, 525; Keturah, 518; Lemuel, 515, 22, 6; Lois, 513, 14, 18; Louis, 524, 6; Love, 512; Lucious, 525; Lucretia, 515, 16, 18, 22; Lucy, 513, 15, 16, 17, 18, 19, 20, 1, 2, 6; Luke, 520, 5; Luther, 522, 5; Lydia, 512, 16, 19, 23; Maria, 519, 23; Margaret, 515, 21; Mary, 509, 10, 11, 12, 13, 14, 15, 16, 17, 18, 20, 21, 1, 2, 4, 5; Martha, 509, 20, 1; Marvin, 516, 18, 20; Matilda, 526; Mehitable, 511; Mercy, 510, 25; Michael, 517; Moses, 508, 9, 13, 14, 26; Namiah, 511; Nathaniel, 513, 16, 20, 2, 4; Naomie, 517; Nancy, 519, 22, 5; Nathan, 512, 14, 15, 18, 22; Nehemiah, 508, 9, 11, 12, 14, 15, 19; Noyes, 513, 16, 19, 20, 2, 3; Othnid, 517; Paul, 526; Peleg, 516, 19; Perez, 515; Phebe, 511, 14, 15, 17, 18, 21, 2, 5; Polly, 520; Priscilla, 522; Prudence, 512, 13, 16, 17, 18, 26; Rebecca, 508, 9, 10, 11, 12, 13, 18, 22, 6; Reuben, 514, 17; Rhoda, 519; Richard, 518; Robert, 516, 18, 19, 25, 6; Roswell, 518, 22, 6; Rowland, 521; Rufus, 512; Ruth, 511; Sabra, 515, 17, 18; Sally, 525; Samuel, 508, 11, 12, 15, 19, 26; Sarah, 512, 14, 17, 18, 19, 25; Sanford, 522; Saxton, 512, 15, 16; Seth, 511; Shubel, 511; Sophia, 518; Stephen, 512, 15, 24; Stuckley, 520; Simeon, 516, 19; Submit, 513, 14; Susan, 519; Susannah, 515; Sylvia, 521; Thankful, 513; Theodore, 525; Thomas, 512, 15, 16, 19, 22, 3, 5, 6; Walter, 504, 6, 7, 10, 14; Wait, 514, 16, 20; Warren, 520, 2; Wealthia, 511, 18, 20; William, 507, 10, 11, 13, 14, 15, 18, 21, 2, 4, 5, 6; Zeba, 520, 4; Zebediah 516; Zerviah, 517, 21; Zebulon, 514; Zipporah, 517.

PARK.—Alice, 528; Ann, 527; Deborah, 528; Dorothy, 528; Hannah, 528; John, 528; Martha, 528; Nathaniel, 528; Robert, 527, 8; Samuel, 527, 8; Sarah, 528; Theora, 528; Thomas, 527, 8; William, 527, 8.

PEABODY.—Abigail, 530; Amie, 529, 30; Benjamin, 529, 30; Elizabeth, 529; Fanny, 530; Frances, 529, 30; George, 530; Giles, 530; Hanna, 529; James, 530; Jerusha, 530; John, 529, 30; Joseph, 529, 30; Judith, 529; Lemuel, 530; Lucy, 530; Lydia, 529, 30; Martha, 529, 30; Mary, 529, 30; Mercy, 529; Nancy, 530; Priscilla, 529; Rachel, 529; Rebecca, 529, 30; Ruth, 529, 30; Samuel, 529; Sarah, 529; Susanna, 530; Thomas, 529, 30; William, 529, 30.

PENDLETON.—Abel, 535; Acors, 533; Alice, 534; Amelia, 533, 4; Amos, 532, 3; Ann, 531; Andrew, 533, 4; Averill, 535; Benjamin, 532, 3, 4, 5; Brian, 531; Caleb, 531; Caroline, 534, 6; Catharine, 534; Charles, 533, 4, 5, 6; Charlotte, 533; Damaris, 534, 5; Deborah, 532; Deney, 534;

Dewitt, 535; Dorothy, 531; Edmund, 531; Eleanor, 531; Ellet, 534; Elizabeth, 534; Emma, 536; Emeline, 535; Emily, 535; Enoch, 535; Ephraim, 532; Eunice, 534, 5; Fanny, 534; Frank, 535; Francis, 535; Frederick, 533, 5; Freelove, 532; Gilbert, 533; Gurdon, 534, 5; Hannah, 531; Harris, 533, 5; Isaac, 532, 3; James, 531, 2, 5; John, 532, 6; Joseph, 531, 2, 4, 6; Joshua, 532; Jonathan, 533, 5, 6; Keturah, 532, 3, 5; Lucy, 532, 4, 5, 6; Lydia, 532, 3, 5; Maria, 534; Martha, 534; Mary, 531, 4, 6; Molly, 533; Moses, 534, 5; Nancy, 533, 5; Nathan, 532, 3, 5; Otis, 533; Patience, 531; Peleg, 532, 4; Phebe, 535; Richard, 535; Rowland, 534; Sally, 533, 5, 6; Sarah, 531; Simon, 534; Susan, 535; Wait, 535; William, 532, 3, 4, 5, 6; Zebulon, 533.

PHELPS.—Abigail, 537; Ann, 537, 8, 9; Anne, 539; Ashbell, 538; Benjamin, 538; Bethuel, 538; Charles, 538, 9; Cornelius, 537, 8; Edmund, 539; Elizabeth, 539; Emily, 539; Erskine, 539; Francis, 539; George, 539; Hannah, 537, 8; Harriet, 539; Hepzibah, 538; Horace, 539; James, 538, 9; John, 538; Joseph, 537, 8, 9; Jonathan, 538, 9; Martha, 537, 8, 9; Mary, 537; Nancy, 538, 9; Nathaniel, 537; Noah, 538; Peleg, 539; Polly, 538; Sally, 538; Samuel, 537; Sarah, 537, 9; Stiles, 538, 9; Swan, 538; Timothy, 537.8; William, 537, 8, 9; Zeruiah, 538.

POLLARD.—Abigail, 540; Ann, 540; Benjamin, 540; Betsey, 540; Deborah, 540; Hannah, 540; John, 540; Joseph, 540; Lydia, 540; Mary, 540; Phebe, 540; Samuel, 540; William, 540.

POMEROY.—Anna, 542; Benjamin, 541; Cyrus, 542; Elihu, 541, 2; Eltweed, 541; Frances, 542; Isaac, 542; Jerusha, 542; Joseph, 541; Lydia, 542; Medad, 541; Phebe, 542; Rebecca, 542.

PRENTICE.—Abigail, 544; Amos, 544; Amy, 545; Asa, 544, 5; Asher, 545; Betsey, 544; Charles, 545; Chester, 545; Daniel, 544; Dorothy, 544; Ebenezer, 544; Elizabeth, 543, 5; Eliza, 545; Esther, 543, 4; Eunice, 543, 5; Grace, 543, 4; Hannah, 543; Henry, 545; Jesse, 544; John, 543, 4, 5; Jonas, 543, 4; Joseph, 543; Joshua, 544, 5; Lucy, 543, 5; Lucinda, 544; Mary, 543, 4, 5; Martha, 545; Nancy, 544; Nathan, 544; Oliver, 543, 5; Phebe, 544, 5; Polly, 545; Rebecca, 544, 5; Sally, 544; Samuel, 543, 4, 5; Sophia, 545; Thomas, 453, 4, 5; William, 545.

RANDALL.—Abby, 549; Abigail, 546, 7, 8; Adelia, 553; Almira, 551; Amos, 548; Amy, 548; Benjamin, 546, 7; Betsey, 549; Charles, 549, 51, 2, 3; Chesebrough, 549; Cyrus, 550; Darius, 552; David, 547; Denison, 551; Desire, 549; 50, 1; Dorothy, 546, 8; Dudley, 549, 51; Eleanor, 547, 8; Elias, 551; Elizabeth, 546, 7, 53; Elisha, 551; Eliza, 552; Emily, 552; Erastus, 552; Esther, 547, 9, 51; Eunice, 550; Frances, 552; George, 553; Greenfield, 547; Hannah, 549, 50, 2; Harriet, 551; Henry, 551, 2; Ichabod, 546; Isaac, 552; Jedediah, 549, 50, 2, 3; Jonas, 548; Joseph, 546, 8; Joshua, 547, 9; John, 546, 7, 8, 51, 3; Jonathan, 547, 52; Julia, 553; Keturah, 547, 9; Lucy, 547, 8, 50, 1; Lydia, 548, 9; Martha, 551; Mary, 546, 7, 51, 2; Mathew, 546, 7; Mercy, 547; Nancy, 549; Nathan, 546, 8, 53; Patty, 549; Patience, 547; Peter, 546, 7; Peleg, 548; Peyton, 549, 51; Phebe, 547, 50; Polly, 549, 50; Prudence, 547, 9; Rebecca, 546; Reuben, 548; Rhoda, 549; Robert, 547; Roswell, 549, 51; Russell, 550; Sally, 551; Samuel, 547; Sarah, 546; Silas, 552; Stephen, 546, 7; Thankful, 547, 50; Thomas, 547, 9, 51; Warren, 551; Wealthy, 552; William, 547, 9, 50, 1, 2; Zebulon, 549.

RHODES.—Abigail, 555, 6; Anne, 555, 6; Charles, 554, 5, 6; Christopher, 556; Dudley, 555, 6, 8; Emma, 555; Francis, 554; Godfrey, 554; Hannah, 556; Henry, 555; James, 554, 5; John, 554, 5, 6; Joseph, 556; Lucy, 555; Mary, 555; Nancy, 555, 6; Oliver, 556; Paul, 556; Sally, 554; Sarah, 556, Simon, 554, 5; William, 556.

ROSSITER.—Andrew, 558; Asa, 558; Ebenezer, 557, 8; Edward, 557, 8; Eliakin, 558; Elnathan, 557; Gilbert, 558; Hannah, 557, 8; Hettie, 557; Josiah, 557; John, 557, 8; Mehitable, 557, 8; Mary, 557; Molly, 557; Phebe, 558; Prudence, 557; Robert, 557; Russell, 557; Sarah, 557, 8; White, 557; William, 558.

RUSSELL.—Benjamin, 559; Daniel, 559; Ebenezer, 561; Esther, 559; Giles, 559; Hannah, 559, 61; James, 559; John, 559; Lydia, 559; Mary, 559; Mehitable, 559; Nathaniel, 559; Samuel, 559; William, 559.

SEARLE.—Benoni, 562, 3; Betsey, 564; Comfort, 564; Content, 563; Constant, 564, 6; Daniel, 564; Davis, 565; Deborah, 564; Ebenezer, 562, 3; Edna, 564; Elizabeth, 562, 5; Hannah, 564; Jabez. 564; James, 563, 4, 5; John, 562, 3 4; Josephine, 565; Katharine, 565; Kittie, 565;

Mary, 562, 3; Margaret, 563; Nathaniel, 564; Robert, 564; Roger, 565; Ruth, 564, 5; Salter, 564; Sarah, 564, 5; William, 565.

SHEFFIELD—Abel, 567; Amos, 566, 7; Benjamin, 566; Catharine, 567; Dorcas, 567; Edmund, 566; Elizabeth, 566; Francis, 567; George, 566, 7; Hannah, 567; Henry, 567; Ichabod, 566; James, 567; Joseph, 566, 7; Maria, 567; Mary, 566; Martha, 566; Nancy, 567; Nathaniel, 566, 7; Samuel, 567; Thomas, 566, 7; William, 566, 7.

SISSON.—Abigail, 568, 9; Ann, 568; Anne 568; Benajah, 568; Benjamin, 569; Betsey, 569; Charles, 569; Cyrus, 569; Elizabeth, 568; Emily, 569; Esther, 569; Eunnice, 569; George, 568; Gilbert, 569; Giles, 568; Hannah, 568, 9; Hope, 568; Huldah, 569; James, 568; John, 568; Jonathan, 568; Joseph, 569; Julia, 569; Lucy, 569; Marcy, 569; Mary, 568, 9; Martha, 569; Nancy, 569; Nathan, 568; Noyes, 569; Oliver, 568, 9; Peleg, 568; Polly, 569; Polly, 569; Rebecca, 568, 9; Richard, 568; Ruth, 568; Thomas, 568; William, 568, 9.

SMITH.—Abigail, 570; Amy, 572, 3; Anna, 571, 4; Anne, 572, 5; Anteneta, 574; Archaleus, 574; Betty, 574, 5; Benjamin, 572, 5; Catharine, 574; Charles, 575; Chester, 573, 5; Charlotte, 574, 5; Cotterill, 572; Daniel, 570, 1, 2, 3, 4; David, 572; Delia, 574; Edward 575; Elias, 572, 4; Elisha, 574; Eliphal, 572; Elizabeth, 570, 2, 4, 5; Ephraim, 571, 2; Erastus, 574; Esther, 571; Ejesta, 574; Fidelia, 574; Gilbert, 572, 3; Giles, 575; Grace, 570, 1; Hannah, 571; Harriet, 574; Henry, 575; James, 572, 4; Jedediah, 574; Jerusha, 571; John, 570, 1, 3, 4; Jonah, 572; Joseph, 570, 1, 2, 3, 5; Josiah, 571, 2; Kezia, 574; Lawrence, 574; Lemuel, 572, 4; Lucinda, 574; Lucy, 571, 2, 4; Lydia, 572; Maria, 574, 5; Margaret, 570; Mary, 571, 2, 4, 5; Martha, 572; Melania, 574; Melvina, 574; Moses, 573; Nancy, 575; Nathan, 575; Nathaniel, 572; Oliver, 572, 4; Parker, 573; Phebe, 572, 4; Polly, 573, 5; Priscilla, 574; Rebeker, 574; Ruth, 574; Sabra, 573; Samuel, 575; Sarah, 570, 2; Sanford, 572, 4; Seth, 571, 3; Shubal, 573; Silas, 571; Squier, 574; Susan, 575; Susannah, 570, 1, 3; Thankful, 571, 2; Thomas, 573; Ursula, 574; Walter, 572; Zerviah, 574; Zipporah, 571, 3.

STANTON.—Abby, 594, 5, 603; Abigail, 583, 588, 93, 6, 600, 2; Adams, 581; Althea, 585; Alfred, 582; Alexander, 598; Amariah 596, 7; Amelia, 581, 600; Amos, 579, 80, 1, 3, 4, 5, 603; Ann, 580, 2, 3; Anna, 578, 9, 81, 3, 4, 5, 92, 3, 5, 6, 7; Asa, 597; Andrew, 595, 6, 9; Avery, 581; Augustus, 585; Azariah, 580; Bathsheba, 603; Benjamin, 585, 98, 601, 2, 3; Betsey, 581, 97, 8; Borodel, 595; Bridget, 579, 80, 93, 4; Caroline, 581; Casinda, 584; Celia, 581; Charles, 582, 5, 98, 602, 3; Charlotte, 585; Christopher, 602; Content, 601; Cynthia, 593; Daniel, 578, 82, 5, 6, 7, 9, 90, 5, 6, 7, 9, 600, 2, 3; David, 582, 96, 600, 2; Densey, 580; Desire, 583, 93; Delight, 597; Dorothy, 578, 9, 82, 3; Ebenezer, 580, 96, 7; Edward, 596, 7, 600; Edmund, 597; Eldredge, 599; Eli, 579, 85; Elias, 594, 5, 600; Elizabeth, 579, 85, 7, 8, 93, 6, 7, 8, 9, 602; Eliza, 585, 600; Elisha, 600; Emma, 603; Enoch, 597, 603; Erastus, 584; Esther, 585, 8, 98, 9, 600; Eunice, 583, 8, 95, 6; Ezra, 594; Fanny, 599, 603; Gardiner, 588, 92; George, 587, 8, 98, 600; Grace, 603; Hannah, 578, 80, 1, 3, 6, 7, 8, 93, 4, 5, 7, 601, 2, 3; Harriet, 594, 7; Henry, 580, 2, 4, 5, 8, 98, 601, 3; Hiram, 585; Horatio, 598; Horace, 585; Hosea, 581, 5; Hulda, 582; Isaac, 583, 4, 94; Isabel, 587; Jabez, 582, 5, 97, 8, 9; James, 581, 4, 96, 9; Jane, 595, 603; Jeremiah, 580, 3; Jesse, 579, 85; Joannna, 579, 92; Job, 602; John, 576, 9, 80, 1, 2, 3, 5, 7, 8, 95, 600, 2, 3; Jonathan, 597, 8, 602; Joseph, 578, 9, 82, 3, 4, 6, 7, 8, 98, 602; Joshua, 579, 80, 1, 4; Keturah, 581; Latham, 602; Lois, 595, 6, 9; Lodowick, 580, 1, 8, 98; Lucy, 579, 81, 5, 7, 92, 6, 600; Lucretia, 580, 5; Lydia, 581, 2, 94, 5; Marlborough, 588; Maria, 585, 94, 5, 600, 3; Martha, 582, 3, 5, 97, 8, 600; Mary, 578, 9, 80, 2, 3, 4, 5, 7 8, 92, 3, 5, 6, 7, 8, 9, 600, 1, 2; Mason, 604; Mercy, 593, 4, 9; Nancy, 581, 7, 94; Nathan, 579, 83, 5, 93, 4, 5, 6, 8; Nathaniel, 583, 602, 3; Oliver, 581, 603; Patty, 581; Palmer, 581; Patience, 600; Paul, 604; Peleg, 593, 4; Persis, 600; Phebe, 596; Phineas, 596, 7, 8, 9, 600; Polly, 584, 99; Prudence, 579, 84, 93, 9; Randall, 581; Rebecca, 580, 2, 7, 93; Rhoda, 579; Robert, 578, 9, 80, 1, 2, 4, 9, 92, 3, 4, 601, 2; Roswell, 581, 5; Rowland, 594, 5; Richard, 589, 90, 1; Ruth, 584; Sabra, 602; Samuel, 579, 80, 1, 2, 3, 6, 8, 9, 91, 5, 6, 7, 8, 9, 602; Sarah, 578, 9, 80, 2, 3, 7, 8, 93, 5; Sophia, 585, 94, 5; Sophronia, 581; Stiles, 597; Susan, 581; Susanna, 580, 1, 602; Thankful, 584, 93, 4; Theophilus, 582; Thomas, 576, 7, 8, 9, 80, 2, 6, 7, 9, 90, 1, 2, 3, 4, 8, 600; Warren, 595; William, 578, 9, 80, 1, 3, 4, 96, 8, 603; Zebulon, 597, 8; **Zerviah, 583, 99.**

STEWART.—Anna, 606; Apphia, 606; Barbary, 606; Betsey, 606, 7; Charles, 608; Content, 605; Cyrus, 606, 7, 8; Cynthia, 607; Deborah, 606; Denison, 607, 8; Dudley, 607; Edward, 606, 7, 8; Ella, 608; Eliphalet, 605, 6; Elizabeth, 605, 7; Elisha, 605; Emily, 607; Emeline, 607; Ephraim, 606; Esther, 606; George, 606, 7, 8; Gilbert, 606; Harriet, 607; Isabel, 608; John, 606; Julia, 607; Lemuel, 605, 6; Lucy, 605; Lucretia, 605; Lydia, 606; Mary, 605, 7; Margaret, 606; Martha, 606; Mercy, 606; Nancy, 607; Nathan, 605, 6, 7; Oliver, 605; Phebe, 606, 7; Phineas, 605, 6; Priscilla, 606; Rebecca, 607; Russell, 606, 7; Sarah, 605, 6, 7; Wealthy, 606; William, 605, 6, 8.

SWAN.—Abby, 613; Abigail, 611, 13, 16; Adam, 613, 14, 15; Adin, 613; Amos, 612, 13, 16; Amy, 613; Angeline, 616; Anna, 612, 14; Anne, 611; Ann, 610; Asa, 611, 12, 17; Betsey, 615, 16, 17; Caleb, 610; Charles, 612, 15, 16; Christopher, 616; Clarissa, 617; Coddington, 616; Courtland, 616; Cyrus, 613, 17; Cynthia, 612, 17; Daniel, 613, 16; Denison, 616; Desire, 611; Dorothy, 610; Edward, 611, 13; Elias, 612; Elisha, 612, 14; Elizabeth, 610, 11, 12, 13, 14, 15; Ephraim, 616; Esther, 614, 15; Eunice, 611, 12, 13, 14; Fanny, 612, 15; Frances, 609; Frederick, 616; George, 611, 13, 14, 16; Gilbert, 613, 14; Giles, 614; Hannah, 613; Harriet, 615, 16; Henry, 613, 16; Hurlburt, 617; Isaac, 611; Jabez, 612, 15, 16; James, 617; Jedediah, 612, 14; Jesse, 612, 14; John, 609, 10, 11, 12, 13, 14; Jonathan, 609; Joshua, 610, 11, 13, 15; Jonas, 612; Joseph, 611, 13, 14, 15; Lavinia, 614; Lois, 612, 13, 14; Louisa, 616; Lucretia, 616; Lucy, 611, 12, 13, 14, 15, 16; Lucinda, 614; Mary, 611, 12, 14, 15, 17; Martha, 615; Mehitable, 613, 17; Miner, 614; Moses, 613; Nathan, 612; Nathaniel, 611, 12, 14; Oliver, 612, 14; Peleg, 613, 14; Perez, 611, 12; Phebe, 616; Polly, 614, 17; Priscilla, 612, 14; Rebecca, 613; Richard, 609, 10; Robert, 609, 10, 12, 14; Roswell, 614, 15; Russell, 614; Rufus, 617; Ruth, 611, 12; Sabra, 616; Sally, 613; Samuel, 610, 12; Sarah, 609, 10, 15; Susan, 609; Susannah, 612; Thankful, 611; Thomas, 611, 13, 15, 16, 17; Timothy, 610, 11, 12, 14; William, 611, 15, 16, 17; Ziba, 614, 16.

THOMPSON.—Amos, 619; Bridget, 618, 20; Catharine, 618; Charles, 618, 19; David, 618; Dorothy, 620; Elihu, 618; Eunice, 619; James, 619; Jedediah, 618; John, 618, 19, 20; Jonathan, 618; Joseph, 618; Mary, 620; Martha, 620; Nathan, 619; Nathaniel, 618, 20; Samuel, 618; Sarah, 619; William, 618; Zerviah, 619.

TRUMBULL.—Andrew, 622; Anna, 623; Charles, 622, 3; Edwin, 623; Eliza, 623; Elizabeth, 621, 2; Frances, 622; Gurdon, 622, 3; Hannah, 621; Harriet, 623; Henry, 622, 3; Horace, 622; James, 621, 2, 3; John, 621, 2, 3; Lucinda, 622; Mary, 621, 2, 3; Maria, 622, 3; Nathaniel, 622; Sally, 622; Samuel, 621, 2; Stiles, 623; Thomas, 622, 3; Timothy, 621, 2; William, 621, 2.

VINCENT.—Albert, 625; Asa, 625; Benjamin, 625; Charles, 625; Deborah, 624; Elizabeth, 624; Eunice, 625; Ezra, 625; Frank, 625; Hannah, 624; Henry, 625; Ira, 625; Jemima, 624; Joanna, 625; John, 625; Joshua, 624; Joseph, 624; Mary, 624, 5; Martha, 625; Mercy, 624; Nicholas, 624; Sally, 624; Samuel, 625; Surviah, 624; Susanna, 624; Thomas, 624, 5; Walter, 625; William, 624, 5.

WEST.—Abby, 634, 5; Abner, 627; Abigail, 626, 7, 32, 3; Alfred, 635; Amy or Amie, 628, 32, 3, 4, 5; Amassa, 627, 8; Amos, 627, 35; Ann, 627, 9; Anna, 633; Anne, 626, 7, 34; Arnold, 632; Asa, 634; Bartholomew, 631; Bathsheba, 626, 8; Benjamin, 626; Bridget, 633; Caroline, 635; Celia, 625; Christopher, 627, 9; Damarius, 633; Daniel, 629, 35; David, 634; Deborah, 628; Desire, 629; Ebenezer, 626; Edward, 630; Edwin, 635; Eleazer, 629; Elisha, 626, 7, 33, 5; Elijah, 629; Elizabeth, 629, 33, 5; Emily, 635; Ephraim, 628; Esther, 626, 33, 5; Eunice, 629, 33; Frank, 635; Frances, 635; Francis, 626, 7, 8, 9, 30, 1, 2, 4; George, 634; Hannah, 629, 33; Henry, 633, 4, 5; Jabez, 628; James, 632; Jason, 635; Jeremiah, 629; Jerusha, 629; Jesse, 634. 5; Jeuen, 626; Joanna, 627, 8; Joseph, 627, 8, 32, 4, 5; Joan, 631; John, 626, 30, 1, 2, 3, 5; Jonathan, 629, 31; Levi, 634; Lois, 629; Lucy, 635; Lucia, 628; Lucretia, 635; Lydia, 632, 3, 4, 5; Mary, 626, 9, 31, 2, 3; Martha, 631, 5; Margery, 626; Marcy, 628. Matthew, 631; Mercy, 627, 8; Mehitable, 628; Michael, 632, 4; Miner, 629; Moses, 627; Nancy, 634; Nathan, 627; Nathaniel, 629, 31; Oliver, 628; Peleg, 633, 5; Pelatiah, 626, 7, 9; Peter, 626, 31; Phebe, 628; Priscilla, 629; Prudence, 627, 9, 34; Rebecca, 628; Richard, 626, 30, 1; Robert, 631, 2; Ruby, 634; Rufus, 628; Ruth, 627; Sally, 634, 5; Salome, 635; Samuel, 626, 7, 31, 2, 3, 4; Sanford, 633;

Sarah, 627, 9, 32, 4; Simeon, 633; Sophia, 633; Stephen, 629; Susan, 628; Susannah, 629, 31, 2; Thankful, 629; Thomas, 630, 1, 2, 3, 4, 5; Timothy, 632, 3, 4, 5; Twiford, 630; Washington, 635; William, 626, 30, 1, 2, 3, 4 5; Zebulon, 627, 8; Zerviah, 629.

WHEELER.—Abigail, 640, 42; Ada, 656; Adeline, 646, 50, 4; Adrian, 656; Albert, 646, 9, 55; Allen, 652, 5; Alexander, 654; Amos, 641, 3; Andalucia, 649; Ann, 644, 6, 8, 9; Annette, 649; Anna, 637, 9, 41, 2, 52, 5, 6; Arthur, 647; Asa, 644, 7, 51, 4; Asher, 652; Betsey, 643; Benjamin, 651, 5; Billings, 647, 9; Bridget, 641, 3, 4, 5, 7, 53; Calvin, 646, 7, 9; Caroline, 647, 56; Celia, 654, 7; Charles, 640, 2, 3, 5, 6, 7, 8, 9, 50, 4, 5, 7; Chauncey, 648, 57; Christopher, 652, 5; Clinton, 656; Ciarissa, 645; Coddington, 652, 6; Content, 650; Cynthia, 642, 6, 53, 7; Cyrus, 640, 2, 4, 5, 8, 9; Daniel, 640, 53; David, 650, 1, 2, 4, 5; Dean, 650; Desire, 641, 2, 3, 7, 57; Delia, 647, 8, 57; Denison, 651; Dorothy, 637, 9, 44; Dudley, 645, 8, 53, 7; Ebenezer, 638; Ede, 647; Edgar, 648; Edward, 648, 52; Edwin, 648, 9, 54; Elam, 653, 4; Eleazer, 651, 2, 3; Elias, 644, 51, 3; Elisha, 643, 51, 2, 5; Eliza, 643, 9, 54, 5; Ellen, 647, 9, 55, 7; Elizabeth, 636, 8, 9, 40, 2, 6, 55; Emeline, 644, 54, 5; Emma, 647, 8, 55; Emily, 646, 54, 7; Ephraim, 640, 2, 4, 7; Erastus, 651, 3, 7; Esther, 639, 45, 6, 7; Eunice, 639, 41, 2, 5, 6, 50, 2, 4; Experience, 638, 9, 40; Ezra, 648; Fanny, 644, 5, 7, 52, 6; Frances, 646, 55; Francis, 643; George, 642, 5, 6, 50; Gilbert, 646, 52, 6; Giles, 647, 50; Gurdon, 643; Hannah, 639, 40, 2, 4, 5, 51, 3, 6, 7; Harriet, 643, 5, 6, 8, 55, 6; Henry, 648, 9, 50, 5; Hiram, 653; Horace, 650, 6; Hosea, 641, 4, 7; Homer, 646; Huldah, 652; Ira, 651; Irvin, 647; Isabella, 643, 54; Isaac, 636, 7, 8, 9, 40, 1, 2, 3, 5, 6; Jabez, 639; James, 646, 9, 51, 4, 5; Jane, 648; Jedediah, 645, 8; Jeremiah, 640, 1, 3; Jennie, 657; Jerusha, 646; Jesse, 651, 2, 3, 5; Jemima, 653; Job, 643; Joanna, 649; John, 639, 41, 2, 3, 4, 5, 50, 1, 3, 4, 5, 7; Jonathan, 639, 50, 1, 2, 4, 5; Joseph, 640, 6, 9, 52, 6; Joshua, 650; Leonard, 646; Lester, 651, 2; Lodowick, 643; Lois, 652; Louise, 648, 57; Lucy, 640, 1, 2, 3, 4, 5, 6, 8, 9, 53, 7; Lucinda, 644, 7; Luke, 644, 7; Lydia, 639, 41, 2, 7, 8, 53, 7; Matilda, 643, 52; May, 654; Maria, 648; Mary, 637, 8, 9, 40, 1, 2, 3, 6 7, 8, 9, 53, 4, 5, 6, 7; Martha, 637, 9, 40, 1, 2, 5, 6, 7, 8, 9, 50, 1, 2, 4, 5; Margaret, 638, 54; Mercy, 640,, 2, 3, 52; Mehitable, 640, 1, 2; Melissa, 654; Miner, 651; Nabby, 644; Nancy, 643, 4, 6, 7, 53; 4, 6, 7; Nathan, 639, 44, 7, 8, 9; Nathaniel, 651, 3; Nelson, 656; Noyes, 643, 6; Oliver,· 643, 6, 55; Patty, 653; Patience, 650, 1, 2; Paul, 640, 1, 4; Perez, 642, 4, 5, 8, 9; Peleg, 643, 6; Phebe, 649, 56, 7; Phineas, 644, 52, 5; Pitts, 646; Polly, 643, 5; Priscilla, 652, 3; Prentice, 646; Prudence, 639, 41, 50, 1, 2, 3, 6; Ralph, 656; Randall, 647; Rebecca, 642, 4, 7, 8; 56; Reuben, 652; Richard, 637, 8, 9, 50, 1, 3, 5, 6; Robert, 642, 5, 8, 9; Roswell, 646; Rufus, 641, 4; Russell, 644, 7, 8, 54; Ruth, 643; Sally, 646, 57; Samuel, 640, 7, 50, 2, 6; Sanford, 652; Sarah, 636, 9, 41, 6, 8, 9, 55, 6; Saxton, 654; Shepard, 640, 1, 4; Silas, 643, 51, 3, 6; Smith, 647; Sophia, 645; Soloman, 645; Stanton, 652; Stephen, 651, 4, 5; Stiles, 646; Susannah, 641, 2, 4; Tabitha, 644; Thankful, 641, 50; Theresa, 650; Thomas, 636, 7, 8, 40, 1, 2, 5, 6, 8, 9, 55, 6; Timothy, 643, 6; Walter, 643; Warren, 647, 56; Wealthy, 642; William, 637, 9, 40, 2, 3, 5, 6, 9, 52, 4, 5; Zerviah, 642, 5, 50, 2, 4.

WILCOX.—Abigail, 660; Abraham, 659; Allen, 661; Amey, 658, 9, 60; Anna, 659; Asa, 660; Caleb, 660; Daniel, 658, 9, 60; David, 661; Desiah, 661; Dorothy, 659, 60; Ebenezer, 661; Edward, 658, 9, 61; Elias, 661; Elisha, 658, 9, 61; Elizabeth, 660; Elnathan, 661; Francis, 661; George, 659; Hannah, 658, 9, 60; Hezekiah, 658, 9, 60; Ianatha, 661; Jared, 661; Jeffrey, 659; Jemima, 659; Jeremiah, 658, 9; Jesse, 660; John, 658, 9, 60, 1; Lodowick, 660; Lucy, 661; Mary, 658, 9, 60, 1; Martha, 660, 1; Mason, 661; Nancy, 660; Nathan, 659, 60, 1; Peleg, 660; Phineas, 660; Prudy, 661; Prudence, 660, 1; Robert, 659; Samuel, 660; Sarah, 658, 9, 61; Silas, 661; Stephen, 658, 9, 60; Susannah, 658, 60; Sylvester, 660, 1; Tabitha, 661; Thomas, 658, 9, 60; William, 658, 9, 60, 1.

WILLIAMS.—Abby, 666, 81, 2, 5; Abigail, 663, 5, 6, 70, 7, 9, 80, 4; Adin, 665; Albert, 668, 74; Alfred, 672, 80, 1; Allen, 680, 1; Alonza, 674; Allyn, 665; Althea, 665; Amariah, 671, 4; Amie, 665, 6; Amanda, 683; Amelia, 674; Amos, 671, 6, 9, 80, 4; Ann, 675, 7, 82; Anna, 665, 6, 72; Aseneth, 684, 5; Asa, 670, 3; Atwood, 668, 9; Augustus, 677; Austin, 680; Avery, 671, 3; Bela, 677; Benjamin, 666, 7, 85; Benajah, 668, 9; Benadam, 670, 2, 3; Bessie, 676; Bethia, 684; Betsey, 667,

80, 1; Bridget, 672; Caleb, 669, 71, 2, 4; Calvin, 675, 8, 81; Caty, 669, 73; Caroline, 664, 76; Celia, 682; Charles, 666, 7, 70, 2, 3, 4, 6, 8, 80; Charlotte, 674; Christopher, 679; Charity, 685; Clark, 667; Clarissa, 674; Courtland, 681; Cyrus, 673, 7; Cynthia, 674, 7, 81; Daniel, 666, 79, 80; Deborah, 662, 3, 5, 6, 8, 79, 81; Desire, 669, 70, 1, 2; Denison, 667, 80, 2; Diadama, 674; Dorothy, 664; Dudley, 665, 7, 8, 71, 84; Dyer, 671, 4; Earl, 671; Ebenezer, 662, 3, 4, 5, 7, 74; Edmund, 672; Edward, 669, 71, 6, 81; Elam, 679, 82; Elias, 672, 5, 6, 84; Eliakin, 667; Eldredge, 666; Elisha, 664, 5, 7, 8; Eleazer, 663, 78, 9, 80, 2; Elizabeth, 662, 3, 4, 5, 9, 70, 3, 4, 7, 8, 81, 5; Eliza, 674, 5, 80, 4; Ellen, 668, 75; Elihu, 670, 2; Elijah, 665, 6; Emma, 666, 76; Emeline, 676; Emily, 673, 7; Ephraim, 663, 70, 3, 6; Erastus, 667, 83; Esther, 667, 70, 2, 81; Eunice, 665, 7, 8, 72, 3, 4, 5, 9, 80, 2, 4, 5; Fanny, 667, 73, 9, 80; Frank, 680, 2; Frances, 674, 81; Franklin, 675, 8; Frederick, 674, 88; Freelove, 671; George, 667, 9, 71, 2, 3, 4; Georgia, 676; Giles, 666, 80, 2; Gilbert, 679; Grace, 674; Gurdon, 672, 5, 84, 5; Hannah, 663, 8, 70, 1, 3, 5, 6, 7, 8, 9, 84; Harriet, 675, 7, 8, 85; Harrietta, 671; Henry, 666, 83, 4, 5; Hepzibah, 676; Hezekiah, 685; Horace, 674, 8; Ira, 680; Isaac, 662, 3, 8, 9, 70, 3, 7, 81; Israel, 664, 5, 70; Jabez, 669, 71; James, 665, 7, 75, 8, 81, 3; Jane, 667, 85; Jefferson, 683; Jemima, 664; Jesse, 664, 7, 72; Jerusha, 673; Jennette, 683; Joanna, 677; Joel, 677; John, 662, 3, 4, 6, 7, 8, 9, 70, 2, 3, 5, 7, 81; Joseph, 669, 72, 3, 5, 6, 84, 5; Joshua, 669, 71, 7; Josephene, 682; Julia, 676, 85; Keturah, 672; Lathrop, 673; Laura, 683; Leonard, 681; Lois, 665; Lucy, 667, 9, 70, 3, 4, 5, 7, 85; Lucretia, 668, 78, 9; Luke, 670, 82; Lydia, 670, 2, 4, 8; Maria, 666, 8, 74; Mary, 663, 4, 6, 7, 9, 71, 4, 6, 7, 8, 80, 1, 2, 3; Martha, 662, 3, 4, 8, 9, 70, 2, 3, 6, 7, 8, 9; Matilda, 667, 80; Melinda, 683; Mercy, 667, 9, 70, 4, 5; Miner, 672; Nancy, 666, 7, 74, 7, 81; Nathan, 668, 9, 71, 85; Nathanel, 664, 5, 6; Nehemiah, 678, 9, 80; Nicholas, 671, 4; Noyes, 680; Oliver, 671; Orren, 685; Oscar, 674; Park, 663, 79, 80, 1, 2; Peleg, 665, 7, 84; Perry, 681; Peter, 663, 6; Phebe, 667, 8, 70, 2, 3, 7, 80; Polly, 672, 80, 1; Prentice, 679, 80, 1; Priscilla, 669, 78, 9; Prudence, 669, 70, 1, 9, 84; Randall, 672; Rebecca, 671, 3; Richard, 678, 83; Robert, 662, 9, 70, 1, 4; Robinson, 670; Roger, 684; Rhoda, 675; Rouse, 675, 81; Roxanna, 684; Rufus, 673, 5;

Russel, 680, 4; Salina, 683; Sally, 666, 7, 73, 84; Samuel, 662, 4, 5, 9; Sanford, 680, 1; Sarah, 663, 5, 6, 7, 8, 71, 3, 6, 7, 81, 3, 4, 5; Seth, 684, 5; Silence, 664; Simeon, 665; Soloman, 664, 71; Sophia, 666; Stanton, 672; Stephen, 662 77, 83, 4; Susan, 677; Thankful, 665, 7, 9, 74; Theoda, 662, 4; Thomas, 662, 3, 5, 6, 7, 9, 70, 5, 7, 8; Tirzah, 677; Warren, 676, 84, 5; Warham, 668, 9, 70, 2; Welthia, 671; William, 663, 4, 6, 8, 9, 70, 2, 3, 4, 5, 6, 7, 8, 83, 4, 5; Youngs, 682; Zerviah, 670.

WITTER.—Abigail, 687; Anna, 689; Annie, 690; Daniel, 688; Davis, 689; Dorothy, 687; Ebenezer, 687, 8; Elijah, 688; Elisha, 688; Elizabeth, 687, 8, 90; Esther, 688; Eunice, 688, 90; Ezra, 688, 9; Hannah, 686, 7, 8, 90; Holly, 690; Huldah, 689; Isaac, 689; Jacob, 688; James, 688; John, 687, 8, 90; Joseph, 687, 8, 9, 90; Josiah, 686, 7, 8, 9, 90; Lois, 690; Mary, 687, 8, 9, 90; Martha, 687, 90; Nathan, 688; Paul, 690; Phebe, 690; Samuel, 688, 9, 90; Sarah, 687, 8, 90; Susannah, 690; Tacy, 690; Weeden, 690; Wealthy, 690; William, 686, 7, 8, 9, 90; Zerviah, 688.

WOODBRIDGE.—Anne, 692; Augustus, 693; Benjamin, 692, 3; Charlotte, 693, 4; David, 693; Dorothy, 692; Dudley, 693, 4; Elizabeth, 693; Emma, 694; Ephraim, 692; Hannah, 693; John, 691, 2, 3; Joseph, 692, 3, 4; Julia, 694; Lucia, 692; Lucy, 693, 4; Martha, 692; Mary, 692, 3; Oliver, 693; Paul, 693; Samuel, 693; Sarah, 692, 3; Thomas, 692; Timothy, 692; William, 693, 4.

YORK.—Abby, 703; Abigail, 695; Abel, 702; Allen 697, 9; Albert, 701; Alice, 701; Amos, 697, 703; Anna, 696, 7, 8, 9; Annie, 702; Asenath, 700; Augustus, 699; Avery, 703; Bell, 697, 8, 9; Benjamin, 699, 700; Brinthia, 703; Calvin, 702; Caroline, 700, 1; Charles, 699; Charlotte, 697; Christopher, 698; Coddington, 700; Collins, 697, 8, 9; Content, 699; Courtland, 701; Cynthia, 701; Daniel, 700; Deborah, 696, 7, 9, 792; Dorothy, 696, 7; Ecmina, 703; Edwin, 701; Edward, 696, 7, 700; Electa, 700; Elisha, 702; Elizabeth, 696, 7, 9, 701; Eliza, 702, 3; Emma, 702; Emeline, 702; Esther, 698, 9, 703; Eunice, 698, 702, 3; Fannie, 700; Frances, 701; Francis, 701; Gershom, 698; Hannah, 696, 7, 8, 9, 700, 3; Harriet, 701, 3; Henry, 696; Harbert, 701; Hiram, 700; Horace, 702; Ichabod, 699; Isaac, 699; 700, 1; Jabish, 697, 702; James, 695, 6, 7, 8, 9, 700, 1; Jane, 701; Jesse, 697, 9, 701

2; Jeremiah, 698, 700; John, 697, 9, 700, 3; Jonathan, 697, 701; Joshua, 701; Joannah, 696; Joseph, 696, 7, 8, 701; Keturah, 699; Keziah, 703; Lois, 699, 702; Lucinda, 699, 703; Lucy, 698, 9, 700; Lydia, 698, 700, 1; Manassah, 703; Manita, 702; Marvin, 699; Martin, 700; Martha, 698, 9, 700, 1, 2; Mary, 696, 7, 8, 700, 2; Maryetta, 702; Nabby, 700; Naomi, 702; Nancy, 701; Nathan, 699, 701, 2; Oliver, 698, 702; Paltsey, 699; Phebe, 698; Polly, 699; Randall, 700; Ray, 702; Rebecca, 702; Reuben, 699, 702; Robert, 698; Ruth, 698, 9, 700; Samuel, 697, 700, 2; Sarah, 698, 9, 702, 3; Saunders, 700; Speda, 702; Stanton, 696; Stephen, 697, 702; Stiles, 703; Susan, 701; Susanna, 700; Thankful, 696, 7, 700; Temperance, 703; Thede, 698; Thomas, 696, 7, 9, 702; Walbert, 701; Wealthy, 703; Welcome, 700; William, 696, 7, 8, 9, 701, 2; Yeomans, 698, 700; Zebulon, 699, 703; Zerviah, 699.

INDEX TO APPENDIX.

Copy of Agreement between James Babcock and his Mother, page 707.

Distribution of the estate of John Babcock by Town Council, page 707.

List of Stonington Men who served in the Colonial Indian Wars of New England, page 708.

Will of Nicholas Cottrell, Sr., page 709.

Will of William Chesebrough, page 709.

Will of Mrs. Anna Chesebrough, page 710.

Jointure of Capt. George Denison, page 711.

Will of Capt. George Denison, page 711.

Deed of William Denison to John Smith, page 715.

Will of Major Israel Hewitt, page 716.

Abstract of the Will of Mrs. Anne Parker Noyes, page 718.

Will of the Rev. James Noyes, page 718.

Will of Capt. Thomas Noyes, page 720.

Will of Brian Pendleton, page 722.

Will of Walter Palmer, page 723.

Marriage contract between Joseph Saxton and Hannah Chesebrough, page 724.

Will of Daniel Smith, page 725.

Will of John Smith, page 726.

Will of Joseph Smith, page 727.

Will of Isaac Wheeler, Sr., page 728.

Will of Thomas Wheeler, page 730.

Inventory of Capt. Thomas Wheeler, page 731.

Will of Robert Williams, page 734.

www.ingramcontent.com/pod-product-compliance
Lightning Source LLC
Chambersburg PA
CBHW052037290426
44111CB00011B/1533